Sale, Lease, and Advanced Obligations

Sale, Lease, and Advanced Obligations

Cases and Readings

Melissa T. Lonegrass
HARRIET S. DAGGETT-FRANCES LEGGIO LANDRY PROFESSOR OF LAW,
BERNARD KEITH VETTER PROFESSOR IN LOUISIANA CIVIL LAW STUDIES,
AND WEDON T. SMITH PROFESSOR IN CIVIL LAW
LOUISIANA STATE UNIVERSITY PAUL M. HEBERT LAW CENTER

Sandi Varnado
ASSOCIATE PROFESSOR OF LAW
LOYOLA UNIVERSITY NEW ORLEANS COLLEGE OF LAW

Christopher K. Odinet
ASSOCIATE PROFESSOR OF LAW
UNIVERSITY OF OKLAHOMA COLLEGE OF LAW,
AFFILIATE ASSOCIATE PROFESSOR IN ENTREPENEURSHIP
UNIVERSITY OF OKLAHOMA PRICE COLLEGE OF BUSINESS,
AND AFFILIATE FACULTY MEMBER
SOUTHERN UNIVERSITY LAW CENTER

CAROLINA ACADEMIC PRESS
Durham, North Carolina

ISBN 978-1-5310-0249-7
eISBN 978-1-5310-0250-3
LCCN 2018962057

Carolina Academic Press, LLC
700 Kent Street
Durham, North Carolina 27701
Telephone (919) 489-7486
Fax (919) 493-5668
www.cap-press.com
Printed in the United States of America
2022 Printing

Contents

v

Part II · Lease

Acknowledgements

This textbook is a project many years in the making. It has been deeply influenced by our students, by our own teachers, and by our many friends and colleagues with whom we have shared materials and ideas for this course over the years. We would like to acknowledge the editorial advice, encouragement, and inspiration of those without whom this textbook would not have been possible, including Dian Tooley-Knoblett, John A. Lovett, David W. Gruning, Ronald J. Scalise Jr., J. Randall Trahan, Alain Levassuer, Patrick S. Ottinger, Wendell Holmes, L. David Cromwell, Peter S. Title, Shael Herman, Nikolaos A. Davrados, and, without question, Saúl Litvinoff, the chief architect of Louisiana's modern law of sales, and Symeon Symeonides, the principal draftsman of the revised law of lease. We are also indebted to our excellent research assistants: Malerie Bulot (LSU, Class of 2018), Endya Hash (LSU, Class of 2018), Jourdan Curet (LSU, Class of 2019), and M.J. Hernandez (LSU, Class of 2019).

MELISSA T. LONEGRASS,
Louisiana State University Law Center

SANDI S. VARNADO,
Loyola University New Orleans College of Law

CHRISTOPHER K. ODINET,
University of Oklahoma College of Law / Southern University Law Center

Part I

Sale

Chapter 1

The Nature of the Contract of Sale

A. Introduction

La. Civ. Code arts. 2438–2439

Article 2439 defines the contract of sale:

> Sale is a contract whereby a person transfers ownership of a thing to another for a price in money. The thing, the price, and the consent of the parties are requirements for the perfection of a sale.

LA. CIV. CODE art. 2439. Notice that Article 2439 provides that a sale is, first and foremost, a contract. This means that the rules of conventional obligations and obligations in general (found in Titles III and IV of Book III of the Civil Code) provide the foundation for Louisiana sales law. In fact, Article 2438 explicitly states so:

> In all matters for which no special provision is made in this title [Title VII], the contract of sale is governed by the rules of the titles on Obligations in General and Conventional Obligations or Contracts.

LA. CIV. CODE art. 2438. This article places the contract of sale "in its context." ALAIN LEVASSEUR & DAVID GRUNING, LOUISIANA LAW OF SALE AND LEASE: A PRÉCIS 1 (2007).

In addition, a sale is a nominate contract, i.e., one given a special designation. LA. CIV. CODE art. 1914. Nominate contracts like sales, matrimonial agreements, exchanges, leases, and partnerships (among others) are governed by the "special rules of the respective titles when those rules modify, complement, or depart from" the obligations rules. LA. CIV. CODE art. 1916. Ultimately, then, the contract of sale is governed by the Titles on Obligations in General and Conventional Obligations or Contracts, as well as by the specific Title on Sale.

Article 2439 also makes clear that in addition to being classified as a nominate contract, a sales contract is also an onerous, bilateral, and commutative contract. Each party to the sale obtains an advantage in return for his or her obligation, and the contract involves performances that are reciprocal or correlative to one another. *See* LA. CIV. CODE arts. 1908, 1909, 1911.

B. Contrast with Other Contracts

The foregoing discussion makes clear that the classification of a contract dictates the rules applicable to the parties' agreement. Indeed, because each nominate contract is governed by a unique set of provisions, proper characterization of a contract as to its kind is of paramount importance. Moreover, the nominate contracts contained in the Civil Code are not the only contracts recognized under Louisiana law. Parties are free to make any contract that suits their needs (assuming, of course, that those contracts do not derogate from laws enacted for the protection of the public interest, *see* La. Civ. Code art. 7). In the event that their contract does not fit within any of the nominate contract schemes, the contract is known as an "innominate" contract, i.e., one with no special designation. Innominate contracts are expressly recognized by the Louisiana Civil Code, La. Civ. Code. art. 1914, but the Code provides no suppletive rules for them. Therefore, they are governed by the rules of Obligations in General and Conventional Obligations, and by rules of nominate contracts that apply by analogy. *See* La. Civ. Code arts. 1915, 1917.

In general, what distinguishes the sale from other types of contracts is its principal object: it involves the *transfer of ownership of a thing* in return for a price in money. However, as illustrated in the Subparts below, determining whether a contract is properly characterized as a sale or some other type of contract, such as a contract to build, contract of lease, or contract of security, can be quite difficult in practice.

1. Sale Distinguished from Contract to Build
La. Civ. Code art. 2756

The contract to build is a common example of one that is difficult to distinguish from a contract of sale. The contract to build differs from a contract of sale in many ways, but ultimately, the fundamental obligation of each is different. A sale's fundamental obligation is one to give, i.e., to transfer ownership of a thing, whereas a contract to build's fundamental obligation is one to do, i.e., to perform labor to construct a thing. The difficulty in characterization lies in the fact that a single contract can sometimes give rise to both an obligation to give and an obligation to do. When this occurs, it is necessary to first determine which obligation is paramount or fundamental to the nature of the contract and then classify the contract accordingly. For example, in *Hunt v. Suares*, 9 La. 434 (1836), the plaintiffs wanted marble mantle pieces and hearths for their home, so they hired the defendant to provide and install them. The question arose as to which of the defendant's obligations—providing the materials (obligation to give) or installing the materials (obligation to do)—was fundamental. Likewise, in *Austin's of Monroe v. Brown*, 474 So. 2d 1383 (La. App. 2 Cir. 1985), the plaintiff wanted a computerized cash register system for its restaurant. It hired the defendant to provide the system, install it, and provide training on how to use it. Again, the question was what obligation—providing the system (obligation to give) or installing it and providing training (obligation to do)—was fundamental. *See also Hebert v. McDaniel*, 479 So. 2d 1029 (La. App. 3 Cir. 1985), and *Papa v. Louisiana Metal Awning* Co., 131 So. 2d 114 (La. App. 2 Cir. 1961), for additional illustrations of this problem.

Properly characterizing a contract as one of sale versus one to build is extremely important, as it determines both the effects of the contract and the obligations of the parties. For example, in *Hunt*, 9 La. 434, the characterization determined who would bear the risk of loss—that is, whether the plaintiff was required to pay for the marble pieces and hearths when they were destroyed by a fire prior to the contract's completion. Under the law that existed at the time, if the contract was properly classified as a sale, then the buyer was not relieved of paying the price even though the object of the contract was destroyed. In contrast, if the contract was properly classified as a contract to build, then the buyer was not obligated to pay as a result of the destruction. In *Austin's of Monroe*, 474 So. 2d 1383, and *Hebert*, 479 So. 2d 1029, the characterization of the contract determined what warranty obligations would be implied in connection with the contract. Contracts of sale carry an implied warranty against redhibitory defects (*see* La. Civ. Code arts. 2520–2548); contracts to build carry an implied warranty of good workmanlike manner (*see* La. Civ. Code art. 2762). Naturally, the implied warranties differ. For instance, the warranty against redhibitory defects involves unique remedies for breach, namely the potential for *quanti minoris*, i.e., a reduction in price (*see* La. Civ. Code art. 2520), as well as unique prescriptive periods (*see* La. Civ. Code art. 2534).

In order to distinguish between a contract of sale and a contract to build, courts have employed various analyses. One approach, referred to as the "value test," involves the determination of whether the principal value of the contract consists of the labor expended in constructing the item (indicating that the contract is one to build) or of the cost of the materials incorporated into the thing (indicating that the contract is one of sale). In *Hunt*, 9 La. 434, the court resolved the issue by comparing the value of the marble pieces and hearths to the value of the installation. Because the value of the work was "trifling" in comparison to the value of the marble pieces and hearths, the court held the contract to be one of sale. In *Austin's*, the court used the same method and found that although the value of the work (1/5 of the total cost) was more than trifling when compared to the value of the cash register system, the contract should still be characterized as one of sale due to the relative values of the labor and materials.

The value test is not the only method used by courts to distinguish between contracts to build and contracts of sale. A different method was employed in the case below. As you read this case, consider whether the court's approach is more or less useful than the value test in determining the contract's fundamental obligation.

Duhon v. Three Friends Homebuilders Corp.

396 So. 2d 559 (La. App. 3 Cir. 1981)

Domengeaux, Judge.

This is a redhibition action. The plaintiffs, Nolan and Patricia Duhon (Duhons), appeal from a judgment of the trial court granting a motion for summary judgment in favor of the defendant, Three Friends Homebuilders Corporation (Three Friends). We affirm.

The sole issue on appeal is whether the contract entered into between the Duhons and Three Friends is a contract of sale or a contract to build.

The parties concurred and submitted at trial of the motion that the determination of whether the transaction is a sale or a building contract would be dispositive of the motion for summary judgment, i.e., if a sale, the summary judgment should be denied, and if a building contract, the summary judgment should be granted because in the latter case the remedy of redhibition would not be available to the Duhons inasmuch as redhibition is the avoidance of a sale; without a sale, there can be no redhibition. La.C.C. Article 2520 [R.C.C. 2520].

The facts, disclosed by affidavits, were undisputed.

Three Friends is in the business of constructing and selling houses. Prospective "buyers" select a floorplan and choose the color schemes, appliances, etc., that they desire. Thereafter, the house is virtually completely constructed on Three Friends' premises. When the house is completed, it is then moved onto the purchaser's lot.

On April 26, 1978, the Duhons negotiated with Three Friends to build a house. On that date, they chose which floorplan and color scheme they desired. After these negotiations were complete, Three Friends began constructing the house. The house was completed on or about July 25, 1978 and moved onto the Duhons' lot. Thereafter, the Duhons noticed several severe defects in the house. After several unsuccessful attempts by Three Friends to remedy the defects, the Duhons filed this suit demanding a rescission of the sale, or in the alternative, a reduction in the price, plus attorney fees. Three Friends then filed a motion for summary judgment contending the contract entered into between the parties was a contract to build, and therefore, the Duhons could not recover in redhibition. The trial court held the contract was a contract to build and granted Three Friends' motion for summary judgment.

The Duhons contend the contract was a contract to sell a future thing, the sale becoming effective upon the completion of the house. They cite *Plaquemines Equipment & Machine Co. v. Ford Motor Company*, 245 La. 201, 157 So.2d 884 (1963), and *Succession of Schieffler v. Belair Trailer Sales, Inc.*, 242 So.2d 285 (La.App. 4th Cir. 1970) to support their contention. We find these cases distinguishable because both involved a sale through a dealership which purchased the desired object from the manufacturer. The contract between the purchaser and the seller (dealer) involved the transfer of a movable object which was essentially complete by the time it was acquired by the dealer. Thereafter, it was transferred to the buyer in essentially the same state as when it arrived from the manufacturer.[1]

---

1. Apart from a few modifications which were to be made by the dealer at the purchaser's request, the truck involved in the Plaquemines Equipment & Machine Co. case was constructed entirely by the manufacturer, with whom the purchaser had no contract.

The contract of sale is defined in La.C.C. Article 2439 [R.C.C. 2439] as follows:

> "The contract of sale is an agreement by which one gives a thing for a price in current money, and the other gives the price in order to have the thing itself.
>
> Three circumstances concur to the perfection of the contract, to wit: the thing sold, the price and the consent."

The Duhons contend that they gave money in exchange for the completed house and because there was consent as to the object and the price, the sale was perfected.

However, the present undertaking can also be construed to fit under the definition of a contract to build as defined by La.C.C. Articles 2756 and 2757:

> "To build by a plot, or to work by the job, is to undertake a building or a work for a certain stipulated price."
>
> "A person, who undertakes to make a work, may agree, either to furnish his work and industry alone, or to furnish also the materials necessary for such a work."

Three Friends contends that this case involves a contract to build because they agreed to construct the house for a certain stipulated price and to furnish the labor, industry and materials necessary for such a work. Because both a contract of sale and a contract to build require an object, a price, and consent, we must look to the jurisprudence to determine what factors distinguish the two types of contracts. There we find support for Three Friends' contention.

The object of the contract in the instant case is a house. In *Broussard v. Pierret*, 215 So.2d 136 (La.App. 3rd Cir. 1968), a prospective buyer negotiated with a contractor to build a house on a lot owned by the contractor. An "act of sale" was passed after the house was built, purporting to convey the title to the house and lot to the buyer. The court held that the contract was a contract to build.

In *Henson v. Gonzalez*, 326 So.2d 396 (La.App. 1st Cir. 1976), a jeweler contracted with a cabinetmaker to make some display cases. The jeweler supplied the plans. The cases were made at the cabinetmaker's shop and were then delivered to the jeweler. Upon delivery, the jeweler refused to accept the cases contending they were unfit for their intended use. The cabinetmaker sued in contract. The court held that the contract was a contract to build rather than a contract to sell.

A reading of the above cases reveal [sic] three major factors in determining whether a contract is a contract of sale or a contract to build. First, in a contact to build, the "buyer" has some control over the specifications of the object. Second, the negotiations in a contract to build take place before the object is constructed. Third, and perhaps most importantly, a building contract contemplates not only that one party will supply the materials, but also that that party will furnish his skill and labor in order to build the desired object. In this respect, see *Kegler's, Inc. v. Levy*, 239 So.2d 450 (La.App. 4th Cir. 1970), writ denied 241 So.2d 253 (La. 1970); *Airco Refrigeration Service, Inc. v. Fink*, 242 La. 73, 134 So.2d 880 (1961).

In the instant case, the Duhons had some control over the construction of the house in that they specified which floor plan and color scheme they desired. The negotiations were conducted before construction of the house commenced and a large degree of skill and labor was required of Three Friends to construct the house. We therefore hold that the contract entered into between the Duhons and Three Friends is a contract to build and that the Duhons cannot recover in redhibition. We express no opinion as to any other rights which plaintiffs might have.

For the reasons stated above, the judgment of the trial court dismissing the plaintiffs' claims is affirmed. The costs of this appeal are taxed to the plaintiffs, Nolan and Patricia Duhon.

Notes and Questions

1. Both the "value test" and the "*Duhon* test" remain prevalent in the jurisprudence. In fact, some courts apply both tests simultaneously. *See, e.g., Morris & Dickson Co. v. Jones Bros. Co.*, 691 So. 2d 882 (La. App. 2 Cir. 1997); *Alonzo v. Chifici*, 526 So. 2d 237 (La. App. 5 Cir. 1988). Other courts apply neither test and simply reference the general rule that a contract "must be characterized by its predominant or fundamental obligation." *See, e.g., Calandro's Supermarket, Inc. v. Hussman Refrigeration, Inc.*, 525 So. 2d 316 (La. App. 1 Cir. 1988). As these differences in approach illustrate, the proper classification of a contract is far from an exact science.

2. For additional discussion of the distinction between contracts of sale and contracts to build, see generally Alain A. Levasseur, *Sale of a Thing or Letting and Hiring of Industry*, 39 La. L. Rev. 705 (1979).

2. Sale Distinguished from Lease
La. Civ. Code art. 2668

Another contract that generates confusion in characterization is the contract of lease. A lease is defined as "a synallagmatic contract by which one party, the lessor, binds himself to give to the other party, the lessee, the use and enjoyment of a thing for a term in exchange for a rent that the lessee binds himself to pay." La. Civ. Code art. 2668. Like the contract of sale, a lease is a nominate, bilateral, onerous, and commutative contract. Unlike a sale, however, a lease does not involve a transfer of ownership. Instead the lessor allows the lessee to use and enjoy the thing in exchange for rent. Typically, the difficulty in classifying a contract as one of sale or one of lease arises when the parties allow for payments to be made in installments. If a party binds himself to pay a certain amount in installments for the use of a thing with the understanding that he or she may become the owner of the thing by paying a further sum (for which he is not bound absolutely), the transaction is a lease with an option to purchase. *See* La. Civ. Code art. 2620. By contrast, historically, courts have regarded an alleged lease as a sale when it provides that the lessee will become the owner of the thing at the end of the term for the rent already paid. *See Byrd v. Cooper*, 117 So. 441 (La. 1928) (holding that the agreement concerning

thirteen mules was a sale, since no additional sum would be due after the installments were paid). The modern-day distinction between the sale and the lease with
an option to purchase is a complex topic that is explored fully in Chapter 7: Effects
of the Contract of Sale.

3. Sale Distinguished from Security
La. Civ. Code art. 3136

It may also be difficult to distinguish a sale from a simulated sale functioning
as a security interest. Again, a sale involves the transfer of ownership of the thing
sold. Security, though, is an accessory right that operates to secure performance of a
principal obligation. La. Civ. Code arts. 1913, 3136. It does not transfer ownership.
Collins v. Pellerin, 5 La. Ann. 99 (1850), illustrates the difference between the two
types of contracts. In that case, the parties executed a bill of sale wherein the defendant sold cotton presses to the plaintiffs for $1500.00, a price significantly less than
the value of the presses. However, a counterletter showed that plaintiffs had lent the
defendant $1500.00 and that the bill of sale was simply collateral security to ensure
repayment. In the event of defendant's default on the debt, the bill of sale would
transfer ownership of the presses to the plaintiffs; in the event of defendant's full
repayment, the bill of sale was to be unenforceable. At all times, the defendant kept
possession of the presses, which indicated that the sale was merely a simulation. The
court held that given the low sale price and the fact that defendant remained in possession of the presses, the bill of sale was not a true a sale but was instead a security
interest.

Due to the complexity and sophistication of modern security devices law, the
problem of distinguishing between sales and security devices has grown less prevalent than it was at the time *Collins* was decided. Nonetheless, the Civil Code contains two provisions that are useful in distinguishing between sale and security.
First, Article 2480 provides in part that "[w]hen the thing sold remains in the corporeal possession of the seller the sale is presumed to be a simulation . . . ." La. Civ.
Code art. 2480. Second, Article 2569 provides that a sale made subject to the seller's
right to redeem the thing sold by returning the price (a right known as the "right of
redemption" and discussed more fully in Chapter 7: Effects of the Contract of Sale)
"is a simulation when the surrounding circumstances show that the true intent of
the parties was to make a contract of security." La. Civ. Code art. 2569. Both of
these provisions are addressed more fully in the Chapters that follow.

Chapter 2

Capacity and Authority

Like any contract, a sale requires the capacity of the parties; the consent of the parties established through offer and acceptance; a lawful, possible, and determined or determinable object; and a lawful cause. *See generally* LA. CIV. CODE arts. 1918–1982. The focus of this Chapter is capacity and authority. Capacity refers to a person's own ability to enjoy and/or exercise a right; authority refers to a person's ability to act on behalf of another.

A. Capacity

La. Civ. Code arts. 27–28

The Louisiana Civil Code provides for two different types of capacity. The first is general capacity (also known as capacity of enjoyment), which is the ability to have rights and duties. LA. CIV. CODE art. 27. The second is capacity of exercise, which is the ability to exercise rights and duties by juridical act (including contracts). LA. CIV. CODE art. 28.

1. Capacity of Exercise

La. Civ. Code arts. 1918–1926

The rules for capacity to enter a contract of sale are no different than those for capacity to enter any contract. The Civil Code provides that the capacity to enter a contract is granted to all persons except unemancipated minors, (some) interdicts, and persons deprived of reason at the time of contracting. LA. CIV. CODE art. 1918.

Minors (those under the age of eighteen per Louisiana Civil Code Article 29) lack capacity to contract as a general rule. However, a minor who is emancipated may be allowed to enter a contract. Recall that emancipation may be full or limited. *See* LA. CIV. CODE arts. 365–368. Fully emancipated minors have capacity to enter contracts. LA. CIV. CODE art. 1922. Full emancipation may occur by court order, LA. CIV. CODE art. 366, or by marriage, LA. CIV. CODE art. 367. Minors subject to limited emancipation have the capacity to contract to the extent provided for in the act or judgment of limited emancipation. Limited emancipation may occur by court order, LA. CIV. CODE art. 366, or by an authentic act executed by the minor and his or her parents or tutor. LA. CIV. CODE art. 368. For more detail, see generally Louisiana Civil Code Articles 365 through 371.

Interdicts also lack capacity to contract as a general rule. An interdict is a major or emancipated minor who has been judicially declared an interdict because of an infirmity that renders him or her unable to consistently make or communicate reasoned decisions regarding the care of his or her person and/or property and whose interests cannot be protected by less restrictive means. LA. CIV. CODE arts. 389–390, 392. Like emancipation, interdiction may be full or limited. LA. CIV. CODE arts. 389–390. Full interdicts completely lack capacity to make juridical acts, including contracts, whereas limited interdicts' capacity to do so is dictated by the parameters of the order of limited interdiction. LA. CIV. CODE art. 395.

Finally, persons deprived of reason at the time of contracting lack capacity to contract. "The expression 'persons deprived of reason' is designed to include all of the varieties of derangements that have been recognized by the Louisiana jurisprudence[]," such as maladies affecting intelligence, senility, habitual drunkenness, and drug sedation. LA. CIV. CODE art. 1918 cmt. b.

Notably, capacity of exercise is presumed. *See* LA. CIV. CODE art. 1918. Lack of capacity must be proven "quite convincingly and by the great weight of the evidence." *Meadors v. Pacific Int'l Petroleum, Inc.*, 449 So. 2d 26, 28 (La. App. 1 Cir. 1984). Provided this burden of proof is satisfied, a contract formed by a person without capacity is relatively null. LA. CIV. CODE art. 1919. For the distinction between a relative and absolute nullity, see Louisiana Civil Code Articles 2029 through 2035. As a general rule, a contract executed by an incapable person may be rescinded at the request of that person or his or her legal representative. LA. CIV. CODE art. 1919. There are situations, however, under which the Civil Code provides exceptions to that general rule in order to protect the interests of the other party to the contract. *See, e.g.*, LA. CIV. CODE arts. 1923–1926.

2. Capacity of Enjoyment; Sale of Litigious Rights
La. Civ. Code arts. 2447, 2652

Incapacities of exercise, such as those discussed above, are typically the focus of discussions of contractual capacity. However, capacity of enjoyment, granted to all natural persons per Article 27, is also important in the context of sales because of rules involving the sale of litigious rights.

Article 2447 provides: "Officers of a court, such as judges, attorneys, clerks, and law enforcement agents, cannot purchase litigious rights under contestation in the jurisdiction of that court." LA. CIV. CODE art. 2447. This article was the subject of *McClung v. Atlas Oil Co.*, 87 So. 515 (La. 1921). In that case, W.M. McClung and Atlas Oil Company both claimed to own a one-half interest in certain mineral rights. Before any legal action was taken by either party, McClung hired Huey P. Long to represent him in the dispute, and in exchange for Long's legal services and payment of court costs, McClung transferred a one-half interest in the mineral rights to Long. Long then filed suit against Atlas Oil, naming himself and McClung as plaintiffs. Atlas Oil filed an exception claiming that Long had violated Article 2447 and, thus, had no right of action. The Louisiana Supreme Court disagreed. It found the transaction between McClung and Long to be "a present conveyance of a fixed undivided interest in such title as McClung then owned in the mineral rights of the property described." 87 So. at 518. The Court went on to state: "Until there is a lawsuit actually pending, no right is litigious, no matter how apparently necessary one may be to enforce it." *Id.* It reasoned that the term "litigious right" is defined in Article 2652 as a right that "is contested in a suit already filed[,]" and that the term has the same meaning in Article 2447. Since no suit had been filed at the time of the contract between McClung and his attorney, Long, there was no violation of Article 2447.

In *McClung v. Atlas*, the Court clearly defined the term "litigious right." This definition was affirmed in the Court's later decision in *Gautreaux v. Harang*, 190 La. 1060 (1938). However, 60 years after *Gautreaux*, the Court would again consider the sale of litigious rights. In connection with the following case, consider the following:

La. Rev. Stat. § 37:218. Contract for fee based on proportion of subject matter; stipulation concerning compromise, discontinuance, or settlement

A. By written contract signed by his client, an attorney at law may acquire as his fee an interest in the subject matter of a suit, proposed suit, or claim in the assertion, prosecution, or defense of which he is employed, whether the claim or suit be for money or for property. Such interest shall be a special privilege to take rank as a first privilege thereon, superior to all other privileges and security interests under Chapter 9 of the Louisiana Commercial laws. In such contract, it may be stipulated that neither the attorney nor the client may, without the written consent of the other, settle, compromise, release, discontinue, or otherwise dispose of the suit or claim. Either party to the contract may, at any time, file and record it with the clerk of court in the parish in which the suit is pending or is to be brought or with the clerk of court in the parish of the client's domicile. After such filing, any settlement, compromise, discontinuance, or other disposition made of the suit or claim by either the attorney or the client, without the written consent of the other, is null and void and the suit or claim shall be proceeded with as if no such settlement, compromise, discontinuance, or other disposition has been made.

B. The term "fee", as used in this Section, means the agreed upon fee, whether fixed or contingent, and any and all other amounts advanced by the attorney to or on behalf of the client, as permitted by the Rules of Professional Conduct of the Louisiana State Bar Association.

Louisiana State Bar Association, Rules of Professional Conduct
Rule 1.8. Conflict of Interest: Current Clients: Specific Rules

* * * * *

(i) A lawyer shall not acquire a proprietary interest in the cause of action or subject matter of litigation the lawyer is conducting for a client, except that the lawyer may:

> (1) acquire a lien authorized by law to secure the lawyer's fee or expenses; and

> (2) contract with a client for a reasonable contingent fee in a civil case.

Succession of Noah Cloud
530 So. 2d 1146 (La. 1988)

LEMMON, Justice.

This litigation began as an action by four of the five children of Noah Cloud to set aside as a simulation the purported cash sale of immovable property from Cloud to B.M. Hatch, the then husband of Cloud's fifth child, Urzula C. Hatch. The suit also sought to set aside a subsequent transfer of the property from Hatch to his ex-wife as part of the community property settlement, as well as two transfers of mineral interests from Mrs. Hatch to Martin Sanders, her attorney, and a later transfer of the property from Mrs. Hatch to Urzula, Inc. The sale from Cloud to Hatch was ultimately set aside as a simulation by a portion of a judgment which is now definitive on that issue. We granted certiorari to review the portion of the judgment which upheld Sanders' mineral interest in the property.

On August 21, 1964, Noah Cloud, then eighty-four years old, executed a deed which purported to transfer a twenty-acre tract of land for $250 to his son-in-law, B.M. Hatch. Shortly thereafter Cloud and his wife moved into the residence of their daughter, Mrs. Hatch. At the time the twenty-acre tract was subject to a mineral lease in favor of Placid Oil Company. When production was obtained in 1965, Placid paid royalties under the lease to Cloud.

Cloud died in 1966, and his wife was interdicted shortly thereafter. Mrs. Hatch was appointed administratrix of Cloud's succession. At the direction of the succession attorney Placid began paying the monthly royalties to the administratrix.

During the administration of the succession Mrs. Hatch filed two descriptive lists, each listing the past and future royalty payments from Placid (but not the twenty-acre tract) as succession property. She also filed twenty-eight tableaus of distribution between the opening of the succession and her mother's death on March 11, 1980. In each tableau she listed her mother as the owner of one-half of the succession funds from Placid's royalty payments and the usufructuary of the other one-half.

In the meantime Mrs. Hatch and her husband were divorced in 1974. The husband was represented in the divorce proceeding by attorney Martin Sanders. In

1976 Mr. and Mrs. Hatch entered into a community property settlement (handled by Sanders) which awarded the twenty-acre tract to Mrs. Hatch.

After Mrs. Hatch's mother's death in March, 1980, the attorney for the succession prepared a document dividing the ownership of the twenty-acre tract and the accumulated royalties equally among the five children. Mrs. Hatch refused to sign, believing that she deserved a larger share because she had taken care of her mother for almost seventeen years after her father's death.

Two or three months after her mother's death, Mrs. Hatch consulted attorney Sanders about her dispute with her siblings over the property and the accumulated royalty funds. Sanders advised her that she was the record owner of the property and as such was entitled to all of the mineral revenues. She employed Sanders to represent her in the dispute and executed a deed, dated June 20, 1980, which transferred a one-fourth mineral interest in the twenty-acre tract to Sanders for the consideration of $10,000 "in legal services". At trial Sanders admitted (as he had in his deposition) that the consideration for the transfer was legal services "to be rendered" because Mrs. Hatch did not have any money to pay for the services which he had been hired to perform.[3]

In April, 1981, Sanders furnished Placid with certified copies of the 1964 sale from Cloud to Hatch, the community property settlement, and the mineral transfer from Mrs. Hatch to him. In accordance with Sanders' request Placid began paying the monthly royalties to Mrs. Hatch and Sanders.[4]

On May 19, 1981, Mrs. Hatch's siblings filed a rule to remove her as administratrix of the succession and to require an accounting. On behalf of Mrs. Hatch, Sanders filed an answer and an exception, claiming ownership of the property and the accumulated royalties on the basis of the 1964 sale from Cloud to Hatch and the subsequent community property settlement. After a hearing the trial judge on July 17, 1981 ordered Mrs. Hatch to file an accounting before September 7.

On August 31, 1981, Mrs. Hatch transferred an additional one-twelfth mineral interest in the twenty-acre tract to Sanders for the consideration of $10,000 "in legal services", which Sanders explained at trial was legal services already performed and to be performed. The next month he filed the accounting ordered by the court.

On November 20, 1981, Mrs. Hatch's siblings filed another rule to traverse the accounting and to remove her as administratrix.

Except for the transfer of the twenty-acre tract by Mrs. Hatch to Urzula, Inc., a corporation formed for her by Sanders, the record does not show any other activity

3. In his deposition Sanders stated that he based the fee on his estimation of the present value of the total mineral interest (which was then yielding about $30,000 per year), adding that "it was just a question of getting paid for the work that [he was] fixing to do".
4. At the time of Sanders' request Placid had paid $221,992.96 in royalties to the administratrix of the succession. Thereafter, Placid paid $249,809.95 to Mrs. Hatch and $108,945.51 to Sanders until payments were stopped in February 1985 because of pending litigation.

relative to the property until December 8, 1983, when Cloud's five children filed a joint motion to withdraw the accumulated royalty payments which were being held in the succession account. In the settlement agreement the five children agreed to divide the funds equally in order to close the succession, without prejudice to any party as to any other claim relating to the successions of Cloud and his wife.

On May 7, 1984, Mrs. Hatch's siblings filed the present action attacking the 1964 sale from Cloud to Hatch as a simulation and seeking to set aside the subsequent transfers. Mr. and Mrs. Hatch, Sanders, Urzula, Inc. and Placid were made defendants.

After a trial on the merits the trial judge dismissed the action. Reasoning that the plaintiffs had the burden of proving a simulation because Hatch was not an heir and because Cloud did not remain in possession, reserve a usufruct or retain possession by precarious title, the judge ruled that plaintiffs did not meet this burden.

The court of appeal reversed. 508 So.2d 577 (1987). On original hearing the intermediate court set aside the 1964 sale from Cloud to Hatch as a simulation and held that the twenty-acre tract belonged to the succession of Noah Cloud.[6] Because the court had not discussed or expressly ruled on the question of how the declaration of simulation affected Sanders' recorded mineral interest in the property, a rehearing was granted.[7]

On rehearing the court amended its prior decision and ruled that Sanders' mineral interest was not affected by the declaration of simulation. The court reasoned that the mineral deeds were not simulations because some consideration in the form of legal services had been given. The court further concluded that Sanders did not violate either La.C.C. art. 2447 [R.C.C. 2447], which prohibits the purchase of a litigious right by an attorney, or DR 5-103(A) of the Code of Professional Responsibility [the predecessor to current Rule of Professional Conduct 1.8(i)], which generally prohibits an attorney from acquiring a proprietary interest in his client's cause of action, because no suit was pending at the time of the transfer.[8] The court noted also that Sanders was a third party relying on Mrs. Hatch's ownership status reflected

---

6. The court reasoned that the exercise of dominion by Cloud and his succession over the mineral royalties from the property raised a presumption that the sale was simulated, especially when considered with Mrs. Hatch's admissions in the descriptive lists and the petitions relating to the tableaus of distribution and with her testimony in an alimony rule in her divorce proceeding that she did not own any property in Natchitoches Parish and that neither she nor her husband had paid for the purchase of the oil producing property. The court concluded that Hatch's testimony that he paid $2,000 for the tract, weakened by the absence of supporting documentation and by his wife's admission that she did not know of any consideration paid for the property by her husband, was insufficient to overcome the inference of simulation.

7. When the case was pending on rehearing, Mrs. Hatch compromised the ownership issue with her siblings and withdrew (through new counsel) her rehearing application, reserving any rights with respect to the issue of Sanders' mineral interest. Mrs. Hatch later aligned herself with her siblings in applying to this court for certiorari.

8. The Code of Professional Responsibility has been replaced by the Rules of Professional Conduct, effective January 1, 1987. However, the conduct in question occurred before the effective date.

by the public records. We granted certiorari to review these rulings. 513 So.2d 280 (La.1987).

Several members of this court were inclined to reconsider *Gautreaux v. Harang,* 190 La. 1060, 183 So. 349 (1938), which held that La.C.C. art. 2447 [R.C.C. 2447] did not prohibit an attorney from purchasing an interest in his client's genuinely disputed claim to immovable property when no suit was pending at the time of the purchase. Because Article 2447 [R.C.C. 2447] also applies to other public officers and because we conclude that Sanders' purchase of mineral rights in the present case was invalid for other reasons, it is unnecessary to address the Article 2447 [R.C.C. 2447] issue.[9]

At the time of the mineral transfer to Sanders an attorney was prohibited by the Code of Professional Responsibility from acquiring a proprietary interest in the cause of action being handled for the client except by means of a reasonable contingency fee contract or by a lien granted to secure his fee and expenses.[10] The purpose of DR 5-103(A) is to prevent a lawyer from speculating on the outcome of a lawsuit by purchasing a percentage of his client's hoped-for recovery at a discounted figure. See generally G. Hazard & W. Hodes, The Law of Lawyering: A Handbook on the Model Rules of Professional Conduct, Rule 1.8(e) and (j) (1985). The rule was designed not only to prevent lawyers from stirring up litigation, but also to minimize the possible adverse effect of the purchase upon the lawyer's exercise of judgment on behalf of his client during litigation. If a lawyer were allowed generally to purchase a proprietary interest in his client's cause, he would first have to negotiate with the client on the amount to which the value of the claim should be discounted. Later, his judgment might be impaired by his conflicting interest in protecting his paid-for investment when an inadequate settlement is offered in a meritorious but close case.

---

9. The *Gautreaux* decision has been criticized in scholarly commentary. Comment, *The Transfer of Litigious Rights in Louisiana Civil Law,* 1 La.L.Rev. 593 (1939); Comment, *The Sale of Litigious Rights,* 13 Tul.L.Rev. 448 (1939). The purchase of a litigious right gives rise to two possible remedies. The person against whom the right has been transferred may redeem the right by paying the price of the transfer. La.C.C. art. 2652 [R.C.C. 2652]. But since the purchase of a litigious right by certain public officers is absolutely prohibited, such a purchase may be annulled. La.C.C. art. 2447 [R.C.C. 2447]. Immediately following Article 2652 is the definition of a litigious right as one where "there exists a suit and a contestation on the same". La.C.C. art. 2653 [R.C.C. 2652]. However, La.C.C. art. 3556(18) [Repealed] ["Litigious rights are those which can not [sic] be exercised without undergoing a lawsuit"], which was adopted at the same time that Article 2447 [R.C.C. 2447] was first included in the Code, contains a definition which arguably could be interpreted as not requiring pending litigation. It has been suggested that the definition in Article 3556(18) [Repealed] was intended to apply only to the purchase prohibited by Article 2447 [R.C.C. 2447], while the definition in Article 2653 [R.C.C. 2652] applies only to a purchase redeemable under Article 2652 [R.C.C. 2652]. Comment, *supra,* 1 La.L.Rev. at 596.
10. Disciplinary Rule 5-103(A) (then in effect) provided:
"(A) A lawyer shall not acquire a proprietary interest in the cause of action or subject matter of litigation he is conducting for a client, except that he may:
(1) Acquire a lien granted by law to secure his fee or expenses.
(2) Contract with a client for a reasonable contingent fee in a civil case."

The exceptions listed in DR 5-103(A) do not solve these conflict of interest problems, but represent a compromise designed to balance countervailing factors. Allowing acquisition of a lien by the lawyer to secure his fee and expenses produces a danger of a conflicting interest by the lawyer to protect his investment, but eliminates a possible source of friction in the lawyer-client relationship. Contingency fee contracts, although not without problems, have the desirable effect of encouraging lawyers to represent clients with meritorious claims that the clients could not otherwise afford to litigate. Of course, the lawyer must enter into such an arrangement in good faith and only when it is beneficial to the client.

In the present case the attorney, shortly after he was employed to represent the client in defending her disputed claim against her siblings, acquired a proprietary interest in that claim in clear violation of DR 5-103(A). The difficult question is whether the client and her co-owners can assert this violation of DR 5-103(A) as a basis for nullifying the transfers and recovering the mineral interests from the attorney. We hold that the plaintiffs can do so, at least as long as the acquired interest is still in the name or control of the attorney.

The standards in the Code of Professional Responsibility which govern the conduct of attorneys have the force and effect of substantive law. *Louisiana State Bar Association v. Connolly*, 201 La. 342, 9 So.2d 582 (1942); *Saucier v. Hayes Dairy Products, Inc.*, 373 So.2d 102 (La.1979); *Leenerts Farms, Inc. v. Rogers*, 421 So.2d 216 (La.1982); *Moody v. Arabie*, 498 So.2d 1081 (La.1986); *City of Baton Rouge v. Stauffer Chemical Co.*, 500 So.2d 397 (La.1987). The disciplinary rules are mandatory rules that provide the minimum level of conduct to which an attorney must conform without being subject to disciplinary action. When an attorney enters into a contract with his client in direct and flagrant violation of a disciplinary rule and a subsequent civil action raises the issue of enforcement (or annulment) of the contract, this court, in order to preserve the integrity of its inherent judicial power, should prohibit the enforcement of the contract which directly contravenes the Code adopted by this court to regulate the practice of law. *Saucier v. Hayes Dairy Products, Inc., supra*, (Dennis, J., dissenting on original hearing). Otherwise, this court's authority to regulate attorney conduct will be substantially undermined.

Furthermore, the prohibition in the disciplinary rule does not apply only when there is a pending lawsuit. When the client consults the lawyer about a right which is genuinely disputed and likely to become the subject of litigation, and the attorney agrees to pursue the claim, the prohibition applies. Otherwise, there would be too much potential for abuse by the attorney who has substantial control over the filing or the answering of a suit.

In the present case the attorney's contracts of acquisition of a proprietary interest in his client's genuinely disputed claim to the property was a direct violation of

DR 5-103(A).[11] The attorney here seeks to maintain his mineral interest by enforcing the contracts which contravene DR 5-103(A). This court cannot place its stamp of approval on such contracts and must declare them null. In doing so, we note that the attorney could have acquired an interest in the client's property claim by entering into a contingency fee contract for a percentage of the client's recovery in excess of her uncontested one-fifth interest as an heir.[12] Also, the attorney could have taken a lien to secure his fixed fee of $20,000. His totally impermissible conduct in contracting to acquire an interest in the client's genuinely disputed claim in violation of DR 5-103(A) has now yielded him funds in excess of $108,000, and the contract simply cannot be allowed to stand.

Accordingly, the judgment of the court of appeal is reversed. The case is remanded to the district court to issue a judgment annulling the transfers of the mineral interests from Urzula Cloud Hatch to Martin S. Sanders, Jr.

COLE, J., concurs in the result.

Notes and Questions

1. The attorney in the foregoing case, Martin S. Sanders, was suspended from the practice of law for nine months. *Louisiana State Bar Ass'n v. Sanders*, 568 So. 2d 1025 (La. 1990).

2. Article 2447 states that the effect of its violation is that the purchase is "null." Is the nullity decreed by Article 2447 absolute or relative? *See* LA. CIV. CODE arts. 2029–2035, 2447 cmt. b.

3. Additional special limitations on the capacity to purchase exist for succession representatives, tutors, and curators. Read the following statutes and consider why the transactions referenced in them are prohibited. The provisions state that these transactions are "voidable" or "null." In each case, is the nullity absolute or relative?

La. Code Civ. Proc. art. 3194. Contracts between succession representative and succession prohibited; penalties for failure to comply

A succession representative cannot in his personal capacity or as representative of any other person make any contracts with the succession of which

---

11. Whether or not the client's claim is genuinely in dispute is a question of fact in each case. Here, there was clearly a genuine dispute over the ownership of the property. Mrs. Hatch consulted the attorney to represent her after her siblings indicated they would not recognize her claim. At the trial after this action was filed by the siblings, Hatch testified that he paid $2,000 for the property, but allowed the royalties to go first to Cloud and then to the succession because the money was used to take care of them without his having to pay taxes on the income. Cloud's other children testified that he had become senile and that they arranged to have the title placed in Hatch's name in order to prevent their father from signing away his interest to royalty buyers who descended on the area in the wake of the discovery of the Black Lake Field. In her divorce proceeding under cross-examination by Sanders, Mrs. Hatch testified that neither she nor her husband had paid for the oil producing property.

12. Because the client did not recover any additional amount, the fee would have been zero.

he is a representative. He cannot acquire any property of the succession, or interest therein, personally or by means of third persons, except as provided in Article 3195.

All contracts prohibited by this article are voidable and the succession representative shall be liable to the succession for all damages resulting therefrom.

La. Code Civ. Proc. art. 3195. Contracts between succession representative and succession; exceptions

The provisions of Article 3194 shall not apply when a testament provides otherwise or to a succession representative who is:

(1) The surviving spouse of the deceased;

(2) A partner of the deceased, with respect to the assets and business of the partnership;

(3) A co-owner with the deceased, with respect to the property owned in common;

(4) An heir or legatee of the deceased; or

(5) A mortgage creditor or holder of a vendor's privilege, with respect to property subject to the mortgage or privilege.

La. Code Civ. Proc. art. 4263. Contracts between tutor and minor

A tutor cannot in his personal capacity or as representative for any other person make any contracts with the minor. He cannot acquire any property of the minor, or interest therein, personally or by means of a third person, except as otherwise provided by law.

Contracts prohibited by this article shall be null, and the tutor shall be liable to the minor for damages resulting therefrom.

La. Code Civ. Proc. art. 4566. Management of affairs of the interdict

A. Except as otherwise provided by law, the relationship between interdict and curator is the same as that between minor and tutor. The rules provided by Articles 4261 through 4269, 4270 through 4274, 4301 through 4342, and 4371 apply to curatorship of interdicts. Nevertheless, provisions establishing special rules for natural tutors and parents shall not apply in the context of interdiction.

B. A curator who owns an interest in property with the interdict or who holds a security interest or lien that encumbers the property of the interdict may acquire the property, or any interest therein, from the interdict upon compliance with Article 4271, with prior court authorization, and when it would be in the best interest of the interdict. Except for good cause shown, the court shall appoint an independent appraiser to value the interest to be acquired by the curator.

B. Authority

In addition to the rules on capacity, contracts of sale can also be affected by the rules on authority that dictate the parameters of the right of one person to act on behalf of another. This section addresses authority in the contexts of mandate and the management of community property.

1. Mandate

La. Civ. Code arts. 1843, 2989, 2993, 2996–2998

Under Louisiana law, representation is the idea that "[a] person may represent another person in legal relations as provided by law or by juridical act." La. Civ. Code art. 2985. A mandate is one such juridical act. "A mandate is a contract by which a person, the principal, confers authority on another person, the mandatary, to transact one or more affairs for the principal. La. Civ. Code art. 2989. Under a valid mandate, the mandatary acts on behalf of the principal." It is important to know, then, the parameters of the mandatary's authority. The assessment of a mandatary's authority involves at least two inquiries: first, is the act of mandate valid in form, and second, what is the scope of the mandatary's authority?

In general, an act of mandate need not be made in any particular form; however, when the law prescribes a certain form for an act, a mandate authorizing that act must also be in that form. La. Civ. Code art. 2993. This rule is commonly referred to as the "equal dignities doctrine." For example, sales of immovable property generally must be made in writing to be enforceable. La. Civ. Code arts. 1839, 2440. Under the equal dignities doctrine, a mandate authorizing the sale of immovable property must likewise be made in writing. In contrast, a sale of a movable thing does not require a writing and may therefore be made verbally. As a result, a mandate authorizing a sale of movable property may be verbally made.

Assuming an act of mandate is valid in form, it must be assessed to ensure that it substantively grants the requisite authority for the mandatary to make a particular act on behalf of the principal. In most situations, the principal may confer on the mandatary general authority to do whatever is appropriate under the circumstances. La. Civ. Code art. 2994. However, for certain transactions, the principal must give express authority. *See, e.g.,* La. Civ. Code arts. 2996 (authority to alienate, acquire, encumber, or lease a thing), 2997 (authority to make an inter vivos donation, accept or renounce a succession, contract a loan, acknowledge or make remission of a debt, or become a surety, draw or endorse promissory notes and negotiable instruments, enter into a compromise or refer a matter to arbitration, or make health care decisions), and 2998 (authority to self-deal). Given that all sales involve the alienation of a thing by the seller and the acquisition of that thing by the buyer, a mandatary acting on behalf of either the buyer or the seller must have express—i.e., explicit—authority to do so.

When a mandatary contracts on behalf of the principal without the appropriate authority, the contract is relatively null. However, several exceptions apply to this rule. Read the case below for a discussion of two such exceptions: the doctrines of apparent authority and agency by estoppel.

Tedesco v. Gentry Development, Inc.

540 So. 2d 960 (La. 1989)

LEMMON, Justice.

This is an action against Gentry Development, Inc. to compel specific performance of a contract to sell immovable property executed by James Winford, Gentry's president, without actual authority from the corporation. The principal issue is whether the doctrine of apparent authority is applicable in a case involving a contract to sell immovable property.

In 1979 Gentry purchased a tract of land containing several acres. Gentry subdivided the tract in 1981 into several lots comprising the Gentry subdivision. Lots 1 and 2, the latter being the property at issue in this litigation, faced U.S. Highway No. 71, and Gentry's directors intended to use these lots as a location for a branch bank.

On April 7, 1983, Winford, under authority given by Gentry's board of directors, signed six-month listing agreements with Montgomery Realty to sell Lots 2, 4, 5, 7, 8 and 9. The listing on Lot 2 provided for a sale price of $50,700.00.[3] When Montgomery placed a "For Sale" sign on the subdivided tract, the sign was located on Lot 2.

Winford renewed the listing agreements for additional six-month periods on November 18, 1983 and June 18, 1984, but was not specifically authorized by the board of directors to extend the listing agreements beyond the original term.

Montgomery eventually obtained a prospective purchaser for Lots 4 and 5. Winford accepted an offer to purchase Lots 4 and 5 on June 18, 1984. The acts of sale for these lots were executed by Winford as Gentry's president on August 30, 1984, pursuant to a written resolution of Gentry's board of directors, adopted at an August 21 meeting, which authorized Winford to execute the particular sales.

In the meantime plaintiffs had contacted Montgomery Realty on July 23, 1984, and had signed an offer to purchase Lot 2 for $45,000. Winford rejected the offer, but indicated he would accept $50,700.

On August 25, plaintiffs executed a written offer to purchase Lot 2 for $50,700. Winford signed the acceptance on August 30 after making certain modifications which were subsequently approved by plaintiffs.[4]

---

3. All of Gentry's directors testified that the inclusion of Lot 2 in the listing was in error, because Lot 2 was to be used for a branch bank.

4. Three members of Gentry's board of directors testified they informed Montgomery's president on August 21 (the same day the board adopted the resolution for the sale of Lots 4 and 5) that

Gentry informed plaintiffs' agent that Winford had not been authorized to extend the listing agreement or to accept the offer to purchase. Gentry accordingly declined to sell the property. Hence this action for specific performance.

After a trial on the merits the district court rendered a judgment ordering specific performance. The court found that Winford was Gentry's agent and that he acted with apparent authority for Gentry when he accepted plaintiffs' offer on Lot 2 on August 30, 1984. The court further found that plaintiffs were third parties who totally relied on Winford's apparent authority as a result of Gentry's manifestations.[5]

The court of appeal reversed. 521 So.2d 717. The court concluded that Winford, as president of Gentry, could only be empowered to sell the corporation's immovable property by an express grant of power in writing. Since Winford was not authorized in writing to sell the immovable property belonging to Gentry, he had no authority to bind Gentry to the contract with plaintiffs. The court concluded that the doctrine of apparent authority is inapplicable in the area of real estate sales.[6]

_____

Gentry was not interested in selling any more lots. Montgomery's president testified the meeting was after August 30, insisting the directors contacted him in an attempt to get out of the contract with plaintiffs.

5. The court found the following manifestations by Gentry of Winford's apparent authority:

(1) Winford had prior dealings with Montgomery Realty during which Gentry had completed sales transactions on Lots 4 and 5 without raising the issue of Winford's authority.

(2) Gentry allowed Montgomery to place a "For Sale" sign on Lot 2, and this sign attracted plaintiffs to the property.

(3) Gentry had Lot 2 appraised by Mark Montgomery without written authorization, but later ratified the appraisal by payment of Montgomery's fee at the completion of the appraisal.

(4) Gentry knew that Montgomery Realty was acting in its behalf, but took no action to tell Montgomery that Winford was not authorized to renew the listing agreements on the property.

(5) Gentry ratified Winford's signing of the subdivision plat as owner, rather than as President of Gentry, on the same day that Winford signed the sales agreement with plaintiffs. The Board ratified the execution of the subdivision plat by Winford by executing an affidavit signed by Winford as President of Gentry Development, Inc.

(6) Gentry's attorney acknowledged in a September 21, 1984 letter the fact that the Gentry board had authorized Winford to sign listing contracts, and the attorney stated his understanding that the listing contract was renewed on June 18, 1984, without Board authorization. Notwithstanding these facts, the Board took no action prior to August 30, 1984 to stop Montgomery Real Estate from offering the property for sale.

(7) Winford testified that he believed he had corporate authority, acted for the corporation at all times, and believed he acted in conformity with the Board's wishes when he signed the instruments.

(8) The same day that Winford signed the sales agreement with plaintiffs on August 30, he signed two deeds, as President of Gentry, for the sales of Lots 4 and 5. Harold Holley, Secretary of Gentry, signed a resolution indicated [sic] that Winford was authorized to execute these acts of sale.

6. The court noted that even if the doctrine of apparent authority was applicable in cases involving real estate, the doctrine would not apply, because Winford's previous actions could not have reasonably been relied upon by plaintiffs as a grant of authority by Gentry to sell another specific tract of land for a specific price. Chief Judge Hall concurred, observing that while he did not necessarily agree that the doctrine of apparent authority could never apply to a corporate transaction involving immovable property, he agreed that the doctrine was not applicable in this case. He observed that the corporation made no manifestations of the president's authority directly to plaintiffs and that plaintiffs were not justified by any manifestations of other corporate officials in

We granted certiorari to address the issue of the applicability of the doctrine of apparent authority in contracts involving the sale of immovable property. 523 So.2d 1313.

Apparent authority is a doctrine by which an agent is empowered to bind his principal in a transaction with a third person when the principal has made a manifestation to the third person, or to the community of which the third person is a member, that the agent is authorized to engage in the particular transaction, although the principal has not actually delegated this authority to the agent.[7] Restatement (Second) of Agency § 8 (1958); W. Seavey, Law of Agency § 8(D) (1968); F. Mechem, Law of Agency § 84 (4th ed. 1952); Comment, *Agency Power in Louisiana*, 40 Tul.L.Rev. 110 (1965) [hereinafter cited as Comment, *Agency Power*]. In an actual authority situation the principal makes the manifestation first to the agent; in an apparent authority situation the principal makes this manifestation to a third person. However, the third person has the same rights in relation to the principal under either actual or apparent authority. Further, apparent authority operates only when it is reasonable for the third person to believe the agent is authorized and the third person actually believes this. Restatement, *supra* § 8, comments a and c.

There is no express codal or statutory authority for the doctrine of apparent authority in Louisiana. This doctrine of unprivileged agency power, however, is an important part of the modern law of agency. A. Yiannopoulos, Civil Law in the Modern World 88 (1965).

Louisiana courts have utilized the doctrine of apparent authority to protect third persons by treating a principal who has manifested an agent's authority to third persons as if the principal had actually granted the authority to the agent. See Restatement, *supra* § 8, comment d; Comment, *Agency Power, supra*; Conant, *The Objective Theory of Agency: Apparent Authority and the Estoppel of Apparent Ownership*, 47 Neb.L.Rev. 678 (1968).

*   *   *   *   *

The Louisiana decisions have sometimes used language of estoppel, but have not distinguished between the concepts of apparent authority and agency by estoppel. The Restatement, however, makes a clear distinction. According to the Restatement, apparent authority is based on the objective theory of contracts that a party ought to be bound by what he says and manifests rather than by what he intends, so that a third person who contracts with an agent need only prove reliance on the appearance of authority manifested by the principal. Because an enforceable contract results from

---

believing that Winford had authority to bind the corporation for this contract. Judge Sexton dissented, believing that the trial court's judgment should be affirmed based on this court's decision in *Ideal Savings & Homestead Association v. Kerner*, 208 La. 513, 23 So.2d 200 (1945).

7. Restatement (Second) of Agency § 8 (1958) contains the following definition:
  "Apparent authority is the power to affect the legal relations of another person by transactions with third persons, professedly as agent for the other, arising from and in accordance with the other's manifestations to such third persons."

the agreement with the agent after the principal's conduct has manifested his consent, the third person need not prove any change of position induced by the reliance. On the other hand, agency by estoppel is based on tort principles of preventing *loss* by an innocent person. The third person not only must show reliance on the conduct of the principal, but also must show such a change of position on his part that it would be unjust to allow the principal to deny the agency. Restatement, *supra* §8, comment d.

Professor Mechem prefers the estoppel approach. F. Mechem, *supra* §85–89. He argues that it is conceptually difficult to see how a real contract can be made between the principal and a person of whose existence the principal is unaware, in the absence of an actual agency, but it is not difficult to understand why the law treats such a person for many purposes as if he had made a real contract. See also Cook, *Agency by Estoppel,* 5 Colum.L.Rev. 36 (1905); Ewart, *Agency by Estoppel,* 5 Colum.L.Rev. 354 (1905); and Cook, *Agency by Estoppel: A Reply,* 6 Colum.L.Rev. 34 (1906).

Two situations come to mind in which the distinction between apparent authority and agency by estoppel may be important. First, it may not be possible in some apparent authority situations to show a change of position. Restatement, *supra* §8B points out that a third person who enters into a contract with an agent in reasonable reliance on the principal's manifestations of the agent's authority should be entitled to enforce the contract without regard to losses or changes in position. If the concepts of apparent authority and agency by estoppel are viewed as identical or coextensive, another element of required proof would be added in apparent authority cases, thus reducing without a conceptually necessary purpose the number of situations in which a third person may hold the principal responsible for the acts of his apparent agent. Comment, *Agency Power, supra.*

The second situation in which the distinction may be important is presented in the present case. In the sale of immovable property, written authority is required for an agent to execute either an agreement to sell or a contract of sale. La. C.C. art. 2996 [R.C.C.2996], 2997 [R.C.C. 2996–2997], 2440 [R.C.C. 2440]; *Bordelon v. Crabtree,* 216 La. 345, 43 So.2d 682 (1949); *Rebman v. Reed,* 335 So. 2d 37 (La.App. 4th Cir. 1976). If a principal authorizes the agent orally to sell property and tells a third person of the agent's authority, the agent's contract with the third person is not enforceable, either on the basis of actual authority or apparent authority, because of the absence of the formal requirement of written authorization. Just as testimonial proof cannot be used to prove the sale of immovable property (or the agreement to sell such property), testimonial proof cannot be used to prove the agent's authority to execute the contract, whether that authority was actual or apparent. Nevertheless, the principal may be estopped from asserting the defense of lack of written authority if the third person can show a change of position in reliance on the representation.[8] Restatement, *supra* §8, comment d.

---

8. The case of *Ideal Savings & Homestead Association v. Kerner,* 208 La. 513, 23 So.2d 200 (1945), was an action to cancel an act of sale from the association to the defendant on the basis that the association did not authorize its president to execute the sale. The sale was passed by the

Change of position includes payment of money, expenditure of labor, suffering of loss, or subjection to legal liability in reliance on the belief of agency. Restatement, *supra* §8B. There is generally no change of position, however, when a third person merely enters into an executory contract which he believes has been authorized by the principal. If the contract is immediately repudiated by the principal (as occurred in the present case) and is ultimately declared unenforceable, the parties are in the exact position they occupied before the contract was executed. However, a change of position has occurred when money has been paid to the agent or other transactions have been undertaken or abandoned in reliance on the contract. Restatement, *supra* §8B.

In the present case, it is not necessary for this court to consider adopting a distinction between the doctrines of apparent authority and agency by estoppel. Even if plaintiffs proved the elements normally necessary for enforcement of a contract on the basis of apparent authority, the absence of Gentry's written authorization for Winford's signing the executory contract renders the contract unenforceable. Furthermore, plaintiffs are not entitled to relief under the doctrine of agency by estoppel (or under the estoppel theory of apparent authority) because they did not change their position in any manner in reliance on Gentry's conduct. They do not claim that they suffered any loss or detriment, expended any money or labor, or incurred any legal liability before Gentry's prompt repudiation of Winford's authority. Plaintiffs simply seek to require performance by Gentry so that they may obtain an apparent "bargain". There is no loss which would justify this court's reliance on equitable principles to make whole.

Accordingly, the judgment of the court of appeal is affirmed.

Notes and Questions

1. The Court in *Tedesco* held that "[i]n the sale of immovable property, written authority is required for an agent to execute either an agreement to sell or a contract to sell," citing the predecessor provisions of Civil Code article 2996. Recall that the equal dignities doctrine applies to contracts of mandate; that is, the act of mandate must be made in the same form required for the act that the mandatary is authorized to make.

While the equal dignities doctrine may seem straightforward, courts occasionally have difficulty applying it. For example, in *Rutledge v. Hibernia Corp.*, 808 So. 2d

---

association's notary (who was a director) after the association's attorney (who was also a director) examined the title, but the resolution of the board of directors was not attached to the act. At the sale the defendant handed a blank check to the president, requesting that he complete it with the correct amount due. The president made the check payable to himself, and he kept the funds and did not record the sale. The deceit was not discovered for more than a year.

This court held that the defendant was entitled to rely on the president's ostensible and apparent authority because of the homestead's manifestations to the defendant. The issue of the lack of written authority required in sales of immovable property was not raised, but the case clearly presented a situation for applying agency by estoppel based on the defendant's change of position in reliance on the association's representations. The court used language of estoppel in the opinion.

765 (La. App. 4 Cir. 2002), the court refused to entertain the argument that a mandatary was verbally authorized to make a donation of a certificate of deposit (the transfer of which generally does not require a writing). The court, citing *Tedesco*, reasoned as follows:

> Citing the then Civil Code articles 2996, 2997, and 2440, the Supreme Court held that "in the sale of immovable property *written* authority is required for an agreement to sell or a contract of sale." (Emphasis added). It is at once apparent that the Supreme Court considered the word "express" to mean "written" authority. We note that this holding has been criticized because former articles 2996 and 2997, while requiring "express" authority such authority could be oral as well as written [internal citations omitted]. However, when the legislature revised these laws in 1997 it did nothing to change the authoritative construction of the words "express authority" in articles 2996 and 2997. We therefore conclude that the legislature intended for the word "express" authority to mean "written" authority in the revised articles.

Id. at 770–71. Can you identify the flaw in the court's reasoning? Compare *Fernandez v. Hebert*, 961 So. 2d 404 (La. App. 1 Cir. 2007), in which the court upheld a donation of shares of stock by a mandatary with verbal, but not written, authorization to do so. The court refused to follow *Tedesco* and *Rutledge*, stating "[r]ather, it is the provisions of Article 2993, which state that the contract of mandate is not required to be in any particular form but that nevertheless, when the law prescribes a certain form for an act, the mandate authorizing the act must be in that form, which are instructive." *Id.* at 411. The court correctly reasoned that, because the transfer of shares did not require a writing, the authority to donate the shares likewise did not require a writing.

2. At the time *Tedesco* was decided, the Louisiana Civil Code did not expressly recognize the doctrine of apparent authority and indeed expressly negated the existence of such a doctrine. *See* LA. CIV. CODE arts. 3010, 3021 (1870). And yet, as *Tedesco* makes clear, Louisiana courts routinely applied the common law theory of apparent authority in cases of a mandatary exceeding his or her authority. The Louisiana legislature introduced the concept of apparent authority to the Civil Code during the 1997 revision of the Title on Representation and Mandate. Article 3021, titled "Putative mandatary," now provides: "One who causes a third person to believe that another person is his mandatary is bound to the third person who in good faith contracts with the putative mandatary." LA. CIV. CODE art. 3021. For a detailed discussion of this article and the state of the doctrine of agency by estoppel following the revision, see Wendell H. Holmes & Symeon C. Symeonides, *Representation, Mandate and Agency: A Kommentar on Louisiana's New Law*, 73 TUL. L. REV. 1087, 1150–58 (1999).

3. Apparent authority and agency by estoppel both allow for a third party to enforce a contract that a mandatary entered into on behalf of the principal when the mandatary lacked actual authority. A third means of enforcing a contract made by

a mandatary who lacks actual authority is ratification. "Ratification is a declaration whereby a person gives his consent to an obligation incurred on his behalf by another without authority." La. Civ. Code art. 1843. This can happen expressly, in which case the ratification must evidence the intention to be bound by the ratified obligation. *Id.* It can also happen tacitly when a person, with knowledge of an obligation incurred on his or her behalf by another, accepts the benefit of that obligation. *Id.* When a principal ratifies a contract made by a mandatary who lacks the authority to act, the contract is treated as though it was always enforceable. This is so because the effects of ratification are retroactive to the date of the ratified act. La. Civ. Code art. 1844.

The principal's ratification of an otherwise unenforceable contract must be clearly proven by the party seeking its enforcement. *Rebman v. Reed*, 335 So. 2d 37 (La. App. 4 Cir. 1976), illustrates the difficulty of proving ratification in the context of sale. In that case, a real estate agent presented to the prospective seller, Reed, a standard form offer to purchase submitted by the prospective buyer, Rebman. Reed rejected the offer, in part because it was conditioned on the buyer obtaining financing. In a telephone conversation with the agent, Reed agreed to allow two days for the buyer to obtain financing and, after learning that the buyer successfully procured a loan, he agreed to the sale, again via telephone conversation with the agent. The agent subsequently accepted the buyer's offer on Reed's behalf. The next day, Reed sent a letter to the agent authorizing her to accept the offer; however, the letter specified that the sale was to be "all cash." The parties conceded that the agent lacked authority at the time she accepted the offer on Reed's behalf, since any such authorization would be required to be in writing. However, Rebman argued that Reed's letter ratified the agent's act. The court disagreed. The court held that since the letter did not "expressly confirm acceptance of the previously rejected term of the contract, it cannot provide conclusive proof that Reed accepted the previously rejected offer . . . ." *Id.* at 42.

4. With respect to sales of immovable property, there exists a split in the authority on whether a ratification of a sale made by an agent who lacked written authority to sell must be made in writing. Some courts have opined that an agreement to purchase immovable property must be made in writing, and thus, parol evidence of ratification cannot be considered. *See, e.g., Daigle & Associates, Inc. v. Coleman*, 385 So. 2d 349 (La. App. 1 Cir. 1980). The Supreme Court has suggested otherwise. *See Bolding v. Eason Oil Co.*, 248 La. 269 (La. 1965) (opining that even if mandatary did not have actual authority to acquire immovable property on behalf of the principal, principal's heirs ratified the purchase when they later leased the property to a third person). *See also* 1 Peter S. Title, Louisiana Practice Series, Louisiana Real Estate Transactions § 6:113 (2017–18 ed.) (concluding that "[o]nce the act of sale has been executed and the principal has received the sale proceeds, however, acceptance of benefits should preclude repudiation of the sale by the principal.").

5. Louisiana Revised Statutes Section 9:5647 provides a five-year prescriptive period for an action to annul a contract made by a mandatary without the requisite

authority. La. Rev. Stat. § 9:5647. This prescription begins to run on the date on which the instrument is recorded in the conveyance or mortgage records. *Id.* Louisiana Revised Statutes Section 9:5646 provides an identical rule for transactions affecting immovable property made by a legal entity or unincorporated association through an officer or agent who lacked the requisite authority. La. Rev. Stat. § 9:5646.

2. Management of Community Property
La. Civ. Code arts. 1843, 2346–2348, 2350–2353, 2355–2355.1

Another area in which one may exceed his or her authority to act on behalf of another is the management of community property. As a general rule, spouses subject to the Louisiana regime of acquets and gains may each, acting alone, "manage, control, or dispose of community property unless otherwise provided by law." La. Civ. Code art. 2346. In other words, Louisiana's community property regime is one of equal management.

That said, certain transactions require the concurrence of both spouses. This is true for the alienation, encumbrance, or lease of community immovables; standing, cut, or fallen timber; furniture or furnishings while located in the family home; all or substantially all of the assets of a community enterprise; and movables issued or registered as provided by law in the names of the spouses jointly. La. Civ. Code art. 2347. Concurrence is also required to harvest community timber and to donate community property to a third person unless the donation is a usual or customary gift of a value commensurate with the economic position of the spouses at the time of the donation. La. Civ. Code arts. 2437, 2349. Note, however, that a spouse may renounce his or her right to concur in certain transactions. La. Civ. Code art. 2348. Also, in some circumstances, a spouse may obtain judicial authorization to act without the concurrence of the other spouse. La. Civ. Code art. 2355.

Furthermore, certain transactions are within the exclusive management rights of one spouse alone. This includes the ability of the spouse who is the sole manager of a community enterprise to alienate, encumber, or lease its movables unless the movables are issued in the name of the other spouse or the concurrence of the other spouse is required by law. La. Civ. Code art. 2350. Likewise, a spouse has exclusive management of movables issued or registered in his or her name as provided by law. La. Civ. Code art. 2351. Finally, a spouse who is a partner of a partnership or a member of a limited liability company has the exclusive right to manage, alienate, encumber, or lease the partnership or limited liability company interest. La. Civ. Code art. 2352. Note, however, that if a spouse is an absent person, the other spouse may, upon a showing that it is in the best interest of the family, obtain judicial authorization to alienate, encumber, or lease community property that the absent spouse has the exclusive right to manage, alienate, encumber, or lease. La. Civ. Code art. 2355.1.

Should a spouse who lacks authority and who has not obtained the requisite judicial authorization enter into a contract, it is a relative nullity. La. Civ. Code art. 2353. However, like in the context of mandate, one spouse may ratify the unauthorized actions of the other. In *Zeller v. Webre*, 17 So. 3d 55 (La. App. 5 Cir. 2009), Mr. Webre agreed to lease a community immovable to the Zellers and granted them an option to purchase the property. Mrs. Webre did not sign the agreement. In fact, she did not even know about it, and when she found out, she was angry. The court recognized that Mr. Webre acted without Mrs. Webre's concurrence, which was required given that the property in question was a community immovable, and it noted that Mrs. Webre did not renounce her right to concur. However, it held that Mrs. Webre, who had experience in real estate transactions, ratified Mr. Webre's actions by voluntarily accepting thirty-eight payments from the Zellers after becoming aware of the agreement, as well as by stating in the answer to the petition that she and Mr. Webre had agreed to sell the property to the Zellers. Furthermore, the court held that Mrs. Webre's ratification of the contract to sell did not require written consent to the agreement; rather, her actions sufficed to bind her. In so holding, the court relied on Article 1837, comment (b), which recites the well-known rule that an act under private signature signed by only one party is valid when the party who did not sign availed himself of the contract through his or her conduct. This important nuance to the rule that contracts involving the transfer of immovables must be made in writing is addressed further in Chapter 6: Form.

Chapter 3

Consent

___

La. Civ. Code arts. 1927, 1943, 2438

Consent is a prerequisite to the formation of every contract, including every sale. The Obligations course covers the intricacies of consent, including the rules governing offer and acceptance. *See* LA. CIV. CODE arts. 1927–1947. While this Chapter does not address the *mechanics* of consent, it does consider the *substance* of consent in the context of sale. The central question examined here is this: *to what, exactly, must the parties to a sale agree?*

A. Consent to Essential Elements: Thing and Price

Article 2439 makes clear that, at a minimum, "[t]he thing, the price, and the consent of the parties are requirements for the perfection of a sale." LA. CIV. CODE art. 2439. The following two cases illustrate the necessity of the parties achieving a concurrence of wills with respect to the essential elements of the sale.

Marcantel v. Jefferson Door Co.

817 So. 2d 236 (La. App. 5 Cir. 2002)

GOTHARD, Judge.

Plaintiffs, Thomas and Elaine Marcantel (the Marcantels), filed suit for breach of contract alleging that defendant, Jefferson Door Company, Inc. (Jefferson Door), delivered kitchen cabinets inferior to those ordered by plaintiffs, and failed to refund plaintiffs' deposit when the mistake was brought to its attention. Jefferson Door filed an answer and reconventional demand which asserted that the Marcantels received the cabinets exactly as ordered and failed to pay the balance due. In due course, the matter went before the bench for a trial on the merits. After hearing the testimony and considering the documentary evidence, the trial court rendered judgment in favor of the plaintiffs, ordering defendant to refund the deposit. The judgment further dismissed defendant's reconventional demand. It is from that judgment that defendant appeals.

The record shows that the Marcantels, as part of a kitchen renovation in their home, selected cabinets from Jefferson Door. The Marcantels thought they were ordering cabinets constructed of all wood. However, when the cabinets were delivered, the Marcantels discovered that the interior of the cabinets were constructed of laminated particle board. They called the sales representative at Jefferson Door, to complain of the problem. Conversations between Mr. Marcantel and representatives of Jefferson Door failed to resolve the dispute and this suit was filed.

At trial, the court heard testimony from Mr. Marcantel who stated that he and his wife went to Jefferson Door to select kitchen cabinets. They spent a considerable amount of time with Mary Jane Ziefel, the cabinet designer for Jefferson Door. The Marcantels told Ms. Ziefel that they wanted cabinets of all wood construction and were shown various possibilities. During the conversation Ms. Ziefel showed them custom made cabinets which featured all wood construction. However, these cabinets were considerably more expensive and would take much longer than the six to eight weeks the Marcantels had until the cabinets would be needed. They ultimately selected from the cabinets on display at the showroom. However, they wished to upgrade to all wood. Mr. Marcantel testified that Ms. Ziefel assured him that in the upgrade the construction would be all wood. Mr. Marcantel testified that he understood he was not ordering custom made cabinets, but thought that he was ordering manufactured cabinets which were constructed of solid wood doors, drawers and toe kicks and plywood interior. When the cabinets were ordered, the Marcantels paid a $2900.00 deposit toward the total purchase price of $5,955.93.

When the cabinets were delivered, the Marcantels opened the boxes and found that the interior construction was of laminated particle board. Because it was a Saturday, Mr. Marcantel was unable to reach Ms. Ziefel, so he left a message for her. On Monday morning he stopped payment of the check he had given to Jefferson Door upon delivery of the cabinets. He spoke to Ms. Ziefel later that day, but was told there was nothing she could do. Mr. Marcantel asked to speak to a supervisor and had a conversation with Mr. Weasly, who offered several options including a return of the cabinets for a full refund. However, Jefferson Door did not pick up the cabinets as scheduled and Mr. Marcantel did not receive a refund of his deposit. The Marcantels did receive a demand letter from an attorney representing Jefferson Door seeking to collect the balance due on the cabinets.

Mrs. Marcantel also testified at trial. Her testimony corroborates that of her husband on the significant factual issues. She testified that they wanted cabinets of all wood construction and thought that was what they had ordered. She recalled looking at the cabinets on display and being shown the solid wood doors and drawers. She did not actually open the cabinet to verify that the interior was also wood, although Ms. Ziefel did open a drawer to show the all wood construction and dovetailing.

Mary Jane Ziefel testified that she recalled the meeting with the Marcantels. Ms. Ziefel stated that the Marcantels did indeed want all wood cabinets. However, when they explored the possibilities, the Marcantels decided that all wood custom made cabinets would not fit into their budget or time frame, so they settled on manufactured cabinets with some upgrades. The Marcantels ordered from the display in the showroom, and those cabinets have particle board interiors. Ms. Ziefel admitted that one would have to open the cabinet to see the particle board because the exposed areas of the cabinets are constructed of solid wood.

The documentary evidence introduced at trial includes photos of the display cabinets and documents used to evidence the sale and the order. There is an invoice from Jefferson Door which gives a sales order number and reflects the total price, the deposit, and the remaining balance. It refers to an attachment in which the cabinets ordered are itemized. However, there is nothing in any of the documents which indicates the type of construction. The itemized list of the cabinets identifies the manufacturer and the appropriate number for each cabinet ordered. The descriptions of the cabinets are nothing more than manufacturer's numbers.

At the conclusion of the trial, the court rendered judgment in favor of plaintiffs, and in reasons for judgment found that no contract of sale was perfected as there was no meeting of the minds as to the "thing" represented by the contract. In support of that position, the trial court made findings of fact as follows:

> In the case *sub judice,* Mr. Marcantel stated that he made it clear to the salesperson that he was interested only in cabinets of a wood construction. Moreover, the court finds that the totality of the circumstance supports this position. That is, Jefferson representatives testified that Mr. Marcantel wanted wood cabinets, but that he could not afford them. Admittedly however, Jefferson never quoted Mr. Marcantel a price for wood cabinets. Additionally, the court finds that there was evidence submitted that Mr. Marcantel was *shown* wood display cabinets which were factory made, but then he was *told* that he could only custom order all-wood cabinets. Thus, the court finds defendant's argument that Mr. Marcantel knew the cabinets he was purchasing were not wood to be without merit. (Footnote omitted, emphasis in original).

In brief to this Court, Jefferson Door asserts that the trial court erred in making certain factual findings and, consequently, incorrectly found that a contract of sale did not exist. Specifically, defendant argues the trial court incorrectly stated:

(1) That the only evidence submitted which evidenced the purchase of the cabinets was a receipt allegedly delivered with the cabinets.

(2) That the plaintiffs were shown a non-custom all-wood display cabinet at Jefferson Door.

Defendant also asserts the trial court erred in failing to find that Jefferson Door had proven its reconventional demand and, in the alternative, in failing to order the cabinets returned to Jefferson Door.

LSA-C.C. art. 2439 defines a contract of sale and lists three requirements for its perfection. Those requirements are the thing, the price, and the consent of the parties. LSA-C.C. art. 2456 requires a meeting of the minds on the thing, and the price, to perfect a contract of sale and transfer ownership. LSA-C.C. article 2438 provides that the contract of sale is governed by the rules of general obligation and contract law where no special provision is made. *Gulf Container Repair Services, Inc. v. FIC Business & Financial Centers, Inc.,* 98-1144 (La.App. 5 Cir. 3/10/99), 735 So.2d 41, 43.

LSA-C.C. art. 1927 provides that a contract is formed by the consent of the parties established through offer and acceptance. *Philips v. Berner,* 00-0103 (La.App. 4 Cir. 5/16/01), 789 So.2d 41, 45, *writ denied,* 2001-1767 (La.9/28/01), 798 So.2d 119, *reconsideration denied,* 2001-1767 (La.11/9/01), 801 So.2d 1066. Under Louisiana law, formation of a valid and enforceable contract requires capacity, consent, a certain object, and a lawful cause. *Id.* The court must find there was a meeting of the minds of the parties to constitute the requirement of consent. *Id.*

It is well settled that a court of appeal may not set aside a trial court's finding of fact in the absence of "manifest error" or unless it is "clearly wrong," and where there is conflict in the testimony, reasonable evaluations of credibility and reasonable inferences of fact should not be disturbed upon review, even though the appellate court may feel that its own evaluations and inferences are as reasonable. *Rosell v. ESCO,* 549 So.2d 840, 844 (La.1989).

In the matter before us, there is no written contract. There is an invoice which shows that Jefferson Door placed an order for cabinets for the Marcantels for a set price. The invoice refers to an attached itemization which gives the quantity and description of the cabinets ordered. However, nothing in any of the documentation indicates type of construction. Jefferson Door also introduced pictures of display cabinets which it maintains was ordered by the Marcantels. All exposed parts appear to be solid wood. In one photograph a door is open to reveal the interior of the cabinet. Testimony at trial shows that the interior is particle board.

The remainder of the evidence is testimony given by the parties. It is undisputed that the Marcantels went to Jefferson Door and requested kitchen cabinets constructed of all wood. The difference in testimony between the Marcantels and Jefferson Door is whether the Marcantels changed their criteria when they discovered the additional cost and time required to get the all wood cabinets, and ultimately ordered cabinets with particle board interior. It is in this regard that the testimony is conflicting. The trial judge accepted the Marcantels' testimony that they thought they were ordering all wood cabinets and, therefore, found there was no meeting of the minds of the parties. Jefferson Door argues, and we agree, that in making that determination the trial judge incorrectly found that the Marcantels were shown all wood, non-custom cabinets in the showroom when they placed their order. The record shows that they were shown cabinets on which all exposed parts were solid wood, and one would only see the particle board interior upon opening the door. Mrs. Marcantel testified she did not look at the interior of the cabinet and Ms. Ziefel only opened a drawer, which was all wood construction, to show the dovetail construction.

Considering our standard of review, and the evidence presented at trial, we cannot find the trial court was manifestly erroneous or clearly wrong in its ultimate finding that no meeting of the minds of the parties occurred, the misstatement of fact notwithstanding. Accordingly, we affirm the trial court's ruling in this regard. Because we find no contract existed between the parties, we also find the trial court's decision to dismiss Jefferson Door's reconventional demand correct. Nevertheless, we find merit in defendant's assertion that the trial court erred in failing to order the Marcantels to return the cabinets. Because there was no contract perfected, ownership of the cabinets did not transfer to the Marcantels. LSA-C.C. art. 2456. Accordingly, we amend the judgment to order the Marcantels to timely return the cabinets to Jefferson Door, and affirm the judgment as amended.

All costs of this appeal are assessed to appellant.

DB Orban Co. v. Lakco Pipe & Supply, Inc.
496 So. 2d 1382 (La. App. 3 Cir. 1986)

DOUCET, Judge

Plaintiff, DB Orban Company, instituted this suit to collect on the unpaid purchase price for steel pipe alleged to have been sold to defendant, Lakco Pipe & Supply, Inc. In its answer, Lakco claimed that the parties failed to agree on a price for the pipe and thus no contract of sale was perfected.

* * * * *

After trial on the merits, the district court rendered a judgment in favor of Lakco on the principal demand, finding that the contract of sale was never perfected. Orban was ordered to pick up the pipe remaining in Lakco's possession and credit Lakco's account for it.

* * * * *

The testimony established that in April 1982, the parties entered into what each believed to be an agreement for the sale of pipe from Orban to Lakco. The parties agreed that the price for the pipe would be $400.00 per net ton based on the actual weight of the pipe.

Lakco picked up a total of 103 segments of pipe between April 29 and June 8, 1982. 73 segments remain in Lakco's possession, the balance having been sold or otherwise disposed of by Lakco. Two invoices, dated May 7 and May 27, 1982, for a total of 28 segments, were paid by Lakco. Upon reviewing the accounts, Rodney Webre, a purchasing agent for Lakco, discovered that Orban was billing Lakco based upon the theoretical weight of the pipe rather than its actual weight.

Lakco was overcharged $730.88, approximately 8%, on the first invoice. A third invoice, dated June 2, 1982, purported to bill Lakco approximately $14,000.00, or 23%, over the correct price as based upon the actual weight of the 73 segments of pipe. This third invoice contained a notation that the billing would be adjusted after all of the pipe has been shipped.

Mr. Webre was informed that Orban billed based on the theoretical weight of the pipe. Later, after all of the pipe had been shipped and weight scale tickets were attained, Orban would compute the sale price based upon actual weight and credit Lakco's account. Mr. Webre was told Lakco would have to pay accordingly. Mr. Webre informed Orban that if Lakco was not billed as agreed upon, Lakco wished to return any pipe in its possession and settle the account. Orban eventually agreed to accept the pipe with freight pre-paid to Houston plus a 15% restocking charge. Lakco would not agree to this or pay for the pipe, and Orban filed this suit.

Orban contends that the trial court incorrectly found that there had been no agreement between the parties as to the price of the pipe, and thus no contract. Orban argues that there was only a misunderstanding regarding the method of billing, not the price. It points out that, based on bills of lading, the difference in price for the pipe received by Lakco is only $2,088.00, or approximately 2½%.

Three circumstances must concur for the perfection of a contract of sale: the thing sold, the price, and the consent. LSA-C.C. art. 2439. In a sale, it is essential that the price be fixed and determined between the parties, otherwise no sale exists. LSA-C.C. art. 2464; *Patton's Heirs v. Moseley*, 186 La. 1088, 173 So. 772 (1937); *Mount Olive Bank v. Jackson Air Taxi, Inc.*, 356 So.2d 1090, (2nd Cir. 1978), writ denied, 359 So.2d 207 (La. 1978). A contract of sale requires that both parties intend the same thing. *Jacob Cohen & Son v. Friedman's Estate*, 13 La.App. 154, 127 So. 412 (La.App. 2nd Cir. 1930).

The evidence establishes that Lakco intended to pay Orban $400 per net ton based on the actual weight of the pipe. Orban, on the other hand, intended to require that Lakco pay $400 per net ton based on the theoretical weight of the pipe with a credit to be issued later. The trial court found that Orban indicated that there was no agreement as to price by its failure to properly invoice Lakco after Lakco protested the amount billed.

The record also reflects a disagreement between the parties concerning what quality pipe was intended to be sold and purchased, J–55 pipe or the lighter grade A–53, or both, and also the quantity of pipe. Orban contends that the sale to Lakco was a "cleanout" sale of all the pipe it had on hand for the reduced actual weight price. However, Lakco denies such was the agreement, maintaining that it only agreed to selectively order the heavier J–55 pipe as needed. Considering all the circumstances, we can find no clear error in the trial court's conclusion that there was no meeting of the minds and therefore no contract between the parties.

* * * * *

Notes and Questions

In each of the foregoing decisions, the court determined that no contract of sale existed. What, exactly, defeated formation of the contract in each case? Could the parties' misunderstandings be characterized as incidents of "error" as contemplated by Articles 1949 through 1952? How does the characterization of a misunderstanding between the parties as bilateral error differ from the characterization of that same misunderstanding as a failure of the "meeting of the minds"? Consider the following commentary of Professor Ronald J. Scalise on the matter.

Ronald J. Scalise Jr., *Rethinking the Doctrine of Nullity*
74 La. L. Rev. 663, 700–03 (2014) (internal citations omitted)

i. A Case Study in Contract Formation

It is hornbook law that "[i]n order to form a valid contract, the parties must have sufficient capacity, give their consent freely for a certain object, and the contract must have a lawful purpose." Omission of or defect in any of the above elements results in nullity, but not all defects or omissions are of equal significance. Where consent to a contract is obtained under duress, the contract is not void ab initio but results in an enforceable contract that must be annulled to deprive it of its effect. A mistake as to price or thing in a sale, on the other hand, may result in no "meetings of the minds" and thus "no enforceable contract" at all. * * * In other words, contracts lacking formative elements are void or absolutely null, whereas those confected defectively are merely voidable or relatively null.

The theory and concept of inexistence is necessary for a complete understanding of juridical acts. As will be demonstrated below, the absence of an element of contract formation—capacity, consent, cause, and object—prevents the formation of a contract or juridical act, so the concept of inexistence is needed for a proper explanation.

* * * * *

(b) Consent

By far, the most common instances of problematic consent involve fraud, duress, or certain types of error, which vitiate consent and render the contract relatively null. For example, when jewelry store employees scheme to make a customer think a ring is worth less than its actual value, fraud can vitiate the contract and render it relatively null.

Be that as it may, there are some vices of consent that prevent contract formation and thus result in absolute nullities or inexistent acts. French doctrine sometimes refers to these kinds of vices that prevent formation of a contract as *erreur-obstacle* because the error serves as an obstacle to the creation of a contract. Although common in French doctrine, the concept of *erreur-obstacle* is not well accepted in Louisiana scholarship. Professor Litvinoff stated that "since the revision of 1825, there is no room in the Louisiana Civil Code for the doctrine of *erreur-obstacle*, because of its careful enumeration of different categories of error, all of which are just vices of consent and give rise to a nullity which is only relative."

Louisiana courts, however, have recognized a kind of error that prevents contract formation, though under the Anglo-American concept rather than the French. What the French consider *erreur-obstacle*, Anglo-American courts find a lack of a "meeting of the minds." Or, "[t]o put the argument in the form in which it is familiar in English law, *erreur-obstacle* is not so much a mistake as a failure of the acceptance to coincide with the offer."

Whatever the name given to the kind of error that prevents contractual formation, the concept is a useful one that has been recognized in the jurisprudence. In
the famous case of *Lyons Milling Co. v. Cusimano*, the plaintiff needed high gluten flour to make macaroni and ordered from the defendant Telegram flour, "f.o.b.
Lyons," Kansas, by which he intended Telegram flour from the Lyons mill. The
defendant, however, sent him Telegram flour from his mill in Hudson, Kansas
(which had a lower gluten content) but paid the freight to transport it from Lyons
to New Orleans. In short, the plaintiff meant one thing, and the defendant meant
another. Thus, the contract lacked the essential element of consent from its formation. In other words, the parties did not have a meeting of the minds on the type of
flour to be bought and sold, or suffered from an *erreur-obstacle*.

Moreover, in *Kaufman v. Audubon Ford/Audubon Imports, Inc.*, the court considered a situation in which one party to an automobile sale contract concealed that he
was the agent for a third party from Taiwan to whom the cars would be exported in
violation of the manufacturer's export agreement policy. The district court found
that the concealment "was sufficient to vitiate the contract for want of consent on
the part of the Appellant." In affirming the district court's opinion, the court of
appeal stated that "there must be a meeting of the minds" and that error could vitiate the necessary consent. In conclusion, the court stated:

> [T]he concealment by the Appellant of the fact that Mr. Vee was the
> intended purchaser and that the Appellant intended to export the vehicles
> was sufficient, therefore, in the case at bar, to vitiate the contract for want of
> consent on the part of the Appellee; thus, there is no valid contract.

* * * * *

Notes and Questions

As the foregoing excerpt explains, certain misunderstandings—those pertaining to
the essential elements of a contract—result in absolute nullity rather than relative nullity. French doctrine refers to this type of misunderstanding as *erreur-obstacle*, because
the error serves as an obstacle to the very creation of the contract. Although common
in French doctrine, the concept of *erreur-obstacle* is not well developed in Louisiana
law; rather, according to our Civil Code, all errors result in relative nullity. La. Civ.
Code arts. 1952, 2032. Louisiana courts thus use an approach similar to the American
common law framework of the "meeting of the minds" to describe problems of error
so profound that the contract never comes into existence in the first place.

B. Consent to Auxiliary Terms

The law of conventional obligations requires that the parties to a contract generally must consent to not only essential terms but to each and every term of the
agreement, no matter how insignificant those terms may seem relative to the contract as a whole. As provided by Article 1943, "An acceptance not in accordance

with the terms of the offer is deemed to be a counteroffer." La. Civ. Code art. 1943. In the law of sales, transactions involving immovable property are governed by this general rule. However, as will be discussed further below in Subpart B.2, the same is not true with respect to sales of movable things.

1. Sales of Immovables
La. Civ. Code art. 1943

Lasalle v. Cannata Corp.
878 So. 2d 622 (La. App. 1 Cir. 2004)

Gaidry, J.

This case involves an alleged agreement to sell a tract of land. The trial court granted summary judgment in favor of defendant, and plaintiff has appealed. For the following reasons, we affirm.

FACTS AND PROCEDURAL HISTORY

Defendant, The Cannata Corporation (Cannata), is the owner of lots 6, 7, and a portion of Lot 8 on the corner of Bernard Street and Highway 90 West in Morgan City, Louisiana. Cannata entered into a listing agreement with A.F. Sauls Real Estate for the sale of that property on September 6, 2001. The listing agreement provides that the price of the property shall be $45,000.00 CASH. The agreement is effective September 6, 2001 and expires on March 30, 2002.

On January 30, 2002, plaintiff, Patrick LaSalle, signed a "Residential Agreement to Purchase and Sell," in which he offered to purchase the property for $43,000.00. This document provided that the sale would be conditioned upon the following: LaSalle's ability to obtain a conventional mortgage and borrow the sum to be determined by the lender at a fixed per annum rate of interest, an appraisal being equal to or greater than the sales price, and acceptance in writing by Cannata with notice given to LaSalle. The document is signed by LaSalle. The listing agent, Robert Businelle, Jr., signed the document as having been received by him at 2 p.m. on January 30, 2002. LaSalle gave Businelle a check in the amount of $1,000.00 as a deposit on the purchase of the property on January 30, 2002, and Businelle deposited the check into the account of A.F. Sauls Real Estate at that time. There is no signed acceptance, nor any evidence of a verbal acceptance of this offer.

On March 18, 2002, LaSalle prepared another document entitled "Seller's Counter Offer to Agreement to Purchase and Sell." This document provides that "the 'Residential Agreement to Purchase and Sell' is acceptable, provided PURCHASER agrees to the following changes: new sales price to be $45,000.00." This "counteroffer," which was signed only by LaSalle, further stated that "ALL OTHER TERMS REMAIN UNCHANGED."

Cannata never signed either document, nor is there any evidence of a verbal acceptance.

LaSalle offered, by certified letter dated April 9, 2002, to close the sale of the property on April 22, 2002, or another date acceptable to the parties. On April 11, 2002, Cannata's counsel informed LaSalle's counsel that there was no sale or agreement to sell. In this letter, Cannata also offered to sell the property to LaSalle for a new sale price of $91,008.00, explaining that the tract of land contained more property than they previously believed.

LaSalle filed this suit, seeking specific performance under the purchase agreement since Cannata refused to sell him the property for $45,000.00. Cannata filed a motion for summary judgment and a hearing was held on November 27, 2002, after which the court granted Cannata's motion for summary judgment, dismissing LaSalle's suit.

LaSalle appealed, asserting that the trial court erred in the following particulars:

1. In granting the motion for summary judgment denying the sale after LaSalle and Cannata agreed on the sale price;

2. In finding that the acceptance by LaSalle was actually a counteroffer;

3. In failing to find that there were sufficient writings to establish a written agreement to sell the property;

4. In failing to find that Cannata should be estopped from refusing to complete the sale; and

5. In failing to find that the real estate broker, as Cannata's agent, bound Cannata to the sale of the property.

DISCUSSION

* * * * *

In order for a contract to be formed, an acceptance must be in all things conformable to the offer. An offer must be accepted as made to constitute a contract. A modification in the acceptance of an offer constitutes a new offer which must be accepted in order to become a binding contract. *Rodrigue v. Gebhardt,* 416 So.2d 160, 161 (La.App. 4 Cir.1982).

LaSalle asserts that Cannata's signing of the listing agreement for the price of $45,000.00 cash was an offer to sell the property for $45,000.00 cash, which LaSalle asserts he accepted in his counter proposal of March 18, 2002. However, both the original "offer" by LaSalle and the "counteroffer" contained conditions which were never accepted by Cannata. The conditions regarding the mortgage and financing, the appraisal, and written acceptance by Cannata varied the terms of the original offer. Thus, acceptance by Cannata was required before an agreement was formed. This acceptance never occurred; therefore, there was no agreement to sell.

There is no genuine issue as to material fact in this case, and summary judgment was appropriate.

DECREE

The December 16, 2002 judgment of the trial court granting Cannata's motion for summary judgment is affirmed. Costs of this appeal are assessed to plaintiff, Patrick LaSalle.

Notes and Questions

1. The requirement of Article 1943 that an acceptance be fully in accordance with the offer, even with respect to nonessential terms, is consistent with the so-called "mirror image rule" of the American common law. Although not directly stated by Article 1943, implicit therein is the notion that an acceptance that does not conform to the offer in every respect is not merely a counteroffer, but also a rejection of the original offer. *See* Saúl Litvinoff, *Consent Revisited: Offer Acceptance Option Right of First Refusal and Contracts of Adhesion in the Revision of the Louisiana Law of Obligations*, 47 LA. L. REV. 699, 739–40 (1987).

2. In sales of immovables, the mechanics of offer and acceptance are often streamlined through the use of a single form to memorialize the parties' consent. In a typical residential real estate transaction, for example, the buyer (often with the assistance of an agent) completes a standard form agreement by filling in the address of the residence and the price the buyer is willing to pay, along with other terms and conditions of the proposed sale. The document, now an offer, is then presented to the seller. If the seller consents to the terms proposed by the buyer, the seller will sign the offer, transforming it into a contract *to sell* (a contract that serves as a precursor to a contract *of sale* and which is addressed fully in Chapter 12: Contracts Preparatory to Sale). If the seller objects to one or more of the buyer's terms, the seller may so indicate on the form itself by striking through text or otherwise amending the document. The form, now a counteroffer, is returned to the buyer for further consideration. This process continues until either a contract to sell is formed or the parties' negotiations fail.

3. Unlike sales of immovables, sales of movables often involve the use of competing forms, which may, and often do, vary from one another. Louisiana's solution to the "battle of the forms" is presented in the next Subpart of this Chapter.

2. Sales of Movables
La. Civ. Code arts. 2601–2602

a. Introduction

In many transactions involving the sale of movables, the communications of the buyer and seller are rarely "mirror images" of one another. Instead, each party typically transmits to the other a preprinted form that recites various terms on which the party purports to agree to be bound. The buyer's "purchase order," for example, may contain language regarding the manner of delivery of the goods, penalties for late delivery, and applicable warranties of quality. The seller's "acknowledgment" may contain terms relating to the manner of payment, interest fees applicable to late payments, and warranty disclaimers or limitations of liability. One or both parties may provide that disputes between the parties shall be arbitrated, provide for a choice of forum for litigation, or provide for choice of law. These forms are usually drafted by attorneys and consist largely of dense, boilerplate language that the parties may not consider as essential to their agreements. Recall that the problem of the exchange of these mismatched forms is known in the American common law as the "battle of the forms."

Under Article 1943, an exchange of such forms that do not match perfectly in every respect does not result in the consummation of a contract, even if the parties' communications agree as to the thing to be sold and the price to be paid. Rather, whereas the first form transmitted between the parties constitutes an offer, the second form, not conforming in every respect to the offer, constitutes a rejection and counteroffer. However, it is seldom the case in commercial transactions that the parties regard their competing communications as a failed contract. Instead, the parties often perform as if a contract existed: the seller ships the goods requested by the buyer and the buyer accepts delivery and pays the price.

Louisiana Civil Code Articles 2601 and 2602 recognize the practical reality that in sales of movables, while the communications of the parties rarely match, the parties generally intend to be bound. Thus Article 2601 articulates a general rule (which admits an exception discussed below) that if the communications of the parties to a potential sale of a movable agree as to *thing* and *price*, a contract of sale is formed, even if the purported acceptance contains terms that vary from those contained in the offer. La. Civ. Code art. 2601. Article 2602 further recognizes that even when the parties' communications do not suffice to form an agreement, a contract nonetheless may be established through the parties' conduct. La. Civ. Code art. 2602.

Articles 2601 and 2602 do not merely address the question of whether a contract of sale exists between the parties. They were also designed to address a problem known in the American common law as the "last shot" doctrine. Under traditional rules of offer and acceptance, if after receiving a counteroffer, the original offeror performs the contemplated contract, that performance constitutes an acceptance of the counteroffer's terms. Since a contract is formed by the document last transmitted (offer) and the performance of the party receiving that document (acceptance), the party who sends the last document has the "last shot" at dictating the contract's terms. This outcome is largely arbitrary and unfairly advantages one party over the other. To alleviate this unfairness, Articles 2601 and 2602 provide several mechanisms for determining what terms from the parties' respective communications will come into the contract. In most cases, the "last shot" doctrine is avoided.

While the fundamental aim of Articles 2601 and 2602 is straightforward, the application of these articles can be challenging. To simplify matters, it is analytically useful to approach the application of these articles by asking two distinct questions: (1) *Is there an enforceable contract between the parties?* and (2) *What are the terms of that contract*? Question 1 is a threshold question that must be answered in the affirmative before the second question can be addressed. Quite obviously, it is unnecessary to address what terms bind the parties if the parties are not bound to a contract of sale at all.

With respect to Question 1—*is there an enforceable contract between the parties?*— the starting point is to examine the communications of the parties under Article 2601. As stated above, that article provides a general rule that if the parties to a potential sale of movables agree on the thing and the price, a contract of sale is formed even if the purported acceptance contains terms additional to or different from those contained in the offer. LA. CIV. CODE art. 2601. The traditional mirror image rule is thus rejected here. Assume, for example, that a prospective purchaser of microchips sends the seller a purchase order requesting 100 microchips of a particular type at the list price provided on the seller's website. In return, the seller sends an acknowledgment in which it agrees to provide 100 microchips at the list price but which also contains a boilerplate arbitration agreement. Under Article 1943 alone, the inclusion of the arbitration clause in the purported acceptance would thwart the formation of the contract. In contrast, Article 2601 now yields a different result: a contract is formed. As explained in more detail below, whether the resulting contract includes the arbitration clause requires additional analysis.

The general rule of contract formation under Article 2601 admits an important exception: if the purported acceptance is "made conditional" on the offeror's acceptance of the additional or different terms, then it does not conclude a contract but operates instead as a *counteroffer*. LA. CIV. CODE art. 2601. This counteroffer must be accepted by the original offeror before a contract of sale is formed. If the counteroffer is accepted by the offeror in a subsequent communication, then a contract of sale is formed through the parties' communications. The rationale for this exception is a simple one: the law will not force a contract on a party who desires to be bound *only if* the other party consents to certain auxiliary terms. Returning to the example of the sale of microchips, if the seller's response to the buyer's offer contains language indicating that the seller will be bound *only if* the buyer agrees to arbitrate disputes, then the buyer's consent to that term will be required for the formation of a contract based on those communications.

If the communications of the parties do not agree with respect to the thing or the price, or if a purported acceptance is "made conditional" on the offeror's acceptance of additional or different terms and the original offeror does not then accept, the question of whether a contract exists requires examination of the parties' conduct, which is called for by Article 2602. Under that provision, even when the communications exchanged by the parties do not suffice to form a contract, a contract of sale may be established "by conduct of both parties that recognizes the existence of the contract." LA. CIV. CODE art. 2602. Thus, if the parties behave as though a contract exists by performing their respective obligations under a purported contract of sale, the law gives effect to their behavior through the recognition of a binding agreement.

The answer to Question 2 — *what are the terms of the contract?* — varies depending upon whether the contract between the parties was formed through their communications (Article 2601) or through their conduct (Article 2602), and, if the contract was formed through the parties' communications, whether the parties are "merchants." Under Article 2601, in a contract formed through the communications of the parties, if at least one party is not a merchant, then additional or different terms contained in the acceptance are regarded as "proposals for modification" that must be accepted by the offeror in order to become a part of the contract. La. Civ. Code art. 2601. This rule rejects the "last shot" doctrine, by preventing the terms in the last document transmitted from automatically controlling the contract. Instead, a "first shot" doctrine is adopted: the terms of the offer will generally control. Returning to the example of the sale of microchips, assume the buyer is not a merchant. If the seller's acknowledgment conforms to the buyer's offer with respect to the number and type of microchips to be sold and the price to be paid but includes an arbitration clause, while a contract is formed between the parties, that contract does not include an agreement to arbitrate. Rather, the arbitration clause is now a "proposal for modification" which must be accepted by the buyer. The same result would apply to any other nonconforming term contained in the seller's acknowledgement. If, for example, the buyer's purchase order states that the chips will be delivered to the buyer's place of business, but the seller's acknowledgment states that buyer must retrieve the chips from the seller's warehouse, then the buyer's communication — the offer — will control.

If *both* parties are merchants, a different rule applies — the additional terms in the acceptance become part of the contract automatically, without the need for the offeror's express consent, unless one of three exceptions applies. First, if additional terms in the acceptance "alter the offer materially," then they do not become part of the contract without the offeror's assent. La. Civ. Code art. 2601. According to the last sentence of Article 2601, terms "alter the offer materially" when their nature is such that it must be presumed that the offeror would not have contracted on those terms. *Id.* Article 2601 comment (g) suggests that arbitration clauses and limitation of liability clauses are examples of such terms. La. Civ. Code art. 2601 cmt. g. Returning again to the example of the sale of microchips, if a seller's acknowledgment conforms to the offer with respect to the number and type of microchips to be sold and the price to be paid, but includes an arbitration clause, while a contract is formed between the parties, that contract does not include an agreement to arbitrate, because that term likely "alter[s] the offer materially."

Second, if the offer "expressly limits the acceptance to the terms of the offer," then additional terms do not become part of the contract without the offeror's assent. La. Civ. Code art. 2601. This exception allows the offeror to avoid being bound by unwanted terms by clearly limiting the possibility of acceptance to the terms the offer contains.

Third, if the offeree is "notified of the offeror's objection to the additional terms within a reasonable time," then the additional terms do not become a part of the contract. *Id.* Instead, they are regarded as proposals for modification that must be accepted by the offeror in order to become part of the agreement.

If the parties' contract was formed not through their communications but instead through their conduct, then Article 2602 provides that the terms of the contract are those "on which the communications of the parties agree" and "any applicable provisions of the suppletive law." LA. CIV. CODE art. 2602. When is a contract formed through the parties' conduct as opposed to the parties' communications? This occurs in two instances. First, this occurs when if the parties' communications do not agree as to thing or price, and yet the parties ultimately perform as if a contract exists. Second, this occurs also when an acceptance is "made conditional" on the offeror's assent to additional or different terms, and, while the offeror does *not* assent to those terms, the parties behave as though a contract exists.

Use Articles 2601 and 2602 to answer the following hypotheticals:

i. Buyer, a distributor of widgets, emails to Seller, a manufacturer of widgets, a purchase order requesting 100 widgets at the list price of $100 each. Seller emails an acknowledgment confirming the order of 100 widgets at the list price. Seller's acknowledgment contains a boilerplate choice of law provision. Buyer's purchase order is silent with respect to the choice of law. *Is there a binding contract of sale? Why or why not? If yes, is the choice of law provision a term of the parties' agreement? Why or why not?*

ii. Buyer, a distributor of widgets, emails to Seller, a manufacturer of widgets, a purchase order requesting 100 widgets at the list price of $100 each. Seller emails an acknowledgment confirming the order of 100 widgets at the list price. Seller's acknowledgment contains a boilerplate arbitration provision. Seller's acknowledgment also states: "Acceptance is conditioned on the buyer's acceptance in writing of all terms contained in this Acknowledgment. To accept the terms contained in this form, sign this document and return to Seller within 10 days of receipt." Buyer does not respond to Seller's Acknowledgment. Seller ships the goods. Buyer accepts delivery and pays the price. *Is there a binding contract of sale? Why or why not? If yes, is the arbitration provision a term of the parties' agreement? Why or why not?*

b. Comparison to the Common Law

Articles 2601 and 2602 were heavily influenced by Uniform Commercial Code section 2-207 ("U.C.C. § 2-207"). Therefore, a complete understanding of these articles and the policies they seek to further requires an appreciation of their common law sources. Carefully read U.C.C. § 2-207 and the excerpt of the law review article that follows comparing U.C.C. § 2-207 to the Louisiana articles. Consider the significance of the slight variations between Louisiana law and U.C.C. § 2-207.

Uniform Commercial Code § 2-207. Additional Terms in Acceptance or Confirmation.±

(1) A definite and seasonable expression of acceptance or a written confirmation which is sent within a reasonable time operates as an acceptance even though it states terms additional to or different from those offered or agreed upon, unless acceptance is expressly made conditional on assent to the additional or different terms.

(2) The additional terms are to be construed as proposals for addition to the contract. Between merchants such terms become part of the contract unless:

(a) the offer expressly limits acceptance to the terms of the offer;

(b) they materially alter it; or

(c) notification of objection to them has already been given or is given within a reasonable time after notice of them is received.

(3) Conduct by both parties which recognizes the existence of a contract is sufficient to establish a contract for sale although the writings of the parties do not otherwise establish a contract. In such case the terms of the particular contract consist of those terms on which the writings of the parties agree, together with any supplementary terms incorporated under any other provisions of this act.

N. Stephan Kinsella, *Smashing the Broken Mirror: The Battle of the Forms, UCC 2-207, and Louisiana's Improvements*, 53 La. L. Rev. 1555, 1557, 1560–1565, 1566–1572 (1993) (internal citations omitted)

* * * * *

II. The Mirror Image Rule and the Last Shot Principle

Under the mirror image rule, a purported acceptance which does not perfectly "mirror" the terms of the offer is not an acceptance; instead, it is a rejection and counteroffer. An ostensible acceptance of *this* counteroffer may, by the same token, be instead a counter-counteroffer. The true acceptance occurs when a party finally starts performing, after receiving the latest counteroffer of the other party. By the performer's acceptance, the contract embodies the terms of the last counteroffer.

In this way the mirror image rule leads to the last shot principle: he who makes the last offer (i.e., the "last shot") before performance/acceptance has his terms locked into the contract.

* * * * *

The last shot principle was largely eliminated by the enactment of UCC section 2-207. Some vestiges of the last shot principle have, however, escaped total elimination; also, the application of section 2-207 is not without uncertainty. Section 2-207 is not yet perfect.

* * * * *

IV. UCC Section 2-207 Problems and Civil Code Solutions

A. Where Acceptance is "Expressly Conditional"

1. The Meaning of "Expressly Conditional"

UCC section 2-207 attempts to solve problems arising from the mirror image rule by eliminating the rule. Under subsection 2-207(1), an "expression of acceptance ... operates as an acceptance even though it states terms additional to or different from those offered . . . ." Thus, the mere fact that an ostensible acceptance does not perfectly mirror the offer does not mean that it cannot operate as an acceptance. By this provision the traditional mirror image rule is eliminated. However, under subsection 2-207(1) the offeror can invoke the mirror image rule, preventing the reply from being an acceptance, if the "acceptance is expressly made conditional on assent to the additional or different terms."

The courts have encountered some problems in deciding whether a purported acceptance was "expressly" made conditional on the offeror's assent to the additional or different terms. For example, in *Roto-Lith, Ltd. v. F.P. Bartlett & Co.*, the court held that a responding document which contained a condition (a disclaimer) was expressly conditional and thus did not operate as an acceptance, even though, according to White and Summers, this holding was inconsistent with the policies embodied in UCC section 2-207. Professor Hawkland suggests that courts should "emphasize the words 'expressly made conditional.'" Thus, to be "expressly conditional," a purported acceptance would have to explicitly state, in unambiguous language, and in a conspicuous position on the form, that acceptance is "expressly conditioned" upon the offeror's assent to such conditions.

Under UCC subsection 2-207(1), an "acceptance" which contains the "expressly conditional" language buried in small type or in an inconspicuous place on the form usually will not be sufficient to prevent the form from being a true acceptance.

> The placement and nature of the qualifying language in the purported acceptance is critical in determining whether or not there is an acceptance under the first part of section 2-207(1), or a rejection and counter-offer under the second part. The qualifying language does not have to use the word "condition" to become expressly conditional within the meaning of the proviso, but it must be stated in such a place, manner and language that the offeror will understand in the commercial setting of the transaction that no acceptance has occurred, despite initial language stating that the offeree is happy to accept.

The jurisprudence is consistent with this reading of subsection 2-207(1). In *Clifford-Jacobs Forging Co. v. Capital Engineering & Manufacturing Co.*, the court stated that an acceptance will be considered a counteroffer only if the acceptance is *expressly* made conditional on *assent* to the additional terms. This provision of the statute has been construed narrowly to apply only to an acceptance which clearly shows that the offeree is unwilling to proceed absent assent to the additional or different terms.

In *Mace Industries, Inc. v. Paddock Pool Equipment Co.*, the court held that to convert an acceptance into a counteroffer under UCC subsection 2-207(1), the conditional nature of the acceptance must be clearly expressed, in a manner sufficient to notify the offeror that the offeree is unwilling to proceed with the transaction unless the additional or different terms are included in the contract.

2. Article 2601 — Omission of "Expressly" — Apparent Disadvantages

Article 2601, in stating that an "expression of acceptance . . . suffices to form a contract . . . unless acceptance is made conditional on the offeror's acceptance of the additional or different terms," does not require the acceptance to be *expressly* conditional, unlike UCC subsection 2-207(1). This appears to be, at first glance, a major and unfortunate change from the wording of section 2-207, for it will be easier for an "acceptance" to fail to be a true acceptance, because the conditioning need not be express.

Thus, under Article 2601, the communications between the parties will fail to form a contract more frequently than under the UCC. Where subsequent conduct of the parties nevertheless recognizes the existence of a contract, suppletive terms, not those of (one of) the parties, will define the contract. Consequently, there will be more resort to Article 2602, which covers this situation and supplies suppletive terms, than there is to subsection 2-207(3) under the UCC, which also provides for suppletive terms.

An advantage of the "expressly conditioned" language in UCC subsection 2-207(1) is that it allows an ambiguous acceptance — e.g., one which is conditional, but not expressly so — to be held against the offeree. Under Article 2601, a similarly "ambiguous" acceptance possibly would not be held against the offeree, but would instead prevent acceptance altogether, because Article 2601 does not require the conditioning of acceptance to be express; i.e., the absence of the word "expressly" allows more ambiguous conditioning of acceptances to bar formation of a contract. Courts may still attempt to hold ambiguous conditioning of acceptances against the offeree, but will be less able to do so because the removal of the word "expressly" clearly indicates that a court should more often find that there was no acceptance. Lack of the word "expressly" in Article 2601 will allow offerees to condition more ambiguously — i.e., less expressly — their "acceptances" and still avoid the contract being formed on the offeror's terms.

3. Article 2601—Omission of "Expressly"—Advantages

There is, however, some reason in support of such an eased standard for conditioning one's acceptance. Conditions attached to an acceptance (though not expressly), in a sense, still convey a rejection of the offer. If the conditioned acceptance were to form a contract on the offeror's terms, there would exist a situation similar to that arising under the "last shot principle" that revocation of the mirror image rule was meant to eliminate. When an offeree's "acceptance" is, indeed, "conditioned" on the offeror's assent to additional or different terms—even if not "expressly" conditioned—the offeree's "acceptance" is not a true acceptance, technically speaking. Thus, omission of the word "expressly" is an improvement because it will actually remove some of the remaining vestiges of the last shot principle.

Some courts have worried that a more lenient standard for finding no true acceptance, because the acceptance was conditioned, would actually lead to a *resurgence* of the mirror image rule. For example, in *Boese-Hilburn Co. v. Dean Machinery Co.*, the court stated:

> [T]his court believes that the drafters of the Uniform Commercial Code, by use of the language "expressly made conditional," clearly intended that an acceptance which merely implied that it was "conditional" on an offeror's assent to a different or additional provision was insufficient to convert an acceptance into a rejection and a counteroffer. Otherwise, many of the problems which prompted the drafting and adoption of U.C.C. § 2-207 would not be alleviated and the specter of the "mirror image" rule would still haunt the marketplace.

In this case, the court was concerned that a looser standard for finding that an acceptance is "conditional" may lead to an increase in mirror image results.

The court's concern appears to be unfounded, for, rather than finding that a failed acceptance is a counteroffer—whose terms will rule if the offeror then performs (an example of the last shot principle)—the court could find that there has been no contract formed at all by the writings of the parties, and instead resort to suppletive law, as provided in UCC subsection 2-207(3) and in new Louisiana Civil Code article 2602. That is, when a reply to an offer is conditioned so that it is not an acceptance, the offeree does not get his terms embodied in the contract if the offeror then performs; rather, suppletive terms are applied.

Let us assume a situation where no contract exists under UCC subsection 2-207(1), but the parties nevertheless perform. A court can proceed to analyze contract formation in one of two ways.

> First, a court can take the common law, *Roto-Lith,* approach and find that the second document is a counteroffer and hold that subsequent performance by the party who sent the first document constitutes acceptance. This approach gives one party (who fortuitously sent the second document) all of his terms. In our view, Code draftsmen did not choose to take this approach. Instead, they proceeded on to contract formation via section 2-207(3) . . . .

Similarly, under Articles 2601 and 2602, if an "acceptance" fails to form a contract because it is conditioned on additional or different terms, instead of being a counteroffer and the offeree getting his terms under the last shot principle if the offeror were to perform, Article 2602 would instead look to the suppletive law to determine the terms of the ensuing contract. Thus, making it easier to condition one's acceptance by not requiring it to be "express" will lead to greater use of the suppletive law, not to increased last-shot results. And while increased occurrence of last-shot results may be undesirable, increased resort to suppletive law may, in many situations, be a beneficial change in the law, because it would in some situations prevent the counterofferor from getting the "last shot."

If the parties go on to perform the contract, where the offeree conditioned his acceptance (though not expressly), there is some justice in holding them equally "at fault" for failing to reach an agreement by their communications, so that neither is in a position to complain about suppletive law determining the terms of the contract. In a sense, then, a more equitable system results from the removal of the word "expressly" and the corresponding increased ability of an offeree to condition his offer, because neither offeror nor offeree receives an inordinate advantage; rather, where there has been acceptance only by performance, both parties, having performed, are subjected to the suppletive law as mandated in Article 2602.

*　*　*　*　*

C. Additional and Different Terms as Proposals for Modification

When a UCC subsection 2-207(1) expression of acceptance has been found, the rules of subsection 2-207(2) govern the fate of the additional and different terms in the acceptance. Where the contract is not "between merchants," subsection 2-207(2) provides that "additional terms are to be construed as proposals for addition to the contract." The subsection is silent with respect to the manner of acceptance of these proposals, but apparently they can be accepted in the ordinary manner by the offeror.

Although the words "different terms" are not included in UCC subsection 2-207(2), presumably any different terms in the offeree's reply are also to be treated as proposals which can be accepted by the offeror. The wording of section 2-207 is somewhat unclear here, but it is likely that omission of the "different terms" language, if it was intended at all, relates to the second sentence of subsection 2-207(2), which applies to a contract between merchants.

However, there is another possible explanation for the lack of the "different terms" language in UCC subsection 2-207(2). "Why the failure to treat 'different' terms? The answer is simple and startling—*the present Code contains a critical printer's omission.*" It appears that subsection 2-207(2) was supposed to include the "or different" language, but "[i]t was lost as the result of a typographical or printer's error."

In any event, it appears that, under UCC section 2-207, if an acceptance (not between merchants) contains additional or different terms, these terms are to be treated as proposals for modification, which may be accepted or not by the offeror.

Article 2601 is drafted in more explicit language, providing that "the additional or different terms" in an acceptance "are regarded as proposals for modification and must be accepted by the offeror in order to become a part of the contract." Thus, mere implications in UCC section 2-207—that additional terms are proposals for modification that may be accepted by the offeror, and that different terms are also proposals for modification—are made explicit in Article 2601. This reduction of uncertainty and ambiguity is an improvement.

D. Additional Terms that "Materially Alter" the Contract

1. "Different Terms" and Acceptance by Silence

Under UCC section 2-207, between merchants, additional terms—but not different terms—can become accepted, effectively, by the silence of the offeror, unless the offeror in some manner objects to the additional terms, or the terms "materially alter" the contract. Presumably, under current interpretations of section 2-207, different terms by their nature "materially alter" the contract and thus cannot be accepted by the mere silence of the offeror. However, as discussed above, there is some reason to think that it should be possible for different terms, as well as additional terms, to be accepted by silence, because the "or different terms" language may have been erroneously left out of subsection 2-207(2).

Article 2601, paragraph 2—the analog of UCC subsection 2-207(2)—provides that, between merchants, "additional terms become part of the contract unless certain events occur." If it is true that the drafters of the UCC originally intended to include the "or different terms" language in subsection 2-207(2), it is unfortunate that this omission is continued in Article 2601. It is not obvious that there is any reason for allowing "additional," but not "different," terms to be accepted by silence, except perhaps for the weak reason that an offeror may be presumed to object to any different term as it contradicts his offer. However, "additional" terms appear to contradict the offer also, yet they may be accepted by silence. It is suggested that the silence of the offeror should operate as an acceptance of "different" terms under paragraph 2 of Article 2601 in the same manner as the silent acceptance of "additional" terms. To this extent, Article 2601—as well as, of course, UCC section 2-207(2)—should be amended.

2. "Materially Alter"

In considering whether the offeror has accepted additional terms by silence, the principal difficulty has been in deciding whether the additional terms "materially alter" the contract. As Professor Hawkland explains,

> [t]he concept "materially alter" is not defined by section 2-207(2), but it is explained by comment 4. That comment suggests that any term is a material alteration if its incorporation into the contract without express awareness by the other party would result in surprise or hardship . . . .
>
> Comments 4 and 5 give examples of terms in the offeree's form which do and do not materially alter the contract created by the exchange of forms,

but they are not particularly helpful . . . because they merely indicate the
way trade usage functions under the Code.

Thus, UCC section 2-207 does not define "materially alter," and the comments do
not make the language much clearer.

Article 2601 also provides a definition of "materially alter" that is an improvement over the indefinite wording of UCC section 2-207. Article 2601 states that
"[a]dditional terms alter the offer materially when their nature is such that it must
be presumed that the offeror would not have contracted on those terms." This functional test should make it easier for courts and merchants to predict whether a contract has been formed.

Comment (g) to Article 2601 elaborates on the text of the article. It states that a
term materially alters an offer when it can be presumed that "the offeror would not
enter a contract with that term." This wording is not as accurate as the wording of
Article 2601, paragraph 2, because of the use of the word "a." It would be beneficial to
substitute the word "the" for "a" in the comment. It is not true that a term is material
because the offeror would *never* contract with that term, in "a" contract. Certainly,
"a" contract could be written, which would include the "material" term, but which
would also be acceptable to the offeror given other terms to complement and make
up for the "material" term. Rather, a term should be considered material if *the* contract under consideration would not be accepted if it contained the material term.

While containing some minor semantic problems, however, the material alteration test in Article 2601 is helpful.

3. Is it the Offer, or is it the Contract, that is "Materially Altered"?

A final comment can be made here. UCC subsection 2-207(2) states that additional terms "become part of the contract unless . . . they materially alter it." The
word "it" apparently refers to the *contract*. However, it is not obvious whether the
offeree's additional terms (may) materially alter the offer, or the contract. If the
additional term is so material that it prevents formation of a contract, there is, it
would seem, no contract to alter. There is, however, an offer, and thus it is better to
speak of terms materially altering the *offer*.

Article 2601, in a change from the wording of UCC subsection 2-207(2), states
that "[b]etween merchants . . . additional terms become part of the contract unless
they alter the *offer* materially." While this distinction is somewhat technical, it does
improve the clarity and structure of the law.

E. Where the Offer Limits Acceptance to the Terms of the Offer

Between merchants, by UCC subsection 2-207(2), additional, but not different,
terms can be accepted by silence of the offeror, unless "the offer expressly limits acceptance to the terms of the offer" or "notification of objection to them has
already been given." If the offer prohibits the formation of a contract on any terms
other than those in the offer, such restriction would be an objection by the offeror
to any additional terms, which is contemplated in subsections 2-207(2)(a) and (c).

Thus, any additional terms in the offeree's acceptance would fall, under these subsections, because objection to them would have already been made by the offeror.

1. Ambiguity of Offer-Restrictions in UCC Subsections 2-207(a) and (c) Abolished

White and Summers offer another possible interpretation of such restrictive language in the offer:

> On the other hand if the offer is read to mean "This offer can be accepted only by a document that contains neither additional nor different terms," any response that contains either additional or different terms would not constitute an acceptance and the case would fall entirely outside 2-207(1) and 2-207(2).

A similar interpretation is less plausible under the language of Article 2601, which states that "[b]etween merchants . . . additional terms become part of the contract unless . . . the offer expressly limits the acceptance to the terms of the offer . . . in all of which cases the additional terms do not become a part of the contract." This language implies that, even where the offeror restricts his offer, and the offeree nevertheless includes additional terms in his acceptance, the additional terms do not become part of the contract, but "the contract" would still exist. Comment (e) to Article 2601 supports this reading: "when both parties are merchants and the offer limits the acceptance to the terms of the offer . . . the contract is formed in the original terms of the offer." Thus, Article 2601 is less ambiguous in this respect than is UCC subsection 2-207(2) because the second possible interpretation of offer-restrictions is ruled out.

2. Reduction in Redundancy

UCC subsection 2-207(2)(a) prevents any additional terms from becoming part of the contract where "the offer expressly limits acceptance to the terms of the offer." Subsection 2-207(2)(c) has an identical effect on additional terms when "notification of objection to them has already been given." There is a redundancy here because, if the offer limits acceptance to its terms (satisfying subsection 2-207(2)(a)), the restriction is also a "notification" of objection to additional terms (satisfying subsection 2-207(2)(c)). Thus, under both subsections, the additional terms would not become part of the contract where the offer limits acceptance to its terms.

Article 2601 is very similar in operation to these two provisions; however, it slightly simplifies the redundancy by providing that, "between merchants . . . additional terms become part of the contract unless . . . the offeree is notified of the offeror's objection to the additional terms within a reasonable time." Article 2601 omits the unnecessary language of UCC subsection 2-207(2)(c) which addresses the situation where notification of objection has already been given, because this situation is already covered where Article 2601 provides "the offer expressly limits the acceptance to the terms of the offer," which is the analog of 2-207(2)(a). Thus, Article 2601 combines the redundant aspects of subsections 2-207(2)(a) and (c) into a more general rule.

* * * * *

Notes and Questions

1. As the foregoing reading suggests, one of the more challenging issues faced by courts applying U.C.C. § 2-207 is the question of whether a purported acceptance is "expressly made conditional" on the offeror's assent to additional or different terms and thereby transformed into a counteroffer. In *Dorton v. Collins & Aikman Corp.*, 453 F.2d 1161 (6th Cir. 1972), the court was called upon to determine if an arbitration provision contained in a communication sent by a seller in response to a buyer's offer to purchase carpets was part of the parties' contract. The document stated, "The acceptance of your order is subject to all of the terms and conditions on the face and reverse side hereof, including arbitration . . . ." *Id.* at 1164. The document did not require that the buyer accept the terms of the document expressly, but provided that assent to such terms could occur through a number of means, including "when buyer has received delivery of the whole or any part thereof, or when buyer has otherwise assented to the terms and conditions . . . ." *Id.* The buyer did not respond to the seller's communication but did accept and pay for the carpets. When a dispute later arose regarding the quality of the carpets, the seller insisted that the matter must be resolved in arbitration.

The court held that for an acceptance to be "expressly made conditional" on the offeror's assent to additional or different terms, the acceptance must "clearly reveal[] that the offeree is unwilling to proceed with the transaction unless he is assured of the offeror's assent to the additional or different terms therein." *Id.* at 1168. Applying this standard, the court held that the seller's document was not "expressly made conditional" on the buyer's asset to its terms; rather, the seller's communication was an "acceptance" of the buyer's offer. Because both parties were merchants, the question of whether the arbitration provision — an additional term — became part of the contract turned on whether it "materially alter[ed]" the offer. The court remanded for a determination on that issue, which it characterized as a question of fact.

In another case, *Diamond Fruit Growers, Inc. v. Krack Corp.*, 794 F.2d 1440 (9th Cir. 1986), two parties involved in a sale of metal tubing disputed whether a limitation of liability for defects appearing in a document sent by the seller to the buyer was contained in the parties' agreement. In response to the buyer's order, the seller sent a form stating that its acceptance was "expressly made conditional to purchaser's acceptance of the terms and provisions of the acknowledgment form." *Id.* at 1441. Noting that the language in the seller's document tracked exactly the language of U.C.C. § 2-207(1), it held that the seller's acceptance was indeed "expressly made conditional" on the buyer's acceptance of its terms and conditions, and thus properly characterized as a counteroffer. However, the court went on to hold that the buyer had not "assented" to the terms of the counteroffer as required to form a contract on those terms. Rejecting the seller's argument that the buyer had accepted its terms through its behavior — accepting delivery of and paying for the tubing — the court found that a contract was formed not through the parties' *communications*, but through the parties' *conduct*, and thus the terms of the contract were those on which the parties' communications agreed and the terms of suppletive law. As a result, the limitation of liability was not enforceable. The court premised its holding on the policies implicit in U.C.C. § 2-207, stating:

> One of the principles underlying section 2-207 is neutrality. If possible, the section should be interpreted so as to give neither party to a contract an advantage simply because it happened to send the first or in some cases the last form. . . . At common law, the offeree/counterofferor gets all of its terms simply because it fired the last shot in the exchange of forms. Section 2-207(3) does away with this result by giving neither party the terms it attempted to impose unilaterally on the other. Instead, all of the terms on which the parties' forms do not agree drop out, and the U.C.C. supplies the missing terms.
>
> Generally, this result is fair because both parties are responsible for the ambiguity in their contract. The parties could have negotiated a contract and agreed on its terms, but for whatever reason, they failed to do so. Therefore, neither party should get its terms. . . . Application of section 2-207(3) is more equitable than giving one party its terms simply because it sent the last form. Further, the terms imposed by the code are presumably equitable and consistent with public policy because they are statutorily imposed.

Id. at 1444–45 (internal citations omitted).

As is discussed in the foregoing law review article, Article 2601 deviates from U.C.C. § 2-207 in a significant way. U.C.C. § 2-207(1) states that an acceptance that is "expressly made conditional" on the offeror's acceptance of additional or different terms is not an acceptance at all but is instead a counteroffer. Article 2601 does not use the term "expressly," but rather states that an acceptance that is "made conditional" on the offeror's acceptance of additional or different terms is not an acceptance. Scholars suggest that this variation in language means that it is easier to condition one's acceptance on the offeror's assent to additional or different terms. However, like U.C.C. § 2-207, Article 2601 fails to state what is required for the offeror's acceptance of those terms to be effective. Is an express acceptance of the additional or different terms required? Will the offeror's mere silence or performance of the contact suffice? Which approach is more in line with the intent of U.C.C. § 2-207?

2. Article 2601 provides that between non-merchants, "additional *or different* terms are regarded as proposals for modification and must be accepted by the offeror in order to become a part of the contract" (emphasis added). La. Civ. Code art. 2601. Between merchants, "additional terms become part of the contract," but *different* terms are not mentioned. *Id.* Should different terms be treated identically to additional terms in contracts between merchants? What does it mean to say that a different term is regarded as a "proposal for modification"? The treatment of different terms in the common law is summarized in the following case.

Gardner Zemke Co. v. Dunham Bush, Inc.

850 P.2d 319 (N.M. 1993)

FRANCHINI, Justice.

* * * * *

I.

Acting as the general contractor on a Department of Energy (DOE) project, Gardner Zemke issued its Order to Dunham Bush for air-conditioning equipment, known as chillers, to be used in connection with the project. The Order contained a one-year manufacturer's warranty provision and the requirement that the chillers comply with specifications attached to the Order. Dunham Bush responded with its preprinted Acknowledgment containing extensive warranty disclaimers, a statement that the terms of the Acknowledgment controlled the parties' agreement, and a provision deeming silence to be acquiescence to the terms of the Acknowledgment.

The parties did not address the discrepancies in the forms exchanged and proceeded with the transaction. Dunham Bush delivered the chillers, and Gardner Zemke paid for them. Gardner Zemke alleges that the chillers provided did not comply with their specifications and that they incurred additional costs to install the nonconforming goods. Approximately five or six months after start up of the chillers, a DOE representative notified Gardner Zemke of problems with two of the chillers. In a series of letters, Gardner Zemke requested on-site warranty repairs. Through its manufacturer's representative, Dunham Bush offered to send its mechanic to the job site to inspect the chillers and absorb the cost of the service call only if problems discovered were within any component parts it provided. Further, Dunham Bush required that prior to the service call a purchase order be issued from the DOE, to be executed by Dunham Bush for payment for their services in the event their mechanic discovered problems not caused by manufacturing defects. Gardner Zemke rejected the proposal on the basis that the DOE had a warranty still in effect for the goods and would not issue a separate purchase order for warranty repairs.

Ultimately, the DOE hired an independent contractor to repair the two chillers. The DOE paid $24,245.00 for the repairs and withheld $20,000.00 from its contract with Gardner Zemke. This breach of contract action then ensued, with Gardner Zemke alleging failure by Dunham Bush to provide equipment in accordance with the project plans and specifications and failure to provide warranty service.

II.

On cross-motions for summary judgment, the trial court granted partial summary judgment in favor of Dunham Bush, ruling that its Acknowledgment was a counteroffer to the Gardner Zemke Order and that the Acknowledgment's warranty limitations and disclaimers were controlling. Gardner Zemke filed an application for interlocutory appeal from the partial summary judgment in this Court, which was denied. A bench trial was held in December 1991, and the trial court again ruled the Acknowledgment was a counteroffer which Gardner Zemke accepted by silence and that under the warranty provisions of the Acknowledgment, Gardner Zemke was not entitled to damages.

On appeal, Gardner Zemke raises two issues: (1) the trial court erred as a matter of law in ruling that the Acknowledgment was a counteroffer; and (2) Gardner Zemke proved breach of contract and contract warranty, breach of code warranties, and damages.

III.

[The court reviewed the issue of whether Dunham Bush's Acknowledgment was "expressly made conditional" on Gardner Zemke's assent to the terms and conditions contained therein. The court ultimately remanded the issue to the trial court for further consideration.]

In the event the trial court concludes that the Dunham Bush Acknowledgment constituted an acceptance, it will face the question of which terms will control in the exchange of forms. In the interest of judicial economy, and because this determination is a question of law, we proceed with our analysis.

IV.

The Gardner Zemke Order provides that the "[m]anufacturer shall replace or repair all parts found to be defective during initial year of use at no additional cost." Because the Order does not include any warranty terms, Article 2 express and implied warranties arise by operation of law. Section 55-2-313 (express warranties), § 55-2-314 (implied warranty of merchantability), § 55-2-315 (implied warranty of fitness for a particular purpose). The Dunham Bush Acknowledgment contains the following warranty terms.

> WARRANTY: We agree that the apparatus manufactured by the Seller will be free from defects in material and workmanship for a period of one year under normal use and service and when properly installed: and our obligation under this agreement is limited solely to repair or replacement at our option, at our factories, of any part or parts thereof which shall within one year from date of original installation or 18 months from date of shipment from factory to the original purchaser, whichever date may first occur be returned to us with transportation charges prepaid which our examination shall disclose to our satisfaction to have been defective. THIS AGREEMENT TO REPAIR OR REPLACE DEFECTIVE PARTS IS EXPRESSLY IN LIEU OF AND IS HEREBY DISCLAIMER OF ALL OTHER EXPRESS WARRANTIES, AND IS IN LIEU OF AND IN DISCLAIMER AND EXCLUSION OF ANY IMPLIED WARRANTIES OF MERCHANTABILITY AND FITNESS FOR A PARTICULAR PURPOSE, AS WELL AS ALL OTHER IMPLIED WARRANTIES, IN LAW OR EQUITY, AND OF ALL OTHER OBLIGATIONS OR LIABILITIES ON OUR PART. THERE ARE NO WARRANTIES WHICH EXTEND BEYOND THE DESCRIPTION HEREOF. . . . Our obligation to repair or replace shall not apply to any

apparatus which shall have been repaired or altered outside our factory in
any way . . . .

* * * * *

The language of the statute makes it clear that "additional" terms are subject to
the provisions of Section 2-207(2). However, a continuing controversy rages among
courts and commentators concerning the treatment of "different" terms in a Section 2-207 analysis. While Section 2-207(1) refers to both "additional or different"
terms, Section 2-207(2) refers only to "additional" terms. The omission of the word
"different" from Section 55-2-207(2) gives rise to the questions of whether "different" terms are to be dealt with under the provisions of Section 2-207(2), and if not,
how they are to be treated. That the terms in the Acknowledgment are "different"
rather than "additional" guides the remainder of our inquiry and requires that we
join the fray. Initially, we briefly survey the critical and judicial approaches to the
problem posed by "different" terms.

One view is that, in spite of the omission, "different" terms are to be analyzed
under Section 2-207(2). 2 Hawkland, § 2-207:03 at 168. The foundation for this
position is found in Comment 3, which provides "[w]hether or not additional or
different terms will become part of the agreement depends upon the provisions of
Subsection (2)." Armed with this statement in Comment 3, proponents point to the
ambiguity in the distinction between "different" and "additional" terms and argue
that the distinction serves no clear purpose. *Steiner v. Mobile Oil Corp.*, 20 Cal.3d
90, 141 Cal.Rptr. 157, 165-66 n. 5, 569 P.2d 751, 759-60 n. 5 (1977); *Boese-Hilburn
Co. v. Dean Machinery Co.*, 616 S.W.2d 520, 527 (Mo.Ct.App.1981). Following this
rationale in this case, and relying on the observation in Comment 4 that a clause
negating implied warranties would "materially alter" the contract, the Dunham
Bush warranty terms would not become a part of the contract, and the Gardner
Zemke warranty provision, together with the Article 2 warranties would control.
§ 55-2-207(2)(b).

Another approach is suggested by Duesenberg and King who comment that the
ambiguity found in the treatment of "different" and "additional" terms is more
judicially created than statutorily supported. While conceding that Comment 3
"contributes to the confusion," they also admonish that "the Official Comments
do not happen to be the statute." Duesenberg & King, § 3.05 at 3-52. Observing
that "the drafters knew what they were doing, and that they did not sloppily fail to
include the term 'different' when drafting subsection (2)," Duesenberg and King
postulate that a "different" term in a responsive document operating as an acceptance can never become a part of the parties' contract under the plain language of
the statute. *Id.* § 3.03[1] at 3-38.

The reasoning supporting this position is that once an offeror addresses a subject
it implicitly objects to variance of that subject by the offeree, thereby preventing
the "different" term from becoming a part of the contract by prior objection and
obviating the need to refer to "different" terms in Section 55-2-207(2). *Id.* § 3.05[1]

at 3-77; *Air Prods. & Chems. Inc. v. Fairbanks Morse, Inc.*, 58 Wis.2d 193, 206 N.W.2d 414, 423-25 (1973). Professor Summers lends support to this position. White & Summers, § 1-3 at 34. Although indulging a different analysis, following this view in the case before us creates a result identical to that flowing from application of the provisions of Section 2-207(2) as discussed above—the Dunham Bush warranty provisions fall out, and the stated Gardner Zemke and Article 2 warranty provisions apply.

Yet a third analysis arises from Comment 6, which in pertinent part states:

> Where clauses on confirming forms sent by both parties conflict each party must be assumed to object to a clause of the other conflicting with one on the confirmation sent by himself. As a result the requirement that there be notice of objection which is found in Subsection (2) is satisfied and the conflicting terms do not become a part of the contract. The contract then consists of the terms originally expressly agreed to, terms on which the confirmations agree, and terms supplied by this act, including Subsection (2).

The import of Comment 6 is that "different" terms cancel each other out and that existing applicable code provisions stand in their place. The obvious flaws in Comment 6 are the use of the words "confirming forms," suggesting the Comment applies only to variant confirmation forms and not variant offer and acceptance forms, and the reference to Subsection 55-2-207(2)—arguably dealing only with "additional" terms—in the context of "different" terms. Of course, Duesenberg and King remind us that Comment 6 "is only a comment, and a poorly drawn one at that." Duesenberg & King, § 3.05[1] at 3-79.

The analysis arising from Comment 6, however, has found acceptance in numerous jurisdictions including the Tenth Circuit. *Daitom, Inc. v. Pennwalt Corp.*, 741 F.2d 1569, 1578-79 (10th Cir.1984). Following a discussion similar to the one we have just indulged, the court found this the preferable approach. *Id.* at 1579; *accord Southern Idaho Pipe & Steel Co. v. Cal-Cut Pipe & Supply, Inc.*, 98 Idaho 495, 503-04, 567 P.2d 1246, 1254-55 (1977), *appeal dismissed and cert. denied*, 434 U.S. 1056, 98 S. Ct. 1225, 55 L.Ed.2d 757 (1978). Professor White also finds merit in this analysis. White & Summers, § 1-3 at 33-35. Application of this approach here cancels out the parties' conflicting warranty terms and allows the warranty provisions of Article 2 to control.

We are unable to find comfort or refuge in concluding that any one of the three paths drawn through the contours of Section 2-207 is more consistent with or true to the language of the statute. We do find that the analysis relying on Comment 6 is the most consistent with the purpose and spirit of the Code in general and Article 2 in particular. We are mindful that the overriding goal of Article 2 is to discern the bargain struck by the contracting parties. However, there are times where the conduct of the parties makes realizing that goal impossible. In such cases, we find guidance in the Code's commitment to fairness, Section 55-1-102(3); good faith, Sections 55-1-203 & -2-103(1)(b); and conscionable conduct, Section 55-2-302.

While Section 2-207 was designed to avoid the common law result that gave the advantage to the party sending the last form, we cannot conclude that the statute was intended to shift that advantage to the party sending the first form. Such a result will generally follow from the first two analyses discussed. We adopt the third analysis as the most even-handed resolution of a difficult problem. We are also aware that under this analysis even though the conflicting terms cancel out, the Code may provide a term similar to one rejected. We agree with Professor White that "[a]t least a term so supplied has the merit of being a term that the draftsmen considered fair." White & Summers, § 1-3 at 35.

Due to our disposition of this case, we do not address the second issue raised by Gardner Zemke. On remand, should the trial court conclude a contract was formed under Section 2-207(1), the conflicting warranty provisions in the parties' forms will cancel out, and the warranty provisions of Article 2 will control.

* * * * *

Notes and Questions

1. As the foregoing case makes clear, the treatment of different terms in contracts between merchants is somewhat uncertain under the common law. Common law scholars generally agree that different and additional terms should be treated identically in contracts between non-merchants; that is, different terms, like additional terms, are to be treated as proposals for addition to of the contract. In contrast, quite a bit of conflict surrounds the question of how different terms should be treated in contracts between merchants. The minority position espouses the view that, between merchants, different terms should be treated in the same manner as additional terms—that is, they should become part of the contract automatically unless one of the three exceptions previously discussed applies. The majority view is that different terms should *not* automatically become part of the contract but should instead always be treated as proposals for addition which must be accepted by the offeror. What reasons can you think of to support the majority view? The minority view? Read Article 2601 and the accompanying comments carefully. Does the language of Article 2601 suggest that the majority or the minority view is more appropriate in Louisiana? Note that if different terms are not uniformly regarded as "proposals for modification," then they will become part of a contract between merchants automatically unless one of the three exceptions articulated in the second paragraph of Article 2601 applies. Consider how, practically, this could be accomplished.

2. In all cases in which a different term is regarded as a proposal for addition to the contract, additional questions remain regarding the effect that this proposal has on the terms of the contract. A minority of common law courts and scholars espouse the "fallout rule." Under the fallout rule, if an acceptance contains a term different from one contained in the offer, the term provided by the acceptance falls out of the contract, and the term contained in the offer controls. A majority of common law courts and scholars reject the fallout rule and instead espouse the "knockout rule."

Under the knockout rule, the conflicting terms in the offer and acceptance cancel each other out entirely, leaving the issue addressed by those terms to be governed by suppletive law. What reasons can you think of to support the majority view? The minority view? Which view does Louisiana law appear to endorse? Read Article 2601 and the accompanying comments carefully.

3. In 2003, the National Conference of Commissioners on Uniform State Laws ("NCCUSL") and the American Law Institute ("ALI") approved a set of revisions to Article 2 of the Uniform Commercial Code. Included in these revisions was a wholesale revision of U.C.C. § 2-207. The proposed revision retained the Uniform Commercial Code's rejection of the mirror image rule but attempted to simplify the question of what terms are included in a contract for the sale of goods. Instead of providing a specific mechanism for the inclusion of certain terms, revised U.C.C. § 2-207 adopts a more neutral approach under which conflicting terms are not included in the contract no matter how it is formed.

Proposed 2003 Revision Uniform Commercial Code § 2-207. Terms of Contract, Effect of Confirmation[±]

Subject to Section 2-202 [writing requirements], if (i) conduct by both parties recognizes a contract although their records do not otherwise establish a contract, (ii) a contract is formed by offer and acceptance, or (iii) a contract formed by any manner is confirmed by a record that contains terms additional to or different from those in the contract being confirmed, the terms of the contract are: (a) terms that appear in the records of both parties; (b) terms, whether in a record or not, to which the parties agree; and (c) terms supplied or incorporated under any provision of this Act.

Although considerable time was spent drafting this proposal, the 2003 revisions to Article 2 were never adopted by any state and were ultimately withdrawn by its sponsors. The official text of U.C.C. § 2-207 now matches the original, pre-revision law.

4. The Convention on the International Sale of Goods ("CISG"), like the Uniform Commercial Code, contains a provision aimed at addressing the problem of competing forms exchanged between buyers and sellers of goods. Consider how the approach of the CISG differs from that of the Uniform Commercial Code and Louisiana law.

United Nations Convention on the International Sale of Goods art. 19[±]

(1) A reply to an offer which purports to be an acceptance but contains additions, limitations or other modifications is a rejection of the offer and constitutes a counter-offer.

[±] Uniform Commercial Code, Copyright © by The American Law Institute and the National Conference of Commissioners on Uniform State Laws. Reproduced with the permission of the Permanent Editorial Board for the Uniform Commercial Code. All rights reserved.

[±] Reprinted with permission of the UNCITRAL Secretariat.

(2) However, a reply to an offer which purports to be an acceptance but contains additional or different terms which do not materially alter the terms of the offer constitutes an acceptance, unless the offeror, without undue delay, objects orally to the discrepancy or dispatches a notice to that effect. If he does not so object, the terms of the contract are the terms of the offer with the modifications contained in the acceptance.

(3) Additional or different terms relating, among other things, to the price, payment, quality and quantity of goods, place and time of delivery, extent of one party's liability to the other or the settlement of disputes are considered to alter the terms of the offer materially.

Chapter 4

Things Which May Be Sold

A. In General

La. Civ. Code art. 2448

11 Beudant, *Cours de Droit Civil Français* §§ 5, 9 (2d ed. 1938) (*translated in* Saúl Litvinoff, Sale and Lease in the Louisiana Jurisprudence 2–3 (4th rev. ed. 1997) (footnotes omitted))

5. Legal Definition. By the terms of Article 1582, Line 1 [La. C.C. art. 2439], the contract of sale is an agreement by which one party obligates himself to deliver a thing and the other to pay for it.

* * * * *

9. Our two articles unduly restrict the role of the sale by presenting it exclusively as a contract translative of movable or immovable property. One may sell or buy anything, either "goods" in the technical sense or the word or "rights"; consequently, all rights of which things are the object may be bought and sold and not only movable or immovable property. [*Cf.* La. C.C. art. 2448.]

The owner of a movable or immovable object may sell it. He may also sell the usufruct of the thing and reserve the property; he may sell a servitude on a thing if it is an immovable, in a word transfer any real right; the sale is the method for constituting or transferring by onerous title any dismemberments of property. Thus Article 579 mentions the will as a method of establishing a usufruct. [*Cf.* La. C.C. art. 544.] Article 690 includes "by title" in the number of methods for creating servitudes. [*Cf.* La. C.C. art. 740.] The contract is a title. If the owner establishes the servitude without asking a price it is a donation. If he establishes it in return for a price it is a sale. Furthermore, the owner of a right of usufruct may sell the right that he owns.

Real rights are not the only ones that are susceptible of being sold. A creditor may sell the credit that he has against a third party (Article 1689). [*Cf.* La. C.C. art. 2642.] One to whom a rent is due may sell his right to the rent (Article 1968 and the following). In a word, the sale may have for its object not only things but any property whatever including all kinds of rights. It is inaccurate, therefore, for Article 1582 and 1583 to limit their application to one kind of property.

* * * * *

Notes and Questions

Article 2448 makes clear that "[a]ll things corporeal or incorporeal, susceptible of ownership, may be the object of a contract of sale, unless the sale of a particular thing is prohibited by law." LA. CIV. CODE art. 2448. Thus, the object of a sale may be a corporeal thing, such as a tract of land or an automobile. Also, the object of a sale may be an incorporeal. Incorporeals include rights in things such as predial and personal servitudes as well as personal rights, such as contractual rights. When personal rights are the object of a contract, the parties' agreement is governed by the rules on Assignment of Rights. LA. CIV. CODE arts. 2642–54. Those provisions are covered at the end of this Chapter.

The sole limitation mentioned in Article 2448 is a prohibition of sales of things "prohibited by law." This mirrors the general rule for contracts, found in Article 1971, which provides that the parties are "free to contract for any object that is lawful . . . ." Thus, the sale of the succession of a living person is absolutely null, LA. CIV. CODE art. 1976, just as is a sale of illegal drugs. *See, e.g.,* LA. REV. STAT. §§ 40:966–70 (providing criminal penalties for distribution of certain narcotic drugs). Recall too that the unlawfulness of a contractual object encompasses not only legal prohibitions but also prohibitions based on public policy. *See, e.g., McGowan v. City of New Orleans,* 43 So. 40 (La. 1907) (finding a public officer's sale of his unearned salary contrary to public policy and therefore unenforceable); *see also* LA. CIV. CODE art. 1968 ("The cause of an obligation is unlawful when the enforcement of the obligation would produce a result prohibited by law or against *public policy.*") (emphasis added).

It is imperative to keep in mind that the object of a sale must conform also to the rules governing contractual objects found in the Title on Conventional Obligations or Contracts. Thus, the object of a sale must not only be lawful, but also "possible, and determined or determinable." LA. CIV. CODE art. 1971. According to Article 1972, "A contractual object is possible or impossible according to its own nature and not according to the parties' ability to perform." LA. CIV. CODE art. 1972. Provided the thing that is to be sold is in existence at the time of the parties' agreement, it is an object that is "possible." Even sales of future things — i.e., things not yet in existence — are valid, provided they involve objects which are possible to bring into being. Sales of future things are explored later in Part B of this Chapter.

In addition, the object of a contract of sale must be determined — at least to its kind — and determined or determinable with respect to its quantity. LA. CIV. CODE art. 1973. A "determinable" quantity may be one that is left to the discretion of a third person, LA. CIV. CODE art. 1974, but it may not be left up to the discretion of one of the parties to the contract. And, when the parties agree that a third person may determine the quantity of the object of the sale, if they later fail to name the third person or if the person named is unable or unwilling to make that determination, the quantity may be determined by the court. *Id.* Another significant nuance to the determinability requirement involves the validity of "output" and "requirements" contracts. Article 1975 provides that "[t]he quantity of a contractual object may be determined by the output of one party or the requirements of the other. In such a case, output or requirements must be measured in good faith." LA. CIV. CODE art. 1975. For example, in a requirements contract, one party may not extract from the other a performance far in excess of a reasonably foreseen amount. *See, e.g., C.A. Andrews Coal Co. v. Board of Directors of Public Schools*, 92 So. 303 (1922) (holding that in a contract for the purchase of all of the bituminous coal required by the schools of a city, the school board, by discontinuing the use of other forms of fuel, could not impose on the seller the duty of furnishing practically double the amount previously necessary under the conditions prevailing at the time of the contract).

B. Sales of Future Things and Sales of Hopes

La. Civ. Code arts. 1912, 1976, 2450–2451

1. Sale of a Future Thing

As mentioned previously, the sale of a future thing—that is, a thing that is not yet in existence—may be the object of a contract of sale. When the parties agree to such a contract, their rights are governed by Article 2450. Read that article carefully, then read the materials that follow.

Louisiana State Law Institute, Proposed Louisiana Civil Code Revision of Sales 4 (1992) (Exposé des Motifs)

SALE OF A FUTURE THING

The sale of a future thing presents two problems. First, there is a possibility of confusion between such a sale and a contract for work by the plot or job. See C.C. Art. 2756 (1870). Second, there is a need to avoid the danger of over-generalizing the implied suspensive condition of the coming into existence of the thing.

Concerning the first problem, even without attempting a definitive solution at this time, it is clear that practical experience shows many instances of sales of things not yet in existence, as is the case of manufacturers who either have run out of stock or simply produce upon orders. Sales of that kind are readily distinguishable from building contracts for the lack of specifications furnished by the buyer.

Concerning the second problem, French writers have shown little concern for the matter. See 10 Planiol et Ripert, Traité pratique de droit civil Francais—De la vente et du louage 25-26 (1932); Beudant, Cours de droit civil Francais—La vente et le louage 56-58 (1908); Pothier, Traité du contrat de vente 3-5 (Bugnet ed. 1861). No doubt, Article 2450 of the Louisiana Civil Code of 1870, like its French ancestor, had been drafted for transactions having as object[s] [sic] things produced as the result of natural processes. When that is the case it is reasonable to imply that the coming into existence of a thing is a suspensive condition of the sale. It is different, however, with things to be produced by the labor or industry of the seller, since in such a situation the seller's failure to make the thing he promised would result in breach rather than in nullity of the contract. Revised Article 2450 addresses this problem by providing that "a party who, through his fault, prevents the coming into existence of the thing, is liable in damages."

Plaquemines Equip. & Machine Co. v. Ford Motor Co.

157 So. 2d 884 (La. 1963)

SANDERS, Justice.

In this action, the plaintiff, Plaquemines Equipment & Machine Co., Inc., asserts ownership of a Ford truck, which it caused to be seized under a writ of sequestration in the possession of The Ford Motor Company. The district court found that the plaintiff had no title to the truck and dissolved the writ of sequestration. On appeal, the Court of Appeal affirmed, but remanded the case for a hearing on the entitlement of The Ford Motor Company to damages resulting from the wrongful sequestration. We granted a writ of certiorari to review the judgment of the Court of Appeal.

The facts in the instant case are not in serious dispute. On January 19, 1961, Plaquemines Equipment entered into a contract to purchase a specially built Ford truck from Pearce Ford, Inc., a New Orleans dealer. The cab and chassis (assembled with special parts and equipment) were to be secured by the dealer from The Ford Motor Company. Pearce Ford was then to have installed on the chassis a special oil field body, a heavy winch, and other mechanical equipment. The price of the unit, composed of the cab, chassis, oil field body, and special equipment, was $6,029.18. Plaquemines Equipment made an initial deposit of $707.30 on the purchase price. Upon delivery of the new unit, Plaquemines Equipment was to transfer to the dealer a used Ford truck for a trade-in allowance of $800.00 and pay the balance of the price in cash.

After The Ford Motor Company had assembled the cab and chassis at the factory, it shipped the equipment to Pearce Ford, where it arrived on or about March 11, 1961. The equipment was accompanied by a "Manufacturer's Statement of Origin," evidencing a transfer of the cab and chassis to Pearce Ford. In the meantime, all of the automotive stock of Pearce Ford had been seized by Associates Discount Corporation, in execution of mortgages held by it under the dealer's financing plan. Subsequently, Pearce Ford went into judicial liquidation.

Having terminated its finance plan with the dealer, Associates Discount Corporation declined to pay The Ford Motor Company for the cab and chassis. In keeping with its policy of maintaining dealer transactions on a cash basis, The Ford Motor Company notified Pearce Ford that the cab and chassis would be picked up. On March 30, 1961, the employees of Pearce Ford delivered the certificate of origin and the truck keys to The Ford Motor Company representative. The Ford Motor Company representative then removed the truck from the dealer's establishment. The truck remained in the possession of The Ford Motor Company until it was sequestered in this proceeding about eight days later. On June 2, 1961, Plaquemines Equipment bonded the sequestration and the truck was released to it.

The legal issue presented by the instant case is the ownership of the cab and chassis at the time of the institution of this suit. If plaintiff had title, then its demand should be sustained and the writ of sequestration maintained. If, on the other hand, it did not own the cab and chassis, its demands should be rejected and the writ of sequestration dissolved.

The plaintiff, Plaquemines Equipment, contends that the sale had been perfected and that upon delivery of the cab and chassis to Pearce Ford, title to the equipment immediately vested in it. The plaintiff relies principally upon Articles 2439 [R.C.C. 2439] and 2456 [R.C.C. 2456] of the Louisiana Civil Code, LSA.

The Ford Motor Company asserts that the object of the sale was a specially built truck and that the transfer of ownership could not become operative until the truck came into existence in deliverable form. Since the fabrication of the truck was never completed, it contends that the contract remained executory and no title passed to the purchaser.

It is clear that future things may be the object of a sales contract. Commercial transactions involving objects to be manufactured or fabricated are quite common. Such a contract is not aleatory, but certain, since the price is to be paid for a specific future object, the production of which depends upon the will of the seller.

In the absence of an expression of intent to the contrary, such a contract is not immediately translative of the ownership of any property. Title to the future thing cannot pass for it is not yet in existence. Title to the component parts does not vest in the purchaser because they are not the object of the contract.

In the instant case, the object of the contract was a specially built truck to be produced. The agreement of the parties specified in detail the body type and other equipment to be installed on the cab and chassis. The body and other special equipment represented a major factor in the cost.

The dealer surrendered the cab and chassis to The Ford Motor Company without making the installation required to place the truck in deliverable form. It follows that the contract remained executory. It did not ripen into a sale. Title did not pass to the purchaser.

Articles 2439 [R.C.C. 2439] and 2456 [R.C.C. 2456] of the Louisiana Civil Code, LSA, provide:

> "Art. 2439 [R.C.C. 2439]. The contract of sale is an agreement by which one gives a thing for a price in current money, and the other gives the price in order to have the thing itself.

> "Three circumstances concur to the perfection of the contract, to wit: the thing sold, the price and the consent."

> "Art. 2456 [R.C.C. 2456]. The sale is considered to be perfect between the parties, and the property is of right acquired to the purchaser with regard

to the seller, as soon as there exists an agreement for the object and for the price thereof, although the object has not yet been delivered, nor the price paid."

In express terms, Article 2439 [R.C.C. 2439] requires the concurrence of the thing sold, the price and the consent for the perfection of the contract of sale. If the thing sold has not come into existence, as in the instant case, the concurrence is lacking.

Article 2456 [R.C.C. 2456] provides for the vesting of title in the purchaser by operation of the law prior to actual delivery. For the transfer of title to be operative under the Article, the object of the contract must exist in a deliverable state. The law does not presume to pass title to anything other than the object of the contract.

* * * * *

We conclude, as did the Court of Appeal, that the plaintiff, Plaquemines Equipment & Machine Co., Inc., has no title to the property in controversy.

For the reasons assigned, the judgment of the Court of Appeal is affirmed.

Notes and Questions

1. In the foregoing case, the Court reasoned that "[f]or the transfer of title to be operative under the Article, the object of the contract must exist in a deliverable state." *Plaquemines Equipment*, 157 So. 2d at 886. What was the "deliverable state" of the truck as contemplated by the parties? Why did the failure of the dealer to make the installation required to place the truck in deliverable form prevent the transfer of ownership of the cab and chassis?

2. Can an argument be made that the seller was at fault in failing to make the installation required to place the truck in the deliverable form contemplated by the parties? Read carefully the last sentence of Article 2450 and Article 1772. What effect would such a finding have on the rights of the parties in this case?

3. Although not an issue before the Court, the distinction between a sale and a contract to build (discussed in Chapter 1: The Nature of the Contract of Sale) is raised by the facts of this case. Can you make an argument that the contract at issue in *Plaquemines Equipment* was a contract to build as opposed to a contract of sale? What information do you need to further analyze this issue?

4. Note that the litigation in *Plaquemines Equipment* commenced with a writ of sequestration. The writ of sequestration is a procedural device described in Articles 3571 through 3576 of the Louisiana Code of Civil Procedure. As Code of Civil Procedure Article 3751 explains, "When one claims the ownership or right to possession of property . . . he may have the property seized under a writ of sequestration, if it is within the power of the defendant to conceal, dispose of, or waste the property or the revenues therefrom, or remove the property from the parish, during the pendency of the action." LA. CODE CIV. PROC. art. 3751. A writ of sequestration thus may be sought by a party seeking revindication—recognition of ownership and

return of possession—of a thing. In such a case, the substantive relief sought by the plaintiff is an adjudication of ownership and possession; the writ of sequestration merely preserves the property and prevents it from being lost, destroyed, or conveyed during the litigation.

2. Sale of a Hope

According to Article 2451, "A hope may be the object of a contract of sale." La. Civ. Code art. 2451. The materials that follow explore the meaning of the term "hope" and contrast the sale of a "hope" from the sale of a future thing.

Louisiana State Law Institute, Proposed Louisiana Civil Code Revision of Sales 5 (1992) (Exposé des Motifs)

SALE OF A HOPE

Former Article 2451 was one of the staples of the Louisiana Civil Code. Yielding to the weight of tradition, the language of that article has been preserved in the revised Article with only slight modifications.

The sale of a hope presents two problems, however. In the first place, a treasure, rather than the originally hoped-for fish, may be caught in the net. In the second, a fortuitous event may prevent the casting of the net. The two problems revolve around the extension of the risk assumed by the parties.

Concerning the problem that things other than fish are caught in the net, various solutions are possible. Thus, one may take the approach that he who bears the risk should also obtain the benefit of an unexpected profit; or, conversely, one may argue that the buyer is only entitled to what was in contemplation of the parties at the time of the agreement—which, in the example given by the article is fish—and, possibly, things of a similar type—Ejusdem Generis. If the Ejusdem Generis approach is used, the buyer would probably be entitled to an octopus or a crab caught in the net, but certainly not to a treasure.

Where a fortuitous event prevents the casting of the fisherman's net, the answer to the question about who should bear the loss would seem to depend upon the particular nature of the hope that was sold. Thus, the hope may be based on a condition of things expected to exist in the future—that is, a readily available net that the fisherman proposes to, and is capable of, casting. Or, the sale may be of the hope both that the net will be cast and, if so cast, that fish will be caught therein. In the first factual situation, the seller bears the risk of a fortuitous event that prevents the casting of the net. In the latter case, the risk of a fortuitous event preventing the casting of the net is born by the buyer. See *Losecco v. Gregory*, 108 La. 648, 32 So. 985, 996 (1901).

Nevertheless, whatever solution may be deemed proper to this latter problem, its place is not in revised Article 2451, but rather as part of the doctrine of impossibility of performance.

Notes and Questions

Losecco v. Gregory, 32 So. 985 (La. 1901), is the seminal Louisiana Supreme Court case addressing the distinction between a sale of a hope and a sale of a future thing. The case involved a contract for the sale of two years' worth of an orange farmer's crop that was ultimately destroyed as a result of an unprecedented freeze that killed not only the oranges but the trees as well. The buyer sought the return of the price, part of which he had paid up front. The central question on appeal was whether the contract was a "certain" contract for the sale of future oranges (in which case, the obligations of the parties were extinguished as a result of a fortuitous event, and the seller was required to return the price) or an "aleatory" contract for the sale of a hope of oranges (in which case, the buyer assumed the risk that the oranges would be destroyed as a result of a fortuitous event). On its first hearing of the matter, the Court held that the sale was a "certain" contract for the sale of a future crop, stating, "The orange grove having been destroyed by a fortuitous event, a vis major, the purchaser of the crops of oranges which the grove was expected to grow in the contract years, had the right to recede from the contract. This being so, the seller is bound to make him restitution of that portion of the price received." *Id.* at 988.

Two applications for rehearing were made, and the Court issued lengthy opinions on each application. Both opinions are reproduced in part below so as to illustrate the facts that were most important to the Court in determining whether the contract in this case was a sale of a future crop or merely a sale of a hope of a crop.

Losecco v. Gregory

32 So. 985 (La. 1901)

On Application for Rehearing
(March 31, 1902)

Provosty, J.

Defendant owned an orange grove in the parish of Plaquemines, about 60 miles south of the city of New Orleans. Plaintiff was, and had been for 25 years, an orange-crop buyer. He had frequently bought orange crops in advance, some of which, as a result of cold weather, had failed entirely. Plaintiff had been known to buy crops as far in advance as three years. The parties entered into the following contract:

> "I have this day, in consideration of the terms hereinafter named, sold unto Vincent Losecco, of the city of New Orleans, two crops of oranges on my place, as follows, i.e.: 1st. All oranges that my trees may produce in the year (1899) eighteen hundred and ninety-nine. 2nd. All oranges that my trees may produce in the year (1900) nineteen hundred. For the sum of eight thousand dollars ($8,000). Four thousand dollars paid cash down, and the balance, four thousand dollars, to be paid on the first day of December, 1900. Purchaser assumes all risks. Vendor to furnish teams and carts and drivers to move the 2 (two) crops."

Within three months after the execution of this contract, and therefore during the same winter, and before the trees had had a chance to even put out the blossoms of the crop of 1899, a freeze came that killed the trees, root and branch. Cold weather had been known to destroy the crops of the year, and even to kill the trees halfway down; but never, within the memory of the oldest inhabitant, had the trees been killed entirely, or even so injured as not to produce a crop the following year. In the several histories of Louisiana, mention is made of such a killing frost having occurred in 1748, 1768, and 1830, but whether the trees then killed were so far south as these of defendant's, does not appear; and nothing shows that the parties, when they entered into their contract, had any knowledge of these events of the distant past.

Plaintiff claims back the $4,000 paid under the contract, and defendant demands in reconvention the $4,000 payable on the 1st day of December, 1900. Plaintiff contends that the subject of the sale was the future crops, and that the contract was conditional upon these crops eventually coming into existence, and that the failure of this condition annuls the contract. He contends further that so long as crops continue to be attached to the realty they are part of the realty and belong to the owner of the soil, and if they perish by *cas fortuit extraordinaire*, or *vis major*, their loss falls upon such owner, and not upon the purchaser, unless the latter has specially assumed such risk; the presumption, otherwise, being that he has assumed only ordinary risks. Defendant contends that the subject of the sale was not the crops themselves, but only the hope of them, coupled with the right to take them in case they materialized, and that, even if the sale was of the crops themselves, plaintiff assumed the risk of their loss.

We do not see how the doctrine of the immobility of growing crops can cut any figure in the case. If the sale was of the hope, merely, then plaintiff got what he bargained for, and there is an end of the matter. If, on the other hand, the sale was of the crops themselves, then the loss must fall upon one or other of the parties according to the interpretation placed upon the risk clause. It cannot be, and is not, contended that the plaintiff could not validly assume the risk of the trees being destroyed by cold. The question must be, therefore, simply whether or not he made the assumption. It was possible, under our Code, for the parties to make either the crops themselves, or the hope of them, the subject of their contract. Civ. Code, arts. 2450, 2451. Had they made the crops themselves the subject of their contract, the sale, in the absence of contrary stipulation, would have been conditional upon the crops eventually coming into existence, as contended by plaintiff. . . . Had they made the mere hope of the crops the subject of their contract, the sale would have been proof against all eventualities, as contended for by defendant. . . .

Plaintiff argues that, even if the sale was merely of a hope, there went along with it a certain warranty of the continued existence of the trees during the time required for the production of the crops; that even in the case of the sale of the cast of the fisherman's net, which is the example given by the Code as an illustration of the sale of a hope, there goes with the sale a warranty that the net shall continue in being until the time shall arrive for the casting of it. . . . . We do not think that anything further is meant here than that the fisherman warrants that he shall not refuse to cast the net or to give up the fish.

* * * * *

The question of whether the crops, or the mere hope of them, was the subject of the sale, is to be determined by the terms of the contract, read in the light of the attending circumstances. Chief among these, according to the unanimous sentiment of the civil-law writers, is the comparison between the price agreed upon and the value of the thing; the inference being one way or the other accordingly as the disparity between price and value is wide or narrow. Unfortunately, in this case, the question of this value has been left by the evidence as much in doubt as the main question itself, by the contract. Both sides argue from this value in favor of their own theory; one placing the value low, and the other high.

* * * * *

[The Court here engaged in an exhaustive analysis of the evidence relating to the value of the orange trees. *Eds.*]

Therefore, not knowing with any degree of certainty what was the number of the trees, and knowing still less what was the value of the average crop of an orange tree eight years old, we are not in a position to establish a comparison between the value of the crops and the price of the sale.

Another circumstance on which defendant places reliance is the fact that plaintiff had made it part of his business to buy orange crops in advance, on a speculation, as he himself testifies. He was a speculator in orange crops, says defendant, assuming all risks, and securing thereby a material reduction in the price. But there is no proof as to how the prices of the crops thus bought in advance compared with the value of the crops after maturity; nor is there any proof that payment was exacted for the lost crops, nor of any local custom in that connection. Orange crops, like all other crops, vary in quantity and quality, affording a margin for speculation irrespective of the risk of total failure from extreme cold; and, besides, assumption of risk of loss of crop would not necessarily mean assumption of risk of loss of grove. Then, again, there is a broad and marked distinction between the purchase of a crop in advance, and the purchase of the hope of the same crop. As already stated, the one sale is valid only if the crop materializes, whereas the other is valid whatever befall. These previous purchases go to show that plaintiff must have been well up in the knowledge of what risks an orange crop was exposed to, but do not show that he consented to assume risks so extraordinary as to amount clearly to vis major or cas fortuit extraordinaire. The salient feature of the case, outside of the contract itself, is that the obvious thing for the parties to deal about was the crops themselves, and not the mere hope of them, and that therefore the natural inference would be that they had made the crops, and not the hope, the subject of the sale.

Coming to the contract, there is no denying that the wording of it is peculiar. After the statement that what is sold is two crops of oranges, there is added, as if by way of explanation, the *videlicet*, "all the oranges that my trees may produce";

not what the trees will, but what they may; the use of the subjunctive from of the verb expressing uncertainty; implying that the trees might and might not produce any oranges, and that the plaintiff took his chances in that regard; and there is no denying that this peculiarity of language, when considered in connection with the sweeping assumption of risks, gives rise to an implication of considerable strength that the mere hope of the crops was the subject of the sale.

Of course, if given the latitude of construction that its terms call for, this clause of assumption of all risks would show beyond a peradventure that nothing more than a mere hope was sold, for one who assumes literally all risks does not buy anything more than a mere chance, but when we come to consider later on, in another connection, the extent of the assumption of risks under this clause, we shall show, we think, that clauses couched in such general terms are not to be construed according to their very letter, but according to what, under all the circumstances of the matter, was most probably the intention of the parties, and that by this clause the purchaser did not intend to assume any other risks than such as the crops were at that time supposed to be liable to. So construing this clause, the theory of the sale's having been of nothing more than a mere hope finds neither in the surrounding circumstances, nor in the terms of the contract, any support, other than the implication arising, as stated, from the peculiarity of the wording of the contract. This implication stops short of legal certainty. It leaves the mind in doubt, and hesitation in the premises must forebode failure to the defendant's theory. "The seller," says the Code (article 2474) [R.C.C. 2474], "is bound to express himself clearly respecting the extent of his obligation; any obscure or ambiguous clause is construed against him." We do not forget that the rule of interpretation by which uncertainty is construed against the vendor is to be applied only in last resort, when all other means of knowing the intention of the contracting parties have failed; but has not that extremity been reached in the present case? Have we not, both on the submission of the case and on this application for a rehearing, exhausted all known means of interpretation in the vain endeavor to reach a satisfactory conclusion on this question? We shall give heed to the conservative wisdom of our predecessors, who, after deciding against the vendor in a case of considerable analogy with the present one, added the following: "But even were the case doubtful with us, we would come to the same conclusion. The price stipulated for plaintiff's pretensions was a large one, and, in a case of doubt, would incline in favor of a party striving to avoid a loss against one seeking to obtain a gain." *Theriot v. Chandoir*, 17 La. 448. A consideration of this kind does not look strong from the standpoint of pure logic, but it addresses itself strongly to the conscience of the court.

Relinquishing as hopeless the attempt to determine, except by means of the presumption enforced above, the question of what, as between the crops themselves and the mere hope of them, formed, in reality, the subject of this sale, we address ourselves to the task of ascertaining what risks the parties intended that the purchaser should assume; in other words, what scope should be given to the clause "purchaser assumes all risks." Writings designed to express the conditions of an agreement are not to be read in the abstract, and to be construed by mere verbal criticism, but are to be read in connection with the facts of the case, and to be construed according to what, all things considered, was most probably the intention of the contracting parties. The clause now in question, for instance, taken in its literal meaning, would embrace such unforseen [sic] risks as those pointed out in our original opinion, namely, the invasion of the country by a foreign foe, or the irruption of the mighty river flowing near by [sic], and the consequent destruction of the grove; and yet it must be clear to any one that nothing could be more improbable than that the contractants should have given a single thought to any such contingencies as these, in connection with their contract. The clause, then, is not to be construed according to its literal meaning. "However general may be the terms in which a contract is couched," says article 1959 of the Civil, Code [R.C.C. 2051], "it extends only to the things concerning which it appears the parties intended to contract." "The reason of this rule," says Poth. Obl., No. 86, "is evident. The contract being formed by the will of the contracting parties, it can have effect only in regard to what the contracting parties have intended, or have had in contemplation."

Our question, then, is, what risks did the contracting parties have in contemplation? Or, more specifically, did they have in contemplation a freeze that, occurring before the end of the same winter, would cut off the crops bargained for? That question resolves itself into another: Had such a thing happened before? In so far as the cutting off of one crop is concerned, it had. According to plaintiff's witness [the] crop of 1881 failed as the result of a freeze that occurred on the 10th of January, 1881, and it failed entirely. The freeze that cut off the crop of 1899 came on the 12th-14th of February, — one month later than that of 1881. True, 17 years had gone by without a recurrence of this experience, but speculators in orange crops had nevertheless to keep note of it and govern themselves accordingly. It had to enter as one of the prime factors in their calculations. They had to know that what had happened might happen again, and that the crop ran the risk, and that the purchaser would assume it if he assumed the risks to which the crop was exposed. This fatal freeze of 1881 had happened within plaintiff's own experience, and therefore he had double reason to know of it, and to be guided accordingly; and, besides, there had been other years when the temperature had fallen low enough to kill the crops, — notably in 1886 and 1895. We hold that plaintiff assumed this risk, and that he must abide the consequences. But in his 25 years' experience, plaintiff had not known the trees to be killed, or even to be so injured as not to produce a crop the following year; nor had the oldest inhabitant known of such a thing. Some of the trees on the adjoining farm were 38 years old. Under the circumstances, we think it would be putting a most strained construction on the situation to hold that the parties, in making this contract, took into consideration the contingency of the trees being thus killed or injured. The most prudent and cautious speculator would hardly have done so. If he had thought of the matter at all, he would have assumed that nature would not deviate from her usual course. We hold, therefore, that the parties did not contemplate this risk, and that, as a consequence, plaintiff did not take it upon himself.

* * * * *

On Application for Second Rehearing
(Nov. 17, 1902)

PROVOSTY, J.

* * * * *

The question of the distinction between the sale of a future crop as contradistin-guished from the sale of the mere hope of such crop, is treated more or less copi-ously by all the French writers on the civil law; and it may be well to insert here some extracts from their books, taken from the places referred to in the opinion handed down on the rehearing:

[The Court here quoted extensively from several French authors. *Eds.*]

From these quotations it is very evident that the question of what formed the subject of the sale,—the future crop, or the hope thereof,—is one of what was the intentions of the parties; that is, of the interpretation of the contract. Contracts must be interpreted from the terms of the writings evidencing them, and from the circumstances surrounding them. In contracts of the nature of the one here in ques-tion, the main circumstance would be the comparison between the value of the crop if it materialized and the price fixed in the contract. Of the benefit of this circumstance the court is deprived in the present instance, as was fully explained in the opinion handed down on the rehearing. The other notable circumstances are pointed out in the same opinion. They are, on the one part: First, that the purchaser had been in the habit of buying orange crops in advance on a speculation, and that not unfrequently these crops had perished entirely from cold weather, which in that locality hung ever as a Damocles sword over the head of the orange grower; and, second, that the purchaser paid the large sum of $4,000 cash, without a word of stipulation for its return on any contingency; and they are, on the other part, that never before, within the memory of the oldest inhabitant, had the trees been killed outright, or so injured as not to produce a crop the second year following, and that the purchaser stipulated that the vendor should furnish the teams and carts and drivers for moving the two crops.

First, as to the terms of the contract: It is undeniable that the wording of the con-tract is peculiar, and that a strong inference arises of its having been so made advis-edly. In describing the crops, the vendor might have said, simply, "The two orange crops of the years 1899 and 1900 on my place," or, "The two orange crops that the trees on my place will produce in the years 1899 and 1900." Instead of this, he industri-ously explains what is meant by "the two crops sold." After saying that he has sold two crops of oranges on his place, he goes on and adds the *videlicet*, "i.e.: 1st. All oranges that my trees may produce in the year 1899. 2nd. All oranges that my trees may pro-duce in the year 1900." This specification must unquestionably be held to control the more general terms made use of previously. They were inserted in the contract for that very purpose. Now, why, if simply the future crops were in contemplation, the simple future form of the verb should not have been used? Why should the conditional future or potential form of the verb have been used, as if mere potential crops, or, in other words, the hope of crops, had been in contemplation? In the above extracts the simple future is invariably used in describing the future crops. Thus Pothier, "la récolte de vin que nous receuillerons" ("the wine crop that we shall gather"); thus Duranton, "vente des fruits que produira tel fonds" ("sale of the crops that such a tract of land shall produce"); thus Troplong, "vente des fruits qui naîtront" ("sale of the fruit that will be produced"); thus Baudry-Lacantinerie, "la récolte que je ferai Pannée prochaine dans ma propriété" ("the crop I shall make next year on my property"); thus Delsol, "la récolte de l'an prochain" ("the crop of next year"); thus Baudry-Lacantinerie again, "la récolte que mon vignoble produira l'année prochaine" ("the crop my vineyard shall produce next year"); thus Mourlon, "la récolte de tel vignoble" ("the crop of such a vineyard"); thus Pardessus, "tout ce que produira le champs" ("all that the field shall produce"). In all these cases the form of expression is such as to give rise to the inference that the parties had in mind a crop that would come into existence, whereas the form, "all oranges that my trees *may* produce," raises no such inference, but, on the contrary, from the fact that the simple form is made to give place to this peculiar one, gives rise to an inference, and an inference, at that, of considerable strength, that the parties made use of the potential mood, instead of the simple indicative, advisedly, in order to describe crops not simply future, but also merely potential.

Delsol, in the extract above, says that the sale must be held to have been of a mere hope, where the parties have contracted "*à tout évènement.*" The literal translation of this would be, "at all events"; a freer and more idiomatic translation would be, "subject to all contingencies," or "on the assumption of all contingencies," or, again, "the purchaser taking all chances," or "assuming all risks." This last translation would make this authority fit exactly the case in hand. Baudry-Lacantinerie, in the extract above, says that the sale must be held to have been of the mere hope where the parties have contracted "moyennant un prix ferme qui me sera payé quoiqu'il arrive"; *anglice,* "in consideration of a lump price to be paid me, no matter what happens." In the case in hand the price was of that character, and the purchaser "*assumed all risks,*" which may be said to be fully the equivalent of "*no matter what happens.*" Thus authority, again, would seem to fit the case. The purchaser, knowing full well that the crop might never materialize, paid cash, and unconditionally, $4,000, and bound himself to pay at a fixed date, and likewise unconditionally, the balance of the price; and he assumed all risks. On further consideration, the court is satisfied that this assumption of all risks meant that the purchaser assumed the risk of the crops never materializing, and that therefore the sale was merely of the hope of the crops. At the time this contract was entered into, the defendant had the hope or chance that his orange trees would produce crops of oranges in 1899 and 1900. His chance in that regard he conveyed to the purchaser. In consideration of the price paid and to be paid, the purchaser stepped into his shoes. From that moment he had no further chance in connection with the crop and no further risk, and from the same moment the purchaser had all the chance and all the risk.

* * * * *

As attempted to be shown in the opinion handed down on rehearing, the parties clearly contemplated that the crops might prove a total failure. They had proven so before, not unfrequently. It is safe, therefore, to say that by assuming all risks the purchaser assumed this risk of total failure. From this it would follow that the clause obligating the vendor to furnish teams, carts, and drivers to move the crops is not inconsistent with the view that within the contemplation of the parties, and within the meaning of the contract, the crops might prove total failures, and there be no crops to move. This clause, therefore, is not inconsistent with the theory of the sale's having been merely of the hope of the crops.

It is therefore ordered, adjudged, and decreed that the plaintiff's suit be dismissed at his cost, and that he be condemned to pay to the defendant the sum of $4,000, with legal interest thereon from the 1st day of December, 1900, and that the plaintiff pay the costs of this appeal.

* * * * *

Notes and Questions

1. After having read the opinions on rehearing in the foregoing case, can you articulate what circumstances surrounding a contract of sale are most significant to the determination of whether the thing sold is a future thing or a hope? The relative values of the contractual object and the price paid? The prior dealings of the parties? The language of the contract? Other circumstances surrounding the contract?

2. A fundamental difference between the two types of contract is this: whereas the sale of a future thing is a "certain" contract, the sale of a hope is an "aleatory" contract. Recall that an aleatory contract is one in which the performance of either party's obligation, or the extent of that performance, depends upon an uncertain event. LA. CIV. CODE art. 1912. In contrast, in a certain contract, neither party's performance is conditional.

3. A more recent case involving the distinction between a sale of a future thing and a sale of a hope is *Springs Thunder Agency, Inc. v. Odom Ins.*, 237 So. 2d 96 (La. App. 1 Cir. 1970). In that case, the defendant contacted plaintiff, which operated a fire and casualty insurance agency, regarding the purchase of the plaintiff's business. The parties entered into a written contract which contained the following clause: "Things sold: Seller conveys all records and files of the agency sold to Buyer and the exclusive right to the renewals on existing active accounts of the agency." *Id.* at 97. The contract also included a non-compete agreement under which the seller agreed not to engage in the fire and casualty insurance business in competition with the buyer. The buyer agreed to pay $4,016.71 for the "renewals on existing active accounts" and $5,000.00 for the covenant not to compete, or a total price of $9,016.71. One of the seller's accounts was that of the Livingston Parish School Board, which made up over 40% of the premium income of the agency. The school board business was let by bids and had been awarded to the seller for several years.

Shortly after the sale, the buyer bid on the school board business but was unsuccessful. The buyer then demanded a reduction in the purchase price by the amount of the premiums lost, which the seller refused. A lawsuit ensued when the buyer stopped paying on the note for the price. Affirming the trial court's finding that the price should not be reduced, the First Circuit Court of Appeal held that the sale was a sale of a hope as opposed to a sale of a future thing. The court's reasoning, which was sparse, focused exclusively on the language in the contract describing the "thing sold" as the right to the renewals on existing contracts, not the renewals themselves.

C. Assignment of Rights

As was pointed out at the outset of this Chapter, a sale may involve a corporeal thing, or it may involve incorporeal rights. When the object of a sale is an incorporeal right, it is properly characterized as an "assignment of rights"—a topic that is addressed in Articles 2462 through 2654. After a brief introduction of the notion of assignment of rights in general, the remainder of this Part will focus on the assignment of so-called "litigious" rights.

1. Assignment of Rights in General

La. Civ. Code arts. 2642–2654

Although much of the law of sales deals with the transfer of corporeal property, *incorporeal* rights are often objects of sales. In the secondary mortgage market, for instance, a lender's right to recover from the borrower frequently becomes the object of a contract of sale. Consider the following example: Bank makes a loan to Debtor in the amount of $250,000, which is to be repaid by Debtor over the course of 30 years. Bank, however, does not want to wait the full 30 years to collect. Credit Buyer, on the other hand, is willing to collect the sum owed over time, provided that it can make a profit by doing so. Credit Buyer enters into a contract of sale with Bank in which it pays a discounted price of $175,000 for Bank's right to collect from Debtor for the remaining life of the loan. Although the loan may be represented by a promissory note and may be secured by a mortgage, the actual object of the contract of sale between Credit Buyer and Bank is the incorporeal right of Bank to demand performance from Debtor.

The Civil Code contains specific rules that govern sales of incorporeal rights. These are contained in Chapter 15 of the Title on Sales, which is titled "Assignment of Rights." Before delving into the provisions in that chapter, it must be noted that the placement of the provisions on assignment of rights within the title of sale is somewhat misleading. Although an assignment of rights may take the form of a sale (i.e., the transfer of a thing—the right—in return for a price in money), an assignment of rights may also be accomplished through other means, including by donation inter vivos, donation mortis causa, exchange, or even innominate contract. Nevertheless, given that many assignments of rights do take the form of a sale, the study of assignments in connection with the law of sale is appropriate.

Article 2642 provides that "[a]ll rights may be assigned, with the exception of those pertaining to obligations that are strictly personal." LA. CIV. CODE art. 2642. Naturally, strictly personal rights may not be assigned; recall, however, that there is a general presumption that *all* rights are transferable or "heritable." LA. CIV. CODE art. 1765. Thus, absent evidence that the performance of an obligation is intended for the benefit of a particular obligee exclusively, the right to enforce that obligation may be transferred freely by one obligee to another. *See* LA. CIV. CODE art. 1766. This general rule admits several exceptions. For one thing, a right cannot be assigned where assignment is prohibited by law. LA. CIV. CODE art. 2642 cmt. c. In addition, "A right cannot be assigned when the contract from which it arises prohibits the assignment of that right." LA. CIV. CODE art. 2653. In such a case, the right, though heritable in nature, has been made strictly personal by agreement. *See* LA. CIV. CODE art. 1765. Nevertheless, a prohibition on assignment "has no effect against an assignee who has no knowledge of its existence." LA. CIV. CODE art. 2653.

When a right is assigned, the assignor is bound to deliver to the assignee "all documents in his possession that evidence the right." LA. CIV. CODE art. 2654. Even when a right is assigned only in part, "the assignor may give the assignee an original or a copy of such documents." *Id.* However, while the duty to deliver documents evidencing the right arises from the assignment, it is not a prerequisite to the assignment. As the Civil Code states clearly, "a failure by the assignor to deliver such documents does not affect the validity of the assignment." *Id.* Again, this is because the object of the sale is not the documents but the rights evidenced by them.

Article 2642 states the effects that the assignment has for the assignee: "The assignee is subrogated to the rights of the assignor against the debtor." LA. CIV. CODE art. 2642. Subrogation, of course, is the *substitution* of one person to the rights of another. LA. CIV. CODE art. 1825. The assignee steps into the legal shoes of the assignor and acquires the right to enforce the obligation against the obligor. *See* LA. CIV. CODE art. 1826. With respect to the assignor, the obligation is extinguished. *Id.* Thus, in the example above regarding Bank's assignment of its rights against Debtor to Credit Buyer, the assignment provides Credit Buyer with the right to enforce the loan against Debtor, while simultaneously extinguishing Bank's right of enforcement. Further, as provided by Article 2645, "The assignment of a right includes its accessories such as security rights." LA. CIV. CODE art. 2645. Thus, in the above example, the transfer of the loan, evidenced by the promissory note and secured by the mortgage, includes both the right to enforce the note and the right to enforce the mortgage securing the debt.

What effects does an assignment of rights have for the obligor and for third persons? Article 2643 provides that "[t]he assignment of a right is effective against the debtor and third persons only from the time the debtor has actual knowledge or has been given notice of the assignment." LA. CIV. CODE art. 2643. The practical effect of this article is significant. Returning to the example above regarding Bank's assignment of its rights against Debtor to Credit Buyer, as long as Debtor neither knows nor has been given notice of the transfer, it may continue to treat Bank as its lawful obligee. Moreover, as provided in Article 2644, "When the debtor, without knowledge or notice of the assignment, renders performance to the assignor, such performance extinguishes the obligation of the debtor and is effective against the assignee and third persons." La. Civ. Code art. 2644. Thus, if Debtor, without knowledge or notice of the assignment, continues to make installment payments on the loan to Bank, that performance reduces the principal value of the loan. Further, Credit Buyer cannot seek payment on those installments from Debtor, but instead must proceed against Bank for those payments.

The Civil Code's treatment of assignment of rights also includes several articles detailing the warranty obligations of the assignor. According to Article 2646, while the assignor of a right warrants the right's "existence at the time of the assignment," the assignor does not warrant "the solvency of the debtor . . . unless he has agreed to give such a warranty." La. Civ. Code art. 2646. Article 2648 further provides that an assignor of a right who agrees to warrant the solvency of the debtor "warrants that solvency at the time of the assignment only and, in the absence of an agreement to the contrary, does not warrant the future solvency of the debtor." La. Civ. Code art. 2648. The assignee's rights upon breach of a warranty as to the debtor's solvency are governed by the rules contained in the Civil Code's chapter on "Eviction," a topic which is addressed in detail in Chapter 9 of this Textbook: The Warranty Against Eviction. Even when the assignor does not warrant the solvency of the debtor, the assignee may have recourse in the event of the debtor's insolvency: Article 2649 provides that "[w]hen the assignor of a right did not warrant the solvency of the debtor but knew of his insolvency, the assignee without such knowledge may obtain rescission of the contract." La. Civ. Code art. 2649.

The assignment of succession rights—that is, the rights of the assignor to the estate of a deceased person—is also the subject of special treatment. According to Article 2650, "A person who assigns his right in the estate of a deceased person, without specifying any assets, warrants only his right of succession as heir or legatee." La. Civ. Code art. 2650. Thus, in a sale of a right of succession, the warranty against eviction "extends only to the right to succeed the decedent, which entitles the buyer to those things that are, in fact, a part of the estate, but it does not extend to any particular thing." La. Civ. Code art. 2513.

The assignment of litigious rights is also the subject of specialized rules. The rights of the parties to such an assignment are addressed in the following Subpart.

2. Sale of Litigious Rights
La. Civ. Code art. 2652

Article 2652 addresses the assignment of "litigious" rights. Under this article, "When a litigious right is assigned, the debtor may extinguish his obligation by paying to the assignee the price the assignee paid for the assignment, with interest from the time of the assignment." La. Civ. Code art. 2652. Thus, the debtor of a right that has been assigned may, under certain circumstances, extinguish the debt by paying the assignee the *price* paid for the debt rather than the debt itself. The right of the debtor to extinguish his obligation in this manner is known as the right of litigious redemption.

A simple example illustrates the rule. Creditor makes a loan to Debtor in the amount of $2,000, which is to be repaid in full one year from the date the loan is made. When the term for repayment expires, Debtor does not pay. Creditor thereafter files suit against Debtor to collect the sum owed. During the course of the litigation, Third Person approaches Creditor and offers to buy Creditor's right to collect the debt for a discounted price of $1,200; Creditor agrees. According to the general rules governing assignments of rights, the assignee is subrogated to Creditor's rights against Debtor and may be substituted as plaintiff in the lawsuit. *See* LA. CODE CIV. PROC. art. 698. However, the right of litigious redemption gives Debtor the right to pay Third Party the amount that Third Party paid to purchase the litigation from Creditor, plus interest (i.e., $1,200 plus interest) and thereby terminate the lawsuit.

To qualify for this treatment, the right in question must be "litigious"—that is, "contested in a suit already filed." LA. CIV. CODE art. 2652. Louisiana courts have elaborated upon this definition to hold that "a right is contested once an answer or defense has been filed in response to the petition." *First Nat'l Bank v. Keyworth*, 670 So. 2d 1288, 1291 (La. App. 5 Cir. 1996). Rights that are not "litigious" when assigned may not be redeemed by the payment of the price for which the right is assigned; rather, satisfaction of the obligation requires performance of the *entire* obligation originally incurred.

The following case addresses both the rationale for the right of litigious redemption and the mechanics of its application in a lawsuit. As you read this case, consider what policy interests support the right of litigious redemption.

Clement v. Sneed Bros.
116 So. 2d 269 (La. 1959)

McCALEB, Justice.

The original plaintiff, Ella Townsen Clement, sued defendants for cancellation of an oil and gas lease covering her property and for the damages she sustained by reason of their failure to drill a well. After a trial on the merits, but before judgment, Mrs. Clement died and the administrator of her succession was substituted as party plaintiff. Judgment was subsequently rendered cancelling the lease and awarding the administrator $60,000 damages, from which judgment defendants prosecuted this appeal.

On June 29, 1959 the four heirs of Mrs. Clement were sent into possession of her estate. Shortly thereafter, two of these heirs transferred their interest in the pending litigation to one James B. Branch, Jr. and notified defendants by letter of this transfer, stating that the consideration therefor was $5,062.50.

By order of this Court dated July 13, 1959, the four heirs of Mrs. Clement were substituted as plaintiffs-appellees and, on the same date, another order was issued substituting Branch as party plaintiff for the two heirs whose interest he had purchased.

On September 14, 1959 defendants filed a motion to remand the cause to the district court so that they could institute proceedings for the purpose of paying Mr. Branch for the litigious rights acquired by him and obtain from him the release provided for in Article 2652 of the Civil Code [R.C.C. 2652], which reads as follows:

> "He against whom a litigious right has been transferred, may get himself released by paying to the transferee the real price of the transfer, together with the interest from its date".

The two plaintiffs who have not assigned their interest, joined by Branch, made written reply to the motion urging certain objections thereto and further declared that a remand of the case would be inequitable with respect to the plaintiffs who have not sold their interest, as the appeal would lose its preference position on the docket of this Court and its disposal would thereby be unseasonably delayed.

Defendants' right to a remand of the cause for the purposes set forth in their motion is well settled in our jurisprudence, the cases holding that the privilege conferred by Article 2652 of the Civil Code [R.C.C. 2652] to a party against whom a litigious right has been transferred may be exerted pendente lite [during litigation], either in the lower court or on appeal, provided it will end the litigation. *Smith v. Cook*, 189 La. 632, 180 So. 469 and authorities there cited. Of course, a remand in this case will not end the litigation completely, since the rights of plaintiffs who have not transferred their interest to Branch remain unaffected. However, it suffices that the right which may be availed of by defendants will end the suit insofar as Branch is concerned, it having been held in *Smith v. Cook* that a defendant may invoke the provisions of Article 2652 [R.C.C. 2652] when some, but not all, of the plaintiffs have sold their interest in the litigation.

On the other hand, it is equally well established that the party seeking to redeem the litigious right must be reasonably prompt in making known his intention and that, if after learning of the transfer he continues to contest the suit and protracts the litigation, he will not be permitted to redeem because he has, by his conduct, defeated one of the objects of Article 2652 [R.C.C. 2652], which is the prevention of unnecessary litigation. *Leftwich v. Brown*, 4 La.Ann. 104; *Pearson v. Grice*, 6 La.Ann. 232; *Rhodes v. Hooper*, 6 La.Ann. 355; *Salbadore v. Crescent Mut. Ins. Co.*, 22 La.Ann. 338; *Evans v. DeL'isle*, 24 La.Ann. 248 and *Crain v. Waldron*, 210 La. 561, 27 So.2d 333.

Plaintiffs contend that defendants have not acted timely since they received notice of the transfer on July 9, 1959 and did not take action until September 14, 1959, when they filed the motion now under consideration.

There may be instances in which a delay of two months before taking action would be considered as untimely. But this is not true under the facts of this case. Defendants have not taken affirmative action inconsistent with the right they invoke. Nor can the fact that they permitted a two-month period to elapse from the date they were informed of the transfer to the date of the filing of their motion preclude them from asserting their right under Article 2652 of the Code [R.C.C. 2652]. So long as the delay does not serve to prolong the litigation, it is improper to say that the party has perferred [sic] to continue the lawsuit rather than to take advantage of his right under the codal article.

Plaintiffs also assert that the two heirs who transferred their interests to Branch were compelled to do so because defendants had refused to compromise separately with them and that, under these circumstances, defendants are not entitled to a remand of the case.

We see no merit in the point. The object of Article 2652 of the Code [R.C.C. 2652], as stated in *Smith v. Cook, supra* (189 La. 632, 180 So. 473), "* * * was primarily to prevent the purchasing of claims from avarice or to injure the debtor * * *" and also "* * * to favor the party against whom the matter in litigation is transferred over one who speculates in law suits". Hence, it matters not that defendants refused to compromise separately with Branch's transferors as this affords no ground for denying defendants their legal rights.

Plaintiffs declare that defendants' motion should be denied since they have not alleged a tender of the price Branch paid for the litigious rights and also because they have not unequivocally pleaded that they will pay him the real price of the transfer, together with interest.

These contentions have no substance. Defendants cannot be required to redeem the litigious right until they are able to ascertain "the real price of the transfer" as provided by Article 2652 [R.C.C. 2652]. The situation here is unlike that obtaining in *Winchester v. Cain*, 1 Rob. 421; *Pearson v. Grice, supra*; *Rhodes v. Hooper, supra*; *Crain v. Waldron, supra* and other matters in which the transfer of the litigious right was made while the case was pending before the district court. In such cases, evidence may be immediately received to establish "the real price" of the litigious right. Then a tender can be made at that time as is required (see *Crain v. Waldron, supra*) and the proper litigants released by the Court.

Conversely, if the litigious right is transferred after judgment of the district court, as in this case, the party seeking the benefit of the codal article has no way of being legally certain of the real price of the transfer unless the case is remanded and evidence of such price is adduced, since he cannot be sure that the price stated by his adversary was the price actually paid.

Finally, the two plaintiffs who have not transferred their interest assert that, if we grant the motion to remand, they will be denied the right of having this litigation concluded in its ordinary course for the reason that the remand will occasion a delay in the hearing of the appeal.

This plea is impressive and we think it our duty to obviate any undue delay in the hearing of the appeal which may be sustained as a result of the remand. While we cannot deny defendants legal right to a remand or hear the case in this Court until defendants are able to determine whether they will redeem the litigious right purchased by Branch, we believe that the remand of the case for the limited purpose of hearing the evidence respecting the real price of the transfer and the exercise by defendants of their rights can be completed and the record returned to this Court within sixty days from the finality of our order. To facilitate compliance, the trial judge is instructed to hear the evidence as soon as possible, when the record is returned for the restricted purpose hereinabove stated. Meanwhile, the appeal will remain in its present position on the preference docket of this Court.

It is therefore ordered that this case be remanded to the lower court so that evidence may be adduced respecting the real price of the transfer to James B. Branch, Jr. so that defendants may elect, if they desire, to release themselves from any liability to said Branch in accordance with the [proviso] [sic] that the record is returned to this Court not later than sixty days from the finality of this decree. Taxation of costs of this remand is to be delayed until final disposition of the case insofar as the interest of Branch is affected.

Notes and Questions

1. The foregoing case provides a helpful synopsis of some of the more important jurisprudential rules of litigious redemption. The litigation here concerned cancellation of an oil and gas lease and for damages sustained by the lessor as a result of the lessees' failure to drill. After the original plaintiff instituted the litigation, she died, and her four heirs inherited her claim. Following trial in favor of the plaintiff (now the succession representative) and while an appeal was pending, two of the heirs transferred their interests in the pending litigation. Two months later, defendants filed a motion to remand so that they could bring an end to the litigation as to the purchaser by paying him the price he paid to the heirs for their interests. How, if it all, did it impact the defendants' claim that (a) the heirs assigned their rights after the trial court judgment was rendered but while an appeal was pending? (b) not all of the heirs transferred their rights in the litigation? (c) the defendants waited two months after the assignee was substituted as party plaintiff (for the two heirs whose interest he had purchased) before seeking to exercise their right to litigious redemption? (d) remand was required to determine the "real price" by the assignee for the assignment?

2. A more recent case involving litigious redemption is *Luk-Shop, L.L.C. v. Riverwood LaPlace Assoc., L.L.C.*, 802 So. 2d 1291 (La. 2002). In that case, a creditor, CFSC Capital Corp., XXVII ("CFSC"), filed suit in federal court against Riverwood LaPlace Associates, L.L.C. ("Riverwood") seeking a judgment against Riverwood for sums allegedly due on promissory notes, mortgage notes, and guarantee agreements. In connection with those claims, CFSC obtained a writ of sequestration to seize the revenues and rents from Riverwood's shopping center operations. Riverwood filed a motion to dissolve the sequestration but then dismissed that motion during efforts to negotiate a settlement with CFSC. Those settlement negotiations

apparently failed, and Riverwood later answered the lawsuit, denying liability on the promissory notes. Riverwood then filed a petition in bankruptcy, which resulted in the imposition of an automatic stay in the pending federal court suit. Thereafter, CFSC assigned its claims against Riverwood to Luk-Shop, L.L.C. ("Luk-Shop"). After Riverwood emerged from bankruptcy, Luk-Shop filed suit against Riverwood in state court, seeking judgment on the promissory notes, mortgage notes, and guarantee agreements that were assigned by CFSC, as well as a writ of sequestration to seize the revenues and rents from Riverwood's shopping center operations. Riverwood responded, claiming it was entitled to litigious redemption and seeking to terminate the litigation by paying to Luk-Shop what Luk-Shop had paid to CFSC. The trial court found that CFSC's assignment to Luk-Sop was not the sale of a litigious right because Riverwood had dismissed its motion to dissolve the writ of sequestration in the prior federal court litigation. The Louisiana Supreme Court disagreed, holding that that while the writ of sequestration was not contested at the time of the assignment, the "underlying monetary obligation, i.e., Riverwood's liability on the promissory notes, mortgage notes, and guarantee agreements" was indeed contested at that time because Riverwood never withdrew its answer denying liability on the promissory notes. 802 So. 2d at 1293. Moreover, the Court distinguished between the writ of sequestration and the underlying debt, noting: "The sequestration is simply a procedural mechanism for enforcing the underlying obligation." *Id.* That the sequestration was no longer contested did not prevent the underlying obligation from remaining litigious.

3. The right of litigious redemption is civilian in origin, its roots grounded in Roman law. Indeed, the right of litigious redemption appeared in the Codex of Justinian's Corpus Juris Civilis. *See* THE CODEX OF JUSTINIAN: A NEW ANNOTATED TRANSLATION, WITH PARALLEL LATIN AND GREEK TEXT 970–975 (Bruce W. Frier et al. eds. 2016). Noted Roman Law scholar Ferdinand Mackeldey described the policy underpinning the ancient rule as follows:

> To prevent the purchasing of claims from avarice or to injure the debtor, Anastasius ordained that whoever purchased a claim for a less price than its true value shall not sue the debtor for more than he paid for it in addition to the lawful interest. This ordinance was afterwards renewed by Justinian, and in several points more precisely determined and elucidated. From the combination of these two ordinances arise the following principles: . . . In the cases where the debtor can invoke the *Lex Anastasiana* against the cedée, the effect is that where the claim amounts to more than the price paid for it with interest, the debtor shall have such advantage. And therefore the cedée must also always show how much he paid for the ceded claim, because he is only to be reimbursed the amount of such payment and interest for it.

FERDINAND MACKELDEY, HANDBOOK OF THE ROMAN LAW 294–295 (1833) (internal citations omitted). These Roman law principles were carried forward in the French *Code Civil* promulgated by the Emperor Napoleon in the 19th century. French civil law scholar Robert Joseph Pothier gave the following comments on the policy underlying litigious redemption in France:

> The right which is accorded by these laws to the one who owes the litigious debt assigned to a third person is a kind of right of recovery of the litigious debt which is accorded to him against the assignee. The debtor by reimbursing the assignee is allowed to take [the assignee's] bargain. *The assignee's purchase of the litigious debt is destroyed with respect to the assignee, and passes to the debtor who is considered as having directly redeemed his obligation from the creditor, and having compromised with him for the price furnished for the assignment. . . .*
>
> This redemption is very equitable. Public policy requires that the debtor who, by taking for himself the bargain extinguishes the law suit to which the litigious debt was to give rise, should be preferred for this bargain to an odious purchaser of litigation.

Smith v. Cook, 180 So. 469, 472–73 (La. 1937) (translating ROBERT JOSEPH POTHIER, TRAIT DU CONTRACT DE VENTE 342–343 (1806)) (emphasis in Court's citation). In turn, the redactors of the Louisiana Digest of 1808 adopted the right of litigious redemption, and the rule has appeared in every revision of the Civil Code since then.

Despite the longevity of the right of litigious redemption, a question arises as to whether those who purchase litigious rights are truly "odious," as Pothier so dubs them. Indeed, transactions in litigious rights may be economically beneficial to both the creditor and the third party, without imposing any undue burden on the debtor. Perhaps for these reasons, states other than Louisiana do not provide for a right of litigious redemption or place other limitations on sales of rights that are being litigated. Is the right of litigious redemption an outmoded institution, or does it have a place in modern commercial life? Is the assignee of a litigious right harmed by litigious redemption? What might the assignee of a right do to protect himself or herself against the obligor's right of redemption?

D. Sale of a Thing Already Owned

La. Civ. Code art. 2443

According to Article 2443, "A person cannot purchase a thing he already owns. Nevertheless, the owner of a thing may purchase the rights of a person who has, or may have, an adverse claim to the thing." LA. CIV. CODE art. 2443. The statements made by this article may seem so obvious as to not merit special treatment in the Civil Code. The first sentence states a consequence of the nature of the sale as a contract whereby one person transfers ownership of a thing to another; quite obviously, a person cannot transfer to himself or herself ownership of a right that he or she already owns. Nevertheless, the second sentence, which was added in the 1995 revision of the Title on Sale, makes clear that while a person may not purchase a thing that he or she already owns, a person may purchase the rights of those who own claims adverse to his or her property rights.

Consider, for instance, a situation in which Annie owns a tract of land known as Blackacre. Annie learns that Beatrice has an adverse claim to a portion of the property stemming from an ancestor-in-title's acquisitive prescription. Annie is uncertain as to the merits of this claim but does not wish to litigate, so she instead offers to purchase Beatrice's adverse claim, thereby extinguishing Beatrice's right to assert this right against Annie. This transfer is characterized as an assignment of rights and more particularly as a quitclaim deed (which is discussed in Chapter 9: The Warranty Against Eviction). Article 2443 makes clear that this transfer is valid and enforceable, even if, through litigation, the parties would have determined that Beatrice never had a valid claim to any portion of Blackacre.

E. Sale of a Thing of Another

1. In General

La. Civ. Code art. 2452

Article 2452 provides simply: "The sale of a thing belonging to another does not convey ownership." LA. CIV. CODE art. 2452. Compare the text of current Article 2452 to that of its source provisions below. What differences do you see? Consider the excerpt of the *Exposé des Motifs* on the revision of the Title on Sales that follows. What reasons explain the changes made in the 1995 revision of the law?

> **French Civ. Code art. 1599.** The sale of a thing of another is null; it can give rise to damages when the buyer was ignorant that the thing belonged to another.

> **La. Civ. Code art. 2452 (1870).** The sale of a thing belonging to another person is null. It may give rise to damages, when the buyer knew not that the thing belonged to another person.

Louisiana State Law Institute, Proposed Louisiana Civil Code Revision of Sales 7 (1992) (Exposé des Motifs)

French authorities agree in asserting that Article 1599 of the Code Napoleon, equivalent to former Civil Code Article 2452 (1870), contained an overstatement. That overstatement is attributed to the drastic change effected by the Code Napoleon in matters of sale, consisting in turning a contract that, under Roman law and the ancien regime only gave rise to an obligation to effect a transfer, into a contract that accomplished an immediate transfer. See C.C. Arts. 2439, 2456 (1870). Taking a step further, it is possible to realize that former Civil Code Article 2452 (1870) stated an incomplete conclusion. In fact, the sale of the thing of another, rather than being null, may effect a transfer through application of the public records doctrine, where immovable property is concerned, and through operation of the bona fide purchaser doctrine, where movables are concerned. A null juridical act would produce no effects at all, while the sale of a thing belonging to another may give rise to damages, in the first place, and may create a just title for purpose of the short acquisitive prescription, in the second. See C.C. Arts. 3473, 3483; Beudant, op. cit. at 71. Both such consequences are important legal effects that seem to deny the nullity that former Article 2452 asserted.

Notes and Questions

While Article 2452 provides that the sale of a thing of another does not convey ownership, such a sale can have important effects for the parties, as well as for the true owner. In addition, the law occasionally makes exceptions to the general rule, according to which the sale of a thing of another *does* in fact convey ownership of that thing to the buyer, despite the seller's lack of an ownership interest. The precise effects of a sale of a thing of another vary depending on whether the thing sold is movable or immovable. If the object of the sale is movable, then the so-called bona fide purchaser doctrine may be applicable. If the object of the sale is immovable, then the public records doctrine may govern the parties' rights. The bona fide purchaser doctrine is the subject of Part E, Subpart 2 of this Chapter. The public records doctrine and its effects in sales of immovable property are explored in Part E, Subpart 3.

2. Movables — Bona Fide Purchaser Doctrine
La. Civ. Code arts. 518, 521–525, 530, 2035, 2477, 2452

When a seller has sold a movable thing that the seller did not own and did not have the right to sell, the rights of the buyer are governed by a body of rules known collectively as the bona fide purchaser doctrine. The bona fide or "good faith" purchaser doctrine seeks to balance the rights of the true owner of the thing, who has been wrongfully dispossessed, with those of the purchaser, who may be unaware that the seller did not own the thing.

The fundamental rule is to protect the right of the true owner to recover the property. This principle is embodied in Article 2452, which states in part that "[t]he sale of a thing belonging to another does not convey ownership." LA. CIV. CODE art. 2452. Thus, in general, when a seller has sold a movable thing that the seller did not own and did not have the right to sell, the true owner is not divested of ownership and may recover the thing from the buyer. The buyer, in turn, may have recourse against the seller in the form of an action for damages. The buyer's recourse against the seller derives from the implied warranty against eviction, which is covered in Chapter 9: The Warranty Against Eviction.

The protection of the true owner at the expense of a purchaser from one who did not own the thing sold is not absolute. Exceptions are made to the general rule in order to protect innocent purchasers and to promote the stability of commerce. The precise balance of the parties' rights depends upon whether the sale involves (a) a double-dealing seller; (b) a lost or stolen thing; (c) a thing obtained through a contract which is relatively null due to a vice of consent; (d) a thing which the true owner placed in the seller's possession voluntarily; (e) a registered movable; or (f) the sale of a thing that is the subject of litigation. Each of these circumstances and the applicable law are explored in detail below.

a. The Double-Dealing Seller

When the seller of a movable thing enters into a contract of sale first with one buyer and then subsequently sells the same thing to another buyer, the rights of the parties are governed primarily by Article 518. Read that article and the comments thereto carefully before reading the case that follows.

Cameron Equipment Co. v. Stewart and Stevenson Servs., Inc.

685 So. 2d 696 (La. App. 3 Cir. 1996)

Knoll, Judge.

In this revendicatory action against the seller and subsequent purchasers of two diesel engines, Cameron Equipment 1987, Inc. d/b/a/ Cameron Equipment appeals the judgment of the trial court. We affirm.

FACTS

On June 12, 1987, Cameron Equipment purchased two used General Motors EMD-12-645-E-1 diesel engines from Petroleum Services, Inc. The two engines were purchased along with other used oil field equipment for a total price of $73,000. At the time of this sale, the two diesel engines were located in the equipment yard of Power Rig Drilling Company in Scott, Louisiana.

For two years following the sale, Cameron Equipment left the engines where they were at Power Rig. The engines were not removed from the yard or marked as property of Cameron Equipment.

On June 12, 1989, Petroleum Services sold the engines to another company, Power International, Inc. for $38,000. Power International immediately resold the engines to American General Transportation Co., Inc. for $60,000. On June 14, 1989, American General brokered the engines to Stewart & Stevenson Services, Inc. for $75,000. Stewart & Stevenson needed the engines for use in a towboat it had contracted to build.

On June 15, 1989, American General removed the engines from the Power Rig yard and transported them to Stewart & Stevenson's facility in Harvey, Louisiana. Coincidentally, Cameron Equipment arrived to remove the engines from the Power Rig yard just hours after they had been taken by American General.

On August 10, 1989, Cameron Equipment filed suit against Stewart & Stevenson and Travis Ward, the president and sole shareholder of Petroleum Services, Inc. In its petition, Cameron sought the return of the engines and damages for their conversion. Eventually, Petroleum Services, American General, and Power International (the subsequent purchasers) were added as defendants.

A bench trial on the merits was held on October 18–27, 1994. The trial court rendered judgment in favor of Cameron Equipment and against Petroleum Services for conversion in the amount of $50,000, which the court determined to be the fair market value of the engines at the time of the second sale. The trial court denied Cameron Equipment's claims against the subsequent purchasers, finding that since Cameron Equipment never took possession of the engines, La.Civ.Code art. 518 operated in favor of the subsequent purchasers, whom it determined were in good faith. The trial court refused to pierce the corporate veil and hold Travis Ward personally liable for the conversion damages awarded against his company, Petroleum Services.

Cameron Equipment appeals, assigning as error the trial court's determination that it did not take possession of the engines following the initial sale, the trial court's application of La.Civ.Code art. 518 in favor of the subsequent purchasers, and the trial court's failure to pierce the corporate veil.

CIVIL CODE ARTICLE 518

The trial court held that Power International, American General, and Stewart & Stevenson were superior in title to Cameron Equipment under La.Civ.Code art. 518, which states:

> The ownership of a movable is voluntarily transferred by a contract between the owner and the transferee that purports to transfer the ownership of the movable. Unless otherwise provided, the transfer of ownership takes place as between the parties by the effect of the agreement and against third persons when the possession of the movable is delivered to the transferee.

> When possession has not been delivered, a subsequent transferee to whom possession is delivered acquires ownership provided he is in good faith. Creditors of the transferor may seize the movable while it is still in his possession.

This appeal raises two questions with regard to Article 518: first, whether possession was delivered to Cameron Equipment sufficient to perfect the sale with regard to third parties, and second, whether Article 518 vested the subsequent purchasers with title superior to Cameron Equipment.

POSSESSION

The 1979 Revision comments to Article 518 indicate that "possession" contemplates both actual delivery and constructive delivery. La.Civ.Code art. 2477 provides the following methods for making delivery with regard to movables:

> Delivery of a movable takes place by handing it over to the buyer. If the parties so intend delivery may take place in another manner, such as by the seller's handing over to the buyer the key to the place where the thing is stored, or by negotiating to him a document of title to the thing, or even by the mere consent of the parties if the thing sold cannot be transported at the time of the sale or if the buyer already has the thing at that time.

Cameron Equipment first asserts that it took actual possession of the engines when Baker Littlefield, the owner of Power Rig, possessed the engines as Cameron Equipment's agent. The record reflects that the engines were originally purchased in 1986 as a joint venture between Petroleum Services and Baker Littlefield. Soon thereafter, Petroleum Services bought out Baker Littlefield's interest in the engines, but Littlefield continued to store the engines at Power Rig on behalf of Petroleum Services.

Baker Littlefield never agreed to store the engines on behalf of anyone other than Petroleum Services. He testified that had he known the engines had been sold by Petroleum Services, he would have told the new owner to remove them from his yard. Travis Vollmering, an agent for Cameron Equipment, knew that Baker Littlefield would not allow the engines to remain at Power Rig if he was aware of the sale. The record evidence clearly indicates that Baker Littlefield did not take possession of the engines as an agent of Cameron Equipment.

Cameron Equipment alternatively asserts that it took constructive possession of the engines under La.Civ.Code art. 2477. Cameron Equipment asserts that Petroleum Services "handed over the keys" to the building where the engines were kept when Petroleum Services made arrangements with Baker Littlefield to store the engines indefinitely at Power Rig. In effect, Cameron Equipment asserts that Petroleum Services transferred its storage agreement with Baker Littlefield incident to the sale. This assertion is also without merit. Petroleum Services had limited access to the Power Rig yard, extended only as a courtesy by Baker Littlefield. As noted above, Baker Littlefield was kept in the dark about the sale to Cameron Equipment, and he never agreed to store the engines at Power Rig for Cameron Equipment. The record amply reflects that Baker Littlefield would not have allowed the engines to remain in the Power Rig yard if they belonged to anyone other than Petroleum Services. We find the record supports the trial court's conclusion that there was no act between Cameron Equipment and Baker Littlefield which would equate to "handing over the keys," or that would put a third party on notice that Cameron Equipment was owner of the engines.

Cameron Equipment asserts that because of the enormous size and weight of the engines, they were insusceptible of transport at the time of the sale. Cameron Equipment therefore alleges that possession of the engines was transferred by the mere consent of the parties under La.Civ.Code art. 2477. The record clearly shows that although the engines were very heavy, they were susceptible of transport. We note with significance that after American General sold the engines to Stewart & Stevenson it took only one day to transport the engines from the Power Rig yard in Scott, Louisiana to Stewart & Stevenson's yard in Harvey, Louisiana. We find that because the engines were susceptible of transport, ownership could not be transferred by mere consent of the parties under La.Civ.Code art. 2477.

Cameron Equipment never took possession of the engines, and its purchase of the engines was never perfected with respect to third parties. Petroleum Services was never divested of possession and Baker Littlefield continued to store the engines for Petroleum Services. Ownership of the engines was never transferred vis-à-vis third parties, and any third party in good faith was entitled to assume that Petroleum Services, who never lost possession, was still owner of the engines.

Cameron Equipment argues that Power International, American General, and Stewart & Stevenson are not entitled to the protection of Article 518 because they each purchased from a vendor who was not in possession of the engines at the time of the sale. Cameron Equipment argues that it already was the owner of the engines and cites the provision contained in La.Civ.Code art. 2452 that: "the sale of a thing belonging to another person is null" to support its superior title to the engines.

Cameron Equipment's argument and reliance on Article 2452 are misplaced. In *Frey v. Amoco Production Co.*, 603 So.2d 166 (La.1992), the Supreme Court stated:

> We also note one need not own a thing in order to perfect a sale. The sale of a thing belonging to another is not absolutely null, but only relatively so, and such nullity is in the interest of the purchaser. *See* La.Civ.Code art. 2452; *Wright v. Barnes*, 541 So.2d 977 (La.App. 2d Cir.1989); S. Litvinoff, [2] Obligations § 36.

Frey, 603 So.2d at 177.

The sale of a corporeal movable without tradition of the movable is insufficient to transfer ownership. Until he receives possession of the movable, the purchaser only has the right to require delivery of the thing from the seller upon payment of the price. *See* Litvinoff, Obligations, 7 Louisiana Civil Law Treatise § 75, at 126 (1975). In the case *sub judice*, Cameron Equipment merely had the right to require delivery, it did not acquire ownership with regard to third parties. In the same fashion, the subsequent purchasers acquired the right to require delivery of the engines from Petroleum Services. While the sale of the engines alone was insufficient to transfer ownership to the subsequent good faith purchasers, the sale combined with the subsequent good faith purchasers' corporeal possession of the engines was sufficient to transfer ownership. The subsequent purchasers were able to acquire full ownership of the engines when they purchased them in good faith and subsequently took possession.

Accordingly, we find that Cameron Equipment never took possession of the engines and that the subsequent good faith purchasers were entitled to the protection of La.Civ.Code art. 518.

* * * * *

Affirmed.

Notes and Questions

1. Under Article 518, a seller of a movable thing who has already sold it may transfer ownership of that same thing to a third person, provided that possession has not yet been delivered to the first transferee. LA. CIV. CODE art. 518. Thus, in this context, the bona fide purchaser doctrine works as a "race to possession" — the

first transferee to take possession of the thing sold acquires ownership. This is a clear departure from the general rule governing the sale of a thing of another articulated by Article 2452. What policies are served by this rule?

2. The term "delivery" as it is used in Article 518 is a term of art which is defined in Article 2477. Note the various methods by which delivery of a movable thing may be accomplished. In *Cameron Equipment,* was delivery to the first transferee accomplished? Was delivery to the second transferee accomplished?

3. In order for the subsequent transferee to acquire ownership of the thing, that transferee must be in "good faith." Article 523 provides the definition of good faith as it applies in this context. Note that an acquirer of a corporeal movable is presumed under this article to be in good faith; thus, a first transferee seeking to avoid the application of Article 518 bears the burden of proving that the subsequent transferee was *not* in good faith.

4. An additional presumption applicable in circumstances involving the sale of a thing of another is found in Article 530. That article provides that "[t]he possessor of a corporeal movable is presumed to be its owner." LA. CIV. CODE art. 530. Notably, this presumption does not apply "against a previous possessor who was dispossessed as a result of loss or theft." Lost and stolen things are the subject of the next section of this Chapter.

b. Lost or Stolen Things

When a thing that has been lost or stolen is sold to another, the rights of the true owner against the buyer are governed by Articles 521 and 524. Read those articles and their comments before reading the following case which illustrates their application.

Brown & Root, Inc. v. Southeast Equip. Co.
470 So. 2d 516 (La. App. 1 Cir. 1985)

GROVER L. COVINGTON, Chief Judge.

The plaintiff, Brown and Root, Inc. (Brown), appeals a judgment requiring it to reimburse the defendant, Southeast Equipment Company, Inc. (Southeast), the purchase price paid for a stolen Caterpillar wheeled loader, under LSA-C.C. art. 524, before recovering possession of it.

The facts surrounding this matter are undisputed. Brown is the owner of a wheeled loader, and it was stolen in Houston in April, 1982. Southeast purchased the loader from a Houston equipment dealer in May of 1982 for $23,000.00 and had it delivered to Louisiana. As the result of a police investigation of the equipment dealer by the Houston police department, the Louisiana State Police tracked the loader to a construction site in Convent, Louisiana, obtained a search warrant and seized the machine. Suit was brought by Brown seeking recognition of its ownership and seeking possession of the loader without being required to pay the defendant,

Southeast, its purchase price. After a hearing on a rule filed by plaintiff, a stipulated partial judgment was signed recognizing Brown as owner and allowing it to obtain possession of the loader by posting a $23,000.00 bond.

The evidence left no doubt that the loader was stolen and that Southeast's vendor was a seller customarily engaged in the used equipment business. Accordingly, the only issue to be decided is whether Southeast is entitled to the proceeds of the bond as reimbursement of the purchase price as a good faith purchaser.

Articles 523 and 524 of the Civil Code are dispositive of cases involving the recovery of stolen movable property.

> Art. 523:
>
> An acquirer of a corporeal movable is in good faith for purposes of this Chapter unless he knows, or should have known, that the transferor was not the owner.
>
> Art. 524:
>
> The owner of a lost or stolen movable may recover it from a possessor who bought it in good faith at a public auction or from a merchant customarily selling similar things on reimbursing the purchase price.
>
> The former owner of a lost, stolen, or abandoned movable that has been sold by authority of law may not recover it from the purchaser.

These articles reflect a change in public policy, as enunciated by the legislature, to the effect that the good faith purchaser of a stolen movable is to be protected at the expense of the true owner. *Southeast Equipment Co., Inc. v. Office of State Police*, 437 So.2d 1184 (La.App. 4th Cir.1983).

In this case the only question is the good faith of Southeast. LSA-C.C. art. 523 defines good faith in terms of the knowledge of the purchaser. If the purchaser knows that the object is stolen prior to purchasing it, there is no good faith and these articles do not apply. But, where actual knowledge is absent, the article imputes knowledge if the purchaser has access to facts which would lead a prudent man to question the ownership of his vendor.

Since good faith is presumed, the true owner must establish sufficient facts to show the purchaser was put on notice his seller's ownership was questionable. In this case Brown attempted to show that Southeast had access to sufficient facts prior to purchasing the loader to indicate the movable might be stolen. The serial number plate on the front of the vehicle was glued on and the manufacturer's secret serial number under the identification number plate had been gouged out of the metal frame. Plaintiff also tried to show that the price Southeast paid was so low as to have put it on notice of the questionable ownership of the transferor. However, other testimony showed that Brown was selling similar loaders from its stock at prices even lower than what defendant paid for the loader in question. After a thorough review of the evidence in this case, we cannot say that the trial court erred in its decision that the plaintiff failed to carry its burden of proof that Southeast was in bad faith when it purchased the loader from the dealer. *Arceneaux v. Domingue*, 365 So.2d 1330 (La.1978).

For the reasons assigned the judgment of the district court is affirmed at appellant's costs.

AFFIRMED.

Notes and Questions

1. Articles 521 and 524 do not so much create an *exception* to the rule articulated in Article 2452 as they provide a *variation* on the general rule. That is, the acquirer of a lost or stolen movable does not become owner of it at the expense of the true owner. However, depending on the circumstances, the true owner may be required to *reimburse* the acquirer for the price paid for the lost or stolen thing as a prerequisite to recovering possession of it. Does this rule effectively balance the rights of the true owner and the acquirer of a lost or stolen thing from a person who was not the owner?

2. When is a thing "stolen" or "lost" for purposes of Article 524? Article 521 provides a definition for "stolen things." Lost things are not defined in the Civil Code but are contrasted with things that have been abandoned in Articles 3418 through 3419. A close reading of these articles makes clear that a thing is "lost" when the owner relinquishes possession of it without the intent to give up ownership.

3. How, if at all, does the acquirer of a lost or stolen movable acquire ownership of it? *See* LA. CIV. CODE arts. 3419, 3489–3491.

4. Article 521 provides that when "the owner [of a thing] delivers it or transfers its ownership to another as a result of fraud," that thing is not stolen. LA. CIV. CODE art. 521. The sale of a thing obtained through fraud is addressed below.

c. Things Obtained Through Vice of Consent

As Article 521 makes clear, the sale of a thing obtained through fraud is not governed by the regime in place for lost or stolen things. Instead, such a sale is governed by Article 522. According to that provision, "A transferee of a corporeal movable in good faith and for fair value retains the ownership of the thing even though the title of the transferor is annulled on account of a vice of consent." LA. CIV. CODE art. 522. Few cases have addressed this article since its introduction into the Civil Code in 1980. However, the following two cases, which predate the revision of the law, illustrate the manner in which courts previously assessed the rights of an owner who has been dispossessed of a thing through the fraud of another versus those of a third person who purchased the thing from the fraudulent transferee.

Jeffrey Motor Co. v. Higgins

89 So. 2d 369 (La. 1956)

VIOSCA, Justice ad hoc.

Defendant, A.T. Higgins, Jr., appeals from a judgment which recognized plaintiff, Jeffrey Motor Company, to be the owner of a 1953 Oldsmobile Automobile, Model 98, ordered A.T. Higgins, Jr., to return the automobile to plaintiff, and, alternatively, ordered A.T. Higgins, Jr., to pay plaintiff the sum of $2,650, with legal interest.

Judgment by default was alternatively rendered in a like amount against the defendant, Arthur Dabbs, d/b/a Arthur Dabbs Auto Sales. Dabbs did not appeal.

The facts of record are that on or about October 1, 1953, Arthur Dabbs, a New Orleans used car dealer, visited the Jeffrey Motor Company in Linden, Alabama. He negotiated with one of the partners, Clyde G. Jeffrey, for the purchase of several automobiles. The purchase included the 1953 Oldsmobile herein involved, for which a price of $2,650, cash on delivery to New Orleans, was agreed upon.

E.E. Ross, a retail salesman for Jeffrey Motor Company, drove the Oldsmobile to New Orleans on Friday, October 2, 1953, and two other cars were driven to New Orleans at the same time for delivery to Dabbs. A fourth car made the trip to return the drivers to Alabama. When Ross reached Slidell, Louisiana, he telephoned Arthur Dabbs Auto Sales Company, and, by arrangement, Edward Dabbs, son of Arthur Dabbs and an employee of the company, met Ross at Martin's Cafe on Louisiana Highway No. 90. After discussion, Edward Dabbs paid Ross for the Oldsmobile by draft, dated October 2, 1953, payable two days after date, drawn by Arthur Dabbs Auto Sales on the Louisiana Bank & Trust Company, Carrollton Branch, New Orleans, Louisiana, to the order of Jeffrey Motor Company for the sum of $2,650. Ross had been instructed to receive cash, but he did not know what a draft was and considered it the same as cash. He delivered the Oldsmobile to Edward Dabbs and turned over to him a bill of sale and the Alabama registration certificate.

Ross returned to Linden, Alabama, and the next morning, October 3, 1953, he turned the draft over to his employer, who deposited it in the Sweetwater State Bank, Sweetwater, Alabama, on October 8, 1953. The draft arrived at the Selma National Bank, Selma, Alabama, on October 10, 1953, and was returned unpaid to the Sweetwater State Bank on October 20, 1953, and charged to the account of Jeffrey Motor Company. Dabbs' bank account was never large enough during the month of October, 1953, to cover the draft.

Dabbs applied for the necessary Louisiana title certificate for the Oldsmobile, and on October 7, 1953, he sold the car to A.T. Higgins, Jr., for the trade-in of his old car and $1,500 cash. Higgins accepted the Oldsmobile and surrendered his old car to Dabbs on October 7, 1953, and he paid the $1,500 cash on October 8, 1953. A Louisiana certificate of title was issued to Higgins on October 22, 1953.

The record is uncontradicted that plaintiff took no action in the matter until the draft was returned unpaid. He then called Dabbs, who told him that he could not pay it. Criminal charges were preferred with the New Orleans District Attorney, and Dabbs was convicted under LSA-Revised Statutes 14:67. The instant suit was filed on November 4, 1953, for the return of the Oldsmobile or a money judgment.

Dabbs and Higgins each filed exceptions of vagueness to plaintiff's petition, and Higgins also filed exceptions of lack of verification and no cause of action. We believe that the trial judge was correct in overruling all exceptions.

Plaintiff alleges that, under Article 2452 [R.C.C. 2452] of the LSA-Civil Code, which provides that the sale of a thing belonging to another is null, it is entitled to the return of the Oldsmobile or its sale price. It argues that no title passed to Dabbs, and, accordingly, none passed to Higgins, and that since Jeffrey Motor Company was an innocent party it should not have to suffer the loss. In its assertion that Dabbs sold stolen property, acquired no title to it, and could convey no title to Higgins, plaintiff relies on Dabbs' conviction of the theft of three automobiles, which included the instant Oldsmobile.

In the case of *State of Louisiana v. Dabbs*, 228 La. 960, 84 So.2d 601, 603, we affirmed the trial court's ruling which denied a motion to quash the Bill of Information. We held that LSA-R.S. 14:67 (1942) broadened the concept of theft to include all offenses of larceny, embezzlement and obtaining by false pretenses, and thereby abolished the distinction between these common law concepts. Because of the broad definition of theft in LSA-R.S. 14:67, we do not believe that the case of *State of Louisiana v. Dabbs, supra*, governs this controversy.

LSA-Revised Statutes 14:67 is part of the Substantive Criminal Law of Louisiana, and the broad definition of theft for purposes of criminal prosecution, does not alter the provisions of the Civil Code of Louisiana and other civil statutes relating to sales and the transfer of title. The learned trial judge apparently considered that he was bound by the ruling of the Court of Appeal, Parish of Orleans, in *Port Finance Co., Inc., v. Ber*, 45 So.2d 404, which applied LSA-R.S. 14:67 to sales in civil proceedings. Insofar as that case conflicts with our opinion herein, it is disapproved.

When Ross submitted the two day draft to Jeffrey on October 3, 1953, Jeffrey was fully cognizant that Ross had not carried out his instructions to receive cash. Jeffrey remained silent, exercising no immediate diligence to secure the return of his car or annul the sale. He did not telephone Dabbs until October 20, 1953, or thereafter (some seventeen days after he received the draft). Therefore, Jeffrey's actions, in not repudiating the payment by draft payable at a future date, and in depositing the draft in the Sweetwater State Bank for collection, constituted his ratification of Ross' acceptance of the draft and converted the transaction to a credit sale. See *Fred G. Jones & Co. v. Sanford*, 163 La. 799, 112 So. 726, 727; LSA-C.C. Art. 3010 [R.C.C. 3008]; LSA-C.C. Art. 1840 [No Corresponding Article].

The sale to Dabbs was complete when Jeffrey accepted the draft, as there then existed an agreement for the object and for the price thereof. It follows that Dabbs had title and could transfer such title. When Higgins made his payment to the Dabbs Auto Sales on October 8, 1953, his contract with Dabbs was complete.

Jeffrey's ratification was, likewise, complete on that date. *I. Szymanski v. Plassan*, 20 La.Ann. 90.

Counsel for defendant Higgins has urged that plaintiff is estopped by his acts from bringing this action. Since we have held that Jeffrey ratified the acts of his agent, Ross, we do not feel that it is necessary to discuss the doctrine of 'Equitable Estoppel.' See *Cleveland v. Westmoreland (Cleveland v. Butler)*, 191 La. 863, 186 So. 593, 596, in which case we held that there was no need for a plea of estoppel where there was ratification.

The cases of *Fisher v. Bullington*, 223 La. 368, 65 So.2d 880; *Packard Florida Motors Co. v. Malone*, 208 La. 1058, 24 So.2d 75; *Freeport & Tampico Fuel Oil Corp. v. Lange*, 157 La. 217, 102 So. 313; *Overland Texarkana Co. v. Bickley*, 152 La. 622, 94 So. 138; *Lynn v. Lafitte*, La.App., 177 So. 83; *Hub City Motors v. Brock*, La.App., 71 So.2d 700; *Holloway v. A.J. Ingersoll Co., Inc.*, 16 La.App. 494, 133 So. 819; and *Moore v. Lambeth*, 5 La.Ann. 66, cited by plaintiff are all inapplicable. In none of them was there a ratification by the vendor, of the unauthorized acts of his agent, after he had knowledge of the facts.

For the reasons assigned, the judgment of the trial court is reversed and set aside, and it is now ordered that plaintiff's suit be dismissed and its demands rejected; plaintiff to pay all costs of both courts.

* * * * *

Flatte v. Nichols

96 So. 2d 477 (La. 1957)

PONDER, Justice.

Plaintiff brought suit for the return of a 1951 Cadillac convertible, Motor No. 5162-99705, or judgment for its value being the sum of $4,375, with legal interest from judicial demand until paid. Plaintiff alleged that it is the owner of the automobile and that one Pat Murphy, through fraud and misrepresentation, took possession of the automobile and thereafter sold it to the defendant in Louisiana. Defendant answered alleging that the plaintiff is estopped from demanding either the return of the car or the price thereof alleging that it was a bona fide purchaser in good faith. After trial on the merits, there was judgment dismissing the plaintiff's suit on the ground that the defendant's plea of estoppel was well founded in law and the plaintiff has appealed from this judgment.

The record shows that the automobile in question was purchased by W.A. Carley, a resident of Texas, on December 7, 1951 from Cargile Motor Company of Texarkana, Arkansas, and Carley was given a manufacturer's certificate. On the date of the purchase, Carley filed an application in Texas for a title certificate, attaching to the application the manufacturer's certificate, and obtained a Texas automobile license. Because his wife was dissatisfied with the car, Carley, on December 14, 1951, sold or traded the car to the plaintiff, Flatte Motor Company, a dealer in Texas.

Carley delivered to Bill Flatte, the owner of Flatte Motor Company, the receipt for the Texas license, these being the only muniments of title which Carley possessed on the car. On the same day, December 14, 1951, Bill Flatte sold the car to Pat Murphy, a dealer in Cleveland, Mississippi, with whom the plaintiff was acquainted and with whom he had previously done business. Plaintiff delivered the car personally to Murphy in Mississippi and gave Murphy the same title papers he had received from Carley and in addition the plaintiff gave Murphy an invoice-bill of sale signed by Ira Allen, bookkeeper of Bill Flatte Motor Company, which invoice was notarized by Bill Flatte himself. This invoice stated that the automobile was sold for the sum of $4,050 cash, and that there were no notes and conditioned sale contracts held by the motor company. In payment for the car, Murphy gave Flatte a check on the Bank of Cleveland, Mississippi and plaintiff company never determined if Murphy's check was good. The Flatte Motor Company at the time of the sale to Murphy knew that Murphy was an automobile dealer in Mississippi and that the car would be resold.

On December 17, 1951 Murphy paid a Mississippi Road and Bridge Privilege Tax and obtained a 1952 Mississippi automobile license, there being no requirement in Mississippi that a title certificate be issued. On December 22, 1951 Murphy sold the Cadillac to Nichols Motor Company, defendant herein, and delivered to it all of the above listed documents of title which Carley had given to Flatte, the invoice signed by Flatte, and the muniments of title in Mississippi. At this time no title certificate had been issued by Texas as applied for by Carley but the defendant was informed by Murphy that same would be forwarded when issued. Nichols Motor Company, defendant herein, sold the car to a dealer in Bridgeport, Connecticut and from there it was finally sold to a man named Robertson in Pennsylvania.

Murphy's check was deposited by Flatte in Texarkana on December 15, 1951 and payment was refused on December 22, 1951. Plaintiff contacted Murphy who told him to re-deposit the check which he did on December 26, 1951 and it was again refused for insufficient funds on January 3, 1952. It was not until January 10, 1952 that a title certificate was issued by the State of Texas and this certificate was delivered to Flatte.

The record shows that Flatte instituted proceedings in Pennsylvania against Robertson, then abandoned same. The present suit was then instituted by plaintiff against the defendant for the recovery of the car or the value thereof. No proceedings have ever been brought against Murphy, hence in this suit we are concerned only with the sale from Flatte Motor Company to Murphy and Murphy to Nichols Motor Company.

It is the contention of the plaintiff-appellant that title to the Cadillac did not pass and that since the defendant, a Louisiana dealer, did not obtain a certificate of title as required by Louisiana law, LSA-R.S. 32:705, it was not a purchaser in good faith. Appellant contends that the doctrine of estoppel cannot be applied where there is positive law and that the provisions of the Civil Code pertaining to the sale of movables have been modified in so far as they affect the sale of motor vehicles by LSA-R.S. 32:705.

The defendant-appellee contends that the sale by Flatte to Murphy was a valid sale passing title and the documents of title and indicia of ownership which Flatte gave to Murphy, who in turn gave to defendant, were sufficient to make the defendant a purchaser in good faith and hence the plaintiff is estopped by its own actions to now claim that Murphy did not acquire title to the automobile in question.

The contention of plaintiff-appellant that the agreement between it and Murphy was a conditional sale conditioned upon the clearing of the check is contradicted by the invoice given by the plaintiff to Murphy which specifically stated that the sale was for 'cash' and carried the notation 'notes and conditioned sales contracts held by none.' It is clear from the decision of this court in *Jeffrey Motor Company v. Higgins*, 230 La. 857, 89 So.2d 369 that this was a credit sale and title passed. The court therein pointed out that under Article 2456 [R.C.C. 2456] of the LSA-Civil Code the sale was complete when Jeffrey accepted the draft, which was given in that case, as there then existed an agreement for the object and for the price thereof. From this, the court stated, it followed that title passed and could then be transferred to another person.

Plaintiff-appellant relies upon the holding in the case of *Packard Florida Motors Co. v. Malone*, 208 La. 1058, 24 So.2d 75. An examination of that case shows that it is inapplicable herein as the car in that case was actually stolen. The Jeffrey case pointed out that the Packard case was inapplicable to a situation like the present one.

It is argued by the plaintiff-appellant that the Louisiana Motor Vehicle Title Certificate Law, LSA-R.S. 32:705, repeals, modifies and alters the basic provisions of Article 2456 [R.C.C. 2456] of the LSA-Civil Code. This contention has been answered in *Transportation Equipment Company v. Dabdoub*, La.App., 69 So.2d 640 wherein it was clearly stated that LSA-R.S. 32:701 et seq. do not make the sale of a motor vehicle void if the transfer is not executed in conformity with the statute, but simply causes the title to be imperfect until the certificate is acquired, nor do the provisions of LSA-R.S. 32:701 et seq. directly or by implication repeal the provisions of Article 2456 [R.C.C. 2456] of the LSA-Civil Code. The court stated that title to motor vehicles, although imperfect, may still be transferred in accordance with provisions of Article 2456 [R.C.C. 2456] as between the parties even though the purchaser did not comply with LSA-R.S. 32:701. In *Hamner v. Domingue*, La.App., 82 So.2d 105 it was held that failure to comply with the administrative regulation of LSA-R.S. 32:705 does not invalidate the sales themselves but such failure only prevents a 'marketable title' from being obtained until such time as the provisions of the statute are complied with but a valid title is perfected even before the purchaser obtains a title certificate. To the same effect are the cases of *Nettles v. General Accident Fire & Life Assurance Corporation*, 5 Cir., 234 F.2d 243; *Bedsole v. Lee*, La.App., 78 So.2d 434; *Hammond Finance Co. v. Carter*, La.App., 83 So.2d 682; *H.G. Williams Motor Co. v. Zeagler*, La.App., 92 So.2d 291.

Defendant-appellee pleads estoppel invoking the principle that when one of two innocent persons must suffer loss, it must be borne by that one of them who by his conduct has rendered the injury possible.

In the instant case the plaintiff knew that Murphy was a dealer and would resell the automobile. Plaintiff gave to Murphy, without ascertaining if the check given by Murphy was good, the application for a title certificate filed in Texas by Carley, the Texas license papers, and an invoice-bill of sale stating that there were no conditioned sales contracts outstanding and that cash had been paid for the car. Thus plaintiff not only gave Murphy possession of the movable but clothed him with every possible indicium of ownership.

It is settled jurisprudence that where one of two innocent parties must suffer loss through the fraud of another, the burden of the loss should be imposed on him who most contributed to it. *Thompson v. Hibernia Bank & Trust Co.*, 148 La. 57, 86 So. 652; *Haley v. Woods*, 163 La. 911, 113 So. 144; *Young v. Gretna Trust and Savings Bank*, 184 La. 872, 885, 168 So. 85, 90; *Theard v. Gueringer*, 115 La. 242, 38 So. 979, 981; *Reed v. Eureka Homestead Society*, La.App., 143 So. 891; *Continental Jewelry Co. v. Weilbacher*, 17 La.App. 420, 136 So. 110; *Whittington Co. v. Louisiana Paper Co.*, 224 La. 357, 69 So.2d 372; *Clark-Kelley Livestock Auction Co. v. Pioneer Bank & Trust Co.*, 228 La. 224, 81 So.2d 869.

The case of *Jackson v. Waller*, 190 Tenn. 588, 230 S.W.2d 1013 from the Supreme Court of Tennessee is almost identical to the case at bar. Therein the purchaser gave a check in payment and the seller gave possession of the car and a carbon copy of an order blank showing that the car had been purchased and paid for. This order blank was signed by the seller as in the instant case. The purchaser then took the car and sold it to another presenting the carbon copy of the order as evidence of his title. A plea of estoppel was upheld by the court saying that the loss was due to the seller's negligence in arming another with a clear indicia of ownership. To the same effect is the case of *Woods v. Thompson*, 159 Fla. 112, 31 So.2d 62. In the *Woods* case the court pointed out that as between the parties the sale was voidable but considering the fact that the plaintiff gave his vendee an invoice reciting that there was no collateral agreement or understanding between the parties, then plaintiff would be estopped as against the defendant who was a bona fide purchaser.

The trial judge was correct in maintaining the plea of estoppel filed by the defendant.

For the reasons assigned, the judgment of the lower court is affirmed at appellant's cost.

Notes and Questions

1. How do the approaches of the foregoing cases differ in their analyses of the rights of the true owners vis-à-vis the subsequent purchasers of the vehicles in question? How do the courts' approaches differ from the approach now mandated by Article 522? Before answering these questions, consider the following synthesis of the jurisprudence that predated Article 522:

> In the absence of clear legislative direction, the Louisiana courts sought to balance the conflict between security of ownership and security of

transaction. Recognizing that strict adherence to the principle that no one can transfer a greater right than he has would impede commerce and result in harsh consequences for good faith purchasers, the courts developed certain exceptions to the rule, similar to the common law bona fide purchaser doctrine. The requirements for the application of these exceptions were that the purchaser have acquired the thing in good faith, without notice that the seller was not the true owner, and for valuable consideration.

A study of the jurisprudence reveals two lines of reasoning used by the courts to avoid application of the rule in article 2452 that the sale of a thing belonging to another is absolutely null. Under one approach, the courts utilized the theory under which certain contracts are deemed to be burdened with a relative nullity. This generally involved cases in which title to the movable had passed from the original owner to the intermediate seller, but such title was deemed to be relatively null. Examples include cases in which there existed a vice of consent, such as fraudulent impersonation, and cases involving dishonored checks. The courts determined that, since title had passed, article 2452 did not apply, because the movable did not belong to another. The action to assert a relative nullity could only be brought by the original owner, who could assert it only against his vendee. Therefore, the person who acquired the movable from the original owner could validly pass title to the third party bona fide purchaser, who was protected from the claims of the original owner.

Under the second line of cases, the exception of equitable estoppel was applied in instances where title had not passed, but the owner had turned over possession to another along with some other indicia of ownership. This doctrine is based on the theory "that where one by his words or conduct willfully causes another to believe the existence of a certain state of things, and induces him to act on that belief so as to alter his own previous position, the former is precluded from averring against the latter a different state of things as existing at the same time." The owner must have surrendered not only possession to the seller but must have also clothed him with some indicia of ownership or authority to sell the thing, which induced the purchaser's reliance. These cases typically involved a breach of confidence by an agent or fiduciary. The owners were held to have contributed to their own loss by negligence in their dealings, and could not be heard to complain against an innocent purchaser.

Thus, as of 1979, the general rule was that the sale of a thing belonging to another was null, subject to certain jurisprudentially developed exceptions.

Tayna Ann Ibieta, Comment, *The Transfer of Ownership of Movables*, 47 La. L. Rev. 841, 843–45 (1987) (internal citations omitted).

2. Recall that Article 2035, which was enacted after the introduction of new Article 522, states a rule similar to that set forth in Article 522: "Nullity of a contract

does not impair the rights acquired through an onerous contract by a third party in good faith." La. Civ. Code art. 2035. According to comment (a) of Article 2035, "This Article . . . merely articulates the doctrine[] of bona fide purchase . . . ." *Id.* at cmt. a.

d. Sales of Things by Precarious Possessors

Articles 521 through 525 do not address the sale of a thing by a person who is not the owner, but who has possession with the owner's consent—that is, a precarious possessor. Consider the following hypothetical:

> Owner leases his bicycle to Lessee, in return for which she pays $50 per week in rent. Short on cash, Lessee decides to sell the bicycle without first consulting Owner. Lessee sells the bicycle to Buyer, who does not realize that Lessee is not the owner, for $200. Owner later discovers the sale and seeks to recover his bicycle from Buyer. Will he prevail?

As the following materials demonstrate, the law governing this circumstance is somewhat unsettled. Recall that, prior to the 1979 revision of the provisions that make up the bona fide purchaser doctrine, Louisiana courts applied the doctrine of equitable estoppel in circumstances in which the owner of a thing voluntarily turned over possession to another who thereafter sold to a third person. When Louisiana Civil Code articles 517 through 525 were revised, the legislature enacted Article 520, which dealt specifically with the sale of a thing by a person who, though not the owner, had possession of the thing with the owner's consent. As discussed in the law review article excerpted below, although Article 520 was enacted, it was never effective, and it was eventually repealed.

La. Civ. Code art. 520, repealed by La. Acts 1981, No. 125

A transferee in good faith for fair value acquires the ownership of a corporeal movable, if the transferor, though not owner, has possession with the consent of the owner, as pledgee, lessee, depositary, or other person of similar standing.

Tanya Ann Ibieta, *Comment, The Transfer of Ownership of Movables*
47 La. L. Rev. 841, 848–51 (1987)

1981-Article 520 is Repealed

Article 520 was the keystone of the revision of the articles relating to the transfer of movables. It marked the most significant change in Louisiana law, by virtue of the broad exception it established to the principle of article 2452 that no one can transfer a greater right than he himself has. It allowed one who did not own a thing to transfer ownership to another. Although article 520 was effective as of January 1980, the legislature suspended its operation during the 1980 Regular Session, and repealed it in 1981. The repeal was in response to the confusion and apprehension generated by the article among Louisiana retailers and equipment leasing companies. Concerned with the ability of lessees to transfer ownership of leased equipment to third parties, representatives of these groups lobbied for the repeal of article 520. In enacting that repeal, the legislature intended to eliminate potential abuse by lessees and others who hold movables for owners; unfortunately, what appeared to be a simple remedy could potentially produce unintended consequences.

Effect of the Repeal of Article 520

Article 520 codified a rule similar to but broader than the jurisprudential doctrine of equitable estoppel. Unlike equitable estoppel, which is based on the express or implied representation by the owner that the seller has the authority to sell the thing, article 520 was to be applied regardless of the nature of the original owner's actions in relinquishing possession of the thing. Its repeal may be seen as a rejection of the entire estoppel exception, or more probably, a return to the case by case approach to determining the effect of an owner's negligence on the validity of the sale of his property by another. In addition, it is reasonable to conclude that the repeal of article 520 indicates a legislative intention that a person who acquired possession of a movable from a transferor who had possession of such movable with the owner's consent should not acquire ownership. However, the force of such a conclusion is weakened by the failure of the legislature to repeal or amend the other articles of the revision that supported article 520.

In testimony before the Senate Judiciary A Committee, Professor Yiannopoulos characterized the repeal of article 520 as a "half-hearted" repeal of the law. Professor Litvinoff, at that same hearing, testified that "the repeal of article 520 would not extend those persons [retailers and lessors] as much protection as they feel it would." He added that the elimination of article 520 would only deprive Louisiana courts of the guidance it provides.

The problem to which these statements refer is that article 520 was originally passed not as an isolated provision, but as a part of an entire scheme of law; it was meant to be read *in pari materia* with the articles enacted in conjunction with it. The repeal of that single article ignored the rest of that scheme. Article 521 was enacted as an exception to 520. The other articles in the revision and in other parts of the code modified and qualified article 520. How does that scheme work without article 520?

Article 520 was intended mainly to handle the problem of breaches of confidence in instances in which the owner entrusted the thing to a person, as lessee, depositary, pledgee, or other agent, who subsequently sold it to someone else. For example, suppose *A* buys a bicycle from a dealer. *A* then loans his bicycle to *B*, who sells it to *C*. If *C* was in good faith and paid fair value, article 520 would have placed ownership of the bicycle in *C*. In the absence of article 520, there is no positive authority to support the conclusion that *C* keeps the bicycle. The repeal of article 520 implies a legislative intent to deny ownership by *C*. However, article 521 remains in effect, and it states that one who has possession of a lost or stolen thing may not transfer ownership. The negative implication of that proposition is that if the thing is not lost or stolen, the possessor may transfer it. In this hypothetical, the bicycle was not "stolen" for purposes of article 521, because *B* had possession of it with *A*'s consent. Thus, two negative implications emerge. One suggests that *C* is the owner, and the other suggests he is not.

The repeal of article 520 suggests that *A*, the original owner of the bicycle, would be able to recover it. In searching for positive authority to support this result, one might turn to article 2452, which provides that the sale of a thing belonging to another is null. One might also turn to article 526, which states that "the owner of a thing is entitled to recover it from anyone who possesses or detains it without right." By contrast, article 530, which states that "the possessor of a corporeal movable is presumed to be its owner," gives to C, the possessor, rights to the bicycle by virtue of his possession. The continued presence of article 530 is what led Professor Yiannopoulos to term the repeal of article 520 "half-hearted."

Article 530's presumption in favor of the current possessor does not avail against the previous possessor, if he can prove that he was dispossessed as a result of theft or loss. However, the facts of the hypothetical indicate that since *A* turned over possession to *B* with consent, the bicycle was not stolen. Or was it?

Notes and Questions

Following the repeal of Article 520, Louisiana courts have struggled to determine what rules should apply to circumstances in which a thing is sold by a precarious possessor who did not have the authority to sell on behalf of the owner. As the following cases make clear, the approach of the courts has been far from uniform.

Livestock Producers, Inc. v. Littleton

748 So. 2d 537 (La. App. 2 Cir. 1999)

GASKINS, J.

This case involves the sale of stolen cattle. The trial court allowed recovery to those who were damaged by the wrongful conduct of the cattle seller, but also applied the principles of comparative fault to reduce their recovery. Most of the parties have appealed the trial court judgment or have answered the appeal. For the following reasons, we reverse in part and affirm in part the trial court judgment.

FACTS

For a number of years, Danny Smith and Charles Glasscock, Sr. had a partnership known as McDade Cattle Company, which engaged in raising cattle in Bossier Parish. In 1992, Mr. Glasscock died and his children, Robert Edward "R.E." Glasscock, Charles W. Glasscock, Jr., and Dorothy Ann Glasscock Dupree, were substituted as partners. R.E. Glasscock, a resident of Houston, was mainly involved in managing the partnership with Smith. He also engaged in a cattle operation with Smith separate from the McDade Cattle Company. This operation was conducted at Shady Grove Farm, located on property owned by the Glasscock family in Bossier Parish. Smith leased the Shady Grove property from the Glasscock family for $12,000, and was paid by Mr. Glasscock for the use of this property in their enterprise. Under their arrangement, Mr. Glasscock provided all the money and property for a cow/calf operation and Mr. Smith supplied the labor. The profits were then divided between the two.

In 1994, Danny Smith told B.L. Littleton, an out-of-state rancher, that he and R.E. Glasscock owned 250 head of Brangus cattle that were for sale. Actually, Glasscock was the sole owner of the cattle which were at the Shady Grove farm. These cattle were not connected with the McDade Cattle Company. After Littleton provided bull semen to artificially inseminate the cows, he then purchased the 200 cows that were pregnant. This sale occurred on August 1, 1994. Littleton paid $150,000 for the cows. Smith asked for two checks, one for $75,000 to Danny Smith Farms and the other for $75,000 to R.E. Glasscock. However, it appears that Smith gave Glasscock the entire proceeds from the sale. When the cows began calving earlier than expected, Littleton and Smith entered into an agreement whereby the cattle were to stay at the Shady Grove farm from November 1, 1994 until February 28, 1995. In exchange for pasturing the cattle, Littleton paid Smith $11,000. Shortly after the purchase of the cows in August 1994, Littleton re-branded them with his "BL" brand, which is registered in Texas. He also placed ear tags on the cows, sequentially numbered from one to two hundred.

At about this time, Smith began experiencing financial difficulties caused largely by a gambling problem. Without Littleton's knowledge or approval, Smith began selling Littleton's cows at Livestock Producers, Inc., (LPI) an auction business run by Ronnie Stratton. A total of 126 cows, some with their calves, were disposed of by Smith. This was accomplished in several separate sales, beginning in September 1994. In January 1995, Smith contacted Stratton, anxious to quickly dispose of the remaining 74 cows. On January 16, 1995, Stratton personally purchased the cows and was reimbursed by LPI, which immediately resold them to Don Sonnier. The cows were taken to Sonnier's farm.

On February 16, 1995, Littleton received an anonymous phone call at his office in Hot Springs, Arkansas, that the cows were gone and that Danny Smith had disappeared. A criminal investigation ensued and Danny Smith was arrested and charged with theft. The Bossier Parish Sheriff's Office determined that the 74 cows should remain on the Sonnier farm until the matter was settled. When the ownership of the cows was called into question, LPI refunded Sonnier's purchase price. Then, the two civil suits at issue here were instituted.

On February 23, 1995, LPI and Ronnie Stratton filed a petition for a temporary restraining order, injunction, declaratory judgment, or in the alternative, money damages. LPI claimed to be the owner of the 74 cows purchased from Smith on January 16, 1995. LPI sought an injunction prohibiting the removal of the cattle until ownership could be determined by the court. In the alternative, LPI and Stratton sought money damages if they should be determined not to be the owners of the cattle or if the cows were encumbered with a priming security interest. Named as defendants were B.L. Littleton, Danny Smith d/b/a Smith Farms, McDade Cattle Company and R.E. Glasscock, individually.

Littleton answered and filed a cross-claim against Danny Smith d/b/a Smith Farms, and against McDade Cattle Company, asserting that Smith and McDade fraudulently sold the 200 cows he had previously purchased. He sought to recover the $150,000 purchase price as well as expenses incurred in the keeping of the cattle. He also asserted his ownership right to the 74 cows remaining with Sonnier and sought reimbursement from LPI and Stratton for the other cows that were disposed of at auction.

The Glasscocks and McDade Cattle Company answered, claiming that the partnership with Smith was dissolved. They contended that LPI did not buy the 74 cows from McDade and that McDade got no money from that sale.

On February 6, 1996, B.L. Littleton filed suit against LPI, Ronnie Stratton, Danny Smith, McDade Cattle Company as well as R.E. Glasscock, individually. Littleton alleged that LPI and Ronnie Stratton sold the cows without checking their ownership, even though the cows had a new and unfamiliar brand and even though Danny Smith was not a regular customer of the auction. He further alleged that Smith and Glasscock were partners in McDade Cattle Company and that they wrongfully received the proceeds from the sale of the cattle and should return the money to him.

On May 8, 1997, Donald E. Sonnier filed a petition of intervention naming as defendants LPI, Ronnie Stratton, B.L. Littleton, Danny Smith d/b/a Smith Farms, McDade Cattle Company and the Glasscocks, seeking to recover expenses for the 74 cows left in Sonnier's care. He later amended his petition of intervention to add as a defendant Larry Deen, Bossier Parish Sheriff, asserting that the sheriff's office determined that the cows should remain on Mr. Sonnier's farm. The claim against the Bossier Parish sheriff was severed from these proceedings at trial because it had not been filed in time for the sheriff's office to respond.

* * * * *

The two suits were consolidated and the trial was held on June 10, October 10 and October 15, 1997. During the trial, the court entered an order dissolving the restraining orders and injunctions and authorizing release of the 74 cows to B.L. Littleton. On May 7, 1998, the trial court issued its original opinion in this case.

* * * * *

The court found that Stratton and LPI were good faith purchasers of the 74 cows from Smith, but that Stratton should have been more careful in examining the brands and in getting more information and corroboration of their ownership. The court found that Stratton was entitled to recover his purchase price for the cows, but that he was 40% at fault, therefore he was entitled to recover only $32,190 of his original purchase price of $53,650. The court found that Smith and Glasscock were solidarily liable to Stratton for $32,190. The court then found that Stratton was entitled to a judgment of $53,650 from Smith.

* * * * *

B.L. Littleton appealed the trial court judgment . . . assert[ing] that LPI and Stratton are not good faith purchasers of the 74 cows remaining at Shady Grove farm. Therefore, Littleton should not have to reimburse them for the price paid to Smith for those cows.

* * * * *

GOOD FAITH PURCHASER

Following the sale at auction of 126 cows, Stratton, in his personal capacity, purchased the remaining 74 cows and was reimbursed by LPI. Littleton argues that Stratton and/or LPI were not good faith purchasers and the trial court erred in ordering that Littleton reimburse LPI and/or Stratton the purchase price of the 74 cows, $53,650.

LPI argues that not only was it entitled to reimbursement for this amount, but the trial court should have ordered that Littleton make reimbursement for this amount before the remaining cows in Sonnier's care were returned to Littleton. According to LPI, it was a good faith purchaser when the 74 cows were purchased from Smith in January 1995 and, under La. C.C. art. 524, it is entitled to recover the purchase price.

La. C.C. art. 524 provides in pertinent part:

> The owner of a lost or stolen movable may recover it from a possessor who bought it in good faith at a public auction or from a merchant customarily selling similar things on reimbursing the purchase price.

La. C.C. art 523 provides that an acquirer of a corporeal movable is in good faith unless he knows, or should have known, that the transferor was not the owner. If the purchaser knows that the object is stolen prior to purchasing it, there is no good faith. But, where actual knowledge is absent, the article imputes knowledge if the purchaser has access to facts which would lead a prudent man to question the ownership of his vendor. *Brown and Root, Inc., v. Southeast Equipment Company, Inc.,* 470 So.2d 516 (La.App. 1st Cir.1985). In *Brown and Root, Inc.,* the purchaser of equipment from a dealer was found to be in good faith even though the serial number on the piece of equipment had been tampered with and the price was low. The facts showed that the tampering was concealed, the purchase was made from an equipment dealer and other equipment was for sale at the establishment at similar or lower prices.

We find that the facts of the present case are distinguishable from those in *Brown and Root, Inc.* Regarding the purchase of the 74 cows, Stratton and/or LPI were not in good faith, as that term is construed under the provisions discussed above. Stratton had sufficient notice that something was amiss when Smith sought to quickly consummate a private sale of cattle that had a new brand that was not attributable to Smith or any of the concerns with which he was associated. According to Littleton, his "BL" brand was registered in Texas. Stratton testified that the brand on the cattle was referenced in a Louisiana brand book and determined to belong to a farmer in

Coushatta with no connection to Smith, Glasscock or the McDade operation. Even though the brand actually belonged to Littleton and was registered in Texas, not only did Stratton fail to check the brand registry in neighboring states, but when the brand did not seem to fit with Smith, he made no further inquiry. Given the freshness of the brand, Stratton should have at least questioned the ownership of the cattle. Smith was pressing for a quick, private sale of the last of the cows from the herd. Stratton moved forward to purchase the cows and immediately resell them for a quick profit. Therefore, we find that, limited to the facts presented herein, and as construed under La. C.C. art. 523 et seq., Stratton and/ or LPI were not in good faith in purchasing the 74 cows, and are not entitled to reimbursement from Littleton for the purchase price of those cows. However, LPI may recover the amount paid from Smith, who knowingly sold property that he did not own.

* * * * *

CONCLUSION

We find that ... [n]either Stratton nor LPI were good faith purchasers of the 74 cows and are not entitled to recover the purchase price from Littleton under La. C.C. art. 524. The trial court judgment to the contrary is reversed. However, LPI is entitled to recover solely from Smith the amount it paid Smith for the 74 cows, $53,650.

* * * * *

Louisiana Lift & Equip., Inc. v. Eizel

770 So. 2d 859 (La. App. 2 Cir. 2000)

STEWART, J.

The defendants, Robert Creamer and Creamer Brothers, Inc., appeal from a judgment awarding the plaintiff, Louisiana Lift and Equipment, Inc., either the return or the value of a forklift bought by the defendants from plaintiff's lessee. For the following reasons, we reverse and remand.

FACTS

In April 1994, Mr. Robert C. Eizel, d/b/a R.C.E. Equipment Company (R.C.E.), approached Louisiana Lift and Equipment Co. (Louisiana Lift) to negotiate the acquisition of a new forklift for Mr. Eizel's business. A credit check on Mr. Eizel was not favorable, so Louisiana Lift elected to enter into a "Rental Purchase Transaction Agreement" with Mr. Eizel. On April 25, 1994, Eizel signed the agreement as lessee for a "New Daewoo" forklift. The agreement listed the lessor as "Louisiana Clark-lift, Inc." The price of the forklift was $16,400.00. The lease agreement had a term of 36 months at $537.56 per month and further specified:

(12) Twelve Month Guarantee

$455 applies to [] principle [sic] each month

Georgia Owens, accounts receivable coordinator for Louisiana Lift, testified that R.C.E. paid 11 of the 36 lease payments before going into default.

The contract also contained a provision forbidding the lessee from selling the forklift. Nevertheless, on October 9, 1995, R.C.E. sold the forklift. Exhibits in the record include an automobile bill of sale which states that the buyer of the forklift is Creamer Furniture (sic) represented by Robert Creamer. According to Robert Creamer, Creamer Furniture is a trade name of a Louisiana corporation, "Creamer Brother's, Inc.," (Creamer Brothers). Creamer testified that he is the owner of Creamer Brothers. This bill of sale gives the price as $9,000.00. Another exhibit is an invoice, signed by Robert Creamer with no indication of his representative capacity. This invoice gives the forklift price as $9,500.00. The invoice specifies that the forklift was sold to Creamer Furniture.

Robert Creamer testified that he negotiated with Robert Eizel to purchase the forklift when Mr. Eizel was in the process of going out of business. Mr. Creamer bought all of Mr. Eizel's office furniture and a load of pallet racks before Eizel agreed to sell the forklift. Creamer said that he thought that $9,000 was a good price for the forklift and that he thought he could make a $1,000 profit by reselling the machine. Creamer testified that he contacted an equipment dealer, James Pharr, before buying the forklift and asked Mr. Pharr to ensure that no liens were outstanding on the machine. Creamer testified that he never had any indication that the machine was leased to Eizel.

On October 26, 1995, Louisiana Lifts, Inc. filed suit in Shreveport City Court against Mr. Eizel. The lawsuit alleged that the defendant was then $2,495.38 behind in rental payments and now owed the balance due under the lease, $14,514.00.

* * * * *

On June 24, 1996, Louisiana Lift filed a rule to show cause in city court stating that Robert Eizel had appeared in the office of the plaintiff's lawyer and admitted that he sold the forklift to "Mr. Creamer of Creamer Furniture." The rule sought an order directing Mr. Creamer to deliver the forklift to Louisiana Lift.

* * * * *

Trial of the matter was held on January 12, 1999. Robert Eizel did not testify or appear at the trial; plaintiff was unable to obtain service upon him. The trial court's reasons for judgment indicate that Mr. Eizel cannot be located and has numerous suits and liens pending against him. No evidence of such suits or liens was introduced at trial, although in its brief, appellee refers to several specific judgments in the mortgage records of Caddo Parish on the date of the sale from Eizel to Creamer.

At the close of the plaintiff's evidence, defendants moved for an involuntary dismissal on the grounds that the plaintiff had no right of action because the original seller of the forklift had been "Louisiana Clarklift, Inc." The trial court denied this motion. On July 30, 1999, the court signed a judgment:

— ordering Robert Creamer and Creamer Brothers, Inc. to submit the forklift for inspection and appraisal by plaintiff's representatives; and

—casting Robert Creamer and Creamer Brothers, Inc. in judgment in solido for the fair market value of the forklift as determined by the appraisal plus legal interest from judicial demand or, at the option of plaintiff, the return of the forklift after inspection.

Robert Creamer filed a motion for a new trial limited to re-argument on the question of his personal liability. The trial court denied this motion for the stated reason that "Mr. Creamer is the head of Creamer Brothers, Inc."

Robert Creamer and Creamer Brothers now appeal from the judgment.

* * * * *

Plaintiff's other remedy is governed by La. C.C. art. 524. Article 524 provides, in part:

The owner of a lost or stolen movable may recover it from a possessor who bought it in good faith at a public auction or from a merchant customarily selling similar things on reimbursing the purchase price.

La. C.C. art. 523 provides:

An acquirer of a corporeal movable is in good faith for purposes of this Chapter unless he knows, or should have known, that the transferor was not the owner.

In *Brown and Root, Inc. v. Southeast Equipment Co., Inc.* 470 So.2d 516, 517 (La. App. 1st Cir.1985), the court considered the effect of articles 523 and 524 on the rights of a good faith purchaser against the owner of a stolen movable. In *Brown and Root*, the court held:

These articles reflect a change in public policy, as enunciated by the legislature, to the effect that the good faith purchaser of a stolen movable is to be protected at the expense of the true owner.

In *Brown and Root*, the purchaser bought a stolen Caterpillar loader from an equipment dealer. The original owner located the loader and had it seized from the purchaser. The original owner then sued the purchaser. The question presented was whether the purchaser was in good faith. At trial, the original owner showed that the price was low and that the serial number plate on the front of the vehicle had been glued on and the manufacturer's secret serial number under the identification number plate had been gouged out of the metal frame.

Despite this evidence, the appellate court affirmed the trial court's decision that the buyer was in good faith because the tampering was concealed, the purchase was made from an equipment dealer, and other equipment was for sale at the establishment at similar or lower prices. In *Southeast Equipment*, the purchaser's good faith was not at issue.

Under La. C.C. art. 523, Creamer was in good faith unless he knew or should have known that R.C.E. was not the owner. Steven Crosby testified that Louisiana Lift usually puts a sticker "that has our name and number" on the machine but did not recall whether the forklift in question had this sticker. There was no testimony that the sticker, if it was on the machine, indicated that the lift was the property of Louisiana Lift. Mr. Creamer said that the machine bore no indicia either that it was leased, or of the identity of the true owner. As noted, Mr. Creamer testified that he had a friend in the equipment business check to see if the machine had a lien against it; no evidence was introduced to show that such a lien existed in the records of the district court.

Mr. Creamer further testified about the appearance of Mr. Eizel's business at the time of the sale:

A: He had a nice place of business over there, nice building, nice enclosed fenced yard with a bunch of equipment and pallet racks and whole business full of stuff over there.

Q: He had other equipment there that you could see?

A: Yes, sir.

Q: In fact he had a sign out there . . . RCE Equipment?

A: Yes, sir.

Steven Crosby gave similar testimony. The mere fact that Eizel was liquidating his business is insufficient on this record to show that Creamer should have known that Eizel did not own the forklift.

According to La. C.C. art. 524, Louisiana Lift may recover the forklift from Creamer Furniture on reimbursing the purchase price. Because the article is permissive, we believe that the best remedy in this case is to allow representatives of Louisiana Lift to inspect the forklift and determine whether they want to recover the machine.

We note the confusion in the record as to the amount of the purchase price. Mr. Creamer testified:

Q: Can you tell the Court why you would list the price of the forklift as $9,500.00 in your invoice and it's $9,000 in the bill of sale if they were done on the same day?

A: Yes, sir. . . . $600 worth of stuff was bought over here. You are the one that put $9,500 in your papers.

We therefore find that the purchase price was $9,000.00.

Because we decide the case on the aforementioned grounds, we do not reach appellant's argument under La. R.S. 10:1-201(37) that Louisiana Lift's failure to file a UCC-1 financing statement precluded judgment in plaintiff's favor.

CONCLUSION

For the reasons just discussed, we hereby reverse the judgment of the trial court. We remand this case to the trial court with instructions to issue an order allowing representatives of Louisiana Lift and Equipment, Inc. to inspect and examine the forklift for purposes of determining whether to exercise its right under Article 524 to recover the forklift on reimbursing the purchase price. Costs of this appeal are assessed 75% to Louisiana Lift and Equipment, Inc. and 25% to Creamer Brothers, Inc.

REVERSED AND REMANDED WITH INSTRUCTIONS.

Caraway, J., dissents with written reasons.

Brown, J., dissents for the reasons assigned by Judge Caraway.

Caraway, J., dissenting.

I respectfully dissent from the majority's application of La. C.C. art. 524 for the resolution of this dispute. Without consideration of the important legislative history for Article 524, the majority has reached for a remedy which neither party requested. Article 524 has no application to this dispute between the owner of a movable (Louisiana Lift) and one who has acquired that movable in good faith without the owner's consent (Creamer Brothers).

With the revision of the Civil Code title regarding Ownership by Act No. 180 of 1979, "Articles 518 through 525 . . . dealing with the voluntary transfer of the ownership of movables established significant change in the law in an effort to re-align Louisiana law with modern civil law and the Uniform Commercial Code." La. Civ.Code Ann. arts. 477-532, *Exposé des Motifs* (West 1980). The code's protection of ownership, as reflected in La. C.C. art. 2452, was tempered by the legislative enactment of these articles which gave protection in specific circumstances to good faith purchasers who acquire from non-owners in possession of the movable.

Under the 1979 legislation, Article 521 reflects the longstanding general principle for the protection of the true owner, while Articles 520 and 524 provided exceptions in favor of transferees in good faith. Those articles as originally enacted provided, in pertinent part, as follows:

Art. 520. Transfer of ownership by possessor

A transferee in good faith for fair value acquires the ownership of a corporeal movable, if the transferor, though not owner, has possession with the consent of the owner, as pledgee, lessee, depositary, or other person of similar standing.

Art. 521. Lost or stolen thing

One who has possession of a lost or stolen thing may not transfer its ownership to another. For purposes of this Chapter, a thing is stolen when one has taken possession of it without the consent of its owner.

Art. 524. Recovery of lost or stolen things

The owner of a lost or stolen movable may recover it from a possessor who bought it in good faith at a public auction or from a merchant customarily selling similar things on reimbursing the purchase price.

While Article 520 specifically addressed the transfer of the movable by a lessee such as R.C.E. and gave protection to a purchaser such as Creamer Brothers, the article was repealed in 1981. Nevertheless, the narrowness of the definition of stolen things in Article 521, which remains the law, is more clearly understood in light of the article's initial context with former Article 520. Under Article 521's definition, a thing is stolen "when one has taken possession of it *without* the consent of the owner," while the lessee originally addressed in Article 520 was recognized as having possession of the movable "*with* the consent of the owner." Because Louisiana Lift placed R.C.E. in possession of the forklift, it does not matter that R.C.E. became delinquent in its payments to Louisiana Lift. Such delinquency reflects a bad credit decision on the part of Louisiana Lift, but is not considered a theft under Article 521's narrow definition for stolen things and as interpreted in the prior jurisprudence before the new code articles were enacted. See, *Exposé des Motifs, supra* and *Jeffrey Motor Co. v. Higgins,* 230 La. 857, 89 So.2d 369 (1956).

In summary, the history of La. C.C. arts. 521 and 524 reveals that the legislature never intended for these articles to apply to the present situation, which originally was to have been covered by former Article 520. The repeal of Article 520 did not make R.C.E.'s sale of Louisiana Lift's property a theft within the meaning of Article 521. The choice for the proper remedy in this case is either (i) total protection of Louisiana Lift's ownership under the principle of La. C.C. art. 2452 or (ii) protection of the innocent purchaser, Creamer Brothers, resulting from the failure of Louisiana Lift to have protected its financed lease under the U.C.C. by perfecting a security interest in the forklift. Since the majority's analysis has not even come to this choice, I pretermit discussion of whether the transaction between Louisiana Lift and R.C.E. created a lease or a financed lease intended as a security interest under the test of La. R.S. 10:1-201(37).

Notes and Questions

1. Were the courts in *Littleton* and *Eizel* correct in holding that the things sold in these cases were "stolen"? Or are these sales more properly classified as sales made by precarious possessors?

2. Should the sale of a thing by a precarious possessor be governed by Civil Code article 2452, which states that "[t]he sale of a thing of another does not convey ownership"? La. Civ. Code art. 2452. Or, instead, should courts analogize the sale of a thing made by a precarious possessor to the sale of a stolen thing? To the sale of a thing obtained through a vice of consent, such as fraud? Which analogy is more appropriate? Can you make an argument that the pre-revision jurisprudential doctrine of equitable estoppel should apply? Why or why not? How would the outcomes of *Littleton* and *Eizel* differ under each of these frameworks?

3. In *Eizel,* the parties who purchased the forklift from the precarious possessor argued that they were protected in their ownership by virtue of the true owner's "failure to file a UCC-1 financing statement." *Eizel,* 770 So. 2d at 867. While the court determined that it was not necessary to address this argument, this holding

may have been in error. The court characterized the contract at issue in this case as a "lease," but it may be more properly characterized as a "financed lease," a transaction that is covered in detail in Chapter 7: Effects of the Contract of Sale. Once you have completed Chapter 7, return to *Eizel* and consider how the classification of the contract as a "financed lease" would have impacted the parties' rights.

4. Consider the common law good faith purchaser doctrine as provided by Uniform Commercial Code Section 2-403. How does the approach espoused by this provision compare to that of Louisiana?

Uniform Commercial Code § 2-403. Power to Transfer; Good Faith Purchase of Goods; "Entrusting"[±]

(1) A purchaser of goods acquires all title which his transferor had or had power to transfer except that a purchaser of a limited interest acquires rights only to the extent of the interest purchased. A person with voidable title has power to transfer a good title to a good faith purchaser for value. When goods have been delivered under a transaction of purchase, the purchaser has such power even if:

(a) the transferor was deceived as to the identity of the purchaser;

(b) the delivery was in exchange for a check which is later dishonored;

(c) it was agreed that the transaction was to be a "cash sale";

(d) the delivery was procured through criminal fraud.

(2) Any entrusting of possession of goods to a merchant who deals in goods of that kind gives the merchant power to transfer all of the entruster's rights to the goods and to transfer the goods free of any interest of the entruster to a buyer in ordinary course of business.

(3) "Entrusting" includes any delivery and any acquiescence in retention of possession regardless of any condition expressed between the parties to the delivery or acquiescence and regardless of whether the procurement of the entrusting or the possessor's disposition of the goods was punishable under the criminal law.

5. Louisiana's bona fide purchaser doctrine is complex, particularly following the repeal of Article 520. For an excellent additional discussion of this area of the law, see 24 Dian Tooley Knoblett & David Gruning, Louisiana Civil Law Treatise, Sales §§ 7:1–7:17 (2017); John A. Lovett, *Good Faith in Louisiana Property Law*, 78 La. L. Rev. 1163 (2018); Spencer C. Sinclair, Comment, *The Louisiana Good Faith Purchaser Doctrine: Codified Confusion*, 89 Tul. L. Rev. 517 (2014); Marie Breaux Stroud, *The Sale of a Movable Belonging to Another: A Code in Search of a Solution*, 4 Tul. Civ. L.F. 41 (1988).

---

e. Registered Movables

La. Civ. Code art. 525

Article 525 appears to exclude from the bona fide purchaser doctrine all sales of registered movables, such as vehicles, mobile homes, and other larger movables. Presumably, special legislation governing the registry of those movables would instead apply to determine ownership. For example, registration of motor vehicles is governed by the Vehicle Certificate of Title Law, Revised Statutes Sections 32:701 through 32:749. The requirement of registration is described in section 32:705:

> A. No person shall sell a vehicle without delivery to the purchaser thereof, whether such purchaser be a dealer or otherwise, a certificate of title issued under this Chapter in the name of the seller with such signed endorsement of sale and assignment thereon as may be necessary to show title in the purchaser . . . .

LA. REV. STAT. § 32:705. The Vehicle Certificate of Title Law statute suggests that the certificate of title will govern ownership of motor vehicles. However, a long line of jurisprudence suggests otherwise. For example, in *Flatte v. Nichols*, 96 So. 2d 477 (1957), reproduced earlier in this Chapter, the Louisiana Supreme Court held that the failure to issue a certificate of title does not prevent the transfer of ownership in a sale of a motor vehicle. Instead, failure to comply with the title law only prevents the title from being "marketable."

In line with this view, most Louisiana courts addressing disputes between a true owner of a motor vehicle and a subsequent transferee prior to the enactment of Article 525 relied upon the doctrine of equitable estoppel to settle the matter. Take as an example *Theriac v. McKeever*, 405 So. 2d 354 (La. App. 2 Cir. 1981). In that case, the owner of a truck gave possession of the vehicle to his employee. The employee later sold the truck to a third person without the consent of the owner. When the owner learned of the sale, he seized the truck, and the third person sued for a determination of ownership. The court held that the third-party purchaser was the owner of the truck. In so holding, the court applied an equitable estoppel framework, emphasizing that the owner had not only placed his employee in possession of the truck, he had also given him an endorsed certificate of title and a signed bill of sale. Thus, the employee had all the "indicia of ownership" necessary to convey ownership of the truck to the third person.

While many courts prior to the enactment of Article 525 utilized an equitable estoppel doctrine to determine the rights of parties to the sale of a motor vehicle sold by someone other than the owner, this approach was not uniform. At least one pre-revision court questioned the application of equitable estoppel to cases involving registered movables. *See Yorkwood Savings & Loan Ass'n v. Charlie Hardison & Sons, Inc.*, 383 So. 2d 1266 (La. App. 1 Cir. 1980).

Since the enactment of Civil Code article 525, few cases have examined the effect of the Vehicle Certificate of Title Law on determinations of ownership. Moreover, those that have considered the issue are inconclusive. For example, in *Lambert v. Ray Brandt Dodge, Inc.*, the court held that the registration is not a prerequisite for a valid sale of a motor vehicle, and that title is merely *prima facie*, and not conclusive, evidence of ownership. 31 So. 3d 1108, 1112 (La. App. 5 Cir. 2010). In contrast, in *Stepter v. Verele*, the court held that the sale of a motor vehicle is invalid unless title has been issued in the name of the transferee. 2011 WL 2462023, at *4 (E.D. La. 2011).

f. Sale of a Movable Pending Litigation

As evidenced by the foregoing materials, contests surrounding the ownership of movables frequently result in litigation. Article 2453 makes clear that "[w]hen the ownership of a thing is the subject of litigation, the sale of that thing during the pendency of the suit does not affect the claimant's rights." La. Civ. Code art. 2453. Thus, if a possessor of a movable thing sells it after the dispossessed owner brings a lawsuit against the possessor for its recovery, the sale does not in any event affect the owner's rights. What is not clear from the text of the article is that Louisiana courts have interpreted it (and its predecessor article) as meaning "that law [makes] the mere filing of the suit *constructive notice* to all the world that the plaintiff claimed the property, and thus charge[s] every one, however innocent, with knowledge of that fact, with the ensuring consequence that he then purchased at his peril, even 'though * * * there was no outward sign of defect in the title' of his vendor." *Richardson Oil Co. v. Herndon*, 102 So. 310, 312 (La. 1924). Said another way, once a dispossessed owner of a movable files a lawsuit against a possessor for the revindication of the thing, a subsequent purchaser is charged with knowledge of the claimant's rights and cannot acquire any right in the thing contrary to that of the claimant.

As will be explained later in this chapter, the rule announced in *Richardson Oil* is likely no longer applicable with respect to immovable property. However, the rule has apparently not been altered with respect to movables.

3. Immovables — The Public Records Doctrine

a. Introduction and General Provisions of the Law of Registry
La. Civ. Code arts. 517, 1839, 2442, 2452, 3338–3342

When a seller has sold an immovable that he or she did not own and did not have the right to sell, the rights of the buyer are governed by a body of rules known collectively as the law of "registry" or the "public records doctrine." The central tenet of this body of law provides that written instruments involving immovable property must be recorded in the appropriate public records to affect third persons. *See* La. Civ. Code arts. 1839, 3338. More particular to the law of sales, whereas ownership of an immovable thing is transferred between the parties to the sale by the effect of their agreement, the transfer of ownership is not effective against third persons until the contract is filed for registry in the conveyance records of the parish where the immovable is located. LA. CIV. CODE arts. 517, 2442, 3338. This principle amounts to a clear departure from the general rule governing the sale of a thing of another articulated by Article 2452—whereas under that provision, the sale of a thing of another does not convey ownership, under the public records doctrine, a seller who sells an immovable that he or she has already sold may indeed convey ownership, provided that the first transfer has not yet been properly recorded.

Consider the case of the double-dealing seller. Assume that Seller first sells Blackacre to Buyer 1 on Monday. Buyer 1 does not record the Act of Sale. On Tuesday, Seller conveys Blackacre to Buyer 2, who promptly records the Act of Sale. Because the sale from Seller to Buyer 1 had not been recorded at the time of Seller's conveyance to Buyer 2, it had no effects against third persons, including Buyer 2. Said another way, while Seller was no longer the owner of Blackacre on Tuesday vis-à-vis Buyer 1, Seller was indeed still the owner of Blackacre on Tuesday vis-à-vis the rest of the world. Thus, despite the prior sale to Buyer 1, Seller could convey ownership of Blackacre to Buyer 2. By recording the Act of Sale executed by Seller and Buyer 2, Buyer 2 ensured its effects against third persons, including Buyer 1. Note that while Buyer 1 has lost ownership vis-à-vis Buyer 2, Buyer 1's failure to record does not impact the enforceability of his contract with Seller. Seller, now unable to fulfill the obligations of the contract of sale, may be liable for breach of the implied warranty against eviction, which is covered in Chapter 9: The Warranty Against Eviction.

Think back to the example of the double-dealing seller of movables in Subpart E.2 of this Chapter. Recall that the transfer of ownership of a movable thing is effective against third persons when possession of the thing is delivered to the transferee. LA. CIV. CODE art. 517. Recall also that when possession has not yet been delivered, a subsequent transferee to whom possession is delivered acquires ownership provided he is in good faith. *Id.* Compare the rules governing movables with the law of registry described above. Whereas the bona fide purchaser doctrine, at least in this context, works as a "race to possession" (where the first transferee to take possession of the thing sold acquires ownership), the law of registry works as a "race to record" (where the first transferee to record the instrument evidencing the transfer of the thing acquires ownership).

Another significant difference between the two doctrines exists—whereas in the case of movable things, the subsequent transferee acquires ownership only if he or she is in "good faith," the good or bad faith of the subsequent transferee of an immovable is practically irrelevant in the operation of the public records doctrine. The following landmark case, decided over a century ago, demonstrates the application of the public records doctrine in a contest involving immovable property.

McDuffie v. Walker

51 So. 100 (La. 1909)

MONROE, J.

In 1907 plaintiff purchased a small tract of land at a sale made by order of court in the succession of Emma McClelland, and, finding that defendant was occupying a parcel (consisting of about an acre and a half) included in the tract so purchased, brought this petitory action for its recovery. Defendant answers, alleging that he bought the parcel in question by notarial act from Emma McClelland on September 23, 1899, and has been in open possession as owner, and has paid the taxes, since that time; that "for some reason" the act was not recorded, but that he has recently (May 30, 1908) had it recorded; that there was, however, on record a plat of the tract owned by Emma McClelland, on which the parcel in question is shown as belonging to "Sam Wallace," which should be "Sam Walker" (defendant herein); that said plat, with defendant's possession, was sufficient notice of his title; that plaintiff purchased with full knowledge of the fact that respondent was in possession as owner; that the sale by which plaintiff pretends to have acquired is void for want of proper notice[.]

* * * * *

Opinion.

It appears to be undisputed at this time that the parcel of land here claimed was included in the tract offered for sale, and adjudicated to plaintiff by order of court, in the succession of Emma McClelland . . . The acts of sale (presumably from Emma McClelland) to "Dan Johnson," "Goldbell Society," and "Allen," and from "Fred Dennis," were offered for the purpose of showing that Emma McClelland had sold certain parcels of land from the original tract to different persons according to the "Barber" map, which was placed on file or deposit in the office of the recorder, and that one or more sales had been made, either by her or by someone holding under her, according to a description or descriptions, which recognized defendant as the owner of the parcel herein in dispute, and, for the purposes of this opinion, it will be assumed that those facts are proved. It is not disputed that the copy of the deed from the succession of Emma McClelland to L.M. McDuffie offered in evidence by plaintiff is as described in the petition, and as there is no suggestion, either in the opinion of the Court of Appeal or in the brief of defendant's counsel, that it was not registered prior to the registry of the sale upon which defendant relies, we will assume that it was so registered.

* * * * *

It is proved and admitted that the sale by Emma McClelland to defendant, though made in 1899, was not recorded until May 30, 1908, and we take it to be proved and admitted that the sale to plaintiff was made and recorded in 1907.

It can hardly be said that the Court of Appeal finds that plaintiff had actual knowledge of the defendant's title at the time that he made his purchase. The judgment of that court is predicated upon the presumption that plaintiff knew that which (it holds) he might have known, or ought to have known. Thus the first paragraph of the opinion upon this branch of the case reads:

> "However, a consideration of the facts and circumstances of the case has led us to the conclusion that, if the plaintiff did not actually know that the defendant had claims against the property under a prior deed thereto from Emma McClelland, it was because he did not choose to know it."

* * * * *

Plaintiff testifies that he did not know defendant, and did not know and had never heard that he was the owner of the property here in dispute, and there is no testimony to the contrary. He says that he was guided in making his purchase by a sketch which he had made by an engineer (who as we take it was guided in making the sketch by the inventory on file in the succession) and by the statement made to him by the representative of the abstract company employed by the attorney of the succession for that purpose, to the effect that the title had been examined and was all right.

* * * * *

On investigating the law applicable to the facts thus disclosed, it will be found that by Act March 24, 1810, c. 25, §7 (3 Martin's Dig. p. 140), it was provided that "no notarial act concerning immovable property has effect against third persons until the same shall have been recorded in the office of the judge of the parish where such immovable is situated;" that the Code of 1825 did not repeal that provision of the act of 1810, and hence that, under the Code of 1825, as under the pre-existing law (save in the parish of Orleans) sales of land not recorded as required by the section above quoted were held to be void as to third persons. *Carraby v. Desmarre et al.*, 7 Mart. (N. S.) 663; *Gravier et al. v. Baron et al.*, 4 La. 241; 2 Hen. Dig. p. 1300, No. 2.

* * * * *

In 1855, [] the General Assembly took the matters up, and passed the Acts Nos. 259 (page 320), 274 (page 335), and 285 (page 345), which . . . were subsequently incorporated in the Revised Civil Code of 1870 under the title, "Of Registry," as articles 2251 to 2266 [R.C.C. 3338–3368]. Act No. 259 was entitled "An act relative to notaries in the city of New Orleans." Act No. 285 was entitled "an act creating a register of conveyances for the parish of Orleans." Act No. 274 was entitled "An act relative to registry," and was of general application throughout the state. It has been incorporated in the revised Civil Code as articles 2264 [R.C.C. 3338], 2265 [R.C.C. 3338], and 2266 [R.C.C. 3338], with an addition (to the latter article) which will be noted. Section 1 of the act (now Civ. Code, 2264 [R.C.C. 3338]) provides:

> "That no notarial act concerning immovable property shall have any effect against third persons until the same shall have been deposited in the office of the parish recorder [an officer created by Act of 1846, p. 71, No. 104]

or register of conveyances of the parish where such immovable property is situated."

* * * * *

In the case of *Swan v. Moore*, 14 La. Ann. 833, the acts of 1855 thus referred to, as also certain provisions then contained in the Civil Code, were carefully considered, and a majority of the court (Merrick, C. J., dissenting) reached the conclusion that:

"Actual knowledge of an unrecorded title on the part of a creditor is equivalent to knowledge or notice resulting from the registry of such title."

In the course of the opinion it was said:

"The question under consideration is, not whether an unrecorded title is without effect as to the third persons, for that is fully admitted and our registry laws are so plain on the subject that argument but obscures and clouds the text, but the question is whether actual knowledge of an unrecorded title on the part of a creditor is equivalent to knowledge or notice resulting from the registry of the act, for, if this be so, then the act of sale is in the eye of the law a recorded title in relation to the creditor having knowledge of its existence."

In reaching the conclusion stated, the court attached some importance to article 2242 (now article 2246) of the Civil Code, which then read as follows:

"Sales or exchanges of real property and slaves by instruments made under private signature are valid against bona fide purchasers and creditors only from the day on which they are registered in the office of a notary or from the time of the actual delivery of the thing sold or exchanged."

That view of the matter was, however, controverted in the dissenting opinion of the Chief Justice, who, moreover, called attention to the fact that, as the laws were on different subjects, it was immaterial for the purposes of the case whether the article in question was repealed or not.

But the article 2242, to which the court referred, no longer exists, and the argument predicated on it, as it existed when the case cited was decided, has now nothing to rest on. To the contrary, it appears to have been altered by the revisers of the Code in order to meet that very argument and to reconcile any supposed difference between it and the act of 1855. It now reads as follows, to wit:

"Art. 2246 (2242). Sales or exchanges of immovable property by instruments made under private signature are valid against bona fide purchasers and creditors only from the day on which they are registered in the manner required by law."

In *Harang v. Plattsmier et al.*, 21 La. Ann. 426, the decision in *Swan v. Moore*, *supra*, was overruled, and the views expressed in the dissenting opinion of the Chief Justice were adopted. Thus it appeared that a defendant had executed two

mortgages, which had not been recorded, and that he then executed a third mortgage, which was recorded, and in which the two preceding mortgages were referred
to. The property having been sold, there was a contest between the different mortgagees over the proceeds, and this court said:

> "The act of the General Assembly [referring to Act No. 285 of 1855]
> declares that acts 'whether they are passed before a notary public or other-
> wise, shall have no effect against third persons but from their registry.'
> Section 9. Another statute, No. 274, entitled 'An act relative to registry,'
> declares that 'no notarial act concerning immovable property shall have
> any effect against third persons until the same shall have been recorded,'
> etc. The second section directs how and where the acts shall be recorded
> and it provides, further, 'that all sales, contracts and judgments which shall
> not be so recorded shall be utterly null and void, except between the par-
> ties thereto. The recording may be made at any time, but shall only affect
> third persons from the time of recording.' Acts 1855, p. 335, No. 274. 'This
> is the last expression of the legislative will upon the subject, and it is clear,
> precise, and contains no exception or qualification.' Whether the laws be
> good or had is immaterial. Courts are bound by them and must determine
> the rights of litigants in accordance with their provisions. The lawgiver, it
> would seem, was determined to settle the vexed question whether knowl-
> edge was equivalent to registry in Louisiana, and he declared that it was not.
> 'All sales, contracts, and judgments which shall not be so recorded shall be
> utterly null and void, except between the parties.' It cannot be pretended
> that Weaver [the last mortgagee] was a party to the mortgages in favor of
> Baquié or Hauck [the two preceding mortgagees]. They were therefore null
> as to him, and could not affect his rights. We concur in the views expressed
> by Mr. Chief Justice Merrick in the dissenting opinion in *Swan v. Moore*, 14
> La. Ann. 838."

* * * * *

It is evident that whether a person acquires an interest in real estate to the extent
of its value or part of its value as a mortgagee or as a vendee the principle involved
in the application of the law of registry is the same; and hence if it be true that one
may acquire a valid first mortgage, though he know at the time that as between the
mortgagor and another there already exists an unrecorded mortgage upon the same
property, it must also be true that one may acquire a valid title to such property,
though he know that as between his vendor and another an unrecorded title has
already been passed. The law makes no distinction between mortgages and sales
or between creditors and vendees or mortgagees; nor does it discriminate between
those who acquire property with knowledge of unrecorded contracts and those who
acquire without such knowledge. Its purpose is to establish and enforce as a matter
of public policy upon the subject of the most important property right with which
it deals the rule that unrecorded contracts affecting immovable property "shall be
utterly null and void, except between the parties thereto."

No language could be plainer or more emphatic, and the courts have no more power to read into the rule established by it an exception, not contained in it, than they would have to read such an exception into the rule that a verbal sale of immovable property shall not affect third persons. It is true that "fraud cuts down everything," and, if it were alleged and proved in a given case that a mortgagee had been induced by fraudulent representation or device to leave his mortgage unrecorded or to abstain from reinscribing it, or that a vendee had been so induced to leave his title unrecorded and that loss had thereby resulted, such mortgagee or vendee would no doubt be granted relief as against the perpetrator of the fraud. But it cannot be said that one perpetrates a fraud who merely treats as utterly null and void a contract which the law in terms declares "shall be utterly null and void." To hold such doctrine is necessarily to hold that one who knows a particular contract to be denounced by the law as utterly void is bound in spite of the law to respect it as valid and binding, a paradox to which a court of justice would be unwilling to commit itself as an interpretation of law.

Beyond that, as appears from the statement which precedes this opinion, the plaintiff herein is not shown to have had actual knowledge when he purchased the property in question of the title thereto which the defendant sets up, and it is not easy to see how the "facts and circumstances" to which our learned brethren of the Court of Appeal refer (even assuming that he was informed of them all, which does not appear to us to be proved) can be said to bring such actual knowledge home to him. It is not pretended that he ever saw defendant's title deed until it was filed in court on the trial of this case or that he had ever until after he had purchased the property seen the defendant. More than that, he testifies, and no one attempts to contradict him, that he did not know, and had never heard, that defendant claimed to be the owner of the property. It does not appear except by inference (not a necessary one) that he knew that defendant was living on the property which he expected to be included in his purchase, or that he ever saw or knew of the "Barber" map. But if he knew that defendant was living on the property, and if he saw the "Barber" map, he was not obliged to conclude that defendant was or claimed to be the owner of the property, since he was assured to the contrary by the representative of the abstract company, which company, as we suppose, is engaged in the business of examining and reporting on titles to real estate, and having been employed for that purpose by the attorney of Emma McClelland's succession, had reported that the title to the parcel in question was vested in that succession.

It may be here remarked, however, that long before it was so declared in the case of *Harang v. Plattsmier, supra*, it had been held by this court that knowledge, unaccompanied by fraud, was not equivalent to registry in Louisiana. Thus in *Crear v. Sowles*, 2 La. Ann. 598, Mr. Justice Rost, as the organ of the court, said:

> "Registry laws ought not to be so interpreted as to enable third persons to commit frauds upon bona fide purchasers. But fraud is not alleged in this case. The fact of knowledge of the transfer by the defendant is not even put at issue, and is only mentioned in the affidavit made to obtain a new trial. If

it had been, knowledge by itself is not a badge of fraud. The defendant may well have believed that the sale was simulated, and, if it was, he was justified in treating it as a nullity."

* * * * *

As we have already noted, it was held in the case of *Harang v. Plattsmier* that the difficulty thus referred to had been solved by the General Assembly in the passage of the acts of 1855. Said the court in that case:

> "The lawgiver, it would seem, was determined to settle the vexed question whether knowledge was equivalent to registry in Louisiana, and he declared that it was not."

For the reasons thus given, we are of opinion that plaintiff should have judgment as prayed for. It is therefore ordered, adjudged, and decreed that the judgments herein rendered by the Court of Appeal and by the district court be avoided and annulled, and that there now be judgment in favor of the plaintiff decreeing him to be the owner, entitled to possession, of the parcel of ground described in the petition . . . .

* * * * *

Notes and Questions

1. *McDuffie v. Walker* stands firmly for the proposition that a third person is not bound by an unrecorded instrument affecting immovable property even if the third person had actual knowledge of the instrument. This proposition has been described by commentators as "the core of the Louisiana public records doctrine." 24 Dian Tooley-Knoblett & David Gruning, Louisiana Civil Law Treatise, Sales § 8:8 (2017). While *McDuffie* is frequently cited for the principle that actual knowledge is not the equivalent of registry, it was not the first case to so hold. Indeed, the Supreme Court held in 1869 that a third recorded mortgage outranked two earlier but unrecorded mortgages despite the fact that the act creating the third mortgage actually referred to the first two. *Harang v. Plattsmier*, 21 La. Ann. 426 (1869).

2. While holding that a third person's actual knowledge of an unrecorded instrument does not amount to registry, the Court in *McDuffie* acknowledged that a third person's "fraud" may be an exception to the general application of the public records doctrine. Care should be given not to read the Court's statements regarding "fraud" too expansively. The Court was careful to differentiate between a third person who had fraudulently induced a buyer or mortgagee not to record the instrument evidencing that person's rights and a third person who merely used non-record knowledge to his or her advantage:

> If it were alleged and proven in a given case that a mortgagee had been induced by fraudulent representation or device to leave his mortgage unrecorded or to abstain from reinscribing it, or that a vendee had been so induced to leave his title unrecorded and that loss had thereby resulted, such mortgagee or vendee would no doubt be granted relief as against the

perpetrator of the fraud. But it cannot be said that one perpetrates a fraud who merely treats as utterly null and void a contract which the law in terms declares "shall be utterly null and void." To hold such a doctrine is necessarily to hold that one who knows a particular contract to be denounced by the law as utterly void is bound in spite of the law to respect it as valid and binding, a paradox to which a court of justice would be unwilling to commit itself as an interpretation of law.

McDuffie, 51 So. at 105.

A somewhat recent case involving a third person's "fraud" is *First National Bank of Ruston v. Mercer*, 448 So. 2d 1369 (La. App. 2 Cir. 1984). In that case, after the First National Bank of Ruston ("the Bank") foreclosed on a piece of immovable property, the president of the Bank contacted Mercer, with whom he had previously done business, to inquire whether Mercer would like to buy the property. Mercer did not want to purchase the property in his own name for two reasons: first, the property was leased to a restaurant that was run by a competitor of his wife's family's restaurant, and second, he was already indebted to the Bank for the maximum amount allowed by the bank's supervising agency. Mercer therefore convinced his employee, Craig, to stand in for him as buyer. At the closing, which was attended by both Craig and Mercer, there was some confusion surrounding the price that would be paid for the property; nevertheless, an Act of Sale was ultimately filed in the public records showing a sale from the Bank to Craig. Craig later failed to make payments on the price, and the Bank initiated foreclosure proceedings. After that, Mercer bought the property from Craig and filed his Act of Sale. Ultimately, a court held that the sale from the Bank to Craig was absolutely null due to a failure of the meeting of the minds as to the price. Mercer attempted to rely on the public records doctrine, citing his status as a third person entitled to rely on the absence of any indication in the public records that the sale was null. The court gave several reasons for rejecting Mercer's argument, relying in particular on its finding that Mercer had attempted to use the public records doctrine to "perpetrate a fraud":

> Without further elaboration, sufficeth to say that we are convinced that any fair reading of this record will convince anyone that a prima facie case of fraud was proven by clear and convincing evidence. It is obvious that Craig and Mercer, knowing all the facts surrounding the initial transaction became aware of the Bank's vulnerable position after which they conspired and schemed to deprive the Bank of this property without paying for it. In actuality, Mercer does not attempt to rely on the public records to protect himself but in fact attempts to use them as a cloak in furtherance of his fraudulent scheme. The rule is well established that fraud vitiates all things, notwithstanding the public records doctrine. A party to a fraudulent transaction can never take advantage of the fraud. The rule has always been that the public records doctrine does not protect a third party purchaser, where there has been fraud or forgery. Accordingly, we conclude that Mercer can find no protection for his actions by relying on the public records doctrine

because we hold that a person can not [sic] use the public records doctrine to perpetrate a fraud.

Id. at 1378–79 (internal citations omitted).

3. *McDuffie*'s assertion that an unrecorded instrument is without effect even to third persons who have actual knowledge thereof may seem surprising, even harsh. However, any criticism of the rule must be conducted with a thorough understanding of the public policies underpinning the land registry and the various recording systems that are used throughout the United States. The following excerpt describes the three systems of land registry used in this country: (1) the pure-race system, (2) the notice system, and (3) the race-notice system.

Michael Palestina, *Of Registry: Louisiana's Revised Public Records Doctrine*
53 Loy. L. Rev. 989, 995–98 (2007) (citations omitted)

B. Philosophical Foundation and Basic Rules

The purpose of any recordation system is two-fold and represents a balance between two otherwise competing objectives. First, a system of public recordation should provide both security and stability for the property rights of owners. Second, it should facilitate the transfer of property between buyers and sellers such that property remains in commerce.

In order to accomplish these objectives, the American common law of property traditionally operated by a single rule: first in time, first in right. This system was very simple: whoever first acquired their interest prevailed over any interest later acquired. Over time, however, most states recognized the injustice inherent in such a draconian, absolute system, and adopted modified systems to deliver a sense of fairness by affording protection to recording first purchasers and by creating the bona fide (subsequent) purchaser doctrine. Generally, a bona fide purchaser is a subsequent purchaser who pays value for the property and has no notice of any kind of prior unrecorded claim on said property. Louisiana, however, did not evolve like most states, and today uses a modified version of the original common law system known as the pure-race system, wherein the first person to record is considered the owner of record. The pure-race system could be described as "first in time (to record), first in right."

Pure-race systems, however, are not all the same. Under the traditional pure-race system, the first purchaser for value to record his interest prevails, and non-record notice is irrelevant. Thus, traditional pure-race systems require a subsequent transferee to be a purchaser, but not to be bona fide. However, under the post-Revision recordation provisions, Louisiana is now one of only two states—the other being Delaware— that requires neither bona fide status nor value to invoke the protection of the PRD.

One hallmark of Louisiana's pure-race system, as with all pure-race systems, is the irrelevancy of non-record notice. With the Revision, Louisiana has conclusively legislated the "bona fide" requirement out of the bona fide purchaser doctrine. A subsequent purchaser is imputed to have only record notice, and is required only to check the public records for prior interests; he can assume, for all legal purposes, that the owner of record is the owner, regardless of any non-record notice he might have to the contrary, even actual notice that another person has a prior, unrecorded interest in the property. Thus, for third parties, an unrecorded instrument, for all intents and purposes, does not exist. Rather, third parties "need look only to the public records to determine [the existence of] adverse claims." To illustrate, assume Owner (O) sells Blackacre to Purchaser 1 (P1), who does not record his interest, and O subsequently resells Blackacre to Purchaser 2 (P2), who records his interest. Because Louisiana recognizes only record notice, P2 is the owner of Blackacre, even if he had non-record notice that O had previously sold Blackacre to P1. However, if P1 had recorded his interest, P2 would be without recourse, because he would have had record notice.

The other hallmark of Louisiana's pure-race system, shared by only one other state, is the irrelevancy of value in the face of record notice. The traditional purpose of any recordation system, pure-race or otherwise, is the protection of either the current owner who recorded or a subsequent purchaser who relied on the record, the theory being that the subsequent purchaser deserves protection because he has relied on the public records to his detriment (i.e., to his financial risk). With the Revision, Louisiana has legislated the purchaser requirement out of the bona fide purchaser doctrine. In other words, under Louisiana's revised pure-race system, O can sell Blackacre to P1; and if P1 were to fail to record his purchase, O could then give Blackacre to Anyone (A), and A would become owner of Blackacre upon recordation. Under this system, A is protected despite the fact that he has not purchased for value—i.e., despite the fact that he has not relied on the public records to his detriment.

Therefore, under post-Revision Louisiana law, a subsequent transferee need not be bona fide in status nor pay value for his interest, thereby removing the only protections afforded a Louisiana first purchaser—protections that first purchasers in notice and race-notice jurisdictions still enjoy. In these alternative jurisdictions, a subsequent purchaser would have to both pay value and have no notice of any kind (record or actual) of any prior claim to the property to receive the protection of the PRD.

Nonetheless, despite this apparent injustice, the pure-race system has its benefits. Pure-race statutes are easier to administer because they minimize the potential for confusion. The criterion for determining ownership is simple, objective, and not open to judicial determination: whoever recorded first is the owner. This system also reduces the amount of litigation involved in title disputes, and, for the most part, is the best means of ensuring clear and unencumbered title such that property can remain in commerce. Consequently, land titles are almost always straightforward and seldom subject to litigation. Because it "limits inquiry to matters of record only and does not require [a] subsequent purchaser to establish that he took title without notice," the pure-race system is, in fact, the most judicially efficient and economical system available.

* * * * *

D. Alternative Options

* * * * *

Following the large-scale rejection of the traditional pure-race system, many states moved to the other extreme, the notice system.

The notice system operates under a simple theory: where a first purchaser has failed to record his claim in an immovable, a subsequent purchaser will prevail over that first purchaser only if he had no notice of any kind of the earlier conveyance to the first purchaser. In that instance, the subsequent purchaser is considered a bona fide purchaser, and can thus avail himself of the public records as he finds them, even if he does not record his interest first.

To qualify as a bona fide purchaser under the notice system, and thus receive the protection of the public records, a subsequent purchaser must (1) be a subsequent purchaser, (2) purchase for value, and (3) purchase without notice of any kind of any prior claim. Notice systems typically recognize all four kinds of notice [actual, constructive, inquiry, and imputed], and notice is determined at the time the subsequent purchaser purchased his interest in the immovable.

Notice statutes are significantly more prevalent than pure-race statutes. They reward the bona fide subsequent purchaser while penalizing the unscrupulous subsequent purchaser who possesses any notice of a prior interest instead of allowing him "to profit by winning the race to record first." Notice statutes tend to "correct the inequality in allowing later buyers to prevail over earlier buyers when they know about the earlier conveyance . . . thereby prevent[ing] later buyers from fraudulently snatching property away from earlier buyers just because they recorded first."

However, notice statutes also have significant disadvantages. Although they do protect innocent purchasers against unscrupulous ones, they do so at the significant cost of clarity, coherence, and predictability of land transfers and titles. The stability of the land system is markedly reduced because of the uncertainty associated with judicial discernment of parties' factual notice. In essence, the clarity of title becomes vulnerable to time-consuming litigation regarding the litigants' subjective knowledge. Notice statutes also cause significant complications in a title search by a later purchaser because they give priority to "the first party who buys without notice even if [that party] records second." Finally, these systems tend to empirically decrease the actual incentives to record one's purchase because earlier purchasers can always claim that a subsequent purchaser had one of the four kinds of notice. In this way, notice systems purportedly dramatically increase litigation, thereby significantly decreasing the efficiency of the recording system by requiring parties to litigation to seek proof of their claims outside of the public records. Thus, although notice statutes remain popular, they tend to diminish the security of titles and retard the transfer of immovables.

Recognizing the inherent shortcomings of both pure-race and notice statutes, almost half of the states have switched to a hybrid system known as the race-notice statute. Under this framework, a subsequent purchaser qualifies as a bona fide purchaser, thereby receiving the protection of the public records, when he (1) is a subsequent purchaser, (2) purchases for value, (3) has no notice of any prior interest, and (4) records his interest first. Therefore, any subsequent purchaser must satisfy both the requirements of the pure-race system (i.e., that one record first) and also the requirements of the notice system (i.e., that one have no notice of any prior interests).

Generally, such statutes "represent a compromise between the predictability of race statutes and the fairness of protecting only those who buy without notice of the prior claim." In so doing, race-notice statutes do not fall prey to the inefficiencies associated with subjective knowledge determinations in notice litigation because they require the would-be bona fide subsequent purchaser to record his interest before a first purchaser to prevail. Therefore, if a first purchaser records within a reasonable amount of time, or perhaps records even as a result of a visit by some potential subsequent purchaser, litigation rarely comes to fruition. Accordingly, race-notice statutes, by incorporating the benefits of both pure-race and notice statutes, strike a happy balance such that substantial justice is done.

Notes and Questions

1. Do you agree with the author's assessment that race-notice systems are superior to pure-race systems like the one used in Louisiana? Why or why not? What are the benefits of Louisiana's pure-race system? What are the downsides of such a system?

2. Article 3338 provides a list of specific instruments that are "without effect as to a third person unless the instrument is registered by recording it in the appropriate mortgage or conveyance records . . . ." LA. CIV. CODE art. 3338. Those instruments include not only (1) an instrument that transfers an immovable or establishes a real right in or over an immovable, but also (2) the lease of an immovable, (3) an option or right of first refusal, or a contract to buy, sell, or lease an immovable or to establish a real right in or over an immovable, and (4) an instrument that modifies, terminates, or transfers the rights created or evidenced by the instruments described above. Id. Leases, options, rights of first refusal, and contracts to buy or sell are all subjects of subsequent Chapters in this Textbook, and the rules of recordation as they apply to those contracts will be addressed in more detail there.

3. Article 3340 further recognizes that special legislation may require the recordation of an instrument that is not specifically described by Article 3338. In such a case, "such act or instrument is not effective as to a third person until it is recorded." LA. CIV. CODE art. 3340. Moreover, the same article provides, "The recordation of

a document, other than an instrument described in article 3338, that is required by law to be registered, filed, or otherwise recorded with the clerk of court or recorder of conveyances or of mortgages or in the conveyance or mortgage records shall have only the effect provided for by such law." *Id.* An example of an instrument that is not referenced but that nevertheless must be recorded to have effects against third persons is a notice of lis pendens—the purpose and effect of which are both explored below in Part 3.e.ii of this Chapter.

4. As Article 3339 makes clear, not *every* right involving immovable property must be evidenced in the public records to affect third persons. According to that article, "A matter of capacity or authority, the occurrence of a suspensive or a resolutory condition, the exercise of an option or right of first refusal, a tacit acceptance, a termination of rights that depends upon the occurrence of a condition, and a similar matter pertaining to rights and obligations evidenced by a recorded instrument are effective as to third persons although *not* evidenced of record." La. Civ. Code art. 3339 (emphasis added). In addition, the public records doctrine admits a number of significant exceptions according to which a right in an immovable is enforceable against third persons even though not evidenced in the public records. Some of these exceptions are addressed below in Subpart E.3.d of this Chapter.

5. The public records doctrine is often described as a "negative" doctrine, because it denies effects to certain unrecorded instruments by allowing third persons to act as if those unrecorded instruments do not exist. Consider the example of *McDuffie v. Walker* reproduced above. There, because Walker failed to file an instrument evidencing a transfer of the land in question from McClelland to him, McDuffie (a third person to the sale between McClelland and Walker) was allowed to regard it as a "nullity." Indeed, McDuffie was allowed to ignore the previous transfer altogether, even though he may have known that the transfer took place. It was the *absence* of Walker's Act of Sale on which McDuffie was entitled to rely.

Citing the negative character of the public records doctrine, courts and commentators frequently make statements to the effect that "recordation . . . is not itself the source of rights." *See, e.g.,* William V. Redmann, *The Louisiana Law of Recordation: Some Principles and Some Problems*, 39 Tul. L. Rev. 491, 496 (1965). In other words, recordation of an instrument does not necessarily ensure the instrument's enforceability, whether against third persons or between the parties thereto. Article 3341 is careful to circumscribe the effects of recordation, stating, "The recordation of an instrument (1) Does not create a presumption that the instrument is valid or genuine, (2) Does not create a presumption as to the capacity or status of the parties, (3) Has no effect unless the law expressly provides for recordation, and (4) Is effective only with respect to immovables located in the parish where the instrument is located." La. Civ. Code art. 3341.

6. Article 3342 provides, "A party to a recorded instrument may not contradict the terms of the instrument or statement of fact it contains to the prejudice of a third person who after its recordation acquires an interest in or over the immovable to which the instrument relates." La. Civ. Code art. 3342. Under this article, third

persons are generally entitled to rely on the absence of any indication in the public records that a recorded instrument is null or otherwise unenforceable according to its terms. The public records' protection against nullity and other "secret claims and equities" of the parties is further discussed below in Subpart E.3.e of this Chapter.

b. Third Person Defined
La. Civ. Code art. 3343

As the foregoing materials make clear, the law of registry provides that unrecorded instruments involving immovables are without effect as to "third persons." LA. CIV. CODE art. 3338. An understanding of who qualifies as a third person to an instrument is thus crucial to the proper application of the public records doctrine.

Article 3343 provides a definition of the term "third person," which begins with the statement that "[a] third person is a person who is not a party to . . . an instrument." LA. CIV. CODE art. 3343. Quite obviously, a person who is a party to an unrecorded instrument is not a "third person" with respect to that instrument and may not rely on the fact that the instrument is not recorded to avoid its effects. LA. CIV. CODE art. 3343; see also LA. CIV. CODE art. 2442. Assume, for example, that Alice sells Blackacre to Betty, who fails to record her Act of Sale. Although the sale has no effects to persons not parties to the instrument, the sale is fully enforceable against Alice, as seller, and Betty, as buyer. If Alice brings a petitory action against Betty, asserting that she is owner of Blackacre by virtue of Betty's failure to record, she will not prevail.

Third persons also include persons "not . . . personally bound by an instrument." LA. CIV. CODE art. 3343. Who may be personally bound by an instrument despite not being a party to it? For one, the universal successors of a party to an instrument are personally bound thereby. See Butler v. Butler, 212 So. 2d 213 (La. App. 2 Cir. 1968) (heirs of seller estopped from asserting interest in property contrary to buyer under unrecorded deed). In addition, when one spouse in community acquires an immovable, the other spouse, though perhaps not bound to the obligations expressed in the instrument to the same extent as a universal heir, is not a "third person" for purposes of the public records doctrine. See Bordelon v. Bordelon, 499 So. 2d 1050 (La. App. 3 Cir. 1966) (spouse whose husband purchased immovable under deed later found to be null could not claim reliance on the public records doctrine to avoid rescission).

Many written instruments affecting immovables contain the signature of persons other than the parties to the contract. For example, if an Act of Sale is executed in authentic form, it will be signed by a notary and at least two witnesses in addition to the buyer and the seller. The question of whether witnesses are "third persons" with respect to the instruments they sign for purposes of the law of registry is answered directly by Article 3343: "A witness to an act is a third person with respect to it." LA. CIV. CODE art. 3343. The Article is silent with respect to notaries; however, given the importance of the role of notaries in Louisiana law, notaries are not considered "third persons" with respect to the acts executed by them. 1 PETER S. TITLE, LOUISIANA PRACTICE SERIES, LOUISIANA REAL ESTATE TRANSACTIONS § 8:20 (2017-18 ed.). Assume that an Act of Sale is executed in authentic form transferring Blackacre from Alice to Betty and is signed by Carlos as Notary and Diangelo and Erica as witnesses. If the Act of Sale is not thereafter recorded, whereas either Diangelo or Erica could acquire the same property from Alice in a valid sale, the same is not true of Carlos.

The third paragraph of Article 3343 contemplates two additional types of persons who, although not parties to an instrument, are not "third persons" with respect to it for purposes of the law of registry. First among these is "[a] person who by contract assumes an obligation[.]" LA. CIV. CODE art. 3343. Assumption, you will recall, is the transfer of an obligation from one obligor to another. *See* LA. CIV. CODE arts. 1821, 1823. Assumption may be accomplished either through an agreement between the original obligor and the third person (LA. CIV. CODE art. 1821) or through an agreement between the obligee and the third person (LA. CIV. CODE art. 1823). In either case, the third person acquires the position of obligor by virtue of the assumption and, with respect to the law of registry, ceases to occupy the position of "third person" to an instrument evidencing the obligation. This rule frequently applies in sales of immovable property burdened with either a mortgage or a lease. Consider the following example: Alice leases Blackacre to Betty for a term of five years. The parties execute a written instrument of lease, but neither party records it. Before the first year of the lease expires, Alice sells Blackacre to Carlos, who agrees in the Act of Sale to assume Alice's obligations under the lease between Alice and Betty. Although the lease between Alice and Betty is unrecorded and therefore unenforceable against third persons, because Carlos assumed Alice's obligations under the lease, he is no longer regarded as a third person with respect to the unrecorded instrument. Instead, he must honor the lease for the remainder of its term and, also by virtue of his assumption agreement, fulfill the obligations of a lessor. (As will be shown in Chapter 14: Obligations of the Lessor and the Lessee, the obligations of the lessor are extensive, and include, among other things, the obligation to maintain the premises and the obligation to maintain the lessee's peaceful possession.)

According to Article 3343, another person who, though not a party to an instrument, is not a "third person" with respect to it is "[a] person who . . . is bound by contract to recognize a right." LA. CIV. CODE art. 3343. This language describes a person who has agreed to honor the rights of a party to an instrument, even if that instrument is unrecorded. Again, this situation arises frequently in the context of lease. Take the example of Alice leasing Blackacre to Betty for a term of five years by virtue of an unrecorded lease. When Alice sells Blackacre to Carlos, he may agree to recognize the unrecorded lease, foregoing his rights under the public records doctrine to disregard the unrecorded instrument, without also agreeing to assume Alice's obligations under the lease. A provision in an Act of Sale by which a purchaser of an immovable agrees to honor unrecorded leases without assuming the obligations of a lessor is known in practice as a "subject to" clause (i.e., the purchaser acquires the immovable "subject to" unrecorded leases). The "subject to" clause differs from an assumption in that, under the former, the purchaser does not agree to take on the obligations of the original lessor (which again, as you will see in Chapter 14: Obligations of the Lessor and the Lessee, include extensive repair and warranty obligations).

The following case provides another example of a person "bound by contract to recognize a right" as the phrase is used in Article 3343.

Bradley v. Sharp
793 So. 2d 500 (La. App. 2 Cir. 2001)

CARAWAY, J.

This case involves a dispute between the owner of standing timber, the plaintiff, and the owner of the land, the defendant. Both owners acquired their property from a common ancestor-in-title by purchases that occurred within two days of each other. The sale of the pine timber occurred first, and the deed to the land to defendant made reference to the prior timber sale. Defendant recorded his deed before the recordation of plaintiff's timber deed. Although plaintiff was allowed to harvest some timber during the term of his 18-month contract, defendant ultimately blocked plaintiff from cutting all of the pine timber, and this suit was filed. Claiming that the public records doctrine protects him and that plaintiff damaged his property and the hardwood timber, defendant appeals the trial court's ruling awarding damages to plaintiff. We affirm the ruling.

Facts

Plaintiff, O. Kyle Bradley, d/b/a Kyle Bradley Logging ("Bradley") brought this suit after he was denied access to a tract of land by defendant, H. Wayne Sharp, Jr. ("Sharp"), to harvest timber that Bradley purchased from Charlotte Brown Bonham, Sandra J. Brown Kenna and Richea Kaye Brown Gaston (the "Browns"). Sharp bought the tract of land from the Browns and recorded his deed to the property nearly two weeks before Bradley's recordation of the timber deed.

The disputed transactions arose after the Browns announced their intention to sell certain property in an October 9, 1997 prospectus letter entitled "Timber/Land Sale on Cross Lake." The timber land consisted of approximately 159 acres near Cross Lake in Caddo Parish. The prospectus instructed Bradley, Sharp and other interested bidders that they could bid on the tract for the land or timber or a combination thereof, including the purchase of the pine timber only on the 159 acres, or the purchase of the hardwood and land. Furthermore, in reference to bid option No. 4, the hardwood and land option, the prospectus stated that bidders "will assume the pine is being sold separately with an 18 month harvest contract." Sharp submitted a bid, in accordance with the prospectus for options 4 and 6, regarding the hardwood timber only and the land on the 159-acre tract plus an adjacent 3-acre tract on the lake with a brick home.

On November 11, 1997, Bradley entered into a Timber Deed with the Browns, purchasing all merchantable pine trees on the 159-acre tract for $227,650. The Timber Deed recited several terms and conditions. First, Bradley was granted the right of ingress and egress upon the land to "cut and fell trees and to carry the same away," until May 10, 1999. After May 10, 1999, any merchantable timber remaining on the tract was to revert to the Browns as sellers of the timber. Secondly, Bradley agreed to conduct all of his logging operations in accordance with Forestry Best Management Practices, agreeing not to litter the tract and to minimize damage to the property. The Timber Deed further provided for specific damages to trees wrongfully cut as follows: Hardwood Saw timber—$450/MBF and Hardwood Pulpwood—$45/cord. The parties agreed that the volume of hardwood timber wrongfully cut was to be determined by Bayou State Timber Services, Inc. ("Bayou State"). Bradley did not record the Timber Deed until December 22, 1997.

Sharp entered a $95,000 bid and signed a purchase agreement with the Browns for the 159-acre tract and hardwood timber on November 13, 1997. In the purchase agreement, the Timber Deed is referred to as follows:

> "Closing date shall be prior to December 1, 1997 but no sooner than 15 days after acceptance by all parties. *This date is contingent upon completion of an attorney's title opinion, survey and a current timber contract which expires May 10, 1999. All rights in timber contract are to be assigned in land sale.*
>
> * * * * *
>
> *Buyer is aware that the pine timber is sold on an 18 month contract.*" (Emphasis ours)

The 159-acre tract was sold by a cash sale deed in accordance with the purchase agreement on November 24, 1997, and was recorded on December 9, 1997. The deed, which was drafted by Sharp's attorney, acknowledges the existence of the Timber Deed as follows:

> "PURCHASER hereby acknowledges the existence of a timber contract between SELLER and O. Kyle Bradley Logging of Texas (hereinafter "TIMBER BUYER"). SELLER herein agrees that the rights of timber and trees revert at the expiration of the timber contract to SELLER are hereby specifically transferred and assigned to PURCHASER.
>
> * * * * *
>
> SELLER agrees to and shall indemnify and hold harmless PURCHASER and subsequent landowners, their officers, agents, employees, heirs and assigns from and against any and all claims, losses, damages causes of action, suits and liability of every kind, including all expenses of litigation, court costs and attorney's fees, for injury to or death of any person, or for damage to any property, arising out of or in connection with the operations under the timber contract executed between SELLER and TIMBER BUYER whether or not such injuries, death or damages, are caused by TIMBER BUYER or

SELLER's sole negligence or the joint negligence of TIMBER BUYER and any other person or entity."

Bradley removed the timber in accordance with the Timber Deed until November 28, 1997. Rain forced the operation to halt from November, 1997, until July 10, 1998. On July 27, 1998, Sharp denied Bradley access to the Tract, claiming that Bradley damaged too many hardwood trees, as well as a cemetery on the northern part of the tract which was specifically flagged as a no logging area. Pursuant to negotiations with Sharp, Bradley paid a $3,400 "deposit" to cover potential damages to the property and/or the hardwood trees that could occur during harvesting of the pine timber. Ultimately, in late July 1998, Sharp blocked the access road leading to the remaining pine timber and informed Bradley that he could no longer harvest the timber on the tract, unless he returned with a court order. Efforts to negotiate any type of agreement to allow Bradley to continue harvesting the land failed. Bradley subsequently filed suit on May 8, 1999, claiming that his rights under the Timber Deed had been violated and seeking damages.

At trial, Sharp's testimony revealed that before he submitted his bid on the property, he expressed concern about the language of the Timber Deed. Sharp never denied knowing about the Timber Deed, nor did he claim that the reference to Bradley's deed in his purchase agreement and deed were in error. In fact, Sharp stated that upon his request, Harvey Bryant ("Bryant"), a Bayou State forester, gave him a copy of a timber deed with a different logger, and that he knew the rates he would be paid for damaged hardwood. Sharp further stated that he considered this information when preparing his bid.

Following a bench trial, the trial court rejected Sharp's claim that the public records doctrine allowed him to disregard Bradley's Timber Deed. The court found that Sharp interfered with Bradley's right to cut the pine timber during the term provided in the Timber Deed and awarded damages to Bradley in the amount of $46,512.30 for the unharvested timber, as well as damages for lost crew time in the amount of $3,500, for a total of $50,012.30. The trial court awarded Sharp $1,500 on his defense and reconventional demand concerning damage to the hardwood timber resulting from Bradley's operations on the property. Sharp appeals the trial court's ruling.

Discussion

I.

Sharp's first assignment of error pertains to his defense that, having recorded his deed to the property 13 days before the recordation of Bradley's Timber Deed, he was a third party purchaser protected by the public records doctrine. He claims that since he did not expressly assume the obligations of the Timber Deed, he was unaffected by the timber sale and thus acquired ownership of the land and pine timber. To the contrary, the trial court ruled that despite the lack of Sharp's express assumption of the personal obligations of the Timber Deed, his acknowledgment of Bradley's unrecorded rights made Sharp's acquisition of the land subject to Bradley's ownership of the pine timber. From our review of the following authorities regarding the ownership of standing timber and the public records doctrine, we affirm the trial court's ruling.

The Civil Code articles pertaining to the ownership of standing timber are as follows:

> La. C.C. art. 464: Buildings and standing timber are separate immovables when they belong to a person other than the owner of the ground.

> La. C.C. art. 491: Buildings, other constructions permanently attached to the ground, standing timber, and unharvested crops or ungathered fruits of trees may belong to a person other than the owner of the ground. Nevertheless, they are presumed to belong to the owner of the ground, unless separate ownership is evidenced by an instrument filed for registry in the conveyance records of the parish in which the immovable is located.

The Louisiana law embodying the principles of our public records doctrine is as follows:

> La. C.C. art. 1839: A transfer of immovable property must be made by authentic act or by act under private signature. Nevertheless, an oral transfer is valid between the parties when the property has been actually delivered and the transferor recognizes the transfer when interrogated on oath.

> An instrument involving immovable property shall have effect against third persons only from the time it is filed for registry in the parish where the property is located.

> La. R.S. 9:2721(A) [R.C.C. 3338, 3342]: No sale, contract, counter letter, lien, mortgage, judgment, surface lease, oil, gas or mineral lease, or other instrument of writing relating to or affecting immovable property shall be binding on or affect third persons or third parties unless and until filed for registry in the office of the parish recorder of the parish where the land or immovable is situated. Neither secret claims or equities nor other matters outside the public records shall be binding on or affect such third parties.

The Civil Code recognizes that standing timber may be a separate immovable belonging to a person other than the owner of the land. However, the ownership of both immovables, the land and the standing timber, are interrelated and are not of equal rank in a manner which is analogous in many respects to the ownership of predial servitudes. *Willetts Wood Products Co. v. Concordia Land & Timber Co.,* 169 La. 240, 124 So. 841 (La.1929), *cert. denied,* 281 U.S. 742, 50 S.Ct. 348, 74 L.Ed. 1156 (1930). For example, the owner of the land must subordinate the use of the land to the timber owner's dominant rights to grow and eventually harvest the timber. This horizontal division of land ownership gives rise to duties that are attached to the land, which are similar to those owed by the owner of a servient estate to the owner of a predial servitude. *See* La. C.C. art. 651. Likewise, our supreme court has said that a timber owner's dominant rights are not perpetual so as to burden the full ownership and use of the land indefinitely and "put the land out of commerce." *Willetts*, 124 So. at 842. Therefore, the subordination of the landowner's use of the property is for a term fixed in the timber deed or set by a court. *Id.; see also*, A. Yiannopoulos, *Property* § 135, in 2 *Louisiana Civil Law Treatise*, 302-303 (3d ed.1991). This rule serves a purpose similar to that of the prescription of non-use which frees the ownership of the servient estate from the burden of the predial servitude. *See* La. C.C. art. 753.

The Civil Code articles on ownership make clear that Bradley acquired a real right in immovable property through the Timber Deed. La. C.C. arts. 476 and 477. Furthermore, Bradley's real right of ownership of the standing timber burdened the ownership of the land, thereby giving rise to real obligations or duties attached to the land. La. C.C. art. 1763. Those real obligations, as discussed above, made the Browns' ownership of the land subject to Bradley's rights to continue to grow the pine timber and to access the property to harvest the pine timber.

La. C.C. art. 1764 describes the effects of real obligations when the land burdened by such obligations is transferred:

> A real obligation is transferred to the universal or particular successor who acquires the movable or immovable thing to which the obligation is attached, without a special provision to that effect.

But a particular successor is not personally bound, unless he assumes the personal obligations of his transferor with respect to the thing, and he may liberate himself of the real obligation by abandoning the thing.

From this article, it can be seen that Sharp could acquire the land from the Browns and be subject to the real obligations arising from the Timber Deed, without assuming any personal obligations under the Timber Deed, such as the Browns' personal obligation of warranty of title. Therefore, the fact that Sharp's deed to the property did not employ language assuming the personal obligations of the timber contract is not dispositive.

The evidence at trial overwhelmingly revealed that Sharp and the Browns intended to recognize Bradley's ownership of the standing timber. In two written contracts, the purchase agreement and the cash sale deed, Sharp effectively acknowledged that his acquisition of the land would be subject to the real obligations flowing from Bradley's ownership of the timber. To that extent, the jurisprudence cited below indicates that under the public records doctrine, Sharp is not considered to be in the position of a protected third party purchaser who can acquire ownership of the land free from the unrecorded document evidencing Bradley's ownership rights. Just as the public records doctrine is unnecessary to protect Bradley's ownership rights in the timber *vis-a-vis* the Browns, the doctrine is likewise inapplicable to afford Sharp protection, since the Browns contractually required Sharp to recognize Bradley's ownership rights as a burden or real obligation on the land which he was acquiring.

* * * * *

In the present case, the contractual intent was evidenced in the three written agreements pertaining to the sale of the land to Sharp: the prospectus, the purchase agreement, and the cash sale deed. Therefore, we reject as irrelevant Sharp's legal argument that he did not assume any personal obligation under the Timber Deed. We hold that Bradley's failure to timely obtain protection from the proper recordation of the Timber Deed was unnecessary because of Sharp's contractual acknowledgment of Bradley's rights. Sharp acquired the land subject to the real obligations owed to the owner of the pine timber.

* * * * *

Conclusion

For the reasons stated above, we affirm the ruling of the trial court in favor of plaintiff, O. Kyle Bradley, d/b/a Kyle Bradley Logging. Costs of this appeal are assessed to defendant, H. Wayne Sharp, Jr.

AFFIRMED.

Notes and Questions

1. Although *Bradley v. Sharp* predates the 2005 revision of the law of Registry, the result of this case would be no different under Article 3343 than under prior law. Read the excerpt of the parties' Act of Sale that is reproduced in this case carefully. What language indicates that the purchaser bought "subject to" the pre-existing but unrecorded timber deed?

2. Prior to the 2005 revision of the law of registry, some courts held that that only a "purchaser for value" was entitled to the protection of the public records doctrine. *See, e.g., Mathews v. Mathews*, 817 So. 2d 418 (La. App. 2 Cir. 2002). According to this rationale, while an unrecorded sale of an immovable would be ineffective against a subsequent purchaser of the same property, the same unrecorded sale of an immovable would be binding against a subsequent *donee* of the same property. It is well-accepted that, under the revision, unrecorded instruments have no effects against any third person who acquires an interest in immovable property, whether by onerous or gratuitous title. *See* 24 Dian Tooley-Knoblett & David Gruning, Louisiana Civil Law Treatise, Sales § 8:26 (2017).

c. The Place and Manner of Recordation
La. Civ. Code arts. 3344–3353

A party seeking to ensure that an instrument affecting immovable property will be enforceable against third persons must take care that the instrument is properly recorded. Although the rules surrounding the mechanics of recordation may seem tedious and uninteresting, they are of paramount importance — an instrument that is improperly filed is just as ineffective against third persons as one that was not filed at all.

A foremost consideration is the *place* of filing. To have effects against third persons, an instrument affecting an immovable must be recorded in the parish in which the immovable is situated. *See* LA. CIV. CODE art. 3346. If the property spans multiple parishes, the instrument must be filed in each parish in which a portion of the property lies. For example, an instrument evidencing a sale of a tract of land lying partly in Jefferson Parish and partly in Orleans Parish must be filed in both Jefferson and Orleans Parishes; if it is filed in Jefferson Parish alone, then recordation is effective against third persons with respect to the portion of the tract lying in Jefferson Parish only.

It is not enough, however, to know the parish in which to file. The law of registry contemplates that within each parish, the clerk of court maintains two distinct sets of records: the conveyance records and the mortgage records. *See* LA. CIV. CODE art. 3346. As these names suggest, conveyances are to be recorded in the conveyance records; mortgages in the mortgage records. As the following case makes clear, filing in the correct parish but the incorrect set of records is tantamount to not filing at all.

Wede v. Niche Marketing USA, LLC
52 So. 3d 60 (La. 2010)

WEIMER, Justice.

This court granted plaintiff's writ application to determine whether an enforceable judicial mortgage existed when the clerk of court received a money judgment for recordation, but admittedly processed the judgment as a conveyance document rather than as a mortgage document within the clerk's computerized immovable property records system. Plaintiff sought to enforce the judgment against defendant purchasers who bought immovable property consisting of a home from the judgment debtor. The defendant purchasers bought this immovable property after the judgment was processed as a conveyance document, rather than as a mortgage document. Finding that this issue is squarely addressed by LSA–C.C. art. 3338 (which requires that a mortgage be recorded in the mortgage records to affect third persons), we affirm the decision of the court of appeal finding that the money judgment cannot be enforced as a judicial mortgage against the defendant purchasers based on the facts of this case.

FACTUAL AND PROCEDURAL BACKGROUND

On August 19, 2005, a North Carolina court awarded Hans Wede a money judgment against Rodney Whitney, Jr. and Niche Marketing USA, LLC. Later, Mr. Wede filed suit in the Fortieth Judicial District Court for St. John the Baptist Parish to make the judgment executory in Louisiana. On December 8, 2005, the district court entered its judgment, and the North Carolina court judgment was made executory.

In St. John the Baptist Parish, the clerk of court is also the recorder of conveyances and of mortgages. The clerk's office has a longstanding policy that, absent contrary instruction from the judgment creditor, all money judgments rendered by the district court are taken to the clerk's "recordation department" to be entered into the parish mortgage records.

Following that policy, on December 8, 2005, a deputy clerk received Mr. Wede's judgment from the district court, made a certified copy of the judgment, and delivered the copy to the recordation department. The recordation department of the clerk's office no longer maintains physical books for recording mortgage and conveyance documents; the records are now kept electronically. During the relevant time period, the records were kept electronically. To record a document electronically, personnel assign and place an instrument number upon the physical document, and scan it. Then personnel select within the office's computer system between the options of "MO" for designating the scanned image as a mortgage document and "CO" for designating the image as a conveyance document.

When Mr. Wede's judgment against Mr. Whitney was processed, however, instead of selecting "MO" on the computer screen, the clerk's office identified the judgment by "CO" as a conveyance document.

The computer system is the sole portal for accessing immovable property records in the parish. Prior to adopting this computer system, clerk's personnel would create an index for each set of conveyance and mortgage records. Now, indices can be created based upon how documents are identified within the computer system (as "MO" or "CO").[3] A clerk's office employee testified that it was possible to run a search of the computer records that would retrieve both mortgage and conveyance records, but it was also possible to run a search that was confined to retrieve only mortgage records. If the search was confined to mortgage records, as a result of being erroneously identified by "CO" within the system, Mr. Wede's judgment against Mr. Whitney would not be revealed to a computer system user.

On December 8, 2005, at the time Mr. Wede's judgment was processed by the clerk's office, the judgment debtor, Mr. Whitney, and his wife owned immovable property upon which was located a home in St. John the Baptist Parish. The Whitneys later sold this property to Robert and Deborah James on January 31, 2007. No provision was made for satisfying Mr. Whitney's indebtedness to Mr. Wede when the act of sale was executed. The act of sale between the Whitneys and Jameses was recorded in the parish records as a conveyance document on February 2, 2007.

Later, an attorney for Mr. Wede sought to enforce the judgment against Mr. Whitney, but the attorney then learned the Whitneys had sold the property to the Jameses. It was also then learned by Mr. Wede's attorney that Mr. Wede's judgment had been identified as a conveyance document, rather than a mortgage document, in the computer recordation system.

On May 3, 2007, another attorney, Lloyd LeBlanc, approached the chief deputy clerk in charge of the recordation department, and inquired about the recordation

---

3. Testimony indicates that twice a year, a printed index of mortgage and conveyance records is made and bound for persons who do not wish to use the computer system. However, the index is generated by the computer system, and not by any separate process. The computer system is, therefore, the only system for organizing the documents and the only portal for accessing the records.

of Mr. Wede's judgment and its apparent designation as a conveyance record. After reviewing the matter, the chief deputy clerk, on that same day, accessed the computer recordation system and selected "MO" as the system's designation for Mr. Wede's money judgment. The judgment itself was not re-scanned, and no new instrument number was created for the judgment.

Asserting that a judicial mortgage existed notwithstanding the original, mistaken designation of the judgment as a conveyance record, Mr. Wede sought enforcement. In the district court, Mr. Wede filed a motion asking for authority to seize the property the Jameses had bought from the Whitneys. Mr. Wede filed his motion naming the Jameses as "defendants-in-rule." The Jameses appeared and opposed the motion.

The trial court granted Mr. Wede's motion, and in well-written reasons, found that the error of the clerk's office (selecting "CO" instead of "MO" in the computer system) was one of indexing. While noting that the Jameses are entitled to rely upon the public records, the trial court pointed out that the indices are not part of the public record, and ruled that erroneous indexing does not affect the validity of recordation. According to the trial court's ruling, Mr. Wede could proceed with seizure of the property from the Jameses.

The Jameses appealed, and the court of appeal reversed. The appellate court disagreed that the error by the clerk's office was one of indexing. The appellate court reasoned that the recorder had erroneously placed Mr. Wede's judgment into the conveyance records, and the money judgment could not therefore be enforced as a mortgage.

Mr. Wede applied to this court for a writ of review, and this court decided to consider the matter. *See Wede v. Niche Marketing USA, LLC*, 2010-0243 (La. 4/16/10), 31 So.3d 1069.

LAW AND ANALYSIS

In the record before us, there is no evidence that the judgment creditor, Mr. Wede, requested his money judgment be designated as a conveyance record instead of as a mortgage record. The record in this case is clear that the clerk of court's office assumed the responsibility of recording the judgment. The record also establishes the copy of the judgment received by counsel for Mr. Wede did not indicate where in the clerk's records the judgment was recorded; the document only indicated a sequential instrument number. Likewise, there is unrefuted testimony that the third-party purchasers, the Jameses—or anyone else who might have reviewed the St. John the Baptist Parish computerized recordation system at the time the Jameses purchased the property from the Whitneys—would have seen no evidence of Mr. Wede's judgment when checking the parish mortgage records.[5]

---

5. According to the testimony of a chief deputy clerk, after the incorrect designation was pointed out to her office, she went back to the computer system and changed the designation of Mr. Wede's

This case, therefore, presents the vexing question of whether the judgment creditor or the third-party purchaser should prevail when both invoke the protections of the public records and both appear to have satisfied the requirements for protection.[6]

Deciding how to resolve this matter is made difficult because both the judgment creditor and the purchasers point to the same event, i.e., an admitted mistake by the recorder/clerk, as a reason for their protection. While both parties may be victims of a mistake,[7] and both have presented cogent arguments, in our view the law of recordation inherently favors the third-party purchaser over the creditor based on the facts of this case.

In reviewing the law of recordation, civilian methodology and the civil code instruct that the sources of law are legislation and custom, and that legislation is the superior source of law. *See* LSA-C.C. arts. 1, 3. Legislation, which is defined as the solemn expression of legislative will, LSA-C.C. art. 2 is to be interpreted according to the rules set forth in the civil code. *See* LSA-C.C. arts. 9-13. Chief among those rules is the admonition in LSA-C.C. art. 9 that "[w]hen a law is clear and unambiguous and its application does not lead to absurd consequences, the law shall be applied as written and no further interpretation may be made in search of the intent of the legislature." Additionally, LSA-C.C. art. 11 instructs that "[t]he words of a

---

judgment from "CO" to "MO." This change was made because "if someone only ran the name in the Mortgage records, they could find it [the judgment]."

6. Louisiana's public records doctrine includes the use of a "race to the courthouse" system of recordation: "Instruments take effect as to third persons in the order in which the instruments are filed." 1 Peter S. Title, Louisiana Real Estate Transactions § 8:16 (2017-18 ed.). The public records doctrine "does not create rights in the positive sense, but rather has the negative effect of denying the effectiveness of certain rights unless they are recorded." *Id.* A well-established consequence of these two principles is illustrated in *McDuffie v. Walker*, 125 La. 152, 51 So. 100, 105–106 (1909), in which this court ruled that an unrecorded contract affecting immovable property has no effect as to third persons, even when a third person has actual knowledge of that unrecorded contract.

7. The chief deputy clerk testified as follows regarding the mistake:
Q. How then is it determined how these particulars [sic] documents are to be recorded?
A. It's just known that judgments go in the Mortgage records; anything dealing with money we put in Mortgage.
Q. Now, based on your research into this particular judgment, do you know what happened to this judgment when it was handed to the Mortgage Office on December 8, '05?
A. When it was recorded, it will look the same way. When it was indexed, the way the computer works, you have to click on "MO" or "CO" and then you index it. And whoever indexed it, they didn't click on "MO", it stayed as a "CO", but they indexed it as if it was a mortgage. But it didn't say that in the computer.
Q. You're looking at a book. I'm going to ask you if you can tell me what that book is.
A. This is the book that we keep the notations in and, if we have any type of errors or anything that needs to be changed, we write it in the book also.
Q. And did you make that notation when Mr. Leblanc talked to you about it [the judgment]?
A. Yes, I did.
It should be noted that this court expresses no view as to the legal consequences of this testimony or of any other testimony in this case beyond the narrow legal issue before us.

law must be given their generally prevailing meaning." Further, LSA-C.C. art. 13 provides: "Laws on the same subject matter must be interpreted in reference to each other." Reading the various codal provisions involved and giving effect to each is the key to resolving this matter.

We begin, therefore, with the words of the codal provisions. *See Dumas v. State, Department of Culture, Recreation & Tourism*, 2002-0563, p. 11 (La. 10/15/02), 828 So.2d 530, 536. In this action to enforce a judicial mortgage, it is worthy to recall that LSA-C.C.art. 3299 describes the effect of a judicial mortgage: "A judicial mortgage secures a judgment for the payment of money." Turning next to LSA-C.C. art. 3300, which provides that "[a] judicial mortgage is created by filing a judgment with the recorder of mortgages," it is implicit in this article that a judicial mortgage owes its very existence to being in the mortgage records. Similarly, from this same article it follows that if a party must present a judgment to the recorder of mortgages for the creation of a mortgage, then the judgment must be within the mortgage records else third parties are unaffected by it.

Preferring a literal view of the law, however, we do not have to rely upon these obvious inferences from Article 3300 to ascertain how a judicial mortgage might affect the rights of third parties. That article does not directly address the rights of third parties, but LSA-C.C. art. 3338 does:

Art. 3338. Instruments creating real rights in immovables; recordation required to affect third persons

The rights and obligations established or created by the following written instruments are without effect as to a third person unless the instrument is registered by recording it in the appropriate mortgage or conveyance records pursuant to the provisions of this Title:

(1) An instrument that transfers an immovable or establishes a real right in or over an immovable.

(2) The lease of an immovable.

(3) An option or right of first refusal, or a contract to buy, sell, or lease an immovable or to establish a real right in or over an immovable.

(4) An instrument that modifies, terminates, or transfers the rights created or evidenced by the instruments described in Subparagraphs (1) through (3) of this Article.

Clearly, a judicial mortgage is an "instrument that ... establishes a real right in or over an immovable." LSA-C.C. art. 3338. Notwithstanding that this article is directed to the rights of third parties, Mr. Wede, the judgment creditor, argues that another article, LSA-C.C. art. 3347, is more specifically on point. Article 3347 provides:

Art. 3347. Effect of recordation arises upon filing

The effect of recordation arises when an instrument is filed with the recorder and is unaffected by subsequent errors or omissions of the recorder. An instrument is filed with a recorder when he accepts it for recordation in his office.

The crux of the judgment creditor's argument is that because the clerk's office admittedly made an error in selecting "CO" instead of "MO" when processing his judgment, that LSA-C.C. art. 3347 nevertheless gives him a judicial mortgage enforceable against the Jameses.

However, this argument figuratively puts the cart before the horse. Twice, Article 3347 speaks to "when" a document gains the effect of recordation. Not at all, however, does Article 3347 speak to the threshold matter of "where" a document must be recorded to gain that effect.[9] But Article 3338, which is addressed to the rights of third parties — the ultimate issue in this case — specifies "where" a document must be recorded to gain effect as to third parties. Specifically, Article 3338 provides a document must be recorded "in the appropriate mortgage or conveyance records," or the instrument is "without effect as to a third person."

In Article 3338, therefore, there is an emphatic, clear, and absolute imperative that a judicial mortgage is "without effect as to a third person unless the instrument is registered by recording it in the appropriate mortgage . . . records." To adopt the judgment creditor's argument that Article 3347 trumps Article 3338 would require this court to interpret Article 3347 to mean that the clerk of court's acceptance of the judgment conferred, not just the effects of recordation, but also "the effect of recordation within the mortgage records." The civilian tradition requires this court to avoid adding the underlined words, or any other words not enacted by the legislature, into Article 3347. *See* LSA-C.C. art. 9.[10]

---

9. The absence of language in Article 3347 regarding "where" a document must be filed to gain effect is dispositive, but reading Article 3347 in pari materia with other provisions in the civil code lends further support for our interpretation. According to the previous article, LSA-C.C. art. 3346(A), "An instrument creating, establishing, or relating to a mortgage or privilege over an immovable is recorded in the mortgage records of the parish in which the immovable is located. All other instruments are recorded in the conveyance records of that parish." The specific mention in Article 3346 of the place of recordation persuades us that the absence of such a mention in Article 3347 means that Article 3347 is directed to "when" not "where." And because Article 3347 twice mentions "when," and the next three consecutive articles (LSA-C.C. arts. 3348, 3349, and 3350) are all addressed to timing, and two of these articles (LSA-C.C. arts. 3349 and 3350) actually deal with resolving mistakes or ambiguities in timing, we are further persuaded that the "errors or omissions of the recorder" described in Article 3347 refer to errors of timing, not of place.

10. Because we refrain from interpreting "[t]he effect of recordation" to mean "[t]he effect of recordation in the mortgage records," it is unnecessary for us here to opine on what might be included within the complete spectrum of "subsequent errors or omissions of the recorder" mentioned later in Article 3347. But to hold that placing an instrument outside of the mortgage records and into the conveyance records is an error or omission contemplated by Article 3347 would place Article 3347 into conflict with the clear, absolute imperative for the effectiveness of a judicial mortgage that we have observed in Article 3338. Our prior jurisprudence counsels against interpreting statutes to be in conflict, and prefers reconciling statutes instead. See *Pumphrey v. City of New Orleans*, 05–979, p. 10–12 (La.4/4/06), 925 So.2d 1202, 1209–10. We find Article 3347

Though we find that giving effect to the plain language of Article 3338 resolves the unusual matter before us, our interpretation is supported by other legislative pronouncements. Article 3338 is part of a larger legislative reworking of the law of registry by 2005 La. Acts, No. 169, § 1. Numerous provisions of the civil code and the revised statutes were thereby consolidated. The legislature did not, however, change paragraph C of LSA-C.C. art. 3320: "Recordation has only the effect given it by legislation." The revision comments from the year 1992, when paragraph C of Article 3320 was enacted, speak to the situation at hand and its resolution:

> Paragraph C of this Article restates three well-established principles. The first is that recordation is only given such effect as the law provides. Louisiana's registry system is not based upon knowledge, actual or implied. A document recorded in the mortgage records has effect as to third persons not because they have or are deemed to have notice of it, but merely because the law provides it has such effect. Conversely, an unrecorded instrument that is required to be recorded has no effect as to third persons, whether or not they are aware of its existence. *See* Art. 3308. Under that system, to be effective, an instrument also must be filed in the place prescribed by law. *Thus, a mortgage recorded in the conveyance records, or a sale recorded in the mortgage records, is without effect as to third persons. . . .* [Emphasis added.]

Thus, because the legislature left intact Article 3320 and the principles espoused in these revision comments when recently revising the law of recordation, we are bound to continue to recognize these principles. *Cf.* LSA-C.C. art. 8 ("Laws are repealed, either entirely or partially, by other laws. A repeal may be express or implied. It is express when it is literally declared by a subsequent law. It is implied when the new law contains provisions that are contrary to, or irreconcilable with, those of the former law . . . .").

The judgment creditor also argues that the jurisprudence counsels for enforcing a judicial mortgage under the circumstances where the recorder intended to process the judgment as a mortgage document, but instead processed it as a conveyance document. This argument, however, fares no better than his reliance upon Article 3347 because the jurisprudence cited has no direct applicability to the unique situation at hand.

For example, the judgment creditor first relies upon *Kinnebrew v. Tri-Con Production Corp.*, 224 La. 879, 884, 154 So.2d 433 (1963). But *Kinnebrew* involved only a question of when, not of where, recordation had occurred: "the only legal issue properly before the Court of Appeal (and now before us) was whether the actual inscription of . . . encumbrances became effective from the time of the filing with the Clerk of Court." *Id.* at 435. As noted earlier in our analysis of Articles 3338 and 3347, the present case does not turn upon a question of timing, so much as it turns

---

and Article 3338 easily reconcilable from the meanings we have discerned each to have here. *See* LSA-C.C. art. 13

upon where a judgment was recorded. In this matter, Article 3338 clearly indicates the judgment has no efficacy unless it is in the mortgage records. Mr. Wede's reliance upon *Kinnebrew* is misplaced.

Of the other authorities cited, only one case arguably examines "where" a document should be recorded in order to have effect against third parties. The judgment creditor cites — without elaboration — the ancient case of *Lewis v. Klotz*, 39 La. Ann. 259, 268, 1 So. 539, 542 (1887), in which this court stated:

> The contract of lease was duly deposited in the recorder's office, and the required indorsement to that effect was made upon it. It was recorded in the book kept by the officer for the recording of leases. Whether it should have been recorded in the book of conveyances it is unnecessary to consider, since the deposit in the proper office, and the proper indorsement by the officer, fully protected the parties.

It appears that in *Lewis* this court analyzed a practice of redundant recordation, and gave effect when a lease document was recorded in only one place (a book specifically for leases) though a third party would expect to also find the lease in a conveyance book. But in the 123 years since this court decided *Lewis*, obviously much in the law of recordation has changed (e.g., Book III, Title XXII-A of the current civil code makes no provision for a lease book). Also, *Lewis* does not concern recordation of a judgment, and whether a judgment should be given effect as a judicial mortgage. For these reasons, we find that *Lewis* is so different from the case at hand as to be of no assistance in its resolution.

Thus, we return to the plain language of Article 3338. In the words of that article, Mr. Wede's money judgment is purportedly "[a]n instrument that modifies, terminates, or transfers the rights created or evidenced by the instruments" that "establishes a real right in or over an immovable." LSA-C.C. art. 3338(4) and (1). Of course, as a money judgment, on its face it said nothing about establishing or transferring any real rights in Mr. Whitney's immovable property. The money judgment could not be transformed into a document affecting real rights as to third parties "unless the instrument [was] registered by recording it in the appropriate mortgage . . . records." LSA-C.C. art. 3338.

CONCLUSION

We find that owing to its entry in the parish's computer recordation system as "CO" for conveyance rather than "MO" for mortgage, Mr. Wede's judgment could not operate as a judicial mortgage against the Jameses. We note that the parties and the courts below have labored at great length to establish whether the mistaken entry of "CO" rather than "MO" was one of indexing or of recordation itself.[13] The

---

13. The clerk is statutorily required to maintain two records, one for mortgages and the other for conveyances. *See* LSA-R.S. 44:185 ("The clerk of court as the parish recorder shall keep a book of conveyances, a book of mortgages, and other recordation books as provided by law. He shall keep indexes as required by law."). The clerk's computer recordation system, by using the designations

trial court's written opinion is particularly commendable for its efforts in grappling with this issue. In our view, however, focus upon the recorder's own intent and understanding has become a metaphysical debate too speculative to be of value.

On the particular facts before us, the designation of the money judgment with "CO" as a conveyance document and the unrefuted testimony that a user of the parish computer system who searched only for mortgages would not find the judgment, are sufficient reasons for us to determine that the judgment was not "registered by recording it in the appropriate mortgage . . . records" for purposes of Article 3338. The Jameses purchased the property in question from the Whitneys unencumbered by a judicial mortgage.

The judgment of the court of appeal is hereby affirmed.

AFFIRMED.

Notes and Questions

1. Article 3347 provides, "The effect of recordation arises when the instrument is filed with the recorder and is unaffected by subsequent errors or omissions of the recorder. An instrument is filed with a recorder when he accepts it for recordation in his office." LA. CIV. CODE art. 3347. Although the law contemplates separate "offices" of recordation (an office of the recorder of mortgages and an office of the recorder of conveyances), these roles are united in the same person in each parish—the clerk of court. Prior to the Louisiana Supreme Court's decision in *Wede*, it was well-accepted that when an instrument, whether a conveyance or mortgage, was deposited in the office of the clerk of court, it was "filed with the recorder" as required by law. Nevertheless, it has always been necessary for a person filing an instrument to specify whether the instrument is to be filed in the conveyance records or the mortgage records. How, if at all, does the Court's decision in *Wede* change this long-held view?

2. The recorder is required to "maintain" instruments filed in the public records in separate books for mortgages and conveyances. *See* LA. CIV. CODE art. 3346(B); LA. REV. STAT. § 44:185. Historically, the distinction between conveyance and mortgage records was very clear. In the earliest days, once an original document was filed with the recorder's office, the clerk or an employee would inscribe the entire

---

"MO" for "mortgage" and "CO" for "conveyance" appears to have been designed to comply with LSA-R.S. 44:185 and with numerous other statutes designating whether an instrument must be recorded in mortgage records, in conveyance records, or in both. *See, e.g.*, LSA-R.S. 3:210(B) (agricultural credit corporations may "execute mortgages of realty" which must be "recorded in the recorder's office of the parish in which the mortgaged property is located, in the mortgage records"); LSA-C.C. art. 467 ("The owner of an immovable may declare that machinery, appliances, and equipment owned by him and placed on the immovable, other than his private residence, for its service and improvement are deemed to be its component parts. The declaration shall be filed for registry in the conveyance records of the parish in which the immovable is located."); and LSA-C.C. art. 357 ("If the prayer for continuing or permanent tutorship be granted, the decree shall be recorded in the conveyance and mortgage records of the parish of the minor's domicile, and of any future domicile, and in such other parishes as may be deemed expedient.").

document in longhand into a physical book of either mortgages or conveyances. Later, typewriters were used to copy original documents, which were then bound into the appropriate books. More recently, the physical books have consisted of photocopies of originals. However, as *Wede* indicates, parishes have increasingly turned to electronic databases for the maintenance of recorded instruments. What are the benefits of maintaining instruments affecting immovable property in electronic form? What are the disadvantages of electronic record-keeping?

3. Note that Article 3347 provides that after the recorder accepts an instrument for recordation in his office, the effect of recordation "is unaffected by subsequent errors or omissions of the recorder." La. Civ. Code art. 3347. Thus, although the recorder is bound, upon acceptance of an instrument, to assign a registry number to it and to write upon or stamp it with both the registry number and the date and time of filing, La. Civ. Code art. 3348, the recorder's failure to do either of these does not negate the effect of recordation. Indeed, once an instrument is filed with the recorder, it is immaterial whether the instrument is ever actually inscribed in the mortgage or conveyance records. *See Delerno v. Coastal States Gas Producing Co.*, 429 So. 2d 183, 191 (La. App. 1 Cir. 1983). Furthermore, the Civil Code contains rules to assist in determining the rank-ordering of an instrument that is not properly marked with the date and time of filing or that bears the same date and time as another instrument. In such cases, "it is presumed that the instrument was filed with respect to other instruments in the order indicated by their registry numbers and that the filing of the instrument occurred immediately before an instrument bearing the next consecutive registry number." La. Civ. Code art. 3349. If the date and time of filing cannot be determined using that rule, "it is presumed that the instrument was filed at the first determinable date and time that it appears in the records of the recorder." La. Civ. Code art. 3350.

4. The trial court in *Wede* found that the designation of the judgment using "CO" rather than "MO" was an error of "indexing" that did not affect the validity of recordation. The Supreme Court disagreed, finding the selection of "CO" or "MO" to be an element of filing, not indexing. Because instruments are recorded in the conveyance and mortgage records in the order in which they are filed, a system of indexing was developed to assist in locating recorded instruments. Without the indices, a person conducting a search of the public records would have no way of locating instruments associated with an immovable. Instruments are indexed using the names of the parties—conveyances are indexed by vendor and vendee, and mortgages are indexed by mortgagor and mortgagee. One searching the public records can trace the chain of title for a specific piece of real estate, beginning with the current owner and working backward to discover prior owners and other right holders, including mortgagors, lienholders, and lessees. In some parishes, some instruments are also indexed by property description, which further eases searching. Importantly, a recorder's failure to properly index an instrument has no impact whatsoever on the validity of its filing. This is so even though an improperly indexed instrument may never be identified through a search of the public records.

5. A clerk may refuse to record an instrument that does not bear the original signature of a party or, if the instrument is a judgment, administrative decree, or other act of a governmental agency, is not properly certified in the manner provided by law. LA. CIV. CODE art. 3344. Nevertheless, if the clerk accepts and records a duplicate that does not bear the original signature of a party, that instrument shall produce the same effect as recordation of the original instrument. LA. CIV. CODE art. 3345.

6. Although Article 3352 contains an extensive list of information that an instrument "shall contain" (including the full name, domicile, mailing address, and marital status of the parties to the instrument, the municipal number or postal address of the property, and the last four digits of the social security number of a mortgagor), the recorder is not permitted to refuse to record an instrument that does not contain this information. LA. CIV. CODE art. 3352. As a general rule, the omission of the required information from the instrument does not impair its validity or the effects of recordation. *Id.* However, if the name of a party is incomplete or incorrect, recordation may be ineffective as to third persons. Article 3353 provides the standard: "A recorded instrument is effective with respect to a third person if the name of a party is not so indefinite, incomplete, or erroneous as to be misleading and the instrument as a whole reasonably alerts a person examining the records that the instrument may be that of the party." LA. CIV. CODE art. 3353.

d. Exceptions to the Law of Registry

It can be tempting to think of the public records doctrine as negating any right to immovable property that is not properly recorded. However, this characterization of the law of registry is far too broad. Keep in mind that Article 3339 enumerates a list of matters that, though not evidenced of record, are effective against third persons. In addition, rights in immovables that arise by operation of law — including inheritance rights and rights in community property — need not be recorded to be enforceable against others. The remainder of this Subpart explores these latter exceptions to the public records doctrine.

i. Inheritance Rights

La. Civ. Code arts. 870–876; 934–938; La. Code Civ. Proc. arts. 3062, 3393; La. Rev. Stat. § 9:5630

Louisiana courts have long held that the enforceability of inheritance rights is in no way dependent upon whether a successor has filed evidence of those rights to inherit in the public records. *See, e.g., Bishop v. Copeland*, 62 So. 2d 486 (La. 1953). The reason given for this rule is that, under Louisiana law, succession — the transmission of the estate from the decedent to the successors — occurs by operation of law at the moment of the decedent's death. LA. CIV. CODE arts. 871, 934. This is true whether the succession is testate or intestate. According to the maxim *le mort saisit le vif* ("the dead give seizin to the living"), successors acquire ownership of the estate immediately at the decedent's death, and at the same time, acquire the right to act as owner with respect to the property that they inherit. *See* La. Civ. Code arts. 935, 938. And, while succession proceedings normally culminate with a "judgment of possession" that names the successors and their inheritance rights, the transfer of the estate from the decedent to the heirs results from succession, not from the judgment of possession. Indeed, the Louisiana Code of Civil Procedure recognizes that the judgment of possession is merely "prima facie evidence of the relationship to the deceased of the parties recognized therein . . . and of their right to the possession of the estate of the deceased." La. Code Civ. Proc. art. 3062. As such, the judgment of possession may be amended to include previously unrecognized successors or property of the estate. *See* La. Code Civ. Proc. art. 3393.

The case that follows illustrates the application of these rules.

Knighten v. Ruffin
255 So. 2d 388 (La. App. 1 Cir. 1971)

Lottinger, Judge.

This is a suit filed by Lillie Knighten against Henry Ruffin and Allstate Finance Corporation in which she seeks to be declared the owner of an undivided one-fourth interest in certain real estate. The Lower Court rendered judgment in favor of defendants and dismissing petitioner's demand at her costs. Petitioner has taken an appeal.

The facts show that Sarah Browdon was the record owner of an undivided one-half interest in the property subject to this law suit and her son, Calip Browdon, was the record owner of the other undivided one-half interest in said property. On May 19, 1961, Sarah Browdon, in the presence of petitioner, executed a last will and testament leaving to her "son Calip Browdon and my granddaughter Lillie Knighten, one half to each, share and share alike, all my real property will improvements thereon and all the furniture and fixtures contained in my residence. It direct that all my just debts be paid and that any cash money remaining after my debts are paid I give and bequeath to Willie Johnson, Rose Lee Maxie, Ella Jean Wheelock and Jenifer McCoy, in equal proportions to each." Calip Browdon had no knowledge that this will had been executed or that Sarah in fact had ever executed any will.

On October 29, 1964, Sarah Browdon died and on February 2, 1965, an ex parte judgment was rendered putting Calip Browdon into possession of the property as the sole heir of his mother. Subsequently, on February 2, 1965, Calip mortgaged the subject property to Allstate Finance Corporation.

On June 9, 1965, Lillie Knighten instituted proceedings to probate Sarah's will and filed in conjunction therewith, a notice of lis pendens in the parish mortgage records. This notice was the first indication on the public records of Lillie's claim to the property. On June 10, 1965, the will was probated.

On July 9, 1965, Calip having failed to make payments on his mortgage loan, Allstate foreclosed its mortgage and, subsequently, on September 15, 1965, bought in the property at sheriff's sale. On the same date, namely September 15, 1965, Lillie filed a petition to amend the judgment of possession in favor of Calip and to secure judgment declaring her to be the owner of an undivided one-fourth interest in the subject property. Neither Allstate or Henry Ruffin was a party to that suit and no notice of lis pendens was filed in conjunction therewith.

On October 21, 1965, Allstate, by warranty sale, transferred the property to Henry Ruffin, appellee herein. On January 11, 1967, at the trial of Lillie's suit of September 15, 1965, judgment was rendered in Lillie's favor and against Calip recognizing her undivided one-fourth interest in the property.

On June 28, 1967, Lillie instituted this present action against Allstate and Henry Ruffin, claiming an undivided one-fourth interest in the property and seeking a partition of the property by licitation. This suit was the first notice to Allstate and Henry Ruffin of Lillie's claim to the property. Following trial, judgment was rendered in favor of defendants dismissing petitioner's suit and petitioner had taken this appeal.

Article 3062 of the Louisiana Code of Civil Procedure sets forth the effect of a judgment of possession as follows:

> "The judgment of possession rendered in a succession proceeding shall be prima facie evidence of the relationship to the deceased of the parties recognized therein, as their, legatee, surviving spouse in community, or usufructuary, as the case may be, and of their right to the possession of the estate of the deceased."

In the official revision comments following Article 3062, it set forth the fact that the said Article is merely declaratory of the prior jurisprudence and a number of cases are cited.

A factual situation similar to the one here presented, was before the Court in *Vaughan v. Housing Authority of New Orleans*, La.App., 80 So.2d 561. In that case the Court said:

> "There are two legal principles which are recognized in Louisiana and are not in dispute—one is that the rights of legal heirs, and especially forced heirs, are sacred and cannot be divested except by proper legal proceedings against those heirs, and the other is that the law of registry, Articles 2251-2266 of our LSA-Civil Code [R.C.C. 3338–3368], has no application where the ownership of immovable property becomes vested by operation of law. In *Bishop v. Copeland*, 222 La. 284, 62 So.2d 486, 488, appears the following:
>
> > '* * * Defendant's initial contention, which is reurged here under his exception of no cause of action, is that plaintiffs' demand should nonetheless be rejected for the reason that their ownership has not been registered and that he, being a third person dealing with immovable property, was entitled to depend on the faith of the public records.'

'There is no merit in the point. It is well settled that our law of registry, Articles 2251 through 2266 of the LSA-Civil Code [R.C.C. 3338-
3353], is not applicable when the ownership of, or claim affecting in the
immovable has become vested in the claimant by mere operation of law.
See Long v. Chailan, 187 La. 507, 175 So. So. 42 and *Dugas v. Powell*, 207
La. 316, 21 So.2d 366. * * *'

We thus find that the rights of the plaintiffs, who were legal heirs of the
deceased, were fixed by operation of law; they were his forced heirs and
became joint owners by the mere fact of his death, and their rights depended
in no way upon any public registration or recordation of their inheritance of
the property. And we find too that, if the codal article be interpreted as the
Housing Authority would have us interpret it, these children were deprived
of their rights without notice, without hearing, and without being afforded
an opportunity to be heard and, therefore, according to the meaning of the
due process clause of either Constitution, without due process of law."

The petitioner herein, as were the heirs in the *Vaughan* case, came into ownership of the one-fourth interest in the property by the mere fact of the death of her
grandmother. Article 940 of the Louisiana Civil Code [R.C.C. 935] dealing with
seisin provides:

"A succession is acquired by the legal heir, who is called by law to the
inheritance, immediately after the death of the deceased person to whom
he succeeds.

This rule applies also to testamentary heirs, to instituted heirs and universal legatees, but not to particular legatees."

See also LCC Art. 941 [R.C.C. 935. Note—under current law, all successors, including particular legatees, acquire ownership of the estate and seizin upon the decedent's death, *Eds.*]

The petitioner herein was a universal legatee of the decedent, and she became
seized of her interest in the property immediately on the death of her grandmother.

In *Succession of Rosinski*, La.App., 158 So.2d 467, where the facts were again similar to the ones presently before us, the Lower Court, relying on *Succession of Deri-
gny*, 156 La. 142, 100 So. 251, sustained an exception of no cause of action filed
by defendants and based on the grounds that they were good faith purchasers for
valuable consideration who had a right to rely on the public records which showed
their vendor, Mrs. Strom, to be the owner of the property. On appeal, the Court distinguished the holding in the Deringny case because there, the Court was involved
with absent heirs whose existence was unknown at the time the succession was
opened and the apparent heirs put into possession under the provisions of Civil
Code Article 76 through 79 [No Corresponding Articles]. After citing *Vaughan v.
Housing Authority of New Orleans (supra)* the Court there said:

"The defendants, Touchet and Dugas, even if they are admitted to be good
faith purchasers relying on the public record, a fact which we are not called

upon at this time to determine, are not protected by the ex parte judgment probating the will, nor by the ex parte judgment placing Mrs. Strom in possession of estate, as against the claim of these petitioners who allege themselves to be heirs by operation of law."

In an excellent article dealing with the effect of judgments of possession in 35 Tulane Law Review 567, the author concludes with the following statement:

"Finally, a judgment of possession is prima facie correct and the presumption that it is correct must, of course, be overcome of the judgment is to be attacked."

The property, which is the subject of this proceeding, has a 40 foot front on the South side of public road known as Stanacola Street by a depth of 120 feet. The evidence discloses that there is a residence situated on the property and, as we have determined that petitioner owns as undivided ¼ interest therein and Henry Ruffin owns an undivided ¾ interest therein, it is obvious that the property is not susceptible to a partition in kind. A partition by licitation as prayed for by petitioner will, therefore, be ordered.

For the reasons hereinabove assigned, the judgment of the Lower Court will be reversed and there will be judgment herein in favor of petitioner and against defendant declaring petitioner to be the owner of an undivided ¼ interest in the following described property, to-wit:

"One certain lot or parcel of ground, together with all buildings and improvements thereon and all the rights, ways, privileges, servitudes thereunto belonging or in anywise appertaining, situated in the Parish of East Baton Rouge, State of Louisiana, in that subdivision known as SUBURB NORTH BATON BOUGE, which lot or parcel of ground is located in the Southwest part of lot number THIRTY-NINE (39), said Suburb North Baton Rouge, said lot or parcel of ground measuring Forty (40) feet front on the South side of a public road now known as Stanacola Street, leading to the Scotland-Baker Road (formerly known as Washington Avenue or Washington Street), by a depth between parallel lines of ONE HUNDRED TWENTY (120) feet, more or less, said lot or parcel of ground bounded now or formerly North by said Stanacola Street, South by lot number Thirty-seven (37) of said Suburb North Baton Rouge, West by the parcel of ground conveyed by Mrs. Sarah Ball to Avery Realty Company, Inc. by act of sale of record in Conveyance Book 95, Page 179, said Parish and State."

and further that a partition by licitation of the above described property be effected in accordance with the instructions herein and that this matter be remanded to the Lower Court so that the partition by licitation might be effected. All costs of this appeal shall be paid by defendants.

Judgment reversed.

Sartain, J., takes no part.

On Application for Rehearing.

Rehearing Refused en banc.

In our original opinion, we erroneously characterized plaintiff as a universal legatee under the will herein, when she is actually a legatee under universal title under Article 1612 of the Civil Code [R.C.C. 1586]. However, she is a testamentary heir and entitled to the benefit of the provisions of Article 940 of the Civil Code [R.C.C. 935], to the same extent as a universal legatee.

Sartain, J., takes no part.

Notes and Questions

1. As illustrated by *Knighten*, the rule that inheritance rights need not be recorded to be enforceable against others presents challenges for those who wish to purchase or acquire rights in immovable property. Here, Ruffin purchased a subdivision lot from someone whom he presumably believed to be the owner, only to later learn that an heir of the previous owner in fact owned an undivided one-fourth interest in the property. Although Ruffin was not protected by the law of registry, Ruffin was not completely without protection, as the warranty against eviction (described in Chapter 9 of this Textbook: The Warranty Against Eviction) affords an evicted buyer the right to rescission of the sale and damages.

2. Persons acquiring interests in immovable property do so at the risk that successors may surface many years later to assert their rights. Admittedly, successors' rights do not last forever. For one thing, successors' rights in immovable property are real rights that may be lost through acquisitive prescription. *See* La. Civ. Code arts. 3473, 3486. In addition, a liberative prescription of 30 years applies to an action for the recognition of a right of inheritance. *See* La. Civ. Code art. 3502. However, these lengthy prescriptive periods may offer little consolation to a potential purchaser of immovable property, particularly when the property is being sold soon after the death of the record owner. This is especially so because the judgment of possession is not an act translative of title, but merely declarative of rights that arise through inheritance. Thus, a judgment of possession is not a "just title"—a prerequisite for the acquisitive prescription of ten years. *Everett v. Clayton*, 29 So. 2d 769, 772 (La. 1947).

In 1960, the Louisiana legislature enacted Louisiana Revised Statutes Section 9:5682, which provided that any claim by a successor who was not recognized in a judgment of possession against a third person who acquired property formerly owned by the deceased from a successor who was recognized in the judgment of possession prescribes in ten years following the registry of the judgment of possession in the conveyance records of the parish where the property is situated. La. Rev. Stat. § 9:5682 (1960). The statute was enacted to provide a measure of protection for third persons against claims of successors who had acquired rights through inheritance but whose rights were not evidenced in the judgment of possession. The statute has been revised several times, and significantly so, and in 1981, redesignated as Louisiana Revised Statutes Section 9:5630. Read the current text of this statute below. How, if at all, would this provision have changed the result in *Knighten*?

La. Rev. Stat. §9:5630. Actions by unrecognized successor against third persons

A. An action by a person who is a successor of a deceased person, and who has not been recognized as such in the judgment of possession rendered by a court of competent jurisdiction, to assert an interest in an immovable formerly owned by the deceased, against a third person, or his successors, who has acquired an interest in the immovable by onerous title from a person recognized as an heir or legatee of the deceased in the judgment of possession is prescribed in two years from the date of the rendering of the judgment of possession.

B. This Section establishes a liberative prescription, and shall be applied both retrospectively and prospectively; however, any person whose rights would be adversely affected by this Section, shall have one year from the effective date of this Section within which to assert the action described in Subsection A of this Section and if no such action is instituted within that time, such claim shall be forever barred.

C. "Third person" means a person other than one recognized as an heir or legatee of the deceased in the judgment of possession.

D. For the purposes of this Section, after thirty years from the date of recordation of a judgment of possession there shall be a conclusive presumption that the judgment was rendered by a court of competent jurisdiction.

ii. Community Property Rights
La. Civ. Code arts. 2334, 2336, 2338–2339, 2346–2348, 2353

As a general rule, property purchased by either spouse during the marriage is classified as community property—property in which each spouse owns a present undivided half interest. *See generally* LA. CIV. CODE arts. 2334, 2336, 2338. Much like a successor's right to the immovable property of the decedent, the spouse of one who acquires immovable property that is classified as community property acquires an interest in that immovable by operation of law. In keeping with the approach that interests in immovable property acquired through operation of law need not be evidenced of record to be enforceable, Louisiana courts have long held that a spouse's rights in community immovables is enforceable despite the fact that neither a marriage license nor other instrument evidencing the spouse's right is filed in the public records. *See, e.g., Succession of James*, 86 So. 403 (1920); *Camel v. Waller*, 526 So. 2d 1086 (La. 1988). Consider the following hypothetical: Husband, during the marriage, purchases Blackacre with community funds. The Act of Sale is silent with respect to Husband's marital status. Nevertheless, because Blackacre is classified as community property, Wife owns an undivided one-half interest in the immovable despite the lack of any indication in the public records of her rights.

Now assume that Husband, without consulting Wife, sells Blackacre to Buyer. What rights, if any, does Wife have with respect to Blackacre following the sale? To answer this question, one must consult the rules governing the management of community property by the spouses. In general, Louisiana provides for equal management of community property by the spouses. Thus, "[e]ach spouse acting alone may manage, control, or dispose of community property unless otherwise provided by law." La. Civ. Code art. 2346. However, one of the more significant exceptions to the rule of equal management is that "[t]he concurrence of both spouses is required for the alienation, encumbrance, or lease of community immovables . . . ." La. Civ. Code art. 2347. If one spouse alienates, encumbers, or leases a community immovable without the concurrence of the other spouse, the transaction is relatively null unless that spouse has renounced the right to concur. La. Civ. Code arts. 2348, 2353. Thus, the non-concurring spouse may rescind the transaction in its entirety. Again, the non-concurring spouse's right to rescind an alienation, encumbrance, or lease is not dependent upon any evidence in the public records of the spouse's right in the immovable.

Like the rules governing the non-record interests of successors, the protection given to non-record community property interests in immovable property may have deleterious effects for those transacting in immovables. Persons seeking to acquire immovable property may have no way of knowing whether the present owner is married or, if married, whether the property is classified as community or separate. Worse, the public records may contain inaccurate information regarding the marital status of the record owner. While the warranty against eviction and title insurance offer some protection against the risk of rescission by a non-concurring spouse, these safeguards are not absolute. In an effort to protect those transacting in community immovables from the non-record rights of spouses, the legislature enacted Louisiana Revised Statutes Section 35:11 ("La. Rev. Stat. § 35:11") in 1987:

La. Rev. Stat. § 35:11. Marital Status of Parties to be Given

A. Whenever notaries pass any acts they shall give the marital status of all parties to the act, viz: If either or any party or parties are men, they shall be described as single, married, or widower. If married or widower the christian and family name of wife shall be given. If either or any party or parties are women, they shall be described as single, married or widow. If married or widow, their christian and family name shall be given, adding that she is the wife of or widow of . . . the husband's name.

B. A declaration as to one's marital status in an acquisition of immovable property by the person acquiring the property creates a presumption that the marital status as declared in the act of acquisition is correct and, except as provided in Subsection C of this Section, any subsequent alienation, encumbrance, or lease of the immovable by onerous title shall not be attacked on the ground that the marital status was not as stated in the declaration.

C. Any person may file an action to attack the subsequent alienation, encumbrance, or lease on the ground that the marital status of the party as stated in the initial act of acquisition is false and incorrect; however, such action to attack the alienation, encumbrance, or lease shall not affect any right or rights acquired by a third person acting in good faith.

D. The presumption provided in Subsection B of this Section is hereby declared to be remedial and made retroactive to any alienation, encumbrance, or lease made prior to September 1, 1987. Any person who has a right as provided in Subsection C of this Section, which right has not prescribed or otherwise been extinguished or barred upon September 1, 1987 and who is adversely affected by the provisions of Subsection C of this Section shall have six months from September 1, 1987 to initiate an action to attack the transaction or otherwise be forever barred from exercising his right or cause of action.

Notes and Questions

1. LA. REV. STAT. § 35:11 gives effect to a recitation of marital status contained in the act by which a spouse *acquires* a community asset. LA. REV. STAT. § 35:11. The recitation of marital status in an act by which a spouse *alienates* a community asset has no effect on the rights of third persons acquiring rights in the immovable. Do you see why? Consider the following hypotheticals:

i. Husband, during the marriage, purchases Blackacre with community funds. The Act of Sale by which Husband acquires the immovable inaccurately states that Husband is not married. Husband later sells Blackacre to Buyer without consulting Wife. The Act of Sale by which Husband sells Blackacre to Buyer states that Husband is married to Wife. Can Wife rescind the sale to Buyer? Why or why not?

ii. Husband, during the marriage, purchases Blackacre with community funds. The Act of Sale by which Husband acquires the immovable accurately states that Husband is married to Wife. Husband later sells Blackacre to Buyer without consulting Wife. The Act of Sale by which Husband sells Blackacre to Buyer states that Husband is not married. Can Wife rescind the sale to Buyer? Why or why not?

Note also that LA. REV. STAT. § 35:11(A) sets forth a directive for notaries, not the parties to a sale. While a notary will be involved in the execution of a sale that is made in authentic form, an Act of Sale need not be notarized to be valid; an act under private signature is sufficient for an onerous transfer of an immovable. *See* LA. CIV. CODE art. 2440. Even if the Act of Sale is notarized, the failure to insert the marital status of the parties does not invalidate the act. *See American Bank and Trust Co. v. Michael*, 244 So. 2d 882, 884 (La. App. 1 Cir. 1971). However, such conduct has been held to be an act of negligence on the part of the notary. *See Succession of LaSalle v. Clark*, 503 So. 2d 694, 696 (La. App. 3 Cir. 1987).

Finally, note that the effects given by LA. REV. STAT. § 35:11 to a recitation of marital status in an act of acquisition of an immovable do *not* depend on whether the act of acquisition is filed for registry.

2. Consider Article 2342. This article contemplates a "declaration in an act of acquisition that things are acquired with separate funds as the separate property of the spouse." LA. CIV. CODE art. 2342. Like LA. REV. STAT. § 35:11, this article gives effects to a declaration in an act of acquisition and does so regardless of whether the act of acquisition is filed for registry, but the scope and effect of Article 2342 are quite different from that of LA. REV. STAT. § 35:11.

Under Paragraph A of Article 2342, "A declaration in an act of acquisition that things are acquired with separate funds as the separate property of a spouse may be controverted by the other spouse unless he concurred in the act . . . ." LA. CIV. CODE art. 2342(A). However, Paragraph B of the same article goes on to state that "an alienation, encumbrance, or lease of the thing by onerous title, during the community regime or thereafter, may not be set aside on the ground of the falsity of the declaration." LA. CIV. CODE art. 2342(B). In other words, while one spouse may challenge the other spouse's declaration that he or she has acquired property with separate funds, an alienation, encumbrance, or lease by onerous title will not be affected as a result of the challenge.

Consider the following example. Wife acquires Blackacre during the marriage with community funds and recites falsely in the Act of Sale that she purchased the property as separate property with separate funds. Husband is entirely unaware of the transaction and does not concur in the act of acquisition. Wife sells Blackacre to Buyer. Husband and Wife later divorce, and Husband seeks rescission of the sale to Buyer, arguing that Blackacre was properly classified as a community asset that Wife lacked the authority to sell without his concurrence. While Husband may prevail in his argument that the property was properly classified as a community asset, under Paragraph B of Article 2342, Husband may not rescind the sale to Buyer. As stated by Article 2342, comment (a), a determination that an asset declared to be separate property is in fact community "is without effect as to things that have been transferred by onerous transaction to a third person. That person acquires ownership from the transferor spouse in reliance on the declaration in the act by which the transferor acquired the thing that is separate property." LA. CIV. CODE art. 2342 cmt. a.

3. Another provision of community property law that relates, albeit indirectly, to the law of registry is Article 2339. This article deals with the classification of certain marital property as community or separate. The first paragraph of the provision states a general rule that the natural and civil fruits of a spouse's separate property are community in nature. LA. CIV. CODE art. 2339. However, this rule admits an exception—a spouse may "reserve" fruits of separate property as the separate property of that spouse by a declaration made in an authentic act or an act under private signature. *Id.* To be enforceable—either against the other spouse or anyone else—the declaration must be provided to the other spouse and properly filed in the public

records. *Id.* As to fruits and revenues of immovables, the declaration must be filed for registry in the conveyance records of the parish in which the immovable property is located. *Id.* As to fruits of movables, the declaration must be filed for registry in the conveyance records of the parish where the declarant is domiciled. *Id.*

4. Louisiana courts have held that third persons may rely on the absence of a judgment of divorce or separation in the public records. The seminal case announcing this rule, *Camel v. Waller*, 526 So. 2d 1086 (La. 1988), predated the current rule that spouses must concur in alienations, encumbrance, and leases of community immovables. The applicable law in *Camel* was instead the rule of head and master, according to which the husband had complete authority to alienate community immovables without the need for the concurrence of his spouse from whom he was not judicially separated. In *Camel*, a husband acquired an immovable during his marriage. Later, the wife obtained a legal separation from her husband, which terminated the community property regime. She failed to record the judgment of separation. After the judgment was rendered, the husband sold the property to a third person. The wife then obtained and recorded a judgment of divorce. Thereafter, she asserted an ownership interest in the property, alleging that her former husband had sold the property without legal authority because they were separated at the time of the sale. The Court disagreed, holding that although vis-à-vis his wife, the husband's right to alienate community property without her consent ceased upon their separation, he retained this right vis-à-vis third persons until the judgment of divorce was recorded.

The precise facts in *Camel* will not repeat themselves under the current rules of community property management, according to which the spouses must concur in the alienation of community immovables. Note also that the Louisiana legislature revised family law after the *Camel* decision and eliminated the regime of separation from bed and board (except in the context of covenant marriage). Nevertheless, the requirement that judgments of separation and/or divorce must be recorded to be enforceable against third persons may still have effects in other contexts. For example, assume Husband and Wife own Blackacre as community property, and that Wife executes a renunciation of her right to concur in any sale of the property. Husband and Wife later divorce, but a Judgment of Divorce is not filed in the conveyance records. Before the former community property is partitioned, Husband sells Blackacre to Third Person without Wife's concurrence. Is Wife entitled to enforce her rights in Blackacre against Third Person? Why or why not?

e. Special Problems in the Law of Registry

As with any area of the law, there are several contexts in which the proper application of the rules of registry are particularly complex or even unclear. This Subpart explores two problem areas in the law of registry that merit special attention: (1) the effects on third persons of the "secret claims and equities" of the parties to a recorded instrument, and (2) the effects on third persons of pending litigation concerning an immovable.

i. Secret Claims and Equities of the Parties

La. Civ. Code art. 3342

According to Article 3342, "A party to a recorded instrument may not contradict its terms or any statements of fact it contains to the prejudice of a third person who, after its recordation acquires an interest in or over the immovable to which the instrument relates." LA. CIV. CODE art. 3342. Article 3342 recodifies a portion of Louisiana Revised Statutes Section § 9:2721, which was repealed in 2005 when the law of registry was comprehensively revised. That provision stated in part that "neither secret claims or equities nor matters outside the public records shall be binding on or affect . . . third parties." LA. REV. STAT. § 9:2721 (repealed). Generally speaking, the "secret claims or equities" of the parties include any claim between the parties to the instrument that is not evidenced in the instrument itself. One such claim is that the contract evidenced by a recorded instrument is either relatively or absolutely null. Another such claim is an assertion that the contract evidenced by a recorded instrument is a "simulation"—an agreement that does not express the true intentions of the parties. A third such claim is that the contract evidenced by a recorded instrument should be dissolved due to a party's failure to perform. In all of these cases, unless the grounds supporting the claim are evidenced on the face of the recorded instrument, the claim may not be asserted against a third person. Said another way, third persons are entitled to rely upon the *absence* from the public records of a party's claim to the immovable.

The following Subparts address, in detail, the relationship between the law of registry and simulations, nullities, and dissolution.

(a) Nullity

La. Civ. Code arts. 2033, 2035

Louisiana courts have long held that the nullity of an instrument, whether absolute or relative, may not be asserted against third persons unless the grounds for nullity are evidenced on the face of the recorded instrument. Since the 1984 revision of the law of Obligations, this rule has been codified in Article 2035, which presently provides:

> Nullity of a contract does not impair the rights acquired through an onerous contract by a third party in good faith.
>
> If the contract involves immovable property, the principles of recordation apply to a third person acquiring an interest in the property whether by onerous or gratuitous title.

LA. CIV. CODE art. 2035. The most central tenet of the "principles of recordation" is the *McDuffie* rule, which holds that unrecorded interests in immovable property are entirely without effect as to third persons. This notion is undoubtedly among the "principles of recordation" to which Article 2035 refers. *See* LA. CIV. CODE art. 2035 cmt. a. (citing *McDuffie v. Walker*, 51 So. 100 (1909)). Thus, as a general rule, unless the grounds for nullity of a recorded instrument appear in the public records, the nullity of that instrument is not effective against third persons who have acquired rights in that immovable.

Assume, for example, that Seller conveys Blackacre to Buyer, who records the Act of Sale. Buyer then conveys the property to Third Person. Assume further that Seller later brings a claim against Buyer for rescission of the sale on grounds of error and prevails. Although Seller has a valid claim against Buyer, Third Person is protected against Seller's claim by virtue of the public records doctrine. Thus, Third Person will retain ownership of Blackacre, and Seller's recovery will be limited to a damages award against Buyer. *See* LA. CIV. CODE art. 2033. (If it is impossible or impracticable to make restoration in kind, it may be made through an award of damages.)

Assume now that Donor attempts to donate Blackacre to Donee in a written Act of Donation that is neither witnessed nor notarized. The Act of Donation, failing to be in authentic form, is absolutely null. *See* LA. CIV. CODE arts. 1541, 1833. Because the nullity of the donation is apparent on the face of the recorded instrument and therefore evidenced in the public records, it may be asserted against both Donee and any third person who acquires rights in the property from Donee.

The rule that grounds for nullity that are not evidenced on the face of a recorded instrument may not be asserted against third persons admits a significant exception: an allegation that a recorded instrument is a *forgery* may always be enforced against third persons, even if the fraudulent nature of the instrument is not apparent on its face. *See Gulf South Bank & Trust v. Demarest*, 354 So. 2d 695, 697 (La. App. 4 Cir. 1978). The reason for this exception should be obvious: without it, a person could acquire an immovable (and thereby deprive the true owner of his or her rights) simply by filing a forged Act of Sale in the public records. While the law of registry seeks to ensure the stability of land titles, it does not protect such a blatant act of theft.

(b) Simulations

La. Civ. Code arts. 2025–2028

Once an instrument affecting immovable property is properly recorded, third persons are protected against any claim of the parties or their universal successors that the agreement evidenced by the instrument is, in fact, a simulation. Recall that a contract is a simulation when, by mutual agreement, it does not reflect the true intent of the parties. LA. CIV. CODE art. 2025. A simulation is relative when the parties intend that their act shall produce effects between them although the effects are different from those recited in the contract. LA. CIV. CODE art. 2027. In contrast, a simulation is absolute when the parties intend that their contract shall produce no effects between them. LA. CIV. CODE art. 2026. Whereas an absolute simulation produces no effects between the parties, *id.*, a relative simulation produces the effects that they intended if all requirements for those effects have been met, LA. CIV. CODE art. 2027.

The distinctions between relative and absolute simulations are best illustrated through examples. Assume first that Alice wishes to donate Blackacre to one of her five children—her daughter Betty. Out of concern that her other four children will be jealous that Betty received a benefit that the others did not, Alice and Betty decide to disguise the donation as a sale. Alice and Betty sign a document titled "Act of Sale" whereby Alice purports to sell Blackacre to Betty for $200,000. The contract indicates an agreement on thing (Blackacre) and a price ($200,000) and is signed by both parties, but it is not notarized. By all outward accounts, this looks like a sale. However, because Alice and Betty in fact intended a donation, their agreement is a relative simulation and is properly classified as a donation. Moreover, their agreement is enforceable as a donation only if all substantive and formal requirements for a donation are satisfied. Because Alice and Betty's agreement was not made in authentic form (as is required for the donation of an immovable, La. Civ. Code art. 1541), it is absolutely null.

Assume now that Alice is suffering from diminished capacity and that she and her children share concerns that Alice may fall victim to exploitation. Alice decides to place Blackacre in her daughter Betty's name so that Alice, acting alone, will not be able to convey rights to Blackacre to anyone else. The two parties sign a document titled "Act of Sale" whereby Alice purports to sell Blackacre to Betty for $200,000. Although this agreement, like the one in the preceding paragraph, by all accounts appears to be a sale, in fact Alice and Betty did not intend for ownership of Blackacre to transfer to Betty, nor did they intend for Betty to pay the price. They instead intend only to create a "sham" or "paper" transaction to remove the property from Alice's name. This agreement is an absolute simulation and will produce no effects between the parties.

Consider now the effects of simulations against third persons. Assume that after Alice purports to sell Blackacre to Betty, Betty executes an Act of Sale transferring ownership of Blackacre to Clark. Following this, Alice dies, and Betty's siblings, who are now Alice's heirs, bring an action seeking a declaration that the "sale" was either (a) in fact a donation invalid in form (as in the first hypothetical above) or (b) an absolute simulation (as in the second hypothetical above). Either declaration would, of course, benefit the siblings by increasing the size of Alice's estate. Assuming that the siblings are successful in proving that the agreement between Alice and Betty was, in fact, a simulation, will they be able to recover the property from Clark? Article 2028 explains the effects simulations may have against third persons:

> Any simulation, whether absolute or relative, may have effects against third persons.

> Counterletters can have no effects against third persons in good faith. Nevertheless, if the counterletter involves immovable property, the principles of recordation apply with respect to third persons.

La. Civ. Code art. 2028. Consider also comment (c) to Article 2028: "Under this Article, an act may not be attacked as a simulation against the interest of a third person who has relied on the public records." *Id.* cmt. c. The following case provides an example of the application of these principles.

Owen v. Owen

336 So. 2d 782 (La. 1976)

CALOGERO, Justice.

This is a lawsuit by six of the seven children of I.M. and Henrietta Owen, including one J.B. Owen, against their brother (the seventh child W.H. Owen) and his vendees (Wayne S. Bush and Charles Wayne Bush) to have two transfers from their father, I.M. Owen, one to W.H. Owen and the other to W.H. Owen and J.B. Owen jointly, declared simulations, or, alternatively, nullified because they were donations in disguise and donations Omnium bonorum, or, alternatively, to have such property collated in a partition.±

On March 22, 1957, I.M. Owen executed three separate deeds of sale covering tracts composed respectively of 40 acres, 40 acres, and 15 acres. He conveyed 40 acres to his son W.H. Owen for a stated consideration of $100, 40 acres to a second son J.B. Owen for a stated consideration of $720, and 15 acres to both W.H. Owen and J.B. Owen for a stated consideration of $300. The property descriptions are more fully given in the Court of Appeal opinion, *Owen v. Owen*, 325 So.2d 283 (La. App.2nd Cir. 1975), and are incorporated herein by reference. The properties are here referred to respectively as tracts one, two, and three. Ownership of tracts one and three are those at issue in this lawsuit.

In October 12, 1957, I.M. Owen died intestate, and on February 1, 1970 his widow, Henrietta Owen, died intestate. In 1972, following the deaths of Mr. and Mrs. Owen and, of course, subsequent to the execution of the three deeds mentioned above, one of the plaintiffs, J.B. Owen, conveyed all of his interest in tract three to his brother W.H. Owen for $1500. Thereafter, on January 29, 1973, W.H. Owen conveyed the acreage made up of tracts one and three in the following manner: twenty-seven and one-half acres comprising the western half thereof to defendant, Wayne S. Bush for $7,837.50, and twenty-seven and one-half acres comprising the eastern half thereof to defendant Charles Wayne Bush, Wayne S. Bush's son, for $7,837.50. Some nine months thereafter this suit was instituted by six of the Owen children against the seventh child, W.H. Owen, and his vendees Wayne and Charles Bush. Plaintiffs asked that the court set aside the transfers from I.M. Owen to his sons, and order the property returned to the decedent's estate or declare that each of the forced heirs own an undivided one-seventh interest in the property. Alternatively, plaintiffs asked that the property be collated under the provisions of Article 1227 *et seq.* of the Civil Code.

± [Collation refers to the right of certain heirs to demand that their coheirs return to the succession gifts given to them by the decent so that they may be shared equally among all of the heirs. *See generally* LA. CIV. CODE arts. 1227–1288. *Eds.*]

After trial on the merits the Second Judicial District Court rendered judgment in favor of plaintiffs declaring that the two deeds attacked were null and void. In his reasons for judgment the trial judge described the transfers as "simulations and donations in disguise." The trial court judgment further declared that each of the seven children owned an undivided one-seventh interest in the designated tracts at issue in this suit.

From this judgment defendants W.H. Owen, Wayne Bush, and Charles Bush appealed to the Second Circuit Court of Appeal alleging error in the trial court's judgment. The Second Circuit Court of Appeal affirmed the trial court's decision, holding that the conveyances from I.M. Owen of the controverted tracts one and three were donations in disguise, donations *omnium bonorum* and consequently absolutely null. *Owen v. Owen, supra.*

We granted writs upon defendants' application. 326 So.2d 376 (La.1976). In this Court, defendants allege that the Court of Appeal erred in finding that the conveyances by I.M. Owen were donations in disguise and donations *omnium bonorum*, that they erred in concluding that a donation *omnium bonorum* is an absolute nullity, and that they erred in decreeing that the seven heirs of Mr. and Mrs. I.M. Owen were owners each of an undivided one-seventh interest in the subject property.

The following facts are borne out by the record and are not seriously contested. In March 1957, at the time I.M. Owen purported to sell the land in question to his sons, he sold tract number three, comprising 15 acres, for $300, although the property was worth $45 per acre, or $675. On that same date he purported to sell tract one, comprising 40 acres, for a stated consideration of $100, although it was worth $45 per acre, or $1800.

In 1970 the fifty-five acres owned by W.H. Owen were valued at $10,725. He sold the land to the Bushes in 1973 for approximately $16,000. In 1975, that same property was worth $18,700. Although neither of the courts below reached this issue, it is clear that the Bushes purchased the disputed property for a fair price.

The acts of sale by which I.M. Owen conveyed the three tracts in 1957 identified the vendor as I.M. Owen and the vendees as W.H. Owen and J.B. Owen. The deeds, in authentic form, recite that the properties were sold to the respective vendees for the stated consideration "cash in hand paid, the receipt of which is hereby acknowledged." The deeds do not indicate that I.M. Owen was the father of W.H. and J.B., nor that these three properties constituted all of the property owned by Mr., or by Mr. and Mrs., Owen.

The only contested issue of fact in the case is whether the sons actually paid their father for the property. J.B. judicially confessed that he paid nothing for the property. W.H. claimed that he did pay for the property which was transferred to him, but could produce no evidence to support his assertion. The trial court found that nothing was paid by either brother for the land, a finding the Court of Appeal upheld. There is no error in this finding, and we agree with the courts below that the March 22, 1957 sales of tracts one and three to W.H. Owen and to J.B. Owen and W.H. Owen, respectively, were not sales but were disguised donations under Article 2444 of the Civil Code [repealed].

It was established at the trial that before the Bushes purchased the property in question from W.H. Owen they were told by J.B. Owen that there was some question as to whether W.H. Owen could transfer a "clear deed," but they were given no reason for J.B.'s assertion. Wayne Bush also learned from W.H. Owen that he had bought the property from his father. However, there is no evidence that the Bushes ever had any knowledge of Mr. and Mrs. I.M. Owen's financial condition (at any time) nor any knowledge of the value of the property in March of 1957, some fifteen years before their purchase of the property.

The plaintiffs established at trial that at the time of the transfers in question Mr. and Mrs. Owen were living on social security and welfare payments, and that they owned no immovable property other than the three tracts transferred; but there was no evidence as to the amount of income they were receiving, nor was there any evidence as to what their living expenses were. It was established that I.M. Owen had $600 when he died in late 1957, a sum W.H. Owen kept in an account "for his mother."

The plaintiffs contend, and the courts below found, that when I.M. Owen sold these two tracts he had divested himself of all of his property without reserving to himself enough for subsistence. Article 1497 [R.C.C. 1498] prohibits such a donation in the following language:

> "The donation *inter vivos* shall in no case divest the donor of all his property; he must reserve to himself enough for subsistence; if he does not do it, the donation is null for the whole."

In order to sustain an attack on a gift as a donation *omnium bonorum*, the heirs must prove conclusively that the donation divested the donor of all of his property. *Whitman v. Whitman*, 206 La. 1, 18 So.2d 633 (1944); *Potts v. Potts*, 142 La. 906, 77 So. 786 (1918); *Hearsey v. Craig*, 126 La. 824, 53 So. 17 (1910); *Hinton v. May*, 241 So.2d 583 (La.App.2nd Cir. 1970). In light of the stringent requirements set forth in the aforementioned cases, we are not as certain as were the lower courts that the requirements of Article 1497 [R.C.C. 1498] were met so as to brand I.M. Owen's disguised donations as donations *omnium bonorum*. We nonetheless accept the finding of the lower courts, for, even assuming the donations were *omnium bonorum*, the decision of the Court of Appeal in our view must be reversed for the reasons we relate thereinafter.

The plaintiffs allege first that the transfers from parent to sons were simulations. In our law, a simulation is a transfer of property which is not what it seems. Simulations are of two types: pure simulations, and disguised transfers. In a pure simulation, sometimes called a non-transfer, the parties only pretend to transfer the property from one to the other, but in fact both transferor and transferee intend that the transferor retain ownership of the property. When this type of simulation is successfully attacked, the true intent of the parties is revealed, which was that no transfer had in fact taken place. In a contest between a vendor and vendee in this situation the true intent of the parties is effectuated and the courts hold that no transfer took place because the simulated sale is an absolute nullity. *Successions of Webre*, 247 La. 461, 172 So.2d 285 (1965); *Schalaida v. Gonzales*, 174 La. 907, 142 So. 123 (1932); *Milano v. Milano*, 243 So.2d 876 (La.App.1st Cir. 1971). The other type of simulation is a disguised transfer which seems on its face to be a valid sale, but which is intended by the parties to be a gift rather than a sale. When this sort of simulation is attacked successfully, as it has been here under Article 2444 [Repealed] the true intent of the parties is likewise effectuated by the law. A valid transfer has taken place, but its form is a donation rather than a sale and the Code articles on donations apply to the transfer. *Stevens v. Stevens*, 227 La. 761, 80 So.2d 399 (1955); *Carter v. Bolden*, 13 La.App. 48, 127 So. 111 (La.App.2nd Cir. 1930); 35 La.L.Rev. 192 (1974); 25 La.L.Rev. 313 (1965).

However, when the property is no longer held by the original vendee but has passed into the hands of an innocent third party who has purchased for value and in reliance on the public records, the result is much different. In the case of *Chachere v. Superior Oil Co.*, 192 La. 193, 187 So. 321 (1939), this Court upheld the rights of third party purchasers to retain the land in question even though the transfer to their vendor had been a disguised donation. The Court held that because the transfer from the original vendor (the parent of the plaintiff-forced heirs) to the original vendee (who in turn sold to the defendant-third party purchasers) was on its face a valid sale, the plaintiffs were not allowed, after the property had passed into the hands of third parties, to introduce evidence that the transfer was not a sale. The Court stated that:

> "It is the well settled jurisprudence of this state that third persons dealing with immovable property have a right to depend upon the faith of the recorded title thereof and are not bound by any secret equities that may exist between their own vendor and prior owners of the land." 187 So. 321.

In the case of *Thompson v. Thompson*, 211 La. 468, 30 So.2d 321 (1947), this Court reaffirmed *Chachere* and held that, when a third person acquires title to land prior to the assertion by forced heirs of their rights to have the disguised donation annulled, and third party who had purchased for value on the strength of the public records will defeat the claim of the forced heir. The Court stated that:

> "[W]hereas our system of law has protected the forced heirs against acts designed to deprive him of his legitimate portion, the rights granted to such forced heir cannot be extended so as to defeat the subsequently acquired rights of third persons who have bought property on the faith of the public records and under the belief that their vendor acquired a valid title by purchase. In fine, considerations of public policy, respecting a stability of titles, makes it necessary that innocent third parties prevail over the forced heir

even though it results in the denial of the heir's right which our law has so carefully guarded." 30 So.2d at 329.

Likewise, when immovable property which has been the subject of a "pure" simulated sale is later sold to third persons who rely on the public records, in a case where the records show that the transfer was a proper sale, and where the records reveal no counterletter, the rights of the third party cannot be affected by subsequent proof that the original transfer was a pure simulation. *Beard v. Nunn*, 172 La. 155, 133 So. 429 (1931); *Jackson v. Creswell*, 147 La. 914, 86 So. 329 (1920); *Vital v. Andrus*, 121 La. 221, 46 So. 217 (1908); *Gordon v. Culbertson*, 296 So.2d 401 (La.App.2nd Cir. 1974); Redmann, *The Louisiana Law of Recordation: Some Principles and Some Problems*, 39 Tul.L.Rev. 491 (1965); 35 La.L.Rev. 192 (1974); 17 Tul.L.Rev. 457 (1943). It is clear then from the jurisprudence that in the situation where the original transfer was a pure simulation (and *not* therefore effective to pass title) *and* in the situation where the original transfer was a disguised donation (and *did* therefore effectively pass title to the transferee) that the rights of a third party are protected if he purchased on the basis of a public record evidencing an apparently valid sale. Since the third party purchasers here, the Bushes, did purchase for value and in reliance on public records which evidenced a valid sale, they are protected against the claims of the plaintiff forced heirs notwithstanding the fact that the transfer was actually a donation in disguise.

However, plaintiffs urge alternatively that the transfer was a disguised donation which purported to give away all that the donor (I.M. Owen) had, without retaining enough for his subsistence, in contravention of Article 1497 [R.C.C. 1498], and therefore "null for the whole." Plaintiff argues that if the vendee received only a null title, one that was ineffective to transfer title, he could not validly pass title on to the Bushes.

We find, however, that even if the title which passed to the sons could be declared absolutely null while the property remained in their hands, when the property passed into the hands of an innocent third party purchasing in reliance on the public records, the claimants could no longer recover the property. In the case of *Rocques v. Freeman*, 125 La. 60, 51 So. 68 (1909), a widow transferred to her children through a partition her undivided interest in her community property. The children subsequently sold the property to third parties. The mother later attempted to nullify her transfer as a donation in disguise and as a donation *omnium bonorum*, but this Court affirmed the dismissal of her petition. The Court found that her transfer was null because it was a donation in disguise and a donation *omnium bonorum*, but held that the nullity could be asserted only against the donees, not against innocent third parties who had dealt with the property on the faith of the public records.

The Court stated:

"The act which is sought to be annulled in this case as a donation does not appear on its face to possess that character. On its face, it is a partition between Charles F. Metoyer and his sister [plaintiffs' children]. It was no more calculated to put innocent third parties on their guard against defects in the title than would have been a donation in the form of a sham sale. *And we do not imagine any one* [sic] *would say that a donation in the form of a sham sale could be annulled to the detriment of innocent third persons who had dealt with the property in the faith of the public records."* 51 So. at 70. (emphasis added)

We hold, therefore, that where there is nothing of record to indicate that the transfer to the original vendee could have been annulled as a donation *omnium bonorum* and when an innocent party has purchased the land for valuable consideration relying upon the public records, the third party takes the property free of these unrecorded and secret equities.

Plaintiffs, however, claim that the Bushes were not innocent third party purchasers because they had certain actual knowledge about the original transfers, namely, that the transfers were from father to children and that one of the brothers felt there was some doubt as to whether they (the Bushes) could get a "clear deed."

It is uncontroverted that the Bushes were arms length purchasers who were buying the property for value, and that they were not participants or co-participants in any attempt at fraud. The legal issue here is whether the actual knowledge which they had of the previous transfer placed them in such a position that they could not rely on the public records. We hold that it did not.

A third party purchaser can rely on the public records so long as he does not participate in fraud. *Jackson v. Creswell*, 147 La. 914, 86 So. 329 (1920); *Kinchen v. Kinchen*, 244 So.2d 316 (La.App.1st Cir. 1970), *writ not considered*, 257 La. 854, 244 So.2d 608; *Dugas v. Talley*, 109 So.2d 300 (La.App.1st Cir. 1959). Even if he has some actual nonrecord knowledge of a preceding transfer which might have made him suspicious of a deed's validity, he may still rely on the public records if they reveal an apparently valid sale. In the case of *Prather v. Porter*, 176 La. 324, 145 So. 675 (1933), this Court upheld the dismissal of a suit by the forced heir of the original vendor on defendants' exception of no cause of action (defendants were third party purchasers) where the plaintiff contended that defendants were chargeable with knowledge that the transfer was a donation, because the defendants knew the following things: the original vendees were stated in the recorded instrument to be the daughter-in-law and grandson of the vendor; the consideration was stated to be "whatever amount"; and the transfer actually divested the transferor of all of his property. The Court held that these allegations were insufficient to charge the defendants with bad faith because, as it stated:

"the conveyance records are the only things to which one dealing with real estate or real rights needs to look. Notice or knowledge dehors the public records on the part of a third person is not equivalent to registry." 145 So. at 677.

As to plaintiffs' contentions as to the family relationship and the price, the Court stated:

> "There is no law prohibiting the owner of real property from selling the property to his daughter-in-law and grandson. The price as finally expressed in an act of sale represents the stated consideration for the sale. And a vendee who has paid an adequate price cannot be dispossessed of his property because a prior vendor has chosen to part with his title for an inadequate consideration." *Id.*

The actual knowledge which the Bushes had of the transfer to their vendor was far less than the Court in *Prather* assumed that the defendants had there. Of record, defendants Bush knew only that the vendor and vendee had a common surname, and that fifteen acres had been sold ostensibly for $300 and forty acres ostensibly for $100. Although the price of the forty-acre tract might have seemed unusually low (had the Bushes known the land values some fifteen years before), the stated consideration of the smaller tract was later established as a full 44% [o]f its true fair market value, and, as this Court stated in *Prather*, "a vendee who has paid an adequate price cannot be dispossessed of his property because a prior vendor has chosen to part with his title for an inadequate consideration." Beyond the record, the Bushes were aware that the original vendor-vendees were father and sons, and that one of the sons felt they could not get a clear deed. However, no suggestion has been made that the Bushes had any reason to believe that the sons had not paid for the property or that the sales in March of 1957 comprised all that the father had for his subsistence. It can therefore hardly be said that the Bushes were put on notice, either by the record or in fact, that the sales in question were donations, much less donations *omnium bonorum*.

Therefore we conclude that a third party, who is not participating in fraud, and who plans to purchase for value property which according to the public records was properly [s]old to his prospective vendor, may rely on those records even though he has some actual knowledge on which he could speculate that a timely prosecuted legal attack upon his vendor's title might be successful.

* * * * *

Plaintiffs do not suggest that the reconveyances evidence fraud or collusion on the part of the Bushes. The deeds tend to establish that the initial transfers were armslength [sic] transactions rather than the reverse, because the monthly payments on the credit portion of the original acquisition price, seemingly at least, were made by the purchasers between acquisition and reconveyance. Furthermore, motivation for the reconveyance, we can properly surmise, is found in the (interim) adverse decision (to defendants) in the Court of Appeal and in W.H. Owen's warranty obligation arising from the original transfers. More important than these considerations, however, is the fact that plaintiffs do not allege the reconveyances are evidence of fraud or some sort of fraudulent complicity on the part of the Bushes.

This phase of the litigants' controversy should and will be concluded on the present record. Conveyance of the property following the Court of Appeal's denied of rehearing, not reprobated by law or otherwise inhibited, and if no evidentiary or other value insofar as it concerned resolution of the joined issues in this litigation, is legally of no moment. The matter of the defendant Bushes acquisition on the strength of the public record is not moot. This motion is denied.

For the foregoing reasons, the judgment of the Court of Appeal is set aside and the plaintiffs' suit is dismissed at their cost.

Notes and Questions

1. In the foregoing case, the plaintiffs alleged that two "sales" of immovable property made by their father before he died to one of his children were in fact donations. A declaration that the sales were donations in disguise would have permitted the plaintiffs to make two alternative claims to the property conveyed. First, the plaintiffs, as heirs of their father, demanded that the donations be collated, or returned to the succession to be divided equally among the heirs. *See* La Civ. Code arts. 1227–1288. Alternatively, the plaintiffs alleged that the transactions were "donations omnium bonorum" — donations in which the donor gives away all of his property without reserving for himself enough for subsistence. *See* La. Civ. Code art. 1498. Relying on the rule that donations omnium bonorum are absolutely null, the plaintiffs essentially contended that the property "conveyed" in fact never left the patrimony of the decedent and was still a part of his estate.

2. The Court in *Owen* noted that although a claim that a recorded act transferring an immovable is a simulation generally has no effects against third persons, the same is not true when the parties have executed and filed a counterletter. A counterletter is an instrument executed by the parties to a simulation that expresses their true intentions. La. Civ. Code art. 2025. If a counterletter is not recorded, third persons may rely upon its absence from the public records. In contrast, once a counterletter is recorded, it becomes effective against third persons. *See* La. Civ. Code art. 2028. Assume, for example, that Seller and Buyer agree to a "sale" of Blackacre, executing and recording an Act of Sale purporting to convey the property to Buyer in return for a stated price. Assume further that despite executing and recording the Act of Sale, Buyer and Seller do not intend for any transfer of ownership to take place; their agreement is an absolute simulation. Now assume that contemporaneously with the Act of Sale, the parties execute a document titled "Counterletter" in which they state that they do not intend for the Act of Sale to have any effects. Under Article 2028 and the principles of recordation, if the Counterletter is not recorded, third persons may rely upon its absence from the public records. Thus, if Buyer sells Blackacre to Third Person before either Buyer or Seller records the Counterletter, Third Person is protected against any claim to Blackacre that Seller may later raise on grounds that the sale to Buyer was a simulation. On the other hand, if before the sale to Third Person, Seller records the Counterletter, Seller's right to reclaim the property from Third Person would be preserved.

(c) Dissolution

A party's right to dissolve the transfer of an immovable evidenced by a recorded instrument likewise may not be asserted against third persons. Article 2021 mirrors the rules set forth by Articles 2035 (on nullity) and 2028 (on simulations), stating:

> Dissolution of a contract does not impair the rights acquired through an onerous contract by a third party in good faith.
>
> If the contract involves immovable property, the principles of recordation apply to a third person acquiring an interest in the property whether by onerous or gratuitous title.

La. Civ. Code art. 2021. For example, as will be shown in Chapter 11: Obligations of the Buyer, when the buyer fails to pay the price, the seller has the right to dissolution of the sale. This right is retained against third persons only if the right to dissolution is evidenced in the public records. Thus, if a recorded Act of Sale recites that the price is unpaid, then the Seller's right of dissolution will be enforceable against third persons who have, after recordation, acquired rights in the property. However, if the recorded Act of Sale recites that the price was paid, the seller's right to dissolution cannot impact third persons. *See* La. Civ. Code art. 2561 cmt. g; *LeBlanc v. Bernard*, 554 So. 2d 1378, 1381 (La. App. 1 Cir. 1989).

ii. Pending Litigation Affecting Immovables

La. Civ. Code art. 2453; La. Code Civ. Proc. arts. 3751–3753

A final matter relating to the public records that merits special attention is the effect of litigation on the rights of a person acquiring an interest in immovable property. Consider the following example. Buyer purchases Blackacre from Seller via an Act of Cash Sale. Although Buyer has not yet paid the price, the Act of Cash Sale gives no indication that the price has not been paid. Later, Seller brings a claim against Buyer for dissolution of the sale on account of Buyer's failure to pay the price. After the lawsuit is filed, but before the case is resolved, Buyer sells the property to Third Person. Later, Seller prevails in the suit for dissolution. As the foregoing discussion of the "secret claims and equities" of the parties makes clear, Seller's right to dissolution, which is absent from the public records, is not enforceable against Third Person. Thus, despite the fact that Seller prevails in his claim against Buyer, Third Person remains secure in ownership of Blackacre, and Seller must be content to recover damages from Buyer. What, if anything, could Seller have done prior to the sale to Third Person to secure his right in Blackacre?

The Civil Code contains a single article addressing the effects of the sale of a thing that is the subject of ongoing litigation. While Article 2453 provides a general rule that the sale of a thing pending litigation "does not affect the claimant's rights[,]" the article states that with respect to immovable property, "the rights of third persons are governed by the laws of registry." La. Civ. Code art. 2453. The "laws of registry" referenced in this article include not only the provisions already discussed in this Chapter, but also special legislation in the Louisiana Code of Civil Procedure governing the effects of the notice of lis pendens ("pending litigation"):

La. Code Civ. Proc. art. 3751. Notice to be recorded to affect third persons

The pendency of an action or proceeding in any court, state or federal, in this state affecting the title to, or asserting a mortgage or privilege on, immovable property does not constitute notice to a third person not a party thereto unless a notice of the pendency of the action or proceeding is made, and filed or recorded, as required by Article 3752.

La. Code Civ. Proc. art. 3752. Requirements of notice; recordation

A. The notice referred to in Article 3751 shall be in writing, signed by the plaintiff, defendant, or other party to the action or proceeding who desires to have the notice recorded, or by a counsel of record for such party showing the name of the persons against whom it is to be effective, the name of the court in which the action or proceeding has been filed, the title, docket number, date of filing, and object thereof, and the description of the property sought to be affected thereby.

B. This notice shall be recorded in the mortgage office of the parish where the property to be affected is situated and has effect from the time of the filing for recordation. The notice shall cease to have effect after ten years from the date of its filing for recordation. Nevertheless, if the action or proceeding is still pending, the notice may be reinscribed by refiling the notice. A reinscription of the notice that is filed before the effect of recordation ceases continues that effect for five years from the day the notice is reinscribed.

La. Code Civ. Proc. art. 3753. Cancellation of notice of pendency

When judgment is rendered in the action or proceeding against the party who filed the notice of the pendency thereof, the judgment shall order the cancellation of the notice at the expense of the party who filed it, and as part of the costs of the action or proceeding. Nevertheless, the notice of pendency filed in connection with the proceeding which gave rise to the judgment shall be canceled at the request of any interested party if the judgment has been canceled or if the action or proceeding has been dismissed.

The following case addresses the question of whether a third person with *actual knowledge* of pending litigation concerning immovable property is affected by the outcome of that litigation if a notice of lis pendens is not properly filed. After having read *McDuffie v. Walker*, the result of this case may surprise you.

Cannata v. Bonner

982 So. 2d 968 (La. App. 3 Cir. 2008)

EZELL, Judge.

Anthony Cannata appeals a trial court judgment granting a permanent injunction in favor Robert Foreman which enjoined the Sheriff of Calcasieu Parish from selling property pursuant to executory process proceedings started by Mr. Cannata. The trial court granted the permanent injunction finding that the north half of the property was owned by Mr. Foreman and not Lori and Rodney Bonner who had executed a mortgage on both the north and south halves of the property in favor of Mr. Cannata.

FACTS

In 1999, the Bonners filed a petition seeking to enforce an agreement to sell immovable property in a lease-purchase agreement they had entered into with Mr. Foreman. On October 15, 2001, a stipulated judgment was entered into ordering Mr. Foreman to execute a deed conveying the property to the Bonners for the sum of $13,250. Mr. Foreman refused to comply with the stipulated judgment, so the Bonners filed a rule for contempt. Judgment was signed on June 7, 2002, declaring them owners of the property.

On May 11, 2005, Mr. Foreman filed a motion to amend judgment. He sought to amend the judgment declaring the Bonners the owners of the following described property:

> Commencing at a point 662 feet East of the Northwest Corner of the Northeast quarter of the Northwest quarter of Section 12, Township 8, Range 8, thence South 640 feet, thence East 331.4 feet, thence North 640 feet, thence West 331.4 feet to a point of commencement.

Mr. Foreman claimed that the property description should have declared that it was the *south half* of the above described property. He argued that he never intended to sell the *north half* and that the Bonners only intended to buy the south half. Apparently, this mistake began with the lease-purchase agreement and continued to be copied in other documents[.] The trial court denied the motion to amend as untimely.

Mr. Foreman suspensively appealed the decision to this court. This court agreed that it was too late to attack to the judgment. However, we found that his motion to amend was in the nature of an action for reformation of a deed which has a prescriptive period of ten years pursuant to La.Civ.Code art. 3499. Finding that all parties were well aware of the erroneous description, this court ordered that the description of the property be reformed to reflect that only the south half of the property described was sold to the Bonners. In an unpublished opinion, judgment was rendered by this court on December 6, 2006.

Between the judgment of the trial court and this court's judgment, while the appeal was pending, the Bonners executed a bearer mortgage on July 14, 2006, covering both the south and north halves of entire property. On February 14, 2007, two months after judgment of this court, Mr. Cannata filed a petition for executory process on the property based on the ownership claim because the mortgage provided that it became due if there was the institution of any legal proceedings to enforce a mortgage, lien, privilege, or claim against the property.

Mr. Foreman filed a petition for injunction as owner of the north half of the property. On April 18, 2007, a temporary restraining order was issued restraining the sheriff from proceeding with the sale set for April 25, 2007. Mr. Cannata filed a motion to dissolve the temporary restraining order which was granted on April 25, 2007.

A hearing was held on June 25, 2007. The trial court granted a permanent injunction enjoining the sale of the north half of the property. The trial court ruled that the sale of the south half of the property could proceed. Judgment was signed on July 18, 2007. Mr. Cannata appealed the judgment.

DISCUSSION

* * * * *

Mr. Cannata claims that he has a valid note and mortgage over both halves of the property. Relying on the public records doctrine, he claims that he is an innocent third party whose rights could not be affected by the pending litigation over ownership. Mr. Cannata points out that when the note and mortgage were executed, the Bonners had a trial court judgment which recognized them as owners of both halves of the property.

We agree with Mr. Cannata that a description of property can be reformed to reflect the intent of the parties as long as the rights of innocent third parties have not intervened. *W.B. Thompson & Co. v. McNair*, 199 La. 918, 7 So.2d 184 (1942); *Marsh Cattle Farms v. Vining*, 30,156 (La.App. 2 Cir. 1/23/98), 707 So.2d 111, *writ denied*, 98–478 (La.4/24/98), 717 So.2d 1167; *M.R. Bldg. Corp. v. Bayou Utils., Inc.*, 25,759 (La.App. 2 Cir. 5/4/94), 637 So.2d 614. However, for the following reasons, we find that Mr. Cannata was not an innocent third party.

The Bonners did receive judgment in the trial court which designated them as owners of both the north and south halves of the land. Mr. Foreman suspensively appealed the judgment. Therefore, the appeal suspended the operation of the judgment. *Hollingsworth v. City of Minden*, 01–2658 (La.6/21/02), 828 So.2d 514; *Wetherbee v. Lodwick Lumber Co., Inc.*, 194 La. 352, 193 So. 671 (1940). We do note that a lis pendens was not filed pursuant to Louisiana Code of Civil Procedure Article 3751. Filing a notice of lis pendens would have definitely put any third party on notice that there was pending litigation affecting title to the property, and the outcome of the litigation would be binding on the third party. *Campbell v. Melton*, 01–2578 (La.5/14/02), 817 So.2d 69.

Regardless, at the hearing it was revealed that counsel for Mr. Cannata had also represented the Bonners in their dispute as to ownership of the property. The mortgage and note between the Bonners and Mr. Cannata was also executed in the same attorney's office.

Notice or knowledge of an agent, while the agency or relationship exists and while the agent is acting within the scope of his authority, is notice and knowledge to his principal. *Marpco, Inc. v. South States Pipe & Supply*, 377 So.2d 525 (La.App.

3 Cir.1979). Therefore, Mr. Cannata's counsel's knowledge of the pending lawsuit affecting ownership of the property constituted actual knowledge on Mr. Cannata's behalf when Mr. Cannata entered into the mortgage at the attorney's office. *Id.; Smart Document Solutions, LLC v. Miller*, 07–670 (La.App. 3 Cir. 10/31/07), 970 So.2d 49, *writ denied*, 08–210 (La.3/28/08), 978 So.2d 308; *Bell v. Demax Mgt. Inc.*, 01–692 (La.App. 4 Cir. 7/24/02), 824 So.2d 490. A lis pendens is not necessary when the third person has actual notice of the pending litigation. *Richardson Oil Co. v. Herndon*, 157 La. 211, 102 So. 310 (1924).

We find that the trial court was correct in granting a permanent injunction. Mr. Foreman was declared owner of the north half of the property by this court in its previous decision. Mr. Cannata had knowledge that there was litigation affecting title to this property when he entered into the note and mortgage with the Bonners. Therefore, Mr. Foreman was entitled to a permanent injunction to prevent the sale of the north half of the property he owned.

The judgment of the trial court is affirmed. Costs of this appeal are assessed to Anthony Cannata.

AFFIRMED.

Notes and Questions

In holding that "[a] lis pendens is not necessary when the third person has actual knowledge of the pending litigation[,]" the court in the foregoing case cites to *Richardson Oil Co. v. Herndon*, 102 So. 310 (La. 1924). In that case, Herndon executed an oil lease in favor of Dunson on certain lands in Caddo Parish. The lease was recorded on December 20, 1916. In 1917, Herndon sued to annul the lease on the grounds that Dunson had failed to "give consideration" for the lease and had obtained it through fraud. No notice of lis pendens was recorded. While litigation surrounding the lease was pending, Dunson assigned the lease to Harrell, who thereafter assigned it to the Richardson Oil Company ("Richardson"). The court eventually annulled the lease from Herndon to Dunson, and a dispute arose between Herndon and Richardson as to whether the annulment was enforceable against Richardson. Relying on the public records doctrine, Richardson argued that because a notice of lis pendens was never filed, the outcome of the litigation had no effect on Richardson. The Supreme Court disagreed, holding that the lis pendens statute then in effect had no bearing on the case because Richardson had *actual knowledge* of the litigation between Herndon and Dunson.

To understand how the *Richardson Oil Co.* Court could arrive at a conclusion so contrary to *McDuffie v. Walker*, one must explore the history of Article 2453 and the lis pendens statute, which was first introduced into the law in 1910. Prior to that time, Article 2453 provided:

> The thing claimed as the property of the claimant, cannot be alienated pending the action so as to prejudice his right. If judgment be rendered for him, the sale is considered as a sale of another's property, and does not prevent him from being put in possession by virtue of such judgment.

La. Civ. Code art. 2453 (1870). In *Richardson Oil Co.*, the Court noted that, in interpreting this article, Louisiana courts had long held that the mere filing of a lawsuit served as "constructive notice" to the world of the plaintiff's claim, such that anyone acquiring a right in the property while litigation was pending did so subject to the right of the claimant. In other words, although rights in immovable property that were not evidenced of record were generally not enforceable against third persons, once a lawsuit to enforce that right was filed, any third person acquiring rights in the immovable was bound by the outcome of that litigation. The legislature enacted the first lis pendens statutes in 1898 and 1904 in order to alter this rule. The Court observed that the lis pendens statutes did not state that the filing of a lawsuit "shall *have no effect* against third persons" or "shall be *utterly null and void*" (as did other legislation providing for the registry of sales, mortgages, privileges, judgments, and other acts concerning immovable property), but instead it provided only that the filing of a lawsuit "shall not be . . . *construed* as notice to third persons." 102 So. at 312–13. This difference, the Court determined, was intentional and significant, and the Court therefore held that the lis pendens statute "does not pretend to say that the filing of a suit shall *have no effect* against third persons even with *actual* notice, it simply says that the mere filing of such shall not suffice as *constructive* notice thereof to third persons." *Id.* at 313.

While *Richardson Oil Co.* may have been correctly decided at the time the court's opinion was rendered (1924), its continuing vitality must be viewed in light of subsequent amendments to the lis pendens statute. When the lis pendens statute was incorporated into the Code of Civil Procedure in 1960, instead of stating that the pendency of an action affecting immovable property "shall not be considered or construed as notice, absent the filing of a notice of lis pendens" the new law provided that the mere pendency of an action "does not constitute notice to a third person not a party" to the litigation. La. Code Civ. Proc. 3751 (1960). Although the redactor's comment states that the change "is intended to overrule legislatively the contrary decision in *Richardson Oil Co. v. Herndon*," a leading commentator on the law of registry questioned whether the overruling was accomplished, noting that "the new language still falls short of saying that the pendency of an action 'shall have no effect against third persons' as *Richardson Oil* thought was necessary." William V. Redmann, *Louisiana Law of Recordation: Some Principles and Some Problems*, 39 Tul. L. Rev. 491, 510 (1965). Thus, at least in the years immediately following the promulgation of the Code of Civil Procedure, some question remained regarding whether a person with actual knowledge of pending litigation concerning immovable property was bound thereby.

Article 2453 was amended in 1995 as part of the revision of the Sales Title. The first sentence of the revised article updates the language of the original, stating, "When the ownership of a thing is the subject of litigation, the sale of that thing during the pendency of the suit does not affect the claimant's rights." La. Civ. Code art. 2453. Although a new, second sentence provides, "When the thing is immovable, the rights of third persons are governed by the law of registry," the redactors apparently did not intend to introduce any change in the law. *Id.* cmt. ("This Article . . . does not change the law.").

In light of the foregoing discussion, what do you think of the Louisiana Third Circuit Court of Appeal's holding in *Bonner v. Cannata*? Is the court's opinion correct? If so, is the result consistent with the principles of the law of registry? For additional discussion of *Herndon v. Richardson Oil*, including alternative explanations for the Court's holding, see William V. Redmann, *Louisiana Law of Recordation*: *Some Principles and Some Problems*, 39 Tul. L. Rev. 491, 509–511 (1965).

Chapter 5

Price

A. In General

La. Civ. Code arts. 2439, 2464–2466

Article 2439 defines a sale as the transfer of "ownership of a thing to another for a price in money." LA. CIV. CODE art. 2439. With respect to the essential elements of the sale, Article 2439 goes on to provide: "The thing, the price, and the consent of the parties are requirements for the perfection of a sale." *Id.* It is clear that without a price, there can be no sale. *See* LA. CIV. CODE art. 2464 ("There is no sale unless the parties intended that a price be paid.").

Louisiana law requires not only that the sale be for a price, but that the price be a sum of money, and that it be "fixed by the parties in a sum either certain or determinable through a method agreed by them." *Id.* The requirements for a valid price are explored in detail in the Subparts that follow.

1. Price in Money

Louisiana State Law Institute, Proposed Louisiana Civil Code Revision of Sales 3 (1992) (Exposé des Motifs)

Article 2439 preserves the idea that a price must consist of a sum of money, an idea that has been challenged in modern times. *See* T.B. Smith, *Exchange Or Sale?*, 48 TUL. L. REV. 1029 (1974). In fact, the Uniform Commercial Code has completely eliminated the requirement that the price of a sale be stipulated in terms of money. *See* U.C.C. § 2-304. It is also worth noting that modern civil codes exclude from the definition of sale the notion that the price must consist of a sum of money. *See* Article 1470 of the Italian Civil Code; Article 433 of the German Civil Code.

* * * * *

Notes and Questions

As indicated in the foregoing excerpt of the *Exposé des Motifs* for the 1995 revision of the Title on Sale, Louisiana law continues to require the price to be "in money" despite the fact that other jurisdictions—both civil law and common law—do not. What purpose is served by requiring that the price be in money? What if the recipient of the thing "sold" provides something other than money in return for the thing "sold"? *See* LA. CIV. CODE art. 2660 (exchange); LA. CIV. CODE art. 2665 (giving in payment); *Thielman v. Gahlman*, 44 So. 123 (La. 1907) (finding an innominate contract).

2. Price Certain or Determinable

Article 2464 requires that the price "must be fixed by the parties in a sum either certain or determinable through a method agreed by them." La. Civ. Code art. 2464. The following materials address the requirement that the parties "fix" the price.

Princeville Canning Co. v. Hamilton
159 So. 2d 14 (La. App. 1 Cir. 1963)

Reid, Judge.

These cases were brought by the Princeville Canning Company, a canner of sweet potatoes, against two sweet potato growers, Calhoun B. Hamilton and Joe Morris, for damages resulting from an alleged breach of written contract. By supplemental petition in the Hamilton case the plaintiff sought redress against Hamilton for the loss of potato crates. The defendants filed exceptions of no cause or right of action alleging the contracts were vague and indefinite, the contract price provision was indefinite and there was no agreement between the parties as to price. The defendants admitted signing the agreement of sale and admitted the sale of sweet potatoes to another cannery but denied any breach of contract. The two cases were consolidated for trial and for written reasons assigned there was a judgment rendered in each case dismissing plaintiff's suit at its cost.

* * * * *

It is from these judgments that the plaintiff has appealed.

The issue before this Court arises out of an interpretation of a formal contract prepared by plaintiff which is used by plaintiff in securing sweet potatoes from growers. The pertinent part of the contract reads thus:

> "This contract made and entered into this __ day of __ 1960, by and between Princeville Canning Company, St. Francisville, La., hereinafter called the Company and the Grower whose name and signature appear above and below, hereinafter called the Grower,
>
> WITNESSETH:
>
> The Company agrees to purchase and the Grower agrees to sell and deliver to the Company Plant the Sweet Potatoes covered by the contract, at the prices and in accordance with the laws and conditions hereinafter set forth.
>
> __ Bushels of Sweet Potatoes at $1.80 per CWT. Minimum Delivered Price.
>
> *This Contract is for Gold Rush Variety only.*

Contract Prices will Increase According to Market Rise.

Specifications for Suitable Potatoes."

⋆ ⋆ ⋆ ⋆ ⋆

The defense of these cases is based upon the proposition that the price actually paid for the sweet potatoes was never agreed upon by the parties; that the portion of the contract which reads "contract prices will increase according to market rise" does not fix any definite criteria as to how the price would be determined; that there was no evidence introduced at the trial to show the parties had agreed on a formula for fixing the price; and that the price paid defendants was based not upon market price or market value, but was unilaterally set by the plaintiff without the agreement of defendants.

The Louisiana law is clear that in order to have a valid contract it is necessary there be an agreement between the parties as to price and the price must be fixed and determined by the parties. This is clearly set forth in LSA-C.C. Article 2439 [R.C.C. 2439] which provides:

> "The contract of sale is an agreement by which one gives a thing for a price in current money, and the other gives the price ⋆ ⋆ ⋆ to have the thing itself. There circumstances concur to the perfection of the contract, to wit: the thing sold, the price and the consent."

and in LSA-C.C. Article 2464 [R.C.C. 2464] which reads as follows:

> "The price of the sale must be certain, that is to say, fixed and determined by the parties. It ought to consist of a sum of money, otherwise it would be considered as an exchange. It ought to be serious, that is to say, there should have been a serious and true agreement that it should be paid. It ought not to be out of all proportion with the value of the thing; for instance the sale of a plantation for a dollar could not be considered as a fair sale; it would be considered as a donation disguised."

As set forth by defendants in their brief, it appears the term "market rise" has no well defined or commonly accepted meaning in law. However, it is clear from a reading of the agreements and from the evidence introduced in this case that what was meant by "market rise" was should the market for sweet potatoes rise to a certain price at a given time, that would be the price to be paid under the contract. The price to be paid under the contract was really the market value or price of the commodity.

"Market value" is defined in Black's law dictionary as follows:

> "The market value of an article or piece of property is the price which it might be expected to bring if offered for sale in a fair market; not the price which might be obtained on a sale at public auction or a sale forced by the necessities of the owner, but such a price as would be fixed by negotiation and mutual agreement, after ample time to find a purchaser, as between a vendor who is willing (but not compelled) to sell and a purchaser who

desires to buy but is not compelled to take the particular article or piece of property."

and has been interpreted by the Louisiana Courts as follows:

"* * * the market value—that is, a price which would be agreed upon at a voluntary sale between a willing seller and purchaser." *City of New Orleans v. Noto*, 217 La. 657, 47 So.2d 36, 37.

"* * * the term "market value" means the fair value of the property between one who wants to purchase and one who wants to sell under usual and ordinary circumstances." *Henderson v. Dyer*, La.App. (1st Cir. 1953) 68 So.2d 623, 625.

"Market price" is defined by Black's law dictionary as follows:

"The actual price at which the given commodity is currently sold, or has recently been sold, in the open market, that is, not at a forced sale, but in the usual and ordinary course of trade and competition, between sellers and buyers equally free to bargain, as established by records of late sales."

and by American Jurisprudence thus:

"Market price within the meaning of the contract is proved, when possible, by actual sales."

In order for plaintiff to recover it is necessary that either the contract itself show the price is certain, that is, fixed and determined by the parties, or it must be shown by extrinsic evidence that a market price or value had been established by the parties and an agreement had been made between the parties as to how the market value or market price was determined. Being silent as to what market would be used to determine the market rise, or how the market price was to be determined, or by whom the market price was to be determined, the contract here concerned does not in itself fix the price with that degree of certainty required by our law, and therefore, plaintiff must rely upon extrinsic evidence.

Plaintiff alleges it based its determination of the market price upon 15 market reports from the Louisiana Department of Agriculture covering the period of September 20, 1960 to November 15, 1960. The said reports were introduced in evidence and contained under the heading "Sweet Potatoes for Processing" a price quotation representing the low and the high paid that day by canneries throughout the State. According to plaintiff's witnesses, several of the company's men would sit down and establish the company's price, using the said market reports as a guide. They would use the low and the high and take an average of the two to set their price and then they would add the cost of the crate. An example of how this was done, as taken from plaintiff's brief, is as follows:

Date	Report No.	Low	High	Average	Price	Cost	¢ above or below average
9/20	13	$2.00	$2.20	$2.100	$2.15	$0.06	+11
9/30	21	$2.00	$2.30	$2.150	$2.15	$0.06	+06

Date	Report No.	Low	High	Average	Price	Cost	¢ above or below average
10/4	23	$2.00	$2.60	$2.300	$2.15	$0.06	−9
10/21	36	$2.00	$2.70	$2.350	$2.15	$0.06	−14
10/23	38	$1.85	$2.55	$2.200	$2.15	$0.06	+1

Plaintiff argued an examination of the market quotations show that although there was a high and a low, there nevertheless was a market quote and the price could be made certain. Plaintiff pointed out that an examination of the 15 reports shows that throughout the period the plaintiff paid more than the low market price and on six occasions paid more than the average market price. It is upon that schedule plaintiff bases its contention the price was certain. Plaintiff fails to show, however, there was any agreement by both parties to the contract that this was the method to be used to determine the price.

Mr. J.A. Swindler, Jr., the market reporter for the Department of Agriculture testified these reports were published twice weekly, on Tuesday and Thursday; he normally contracted four or five producers and the reports reflected the lowest price paid by one of the canneries and the highest paid by another. Mr. Swindler further testified there were approximately 25 canners in the State but the market report was made up from four to five. It is apparent, however, the four or five used were the larger canneries.

Mr. Gordon Truitt, Chief Executive Officer of the plaintiff, testified plaintiff established the price on Monday for each week and would pay that price until further notice. According to the record plaintiff paid only two prices during the entire season despite the fact the market price reflected in the reports changed almost every day.

Mr. Edward Daniels, plaintiff's manager, testified the company met usually on Saturday and made up the price for the following week. Mr. Daniels testified:

XQ: The development of the market price is done at Princeville?

A: As far as we're concerned, the price that we set up is.

An examination of the schedule of market reports set forth by plaintiff in its brief shows regardless of the high or the low, or the average, the plaintiff had a constant price, namely, $2.15, which never varied. Only once during the entire period covered by the reports did plaintiff's price equal the highest price paid. On all other 14 occasions the price paid by plaintiff was below that shown as the high—on one occasion by as much as 55¢. It is apparent the $2.15 figure was an arbitrary figure set by plaintiff and bears little relation to the market reports on which it is supposedly based.

In support of its contention that the plaintiff did not base its price upon the market value of the potatoes, defendants introduced evidence to show during the period in dispute another buyer, B.F. Trappery & Sons, Inc., came into the area and offered more for sweet potatoes than plaintiff was paying. The record shows on several occasions while plaintiff was paying $2.15 per crate, B.F. Trappery was offering $2.40 per crate. Further evidence that plaintiff's basis for setting the price bore little relationship to the market price is shown by the testimony of plaintiff's witness Mr. Truitt who testified on November 17 and 18, 1960, he purchased potatoes for plaintiff from a non-contract source for $2.80—only two days after the plaintiff, by its own admission, set $2.15 as its contract price.

It is thus apparent from an examination of all the evidence in these cases that the determination of the market rise to be paid was unilaterally fixed by plaintiff without agreement by defendants and although the price was allegedly based upon the market reports of the Louisiana Department of Agriculture, the price remained unchanged during that period despite the fluctuations in the market reports and actually bears no relationship to the market reports. There is nothing in the record to indicate that there was at any time a meeting of minds between plaintiff and defendants as to how the market price was to be determined.

After examining the evidence the Trial Court concluded:

> "The conclusion reached by this Court must be that the phrase market rise or market price of sweet potatoes, unqualified and unexplained, cannot provide an objective method by which the price of a sale can be established with certainty. Plaintiff in its brief demonstrates its inability to fix any sum as the market price by suggesting the Court use a theory of fair market price or average market price."

It is the opinion of this Court that this statement of the Trial Court is correct.

Wall v. United Gas Public Service Co., 178 La. 908, 152 So. 561, contains an excellent discussion of the test which should be applied in cases such as this. In that case the Court held:

> "The term 'market price' does not mean an arbitrary price fixed by the lessee. 'Market price' means, according to Webster, 'the price actually given in current market dealings.'"

The Court then went on to cite the case of *Louisville & Nashville R.R. Company v. R.E.E. DeMontluzin Co.*, 166 La. 211, 116 So. 854, 855, thus:

> "The market value means the fair value of the property between one who wants to purchase and one who wants to sell, under usual and ordinary circumstances.
>
> "The 'market value' of a commodity is the 'price at which the owner of the goods or the producer holds them for sale; the price at which they are freely offered in the market to all the world; such prices as dealers in the goods are willing to receive, and purchasers are made to pay, when the goods are bought and sold in the ordinary course of trade.' *Muser v. Magone*, 155 U.S. 240, 15 S.Ct. 77, 81, 39 L.Ed. 135. *See* Words and Phrases, First Series, page 4383, under the heading 'Market Value.'"

It is, therefore, the opinion of this Court that the contract sued upon here is so indefinite as to price as to be null and void. We further observe the contract was prepared by plaintiff and it is well established when there is doubt as to its meaning a contract will be construed against the party who formed it. *Muse v. Metropolitan Life Insurance Co.*, La.App., 192 So. 72.

In regard to plaintiff's claim against Hamilton as to crates, we agree with the Trial Court's conclusion that plaintiff failed to offer any proof in this regard.

For the foregoing reasons, the judgment of the Trial Court is affirmed.

Affirmed.

Notes and Questions

1. The principles expressed in Articles 2464 and 2465 relating to the requirement that the price be "fixed" or "determinable" are not unique to the law of sales. Rather, Articles 1973 and 1974 articulate similar principles for all conventional obligations. Read those articles carefully.

2. The court in *Princeville Canning* found the price too indefinite to support an enforceable contract of sale. Would the result have been different if the plaintiff had put on evidence that the parties explicitly agreed that the price would be an average of the high and low prices in the most recently published report of the Louisiana Department of Agriculture? Why or why not?

3. In *Louis Werner Sawmill Co. v. O'Shee*, the Louisiana Supreme Court considered the requirements for a price to be fixed as required by the Civil Code. 35 So. 919 (La. 1904). Quoting doctrine expounding upon the French *Code Civil*, the Court stated:

> What is essential . . . is that the parties should have bound themselves in such a way that the price may be thereafter demanded as a mere consequence of the consent given by them, without any new act of volition on their part.

Id. at 921 (quoting Victor-Napoléon Marcadé, 6 Explication du Code Napoléon 175–83 (5th ed. Cotillon, Libraire Du Conseil D'Etat 1859)). How does this language aid in your understanding of what is required for a valid price under Articles 2464 and 2465?

4. In lieu of fixing the price as a sum certain or through a method agreed upon by the parties, the parties may leave the price to the discretion of a third person. La. Civ. Code art. 2465. If after the parties manifest an intention to fix the price through this method, they fail to appoint a third person or the third person fails to fix the price, the sale remains enforceable, and the price may be determined by the court. *Id.* What is the justification for permitting the court to decide the price? How does the court go about setting a price in a contract of sale? Can the court appoint its own expert to aid in the determination of the price? *See* La. Code of Evid. art. 706 (Court Appointed Experts).

5. The 1995 revision of the Title on Sale introduced Article 2466, which provides that in certain sales of movables, if the parties say nothing about the price or leave it to be agreed later and they fail to agree, the price is a "reasonable price at the time and place of delivery." LA. CIV. CODE art. 2466. This article applies only when the thing sold is a movable "of the kind that the seller habitually sells." *Id.* As the legislative commentary suggests, Article 2466 gives legislative formulation to a rule previously expressed by the following case.

Benglis Sash & Door Co. v. Leonards

387 So. 2d 1171 (La. 1980)

LEMMON, Justice.

This suit to collect the reasonable retail value of bay windows ordered by defendant Leonards' architect (with admitted authority) presents the issue of whether a valid contract was struck although the parties at the time of contracting did not state a price certain in money.

Leonards had employed the architect in connection with the renovation of a building into apartments. While Leonards was out of the country, his wife selected certain bay windows for the building, and the architect contacted plaintiff, a building material wholesale dealer, to furnish the windows. Plaintiff had previously furnished other materials to defendant for this and other jobs. Since the desired windows were not stock items, it was necessary to order them specially from the manufacturer. Plaintiff estimated that delivery would take about eight to ten weeks, and the architect indicated satisfaction, without requesting a guaranteed delivery date or otherwise indicating a need for delivery within a certain period. The price of the windows was not discussed, and plaintiff did not require the usual deposit for a special order because of the previous dealings between the parties. Plaintiff placed the order on July 22, 1977 and received delivery on October 6, about 11 weeks later.

In the meantime Leonards had returned home and, being displeased with the progress of the renovation, fired his office manager. Leonards claimed he wrote a letter to plaintiff on September 24, cancelling the order because of failure to deliver within the time promised, but plaintiff denied receiving the letter. When the windows arrived, plaintiff contacted Leonards for delivery instruction, whereupon Leonards refused to accept the windows. This suit ensued, with Leonards' sole defense being that the windows were not delivered within the agreed time.

After trial on the merits the trial court found that delivery was timely and rendered judgment awarding plaintiff the invoice price of the windows and interest, but denying attorney's fees and other items of damages. The court of appeal reversed and dismissed the suit, holding that there was never an enforceable contract, since the parties had never agreed upon a price as required by C.C. arts. 2439 [R.C.C. 2439] and 2464 [R.C.C. 2464]. 378 So.2d 992. We granted certiorari. 380 So.2d 97.

The four requisites of a valid contract are capacity of the parties, their consent, a certain object and a lawful purpose. C.C. art. 1779 [No Corresponding Article]. Particular types of contracts, such as a contract of sale, may have other requisites, and if the requisite is missing there is either no contract or a contract of another description. C.C. art. 1764 [No Corresponding Article].

C.C. art. 2439 [R.C.C. 2439] defines the contract of sale and states the circumstances which must concur for the perfection of the contract. Thus, the contract of sale is perfected when one party consents to give a certain thing for a price in money and the other consents to give the price in order to have that thing. Although there must be consent to give and to accept a price, it is not essential that the specific sum of the sales price be stated at the time of contracting. The parties can agree that the price may be ascertained by computation or that the price may be fixed by arbitration. Or the parties can consent to buy and to sell a certain thing for a reasonable price, and when they do, the contract of sale has been perfected. The essential thing is that there be a meeting of the minds (as opposed to a disagreement) as to price.

The crucial question in this case is whether the parties expressly or impliedly agreed to buy and to sell these specific windows at a reasonable price, or stated otherwise, whether there was a meeting of the minds as to price. Since the parties did not discuss price at all at the time of contracting, there was no express agreement to buy and to sell at a reasonable price. However, C.C. art. 1811 [No Corresponding Article] provides that the proposition and the assent to a contract may be either express or implied, and there are factors indicating the parties consented to buy and to sell those windows at a reasonable price.

The parties had a history of dealings in which Leonards ordered materials and paid the price stated on the delivery invoice. In the present transaction, moreover, Leonards' authorized agent ordered a specific item which had to be specially ordered from the manufacturer. Although an exact price was not immediately ascertainable, Leonards did not object to the price which was eventually charged. Under these circumstances one could reasonably infer that Leonards and plaintiff intended to buy and sell these particular windows at a reasonable price. Thus, the case differs from those cases relied on by defendant such as *Stupp Corp. v. Con-Plex, Div. of U. S. Indus.*, 344 So.2d 394 (La.App. 1st Cir. 1977), in which the parties negotiated price but failed to agree, thereby creating circumstances under which one could not reasonably infer the parties' implied consent to a reasonable price.

We accordingly hold that consent of the parties to buy and sell the specific item at a reasonable price may be implied from the circumstances of this case and that the contract of sale was perfected before plaintiff ordered the windows from the manufacturer in reliance thereon. The contract was valid and may be enforced by plaintiff.

* * * * *

Accordingly, the judgment of the court of appeal is reversed, and the judgment of the trial court is reinstated, except that interest is awarded from October 6, 1977. All costs are assessed against defendant.

REVERSED AND RENDERED.

DENNIS, J., concurs with reasons.

DENNIS, Justice, concurring.

I respectfully concur in the result reached by the majority, but I respectfully decline to join in the conclusion that the contract between the parties was that of a sale. There is ample codal, jurisprudential and doctrinal authority that a contract which cannot be considered a sale for the lack of certain price can, nevertheless, be construed as an enforceable innominate contract. La.C.C. arts. 1777 [R.C.C. 1915], 1778 [R.C.C. 1916]; *Thielman v. Gahlman*, 119 La. 350, 44 So. 123 (1907); *Helluin v. Minor*, 12 La.Ann. 124 (1857); 1 S. LITVINOFF, OBLIGATIONS §§ 113–115 in 6 LOUISIANA CIVIL LAW TREATISE 197-99 (1969); Hebert and Lazarus, *Some Problems Regarding Price in the Louisiana Law of Sales*, 7 LA. L. REVIEW., 378, 384-87 (1942); Mashaw, *A Sketch of the Consequences for Louisiana Law of Adoption of "Article 2: Sales" of the Uniform Commercial Code*, 42 TUL. L. REV. 740, 746-47 (1968). *See also H.T. Cottam & Co. v. Moises*, 88 So. 916 (La. 1921).

MARCUS, J., dissents and assigns reasons.

WATSON, J., recused.

MARCUS, Justice (dissenting).

I agree with the court of appeal that there was never an enforceable contract since the parties had never agreed upon a price as required by La.Civ.Code arts. 2439 [R.C.C. 2439] and 2464 [R.C.C. 2464]. Section 2-305 of the Uniform Commercial Code provides in pertinent part that the parties may conclude a contract for sale even though the price is not settled. In such a case, the price is a reasonable price at the time of delivery if nothing is said as to the price. However, the Louisiana legislature did not adopt this section of the Uniform Commercial Code. Accordingly, the articles in the Civil Code on sales should control.

I respectfully dissent.

Notes and Questions

1. Though criticized by the dissent, the result reached in *Benglis Sash* was supported by Article 1816 of the Code of 1870:

> Actions without words, either written or spoken, are presumptive evidence
> of a contract, when they are done under circumstances that naturally imply
> a consent to such contract. To receive goods from a merchant without any
> express promise, and to use them, implies a contract to pay the value.

LA. CIV. CODE art. 1816 (1870). This article was not reproduced in the 1985 revision of the law of Obligations, and yet, it is undoubtedly one of the sources of new Article 2466.

2. How should a court ascertain a "reasonable price" at the time and place of delivery? Article 2466 states that "quotations or price lists of the place of delivery . . .

are a basis for the determination of a reasonable price." LA. CIV. CODE art. 2466. What other considerations might be relevant? *See* LA. CIV. CODE arts. 2054–2055; *Morphy, Makofsky & Masson, Inc. v. Canal Place 2000*, 538 So. 2d 569, 575 (La. 1989) (holding that a "reasonable sum" in a contract for services includes "actual cost, including general overhead attributable to the project, and a reasonable profit").

3. Can parties to a sale of movable things avoid the application of Article 2466? What if the parties agree that they will determine the price at a later time but do not wish to be bound to a contract of sale unless they can so agree?

4. The provisions of the Uniform Commercial Code relating to price appear below. How do these provisions differ from Articles 2464 through 2466?

Uniform Commercial Code § 2-304. Price Payable in Money, Goods, Realty, or Otherwise.[±]

(1) The price may be made payable in money or otherwise. If it is payable in whole or in part in goods, each party is a seller of the goods that the party is to transfer.

(2) Even if all or part of the price is payable in an interest in real property the transfer of the goods, and the seller's obligations with reference to them are subject to this Article, but not the transfer of the interest in real property or the transferor's obligations in connection therewith.

Uniform Commercial Code § 2-305. Open Price Term.[±]

(1) The parties if they so intend may conclude a contract for sale even if the price is not settled. In such a case the price is a reasonable price at the time for delivery if:

(a) nothing is said as to price;

(b) the price is left to be agreed by the parties and they fail to agree;

(c) the price is to be fixed in terms of some agreed market or other standard as set or recorded by a third person or agency and it is not so set or recorded.

(2) A price to be fixed by the seller or by the buyer means a price to be fixed in good faith.

(3) If a price left to be fixed otherwise than by agreement of the parties fails to be fixed through fault of one party, the other may at the party's option treat the contract as canceled or the party may fix a reasonable price.

(4) If, however, the parties intend not to be bound unless the price is fixed or agreed and it is not fixed or agreed, there is no contract. In such a case the buyer must return any goods already received or if unable to do so must pay their reasonable value at the time of delivery and the seller must return any portion of the price paid on account.

B. Price Out of Proportion with the Value of the Thing Sold

La. Civ. Code arts. 1848–1849, 2025–2028, 2464

According to Article 2464, "The price must not be out of all proportion with the value of the thing sold. Thus, the sale of a planation for a dollar is not a sale, though it may be a donation in disguise." La. Civ. Code art. 2464. This provision cautions that if the price is not "serious," the contract may be a simulation, whether absolute or relative. *See id.* at cmt. d. The following case addresses the consequences of an inadequate price.

Moore v. Wilson
772 So. 2d 373 (La. App. 2 Cir. 2000)

Caraway, J.

This is a suit to set aside a cash sale deed. The case was tried after the death of the "vendor" and thus without any testimony of his intentions for the transaction. Although the purchasers admitted at trial that the price stated in the deed ($10.00 cash) was never paid, they asserted that a donation was intended. The trial court found that although the deed (an authentic act) was valid as to form for a donation, it was nevertheless null because the donor lacked the requisite donative intent. The judgment ordered the deed set aside and cancelled from the conveyance records. For the reasons expressed herein, we affirm the ruling of the trial court regarding the cancellation of the deed, but remand the case for further consideration of appellants' reconventional demand which the trial court's judgment neglected to address.

Facts

On March 4, 1997, Jimmy Moore filed suit to rescind a deed dated March 4, 1996, in favor of his granddaughter, Vicki Moore Wilson and her husband, Freddy Lee Wilson, which purportedly conveyed for $10.00 an undivided one-fifteenth interest in 119 acres of land located on Lake Bistineau in Bienville Parish, Louisiana. Plaintiff's daughter, Willie Alice Moore Green, signed a verification of Moore's petition as his agent and attorney-in-fact. Subsequently, Moore died on October 25, 1997. He was reputedly 107-years-old, and it was established at trial that he was illiterate. Green, as Executrix of the Succession of Jimmy Moore, was substituted as party plaintiff on May 7, 1998.

The suit alleged that the deed was a sham and fraud since Moore never intended to sell his interest in the property, nor did he remember signing the deed. Alternatively, the petition alleged that the sale should be rescinded for lesion. At trial, the Wilsons admitted that the $10.00 consideration recited in the deed was never paid.

The deed was executed by Moore and the Wilsons in Shreveport and notarized by Robert McLane, a Caddo Parish notary. Plaintiff's counsel subpoenaed the notary, who appeared in court on the day of trial and was sworn. Before he was called to testify, McLane left the courthouse on the first day of trial without notice. Despite the issuance of a bench warrant for his contempt and a delay in the trial for 4½ months, McLane never testified.

After Moore died, Green filed a supplemental petition, alleging that the defendants coerced Moore into signing the deed in question by threatening that the property may somehow be lost by "HooDoo." Defendants responded with a reconventional demand alleging, alternatively, their entitlement to compensation for the value of improvements made on the property.

At trial, defendants testified that they began working on the property in 1994, two years before the deed was executed. They cleared overgrowth and did bulldozer work. In February 1997, they expended $3,523 for fill dirt, fencing and water well installation. However, they did not begin living there until January of 1999, after they moved a mobile home onto the land.

The property was co-owned by Moore and his siblings, and the disputed 1/15th interest was his entire undivided interest in the land. Moore did not live on the 119-acre tract. Prior to his death, he was living with his granddaughter Green, who testified that she was his primary caregiver. Vicki testified that another individual named Aunt Dolly, apparently a co-owner, lived on the property. The Wilsons testified at trial that Moore wanted them to have the land.

In its reasons for judgment, the trial court found that the evidence failed to establish Moore's donative intent. Furthermore, the trial court stated that it "was not convinced there was even a close relationship" between Moore and the alleged donees, Vicki and Freddy Wilson. Accordingly, the trial court ordered that the deed be set aside and erased from the public records.

Discussion

The disputed sales contract in this case states a price which is merely nominal. As expressed in La. C.C. art. 2464:

> The price must not be out of all proportion with the value of the thing sold. Thus, the sale of a plantation for a dollar is not a sale, though it may be a donation in disguise.

Recognizing this fatal flaw in the "sale," the Wilsons admitted the non-existence of a price and attempted to defend the suit by claiming that a donation nevertheless occurred. They now argue that the trial court was manifestly erroneous in failing to recognize Moore's donative intent.

La. C.C. art. 1970 addresses the misstatement of cause in a contract and provides:

> When the expression of a cause in a contractual obligation is untrue, the obligation is still effective if a valid cause can be shown.

In *Reinerth v. Rhody*, 28 So. 277 (La.1900), a granddaughter filed suit to annul a deed conveying a portion of her grandmother's property to a caretaker, who was also a relative. The deed was signed two days before the grandmother died. The court first noted that "one dollar and other valuable consideration" recited as the price "was no consideration at all." The court then concluded that the act was not a simulated sale since the ill-stated price did not conceal anything. Nevertheless, the testimony showed that the grandmother, although weak and feeble, understood what she was signing. Finding that the evidence proved the donor's intent to donate, the court upheld the instrument as a valid *inter vivos* donation between the parties. The court stated:

> The act complies with all the forms necessary to an act of donation. The act differs from an act of donation in that it sets out that vendor "sells, transfers, and conveys." If the word "donates" had been used instead, the act would have been complete and legal beyond all question. The act may import a donation if there is no price. Such an act may be valid as a donation if it contains all the formality required in a donation. The law requires that in the matter of donations the act be in authentic form. If it be in that form, and there be no price, it may yet be held valid as a donation when it contains all the requisite formalities and the donee at once goes into possession, though the act would be null as a sale.

Id. at 277, 278.

Another case where the transferee of the property was allowed to prove the existence of a donation was *Nofsinger v. Hinchee*, 199 So. 597 (La.App. 1st Cir.1941), where a brother and sister sued to set aside a deed conveying their undivided one-half interest in farmland to their cousin, alleging that no consideration was paid therefor. The deed recited as consideration for the sale the sum of "$1,000 cash and other valuable consideration." Defendant admitted this was not paid nor intended to be paid. The deed was executed by the parties shortly after plaintiffs' mother's death, along with other matters relating to the succession. Plaintiffs alleged that they did not know what they signed and did not intend to donate any property to defendant. The "notary-attorney" who prepared the deed testified that all of the parties signed the act after it had been read and explained to them as an act which was in keeping with the decedent's desires. The trial court noted that the instrument could not stand as a sale because it lacked consideration; nevertheless, the act was in authentic form. In light of the notary's testimony and viewing the evidence as a whole, the court upheld the transfer as a valid donation.

In this case, although the contract was executed as an authentic act, which is the form required for a donation, the trial court determined that Moore's donative intent was not proven by the Wilsons. From our review of the record, we find no error in the trial court's ruling. The evidence did not show that Vicki's relationship with her grandfather was close. The Wilsons did not show that they had rendered services to Moore. Moore was allegedly 107-years-old and illiterate. Moore's daughter and caretaker at the time the instrument was executed was unaware that the trip to Shreveport and the transaction had occurred. Since the Wilsons did not produce testimony from the notary and witnesses to the transaction to describe the circumstances of the act, the trial court could reject the Wilsons' self-serving testimony which was the only evidence of Moore's donative intent.

Moore's donative intent was also not reflected by any significant change in corporeal possession of the property. If Moore had solely owned and occupied the tract and had placed the Wilsons into corporeal possession, the delivery of corporeal possession coupled with the language of conveyance in the authentic act would strongly imply donative intent.

* * * * *

Conclusion

Based on the foregoing, the ruling of the trial court to set aside and cancel the cash sale deed is hereby affirmed. The case is remanded to the trial court for consideration of the appellants' reconventional demand and the joinder of all parties needed for the adjudication of such demand. Costs of these proceedings are assessed to appellants.

AFFIRMED AND REMANDED.

Notes and Questions

1. The parties to a purported "sale" may intend a donation despite the designation given to their contract. Why would the parties to a gratuitous contract style their transaction as a "sale" rather than as a donation? As the foregoing case illustrates, when the price for the purported sale is out of all proportion with the value of the thing sold, the parties' agreement is enforceable only if the formal and substantive requirements for a donation are satisfied. *See* La. Civ. Code art. 2027. What are those requirements? *See* La. Civ. Code art. 1468, 1541.

2. The parties to a purported "sale" may not intend for *any* transfer of ownership to occur. When this is the case, the contract is an absolute simulation. Such a contract is enforceable according to the parties' true cause — that is, the contract will have no effect whatsoever between the parties. *See* La. Civ. Code art. 2026. Why would anyone enter into a "sale" of property when they intend for their contract to have no legal effects?

3. The parol evidence rule plays an important role in the enforcement of simulated contracts. Article 1849 provides as follows:

> In all cases, testimonial or other evidence may be admitted to prove the existence or a presumption of a simulation or to rebut such a presumption. Nevertheless, between the parties, a counterletter is required to prove that

an act purporting to transfer immovable property is an absolute simulation, except when a simulation is presumed or as necessary to protect the
rights of forced heirs.

LA. CIV. CODE art. 1849. Under this article, parol evidence is generally admissible
to prove the existence of a simulation, whether absolute or relative. However, such
evidence is *not* admissible between the parties to prove that a contract purporting to
transfer immovable property was, in fact, an absolute simulation. Do you see why?

4. Article 2480 sets forth a presumption of simulation when the seller of the thing
remains in corporeal possession of it: "When the thing sold remains in the corporeal possession of the seller the sale is presumed to be a simulation, and, where the
interest of heirs and creditors of the seller is concerned, the parties must show that
their contract is not a simulation." LA. CIV. CODE art. 2480.

5. It has been held that rent previously paid pursuant to the lease of a thing may
constitute all or a part of the "price" for the subsequent sale of that thing. *See In re
Succession of Samuel,* 158 So. 3d 27, 33 (La. App. 4 Cir. 2014). In *Samuel,* a father sold
a certain piece of immovable property to his son for a stated price of $250,000. The
Act of Sale specified that $200,000 of the price had been paid through the payment
of rent in connection with a lease previously executed by the father in favor of the
son and that the remaining $50,000 was to be thereafter paid in full. The son paid
the remaining $50,000, after which his father died. The succession representative
sought to rescind the sale on the grounds that "there was no consideration given."
The court disagreed, finding prior rent, together with the $50,000 in additional
payments, sufficient "consideration" to support the sale.

Consider the following critique of *Samuel:*

> [W]hen one applies the law of contract and sale to this case, it is clear that
> a dollar that has been paid and received as rent cannot subsequently serve
> as price of the thing sold. Price is the object of the obligation of the buyer. It
> is what the buyer obligated himself to do primarily. And price is the cause
> of the obligation of the seller; it is, as article 1966 says, the "reason why"
> seller obligates himself. But if the price consists of money that the buyer
> has already paid, it cannot be the object of his obligation: it isn't there. And
> if the price consists of money that the seller has already received because it
> was the cause of another contract—here, a lease—then that money cannot
> be the cause of seller's obligation.
>
> If, on the other hand, the lessor and lessee agree when they execute their
> lease that when the lease ends (upon arrival of its extinctive term) the lessee
> will become owner of the thing leased, then there is in fact a sale, and they
> are merely confused about the nature of their contract [which is not a lease,
> but is in fact a sale in which the parties have agreed that ownership will pass
> upon the payment of the price, in the form of rent, by the buyer].
>
> What about in this case? If Father and Son truly believed that rent
> paid in the past could serve as the price in a sale of the thing leased, even

retroactively re-characterized, then they incorrectly believed they had entered into an effective sale, but they might have entered a different sort of contract. A donation inter vivos is a possible candidate, even perhaps a remunerative or an onerous donation, depending on the circumstances. A difficulty with that approach would be the proof of the donative intent of the Father. The fact that a seller is willing to accept a fictional price, since the seller already has it, for transferring ownership might by itself support a factual determination that the seller intended to make a donation. Indeed, the seller is transferring ownership. That is not a sale; it's a gift.

Having focused on the fictional cash portion of the price to this point, it is well to point out another solution. The Son agreed to pay and did pay an additional $50,000 over time. If the fair market value of the corporeal immovable sold was $250,000, then its sale for $50,000 would have entitled the seller to a claim of lesion beyond moiety. That claim, however, would have been extinguished by peremption one year after the 1998 sale under article 2595 of the Civil Code. This, in our view, provides a solution in the case that would have avoided a confusing reliance upon consideration.

24 DIAN TOOLEY-KNOBLETT & DAVID GRUNING, LOUISIANA CIVIL LAW TREATISE, SALES § 2:2 (2017). The excerpt above contrasted the contract in *Samuel* with one in which the parties agree up front that the buyer of a thing will pay "rent" that will be applied to the price of an eventual sale. For additional discussion of the latter type of transaction, which is termed a "conditional sale," see Chapter 7, Subpart B.4: Effects of the Contract of Sale; Sales Conditioned on Payment of Price (a/k/a "Common Law" Conditional Sales). The foregoing excerpt also suggests that the parties' contract in *Samuel* may have been subject to rescission for "lesion beyond moiety." The doctrine of lesion beyond moiety is the topic of the following Part.

C. Rescission for Lesion Beyond Moiety

1. In General

La. Civ. Code arts. 1965, 2589–2600

Assuming the basic requirements for a valid price are met, must the price also be "fair" or "just"? What recourse, if any, exists for a seller who receives less than fair market value in return for the thing sold? Louisiana law provides the seller with an action to rescind a sale of a corporeal immovable for lesion beyond moiety; that is, when the price paid is less than half of the fair market value of the thing. *See* LA. CIV. CODE art. 2589.

a. The Purpose and Mechanics of Lesion

The right to invoke lesion beyond moiety arises from the Civil Code's pronouncement that the price paid for immovable property must not be out of all proportion to the value of the thing sold. *See* La. Civ. Code art. 2464. This pronouncement is, of course, made in recognition of the fact that the sale is a commutative contract, that is, one in which equivalents are supposed to be given and received. *See* La. Civ. Code art. 1911. It is also inherently tied to the requirement of all conventional obligations that the consent of the parties be free of vices. Indeed, lesion technically is a vice of consent, alongside error, fraud, and duress. *See* La. Civ. Code art. 1965. In this context, lesion is "founded upon the idea that the vendor has been driven by his necessities to make a sacrifice so enormous, as to give rise to the presumption that he has been hardly dealt by." *Copley v. Flint*, 1 Rob. 125, 128 (1841).

At a fundamental level, the action for rescission for lesion beyond moiety seeks to protect the seller who may be unsophisticated in his or her negotiations or who suffers a loss at the hands of a manipulative or cunning buyer. Further, it also seeks to protect the rights of creditors who wish to safeguard against their debtors divesting themselves of their assets for less than that which would otherwise be obtained in the fair and open market. While protection against overreaching may seem like a far-reaching goal, Louisiana's law of lesion is, in fact, quite limited in scope. Article 1965 makes clear that "[a]contract may be annulled on grounds of lesion only in those cases provided by law." La. Civ. Code art. 1965. And, as these materials demonstrate, the law specifies lesion as grounds for rescission only in a handful of cases.

In the context of sales, lesion may be claimed only by the seller and only in sales of corporeal immovables. La. Civ. Code art. 2589. It cannot be alleged in a sale made by order of the court. *Id.* Furthermore, the action for lesion is subject to a strict peremptive period of one year from the time of the sale. La. Civ. Code art. 2595. Nevertheless, the right of rescission for lesion beyond moiety is one that cannot be waived — the seller may invoke lesion even if the right has been renounced in the Act of Sale. La. Civ. Code art. 2589.

Once a seller invokes the right to rescind, the buyer, if still in possession of the thing sold, is presented with an option: the buyer may either return the immovable to the seller or keep the immovable and give to the seller a supplement equal to the difference between the price paid by the buyer and the fair market value of the immovable. La. Civ. Code art. 2591. In this way, the buyer's obligations under the law of lesion are facultative in nature. Alain Levasseur, Louisiana Law of Obligations in General: A Précis § 4.3.1 (4th ed. 2015).

Note that if the buyer elects to pay a supplement, the amount owed is the difference between the price paid and the fair market value of the thing, not the difference between the price paid and the minimum non-lesionary price. A brief hypothetical illustrates the importance of this distinction. If Seller conveys Blackacre (valued at $150,000) to Buyer for a price of $65,000, the supplement which Buyer must pay is $85,000 (the difference between $150,000 and $65,000), *not* $10,000 (the difference between $75,000, the lowest non-lesionary price, and $65,000). This is so despite the fact that a price of $75,000 would have foreclosed a claim of lesion altogether.

If the buyer elects to return the immovable, the seller must return the price with interest from the time the demand for rescission was made. La. Civ. Code art. 2592. In such a case, the buyer must return not only the immovable but also any fruits produced by the immovable from the time the demand for rescission was made. *Id.* The buyer who elects to keep the immovable must pay not only the supplement but also interest on the supplement from the time of the demand for rescission. *Id.*

The law of lesion is highly protective of the rights of *third persons* to the sale who later acquire rights in the immovable. For example, if the buyer has resold the immovable, the seller generally may not bring an action for lesion against the third person who bought the immovable from the original buyer. La. Civ. Code art. 2594. Instead, the seller may recover from the original buyer only whatever profit the buyer realized from the sale to the third person, up to the value of the supplement the seller could have recovered if the original buyer had chosen to keep the immovable. *Id.* Thus, if Seller conveys Blackacre, valued at $150,000, to Buyer for a price of $65,000, and Buyer subsequently conveys Blackacre to Third Person for a price of $160,000, Seller may recover only $85,000 and no more. If, in contrast, Buyer conveys Blackacre to Third Person for a price of $90,000, Seller's recovery against Buyer is limited to $25,000. An exception to the rule limiting the seller's recovery to the buyer's profits, though not found in the legislation itself, is suggested by the comments. According to Article 2594, comment (b):

> Where . . . the vendee has acted fraudulently or in bad faith, the situation is quite different. In such a case, the vendee has knowingly deprived the vendor of a valuable right by intentionally inducing the vendor to sell under false pretenses . . . . In such a situation, as in other instances of fraud, the vendor should be entitled to a damage award, measured, in this instance, by the fair market value of the property at the time of the sale.

La. Civ. Code art. 2594 cmt. b.

In addition, when the buyer has granted a right on the immovable to a third person, rescission may not impair the interest of that person. La. Civ. Code art. 2596. The seller who receives an immovable that has been encumbered by a third person is entitled to recover from the buyer any diminution in value suffered by the immovable because of the encumbrance. *Id.* That recovery may not exceed the supplement the seller would have recovered if the buyer had not encumbered the immovable and had decided to keep it. *Id.*

When rescission is granted for lesion the seller must take the immovable back in the state that it is at that time. La. Civ. Code art. 2597. The buyer is not liable to the seller for any deterioration or loss sustained by the immovable before the demand for rescission was made, unless the deterioration or loss was turned into profit for the buyer. *Id.* The seller must reimburse the buyer for the expenses of the sale and for those incurred in the improvement of the immovable, even if the improvement was made solely for the convenience of the buyer. *Id.* Moreover, the buyer may retain possession of the immovable until the seller reimburses the buyer the price and the recoverable expenses. La. Civ. Code art. 2599.

Article 2600 contemplates the action for lesion in the event that a thing was sold by more than one seller, i.e., co-owners in indivision. In such a case, "each seller may bring an action for lesion for his share." La. Civ. Code art. 2600. Article 2600 recognizes also that a seller's "successors" may bring an action to rescind on grounds of lesion. *See also Rogers v. Read*, 355 So. 2d 46 (La. App. 2 Cir. 1978) (holding that under Article 2600, the right to demand rescission on grounds of lesion is heritable). Further, "if a seller died leaving more than one successor, each successor may bring an action for lesion individually for that share of the immovable corresponding to his right." La. Civ. Code art. 2600.

b. Problems of Valuation

The mechanics of lesion described above are straightforward and, as a result, are not frequently the subject of litigation. Instead, the most frequently litigated issue of the law of lesion is the valuation of the immovable under consideration. The following case is illustrative of the challenge of accurate valuation.

Cook v. Mixon

700 So. 2d 1264 (La. App. 2 Cir. 1997)

Caraway, Judge.

In this case, a disputed sale of a large tract of timberland was held by the trial court to be in violation of Louisiana's lesion principles. Soon after the initial sale, a second sale of the property was made to a large timber company for over two and one-half times the first purchase price. This dispute therefore requires a determination of the "fair market value" of the property under La. Civ. Code art. 2589. Finding that the trial court misapplied the high legal standard for setting aside as lesionary a transaction involving timber as the principal market value component for the land, we reverse the trial court and dismiss the lesion claim.

Facts and Trial Court Ruling

In late September, 1994, the defendants, James Mixon and Floyd Smith, entered a contract for the purchase of a 160-acre tract of timberland in Winn Parish from Mary Alice Barber Cook for $84,215. Approximately six weeks later and after the parties' sale had been consummated, the defendants, in an effort to resell the property, solicited and received bids from other potential timberland purchasers, including Williamette Industries, an adjoining landowner, which had the timber cruised and the property appraised in early November. After receiving Williamette's $192,180 bid on the tract—$60,000 more than the next highest bid—Smith contacted Williamette to assure the accuracy of the bid and was informed that Williamette was upping its bid to $225,934. Defendants quickly accepted Williamette's bid, and the property was deeded in January, 1995.

After becoming aware of Williamette's purchase price, the plaintiff, Mrs. Cook, brought this action pursuant to La. Civ. Code 2594 to recover the profit which defendants realized from their sale to Williamette. Plaintiff's primary witness was Steve

Barham, Williamette's manager of the Dodson Forestry and Logging Division, who had recommended to his management the initial $192,180 bid for the property after reviewing a Williamette estimate of the volumes of marketable timber on the land. Plaintiff attempted to support the Williamette appraisal of the property through the testimony of a real estate appraiser, Randy LaCaze. However, LaCaze, who viewed the property after Williamette had clear-cut the timber, gave no opinion of the disputed timber value based upon his determination of the quantity of timber and timber prices existing in the fall of 1994.

The defendants presented evidence from various sources indicating that at the time of the September, 1994 contract to sell, the land with the standing timber was worth no more than $133,000, which was much less than the $168,500 lesionary threshold. Defendants' evidence included four timber cruises of the property made by foresters for different companies conducted at various times between January, 1994 and late October, 1994. There was a difference of 94,000 board feet of pine saw logs between Williamette's cruise obtained by Barham and the next highest estimate obtained by Greg Wilbanks. Significantly, Wilbanks, a real estate appraiser, prepared his appraisal in October before this controversy and submitted it as his opinion to a bank which was loaning money to Mixon for the purchase. Wilbanks, who reported a $123,500 appraisal, found the value of the raw land to be $285 per acre based upon comparable sales of other cut-over timber tracts in Winn Parish. He valued the timber after obtaining a cruise by a forester and determining current prices from timber processors in the area.

The undisputed evidence, which Wilbanks and the other witnesses presented, showed that the price for pine saw logs during the last quarter of 1994 was increasing at a rapid rate of 33%, from $300/mbf in late September when the parties entered their contract, to $330/mbf in November at the time of Williamette's bid, and finally, to $400/mbf or more in January, 1995, when Williamette's purchase was complete.

In ruling that lesion applied, the trial judge rested his decision primarily on the fact of the actual sale to Williamette, as seen in the following excerpts from his oral reasons for ruling:

> We are not talking here in the abstract about . . . we are not talking, for example like an expropriation where one appraiser says the land is worth . . . and another appraiser says the land is worth that and the court has to decide how much the state is going to have to pay to expro . . . . This is really valuing the abstract. That is not what the case is here because in this case it is different because the testimony of Mr. LaCaze is supported by what really happened. The difference in this case is that Williamette . . . * * * The difference is that Williamette paid over two hundred and twenty five thousand dollars. Now, that backs up certainly the testimony of Mr. LaCaze as to what this property was worth. * * * What actually somebody pays is hard to dispute that it is not worth what somebody pays. That is the biggest factor, I think, that it was actually done.

* * * * * *

Now, there is evidence to indicate that it would have been a bad buy perhaps for anybody else to pay two hundred and twenty five thousand dollars or even a hundred and ninety two, the original offer. But, market is not determined by what somebody else couldn't make any money on. Market is determined by what it will bring. We can't take that company out. We can't take Williamette out and say we have to determine value based upon everybody except Williamette. * * * Maybe somebody that is not adjoining would not be willing to pay as much. Obviously, that is what the case just about proved. But, they are adjoining and they are there and they were buying property and they did pay it. I can't envision any greater test of value than what actually happens.

Discussion

In the context of lesion and other settings, fair market value is consistently defined as the amount a willing and informed buyer would pay a willing and informed seller for a particular piece of property, with neither being under any compulsion to buy or sell. *See,* for example, *Mullins v. Page,* 457 So.2d 64 (La. App. 2d Cir.1984), *writ denied,* 459 So.2d 538 (La.1984); La. R.S. 47:2321[*] and Treas. Regs. § 20.2031-1(b).[±] A market brings together buyers and sellers who arrive, through their collective force, upon price or fair value.

The trial court's singular focus erroneously made Williamette the market, dismissing from consideration the collective expression of fair value reported by the other witnesses. Despite Williamette's willingness to pay an excessive price and its actual purchase, the market was still required to be measured by the trial court "in the abstract" in terms of what other willing and informed buyers would pay in order to realize an economic benefit or obtain "fair value" from the property. The above ruling of the trial court demonstrates an error of law in that he rejected as "abstract" the undisputed evidence of what other market participants would have paid and the evidence of the quantity of the harvestable timber which overwhelmingly demonstrated that Williamette made a "bad buy."

Historically, our law has maintained a firm policy rejecting lesion as a market impediment in the sale of movables, limiting the doctrine to immovables only. La. Civ. Code art. 2589. Though this land with its component part, the timber, was a

---

[*] [LA. REV. STAT. § 47:2321 defines "fair market value" for purposes of calculating ad valorem taxes on immovable property: "Fair market value is the price for property which would be agreed upon by a willing and informed buyer and a willing and informed seller under usual and ordinary circumstances; it shall be the highest price estimated in terms of money which property will bring if exposed for sale on the open market with reasonable time allowed to find a purchaser who is buying with knowledge of all the uses and purposes to which the property is best adapted and for which it can be legally used." *Eds.*]

[±] [Federal Treasury Regulations likewise define "fair market value" for taxation purposes: "The fair market value is the price at which the property would change hands between a willing buyer and a willing seller, neither being under any compulsion to buy or to sell and both having reasonable knowledge of relevant facts." *Eds.*]

single immovable at the time of the sale and therefore subject to lesion, the appraisal method and market applicable for the harvestable timber are basically the same as employed for movables where protection against lesion is unnecessary. The law does not protect the owner of harvested timber, who presumably can determine the quantity and quality of the product and transport it to a current market for processing, where other sellers also are continuously realizing the going price for similar timber and pulp.

In contrast, the more difficult appraisal of land, for which the law affords the seller protection, must involve a review of other land sales, usually more distant in time from the current sale, with somewhat dissimilar characteristics as to the property and its locality. The appraiser of land reviews prior sales of distinguishable, yet comparable tracts and makes adjustments for the analysis of the subject tract. The appraiser of harvestable timber is dealing more with a commodity of a fungible nature, which, by definition, is more definitely and conveniently measured and priced.

With this distinction between the appraisal processes for the land and the timber, the trial of this case nevertheless involved no controversy over the appraisals for the raw land since clear-cut tracts in nearby rural locations demonstrated a consistent market price in the range of $250-$300 per acre. The trial court's choice of $250 per acre or $40,000 for this land (absent the timber value) has not caused this lesion controversy.

This controversy centered instead on the evaluations for the timber component for this tract. These estimated values varied in the extreme with the primary dispute arising from the disparate assessments of the quantity of the harvestable timber. What was the plaintiff's burden of proof to demonstrate an accurate measure of the quantity of timber and to determine the fair market value of what, in essence, was the commodity element of the value of this tract? The jurisprudence of our highest court holds that before the free commerce between the parties can be thwarted by lesion, the evidentiary burden requires "practical certainty" for the timber value of this land.

The leading case, *Smith v. Huie-Hodge Lumber Co.*, 129 La. 28, 55 So. 698 (1911), arose at a time shortly after the passage of Act No. 188 of 1904 which had made standing timber sold to another by the landowner an immovable. *See,* La. Civ.Code art. 464. Lesion, therefore, had become clearly applicable to the sale of standing timber, contrary to the court's view of the prior Louisiana law and to French law. The court gave the following insight into why lesion claims in a timber sale setting should require "unquestionable proof" of the quantity and price of timber:

> A lesion suit, at best, when unaccompanied, as in the present case, by any suspicion of actual fraud, does not recommend itself to a court of justice. It calls upon the court to set aside a contract to which parties fully capable of contracting, and not alleging any actual error or fraud, have deliberately consented. The law does not countenance such a suit when the property

sold is a movable. "The reason," says Troplong, Com. of article 1674, C.N., "is that the price of movables is less constant than that of immovables . . . ."

It would be impossible to find a point of comparison positive enough to establish the ruling price at the moment of the contract. "For that reason," says the learned author, "rescission is not admitted in the sales of timber." Under stress of a legislative act whereby, with no thought to suits like the present, standing timber has been made to retain its character of immovability, after sale, this court has had to recognize that the sale of timber may furnish ground for an action of lesion; but the same reason which, before the passage of said legislative act, would have defeated an action in such a case, continues to apply to this extent, that it will make the courts all the more careful and exacting in requiring full, complete, and unquestionable proof of the lesion.

Id., 129 La. at 35, 55 So. 698.

While the reasons for volatility in the pricing of timber referred to in the quoted commentary of Troplong and discussed in other portions of the opinion in *Smith* are apparently not the same in this day of modern transportation and available processing facilities for timber, the critical factor wrestled with in *Smith,* as in this case, concerned the determination of the volume of the harvestable timber. Though everyone examined the same forest, the plaintiff's experts in *Smith* (which, like Williamette's appraiser, Mr. Barham, had some obvious bias) estimated a high volume of timber in comparison to the timber cruise of the defendants' experts. The trial court accepted the plaintiff's estimates, and the supreme court reversed, even after assuming no bias on the part of the plaintiff's witnesses. The court ruled:

As to the quantity of the timber, assuming that the interest which Mr. Williams and plaintiff's son had in the result of the suit, with a view to which the estimates were made by them, in no way warped the judgment of the estimators in guessing at the diameter of the trees as they counted them or in determining whether they were merchantable or not, and in no way influenced their action in selecting the particular trees whose average contents should serve as the multiplicand or multiplier for calculating the contents of the trees upon the land, and in guessing the height of these trees, there still remains a wide margin for uncertainty; *and in a case of this kind, where the deliberate contract of parties devoid of all fraud is to be set aside, there ought to be certainty, or practical certainty.*

Id., 129 La. at 38, 55 So. 698 (emphasis supplied). (The companion case with the *Smith* case, *Rogers v. Huie-Hodge Lumber Co.*, 129 La. 40, 55 So. 702 (1911), applied the same rationale to a sale of land with standing timber, such as the subject sale in this dispute.)

Smith's stern test of "practical certainty" for the "appraisal" of the quantity of timber is a recognition that such appraisals involve merely counting, the counting of a finite number of trees. Unlike the *subjective* inferences that must be drawn and interpreted by the experts from comparable land sales in order to appraise the land, the essential task of the appraisers of the timber in *Smith* and in this case involved the *objective* craft of counting. In *Smith,* timber cruises over sample areas of the tract and the *estimated* counts of timber from those cruises resulted in the ruling against the plaintiff in the lesion action where more accurate proof by an *actual* count could have established "practical certainty."

In the instant case, the evidence of the five cruises of the timber reveals a difference of 94,000 board feet of pine saw logs between the Williamette timber cruise and the defendants' highest estimate from the other cruises. Other than the pine saw logs, the differences between the Williamette cruise and the other four cruises regarding the estimated amount of pine pulp and hardwood are not significant enough to tip the lesionary scale. This huge difference in the estimated pine saw log volumes, when priced at the established price of $300/mbf, amounts to $28,200. This is more than enough to reduce Mr. Barham's $192,180 bid which was based upon the Williamette cruise to an amount less than the $168,000 lesionary threshold.

With the *Smith* test for practical certainty, the best evidence of the timber quantities which was established before trial resulted from Williamette's actual harvesting of the timber by the clear-cutting of the property in 1995. On cross-examination, *Mr. Barham testified that he had seen and reviewed the actual amounts of the various volumes harvested from the property but could not recall those amounts at the time of trial.*

Even in the absence of *Smith's* heightened evidentiary burden upon this plaintiff to show with practical certainty the specific amount of timber on this property, the general rule is that the failure of a litigant to produce evidence within his reach raises the presumption that the evidence would have been detrimental to his case. *Johnson v. Department of Public Safety,* 627 So.2d 732 (La.App. 2d Cir.1993). Plaintiff's suggestion in argument against a motion for new trial that defendants should have discovered the actual amount of the harvested timber before trial is a distortion of the high burden of proof in this lesion action.

Moreover, there clearly was a cloud of suspicion, speculation and bias surrounding Mr. Barham's testimony and Williamette's bid. At the time of Williamette's bid, the property was landlocked with an expanse of Williamette's land extending on three sides of the 160-acre quarter section. Though Williamette would not admit to any subjective compulsion to acquire this missing piece of its timberland domain, its management's unexplained $35,000 raise of its initial high bid indicates that Williamette wanted this land badly for reasons extending beyond fair market value. In *Mayard v. Laporte,* 109 La. 101, 33 So. 98, 100 (1902), the court expressly refused consideration of an extremely high price later paid by an adjoining owner for a portion of the disputed lot which was claimed to have been sold months earlier in violation of the lesion principle. Even though the second sale involved the very tract whose market value was in dispute, that sale to the adjoining owner was ruled an "exceptional transaction" that was "dictated more by the special need of the purchaser" and therefore not indicative of fair market value.

Additionally, the testimony showed that the prevailing price for pine saw logs during the last quarter of 1994 was increasing rapidly. A breakdown of Barham's appraisal for the harvestable timber, even after accepting his high estimates for the volumes of the pine and hardwood, reveals that his $143,205 value for the timber was based upon prices which were 20% higher than the late-September prices, and even higher than the prevailing November prices as established at trial.

Williamette's view of the timber prices must therefore be seen as excessively speculative. The late-September prices must determine whether this sale was lesionary, and the trial court's acceptance of Williamette's mid-November appraisal employing prices 20% higher than the prices at the time of the late-September contract between the parties is clear error. La. Civ. Code art. 2590. Indeed, in September, another national timber company, Stone Container, declined to exercise its right of first refusal to meet the defendants' $84,000 price for the property. Stone's foresters had managed the property for the plaintiff in the months immediately preceding this disputed sale under a contractual arrangement which provided Stone with option rights in the property. The detailed maps of the topography and areas of timber growth, which Stone had provided to the plaintiff in rendering its forestry services, placed Stone in the best position to evaluate the property. Yet, Stone declined to acquire for $84,000, a tract which Williamette valued at $225,000.

Finally, Mr. Barham's $192,180 appraisal, upon which his company "heavily" relied, was $60,000 more than the next highest bid presented to the defendants. Moreover, he did not object to his upper management's unexplained raising of the bid to $225,000. If he could not justify his high estimate for the value of timber on the property and if Williamette truly had no special desire to acquire this adjoining 160-acre tract, his company would have been shown to have suffered a loss as the result of his management decisions. This bias cannot be ignored.

In summary, the cloud overhanging Williamette's extremely high price cannot be dismissed when the bids of the rest of the market participants exhibited unquestioned accuracy and collectively centered around a fair value of approximately $125,000, which was $100,000 less than the price paid by Williamette. The trial court's emphasis that Williamette cannot be excluded from the "market" analysis for this property ignores the concept of "fair value." For our law to provide relief under the policy for lesion in a setting closely akin to the sale of movable property which can be counted and priced to determine fair value, the plaintiff was required to establish that Williamette's extremely high estimate of the volume and price for the timber was accurate. The plaintiff's evidence failed to meet that test with practical certainty. Williamette's high appraisal and actual purchase were not indicative of fair market value.

Conclusion

The judgment of the trial court granting the plaintiff's claim of lesion is reversed and the case is dismissed. Costs are assessed to the plaintiff.

REVERSED.

STEWART, J., dissents and assigns written reasons.

HIGHTOWER, J., dissents for the reasons set forth by STEWART, J.

STEWART, Judge, dissenting.

For the following reasons, I respectfully dissent from the majority holding and *de novo* review. After a careful review of the record and pertinent authority, I find that, based on the evidence presented, the trial court properly determined the "fair market value" of the subject property and was not manifestly erroneous in ruling that the sale was lesionary.

Defendant Smith contacted the Cooks in June, 1994, about selling the 160-acre tract of timberland in Winn Parish. By cash deed executed on October 24 and 26, 1994, defendants purchased the property from Mrs. Cook for $84,215.25. Less than two weeks later, defendant Smith contacted Steve Barham, manager of the Dodson Forestry and Logging Division of Williamette Industries, to inquire if Williamette was interested in purchasing the 160-acre tract. On November 7, 1994, Mr. Barham had the tract of timber land cruised and valued the timberland at $192,180.00. Approximately one month after the sale to defendants was consummated, Williamette offered $225,934.00 for the tract, which offer was communicated to, by telephone, and accepted by defendant Smith on November 29, 1994. In the sale to Williamette, defendants received an amount over $140,000 more than defendants paid for the property. I agree with plaintiffs' assertion that the profit made by defendants on selling the property to Williamette was not only lesionary but obscene.

Relying on *Smith v. Huie-Hodge Lumber Company, Ltd.,* the majority concluded that the trial court's determination that the fair market value of the 160-acre tract exceeded $168,430.50 was based on its "singular focus" on Williamette's offer and was erroneous as a matter of law because, in accordance with *Smith,* there "ought to be certainty, or practical certainty" in valuing property in a lesion case. *Smith v. Huie-Hodge Lumber Company, Ltd.,* 129 La. 28, 38, 55 So. 698, 702 (La.1911). That case involved a suit to annul the sale of timber based on lesion. Consequently, the court was concerned solely with the value of the timber, which they deemed to be "purely relative", and not the total value of the property. *Smith v. Huie-Hodge Lumber Company, Ltd.,* 129 La. at 38, 55 So. at 701. As in the instant case, the court determined the value of the timber based, not on "certainty, or practical certainty", but on the estimations of timber volume by several experts whose estimations varied dramatically.

In concluding that the value of the 160-acre tract is less than the lesionary mark, the majority attempts to calculate the value of the timber with mathematical certainty, an impossibility considering the fact that all timber cruises offered at trial reflect only estimates of timber volume. The majority criticizes the Williamette cruise because that cruise examined 10% of the tract. However, there is no evidence to indicate that the other timber cruises, on which the majority places great weight, were not made in precisely the same manner.

Further, the majority discounts Mr. Barham's valuation and estimation of timber volume because "there was a cloud of suspicion, speculation and bias surrounding Mr. Barham's testimony and Williamette's bid." The majority has no reasonable basis for finding any bias in Mr. Barham's testimony. The trial court apparently found Mr. Barham's testimony credible and the best evidence of fair market value. Mr. Barham nor Williamette, his employer, were parties to this action. Neither had any connection to plaintiffs. "Though everyone examined the same forest," unlike the majority, I find no prejudice in Mr. Barham's testimony.

The majority ignores several pertinent facts which indicate "some obvious bias" by defendants' witnesses. B & S Timber, author of one timber cruise, employed defendant Smith. The owner of B & S Timber, a defense witness, testified that he signed a letter, prepared by defendant Smith and dated October 12, 1994, which offered defendant Smith $50,000 for the timber on the 160-acre tract. Also, another defense witness, Greg Wilbanks, a real estate appraiser, was more closely connected to this action than was Mr. Barham because the bank that employed Mr. Wilbanks made the loan to defendants for the purchase of the property.

Even though the majority feels that its own evaluations of credibility and inferences of fact are more reasonable than those of the trial court, the trial court was in a better position to weigh the conflicting testimony and to determine which evidence was most credible. Plaintiffs presented evidence on the total value of the property consisting of Mr. Barham's testimony regarding his valuation and estimation of timber quantity, the initial bid submitted by Williamette, the purchase price paid by Williamette and the testimony of Randy LaCaze, an appraiser, who testified that the price paid by Williamette was indicative of fair market value. Mr. Barham further testified that, had he prepared a valuation of the property in late September, 1994, it would not have been substantially different than the valuation he made in early November, 1994.

Mr. Wilbanks, testifying on behalf of defendants, valued the 160-acre tract at $123,500. Other evidence offered by defendants regarding the total value of the property was their own, unsupported and undocumented, testimony about three other offers for the land.

The five timber cruises presented as evidence of timber volume reflected greatly different volumes for four types of timber. Although Williamette's cruise reported the highest volume of pine saw logs, the Stone Container cruise and the Wilbank's data included higher volumes for the other categories of timber.

The majority characterizes the testimony and evidence regarding the price of timber as "undisputed" and concludes that Williamette's prices are "excessively speculative." Johnny Meredith and Mr. Wilbanks both offered evidence regarding the price of timber in October, 1994. Mr. Meredith testified that the price for pine saw logs was $300/mbf, pine pulp was $25/cord, hardwood pulp was $14/cord, red oak logs was $300/mbf, white oak logs was $200/mbf, and miscellaneous hardwood logs was $100/mbf. Mr. Wilbanks testified that the price for pine saw logs was $330/mbf and hardwood logs was $180/mbf. Clearly, the testimony on timber prices is not "undisputed."

Additionally, Mr. Barham testified that, during September and October, 1994, no dramatic movement of timber prices occurred which would have justified an increased value of the property from the amount of $84,215.25 initially paid by defendants to the amount of $225,934.00 paid by Williamette.

Because the trial court was in a better position to judge the credibility of each witness and to determine the weight to be given each witness' testimony, I believe that the appropriate standard applicable to the instant case is that articulated by the Louisiana Supreme Court in *Stobart v. State Through DOTD*, 617 So.2d 880 (La.1993). An appellate court may not reverse a trial court's find of fact absent manifest error or unless clearly wrong. The Louisiana Supreme Court annunciated a two-pronged test for setting aside the finder of fact's determinations. The appellate court must find from the record that a reasonable factual basis does not exist for the finding of the trial court and, then, must determine that the record establishes the finding is clearly wrong. *Stobart v. State Through DOTD, supra; Mart v. Hill*, 505 So.2d 1120 (La.1987); *Parker v. Centenary Heritage Manor Nursing Home*, 28,401 (La.App.2d Cir. 6/26/96), 677 So.2d 568. Where conflict exists in the testimony, reasonable evaluations of credibility and inferences of fact should not be disturbed on review, even when the appellate court may feel that its own evaluations and inferences are more reasonable that those of the trial court. *Blair v. Tynes*, 621 So.2d 591 (La.1993); *Stobart v. State Through DOTD, supra; Rosell v. ESCO*, 549 So.2d 840 (La.1989); *Parker v. Centenary Heritage Manor Nursing Home, supra*.

In reviewing conflicting expert testimony, the finder of fact has the responsibility to determine which evidence is most credible. *Rosell v. ESCO, supra*. Where two permissible views of evidence exist, the fact finder's choice between them cannot be clearly wrong or manifestly erroneous. *Rosell v. ESCO, supra*.

In an action based on lesion, the standard applied to determine the value of the property is the fair market value at the time of the sale. *La.C.C.* art. 2589; *Mullins v. Page*, 457 So.2d 64 (La.App. 2d Cir.1984). Market value has been defined to mean the amount a willing buyer would pay a willing seller for a particular piece of property. *Mullins v. Page, supra; Valley Land Corporation v. Fielder*, 242 So.2d 358 (La. App. 2d Cir.1970).

In a lesion action, the plaintiff may introduce evidence of the highest and best use of the property rather than solely the actual use of the property at the time of the sale. Such evidence may be considered along with all the other evidence of property value. *Nation v. Wilmore*, 525 So.2d 1269 (La.App. 3d Cir.1988); *Mullins v. Page, supra; Valley Land Corp. v. Fielder, supra*.

When the appraisals vary greatly, the court must examine each appraisal to determine which is more reasonable. The court is not bound to accept or reject one expert's testimony, but parts of each expert's testimony may be accepted when the testimony is based on proper facts and sound reasoning. *Montegut v. Davis*, 473 So.2d 73 (La.App. 5th Cir.1985); *Bisco v. Middleton*, 383 So.2d 1047 (La.App. 1st Cir.1980). The trial court's assessment of appraisers' testimony is entitled to great respect. *Montegut v. Davis, supra; Evergreen Plantation, Inc. v. Zunamon*, 319 So.2d 543 (La.App. 2d Cir.1975). The trial judge is in a better position to determine the weight and credibility to be accorded an expert's testimony where the experts differ, and the trial judge's decision as to the valuation of the property should not be disturbed on appeal unless manifestly erroneous. *Montegut v. Davis, supra; State, Department of Highways v. Wax*, 295 So.2d 833 (La.App. 1st Cir.1974).

The majority's "singular focus" on the value of the timber, which they deem to be "the principal market value component for the land," dismisses other components giving value to the property. Mr. Barham's valuation of the land and the timber considered such other components whereas the valuation by defendants' expert did not. Mr. Barham testified that his value of the property was based on factors in addition to "the standing volume", including "the reproduction that has value to us" and the volume of pre-merchantable timber.

Upon a considered review of the record, particularly the testimony and evidence adduced at trial, I do not conclude that the trial court was clearly wrong or manifestly erroneous in determining that the value of the 160-acre tract exceeded $168,430.50 and, therefore, in concluding that the sale was lesionary. For the foregoing reasons, I would affirm the judgment of the trial court.

APPLICATION FOR REHEARING

Rehearing denied.

Notes and Questions

As the foregoing case makes clear, the valuation of an immovable for purposes of determining whether the price paid for it was lesionary can be a difficult task. Both the Civil Code and the jurisprudence provide several guiding principles for the proper assessment of an immovable's value. First, the Civil Code provides a bright-line rule regarding the timing of valuation: "To determine whether there is lesion, the immovable sold must be evaluated according to the state in which it was at the time of the sale." LA. CIV. CODE art. 2590. Later fluctuations in value are not relevant to the determination of whether the price was lesionary. If the sale was preceded by an option contract or contract to sell, the relevant time for determining the fair market value is the time at which that contract was made. *Id.* How, if at all, did fluctuations in prices of timber complicate the valuation of the property in *Cook v. Mixon*?

Second, Louisiana courts have long allowed evidence of the "best and highest use" of the property when determining the fair market value, even if such a use would differ from the actual use of the property at the time of the sale. *See, e.g.,* *Joiner v. Abercrombie*, 968 So. 2d 1184 (La. App. 2 Cir. 2007) (considering potential residential use of undeveloped timberland); *Montegut v. Davis*, 473 So. 2d 73 (La. App. 5 Cir. 1985) (considering potential residential use of land used for sugarcane production). In *Cook v. Mixon*, the evidence showed that Willamette owned property adjoining the disputed tract. How is Willamette's idiosyncratic use for the property different, if at all, from its "best and highest use"?

What, according to the majority in *Cook v. Mixon*, is the proper burden of proof in a lesion dispute? Note that courts have been somewhat inconsistent in their articulation of the appropriate standard. *See, e.g., Ronaldson & Pucket Co. v. Bynum*, 48 So. 152 (1908) ("reasonable certainty"); *Caillouet v. Zwei Bruderland, L.L.C.*, 746 So. 2d 752 (La. App. 3 Cir. 1999) ("clear and convincing evidence"); *Montegut v. Davis*, 473 So. 2d 73 (La. App. 5 Cir. 1985) ("strong and convincing proof"); *Harruff v. King*, 139 So. 3d 1062 (La. App. 3 Cir. 2014). Although the precise standard differs from opinion to opinion, the trend of requiring more than a mere preponderance of the evidence is clearly established.

2. Variations on Lesion

Lesion applies not only to sales but also to exchanges and certain partitions. Special legislation governs the action for lesion in each of these contexts, supplemented by the general rules of lesion found in the Title on Sales.

a. Exchange
La. Civ. Code arts. 2663–2664

The rules governing lesion in the contract of exchange were revised in 2010. Contracts of exchange are governed by the Civil Code Title on Exchange, which consists only of a handful of articles, as well as the Title on Sale. The Title on Exchange contains a single article on lesion which adapts the formula for a lesionary price to the nature of an exchange, which is a contract in which *each party* transfers ownership of a thing to the other (and thus, occupies a role much like a "seller"). According to Article 2663, "A party giving a corporeal immovable in exchange for property worth less than one-half of the fair market value of the immovable given by him may claim rescission on grounds of lesion beyond moiety." LA. CIV. CODE art. 2663. Under this article, the right to rescind an exchange for lesion is afforded to any transferor of a corporeal immovable, provided the value of the property received in return is worth less than half of the fair market value of the immovable that was transferred. Aside from this rule, the mechanics of lesion are governed by the general rules found in the Title on Sale.

The following hypothetical illustrates the application of Article 2663. Sonya transfers Blackacre (valued at $300,000 at the time of the transaction) to Britton in exchange for shares of stock in Apple, Inc. (valued at $90,000 at the time of the transaction). Because the value of the shares of stock is less than $150,000 or one-half the value of Blackacre, the exchange is subject to rescission on grounds of lesion. The rules governing the timing for valuation, remedies, and peremption are all the same here as in the context of a sale.

Imagine now a different hypothetical. Sonya transfers Blackacre (valued at $300,000 at the time of the transaction) to Britton in exchange for Whiteacre (valued at $900,000 at the time of the transaction). In this case, Britton may rescind the exchange on grounds of lesion because the value of the property received (Blackacre) is $300,000, which is less than one-half of the value of the property transferred (Whiteacre, half the value of which is $450,000). Again, the rules governing valuation, remedies, and peremption found in the Title on Sale are applicable to this exchange.

b. Partition

La. Civ. Code art. 814

Lesion is also available in the context of partition. Most students will remember partition from the course in Civil Law Property. Partition, of course, is the division of co-owned property among the co-owners. Partition may take place by agreement of all of the co-owners, that is, extra-judicially. La. Civ. Code art. 809. In the absence of an agreement to partition, a co-owner may demand a judicial partition, in which a court orders partition of the property either in kind or by licitation or private sale. *See* La. Civ. Code arts. 810–811.

The Civil Code Title on Ownership in Indivision includes a provision on lesion, which states: "An extrajudicial partition may be rescinded on account of lesion if the value of the part received by a co-owner is less by more than one-fourth of the fair market value of the portion he should have received." La. Civ. Code art. 814. Under this article, rescission on grounds of lesion is permitted only in cases of extra-judicial partition, that is, when the co-owners partition the property through an agreement. Further, a co-owner may rescind for lesion only when the value of the part received is "less by more than one-fourth" of the fair market value of the portion he should have received. Said another way, a co-owner is entitled to rescission only when the value of the part received is less than three-fourths the value of the property that he should have received. Note that this formula differs significantly the rules applicable to sales and exchanges.

Consider the following example. Alice, Brady, and Catrina are co-owners in indivision of Blackacre (valued at $120,000). The parties agree to partition the property in equal shares. To accomplish this, they execute a partition agreement in which they extrajudicially partition Blackacre into three tracts, believing the tracts are equal in value (valued at $40,000 each). Immediately after the partition agreement is executed, Alice suspects that her tract is worth less than the value to which she is entitled. She conducts an appraisal and learns that at the time of partition her tract was valued at $28,000. Is Alice entitled to rescind the partition on grounds of lesion? To do so, the value of the part she received must be "less by more than one-fourth" of the fair market value of the property she should have received. Again, said another way, the value of the part received must be less than three-fourths the value of the property she should have received. Alice should have received $40,000, three-fourths of which is $30,000. The value of the portion she received ($28,000) is less than $30,000, and thus she may rescind for lesion. If, on the other hand, Alice had received a tract valued at $32,000, a lesion claim would be foreclosed, as $32,000 is not less than three-fourths of the value of the property that she should have received.

As a final note, remember that lesion does not apply in the context of a judicial partition. *See, e.g., Wurtzel v. Wurtzel,* 864 So. 2d 727 (La. App. 5 Cir. 2003). Thus, if Alice, Brady, and Catrina were not able agree on an extrajudicial partition, but instead one of them sued for partition, lesion would not apply to the resulting judicial partition.

Aside from the rule governing the threshold for lesion, the action for lesion between former co-owners does not differ from that between buyer and seller. As noted in comment (b) to Article 814, the rules governing rescission of a sale on account of lesion are applicable in the context of partition. LA. CIV. CODE art. 814 cmt. b. Thus, the rules of the Title on Sale governing the timing for valuation, remedies, and peremption are all applicable.

3. Exceptions — Transactions to Which Lesion Does Not Apply

While lesion may be raised as grounds for rescinding a sale, exchange, or partition, Article 1965 makes clear that lesion is not grounds for rescinding a contract unless specifically provided by law. LA. CIV. CODE art. 1965. Of the many contracts to which lesion is inapplicable, two merit special attention, if for no other reason than the law *affirmatively* forecloses the application of lesion to these transactions. First, lesion may not be raised as grounds for rescinding a sale or other transfer of a mineral right. Second, lesion may not be raised as grounds for rescinding a compromise. Each of these exceptions is addressed below.

a. Sales of Mineral Rights

According to the Mineral Code, lesion is inapplicable in all sales of mineral rights. The Mineral Code explicitly provides: "A sale of a mineral right is not subject to rescission for lesion beyond moiety." LA. REV. STAT. § 31:17 ("Article 17 of the Mineral Code"). The exclusion of mineral rights from the ambit of lesion is based on a simple premise: the valuation of mineral rights is inherently speculative, both with regard to the presence of minerals, as well as the value that the minerals may have when they are produced. *See Wilkins v. Nelson,* 99 So. 607, 609 (La. 1924); PATRICK S. OTTINGER, LOUISIANA MINERAL LEASES: A TREATISE Ch. 3-41(b), at 277 (2016). Because such rights can be neither valued nor quantified with certainty prior to the time minerals are separated from the land, and because transactions in mineral rights often involve some risk on the part of both parties, lesion may not be invoked by the seller in the event that the minerals that are later discovered or extracted from the property are worth more than the parties anticipated at the time of the sale. Moreover, even if the statute did not exist, lesion should not apply in any event to the sale of a mineral right since lesion "can be claimed . . . only in sales of corporeal immovables." La. Civ. Code art. 2589. As mineral rights are incorporeal immovables, La. Rev. Stat. §31:18, the doctrine of lesion is expressly inapplicable to them.

While the Mineral Code leaves no question that the sale of a mineral right may not be rescinded for lesion, the text does not clearly address a related but distinct question: can the sale of an immovable containing minerals be rescinded on that basis? In Louisiana, absent contrary agreement, the sale of real estate automatically includes the sale of the minerals contained therein. Does the value of the minerals factor into the fair market value calculation for determining whether the price paid was lesionary? Or is the value limited to only the land and its component parts, less the mineral value? Further, does it matter if the minerals at issue are fugacious (migratory), such as oil or natural gas, or non-fugacious (solid), such as gravel or limestone?

Resolution of these questions requires consideration of the nature of mineral rights and the various types of minerals recognized under Louisiana law. In Louisiana, a landowner only owns those minerals lying underneath his or her property that are non-fugacious, as they are considered component parts of the land in which they are situated. See La. Rev. Stat. §31:5. Fugacious minerals, by contrast, are not considered to be owned by anyone. Indeed, the Mineral Code specifically states that the landowner does not have ownership of "oil, gas, and other minerals occurring naturally in liquid or gaseous form, or of any elements or compounds in solution, emulsion, or association with such minerals." La. Rev. Stat. §31:6. That does not mean, however, that the owner of the land has no rights to these minerals at all. Rather, the owner has the *right* to explore the property (usually through drilling or digging) to extract the minerals from the ground, and to reduce them to possession and become owner of them through occupancy. *Id.*

Colloquially it is often said that a landowner "sells his minerals," but in fact, such a transaction is not possible. A landowner cannot convey fugacious minerals which have not been reduced to possession because ownership of the land does not include ownership of those minerals. La. Rev. Stat. §31:6. And while a landowner is also owner of any non-fugacious minerals contained in the land, "[s]olid minerals are insusceptible of ownership apart from the land until reduced to possession." La. Rev. Stat. §31:5. Thus, all that a landowner may convey to another is the "right" to enter the property, explore for minerals, and reduce them to possession. *Id.* This is not done through a sale but is generally accomplished through the granting of a mineral servitude. See La. Rev. Stat. §31:21.

With this background in mind, consider the following case addressing the lesion claim of a seller of an immovable that contained sand and gravel (non-fugacious minerals).

Hornsby v. Slade

854 So. 2d 441 (La. App. 1 Cir. 2003)

KLINE, J.

This is an appeal from a judgment finding the sale of an interest in a tract of land subject to rescission for lesion beyond moiety. For the following reasons, we affirm.

On July 15, 1994, plaintiff/appellee, William (Willie) Hudson Hornsby, sold her 5/18ths undivided interest in 364 acres of immovable property located in East Feliciana Parish to defendant/appellant, Winton L. Slade. Nearly four years later, on May 4, 1998, Ms. Hornsby instituted this lawsuit against defendants/appellants, Winton L. Slade and Dorothy Prevost Slade, to set aside the sale on the basis of lesion, claiming that because of the gravel value in the property, the value of the property was more than twice the amount of the sale price.

* * * * *

DISCUSSION

Lesion. La. Civil Code Art. 2589 provides:

Art. 2589. Rescission for lesion beyond moiety

The sale of an immovable may be rescinded for lesion when the price is less than one half of the fair market value of the immovable. Lesion can be claimed only by the seller and only in sales of corporeal immovables. It cannot be alleged in a sale made by order of the court.

The seller may invoke lesion even if he has renounced the right to claim it.

It is to be emphasized that lesion can be claimed only by the seller and only in sales of corporeal immovables. La. C.C. Art. 2590 requires that to determine whether there is lesion, the immovable sold must be evaluated according to the state in which it was at the time of the sale. The required standard is "fair market value."

Rescission on grounds of lesion differs from rescission on grounds of error, fraud or duress. The latter results in a declaration of nullity while in cases of the former the buyer has an option between returning the thing and recovering the price he paid, which is the effect of rescission, or paying a balance up to the fair price. *See* Saul Litvinoff, *Vices of Consent, Error, Fraud, Duress and an Epilogue on Lesion*, 50 LA. LAW. REV., p. 110 (Sept. 1989).

Lesion is actually an instrument of public policy that, with certain limitations, allows the judicial policing of certain contracts that, because of unfairness that can be objectively shown, are inconsistent with the welfare of the community and therefore contrary to the public order. *Id.*

Legislative framework—Minerals and Mineral Rights.

The Louisiana Mineral Code, LSA-R.S. 31:1, et seq., effective January 1, 1975, states that its provisions are supplementary to those of the Louisiana Civil Code and are applicable specifically to the subject matter of mineral law. LSA-R.S. 31:2.

414

PRICE

Section 2 also provides that in the event of conflict between the provisions of the Mineral Code, the Civil Code or other laws, the provisions of the Mineral Code will prevail. Additionally, if the Mineral Code does not expressly or impliedly provide for a particular situation, then the Civil Code or other laws are applicable. LSA-R.S. 31:2.

LSA-R.S. 31:4 determines the application of the provisions of the Mineral Code. It does not attempt a firm definition of the term "minerals." Comment to LSA-R.S. 31:4. Section 4 provides:

> The provisions of this Code are applicable to all forms of minerals, including oil and gas. They are also applicable to rights to explore for or mine or remove from land the soil itself, gravel, shells, subterranean water, or other substances occurring naturally in or as a part of the soil or geological formations on or underlying the land.

Thus, sand and gravel are substances to which the Mineral Code applies. *Slay v. Smith*, 368 So. 2d 1144, 1146 (La. App. 3 Cir. 1979); LSA-R.S. 31:4.

Ownership of land includes all minerals occurring naturally in a solid state. However, solid minerals are insusceptible of ownership apart from the land until reduced to possession. LSA-R.S. 31:5. Minerals are reduced to possession when they are under physical control that permits delivery to another. LSA-R.S. 31:7. The comment to section 7 provides, in part:

> Despite the fact that Article 5 recognizes that the owner of land also owns solid minerals, such minerals are insusceptible of ownership apart from the land, and the landowner may therefore only convey or lease the right to explore for them and reduce them to possession and simultaneously to ownership. Accordingly, the nature of the substance involved has no impact on the significance of reduction to possession and consequent vesting of title.

A.N. Yiannopoulos, *Property* § 118, at pp. 276–277 in 2 Louisiana Civil Law Treatise (4th ed. 2001), provides a concise analysis, to wit:

> § 118. Ownership of Things Incorporated in, or Attached to, a Tract of Land—Minerals
>
> Deposits of solid minerals are inseparable component parts of the ground, whereas fugacious minerals are in theory *res nullius*. However, the right to possession belongs to the owner of the ground.
>
> The owner of the ground may segregate the mineral rights from the ownership of the land and either retain them himself or convey them to another person. Accordingly, rights in minerals may be regarded as separable component parts of the ownership of land. Mineral rights segregated from the ownership of land ordinarily take the form of the mineral servitude, a mineral lease, or a mineral royalty. (Reference footnotes omitted).

Louisiana Civil Code article 462 states:

> Art. 462. Tracts of land
>
> Tracts of land, with their component parts, are immovables. Louisiana Civil Code article 470, distinguishes from article 462 "rights and actions" that apply to immovables.
>
> Art. 470. Incorporeal immovables.
>
> Rights and actions that apply to immovable things are incorporeal immovables. Immovables of this kind are such as personal servitudes established on immovables, predial servitudes, mineral rights, and petitory or possessory actions.

The nature and creation of mineral rights are provided in La. R.S. 31:15 *et seq.,* to wit:

> Part 5. CREATION OF MINERAL RIGHTS BY THE LANDOWNER
>
> § 15. Right of landowner to convey, reserve, or lease right to explore and develop.
>
> A landowner may convey, reserve, or lease his right to explore and develop his land for production of minerals and to reduce them to possession.
>
> § 16. Basic mineral rights; status as real rights
>
> The basic mineral rights that may be created by a landowner are the mineral servitude, the mineral royalty, and the mineral lease. This enumeration does not exclude the creation of other mineral rights by a landowner. Mineral rights are real rights and are subject either to the prescription of nonuse for ten years or to special rules of law governing the term of their existence.
>
> § 17. Rescission for lesion beyond moiety unavailable
>
> A sale of mineral right is not subject to rescission for lesion beyond moiety.
>
> § 18. Nature of mineral rights
>
> A mineral right is an incorporeal immovable. It is alienable and heritable. The situs of a mineral right is the parish or parishes in which the land burdened is located. All sales, contracts, and judgments affecting mineral rights are subject to the laws of registry.

Plaintiff's contentions:

Plaintiff contends that sand and gravel are solid minerals and by nature corporeal, and that lesion lies in and only in cases of corporeal immovables as distinguished from mineral rights that are classified as incorporeal immovables under Civil Code article 470. Plaintiff urges that the value of the land includes the unmined quantity of sand and gravel deposits determined by precision testing. Plaintiff argues that the trial court was correct in finding under the law that ownership of land includes all minerals occurring naturally in a solid state and that including sand and gravel in the valuation of a tract of land does not constitute an "incorporeal immovable mineral right" so as to preclude lesion, and that the presence of these solid minerals that form the land should be considered in the fair market value of the land.

Defendant's Contentions:

Defendant contends that it has been the doctrine in Louisiana that one did not own mineral interests until they were reduced to possession, and that one simply owned a right to produce them, and that un-produced minerals beneath the surface have little or no intrinsic value and are speculative in nature. Defendant argues that the expert valuation is based on a right to produce and develop gravel, which is a "mineral right" under the Mineral Code. By classifying the right to produce minerals as a mineral right, those rights should be considered incorporeal immovables for all purposes.

Defendant reasons, to wit:

There is no valid reason for treating the valuation of solid minerals owned by the landowner any differently from the valuation of the same minerals when owned by a separate owner as a "mineral right."

It is clear under article 17 of the Mineral Code that the sale of a mineral is not subject to rescission for lesion beyond moiety.

Defendant argues that "Left in place, the sand and gravel add no 'extra value' to the land."

CONCLUSION

The trial court was asked to determine under the statutory scheme of the Civil Code and the prevailing Mineral Code whether the value of sand and gravel or solid mineral deposits in the land sold could be considered in determining fair market value of the land and, thus, subject the sale to cause of action for lesion beyond moiety.

Solid minerals, until reduced to possession, form an integral part of the land. It cannot be said that the presence of solid materials, being a component part of the land and capable of being reduced to possession, is an inconsequential factor in determining fair market value. With other factors being equal, lands with mineral deposits are worth more than lands without them.

Deposits of solid minerals are inseparable parts of the land. However, the owner of the land may segregate the mineral rights from the ownership of the land, and these mineral rights are deemed separable component parts of ownership in the usual form of mineral servitudes, leases, and royalties. These segregated rights are classified as incorporeal immovables. These are the mineral rights that are not subject to a lesionary inquiry because of their speculative character.

Our statutory schemes have distinguished the classification of land with mineral deposits and the classification of the alienation of component parts called mineral rights. The former are corporeal immovables subject to lesionary inquiry and the latter are incorporeal immovables not subject to a lesionary inquiry.

Lands with known mineral deposits may be valued as an entity and that trial judge was correct in permitting that testimony.

* * * * *

DECREE

For the foregoing reasons, the judgment of the trial court is affirmed. Costs of this appeal are assessed against the appellee.

Affirmed.

McCLENDON, J., dissents with reasons.

McCLENDON, J. dissents.

I respectfully dissent from the majority opinion.

Admittedly, if not for the Mineral Code the sale of the property in this matter would be subject to rescission for lesion beyond moiety. Further, land with mineral deposits is clearly more valuable than similar land without mineral deposits. However, that is not the issue before this court. The only issue is whether the Mineral Code is or is not applicable to this sale of property. It is my opinion that the provisions of the Mineral Code do apply and that the sale in question was not lesionary, in accordance with LSA-R.S. 31:17.

The majority of this panel determined that sand and gravel are corporeal immovables, and not incorporeal rights and, therefore, Article 17 of the Mineral Code does not apply. It is my belief, however, that the majority failed to distinguish between the actual sand and gravel, which may be a corporeal immovable, and the mineral right which is clearly an incorporeal immovable. *See* LSA-R.S. 31:18.

Article 4 of the Mineral Code provides:

> The provisions of this Code are applicable to all forms of minerals, including oil and gas. They are also applicable to rights to explore for or mine or remove from land the soil itself, gravel, shells, subterranean water, or other substances occurring naturally in or as a part of the soil or geological formations on or underlying the land.

LSA-R.S. 31:4.

According to Article 5, ownership of land includes all minerals occurring naturally in a solid state. However, solid minerals are insusceptible of ownership apart from the land until reduced to possession. LSA-R.S. 31:5. Minerals are reduced to possession when they are under physical control that permits delivery to another. LSA-R.S. 31:7. The Comment to Article 7 explains:

> In the case of solid minerals, the landowner is regarded by Article 5 as the owner of such substances, but vesting of possession will still determine when minerals extracted become subject to the law of movables. As to others than the landowner, vesting of possession will have the dual effect of marking the vesting of title and mobilization. Despite the fact that Article 5

recognizes that the owner of land also owns solid minerals, such minerals are insusceptible of ownership apart from the land, and the landowner may therefore only convey or lease the right to explore for them and reduce them to possession and simultaneously to ownership. Accordingly, the nature of the substance involved has no impact on the significance of reduction to possession and consequent vesting of title.

Thus, minerals in their natural state cannot be "owned" separately from the land. *United States v. 43.42 Acres of Land*, 520 F. Supp. 1042, 1045 (W.D. La. 1981), *citing Frost-Johnson Lumber Co. v. Salling's Heirs*, 150 La. 756, 91 So. 207 (1921). Ms. Hornsby, however, was able to convey, reserve, or lease the right to explore and develop her land for the production of minerals and to reduce them to possession and simultaneously to ownership. *See* LSA-R.S. 31:15; LSA-R.S. 31:7 and Comment.

Article 17 of the Mineral Code provides that a sale of a mineral right is not subject to rescission for lesion beyond moiety. The Comment to LSA-R.S. 31:17 specifically acknowledges that said article represents existing law as to mineral transactions on undeveloped property finding it appropriate due to the speculative character of such transactions. The Comment went further, however, and recognized that there could be transactions where values could be more accurately determined. It was decided that even in those instances where values are not as speculative, the article should apply. The Comment continues:

> A case could be made for application of the principle of lesion when the rights sold are in fully developed property, thus permitting rather accurate determination of reserves and computations of values. However, considering the nature of transactions in developed properties and the facts that parties to them are usually experienced and lending institutions involved are highly conservative, the opportunities for the kind of overreaching which the concept of lesion was designed to prohibit are small indeed. Thus it is reasonable to make the doctrine of lesion beyond moiety inapplicable to all mineral transactions.

The unproduced minerals beneath the surface have little or no intrinsic value until reduced to actual possession permitting delivery to another. LSA-R.S. 31:7. The only added value to the land resulting from the sand and gravel in the land arises from the right to explore, mine or remove these minerals, and is, therefore subject to the provisions of the Mineral Code. When removed and reduced for possession, the sand and gravel can then be valued subject to the law of movables. *See* LSA-R.S. 31:7 Comment.

The trial court and the majority of this panel viewed the sand and gravel as minerals, and valued them as such, but then determined that the Mineral Code did not apply. I disagree. If sand and gravel are valued apart from the land, I am of the opinion that they are minerals and must be treated as such. Further, if the added value of the land is based simply on the right to remove the gravel below the surface the Mineral Code clearly applies. LSA-R.S. 31:18.

Accordingly, I believe that this sale is not subject to rescission for lesion beyond moiety and I respectfully dissent.

Notes and Questions

1. The majority in *Hornsby v. Slade* held that the value of non-fugacious minerals may be considered in determining the fair market value of the land in which the minerals are situated for purposes of a lesion claim. The Louisiana Third Circuit Court of Appeals examined the same issue in a more recent opinion, *Harruff v. King*, 139 So. 3d 1062 (La. App. 3 Cir. 2014). Without citing *Hornsby*, the court in *Harruff* approved of the trial court's conclusion that "[u]nsevered mineral interests, or rights, are owned as a part of the ownership of the land and constitute a part of the corporeal immovable. If they increase the value of the land alone, they should be considered." *Id.* at 1067. Ultimately, the court determined that the plaintiffs did not satisfy their evidentiary burden of proving by "clear and exceedingly strong" evidence that the price was less than one-half of the fair market value of the property. *Id.* at 1067–68. Nevertheless, the case provides additional support for the approach of the First Circuit in *Hornsby*.

2. Are *Hornsby* and *Harruff* consistent with the general premise of Louisiana law that "[s]olid minerals are insusceptible of ownership apart from the land until reduced to possession"? La. Rev. Stat. § 31:5. Consider also the primary reason for the Mineral Code's exemption of sales of mineral rights from rescission for lesion: the inherently speculative nature of mineral rights. Is the purpose of the rule furthered by the courts' holdings in *Hornsby* and *Harruff*, or does this line of cases impede the policy underpinning the law? For additional discussion and a critique of these cases, see Dakota S. Hawkins, *Comment, To Sell or Not to Sell, That is the Question: The Rescission of Sale on the Basis of Lesion and Its Applicability to Mineral Rights*, 6 LSU J. Energy L. & Resources 273 (2017). *Cf.* Patrick S. Ottinger, Louisiana Mineral Leases: A Treatise Ch. 3-41(d), at 281–83 (2016) (concluding that the court in *Harruff* "correctly held that the value, if any, of minerals *in situ* may be considered in an appraisal of the lands under which the minerals were allegedly situated").

b. Compromise
La. Civ. Code art. 3082

Article 3082 definitively forecloses the ability of a party to raise lesion as grounds for rescission of a compromise, or settlement. Consider the following: Plaintiff and Defendant are engaged in litigation in which Plaintiff claims that Defendant owes her $90,000 in damages resulting from a breach of contract. The parties eventually settle their dispute, and Defendant conveys to Plaintiff a tract of land valued at $230,000 in return for the plaintiff's agreement to dismiss the claim. A few months later, Defendant seeks to rescind the transfer of the tract of land on the ground that the transfer was lesionary due to the fact that the amount of the claim ($90,000) was far less than one-half the fair market value of the land ($115,000). While this might be true, Article 3082 makes quite clear that "[a]compromise cannot be rescinded on grounds of error of law or lesion." LA. CIV. CODE art. 3082. *See also Dornier v. Live Oak Arabians, Inc.,* 602 So. 2d 743 (La. App. 1 Cir. 1992) ("Under the law, a transaction or compromise, having between the interested parties a force equal to *res judicata,* may not be attacked on the basis of lesion."). Do you see why?

4. Comparative Analysis

Lesion is firmly embedded in the law of many civil law jurisdictions. Consider the following civil code provisions of several civil law jurisdictions that recognize lesion. What differences do you note between the law of these jurisdictions and the law of Louisiana? The excerpt of the law review article that follows explains in part why Louisiana law differs from that of other civil law jurisdictions.

Québec Civil Code art. 1406 (*translated in* Gouvernement du Québec, *Civil Code of Québec*, art. 1406 (2018), http://legisquebec.gouv.qc.ca/en /ShowDoc/cs/CCQ-1991.)

Lesion results from the exploitation of one of the parties by the other, which creates a serious disproportion between the performances of the parties; the fact that there is a serious disproportion creates a presumption of exploitation.

In cases involving a minor or a protected person of full age, lesion may also result from an obligation that is considered to be excessive in view of the patrimonial situation of the person, the advantages he gains from the contract and the circumstances as a whole.

Swiss Obligations Code, art. 21 (*translated in* The federal Council, *Federal Act on the Amendment of the Swiss Civil Code*, art. 21 (2017), https://www.admin.ch/opc/en/classified-compilation/19110009 /index.html.)±

Where there is a clear discrepancy between performance and consideration under a contract concluded as a result of one party's exploitation of the other's straitened circumstances, inexperience or thoughtlessness, the injured party may declare within one year that he will not honour the contract and demand restitution of any performance already made.

Italian Civil Code art. 1448 (*translated in* Susanna Beltramo, The Italian Civil Code art. 1448 (2012) (internal citations omitted))

If there is a disproportion between the performance of one party and that of another, and such disproportion was the result of a state of need of one

---

± This is not an official publication. The only authoritative publications are those issued by the Federal Chancellery of Switzerland. Translations provided by the Swiss Confederation are provided for information purposes only and have no legal force.

party, of which the other has availed himself for his advantage, the injured party can demand rescission of the contract.

The action is not admissible if the lesion does not exceed one-half the value that the performance made or promised by the injured party had at the time of the contract.

Christopher K. Odinet, *Commerce, Commonality, and Contract Law: Legal Reform in a Mixed Jurisdiction,* 75 La. L. Rev. 741, 777–780 (2015) (internal citations omitted)

1. History of the Doctrine

Much like redhibition, lesion is long-standing on the civil law island. Although preceded by a more limited Roman law institution for protecting minors called *restitutio in integrum*, lesion beyond moiety first appeared in substantial form during the time of the early Christian Roman emperors. This early form of lesion, called *lasesio enormis*, was meant to protect petty landowners who were often under harsh economic pressure during the later years of the empire to sell their lands to their wealthier, aristocratic neighbors. By preventing a sale that would yield to the improvident landowner less than half the value of his land, Roman law sought to afford protections and a balancing of the equities in these transactions.

Later, as Christianity became more entrenched in early Europe, the idea behind lesion would permeate into the central tenets of Canon Law—which, among other things, demanded that a fair and reasonable return be given in every contract—and eventually began to pervade all forms of contract law. This great wave of Christian legal thinking made its way into other forms of transactions aside from merely those involving property. Contracts for services and interest on loans, as well as any other form of agreements whereby an excessive advantage was given to any one party were also included under lesion.

Turning to early French law, because of the economic and political woes that were a hallmark of 17th and 18th century pre-revolutionary France, litigation dealing with lesion was rampant in the French courts. This sparked a general fear that the institution was causing serious damage to and uncertainty in the stability of private transactions. Thus, during the tumultuous legal reforms brought about by the various post-revolutionary French governments, lesion beyond moiety was eliminated in its entirety.

Finally, the Emperor Napoleon reintroduced the institution of lesion when he promulgated the French *Code Civil*. However, its breadth and substance were much diminished from its earlier canonical form. For instance, the action was made available only in cases of sales and partitions and restricted to only immovable property. At the time, this restricted application was supported by the notion that movable property had little value compared to that of land and that land, as a general rule, was subject to less variability in value. It was at this time that the institution was also limited to only the seller under the theory that only the person giving up the immovable could reasonably be susceptible to necessitous circumstances.

2. Louisiana's Incorporation of the Doctrine

It was in this form, as articulated in the French *Code Civil*, that the institution of lesion beyond moiety was incorporated into Louisiana law and the law of most other mixed jurisdictions. Few changes — such as the time period for bringing an action and the circumstances governing when rescission, as opposed to supplementing the price, may be demanded — have been made to Louisiana's law of lesion, and it remains largely the same as when it was originally enacted into the French *Code Civil*. Nonetheless, this preservation is consistent with Louisiana's strong desire to uphold its traditional institutions, even to the point of allowing them to remain relatively unchanged for multiple centuries.

With lesion, Louisiana courts have declined to augment the circumstances under which it may arise, even when the facts of a case might otherwise merit an equitable expansion of the concept. For instance, courts have rejected using lesion for the sale of incorporeals, regardless of the inadequacy of the price or the vulnerable position of the buyer, such as with the sale of rights of inheritance, obligations, and intellectual property. And, despite the development of markets for property other than real estate — as well as changing economic circumstances that might impact what is deemed a "fair" price — lesion has not been otherwise modified or expanded to take these changing expectations of a modern world into account.

* * * * *

In sum, lesion is largely unchanged since its earliest days in Louisiana. The rationale of the Romans and the French that initially dictated the rules and limitations of lesion have continued to govern its applicability, even when such rationale is arguably no longer valid.

Notes and Questions

1. Louisiana's law of lesion is far more limited in scope and applicability than that of the jurisdictions whose law is excerpted above. Why do you think that this is the case? Note that the Louisiana State Law Institute recently considered an expansion of lesion that would bring the doctrine more into line with the approach of other civil law jurisdictions. While the work of the Lesion Committee is still ongoing, to date the Law Institute has determined not to recommend that the legislature expand lesion to apply to contracts other than sales, exchanges, and partitions, nor has it recommended that the legislature abandon the precise mathematical formulas set forth in Louisiana law in favor of a more subjective test. In the view of a majority of the members of the Law Institute's Council, the Civil Code's current approach — which is both narrow and objective — allows courts to police the most objectionable contracts while simultaneously avoiding the risks of judicial overreaching and increased litigation.

2. While lesion is not recognized in the common law, a functional equivalent to lesion does exist in the doctrine of unconscionability. According to Article 2 of the Uniform Commercial Code:

> (1) If the court as a matter of law finds the contract or any term of the contract to have been unconscionable at the time it was made, the court may refuse to enforce the contract, or it may enforce the remainder of the contract without the unconscionable term, or it may so limit the application of any unconscionable term as to avoid any unconscionable result.

U.C.C. § 2-302. While the provision does not define the term "unconscionable," the official comments state that when determining whether a contract is unconscionable, the relevant inquiry is whether, in the light of the general commercial background and the commercial needs of the particular trade or case, the terms involved are so one-sided as to be unconscionable under the circumstances existing at the time of the making of the contract. *See* U.C.C § 2-302 cmt. 1 (2013). This definition has been further expounded upon by scholars and courts to encompass both "procedural" unconscionability—that is, unfairness in the contracting process, and "substantive" unconscionability—that is, unfairness in the rights and obligations of the parties to the contract. And, although Article 2 of the Uniform Commercial Code is directly applicable only to sales of goods, American courts have expanded the reach of the doctrine into the broader realm of contract law, and the Restatement (Second) on Contracts contains an unconscionability provision nearly identical to the one found in the Uniform Commercial Code. *See* Melissa T. Lonegrass, *Finding Room for Fairness in Formalism—The Sliding Scale Approach to Unconscionability*, 44 Loy. U. Chi. L.J. 1, 8–12 (2012). In what ways is the doctrine of unconscionability similar to the doctrine of lesion? How do the doctrines differ?

3. Lesion is certainly not the only doctrine that protects contracting parties against overreaching and unfairness. For further reading on the many protective doctrines found in Louisiana contract law, *see generally* Ronald L. Hersbergen, *Unconscionability: The Approach of the Louisiana Civil Code*, 43 La. L. Rev. 1315 (1983).

Chapter 6

Form

Recall the general rule of consent found in the Title on Conventional Obligations or Contracts: "Unless the law prescribes a certain formality for the intended contract, offer and acceptance may be made orally, in writing, or by action or inaction that under the circumstances is clearly indicative of consent." LA. CIV. CODE art. 1927. While the Civil Code does not prescribe any formality for the sale of a movable thing, it does for the sale of an immovable thing. The following Parts discuss the specifics of form for both types of things.

A. Movables

La. Civ. Code arts. 1846, 1848, 1927

The Civil Code does not prescribe any formality for the sale of a movable thing; thus, in accordance with the general rule above, the consent of the parties to such a sale may be expressed verbally, in writing, or even through their conduct. LA. CIV. CODE art. 1927.

Because the sale of a movable need not be made in writing, the issue arises as to how one may prove the existence of such a sale. The Civil Code provisions on Proof of Obligations are relevant to this inquiry. *See generally* LA. CIV. CODE arts. 1831–1853.

Before reading the following case, read carefully Article 1846.

Peter Vicari General Contractor, Inc. v. St. Pierre
831 So. 2d 296 (La. App. 5 Cir. 2002)

JAMES L. CANNELLA, Judge.

In a contract dispute, the Defendants, Gator Ready Mix, Inc. (Gator) and Scottsdale Insurance Company (Scottsdale), appeal from a judgment in favor of the Plaintiff, Pete Vicari General Contractor, Inc. We affirm.

In February of 1994, the Plaintiff, a general contractor owned by Pete Vicari (Vicari), began rebuilding Grand Isle High School in Grand Isle, Louisiana, which had been demolished by a tornado. The new school was to be raised above the ground on concrete slabs supported by steel enforced concrete columns. The concrete for the job was mixed, or batched, at the supplier's plant, brought to the site in a cement mixer truck and poured at the site into the molds for the columns and slabs. During the construction, problems arose with the strength of some of the concrete columns, which resulted in the demolition and re-pouring of fifteen columns.

* * * * *

Among the allegations in this lawsuit, the petition claims that Gator and its insurer, Scottsdale, are liable based on the breach of an oral contract to supply the concrete for the Grand Isle job. * * * Gator and Scottsdale filed exceptions of res judicata, prescription, no cause of action, and lack of subject matter jurisdiction. The exceptions were denied and the matter was tried on July 9, 2001. On September 11, 2001, the trial judge rendered a judgment in favor of the Plaintiff for $116,295.23.

On appeal, the Defendants assert that the trial judge erred in denying the exceptions of res judicata, prescription, and lack of subject matter jurisdiction, and in denying their motion for directed verdict (involuntary dismissal). They further contend that the trial judge erred in finding that the Plaintiff proved the existence of an oral contract by a preponderance of the evidence.

* * * * *

ORAL CONTRACT

Under La.C.C. art. 1846, one witness and other corroborating circumstances must prove an oral contract for a price in excess of $500. Only general corroboration is required. *Gulf Container Repair Services, Inc. v. FIC Business & Financial Centers, Inc.*, 98–1144 at p. 6 (La.App. 5th Cir.3/10/99), 735 So.2d 41, 43. It is not necessary that plaintiff offer independent proof of every detail. *Id.* The manifest error standard of review applies to a factual finding by the trier of fact in this regard and will not be overturned unless it is clearly wrong. *Gulf Container Repair Services, Inc.*, 98–1144 at p. 6, 735 So.2d at 43.

Vicari testified that he orally contracted with Gator [owned by Theresa and Eddie St. Pierre] to supply the concrete and that Theresa St. Pierre told him to put St. Pierre's name on the purchase order, that St. Pierre had the trucks, but the batches would be mixed at her plant. He also testified that he thought that the two companies were owned by the same parties and were interchangeable. This was the reason he wrote to St. Pierre about the problems. Furthermore, he continued to talk to Theresa and/or Eddie St. Pierre during the period when the dispute arose. He was never informed that they were not involved and he did not discover that Gator was in liquidation until after the problems with the concrete arose. In addition, the evidence shows that Scottsdale believed that there was an oral contract as evidenced by Scottsdale's letter to Gator after the Plaintiff made a claim. The letter stated that Scottsdale's' investigation indicated that Gator had an oral contract with the Plaintiff. Gator continued to carry commercial general liability insurance into August of 1994 and St. Pierre applied for the same insurance from Scottsdale in May of 1994.

No witness contradicted Vicari's testimony, although Theresa or Eddie St. Pierre could have been called to rebut the evidence. In *Dennis v. Allstate Ins. Co.*, 94–305, p. 5 (La.App. 5th Cir.10/25/94), 645 So.2d 763, 765, we stated:

> When a defendant in a civil case can by his own testimony throw light upon matters at issue which are necessary to his defense and peculiarly within his own knowledge, and he fails to go upon the witness stand, the presumption is raised, and will be given effect, that the facts as he would have then [sic] do not exist.

In *Taylor v. Entergy Corp.*, 01–0805, p. 15 (La.App. 4th Cir.4/17/02), 816 So.2d 933, 944, the court noted:

> The "uncalled witness" rule has been defined as an adverse presumption that arises when "a party has the power to produce witnesses whose testimony would elucidate the transaction or occurrence" and fails to call such witnesses. . . . A party's failure to call such witnesses gives rise to the presumption that "the witnesses' testimony would be unfavorable to him." . . . Although the advent of modern, liberal discovery rules has been recognized to limit this rule, it "remains viable." . . . "[t]he court may consider this presumption as it would any other relevant evidence in the case."

Id. [Citations omitted]

Since Theresa and Eddie St. Pierre owned Gator, Defendants had the burden to call them as witnesses if they could have contradicted Vicari. Their failure to do so raises the presumption that their testimony would have been adverse to Gator's case. *Dennis*, 94–305, at p. 5, 645 So.2d at 765. Based on the evidence, the trial judge concluded that the Plaintiff proved the oral contract. We find no manifest error in that ruling.

* * * * *

Accordingly, the judgment of the trial court is hereby affirmed. Costs of this appeal are to be paid by the Defendants.

* * * * *

DALEY, J., dissents with reasons.

* * * * *

The majority opinion affirms the trial court findings that there was an oral agreement between Peter Vicari General Contractor, Inc. (Vicari) and Gator Ready Mix, Inc. I respectfully dissent. All of the written documentation exchanged between the parties demonstrates that a written contract to supply concrete existed between Vicari and St. Pierre Ready Mix, Inc. If an oral contract existed between Vicari and Gator, that contract was clearly superceded [sic.] by the written agreement between Vicari and St. Pierre Ready Mix, Inc.

The initial bid form, which was a document prepared by Vicari's estimator, identifies, in writing, St. Pierre Ready Mix, Inc. as the supplier of ready mix. While Gator was originally identified on the document as the supplier, Vicari testified that Gator was crossed out and replaced with St. Pierre Ready Mix. Mr. Vicari testified he had no objection to this modification. Thereafter, the written purchase agreement, prepared by Vicari, identified St. Pierre Ready Mix, Inc. as the supplier of ready mix. The purchase agreement is the only document that sets forth the terms and conditions of the sale and the specifications of the ready mix that was to be provided. The purchase agreement is signed by a representative of Vicari and St. Pierre Ready Mix. All invoices and shipping documents were prepared by St. Pierre Ready Mix. All testing and inspection reports identify St. Pierre Ready Mix as the concrete supplier. All payments for the ready mix supplied were made directly to St. Pierre Ready Mix, Inc. All correspondence concerning alleged defects in the ready mix supplied, prepared by Vicari, were addressed to St. Pierre Ready Mix, Inc. None were copied to or addressed to Gator Ready Mix, Inc. Peter Vicari states in a correspondence addressed to St. Pierre Ready Mix, Inc. dated May 19, 1994, "Based on the facts, it is my determination that your firm is the sole party responsible for the failure of the concrete to meet this specification." If, as argued by Vicari, St. Pierre Ready Mix, Inc. was a subcontractor for Gator Ready Mix, Inc. then the purchase agreement, invoicing, payments, and correspondence regarding disputes over quality would identify Gator Ready Mix at some stage. All of the written documentary evidence concerning this commercial transaction are between Vicari and St. Pierre Ready Mix, Inc. No written documentation evidences a contract between Vicari and Gator Ready Mix, Inc.

In the middle of this construction contract, when the problem over the quality of the ready mix presented itself, Vicari and St. Pierre Ready Mix, Inc. renegotiated the terms of the purchase agreement. Gator Ready Mix, Inc. does not participate in this renegotiation in any way.

Counsel for Vicari suggest that if the purchase agreement created a written contract between St. Pierre Ready Mix, Inc. and Vicari, there was also an oral contract between Gator Ready Mix and Vicari to supply the same ready mix under the same terms and conditions. To accept this agreement I would have to ignore all of the written documentation between the parties. Because of the overwhelming documentary evidence in this case, I am forced to conclude that the trial court erred in finding that there was a binding oral agreement between Vicari General Contractor, Inc. and Gator Ready Mix, Inc. For the foregoing reasons, I would reverse the trial court's finding and vacate the judgment against Gator Ready Mix and Scottsdale Insurance Company.

Notes and Questions

1. When interpreting the requirement that an oral agreement pertaining to a thing priced or valued in excess of $500 must be proved by at least one witness and other corroborating circumstances, Louisiana courts have consistently held that a party to the action may be a "credible witness," and the other "corroborating circumstances" need only be general in nature. *See Deubler Electric Inc. v. Knockers of Louisiana, Inc.*, 665 So. 2d 481, 484 (La. App. 5 Cir. 1995). A contract for a price or

value not in excess in $500 may be proved by any competent evidence. *See* La. Civ. Code art. 1846.

2. Although the parties to a sale of movables need not reduce their agreement to writing, if they do so, the sale may no longer be proved by parol evidence. *See* La. Civ. Code art. 1846 ("When a writing is not required by law, *a contract not reduced to writing . . .* may be proved by competent evidence."). Additionally, any written agreement of the parties is subject to Article 1848, which governs the circumstances under which parol evidence may be admitted in a dispute surrounding a written agreement. Under that article, parol evidence may not be admitted to "negate or vary the contents of" the parties' written agreement. La. Civ. Code art. 1848. Nevertheless, testimonial or other proof may be admitted to prove that the written agreement was modified by a subsequent oral agreement, or that the contract formed by the written agreement should be rescinded on the basis of error, fraud, or duress. *Id.* In addition, testimonial or other evidence may be admitted to prove that the contract evidenced by the written agreement is a simulation, whether absolute or relative. *See* La. Civ. Code art. 1849.

B. Immovables

La. Civ. Code arts. 1831–1839, 1848, 2440

Unlike the sale of a movable, the sale of an immovable must be made by authentic act or by act under private signature, as provided by Articles 1839 and 2440. The rule that the transfer of an immovable must be made in writing should be a familiar one, as it is covered in most introductory courses on Obligations and Property. However, the familiarity of the writing requirement for transfers of immovable property tends to mask its complexity. The scope and nuance of the writing requirement for sales of immovable property are the subject of the remainder of this Chapter.

1. The Writing Requirement

a. In General

While the transfer of an immovable may be made by authentic act or act under private signature, the following case addresses the latter of the two: the act under private signature. Before reading the case, read carefully Article 1837 and the comments thereto.

Milliman v. Peterman

519 So. 2d 238 (La. App. 5 Cir. 1988)

Bowes, Judge.

In this action, defendants/appellants, Helen Peterman and Marie Bulgherini, assert that the trial judge erred when he held that the Millimans, plaintiffs and appellees, validly and timely accepted an offer by defendants to purchase immovable property belonging to plaintiffs and that the defendants later breached the contract, thus entitling the Millimans to the deposit and attorney's fees. We disagree and affirm.

When the plaintiffs moved from Kenner, Louisiana, to Bowling Green, Kentucky, they entered into a listing contract with Merrill Lynch Realty, Inc. to market the property.

On August 19, 1985, by which time the Millimans had already moved to Bowling Green, Mr. William Althans, an agent with Merrill Lynch, showed the property to the defendants-appellants and prepared an agreement to purchase. The agreement was signed by Ms. Peterman and Ms. Bulgherini. However, at line 79, the agreement had a provision that the offer remained binding and irrevocable through August 20, _____ at 7:00 p.m. and the year was not inserted in this blank space. The defendants also executed and signed a Real Estate Deposit Note for $9,950 as a partial deposit on the purchase, and, on August 20, 1985, gave Mr. Althans a money order made payable to Merrill Lynch Realty, Inc. in the sum of $1,000.00. Additionally, on August 19, 1985, the defendants signed a lease for use with an Agreement or Option to Purchase, intending to lease the home for a period not exceeding one year commencing on August 21, 1985, and ending the last calendar day of August 1986.[1]

On that same date, August 19, Mr. Althans contacted Mr. Milliman and advised him that the defendants had made this offer to purchase the property. Mr. Althans testified that he read all of the pertinent parts of the contract to Mr. Milliman over the phone. Mr. Milliman testified that he had, in fact, accepted the offer over the phone, but, in discussing the issue with Mr. Althans, it was decided that the acceptance should be put in writing.

The following day, Mr. Milliman sent a telegram, addressed to Bill Althans, which stated:

> WE, RONALD AND PALMA MILLIMAN, ACCEPT THE LEASE PURCHASE OFFER MADE BY HELEN PETERMAN AND MARIE BULGHERINI OF $109,500 WITH A 12 MONTH LEASE AT $850 PER MONTH FOR THE FIRST 6 MONTHS AND $875 PER MONTH FOR THE REMAINING LEASE. ALL OTHER TERMS AND CONDITIONS OF THE CONTRACT DATED AUGUST 19, 1985 ARE ACCEPTED.
>
> RONALD AND PALMA MILLIMAN 12:06 EST

---

1. The defendants were awaiting an insurance settlement and intended to use the proceeds of the settlement to purchase the home. Consequently, if the settlement took place prior to the end of the year lease, the property would be purchased sooner. We note, however, that the purchase of the home was in no way predicated on their receiving the insurance settlement.

On August 21, 1985, the defendants moved into the home and remained there until some time after March 1, 1986, when they notified the plaintiffs and Mr. Althans, in writing, that they did not intend to purchase the home.[2]

Plaintiffs filed this suit and obtained a judgment forfeiting the purchasers' deposit to them, and awarding them attorney's fees under the contract.

On appeal, defendants present five assignments of error:

1. The trial judge was in error in failing to hold that the offer to purchase was to remain binding and irrevocable only through August 20, 1985.

2. The trial judge was in error in ruling that the acceptance by the plaintiffs of the defendants' offer by telegraph was satisfactory.

3. The trial judge was in error in ruling that the action of the defendants in moving into the premises indicated they were satisfied that their offer had been accepted.

4. The trial judge was in error in ruling that the defendants breached a contract and are not entitled to a refund of their deposit of $1,850.00.

5. In the alternative, and only in the event the court should affirm the decision of the trial judge, the trial judge was in error in awarding attorney fees of $2,500.00.

Assignments one, two and three will be discussed together for the sake of continuity.

Appellants argue strenuously that although the purchase agreement stated that "This offer remains binding and irrevocable through (date) *August 20,* _____ (time) *7 p.m.*" (and does not include the year "1985"), nonetheless it is clear what year was intended by the parties. Each of the three witnesses at trial, Mr. Milliman, Mr. Althans and Ms. Bulgherini, testified that August 20, 1985, at 7:00 p.m. was indeed the time limit set by and agreed upon by the parties.

The Louisiana Supreme Court held in *Dixie Campers, Inc. v. Vesely Co.*, 398 So.2d 1087 (La. 1981):

Although parol evidence is inadmissible to vary the terms of a written contract, La. C.C. art. 2276 [now see LSA C.C. art. 1848], when the terms of a written contract are susceptible to more than one interpretation, or there is uncertainty or ambiguity as to its provisions, or the intent of the parties cannot be ascertained from the language employed, parol evidence is admissible to clarify the ambiguity and to show the intention of the parties. [cites omitted]

---

2. In March, 1986, when the defendants' rent check was late in arriving, and Mr. Milliman called regarding the status of the payment, he was told over the phone that the defendants did not intend to purchase the home as they had agreed to do. At some later point, their intention was reduced to writing.

Therefore, although the trial judge stated in his reasons for judgment "since no year was provided in the agreement, the court assumes that the time period was a reasonable period of time which was allowed to the plaintiff/sellers to accept the offer", considering all the testimony and evidence brought out at the trial, we find in the instant case that the date intended for the offer to expire was August 20, 1985 at 7:00 p.m.

The second assignment of error raised by the appellants asserts that the telegram was not a valid acceptance by the appellees of appellants' agreement to purchase. We find this argument without merit. In the case before us, appellants signed the actual agreement to purchase on August 19, 1985. That same day, the real estate agent contacted Mr. Milliman by phone, and, the very next day, several hours before the offer was to expire, the Millimans sent a telegram (contents reproduced supra) with their names typed out at the bottom.

Appellants cite *Morvant v. Arnoult*, 490 So.2d 549 (La. App. 4 Cir. 1986) and *Rebman v. Reed*, 335 So.2d 37 (La.App. 4 Cir.1976), *writ denied*, 338 So.2d 699 (La.1976) for the legal principle that "A contract to sell immovable property, to be enforceable, must be in writing and must be signed by the buyer and seller, and if an agent executes the contract on behalf of the buyer or the seller, the agent's authority must be express and in writing." Based on these cases, the appellants argue that since the agreement was not signed by *both* parties prior to the expiration of the acceptance period, it is invalid and appellees' oral acceptance and telegram do not cure the defect.

The cases cited by appellants to support their position are easily distinguishable from the facts of the instant case. Both of the cases cited by appellants involved a situation in which the seller did not sign the contract or exhibit any other outward manifestation of acceptance to sell except to rely on his agent to sign the agreement for him. In both cases, the court held that the agent did not have express written authority to act on behalf of his principal and for that reason the contract was invalid. This is clearly inopposite [sic] to the case at issue since neither the appellants nor the appellees assert that the telegram sent by the Millimans merely authorized Mr. Althans to accept the offer for them. The telegram and all other actions by the Millimans were done to indicate *their* acceptance of the agreement.

The issue we must decide is whether the written agreement to purchase was valid even though only one party actually signed that document while the other parties sent a telegram confirming their acceptance and provided other outward manifestations of acceptance. The trial judge determined this was a satisfactory acceptance. We agree.

Under Louisiana law, a promise to sell immovable property must be vested with the same formalities as prescribed for sales of immovable property. *Oeschner v. Keller*, 134 La. 1098, 64 So. 921 (La.1914); *Alley v. New Homes Promotion, Inc.*, 247 So.2d 218 (La.App. 4 Cir.1971), [w]rit denied, 248 So.2d 832 (La.1971). The Civil Code requires that all sales of immovable property shall be made by authentic act or under private signature. LSA C.C. Art. 2440 [R.C.C. 2440]. The Civil Code further requires that an act under private signature need not be written by the parties, but must be signed by them. LSA C.C. Art. 1837. However, the "Comments" under this Article, Section (b) states in pertinent part: "This article is not intended to change the jurisprudential rule that an Act under private signature is valid even though signed by one party alone . . . ." The cases which support the proposition expressed in the comments above are legion. See: *Miller v. Douville*, 45 La.Ann. 214, 12 So. 132 (La.1893) (A written promise to sell real property is valid, and may be enforced, although not signed by the obligee.) *Joseph v. Moreno*, 2 La. 460 (1831) (A written promise to sell signed only by the vendor was valid and that acceptance by the vendee could be established by extraneous evidence to the written agreement.) *Miller v. Miller*, 335 So.2d 767 (La.App. 3 Cir.1976) writ denied 338 So.2d 927 (La.1976) (There is no requirement that a written promise to sell be signed by both parties. Acceptance by the vendee could be established by evidence extraneous to the written instrument.) *Cerami v. Haas*, 195 La. 1048, 197 So. 752 (La.1940). (The law does not require that the acceptance of a contract be expressed on its face, nor is it essential that the Act be signed by the party in whose favor it is made. The acceptance may result from his acts in availing himself of its stipulations or in doing some act which indicates his acceptance.) *Succession of Jenkins*, 91 So.2d 416 (La.App. 2 Cir.1956). (The consent and agreement of vendees may be shown otherwise than by the signing of the Act of Sale itself.) *Alley v. New Homes Promotion, Inc., supra.* (An acceptance of a written offer may be proved by some unequivocal act of the offeree, if the terms of the contract are clearly indicated in the written offer.)

Thus, the courts of this state have repeatedly declined to find an agreement to purchase or sell invalid simply because one party failed to sign the instrument but at some point later that same party exhibited some outward manifestation of acceptance beyond oral assent.

The following factors indicate to us that although one party (the seller) did not actually sign the agreement prior to the established deadline, that party did exhibit many acts of outward manifestation of acceptance beyond oral assent, including the following:

1. Appellants signed the agreement to purchase and did not revoke their offer prior to the expiration of the acceptance period as set forth in the agreement.

2. The Millimans were verbally informed of all pertinent points of the agreement to purchase.

3. Within the acceptance period set forth in the agreement, the Millimans sent a telegram stating their intention to be bound by the agreement.

4. The agent for the appellees accepted a Real Estate Deposit Note for $9,950 as a partial deposit and a money order for $1,000 made payable to Merrill Lynch Realty, Inc. both provided by the appellants.

5. The appellants provided the Millimans with an $850 damage deposit on the home.

6. They were allowed to move into the home.

7. The Millimans did actually sign a copy of the agreement as soon as they received it on August 25, 1985.

We note that in this case, as with all of those cited above, the agreement actually was *signed* by the party who now alleges that the agreement is invalid for lack of form, even though the non-signing party manifested his assent to the agreement by unequivocal acts. In this case, we agree with the well-established principle that the party who has given his written assent to an agreement and later asserts that the agreement is invalid for lack of the other party's written assent, is estopped to assert this lack of formality. *Bradford's Heirs v. Brown,* 11 Mart (O.S.) 217 (La.1822); Jones, *An Exception to the Rules of Form and Parol Evidence,* 33 La.L.R. 344 at 349 (1973). The telegram and other outward manifestations of acceptance by the Millimans communicated the intention of the sellers to be bound to the purchase agreement and is sufficient to create a binding and enforceable obligation. Therefore, we find that there was a meeting of the minds, that the written contract was accepted and consented to by both parties, and is valid and binding on each.

* * * * *

Notes and Questions

1. The foregoing case did not involve a contract *of sale*, but rather concerned a contract *to sell*. This agreement is one of several "Agreements Preparatory to the Sale" which will be addressed in Chapter 12: Contracts Preparatory to Sale. The contract *to sell* contemplates that the parties will enter into a contract *of sale* at a later date, or upon the occurrence of a condition, such as the buyer obtaining financing. *See* La. Civ. Code art. 2623. The contract to sell must set forth the thing and the price of the contemplated sale and must "meet the formal requirements of the sale it contemplates." La. Civ. Code art. 2623. Aside from the contract to sell, the Civil Code recognizes two additional agreements preparatory to the sale: the option to buy or sell and the right of first refusal. The Civil Code makes clear that an option contract must "meet the formal requirements of the sale it contemplates." La. Civ. Code art. 2620. Although the Civil Code does not state unequivocally that rights of first refusal affecting immovable property must be made in writing, courts and scholars generally agree that the writing requirement applies to such contracts. *See, e.g., Jones v. Hospital Corp. of America,* 516 So. 2d 1175 (La. App. 2 Cir. 1987) (right of first refusal concerning immovable must be made in writing); 24 Dian Tooley-Knoblett & David Gruning, Louisiana Civil Law Treatise, Sales § 6:17 n. 1 (2017) (discussing uncertainty surrounding writing requirement for rights of refusal affecting immovable property).

2. Although a sale of an immovable may be made by authentic act, there is no requirement that the parties' written agreement be passed before a notary or

witnesses. Nevertheless, many sales of immovable property are made in authentic form. What are the benefits of executing the sale of an immovable in an authentic act? *See* La. Civ. Code art. 1835 ("The authentic act constitutes full proof of the agreement it contains, as against the parties, their heirs, and successors by universal or particular title.").

3. A corollary of the principle that the transfer of an immovable must be made in writing is the rule that parol evidence is not admissible to prove ownership of an immovable. La. Civ. Code art. 1832. *Mitchell v. Clark*, 448 So. 2d 681 (La. 1984), illustrates the seriousness of this rule. *Mitchell* involved a dispute between Isabel Mitchell and her nephew, Willie Clark., Jr., regarding the ownership of a home. Mitchell negotiated the purchase of the home with its former owner and paid the price; however, she instructed the seller to list Clark, rather than herself, as the buyer of the property in the Act of Sale. *Id.* at 683. Mitchell alleged the home was hers, claiming that while she intended to donate the home to Clark at her death, the donation was without effect because it was not made in the form of a valid will. *Id.* at 684. Despite the accuracy of the principle on which Mitchell relied, the Supreme Court held that she was not entitled to relief. *Id.* at 686. In so holding, the Court opined:

> [B]ecause the authentic act effected [sic] the transfer of immovable property, only written evidence was admissible to prove any rights with respect to the property. * * * * * The admissible evidence in this case establishes that Mitchell paid Holmes [the seller] for the lot, and that Holmes followed Mitchell's instructions and executed a deed to Clark. The inadmissible evidence establishes that Mitchell's intention—to make a gift of immovables to take effect upon Mitchell's death—could not be accomplished in the way attempted. We cannot give relief to the plaintiff without abrogating the consistent rule of property that excludes parol evidence to prove that one not named in the deed is the real vendee.

Id. at 686–87.

4. Note because the law requires the parties' *agreement* to transfer an immovable be in writing, extrinsic evidence—even if written—will not suffice as proof of the agreement in the absence of a written act of transfer. In *Shoreline Gas, Inc. v. Grace Resources, Inc.*, 786 So. 2d 137 (La. App. 2 Cir. 2001), the property in question was an interest in a gas lease which, by virtue of the Mineral Code, is properly classified as immovable property. *See* La. Rev. Stat. § 31:16 (classifying a mineral lease as a mineral right) and La. Rev. Stat. § 31:18 (classifying mineral rights as incorporeal immovables). The lessor allegedly sold its interest in the lease to a third person, and a dispute arose surrounding who the lessee was required to pay—the original lessor or the alleged purchaser. To prove that the sale from the lessor to the third person had occurred, a letter was produced during the course of litigation indicating that the original lessor had "sold, transferred and assigned all of its interests" in the pertinent wells to the third person. *Shoreline Gas*, 786 So. 2d at 140. Although the letter was written by the lessor (i.e., the alleged seller), the court refused to recognize the

transfer. The court observed: "[T]he record is devoid of evidence of a valid, written transfer of [the lessor's] interests to [the third person] . . . At best, as the district court reasonably concluded, the July 22 letter was simply parol evidence which cannot establish title in [the third person]." *Id.* at 141. In other words, written evidence indicating that a sale has occurred simply will not suffice; proof of a sale requires a written juridical act of transfer.

5. While an act transferring an immovable must be made in writing, the same is not true with respect to an agreement to *cancel* the sale of an immovable. In *Frank v. Motwani*, 513 So. 2d 1170 (La. 1987), the Louisiana Supreme Court held definitively that neither the writing requirement for transfers of immovables nor the parol evidence rule (found in Article 1848) applies to the cancellation of a contract for the transfer of an immovable. The Court stated:

> There is no reason why a party to a contract that has to be in writing should not be able to offer evidence that the parties verbally agreed to cancel the contract. Clearly, the burden of proof will be on the party asserting that it was canceled. La. Civ.Code art. 1831. Although this may very well be a difficult burden to meet in the face of a signed written contract, the party claiming cancellation should be allowed to present evidence to prove that the contract was verbally canceled.

Id. at 1172. In his concurring opinion, Justice Lemmon emphasized that while the cancelation of the sale of an immovable may be made verbally, any other modification of the sale of real estate must be made in writing, just as if it were the original sale. *Id.* (Lemmon, J., concurring).

6. In 2001 the Louisiana Uniform Electronic Transactions Act was enacted. *See generally* La. Rev. Stat. §§ 9:2602–2620. The Act gives legal recognition to electronic records, signatures, and contracts. La. Rev. Stat. § 9:2607. Although the Act contains a number of exceptions, real estate transactions are subject to the Act. La. Rev. Stat. § 9:2603. However, the Act applies only to transactions between parties who have agreed to conduct their transaction by electronic means. La. Rev. Stat. § 9:2605.

7. When the immovable property sold is residential and one or more of the parties is represented by a licensed real estate broker, the contract to sell must be made using the Louisiana Real Estate Commission's Purchase Agreement Form, titled "Louisiana Residential Agreement to Buy or Sell." This form may be found on the Louisiana Real Estate Commission's website at www.lrec.state.la.us/mandatory -forms/. Although the use of this form is required by law, the requirement is directed to the licensed real estate broker, not the parties. *See* La. Rev. Stat. § 37:1449.1(A). It follows, therefore, that a sale of residential real estate that does not comply with this requirement, though made in written form, is nevertheless enforceable.

8. Recall that the "equal dignities doctrine" applies to the contract of mandate, such that when the law prescribes a certain form for an act, a contract of mandate

authorizing such an act must also be in that form. La. Civ. Code art. 2993. Thus, because an Act of Sale must be made in writing, a mandate authorizing the sale or purchase of immovable property must also be made in writing. See Chapter 2: Capacity & Authority for additional discussion of the "equal dignities doctrine" in the context of mandate.

b. Exception: Delivery Plus Admission

La. Civ. Code art. 1839

The writing requirement for immovables is not without exception. Indeed, since 1825, the Civil Code has recognized that in limited circumstances an *oral* transfer of an immovable may be valid. Read Article 1839 carefully before reading the following case. Under what circumstances is an oral transfer of an immovable enforceable?

Martin v. Brister

850 So. 2d 1106 (La. App. 2 Cir. 2003)

Williams, Judge.

The defendant, John Brister, Jr., appeals a judgment in favor of the plaintiffs, Tommy Martin and Brenda Martin. The trial court found that pursuant to a verbal contract of sale, the plaintiffs had paid $6,000 to purchase a strip of land measuring 40 feet by 200 feet. The court adjudicated title to the property to the plaintiffs, awarded defendant $850 owed by plaintiffs and dismissed all other claims. For the following reasons, we affirm.

FACTS

On January 3, 1997, John Brister, Jr., conveyed to Tommy Martin and his wife, Brenda Martin, a two-acre tract of land, which measured 208.71 feet by 417.40 feet, located along Highway 167 in Winn Parish, Louisiana. The parties executed a "Credit Sale" instrument and deed for the consideration of $75,600 and the seller acknowledged receipt of a $5,600 down payment with a promissory note and mortgage for the balance of $70,000. At the time, the parties did not realize that the property was incorrectly described in the credit sale instrument.

Shortly after the sale, the Martins approached Brister about purchasing an additional 40-foot strip of land adjacent to the tract previously conveyed for use as a driveway. According to the Martins, Brister agreed to sell the strip for $6,000 and to sign a deed correcting the original property description and including the additional 40 feet. Although Brister does not dispute that he agreed to sell an additional 40 feet to the Martins, he denies that there was consent as to the purchase price. There was no written agreement regarding the sale of the 40-foot strip of land.

Subsequently, the Martins borrowed funds from T.J. Kervin to pay the balance owed to Brister. On February 6, 1997, they gave Kervin a mortgage on the land bought from Brister as security for the loan. Kervin then delivered a check for the necessary funds to the Daniel Frazier Trust Account. The following day, the Frazier Trust issued a check to Brister in the amount of $76,466.67 as full payment of the Martins' promissory note. According to the Martins, the amount of the check included $70,000 for the balance due on the note, $6,000 for the additional 40-foot lot and $466.67 for one month's interest. Brister accepted the payment, but did not deliver the cancelled promissory note and mortgage to the Martins. Approximately one year later, in February 1998, the Martins' attorney prepared a "Correction Credit Deed" to correct and amend the original property description and to include the additional 40-foot strip of land. Brister refused to sign this correction deed and sent the Martins' attorney an alternative revised deed, which corrected the original instrument, but did not add the 40-foot lot to the property description.

Subsequently, the plaintiffs, Tommy and Brenda Martin, filed a petition for damages against the defendant, John Brister, Jr., for his failure to execute an act of correction of the credit deed and to cancel the note and mortgage. The plaintiffs requested that the credit deed property description be corrected and amended and that defendant be ordered to convey to them the 40-foot strip of land adjacent to the property originally described. The defendant filed an answer and reconventional demand seeking damages for lost video poker revenue, property damage and payment for a motor boat.

At trial, the parties gave conflicting testimony regarding the circumstances of their transaction. The plaintiffs introduced into evidence the credit sale deed, the checks paid to defendant and the correspondence sent to him by their attorney. In its reasons for judgment, the trial court found that the parties had formed a verbal contract for the sale of the strip of land measuring 40 feet by 200 feet adjacent to the property originally conveyed for the price of $6,000 and that possession of the lot had been transferred to plaintiffs for the construction of a driveway. The court rendered judgment adjudicating title to the 40-foot strip of land to plaintiffs, awarding defendant $850 for the value of a motor boat and dismissing all other claims. The defendant appeals the judgment.

DISCUSSION

The defendant contends the trial court erred in finding that there was an enforceable verbal contract between the parties. Defendant argues that the evidence failed to establish a sale because the parties did not agree on the thing to be sold or the price.

Generally, a transfer of immovable property must be made by authentic act or by act under private signature. Nevertheless, an oral transfer is valid between the parties when the property has been actually delivered and the transferor recognizes the transfer when interrogated under oath. LSA-C.C. art. 1839. The term actual delivery means that the immovable which is the object of the verbal sale has in fact been transferred or placed into the possession of the buyer. A determination of whether actual delivery of an immovable has been made depends on the circumstances of each individual case. *Duhon v. Dugas*, 407 So.2d 1334 (La.App. 3rd Cir.1981). A sale is a contract whereby a person transfers ownership of a thing to another for a price in money. The thing, the price and the consent of the parties are requirements for the perfection of a sale. LSA-C.C. art. 2439.

A court of appeal should not set aside a trial court's finding of fact in the absence of manifest error or unless it is clearly wrong. *Stobart v. State DOTD*, 617 So.2d 880 (La.1993). The task of a reviewing court is to assess whether the fact finder's resolution of conflicting evidence was reasonable in light of the record as a whole. *Fowler v. Wal-Mart Stores, Inc.*, 30,843 (La.App.2d Cir.8/19/98), 716 So.2d 511.

In the present case, defendant argues in his brief that the parties did not agree on the thing to be transferred because he agreed to sell a 40-foot lot, but the plaintiffs' petition and their attorney's correspondence refer to a 48-foot strip of land. However, at trial the plaintiffs and defendant all testified that they had discussed the sale of a strip of land measuring 40 feet by 200 feet adjacent to the tract previously conveyed. Thus, the testimony demonstrated that the parties had agreed on the thing which was the object of the sale.

The defendant also contends that the parties did not agree on the sale price of the 40-foot strip of land. The evidence shows that the January 1997 promissory note stated a balance due of $70,000 and that in February 1997, defendant appeared at the office of Daniel Frazier to collect a check in the amount of $76,466.67 as payment of the note. The plaintiffs testified that the amount of $6,466.67 above the balance owed reflected the $6,000 price of the 40-foot lot and one month's interest. Defendant testified that this amount represented a pre-payment penalty. However, the promissory note did not provide for the assessment of such a penalty. Additionally, in May 1997, the Louisiana Department of Transportation and Development issued a permit for construction of a driveway to Tommy Martin as owner of the land and defendant signed a statement that he did not object to extending the driveway. Defendant's acceptance of the $6,000 payment in excess of the amount due under the 1997 note and his acquiescence in plaintiffs' exercise of ownership over the 40-foot strip of land at issue support a finding that the parties had agreed to the price for the thing sold. Thus, defendant's arguments are not supported by the record.

At trial, the defendant testified as follows:

> It is on the side of the forty feet. But, his forty feet is (sic) built up. You see I sold Tommy forty feet. I said, yeah, Tommy I will sell you the forty feet. There is no question about that in my mind. I sold him forty feet. He just never did pay me for it. That is the reason we are here today.

The above quoted testimony shows that defendant acknowledged under oath that he had made a verbal sale of the 40-foot strip of land to the plaintiffs. Witness testimony that the plaintiffs had built a driveway across the 40-foot lot supports the trial court's determination that the property was placed into the possession of the plaintiffs. Based upon the evidence presented, we conclude that the requirements of

Article 1839 were satisfied by the actual delivery of the property to the plaintiffs and the defendant's recognition of the transfer under oath. Consequently, we cannot say the trial court was clearly wrong in finding that the verbal sale of the 40-foot lot was valid. The assignment of error lacks merit.

Notes and Questions

1. Consider the purposes of heightened form requirements:

> In some instances, the formality of a writing is required by the law *ad solemnitatem*, that is, as a solemnity without which an act cannot have any effect and cannot therefore give rise to any obligation. There is a good policy reason for this turning of a formality into a solemnity whenever a person, through the process of executing the formality, must be given a chance of becoming clearly aware of the consequences of the intended act. In such cases, the formality may be said to perform a *cautionary* function. * * * In other instances the formality of a writing is required by the law *ad probationem*, that is, for evidentiary purposes, in which case the juridical act may produce effects even when the formality has been omitted, although subject to the uncertainty of securing proof other than witnesses or presumptions. That is why such a formality is evidentiary rather than cautionary.

5 Saúl Litvinoff (Deceased) & Ronald J. Scalise Jr., Louisiana Civil Law Treatise, Obligations § 12.12 (2d ed. 2017).± In light of the foregoing discussion, what is the primary purpose of the writing requirement for sales of immovables?

2. In addition to the exception provided in Article 1839, a sale may be proven by verbal testimony if the written instrument has been destroyed, lost, or stolen. La. Civ. Code art. 1832.

3. Although an oral transfer of an immovable may be valid between the parties, such a transfer is not enforceable against third persons. Do you see why? *See* La. Civ. Code art. 3338.

2. The Content of the Parties' Agreement

While the Civil Code is clear that the sale of an immovable must be made in writing, it less clear what the content of such an act must be. In connection with the following materials, consider the language of Article 2439: "The thing, the price, and the consent of the parties are requirements for the perfection of a sale." La. Civ. Code art. 2439.

± Reproduced with permission of Thomson Reuters.

a. The Consent of the Parties

Chauvin v. Bohn

411 So. 2d 442 (La. 1982)

Dixon, Chief Justice.

The central issue presented in this case is whether a notation on the back of a personal check given to the vendor of a residence as a down payment suffices as a written contract to buy an immovable.

The facts are as follows:

Plaintiff-vendor, John Kent Chauvin, placed his residence in the Willowdale Subdivision in Luling, Louisiana, up for sale in the summer of 1976. On Sunday, August 15, 1976, defendant-vendee, C. Robert Bohn, and his wife heard that the house was on the market. They were interested in moving to the area so they telephoned the Chauvins and arranged a tour of the home. After looking at the house, Mr. Bohn inquired about the purchase price. Mr. Chauvin stated that he was asking $85,000.00. Mr. Bohn offered to pay $80,000.00 and Mr. Chauvin responded that he would accept that amount. The parties walked back inside the house where Mr. Bohn wrote a personal check to Mr. Chauvin for $4,000.00. Mr. Chauvin objected to the figure because he believed the deposit should be 10% of the purchase price, or $8,000.00. Mr. Bohn replied that he had already written the number $4,000.00 on the check, that he did not have another check with him, and that this would be a cash sale requiring no financing. Mr. Chauvin testified that he then agreed to accept the $4,000.00 as a down payment. Since Mr. Bohn's attorney was out of town for the week, the parties agreed to wait until the attorney returned to draw up the act of sale.

As the Bohns were leaving, Mr. Bohn jokingly requested that the "For Sale" sign staked up in the front yard be removed. Mr. Chauvin complied and put the sign in the garage. There was some discussion about how soon the Bohns would want to move into the residence. Mrs. Chauvin expressed concern about having to move into an apartment with their three small children because it would be some time before a new home could be built. Mr. Bohn kissed her, said they were not in a hurry to move, and assured her that the Chauvins could stay in the house as long as necessary and just pay rent. Mr. Chauvin volunteered to find out the current rental values in the vicinity.

A few hours later, Mr. Chauvin examined the check and realized that Mr. Bohn had made the check payable to "John Kent," omitting Mr. Chauvin's last name. Mr. Chauvin telephoned the Roussel residence where Mr. and Mrs. Bohn had been visiting. The Bohns were still at the Roussels; Mr. Bohn instructed Mr. Chauvin to simply write in his last name on the instrument. At this point it is clear that one intended to buy, and gave a check to evidence his intention; the other intended to sell. The thing and the price were fairly certain. Each, however, contemplated consulting his lawyer, and assumed there would be a simple cash transaction. It is fair to assume that each would probably follow his attorney's advice.

Mr. Bohn testified that he tried several times during the next few days to reach Mr. Chauvin because Bohn's wife decided she did not want the house. On Thursday, August 19, Mr. Bohn contacted someone at the Chauvin residence. Mr. Bohn testified that he spoke with Mrs. Chauvin in the morning; on the other hand, Mrs. Chauvin testified that she always goes shopping on Thursdays and that Mr. Bohn talked to the baby sitter. In any event, when Mr. Chauvin arrived home his wife told him Mr. Bohn had telephoned earlier in the day. Mr. Chauvin returned the call only to learn that Mr. Bohn no longer wished to go through with the sale.

It is impossible to discern from the testimony exactly when Mr. Chauvin deposited the check given to him by Mr. Bohn on the previous Sunday. Mr. Chauvin admitted that he did not deposit the check immediately after receiving it; he testified that his lawyer advised him on Monday to "hold onto the check." He asserts that the check was deposited, along with his paycheck, on the afternoon of Thursday, August 19, before his conversation with Mr. Bohn; the check was posted to Mr. Chauvin's bank on Friday, August 20. Mr. Bohn argues that Mr. Chauvin deposited the check some time after having been informed that the sale was off. Although Mr. Bohn testified that he went to his bank in New Orleans at 9:00 a.m. on Friday, August 20 to stop payment on the check, the stop payment order is dated August 20 at 2:00 p.m. The $4,000.00 deposit was initially credited to Mr. Chauvin's account on August 20. However, payment was stopped on August 23 and the account later debited on August 26.

Mr. Chauvin filed suit to recover $4,000.00 liquidated damages alleging that the deposit constitutes earnest money pursuant to a valid and enforceable contract to sell.[2] The trial court found in favor of Mr. Chauvin, awarding him $4,000.00 as a forfeit of the deposit. The court held:

> "The Parties confected an oral agreement which was reduced to writing as evidenced by the Defendant's check and deposit, which was deposited prior to the Plaintiff, Chauvin, being advised by the Defendant, Bohn, that the agreement for the purchase and sale of Plaintiff's home (No. 13

---

2. The concept of earnest money is found in C.C. 2463 [R.C.C. 2624]:
   "But if the promise to sell has been made with the giving of earnest, each of the contracting parties is at liberty to recede from the promise; to wit: he who has given the earnest, by forfeiting it; and he who has received it, by returning the double."

It is not necessary to give earnest in order to suspend the transfer of ownership. Rather, earnest money acts as a substitute for performance, allowing either party to withdraw from the contract upon forfeiting the earnest. Earnest money is most often seen in conjunction with a promise of sale, or contract to sell, where the buyer gives a deposit to the seller. The jurisprudence has adopted a rule that any payment made in connection with a contract to sell will be considered earnest money, unless the parties expressly provide otherwise. Smith, *An Analytical Discussion of the Promise of Sale and Related Subjects, Including Earnest Money*, 20 La.L.Rev. 522 (1960); Comment, *Deposits in Contracts to Sell Immovable Property in Louisiana*, 26 Tul.L.Rev. 498 (1952); See also, Hebert, *The Function of Earnest Money in the Civil Law of Sales*, 11 Loyola L.J. 121 (1930).

Weinning Drive, Willowdale Subdivision, St. Charles Parish, Louisiana, for and in consideration of the purchase price of $80,000.00) was being cancelled and awarding to John Kent Chauvin, the Plaintiff herein, the sum of $4,000.00 representing forfeiture of the deposit by C. Robert Bohn for breach of contract."

The judgment was affirmed on appeal. La. App., 400 So.2d 1205. Certiorari was granted to review the disposition of this matter by the lower courts.

A notation on the back of the check, put there by Mr. Bohn, the maker of the check and the prospective purchaser, lies at the center of this controversy:

C.C. 1798 [R.C.C. 1927] provides:

> "As there must be two parties at least to every contract, so there must be something proposed by one and accepted and agreed to by another to form the matter of such contract; the will of both parties must unite on the same point."

Once a contract is confected, each party confers on the other the right of judicial enforcement (See C.C. 1799 [No Corresponding Article]); however, the Code permits the offeror to withdraw the offer so long as the other party has not previously accepted. C.C. 1800 [No Corresponding Article] states:

> "The contract, consisting of a proposition and the consent to it, the agreement is incomplete until the acceptance of the person to whom it is proposed. If he, who proposes, should before that consent is given, change his intention on the subject, the concurrence of the two wills is wanting, and there is no contract."

A preliminary question raised by the facts is, if Mr. Bohn's execution and delivery of the check to Mr. Chauvin amounted to an offer to purchase the property, did Mr. Chauvin's endorsement and deposit of the instrument constitute a timely acceptance of the offer. Both lower courts made a factual determination that Mr. Chauvin deposited the check before Mr. Bohn withdrew his proposal by stopping payment on the instrument. (The check was probably deposited before Bohn's withdrawal from the transaction was communicated to Chauvin). The facts support this finding. Mr. Chauvin testified that he deposited the check on Thursday afternoon, August 19. Since the stop payment order was not issued until some time on Friday, August 20, as late as 2:00 p.m. according to the order itself, it is reasonable to conclude that the deposit preceded issuance of the stop payment order. Thus, if the means employed by Mr. Chauvin to accept the offer to buy satisfy the codal requirements, Mr. Bohn is bound; his attempted revocation came too late.

The court of appeal held that Mr. Chauvin reduced his oral acceptance to writing when he endorsed the check and deposited it. If the contract did not involve immovable property, the form of the acceptance would be less important. However, all contracts regarding transfers of immovables must be in writing. C.C. 2275 [R.C.C. 1839].[4]

In *Louisiana State Board of Education v. Lindsay*, 227 La. 553, 569, 79 So.2d 879, 885 (1955), this court held that an oral acceptance by telephone was insufficient under the mandate of C.C. 2275 [R.C.C. 1839]. The court stated:

> "It is manifest, therefore, that not only must an option to buy immovable property 'be evidenced by a written instrument' but the unqualified acceptance thereof be evidenced in writing, giving full rcognition (sic) to and in accordance with the terms and conditions of the proposal, and formally exercised and tendered to the proposer prior to the expiration of the stipulated time."

Perhaps if the prospective seller could produce a separate writing to evidence the contract between the parties, the insufficiency of the form of acceptance would not be determinative. Here, the mere endorsement and deposit of the check falls short of an "acceptance" of the offer to buy. Nothing in the words on the instrument denotes consent to a sale of the tract on certain terms. Both the offer and the acceptance, if the contract takes that form alone, must be in writing and must declare the parties' intent to be bound.[5]

---

4. Although C.C. 2275 [R.C.C. 1839] literally demands only that transfers of immovable property be in writing, the jurisprudence has construed the article to encompass all contracts concerning immovable property. *Torrey v. Simon-Torrey, Inc.*, 307 So.2d 569 (La.1974); *Little v. Haik*, 246 La. 121, 163 So.2d 558 (1964); *Louisiana State Board of Education v. Lindsay, infra*; *Hoth v. Schmidt*, 220 La. 249, 56 So.2d 412 (1951); *Fox v. Succession of Broussard*, 161 La. 949, 109 So. 773 (1926); see generally, *Comment, Writing Requirements and the Authentic Act in Louisiana Law: Civil Code Articles 2236, 2275 & 2278*, 35 LA.L.REV. 764 (1975).

5. In *Joseph v. Moreno*, 2 La. 460 (1831), the court held that a written promise to sell signed only by the vendor was valid and that acceptance by the vendee could be established by evidence extraneous to the written instrument. The same conclusion was reached in *Miller v. Miller*, 335 So. 2d 767 (La. App. 1976), *writ refused*, 338 So. 2d 927 (1976).

Saunders v. Bolden, 155 La. 136, 98 SO. 867 (1923) and *Succession of Jenkins*, 91 So. 2d 416 (La. App. 1956) have been misinterpreted. See 35 La.L.Rev. 764, 769. Both involved acts of sale, signed by the vendor and not by the vendee; in *Saunders*, the vendee went into possession and the deed was

C.C. 2462 [R.C.C. 2623] reads, in part, as follows:

> "A promise to sell, when there exists a reciprocal consent of both parties as to the thing, the price and terms, and which, if it relates to immovables, is in writing, so far amounts to a sale, as to give either party the right to enforce specific performance of same."

(The first paragraph of C.C. 2462 [R.C.C. 2620] treats a promise of sale, more commonly termed a contract to sell. It may be defined as an agreement to buy and sell where the parties anticipate a sale, but which is not yet a sale as it does not transfer ownership. Litvinoff, *Of the Promise of Sale and Contract to Sell*, 34 La.L.Rev. 1017, 1068 (1974)).

In *Klotz v. Gertrude Gardner, Inc.*, 293 So.2d 601 (La.App.1974), *writ refused*, 296 So.2d 831 (1974), a telegram was wired to the vendor which said: "Reference my offer to purchase 1019 Constantinople. Confirm my verbal agreement of 6 December, counteroffer of $35,000 accepted." The vendor had not signed an agreement to sell at this price. The court correctly held that no binding written contract to sell existed. See also, *Roy O. Martin Lumber Co. v. Saint Denis Securities Co.*, 225 La. 51, 72 So.2d 257 (1954); *Fleming v. Romero*, 342 So.2d 881 (La.App.1977), *writ refused*, 345 So.2d 50 (1977); *Manuel v. Moity*, 313 So.2d 278 (La.App.1975), *writ refused*, 318 So.2d 48 (1975).

Mr. Chauvin relies, as did the court of appeal, on the early decision in *Guice v. Mason*, 156 La. 201, 100 So. 397 (1924), to support the position that the check is adequate. In *Guice*, an oral agreement to sell an 80 acre tract for $400.00 was confected. As part payment, the vendee made a $100.00 payment to the vendor who gave the following receipt:

> "'Received of T.J. Guice, of DeSoto Parish, La., the sum of one hundred dollars ($100) in part payment of a certain 80-acre tract of land laying broadside with the 160-acre tract that he now lives on. This the 7th day of March, A.D., 1889. W. H. Mason.'" 156 La. at 204, 100 So. at 398.

The court noted that the vendor admitted (either in his answer or in testimony) that he sold the property to the vendee and that the vendee took possession of the property. Although the case was not decided on this point, the vendor was bound by virtue of his admission of the sale and delivery to the vendee, regardless of the language in the receipt. See C.C. 2275 [R.C.C. 2620].

The notation on the back of the check is insufficient to satisfy the codal requirements. It represented the prospective purchaser's conception of the transaction, and showed that the sum of $4,000.00 was subtracted from the total price, jotted down

---

held effective; in *Jenkins*, the deed included an act of assumption of a mortgage, was not signed by the vendee and was held not translative of title.

by the buyer. There is no dispute that the parties intended to wait until the attorneys could draft the necessary documents and take care of the details connected with the transaction. There is, however, nowhere on the document the words "I agree to sell" and "I agree to buy" or the equivalent. Language to this effect manifests the reciprocal consent of each party to be bound; it instills solemnity in the transaction and completes the proof. In essence, Mr. Chauvin asks the court to look at extrinsic evidence surrounding the giving of the check to establish the missing elements of a contract to sell. It is the writing and the words that are important in the sale of immovables, not extrinsic evidence.

> "Neither shall parol evidence be admitted against or beyond what is contained in the acts, nor on what may have been said before, or at the time of making them, or since." C.C. 2276 [R.C.C. 1848].

In light of the prohibition in this article, the court is constrained to an examination of the instrument itself; the words found there do not constitute a valid contract to sell.

For these reasons, the judgment appealed from is reversed and the suit dismissed at plaintiff's cost.

MARCUS and LEMMON, JJ., dissent and assign reasons.

MARCUS, Justice (dissenting).

I agree with the courts below that the writing on the back of the check was sufficient to satisfy the requirement that all offers to buy and sell real estate must be in writing and that Chauvin reduced his oral acceptance of Bohn's written offer to writing when he endorsed and deposited the check before Bohn communicated his desire to withdraw from the agreement. Hence, the $4,000 deposit on the purchase price of the home given by check by Bohn was earnest money and was forfeited by him when he receded from the promise to buy Chauvin's home. The courts below properly rendered judgment in Chauvin's favor for this amount. Accordingly, I respectfully dissent.

LEMMON, Justice, dissenting.

A valid contract to sell requires the thing, the price and the consent. C.C. Art. 2456, 2462 [R.C.C. 2456, 2620, 2623]. The thing to be sold and the selling price are clearly set forth in the contract itself (the check), and the buyer's consent is also evidenced on the instrument that he drew.[1]

---

1. The wording on the check, particularly the words "Deposit for 13 Weinning Dr." and "Selling price", clearly indicates the purchaser's consent to buy 13 Weinning Drive for a selling price of $80,000. Although the words "I agree to buy" do not appear anywhere on the instrument, that intent is made evident on the instrument itself.

It is only the seller's consent which is truly at issue.[2] The seller's taking possession of the instrument and his subsequently depositing it clearly evidenced his consent to sell No. 13 Weinning Drive to Bohn for a selling price of $80,000. No other reasonable explanation can be given for his action.

The lower courts correctly found the seller consented to the buyer's written offer prior to the withdrawal of that offer.[3] The judgments of the lower courts should be affirmed.

AFFIRMED.

b. The Property Description

The writing requirement for immovable property extends not only to the consent of the parties but also to the thing to be sold. That is, the parties' written agreement must include a description of the property conveyed. This description is often called a "legal" description of the property. The following materials address two important questions surrounding legal property descriptions: (1) how precisely must the property be described in the Act of Sale; and (2) what happens if the property description, although sufficiently detailed, contains an error?

i. Sufficiency of Descriptions

The question of whether a property description is sufficiently precise to support an enforceable contract of sale is not answered directly by the Civil Code. Instead, the standard for sufficiency of property descriptions has been developed by the jurisprudence. Before exploring that jurisprudence, it is useful to understand that, in Louisiana, land may be properly described in one of three ways: by reference to an official governmental survey, by "metes and bounds," or by reference to the map or plat of a subdivision. These methods of describing property are discussed in the excerpt that follows.

---

2. The buyer also contends that the contract was incomplete because no date was stated for the passing of the act of sale and no terms were given for payment of the amount of the selling price in excess of the deposit. However, the absence of these conditions of the sale does not detract from a conclusion that there was a consensual agreement to the thing and the price. When the parties consent to buy and to sell a certain thing for a certain price, the law presumes that the sale will take place within a reasonable time, and in the absence of a stipulation for terms of credit, the law presumes that the sale will be for cash.

3. The record supports the trial court's factual finding that the seller deposited the check prior to the buyer's withdrawal of the offer. Since it is not the function of this court to substitute its judgment for that of the trier of fact on factual findings which are supported by the record, I accept the fact that the seller's acceptance was made timely before the withdrawal.

1 Peter S. Title, *Louisiana Practice Series, Louisiana Real Estate Transactions* §§ 2:1–2:22 (2017–18 ed.)±

I. Land Descriptions

* * * * *

II. Kinds of Property Descriptions

§ 2.4 Overview

Descriptions of property in Louisiana may be by reference to official governmental surveys, metes and bounds or plats of subdivision. Legal descriptions often combine the three forms of descriptions.

§ 2.5 Governmental Surveys

Rural property is generally described by the rectangular United States Public Land System (USPLS) adopted by the federal surveyors in subdividing the Louisiana public lands in the early 1800's. By Act of Congress on March 2, 1805, two years following the Louisiana Purchase, the Surveyor General of the United States was directed to send surveyors of the United States to survey and subdivide the vacant public lands. The official government surveys resulting from those surveys create, and do not merely identify, the boundaries. Where public lands were disposed of by the government to the State of Louisiana or to private persons according to lines appearing on the official plat of government surveys approved by the Surveyor General, the location of the lines as shown on the official plat is controlling. *State v. Aucoin*, 206 La. 787, 20 So. 2d 136 (1944); *State v. Ward*, 314 So. 2d 383 (La. Ct. App. 3d Cir. 1975) (surveys of public lands).

§ 2.6 Governmental Surveys—The USPLS System or rectangular survey description

Louisiana, along with 29 other states, operates under the USPLS System. To subdivide land under that system, the surveyors established an initial point, a principal meridian, and a base line. The principal meridian runs north and south and the base line runs east and west through that initial point. Monuments were then set by the surveyor every six miles on the principal meridian and base line, north, south, east and west. The additional east-west lines that were monumented at six-mile intervals are called township lines. The additional north-south lines that were monumented at six-mile intervals are called range lines. Hence, townships are numbered north and south of the base line, and ranges are numbered east and west of the principal meridian.

§ 2.7 Governmental Surveys—Medians

There are two principal meridians in Louisiana, the 91st west of the Mississippi River and the 90th east of the Mississippi River, known as the St. Helena Meridian. There is one base line which crosses the State about its center.

± Reproduced with permission of Thomson Reuters.

§ 2.8 Governmental Surveys — Townships

Townships are numbered as tiers in rows running east to west, parallel to the base line and by ranges, numbered east or west of the principal meridian. Each township is 6 miles square or 36 square miles and consists of 36 sections, each section being 1 mile square and containing 640 acres. Commencing in the northeast corner of the township for the first section, sections are numbered from 1 to 36 in the following manner. Sections 1 to 6 from east to west; the northern boundary of section 7 adjoins the southern boundary of section 6; section 7 to 12 from west to east; section 13's northern boundary adjoins section 12's southern boundary; section 13 to section 18 from east to west; and so on. Some townships contain more than 36 sections because of radiating sections that border navigable waters.

Figure One is a diagram of an ideal township, which shows the configuration of 36 sections:

6 MILES

6	5	4	3	2	1
7	8	9	10	11	12
18	17	16	15	14	13
19	20	21	22	23	24
30	29	28	27	26	25
31	32	33	34	35	36

6 MILES

Each section is then subdivided by lines, known as quarter section lines, running north and south, and east and west; so that the section is divided into quarters; northeast quarter, northwest quarter, southeast quarter, and southwest quarter, each containing 160 acres. These quarter sections are further subdivided into quarters containing 1/16 of a section, 40 acres each.

Figure Two which follows shows the division of one of the sections (Section Four) into quarter sections and further subdivisions:

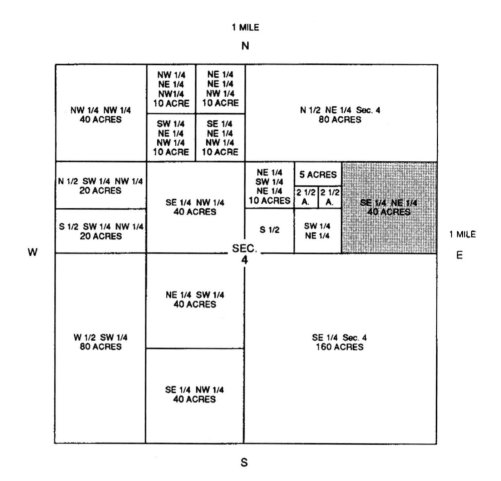

In Figure Two, the shaded area in the Section would be described as the SE ¼, NE ¼, Sec. 4, T.9S., R.3E.

The legal description using the USPLS system would also contain the parish and state.

*　*　*　*　*

§ 2.11 Metes and Bounds

Metes are lengths such as feet, yards and rods. Bounds are boundaries, either natural or artificial. A typical metes and bounds description draws a "picture" of the property beginning with reference to a public and recognizable point, known as the "commencing point." The description then expresses the distance from the commencing point to a point, the "point of beginning" of the parcel itself that is being described. The boundaries of the parcel are then outlined from the point of beginning by distances and often also by courses, or by reference to natural or artificial monuments. A "monument" is a physical structure which marks the location of a corner or other survey point. A "natural monument" is a natural object such as a lake, stream or stone. An "artificial monument" is a man-made object such as a street or surveyor's marker. Courses, also known as bearings or azimuths, are compass directions with reference to a meridian. Thus, a "metes and bounds" description describes a parcel of land by reference to courses and distances and/or by reference to natural or artificial monuments. Metes and bounds descriptions are often combined with descriptions referring to government surveys or to plats of subdivisions.

§ 2.12 Metes and Bounds — Closing the Land

The metes and bounds description must "close the land," i.e., the finishing point of the description must coincide with the point of beginning. If the finishing point of the description is not the point of beginning, the description is incomplete and is said "not to close" or called "not closed."

§ 2.13 Plats of subdivision

Common in urban areas is the description by reference to the plat of subdivision, by square (or block) and lot. Plats or maps of subdivisions are most commonly found in residential areas which have been subdivided by commercial developers, although platted subdivisions can be used in rural areas as well. *Banta v. Federal Land Bank of New Orleans*, 200 So. 2d 107 (La. Ct. App. 1st Cir. 1967).

§ 2.14 Plats of Subdivision — Sufficiency of Description by Square and Lot

When real estate has been platted by square (or block) and lot according to a recorded plat or map as used frequently in metropolitan areas, a description by square (or block) and lot followed by the subdivision is a sufficient legal description without combining a metes and bounds description of the lot, since a conveyance of land according to a recorded plat or map incorporates by reference all of the notes, lines, descriptions and landmarks of the plat. *Cragin v. Powell*, 128 U.S. 691, 9 S. Ct. 203, 32 L. Ed. 566 (1888). In the Parish of Orleans, the square and lot number must be provided in any notarial sales and mortgages. La. Rev. Stat. Ann. § 44:267.

§ 2.22 Buildings and Improvements

It is not necessary to include or refer to buildings or other improvements in a legal description of a tract of land, because they are included as component parts of the tract of land. As a matter of custom, however, many attorneys' legal descriptions include a phrase such as "together with all buildings and improvements thereon" as part of the legal description.

Notes and Questions

As a general rule, Louisiana courts do not require that a written Act of Sale contain a perfect legal description that meets every requirement of one of the types of descriptions discussed above. Instead, courts generally require that "[t]he description [of the immovable property] in a deed must be such that the property intended to be conveyed can be located and identified, and . . . that the description must fully appear within the four corners of the instrument itself, or that the deed should refer to some map, plat, or deed as a part of the description, so that the same may be clear." *Hargrove v. Hodge*, 121 So. 224, 225 (La. App. 2 Cir. 1928); *see also* LA. CIV. CODE art. 2440 cmt. b. How do the following cases aid in your understanding of the legal requirements for a sufficient property description?

Lemoine v. Lacour

34 So. 2d 392 (La. 1948)

HAMITER, Justice.

The main demand of plaintiff herein is for specific performance to compel the defendants to make formal conveyance of a one-acre parcel of land, with improvements thereon, located in Rapides Parish.

He alleges that defendants agreed verbally, during the first part of July, 1944, to sell the property to him for the sum of $350, payable in ten monthly installments of $35 each; that he made nine of the monthly payments, as is fully shown by the receipts therefor attached to the petition, and that the tenth payment, which was tendered to defendants but by them declined, has been deposited in the registry of the court; and that defendants have refused to give him a deed to the property, notwithstanding he has fully complied with the agreement.

Plaintiff prays that defendants be ordered and commanded to execute an appropriate deed. Alternatively, he asks judgment for all sums expended by him in connection with the property.

Defendants excepted to the petition as stating no cause of action. The exception was sustained by the district court, and the suit dismissed, as to the demand for specific performance; it was overruled as to the alternative or money demand. On appeal to the Court of Appeal the judgment was affirmed. The case is presently before us on a writ of certiorari or review granted on plaintiff's application.

The Court of Appeal, as well as the district court, correctly concluded that the petition in its present form states no cause of action. Plaintiff expressly alleges that the agreement of sale, under which he seeks specific performance was verbal. Civil Code Article 2440 [R.C.C. 2440], states:

> "All sales of immovable property shall be made by authentic act or under private signature.
>
> Except as provided in Article 2275 [R.C.C. 1839], every verbal sale of immovables shall be null, as well for third persons as for the contracting parties themselves, and the testimonial proof of it shall not be admitted."

And there is nothing in the petition to bring the case within the provisions of the referred to Civil Code Article 2275 [R.C.C. 1839] reading:

> "Every transfer of immovable property must be in writing; but if a verbal sale, or other disposition of such property, be made, it shall be good against

the vendor, as well as against the vendee, who confesses it when interrogated on oath, provided actual delivery has been made of the immovable property thus sold."

There are nine receipts, of course, attached to and made a part of the petition, which the to be considered in passing upon the exception of no cause of action. All of them are identical, except for their respective dates, and recite:

"Received from Mr. Clifton Lemoine $35.00 for payment on place.

W.L. Lacour

C.P. Lemoine."

Plaintiff's counsel contends that these receipts constitute written evidence of his contract of sale with the defendants and are sufficient to permit the introduction of parol testimony to identify the property. And in support of the contention he cites *Saunders v. Bolden*, 155 La. 136, 98 So. 867, *Guice et al. v. Mason et al.*, 156 La. 201, 100 So. 397, 398, and *Walker v. Ferchaud et al.*, 210 La. 283, 26 So.2d 746, 747. The cited cases are not appropriate here. In each of them the writing relied on contained a substantial description of the affected property. Thus in the Saunders case the property was described as the "Judie Lewis place." In *Guice v. Mason* the description was "a certain 80-acre tract of land laying broadside with the 160-acre tract that he [vendee] now lives on" (brackets ours). And in *Walker v. Ferchaud* the contract of sale made reference to "[]24 Stella Street, on grounds measuring about 60 × 150, as per title." In the instant case, however, each of the receipts merely evidences a "payment on place;" it contains no description whatever of any property.

There is applicable here, we think, the doctrine of *Kernan v. Baham*, 45 La.Ann. 799, 13 So. 155, which was followed in *Jackson v. Harris et al.*, Second Circuit, 18 La.App. 484, 136 So. 166, viz.:

"The writings which defendants present as establishing their title are not only insufficient per se for that purpose, but they are so defective as not to serve as a basis upon which a title could be built up or eked out by parol. The declaration that the promissory note was given as 'the price of certain lands in the parish of St. Tammany' is entirely too general to justify the admission of parol evidence to establish possession of particular property by the party named in the instrument as the vendee, and from such possession to assume or infer it to be that referred to in the writing. Parol evidence to establish identity is allowable, as is likewise parol evidence of possession, in aid of a defective or ambiguous description; but this is only in cases where there is a sufficient body in the description to leave the title substantially resting on writing, and not essentially on parol, as it would have to rest, if at all, in the case at bar. [45 La.Ann. 799, 13 So. 159.]"

But it is our opinion that the Court of Appeal, as well as the district court, after concluding that the petition stated no cause of action, should have granted to plaintiff (as he requested in the alternative) permission to supplement his pleadings and to interrogate defendants on oath regarding the verbal sale, pursuant to the provisions of Civil Code Article 2275 [R.C.C. 1839]. Plaintiff has already alleged that immediately after entering into the contract of sale he moved on to the property and that he has lived there continuously since that time. If he can show also that the defendants, in their answers to interrogatories on facts and articles, have confessed the existence of the asserted agreement, clearly his petition will state a cause of action.

Under our modern jurisprudence, in the interest of justice, the technical rules of pleading have been greatly relaxed, and a plaintiff now is accorded the privilege of amending his petition so as to state a cause of action if he can and thereby prevent the dismissal of his suit. *Drewett et al. v. Carnahan et al.*, 186 La. 243, 172 So. 6; *Pool v. Pool et al.*, La.App., First Circuit, 16 So.2d 132; and *Reagor v. First National Life Insurance Company*,—La.Sup.—, 33 So.2d 521, recently decided by this court and not yet reported in State Reports.

For the reasons assigned the judgments of the Court of Appeal and of the district court, which dismissed plaintiff's suit as to his demand for specific performance, are amended to the extent of reserving to plaintiff the right to supplement his pleadings in the manner above indicated so as to state a cause of action; and the case is remanded to the district court for further proceedings according to law and not inconsistent with the views herein expressed. If, however, the pleadings are not so supplemented within ninety days from the time this decree becomes final, the suit, as to the demand for specific performance, shall stand dismissed. The costs incurred in this court and in the Court of Appeal shall be paid by defendants. All other costs shall await the final determination of the litigation.

O'NIELL, C.J., absent.

City Bank and Trust of Shreveport v. Scott
575 So. 2d 872 (La. App. 2 Cir. 1991)

Marvin, Chief Judge.

In this appeal of a judgment rejecting the plaintiff-seller's demands for specific performance by the defendant-purchaser under a written "Real Estate Purchase Contract," the one issue framed by the litigants is whether parol evidence is admissible to establish the thing or object of the contract which was described only as "Auction Property # 137" and then as "Vacant Land 21 Acres." The auction brochure advertised the property only as:

Property # 137-Gilliam, Louisiana-Vacant Land 21 acres-call for directions.

We agree with the trial court that parol evidence was not admissible and affirm the judgment.

The law requires a sale or contract to sell immovable property to be in writing. Where the purchaser and the seller reciprocally consent in writing to the thing, the price and the terms under which immovable property shall be sold, either party may enforce specific performance. CC Art. 2462 [R.C.C. 2623].

When the law requires a contract to be in written form, the contract may not be proved by testimony . . . unless the written instrument has been destroyed, lost, or stolen. CC Art. 1832. Revision Comments—1984 state that Art. 1832 is new, but does not change the law, the principles and substance of which are derived from former CC Arts. 2275, 2278(4), 2279 and 2280.

This court has noted that there are cases in which parol or extrinsic evidence may be admitted to aid and identify immovable property described in a written contract to sell. Parol evidence has not been allowed, however, to wholly identify the immovable. Parol has been allowed only where the courts have found that there was "sufficient body" in the initial written description so as to leave the title to immovable property "resting substantially on writing and not essentially on parol." *Jackson v. Harris,* 18 La.App. 484, 136 So. 166, 169 (La.App. 2d Cir.1931).

The issue in *Jackson,* above cited, was whether parol was admissible. There Jackson gave Hale $600 for 40 acres in 1925 and obtained a written and signed receipt "in full payment of land ($600)" and went into possession. Parol evidence, which was objected to, showed that Jackson fenced and cultivated 11 acres and cut cross ties from timber on the remainder of the 40 acres from time to time for several years and, that during Hale's last illness, Hale told his niece, who had conveyed to him the land to sell to Jackson in 1925, that the property should not be included in Hale's estate in the event of his death. Hale died sometime before July 16, 1931, the date of the appellate opinion. In a slander of title action, Jackson sued Hale's heir who acquired the 40 acres in a partition of Hale's estate. The court noted:

> . . . [I]f the parol evidence is admissible . . . the plaintiff should recover; but if the evidence should have been excluded, and the plaintiff is left standing upon the naked receipt, we are of the opinion that his case must fall. 136 So. at 167.

The rule in Louisiana then, and now, was stated, citing *Kernan v. Baham,* 45 La.Ann. 799, 13 So. 155 (1893). The court noted that the *Kernan* rule "prevails, with slight modifications, throughout the United States." 136 So. at 168. We shall attempt to paraphrase the rule:

> To aid and establish identity of a defective or ambiguous description of an immovable property in a written contract, parol evidence is admissible only where the written, but defective, description distinguishes the property from other properties so as to allow the conclusion that the mutual or common intent of the parties to the writing was to deal with the particular property and not another property of the same kind or quantity.

> There should be sufficient substance in the written description in question so as to leave the title to the immovable resting substantially on the writing and not on parol.

Kernan, supra, held that the initial description of "certain lands in St. Tammany Parish sold [on March 20, 1848] by the Union Bank to [Baham]," was "too general" and "could not serve as a basis upon which a title could be built up or eked out by parol." 13 So. at 159.

Lemoine v. Lacour, 213 La. 109, 34 So.2d 392 (1948), reiterated the *Kernan* rule, finding that the writing,

Received from Mr. Clifton Lemoine $35.00 for payment on place,

was not a sufficient base upon which to admit parol to establish the identity of immovable property and to require specific performance of the alleged written contract. In *Langevin v. Howard*, 363 So.2d 1209 (La.App. 2d Cir.1978), writ denied, we ruled the written description "use of driveway" also an insufficient base to allow parol.

On the other hand, *Young v. Guess & Swanson*, 115 La. 230, 38 So. 975 (1905), held that the sale of "Dixie Sawmill," by its owners, initially "carelessly drawn" and described as:

One saw mill complete with all the attachments, . . . the lessee's right to all the land in which is owned or leased by the company, houses and lots, . . . altogether with shops and take all things owned by the Dixie Lumber Co., that is in operation at the above date[]

could be aided by "testimony . . . to show the intention of the parties . . . ." and that it "was proper to admit the testimony . . . to prove what property had been delivered to the buyer . . . to be descriptive of the property transferred." 38 So. at 976. The court found that four houses and 200 acres of timber were included in the sale and had been pointed out to and thereafter possessed by the purchaser, according to the extrinsic and testimonial evidence by one or more of the selling partners. 38 So. at 976-977.

In *Tullis v. Aertker*, 352 So.2d 415 (La.App. 3d Cir.1977), the court enforced specific performance on a 1963 written receipt for $100 "Down Payment House Esler Field, Bal 13 months @ $45.00, *Unpaid Balance* $6150.00, $55.00 Per Mo" where defendants placed and allowed plaintiff to remain in possession of the house and accepted $45 monthly payments from her for 12 years through November 1, 1955. Defendants contended on appeal that the receipt was ambiguous as to the sales price and method of payment and did not contain an adequate description of the property.

Where a defendant "confessed" the verbal sale to plaintiff of "five acres located in the SE corner of the SW quarter of the SW quarter, Section 27, Township 23 N, Range 9 W" and allowed plaintiff to go into possession in 1946, parol evidence was admitted to identify the five acres as being in the form of a square. Specific performance was ordered. *See Sexton v. Waggoner*, 66 So.2d 634 (La.App. 2d Cir.1953).

Similarly, these written descriptions have been held to be sufficient written bases upon which to allow parol to identify the immovable property:

124 Stella Street on grounds measuring 60 × 150, as per title. *Walker v. Ferchaud*, 210 La. 283, 26 So.2d 746 (1946), reversing the sustaining of exceptions of no cause of action and no right of action.

[mineral rights under] parcels of property in Sections 43, 52, 53, 27 and 28, T2SR5E, Parish of St. Helena. *Succession of Lindsey,* 477 So.2d 148 (La.App. 1st Cir.1985), upholding a "sharing agreement" of minerals underlying tracts of land partitioned in kind between co-owners.

This court in *Jackson,* discussed supra, expressly "felt," but declined to resort to equitable considerations which would benefit Jackson, explaining:

> [We] are not only constrained . . . by an established jurisprudence, but by the possible consequences of such a precedent. The rule that every transfer of immovable property must be in writing was established by the Legislature to prevent the perpetration of fraud. If it should be held that the identity of the immovable subject of a transfer might be wholly shown by extrinsic evidence, it would defeat the purpose of the statute and invite rather than avert fraudulent transactions involving real estate. The enforcement of the rule that there should be sufficient body in the description of the immovable property to leave the title resting substantially on writing and not essentially on parol may work a hardship occasionally, as in the instant case; nevertheless it is clearly our duty to enforce it.

This court held parol evidence was inadmissible. The trial court's judgment was reversed and judgment was rendered rejecting Jackson's demands. 136 So. at 168-169.

CONCLUSION

We hold the initial description in question here, vacant land, 21 acres, Gilliam, Louisiana, is too general and cannot serve as a base on which title to an immovable might be identified, "built up or eked out," by extrinsic and parol evidence. The Real Estate Purchase Contract upon which the plaintiff bank relies is not a sale or a contract to sell immovable property owned or used or occupied by a *named* thing, such as Dixie Sawmill in *Young v. Guess & Swanson,* supra.

DECREE

At appellant's cost, the judgment is AFFIRMED.

Notes and Questions

1. The phrase "eking out title by parol" describes the use of parol evidence to flesh out a property description that, while incomplete in some way, identifies the property with sufficient certainty to support a valid sale. When a property description is eked out by parol, testimonial and other evidence is taken by the court to determine the precise parameters of the property that the parties intended to convey. Was the description in *Lemoine v. Lacour* sufficient to support a sale if eked out by parol evidence? The description in *City Bank and Trust of Shreveport*? Why or why not?

2. Aside from any defect in the property description, is there another reason why the nine receipts introduced as evidence of the sale in *Lemoine* may not have been sufficient to satisfy the writing requirement for transfers of immovable property?

How, if at all, does this case differ from *Chauvin v. Bohn*, reproduced above in Subpart B.2.a?

3. Might a property description, although sufficient to support a sale *between the parties*, still be so incomplete that the writing in which it appears, though recorded, fails to have effects against third persons? The following two cases address the interaction of the writing requirement for transfers of immovables and the law of registry.

Williams v. Bowie Lumber Co.

38 So. 2d 729 (1948)

McCaleb, Justice.

Plaintiffs, claiming that, as descendants of one Francis Martin, they have inherited ownership of the N ½ of Sec. 17 T. 14 S., R. 8 E., Lafourche Parish, less 40 acres comprising the NW ¼ NW ¼ of that section, filed this suit to have their ownership recognized and the claims of the defendant denied. Proceeding under the provisions of Act No. 38 of 1908, they alleged that the tract is swamp land, not susceptible of actual physical possession; that the defendant, nonetheless, claims possession and that it is also asserting legal ownership under an act, dated November 5th 1900, wherein Francis Martin transferred certain properties to Robert H. Downman (defendant's author in title). In the alternative, it is averred that, should it be found that defendant is in actual possession of the land, petitioners assume the position of plaintiffs in a petitory action.

Defendant resists the demand on the ground (1) that the deed from Francis Martin to its grantor, Downman, conveyed title to the property in suit and (2) that, in any event, it has acquired the land by prescription as it has been in open and notorious possession of the premises since 1906, or for more than 30 years.

On the issues thus formed by the pleadings, the parties stipulated the facts. After a hearing, the trial judge sustained both contentions of the defendant and dismissed the suit. Plaintiffs have appealed.

The salient facts are not in dispute and may be stated as follows: Francis Martin, from whom plaintiffs inherited, was the owner of many large tracts of timberland in Lafourche Parish, including the property in controversy. In April 1900, Martin brought suit in the Federal Court against Robert H. Downman and others, alleging that the defendants had trespassed on his lands and appropriated the standing timber thereon. However, before trial of the case, an agreement of compromise was made whereby Martin promised to transfer all of his property in Lafourche Parish (excepting certain specific tracts not involved herein) for $100,000. Pursuant to this agreement, Martin sold and delivered to Downman by notarial act, dated November 5th 1900, a large quantity of land in Lafourche Parish (19 separate parcels) for the stated consideration of $100,000 and his additional agreement to dismiss the suit in the Federal Court and release Downman from any claims which he might have against him for trespass. The tract in controversy was not specially described in this sale. However, following a detailed description of the 19 tracts, the deed contained the following clause:

> "The vendor herein declares that it is his true intent and purpose to sell to the purchaser herein all the property owned by him in the Parish of Lafourche, except, however, the north half of southwest quarter of section fifteen township fourteen south of range seventeen east, and also such lands as he the vendor may own in section eight of township fourteen south of range seventeen east."

Soon after his purchase of the lands, Downman transferred to the defendant corporation. From its acquisition until 1907, defendant paid taxes on all of the lands including those in Section 17 which were erroneously described as the "NW ¼ of the NW ¼". In 1907, the description was corrected so as to properly designate the lands on the assessment rolls as the N ½ of Section 17. From that year on, or for a period of 41 years, defendant paid all taxes on the property.

Many other acts indicating possession of the lands in full ownership throughout the years have been shown by the defendant but it would be inutile to advert to this evidence since the view we take of the case makes it unnecessary that we pass upon defendant's plea of prescription of thirty years.

The main contention of the defendant is that the deed from Martin to Downman transferred the land in controversy, even though it was not particularly described therein, in view of Martin's expressed intention to convey "all of the property owned by him in the Parish of Lafourche" except certain described land in Section 15 and all land in Section 8.

We think that the point is well taken for the reason that, as between the parties to the contract and their privies, a sale of real property by an omnibus designation is just as effective and binding as though the lands were specifically described.

Under our law, the only prerequisite of form relative to the sale of an immovable is that it must be made by authentic act or under private signature. Article 2440 [R.C.C. 2440] of the Civil Code. As between the parties, the contract of sale is perfected when three circumstances, the thing, the price and the consent, concur. Article 2439 [R.C.C. 2439]. In the case at bar, all of the essentials appear, i.e., conveyance by Martin of all of the property owned by him in Lafourche Parish (with certain specified exceptions), the price and the consent of the vendor and vendee. And, since Martin's intent to convey everything he owned is clearly expressed in the deed, there is no reason to look beyond the four corners of the contract for interpretation. Article 1945 of the Civil Code [No Corresponding Article] provides that "Legal agreements having the effects of law upon the parties, none but the parties can abrogate or modify them" and that the intent "is to be determined by the words of the contract, when these are clear and explicit and lead to no absurd consequences."

Counsel for plaintiffs nevertheless maintain that the clause relied upon by defendant is meaningless and invalid because of the lack of a detailed description of the lands and that, therefore, it conveys absolutely nothing. In support of this proposition, reliance is placed in *Baldwin v. Arkansas-Louisiana Pipeline Co.*, 185 La. 1051, 171 So. 442; *McCluskey v. Meraux & Nunez*, La.App., 188 So. 669; *Cupples v. Harris*, 202 La. 336, 11 So.2d 609; *Snelling v. Adair*, 196 La. 624, 199 So. 782; *Reynaud v. Bullock*, 195 La. 86, 196 So. 29; *United Gas Public Service Co. v. Mitchell*, 188 La. 651, 177 So. 697 and *Daigle v. Calcasieu Nat. Bank*, 200 La. 1006, 9 So.2d 394, 395.

The adjudications depended on do not support the contention of counsel and are not applicable to the situation presented here. All of those cases involved the rights of third persons and they are authority only for the proposition that a sale with an omnibus description does not supply notice to third persons who acquire an adverse interest in the lands. This was clearly pointed out in *Daigle v. Calcasieu Nat. Bank*, supra, where we remarked that, whereas Articles 3306 [R.C.C. 3328] and 3307 [R.C.C. 3328] of the Civil Code require precise description as one of the essentials for the validity of a conventional mortgage, there is no specific article of the Code with such a prerequisite as to sales. But, after referring to Articles 2251 [R.S. 9:2741] and 2259 [R.S. 2749], dealing with the registry of authentic acts by notaries in the Parish of Orleans and those in other parishes, and many authorities, the Court resolved that, to bind third persons, the act must contain a description of the immovables and concluded thus:

> "It seems to be settled now by the jurisprudence in Louisiana that such a vague and indefinite description, in an instrument purporting to convey title to real estate, as all of the land owned by the seller in a named parish, *is not sufficiently specific to give notice to third parties thereafter dealing with the seller.*"

We did not say that such a description rendered the sale invalid as between the immediate parties thereto. On the contrary, we merely held that an omnibus description does not provide adequate notice to third parties.

The difference between the line of cases depended on by plaintiffs and a matter such as this was perceived by the Circuit Court of Appeals for the Fifth Circuit in *Saucier v. Crichton*, 147 F.2d 430, where Judge Lee, as organ of the court, correctly announced that the former are limited in their application to third parties subsequently dealing with the vendor.

Plaintiffs also contend that the only right which defendant acquired under the omnibus description was an action to reform the deed, or for specific performance, and they point out that it is now too late for defendant to pursue either one of these remedies as they are personal actions which prescribe in ten years under Article 3544 of the Civil Code [R.C.C. 3499]. Pursuant to this notion, counsel have filed in this court a plea of prescription.

These postulations are not tenable. Initially, it is not correct to say that defendant acquired only a right to reform the sale or to have a specific performance. Indeed, the act transferred title to Downman in accordance with the clear and expressed intent of Martin. True enough, defendant could have demanded from Martin a precise description of the tract to protect itself from claims of third persons and it would have been entitled to a reformation if Martin had refused the request. See *Daigle v. Calcasieu Nat. Bank, supra,* at page 1019 of 200 La., at page 394 of 9 So.2d. But the fact that defendant has not elected to so do cannot improve the claim of plaintiffs as it is clear that they have no title.

Nor can the lapse of time increase plaintiffs' rights. Defendant is neither attempting to reform the deed, nor is it seeking a specific performance of the contract. Its position is that Martin sold to Downman all of his lands in Lafourche Parish (except certain land specifically designated); that the effect of this deed was to transfer title to the property in controversy and that plaintiffs, as heirs of Martin standing in his shoes, are without right or interest to assert that the sale is invalid because the lands are not described in detail.

The judgment appealed from is affirmed.

Notes and Questions

1. *Williams v. Bowie Lumber Co.* addresses the effects of the so-called "omnibus" description of immovables. What, exactly, is an "omnibus" description and how does it differ from other legal descriptions of immovable property? Was the omnibus description in this case enforceable between the parties?

2. *Williams* stands for the proposition that an omnibus description is not sufficient to put third persons on notice of a sale. In other words, even if properly recorded in the public records, an Act of Sale containing only an omnibus description is not enforceable against third persons. The following case addresses the enforceability against third persons of a property description which, while not omnibus in nature, is incomplete.

Nitro Energy, L.L.C. v. Nelson Energy, Inc.
34 So. 3d 524 (La. App. 2 Cir. 2010)

LOLLEY, J.

Nelson Energy, Inc. and Richard B. Nelson ("appellants") appeal a judgment from the Second Judicial District Court, Claiborne Parish, Louisiana, which granted the motion for summary judgment in favor of Nitro Energy, L.L.C. and Donald Faust. For the following reasons, we affirm the trial court's judgment.

FACTS

The property at issue in this case is a portion of several tracts of land totaling 227 acres in Section 14, Township 19 North, Range 5 West (the "Swift Tract"). Although the parties are disputing that portion of the property that is located only in Claiborne Parish, some of the Swift Tract is also located in Lincoln Parish. The entire tract was identified initially in a deed dated August 26, 2002, from Emmett R. Woodard, Ann Woodard Windsor and Dell Woodard Nichols to Rickey K. Swift, Jeweline Malone Swift, Darren C. Swift and his wife, Cherrie Stallworth Smith (the

"Woodard deed"). The Woodard deed was properly recorded in the conveyance records of both Claiborne and Lincoln Parishes, as it pertained to property located in both parishes.

The appellant, Richard Nelson, obtained a mineral lease purporting to cover the entire Swift Tract on September 30, 2004, from each of the owners of the tract (the "Nelson Lease"). The Nelson Lease was recorded in Lincoln Parish on February 4, 2005. Although it purported to apply to all of the property in Lincoln and Claiborne parishes, Nelson did not record the Nelson Lease in Claiborne Parish, which he concedes was a mistake on his part. The Nelson Lease described the property affected by referring to the Woodard deed and included the Lincoln Parish recording information. The Claiborne Parish recording information was not referred to, and Nelson did not file the lease in the Claiborne Parish records until January 3, 2006.

On December 21, 2005, Donald Faust obtained a mineral lease covering the portions of the Swift Tract only in Claiborne Parish; however, only two of the landowners, Rickey Swift and Jeweline Swift, signed (the "Faust Lease"). Together, Rickey and Jeweline owned two-thirds of the Swift Tract. That lease was recorded in the Claiborne Parish public records on the same day. The Faust Lease contained the following property:

Section 14, Township 19 North, Range 5 West

A tract of land containing 227 acres, more or less, and being the same land described in that deed dated August 26, 2002 from Emmett R. Woodard et al [sic] to Rickey K. Swift, and recorded in Book 1136, Page 363 of the conveyance records of the Lincoln Parish, LA. It is the intention of the Grantors to convey all their interest in that land lying in Claiborne Parish, La. whether more particularly described or not.

The Faust Lease did not state that the property included lands in both Sections 11 and 14, Township 19 North, Range 5 West, because the Faust Lease only pertained to that part of the property in Claiborne Parish. Further, it did not refer to the Claiborne Parish conveyance book and page for the Woodard deed. Notably, on the day the Faust Lease was recorded, December 21, 2005, the Nelson Lease had not been recorded. As stated, the Nelson Lease was not recorded in the Claiborne Parish public records until January 3, 2006.

In 2008, Nitro Energy and Faust filed suit seeking (among other claims) a declaration from the trial court that the Faust Lease was the ranking and valid lease on the portion of the Swift Tract located in Claiborne Parish, Louisiana, as to the two-thirds ownership interest described in the Faust Lease. The parties filed cross motions for summary judgment, agreeing ultimately that there was no dispute regarding the material facts of the case. They also agreed that the sole issue in dispute was the sufficiency of the description contained in the Faust Lease. After a hearing on the matter, the trial court ruled in favor of Nitro Energy and Faust, and this appeal by Nelson Energy and Nelson ensued.

DISCUSSION

There is one issue on appeal: whether the property description stated in the Faust Lease is so inaccurate or faulty as to be actually misleading. Specifically, appellants urge that the Faust Lease contains several errors in the property description that are misleading and conflicting which would prevent a third party from identifying with certainty the property covered by the lease, so as to render the Faust Lease ineffective to third parties. Thus, we are called to determine whether the property description contained in the Faust Lease was sufficient to put third parties on notice. The parties agree that if it is, then the Faust Lease is the ranking and valid lease pertaining to that part of the Swift Tract located in Claiborne Parish.

As stated, the Faust Lease describes the property it intends to affect as follows:

Section 14, Township 19 North, Range 5 West

A tract of land containing 227 acres, more or less, and being the same land described in that deed dated August 26, 2002 from Emmett R. Woodard et al [sic] to Rickey K. Swift, *and recorded in Book 1136, Page 363 of the conveyance records of the Lincoln Parish, LA.* It is the intention of the Grantors to convey all their interest in that land lying in Claiborne Parish, La. whether more particularly described or not. (Emphasis added).

Primarily, it is the emphasized text that the appellants contend makes the property description misleading. We disagree.

* * * * *

Louisiana C.C. art. 3338 now states the public records doctrine under Louisiana law. It states, in pertinent part, as follows:

The rights and obligations established or created by the following written instruments are without effect as to a third person unless the instrument is registered by recording it in the appropriate mortgage or conveyance records pursuant to the provisions of this Title:

(1) An instrument that transfers an immovable or establishes a real right in or over an immovable.

A third person is a person who is not a party to or personally bound by an instrument. La. C.C. art. 3343. Thus, Faust is a third party as to the Nelson Lease and Nelson is a third party as to the Faust Lease. Further, as pointed out by Faust, mineral leases are classified as incorporeal immovable property, and as such, they are subject to the public records doctrine as provided in the Civil Code. La. R.S. 31:18.

The question in this case is whether the Faust Lease contained a sufficient property description as to put third parties on notice. Louisiana jurisprudence has not established precise criteria to determine what description in the public records is sufficient to place third persons on notice, and such determination is to be made on a case by case basis. *Santopadre v. Pelican Homestead and Sav. Ass'n*, 782 F.Supp. 1138 (E.D.La.1992); see also, 1 PETER S. TITLE, LOUISIANA PRACTICE SERIES, LOUISIANA REAL ESTATE TRANSACTIONS § 8:9 (2009). In fact, as long ago as 1872, in the case of *Consolidated Ass'n of Planters of Louisiana v. Mason*, 24 La. Ann. 518 (1872), the Louisiana Supreme Court recognized the impossibility of adopting a standard for distinguishing a description which would be sufficient from one which would not be sufficient, to put third parties on notice, noting that "[w]e are not prepared to fix the line between a valid and invalid or sufficient and insufficient description, which shall serve as a guide in all future cases. Each case must depend on its own circumstances." Notably, however, courts have been liberal in construing the description of property in deeds, so as to sustain, rather than defeat, the conveyance. *Emerson v. Cotton*, 209 La. 1003, 26 So.2d 16 (La.1946). We believe the same standard should hold true for the construction of property descriptions in other acts affecting immovable property as well.

In *Daigle v. Calcasieu Nat. Bank in Lake Charles*, 200 La. 1006, 9 So.2d 394 (La.1942), the supreme court determined that a vague and indefinite description, in an instrument purporting to convey title to real estate, as all of the land owned by the seller in a named parish, is not sufficiently specific to give notice to third parties thereafter dealing with the seller. In *Hargrove v. Hodge*, 9 La.App. 434, 121 So. 224, 225 (La.App. 2d Cir.1928), it was determined that the property description in the instrument must be such that the property intended to be conveyed could be located and identified, and the general rule is that the description must fully appear within the four corners of the instrument itself, or that the instrument should refer to some map, plat, or deed as a part of the description, so that the same may be clear.

We agree with the line of cases relied upon by Faust in support of his motion. Notably, it is well settled that a property description in a conveyance is sufficient if it makes reference to the vendor's deed of acquisition (as in the case at hand). *Lawler v. Bradford*, 113 La. 415, 37 So. 12 (La.1904). We also agree that the case, *H.J. Smith & Sons v. Baham*, 157 La. 524, 102 So. 657 (La.1925), is precisely on point. There, the supreme court deemed sufficient a property description that left blank the section and range that a portion of the property was located in but included information referring to the original acquisition of the property. 157 La. at 528, 102 So. at 658.

We believe the court's reasoning in *Baham* is persuasive here as well. In this case, the property is described by three identifying elements in the Faust Lease. First, it is described as being part of a 227 acre tract of land located in Section 14, Township 19 North, Range 5 West. Second, it is stated to be that part of the tract that is in Claiborne Parish only. Third, and finally, it identified as that tract of land that was conveyed by a deed dated August 26, 2002, from Woodard to Rickey K. Swift. The fact that the Faust Lease goes on to give the recordation information for the Woodard deed in Lincoln Parish is not misleading, i.e., it would not throw someone off the scent of tracking down the Woodard deed in the Claiborne Parish conveyance records, even though the recordation information was not applicable in Claiborne Parish.

The appellants' emphasis on the flaws in the Faust Lease are misdirected since the question is simply whether you can locate the property even with the flaws or the superfluous recordation information for Lincoln Parish. The most important directive included in the property description in the Faust Lease is that it makes an adequate reference to another recorded document that contains a metes and bounds description of the property. The fact that it gives the recordation information for Lincoln Parish rather than Claiborne Parish is immaterial, significantly because the description contained sufficient information for a third person to easily find the Woodard deed in the Claiborne Parish public records—where the entire metes and bounds description would be obtained. The names of the parties to the Woodard deed as well as the date of the instrument are sufficient for a third person to locate the instrument in the Claiborne Parish records. So considering, while not entirely and completely accurate in and of itself, the property in the Faust Lease is described with a degree of particularity as to leave no doubt as to the property intended to be affected. Thus, we conclude that the property description in the Faust Lease was sufficient to put third parties on notice as to which property was affected, and the trial court's judgment was not in error.

CONCLUSION

For the foregoing reasons, we conclude that the trial court properly granted the motion for summary judgement in favor of Nitro Energy, L.L.C. and Donald Faust. All costs of these proceedings are assessed to appellants.

AFFIRMED.

Notes and Questions

1. According to the court in *Nitro Energy*, "The most important directive included in the property description in the Faust Lease is that it makes an adequate reference to another recorded document that contains a metes and bounds description of the property." 34 So. 3d at 528. Incorporation by reference is a common means of describing real estate, particularly in sales of residential property, in which the parties will frequently describe the property in their initial purchase agreement (contract to sell) "as per deed."

2. The Louisiana Supreme Court recently cited *Nitro Energy* with approval. In *Quality Environmental Processes, Inc. v. I.P. Petroleum Co., Inc.*, a case involving the enforceability of a mineral servitude between the parties and against third persons, the Court stressed the "impossibility of adopting a standard for distinguishing a description that would be sufficient from one which would not be sufficient to put third parties on notice." 144 So. 3d 1011, 1020–21 (La. 2014). Reaffirming its view that such determinations must be made on a "case by case basis," the court also observed that "Louisiana courts have been liberal in construing the description of property in deeds, so as to sustain, rather than defeat, the conveyance." *Id.* at 1020.

ii. Reformation of Erroneous Property Descriptions

A description of immovable property, though facially sufficient to support a contract of sale, may not accurately reflect the parties' intentions. When this occurs, the rights and obligations of the parties are dictated by the law governing vices of consent, as the following case illustrates.

Mathews v. Emerson

141 So. 3d 346 (La. App. 2 Cir. 2014)

Brown, Chief Judge.

Plaintiff, Amanda Fontenot Mathews, brought this action to reform a cash sale deed to include a mineral reservation. Finding mutual error, the trial court reformed the cash sale deed to include a mineral reservation in favor of plaintiff. Defendant, Jennifer Lynn Emerson O'Brien Duke, has appealed. We affirm.

Facts

Amanda purchased a two-acre lot next to one owned by her mother in the Woolworth subdivision in DeSoto Parish, Louisiana. On February 20, 2004, plaintiff executed a mineral lease, with a no surface operations clause, with JPD Energy, Inc. A pooled unit was created, and producing wells were drilled in the unit at the Cotton Valley level. Amanda received royalties regularly which she used to pay her house note. Also, because she was at school, she rented the house.

In September of 2006, Amanda listed the property with Realty Executives and wrote on the listing agreement "mineral rights reserved." The official MLS listing showed that the mineral rights were to be reserved. Defendant purchased the property as her separate and paraphernal property on April 24, 2007. The deed made no mention of a mineral reservation. Prior to the purchase, plaintiff executed a "property disclosure document for residential real estate." This disclosure statement consisted of seven pages and included a paragraph with two check marks signifying "rights vested with others." An explanatory notation at the bottom of the page contained the writing "pipeline runs through property, mineral rights reserved-long term lease." On April 3, 2007, both plaintiff and defendant initialed the bottom of each page of the seven-page disclosure statement and signed on the last page. Thereafter, defendant's realtor drafted an offer, in the form of a buy/sell agreement, to purchase the property for less than the listed price. The property was listed for $125,000 with a mineral reservation. Defendant's offer was for $113,500. Defendant signed the offer on April 3, 2007, and Amanda accepted it on April 4, 2007. Although the buy/sell agreement did not mention a mineral reservation, it did contain wording that the "purchaser does acknowledge receipt of the seller's property condition statement." As stated, the disclosure statement included the wording "mineral rights reserved-long term lease."

At closing, plaintiff was presented with a cash sale deed drafted pursuant to defendant's realtor's instructions. Admittedly plaintiff did not read the deed; however, Amanda specifically asked whether her minerals were reserved. Her realtor and the closing agent (in brief defendant refers to a "closing attorney") assured plaintiff that the minerals were reserved. The closing agent/attorney did not testify at trial. At trial neither defendant nor defendant's realtor could remember whether the minerals were discussed.

Plaintiff's mother testified that she was involved in the process, except that she was not present when the deed was executed. She testified, as did plaintiff's realtor, that the minerals were to be reserved was clearly stated to everyone and that no one objected to or questioned this reservation.

For approximately two years after the sale, Amanda continued to receive the mineral royalties without resistance or objection from defendant. In her testimony, defendant indicated that she could see the wells from the back of her house. At no time, until after being contacted by plaintiff, did Jennifer assert ownership of the minerals.

In the summer of 2008, the Haynesville Shale came into play and issues arose concerning the deeper mineral rights below the Cotton Valley formation. At this time, plaintiff learned that the deed did not include a mineral reservation. Amanda and her mother contacted defendant by phone and informed defendant of the error. In that conversation Jennifer expressed concern about a possible right-of-access across the property. At trial Jennifer did not recall these conversations. Plaintiff sent a friend, Chris Procell, who was a landman, to speak with defendant to explain the process if access was sought. Procell also brought an act of correction concerning the minerals. According to Procell, Jennifer admitted that the minerals were to be reserved but this reservation did not get into the deed.

Defendant sent the document to her mother who worked for a law firm in New Orleans. After hearing from her mother, Jennifer refused to sign the act of correction and claimed ownership of the minerals. Plaintiff then filed suit seeking reformation of the deed. At the conclusion of trial, the district court took the matter under advisement and later issued a lengthy and well-reasoned written opinion. The trial court found that plaintiff met her burden of proving that mutual error existed between the two parties at the time the cash sale deed was executed. The court ruled that plaintiff was entitled to reform the deed to provide for a mineral reservation in her favor. Defendant filed this appeal.

Discussion

* * * * *

La. C.C. art. 1949 provides:

> Error vitiates consent only when it concerns a cause without which the obligation would not have been incurred and that cause was known or should have been known to the other party.

As reflected in our jurisprudence and codified in the 1984 Revision of the Civil Code's articles on Obligations, error, which vitiates consent, can manifest itself in two ways: mutually, i.e., both parties are mistaken, or unilaterally, i.e., only one party is mistaken. However, in both situations, the error for which relief may be granted must affect the cause of the obligation, and the other party must know or should have known "the matter affected by error was the cause of the obligation for the party in error; that is, that it was the reason he consented to bind himself." *See* Revision Comments (b) and (c) to La. C.C. art. 1949.

The granting of relief for error presents no problem when both parties are in error, that is, when the error is bilateral. When that is the case the contract may be rescinded. As an alternative, the instrument that contains the contract may be reformed in order to reflect the true intent of the parties. As observed by the supreme court in *Peironnet v. Matador Resources Co.* 12–2292, p. 13 (La.06/28/13), 2013 WL 3752474, 144 So.3d 791, 804:

> When a contract is reduced to writing, an error may occur in the drafting of the instrument so that the written text does not reflect the true intention of the parties. When such is the case, upon proof that the error is mutual, that is, that neither party intended the contract to be as reflected in the writing, the court may decree the reformation of the written instrument, rather than the rescission of the contract, so that the writing, once reformed, will express the parties' true intention.

> In the view expressed by Louisiana courts, an action to reform a written instrument is an equitable remedy, and it lies only to correct errors in a written instrument that does not express the true agreement of the parties....

> ...An action to reform a written instrument is a personal action, even when applied to real estate, and the burden of establishing the mutual error by clear and convincing proof rests on the party seeking reformation.

Litvinoff, *Vices of Consent, Error, Fraud, Duress and an Epilogue on Lesion,* 50 La.L.Rev. 1, 45–46 (1989) (footnotes omitted).

Unlike reformation, which is only available upon mutual error for the explicit purpose of reforming an instrument to reflect the true intent of both parties, rescission is a remedy available for both forms of error. *Peironnet, supra.* Our Civil Code specifically allows for rescission for unilateral error, providing the party who obtains rescission on grounds of his own error is liable for the loss thereby sustained by the other party unless the latter knew or should have known of the error. La. C.C. art. 1952.

In the case of an [sic] unilateral error, to determine whether to grant rescission, our courts have considered "whether the error was excusable or inexcusable, a distinction received by modern civilian doctrine," granting relief when error has been found excusable. *Peironnet, supra* at 14, 144 So.3d at 810; *Franklin v. Camterra Resources Partners, Inc.,* 48,021 (La.App.2d Cir.05/22/13), 123 So.3d 184.

This court concurs with the trial court's finding that plaintiff consistently expressed her intent to reserve the mineral rights. Evidence of this communication is contained in the MLS listing notifying potential buyers, as well as the property disclosure statement. Even the buy/sell agreement references the disclosure statement. The buy/sell agreement was a counteroffer dealing only with the price. The listing by plaintiff reflected a price for the property without the minerals. As the trial court stated, "It is noted that the final purchase price (allegedly with the minerals) was less than the asking price (without the minerals). In other words, defendant got more by paying less." The mineral reservation clearly concerned a cause without which the obligation would not have been incurred. La. C.C. art. 1949.

This case presented a factual question, i.e., was there mutual error? The trial court answered this affirmatively. The trial court found plaintiff and her witnesses to be credible, while it found defendant and defendant's realtor to be equivocal. The overwhelming evidence supports that conclusion. Plaintiff was a student, a single women [sic], who was receiving royalties from her minerals. She had no intention of giving up the minerals or the income derived therefrom. Defendant and her realtor clearly understood plaintiff's intent. Following the sale of the surface, plaintiff continued to receive the royalties for approximately two years uninterrupted and without objection by defendant, who knew that the wells were there and were producing. Defendant admitted as much to Procell.

The trial court wrote, "As noted above, the court finds that the evidence showed that neither Ms. Mathews [n]or Ms. Duke intended a mineral transfer . . . [A]s such, to deny reformation would be to deny the truth of the matter." This record contains a reasonable factual basis for the trial court's factual conclusions, which are neither clearly wrong nor manifestly erroneous. *See Guillory, supra; McGlothlin, supra.* Under the particular and unique circumstances of this case, we affirm.

Conclusion

For the reasons stated above, the trial court's judgment granting reformation of the cash sale deed is affirmed at defendant's cost.

MOORE, J., dissents with written reasons.

WILLIAMS, J., dissents for the reasons assigned by MOORE, J.

MOORE, J., dissents.

I respectfully dissent. I understand the equities of the case and this court's proclivity to restore as many mineral rights as possible to the people who owned them before the Haynesville Shale. The majority cites a portion of the supreme court's recent opinion, *Peironnet v. Matador Resources Co.,* 2012–2292 (La.6/28/13), 144 So.3d 791, for its discussion of rescission and reformation, drawn from Prof. Litvinoff's article. What the majority conspicuously omits, however, is that the high court's decree in *Peironnet* actually reversed another ruling of this court that found mutual error, and reinstated the district court's refusal to reform or rescind a mineral lease. Specifically, the supreme court rejected our theory that a party seeking to reform or rescind a contract need prove only that the other side "should have known" the plaintiff's intent. The burden of proof is actually *clear and convincing evidence. Id.* at 22, 144 So.3d at 809 (quoting Prof. Litvinoff). I do not agree that Ms. Mathews met this burden of proof.

The record amply shows that Ms. Mathews intended to reserve the mineral rights to this two-acre lot, that she discussed this with her realtor, Ms. Allen, and that the reservation was stated on internal MLS documents and the property disclosure executed by Ms. Mathews. However, Ms. Duke (through her realtor, Ms. Ratcliff) made an offer to purchase without reservation of minerals, and Ms. Mathews accepted, making no counteroffer. The buy/sell agreement, the sale-in-process checklist and, critically, the cash sale deed all totally omit the reservation of minerals. Ms. Mathews signed these documents without objection. Notably, this sale occurred in April 2007, before the March 2008 announcement of the Haynesville Shale play and the spike in mineral royalties. Ms. Mathews did not try to revive her reservation of mineral rights until early 2009.

The case is governed by the precepts reiterated in *Peironnet:* "The only error alleged is in signing a written contract without reading it, believing it to contain the terms of an agreement as he had understood them, which, in the absence of any charge or proof of fraud, force or improper influences upon the part of the other contracting party, is not an error from which the law will relieve him." *Id.* at 23–24, 144 So.3d at 810, quoting *Watson v. Planters' Bank of Tennessee,* 22 La.Ann. 14 (1870). "Courts will refuse rescission unless they can conclude that the error besides meeting the requirements already discussed, is also excusable, that is, that the party in error did not fail to take elementary precautions that would have avoided his falling into error, such as making certain that he was reasonably informed. Otherwise the error is regarded as inexcusable, in which case the party does not obtain relief." *Id.* at 24, 144 So.3d at 810, quoting Saúl Litvinoff, *Vices of Consent, Fraud, Duress and an Epilogue on Lesion,* 50 La. L.Rev. 1, 36 (1989). "The most fertile ground for the healthy growth of the notion of inexcusable error is the often-recurring situation where a party claims to have made an error that bears on a cause of his obligation but further explains that he omitted to read the writing to which the contract giving rise to that obligation was reduced. In such a context Louisiana courts have said that a party may not avoid the provisions of a written contract he signed but failed to read or have explained to him. That is so because, 'Signatures to obligations are not mere ornaments.'" *Id.* at 25, 144 So.3d at 811, quoting Litvinoff, *op. cit.,* 37 (internal citations omitted).

With due deference to the trial court's credibility calls and factual findings, this record does not prove, either by a preponderance or by clear and convincing evidence, that Ms. Mathews took the elementary precaution of reading the documents before she signed them, or of asking her realtor or the closing agent why they failed to reserve the minerals. Her error is inexcusable and does not support reformation of the sale. I would reverse and render, dismissing this claim.

Notes and Questions

Consider how the action for reformation of the deed differs from an action for rescission. According to the court in the foregoing case, the claimant must prove mutual error of the parties by clear and convincing evidence. In addition, an action for reformation of the deed is a personal action subject to a ten-year liberative prescription. *See* La. Civ. Code art. 3499; *Agurs v. Holt*, 95 So. 2d 644 (La. 1957).

c. Recitation of Price

La. Civ. Code arts. 1969, 1970

Unlike the property description, the price need not be recited in the written Act of Sale. *See Tremont Lumber Co. v. Powers & Critchett Lumber Co.*, 139 So. 12, 14 (La. 1932) (price recited as "$1 and other valuable considerations"). Parol evidence may be used to establish the true price if necessary. It is customary, however, for parties in Louisiana to recite the actual sales price in the Act of Sale. Those who wish to omit the sales price from the recorded instrument may execute an Acknowledgment of Sales Price, a notarized document that reflects the actual sales price and may serve as proof of the actual price paid. Consider why the parties to a sale would memorialize the price in a separate document in this manner? For one thing, if the Act of Sale recites a sales price of $1, the agreement on its face appears to be a donation under Article 2464. An Acknowledgment of Sales price (together with testimonial evidence) may be used to show that the parties' agreement was, in fact, a sale. *See* La. Civ. Code art. 1849. For another thing, an Act of Sale of an immovable reciting a sales price of $1 is subject to a claim by the seller for lesion. *See* La. Civ. Code art. 2589. The execution of a separate and contemporaneous agreement as to the actual price paid protects the buyer against such a claim.

Finally, note that filing an Act of Sale containing a misrepresentation as to the price paid may have other consequences for the parties. For example, the filing of a document "containing a false statement or false representation of a material fact" is a criminal offense, punishable by imprisonment for not more than five years or a fine of not more than five thousand dollars, or both. La. Rev. Stat. § 14:133.

Chapter 7

Effects of the Contract of Sale

A. General Principles

La. Civ. Code arts. 517–518, 2456, 2461–2462, 2467, 2477

Louisiana State Law Institute, Proposed Louisiana Civil Code Revision of Sales 7–8 (1992) (Exposé des Motifs)

Time of Transfer of Ownership

At Roman law, and under ancient French law, ownership was transferred upon delivery of the thing sold to the buyer. This approach was not followed by the Code Napoleon. Article 1583 of the French Civil Code, the source provision of Article 2456 of the Louisiana Civil Code, provides that ownership is transferred from the seller to the buyer upon consent alone, when there exists an agreement as to the thing and the price of the sale. *See* 2 Litvinoff, Obligations, 136 et seq. (1975). Revised Article 2456 preserves the principle that ownership is transferred by consent alone.

Time of Transfer of Risk

The rule that risk follows ownership, even in the absence of delivery of the thing sold, introduced into modern law by the Code Napoleon, was adopted by the common law and the Uniform Sales Act. This rule has been criticized on several counts, both in continental Europe and in the United States. The argument of the critics is basically two-fold: unfairness in the buyer's bearing the risk of loss of an object which he cannot control, and unpredictability of the moment when ownership is transferred in many practical situations. *See* 3 Mazeud, Lecons de droit civil, Vol. 2, pt. 1 at 173 (1979); White and Summers, Uniform Commercial Code 175-177 (2d ed. 1980).

The U.C.C. abandoned the approach of res perit domino in favor of an approach considered to be more in line with commercial expectations. Under the U.C.C. risk essentially follows possession and control over the thing, regardless of who is deemed to be the owner at the time of the loss. *See* U.C.C. ss 2-509, 510. Modern civil codes uniformly provide that the risk of loss is transferred to the buyer at the moment of delivery. *See* Article 522 of the Greek Civil Code and Article 2324 of the Civil Code of Ethiopia.

The first paragraph of revised Article 2467 follows the modern approach by providing that risk of loss or deterioration of the thing sold is transferred at the moment of delivery.

The second paragraph of that article also changes the law. It provides that, after delivery, risk of loss is transferred to the buyer even if the goods do not conform to the specifications of the contract, if the buyer does not act "in the manner required to dissolve the contract."

When the buyer receives nonconforming goods, if the nonconformity makes the goods unsatisfactory to him, he should promptly notify the seller of that fact. It is reasonable to assume that if the buyer does not seasonably move to either (1) have the contract rescinded, or (2) have the goods replaced by the seller, the goods delivered, though nonconforming, are nonetheless satisfactory to him. In such a situation, basic notions of fairness and good faith would seem to require that the buyer bear the risk of loss or deterioration of the thing sold caused by a fortuitous event. *See* C.C. Arts. 1759, 1983 (rev. 1984).

Notes and Questions

1. Between the parties to the sale, ownership is transferred between the parties as soon as there is agreement on the thing and the price is fixed — even though the thing sold is not delivered nor the price paid. La. Civ. Code art. 2456. Recall, however that the parties' consent does not effectuate a transfer of ownership vis-à-vis third persons. With respect to movables, the transfer of ownership is not effective against third persons until the thing sold is delivered to the buyer. *See* La. Civ. Code art. 518. With respect to immovables, the transfer of ownership is not effective against third persons until the instrument evidencing the sale is filed for registry. *See* La. Civ. Code arts. 517, 2342, 3338.

2. As the foregoing excerpt explains, the rule of *res perit domino* has been abandoned in favor of a more practical rule governing the transfer of the risk of loss owing to a fortuitous event. How, under current law, are the following hypotheticals to be resolved? How would these hypotheticals have been resolved under prior law?

   i. Buyer, a textile manufacturer in New Orleans, purchases cotton from Seller, a farmer in Shreveport. Buyer and Seller verbally agree to a sale of 100 bales of cotton for a total price of $1,000. The parties further agree that Seller will deliver the cotton to Buyer's warehouse in New Orleans the following week. Before Seller delivers the cotton, a fire breaks out in Seller's warehouse and destroys the cotton. Must Buyer pay the price for the cotton, or is Buyer relieved from paying?

   ii. Buyer agrees to purchase Seller's home. On August 1, Buyer and Seller execute a written Act of Sale, valid in form. On August 5, before Buyer moves into the home, the home is completely destroyed by a fire. Must Buyer pay the price for the home, or is Buyer relieved from paying? *Hint:* consider the effect of Article 2477.

3. Note that "[t]he sale of a thing includes all accessories intended for its use in accordance with the law of property." La. Civ. Code art. 2461. Consider the meaning of the term "accessories" in Article 2461. The law of property dictates that for

movables, "an accessory is a corporeal movable that serves the use, ornament, or complement of the principal thing." La. Civ. Code art. 508. For immovables and for movable constructions permanently attached to the ground, accessories are the component parts of the thing sold. La. Civ. Code arts. 469, 508. In addition, in sales of immovable property, this includes predial servitudes, La. Civ. Code art. 650, and real rights, as well as mineral rights, unless expressly reserved. *Texaco, Inc. v. Newton and Rosa Smith Charitable Trust*, 471 So. 2d 877, 882 (La. App. 2 Cir. 1985). By contrast, the term "accessories" does not include the personal rights of the seller, which are never considered accessories of an immovable. Thus, a purchaser has no right to recover from a lessee for property damage sustained before the sale. *See Prados v. South Central Bell Telephone Co.*, 329 So. 2d 744 (La. 1976). For the personal rights of the seller to transfer to the buyer, a specific assignment of those rights is required.

4. According to Article 2463, "The expenses of the act and other expenses incidental to the sale must be borne by the buyer." La. Civ. Code art. 2463. This rule is suppletive in nature; thus, it may be altered by the agreement of the parties. *Id.* cmt. b.

B. Exceptions to the General Rules

Although as a general rule ownership of the thing sold transfers upon the parties' consent to the sale, and risk of loss transfers upon delivery to the buyer, these general rules admit numerous exceptions and variations. In some cases, ownership cannot transfer upon the mere consent of the parties because of indeterminacy as to which of multiple identical items belonging to the seller is the object of the sale, or because of indeterminacy of the price. These problems are treated in Subpart 1, "Things Not Individualized." In other cases, complexities introduced by the fact that the parties to the sale are contracting at a distance from one another and with the assistance of a common carrier require adaptation of the general rules. These variations are the subject of Subpart 2, "Things in Transit." In addition, the operation of conditions imposed upon the sale by the parties' agreement may affect the timing or even permanence of the transfer of ownership and risk of loss. These problems are addressed in Subpart 3, "Sales Subject to Conditions." Finally, a special class of sale in which the transfer of ownership is conditioned upon the buyer's payment of the price poses particular challenges for the application of the general rules. Those sales are discussed in Subpart 4, "Sales Conditioned on Payment of Price (a/k/a 'Common Law' Conditional Sales)."

1. Things Not Individualized
La. Civ. Code arts. 2457–2458

While the general rule is that ownership transfers from the buyer to the seller once there is agreement upon thing and price, this rule admits of a number of exceptions. In some cases, mere agreement as to thing and price does not suffice; instead, additional steps must be taken by the parties to complete the transfer of ownership. One case in which such additional steps are required is when the object of a sale is a thing that is not "individualized."

a. The Problem of Individualization

If the thing being sold "must be individualized from a mass of things of the same kind," then the general rules governing the transfer of ownership and risk do not apply. LA. CIV. CODE art. 2457. Instead, "ownership is transferred when the thing is thus individualized according to the intention of the parties." *Id*. When must a thing sold be individualized from a mass of things of the same kind? Consider the following hypothetical: Seller and Buyer agree over the telephone to a sale of 20 chairs for a price of $100.00 per chair. Seller, being a retailer of chairs, owns hundreds of identical chairs, all of which are stored in a warehouse. When the parties agree as to the object of the sale (20 chairs) and the price ($100.00 per chair), has ownership of the chairs transferred? The answer is "no." Given these facts, it is impossible to know which of Seller's chairs belong to the buyer at the time of the parties' consent. It is only after 20 chairs are "individualized"—i.e., separated out from the mass of identical chairs and identified as the object of the sale—that a transfer of ownership may take place.

Before proceeding further into the meaning of the term "individualization," it is necessary to make one thing clear—once there is agreement on thing and price, an enforceable contract of sale exists. The fact that ownership has not yet transferred to the buyer does not prevent either of the parties from enforcing the terms of the agreement. In the above hypothetical, prior to individualization Seller may not refuse to honor the contract. Instead, Seller is obligated to individualize 20 chairs from his inventory, and Buyer may seek specific performance of the contract if Seller refuses. In common law terms, prior to individualization, the contract of sale is "executory"—meaning that either party can compel the other to execute the bargain.

b. Appropriation

As discussed, Article 2457 requires the seller to individualize the thing sold in certain sales. But how does a seller do that? What does it mean to "individualize"? Prior to the 1995 sales revision, Louisiana courts used a concept termed "appropriation" to describe the act required for individualization to be complete. Appropriation involved something other than merely segregating the object of the thing sold from a mass of identical things. According to one commentator summarizing the jurisprudence, for appropriation to occur, "there must be some act by the vendor isolating the goods from a general mass which involves an element of irrevocability, so that he no longer has complete control over the destination of the goods." Charles S. Weems, Jr., *Passage of Title and Risk of Loss Under the U.C.C. and Louisiana Law*, 27 LA. L. REV. 299, 300 (1967). Said another way, when the object of a sale is a thing that must be individualized from a mass of things of the same kind, it must also be set aside for the buyer in such a way that the seller has lost dominion over it. Although Article 2457 speaks in terms of "individualization" rather than "appropriation," the article codifies the prevision jurisprudence. *See* La. Civ. Code art. 2457 cmts. a, b. In sum, under current law, appropriation is still the means by which the seller individualizes the thing sold.

At the very latest, the seller loses dominion over the thing sold when it is delivered to the buyer. However, delivery to the buyer is not the only way by which appropriation takes place. Two examples drawn from the jurisprudence may assist in clarifying the concept of appropriation. According to *George D. Witt Shoe Co. v. J.A. Seegars & Co.*, 47 So. 444 (La. 1908), appropriation may take place in a sale in which the parties are at a distance from one another when the thing sold is delivered to a common carrier. In that case, a purchaser of shoes (located in Louisiana) placed an order from a manufacturer (located in Virginia). A dispute arose between the parties when the buyer failed to pay the price, and the central issue on appeal was whether Louisiana law or the law of another state governed the parties' agreement. Under the choice of law rules in effect at the time, the issue turned, in part, on whether ownership of the shoes transferred in Virginia or in Louisiana. In its resolution of the issue, the Court held: "[I]n the absence of a more specific agreement on the subject . . . appropriation takes place only when the goods as ordered are delivered to the public carriers at the place from which they are to be shipped, consigned to the person by whom the order is given, at which time and place, therefore, the sale is perfected and title passes." *Id.* at 446. As this case illustrates, delivery to a carrier results in appropriation when the thing sold is "consigned to" the buyer. The notion of consigning movable things to the buyer in contracts involving common carriers is addressed in detail in Part C below; it is sufficient to note here that by consigning goods to the buyer, the seller relinquishes any control over them from the point of delivery to the carrier.

In a later case the Louisiana Supreme Court clarified that appropriation may take place even prior to delivery to a carrier, provided the thing sold is identified as the property of the buyer. *Edgwood Co. v. Falkenhagen*, 92 So. 703, 703 (La. 1922) involved the sale of 20 barrels of whiskey. After receiving the buyer's order, the seller filled the barrels, prepared them for shipment, and marked them with the buyer's name and address. Before the barrels were shipped, a dispute arose between the parties. Holding that ownership of the whiskey had transferred to the buyer despite the fact that the barrels never left the seller's warehouse, the court held, "Any act indicating a definite intention to appropriate the goods to the contract is sufficient, such as setting apart and marking the goods for the buyer." *Id.*

c. Sales by Weight, Tale, or Measure or by Lump

While Article 2457 requires "individualization" as a prerequisite for the transfer of ownership when the thing sold is one of multiple identical items, Article 2458 sets forth guidance regarding the transfer of ownership of things that are sold "by weight, tale, or measure" and things that are sold "in a lump." La. Civ. Code art. 2458. With regard to the former, "ownership is transferred between the parties when the seller, with the buyer's consent, weighs, counts, or measures the things." *Id.* With regard to the latter, "ownership is transferred between the parties upon their consent, even though the things are not yet weighed, counted, or measured." *Id.* The following case elaborates upon the distinction between these two types of sales.

Gulf Rice Milling, Inc. v. Sonnier

930 So. 2d 256 (La. App. 3 Cir. 2006)

Sullivan, Judge.

Gulf Rice Milling, Inc. appeals a jury verdict in favor of Richard Sonnier, a rice farmer in Jefferson Davis Parish, Louisiana, in which the jury determined that Mr. Sonnier did not breach a contract with Gulf Rice Milling, Inc. and awarded Mr. Sonnier damages for its wrongful seizure of his property. For the following reasons, we affirm.

Facts

In November 2003, Gulf Rice Milling, Inc. (Gulf Rice) contacted Mark Tall, a broker with Louisiana Farm Bureau Marketing, seeking to purchase rice. Mr. Tall contacted area farmers and notified them of Gulf Rice's interest in buying rice at $14.00 per barrel. Mr. Sonnier submitted a sample of his rice to Mr. Tall. After the rice was tested, Gulf Rice told Mr. Tall it would purchase Mr. Sonnier's rice. A written confirmation was prepared by Mr. Tall and submitted to Gulf Rice which specified that Gulf Rice would pay $14.00 per barrel and that Gulf Rice would pick up Mr. Sonnier's rice by March 15, 2004.

All rice purchased by Gulf Rice must go through a receiving pit. In February 2004, Gulf Rice experienced a problem with its receiving pit, which took eight days to resolve. As a result, it got behind in its shipping schedule. Mr. Tall testified that he was led to believe Gulf Rice was attempting to pick up the rice by March 15. He also testified that he asked Jay Putt, Gulf Rice's Director of Operations, about paying a storage fee to farmers whose rice was not picked up by March 15. As late as March 15, 2004, Mr. Putt told Mr. Tall that Gulf Rice would not pay storage fees for rice that it did not pick up by that day.

Mr. Sonnier called Mr. Tall in the afternoon of March 15 asking about Gulf Rice picking up his rice. He told Mr. Tall Gulf Rice had until 5:00 p.m. to pick up the rice or "it's mine." Mr. Tall relayed Mr. Sonnier's message to Mr. Putt. Mr. Sonnier testified that he was never told that Gulf Rice would have a problem picking up his rice. Mr. Tall corroborated this testimony, testifying that he only told Mr. Sonnier that Gulf Rice had a problem at the mill, not that it would be late picking up his rice because he did not know himself that Gulf Rice would not pick up his rice as per the confirmation sheet. Mr. Tall also testified that Gulf Rice did not agree to pay storage until after March 15 and that Mr. Putt told him it would only pay storage if asked.

On March 16, Mr. Sonnier contacted another mill about selling his rice. That mill bought his rice on March 22 and began picking it up on March 24. On March 24, Gulf Rice sent a shipping schedule to Mr. Tall which outlined the dates on which it was going to pick up the rice it was to have picked up March 15.

On April 7, 2004, Gulf Rice filed a Petition for Specific Performance and, in the alternative, for Damages and Writ of Sequestration, alleging that it owned the rice stored in bins at Mr. Sonnier's farm. A writ of sequestration issued, sequestering Mr. Sonnier's rice. Thereafter, Gulf Rice also obtained a writ of sequestration, sequestering $100,552.58 in the possession of the mill that bought Mr. Sonnier's rice, which represented the proceeds of Mr. Sonnier's rice the mill had already picked up.

Mr. Sonnier answered Gulf Rice's petition, admitting that he had agreed to sell his rice to Gulf Rice. However, he also asserted that the sale was never completed because Gulf Rice did not pick up his rice by March 15 and had not weighed or tested the rice. He reconvened against Gulf Rice, seeking damages for wrongful sequestration of his rice and money. Mr. Sonnier also asserted a claim for attorney fees.

After a hearing held on May 25, 2004, the trial court issued an order dissolving the writs of sequestration and awarding Mr. Sonnier $1,500.00 in attorney fees for having to obtain a dissolution of the writs of sequestration. On June 17, 2004, Mr. Sonnier received a check from the Jefferson Davis Parish Clerk of Court in the amount of $100,591.81, which represented the sequestered funds plus accrued interest.

The remaining claims were tried before a jury on April 25 and 26, 2005. The jury denied Gulf Rice's breach of contract claim against Mr. Sonnier and awarded Mr. Sonnier $100,000.00 in damages for Gulf Rice's wrongful seizure of his rice and his money.

Gulf Rice appealed, asserting it bought Mr. Sonnier's rice in November 2003. Mr. Sonnier answered Gulf Rice's appeal, urging he is entitled to attorney fees for the work performed by his attorney preparing for and representing him at the trial and on this appeal.

Sale or Promise to Sell

Gulf Rice contends it became the owner of Mr. Sonnier's rice in November 2003. The Civil Code provides that a "[s]ale is a contract whereby a person transfers ownership of a thing to another for a price in money. The thing, the price, and the consent of the parties are requirements for the perfection of a sale." La.Civ.Code art. 2439. The Civil Code further provides that ownership of the thing purchased is "transferred between the parties as soon as there is agreement on the thing and the price is fixed, even though the thing sold is not yet delivered nor the price paid." La. Civ.Code art. 2456. Gulf Rice contends its agreement with Mr. Sonnier satisfies the requirements of Article 2456; therefore, ownership of the rice transferred to it when their agreement was confirmed in November 2003.

Mr. Sonnier contends he did not sell his rice to Gulf Rice.

* * * * *

Mr. Sonnier also argues that the sale was never completed because a price for his rice was never fixed as required by Article 2456 and because his rice was never weighed as required by La.Civ.Code art. 2458, which provides:

> When things are sold by weight, tale, or measure, ownership is transferred between the parties when the seller, with the buyer's consent, weighs, counts or measures the things.
>
> When things, such as goods or produce, are sold in a lump, ownership is transferred between the parties upon their consent, even though the things are not yet weighed, counted, or measured.

Mr. Putt testified that the price a mill will pay for rice is not established until the rice is in the mill's possession and is milled. Milling determines the total rice yield. Mr. Putt explained that milling 100 pounds of rough rice results in 20% rice hulls and ten percent rice bran; the remaining 70% is the total yield. The rice is also sampled and tested to determine its actual grade. Mr. Putt explained that the price to be paid goes up or down as a result of milling and testing. The confirmation sheet establishes that staining also affects the price of the rice, as it provides that one lot of Mr. Sonnier's rice would be discounted $.30 because of stain. After milling and sampling, the rice is then weighed to determine the settling price, the amount to be paid to the farmer.

In *Kohler v. Huth Const. Co.*, 168 La. 827, 123 So. 588 (1929), the supreme court was presented with a situation almost identical to this one. The court determined that a sale of coal at $8.00 per ton was not complete when the barge on which the coal was deposited sank before the coal was weighed. In reaching this determination, the supreme court explained:

> The written contract fixed the price at $8 per ton, and the plaintiff testified that the stuff had to be counted, the tools counted, and the coal measured, and everything checked up. He also testified that the coal at Baton Rouge was never measured or weighed after the defendant agreed to buy.
>
> The Civil Code, art. 2458, declares that, when goods, produce, or other objects are not sold in a lump, but by weight, by tale, or by measure, the sale is not perfect, inasmuch as the things so sold are at the risk of the seller until they be weighed, counted, or measured.
>
> But where the goods, etc., have been sold in a lump, the sale is perfect, though these objects may not have been weighed, counted, or measured. Civ.Code [] art. 2459.
>
> The case here falls squarely under the first article quoted. The coal was not sold in a lump at a price for the whole, but the quantity sold was to be determined by weight or measure, and the price was to be $8 per ton for whatever was found to be on hand.
>
> There was no agreement as to the amount of the coal, and there could be no definite agreement as to the price the defendant would owe the plaintiff

until the coal was measured. Hence the sale was not perfect, because two essential things were lacking—the agreement as to the amount of coal the defendant was to get, and the total price that would be due plaintiff.

Id. at 829–30, 123 So. at 589. The same is true here: the rice had to be weighed, milled, and tested before the final price Gulf Rice would pay Mr. Sonnier was determined.

Gulf Rice argues an earlier supreme court decision, *Penick & Ford v. Waguespack & Haydel*, 148 La. 39, 86 So. 605 (1920), conflicts with *Kohler* and should be applied. The supreme court in *Kohler* refused to follow the court's decision in *Penick*, explaining:

> The court held the contract to be a sale which vested the ownership of the molasses in the plaintiff. The reason given by the court for so holding was that a definite method of determining the exact quantity was fixed by the parties.
>
> It will be observed, however, that the question as to whether the contract of sale was by lump or by tale and measure was not an issue. The case went off in the lower court on an exception of no cause of action, on the theory that defendant was required to deliver only such molasses as the plaintiff requested and for which tank cars were furnished.

Kohler, 168 La. at 830–31, 123 So. at 589. However, the supreme court continued, stating:

> The molasses contract was clearly a sale, in the sense that the plaintiff had a right to compel specific performance, or to sue for damages for the breach of the contract.
>
> And that would be true in this case if the plaintiff had sold his coal to another person and the defendant had been forced to buy coal at a higher price than $8 per ton. In a suit for the difference in price, the court, following the molasses case, would probably have held the contract to be a sale.
>
> The difference between the two cases is obvious.

Id. at 831, 123 So. at 589. We disagree with this reasoning, as the determination of whether or not a sale has occurred is determined by the facts surrounding the transaction, not the relief a party to the transaction seeks.

As noted by the supreme court in *Kohler*, the case was decided on an exception of no cause of action, not on the merits. Additionally, two justices dissented in *Penick*, 148 La. 39, 86 So. 605. Justice O'Neill observed that the decision in *Penick* was in direct conflict with Article 2458 and the decision in *Peterkin v. Martin*, 30 La.Ann. 894 (La.1878). In *Peterkin*, the issue was which party bore the risk of damage to the corn grown by the defendant. The defendant contended that he had sold "all the mixed corn he had in the elevator, being six, seven or eight thousand bushels" at sixty-five cents per bushel because it was a "determined lot" and that the corn was at the risk of the purchaser when it was damaged by heat in storage bins. *Id.* at 895. The court, citing Article 2458, disagreed, explaining:

We apprehend that in a case like this (admitting, for the sake of the argument, it was a purchase of all the mixed corn of Martin in the elevator, though Peterkin seems to deny this), where the quantity was stated between six and eight thousand bushels, at sixty-five cents per bushel, the price was not agreed upon and ascertained in the sense of article 2456. . . . We think the rule of article 2458 governs this case. That by the very terms of that article a sale "by weight, tale, or measure," is not a sale "in lump." We agree with plaintiff's counsel that there can be no sale in lump, except for a lumping price. . . . Nothing short of an express agreement, in a case like this, will put the thing before it is weighed at the risk of the buyer.

Id. at 895–96. The court ultimately concluded that "the sale was not perfect until the weighing and delivery" of the corn. *Id.* at 896.

The evidence established the strong similarities between *Kohler*, *Peterkin*, and this case. Mr. Putt's testimony established that determination of a final price for the rice was not be determined until after milling, testing, and weighing. We find the decisions in *Kohler* and *Peterkin* more accurate interpretations of Article 2458, than the decision in *Penick*. Applying Article 2458 and the rationale of *Kohler* and *Peterkin* to the facts of this case, we find no error with the jury's determination that Mr. Sonnier did not breach a contract with Gulf Rice.

* * * * *

Disposition

The judgment is affirmed. Costs are assessed to Gulf Rice Milling, Inc.

AFFIRMED.

Notes and Questions

1. Article 2458 sets forth two distinct rules: one for sales by weight, tale [number], or measure, and another for sales of things "sold as a lump." LA. CIV. CODE art. 2458. In sales of things "sold in a lump," the general rule for transfer of ownership applies—that is, ownership is transferred upon the parties' consent as to thing and price. Do you see why?

2. Consider what it means, exactly, for things to be "sold as a lump." First, and perhaps most obviously, the object of the sale must be a lump thing—that is, an identifiable body of fungible things (i.e., an entire crop of oranges, a train car full of rice, etc.). Although the parties may not yet know the precise weight, number, or measure of the items contained within the identifiable body, their intention in this type of sale is to transfer the entirety. Note that the parties may contemplate that the identifiable body of things that will be delivered by the seller will contain a certain weight, count, or measure of goods (i.e., an entire crop of oranges to include at least 40 tons of oranges). In such a case, any required weighing, counting, or measuring is conducted only for the purpose of ascertaining whether the seller performed in full. *See* LA. CIV. CODE art. 2458 cmt. c.

In addition, as indicated by the foregoing case, Louisiana courts have held that a lump sale requires not only a lump thing but also a lump price. The reason for this rule is not readily apparent. After all, whether a sale of an identifiable body of fungible things is made at a lump price (i.e., an entire crop of oranges for $10,000) or a unit price (i.e., an entire crop of oranges for $0.25 per orange), there is no uncertainty regarding *which* items are to be sold. Certain French commentators concluded that when a lump thing is sold for a unit price, the uncertainty as to the price prior to its calculation prevents ownership from transferring upon the parties' consent alone. Louisiana adopted this view. *See* 7 SAÚL LITVINOFF, LOUISIANA CIVIL LAW TREATISE, OBLIGATIONS § 46 (1975). The concern of the courts and commentators may have been understandable during the age of *res perit domino*. Consider a sale of an orange crop at a price of $0.25 per orange. Assume that following the parties' consent as to thing and price, but before the oranges are counted, the oranges are destroyed in a fire. If risk of loss passed to the buyer with ownership and upon the parties' consent, how would the parties know the price that the buyer is required to pay? Although the rule of *res perit domino* has been eliminated in the sales revision, the redactors apparently did not intend any change in this understanding of a "lump sale." *See* LA. CIV. CODE art. 2458 cmt. b.

3. Is it clear to which sales Article 2458 applies versus those to which Article 2457 applies? Prior to the 1995 sales revision, the answer was clearer. At that time, the term "sale by weight, tale, or measure" included not only sales of lump things at a price per weight, tale, or measure, but also sales of things that must be individualized from a mass of similar things sold at a price per weight, tale, or measure. Thus, under *prior law*, in a sale of 20 chairs (out of dozens of identical chairs) for $100 per chair, ownership passed once the chairs were counted. Over time, however, as Louisiana courts developed the concept of appropriation, it became clear that mere weighing, counting, or measuring was often not sufficient to identify which goods, out of a mass of goods of the same kind, belonged to the buyer. Under that jurisprudence, mere counting of the chairs would often not be sufficient to transfer ownership; instead, the chairs would also have to be irrevocably allocated to the buyer. Now that the jurisprudence on appropriation has been codified in Article 2457, it seems that Article 2458 has been severely restricted in its scope.

In their authoritative treatise on the law of sales, Professors Dian Tooley-Knoblett and David Gruning suggest that following the revision, Article 2458 should be read as encompassing *only* sales of lump things—identifiable bodies of fungible things. The object of the sale may be the entire mass of goods belonging to the seller (i.e., an entire crop of oranges) or it might be a quantity of things that, while comprising less than the whole, are still discernible as a unit (i.e., the contents of an identified silo of rice). In either case, no question exists regarding *which* goods are the object of the sale. However, if the sale is not for a lump price but is for a price per weight, tale, or measure, then indeterminacy exists as to the price until the things are weighed, counted, or measured. In such a case, the first paragraph of Article 2458 applies: ownership transfers upon the determination of the price through the method agreed upon by the parties, and no additional appropriation is required. If the sale is for a lump thing at a lump price, then the second paragraph of Article 2458 applies, and ownership transfers upon the parties' mere consent. For additional discussion, see 24 Dian Tooley-Knoblett & David Gruning, Louisiana Civil Law Treatise, Sales § 3:9 (2017).

2. Things in Transit
La. Civ. Code arts. 2613–2617

In many sales of movables, the things sold are shipped from the seller to the buyer using a "common carrier." A "common carrier," as the term is used in this context, is "a commercial enterprise that holds itself out to the public as offering to transport freight or passengers for a fee." *Common Carrier*, Black's Law Dictionary (10th ed. 2014). Common carriers include the U.S. Postal Service, as well as commercial shipping companies such as UPS and FedEx. The term also includes commercial shipping companies that may be less well-known to consumers but that are frequently utilized by wholesalers and retailers of movable things. When the parties agree that the things sold will be shipped through a carrier, the Civil Code provides special rules governing the transfer of ownership and risk of loss of those things.

a. Transfer of Ownership

The transfer of ownership of things shipped through a carrier is governed by Article 2613. Understanding the rules set forth in this article requires a general understanding of a document referenced there—the "bill of lading." A bill of lading serves three functions. First, it serves as evidence of the contract of carriage (the shipping contract). Second, it serves as a receipt of the goods that is issued by the carrier to the seller when the goods are delivered to the carrier's possession. Third, it is a document of title that dictates who has the authority to pick up the goods from the carrier at the point of destination. This last function of the bill of lading is the focus of our study in this Chapter.

Consider the following hypothetical: Buyer, who is located in New Orleans, agrees to buy 10,000 widgets from Seller, who is located in Shreveport. The parties agree that the widgets will be shipped by railway. The seller delivers the widgets to the railway company, which issues a bill of lading to Seller. This document serves as the contract of carriage, serves as a receipt for the goods (that is, it evidences that the goods were in fact turned over to the railway), and indicates who has the right to pick up the widgets from the railyard when they arrive in New Orleans. Whether Buyer or some other party has the right to retrieve the widgets in New Orleans will depend on the form of the bill of lading.

Bills of lading are generally either negotiable or nonnegotiable. Negotiable bills of lading include "order" bills of lading and "bearer" bills of lading, and nonnegotiable bills of lading are often called "straight" bills of lading. A straight bill of lading requires the delivery of the goods to a named party, the consignee, and the document is not negotiable. An order bill of lading provides for the delivery of the goods to the order of a named consignee *or* to whomever the consignee may negotiate such rights. An order bill (unlike a straight bill of lading) can be negotiated by the consignee by endorsing the document over to another party. A bearer bill of lading permits any holder of the bill of lading to take delivery of the goods and may be negotiated by simple delivery (no endorsements needed). Returning to the hypothetical above, Buyer will have the authority to retrieve the widgets from the railyard in either of three circumstances: (1) if the widgets are consigned to Buyer on a straight bill of lading, (2) if, although the widgets were consigned to another party on an order bill of lading, the document was negotiated to Buyer (by endorsement of the order bill of lading by the other party), or (3) if Buyer has possession of a bearer bill of lading. For in-depth treatment of the law governing bills of lading, see generally UNIFORM COMMERCIAL CODE §§ 7:101–7:704 ("Documents of Title").

Turning now to the Civil Code's treatment of the transfer of ownership of things in transit, consider Article 2613. This article provides that "the form of the bill of lading determines ownership of the things while in transit." LA. CIV. CODE art. 2613. Elaborating upon this general rule, the article provides different rules depending upon whether the bill of lading consigns the goods to the buyer, the seller, or another party. First, "[w]hen the bill of lading makes the things deliverable to the buyer, or to his order, ownership of the things is thereby transferred to the buyer." *Id*. Under this provision, as soon as the goods are delivered to the carrier and a bill of lading is issued consigning the goods to the buyer or to the buyer's order, ownership is transferred to the buyer. Consider the rationale for this rule in light of the preceding discussion of "individualization." When the seller consigns the goods to the buyer or the buyer's order, the seller thereby loses control over their destination. As Article 2613 comment (f) explains, "Indeed, delivery to a carrier under a bill of lading that makes the things deliverable to the buyer is a clear act of individualization of the contractual object. It is clear that, for the Louisiana jurisprudence, delivery to a carrier amounts to an appropriation. *See Edgwood v. Falkenhagen*, 151 La. 1072, 92 So. 703 (La. 1922)." LA. CIV. CODE art. 2613 cmt. f.

In contrast, "[w]hen the bill of lading makes the things deliverable to the seller, or to his agent, ownership of the things thereby remains with the seller." LA. CIV. CODE art. 2613. Under this latter provision, even though the goods have been delivered to the carrier, if the bill of lading consigns the things to the seller or the seller's agent, the seller remains the owner. Again, consider the rationale for the rule. When the bill of lading makes the things deliverable to the seller, no relinquishment of control—and thus, no individualization—has occurred. Such individualization cannot take place until the seller physically delivers the goods to the buyer following transit, endorses an order bill of lading over to the buyer or the buyer's agent, or delivers a bearer bill of lading to either of them. *See* LA. CIV. CODE art. 2613 cmt. f.

Why, as a practical matter, would a seller make the goods deliverable to the seller or the seller's agent rather than to the buyer? One reason is this: retention of ownership and control over the goods provides a seller with an advantage in the event that the buyer repudiates the contract while the goods are in transit. For instance, if while the goods are in transit the buyer informs the seller that he or she will no longer perform, the seller who has retained control over the goods may direct the carrier to hold the goods at the point of destination for the seller or a substitute buyer. In addition, by retaining ownership, the seller protects his right to payment. Take, for example, a buyer who purchases goods with borrowed funds and grants the creditor a security interest in the goods as collateral. That security interest attaches once the buyer acquires rights in the things sold. La. Rev. Stat. § 10:9-203(b)(2). If, after the buyer has acquired ownership of the goods, the buyer subsequently fails to pay the seller and defaults on the loan, the secured party's rights in the things may be superior to the seller's vendor's privilege. La. Rev. Stat. §§ 9:4770(B), 10:9-322(h). To avoid this eventuality, a seller may wish to retain ownership of the goods until payment is tendered by the buyer, at which time the seller will endorse or hand over a bill of lading to the buyer, thereby relinquishing ownership of the goods. Another reason why the goods would be consigned to the *seller* in the bill of lading is that a creditor of the seller may require it. This would occur, for example, if the seller has granted a security interest in the goods to a creditor. Because the creditor's security interest in the goods will be lost when the buyer obtains ownership of them, the creditor has an interest in the seller retaining ownership until the buyer pays the price.

Note that Article 2613 contemplates that the seller may also protect his or her interest in the goods even when the bill of lading makes the things deliverable to the buyer or the buyer's order: "When the seller or his agent *remains in possession* of a bill of lading that makes the things deliverable to the buyer, or to the buyer's order, the seller thereby reserves the right to retain the things against a claim of the buyer who has not performed his obligations." La. Civ. Code art. 2613 (emphasis added).

The following is a reproduction of the Uniform Straight Bill of Lading, promulgated as part of the U.S. Interstate Commerce Act. Notice that it includes a line for the shipper to indicate to whom the goods are "consigned." This is where the object of the sale is made deliverable either to the buyer or to the seller, which thus determines ownership during the transit period.

Uniform Straight Bill of Landing

49 C.F.R. Pt. 1035, App. A (2016)

Original—Not Negotiable

Shipper's No_____

Agent's No_____

Company_____

Received, subject to the classifications and tariffs in effect on the date of this Bill of Lading:

at _____, 20_____

from_____

the property described below, in apparent good order, except as noted (contents and condition of contents of packages unknown), marked, consigned, and destined as indicated below, which said company (the word company being understood throughout this contract as meaning any person or corporation in possession of the property under the contract) agrees to carry to its usual place of delivery at said destination, if on its own road or its own water line, otherwise to deliver to another carrier on the route to said destination. It is mutually agreed, as to each carrier of all or any of said property over all or any portion of said route to destination, and as to each party at any time interested in all or any of said property, that every service to be performed hereunder shall be subject to all the conditions not prohibited by law, whether printed or written, herein contained, including the conditions on back hereof, which are hereby agreed to by the shipper and accepted for himself and his assigns.

[Mail or street address of consignee—For purposes of notification only.]

Consigned to_____

Destination_____

State of_____

County of_____

Route_____

Delivering Carrier_____

Car Initial_____

Car No_____

Trailer Initials/Number_____

Plan_____

Length_____

Plan_____

Container Initials/Number_____

Length_____

Plan_____

Length_____

Plan_____

No. packages	Description of articles, special marks, and exceptions	*Weight (subject to correction)	Class or rate	Check column	
. . . .	. . . .	. . . .	. . . .	. . . .	Subject to Section 7 of conditions, if this shipment is to be delivered to the consignee without recourse on the consignor, the consignor shall sign the following statement:
. . . .	. . . .	. . . .	. . . .	. . . .	
. . . .	. . . .	. . . .	. . . .	. . . .	
. . . .	. . . .	. . . .	. . . .	. . . .	
. . . .	. . . .	. . . .	. . . .	. . . .	The carrier shall not make delivery of this shipment without payment of freight and all other lawful charges.
. . . .	. . . .	. . . .	. . . .	. . . .	
. . . .	. . . .	. . . .	. . . .	. . . .	(Signature of consignor)
. . . .	. . . .	. . . .	. . . .	. . . .	If charges are to be prepaid, write or stamp here,
. . . .	. . . .	. . . .	. . . .	. . . .	"To be Prepaid."
. . . .	. . . .	. . . .	. . . .	. . . .	Received $___ to apply in prepayment of the charges on the property described hereon.
. . . .	. . . .	. . . .	. . . .	. . . .	
. . . .	. . . .	. . . .	. . . .	. . . .	Agent or Cashier
. . . .	. . . .	. . . .	. . . .	. . . .	Per_____
. . . .	. . . .	. . . .	. . . .	. . . .	(The signature here acknowledges only the amount prepaid.)

*If the shipment moves between two ports by a carrier by water, the law requires that the bill of lading shall state whether it is "carrier's or shipper's weight."

Note. — Where the rate is dependent on value, shippers are required to state specifically in writing the agreed or declared value of the property.

The agreed or declared value of the property is hereby specifically stated by the shipper to be not exceeding — _____ per _____

Charges advanced: _____

Shipper_____

Agent_____

Per_____

Per_____

Permanent post office address of shipper:

b. Transfer of Risk of Loss

The Civil Code chapter on Sales of Movables also includes a provision governing the transfer of the risk of loss when movable things are shipped through a common carrier. Article 2616 provides two distinct rules for transactions of this type. First, the article states that if the contract "does not require [the seller] to deliver the things at any particular destination, the risk of loss is transferred to the buyer upon delivery of the things to the carrier, regardless of the form of the bill of lading." La. Civ. Code art. 2616. In contrast, if the contract "requires the seller to deliver the things at a particular destination, the risk of loss is transferred to the buyer when the things, while in possession of the carrier, are duly tendered to the buyer at the place of destination." *Id.*

At first blush these rules may seem nonsensical; under what circumstances, one might ask, would a buyer request that goods be shipped by a carrier, but not "require[] the seller to deliver the things at a particular destination"? However, the language of Article 2616, which is derived from Article 2 of the Uniform Commercial Code, has an established and sensible meaning.

The first paragraph of Article 2616 refers to a type of contract termed a "shipment" contract. La. Civ. Code art. 2616. As a general rule, all contracts of sale in which goods are transported through a common carrier are considered to be shipment contracts unless the parties agree otherwise. In such a contract, delivery of the goods by the buyer to the seller is deemed to occur when the goods are placed in the possession of the carrier. As a result, the risk of loss transfers to the buyer at that time. In essence, in a shipment contract, the seller avoids the risks of shipping the goods through a carrier. If something happens to the goods during transit (for instance, they are damaged in a storm or fire) then the buyer bears that loss and must still pay the price.

While the language of Article 2616 may seem to suggest otherwise, the seller in a "shipment" contract does not hand the goods over to the carrier without specifying the place to which they will be delivered. Rather, while the seller will still require the carrier to send the goods to the buyer at a certain address, the seller does not guarantee that the goods will in fact be delivered to the buyer.

Although sales of movables in which the goods are shipped through a carrier are, by default, shipment contracts, the parties may alter the default rule by agreement. If the parties agree that the seller will assume the risk of loss of the goods during transit, then the parties' contract is a "destination" contract. In this type of contract, delivery of the goods to the buyer is deemed to occur when the carrier tenders the goods to the buyer at the place of destination. Thus, if something happens to the good during transit, then the seller bears that loss and may not require the buyer to pay the price.

How does one determine whether a particular contract for the sale of movables is a shipment contract or a destination contract? The last paragraph of Article 2616 provides guidance on this issue: "When the parties incorporate well established commercial symbols into their contract, the risk of loss is transferred in accordance with the customary understanding of such symbols." La. Civ. Code art. 2616. The "commercial symbols" referenced in this article are accepted shorthand phrases that have been developed by domestic and international commercial organizations such as the International Chamber of Commerce to streamline contractual negotiation and ensure clear communication between the parties regarding the risks, costs, and other particulars of delivery through carriers.

An exhaustive study of the commercial symbols used in sales of goods (of which there are many) is neither necessary nor appropriate for an introductory course in the law of sales. However, a brief introduction to just one of these symbols will aid in your understanding of when the risk of loss transfers in common commercial transactions. F.O.B., which means "free on board," is among the most commonly-used commercial symbols. When this symbol is used in the parties' agreement, it is followed by a location, for example, a sea or river port (i.e., F.O.B. Port of New Orleans). The designation F.O.B. serves at least two purposes. First, it designates the location at which delivery occurs and the risk of loss is shifted. When the location indicates the place *from which* the goods are being shipped, the contract is a shipment contract. Accordingly, risk of loss is transferred to the buyer when the goods are loaded onto the ship at the port of shipment. When the location indicates the place *to which* the goods are being shipped, the contract is a destination contract. Accordingly, risk of loss is not transferred until the goods arrive at the port of destination. In addition, F.O.B. provides a shorthand for the parties' agreement regarding which of them will be responsible for the costs of delivery. When the contract is a shipment contract, although the seller bears the cost of delivering the goods to the carrier, it is the buyer who bears the cost of freight from the place of shipment to the place of destination. *See* La. Civ. Code art. 2616 cmt. c. In contrast, when the contract is a destination contract, the seller bears the cost of both delivering the goods to the carrier and the cost of freight from the place of shipment to the place of destination. *Id.*

Consider the following example: Buyer is located in New Orleans, Louisiana, and Seller is located in Baton Rouge, Louisiana. The parties agree that Buyer will purchase from Seller a certain number of gallons of oil for a specified price, and that the oil will be transported from Seller to Buyer via barge. The parties agree that the oil will be shipped F.O.B. Port of Greater Baton Rouge on a straight bill of lading under which the oil is consigned to Buyer. When does ownership transfer? When does the risk of loss transfer? Who bears the cost of delivery?

First, the form of the bill of lading determines ownership of the things while they are in transit. La. Civ. Code art. 2613. Because the bill of lading makes the oil deliverable to Buyer, ownership of the oil transferred to Buyer when the bill of lading was issued. Second, the nature of the contract (shipment or destination) determines the shifting of the risk of loss. La. Civ. Code art. 2616. Because the parties' agreement included the commercial symbol F.O.B., which was followed by the location of the point of shipment, the contract is a shipment contract, according to which risk of loss transferred to Buyer when the oil was placed in the possession of the carrier at the Port of Greater Baton Rouge. Finally, the parties' commercial symbol makes clear that Buyer will bear the cost of freight.

3. Sales Subject to Conditions

La. Civ. Code arts. 1767–1776

Article 2457 of the Civil Code of 1870 provided in part that "[t]he sale may be made purely and simply, or under a condition either suspensive or resolutive . . . ." Although this Article was not reproduced in the 1995 revision of the Title on Sales, the principle articulated in the former provision remains true: like any other obligation, the obligations of the parties in a sale may be subject to suspensive or resolutory conditions. Before reading the material that follows, refresh your memory of the general principles of conditional obligations by reviewing Louisiana Civil Code Articles 1767 through 1776.

a. In General

Canal Motors, Inc. v. Campbell

241 So. 2d 5 (La. App. 4 Cir. 1970)

BARNETTE, Judge.

The plaintiff, Canal Motors, Inc., was awarded judgment of $3,137.50 against the defendant, Gerard C. Campbell, after a hearing of rule for judgment on the pleadings, pursuant to LSA-C.C.P. art. 965. The defendant Campbell has appealed devolutively.

* * * * *

The following pleaded facts are not in dispute. On May 28, 1969, the defendant Campbell selected a used automobile for purchase from plaintiff, an automobile dealer. The price was agreed upon, being $3,162.50. Campbell made a down payment or deposit of $25. The plaintiff in Article III of its petition alleged the $25 was "* * * a deposit to hold the said automobile until his loan with his Federal Credit Union had been approved * * *." In his answer Campbell denied the allegations of Article III except the fact that defendant paid the sum of $25 as a deposit on the 1968 Chevrolet station wagon, which he admitted. Therefore for the purpose of the motion under consideration, we must accept as true that the $25 was a "deposit" pending a loan approval. On that date the vehicle was delivered to Campbell and held in his possession and use until June 22, 1969, when it was seriously damaged in an accident. No further payment on the purchase price was made. Attached to plaintiff's petition and made a part thereof by reference are two exhibits showing Campbell as "purchaser" of the described automobile, the price, the "down payment" and "net balance due." One of these is signed by Campbell.

The disputed pleadings are plaintiff's allegation that it was assured by Sealco that Campbell's loan application was approved and in reliance upon that information it delivered possession of the automobile to Campbell on May 28, and that Sealco refused to make the loan to Campbell after the automobile was damaged. Campbell denied this allegation for lack of information sufficient to justify a belief. He reconvened seeking return of the $25 "cash deposit" and alleged: "The balance of $3,137.50 due on the purchase price has not been paid, for reasons beyond the control of defendant; and no terms of credit were extended defendant for the balance of the purchase price."

The foregoing summary of the pertinent pleadings shows a genuine issue of a material fact. If the $25 payment was a "deposit" as alleged to "hold the automobile" until the purchaser's loan application was approved, there was at that time (May 28, 1969) no completed sale, but at most a conditional obligation dependent upon an uncertain event. The condition of loan approval was a suspensive condition. LSA-C.C. arts. 2021 [R.C.C. 1767] and 2471 [No Corresponding Article]; *Jackson Motors, Inc. v. Calvert Fire Insurance Co.*, 239 La. 921, 120 So.2d 478 (1960); *Kershaw v. Deshotel*, 179 So.2d 528 (La.App.3d Cir. 1965).

The plaintiff alleged that it delivered possession of the automobile to Campbell after assurance from Sealco that the loan application had been approved. This is denied by Campbell. Whether or not the suspensive condition was satisfied is therefore an issue of fact material to a determination if there was a completed sale of the automobile to Campbell when possession was delivered to him.

Having concluded that there is a genuine issue of material fact, the motion for judgment on the pleadings cannot be maintained. This conclusion makes unnecessary our consideration of the remaining questions argued and briefed at length by counsel.

For these reasons the judgment maintaining plaintiff's motion for judgment on the pleadings and granting judgment in favor plaintiff, Canal Motors, Inc., and against the defendant, Gerard C. Campbell, in the principal sum of $3,137.50 is annulled and the motion for judgment on the pleadings is denied.

The case is remanded for further proceedings according to law.

Cost of this appeal is cast to plaintiff-appellee. All other costs shall be assessed upon conclusion of the proceedings in the trial court.

Judgment annulled; case remanded.

Notes and Questions

1. The contract in *Campbell* was made subject to a condition. Was the condition suspensive or resolutory? What was the uncertain event upon which the contract depended? Why would the parties condition the existence of their contract on this event? How does the determination of whether the condition was fulfilled affect the rights of the parties to this contract?

2. Recall that Articles 1773 and 1774 govern the fulfillment of conditions. Article 1773 addresses positive conditions and is applicable when the parties have

conditioned their contract on the *occurrence* of an event. Article 1774, in contrast, addresses negative conditions and is applicable when the parties have conditioned their contract on the *nonoccurrence* of an event. Read both articles carefully and then, for each of the following hypotheticals, determine: (a) whether the condition to which the sale is subject is suspensive or resolutory; (b) whether the condition was fulfilled; and (c) whether the sale is enforceable.

i.   On March 1, Buyer and Seller agree to the sale of a car subject to Buyer securing financing for the price by March 15. The parties agree that the Seller will hand over possession of the car once the loan is approved. On March 2, Buyer applies for financing with the Bank. The Bank approves financing on March 16.

ii. On March 1, Buyer and Seller agree to the sale of a car subject to Buyer securing financing for the price. The parties agree that the Seller will hand over possession of the car once the loan is approved. The parties do not discuss a date by which financing must be secured. On March 2, Buyer applies for financing with the Bank. The Bank approves financing on March 16. *Variation:* How would it affect your answer, if at all, if the Bank instead approves financing on May 16?

iii. On March 1, Buyer and Seller agree to the sale of a car, with the proviso that Buyer may return the car if unable to secure financing for the price by March 15. On the day their agreement is made (March 1), Seller delivers the car to Buyer by handing over the keys and allowing Buyer to drive the car off the lot. On March 2, Buyer applies for financing with the Bank. As of March 16, the Bank has not approved financing for the price. *Variation:* How would it affect your answer, if it all, if on March 15 the car was destroyed in a fire at the Buyer's place of business? Continue to assume that, as of March 16, the Bank has not approved financing for the price.

3. Recall that under Article 1772, "A condition is regarded as fulfilled when it is not fulfilled because of the fault of a party with an interest contrary to fulfillment." La. Civ. Code art. 1772. In a sale subject to a suspensive condition, the parties are not bound by the obligations of a contract of sale until the condition is fulfilled. However, while the condition is pending they are juridically linked in such a manner as to be bound by the overriding duty of good faith. *See* La. Civ. Code art. 1759. Thus, if a party to a contract subject to a suspensive condition thwarts the fulfillment of the condition, the condition is regarded as nonetheless fulfilled. Consider the following hypothetical:

> On March 1, Buyer and Seller agree to the sale of a car subject to Buyer securing financing for the price by March 15. On March 2, Buyer discovers the same car available from a different seller at a better price and, in an effort to avoid his contract with Seller, intentionally fails to apply for a loan. On March 16, Buyer notifies Seller that he regards the contract null and void as a result of his failure to secure financing. Is the contract enforceable?

Why or why not? What recourse does Seller have against Buyer as a matter of law? As a practical matter?

4. Article 1775 expresses the principle of retroactivity that applies to conditional obligations: "Fulfillment of a condition has effects that are retroactive to the inception of the obligation . . . ." La. Civ. Code art. 1775. According to this principle, the effects of a condition, once fulfilled, date back to the time the contract was created. This principle has important effects for the transfer of ownership and risk of loss in sales. Consider the following hypotheticals:

i. On March 1, Buyer and Seller agree to the sale of a car subject to Buyer securing financing for the price by March 15. The parties agree that the Seller will hand over possession of the car once the loan is approved. On March 2, Buyer applies for financing with the Bank. The Bank approves financing on March 10. On March 11, Seller delivers the car to Buyer by handing over the keys and allowing Buyer to drive the car off the lot. Identify the time at which ownership and risk of loss transferred to the buyer.

ii. On March 1, Buyer and Seller agree to the sale of a car, with the proviso that Buyer may return the car if he is unable to secure financing for the price by March 15. On that same date, Seller delivers the car to Buyer by handing over the keys and allowing Buyer to drive the car off the lot. Despite his best efforts, Buyer is unable to secure financing for the price by the deadline and returns the car to Seller on March 16. Identify the time at which ownership and risk of loss transferred to the buyer.

Note that Article 1775 articulates important limitations on the principle of retroactivity. Although generally the effects of a condition are retroactive to the inception of the obligation, "[n]evertheless, that fulfillment does not impair the validity of acts of administration duly performed by a party, nor affect the ownership of fruits produced while the condition was pending. Likewise, fulfillment of the condition does not impair the right acquired by third persons while the condition was pending." La. Civ. Code art. 1775.

5. A condition, like a term, may be renounced by the party in whose favor it has been established. *See* La. Civ. Code art. 1780; *id.* cmt. b. Thus, if Buyer and Seller have conditioned their agreement to the sale of a car on Buyer's ability to secure financing, Buyer may renounce the condition and opt to pay cash for the car instead.

b. Sales Subject to Suspensive Conditions

i. Sale on View or Trial

La. Civ. Code art. 2460

The Louisiana Civil Code Title on Sales contains only one article addressing sales made subject to conditions. Article 2460, which is placed among the provisions addressing the transfer of ownership of the thing sold, provides: "When the buyer has reserved the view or trial of the thing, ownership is not transferred from the seller to the buyer until the latter gives his approval of the thing." LA. CIV. CODE art. 2460. While Article 2460 correctly states that "ownership is not transferred" until the buyer has approved the thing, the limited focus on the transfer of ownership obscures the complete picture of this type of sale, wherein the parties agree that the sale itself, and not merely the transfer of ownership, is conditioned upon the buyer's approval. Consider the following excerpt from the writing of Professor Saúl Litvinoff on the sale on view or trial, then consider the case that follows.

7 Saúl Litvinoff, *Louisiana Civil Law Treatise, Obligations § 56*, at 76-78 (1975) (internal citations omitted)±

In terms of article 2460 of the Louisiana Civil Code [R.C.C. 2460] a sale on trial is a form of conditional sale. The condition on which the perfection of the sale depends is defined as suspensive. Before the Code Napoleon, the condition of trying or testing the thing was regarded as resolutory. The sale was perfect upon delivery of the thing which rendered the purchaser the owner; the seller, however, was bound to take back the thing if, after trying it, the buyer declared it unfit for his purpose. Under such an approach the risk belonged, of course, to the buyer. This was precisely the consequence that the redactors of the French Civil Code intended to avoid when they drafted article 1588 [of the French *Code Civil*], which declares that a sale on trial is always presumed to be made under a suspensive condition. . . . [T]his language was introduced into article 2460 of the Louisiana Civil Code.

As a direct consequence of the nature of the condition, the existence of the sale and all its effects are suspended until the thing is viewed, tried, and approved. This is recognized in article 2043 of the Louisiana Civil Code [R.C.C. 1767]. If, after trying the thing, the purchaser refuses it, or if by reason of loss of the thing a trial is no longer possible, the condition does not materialize and the buyer is considered as never having been the owner. If on the contrary the buyer keeps the thing after the view or trial, his right of ownership is retroactive to the moment of the contract. The rule is stated in article 2041 of the Louisiana Civil Code [R.C.C. 1775], according to which the fulfillment or materialization of the condition has a retrospective effect to the day that the engagement was contracted.

* * * * *

By virtue of article 2044 of the Louisiana Civil Code [No Corresponding Article] the thing sold on trial is at the risk of the vendor until tried and approved by the vendee. Even the accidental loss or deterioration of the thing during the trial or test is to be borne by the vendor, as the suspensive condition cannot be regarded as fulfilled until the viewing or trial is completed. This solution accords with the presumed intention of the parties; it seems unlikely that a purchaser would be willing to take responsibility for a thing he has not yet acquired and might very well refuse.

± Reproduced with permission of Thomson Reuters.

The fact that the trial of a thing is characterized as "a kind of suspensive condition" in article 2460 [R.C.C. 2460] also gives the seller a basis for obtaining specific performance of the buyer's obligation, instead of resolution of the contract, when the buyer refuses to try the thing. Indeed, such a refusal prevents fulfillment of the condition, which, under article 2040 of the Louisiana Civil Code [R.C.C. 1772], is considered as fulfilled by way of sanction against the party bound under condition who frustrates its occurrence. Accordingly, upon the buyer's refusal to try the thing, the seller may seek a judgment that the condition is accomplished and the sale is perfect as a consequence[.]

* * * * *

Although Louisiana article 2460 [R.C.C. 2460] speaks of a suspensive condition, it is possible for the parties to stipulate in their agreement that the condition shall be of a resolutory instead of a suspensive nature.

American Creosote Works v. Boland Machine & Mfg. Co.
35 So. 2d 749 (La. 1948)

FOURNET, Justice.

The plaintiff instituted this suit to recover the sum of $1,924.81, the price of certain creosoted fir pilings allegedly sold and delivered to the defendant, and the matter is now before us for a review of the judgment of the Court of Appeal for the Parish of Orleans affirming the judgment of the district court in favor of the plaintiff, as prayed for.

* * * * *

On August 4, 1943, the plaintiff, the American Creosote Works, entered into a contract with the defendant, Boland Machine & Manufacturing Company, a copartnership. This contract is incorporated in one of the plaintiff's order forms. According to its terms the plaintiff agreed to supply the defendant with 24 creosoted fir pilings treated by what is known as the Full Cell Bethel Process and conforming to Navy specifications No. 39P14a (meaning 13 inches in diameter 3 feet from the butt or bottom end of the tree) in four lots of six units each, i.e., six 75' long, six 80' long, six 85' long, and six 90' long, at a price of 95¢ [cents] per lineal foot, f.o.b. the plaintiff's plant at Southport in New Orleans, at which place they were to be loaded on the defendant's truck, subject to inspection and acceptance by the defendant. Subsequently, according to a letter of August 17 confirming a telephone conversation had with the defendant, the contract was amended to provide for the loading of these pilings on the defendant's barge at the plaintiff's Southport plant wharf on Saturday, August 21, 1943. An extra charge of $25 was to be included in the purchase price under this new agreement for the barge loading.

Since the plaintiff did not have these fir pilings in stock, they had to be specially ordered for treatment according to the detailed specifications and after they were processed the plaintiff, on August 20, under the provision in the contract calling for one day advance notice, notified the defendant by telephone to have a barge at its wharf so that loading might begin at seven the next morning, for delivery around noon. Accordingly, the defendant, on Friday afternoon, ordered a barge from the Bisso Coal and Towboat Company and it was tied up at the wharf ready for loading at the specified time. The actual loading was completed about eleven. The defendant, upon advice from the plaintiff, likewise asked the Bisso people to have a tug pick the barge up about noon, but before that time a fire started on the wharf of the plaintiff company and spread to the barge. When the tug did approach the wharf as instructed, the barge had been cut away from the wharf in an effort to save it and was drifting down the river enveloped in flames.

The defendant denied liability, contending that under the contract title did not pass to them until the property was loaded on the barge and tendered to them or their agent for inspection and acceptance.

The plaintiff, relying on Articles 1909 [No Corresponding Article], 2456 [R.C.C. 2456], 2458 [R.C.C. 2457, 2458], 2467 [R.C.C. 2467], and 2468 [No Corresponding Article] of the Revised Civil Code, contends that title to these pilings passed to the defendant the moment they were treated and removed from the processing shed; in any event, that title passed when the pilings were measured, counted, and loaded on the barge.

In passing on these issues, the Court of Appeal found that neither these codal articles nor the cases relied on by the defendant were applicable under the facts of this case, but concluded that title to the pilings had passed to the defendant prior to the fire inasmuch as they were, at that time, loaded on the barge furnished by the defendant in accordance with the court's construction of the contract, the fact that the defendant was not to take possession of them nutil [sic] a later time, i.e., around noon, being immaterial.

We think the court's conclusion with respect to the inapplicability of the codal articles is correct. A mere reference to these articles will show their general tenor to be that the sale of an object is perfect and complete and the article is at the risk of the buyer as soon as there exists an agreement as to the object and price, although actual delivery has not been made and the price has not been paid, and that once the sale is perfected and completed, the only responsibility then resting on the seller is that of guarding the goods as a faithful administrator. But this rule applies only "*if the contract is one of those that purport a transfer.*" Article 1909 [No Corresponding Article]. The contract in this case does not purport to be a transfer of the pilings to the defendant. On the contrary, its terms show very plainly that the pilings are to be transferred to the defendant only after they have been tendered for inspection and have actually been accepted. (Italics ours.)

Under this contract the plaintiff agreed to furnish the defendant with goods that had to meet certain specifications, that is, the pilings had to be of definite lengths and size and they had to be treated with creosote under a special process. While on the reverse side of this contract there is to be found, along with other printed provisions, the general stipulation that the "Buyer agrees to receive material when and as delivered on cars at Seller's plant. It is specifically agreed that there shall be no claims of any kind after material is delivered as above," this general stipulation is not controlling in this case for it has been abrogated by the very positive provision on the face of the contract, where all of the detailed specifications and conditions are clearly set out, that the pilings were to be subject to final inspection and acceptance by the defendant at the plaintiff's plant.

The intention of the parties as to when the pilings would be transferred to the defendant is not only thus clearly shown on the face of the contract itself, but is further demonstrated by the oral and documentary evidence in the record unmistakably showing the property belonged to the plaintiff until delivery was completed and that delivery could not be completed until the defendant, who was given the right to inspect and check it, had actually inspected it and accepted it, such acceptance being evidenced by the defendant's signature on the delivery slip prepared for that purpose which constituted the defendant's acknowledgment that the goods had been received in good condition and accepted.

We think our conclusion that the plaintiff did not consider ownership of the property passed to the defendant until after delivery had been completed is evidenced by its own construction of the contract as expressed in its letter to the defendant on August 27, 1943, a few days after the fire, wherein it is said:

> "Under the terms of our insurance policies *our liability ends with completed delivery,* and both the insurance adjustors and our attorneys have advised me that our policies will not cover this damage. *After delivery is completed,* it is customary for the then owner of the pilings to have them insured * * *."

And the plaintiff's understanding of the time when the delivery could be considered as completed is emphasized by the testimony of Mr. Theester A. Hamby, the plaintiff's secretary-comptroller, to the effect that it was not necessary for the defendant to have the pilings insured until "the time he (defendant) takes possession of them, or when they come under this control—when they leave our control." (Italics and brackets ours.)

And there can be no question but that the defendant had the right to check and inspect the pilings before accepting them, as stipulated in the contract and also in accordance with the custom of the plant. According to the testimony of the plaintiff's employees, the pilings ordered were stored in a pile on the yard after they had been creosoted, pending delivery. After the barge ordered by the defendant was tied up to the wharf the office furnished the yard checker with a card containing pertinent information relative to the specifications of the order being supplied the defendant. The checker measured and counted the pilings against this card to see that they met specifications before they were loaded on flat cars that took them from the yard, across the levee, and down to the wharf where they were turned over to another checker. This checker was also furnished with a card containing the specifications covering the order and he rechecked the pilings as they were loaded on the barge. After the last piling was loaded, this checker went back to the office and there filled out a slip listing the material that had been loaded under his supervision. This slip was left with the office force to be presented to the defendant customer or representative for signature at the time they were taken possession of, signifying the defendant's acceptance and receipt of the goods in good condition.

We therefore conclude that delivery was never completed under the terms of this contract and under the facts of this case and that title had not passed to the defendant at the time the pilings were destroyed by fire; consequently, their loss was at the risk of the plaintiff and not that of the defendant.

For the reasons assigned, the judgment of the district court in favor of the American Creosote Works, as prayed for, and that of the Court of Appeal for the Parish of Orleans affirming the same, are reversed, and it is now ordered, adjudged, and decreed that the plaintiff's suit be dismissed at its cost.

Notes and Questions

1. The court in the foregoing case characterized the sale as incomplete until the defendant inspected and accepted the pilings. What impact did this characterization have on the transfer of ownership and risk of loss? Note that this case was decided before the abandonment of *res perit domino*. Would this case be resolved any differently under current law governing the timing of transfer of risk of loss?

2. Although the parties in a sale on view or trial are not bound to the obligations of a sale until after the buyer approves of the thing, the buyer is not free to reject the thing arbitrarily. Instead, the buyer is bound to view or try the thing according to the intentions of the parties, and the buyer's approval or rejection of the thing must be made in good faith. *See* La. Civ. Code art. 2460 cmt. b. Moreover, if the seller delivers the thing to the buyer for the purpose of viewing or conducting a trial of the thing, a contract of deposit arises. *See* La. Civ. Code arts. 2926–2940. As a result, while the buyer has possession of the thing he or she is held to the standard of "diligence and prudence" and is liable to the seller for any losses sustained because of the buyer's lack of due care. *See* La. Civ. Code art. 2930.

3. The *American Creosote Works* court characterized the sale as one subject to a suspensive condition—i.e., the buyer's inspection and approval of the thing. This characterization may not be entirely accurate, particularly under current law. As you read the following materials on the "buyer's right to inspect," consider whether today the sale in *American Creosote Works* would be characterized as a sale subject to a suspensive condition at all.

ii. Buyer's Right of Inspection
La. Civ. Code arts. 2604–2608

Under Articles 2604 through 2608, the buyer in a sale of movable things has the right to inspect the things, even after delivery, for the purpose of ascertaining whether they conform to the contract. If the buyer determines upon inspection that the things delivered do not conform to the contract, the buyer may reject those things within a reasonable time. This right of inspection—which is implied in every sale of movables and is related to the seller's obligation to deliver "conforming things"—is covered in detail in Chapter 8: Delivery. However, some treatment of the buyer's right of inspection is required here because the buyer's right to inspect movable things delivered by the seller must be distinguished from a sale on view or trial.

Unlike the sale on view or trial, the buyer's right to inspect does not operate as a suspensive condition on the entire contract of sale. Instead, the contract is an unconditional and fully enforceable sale, even before the buyer inspects the things to determine if they conform to the contract. The buyer's right to inspect likewise does not operate as an implied resolutory condition.

Importantly, the buyer's rejection of nonconforming goods shifts ownership and risk of loss of those goods back to the seller, but it does not bring the contract to an end. Rather, the seller's failure to deliver conforming goods may result in liability for damages owing to the seller's failure to perform. *See* La. Civ. Code arts. 2609–2610. Additionally, a merchant buyer who rejects nonconforming goods has continuing duties with respect to the handling of those goods. *See* La. Civ. Code art. 2608.

Historically, courts have had some difficulty distinguishing between the buyer's implied right to inspect movable things and a sale on view or trial. The following case illustrates the challenges in making this determination, as well as a circumstance in which proper classification had important legal consequences.

Tunica Biloxi Tribe of Indians v. Bridges
437 F. Supp. 2d 599 (M.D. La. 2006)

Parker, District Judge.

[At issue in this case is whether the plaintiff, Tunica Biloxi Tribe of Indians, was required under state sales tax law to pay sales tax on the price of a van that it purchased from a dealership located outside of the Tribe's reservation. *Eds.*]

Background

On April 15, 2005, the court denied the Tunica-Biloxi Tribe's motion for preliminary injunction (doc. 51). In its ruling, the court detailed the facts and procedural history of the case up to that point (including the shift in focus from mobile homes to the van) and concluded that the sale of the van was completed for tax purposes when the Tribe bought the van from Bolton Ford, a Lake Charles dealership. At that moment, both the price and specifications for the vehicle were then agreed upon by the parties. Since the "taxable event" occurred off-reservation, the court concluded that the sale of the van should not be excluded from Louisiana sales tax.

* * * * *

A pretrial conference was held on March 21, 2006, during which the court instructed that, if counsel were able stipulate to an agreed statement of facts and authenticity/admissibility of additional exhibits, the matter would be submitted without a formal trial (doc. 104).

* * * * *

[Stipulation of facts omitted. *Eds.*]

The Tribe's essential argument is, of course, that the sale of the van was completed on-reservation and therefore is not subject to Louisiana sales tax on motor vehicles. According to the Uniform Pretrial Order dated March 14, 2006 (doc. 99), the Tribe seeks a refund of the sales tax paid on the van, and declaratory and injunctive relief.

Conclusions of Law

Site of the Sale

The critical question at this stage of the litigation is whether the sale of the van occurred on the Tribe's reservation or whether it took place at Bolton Ford in Lake Charles. For tax purposes, a 'sale' is defined as "any transfer of title or possession, or both, exchange, barter, conditional or otherwise, in any manner or by any means whatsoever, of tangible personal property, for a consideration . . . ." La.R.S. 47:301(12). The court has previously concluded that "[t]he word 'title,' as used in this context, is best understood as being synonymous with 'ownership.'" *Tunica-Biloxi Tribe of Indians v. Bridges,* 365 F.Supp.2d 782, 786 (M.D.La.2005). Therefore, a tax 'sale' is perfected upon the earliest of the transfer of ownership or the transfer of possession. Since "[t]he jurisprudence of Louisiana is quite clear that the sale of a motor vehicle is governed by the articles in the Louisiana Civil Code relating to the sale of movables," *Biggs v. Prewitt,* 669 So.2d 441, 443 (La.App. 1 Cir.1995), *writ denied,* 674 So.2d 264 (La.1996), the court notes that a transfer of ownership occurs "as soon as the price is fixed, even though the thing sold is not yet delivered nor the price paid." La.Civ.Code art. 2456.

Mr. Bertalotto [the Tribe's Transportation Manager] sent out a written solicitation for bids by fax to at least two Louisiana car dealerships, including Bolton Ford in Lake Charles. The Tribe concedes that the solicitation of bids was not an offer, but rather, an invitation for dealerships to make offers to the Tribe. Bolton Ford responded in kind and "offered"-by fax-to sell a van to the Tribe. Bertalotto called Bolton Ford in Lake Charles from his office on the reservation and agreed to pay $32,064 for the van.

The court cannot but comment upon how unhelpful the reply brief on behalf of defendant was to the court. In that brief, the State abandons all prior positions and advances the notion that the sale of a motor vehicle is not complete "until the [S]tate of Louisiana actually issues a paper title" (doc. 117, p. 3). In addition to a radical change in legal position by the State, that assertion contradicts established Louisiana law:

> The jurisprudence of this state does not require that the certificate of title
> to a vehicle be transferred in order for the sale to be a valid one. *Wright*

v. Barnes, 541 So.2d 977 (La.App. 2d Cir.1989); *Shanks v. Callahan,* 232 So.2d 306, 308 (La.App. 1st Cir.1969). Furthermore, sale of a vehicle is not affected by non-compliance with the Vehicle Certificate of Title Law, LSA-R.S. 32:701-738. *Wright,* 541 So.2d 977; *Sherman,* 413 So.2d at 646. Neither does the law require that an agreement to sell a motor vehicle be notarized or even reduced to writing. *See Maloney v. State Farm Ins.Co.,* 583 So.2d 12 (La.App. 4th Cir.), *writs denied,* 586 So.2d 544, 589 So.2d 1058 (1991).

Biggs, 669 So.2d at 443.

"The law in Louisiana is clear that absent contrary intent by the parties, a contract is considered executed at the place where the offer is accepted or where the last act necessary to a meeting of the minds or to completing the contract is performed." *Aetna Ins. Co. v. Naquin,* 478 So.2d 1352, 1354 (La.App. 5 Cir.1985). Bertalotto accepted Bolton Ford's offer from the reservation (and ultimately accepted delivery on the reservation), but the "last act necessary" was for Bolton Ford itself *to receive* the acceptance of its offer. An acceptance means nothing unless it is properly communicated to the offeror. A "meeting of the minds" cannot occur unless both minds are "on the same wavelength" and communication between them is required to accomplish this. Once the acceptance was received by the seller in Lake Charles, the thing, price, and consent all converged and the sale was perfected. The sale having taken place in Lake Charles, the tax on the van was proper but for the Tribe's new argument regarding inspection by the buyer.

Inspection by the Buyer

It is undisputed that Bertalotto ordered the van "contingent on inspection." Therefore, the Tribe argues the applicability of La.Civ.Code art. 2460, which reads as follows: "When the buyer has reserved the view or trial of the thing, ownership is not transferred from the seller to the buyer until the latter gives his approval of the thing." The comments to Article 2460 advise that the situation contemplated by the article "must be distinguished from the buyer's right to inspect things delivered by the seller in performance of a contract of sale. The [view or trial] is incidental to a special kind of sale where the transfer of ownership depends on approval by the buyer. The [usual sale] is the buyer's right to check whether the seller has complied with the contract."

Pertinent to this issue are La.Civ.Code arts. 2604 and 2605. Article 2604 provides that "[t]he buyer has a right to have a reasonable opportunity to inspect the things, even after delivery, for the purpose of ascertaining whether they conform to the contract." Article 2605 adds, in part, that "[a] buyer may reject nonconforming things within a reasonable time. The buyer must give reasonable notice to the seller to make the rejection effective."

Thus, under general sales law, the Tribe had the right to inspect the van even after it was delivered to the reservation and to reject it if it did not meet the Tribe's specifications. The Tribe, as buyer, had that right even without specifically noting that the sale would be "contingent on inspection." The exercise of that right does not bear upon the transfer of ownership of the thing under Article 2456 because at the time of delivery of the van, there already was "agreement on the thing and the price [was] fixed . . . ." The court therefore concludes that this was not a 'special kind of sale." Rather, Bertalotto's "inspection" is more appropriately classified as an exercise of any buyer's right of inspection following any sale under Article 2604.

Ownership was transferred at the moment the Tribe and Bolton Ford agreed upon the thing and the price. That moment occurred in Lake Charles, not on the reservation. Therefore, the sales tax was lawfully imposed on the transaction.

For the foregoing reasons, there shall be judgment herein in favor of defendants and against plaintiff, dismissing this action.

Notes and Questions

In light of the foregoing case, what is required for a sale of a movable to be one "on view or trial" as opposed to one in which the buyer merely enjoys the implied right to inspect and reject the goods? One of the more frequently cited cases involving a sale on view or trial is *Hamilton Co. v. Medical Arts Bldg. Co.*, 135 So. 94 (La. App. 2 Cir. 1931). In this case, the buyer and seller agreed to the sale of refrigeration equipment that was to be installed in the buyer's building. After the equipment was installed, the buyer's building was foreclosed upon by one of the buyer's creditors. The precise issue before the court was whether the seller had a vendor's privilege in the equipment under Louisiana law, a question that—under the conflicts of law principles in effect at the time of the decision—turned on whether ownership of the equipment transferred in Missouri (the place at which the parties' consented to the sale) or Louisiana (the place at which the equipment was delivered and installed). The court determined that the sale was conditioned upon the buyer's approval of the equipment, an event that occurred in Louisiana. In reaching this determination, the court considered the following language in the parties' written contract:

> "The seller shall furnish an engineer to supervise and assist in making installation of said equipment and machinery."

> "The seller shall furnish all labor for ammonia work. Buyer to furnish labor for putting up water lines and cooling tower."

> "It is agreed and understood that a test run of three days must be made on the plant, for the purpose of making adjustments, if any, that may be required."

> "And it is hereby understood and agreed that a failure on the part of the buyer to reject the plant by notifying the seller in writing within three days from completion of installation above mentioned, shall constitute an acceptance on the part of the buyer."

Id. at 511. How does the above-quoted language differ from the parties' agreement in *Tunica Biloxi Tribe of Indians*?

c. Sales Subject to Resolutory Conditions

Unlike a sale subject to a suspensive condition, a sale subject to a resolutory condition is immediately enforceable, but it may come to an end if an uncertain event takes place. *See* LA. CIV. CODE art. 1767. While the Louisiana Civil Code recognizes that the parties may impose any condition on their agreement—whether suspensive or resolutory—that is not illegal or against public policy, the most common types of sales subject to resolutory conditions are (1) the "sale or return," and (2) the sale with the right of redemption.

i. Sale or Return

7 Saúl Litvinoff, *Louisiana Civil Law Treatise, Obligations § 58,* at 80–82 (1975) (citations omitted)[±]

When, by agreement of the parties, the condition is resolutory and not suspensive, the contract of sale effects an immediate transfer of ownership to the vendee, although subject to resolution in case of nonfulfillment of the condition of trial and approval. The risk also passes to the vendee. In French law it is understood that the parties' intention to make the condition resolutory, rather than suspensive, may be implied from the circumstances surrounding the agreement. The parties' freedom to introduce such a resolutory condition, and even the possibility that the condition be implied, are consistent with the language of French article 1588 which states that it is *presumed* that sales on approval are subject to a suspensive condition.

* * * * *

Agreement of "sale or return" and "bargain for sale, or return" are common-law expressions signifying a sale where the buyer's privilege of returning the thing operates as a condition subsequent. Functionally, this kind of transaction is the same as a contract of sale made under the resolutory condition of return by the buyer in the civilian view. The current use of the common-law expressions in the English language amply justifies their use by the Louisiana courts. It should be added here that the return of the thing by the buyer need not be in consequence of his disapproving it, but may be the result of a special relationship between the parties, as between merchants, according to which the buyer is allowed to return the thing if he cannot resell it. That is to say, not every sale of goods under a resolutory condition is of necessity a sale on trial and approval, though obviously some of them are.

* * * * *

± Reproduced with permission of Thomson Reuters.

Manuel v. Shaheen

316 So. 2d 878 (La. App. 3 Cir. 1975)

HOOD, Judge.

Julius R. Manuel claims damages for personal injuries sustained by him when he collided with a wharf while water skiing behind a boat being operated by Jake Shaheen. The original defendants were Joseph Shaheen, Jake Shaheen and Home Insurance Company. The suit was dismissed as to Home Insurance, and Zurich Insurance Company was impleaded as a party defendant. A summary judgment was rendered thereafter by the trial court dismissing the suit as to Zurich. Plaintiff appealed. We affirm.

The issues presented are (1) whether there is a genuine issue of fact as to the ownership of the boat which was involved in the accident, and (2) if not, whether that boat was owned by Joseph Shaheen or by Clay's Marine, Inc., the latter being insured by Zurich, when the accident occurred.

The judgment of the trial court was based on the pleadings, answers to interrogatories, affidavits, depositions and documentary evidence.

The receivable evidence shows that prior to June 5, 1973, Joseph Shaheen owned a 16-foot "Cathedral" boat, powered by a 110 horsepower outboard motor. On or shortly before that date he authorized his 19-year old son, Jake Shaheen, to purchase a new boat and motor from Clay's Marine, and to trade in the old Cathedral boat and motor for the new rig. Pursuant to that authorization, young Shaheen on June 5 selected and purchased from Clay's Marine a new 16.7-foot "Boston Whaler" boat and a new 85 horsepower Mercury outboard motor. They agreed on the price and the amount which was to be allowed for the "trade-in" of the old boat and motor. Clay's Marine picked up the old Cathedral boat and motor on or about June 5, and neither Joseph nor Jake Shaheen have seen or possessed the old boat and motor since that time. The new Boston Whaler boat, with a new 85 horsepower outboard motor, was delivered to Jake Shaheen on June 6 or 7, 1973, and it has been in the possession of Joseph and Jake Shaheen and has been used by them regularly since that time.

On June 5, Clay's Marine invoiced Joseph Shaheen for the purchase price of the new boat, motor and equipment, and on June 19, 1973, Joseph Shaheen paid to Clay's Marine the full amount due as shown on that invoice.

On June 29, 1973, plaintiff Manuel sustained personal injuries as the result of the above mentioned accident which occurred while he was water skiing behind the new Boston Whaler boat being operated by Jake Shaheen. Manuel instituted suit on December 4, 1973, against Joseph Shaheen, Jake Shaheen and Home Insurance Company to recover damages, and in his original petition he alleged that the Boston Whaler boat was owned by Joseph Shaheen at the time the accident occurred, and that the latter was insured by Home Insurance. On motion of Home Insurance, a summary judgment was rendered on March 25, 1974, dismissing the suit as to that defendant on the ground that the policy which it had issued to Shaheen did not cover claims for damages resulting from the operation of the boat involved in the accident. No appeal was taken from that judgment.

About the time that judgment was rendered, plaintiff amended his petition to allege that on June 5, 1973, Joseph Shaheen obtained the boat and motor which later was involved in the accident from Clay's Marine on a 30-day "try-out basis," with the understanding that the sale would be consummated later if the boat and motor proved to be satisfactory. He asserts in his amended pleadings that the sale had not been consummated by the time the accident occurred, and that the boat and motor were still owned by Clay's Marine, insured by Zurich, at the time plaintiff was injured. He took the position in the trial court, and he argues here, that the sale was made with a suspensive condition, that the condition had not taken place by the time the accident occurred, and that the boat and motor thus were still owned by Clay's Marine at that time. He contends that the operator of the boat was an insured under the policy which Zurich had issued to Clay's Marine, and that he is entitled to recover from that insurer.

Zurich filed a motion for summary judgment, and after a hearing the trial court rendered judgment on December 12, 1974, dismissing the suit as to Zurish [sic]. Plaintiff has appealed from that judgment.

Plaintiff contends that there is a genuine issue of material fact relating to the ownership of the boat at the time of the accident, and that accordingly the summary judgment appealed from should be reversed and the case remanded for trial on its merits.

To support that argument, Manuel relies on an affidavit executed by Joseph Shaheen, in which the affiant states that on June 5, 1973, Clay's Marine let the Boston Whaler boat out on a 30-day "try-out basis," so that Shaheen could determine whether he wanted to purchase it. The affidavit recites that Shaheen had not decided whether he wanted to purchase the boat by the time the accident occurred, that "title was not transferred and a bill of sale not completed as of the date of June 29, 1973," and that no document or instrument of any kind, in fact, has ever been signed transferring the new boat to him, or transferring the old Cathedral boat and motor to Clay's Marine. Shaheen stated in that affidavit that he still owned the old Cathedral boat and motor, and that he "was merely furnished the use and benefit of the 16.7 Boston Whaler and motor on a contingent basis."

The above affidavit, on its face, indicates that an issue of fact exists as to the ownership of the boat and motor at the time of the accident. The record, however, contains the testimony of Joseph Shaheen in two separate depositions, in both of which he testified that he was not present when his son purchased the boat and motor, that he has no personal knowledge of the terms of the sale, and that his statements in the affidavit relating to the conditions of the sale were based solely on information he obtained later from his son. In those depositions, Shaheen confirmed the fact that he received the new boat and motor from Clay's Marine on or shortly after June 5, 1973, that he traded in his old boat and motor for the new one at that time, that he paid for the new boat and motor on June 19 (10 days before the accident occurred), and that the boat and motor which he acquired from Clay's Marine were still in his possession and were being used by him when the last deposition was taken on August 30, 1974. He explained that the statement in his affidavit that the sale of the new boat had not been consummated before the accident occurred, was based solely on the fact that he had received no written transfer of title to the boat and motor by that time. The law, of course, does not require that the sale of a boat or motor be evidenced by a written document. LSA-C.C. art. 2441 [No Corresponding Article].

Jake Shaheen testified by deposition that the 85 horsepower motor which he acquired on June 5 was the largest outboard motor Clay's Marine had in stock at that time, and that although he preferred a bigger motor he accepted that one with the understanding that he could trade it in on a larger motor as soon as Clay's Marine got some larger ones in stock. According to young Shaheen, the agreement was that if he decided to trade it in that he would have to pay the difference in the prices of the two motors. He stated that the Boston Whaler boat was the boat he wanted, and that he never considered trading it in for another one. He also testified that, regardless of his own desires, his father would not let him trade in the 85 horsepower motor for a larger one.

The trial judge found that the sale was completed on June 5, 1973, and that the new boat and motor thus were owned by Joseph Shaheen at the time the accident occurred later that month. He concluded that the agreement between Shaheen and Clay's Marine that the 85 horsepower motor could be traded in later for a larger one was a "resolutory condition" relating only to the motor, that title to the boat and motor nevertheless became vested in Shaheen on June 5, 1973, and that the resolutory condition never took place. Since he determined that the boat and motor were not owned by Clay's Marine at the time of the accident, he rendered judgment dismissing the suit as to the latter's insurer, Zurich.

* * * * *

Article 967 of the Code of Civil Procedure provides that affidavits supporting or opposing motions for summary judgment "shall be made on personal knowledge," and that they "shall set forth such facts as would be admissible in evidence." We have pointed out that the affidavit executed by Joseph Shaheen, on which plaintiff relies, contains several statements which were not within the personal knowledge of the affiant and which would not be admissible in evidence. We agree with defendant Zurich that those statements may not be considered in determining whether a summary judgment should be rendered. The additional statements of fact contained in the affidavit, as explained in the depositions of Joseph Shaheen, tend to confirm rather than contradict the other evidence which is in the record.

We find, as the trial judge apparently did, that there is no dispute as to any material fact in this case. Joseph Shaheen, through his son, purchased from Clay's Marine a Boston Whaler boat and an 85 horsepower motor on June 5, 1973. The parties agreed on the boat and motor to be purchased, and on the price which was to be paid for them. They also agreed that Shaheen could trade the motor in for a larger one at a later date, if he desired to do so, by paying the difference in the purchase prices of the two motors. The boat and motor were delivered to Shaheen on June 6 or 7, 1973, and the purchase price was paid in full on June 19. Shaheen has had continuous possession of the boating rig since the date on which it was delivered, and he has used it regularly since that time. He has never decided or sought to trade in the 85 horsepower motor for a larger one. The accident resulting in injuries to plaintiff occurred on June 29, 1973, after the parties had agreed on the objects to be purchased and the price to be paid for it, and after the new boat and motor had been delivered and the agreed purchase price had been paid.

Article 2456 of the Louisiana Civil Code [R.C.C. 2456] provides that a sale is considered to be perfect between the parties "as soon as there exists an agreement for the object and for the price thereof, although the object has not yet been delivered, nor the price paid."

In the instant suit, the parties agreed on the object and the price which was to be paid for that object on June 5, 1973. Applying the provisions of the cited article of the Civil Code, it is apparent that the sale was perfected on that date, and that Joseph Shaheen was the owner of the boat at the time the accident occurred.

Plaintiff argues that the sale was not to be perfected until the expiration of the 30-day try-out period, and that it thus was made on a suspensive condition which had not occurred by the time of the accident. We do not agree with that argument. LSA-C.C. art. 2043 [R.C.C. 1767] defines an obligation contracted on a suspensive condition as one which "can not [sic] be executed till after the event." In the instant suit, we think the sale of the boat and motor was "executed" on June 5, 1973, when the parties agreed on the object and the price. Aside from the fact that the sale was completed on that date the evidence shows that the boat and motor were actually delivered to the purchaser and were paid for before the 30-day period expired and before the accident occurred. Our conclusion is that the sale was not contracted on a suspensive condition.

We make no determination as to whether the sale was made on a "resolutory condition," because such a finding is immaterial to the outcome of the case. LSA-C.C. art. 2045 [R.C.C. 1767] provides that a resolutory condition "does not suspend the execution of the obligation," but it only obliges the creditor to restore what he has received, "in case the event provided for in the condition takes place." The sale thus became effective when the parties agreed on the object and the price, and the evidence shows that the so-called resolutory condition (that is, the decision of the purchaser to trade in the 85 horsepower motor for a larger one) did not occur. Shaheen thus must be held to have been the owner of the boat at the time the accident occurred whether the sale was or was not made on a resolutory condition.

Our ultimate conclusion is that the ownership of the above mentioned boat and motor was transferred from Clay's Marine to Joseph Shaheen on June 5, that Clay's

Marine thus was not the owner of those items when plaintiff was injured on June 29, 1973, and that the trial judge correctly dismissed the suit insofar as it was directed against Zurich Insurance Company, the insurer of Clay's Marine.

For the reasons assigned, the judgment appealed from is affirmed. The costs of this appeal are assessed to plaintiff-appellant.

Affirmed.

Notes and Questions

1. Whether a condition affecting a sale is suspensive, on the one hand, or resolutory, on the other, is a matter of the parties' intentions, whether express or implied. Did the court in the foregoing case find the condition to be suspensive or resolutory? What aspects of the transaction were central to the court's determination?

2. Both the sale on view or trial and the sale or return must be distinguished from a consignment sale. This term is not defined in the Louisiana Civil Code, but it can be understood by the following definition of the term "consign" found in Black's Law Dictionary: "To give (merchandise or the like) to another to sell, usu[ally] with the understanding that the seller will pay the owner for the goods from the proceeds." *See Consign*, BLACK'S LAW DICTIONARY (10th ed. 2014). In a typical consignment sale, the seller of a movable thing places it in the possession of a merchant who sells movables of the same kind. The merchant agrees to sell the thing on behalf of the owner in return for a percentage of the price. In such an arrangement, the seller (or consignor) and the merchant (or consignee) are not bound by a contract of sale. Instead, under Louisiana law the contract is properly characterized as both a contract of deposit (*see* LA. CIV. CODE art. 2926) and a contract of mandate (*see* LA. CIV. CODE art. 2989). As a result of the proper characterization of a consignment sale, as between the parties, ownership and risk of loss of the thing placed in the merchant's possession remains with the seller unless and until the merchant sells the thing to a third person on behalf of the seller. At that point, the third person — and not the merchant — is bound to a contract of sale with the seller.

ii. Right of Redemption
La. Civ. Code arts. 2480, 2567–2588

In a sale with the right of redemption, the parties to the contract agree that the seller shall have the right "to take back the thing from the buyer" upon refunding the price. LA. CIV. CODE art. 2567; *id.* cmt. b. Such a sale is subject to a resolutory condition — the exercise of the right of redemption extinguishes the sale, and the parties are returned to the situation that existed prior to their agreement (with the exception that the buyer is entitled to retain the fruits and products of the thing sold prior to the seller's exercise of the right). LA. CIV. CODE art. 2575. The right of redemption is explored in detail in the following case.

Steib v. Joseph Rathborne Land Co.

163 So. 2d 429 (La. App. 4 Cir. 1964)

HALL, Judge.

Plaintiff, in his capacity as Receiver of The Joseph Webre Co., Limited, prosecutes this appeal from a summary judgment dismissing the Receivership's suit to be decreed to be the owner of certain land located in the Parishes of St. James and St. John the Baptist.

On the 9th day of June, 1909, The Joseph Webre Co., Limited, executed an authentic act in regular form purporting to sell and deliver to The Louisiana Cypress Lumber Company, Limited, certain described lands in said parishes for and in consideration of $114,600.00 cash.

The Act of Sale contains the following provision.

"The Vendor reserves the right to redeem the said lands after the removal of the cypress timber therefrom by the purchaser, said redemption price not to exceed the sum of one hundred dollars for all of said lands."

In addition to this reservation, the vendor therein reserved the right of pasturing cattle free of charge and the right to cultivate, free of charge, the ridges on the land; also the right to drain waters over and across the property; and finally the right to remove at its own expense all the cord wood and manufactured stove wood on the property.

On the 31st day of December, 1927, The Louisiana Cypress Lumber Company, Limited, by an authentic act of sale transferred the same property, among other properties, to the Joseph Rathborne Land Company, Inc. (Now Joseph Rathborne Land & Lumber Co., Inc.) for and in consideration of the price and sum of $100,000.00 cash.

This conveyance contains the following stipulation.

"Purchaser declares that it is familiar with the titles of vendor to the property herein conveyed and takes the same subject to any obligations of the vendor that may be contained in any of such titles but without recognizing the validity thereof or any liability thereupon, and expressly waiving any recourse upon vendor for any loss, damage or liability that purchaser may suffer by reason thereof."

The plaintiff as Receiver for The Joseph Webre Co., Limited, filed this suit praying (a) that the sale of June 9, 1909 to The Louisiana Cypress Lumber Company, Limited, be decreed to be a timber deed only; (b) that plaintiff be recognized as full owner of the fee simple title to all the land therein described; (c) that defendants be allowed a reasonable term to terminate their timber operations under the deed; and (d) that defendants be ordered to account for all revenues received by them resulting from the exercise by them of Acts of Ownership other than with respect to the timber rights.

Made defendants in the suit are The Joseph Rathborne Land and Lumber Company, Inc., certain mineral royalty assignees and certain mineral lessees holding under that corporation.

The Joseph Rathborne Land and Lumber Company, Inc. and its royalty assignees filed answers in which they deny the instrument of June 9, 1909 to be a timber deed and allege that the defendant corporation and its predecessor in title have exercised not only the right to cut and remove timber but during the entire period of time from June 9, 1909 have exercised all the rights of ownership of the said property including possession thereof as owner. The defendants specifically plead the prescription (peremption) of ten years provided by LSA-C.C. Article 2568 [R.C.C. 2568] against the exercise of the right of redemption and the prescription of 30 years Acquirendi causa provided by LSA-C.C. Articles 3499 [R.C.C. 3486], 3500 [R.C.C. 3486] and 3501 [R.C.C. 3486].

The mineral lessees who were joined as defendants plead in addition the protection of the law of registry provided by LSA-R.S. 9:1105 and LSA-C.C. Articles 2251 to 2266 inclusive [R.C.C. 3338–3353].

It is noted that none of the defendants filed any pleas of prescription Liberandi causa, unless the peremption provided in LSA-C.C. Article 2568 [R.C.C. 2568] may be regarded as such.

Both plaintiff and the defendants filed motions for summary judgment as authorized by LSA-C.C.P. Article 966.

The record consisting of the pleadings, answers to interrogatories and requests for admissions, and the affidavits and documentary evidence filed by the parties reveal the following undisputed facts:

Ever since the transfer in 1909 by The Joseph Webre Co., Limited to The Louisiana Cypress Lumber Company, Limited, the property has been assessed in the names of, and taxes have been paid thereof, by the latter company and its successor. The property was surveyed in 1909 and on several other occasions thereafter by them and the corners and boundaries marked with galvanized markers and a red painted line. A path of from six to seven feet wide was cleared and maintained around the outer boundaries. The lands were continuously patrolled by various persons employed for that purpose. Trapping operations were conducted for a number of years under the supervision of a paid supervisor of the corporations. Since 1937 mineral leases have been granted to various oil companies. Drilling for oil in 1956 resulted in a dry hole.

No timber was cut by defendants prior to 1918. From 1918 through 1921 The Louisiana Cypress Lumber Company, Limited, cut and removed 33,500,000 feet of saw timber. By the end of 1921 all of the merchantable cypress timber standing on the property had been cut and removed. Commencing in the year 1930 and continuing through the year 1953 the Rathborne Corporation cut and logged the second growth timber.

The plaintiff corporation from the date of the sale in 1909 has exercised no possession of any nature upon the land.

After a painstaking examination of the record the District Judge held that there was no dispute between the parties as to any material issue of fact and that a summary judgment could properly be rendered. Being of the opinion that the conveyance of June 9, 1909 was a valid sale of land with the right of redemption and not a timber deed or other type of contract, the District Judge maintained defendants' plea of prescription (peremption) of 10 years as provided in LSA-C.C. Article 2568 [R.C.C. 2568] and rendered summary judgment dismissing plaintiff's suit. Plaintiff appealed.

The basic issue presented for our determination is whether the conveyance of June 9, 1909 from The Joseph Webre Co., Limited to The Louisiana Cypress Lumber Company, Limited, was (a) a timber deed only, (b) a sale of land with the right of redemption, or (c) some other and different type of contract.

Plaintiff contends that the instrument is nothing more than a timber deed and should be enforced in accordance with its terms notwithstanding that 52 years has elapsed since the date of the deed. They suggest that if the instrument is not a timber deed that it is a contract *sui generis* to be recognized and enforced as such.

Defendants contend that the instrument is plainly a deed to land in the form of an act of sale with the right of redemption, as held by the District Judge.

(a)

The conveyance of June 9, 1909 contains the usual provisions for the fee transfer of real estate. It recites that the vendor "* * * does by these presents grant, bargain, sell, convey, transfer, assign, setover, abandon and deliver with full warranty and with full substitution and subrogation in and to all the rights and actions of warranty which it has or may have against all preceding owners and vendors unto * * *" the vendee accepting and [] purchasing for itself "* * * its successors and assigns and acknowledging due delivery and possession thereof all and singular the following described property to wit:" (land description follows) "* * * To have and to hold the above described property unto the said purchaser its successors and assigns forever."

The instrument further describes the property transferred as "being the same property which the said vendor acquired by purchaser from" (here follows the name of the former owner, the date of the act of purchase and a recitation of its recordation).

Then follows the reservation to the vendor of the right to repurchase or redeem "*the said lands*" after the removal of the cypress timber therefrom.

Plainly the instrument was a sale of land and not a sale of the timber only. We find no necessity to discuss the arguments advanced by plaintiff in an effort to show that the parties *intended* to transfer the timber only. The arguments are based upon pure speculation. The only proof we have of their intention is the deed itself. The plain language of the deed manifests a positive intent on the part of the parties thereto to transfer and deliver ownership of the *land*, subject to certain designated servitudes such as the right of pasturage, drainage etc. Incidentally, the reservations of these servitudes would be wholly unnecessary had the instrument been merely a timber deed.

(b)

A sale with the right of redemption (*vente à réméré*) is a special and distinct type of sale authorized and governed by special rules (see LSA-C.C. Articles 2567 to 2588 inclusive). [R.C.C. 2567–2588]

The right of redemption is defined in LSA-C.C. Article 2567 [R.C.C. 2567] as being "* * * an agreement or paction, by which the vendor reserves to himself the power of *taking back the thing sold by returning the price paid for it.*" (Emphasis supplied). The reimbursement of the purchase money by the vendor is again alluded to in LSA-C.C. Articles 2586 [No Corresponding Article] and 2587 [R.C.C. 2587].

The first sentence of LSA-C.C. Article 2578 [R.C.C. 2578] provides:

> "The thing sold shall be restored to the seller who exercises the right of redemption, in the state in which it is *at the moment * * *.*" (Emphasis supplied).

This we interpret to mean in the state in which it is at the moment of delivery to the purchaser. But the remainder of the Article as well as LSA-C.C. Articles 2576 [R.C.C. 2577], 2577 [R.C.C. 2577] and 2587 [R.C.C. 2587] show that when the right of redemption is exercised an adjustment between the parties must be made in order to restore them to the position they occupied prior to the sale. The thing sold should not be injured. (See LSA-C.C. Articles 2576 [R.C.C. 2577] and 2577 [R.C.C. 2577]).

"When the right to redeem is exercised in time, it produces the retroactive resolution of the contract of sale and of the transfer of the property which was a consequence of it. The vendor is reputed never to have ceased to be the owner, and the buyer is reputed never to have owned. * * *." Planiol "Civil Law Treatise" Vol. 2, Part 1, Sec. 1582.

Thus we see the *vente à réméré* is based upon two elements viz. (1) the taking back of the thing sold with adjustments made for deterioration and augmentation and (2) the return of the price paid for it.

Without these two elements the contract is not a sale with the right of redemption, although it may be some other valid contract.

In the instant case the vendor did not reserve the right to redeem the thing sold and the reservation did not contemplate returning the purchase price. What he sold was the land which included the growing timber. What he proposed to redeem was the land denuded of the trees. It was contemplated that the thing sold would be *depleted* before the exercise of the right to redeem. It may be appropriate here to observe that growing timber is not a "fruit" which would belong to the purchaser under LSA-C.C. Article 2575 [R.C.C. 2575].

As to the return of the purchase price we are told that some of the French commentators have said the redemption price could be different from the original price while others have held contrary views. Planiol states in his "Civil Law Treatise" Volume 2, Part 1, Section 1579 that the price to by [sic] restored can be inferior or superior to the original price. Our Courts have held that it may be more. See *Levy v. Ward*, 32 La.Ann. 784; *Soulie v. Ranson*, 29 La.Ann. 161. We know of no decision which says it may be less.

We do not find it necessary to decide whether the sum stipulated to be reimbursed to the purchaser in the present case satisfies the element of "return of the purchase price", because in our opinion the other element is lacking (i.e. "the return of the thing sold.")

We hold that the instrument in question here is not a sale with the right of redemption. Consequently, we are not authorized to maintain the special prescription (peremption) applicable to the reservation of the right of redemption (LSA-C.C. Articles 2568 [R.C.C. 2568], 2569 [R.C.C. 2571] and 2570 [R.C.C. 2570]).

(c)

Although the instrument in question is not in our opinion a sale with the right of redemption it nevertheless may well be a valid contract of another sort. It is suggested that it may be a sale with a counter letter written into it, or a sale with a resolutory condition, or a sale with a right to repurchase a portion of the realty conveyed.

We reject the suggestion that the reservation may be a built-in counter letter because it bears no resemblance to a counter-letter and, if enforced, would not have the effect of a counter letter. We are likewise of the opinion that the instrument in question is not a sale with a resolutory condition, because it contains no condition which when accomplished would operate the revocation of the obligation. (LSA-C.C. Articles 2021 [R.C.C. 1767], 2045 [R.C.C. 1767]). Moreover, a retransfer of the land is required.

We are of the opinion that the instrument evidences a sale of realty and the timber which formed a part thereof, which a reservation to the vendor of the right to repurchase the denuded land after the timber had been cut and removed.

Conclusion

Having reached the conclusion that the instrument in question is not merely a timber deed as contended by plaintiff and that it is not a *vente à réméré* as contended by defendants, it becomes necessary for us to consider whether plaintiff is entitled to the relief prayed for when the instrument is viewed as a sale with the right to repurchase the bare land.

The repurchase price for the land was fixed at "not to exceed the sum of one hundred dollars for all of said lands." If this price be regarded as uncertain the reservation of the right to repurchase would be invalid (See LSA-C.C. Article 2464 [R.C.C. 2464]). (The invalidity of the reservation clause would not however affect the remainder of the contract, the contract being separable.) Obviously if the reservation is invalid plaintiff has no rights at all.

If on the other hand the repurchase price be regarded as certain and the reservation clause be regarded as valid and binding it would have been necessary for plaintiff to tender the price before filing suit to be declared the owner of the land. This plaintiff did not do. (Compare *R. E. E. De Montluzin Co., Limited v. New Orleans & N.E.R. Co.*, 166 La. 822, 118 So. 33).

As we have heretofore pointed out none of the defendants filed a plea of prescription Liberandi causa. Although the liberative prescription of 10 years under LSA-C.C. Article 3544 [R.C.C. 3499], or the liberative prescription of 30 years under LSA-C.C. Article 3548 [R.C.C. 3502] might be applicable to the facts of this case when viewed in the light of our appreciation of the instrument of June 9, 1909, we cannot supply such pleas (See *Welch v. Courville*, La.App., 99 So.2d 487).

For the foregoing reasons the judgment appealed from is affirmed.

Affirmed.

ON APPLICATION FOR REHEARING

Per Curiam.

After argument and submission of this case we handed down our opinion and decree on April 6, 1964. Following this, on April 21, 1964, all defendants for the first time filed pleas of 10 and 30 year liberative prescription (LSA-C.C. Arts. 3544 [R.C.C. 3499] and 3548 [R.C.C. 3502]). These pleas are not considered for the reason that the same were filed too late. Under LSA-C.C.P. Art. 2163 we cannot consider the peremptory exception filed for the first time in this court if it is pleaded after submission of the case for a decision.

Plaintiff's application for rehearing is denied.

Rehearing denied.

Notes and Questions

1. The court in *Steib* points out that if the seller has the right to repurchase something other than the thing actually resold, the seller's right is not a "right of redemption" as contemplated by the Civil Code. The court in *Steib* also raised an important question about the right of redemption—whether the redemption price can be different from the original price paid. Prior to its revision in 1995, Article 2567 stated that the right of redemption involved the seller "taking back the thing sold *by returning the price paid for it.*" La. Civ. Code art. 2567 (1870) (emphasis added). This language appeared to require that the parties agree that the seller would return the exact price paid by the buyer—no more and no less. However, as indicated by *Steib*, Louisiana courts did not always read that requirement literally. The language requiring the return of the price was omitted from Article 2567 when it was revised. Article 2567 comment (d) indicates that this change was intentional.

2. Read carefully Article 2567 and comment (b) to that Article. That comment states that "in the usual sale subject to redemption, the vendor must reserve the right to repurchase. If, on the contrary, the right to repurchase is granted by the vendee, the contract is a sale with option to repurchase and not a sale with a right of redemption." LA. CIV. CODE art. 2567 cmt. b. Given that the parties must mutually consent to either type of contract, how does one distinguish between an agreement in which the vendor "reserves" the right of redemption and one in which the vendee "grants" an option to repurchase? For additional discussion of the distinction between the option contract and the right of redemption, see Chapter 12: Contracts Preparatory to Sale.

3. As under prior law, the right of redemption is subject to stringent limitations on duration. Article 2568 provides that the right of redemption may not be reserved for more than ten years if the thing sold is immovable, and for no more than five years if the thing sold is movable. LA. CIV. CODE art. 2568. These periods are peremptive. *See* LA. CIV. CODE art. 2571. What is the purpose of these limitations?

4. At the time *Steib* was decided, while the fruits of the thing sold subject to a right of redemption belonged to the buyer, products of the thing belonged to the seller. *See* LA. CIV. CODE art. 2575 (1870). Recall that "[f]ruits are things that are produced or derived from another thing without diminution of its substance," and include both natural fruits and civil fruits, such as rents. LA. CIV. CODE art. 551. By contrast, "[p]roducts [are things] derived from a thing as a result of diminution of its substance . . . ." LA. CIV. CODE art. 488. The law was changed in 1995 to provide that "[t]he fruits and products of a thing sold with right of redemption belong to the buyer." LA. CIV. CODE art. 2575. This change is consistent with the notion that, prior to the seller's exercise of the right of redemption, the thing is owned by the buyer. The court's holding in *Steib* that the parties' agreement was not a right of redemption turned in part on the fact that, under the contract, the seller only had the right to repurchase the denuded property after the standing timber (a product) was harvested. Would the result of *Steib* be the same today under new Article 2575? Why or why not?

5. Article 2577 is also consistent with the notion that the buyer is the owner of the thing prior to the seller's exercise of the right of redemption. That article provides that the buyer is entitled to all improvements he or she made on the thing that can be removed when the seller exercises the right of redemption, and, if the improvements cannot be removed, the buyer is entitled to the enhancement of the value of the thing resulting from the improvements. LA. CIV. CODE art. 2577.

6. The rights of a third person who acquires an interest in a thing sold subject to the right of redemption must also be addressed. With respect to immovable property, Article 2572 provides that "the right of redemption is effective against third persons only from the time the instrument that contains it is filed for registry in the parish where the immovable is located." LA. CIV. CODE art. 2572. Consider the following hypothetical:

Seller conveys a tract of land to Buyer and in the Act of Sale reserves the right of redemption for a period of five years. Seller properly records the Act of Sale in the appropriate conveyance records. One year after the sale, Buyer sells the same tract of land to Third Person. The following year, Seller attempts to exercise the right of redemption. Can Seller recover the property from Third Person? Why or why not?

With respect to movable things, Article 2572 provides that "the right of redemption is effective against third persons who, at the time of purchase, had actual knowledge of the existence of that right." *Id.*

6. Another classification problem posed by the right of redemption is the distinction between a sale with a right of redemption and a security agreement. The seller in a sale with the right of redemption often intends the price paid by the buyer to serve as a loan, and for the transfer of ownership of the thing sold to serve as a form of security for the buyer's obligation to repay the price. When the seller-borrower repays the loan, the buyer-lender reconveys the thing sold. However, in some cases, the parties to a purported "sale" with the right of redemption may actually intend that ownership will not transfer unless and until the borrower defaults on the obligation to repay the price at the time agreed by the parties. In such a case, the contract is properly classified as a simulated security agreement, under which ownership does not transfer immediately to the "buyer." The following case is illustrative of this classification problem.

Tyler v. Rapid Cash, LLC

930 So. 2d 1135 (La. App. 2 Cir. 2006)

DREW, J.

Willie Tyler appeals from a judgment of the Monroe City Court rejecting his demands against defendants, Rapid Cash, LLC ("Rapid Cash"), and James Hampton. We reverse.

FACTS

This dispute concerns the surrender by Mr. Tyler of his car to Hampton under an agreement executed by these two men at Hampton's place of employment, Rapid Cash, in Monroe. Tyler urges that he is entitled to the return of his car or its value because the agreement was illegal.

Rapid Cash is a small finance company with offices in north Louisiana. At the time of the transaction in question, Hampton was the office manager at the Monroe location. He and three other family members own the company.

Tyler owned a 1991 Toyota Camry that he purchased in 2003 for $2,000.00. Tyler is a cancer patient and testified that he needed the car to drive from his home in Monroe to Shreveport for his cancer treatments. In March of 2004, Tyler met with an acquaintance from his neighborhood, Shawn Wilson, whose home had recently been burglarized. Tyler related that Wilson asked him if she could borrow money from him. She suggested that the two go to Rapid Cash, and Tyler agreed.

According to Hampton, Tyler first dealt with another employee of Rapid Cash but did not bring with him sufficient documentation of income that was required to obtain a loan from the business. Hampton testified that the other Rapid Cash employee then referred Tyler to him. Hampton testified that he then offered, in his individual capacity, to buy Tyler's Camry from him for $225.00, and that Tyler accepted the offer. The two men executed a contract, printed from a Rapid Cash computer, which provided as follows:

Motor vehicle Bill of Sale

March 6, 2004

I Willie James Tyler . . . sell outright to James Hampton . . . one TOYT CAY (White) vin # . . . . Total agreed to price is $225.00. Payment is agreed by Seller and Buyer as: $225.00 non refundable payment, paid by cash on March 6, 2004. Buyer is responsible for all local, city, county and / or state taxes and / or tariffs resulting from purchase.

The above motor vehicle is being purchased by the buyer in an "as is" condition, with no stated or implied warranties by the seller, which is understood by the Buyer and Seller, at the time of this sale, to be no warranties what so ever.

Rapid Cash was not a named party to the transaction and did not loan Tyler any money. The agreement is signed by both Tyler and Hampton and is notarized and witnessed by two witnesses. Tyler acknowledged in court that he signed the agreement. Tyler also endorsed his certificate of title and gave it to Hampton. Tyler said that Wilson received the proceeds of the "sale" and moved away from the area without repaying the money.

Hampton did not take possession of the car at the time. As he explained in his testimony:

A: [O]n the 6th I told Mr. Tyler that I would take future delivery of the car. That he could either repay me the money after 14 days or I, he could drop the vehicle off at my office. And he did not do either. And so, I'm sure of the exact date uh, in between the 20th and say the 27th I uh, went to Mr. Tyler's house and I picked up the vehicle personally. I said I'm here to pick up your, uh, the vehicle you sold me and he gave me the keys and uh . . . .

Q: Because he didn't bring the money to you in 14 days you went down there and picked up the car?

A: Yes, sir.

Q: If he had brought the money to you within 14 days?

A: I would have voided the transaction.

* * * * *

[In early May, well after Hampton picked up the car, Tyler attempted to repay the amount he owed Hampton, but he discovered that his car had been sold. Tyler then filed suit. *Ed.*]

The court found that the transaction was lawful, that it was simply a "bad deal" for Tyler, and that Hampton was entitled to keep the car when Tyler failed to repay the money within two weeks. Tyler now appeals.

DISCUSSION

* * * * *

The written agreement between the parties in this case is a simple contract of sale. Even though the agreement appears to be invalid as an authentic act because no notary was present when the parties and witnesses signed, the agreement appears to be an act under private signature since Tyler acknowledged in court that he signed the document. La. C.C. arts. 1834 and 1836. Testimony may be admitted to prove that such an agreement was, *inter alia,* a simulation. La. C.C. art. 1848.

Both Taylor and Hampton testified that the written agreement did not encompass their entire agreement. Indeed, both testified that the "sale" agreement would be voided if Tyler repaid the loan. Hampton testified that the term of the loan was two weeks from its inception. Tyler did not testify about the term of the loan, but said that at the time Hampton took the car from his house in April, Hampton told him that he could get his car back if he repaid the money. Tyler did not testify about what time limit he understood to apply to this agreement. These two witnesses also disagreed about the dates of other events; Hampton said that he came to get the car in March, but Tyler remembered the event happening in April.

* * * * *

It is significant that Tyler retained possession of the Camry after the sale. La. C.C. art. 2480 provides, "When the thing sold remains in the corporeal possession of the seller the sale is presumed to be a simulation . . . ." Accordingly, given the evidence that Mr. Tyler retained the corporeal possession of the car after the "sale," the sale is presumed to be a simulation. Moreover, La. C.C. art. 2027 provides:

> A simulation is relative when the parties intend that their contract shall produce effects between them though different from those recited in their contract. A relative simulation produces between the parties the effects they intended if all requirements for those effects have been met.

Although the trial court's findings of fact are subject to review under the manifest error standard, *Stobart v. State of Louisiana, through Dep't of Transp. and Development,* 92-1328 (La.4/12/93), 617 So.2d 880, we are convinced that the only reasonable interpretation of the evidence is that this transaction was a simulated sale intended to establish a security interest in Hampton's favor for a loan of $225.00. Both parties agreed that Tyler would not have to surrender the car if he repaid the sale price of $225.00, and the auto was likely worth between $1,000.00 (the actual resale "wholesale" price) and $2,450.00, the NADA Guide value. The "sale" was thus intended to serve only as collateral for the loan.

* * * * *

CONCLUSION

We reverse the judgment of the trial court and award damages of $2,700.00 in favor of Willie James Tyler and against James Hampton and Rapid Cash, LLC. Attorney fees of $1,800.00 and court costs are assessed against James Hampton and Rapid Cash, LLC.

REVERSED.

Notes and Questions

A right of "redemption" also exists in the context of tax sales, although tax redemptions are governed the Louisiana Constitution and Revised Statutes rather than the Civil Code. Pursuant to Article 7, Section 25 of the Louisiana Constitution of 1974, immovable property may be sold due to the owner's failure to pay property taxes. The purchaser of such property pays the delinquent taxes as the price. The prior owner may "redeem" the property within three years after the date of recordation of the tax sale by paying the price paid by the purchaser, a 5% penalty, and interest at 1% per month until the property is redeemed.

4. Sales Conditioned on Payment of Price (a/k/a "Common Law" Conditional Sales)

The parties to a contract of sale may wish to agree that ownership of the thing sold will remain with the seller until the buyer has paid all or a part of the price. Such a sale is referred to in common law jurisdictions as a "conditional sale." The term used in civilian jurisdictions is perhaps more descriptive: "sale with reservation of title." Irrespective of the designation given to this transaction, it has never fit neatly into the framework of Louisiana's law of obligations. As the following materials demonstrate, Louisiana's treatment of these "conditional sales" and more particularly, its willingness to enforce them as written, has varied significantly depending upon whether the thing sold is movable or immovable in nature.

a. Conditional Sales of Movables

Louisiana's treatment of conditional sales of movables has evolved significantly over the course of the last century. Complete understanding of the current approach to transactions of this type requires a brief exploration of historical jurisprudence, followed by an examination of modern-day statutory law. A comparative look is then given to the ways in which Louisiana's approach to conditional sales differs from that of the rest of the United States.

i. The Historical Approach

Ventre v. Pacific Indem. Co.
419 So. 2d 969 (La. App. 3 Cir. 1982)

LABORDE, Judge

Emile K. Ventre, plaintiff-appellant, seeks to recover damages for the total loss of a Fairchild airplane insured by Pacific Indemnity Company, defendant-appellee, which crashed on June 7, 1967, while being flown by Robert Moody. The trial court granted a judgment in favor of Pacific. We affirm.

On April 19, 1967, Ventre purchased the airplane in his name. He subsequently entered into an agreement of sale with Robert Moody which provided that Moody would purchase a one half interest in the airplane on an installment basis. Moody had permission to fly the airplane whenever he desired. Operational costs such as hanger rent, gas and oil, etc., were to be paid by Ventre and Moody.

Ventre obtained a binder for insurance on the airplane. The insurance binder named Ventre and Moody as authorized pilots.

On or about May 24, 1967, Moody gave Ventre a check for $165 representing the first installment payment on their agreement. The check was returned "NSF". Ventre became dissatisfied with Moody, called the insurance agent and had Moody's name removed from the binder of insurance. On June 3, 1967, he called the people at the local airport, Opelousas Flying Service, and told them Moody was not authorized to fly the plane. He followed his phone call by a personal visit to the airport and again told them Moody was not authorized to fly the plane. He told Moody the "deal was off" because Moody had failed to make proper payment on the airplane and had failed to qualify for insurance coverage.

On June 7, 1967, Moody flew the airplane; it crashed, resulting in a total loss. Ventre filed this suit to recover his loss under the policy of insurance issued by Pacific.

Ventre contends that Moody is not a part-owner of the plane and that his unauthorized use of the plane constitutes theft. Under his theory, Ventre is entitled to recover under the terms of his policy with Pacific.

Pacific contends the plane was owned by Ventre and Moody; Ventre was the only insured pilot, but as part-owner Moody was authorized to fly the plane and there is no coverage under the terms of their policy since he was not a named pilot.

In granting judgment in favor of Pacific, the trial judge held, in part, as follows:

"Ventre contends that he is the sole owner of the plane and that Moody's use was unauthorized and constituted theft. This contention is necessary as the policy affords coverage for all damage to the plane resulting from its theft but not from its use by another pilot.

The testimony shows that Ventre and Moody entered into an agreement to jointly purchase the aircraft. This agreement was in the form of a conditional sale—Ventre purchased the plane in his own name and Moody was to pay for his one-half interest in the aircraft on an installment basis. (Transcript p. 40). In the common law, this agreement has the effect of maintaining title in the conditional vendor until the conditions of sale are fulfilled. However, in Louisiana, the effects following from that particular contract are those of a completed sale and title passes to the vendee at that time and cannot be rescinded unilaterally. *Givens v. Southern Farm Bureau Casualty Insurance Co.*, 197 So.2d 380 (La. App. 1967).

Pursuant to their agreement, Moody delivered a check for $165.00 representing the first installment payment on their agreement. Though the check was dishonored, its tender and acceptance indicates that the price of the thing and the terms of the sale had been agreed upon and that the sale was complete. Moody then owned one-half of the airplane and had an absolute right to its use regardless of insurance coverage.

Judgment will be rendered in favor of the defendant."

We agree with the trial judge that the sale of the one half interest in the plane from Ventre to Moody was complete. Even though Louisiana courts have consistently refused to recognize the common law "conditional sale" they have repeatedly held that where all essential elements and conditions for absolute sale are present in a contract between parties, the effect flowing legally from that particular contract follow whether the parties foresaw and intended them or not, and though they may refer to their contract as a conditional sale. LSA-C.C. art. 2439 [R.C.C. 2439]; *Givens v. Southern Farm Bureau Casualty Insurance Co.*, 197 So.2d 380 (La. App. 2nd Cir. 1967), writ refused, 250 La. 902, 199 So.2d 916 (La. 1967).

We conclude that under the above cited jurisprudence, the testimony elicited at trial and specifically the testimony of Ventre, a sale of a one half interest in the plane from Ventre to Moody was complete.

Ventre argues, alternatively, that assuming a sale did occur, ownership of the plane did not pass to Moody because the sale was subject to a suspensive condition, i.e., that Moody had to qualify for insurance coverage. We view this condition as resolutory rather than suspensive, such that the failure to comply with the engagements of one of the parties, does not dissolve the contract of right, but rather provides a means, which consists of a suit for dissolution or a demand for specific performance. LSA-C.C. arts. 2046 [R.C.C. 2013] and 2047 [R.C.C. 2013].

Moody was named as an authorized pilot in the original binder of insurance. When Ventre had Moody's name removed from the binder and decided the "deal was off." because of Moody's NSF check and his failure to qualify for insurance coverage, he could not unilaterally rescind that sale without suit for dissolution. The sale was complete within the intendment of LSA-C.C. art. 2456 [R.C.C. 2456] and Ventre could not impose further conditions, i.e., full payment and/or full insurance coverage.

For the reasons assigned the judgment of the trial court is affirmed at appellant's costs.

Affirmed.

Notes and Questions

1. The foregoing case illustrates that Louisiana courts will not enforce a conditional sale according to the parties' intent when the thing sold is a movable. The Louisiana Supreme Court first expressed its disapproval of sales conditioned on payment of the price in the seminal case of *Barber Asphalt Paving Co. v. St. Louis Cypress Co.*, 46 So. 193 (La. 1908). In *Barber Asphalt*, the plaintiff, Barber Asphalt Paving Co., agreed to sell a steam shovel to Hoyt for $1,200, payable in four equal installments. The parties' agreement provided that the seller would remain the owner of the steam shovel until the buyer had paid the price in full. After making one payment, but before paying the balance of the price, the buyer sold the steam shovel to the defendant, St. Louis Cypress Co. The seller sued the third-party purchaser, claiming that Hoyt had sold a thing that did not belong to him. The seller argued that "under the express terms of the contract the payment of the entire price was a condition precedent to Hoyt's becoming owner, and that inasmuch as the condition was never fulfilled he never became owner, and, in consequence, the sale to defendant was of the property of another, and null." *Id.* at 193. The Supreme Court disagreed with the seller. Although the Court recognized that the agreement intended by the parties would have been enforceable in a common law jurisdiction, it determined that under Louisiana law, the seller's theory was "legally impossible." *Id.* at 194.

According to the Court, because the essentials of a sale are a thing and a price, "[i]t follows from this that to suppose a sale without a transfer of the property in the thing which forms the object of the sale is simply to suppose an impossibility." *Id.* at 196. Moreover, the court rejected the seller's characterization of the sale as one subject to a suspensive condition, "since a sale of that kind has no effect or operation, and the present sale had an effect or operation — it had the effect or operation of making Hoyt debtor of the price and entitled to the possession of the property." *Id.* at 197. With respect to this point, the Court went on to say:

> The supposition that the payment of the price can be made a suspensive condition, or condition precedent, to a sale, is altogether a mistaken idea. A price cannot be paid until there is a price; and there cannot be a price until there is a sale; and there cannot be a sale until the condition precedent to there being one is accomplished. The proposition of the payment of the price being a condition precedent to the sale is on a par with those of putting the cart before the horse, and of not going into water before knowing how to swim. It is the sale which creates the price; the existence of the sale is a condition precedent to there being a price. The payment of the price cannot, therefore, be a condition precedent to the existence of the sale; unless, indeed, two events can be conditions precedent to each other.

Id. at 198. The Court also characterized the parties' obligation as "lopsided"—lacking mutuality—since the buyer was bound unconditionally to pay the price, while the seller was bound only conditionally to transfer ownership of the thing sold. *Id.* at 199.

Finding the contract intended by the parties impossible under Louisiana law, the Court in *Barber Asphalt* went on to hold that the parties' contract was *unconditional*, and as a result, ownership of the steam shovel transferred to Hoyt upon the parties' consent as to thing and price. *Id.* at 196–97. Since Hoyt had become the owner of the thing at the time of the parties' agreement, his subsequent sale to a third person was not a "sale of a thing of another" under the meaning of Article 2452.

2. Since *Barber Asphalt*, Louisiana courts have consistently held that in these so-called "conditional sales," the parties' intent to delay the transfer of ownership should be disregarded in favor of the general rule that ownership of the thing sold transfers upon the parties' consent as to thing and price. In light of the fact that the *Barber Asphalt* Court characterized the condition as "impossible," is this approach appropriate? Why or why not? *See* La. Civ. Code art. 1769. Are there policy reasons that justify the *Barber Asphalt* Court's approach?

3. Louisiana's treatment of sales of movables in which the transfer of ownership is conditioned upon the payment of the price has been the subject of intense criticism by scholars. Do you see why? What arguments can you make that an agreement in which the parties' delay the transfer of ownership until the buyer has paid all or a designated portion of the purchase price is neither "legally impossible" nor "lopsided"? What arguments can you make that such a contract is not subject to a condition at all?

ii. The Modern Approach

La. Rev. Stat. §§ 9:3301–42, 10:1-201(b)(35), 10:1-203

The enactment of two bodies of statutory law since 1985 has profoundly affected the treatment of conditional sales of movables in Louisiana: Article 9 of the Uniform Commercial Code and the Louisiana Lease of Movables Act. While exhaustive treatment of Article 9 of the Uniform Commercial Code and the Lease of Movables Act is beyond the scope of this textbook, some appreciation of these two bodies of law is required for a complete understanding of the modern status of conditional sales of movables in this state.

(a) Article 9 of the Uniform Commercial Code

Louisiana's version of Article 9 of the Uniform Commercial Code is found in LA UCC-9 of Title 10 of the Louisiana Revised Statutes (titled "Commercial Laws") and is thus often referred to as "Chapter 9" or "LA UCC-9." LA UCC-9 governs security interests in movables. Security interests, in most cases, are interests created by contract which secure payment or performance of an obligation. La. Rev. Stat. § 10:1-201(b)(35).

Relevant to conditional sales of movables, LA UCC-9's definition of a "security interest" provides in part: "The retention or reservation of title by a seller of goods notwithstanding perfection of the sale is limited in effect to a reservation of a 'security interest.'" *Id.* Under this provision, when the parties to a sale agree that the transfer of ownership of the thing sold is conditioned upon the buyer's payment of the price, that "retention or reservation of title" creates a security interest in favor of the seller. Compare this rule to the historical jurisprudential treatment of conditional sales of movables. Under *Barber Asphalt* and its progeny, a buyer in a conditional sale of movable property is regarded as the owner from the time of consent, regardless of whether the price has been paid. This rule is unchanged by LA UCC-9. However, LA UCC-9 gives the seller an important right that the jurisprudence did not: a *security interest* in the thing sold.

The seller's security interest in the thing sold pursuant to a conditional sale is enforceable against the debtor and some unsecured creditors from the time of the parties' agreement. However, the seller's security interest creditors must be "perfected" for the seller to obtain maximum protection against the buyer's other creditors. "Perfection" in this context usually requires that a financing statement be filed in accordance with the requirements of LA UCC-9. *See* La. Rev. Stat. § 10:9-310(a).

In sum, since the enactment of LA UCC-9, effective January 1, 1990, while the buyer in a conditional sale of a movable thing acquires ownership of the thing sold according to the general rules governing transfer of ownership, the seller retains a security interest in the thing sold which may be enforced against the debtor and, if properly perfected, against the buyer's creditors.

(b) Louisiana Lease of Movables Act

Since *Barber Asphalt*, Louisiana courts have been faced with the challenge of determining the enforceability of contracts in which the parties have attempted to circumvent the prohibition on conditional sales by *disguising* their contract as a lease with an option to purchase. The Louisiana Lease of Movables Act ("LMA"), enacted in 1985, directly addresses the enforceability of such contracts. An appreciation of the provisions of the LMA requires additional exploration of the classification problem posed by "financed leases" and the historical treatment of such contracts by Louisiana courts.

In a "true" lease with an option to purchase, the lessee of a thing pays rent in return for the use and enjoyment of the thing for a term and has the right to purchase the leased item before the end of the term for an additional sum. In this type of transaction, the lessor remains the owner of the thing that is leased unless and until the lessee exercises the option to buy it. Only when the option is exercised does the lessee become buyer and thereby owner of the thing. This framework of a lease with an option to purchase has been used by parties who wish to avoid Louisiana's prohibition on conditional sales. In such situations, the parties do not intend a lease at all but intend instead a sale with reservation of title. In such a case, the parties agree that the "lessee" is bound to pay the full purchase price of a thing in installments, after which ownership is transferred in return for the lessee's payment of a nominal sum or even no additional sum at all.

One of the earliest cases to address this classification problem is *Byrd v. Cooper*, 117 So. 441 (La. 1928). In this case, one party "leased" thirteen mules to the other in exchange for the execution of six notes, upon payment of which the purported "lessee" was to receive ownership of the mules. Like Hoyt, the purchaser of the steam shovel in *Barber Asphalt*, the "lessee" in *Byrd* sold the mules to a third person prior to having paid all of the notes. And, like the seller of the steam shovel in *Barber Asphalt*, the "lessor" in *Byrd* brought suit against the third-party purchaser, seeking to be declared the owner of the mules. Relying on *Barber Asphalt*, the Louisiana Supreme Court rejected the plaintiff's claim:

> [I]t is clear that a so-called contract of lease by which the lessee binds himself at once and irrevocably for a rental equal to the full value of the thing leased, and is to become owner thereof when the so-called rental is paid in full, and without payment of any further consideration, is nothing else than a conditional sale disguised under the form of a so-called lease; and the effect of such a contract is to vest title in the so-called lessee, [that is, the] purchaser.

Id. at 442. Thus, the court held that the parties' contract, though disguised as a lease, was, in fact, a sale conditioned upon payment of the price and, as a result of the proper classification of the contract, ownership of the mules had transferred to the "lessee" upon the parties' agreement as to thing and "rent." *Id.*

Following *Byrd v. Cooper,* Louisiana courts used a case-by-case approach to determine the true intent of the parties. If a court determined that the parties' intent was to enter into a sale with reservation of title, the court would enforce the contract as a sale with immediate transfer of ownership. As discussed in a student comment summarizing the early jurisprudence on conditional sales:

> The question of whether a contract is a conditional sale or lease depends upon the circumstances attending the transaction. Factors tending to indicate that a so-called "lease" is in reality a sale are: that the "lessee" is given practically all the rights of an owner; that the "rentals" are too large, represent the full value of the thing, and are in fact intended as a purchase price; that it is reasonable to assume the thing will be consumed or will have served its usefulness during the period of the "lease"; that the contract contains a clause by virtue of which, on default in payment of an installment, the entire price of the contract becomes due. Where the parties resort to a lease agreement, with a provision for the payment of an additional sum by the lessee in order to obtain title, the courts subject the transaction to equally close scrutiny. Such a contract "is simply a lease with an option to purchase, and is not a sale." But, even in this type of agreement, the additional payment must be a substantial sum; where it is a merely nominal amount the contract is deemed to be a sale translative of ownership from its very inception.

F. Hodge O'Neal, *The Conditional Sale in Louisiana*, 2 La. L. Rev. 338, 342-43 (1940).

In 1985, the Louisiana legislature enacted the "Louisiana Lease of Movables Act," ("LMA") which dramatically modified the treatment of conditional sales disguised as leases with respect to the transfer of ownership of the leased thing. Indeed, as indicated by the legislation's own "declaration of policy," the LMA was designed in part to depart from the traditional jurisprudential treatment of so-called "financed leases":

> It is declared to be the policy of this state to encourage and foster the leasing of movable property to individuals and businesses, thus promoting economic growth and development. To that end, financed leases, which have previously been construed as conditional sales transactions, are hereby recognized as valid and enforceable in this state.

La. Rev. Stat. §9:3302. To effectuate this policy, the LMA provided at the time of its enactment:

> Financed leases subject to this Chapter shall have the same legal affect [sic] as true leases for purposes of Louisiana law notwithstanding the fact that financed leases of movable property have been previously construed in Louisiana as completed credit sales or conditional sales transactions. The lessor under a financed lease subject to this Chapter shall retain full legal and equitable title and ownership in and to the leased equipment until such time as the lessee exercises his option or complies with his obligation to purchase the leased equipment from the lessor as provided under the lease agreement.

La. Rev. Stat. §9:3310(B)(1985).

The LMA also implemented a number of regulations affecting financed leases. Some of these regulations relate to the lessee's rights following the lessee's default under the financed lease. In the case of such default—such as the lessee's failure to pay the rent as agreed by the parties—the lessor may pursue one of two *mutually exclusive* remedies: the lessor may *either* (i) maintain the lessee in possession of the leased thing and recover accelerated rental payments and additional amounts due and that will become due under the lease; *or* (ii) cancel the lease, recover possession of the leased property, and recover liquidated damages provided for in the contract. La. Rev. Stat. §9:3318. Other regulations in the LMA relate to permissible charges that may be imposed upon the lessee of a financed lease. These provisions regulate, among other things, interest rate charges, late charges, early termination charges, and attorney fees, and generally place restrictions on some of these charges in "consumer" leases (as that term is defined in the LMA) while allowing parties to "commercial" leases to agree freely to charges such as these. La. Rev. Stat. §§9:3312-3317.

The LMA also sought to clarify the manner by which true leases were distinguished from financed leases. When it was first enacted in 1985, the LMA defined a "financed lease" as a contract in which (i) the rent to be paid by the lessee is "substantially equivalent to or which exceeds the initial value of the leased property" and (ii) "the lessee is either obligated to become, or has the option of becoming, the owner of the leased property upon termination of the lease for no additional consideration or for nominal consideration." La. Rev. Stat. § 9:3306(12) (1985). This definition was superseded in 1990 when Louisiana adopted Article 9 of the Uniform Commercial Code. Thus, for contracts entered into since January 1, 1990, a "financed lease" means a lease that is "classified as a security interest" under that statutory regime. La. Rev. Stat. § 9:3306(12)(b).

Unfortunately, the identification of a lease that is "classified as a security interest" under LA UCC-9 is a difficult task that requires familiarity with a dense provision of Louisiana's commercial law: La. Rev. Stat. § 10:1-203, titled "Lease distinguished from security interest." According to this provision, the evaluation of whether a contract is a true lease or a security interest "is determined by the facts of each case." *Id.* This section goes on to state that a transaction in the form of a lease creates a security interest if *both* "the consideration that the lessee is to pay the lessor for the right to possession and use of the goods is an obligation for the term of the lease and is not subject to termination by the lessee" *and* at least one of the following factors is present:

(1) the original term of the lease is equal to or greater than the remaining economic life of the goods;

(2) the lessee is bound to renew the lease for the remaining economic life of the goods or is bound to become the owner of the goods;

(3) the lessee has an option to renew the lease for the remaining economic life of the goods for no additional consideration or for nominal additional consideration upon compliance with the lease; or

(4) the lessee has an option to become the owner of the goods for no additional consideration or for nominal additional consideration upon compliance with the lease.

La. Rev. Stat. § 10:1-203(b)(1)–(4).

The section then goes on to describe circumstances which, in and of themselves, *do not* indicate that a contract in the form of a lease is a security interest. Thus, a "lease" is not characterized as a security interest simply because:

(1) the present value of the consideration the lessee is obligated to pay the lessor for the right to possession and use of the goods is substantially equal to or is greater than the fair market value of the goods at the time the lease was entered into;

(2) that the lessee assumes the risk of loss of the goods;

(3) the lessee agrees to pay, with respect to the goods, taxes, insurance, filing, recording, or registration fees, or service or maintenance costs;

(4) the lessee has the option to renew the lease or to become the owner of the goods;

(5) the lessee has an option to renew the lease for a fixed rent that is equal to or greater than the reasonably predictable fair market rent for the use of the goods for the term of the renewal at the time the option is to be performed; or

(6) the lessee has an option to become the owner of the goods for a fixed price that is equal to or greater than the reasonably predictable fair market value of the goods at the time the option is to be performed.

La. Rev. Stat. § 10:1-203(c)(1)–(6).

As the foregoing discussion makes clear, the determination of whether a given contract is a lease or a sale with a security interest is quite complex. That said, for purposes of understanding generally the effects of the LMA, it is enough to focus on the essential elements of this definition. As articulated by one authority on the matter:

> A so-called "lease" whose original or extended term encompasses the entire economic life of an asset indicates ownership and therefore lacks intent to return the goods to the putative lessor. The lack of a requirement to pay any additional money or an insignificant amount of cash to extend a lease says much the same as to the true intent of the parties to create a security interest.

Michael J. Abatemarco & Anthony Michael Sabino, *"True Lease" Versus Disguised Security Interest: Is the United Trilogy Truly the Last Stand?*, 40 U.C.C. L.J. 445, 449 (2008).

Of course, the fact that a lease is classified as a security interest under LA UCC-9 does not on its own lead to the conclusion that the lessor may retain ownership of the leased goods until the lessee complies with the terms of the parties' agreement. Rather, if under La. R.S. § 10:1-203 a lease is to be regarded as a security interest, then LA UCC-9 applies, and the transaction is treated as a credit sale under which ownership transfers immediately leaving the seller with only a security interest in the thing leased. However, the LMA was revised at the same time LA UCC-9 was enacted (January 1, 1990) to provide an exception to the general rule found in the commercial laws. Thus, the LMA now states:

> Notwithstanding the fact that a financed lease creates a security interest under Chapter 9 of the Louisiana Commercial Laws, the lessor under a properly perfected financed lease shall retain full legal and equitable title and ownership in and to the leased equipment until such time as the lessee exercises his option or complies with his obligation to purchase the leased equipment from the lessor as provided under the lease agreement.

La. Rev. Stat. § 9:3310(B). Said another way, a lessor in a "financed leased" can prevent the transfer of ownership of the leased thing by properly perfecting his or her security interest in the manner provided by law.

A final note on the LMA is that it does not govern "rental-purchase agreements," which are instead governed by Louisiana Revised Statutes sections 9:3351 through 9:3362. A "rental-purchase agreement" is defined as:

> an agreement for the use of personal property by a natural person primarily for personal, family, or household purposes for an initial period of four months or less, that is automatically renewable with each payment after the initial period, but that does not obligate or require the consumer to continue renting or using the property beyond the initial period, and that permits the consumer to become the owner of the property.

La Rev. Stat. §9:3352(6). The Louisiana Rental-Purchase Agreement Act specifically provides that rental-purchase agreements "shall not be governed by the laws relating to . . . [a] conditional sale . . . . " La. Rev. Stat. §9:3353(A)(7). The Act goes on to provide for extensive protection for consumers in such transactions.

iii. Comparative Law

Louisiana's adoption of Chapter 9 of the Uniform Commercial Code brought Louisiana's treatment of conditional sales of movables partially into line with that of the American common law. La. Rev. Stat. §10:1-201(b)(35), which defines the term "security interest" and provides that "[t]he retention or reservation of title by a seller of goods notwithstanding perfection of the sale is limited in effect to a reservation of a 'security interest,'" does not depart in substance from the Uniform Commercial Code. Nor does Section 10:1-203 of the Louisiana Revised Statutes, which provides criteria for distinguishing a lease from a security interest. Thus, LA UCC-9 treats conditional sales disguised as leases in the same manner as other U.S. jurisdictions. However, the Lease of Movables Act departs significantly from Anglo-American law. First, the term "financed lease" is a Louisiana anachronism not used in the common law. (Instead, these leases are referred to colloquially as "dirty leases.") Second, and more significantly, Louisiana is alone in providing that the "lessor" in such a lease may prevent the transfer of ownership of the thing leased by perfecting an Article 9 security interest in the thing "leased." This means that among U.S. jurisdictions, Louisiana is the *only* state in which a seller of goods may retain ownership of the things sold until the buyer satisfies the obligation of paying the price. The Louisiana State Law Institute is currently examining the impact of the divergence between Louisiana law and that of other states, with an eye toward a revision that will promote uniformity on this issue.

b. Conditional Sales of Immovables (a.k.a. "Bond for Deed")
La. Rev. Stat. §§ 9:2941–9:2948

As the foregoing section makes clear, the sale of a movable in which the transfer of ownership is conditioned on the payment of the price is generally disfavored in Louisiana. Such a sale results in the immediate transfer of ownership of the thing sold, despite the intent of the parties otherwise expressed, unless the contract is characterized as a "financed lease" under the LMA *and* the lessor has properly perfected its security interest in the leased property.

In contrast, sales of *immovables* in which the transfer of ownership is conditioned on payment of the price are viewed as enforceable according to the parties' intent—that is, the effect of such a sale is that the seller will retain ownership of the thing sold until the buyer pays all or a portion of the purchase price as intended by the parties. Conditional sales of immovables—designated as "bond for deed" contracts—were first approved by the Louisiana Supreme Court in *Trichel v. Homes Ins. Co.*, which follows.

Trichel v. Homes Ins. Co.
99 So. 403 (La. 1924)

St. Paul, J.

On March 26, 1918, plaintiff insured his house with defendant for $3,000 with a "loss payable" clause in favor of W.P. Hall, mortgagee. On December 27, 1917, plaintiff entered into, with one Mrs. W.G. Cavell, a certain agreement which they styled "contract to sell." On February 28, 1919, the house was destroyed by fire.

As the "loss payable" clause in favor of the mortgagee was *unconditional*, defendant paid the mortgage in full, took a subrogation from the mortgagee, and proceeded to foreclose. Whereupon plaintiff sued out an injunction, which the lower court perpetuated; and defendant appeals.

I.

It may be conceded for the purposes of this case that a contract of insurance may be so written that the mortgagee is protected unconditionally, whilst the owner is protected only conditionally, and that in such case the insurer on paying the mortgage may be subrogated to the latter's rights; and the policy in this case seems to be so written.

The question therefore arises whether in this case the policy has been voided as to owner.

II.

The clause in the policy relied upon by the defendant as voiding the policy as to the owner is as follows:

> This entire policy * * * shall be void * * * if the interest of the insured be other than unconditional and sole ownership * * * or if any change, other than by the death of an insured take place in the interest, title or possession of the subject of insurance (except change of occupants without increase of hazard). * * *

And the fact relied upon as operating a forfeiture under said clause is the aforesaid "contract to sell," which provides, substantially:

> That the said Trichel agrees to convey by deed of warranty to the said Mrs. W.G. Cavell the following described property * * * upon the payment to the said Trichel by the said Mrs. Cavell of $5,750 as follows: $900 cash in hand paid, and the balance at the rate of $50 per month with interest from sale. Whenever the said Mrs. Cavell shall have reduced the principal to such an amount as she can [and will] borrow [from a certain building association], said Trichel agrees to make said warranty deed, on being paid said balance. Failure of said Mrs. Cavell to meet any payment within 60 days after the same becomes due, shall entitle said Trichel to annul this contract and forfeit all previous payments, as rent and liquidated damages for possession of the premises.

It is claimed by the defendant that the foregoing contract operated a change of *title*, or at any rate a change of *interest* in the assured.

The trial judge did not think so; nor do we.

III.

The cases of *Barber Asphalt Co. v. St. Louis Cypress Co.*, 121 La. 152, 46 South. 193, and *Adams Machine Co. v. Newman*, 107 La. 702, 32 South. 38, are not applicable here. Those cases deal with personal property, as to which the sale is complete between the parties by their mere *consent*, and as to the whole world by *delivery*. Hence where the thing sold has been delivered and there remains only to pay the price, it is quite immaterial what name the parties give to such price, rent or what not, the fact remains that there has been a sale and transfer of ownership.

But with real estate the case is different; neither consent, nor delivery, nor payment of price suffice to transfer the ownership; there must be *a deed translative of the title*. And the question in this case is whether there was such a deed.

IV.

In *Geo. P. Caire v. Mutual Building & Homestead Association*, No 7315 of its docket, the Court of Appeal for the Parish of Orleans held that—

> A promise of sale amounts to a sale only in the sense that it entitles either party to enforce specific performance; but a promise of sale is not translative of property, and does not change the ownership of, or dominion over, the thing, even as between the parties, or put the thing at the risk of the promise—citing *McDonald v. Aubert*, 17 La. 449; *Bennett v. Fuller*, 29 La. Ann. 663; *Broadwell v. Raines*, 34 La. Ann. 677; *Thompson v. Duson*, 40 La. Ann. 712, 5 South. 58; *Baldwin v. Morey*, 41 La. Ann. 1107, 6 South. 796; *Collins v. Desmaret*, 45 La. Ann. 108, 12 South. 121; *Peck v. Bemiss*, 10 La. Ann. 160; *Satterfield v. Keller*, 14 La. Ann. 606; *Garrett v. Crooks*, 15 La. Ann. 483; *Knox v. Payne & Harrison*, 13 La. Ann. 361.

And the practical application of that doctrine in that case was that the loss of a building destroyed by the great hurricane of 1915 must fall upon the promisor and not upon the promisee.

A writ of review was applied for to this court, under No. 23193 of its docket, and the writ was refused on November 4, 1918.

In *McDonald v. Aubert*, 17 La. 449, the practical application of the doctrine was this: That a *promise of sale* made by a husband during the life of his wife did not transfer the title to such property, and that accordingly a deed to such property executed by the husband alone after the death of his wife, *even though made in pursuance of said promise of sale*, conveyed only his own half interest therein and not the half interest of his deceased wife.

So that a promise of sale differs widely from a sale; it does not transfer the ownership of the thing, but gives only the right to demand specific performance.

V.

In *Capo v. Bugdahl*, 117 La. 992, 42 South. 478, this court held that a contract reading as follows was a mere promise of sale, and not a sale, to wit: "This is to certify that I have this day *sold* my house No. 1904 St. Louis St., to Thomas Capo, for the sum of $2,300, ten per cent. paid cash, balance *when act of sale is passed*." (Italics ours.)

It will be observed that another deed was contemplated by the parties; hence it follows that the agreement abovesaid could not have vested title in the promisee, since "he who has once acquired the ownership of a thing by one title, cannot afterwards acquire it by another title; unless it be to supply a deficiency in the first title." R.C.C. art. 495 [No Corresponding Article].

A similar holding will be found in *Legier v. Braughn*, 123 La. 463, 49 South. 22; and our conclusion is that any agreement for the sale of real estate, which is not intended to be the final writing between the parties, but, on the contrary, to be followed by another and final deed, is a mere promise of sale and not a sale, and does not transfer the title to said property; unless it clearly appear that the parties contemplated that the new deed should be only a *confirmation* of the first, and not indispensable for the transfer of title. And on the face of the agreement herein entered into between Trichel and Mrs. Cavell, it will be seen that it was not to be final, but was to be followed by a formal deed under certain conditions.

Kinberger v. Drouet, 149 La. 986, 90 South. 367, is in perfect accord with the foregoing; it was there held that an option or right to purchase gave a right to demand specific performance; and that the court would enforce specific performance; indirectly, if it could not do so directly. It will be observed that the court said, not that plaintiff was the owner of the property, but that defendant should make him such, and in default thereof that the judgment of the court should do so.

VI.

Several cases are cited from other jurisdictions which seem to hold that a mere promise of sale on the part of an owner operates such a change in his *interest* in the property as to forfeit the insurance thereon. As to these we say simply that we decline to follow them. We think that such a doctrine is subversive of the whole theory of insurance which (in theory at least) is intended to provide *protection* for the assured. As we have heretofore said, the property insured remains at the risk of the insured, notwithstanding a promise to sell the same; and in dollars and cents (which is the practical side of the question) his interest in the property is precisely the same before and after his promise to sell; his risk not ceasing therein until the actual sale. In *Power v. Ocean Insurance Co.*, 19 La. 28, 36 Am. Dec. 665, this court said: "The nullity mentioned in the clause relied on by defendants, was, in our opinion, intended and understood by the parties for the case where by sale or otherwise an absolute transfer or *termination* of the interest of the insured should take place so as to leave him *without* interest at the time of the loss." (Italics ours.)

We think that doctrine perfectly sound; and we will follow it.

Decree.

The judgment appealed from is therefore affirmed.

Rehearing refused by the WHOLE COURT.

Notes and Questions

1. Recall that in *Barber Asphalt*, the Court stated that "to suppose a sale without a transfer of the property in the thing which forms the object of the sale is simply to suppose an impossibility." 46 So. at 196. The Court in *Trichel* characterized the parties' agreement as a "contract to sell," which allowed the Court to avoid this problem of "impossibility" altogether. A contract to sell is one in which "one party promises to sell and the other promises to buy a thing at a later time, or upon the happening of a condition, or upon the performance of some obligation by either party . . . ." LA. CIV. CODE art. 2623. Contracts to sell are discussed more fully in Chapter 12 of this Textbook: Contracts Preparatory to Sale. When parties enter into a contract to sell an immovable, the transfer of ownership does not take place until the parties execute a written act of transfer.

While the Court was correct in holding that a transfer of immovable property requires "a deed translative of title," the Court's characterization of the contract as a "contract to sell" is arguably flawed. First, in a typical contract *to sell*, the buyer is not bound to pay all or a substantial portion of the price as a prerequisite to the transfer of ownership of the thing sold (although money does frequently change hands in a contract to sell in the form of a deposit or earnest money). The obligation to pay the price does not arise until the parties later enter into the contract *of sale*. Yet, the bond for deed contract contemplates that the buyer will pay all or a substantial portion of the price prior to the transfer of ownership. Second, in a typical contract *to sell*, the seller is not bound to deliver to the buyer the thing which is the object of the anticipated sale. Like the buyer's obligation to pay the price, this obligation does not arise until the parties enter into the contract *of sale*.

Thus, the "impossibility" raised by *Barber Asphalt*—that the parties would be bound by the obligations of a contract not yet in existence—is still present in the bond for deed.

These conceptual difficulties aside, the Court plainly was willing to hold that while the conditional sale of a movable thing is impermissible, the transfer of ownership of an immovable may be conditioned upon the payment of the price. Consider the following explanation for this distinction offered by Professor Saúl Litvinoff:

> It is extremely difficult to find any basis for this distinction [between movables and immovables] in the language of the Louisiana Civil Code, and the lack of convincing support makes the distinction somewhat incongruous. If, however, the court had stressed that the reasons for refusing to recognize the sale of a movable with reservation of title in the original *Barber Asphalt Paving Co.* case were, actually, reasons of public policy, then inconsistency and incorrect reading of the code articles could have been averted. Quite clearly, there is no need to protect further either the vendee or third parties when the object of the sale is an immovable: the public records protect both. The vendor can take no unfair advantage of the vendee because, as soon as the latter records the contract to sell the immovable, it becomes impossible for the former to transfer title to anyone free of the first vendee's right to acquire ownership upon fulfillment of the condition that the price be paid. Third parties in the position of *bona fide* purchasers need only look to the records to determine who owns the property and whether it is freed of an existing obligation. Thus, policy considerations that might dictate that the reservation of title be not allowed in the sale of a movable thing do not exist when the object of sale is an immovable. This, no doubt, is the true—and therefore the more convincing—basis for the distinction.

7 Saúl Litvinoff, Louisiana Civil Law Treatise, Obligations § 71, at 116 (1975) (internal citations omitted).±

Whatever might have been the true rationale of the Court in *Trichel*, courts considering conditional sales of immovables since *Trichel* have consistently found such sales to be enforceable, with the transfer of ownership delayed until the payment of the price as contemplated by the parties' agreement.

2. In 1934, the Louisiana legislature enacted legislation governing the bond for deed contracts. *See* La. Rev. Stat. §§ 9:2941–9:2948 (designated the "Bond for Deed Act"). A "bond for deed" is defined as "a contract to sell real property, in which the purchase price is to be paid by the buyer to the seller in installments and in which the seller after payment of a stipulated sum agrees to deliver title to the buyer." La.

± Reproduced with permission of Thomson Reuters.

Rev. Stat. §9:2941. The Bond for Deed Act thus retains the jurisprudential characterization of the bond for deed as a contract to sell.

The primary aim of the Bond for Deed Act is to regulate bond for deed contracts for the protection of the buyer. In particular, when the property that is the object of the bond for deed is encumbered by a mortgage or a privilege, the buyer is vulnerable to acquiring the property still burdened with the mortgage or privilege or, alternatively, losing the property due to seller defaulting on the obligation which the mortgage or privilege secures. Thus, the Bond for Deed Act provides that it "shall be unlawful" to sell by bond for deed contract property that is encumbered by a mortgage or privilege without first obtaining a written guarantee from the mortgage and privilege holders to release the property upon payment by the buyer of a stipulated release price. La. Rev. Stat. §9:2942. This guarantee must be filed in the mortgage records of the parish where the immovable is situated. *Id.* In addition, the Bond for Deed Act requires that when the property that is the object of the bond for deed contract is burdened with a mortgage or privilege, all payments made by the buyer shall be paid to an escrow agent, who is required to distribute the payments directly to the holder of the mortgage or privilege. La. Rev. Stat. §9:2943.

While the protective provisions of the Bond for Deed Act are laudable, the consequences of noncompliance with the Act are less than clear. The Bond for Deed Act itself provides that any person who sells property burdened by a mortgage or privilege by bond for deed without first recording the required guarantee from the mortgage or privilege holder to release the property upon the buyer's payment of a stipulated price "shall be fined not more than one thousand dollars, or imprisoned for not more than six months, or both." La. Rev. Stat. §9:2947. However, the legislation is silent as to whether failure to comply with this or the other protective measures of the Bond for Deed Act affects the validity or enforceability of the bond for deed contract itself. Courts have routinely held that failures to comply with the requirements of the Act neither invalidate the contract nor prevent the seller from retaining title until the price is paid as required by the contract. *See, e.g., St. Landry Loan Co. v. Etienne*, 227 So. 2d 599 (La. App. 3 Cir. 1969); *Bergeron v. Parker*, 964 So. 2d 1075 (La. App. 1 Cir. 2007).

3. The Bond for Deed Act contains a specialized regime for cancellation of the contract upon the buyer's failure to perform. If the buyer should fail to make payments in accordance with the contract, the seller may cancel the bond for deed and evict the buyer. However, the seller must first serve the buyer with a notice to perform within 45 days by registered or certified mail. La. Rev. Stat. §9:2945. Beyond the requirement of 45 days written notice, the legislation does not provide for the rights of the parties upon cancellation. It has been left to the courts to determine what happens to the installments paid by the buyer if the contract is cancelled. Consider the following summary of the jurisprudence on this issue, discussed in *Montz v. Theard*, 818 So. 2d 181, 187 (La. App. 1 Cir. 2002):

A body of jurisprudence has established appropriate adjustments to be made in the case of a failed Bond for Deed transaction. Regardless of penalty or forfeiture clauses in the contract, the vendor in a Bond for Deed contract is not entitled to retain all monies paid by the purchaser. The law is clear that such forfeiture clauses should be regarded as null and void since they are inequitable, unreasonable and represent an illegal attempt to recover punitive rather than compensatory damages. The purchaser is entitled to the return of all moneys paid on the purchase price, including the down payment and monthly installments, the insurance premiums, and the taxes paid. The same body of jurisprudence establishes that the seller is entitled to an allowance for the fair rental value of the property during the period of plaintiff's occupancy and that a remand is appropriate where the rental value cannot be determined from the record (citations omitted).

4. Amendments to the Bond for Deed Act since its enactment in 1934 have further expanded the rights of buyers. For example, the legislation has been amended to provide that the buyer in a bond for deed contract is deemed eligible for the homestead exemption despite the fact that the buyer is not yet the owner of the property. LA. REV. STAT. §9:2948. In addition, the Bond for Deed Act now provides that a bond for deed contract recorded in the mortgage and conveyance records of the parish where the property is situated shall have effects against third persons and, more specifically, that:

> any sale, contract, counterletter, lease, or mortgage executed by the bond for deed seller, and any lien, privilege, or judgment relating to or purporting to affect immovable property that has not been filed previously for registry or recorded in the mortgage records shall be subject to the rights created by the bond for deed contract.

LA. REV. STAT. §9:2941.1. This provision was added in 2006 in order to overrule the Louisiana Fourth Circuit Court of Appeal's opinion in *James v. Ocean National, L.L.C.*, 905 So. 2d 1096 (La. App. 4 Cir. 2005). In that case, James entered into a bond for deed contract with the Walkers to purchase a piece of immovable property in New Orleans. The bond for deed agreement was properly recorded in the mortgage records in Orleans Parish. Subsequently, two judgments were rendered against the Walkers and filed in the same mortgage records. A question arose as to whether the judicial mortgages burdened the property that was the object of the bond for deed. The court held that the judicial mortgages attached to the property because the bond for deed sellers were the "actual and record owners" of the property at the time the judgments were filed. *James*, 905 So. 2d at 1101. It should be noted that the new legislation requires bond for deed contracts to be filed in *both* the conveyance records and the mortgage records in order to fully protect the bond for deed purchaser. It should further be noted that the rationale of *James* could be applied to other types of contracts that contemplate that future sale of an immovable, including options, rights of first refusal, and contracts to sell (all of which are addressed fully in Chapter 12: Contracts Preparatory to Sale). Obviously, the amendment to the Bond for Deed Act overrules *James* only with respect to bonds for deed.

5. An issue frequently litigated in the area of bond for deed contracts is the threshold question of whether a particular contract is properly classified as a bond for deed or some other type of contract, such as a lease. Because the parties to bond for deed contracts often have access to neither traditional forms of financing nor legal counsel, courts are called upon to interpret written contracts drafted by unsophisticated parties when determining the true nature of the transaction. The following cases are illustrative of the difficulties, and practical significance, of classification.

McCoy v. Robbins

974 So. 2d 170 (La. App. 2 Cir. 2008)

PEATROSS, J.

In this consolidated appeal, the primary issue concerns the effect of a purported buy/sell agreement for the sale of approximately 13 acres and home located thereon in Mansfield, Louisiana, by and between Alton Robbins, through his power of attorney, Loretta Born, as seller, and prospective purchaser, Toni Ford McCoy. The trial court entered judgment ordering Ms. McCoy to vacate the home as requested by Ms. Born. Ms. McCoy appeals. For the reasons stated herein, we affirm.

FACTS

Mr. Robbins, through his daughter and power of attorney, Loretta Born, and Ms. McCoy executed a buy/sell agreement whereby Mr. Robbins would sell and Ms. McCoy would purchase approximately 13 acres of land and home located at 1302 Maple Street in Mansfield. The agreement provided for the payment of a $500 deposit by Ms. McCoy, which she paid. The agreement further provided for a purchase price of $60,000, but the agreement did not provide for any payments, nor did the agreement provide for a closing date. After the agreement was executed, Ms. McCoy made several unsuccessful attempts to secure financing for the purchase of the home. According to Mr. Robbins, Ms. McCoy occupied the residence for about five months while remodeling it and paid no rent or payments during that time because she was bearing the remodeling expenses. Thereafter, Mr. Robbins agreed to accept $200 per month "rent" until Ms. McCoy was able to obtain financing. Three and a half years passed, however, and the parties never closed the sale on the home.

Mr. Robbins ultimately decided to have Ms. McCoy vacate the premises and provided her with notice to vacate. This prompted Ms. McCoy to file a "Petition for Injunction W/TRO" which sought to prevent Mr. Robbins from selling the property. Mr. Robbins, through his agent, Ms. Born, then filed a "Dilatory Exception of Unauthorized Use of Summary Proceedings" followed by a "Petition for Eviction and Possession of Premises." The matters were consolidated and Ms. McCoy's petition was dismissed as an improper use of summary proceedings. After a brief trial, Mr. Robbins' petition for eviction was granted and Ms. McCoy was ordered to vacate the premises and to leave certain items there that were owned by Mr. Robbins. This appeal ensued.

DISCUSSION

La. C.C. art. 2440 states:

> A sale or promise of sale of an immovable must be by authentic act or by act under private signature, except as provided in Article 1839.

Article 1839 provides that an oral transfer is valid when the property has been delivered and the transferor recognizes the transfer when interrogated under oath.

In the case *sub judice*, Mr. Robbins submits that the sale of the property was never closed and title was not transferred to Ms. McCoy because she was unable to secure financing. It is not disputed that Ms. McCoy paid a $500 deposit, but never paid the remaining $59,500 of the purchase price. In addition, Mr. Robbins did not admit under oath a transfer of the property. To the contrary, he argues that, in order to accommodate Ms. McCoy, he agreed to accept $200 per month rent on a month-to-month basis following her renovations of the property while she tried to obtain financing of the purchase price. Ultimately, she was unable to do so and he chose to have her vacate the premises.

The testimony reveals that Ms. McCoy was current with the $200 payments and that there were notations of "house note" on various payment instruments including cancelled checks and money order receipts. Ms. McCoy maintains that this indicates that the payments were house payments to be applied against the purchase price. Ms. Born, however, testified that she agreed as agent for her father to this modification of the memo on the checks out of sympathy for Ms. McCoy because Ms. McCoy had told her ailing mother, who was suffering from cancer, that she was purchasing the home rather than renting it. Ms. Born maintained that the relationship was a month-to-month rental arrangement. She testified that $200 per month was well below the rental value of the home and that, at that rate, it would take over 24 years to pay the purchase price, and with no interest. Mr. Robbins suggests that Ms. McCoy is attempting to salvage a failed buy/sell agreement by turning it into a bond for deed arrangement.

A bond for deed is defined as "a contract to sell real property, in which the purchase price is to be paid by the buyer to the seller in installments and in which the seller after payment of a stipulated sum agrees to deliver title to the buyer." La. R.S. 9:2941. Under this special contract to sell, possession of the immovable is delivered immediately to the prospective purchaser prior to the payment of the bond for deed installments. *Thomas v. King*, 35,857 (La.App.2d Cir.4/3/02), 813 So.2d 1227. The bond for deed has been interpreted by the jurisprudence as a device to circumvent the normal prohibition against conditional sales, i.e., sales under which passage of title is postponed until payment of the price. *Lyons v. Pitts*,

40,733 (La.App.2d Cir.3/8/06), 923 So.2d 962; *Seals v. Sumrall,* 03-0873 (La.App. 1st Cir.9/17/04), 887 So.2d 91; *David Levingston, Bond for Deed Contracts,* 31 La. L.Rev. 587 (1971); F. Hodge O'Neal, *The Conditional Sale in Louisiana,* 2 La. L.Rev. 338 (1940).

Significantly, however, there is no evidence in this record of any written modification of the buy/sell agreement providing for installment payments toward the purchase price of the property. Likewise, there is no evidence of any credit sale deed or bond for deed arrangement for $200 per month or any other amount per month. We can find nothing in this record that indicates the written confection of any credit arrangement between the parties affecting this immovable property. The notations of "house payment" on some of the payment receipts are insufficient to support such a finding, especially in light of Ms. Born's explanation of these notations as explained above.

In summary, we find no error in the trial court's conclusion that the sale of the property was never confected according to the buy/sell agreement between Mr. Robbins and Ms. McCoy. Further, we find nothing in this record that supports a bond for deed arrangement; rather, the arrangement following the execution of the agreement was a verbal month-to-month lease at a rental rate of $200 per month, which lease can be terminated at any time by proper notice. La. C.C. art. 2727, *et seq;* La. C.C.P. art. 4701, *et seq.* Mr. Robbins properly notified Ms. McCoy to vacate and the trial court was correct in ordering the eviction.

CONCLUSION

For the foregoing reasons, the judgment of the trial court is affirmed at the cost of Toni Ford McCoy.

AFFIRMED.

Bergeron v. Parker

964 So. 2d 1075 (La. App. 1 Cir. 2007)

Before: PETTIGREW, DOWNING and HUGHES, JJ.

DOWNING, J.

This matter comes before us on appeal from a judgment on rule for eviction ordering Sharon Parker, defendant/appellant, to vacate certain premises and deliver possession of them to the plaintiff/appellee, H.J. Bergeron, Inc. (Bergeron). Concluding that the trial court erred in mischaracterizing the agreement between Ms. Parker and Bergeron as a lease rather than a bond for deed and entering judgment accordingly, we reverse the trial court's judgment and vacate its orders.

Pertinent Facts

Sharon Parker had entered an agreement with Bergeron regarding certain property entitled, "Lease With Option to Purchase," to become effective on February 5, 2002. Ms. Parker took possession of the property at about that time.

Subsequently, in February 2006, Bergeron filed a lawsuit against Ms. Parker for "back due rent" and for eviction. At the rule for eviction, the trial court ruled in favor of Bergeron and ordered Ms. Parker to vacate the premises and deliver possession of them to Bergeron, failing which a warrant of eviction would issue.

Ms. Parker now appeals, asserting two assignments of error summarized as follows:

> 1) The trial court erred in ruling that the "Lease With Option to Purchase" was not to be considered a bond for deed contract pursuant to La. R.S. 9:2941 *et seq.;*

> 2) The trial court erred in ruling that Ms. Parker was in default of the agreement without properly allowing her to cure the default in accordance with La. R.S. 9:2945, governing cancellation of a bond for deed upon default.

Discussion

The trial court held that a document entitled, "Lease with Option to Purchase," attached hereto, was a lease and not a bond for deed contract as alleged by defendant/appellant. This document stated a price of $19,000 at 9%, described the property, and provided for a $1,200 down payment with $200 monthly payments for 146 months (which would approximately amortize the balance of the "purchase price" of $17,800).

The "Bond for Deed" definition statute, La. R.S. 9:2941, provides:

> A bond for deed is a contract to sell real property, in which the purchase price is to be paid by the buyer to the seller in installments and in which the seller after payment of a stipulated sum agrees to deliver title to the buyer.

Here, we observe that the document at issue, prepared by the purported Lessor, provides a description of real property, a purchase price in installments and an agreement to deliver title after the payment of the "sale Price." Further, in the last paragraph of the document, it specifically refers to the parties as BUYER and SELLER. Similar documents have been held to be "Bond for Deed" contracts. See *Tabor v. Wolinski*, 99–1732 (La.App. 1 Cir. 9/22/00), 767 So.2d 972, and *Smith v. Miller*, 06–1049 (La.App. 1 Cir. 3/23/07), 953 So.2d 206 (table).[2]

---

2. *Smith v. Miller, supra*, correctly notes that "a disguised conditional sale will be regarded as a sale from its inception." However, it then concludes that the agreement was a bond for deed contract. We believe that unless the bond for deed statute is strictly followed, the Civil Code should apply and this document should be considered a sale, and the vendor would have to seek recovery using his vendor's lien. However, we are required to follow existing First Circuit jurisprudence. *See* Internal Rules of Court, First Circuit Court of Appeal, rule 2.1.d(1).

The trial court here incorrectly held that because the document was not recorded pursuant to La. R.S. 9:2941.1 and because the vendee did not apply for a homestead exemption, the document was not a bond for deed contract. However, recordation is for the protection of the vendee and third parties and is not a requirement for the validity of the contract. Likewise, application for a homestead exemption does not affect the validity of the contract.

Accordingly, we conclude that the "Lease with Option to Purchase" is in fact a bond for deed contract. We further conclude that the seller, H.J. Bergeron, Inc., did not comply with La. R.S. 9:2945 and, therefore, the judgment ordering Ms. Parker to vacate the premises and deliver possession of them to Bergeron should not have been issued.

We find merit in Ms. Parker's assignments of error. We will reverse the judgment of the trial court, vacate the orders therein, and remand for further proceedings consistent with this opinion.

Decree

For the foregoing reasons, we reverse the judgment of the trial court and vacate its orders. We remand this matter for further proceedings consistent with this opinion. Costs of this appeal are assessed to H.J. Bergeron, Inc.

REVERSED; ORDERS VACATED; REMANDED

PETTIGREW, J., concurs, and assigns reasons.

PETTIGREW, J., concurring.

I agree with the majority that the specific contract involved in this dispute is a bond for deed contract. I take this opportunity and humbly suggest that the Louisiana Legislature should revisit whether we should rescind legislation on bond for deeds. Louisiana has more adequate alternatives that safeguard both the vendor's and vendee's rights under Louisiana law; such as, a sale with mortgage. In my humble opinion, the bond for deed concept has led to nothing but confusion in real estate titles and abuse of various parties.

Appendix

LEASE WITH OPTION TO PURCHASE *CELL 2 397 756*
638 - 999 30 H/D

STATE OF *Louisiana* EXHIBIT *P-1*
SUIT *# 34,783-D* *7 09 529 7644*
PARISH OF *Point Coupee* LED IN EVIDENCE THIS
2nd DAY OF *March* *618 - 0598 - (Home)*

BEFORE ME, the undersigned duly commissioned and qualified Notary Public, in and for the aforesaid jurisdiction, and in the presence of the witnesses hereinafter named and undersigned, personally came and appeared *H.J. BERGERON II* whose mailing address is *8091 Bayou Fountain # 809, B.R., LA 7488* hereinafter referred to as LESSOR, who declared that he does by these presents, let and grant a Lease unto, *SHARON D. PARKER*, resident of the lawful age of majority of the *8678 ST. CECELIE, NEW ROADS, LA 70760*, hereinafter called LESSEE, on the following terms and considerations, the following described property, to-wit:

ONE (1) CERTAIN LOT OR PARCEL OF GROUND, together with all the buildings and improvements thereon, situated in that subdivision of the *PARISH* of *POINTE COUPEE* State of *Louisiana*, known as *JACKSON SD EAST* SUBDIVISION, and being more particularly described according to the official subdivision map, on file and of record in the office of the Clerk and Recorder for said *PARISH* and state, as LOT *LOT TEN - # 10*, said subdivision; said lot having such measurements and dimensions as shown on said map. *SALE PRICE - $13,000. ⁵⁷ @ 9%*

(12.3 YRS)
This lease is made for a term of *$1,200. DOWN PAYMENT - 146 MONTHS*, commencing on the *5TH* day of *FEB., 2002* Monthly rental payments shall be in the amount of *TWO - HUNDRED - $ 201. ⁵⁷*. The first rental payment shall be due and payable on the *5TH* day of *FEB, 2002*; and the others payable respectively on the same day of each month thereafter until all have been paid. Payments shall be made to LESSOR unless agreed otherwise by all parties in writing. Payments shall be deemed delinquent if not received by the 8th day of each month and subject to a late charge in the amount of twenty-five dollars ($25).

The sole possession and control of the property herein leased shall be and remain in the lessee or tenant during the term hereof, and the tenant covenants and agrees to protect and save harmless the lessor of and from any and all claims for injury, loss or damage to any person or persons, or property in or upon the leased premises, and tenant assumes responsibility for the condition of the premises; lessor will not be liable for injury or property loss caused by any defect therein to the

...ess the lessee knew of should have known the defect or had received ...e thereof and failed to remedy said defect within a reasonable time.

Lessor shall have or be granted reasonable access to inspect said premises upon the giving of reasonable notice to lessee.

All property of every kind, both movable and/or immovable, which may be in or on said leased premises during the term thereof, shall be at the sole risk of the tenant, and in the event of the termination of this lease, lessee shall remove all improvements thereon at lessee's cost and it is further expressly understood that lessor shall not be responsible to lessee for the value of improvements left on the leased premises by lessee. It being further understood and agreed that no improvements shall be made to the property without the prior written consent of the Lessor.

Lessee shall be responsible for all taxes on the leased premised and on all improvements. Lessee shall maintain insurance on the home, including but not limited to liability, hazard/fire, and insurance on the contents of the home. Lessee shall pay to the lessor each year, _ALL PAID BY LESSEE_ dollars ($0.0) for owners liability insurance.

LIABILITY. In addition to maintaining liability insurance on these premises, lessee assumes all liability for injuries suffered by any person on this property and agrees to hold lessor harmless and indemnify lessor for any and all claims filed on behalf of any person, including attorney fees and court costs.

Failure on the part of lessee to pay any monthly installment of rent when due, or to comply with others provisions of this lease within FIVE (5) days after compliance is demanded in writing by lessor, or at lessee's abandoning the leased premises, or lessee being adjudicated a bankrupt, or a receiver being appointed for lessee, shall without any putting in default, give lessor the right at his option to declare the unpaid installments of the rental immediately due and exigible, or, at the option of lessor, to cancel this lease by written notice of the cancellation of the lease and collect rental accrued to date of said cancellation. Lessor shall also have the right, in spite of such delinquency and in spite of any notices of delinquency, to treat the lease as being still in force and to collect the rental thereunder as such becomes due. Any default or delinquency on the part of lessee or any failure of lessor to exercise any option given him or the exercise by the lessor of the right to sue for any accrued rental shall not bar or abridge the right of lessor to exercise any of said options, upon any subsequent delinquency or to insist thereafter upon a strict compliance with said provisions.

This lease is non-assignable, nor shall lessee have the right to sublease the said premises without the express, written consent of the lessor first obtained.

...uld it become necessary to employ an attorney at law to collect any rents
or enforce any claim arising out of lessee's failure to abide by this lease, lessee
agrees to pay reasonable attorney fees to lessor.

OPTION OF PURCHASE: Lessee shall have the option to purchase the
above described property upon payment to lessor the full sum of
NINETEEN THOUSAND DOLLARS hundred fifty dollars ($19,000). Lessee shall
receive credit on each lease payment according to amorization table (attached) at
the rate of 9 % interest made pursuant to this agreement.

In consideration of the granting of this option to purchase, lessee has further paid
unto Lessor this date the sum of _TWELVE HUNDRED_ Dollars($1200). This option to
purchase shall expire upon termination or default of the lease. Further, this option
is extended concurrent with and as a condition of this lease agreement. In the event
lessee should default under the provisions of the agreement resulting in cancellation
or termination of this agreement, then this option to purchase is null and void and
Lessor will retain the previously described sum of principal and interest as
liquidated damages.

BUYER(S) hereby acknowledge and recognize that this sale is in an "AS IS"
condition, and accordingly, hereby relieve and release SELLER and all
previous owners there of from any and all claims for any vices or defects in
said property, whether obvious or latent, known or unknown, easily
discoverable or hidden, and particularly for any claim or cause of action for
redhibition pursuant to _LOUISIANA_ Civil Code Articles _18_ , et seq., or for
diminution of purchase price pursuant to _LOUISIANA_ Civil Code Articles 2541,
et seq. BUYER(S) acknowledge they understand that Louisiana redhibition
law enables them to hold SELLER responsible for any obvious or hidden
defects in the property existing on the act of sale date, and that they are
waiving that right.

THUS DONE, READ AND SIGNED in the presence of the undersigned
competent witnesses, _Joseph B. Major_ .

WITNESSES:

K. Diaxon, Rw. Crochet   _A. J. Blazon_ _INC #72-1353250_
                                  HAL J. BERGERON, LESSOR
Joseph B. Major

                                  Sharon D. Parke SSN 433-33-9867
                                  Sharon D. Parker

_____

NOTARY PUBLIC

Notes and Questions

1. The majority in *Bergeron* suggests in footnote 2 of the decision that unless the Bond for Deed Act is strictly followed, a contract involving a conditional sale of an immovable "should be considered a sale, and the vendor would have to seek recovery using his vendor's lien." 964 So. 2d 1075, 1076 (La. App. 1 Cir. 2007). In other words, the court suggests that if the parties do not comply with the requirements of the Bond for Deed Act, ownership will pass to the buyer immediately despite the parties' intent to delay the transfer of ownership until the price is paid. Would this approach require *Trichel* to be overruled? Why or why not?

2. Some courts have recently taken the approach that a contract purporting to delay the transfer of an immovable until the price is paid but that either fails to comply with the requirements of the Bond for Deed Act or is not styled as a bond for deed contract is best classified as an "innominate contract." Whether such a contract should be governed by some or all provisions of the Bond for Deed Act by analogy is unclear. For example, in *Montz v. Theard*, 818 So. 2d 181 (La. App. 1 Cir. 2002), the court was called upon to classify a contract in which the transfer of ownership was conditioned on the payment of the price, but in which the parties intentionally avoided the "bond for deed" designation in order to prevent a "due on sale" clause in the seller's mortgage from being triggered. The court determined that the contract was best classified as a "hybrid innominate contract," but nevertheless held that the contract was required to conform to the Bond for Deed Act's provisions regarding cancellation. In contrast, in *Keyes v. Brown*, 158 So. 3d 927 (La. App. 4 Cir. 2015), the court held that a contract in which the parties agreed that one would pay "rent" over time in contemplation of the eventual transfer of ownership of the property, but which did not state that the other party was absolutely obligated to transfer title, was neither a bond for deed nor a lease. As a result, when the occupant failed to pay rent, the owner was entitled to evict without complying with either the 45-day notice period in the Bond for Deed Act or the rules applicable to evictions of lessees. Together, these cases evidence that some legislative clarification may be in order.

3. In his concurrence in *Bergeron*, Judge Pettigrew called upon the Louisiana legislature to revisit whether the Bond for Deed Act should be repealed. Would repealing the Bond for Deed Act bring more, or less, clarity to this area of the law? In what alternative ways could the law be improved? For further discussion, see Endya Hash, Comment, *Bond for Deed in Louisiana: 99 Problems but Being a Sale Ain't One*, 78 LA. L. REV. 1289 (2018).

Chapter 8

Delivery

_____

La. Civ. Code arts. 2474–2475

A sale creates obligations for both the seller and the buyer. Under the default scheme of the Louisiana Civil Code, the seller must (1) deliver the thing sold and (2) warrant to the buyer (a) ownership and peaceful possession of the thing, (b) the absence of hidden defects in the thing, and (c) that the thing is fit for its intended use. LA. CIV. CODE art. 2475. While the parties may modify or exclude some of these obligations, they must do so in accordance with the rules of the Louisiana Civil Code. Furthermore, "[t]he seller must clearly express the extent of his obligations arising from the contract, and any obscurity or ambiguity in that expression must be interpreted against the seller." LA. CIV. CODE art. 2474. This Chapter focuses on the first obligation of the seller: the obligation of delivery.

A. Necessity of Delivery

La. Civ. Code art. 2480

The obligation of delivery is required. Quite obviously, if the seller fails to deliver the thing or fails to do so in a timely manner, the buyer may seek either specific performance of the seller's obligation or dissolution of the contract. Article 2485 expressly states so. LA. CIV. CODE art. 2485. Furthermore, that same article also states that "[i]n either case, and also when the seller has made a late delivery, the buyer may seek damages." *Id.* This rule mirrors those provided in the Title on Conventional Obligations. *See, e.g.*, LA. CIV. CODE arts. 1986–2024.

Because delivery of the thing to the buyer is fundamental to the very nature of the contract of sale, if the thing sold remains in the corporeal possession of the seller, the sale is presumed to be a simulation. LA. CIV. CODE art. 2480. Where the interest of the heirs and creditors of the seller is concerned, the parties must show that their contract is not a simulation when delivery does not take place. *Id.* For example, recall that in *Tyler v. Rapid Cash, LLC*, 930 So. 2d 1135 (La. App. 2 Cir. 2006), reproduced in Chapter 7: Effects of the Contract of Sale, Willie Tyler sold his car (worth $1,000–$2,450) to James Hampton for $225. The parties testified that the bill of sale did not constitute their entire agreement; they had also agreed that Hampton would "void" the bill of sale if Tyler gave back the $225. Meanwhile, Tyler kept corporeal possession of the car. After Tyler did not repay the money, Hampton came and got the car. The court held that the agreement in question was a simulated sale and thus did not intend an immediate transfer of ownership from Tyler to Hampton. Instead, the parties actually intended to create a security interest in Hampton's favor for the loan.

B. Time, Place, and Manner of Delivery
La. Civ. Code arts. 2477, 2481–2484

In addition to being required, delivery must be made by an appropriate method. What constitutes an appropriate method depends upon whether the thing sold is movable or immovable, and further, whether the thing is corporeal or incorporeal.

If the thing is a corporeal movable, delivery can be actual, i.e., handing the thing over to the buyer, or, if the parties so intend, delivery can occur in another manner. LA. CIV. CODE art. 2477. "Another manner" of delivery would include such acts as the seller's handing over to the buyer the key to the place where the thing is stored, or by negotiating to the buyer a document of title to the thing, or, even by the mere consent of the parties if the thing sold cannot be transported at the time of the sale or if the buyer already has the thing at that time. *Id.*

For a simple illustration of the application of Article 2477, recall *Cameron Equipment Co., Inc. v. Stewart & Stevenson Servs. Inc.*, 685 So. 2d 696 (La. App. 3 Cir. 1996), reproduced in Chapter 4: Things Which May be Sold. In that case, Cameron Equipment bought two diesel engines from Petroleum Services, Inc. At the time of the sale, the diesel engines were located at Power Rig Drilling (a company owned by Baker Littlefield). They remained there for two years, at which time Petroleum Services, Inc. sold the same two diesel engines to Power International, Inc. The diesel engines were subsequently transferred two more times. Ultimately, the engines were physically delivered to Stewart & Stevenson, the final purchaser. Cameron Equipment sued for the return of the engines, among other things. Realizing that the transfer of ownership of the engines vis-à-vis third persons would hinge on the timing of the delivery of possession of the engines (per Article 518), Cameron Equipment argued that it had received both actual and constructive delivery of the engines before Stewart & Stevenson took possession of them. First, it argued that it had actual possession because Baker Littlefield took possession of and stored the engines as an agent for Cameron Equipment. The court rejected the argument, noting that Baker Littlefield's testimony showed that he stored the engines for Petroleum Services and would not have kept possession of them had he known they had been sold. Cameron Equipment then argued that the engines were constructively delivered. First, it asserted that Petroleum Services "handed over the keys" to the building where the engines were kept when Petroleum Services transferred its storage agreement with Baker Littlefield incident to the sale. The court deemed this assertion without merit, given that Petroleum Services had limited access to the Power Rig yard, extended only as a courtesy by Baker Littlefield who knew nothing about the sale to Cameron Equipment and who never agreed to store the engines for Cameron

Equipment. Finally, Cameron Equipment asserted that the engines, because of their enormous size and weight, were insusceptible of transport at the time of the sale such that possession of the engines was transferred by the mere consent of the parties. The court rejected this argument because the engines were clearly susceptible of transport given that it took only one day for them to be transported to Stewart & Stevenson. Ultimately, then, Cameron Equipment never acquired ownership of the engines as delivery vis-à-vis third persons because delivery was never made in any fashion.

Article 2481 provides the rules governing delivery of incorporeal movable things. Delivery of incorporeal movable things that are incorporated into an instrument, such as stocks and bonds, takes place by negotiating the instrument to the buyer. LA. CIV. CODE art. 2481. The same article further provides that delivery of other incorporeal movables, such as credit rights, takes place upon the transfer of those movables. LA. CIV. CODE art. 2481. Because the sale of an incorporeal movable is also an assignment of rights, Article 2654 additionally mandates that the assignor deliver to the assignee all of the documents in the assignor's possession that evidence the right assigned. LA. CIV. CODE art. 2654.

Delivery of an immovable, by contrast, is deemed to take place upon execution of the writing that transfers its ownership. LA. CIV. CODE art. 2477. The case below illustrates the seller's obligation to deliver in the sale of an immovable thing.

Matthews v. Gaubler

49 So. 2d 774 (La. App. Orl. 1951)

McBRIDE, Judge.

By contract dated November 8, 1945, Morris Matthews, the plaintiff, agreed to purchase from Mr. and Mrs. A. J. Gaubler, and they agreed to sell to him, the property known as 2825 Arts Street, New Orleans, for the price and sum of $3000. It was stated in the contract that the property was not under lease, but was occupied by the owners, and that "possession to be given at act of sale." It was stipulated that the sale would be passed before the purchaser's notary public "on or prior to Dec. 15, 1945." By a subsequent mutual verbal understanding, the parties postponed the time for passing the act of sale to January 2, 1946.

Matthews, to finance the purchase of the property, arranged for a loan from a local homestead, and it was understood that the act of sale was to be passed before Mr. Allain C. Andry, Jr., the notary public for the homestead.

On January 2, 1946, about noon, all of the parties gathered in Mr. Andry's office. After all of the necessary documents were signed by Matthews and Mr. and Mrs. Gaubler, that is to say, the act transferring the property to the homestead, the act of resale from the homestead to the purchaser, and the purchaser's mortgage note evidencing the loan, and after Matthews had written his check for the portion of the purchase price which he would have to advance, he asked the Gaublers for the keys to the premises. They stated that they did not have the keys with them, and informed Matthews that their child was ill, and that they could not move from the premises that day. Matthews then peremptorily refused to go through with the sale. There is some testimony by the Gaublers that they told Matthews the keys could be delivered later that afternoon, but the plaintiff denies this.

Be that as it may, when Matthews insisted upon delivery of the keys and immediate possession, Mr. and Mrs. Gaubler admitted that they were not in position to turn over the keys to him at that particular moment, and after a discussion of the matter, they finally stated that they would move out of the house by eight o'clock the following morning, and would deliver the keys to Matthews then. He refused to accede to this delay.

In connection with his agreement to purchase the property, Matthews deposited with the realtors who negotiated the transaction the sum of $300, and the agreement states that: 'This deposit is to be noninterest bearing and may be placed in any bank of your selection in the City of New Orleans without responsibility on your part in case of failure or suspension of such bank pending settlement. In the event that purchaser fails to comply with this agreement within the time specified, the vendor shall have the right, either to declare the deposit, ipso facto, forfeited, without formality and without placing purchaser in default, time being the essence of this contract; or the vendor may demand specific performance. In the event that the deposit is forfeited, the commission of the agent shall be paid out of this deposit, reserving to the vendor the right to proceed against purchaser for the recovery of the amount of the commission. In the event that the vendor does not comply with this agreement to sell within the time specified, purchaser shall have the right either to demand the return of double the deposit, or specific performance.'

By this suit, Matthews, who alleges that the Gaublers are in default, seeks to recover from them double the amount of the doposit [sic], or $600 plus $250 for his attorney's fee. After their exceptions of vagueness and no right or cause of action had been overruled, defendants answered the suit, denying that they were in default, and averring that plaintiff himself was in default, and was not entitled to the relief which he sought. The trial in the lower court resulted in a judgment in favor of plaintiff for $600, plus a $150 attorney's fee, from which the defendants have appealed.

It might be stated at this point that the stipulation 'possession to be given at act of sale' was incorporated in the agreement at the insistence of Matthews. The evidence also shows that on January 2, 1946, before proceeding to the notary's office, Matthews visited the property to examine it, and upon observing that the furniture and furnishings of the Gaublers were still in the house, he became apprehensive about getting possession at the time of the passage of the sale.

The basis of the exception of no right or cause of action, which was reurged before us, is that the plaintiff is not entitled to a return of double the deposit, as he should have accepted title, paid the purchase price, and then, in the event that the keys were not delivered to him by eight o'clock the following morning, he should have brought an action for damages against defendants. We perceive no merit whatever in the exception.

Counsel for appellants first argues that a decision of the case hinges on the meaning of the phrase, 'possession to be given at act of sale.' His contention is that the stipulation does not mean that a simultaneous delivery of the keys would be made at the signing of the formal act of sale, but that the parties, by employing such language, only intended that there would be a delivery of physical possession of the property within a reasonable time after the act was passed. Says counsel in his brief: 'Now, what are the respective rights of a vendor and a vendee? There can be no question that the vendee is entitled to obtain possession of the premises he purchases when he pays the consideration thereof, but certainly he cannot be unreasonable in his demand. What assurance does the vendor have that the vendee will have sufficient funds to complete the sale or that he will even appear at the time and place fixed for the passage of the act of sale? Must the vendor vacate his house in the absence of such assurance, or should he have a reasonable time to effect compliance with his contract when he is assured that the vendee has complied with his obligations? We submit that when Defendants appeared in Mr. Andry's office on January 2, 1946 and agreed to deliver the keys to Plaintiff not later than either [sic] o'clock on the morning of January 3, 1946, they had effected full compliance with the contract of sale.'

Our opinion is that the words, 'possession to be given at act of sale,' which, it must be remembered, were incorporated in the agreement at the instance of Matthews, were intended to mean, and could only mean, that at the very moment of the execution of the formal act of sale, physical and corporeal possession of the property would be forthcoming to the purchaser.

Counsel states that there are no Louisiana authorities interpreting the clause, or defining the meaning of the words in question. Our research, however, discloses the case of *Warfield v. Cotton*, 149 La. 1004, 90 So. 374, which we think is analogous to the question posed in the instant case. The Supreme Court held that the stipulation, 'possession to be given immediately,' as used in an agreement to purchase, entitled the defendant 'by its express, explicit terms, to immediate possession,' and that when defendant took possession, he was but exercising his legal right.

It is also argued on behalf of appellants that there are extenuating circumstances in the case, which would render inhuman indeed a holding that they should have conveyed their sick child from the house before going to the notary's office, and that, because of the illness of either child, they had the natural right to retain possession of the property for the short period of time until eight o'clock of the following morning.

Again, we cannot agree with counsel. We are not at liberty to disregard the explicit terms of the agreement, which bound the vendors to deliver corporeal possession of the property to the purchaser at the very moment of the passing of the act of sale, merely because it was inconvenient for them to make delivery, or because the making of delivery would have worked a hardship upon them. Legal agreements have the effect of law upon the parties, and courts are bound to give legal effect to all such contracts according to the true intent of all the parties, and that intent is to be determined by the words of the contract, when these are clear and explicit and lead to no absurd consequences. Art. 1945 [R.C.C. 1983, 2045, 2046]

Under the provisions of art. 2475 [R.C.C. 2475], the seller is bound to two principal obligations, that of delivering the thing, and that of warranting the thing which he sells. In *Derbonne v. Burton*, La.App., 189 So. 473, 474, it was said that 'the obligation of delivery is the primary obligation to be fulfilled.'

What is to be considered a delivery of possession is determined by the rules of law, applicable to the situation and nature of the property. Art. 1924 [No Corresponding Article]. The tradition or delivery is the transferring of the thing sold into the power and possession of the buyer, and the law considers the tradition or delivery of immovables, as always accompanying the public act, which transfers the property. Arts. 2477 [R.C.C. 2477], 2479 [R.C.C. 2477].

According to art. 496, [R.C.C. 481], the ownership and the possession of a thing are entirely distinct.

Art. 3434 [No Corresponding Article] provides in part: 'Since the use of ownership is to have a thing in order to enjoy it and to dispose of it, and that it is only by possession that one can exercise this right, possession is therefore naturally linked to the ownership.'

In *Ellis v. Prevost*, 19 La. 251, the Supreme Court said: '* * * Possession is acquired by the actual and corporal detention of the property; this is the natural possession, or possession in fact; * * *'

The penalty for the failure of a vendor to make delivery is stipulated for in R.C.C. arts. 2485 [R.C.C. 2485] and 2486 [R.C.C. 2485], respectively, as follows:

> 'If the seller fails to make the delivery at the time agreed on between the parties, the buyer will be at liberty to demand, either a canceling of the sale, or to be put into possession, if the delay is occasioned only by the deed of the seller.'

> 'In all cases, the seller is liable to damages, if there result any detriment to the buyer, occasioned by the non-delivery at the time agreed on.'

In *Franton v. Rusca*, 187 La. 578, 175 So. 66, it was held that a petition by a purchaser under a warranty deed, for damages for the vendor's failure to deliver possession of part of a tract of land which was in possession of another, stated a cause of action under Rev.Civ.Code, arts. 2475 [R.C.C. 2475], 2486 [R.C.C. 2485].

Matthews was to have immediate physical and corporeal possession at and upon the passage of the formal act of sale, both under the express stipulations of the agreement, any by the plain import of the law. By failing to make delivery of possession at the time agreed upon between the parties, the vendors actively breached their obligation, and Matthews, the purchaser, was within his rights in receding from the agreement and refusing to pay for the property. Under the terms of the agreement, the law between the parties, which provides that in the event the vendors do not comply with their agreement the purchaser shall have the right either to demand return of double the deposit or specific performance, Matthews is entitled to maintain the present action.

* * * * *

Amended and affirmed.

REGAN, J., dissents.

Notes and Questions

1. *Matthews* illustrates that the delivery of an immovable takes place upon the execution of the writing that transfers its ownership. *See* LA. CIV. CODE art. 2477. As a result, the buyer is entitled to immediate corporeal possession of the thing sold. In practice, if the seller is unable to deliver corporeal possession of the property at the time of the sale, the parties may enter into an occupancy agreement under which the seller may remain in possession of the property for a defined period of time. Note that the buyer must consent to any such arrangement.

2. With respect to movables, the Civil Code does not speak to the time at which delivery must be made. In general, when the parties do not specify a term for performance, performance of an obligation is due immediately. *See* LA. CIV. CODE art. 1777. Nevertheless, Louisiana courts have held that in sales of movables, when the parties do not specify a time for delivery, delivery must be made within a "reasonable time." *See Lanier Bus. Prods., Inc. v. First Nat. Bank of Rayville*, 388 So. 2d 442, 445 (La. App. 2 Cir. 1980). What constitutes a "reasonable time" is determined "by the particular circumstances surrounding the particular sale." *Id.*

3. Article 2484 provides a suppletive rule regarding the place at which delivery must occur: "Delivery must be made at the place where the thing is located at the time of the sale." LA. CIV. CODE art. 2484. Of course, the parties may alter this rule by their agreement, in which case delivery must be made at the place agreed by the parties or intended by them. *Id.*

4. The costs of making delivery are generally borne by the seller, and the costs of taking delivery borne by the buyer. LA. CIV. CODE art. 2483. In addition, if the seller is not in possession of the thing sold, he must obtain possession of it and bear the cost of doing so. LA. CIV. CODE art. 2482. These rules, like the rule governing the place of delivery, are suppletive and may be altered by the parties' agreement.

5. Of course, a sale is a commutative contract — one under which the performance of the obligation of each party is correlative to the performance of the other. *See* LA. CIV. CODE art. 1911. Thus, the seller may refuse to deliver the thing sold until the buyer tenders payment of the price, unless the seller has granted the buyer a term for such payment. LA. CIV. CODE art. 2487. If the buyer has become insolvent or has filed for protection under bankruptcy law, then the seller may refuse to deliver the thing sold even if a term for performance has been granted, unless the buyer gives security

for payment of the price. *See* LA. CIV. CODE arts. 2487 cmt. b; 2023. Note also that if the things sold are movable and in the possession of a carrier or other depositary, the seller may stop delivery of the things sold upon learning that the buyer will not perform his obligations or is insolvent. LA. CIV. CODE art. 2614.

C. Conformity

La. Civ. Code art. 2489

The seller must deliver the thing sold in the condition that, at the time of the sale, the parties expected, or should have expected, the thing to be in at the time of delivery, according to its nature. LA. CIV. CODE art. 2489. For example, if Buyer orders a certain product that is new, Seller may not send a used version of that product. If Buyer purchases a thing without having had the opportunity to see it (as when purchased from a distance), the Seller must ensure that the thing is of merchantable quality (assuming, of course, the parties had no agreement to the contrary). LA. CIV. CODE art. 2489 cmt. d.

Beyond this general rule, the Civil Code provides more particular rules for the seller's delivery obligation which vary depending upon whether the thing sold is classified as a movable or an immovable.

1. Movables

La. Civ. Code arts. 2603–2610

Louisiana State Law Institute, Proposed Louisiana Civil Code Revision of Sales 11–17 (1992) (Exposé des Motifs)

OBLIGATION TO DELIVER CONFORMING THINGS

According to Article 2475 of the Louisiana Civil Code of 1870, the seller had two principal obligations: delivery and warranty of the things sold. While the Civil Code of 1870 devoted no less than six articles to regulating the extent and effects of the obligation of delivery with respect to immovables, it was conspicuously silent with respect to the obligation of delivery concerning movables. That silence may have been due to the fact that civil codes were not conceived as instruments to regulate commercial sales. At the time the Louisiana Civil Codes of 1825 and 1870 were enacted, most major European countries had commercial codes regulating, among other things, commercial sales.

Revised Article 2603 provides that the seller must deliver "things conforming to the contract." Clearly, delivery of non-conforming goods would have been a breach of the obligation of delivery and, consequently, a breach of contract under the Civil Code of 1870. However, due in part to the fact that the Civil Code did not regulate at length the seller's obligation of delivery with respect to movables, Louisiana courts experienced some difficulty in distinguishing between problems of faulty performance of the obligation of delivery—i.e., delivery of goods that did not conform to the specifications of the contract—and problems of delivery of defective goods or redhibition. Thus, in *Walton v. Katz & Besthoff, Inc.*, 77 So. 2d 563 (La. App. Orl. Cir. 1955), the plaintiff had bought from the defendant paint advertised as "mildew resistant," a quality verbally re-asserted by the defendant's employee. The paint was fine in every respect, except that it did not resist mildew. The court sustained a plea of prescription over the buyer's objection that the suit was one for breach of contract, which called for application of a 10-year prescriptive period, rather than a suit for redhibition.

That same court held, however, in *Victory Oil v. Perret*, 183 So. 2d 360 (La. App. 4th Cir. 1966), where the plaintiff oil company had contracted to supply to the defendant for use in the latter's truck diesel fuel suitable for that purpose, but had delivered, in part, diesel fuel of a type that caused damage to the truck, that the oil company had failed to fulfill its contractual obligations and that the rules of redhibition were not applicable, stating that the seller did not deliver that for which the parties had contracted.

On the other hand, in *Reiners v. Stran-Steel*, 317 So. 2d 657 (La. App. 3d Cir. 1975), a case involving the supplying of incorrect rafters for the construction of a steel building, another appellate court analyzed the problem as one involving redhibition. The court held, however, that since the "defects" in the supplying of the rafters were corrected prior to the plaintiffs bringing suit, such defects could not properly be grounds for redhibition, but gave rise only to reduction of the price or quanti minoris. *Id.*, at 660.

Revised Article 2603 attempts to solve that conflict in the jurisprudence by stating, categorically, that the seller of movables must deliver things conforming to the contract. Under this article it becomes clear that where the seller delivers goods that do not conform to the specifications of the contract, he has breached the contract of sale regardless of whether the goods actually delivered are defective or not.

BUYER'S RIGHT OF INSPECTION

Revised Article 2604 provides that a buyer has a right to inspect things delivered pursuant to a contract of sale.

The buyer's right of inspection is accessory to his right to receive goods that conform to the specifications of the contract. *See* revised Article 2603. Unless the parties stipulate otherwise the buyer has a right to inspect the goods before making payment.

The right of inspection before making payment does not exist, however, in documentary sales—as, for instance, in a C.I.F. contract—since in such agreements the buyer must make payment upon the seller's tender of the required documents, regardless of whether the goods arrived at the point of destination. Nevertheless, even in the case of documentary sales, the buyer has a right to inspect the goods in order to ascertain whether they are in conformity with the agreement, and may reject them if they do not so conform.

ACCEPTANCE AND REJECTION OF NONCONFORMING THINGS

According to revised Article 2605, a buyer may reject nonconforming things within a reasonable time. To make effective a rejection of such things the buyer must give reasonable notice to the seller. A buyer's failure to make an effective rejection shall be regarded as an acceptance of the things.

After the buyer has had sufficient time to inspect the goods delivered, it is reasonable to require that he either seasonably notify the seller of any nonconformity of the goods to the specifications of the contract or be deemed to have accepted the goods. There are several policy reasons militating in favor of this requirement. First of all, the seller may be able to cure the defect in delivery, and, if he is capable of doing so seasonably, he should be allowed to do so. Second, if promptly notified of the rejection, the seller may be in a better position to sell the goods to another buyer. Third, in many cases the buyer's neglect to inform the seller promptly that the goods are nonconforming amounts to a violation of the overriding duty of good faith. *See* C.C. Arts. 1759, 1983 (rev. 1984); 2 Litvinoff, Obligations 5–9 (1975). Moreover, the buyer should not be allowed to "sit on the goods" and speculate on the market's fluctuations at the seller's peril and risk.

Thus, it appears quite reasonable for the law to provide that when the buyer does not seasonably notify the seller that the goods are rejected due to their nonconformity, the buyer who has had a reasonable opportunity to inspect the goods is deemed to have accepted them.

As the comments to revised Article 2605 indicate, that rule should not be applied to a purchaser of consumer goods. The buyer of consumer goods cannot be held to the same standards of commercial reasonableness as the merchant buyer. That is so because the consumer lacks the resources and "know how" that a merchant buyer is presumed to have. Even the consumer, however, must act reasonably and in good faith. *See* C.C. Arts. 1759, 1983 (rev. 1984).

Where the buyer accepts the delivered goods with knowledge that they do not conform to the specifications, it is fair to preclude him from rejecting the goods thereafter on grounds of nonconformity. In such an instance the buyer, having willingly accepted a variance in the object of the contract, should not be allowed to repudiate his acceptance and reject the goods. Aside from the provisions of this Article, it would seem that, in such a situation, the buyer would be precluded from rejecting the goods on grounds of nonconformity by the overriding principle of good faith and the doctrine of contra factum proprium. *See* C.C. Arts. 1759, 1983 (rev. 1984). *Hebert v. McGuire*, 447 So. 2d 64 (La. App. 4th Cir. 1984). Thus, according to revised Civil Code Article 2606, a buyer who, with knowledge, accepts nonconforming things may no longer reject those things on grounds of that nonconformity, unless the acceptance was made on the reasonable belief that the nonconformity would be cured.

As the comments indicate, the provisions of Article 2606 are consistent with the principle of contractual freedom. Where the buyer accepts the delivered goods with knowledge that they do not conform to the specifications, the buyer may be presumed to consent to an alteration in the object of the sale. It follows that he has agreed to enter into a sale whose object is the thing that was actually delivered. Concerning that—new—sale there are no grounds to rescind for nonconformity, because, by virtue of the acceptance, the thing delivered now conforms to the specifications of the sale. *See* C.C. Art. 1983 (rev. 1984).

Nevertheless, when the buyer reasonably believes that the nonconformity will be cured by the seller, the buyer may subsequently reject the goods on grounds of nonconformity if the nonconformity is not cured. That is so because, in such a situation, the buyer has only conditionally accepted nonconforming goods. The seller's failure to correct the nonconformity constitutes a resolutory condition. *See* C.C. Arts. 1767, 1773, 1775 (rev. 1984).

PARTIAL ACCEPTANCE

It is not unusual for the object of a contract of sale to consist of more than one commercial unit. When a shipment of goods contains several commercial units of a certain thing, one or more of such units may not conform to the specifications of the contract. In such a situation the buyer finds himself with goods that are useful for the intended purpose—the contractually conforming units—and goods that are not—the contractually nonconforming units. In such an instance it seems inequitable, as well as economically inefficient, to make the buyer either accept or reject the entire shipment. Revised Article 2607 allows the buyer to accept those commercial units of the shipment that conform to the specifications of the sale and reject those that do not.

Louisiana courts have on several occasions been confronted with the problem of determining the buyer's right to accept part of the things delivered where a shipment of goods contained both conforming and nonconforming goods. The matter has arisen primarily in redhibition cases. In *Bates v. Lilly Brokerage Co.*, 159 So. 457 (La. App. 2d Cir. 1935), the plaintiff bought 200 second-hand barrels to be used for vinegar. Upon inspection, he discovered that 150 barrels had contained an acid that made them unfit for that use. The court held that the buyer was entitled to keep the contractually conforming units and return the remainder against the defendant's contention that the plaintiff had to return all or none. The court formulated the rule thusly: "If several things sold together are independent of each other and do not form a whole, and if the value of each thing is not increased by its union with the rest, a redhibitory action can be maintained only for those things that are found to be defective, and the contract must stand and be carried into effect in relation to the others." *Id*. at 459.

In *Huntington v. Lowe*, 3 La. Ann. 377 (1848), the purchaser of pork by hogheads discovered that several hogheads were unsound. The Louisiana Supreme Court held that in such a situation the buyer was entitled to retain the sound hogheads and return the unsound ones. *Id*. at 379. It is noteworthy that in *Huntington*, just as in *Bates, supra*, the vendor claimed that the buyer had either to keep or to return the entire shipment. The court in *Huntington* countered the seller's argument thusly: "The rule that the redhibitory vice of one of several things sold together gives rise to the redhibition of all, applies to a limited class of cases; those where one of the things would not have been bought without the other. The illustrations given in the code are a pair of matched horses or a yoke of oxen. The rule is a reasonable one, and we have narrowed it from the Roman law. "Quumautem jumenta paria veneunt, edicto expressum est ut, cum alterum in ea causa sit ut redhiberi debeat, utrumque redhibeatur; in qua re tam emptori quam venditori consulitur, dum jumenta non separantur." But when the things are independent of each other, the redhibitory action lies for that which is affected by the redhibitory vice. The example given by the civilians is a lot of unmatched horses or a flock of sheep. If one proves to be unsound, the partial dissolution of the sale is permitted." *Id.* at 379. Under revised Article 2607, as under these prior decisions, the buyer may accept conforming commercial units and reject nonconforming ones. In case of partial acceptance the buyer "must pay at the contract rate for any things that are accepted."

MERCHANT BUYER'S DUTY UPON REJECTION

When the buyer rejects goods that have been delivered to him by the seller, revised Article 2608 requires that he take certain measures to preserve the integrity of the goods delivered. It should be noted, however, that in such instances the buyer, even though following the seller's instructions in accordance with the provisions of this Article, is not a mandatary of the seller. In other words, the fact that the buyer has exercised the right of rejection does not transform the contract of sale into one of agency. Rather, the buyer at that point becomes a kind of negotiorum gestor. *See* C.C. Arts. 2295–2300 (1870). Thus, the rejecting buyer is held to the standard of a prudent administrator in the care and handling of the goods for the seller's account. *See* C.C. Art. 2298 (1870). As in the case of a gestor, the buyer who undertakes to handle and care for rejected goods pursuant to Article 2608 should be entitled to reimbursement for his expenses. *See* C.C. Art. 2299 (1870).

* * * * *

Consider the following case, which illustrates the obligation to deliver conforming things in the context of movable property. Note that although this case was decided before the 1995 sales revision, it is nonetheless consistent with the current rules on the seller's obligation to deliver conforming goods.

Mabry v. Midland Valley Lumber Co.

47 So. 2d 673 (La. 1950)

LeBlanc, J.

This suit is brought by Sam Mabry Lumber Co., a commercial partnership having its domicile in the town of Liberty, Mississippi, and composed of Sam Mabry and Sam Mabry, Jr., to recover from the defendant, Midland Valley Lumber Co., a Missouri corporation, doing business in Louisiana, an alleged indebtedness in the sum of $4510.81 on a sale of a quantity of rough lumber to be shipped in railroad

cars from Woodville, Mississippi. For the sake of brevity, the plaintiff will be hereafter referred to as "Mabry" and the defendant as "Midland" [sic].

* * * * *

On February 25, 1947, Midland issued six checks payable to the order of Mabry,
all drawn on Mutual Bank and Trust Company, St. Louis, Missouri, the sum total
thereof being $2,268.03, in payment of lumber purchased by it and shipped on its
instructions.

On March 3, 1947, Midland issued "Stop Payment Orders" on the six checks above
mentioned on the ground that the lumber did not conform to the grade required
by shipping releases and instructions. Mabry then instituted this suit on May 28,
1947 for the sum of $4,510.81, as already stated, that sum representing $2,268.03,
the amount of the six checks on which payment had been stopped; $1,929.13, the
amount due for two additional cars of pine lumber and $313.65 for hardwood lum-
ber refused by Midland.

Midland, in its answer, denied liability to the plaintiff in any amount, setting up
as its defense the breach of contract on the part of the plaintiff, in that the several
carloads of lumber shipped did not conform to agreed requirements "because of
inferior grades, improper trimming, and because of the fact that the lumber was
shipped green and not air dried as called for."

Assuming the position of plaintiff in reconvention, Midland claimed damages
because of loss due to shipment of inferior lumber by plaintiffs, and cancelled
orders, and loss of profits, in the sum of $ 9,078.48.

* * * * *

Aside from the fact that the testimony fairly shows that plaintiff was well aware
that rough lumber is not merchantable except for a few specific purposes, and knew
also that the lumber it sold to Midland would have to be re-milled, the proof is
otherwise most convincing that in two essential particulars the lumber did not
comply with the terms of Order No. 1065, or the releases issued, when it reached the
planing mills, both at Memphis and at Jackson and before its form was changed, for
most of it was found to be wet and green and untrimmed.

The evidence further shows that the lumber was never exposed to weather conditions at the mills; that it was taken from one car and after being processed was
immediately loaded in another car and sent on to its destination. There is an abundance of proof in the record that upon reaching destination, in several instances,
it was found on inspection to be not only under grade but also very green and wet.
Upon rejection in some cases, and claims for adjustments in others, it was inspected
by certified inspectors of the SPIB and in all cases the moisture content was found
to be in excess of the minimum 19% allowed under the standards of that Bureau.

We believe therefore, that defendant was justified in stopping payment on the six
checks it had issued in payment of some of the lumber shipped on the original order
of December 4, 1946, and in refusing to pay for the two carloads shipped on the

additional order of January 13, 1947. It was also justified in refusing the hardwood which was never shipped and for which releases were never issued. With regard to this lumber the trial judge had this to say: "I am of the opinion that the preponderance of the evidence is that this hardwood lumber was scattered on the ground (on plaintiff's yard) became wet and off grade and was unusable because it was not restacked."

After a careful review of all the evidence the learned district judge was of the firm opinion that plaintiff had breached the contract and must suffer the consequences.

In considering the defendant's reconventional demand the trial judge analyzed the defendant's statement on which it is based. It is a lengthy, comprehensive statement of the account between the parties beginning with the first advance of cash made to plaintiff and covering every transaction in which a loss was sustained or an expense incurred and in which an adjustment had to be made. It also includes loss of profits on orders which it had and could not fill because of inferior grade of the stock. The claim on this last item amounts to the sum of $4224.50 and the total sum of all other items is $4853.98. The district judge refused the demand for loss of profits on orders which were never filled on the ground that the damages claimed thereunder were too speculative. This item forms the basis of defendant's answer to the appeal asking that the judgment in its favor be amended by increasing the award on its reconventional demand. We are of the opinion that the trial judge was correct in rejecting that item. The general rule is that in cases where damages are claimed for having been deprived of profits, the contemplated profit must be proved to be certain and not merely conjectural or speculative. See *Gebelin v. Hamilton*, 18 La.Ann. 646; *Ferguson v. Britt*, 191 La. 371, 185 So. 287; *Spencer v. Luckenbach Gulf S. S. Co.*, 197 La. 652, 2 So.2d 53.

With regard to the other items the district judge apparently accepted the figures in the statement produced by the defendant which was supported by the testimony of one of its witnesses. The statement was not controverted nor does the amount seem to be questioned on this appeal. In the absence of a showing of manifest error the finding of the trial judge will be sustained.

For the reason stated, the judgment appealed from is affirmed at the costs of the plaintiff, appellant herein.

Notes and Questions

1. How does one determine whether the movables that are delivered conform to the contract? Clearly, things that are different from those selected by the buyer or are of a kind, quality, or quantity different from the one agreed to do not conform to the contract. LA. CIV. CODE art. 2603. But what if the contract lacks clear specifications? Per comment (b) to Article 2603, any determination of a certain kind, quality or quantity as agreed to by the parties must be made in light of prevailing usages and prior dealings between the parties. LA. CIV. CODE art. 2603 cmt. b. The law of obligations in general provides further guidance by dictating that if the thing

has not been determined as to quality, the obligor (here, the seller) need not give one of the best quality but he may not tender one of the worst, either. La. Civ. Code art. 1860. For example, Buyer and Seller agree to the sale of 10 bottles of chardonnay. The parties do not stipulate to a certain quality of chardonnay, and the Seller carries three different types of chardonnay, with prices of $25 per bottle, $50 per bottle, and $75 per bottle. Assuming that this is the parties' first transaction, Seller would be obligated to deliver the $50 bottles, as they are not "one of the best quality," but neither are they "one of the worst."

2. Ultimately, the buyer has the right to inspect the things delivered in order to ascertain whether they conform to the contract, La. Civ. Code art. 2604, and if they do not, the buyer may reject them within a reasonable time by giving the seller reasonable notice. La. Civ. Code art. 2605. If a buyer fails to reject the goods within a reasonable time, then this will be regarded as the buyer's acceptance of the things. *Id.* Why is a seller who delivers nonconforming goods entitled to notice that the goods do not conform to the contract? Note that per Article 2605, comment (b), consumer buyers are subject to a lower standard of diligence than a merchant buyer in the provision of notice to the seller. La. Civ. Code art. 2605 cmt. b.

3. A buyer who has knowledge of the nonconformity and accepts the things anyway may not reject them on grounds of that nonconformity unless the acceptance was made in the reasonable belief that the seller would cure the nonconformity. La. Civ. Code art. 2606. Why does a buyer's acceptance of nonconforming goods prevent the buyer from rejecting them at a later time? *See* La. Civ. Code art. 1881. Note also that if some of the things received by the seller conform to the contract and others do not, the buyer may accept those things that conform and "form a commercial unit," and reject those things that do not conform. The buyer must pay at the contract rate for the things that are accepted. La. Civ. Code art. 2607. What is a "commercial unit" as the term is used in this context?

4. A buyer's rejection of nonconforming goods triggers additional rights and duties for the parties. *See* La. Civ. Code arts. 2608–2610. Are merchants held to the same standards as consumers? Read Article 2608 and comment (f). Comment (b) indicates that a merchant buyer is a "negotiorum gestio" for the seller. What does this mean? *See* La. Civ. Code arts. 2292–2297.

5. Note that the buyer's rejection of nonconforming goods does not automatically result in the dissolution of the sale, but it does shift the risk of loss from the buyer back to the seller. This rule is articulated, albeit indirectly, by the second paragraph of Article 2467: "[The] risk [of loss] is so transferred even when the seller has delivered a nonconforming thing, unless the buyer acts in the manner required to dissolve the contract." La. Civ. Code art. 2467. Presumably, if ownership of nonconforming goods has transferred to the buyer prior to the buyer's rejection, the buyer remains the owner until the contract is dissolved, whether judicially or extrajudicially.

6. When the seller fails to deliver conforming things, the buyer is allowed to purchase substitute things within a reasonable time and in good faith and is entitled

recover the difference between the contract price and the price of the substitute things and also other damages less the expenses saved as a result of the seller's breach. La. Civ. Code art. 2609. Nevertheless, the seller is allowed the right to cure the nonconformity when the time for performance has not expired or when the seller had a reasonable belief that the nonconforming things would be acceptable to the buyer, but the seller must give reasonable notice of his intention to cure to the buyer. La. Civ. Code art. 2610. In light of those rules, how should the hypothetical that follows be resolved? On Monday, Buyer orders 100,000 red widgets from Seller at the list price of $1/widget. When the widgets are delivered on Wednesday, Buyer immediately opens the boxes and discovers that the widgets are green. On the same day, he notifies Seller that he is rejecting the widgets. On Thursday, Buyer orders 100,000 red widgets from another manufacturer at a price of $1.25/widget. On Friday, Seller delivers 100,000 red widgets to Buyer. Is Buyer obligated to pay Seller for the red widgets? Can Buyer recover any damages from Seller?

7. Many of the Civil Code articles on the buyer's right of inspection include a standard of reasonableness. *See* La. Civ. Code art. 2605 (reasonable time and reasonable notice of nonconformity by the buyer), La. Civ. Code art. 2606 (reasonable belief by the buyer that nonconformity would be cured), La. Civ. Code art. 2608 (reasonable instructions from the seller to merchant buyer), La. Civ. Code art. 2609 (reasonable time for the buyer to purchase substitute things), La. Civ. Code art. 2610 (reasonable belief by the seller that the buyer would accept the nonconforming things; reasonable notice of intent to cure nonconformity). How does a court determine whether a party has acted "reasonably" in the performance of these obligations?

2. Immovables

La. Civ. Code arts. 2491–2498

In the context of immovable property, the obligation to deliver a conforming thing means that the seller must deliver to the buyer the full extent of the immovable sold. La. Civ. Code art. 2491. One might think that if the parties agree to a sale of a 20-acre tract of land, then the seller must deliver the entire 20 acres of property—no more and no less. However, the seller's obligation to deliver immovable property depends on whether the sale is classified as (1) one at price per measure, (2) one for a lump price, or (3) one described as a certain and limited body or of a distinct object sold for a lump price. *Id.*

A sale of immovable property is one at a price per measure when it is made with "an indication of the extent of the premises" and the price is set "at the rate of so much per measure." La. Civ. Code art. 2492. Therefore, the sale must be one of immovable property, and the Act of Sale must state the entire extent of the premises in some unit of measure (e.g., 50 acres, 1500 square feet, etc.) and also name a price per unit (e.g., $100 per acre, $100 per square foot, etc.). For example, a sale of 100 acres of land at a price of $100 per acre is a sale per measure. In a sale at a price per measure, if the seller does not deliver the precise amount promised, the parties' rights are governed by Article 2492.

Article 2492 provides that as a general rule, any discrepancy in the extent specified in the contract will result in a proportionate reduction or supplement in price. LA. CIV. CODE art. 2492. Consider the example from above whereby 100 acres of land are sold at a price of $100 per acre. If the seller delivers the entire 100 acres, the buyer owes $10,000. If the seller delivers only 97 acres, then the buyer is only required to pay $9,700. If the seller delivers 103 acres, then the buyer must pay $10,300. However, Article 2492 provides that in the event that the actual extent of the immovable sold *exceeds* by more than 1/20 the extent specified in the contract, the buyer may recede from the sale. LA. CIV. CODE art. 2492. Consider the same hypothetical again. The extent specified in the contract is 100 acres; 1/20 of that extent is 5 acres. Thus, if the seller delivers an immovable that exceeds the 100 acres contemplated by more than 5 acres, the buyer may recede from the sale. So, if the seller delivers 106 acres, the buyer may recede. Note, however, that if the extent of the immovable is *less* than specified, the buyer is not allowed to recede from the sale. Also, in no case does the seller have the right to recede.

A sale of immovable property is one for a lump price when it is made "with indication of the extent of the premises but for a lump price." LA. CIV. CODE art. 2494. Therefore, the sale must be one of immovable property, and the Act of Sale must state the entire extent of the premises (e.g., 50 acres, 150 square feet, etc.) and also name a total price (e.g., $5000, $150,000, etc.). For example, a sale of 100 acres of land at a price of $10,000 is a sale for lump price. In such a sale, if the seller does not deliver the precise amount promised, Article 2494 provides that, as a general rule, there is no remedy at all. The exception is when the discrepancy between the extent specified in the contract and the extent actually delivered exceeds 1/20 of the extent specified in the contract. LA. CIV. CODE art. 2494. In such a case, the price will be adjusted proportionately, or, in the case of a surplus, the buyer may choose to recede from the contract instead. *Id.* Consider the example from above whereby the sale of 100 acres of land is sold for $10,000. If the seller delivers any acreage between 95 and 105 acres to the buyer, neither the buyer nor the seller has a remedy. If the seller delivers less than 105 acres, the buyer is entitled to a proportionate reduction in price. For example, if the seller delivers 93 acres, the buyer owes only $9,300. If the seller delivers more than 95 acres, the buyer may choose to pay a proportionate increase in price or to recede from the contract. For example, if the seller delivers 107 acres, the buyer may choose to pay $10,700 or to recede.

In the case of either a sale by measure or a sale at a lump price, any action for reduction or supplement in price or dissolution of the sale prescribes one year from the date of the sale. LA. CIV. CODE art. 2498. Also, if the buyer recedes from the sale, the seller must return the price if he has already received it and reimburse the buyer for the expenses of the sale. LA. CIV. CODE art. 2497.

If the sale of immovable property is one described as "a certain and limited body or of a distinct object sold for a lump price," there is no remedy for a discrepancy between the extent specified in the contract and the extent actually delivered. LA. CIV. CODE art. 2495. This type of sale is also known as a "sale per aversionem." A sale per aversionem, then, must be one of immovable property and must name a lump price (rather than a unit price). In addition, while the Act of Sale may state the extent of the premises to be delivered (in units or as an indication of the entire extent of the premises), it must also describe the immovable as a "limited body" or a "distinct object." According to the comments to Article 2495, examples of a sale per aversionem include an immovable with indication of boundaries, an immovable designated by the adjoining owners, and an immovable designated by particular property name. *See* LA. CIV. CODE art. 2495. Jurisprudence provides that if the Act of Sale describes the immovable as a subdivision lot number, by street number, or by reference to its location on a plat or map, then it is one per aversionem. *See, e.g., Fitzgerald v. Hyland*, 6 So. 2d 321 (1942) (reproduced below); *Passera v. City of New Orleans*, 118 So. 887 (1928). If the sale describes the immovable in one of those ways, even if it also contains an indication of the extent of the premises, it is treated as a sale per aversionem.

The rules provided by Articles 2492 through 2485 are not arbitrary; rather, they are rooted firmly in the doctrine of cause. As defined, "[c]ause is the reason why a party obligates himself." LA. CIV. CODE art. 1967. Depending on the classification of a sale of immovable property, the parties' cause varies. In a sale by measure, the parties' utmost concern is the transfer of a precise measure of property, as evidenced by their agreement upon a unit price. By contrast, in a sale for a lump price, the parties are less concerned with the transfer of a precise measure, as evidenced by their willingness to utilize a lump price; in such scenarios, the parties would seem to tolerate superficial deviations between the extent of the immovable promised and the extent actually delivered. Finally, in a sale per aversionem, the parties' cause is the transfer of a particular piece of property, as evidenced by their choice to describe the property by its name or by reference to its boundaries or adjoining owners. Thus, they are less interested in the precise contours of the property and presumably are satisfied by the transfer of the property so described even if there is a large discrepancy between its actual acreage and any acreage that was included in the Act of Sale.

In practice, the determination of whether a sale is made with an indication of the extent of the premises, per lump price, or per aversionem can be quite difficult. In the cases below, the courts grapple with the classification of the sales in question.

Lasiter v. Gaharan

670 So. 2d 395 (La. App. 3 Cir. 1996)

YELVERTON, Judge.

This is an appeal by Donald Gaharan and his daughter Phyllis, defendants, from a judgment which ordered them to refund $14,750 to Charles Lasiter, the plaintiff. Lasiter had bought a piece of property from the Gaharans. The property was described as containing 80 acres, more or less. It was discovered after the sale that it actually contained only 43.20 acres. The trial court ordered a diminution of the purchase price for failure of the seller to deliver the full extent of the property. The Gaharans appealed. We affirm.

Lasiter bought the land for $50,000 cash. The Gaharans had inherited the property. What they sold to Lasiter was described in the cash sale instrument as follows:

> A certain piece, parcel or tract of land, together with all buildings and improvements thereon, and all rights, ways and privileges thereto appertaining, being, lying and situated in the Parish of Catahoula, State of Louisiana, and being more particularly described as follows, to-wit:
>
>> That part of the East Half (E1/2) of Babin Ricquet, Section 50, Township 8 North, Range 5 East, Eying North of Louisiana State Highway 8, Catahoula Parish, Louisiana, estimated to contain approximately 80 acres, being the same property acquired by Vendors by Judgment of Possession in the Succession of Philip S. Gaharan, Jr., filed October 12, 1990, under file Number 220295, and recorded in Conveyance Book 158, Page 99, of the records of Catahoula Parish, Louisiana, and by Amended Judgment of Possession, filed October 12, 1990, under File Number 220296, and recorded Under File Number 220296, and recorded in Conveyance Book 158, Page 105 of the records of Catahoula Parish, Louisiana.

Lasiter bought the land mainly for the timber. Before the sale, he hired Mike Albritton, a forestry consultant, to cruise the land for him. Albritton got a map from the tax assessor's office. He physically went to the property and estimated the timber based on the map which showed approximately 80 acres.

After the purchase, Lasiter cut what he thought was his 80 acres of timber. He learned that he had trespassed on neighboring property. Lasiter then had his purchase surveyed. The survey showed that the property he bought was actually 43.20 acres. Albritton returned and counted the stumps on the land that Lasiter had overcut. Lasiter then paid the owners who had suffered the trespass for the overcut trees.

On appeal, the Gaharans claim that this was a sale per aversionem pursuant to La.Civ.Code art. 2495, and that, accordingly, the trial court erred in ordering a diminution of the purchase price when it was discovered that the sale was short on acreage. A sale per aversionem is a sale when the object is designated by the adjoining tenements and sold from boundary to boundary. Article 2495. In such a sale, there can be neither an increase nor diminution of price on account of a disagreement in measure. *Id.* They claim that this was a sale per aversionem because the description of the property was from one fixed boundary to another.

The code articles dealing with the obligation of the seller to deliver the full extent of the immovable sold were amended by Acts 1993, No. 841, § 1, effective January 1, 1995. The sale in this case was in 1991. For our purposes as applied to this case, the only change in the law is that a sale hitherto referred to as a sale per aversionem is now described as a sale of a certain and limited body or a distinct object.

The Gaharans have cited the case of *Cornish v. Kinder Canal Company*, 267 So. 2d 625 (La.App. 3 Cir.), *writ denied*, 268 So. 2d 679 (La.1972), *writ not considered*, 269 So. 2d 248 (La.1972), in support of their position that the above description of property is a sale per aversionem. In the cited case the property sold was described as *follows:*

> "Also all that portion of the North East quarter *of* Section Twenty six in Township No. Six South Range No. Five West, *that lies North of the Calcasieu River Irrigation Co.'s Canal*, containing 5 acres more or less." *Id.* at 628.

In that case the court found that the property conveyed was triangular shaped, with the canal crossing the northeast/northwest corner of the section, thus establishing clear boundaries. It was bounded on the north by the north line of Section 26, on the east by the east line of Section 26, and on the southwest by the canal. The court held that a section line is sufficient to constitute a "fixed boundary," and that that was a sale per aversionem.

In the present case there are only three clear boundaries. Mr. Allbritton cruised what he determined to be 80 acres, finding one good boundary, the southern boundary of La. Hwy. 8. He assumed the section lines of Section 50 on the north and east were boundaries, but there was nothing on the west side to go by except what was necessary to make up 80 acres. In fact, the property was bounded on the north and east by Section 50 and on the south by Highway 8. However, there is no clear boundary for the west. If one boundary of the four-sided tract is not identified in the deed, it is not a sale per aversionem. *Deshotel v. Lachney*, 465 So. 2d 974 (La. App. 3 Cir. 1985). This sale was not one per aversionem.

This was a sale per lump. La.Civ.Code art. 2494. In the present case the cash sale instrument showed that the sale was made in consideration of $50,000. No amount per acre was specified. Pursuant to Article 2494 the purchaser of immovable property for a lump sum cannot claim a diminution of the price on a deficiency of the measure, unless the real measure comes short of that expressed in the contract by one-twentieth. In the present case, the cash sale stated that 80 acres more or less was being conveyed. One-twentieth of 80 acres is four acres. A survey of the property after it was bought revealed that 43.20 acres was actually conveyed. The property conveyed to Lasiter was short 36.8 acres. The trial court was correct in ordering that the sale price of the land be reduced.

The defendants also argue that the trial court awarded too much as a diminution in the sales price. They claim that the trial court should have considered that Lasiter made more money selling the timber than he paid for the land and therefore was not damaged. The fact that Lasiter may have profited by buying this property and selling the timber has no bearing on the agreement he reached with the sellers for the purchase of 80 acres. He bought the land for the timber. The defendants could have sold the timber but chose instead to sell the land. Lasiter simply made a good business deal. His profit would have been greater had he received the full 80 acres. We agree with the trial court that Lasiter is entitled to a diminution of the purchase price.

We also find that the trial court's determination of the amount of diminution of the purchase price was not an abuse of discretion. The trial court made a determination that the value of the land was $750 an acre. It did so based on the value of the timber that Lasiter sold off the land. In oral reasons for judgment the trial judge explained, in general although not in particular, how he arrived at the diminution figure of $14,750. He took into account what Lasiter thought he was buying, and what he actually bought; what he got for the timber; and what he recovered when he conveyed the bare land after the timber was cut. Lasiter testified that what he believed he was getting out of his $50,000 purchase of 80 acres was 80 acres at $625 an acre. Considering that his loss by this measure would have justified a diminution in price of over $20,000, we cannot say that a reduction of only $14,750 was an abuse of discretion.

For the reasons set forth in this opinion the judgment of the trial court is affirmed. All costs of this appeal are assessed against defendants-appellants.

AFFIRMED.

Notes and Questions

1. Was the sale in this case a sale made with an extent of the premises, a sale for a lump price, or a sale per aversionem? How did the court determine the type of sale in this case?

2. Based on the cases discussed in *Lasiter v. Graham,* are township and range and/or section lines considered boundaries?

3. Note that in calculating damages, the trial court estimated the value of the land that the buyer did not receive. This estimation was based upon "what Lasiter thought he was buying, and what he actually bought; what he got for the timber; and what he recovered when he conveyed the bare land after the timber was cut." *Lasiter v. Gaharan*, 670 So. 2d at 397. Do you agree with the court's method of calculation? How would the damages award have differed if the court had employed a simple pro rata approach to reducing the price?

4. Recall that as a result of the Grahams' failure to deliver the full extent of the premises, Lasiter trespassed on his neighbor's land and cut down the neighbor's timber. Lasiter then paid the neighbors for the overcut resulting from the trespass. Are the Grahams required to recompense Lasiter for what Lasiter paid the neighbors? Should they be? Remember that Lasiter's conduct in cutting down the neighbor's timber is a tort (trespass), whereas the Grahams breached a contractual obligation associated with the sale. Is the seller liable for the buyer's resulting trespass on his neighbor's property? Can a breach of contract serve as the basis for indemnification under tort law?

Long-Fork, L.C.C. v. Petite Riviere, L.L.C.

987 So. 2d 831 (La. App. 3 Cir. 2008)

Cooks, Judge.

The Plaintiff, Long-Fork, L.L.C. (Long-Fork), brought this action seeking to compel the buyer of certain property to supplement the purchase price or to return the property. On October 31, 2003, an Agreement to Purchase and Sell Real Estate (Purchase Agreement) was executed between Long–Fork and Petite Riviere, L.L.C. involving a piece of property located in Avoyelles Parish. The property description in the Purchase Agreement provided "said tract estimated to be 2,759 acres more or less and generally described as the South Farm, less seventy-seven acres north of the center line of Little River." The Purchase Agreement set forth a price of $1,050.00 per acre and provided that the "price per acre shall control in the event of a discrepancy between the price stated below and the price as determined by the number of acres conveyed, ..." The Purchase Agreement also provided "that a survey would be performed, by a surveyor mutually agreeable to Vendor and Vendee, of the tract of land . . . in order that the Vendor and Vendee may more accurately calculate the acreage of the property to be conveyed." The Purchase Agreement also provided for the consideration of the sale to be $2,896,950.00, which reflected the $1,050.00 per acre price for 2,759 acres. The Purchase Agreement further provided that the act transferring title was to be executed on or before December 31, 2003. A provision that "the Act of Transfer of the property will include the terms and provisions of this contract" was included.

When the Act of Cash Sale was executed on February 13, 2004, the property was described as "comprising approximately 2759 [acres] more or less." The Act of Cash Sale did not contain any clause with respect to the price per acre controlling as was included in the Purchase Agreement. The sales price was $2,896,950.00. Brown Realty Company of Rayville, Inc. was Long-Fork's realtor for the transaction. The property was subsequently transferred by exchange from Petite Riviere to R. Dugas Family, L.L.C. Six months after the sale it was discovered by Long-Fork that the property sold encompassed more acres (approximately 215) than originally thought.

* * * * *

Judgment was rendered in favor of Long-Fork in the amount of $226,485.00 with interest from the date of judicial demand. Long-Fork's request for attorney fees was denied . . . . This appeal followed, wherein Defendants contend the trial court erred in concluding that La.Civ.Code art. 2495 was inapplicable, that La.Civ.Code art. 2498 applied, and allowing for a supplement of the purchase price and attorney fees. Long-Fork answered the appeal, and argues the trial court erred in ruling that Defendants did not violate the right of first refusal granted to Long-Fork in the Act of Cash Sale.

ANALYSIS

As noted by all the parties and the trial court, the material facts in this case have been stipulated to and, as the trial court stated, "the dispute appears to be application of applicable law." When there is an appellate review of questions of law, we must simply determine whether the trial court was legally correct in its application of the law. *Foster v. ConAgra Poultry Co.*, 95-793 (La.App. 3 Cir. 2/14/96), 670 So.2d 471, *writ denied*, 96-645 (La.4/26/96), 672 So.2d 674. If it is determined the trial court made a reversible error of law, the appellate court will review the record *de novo* and render a judgment on the merits. *Lawson v. White*, 01-1173 (La.App. 3 Cir. 2/6/02), 815 So.2d 958, *writ denied*, 02-668 (La.5/3/02), 815 So.2d 107.

Defendants argue, contrary to what the trial court held, that La.Civ.Code art. 2495 is applicable and controlled the Act of Cash Sale. Louisiana Civil Code Article 2495 provides as follows:

> When an immovable described as a certain and limited body or a distinct object is sold for a lump price, an expression of the extent of the immovable in the act of sale does not give the parties any right to an increase or diminution of the price in the case of surplus or shortage in the actual extension of the immovable.

Article 2495 mentions only the "act of sale" and does not reference purchase agreements. In examining the description of the property in the Act of Cash Sale, it seems clear the property was described as a "certain and limited body or a distinct object." *Id.* The description stated what was being sold was "[a]ll of the Seller's rights, title and interest to a certain piece, parcel, or tract of land ... SOUTH OF THE CENTER LINE OF PETITE RIVIERE ... in Sections 2, 9, 10, 11, 13, 14, & 15."[3]

The Louisiana Supreme Court has long held that when a sale is made pursuant to specific boundaries, it is a sale *per aversionem. Johnston v. Quarles,* 3 La. 90 (1831). To constitute a sale *per aversionem,* the buyer must acquire the land within defined boundaries. *Passera v. City of New Orleans,* 167 La. 199, 118 So. 887 (1928). Such a purchase "conveys all of the land within the boundaries given, whether the measure be correctly stated in the deed or not. The designation of the boundaries controls the enumeration of the quantity." *Id.* at 202, 118 So. 887.

In *Campbell v. Cook,* 151 La. 267, 91 So. 731 (1922), the purchaser sought a credit on the purchase price, because the property was said to contain 177 acres more or less, but in fact only contained 123.53 acres. The act of sale described the property as being bounded by three adjoining properties and the Cane River. The court found the boundaries set forth in the legal description were accurate, even if the measurement was not. The court found ". . . the jurisprudence is settled that where there is error as to quantity and none as to boundary, the purchaser cannot claim a diminution of the price in the absence of concealment and fraud. [*Gugliemi v. Geismar,* 46 La. Ann. 280, 14 So. 501.]" *Id.* at 269, 91 So. 731. Citing La.Civ.Code

---

3. Long-Fork in its brief acknowledges "the description in the Act of Sale was *per aversionem* ...." It argues even though this is so, the "common intent that the subject sale be controlled on a price per acre basis" should override this fact.

art. 2495, the court held the sale was *per aversionem* and that no price adjustment was due.

Long-Fork argued below that the Purchase Agreement is the final expression of the parties' intent, and claims it evidenced a "mutual" intent that the price per acre should control. Defendants maintain that the price per acre was used to determine what the sales price would ultimately be in the Act of Cash Sale. In finding in favor of Long-Fork the trial court determined that the silence in the Act of Cash Sale of the price per acre terms did not preclude proof of the obligation that the sale was to be on a price per acre basis. The trial court found that the "obvious and apparent intent of the parties throughout this entire transaction was that the property was to be sold on a price per acre basis."

The trial court's written reasons for judgment indicate it put great import on the use of the word "approximately" in the Act of Cash Sale. Those reasons provide:

> [D]escribing a tract to be "approximately 2,759[acres] more or less" is certainly an indication that the parties to the act of sale knew that there were other terms potentially applicable concerning price, and quite naturally, those terms are the terms reflected in the purchase agreement, being a price per acre. This confirms the parties['] [sic] intent that the sale be on a "per acre" price.

We do not reach the same conclusion as the trial court. It was incumbent on the parties to set an acreage amount to determine a final sales price in the Act of Cash Sale. It is, at best, pure speculation for the trial court to ascribe the meaning it did to the parties' use of the word "approximately." Defendants asserted that the use of the word "approximately" was a further confirmation, along with the use of the phrase "more or less," that acreage was only incidental rather than essential to the transaction. Certainly, this is as plausible an explanation for the use of the word "approximately" as what the trial court found.

Of much greater significance to this court is the use of the phrase "more or less" when describing the property sold between the parties. A reading of the phrase "approximately 2,759 [acres] more or less" leads to a common sense conclusion that the exact acreage amount was *not essential* to the transaction. It would be difficult to conclude otherwise. Thus, we cannot agree with the trial court and Long-Fork that there was a mutual consent between the parties that the price per acre should control, particularly noting the Act of Cash Sale excluded the price per acre language contained in the Purchase Agreement.

Long-Fork also points to its Certificate of Authority as evidence of the parties' mutual intent that the price per acre provision survived to the Act of Cash Sale. We note that this Certificate of Authority was executed by Long-Fork alone. Further, it lists $2,896,950.00, the price listed in the Act of Cash Sale, as the "*total* sales price."

Defendants, in arguing the Purchase Agreement was not the final expression of the parties' intent, noted that there "were a total of thirteen (13) differences between the Purchase Agreement and the Act of Sale."[4] They point out that such extensive differences between the two are at odds with Long-Fork's assertions that there were no changes or negotiations prior to the perfection of the Act of Cash Sale. We agree.

Long-Fork also dismisses the failure of the Act of Cash Sale to contain any clause with respect to the price per acre controlling as "unfortunate" and an "error." Although alleging "error" as the reason for the absence of any clause with respect to the price per acre controlling, Long-Fork did not sue for reformation of the Act of Cash Sale as was done in *Teche Realty & Inv. Co. v. Morrow,* 95-1473 (La.App. 3 Cir. 4/17/96), 673 So.2d 1145. Reformation is an equitable remedy that is available to correct mistakes when the instruments as written do not reflect the true intent of the parties. *See Agurs v. Holt,* 232 La. 1026, 95 So.2d 644 (1957); *WMC Mortgage Corp. v. Weatherly,* 07-75 (La.App. 3 Cir. 6/13/07), 963 So.2d 413. If Long-Fork believed the Act of Cash Sale did not accurately reflect the true intent of the parties, the appropriate action would have been a suit for reformation.

Furthermore, this court has held that the presence of error is irrelevant to the applicability of La.Civ.Code art. 2495. In *Kile v. Louisiana Limestone Aggregates, Inc.,* 378 So.2d 978 (La.App. 3 Cir.1979), *writ denied,* 380 So.2d 71 (1980), Louisiana Limestone Aggregates (LLA) sought a piece of property of at least three acres to build a facility for storing and selling its products. Representatives of LLA examined a piece of land owned by Kile on foot and viewed it from the air. A purchase agreement describing the property by reference to boundaries was signed. This court determined the property description set forth a certain and limited body such as to fall within the scope of La.Civ.Code art. 2495. After the purchase agreement was signed, LLA discovered the tract only encompassed two acres and was insufficient to build its facility. LLA refused to purchase the property and Kile brought suit for specific performance. This court was faced with a question of what is the effect of a *per aversionem* sale where both parties were mistaken as to the quantity of land. We stated:

> We conclude that the description at hand is "per aversionem," as being within "fixed boundaries." LLA is obligated to purchase the property so described even though the parties to the agreement were under the impression that the area contained three acres instead of approximately two acres as reflected by the survey. LLA's contention that the deficiency in area was an error of fact that would justify the invalidation of the agreement, must yield to the clear law of "per aversionem."

4. Many of the differences between the Purchase Agreement and Act of Cash Sale are significant. The Purchase Agreement states that the property in question would be conveyed "free and clear of any encumbrance, servitudes, conditions or restrictions which would render the property unsuitable for the purposes reasonably intended by the Vendee." However, the Act of Cash Sale contains specific listed exceptions which the property was taken subject to. The Purchase Agreement provides that a survey "will be performed" of the strip between Spring Bayou Road and Little River. The Act of Cash Sale noted the only survey performed was that of the servitude of passage.

Id. at 983. Even though there was acknowledged mutual error between the parties in *Kile,* this court found such error was irrelevant to the applicability of La.Civ.Code art. 2495. Likewise, any error alleged by Long-Fork is equally irrelevant in this case. Long-Fork also argues the language of the Purchase Agreement should control over the language of the Act of Cash Sale. In support of this position, it cites the case of *Hingle Brothers, Inc. v. Bonura,* 248 So.2d 391 (La.App. 4 Cir.1971). We find *Hingle* distinguishable on the facts and find it inapplicable to the situation presented here. In *Hingle,* the issue was whether the purchaser of the land could recover from the seller the cost of certain street improvements that were made before the sale, but which were not assessed against the property until after the sale. *Hingle* did not deal with an action seeking a supplement to the purchase price pursuant to La.Civ.Code articles 2492 through 2495. *Hingle* was decided based upon the legal warranty of title as governed by the Civil Code.

Further, the court in *Hingle* noted the act of sale need not conform to the purchase agreement if "varied by mutual consent." The trial court in the present case concluded there was "absolutely no evidence of mutual consent to change the purchase agreement." We disagree. The description of the property in the Act of Cash Sale and the deposition testimony of Charles Mitchell indicate it was Long-Fork's intent to convey a particular piece of land for a set price. Mitchell, who was a co-managing partner of Long-Fork testified as follows:

> Q. But you came to an agreement to sell all land south of the river?
>
> A. Right.
>
> Q. And that is what you intended to convey both through the purchase agreement and the Act of Sale?
>
> A. Correct.
>
> . . .
>
> Q. So correspondingly, it was your intention, Long-Fork's intention, to convey all land that Long-Fork had south of Little River?
>
> A. Correct.

The jurisprudence holds that the act of sale represents "the conclusion of the negotiation process and embodies the final expression of the parties' intent." *Esplanade Management, Ltd. v. Sajare Interests,* 498 So.2d 289, 292 (La.App. 4 Cir.1986); *see also Teche Realty,* 673 So.2d 1145. An authentic act constitutes full proof of the agreement it contains, as against the parties. La.Civ.Code art. 1835.

The Act of Cash Sale, unlike the Purchase Agreement, did not include any "price per acre" language. The Act of Cash Sale provides the latest and best expression of the parties' intent with respect to price. Thus, we find the presumption provided by La.Civ.Code art. 2495 serves to reinforce the "mutual intent" of the parties in this case.

Applying La.Civ.Code art. 2495 to the Act of Cash Sale confirms that the object of the sale was to include all of the property south of the centerline of Petite Riviere in specified sections. The Act of Cash Sale also states a lump price. Therefore, both requirements are met for the sale of a certain and limited body. Thus, the legal description used in the Act of Cash Sale makes the sale a transaction pursuant to La.Civ.Code art. 2495. We find, contrary to the trial court, that the language of "approximately" 2,759 acres "more or less" supports this conclusion.

Finding this was a sale pursuant to La.Civ.Code art. 2495, the one-year prescriptive period allowed for in La.Civ.Code art. 2498 is inapplicable here. Because La.Civ. Code art. 2495 is the controlling statute, the period of time to seek a supplement of the sales price ends with the act of sale. As Defendants note, since the Purchase Agreement contained the "price per acre shall control" language, Long-Fork did have the right to seek an adjustment of the purchase price prior to the closing of the sale. Had Long-Fork surveyed the property, as was its right, the total price could have been adjusted prior to closing. It is certainly reasonable to conclude that if the price per acre were the controlling factor in the setting of the sales price, Long-Fork would have conducted a survey. However, Long-Fork did not survey its property, further confirming its intent was not to sell a certain quantity of property (which would be governed by La.Civ.Code art. 2492), but to sell all of its property south of the centerline of the Little River regardless of acreage. As such, La.Civ.Code art. 2495 is controlling and Long-Fork was not entitled to "any right to an increase or diminution of the price in the case of surplus or shortage in the actual extension of the immovable the property." The trial court erred in holding otherwise, and we reverse the trial court's judgment awarding Long-Fork a supplement to the purchase price and attorney fees and render judgment granting the Motion for Summary Judgment filed by Defendants.

* * * * *

DECREE

For the foregoing reasons, we reverse the trial court's judgment awarding Long-Fork a supplement to the purchase price and attorney fees and render judgment granting the Motion for Summary Judgment filed by Defendants. We affirm the portion of the judgment holding that Defendants did not violate the right of first refusal. Costs of this appeal are assessed to Plaintiff, Long-Fork, L.L.C.

AFFIRMED IN PART; REVERSED IN PART; AND RENDERED.

Notes and Questions

1. In this case, there were discrepancies between the contract to sell (an agreement that precedes the Act of Sale and determines the parties' rights prior to the passage of the Act of Sale) and the Act of Sale. Which documents controls? Why?

2. According to the court, what is the importance of language in the Act of Sale like "approximately" and "more or less"?

3. How did the court address the seller's argument that the parties to the sale were in error regarding the extent of the premises? How does the law governing vices of consent generally interact with Articles 2491 through 2495?

Fitzgerald v. Hyland

6 So. 2d 321 (La. 1942)

ODOM, Justice.

Defendants own a plot of vacant ground in Jefferson Parish fronting on Jefferson Highway in Square 148 of what is known as the "Harlem Subdivision", as per plan made by Hotard and Webb, civil engineers and surveyors. According to this plan, Square 148 is bounded on the south by Jefferson Highway and on the north by Hawkston Street. The owners appointed J. Wallace Paletou, Inc., realtors, their agents for the sale of the property.

Someone, presumably the realtors, posted a large sign in front of the property on Jefferson Highway, advertising it for sale, the sign reading:

"For Sale
"210 Front By 205 Deep
"Whole or Part
"J. Wallace Paletou, Inc.
"Realtors
"822 Perdido St. Ra. 7117"

Plaintiff and his wife, while driving on Jefferson Highway, saw the sign and stopped. They wanted to establish in that vicinity what plaintiff referred to in his testimony as a 'sea-food restaurant', and they thought this vacant property might be a good location for such establishment. Plaintiff left his automobile and looked at the property. He went from there to the office of the realtor, where he made inquiry as to the price of the property and was told that it was for sale at $35 per front foot on Jefferson Highway. Plaintiff told the realtor that he did not want the entire frontage of 210 feet on Jefferson Highway but would purchase 120 feet frontage and pay therefor $3,500 cash. Plaintiff asked the realtor what the depth of the property was and was told that it ran back a distance of 250 [sic.—205] feet through the square. The realtor suggested to plaintiff that he make his offer to purchase in writing, which offer would be presented to the owners for their acceptance or rejection. The realtor wrote and presented to plaintiff an instrument which reads, in so far as it need be quoted, as follows:

"I offer and agree to purchase Vacant property in square 148 nearest Harlem Ave., fronting on Jefferson Highway running thru square the grounds measuring approximately 120 × 205 or, as per title for the sum of Thirty-five Hundred and no/100 Dollars ($3500.00), on terms of Cash."

The instrument was then and there signed by plaintiff. This was on June 15, 1939, and the owners formally accepted the offer some three or four days later.

Subsequent surveys and measurements of the plot of ground showed that, instead of having a depth of 205 feet, as stated in the advertisement and in plaintiff's offer to purchase, it had a depth, according to surveyors Wadell and Hotard, of not more than 165 feet, which is the distance from the north edge of Jefferson Highway, through Square 148, to the south edge of Hawkston Street; so that the shortage in the depth of the plot, according to these surveyors, is 40 feet.

Plaintiff, on learning that the lot did not have a depth of 205 feet as advertised and as stated in his offer to purchase, refused to accept the property at the agreed price of $3,500, but did agree to accept it provided defendants would allow a diminution in the price proportionate to the difference between the distance of 165 feet, as shown by the surveyors Wadell and Hotard, and the distance of 205 feet, as shown by the advertisement and in the offer to purchase. According to plaintiff's calculation, the shortage amounts to 4,827 square feet, which, on the basis of the price agreed upon, would be worth $675.78, the diminution demanded.

Defendants were willing to make deed to the property at the agreed price of $3,500 cash, but refused the diminution in the price demanded.

This suit followed. Plaintiff in his petition set out the facts above stated, alleging that, before he signed the offer to purchase, he asked the defendants' agent whether the lot had a depth of 205 feet, as advertised, and was told that it did, and that his offer was based upon that assurance; that he bargained for a lot having a depth of 205 feet; that the lot bargained for and tendered to him has a depth of only 165 feet, and that, since defendants do not own, and therefore cannot deliver, the measure of ground or square footage which they declared they owned, they must deliver to him what they have and suffer a diminution in price.

Plaintiff alleged further that, due to defendants' default, he had suffered damages to the extent of $1,700—$1,000 loss of profits which he would have derived from operating the restaurant which he expected to establish, $400 attorney's fees, and $300 for loss of time, etc.

He prayed for judgment ordering defendants to deliver the lot in controversy and ordering them to suffer a diminution in the price amounting to $675.78, thereby reducing the consideration from $3,500 to $2,824.22, and judgment for damages amounting to $1,700.

Defendants filed in limine exceptions of no cause and no right of action, which were, in effect, referred to the merits. They filed answer, admitting the alleged facts relating to the execution of the written offer to purchase by plaintiff and their acceptance of it. They denied that their agent was authorized to represent that said lot had a depth in excess of that shown in their title or in excess of the actual distance through Square 148. They alleged that it was never their intention to sell the lot at so much per measure or per square foot, but that they intended to sell the lot as a whole, running through the square, or from street to street, as is shown by the contract itself, upon which they rely; that the sale was one per aversionem, which admits of no diminution in price.

At plaintiff's request, the case was tried by jury, which rendered a verdict in his favor on all points as prayed for. The verdict was approved by the trial judge, and judgment was signed accordingly. The defendants appealed.

We need not discuss the exceptions filed by defendants. The verdict of the jury and the judgment carrying it into effect are wrong on the merits and must be set aside.

Plaintiff relies mainly upon Articles 2491 and 2492 of the Revised Civil Code to support his case. These articles read as follows:

> "Art. 2491 [R.C.C. 2491] []. Of Immovables; Seller's Obligation. The seller is bound to deliver the full extent of the premises, as specified in the contract, *under the modifications hereafter expressed.*"

> "Art. 2492 [R.C.C. 2492] []. When Premises Include Less Than Quantity Stipulated. If the sale of an immovable has been made *with indication of the extent of the premises at the rate of so much per measure,* the seller is obliged to deliver to the buyer, if he requires it, the quantity mentioned in the contract, and if he can not [sic] conveniently do it, or if the buyer does not require it, the seller is obliged to suffer a diminution proportionate to the price." (Italics are the writer's.)

We here repeat the pertinent portion of the plaintiff's offer to purchase, which was accepted by the defendants:

> "I offer and agree to purchase Vacant property in square 148 nearest Harlem Ave., fronting on Jefferson Highway running thru square the grounds measuring approximately 120×205 or, as per title for the sum of Thirty-five Hundred and no/100 Dollars ($3500.00), on terms of Cash."

This offer and agreement to purchase by plaintiff, having been accepted by defendants, became a contract which is binding upon the parties to it. Each of the parties relies upon it. This lawsuit is the result of a dispute between them as to the correct interpretation of its meaning.

There is no dispute between the parties as to the identity of the lot or plot of ground which plaintiff intended to purchase and defendants intended to sell. They agree that it has a frontage of 120 feet on Jefferson Highway and runs back, or north, between parallel lines through Square 148 to Hawkston Street. They agree that the wording of the contract shows that the lot is bounded on the south by Jefferson Highway and on the north by Hawkston Street. Plaintiff prayed for judgment ordering defendants to transfer to him the lot of ground "as it actually stands and exists, * * * which said property is accurately described and shown on a plan of survey made under date of Sept. 5, 1939 (revised plan), by Hotard and Webb, Civil Engineers and Surveyors, as follows, to-wit".

Then follows a description of the lot described as being "in Square No. 148, bounded by Harlem Avenue, Worthington (Jefferson Highway) Hawkston and Lowerline Streets".

The boundaries referred to are the boundaries of Square 148. It is important to note these boundaries because the contract itself shows that the lot is in Square 148 and runs "thru square". The "plan of survey" of the lots made by Hotard and Webb, which plaintiff alleges accurately shows and describes the lot, is attached to, and made a part of, the petition. This plan of survey is before us, and we note that it shows that the lot is bounded on the south by Worthington Street, now Jefferson Highway, and on the north by Hawkston Street, the street and highway being clearly designated on the plan referred to.

We cannot concur in the view expressed by counsel for plaintiff that the provisions of Article 2492 [R.C.C. 2492] of the Civil Code are applicable to a case of this kind. That article applies to sales of immovable property made "with indication of the extent of the premises at the rate of so much per measure". In other words, the article relates to sales where the "extent of the premises" is to be so many acres or arpents, square feet or yards, and the price is to be "at the rate of so much per measure". That is what the article says. It relates to sales where "quantity" is involved. In such sales, says the Code, the seller is obliged to deliver to the buyer, if he requires it, "the quantity mentioned in the contract", and, if he cannot do so, he is "obliged to suffer a diminution [in price] proportionate to the price".

In this case no "quantity" is mentioned in the contract, and it is not stated that the sale is to be made "at the rate of so much per measure". The buyer was to pay, and the sellers were to get, a named sum of money for the whole of a certain lot or plot of vacant ground. In other words, the lot or plot of ground was to be sold as a whole, or as a unit, and not at a specified price by the foot. Each knew and well understood that the lot was to have a frontage of 120 feet on Jefferson Highway and was to run back, or north, through Square 148 to Hawkston Street. The contract so stated in plain terms. Plaintiff says he read the contract before he signed it, and that he noticed that portion of the description which showed that the lot ran "thru square". He knew, therefore, that the lot he was to get had fixed boundaries on the north and on the south, and that the depth of the lot could not exceed in feet the distance between those boundaries. He knew also, of course, that, regardless of the statement in the contract that the lot had a depth of 205 feet, he could get no more depth than the lot actually had.

We do not have to look beyond the four corners of the instrument itself to learn what was the intent of the parties. That instrument shows on its face that plaintiff intended to purchase, and defendants intended to sell, a certain lot or plot of vacant ground, as a whole, in Square 148 of the "Harlem Subdivision", the lot fronting on the highway and running back through the square. And it is important to note that by his suit plaintiff demands that defendants transfer to him "said property as it actually stands and exists". That is what he intended to get, what he wants now, and that is what defendants intended to deliver, for that is all they had and they could deliver no more. This is clearly shown by the contract itself when it is read as a whole.

"All clauses of agreements are interpreted the one by the other, giving to each the sense that results from the entire act." Revised Civil Code, Article 1955 [R.C.C. 2050].

All the provisions of a contract are to be construed together so as to give effect to each of the provisions, if possible. *Cerniglia v. Kral*, 170 La. 372, 127 So. 872. A contract must be construed as a whole and in the light of conditions and circumstances existing at the time. *Andrews Coal Co. v. School Board*, 151 La. 695, 92 So. 303. A contract containing several clauses evidencing an agreement between the contracting parties is to be viewed as a whole, and the intentions of the parties are to be gathered from all parts of it, to the end of giving practical effect to the instrument in the way in which such contracts are ordinarily understood. *Lozes v. Segura Sugar Co.*, 52 La.Ann. 1844, 28 So. 249.

Counsel for plaintiff says in his brief at page 21, after referring to the above established rules for the interpretation of contracts, that this court "cannot fail to consider the special clause providing for a fixed depth of approximately 205 feet, as specifically provided in the contract under consideration". We have given that clause consideration, and our conclusion is that it does not prevail over other clauses in the contract relating to the description. Under the above stated rules, that clause must be construed with other clauses in order to ascertain the true intent of the parties. Construing the agreement as a whole, it clearly appears to us that the plaintiff intended to purchase, and defendants intended to sell, a certain designated lot with the front and rear boundaries fixed.

Plaintiff did not allege, nor does he now contend, that he was induced to sign the contract through fraud perpetrated by defendants. The testimony shows that neither the reactor nor defendants were quite certain as to the depth of the lot. The record discloses that Square 148 of the "Harlem Subdivision" is bounded on the north by Hawkston Street and on the south by Worthington Street, now Jefferson Highway, and that it originally had a depth of 240 feet between those boundaries. These defendants acquired the property by inheritance from their father, and during their minority their tutor made two sales to the police jury for a right-of-way for Jefferson Highway, each conveying a strip of ground 25 feet in width off the south side of Square 148. This reduced the depth of the square to 190 feet, according to the conveyance records.

The record further discloses that the police jury, or the highway commission, in building Jefferson Highway encroached without authority and probably by mistake upon Square 148 a distance of 25 feet beyond the limits of its purchases, which accounts for the fact that the distance between the north edge of the highway and the south edge of Hawkston Street is now only 165 feet. The fact that defendants were minors at the time the sales were made and that they did not know of the encroachment upon their property by the police jury lends credence to their testimony that they were not quite certain as to the depth of the lot. We have no doubt, therefore, that the representation that the lot had a depth of 205 feet was made in good faith and through error.

The question, then, is whether defendants must suffer a diminution in the price of the lot. We do not think they should. This controversy arose over the depth of the lot, and, as to that dimension, the sale was to be from boundary to boundary, as is clearly shown by the contract. It was therefore to be a sale per aversionem. Article

2495 [R.C.C. 2495] of the Revised Civil Code governs cases of this kind. It reads as follows:

> "Sale Per Aversionem. There can be neither increase nor diminution of price on account of disagreement in measure, when the object is designated by the adjoining tenements, and sold from boundary to boundary."

There is another article of the Code which contains similar provisions. It is Article 854 [No Corresponding Article], which reads as follows:

> "Sales By Metes and Bounds (Per Aversionem). If any one [sic] sells or alienates a piece of land from one fixed boundary to another fixed boundary, the purchaser takes all the land between such bounds, although it give him a greater quantity of land than is called for in his title, and though the surplus exceeded the twentieth part of the quantity mentioned in his title."

Defendants concealed nothing from plaintiff. The back boundary of the lot was a street, and plaintiff knew it. The street was visible, as was a fence along the edge of it. Plaintiff did not allege, and does not now claim, that defendants perpetrated any fraud upon him. In the absence of fraud or concealment, the rule established by the jurisprudence of this state is that, in sales where specific boundaries are given or where the sale includes property from one fixed boundary to another, the sale is per aversionem, and the seller conveys, and the buyer gets, all the property within the boundaries given, whether it be more or less than the measure mentioned in the contract, and that, in sales where fixed boundaries are designated, such measurements and distances as may be mentioned in connection with the description must yield to the designated boundaries.

It would serve no useful purpose to review the jurisprudence which supports this rule. We need cite only two comparatively recent cases, in which this court with precision and at great length cited and reviewed the earlier pertinent cases. The cases to which we refer are *Consolidated Companies v. Haas Land Co.*, 179 La. 19, 153 So. 6 (on rehearing), and *Passera v. City of New Orleans*, 167 La. 199, 118 So. 887. See, also, *Hunter v. Forrest*, 183 La. 434, 441, 164 So. 163.

Our jurisprudence is in accord with that which prevails elsewhere, as shown by the following extract which we quote from 27 R.C.L., Section 146, page 432:

> "And as a general rule, where the sale is of a particular tract for a gross sum to be paid for the whole tract and not at a specified price by the foot or acre, though the tract is also described as containing a certain quantity, it is considered as a sale of the actual quantity within the designated boundaries, without reference to the quantity or measure of the premises mentioned in the contract or conveyance; and where there has been no fraud or misrepresentation the purchaser is neither liable for a surplus nor entitled to a deduction in the price on account of any deficiency in the quantity or measure mentioned."

The last sentence of that section reads as follows:

> "The Louisiana code, however, has in effect adopted the general rule pre-
> vailing in this country and placed the vendor and the purchaser upon an
> equality as regards any surplus or deficiency in the quantity mentioned."

Counsel for plaintiff suggests that this was not to be a sale per aversionem because
the east and west boundaries of the lot were not mentioned. There is no merit in this
suggestion. It is true that the lot or plot of ground was not bounded on either the
east or the west side by streets or by visible markers of any kind. But there is no controversy over the width of the lot. The controversy relates to the depth of the lot, i.e.,
its length from north to south, and as to that dimension the lot has fixed boundary
lines. The plaintiff understood that the lot or plot of ground he was to get was to
run from Jefferson Highway on the south through the square to Hawkston Street,
between parallel lines 120 feet apart.

Counsel for plaintiff cites the following cases to support his contention that this
was not to be a sale per aversionem: *McBride v. Elam*, 8 La.App. 520; *Phelps v. Wilson*, 16 La. 185*; Lesassier v. Dashiell*, 13 La. 151; *Hall v. Nevill*, 3 La.Ann. 326, and
Favrot & Livaudais v. Stauffer, 112 La. 158, 36 So. 307.

The cases are not in point. In the *McBride* case, the property sold was a part of
a larger tract, the larger tract being specifically described by surveys showing distances, angles, etc., the land sold being described as "The part of said tract hereby
sold being that part lying west of said dirt road, containing 7.50 acres, more or less".
It was held that this was not a sale per aversionem, although the court did say that
the tract of land sold had definite boundaries. If in fact the land sold had fixed and
definite boundaries and was sold with reference to them, a fact which is not clear
to us from our reading of the description, we cannot understand how the court
reached the conclusion it did.

In *Phelps v. Wilson*, the court said:

> "In order to be considered as a sale per aversionem, it is necessary that the
> object should be designated by adjoining tenements, and sold from bound-
> ary to boundary; Idem., article 2471 [2495], which circumstance does not
> exist in the sale in question."

In *Lesassier v. Dashiell*, it appears that the seller had led the buyer into error by
fraudulent claims as to the real quantity within the specified boundaries.

In *Hall v. Nevill*, the sale was held not to be one per aversionem, the court saying:

> "This was not a sale per aversionem, the property not being designated by
> adjoining tracts or tenements, nor sold from boundary to boundary."

In *Favrot & Livaudais v. Stauffer*, the description in the deed called for property
"measuring thirty-one feet front on Perdido Street, by a depth between parallel
lines and front on Carondelet Street of one hundred and seventeen feet two inches
and six lines". The measure in dispute was the frontage on Perdido Street, which in
the deed was stated to be 31 feet, when as a matter of fact the property actually had

a frontage on that street of only 21 feet. The court, without discussing the general rules relating to sales per aversionem, stated that this was not such a sale, but was a sale by measurement.

For the reasons assigned, the verdict of the jury and the judgment carrying it into effect are set aside, and it is ordered that plaintiff's demands be rejected and his suit dismissed at his cost.

Notes and Questions

1. In this case, the property description did not include four boundaries, yet the court found the sale to be one per aversionem. How did it reach that result?

2. Note that the dispute in this case arose after the parties executed a contract to sell (purchase agreement) but before the parties executed an Act of Sale. Presumably, if the plaintiff had been successful in arguing that the sale was one for which a remedy is provided under either Articles 2492 or Article 2493, then he could have required the sellers to accept a reduced price in return for the property. As you will see in Chapter 12: Contracts Preparatory to Sale, after the execution of a purchase agreement, the buyer may refuse to consummate an Act of Sale if the title to the property to be conveyed is not "merchantable." After reading Chapter 12, consider how the seller's warranty of "merchantability" differs from the seller's obligation to deliver the extent of the premises promised.

3. As a final note, it should be kept in mind that the classification of the sale for purposes of determining whether the seller has delivered the extent of the premises delivered is governed by the Act of Sale rather than any representations made by the seller in listing documents or signage. Moreover, when the Act of Sale describes the immovable by reference to a recorded plat or subdivision map, the seller's obligation is to deliver the extent of the premises indicated in such plat or map. *Strange v. Kennard*, 763 So. 2d 710 (La. App. 1 Cir. 2000) is illustrative of both of these points. There, the Stranges purchased two lots located in a residential subdivision from the Kennards for a lump price of $170,000. The ReMax flyer described the land as a "2 Acre Tree Shaded Lot (330 × 265)." *Id.* at 711. The contract to sell portrayed the property as "Land measuring approximately 330 × 265 (as per plat)." The Act of Sale ultimately described the property as "Lots Eleven (11) and Twelve (12)" of the Northwoods Subdivision, "said lots having such measurements and dimensions . . . as more particularly described on said subdivision map." *Id.* at 711. Shortly after the sale, the Stranges discovered that the two lots measured only approximately 220 × 243 feet, or about 1.2 acres, and brought suit for a reduction of the price. The court rejected their claim, holding that "[t]he designation of the sale [under Articles 2492 through 2495] should be based exclusively on the written act of sale." 763 So. 2d at 712. Furthermore, the court observed that because "[t]he subdivision plat, filed in the public records and referenced in the act of sale, provided the correct measurements of the lots in question," and "[t]he sellers delivered the property 'as per plat[,]'" the sellers complied with the terms of the agreement and, ultimately, their obligation to deliver. *Id.*

Chapter 9

The Warranty Against Eviction

A. Introduction and Scope of the Warranty Against Eviction

La. Civ. Code arts. 2475, 2500

In addition to the obligation to deliver, the seller owes a number of warranty obligations to the buyer. *See* La. Civ. Code art. 2475. The first such obligation of the seller is the warranty against eviction. This warranty involves, in essence, a promise by the seller to the buyer that the seller is indeed the owner of the thing that is conveyed. *See generally* Robert J. Pothier, A Treatise on the Contract of Sale § 83 (L.S. Cushing Trans. 1839). Article 2500 provides a definition of eviction and elaborates upon the scope of the warranty. According to that article, the definition of eviction contains at least three fundamental concepts. First, an eviction is defined as "the buyer's loss of, or danger of losing, the whole or part of the thing sold because of a third person's right that existed at the time of the sale." La. Civ. Code art. 2500. Second, the warranty also includes "encumbrances on the thing that were not declared at the time of the sale." *Id.* Third, the article states that the warranty applies only to rights and encumbrances "that existed at the time of the sale." *Id.* Any later-arising rights, as a general rule, are not covered. Each of these three aspects of the warranty will be discussed in the Subparts that follow.

1. The Buyer's Loss or Danger of Losing the Whole or a Part of the Thing

Article 2500 makes a distinction between the buyer's "loss" of the thing sold and the "danger of losing" that thing. "Loss" of the thing sold occurs when a court decrees the superior right of a third person. Consider, for example, a sale in which Seller conveys to Buyer a tract of land which, unbeknownst to Seller, is in fact owned by Third Person. After learning of the sale, Third Person brings a petitory action against Buyer and wins. By virtue of this judicial decree, it is clear that Buyer has been evicted.

In contrast to "loss" of the thing, the "danger" of losing the property arises when a third person has a superior interest in the property that has not yet been decreed by any court. Thus, in the case above, Buyer suffered the "danger" of losing the property by virtue of the mere fact that Third Person, not Seller, owned the property at the time of the sale. Even before any court recognized Seller's right as superior, an eviction had occurred.

Consider the following case. Did the buyer suffer a "loss" of the thing sold? The "danger of losing" the thing sold? What is required of a buyer seeking to show the danger of eviction?

Bologna Bros. v. Stephens

18 So. 2d 914 (La. 1944)

Hamiter, Justice.

Bologna Bros. and the individual members of that partnership are suing the widow and the sole heir of Benjamin J. Stephens deceased for the return of the price of $1,500 paid by plaintiffs to decedent in the purchasing of a parcel of ground, and also for the recovery of certain taxes amounting to $855.49 paid thereon by them, they contending that the deceased vendor and recipient of the purchase price had no title to the property which he undertook to convey.

The district court rendered judgment in favor of plaintiffs for $1,500; but it rejected their demands for taxes. Defendants are appealing.

On November 19, 1919, Benjamin J. Stephens acquired from Lewis Gottlieb, by a good and valid title, Lots 21, 22 and 23, of Square 1, Bonnecaze Subdivision, in the City of Baton Rouge.

Sometime later there was organized the Stephens Realty Company, Inc., of which the said Stephens owned 198 shares of its 200 shares of stock, and his wife and daughter, defendants herein, each owned one of the two remaining shares.

In favor of that corporation, which was clearly a family affair and had no bank account, Stephens executed a deed on September 28, 1931, reciting the conveyance to it of Lots 21, 22 and 23 of the Bonnecaze Subdivision in the City of Baton Rouge. No square number was listed or shown in the description of the property conveyed, notwithstanding that the Bonnecaze Subdivision consists of two squares, known as Square, No. 1 and Square No. 2, in each of which there are Lots 21, 22 and 23; neither was reference made to the deed by which Stephens had acquired title from Gottlieb.

On September 13, 1935, Benjamin J. Stephens, in his own name, transferred to the plaintiff partnership of Bologna Bros., for a cash consideration of $1,500, the south 37' of Lot 21 of Square No. 1, of the Bonnecaze Subdivision; and on this parcel of ground the purchaser, at a later date, erected a building at a cost of approximately $10,000. The deed evidencing the transaction correctly described the property intended to be purchased, it reciting the square number and also referred to the instrument by which Stephens acquired from Gottlieb. And the mentioned consideration of $1,500 is the purchase price sought to be recovered in this suit.

In July, 1941, subsequent to the death of Benjamin J. Stephens and after his wife and daughter (defendants herein) had been sent into possession of his estate, the

Stephens Realty Company, Inc., represented by decedent's wife as its president and for a consideration of $4,000, executed a deed conveying to Cecil N. Bankston two parcels of ground. One of these parcels was the south 37' of Lot 21 of Square 1, of the Bonnecaze Subdivision, the same property which had been sold by Benjamin J. Stephen to Bologna Bros. on September 13, 1935.

Following this conveyance Bankston informed Bologna Bros. that he owned the land upon which its building was constructed; and after some negotiations, but without any notice to defendants, he received from that partnership the sum of $1,000 for a deed to the property.

Later this suit was commenced, plaintiffs taking the position in it, to quote from the brief of their counsel, "that at the time that Benjamin J. Stephens purported to sell to plaintiffs he did not own the property, but Stephens Realty Company, Inc., owned it; that the sale from Benjamin J. Stephens to Bologna Bros. was therefore void, and that Stephens' heirs must return the purchase price."

Defendants, on the other hand, are urging, 1 — that plaintiffs have never been evicted and therefore cannot sue for the return of the purchase price; 2 — that in as much as no square number was given in the transfer from Benjamin J. Stephens to the Stephens Realty Company, Inc., the property remained in Stephens, and the sale by him to Bologna Bros. was good and valid; and 3 — that if the partnership had waited for the filing of suit against it by Bankston, and therein defendants had been called in warranty, the defense could have been made that he (Bankston) obtained no title to the property, that he had been guilty of fraud, and that error was made in the transfer of the property to him.

In *Bonvillain v. Bodenheimer*, 117 La. 793, 42 So. 273 (a case cited and relied on by appellees), plaintiff sued to recover the price that he paid to defendant for property which the latter had never owned, and this court, on rehearing, held that he was entitled to restitution of the money, even though he may not have been actually evicted or disturbed in his possession by the true owner. Our conclusion was founded on R.C.C. Article 2452 [R.C.C. 2452], which declares that the sale of a thing belonging to another person is null, and also on the rule announced in *Robbins v. Martin*, 43 La.Ann. 488, 9 So. 108, and *McDonald & Coon v. Vaughan*, 14 La.Ann. 716, to the effect that actual eviction is unnecessary "if a perfect title exists in some third person, whereby it is rendered legally certain that his vendor had no title."

Such doctrine or rule was later recognized and approved in *Kuhn v. Breard*, 151 La. 546, 92 So. 52, in *Bickham v. Kelly*, 162 La. 421, 110 So. 637, and in *Abney v. Levy*, 169 La. 159, 124 So. 766, 767.

Moreover, in the *Abney* case, which was also a suit for the return of the purchase price, it was said:

> "It is a matter of no importance that, in this case, the third person, in whom it is alleged title is vested, is not a party to this suit. He is not a necessary party to it. The court, even in his absence, may inquire to ascertain whether

it appears that a perfect title is vested in him. For the court to be legally in position to do this it is not necessary that the third person to the sale be bound by the decree. The only necessary parties to the suit are the parties to the sale, the plaintiff, and the defendant herein. The third person is not concerned as to whether defendant be ordered to return the purchase price to plaintiff or not."

The discussed principles of law, it will be noticed, are applicable only when a perfect title exists in some third person, thus showing with legal certainty that there is none in the vendor of him who claims the restitution. And from this the question arises: Did Bankston, who has not been made a party to this suit, have a perfect title to the disputed 37' of ground?

"The purpose of registry is that third persons may have notice of the transfer, and, if the description in the deed is so vague, indefinite, and uncertain that the property cannot be located and identified, the sale is void as to third persons who deal upon the faith of the public records." This was a comment in *Hargrove v. Hodge et al.*, 9 La.App. 434, 121 So. 224, 225, a case decided by the Court of Appeal, Second Circuit. And therein the court further observed:

> "The description in a deed must be such that the property intended to be conveyed can be located and identified, and the general rule is that the description must fully appear within the four corners of the instrument itself, or that the deed should refer to some map, plat, or deed as a part of the description, so that the same may be clear."

A writ of certiorari was refused by this court in the *Hargrove* case. Furthermore, in two recent decisions we specifically affirmed its holding. *Daigle v. Calcasieu Nat. Bank in Lake Charles*, 200 La. 1006, 9 So.2d 394; *Cupples v. Harris*, 202 La. 336, 11 So.2d 609.

Applying the test of the *Hargrove* case to Bankston's title, and keeping in mind that Bologna Bros. (a third person) dealt on the faith of the public records, we cannot conclude with certainty that it is perfect. To say the least, it is possibly defective. True the deed by which he acquired from Stephens Realty Company Inc., accurately and correctly described the property; but as to the instrument executed by Benjamin J. Stephens in favor of that corporation, which is a link in Bankston's chain of title, some doubt exists as to the sufficiency of the description, this because of its failure to give the number of the square in which the parcel of ground was situated.

Since we are unable to hold that Bankston's title on its face is perfect, it becomes necessary to and we will remand the case so that plaintiffs can make him a party to the suit; and in this connection the present litigants are granted the privilege of filing supplementary pleadings and of introducing any additional admissible evidence that may be material to the litigation. If we should adjudicate on the title of Bankston while he is not a party hereto and hold it to be invalid, certainly he would not be bound by the decree. Then, too, such would be unfair to him. Furthermore, if that be done, most probably he would bring an action for restitution against these defendants; also these plaintiffs would sue for a return of the $1,000 which they paid him. By making Bankston a party to the proceeding, the controversy will be simplified and a multiplicity of suits avoided. This is in keeping with the adage that the law abhors a multiplicity of suits.

No exception of non-joinder was filed; however, the court of its own motion may take cognizance of the lack of necessary parties. *Succession of Todd*, 165 La. 453, 115 So. 653; *De Hart v. Continental Land & Fur Co.*, 196 La. 701, 200 So. 9.

For the reasons assigned the judgment of the district court is reversed and set aside, and the case is remanded for further proceedings consistent with the views herein expressed and in accordance with law. Costs of the appeal shall be paid by plaintiffs; all others are to await the final determination of the case.

O'Niell, C.J., does not take part.

Notes and Questions

1. The term "eviction" is used in many legal contexts with varying meanings. In the context of lease, "eviction" refers to the lessor's action to regain possession following the termination of the lease. *See infra* Chapter 15: Termination and Dissolution of the Lease for a discussion of the summary eviction procedure. In the basic course in Civil Law Property, students learn that the possessor of an immovable is "evicted" by a disturbance or usurpation sufficient to result in the loss of possession. *See* La. Civ. Code art. 3433. Thus, the term "eviction" often refers to a loss of corporeal possession. However, in the context of sale, it is not necessary that the buyer be physically dispossessed of the thing sold in order to suffer an "eviction." *See* La. Civ. Code art. 2500 cmt. b; *McDonald v. Vaughan*, 14 La. Ann. 716 (La. 1859).

2. Article 2500 provides explicitly that the warranty against eviction extends to the buyer's loss of or danger of losing the thing "because of a third person's *right*...." La. Civ. Code art. 2500 (emphasis added). The seller is not responsible for the acts of persons who do not enjoy a legal right to the thing sold:

> [T]hus, the dispossession of the buyer from the thing sold by a trespasser or other wrongdoer does not constitute eviction. It is only when the third party asserts a lawful claim to the thing sold, under color of title or otherwise, that the seller's obligation to warrant the buyer against eviction comes into play.

Louisiana State Law Institute, Proposed Civil Code Revision of Sales 26 (1992) (Exposé des Motifs).

2. Encumbrances and Other Charges on the Thing Sold

As provided by Article 2500, the warranty against eviction extends to certain "encumbrances" on the thing sold that were not declared by the seller at the time of sale. La. Civ. Code art. 2500.

Importantly, not every encumbrance burdening the property at the time of the sale is included within the scope of the warranty. As provided in Article 2500, the warranty extends only to "encumbrances on the thing *that were not declared at the time of the sale, with the exception of apparent servitudes and natural and legal non-apparent servitudes, which need not be declared.*" *Id.* (emphasis added). This article makes clear that the seller does not unconditionally guarantee that the property conveyed will be free of encumbrances; rather, the seller is bound only to communicate the existence of those encumbrances that are not obvious and that do not arise by operation of law.

Declared encumbrances include those that are communicated by the seller to the buyer in the Act of Sale. Louisiana courts have also held that encumbrances noted in maps or plats that are referenced in the parties' agreement and annexed to it are "declared" under the meaning of this article. *See Werk v. Leland University,* 99 So. 716, 717 (1924) (annexing "the map to the deed, and the reference to it in the description given in the deed, made the map as important a part of the description as if it had been actually copied in the deed."). When an encumbrance is declared, the Act of Sale makes clear that thing sold is the property in its burdened state. Thus, the buyer has no recourse against the seller for the loss of the part that is affected by that burden. Although not stated in the article, it is implicit that the buyer has no recourse against the seller for encumbrances of which the buyer is actually aware, even if they are not declared. *See* 24 DIAN TOOLEY-KNOBLETT & DAVID GRUNING, LOUISIANA CIVIL LAW TREATISE, SALES § 10:11 (2017).

The exclusion of apparent servitudes follows a similar logic. An apparent servitude is one that is "perceivable by exterior signs, works, or constructions; such as a roadway, a window in a common wall, or an aqueduct." LA. CIV. CODE art. 707. If the buyer can see that a servitude exists upon conducting a physical inspection of the property, then the thing sold is the property in its obviously burdened state. The exclusion of apparent servitudes from the warranty against eviction imposes an obligation on the buyer to inspect the premises in order to ascertain whether any apparent servitude exists.

The exclusion of legal and natural servitudes from the scope of the warranty arises not from the buyer's actual or constructive knowledge of their existence, but from the fact that these servitudes are imposed by law rather than any seller of the property. Legal servitudes are "limitations on ownership established by law for the benefit of the general public or for the benefit of particular persons." LA. CIV. CODE art. 659. Although a buyer who purchases a thing burdened with a legal servitude is thereby restricted in his or her use of the property, the buyer has no recourse against the seller. Some common legal servitudes include the obligation to keep one's buildings in repair (LA. CIV. CODE art. 660, 661), the obligation to maintain one's roof to prevent rainwater from falling on a neighbor's property (LA. CIV. CODE art. 664), and the obligation of owners to leave space open on the shores of navigable rivers for public use (LA. CIV. CODE art. 665). Similarly, natural servitudes are ones that "arise from the natural situation of estates." LA. CIV. CODE art. 654. A prominent example of a natural servitude is the servitude of drain found in Article 655, which states that "[a]n estate situated below is the servient estate and is bound to receive the surface waters that flow naturally from a dominant estate situated above unless an act of man has created the flow." La. Civ. Code art. 655. Because this servitude arises as a result of the natural situation of the property, it is not covered by the warranty.

Consider now an example of an encumbrance that *is* included within the scope of the warranty against eviction: an undeclared, nonapparent pipeline servitude. When property is burdened by such an encumbrance, it is a conventional one, i.e., the result of an agreement between the seller or a former owner of the property and a third person — not the law or the natural situation of the property. If the servitude is undeclared, the buyer has no reason to know of its existence, as there are no external signs or markers to indicate its presence. As a result, the buyer has recourse against the seller for breach of the warranty against eviction.

Importantly, servitudes are not the only encumbrances covered by the warranty; rather, all real rights affecting the immovable fall within its scope, including mortgages, privileges, building restrictions, and mineral rights. In addition, the term also encompasses rights that, though classified as personal rights, affect third persons by virtue of the public records doctrine. These rights — occasionally referred to "quasi-real rights" — include leases, option contracts, rights of first refusal, and contracts to sell. *See* 24 Dian Tooley-Knoblett & David Gruning, Louisiana Civil Law Treatise, Sales § 10:8, n.17 (2017).

In the following case, the Louisiana Supreme Court explored the Civil Code's exclusion of apparent servitudes from the scope of the warranty against eviction.

Richmond v. Zapata Development Corp.
350 So. 2d 875 (La. 1977)

Dennis, Justice.

The question presented by this case is whether the presence of drilling structures on land, as visible evidence of a mineral lease, will prevent a buyer of the property, who made no pre-sale inspection, from recovering in warranty from his vendor, who failed to disclose the existence of the lease.

On June 9, 1972, defendant Zapata Development Corporation, conveyed to plaintiff R. Randolph Richmond, Jr., by warranty deed a parcel of immovable property located in Iberville Parish comprising some 640 acres. The act of sale declared a number of charges claimed against the property. Richmond purchased without examining the title or inspecting the premises, and later discovered that the property was being exploited for oil and gas pursuant to a mineral lease by Gay Union Corporation in favor of Gulf Refining Company of Louisiana which had been executed and properly recorded in 1930.

On October 2, 1974, Richmond filed suit against his vendor, Zapata, alleging that the extensive mineral recovery operations conducted under the 1930 Gay-Gulf lease on some 360 acres of the property rendered that portion of the property useless for any purpose other than mineral production and impaired his ability to develop and utilize the remaining 280 acres. Plaintiff alleged that the mineral lessee had placed on the property a network of pipelines, tanks, lines, canals, structures, shacks, offices, houses, drilling equipment, rigs both active and abandoned, roadways and other earthen works, ponds, pits, oil spills and pollutants. Contending that failure to declare the existence of the lease in the act of sale amounted to a breach of Zapata's warranty against eviction, Richmond originally prayed for judgment in the amount of $120,000, but subsequently amended his petition to seek an award of $2,120,000.

Defendant Zapata filed exceptions of no cause of action and prescription, and a motion for summary judgment. In support of the latter motion it attached as exhibits copies of the 1972 act of sale of the property from Zapata to Richmond, a 1971 recorded act of sale of all oil, gas and mineral interests in the property from Southdown, Inc. to Pelto Oil Company, and the 1930 mineral lease from Gay Union Corporation to Gulf Refining Company of Louisiana.

During the six months following the filing of defendant's motion for summary judgment, plaintiff filed no opposing affidavits demonstrating the existence of a material factual dispute. La. C.C.P. arts. 966-67. Subsequently, the district court rendered summary judgment for defendant, finding that Zapata did not warrant the property sold to be free of oil and gas exploration because of the numerous paragraphs in the deed suggestive of mineral activity, especially paragraph (k) which disclosed a 1971 sale of all mineral rights in the property from Southdown, Inc. to Pelto Oil Company. In his reasons for judgment the district judge also expressed his view that, if plaintiff's action were regarded as one in redhibition, it had prescribed.

The court of appeal affirmed, holding that plaintiff Richmond had been apprised, by the inscriptions recited in the deed, of facts sufficient to provoke his examination of the title before purchasing. 339 So.2d 939 (La.App. 4th Cir. 1976). We granted writs to review this decision. 341 So.2d 1126 (La.1977).

In its opinion the appellate court, citing *Juneau v. Laborde*, 219 La. 921, 54 So.2d 325 (1951), stated our jurisprudence holds that, generally a buyer is not obliged to examine title to immovable property, but where certain facts known to him constitute a warning that further inquiry is needed, and such facts are sufficient to excite inquiry, a duty devolves upon him to investigate his vendor's title. Defendant, Zapata, has called our attention to a number of cases it says also stand for this broad proposition. We find the Juneau case and these decisions inapposite to the instant proceeding as the holding in none of them hinges on the vendor's obligation in warranty owed to the vendee.

Juneau v. Laborde, for example, involved a petitory action brought by heirs to immovable property against a possessor claiming the property on the basis of ten-year good faith acquisitive prescription. La. C.C. art. 3478 [R.C.C. 3473]. This Court found that the possessor was aware of facts which were sufficient to excite inquiry into the validity of his vendor's title, and that a duty devolved upon him to investigate the title before purchasing. However, this rule provides no defense against a vendee who seeks to enforce his vendor's obligations under a warranty deed. In fact, to allow its application in such an action would violate basic principles of warranty against eviction in the civil law and a substantial body of jurisprudence interpreting our Civil Code.

Because the registry laws are intended only as notice to third parties and have no application whatever between parties to a contract, a vendee is under no obligation to search the record in order to ascertain what his vendor has sold and what it has not, and the vendee is entitled, as between himself and his vendor, to rely upon his deed as written. *Young v. Sartor*, 152 La. 1064, 95 So. 223 (1923). Moreover, as a general rule, in the absence of a stipulation of non-warranty in the act of sale, knowledge of the danger of eviction does not prevent the purchaser from recovering the purchase price upon disturbance of his possession. *Scott v. Featherston*, 5 La.Ann. 306 (1850) citing Article 2481 of the Louisiana Civil Code of 1825 (La. C.C. art. 2505 [R.C.C. 2503]); *Hall v. Nevill*, 3 La.Ann. 326 (1848). *See*, Comment, *Warranty Against Eviction in the Civil Law: Limitations on the Extent of the Vendee's Recovery*, 23 Tul.L.Rev. 154, 169-70 (1948). Cf. *Collins v. Slocum*, 317 So.2d 672 (La.App. 3d Cir. 1975). *But see, Culver v. Culver*, 188 La. 716, 178 So. 252 (1938), criticized in 23 Tul.L.Rev., supra, at 170.

This accords with the view of a majority of French courts and writers that although such knowledge bars recovery of damages by an evicted buyer who purchases by a deed which does not contain a non-warranty clause, the purchaser is nevertheless entitled to a restitution of the price. 2 M. Planiol, Civil Law Treatise, pt. 1, ss 1504, 1509 (La.St.L.Inst.Transl.1959); 1 M. Troplong, Droit Civil Explique: De La Vente, s 482 (2d ed.1835); *See*, Comment, *Warranty Against Eviction in the Civil Law*, supra, at 160, and authorities cited therein. It is their view that this principle is not provided directly by the warranty provisions of the Code, but results from Article 1599 of the Code Napoleon (La. C.C. art. 2452 [R.C.C. 2452]) which, after declaring that the sale of the thing of another is null, adds that it can give occasion for damages "when the buyer did not know that the thing belonged to another." *See*, Planiol, *id.* at 1509.

An exception to the rule is recognized, however, regarding an alleged eviction resulting from the existence of an apparent servitude on the property. In discussing Code Napoleon Article 1638, the French authorities have declared that the only servitudes which give rise to the warranty are those which at the same time are non-apparent and not declared. 2 M. Planiol, Civil Law Treatise, pt. 1, ss 1493-95. The origin of the distinction drawn between visible servitudes and non-apparent charges against the property was explained by Pothier, who observed:

> "A . . . kind of real charges, of which it is the buyer's business not to be ignorant, and against which consequently he cannot claim any warranty, though they are not expressly declared by the contract, consists of visible servitudes, such as those of light and eaves-dropping; of which the buyer

cannot be ignorant, since in visiting the house before purchasing it, he cannot avoid seeing the windows or the eaves.

"Are we to include amongst the rights, which it is the buyer's duty not to be ignorant of, a right of champart not seignorial? The reason for doubting is, that the perception of the champart being public and known in the country, it is easy for the buyer to inform himself, and to ascertain before purchasing, whether the estate is subject to that charge.

"* * *

"Notwithstanding these reasons, we must decide, that the seller is bound to warrant against a champart, which is not declared by the contract. A buyer does not buy a house without visiting it in person, or sending some one [sic] on his part, nor, consequently, without perceiving the visible servitudes; but, he cannot be instructed of the charge of champart, except by being informed of it, and he may neglect to inform himself, or be deceived in the information, which he receives. * * *" 1 R. Pothier's Treatise on Contracts: Contract of Sale, ss 200-01 at 123-24 (L. S. Cushing transl. 1839).

Louisiana courts also have adopted the view that a vendor does not warrant the property conveyed as free from apparent servitudes. *Lallande v. Wentz & Pochelu*, 18 La.Ann. 289 (1866); *James v. Buchert*, 144 So.2d 435 (La.App. 4th Cir. 1962). *Cf. Collins v. Slocum*, 317 So.2d 672 (La.App. 3d Cir. 1975). This conclusion may be inferred from La. C.C. art. 2515 [R.C.C. 2500], which, as Code Napoleon art. 1638, provides that the seller is bound to warrant against undeclared, non-apparent servitudes. The rule is justified as a practical matter for the reasons stated by the French writers. Pothier, *supra*, and Planiol, *supra*, s 1494.

In the instant case the undisputed material facts are as follows: The buyer acquired by deed containing no general stipulation of non-warranty. The existence of the Gay-Gulf lease as a charge on the property was not declared in the list of inscriptions bearing upon the property included in the act of sale. . . . The extensive mineral development of which plaintiff complains does not flow from any of the charges enumerated in the act of sale, but rather from the 1930 Gay-Gulf lease. The alleged eviction stemmed from an undeclared mineral lease and not an undeclared apparent servitude, but there were on the property ample external signs of mineral production conducted pursuant to this lease.

Hence, if it is the vendee's duty not to be ignorant of apparent mineral leases as well as apparent servitudes, the action in warranty should be refused him, and the vendor would be entitled to judgment as a matter of law. On the other hand, if the vendee is presumed to know only of apparent servitudes, the vendor must respond in warranty because the eviction resulted from a different kind of visible charge which was not declared at the time of the sale.

The Civil Code does not expressly address the issue. It merely indicates that the buyer has a warranty against a servitude which at the same time is non-apparent and not declared. La. C.C. art. 2515 [R.C.C. 2500]. The civilian writers do not seem to have considered whether other charges equally as visible as apparent servitudes are excluded from the vendor's warranty. In discussing the special rules as to servitudes, however, the writers dwell not upon the legal classification of the charge but on the practical question of whether the premises may be examined without perceiving the visible signs of its existence. If the buyer cannot avoid seeing evidence of the charge should he visit the property before the purchase there is no need for the seller to inform him of it. In the event the purchaser is unable to learn of a charge because it is non-apparent, fairness demands that the buyer must either inform him of it before the sale or protect him against eviction.

As the treatise writers, we think paramount importance should be attached to whether the charge produces visible external effects on the property rather than upon the legal classification of the charge. In the present case, for instance, the drilling structures and other artifacts of mineral production would be equally apparent regardless of their source. A simple inspection of the premises would have apprised the buyer of the existence of a significant charge against the property whether it derived from a lease or a servitude. Furthermore, there is probably less difference between a mineral lease and a mineral servitude than between other servitudes and charges. Both are basic mineral rights, and they share many of the same attributes. *See*, La.R.S. 31:16, 31:21 *et seq.*, 31:114 *et seq.*, and comments. For all these reasons we conclude that, just as an apparent servitude, an undisclosed mineral lease which produces on the property ample signs of its existence is a real charge of which it is the buyer's business not to be ignorant and against which he cannot claim warranty.

For the foregoing reasons, we find there is no genuine issue of material fact in this case and that the defendant Zapata is entitled to judgment as a matter of law. Although we do not approve of the reasons given by the trial court and court of appeal, we conclude they reached the correct result. Accordingly, the judgment of the court of appeal is affirmed at appellant's cost.

Affirmed.

SUMMERS, J., concurs.

DIXON, J., concurs with reasons.

CALOGERO, J., dissents and assigns reasons.

DIXON, Justice (concurring).

I respectfully disagree with the holding of the majority, but concur in the result, because the deed disclosed a sale of all minerals and extensive mineral activity, enough to put the purchaser on notice of probable extensive mineral activity which might result in the surface encroachment of which plaintiff complains.

CALOGERO, Justice (dissenting).

Until rendition of this opinion, there has been no statutory or jurisprudential authority for declaring that a vendee, acquiring by deed containing no general stipulation of non-warranty, and ignorant of "apparent mineral leases," should be denied an action in warranty. In fact this Court has said that a buyer who purchases under a warranty deed has no duty to investigate his title by searching the mortgage and conveyance record or by visiting the property. *Young v. Sartor*, 152 La. 1064, 95 So. 223 (1922).

I would not extend to "apparent mineral leases" by analogy or otherwise the Codal (inferentially) and jurisprudential rule that a vendor under warranty deed does not warrant property conveyed as free from apparent servitudes. Accordingly I respectfully dissent.

Notes and Questions

1. Did the court in *Richmond* find that the mineral lease was "declared"? Was it "apparent"? Is a mineral lease a "servitude"? What does the holding of this case suggest about the application of Article 2500 to encumbrances other than servitudes?

2. How, if at all, did the fact that the mineral lease was recorded in the public records affect the *Richmond* court's decision? Is a recorded encumbrance "apparent" or "declared" by virtue of its recordation alone? What if the Act of Sale states that the property is conveyed "subject to" recorded encumbrances? In *Spillman v. Gasco, Inc.*, 110 So. 3d 150 (La. App. 2 Cir. 2012), *writ denied*, 99 So. 3d 652 (La. 2012), the Louisiana Second Circuit Court of Appeal held that language in an Act of Sale stating that the sale was "subject to recorded restrictions, easements, and servitudes of record" was sufficient to negate a claim under the warranty of eviction with respect to a recorded mineral servitude burdening the property. Is this result consistent with *Richmond*? Why or why not? It should be noted that in practice the language "subject to recorded encumbrances" appears in many Acts of Sale (although for good measure the phrase is typically accompanied by an actual listing of the encumbrances and their recording information). The *Spillman* decision has been criticized by commentators. *See* 24 DIAN TOOLEY-KNOBLETT & DAVID GRUNING, LOUISIANA CIVIL LAW TREATISE, SALES § 10:9 (2017), *see also* Martha Thibaut, Comment, *Shale in Sale-Adaptive Resolution of Mineral Rights Disputes Through Warranty Law and Veil-Piercing Remedies*, 74 LA. L. REV. 975 (2014). Do you see why?

3. The Court in *Richmond* discussed the "general rule" that, "in the absence of a stipulation of non-warranty in the act of sale, knowledge of the danger of eviction does not prevent the purchaser from recovering the purchase price upon disturbance of his possession." 350 So. 2d at 878–79. Later in Subpart C.2 of this Chapter, the impact of the buyer's knowledge of the danger of eviction on a claim against the seller will be explored in detail. For now, it should be underscored that the "rule" that the buyer's knowledge does not foreclose his or her claim for a return of the price does *not* apply to encumbrances. By virtue of the plain language of Article 2500, apparent encumbrances or those of which the buyer is aware are excluded entirely from the scope of the warranty. This is why, after holding that "an undisclosed mineral lease which produces on the property ample signs of its existence is a real charge of which it is the buyer's business not to be ignorant," the Court held that the buyer had *no claim* in warranty against his seller, despite the fact that the sale was a full warranty sale. *Id.* at 880.

3. Time at Which Third Person's Right Exists

A central requirement to having a valid cause of action under the warranty against eviction is that the third person's lawful right in the thing sold must exist at the time of the sale. This rule is not without exception, however. Consider the following discussion of French law on this point.

2 Marcel Planiol & George Ripert, *Traite Elementaire de Droit Civil No. 1492* (11th ed. 1939) (*translated in* La. State Law Inst. 1959)

By exception, the vendor sometimes responds for an eviction the cause of which is posterior to the sale. That always presupposes a fault on his part. Examples:

(1) *Prescription Imminent at the Time of Sale.* When the prescription, although posterior to the sale accrues at a time so close to the contract that the buyer does not have the opportunity to learn of it and to interrupt it, the vendor alone is at fault, and as a consequence, responsible for this cause of eviction.

(2) *Eviction Resulting from Personal Act of Vendor.* The vendor also responds for the eviction if it is because of him that a third person has been placed, after the sale, in a position to evict the buyer.

Such a combination may at first sight be surprising for, how can a vendor after having stripped himself of all right to the thing, be able to give to another the means of taking it away from the first purchaser? That can happen in two different ways, according to whether the thing is a movable or an immovable. Suppose the sale of a corporeal movable not yet delivered; the vendor sells it again to another person and puts him in real possession; the second buyer will be preferred to the first (Art. 1141) [R.C.C. 518], but the latter has an action in warranty against the vendor. Suppose now the sale of an immovable. . . . [T]he first sale is by an unrecorded act under private signature; the second [is properly recorded] . . . . [T]he first buyer is obligated to suffer the effect of the second sale and can proceed against the vendor, . . . he is not required to have his title transcribed or recorded.

Notes and Questions

As the foregoing excerpt makes clear, under French law the buyer has recourse against the seller even when an eviction takes place after the sale, provided the eviction was the result of the seller's fault. Although this exception is not clearly articulated in the Louisiana Civil Code, it is implied in two provisions.

First, the second paragraph of Article 2500 states: "If the right of the third person is perfected only after the sale through the negligence of the buyer, though it arises from facts that took place before, the buyer has no claim in warranty." LA. CIV. CODE art. 2500. The right of the third person that "arises from facts" predating the sale but is "perfected only after the sale" is that of acquisitive prescription. As suggested by Planiol & Ripert, when acquisitive prescription accrues so soon after the sale that the buyer is unable to discover and to interrupt it, the buyer's loss of owner-ship is considered to be the fault of the seller, who is therefore answerable for breach of the warranty against eviction.

Consider the following example: Suppose that Seller owns Blackacre and Third Person has been in possession of Blackacre without title for nearly thirty years. On the last day of the 29th year of Third Person's possession, Seller conveys Blackacre to Buyer. The following day, unbeknownst to Buyer, Third Person's right of ownership is perfected through 30-year acquisitive prescription. Although perfection of Third Person's right occurred *after* the sale, because the facts giving rise to Third Person's right predate the sale, the Buyer's claim in warranty against the Seller is preserved. Under Article 2500, the result would be different if Seller conveyed Blackacre to Buyer during the 28th year of Third Person's possession. In such a case, it must be presumed that Buyer should have discovered Third Person's possession of the property and taken steps to remove the possessor from the premises. Because Third Person's right to the property was perfected after the sale only through Buyer's "negligence," Buyer has no claim in warranty against Seller.

Article 2503 also points to the rule that a seller is always liable for an eviction resulting from his or her personal act. The article provides: "In all [] cases the seller is liable for an eviction that is occasioned by his own act, and any agreement to the contrary is null." La. Civ. Code art. 2503. On this point, consider the following case.

Clark v. O'Neal

13 La. Ann. 381 (La. 1858)

Merrick, C. J.

This suit is brought upon two promissory notes given as the price of a tract of land. The defence [sic] to the action is the failure of consideration. It appears that in March, 1849, the plaintiff sold the defendant the land by an act under private signature. The act of sale not having been recorded in November, 1850, one *Robert Burns* instituted a suit by attachment against the plaintiff, before a Justice of the Peace in the parish of De Soto, where the land is situated. After the return of citation and attachment was made, showing that they had been served, judgment was rendered against the defendant in that suit. Execution having issued on the judgment, directed to the Sheriff, he seized the tract of land as the property of *Mrs. Clark*, and after advertising the sale, sold it for the sum of $75 cash.

In regard to the judgment, it does not appear that *Mrs. Clark* ever made any effort to have it set aside, or even took an appeal from it. It acquired the force of the thing adjudged, and must be held to have been rendered in conformity to law and for a just debt. As between herself and *Burns*, it was her duty to pay the debt; to acquit and discharge her obligation resulting from her debt, and the judgment of the court and the law. Instead of fulfilling her obligation in this respect, she suffered the property which she had sold, and which she had covenanted to warrant and defend, to be seized to pay her debt. The record does not show that she made any effort to relieve the property or even to substitute the promissory notes given as the price (and which she still held), in the place of the seizure of the land.

The mere fact that the vendee had neglected to record the act of sale did not release the plaintiff from her obligation to warrant the title. The unregistered act has its full force between the contracting parties, so much so[,] that a second sale of the same property to a third party is viewed as a fraudulent act. C. C. 2417 [No Corresponding Article]; Rev. Stat. 453.

The sale being valid between the parties, and having force as such, the rules of law in regard to warranty, have their application.

The seller is bound to deliver and warrant the thing which he sells. C.C. 2450 [R.C.C. 2450]. The warranty respects the buyer's peaceable possession of the thing sold (C.C. 2451 [R.C.C. 2451]) and the vendor warrants the buyer against the eviction of the whole or a part of the same. C.C. 2477 [R.C.C. 2477].

The proof shows that the defendant has violated this obligation by a neglect of her own duties, and she has suffered the property to be sold for her own debt, and thus has she been instrumental in evicting her own vendee, and thus has she bound herself to maintain the *new vendee* in possession. C.P. 711, 712, 713; 6 La. 737.

But it is said that Art. 2478 C.C. [R.C.C. 2477] exempts the defendant from this sort of eviction. This Article, it is true, declares that in order that the warranty should have existence, the right of the person evicting should exist before the sale. But this evidently applies to some right acquired of persons other than the vendor himself. The last paragraph of the Article says: "If, therefore, this right before the sale was only imperfect and is afterwards perfected by the *negligence* of the *buyer*, he has no claim for warranty." Now an example or two will at once show that the Article has no application to the acts and omissions of duty of the *vendor*. Take this case: A sells a tract of land to B for $10,000, B, having the utmost confidence in A's integrity, omits or is prevented from recording his act of sale. Thereupon A sells the same land to C, an innocent purchaser, for $11,000, and C records his title. C sues B to recover the land. B cites A in warranty. A defends the demand of B in warranty on the ground, that C's right did not exist at the date of the sale, and cites the Article 2478 in support of his position. Will it avail him? Again, D sells E a tract of land for $10,000, but before the act is recorded, a recent judgment creditor of D seizes the land and sells the same and pays a debt of D's of $10,000. Is E to lose his money? It is apparent to every one [sic] how these questions must be answered. We think, therefore, that the obligation of warranty continued upon the plaintiff, although the act of sale was not recorded, and that the defendant has a valid defence [sic] to the notes, both under the Civil Code and the commercial law. 8 La. 547.

It is, therefore, ordered, adjudged and decreed by the court, that the judgment of the lower court be avoided and reversed, and that there be judgment in favor of the defendant, and against the demand of the plaintiff; and that the plaintiff pay the costs of both courts.

SPOFFORD, J., took no part in the decision of this case.

Notes and Questions

A more recent case involving the perfection of a third party's right after the sale is *Hingle Bros., Inc. v. Bonura*, 248 So. 2d 391 (La. App. 4 Cir. 1971). In that case, Hingle purchased two lots on Aviator Street in New Orleans from Bonura. More than three months after the sale, the City of New Orleans filed a paving lien in the mortgage records office of Orleans Parish relating to the paving of Aviator Street, which took place during the year before the sale. Ordinances of the City of New Orleans authorizing the paving of Aviator Street, together with an estimate of the total cost of the project, had been filed in the mortgage records prior to the sale. Notice of the paving assessment was sent by the City of New Orleans to Bonura, who in turn forwarded it to Hingle. A dispute arose over who was responsible for payment of the lien. The court stated:

> The filing of these ordinances coupled with the actual paving of the street covered thereby, created an encumbrance against the property of which the vendor, under his duty to deliver a merchantable title, either had to remove by payment or exclude from his warranty. He did neither. These actions constituted an encumbrance in that they would later serve as the basis for the imposition of the lien assessment. The fact that the recorder of mortgages failed to reflect the recordation of these ordinances on his certificates, or that no specific lien had been filed as of the date of sale, does not destroy the character of these charges as an encumbrance adversely affecting the title to the property.

Id. at 394. Although the court phrased its conclusion in terms of "merchantable title," the court plainly held that Hingle had a valid claim against Bonura for breach of the warranty of eviction. (The seller's obligation to deliver merchantable title is related to, but distinct from, the obligation to warrant against eviction, and is discussed further in Chapter 12: Contracts Preparatory to Sale.) Did *Hingle* involve a circumstance under which the right of the third person (here, the City of New Orleans), though perfected after the sale, arose from facts that took place before? Is this a case involving an eviction occasioned by an act of the seller?

B. Rights of the Buyer

La. Civ. Code arts. 2506–2511, 2517, 2557, 2560

1. In General

The primary remedies available to a buyer who has suffered an eviction from the property are rescission and damages. Article 2506 provides: "A buyer who avails himself of the warranty against eviction may recover from the seller the price he paid, the value of any fruits he had to return to the third person who evicted him, and also other damages sustained because of the eviction with the exception of any increase in value of the thing lost." La. Civ. Code art. 2506.

With respect to rescission, the buyer is entitled to the return of the price the buyer has paid (although the buyer may receive less than the full price in the case of a partial eviction as described below). The "price" to which the buyer is entitled is the actual sales price, regardless of any fluctuation in value of the thing sold since the date of the sale. As Article 2507 provides, "A seller liable for eviction must return the full price to the buyer even if, at the time of the eviction, the value of the thing has been diminished due to any cause including the buyer's neglect." La. Civ. Code art. 2507. Note, however, that the buyer's recovery may be reduced if the buyer has benefited from a diminution in value caused by his or her own act: "Nevertheless, if the buyer has benefitted from a diminution in value caused by his own act, the amount of his benefit must be deducted from the total owed to him by the seller because of the eviction." *Id.* Assume, for example, that Buyer purchased a car from Seller for a price of $25,000, only to learn six months later that the car, in fact, belonged to Third Person. In a suit for rescission of the sale, Buyer's recovery will be reduced by the value derived from using the car for six months — ostensibly, the fair rental value of the same vehicle.

Although Article 2506 is silent on the matter of interest on the price, leading commentators agree that the buyer may recover interest on the price from the date on which he or she was evicted. *See* Alain Levasseur, Louisiana Law of Sale and Lease: A Precis 67 (3rd ed. 2015); 24 Dian Tooley-Knoblett & David Gruning, Louisiana Civil Law Treatise, Sales § 10:33 (2017).

If the buyer has not yet paid the price at the time he or she is evicted, the Code provides the buyer with the right to suspend payment. "A buyer who is evicted by the claim of a third person may withhold payment of the price until he is restored to possession . . . ." La. Civ. Code art. 2557. This rule rests on the correlative nature of the obligations of buyer and seller. *See* La. Civ. Code art. 2022. The seller may avoid this rule by posting security for "any loss the buyer may sustain as a result of the eviction." La. Civ. Code art. 2557. If the seller cannot or will not give security, the Code provides the seller with an alternative: "A seller who, in such a case, is unable or unwilling to give security may compel the buyer to deposit the price with the court until the right of the third person is adjudged." *Id.* The buyer may also voluntarily opt to deposit the price with the court in order to prevent the accrual of interest. *Id.* Note that the buyer does not have the right to withhold the price "when the seller is not liable for a return of the price in case of eviction." *Id.* The circumstances under which the seller is not liable for a return of the price in case of eviction are described below in Part C. Note also that while the buyer may withhold payment of the price as soon as the buyer is disturbed in his or her possession, the buyer may not demand the return of any part of the price that was paid prior to the eviction or demand security for it. La. Civ. Code art. 2560.

The buyer may recover, in addition to the price, damages occasioned by the eviction. The seller's liability for damages is governed by the general rules found in the title on Conventional Obligations or Contracts. *See generally* La. Civ. Code arts. 1994–2004. The only special rule on damages found among the Civil Code articles on the warranty against eviction is the admonition in Article 2506 that the damages recoverable by the buyer do *not* include "any increase in value of the thing lost." LA. CIV. CODE art. 2506.

The seller also must reimburse the buyer for the cost of improvements. The extent of this obligation depends upon whether the seller knew at the time of the sale that the thing belonged to a third person, i.e., whether the seller was in good faith or bad faith. Article 2509 provides:

> A seller liable for eviction must reimburse the buyer for the cost of useful improvements to the thing made by the buyer. If the seller knew at the time of the sale that the thing belonged to a third person, he must reimburse the buyer for the cost of all improvements.

LA. CIV. CODE art. 2509. "Useful" improvements are those that enhance the value of the thing. *See* LA. CIV. CODE art. 1259; 24 DIAN TOOLEY-KNOBLETT & DAVID GRUNING, LOUISIANA CIVIL LAW TREATISE, SALES § 10:33 (2017). Thus, a good faith seller is liable only for the cost of improvements that enhance the value of the thing sold, while a bad faith seller is liable for the cost of all improvements. Regardless of the seller's good or bad faith, the seller must reimburse the buyer for the value of any fruits the buyer had to return to the third person who evicted him. LA. CIV. CODE art. 2506.

Finally, a buyer who is threatened with eviction has both the right and the duty to timely notify the seller and call upon the seller to do whatever is needed to protect against the potential eviction. This notification is referred to as the "call in warranty" and is described in Article 2517. If a lawsuit has been brought against the buyer by a third person, the buyer must notify the seller so that the seller may defend the suit. LA. CIV. CODE art. 2517. Alternatively, if the buyer elects to bring a lawsuit against a third person who has disturbed the buyer's peaceful possession of the thing sold, the buyer must give timely notice of that suit to the seller. *Id.*

> In either case, a buyer who fails to give such notice or who fails to give it in time for the seller to defend himself forfeits the warranty against eviction if the seller can show that, had he been notified in time, he would have been able to prove that the third person who sued the buyer had no right.

Id.

2. Partial Eviction

Although the buyer may be evicted from the entirety of the thing sold, the more common scenario involves a so-called "partial" eviction — the buyer's loss of only a part of the property either because of a third person's ownership of a portion or an undivided interest in the thing sold or because of the existence of an encumbrance burdening the property. In cases of partial eviction, the buyer's right to rescission may be limited. Under Article 2511,

> When the buyer is evicted from only a part of the thing sold, he may obtain rescission of the sale if he would not have bought the thing without that

part. If the sale is not rescinded, the buyer is entitled to a diminution of the price in the proportion that the value of the part lost bears to the value of the whole at the time of the sale.

LA. CIV. CODE art. 2511. Thus, in cases of partial eviction, the buyer's recovery will be limited to a diminution of the price unless the buyer can show that he or she would not have bought the thing without the part from which he or she was evicted (in which case the buyer is entitled to rescission of the sale). The following case illustrates the application of this rule.

Taylor v. Fuselier

915 So.2d 1030 (La. App. 3 Cir. 2005)

THIBODEAUX, Chief Judge.

Plaintiff-Appellant, Gloria Taylor, sought rescission of her agreement to purchase land from Defendant, Conley Fuselier, because she discovered after the sale that Mr. Fuselier had sold a portion of the property to the town of Oberlin before selling the lot to her. She argued she had been evicted from that portion of the lot. The trial court denied Ms. Taylor's request for return of the purchase price of the property, finding that the portion from which she had been evicted was insignificant in relation to the whole. We reverse the judgment of the trial court because, although the relative size of the portion sold to Oberlin compared to the entire lot may not be large, the significant location and use of that portion deprived Ms. Taylor of her full enjoyment of the property she believed she had purchased.

I. ISSUE

We must consider whether the trial court was correct to award Ms. Taylor only a diminution of her purchase price, or whether she is entitled to full rescission of the purchase price of the property.

II. FACTS

On October 2, 2002, Gloria Taylor signed a cash warranty deed for the purchase of a tract of land from Conley Fuselier in the town of Oberlin. The tract she purchased measured 150 feet by 100 feet. She specifically chose a corner lot, she testified, because she thought it would look better when she built a house on it, and believed a corner lot would ultimately have a higher resale value. Ms. Taylor stated that she told Mr. Fuselier her reasons for choosing the corner lot. Ms. Taylor installed a culvert, which cost $167.00, and planted trees, which cost $90.00.

After she planted the trees in January 2003, she noticed construction on part of her land, and called Mr. Fuselier to find out what was happening. She testified Mr. Fuselier told her that before he had sold her the lot, he had sold a 20 square foot portion of it to the Town of Oberlin to construct a sewerage pumping station. Ms. Taylor testified that, when completed, the sewerage pumping station included a seven-foot-high hurricane fence with barbed wire at the top, measuring ten by fifteen feet. Inside the fence, the pumping apparatus included a blinking red light. Ms.

Taylor and her next door neighbor, Donette Taylor, both testified that the station was aesthetically unappealing and also caused a noisome odor.

Ms. Taylor filed a Petition to Rescind the Sale of Immovable Property. After a trial in March 2004, the court found that the section of land sold to Oberlin was inconsequential in relation to the whole and awarded Ms. Taylor a reduction in price of $266.00, plus an additional $300.00 to erect a privacy fence around the station. Ms. Taylor appeals the judgment of the trial court, arguing that the court erred in finding she was not entitled to rescission because the tract of land sold to the city was inconsequential in relation to the whole.

III. LAW AND DISCUSSION

Mr. Fuselier claims that because there is no evidence contradicting Ms. Taylor's clear title search, we cannot find that a prior sale occurred. He argues that Ms. Taylor's parol evidence is insufficient to establish that a sale to Oberlin occurred and, if it occurred, that it was recorded. In general, a court may not rely on parol evidence to define an agreement regarding the sale of real property, as "[t]he designation of the sale should properly be based exclusively on the written act of sale." *Strange v. Kennard*, 99-406, p. 4 (La.App. 1 Cir. 3/31/00), 763 So.2d 710, 712. Ms. Taylor, however, did not attack the validity of any purported sale to Oberlin, nor did she dispute any instrument transferring property from Mr. Fuselier to Oberlin. The issue, in other words, is not the contents of the agreement between Mr. Fuselier and Oberlin. Moreover, her testimony that Mr. Fuselier admitted the prior sale of the portion of the lot to Oberlin went uncontradicted.

Mr. Fuselier further argues that because an instrument involving immovable property does not affect third parties until it has been recorded, and there is no record of the sale to Oberlin, Ms. Taylor's rights in the property trump those of Oberlin to the property; therefore, she may rightfully evict the municipality of Oberlin. La .Civ.Code art. 1839; *see also King v. Strohe*, 95-656 (La.App. 3 Cir. 5/8/96), 673 So.2d 1329 (finding that agreements involving immovable property affect third parties only after they are filed for recordation and that they are a nullity as to third parties until that time). However, Mr. Fuselier's attempt to deflect the legal conflict onto Oberlin does not extinguish Ms. Taylor's ability to obtain rescission on grounds of eviction. Ms. Taylor had a title search performed at her request and her expense. The title search did not provide any information that would lead her to suspect that she was not purchasing the entire lot Mr. Fuselier offered for sale. Ms. Taylor was entitled to rely on the results of her title search. La.R.S. 9:2721; *see also Mortgage Elec. Registration Sys., Inc. v. Bynum*, 03-1671 (La.App. 1 Cir. 5/14/04), 879 So.2d 807, *writ denied*, 04-1926 (La.11/15/04), 887 So.2d 479 (noting that a third party purchasing immovable property is entitled to rely on the absence from public records of any unrecorded interest in the property). Mr. Fuselier is correct that the lack of record of the sale does not adversely impact Ms. Taylor's title to the property. Whether or not Ms. Taylor had the option of taking action against Oberlin does not alter Ms. Taylor's claim based on eviction vis à vis Mr. Fuselier.

Louisiana Civil Code Article 2500 states in part that "[t]he seller warrants the buyer against eviction, which is the buyer's loss of . . . part of the thing sold because of a third person's right that existed at the time of the sale."

* * * * *

Louisiana Civil Code Article 2511 states: "When the buyer is evicted from only a part of the thing sold, he may obtain rescission of the sale if he would not have bought the thing without that part. If the sale is not rescinded, the buyer is entitled to a diminution of the price in the proportion that the value of the part lost bears to the value of the whole at the time of the sale." *See also* La.Civ.Code art. 2506 ("A buyer who avails himself of the warranty against eviction may recover from the seller the price he paid, the value of any fruits he had to return to the third person who evicted him, and also other damages sustained because of the eviction with the exception of any increase in value of the thing lost").

Ms. Taylor testified she would not have purchased the land from Mr. Fuselier had she known he had already sold a portion to the town of Oberlin. Although Mr. Fuselier implies this is merely self-serving testimony, there is nothing to suggest that this assertion is untrue. In fact, she explained to Mr. Fuselier that she wanted a corner lot because she wished either to build a home or to move a trailer onto the property, and she believed that a home would look more appealing on a corner lot, benefit from better road access, and have an increased resale value. She paid an extra $2,000.00 for the corner lot. Furthermore, she declined Mr. Fuselier's offer of additional property to compensate for the portion that later turned out to belong to Oberlin. The record makes clear that Ms. Taylor specifically wanted the corner lot, and nothing else would do.

While the trial court considered only the relative proportion of the area belonging to Oberlin compared to the remaining parcel Ms. Taylor owned, it failed to consider that the piece owned by Oberlin is, as it were, on the corner of this corner lot. In light of Ms. Taylor's desire for the corner lot, the placement of the sewerage lift station is significant. Furthermore, the trial court should have considered more than just the size of the piece belonging to Oberlin. The testimony at trial showed that the apparatus is aesthetically unappealing. It includes a blinking light and has produced a troublesome and noxious odor.

Although the physical size of Oberlin's portion may not be large, it has clearly impinged on Ms. Taylor's enjoyment of the property. Furthermore, Mr. Fuselier attempts to argue that the station is actually a benefit, since lots with sewerage access are more valuable than lots which require installation of a septic system. Ms. Taylor, however, as the buyer of the property, has the right to make that judgment. In fact, she testified that, given the choice, she would prefer a concealed septic system, notwithstanding the convenience of the sewerage lift station in her front yard.

The first part of La.Civ.Code art. 2511 states that if the buyer shows she would not have bought the property had she known of the defect, she may obtain rescission. Because Ms. Taylor has clearly shown she would not have purchased the property had she known that Oberlin owned the front corner of the lot, there was no legal justification to deny rescission of the sale and opt instead for diminution of the price.

IV. CONCLUSION

For the above reasons, the judgment of the trial court is reversed. Costs of appeal are assessed to appellee, Conley Fuselier.

REVERSED AND RENDERED

Notes and Questions

1. As *Fuselier* demonstrates, whether the buyer who suffers a partial eviction is entitled to rescission of the sale or a reduction of the price depends upon the importance to the buyer of the portion of the property lost as a result of the eviction. The analysis is closely tied to the doctrine of cause. *See* LA. CIV. CODE art. 2511 cmt. b. A buyer who can demonstrate that the eviction has resulted in a total failure of cause is entitled to rescission. In contrast, a buyer whose cause has failed only in part is entitled to damages only.

2. Note that in *Fuselier*, the defendant argued that the plaintiff had no cause of action because the Act of Sale between defendant and the City of Oberlin was unrecorded. The court rejected that argument. Was the court correct in doing so? Was the conveyance to the City of Oberlin enforceable against Ms. Taylor under the law of registry? Under the plain language of Article 2500, was Ms. Taylor "evicted" from the thing sold? Why or why not? Is there another reason for finding this seller answerable for breach of the warranty?

3. The court discussed at some length the impact of Taylor's title examination, which revealed no evidence of a prior sale to the Town of Oberlin. The portion of the Court's opinion in which it addressed this issue was redacted from the excerpt above. Consider its analysis of the issue:

> However, La.Civ.Code art. 2521 states that "[t]he seller owes no warranty for defects in the thing that were known to the buyer at the time of the sale, or for defects that should have been discovered by a reasonably prudent buyer of such things." Ms. Taylor testified that, at her request and expense, a deputy clerk in the clerk's office performed a title search. The title search did not reveal the prior transfer of the property to Oberlin, leading Ms. Taylor to believe that she was purchasing the full 150 × 100 foot lot. Because Ms. Taylor was entitled to rely on the results of her title search, and had no reason to suspect the title to the property was not as it appeared to be, Mr. Fuselier continues to owe her the warranties contained in their contract.
>
> Mr. Fuselier cites *Collins v. Slocum,* 284 So.2d 98, 100 (La.App. 3 Cir.1973), for its statement that "all persons have constructive notice of the existence and contents of recorded instruments affecting immovable property," and then explains that a later case, *Collins v. Slocum,* 317 So.2d 672, 681 (La. App. 3 Cir.), *writs denied,* 321 So.2d 362, 363, 364 (La.1975) modified this statement by finding that "a title examination prior to purchase [does not]

defeat[ ] the warranty action." He argues that this is an unresolved point of law. In those cases, the defendant argued that Collins could not rescind the sale of property and recover the purchase price because he had constructive knowledge of the existence of a servitude on the property, since the servitude had been recorded. The trial court rejected this argument, and the third circuit noted on appeal that the record supported this finding. Although Collins himself did not have the title examined before purchasing the property, the Savings & Loan from which Collins borrowed money to finance construction of a home on the property had the title examined at Collins' expense. Nevertheless, the third circuit concluded there was no evidence indicating Collins had either actual or constructive knowledge of the existence of the servitude on the property, and that therefore the trial court correctly awarded Collins the purchase price of the property.

The key distinction, however, is that in *Collins,* the servitude had been recorded. While the title had been examined, and the title reflected the existence of the servitude, the person hired to examine the title failed to render an accurate opinion as to the impact of the servitude on title to the property. In contrast, Ms. Taylor had the title examined, and the title did not indicate the transfer to Oberlin.

915 So. 2d at 1032–1033. This excerpt reflects some confusion on the part of the court regarding what effect, if any, a title examination may have on a buyer's claim under the warranty against eviction. Note that the court incorrectly references Article 2521, which is applicable to the warranty against redhibitory defects (discussed in Chapter 10: The Warranty Against Redhibitory Defects). While a buyer may not maintain an action against the seller for breach of the *warranty against redhibitory defects* if the defect should have been discovered upon a reasonable inspection, the *warranty against eviction* does not require that the buyer inspect the public records prior to the sale. This point was made plain in *Richmond v. Zapata Develop. Corp.* when the Court stated:

> Because the registry laws are intended only as notice to third parties and have no application whatever between parties to a contract, a vendee is under no obligation to search the record in order to ascertain what his vendor has sold and what it has not, and the vendee is entitled, as between himself and his vendor, to rely upon his deed as written.

350 So. 2d 875, 878. Of course, if a buyer conducts a title examination and learns of the existence of a third person's right, that knowledge may have consequences. If the right of the third person is an *encumbrance*, then the buyer's knowledge defeats his or her claim entirely. If, in contrast, the right of a third person is one in *ownership*, then the impact of the buyer's knowledge on his claim depends upon whether the sale made with the full implied warranty against eviction or whether the warranty was modified or excluded by the parties. The impact of the buyer's knowledge of the danger of eviction on his or her claim is more fully addressed in Subpart C.2 of this Chapter.

4. Consider the manner in which the diminution of the price is calculated under Article 2511: "[T]he buyer is entitled to a diminution of the price in the proportion that the value of the part lost bears to the value of the whole at the time of the sale." LA. CIV. CODE art. 2511. The amount of the buyer's recovery in a case of a partial eviction is not solely dependent upon the extent of the premises from which the buyer has been evicted nor is it calculated as a pro rata percentage. Instead, the buyer's recovery depends upon the *relative value* of the part from which he or she has been evicted.

Consider a sale in which Buyer purchases 100 acres of swampland, 5 of which border on a navigable waterway, for $50,000. If Buyer is evicted from the acreage bordering on the waterway, the buyer's recovery will likely exceed 5/100, or 5%, of the purchase price ($2,500) because the relative value of the frontage property far exceeds that of the inaccessible swampland. How does this calculation differ from the calculation of damages when the seller breaches his obligation to deliver the full extent of the premises promised (LA. CIV. CODE arts. 2491–95), discussed in Chapter 8: Delivery?

Guthrie v. Rudy Brown Builders, Inc.

416 So. 2d 590 (La. App. 5 Cir. 1982)

GRISBAUM, Judge.

This case is concerned with the issues of damages for mental anguish and attorney's fees in an action styled as redhibition or "quanti minoris" involving a surveying error on the part of a builder-vendor's surveyor. The survey did not note the improper placement of a house in violation of parish ordinances and the subdivision's restrictive covenants. Relying on the erroneous survey, one home owner built a fence on his neighbor's property.

Plaintiffs in this case, Sharon and Joseph M. Guthrie, Jr., initially sought to have the trial court enjoin defendants, Mr. and Mrs. Ralph Ragusa, from maintaining and occupying the Ragusa residence at 5108 Tusa Drive, Marrero, Louisiana, alleging that the Ragusa house was placed such that it was in violation of parish ordinances and subdivision restrictive covenants. They also requested the Ragusas remove a fence they had erected which allegedly encroached on the Guthries' property. A preliminary injunction was granted by the trial court on March 27, 1979.

This action for injunction was followed by a "Petition for Damages" brought by plaintiffs, Mr. and Mrs. Guthrie, against the Ragusas, Rudy Brown Builders, Inc. (their vendor) and Don Garland (the surveyor of both the Guthrie and Ragusa property). The defendants, Ragusas, filed a "Third-Party Demand" against Rudy Brown Builders, Inc. and Don Garland. Rudy Brown Builders, Inc. also filed a "Third-Party Demand" against the Ragusas and Don Garland.

Prior to the trial on the merits the following stipulations were made: (1) Since the gutter of the Ragusa house encroached on the property of the Guthries, a resubdivision of the property between the parties was agreed upon which would cure the encroachment; (2) Rudy Brown Builders, Inc. would pay the sum of $525.00 to the Guthries, on behalf of the Ragusas, to purchase a portion of the Guthries' property in order to cure the encroachment; (3) Rudy Brown Builders, Inc. would pay for the cost of effecting said resubdivision and transfer.

The only issues to be resolved at trial were that of damages for mental anguish and attorney's fees. After trial on the merits, the trial judge confirmed the stipulation made prior to trial and answered a judgment in favor of Mr. and Mrs. Guthrie and against Rudy Brown Builders, Inc. in the sum of $775.00, and in favor of Mr. and Mrs. Ralph Ragusa and against Rudy Brown Builders, Inc. in the sum of $500.00. Judgment was further entered in favor of Rudy Brown Builders, Inc. over against third-party defendant, Don Garland, in the amount of $1,275.00. The court held that there was a good faith error in surveying by Mr. Garland, the surveyor of the properties in question, which was imputed to Rudy Brown Builders, Inc., therefore, no attorney's fees were granted. The claim of the Guthries and Ragusas for mental anguish was not allowed by Judge Eason who cited the Supreme Court decision in *Meador v. Toyota of Jefferson, Inc.*, 332 So.2d 433 (La. 1976) to support his denial.

The Guthries and Ragusas have appealed from that part of the trial court's decision which denies damages for mental anguish and attorney's fees.

FACTS

Plaintiffs-appellants, Mr. and Mrs. Guthrie, purchased a house and lot from defendant-appellee, Rudy Brown Builders, Inc., in October of 1977. Their neighbors, Mr. and Mrs. Ragusa, also bought their home from Rudy Brown Builders, Inc. some five months before in May of 1977. Rudy Brown was the builder as well as vendor of both of these homes. Don Garland, defendant in this suit, was hired by Rudy Brown and had prepared the surveys used at the respective acts of sale.

In approximately June of 1977, Mr. Ragusa attempted to fence his lot in accordance with the Don Garland survey dated December 3, 1976, which was used in the act of sale of his property. Testimony at trial is conflicting, but it seems that while constructing the fence Mr. Ragusa ran into difficulty when his measurements did not agree with stakes placed on his property. Mr. Ragusa testified that he informed the office of Rudy Brown Builders, Inc. of this discrepancy and Rudy Brown spoke to his wife by telephone. Rudy Brown testified he went out to the Ragusa property and advised Mr. Ragusa that the stakes on the Ragusa property designated the correct property line and that Mr. Ragusa's fence was incorrectly placed. In any case, the fence was completed using the Don Garland survey for reference.

After purchasing the adjoining lot and house in October 1977, Mr. and Mrs. Guthrie also attempted to construct a fence. While measuring his property, Mr. Guthrie found the Ragusa fence seemed to encroach upon his property. The Guthries hired a surveyor who discovered that a second Don Garland survey made July 20, 1977 did not reflect the incorrect placement of the Ragusa fence and a gutter encroachment on the Guthrie property. It seems Rudy Brown Builders, Inc. had incorrectly placed the Ragusa house upon its lot. This placement caused the gutter encroachment and violated the subdivision's restrictive covenants and the parish ordinances.

The Don Garland survey in December 1976 did not reflect the actual placement of the Ragusa home but instead indicated the house was situated approximately five feet from the property line. The monumentation aspect by Don Garland on the Ragusa property was correct; the actual drawing which Mr. Garland signed as the survey was incorrect; thus, by relying upon this incorrect survey made in December 1976, Mr. Ragusa constructed his fence upon property which would eventually become that of the Guthries. The second Don Garland survey (made in July 1977) used in the Guthrie sale also contained this error. The trial court determined Rudy Brown, president of Rudy Brown Builders, Inc., had no knowledge of this survey error before the sale of the adjoining property to the Guthries.

ATTORNEY'S FEES AND MENTAL ANGUISH DAMAGES

* * * * *

As a seller Rudy Brown Builders, Inc. has two principal obligations, that of delivering and that of warranting the thing which he sells. La.C.C. Article 2475 [R.C.C. 2475]. It is primarily the breach of the second obligation that of "warranting" the thing which is sold that is the concern of this suit. Article 2476 [R.C.C. 2476] states:

> "The warranty respecting the seller has two objects; the first is the *buyer's peaceable possession* of the thing sold, and the second is the hidden defects of the thing sold or its redhibitory vices." (Emphasis added)

The central question is whether the improper placement of a home on its lot causing a gutter encroachment and a fence encroachment upon the adjacent property is covered by Articles 2500 [R.C.C. 2500] through 2519 [R.C.C. 2517] which deal with warranty against eviction or whether the improper placement of the house should be considered a "vice" in the thing sold and thereby covered by Articles 2520 [R.C.C. 2520] through 2548 [R.C.C. 2548]. We find the improper placement of a house on a lot which causes encroachments upon adjoining property is more appropriately covered by the articles on warranty against eviction.

The articles under the eviction section of the Code contemplate two types of eviction; the first is the "loss suffered" from acts of third persons. Article 2500 [R.C.C. 2500] and 2501 [R.C.C. 2500] state respectively:

> "Eviction is the loss suffered by the buyer of the totality of the thing sold, or of a part thereof, occasioned by the right or claims of a third person."

> "Although at the time of the sale no stipulations have been made respecting the warranty, the seller is obliged, of course, to warrant the buyer against the eviction suffered by him from the totality or part of the thing sold, and against the charges claimed on such thing, which were not declared at the time of the sale."

Under the facts of this case, the Guthrie claim is covered by these articles and Article 2514 [R.C.C. 2511] on partial eviction which states:

> "If in case of eviction from a part of the thing, the sale is not canceled, the value of the part from which he is evicted, is to be reimbursed to the buyer

according to its estimation, proportionably [sic., proportionately] to the total price of sale."

The Ragusa fence and gutter have caused them to suffer a "loss" of a portion of their property. It is this situation, namely the loss of a portion of the Guthries' property caused by the fence and gutter encroachments, that the eviction articles were designed to cover. The Ragusa fence has thus interrupted their peaceful possession of their property.

The second type of eviction found in Article 2504 [R.C.C. 2503] is that of the "loss suffered" from acts of the vendor. This article states:

"Although it be agreed that the seller is not subject to warranty, he is, however, accountable for what results from *his personal act*; and any contrary agreement is void." (Emphasis added).

The Ragusa claim is in essence a claim against their vendor, Rudy Brown Builders, Inc., for eviction. By improperly placing their home and by providing them with an improper survey drawing, Rudy Brown Builders, Inc. exposed the Ragusas to suit by the adjoining landowners and thus to the requirement of either removing the fence and gutter encroachments or buying that portion of the Guthrie property that had these encroachments. This factual situation is similar to that of *Katz v. Katz Realty Co.*, 228 La. 1008, 84 So.2d 802 (1955). In that case plaintiffs were reimbursed by their vendor for the amount they paid to purchase a portion of an adjoining landowner's property which had encroachments of their walls and foundation upon it. The *Katz* court analogized the reimbursement demand in that case to similar factual situations presented in earlier cases which allowed "reimbursement." *See Katz*, 84 So.2d 802, 804-05. Similarly, the reimbursement under eviction articles that *Katz* allows has been effected by the pre-trial stipulation that provides for the Ragusa purchase of that portion of the Guthrie property with the fence and gutter encroachments and reimbursement for that amount from Rudy Brown Builders, Inc.

Since both the claims of the Guthries and Ragusas are eviction claims, attorney's fees are not considered part of the "costs occasioned by the eviction" and cannot be recovered. La.C.C. Article 2506.3 [R.C.C. 2506]; *Calvary Tabernacle v. Louisiana Central Bank*, 393 So. 2d 708, 710 (La. 1981).

With respect to mental anguish damages, the obligation of warranty is one "to do," i.e., to come to the vendee's rescue. La.C.C. Article 1926 [R.C.C. 1986] states:

"On the breach of any obligation to do, or not to do, the obligee is entitled either to damages, or, in cases which permit it, to a specific performance of the contract, at his option, or he may require the dissolution of the contract, and in all these cases damages may be given where they have accrued, according to the rules established in the following section."

In the following section Article 1934.3 [R.C.C. 1998] is applicable; it states in part:

"Although the general rule is, that damages are the amount of the loss the creditor has sustained, or of the gain of which he has been deprived, yet there are cases in which damages may be assessed without calculating altogether on the pecuniary loss, or the privation of pecuniary gain to the party. Where the contract has for its object the gratification of some intellectual enjoyment, whether in religion, morality or taste, or some convenience or other legal gratification, although these are not appreciated in money by the parties, yet damages are due for their breach; a contract for a religious or charitable foundation, a promise of marriage, or an engagement for work of some of the fine arts, are objects and examples of this rule."

Article 1934.3 [R.C.C. 1998] has been interpreted by the Louisiana Supreme Court in *Meador v. Toyota of Jefferson, Inc.*, 332 So. 2d 433, 437 (La. 1976) to mean that:

"Where an object, or the exclusive object, of a contract, is physical gratification (or anything other than intellectual gratification) nonpecuniary damages as a consequence of nonfulfillment of that object are not recoverable.

On the other hand, where a principal or exclusive object of a contract is intellectual enjoyment, nonpecuniary damages resulting from the nonfulfillment of that intellectual object *are* recoverable."

Applying these principles to the instant case, we find that the Guthries and Ragusas are not entitled to recover damages for mental anguish. Although some aesthetic enjoyment may be important, the object of the contract of sale of a house is primarily physical gratification. According to *Webster's New Collegiate Dictionary* a "house" is "a building that serves as living quarters . . . a shelter or refuge . . . [.]" Like the automobile repair in *Meador*, the primary purpose in purchasing the houses and lots involved in this suit was the procurement of living quarters and, thus, the "utility" of these structures or physical gratification was the principal object of the contracts. *See Meador*, 332 So.2d 433, 437-38. Nonpecuniary damages, therefore, are not recoverable.

For the reasons assigned, the judgment of the trial court is affirmed. The costs of this appeal are assessed to the appellants.

AFFIRMED.

Notes and Questions

1. How is the "eviction" that occurred in this case similar to that in *Taylor v. Fuselier*? Under the plain language of Article 2500, were the Ragusas "evicted" from the thing sold as a result of a third person's right that existed at the time of the sale? Why or why not? Is there another reason for finding the seller answerable for breach of the warranty?

2. The parties in this case entered into a pre-trial stipulation under which the Guthries purchased the portion of the Ragusa property with the fence and gutter encroachments and Rudy Brown Builders, Inc. reimbursed the Guthries for the price they paid to the Ragusas. As the court notes, this result is consistent with Louisiana

jurisprudence holding that when a buyer cures a partial eviction by purchasing the part from which the buyer was evicted from a third person, reimbursement by the seller is the appropriate remedy. A case with facts similar to *Guthrie* is *Fuselier v. Comeaux*, 425 So. 2d 298 (La. App. 3 Cir. 1982). In that case, the buyers purchased a parcel of land by warranty deed and the price included a 20' × 30' house, already constructed and located elsewhere. The parties' agreement required the seller to move the house onto the exact center of the property, to erect an addition to the house once it was placed on the lot, and to install a septic tank on the property. After this work was complete and the buyers took possession of the property, they constructed a driveway, built a garage, and put in a garden. It was later discovered that due to the seller's misplacement of the house on the lot, the septic tank and the improvements constructed by the buyers encroached on their neighbor's land. The neighbors instituted suit against the buyers seeking an order that would require them to move the house and won. In the same proceedings, the buyers filed a third-party demand against their own seller. In determining that the seller's improper placement of the house amounted to a breach of the warranty against eviction, the court reasoned as follows:

> There is no special provision for damages among the articles dealing with delivery in the title: *Of Sale*. However, art. 2438 [R.C.C. 2438] says that in such a case, the contract of sale is subjected to the general rules established under the title: *Of Conventional Obligations*. Among the articles dealing with warranty in case of eviction there are special articles dealing with damages. But none apply specifically to the instant facts. Article 2506 [R.C.C. 2506] provides for damages for a total eviction, which this is not. Nor is this a partial eviction of such consequence as to justify cancellation of the sale envisioned by article 2511 [R.C.C. 2511]. Nor is it a partial eviction such that the purchaser can be restored by proportionate reimbursement of the purchase price as provided by article 2514. [R.C.C. 2511]. However, these articles were not intended to be the exclusive rules for deciding claims for damages in eviction cases, as article 2516 [No Corresponding Article] demonstrates, as follows: . . . "Other questions arising from a claim for damages, resulting from the non-execution of the contract of sale, shall be decided by the general rules established under the title: *Of Conventional Obligations*."

> Like *Katz v. Katz Realty Co.*, 228 La. 1008, 84 So.2d 802 (1955) and *Guthrie v. Rudy Brown Builders, Inc., supra*, we find that damages in these circumstances should be based on La.Civ.Code arts. 1926 [R.C.C. 1986] and 1934(3) [R.C.C. 1995–1997, 1999, 2003]. In *Katz*, it was held proper that plaintiffs be reimbursed by their vendor for the amount they paid to purchase a portion of an adjoining landowner's property which had encroachments of their walls and foundation upon it. The *Katz* plaintiffs went about solving their potential eviction problems on their own without prior approval of either the court or their vendors. In the instant case, where the eviction was forced upon the Comeauxs and their loss determined by judgment after assertion of the rights and claims of third persons, we perceive

no difficulty in holding that the damages required to "fully indemnify the creditor" (La.C.C. 1934(3) [R.C.C. 1997–1999, 1999, 2003]) justifies affirming this award. For the same reasons we feel that the imposition of the further burden on Berzas that he pay for the reinstallation of the septic tank, is proper.

Comeaux, 425 So. 2d at 302.

3. The plaintiffs in *Guthrie* argued that their case involved a breach of the warranty against redhibitory defects. The reason for this is that a claim under redhibition can give rise to attorney fees. *See* La. Civ. Code art. 2545. However, the same is not true of a claim under the warranty against eviction, although the buyer is entitled to recover from the seller the costs of the eviction, including the costs of any lawsuit with the third person who evicted the buyer and those of any lawsuit with the seller. *See* La. Civ. Code art. 2506 & cmt. b. The court in *Guthrie* rightly rejected the plaintiffs' claim for attorney fees, stating: "Since both the claims of the Guthries and Ragusas are eviction claims, attorney's [sic] fees are not considered part of the 'costs occasioned by the eviction' and cannot be recovered." *Guthrie*, 416 So.2d at 594.

4. The plaintiffs in *Guthrie* sought also to recover nonpecuniary damages (i.e., damages related to emotional distress and mental anguish). The availability of such damages is governed by Article 1998. Under that article, damages for nonpecuniary loss may be recovered under two circumstances. First, such damages are available "when the contract, because of its nature, is intended to gratify a nonpecuniary interest *and*, because of the circumstances surrounding the formation or the nonperformance of the contract, the obligor knew, or should have known, that his failure to perform would cause that kind of loss." La. Civ. Code art. 1998 (emphasis added). The Louisiana Supreme Court has emphasized that a buyer seeking to recover nonpecuniary damages on this basis must show that his or her nonpecuniary interest in the contract was *significant. See Young v. Ford Motor Co.*, 595 So. 2d 1123 (La. 1992). A buyer seeking nonpecuniary damages on the basis of the nature of the contract must therefore show that the sale was made to gratify a significant intellectual or aesthetic interest, not mere physical or economic need, and that the seller "knew or should have known" that the buyer would suffer a nonpecuniary loss in the event of an eviction. In *Guthrie*, the court, in rejecting the plaintiffs' claim for nonpecuniary damages, observed that a contract for the purchase of a home generally involves satisfaction of the buyer's physical need for shelter. Similarly, in *Young*, the Louisiana Supreme Court observed that the sale of a truck generally involves satisfaction of the buyer's physical need for a mode of transportation. 595 So. 2d 1123 (La. 1992). While these decisions do not foreclose the possibility that a buyer who suffers an eviction may recover nonpecuniary damages, they do require that the buyer show that the sale was made to satisfy a specific and significant nonpecuniary interest.

Note that damages for nonpecuniary loss are also available under Article 1998 when the obligor "intended, through his failure, to aggrieve the feelings of the obligee." La. Civ. Code art. 1998. A buyer seeking to recover nonpecuniary damages on this basis would be required to show that the seller intended to cause the buyer's nonpecuniary losses through an eviction.

C. Modification of the Warranty Against Eviction

The warranty against eviction, although implied in every sale, can be modified by the parties or excluded by the agreement of the parties. Although the remedies discussed in the foregoing section are available to a buyer who purchases with the full protection of the warranty against eviction, the rights of a buyer who agrees to a modification or exclusion of the warranty are likely to be reduced. Consider the text of Article 2503:

> The warranty against eviction is implied in every sale. Nevertheless, the parties may agree to increase or to limit the warranty. They may also agree to an exclusion of the warranty, but even in that case the seller must return the price to the buyer if eviction occurs, unless it is clear that the buyer was aware of the danger of eviction, or the buyer has declared that he was buying at his peril and risk, or the seller's obligation of returning the price has been expressly excluded.
>
> In all those cases the seller is liable for an eviction that is occasioned by his own act, and any agreement to the contrary is null.

La. Civ. Code art. 2503. As the following discussion makes clear, the buyer's recovery for eviction is impacted not only by the extent to which the warranty is modified, but also by the buyer's knowledge of the danger of eviction at the time of the sale. In addition, the fault of the seller in occasioning the eviction impacts the buyer's rights.

1. Categories of Sale

Article 2503 contemplates three types of sale: one in which the warranty against eviction applies fully (the "warranty sale" or "full warranty sale"), one in which the parties exclude the warranty (the "non-warranty" sale), and one which is at the buyer's "peril and risk" ("the sale at buyer's peril and risk"). In addition to these three categories, in practice a fourth category of sale is recognized: the "limited warranty sale" or "special warranty sale." Each of these categories will be explained below.

a. Warranty Sale

In a "warranty sale," the parties either say nothing about the warranty against eviction or expressly provide for such a warranty in the Act of Sale. A buyer in a warranty sale who is evicted is generally entitled to the full remedies allowed by law, specifically rescission of the sale and damages (as described above in Part B). *See* La. Civ. Code art. 2506.

b. Non-warranty Sale

A "non-warranty" sale is one in which the parties agree to an exclusion of the warranty against eviction. Importantly (and perhaps counter-intuitively) a buyer in a non-warranty sale who suffers an eviction is not entirely without recourse against the seller. Rather, while such a buyer is not entitled to recover any damages against the seller, the buyer is nonetheless entitled to a return of the price. *See* La. Civ. Code art. 2503. The rule here is tied to the doctrine of cause: when the parties agree to the sale of a specified thing, an eviction of the buyer results in a failure of cause which entitles him or her to rescission of the sale, even when the parties have excluded the warranty. *See, e.g., Montgomery v. Marydole Land & Lumber, Ltd.*, 15 So. 63, 65 (La. 1894).

c. Sale at Buyer's Peril and Risk

When the sale is made at the buyer's "peril and risk," the buyer has no recourse in the event of an eviction. Article 2503 makes clear that there are three circumstances in which a sale at the buyer's peril and risk takes place.

The first is when the parties exclude the warranty *and* the buyer is aware of the danger of eviction. When the buyer agrees that the sale is one without warranty and is aware of the possibility of his or her eviction, the sale is not of the thing itself, but of the hope of acquiring that thing. *See* La. Civ. Code art. 2451. Thus, if a third person has a right superior to that of the buyer, the buyer has not suffered a failure of cause and should be afforded no remedy. *See, e.g., Lyons v. Fitzpatrick*, 52 La. Ann. 697 (La. 1900).

Second, quite obviously, if the buyer declared that he or she was buying at his or her peril and risk in the Act of Sale, then the parties are bound by the consequences of that declaration. The buyer in such a case has expressly agreed to the sale of a hope. "In that case . . . the object of the sale is not properly the thing itself, but merely the pretensions and claims which the vendor may have upon this thing." *New Orleans & Carrollton Railroad Co. v. Jourdain's Heirs*, 34 La. Ann. 648, 650 (La. 1882) (internal citations omitted).

Third, if the parties expressly exclude the seller's obligation of returning the price, they are bound by the consequences of a sale at buyer's peril and risk even without having used that designation. As stated by the Louisiana Supreme Court, when the parties expressly foreclose the return of the price, "[the buyer] merely bought a hope which he was willing to gamble on and he cannot now, after having failed in his undertaking, recover the purchase price . . . . The contract is a valid one and contains nothing against public policy." *In re Canal Bank & Trust Co.*, 59 So. 2d 115, 118–19 (La. 1952).

d. Limited Warranty Sales

Although the Civil Code describes only three categories of sale in the context of the warranty against eviction, in practice, a fourth category exists—the "special warranty" or "limited warranty" sale. In this type of sale, the seller warrants against any alienation or encumbrance made during the seller's ownership of the thing but not by prior sellers in the chain of title. Though not expressly recognized in the Civil Code, this type of modification of the warranty against eviction should be enforceable, as it offends no rule of public policy. *See* 1 Peter Title, Louisiana Practice Series, Louisiana Real Estate Transactions § 10:45 (2017–18 ed.); *see also* La. Civ. Code art. 7. In such a case, if the buyer is evicted by a third person whose right in the thing sold derived from an owner other than the buyer's immediate seller, the sale should be treated as a non-warranty sale or a sale at the buyer's peril and risk, depending upon the buyer's knowledge of the danger of eviction and the precise language in the Act of Sale.

2. Knowledge of the Danger of Eviction

In addition to the type of sale involved, the buyer's knowledge of the danger of eviction has significant consequences. First, recall that if the buyer is evicted by an *encumbrance* of which the buyer was aware, the warranty against eviction does not even apply, leaving the buyer with no recourse whatsoever against the seller. *See* La. Civ. Code art. 2500; *Richmond v. Zapata Develop. Corp.*, 350 So. 2d 875 (La. 1977) (*See* Subpart A.2, above, for a discussion of the buyer's knowledge in the context of eviction due to an encumbrance.) In contrast, if the buyer is evicted by a third person with an *ownership interest in the thing sold*, the warranty against eviction generally applies *even if the buyer was aware* of the third person's right at the time of the sale. However, the buyer's knowledge of the third person's right affects the extent of the buyer's remedies and depending upon whether the sale was a full warranty sale, non-warranty sale, or sale at the buyer's peril and risk, may foreclose the buyer's claim altogether.

As stated by the Court in *Richmond*, when a buyer in a *full warranty sale* has knowledge of the danger of eviction, the buyer is precluded from recovering damages, but may still receive the return of the price paid. *Id.* at 878–89. Although the Civil Code provisions on the warranty against eviction do not directly address this effect, Louisiana courts historically arrived at this approach by application of Article 2452 (1870). Recall that prior to the 1995 revision of the sales articles, Article 2452 stated: "The sale of a thing belonging to another person is null. It may give rise to damages, when the buyer knew not that the thing belonged to another person." La. Civ. Code art. 2452 (1870). Under this provision, although a buyer who is aware that the thing sold belongs to another may not recover damages, the buyer is entitled to the return of the price paid as a result of the nullity of the sale. When Article 2452 was revised in 1995, the redactors changed the language to remove the reference to damages. In addition, the phrase "is null" was replaced with "does not convey ownership" in order to make clearer that the sale of a thing belonging to another may have consequences for both buyer and seller. Louisiana State Law Institute, Proposed Louisiana Civil Code Revision of Sales 7 (1992) (*Exposé des Motifs*). Despite the change in language, no substantive change to the law of eviction was intended by the redactors. *See* La. Civ. Code art. 2452 cmt. a ("This article is new. In spite of its different language it does not change the law as stated in the source article."); 2452 cmt. d ("Under this Article, a seller who purports to sell a thing he does not own is liable for damages if the buyer did not know that the thing did not belong to the seller."). Although the law on this point may be less than clear, it is widely accepted that the approach described in *Richmond* prevails under current law. *See* 24 Dian Tooley-Knoblett & David Gruning, Louisiana Civil Law Treatise, Sales § 10:26 (2017).

What is the impact of the buyer's knowledge of the danger of eviction in a *non-warranty sale*? Article 2503 makes clear that the buyer's knowledge forecloses a claim against the seller entirely. Indeed, by virtue of the seller's knowledge of the danger of eviction, the sale is transformed into a sale at the buyer's peril and risk, whose true nature is the sale of a hope. And, because a sale at buyer's peril and risk affords the buyer with no recourse against the seller, it is not necessary to explore the consequences of the buyer's knowledge of the danger of eviction on the buyer's claim when the Act of Sale declares that the buyer is purchasing at his or her peril and risk or that the seller's obligation to return the price is foreclosed. In either case, the buyer is in no worse a position if he or she is aware of the danger of eviction or ignorant of it.

A final point to consider is this: what level of knowledge of the danger of eviction is required to impact the buyer's claim in the ways described above? The Louisiana Supreme Court has announced that only actual knowledge and not merely constructive knowledge of the danger of eviction is required. *See New Orleans & Carrollton Railroad Co. v. Jourdain's Heirs*, 34 La. Ann. 648, 652 (1882). Constructive knowledge would include, of course, knowledge based upon the mere recordation of the third person's right.

3. Seller's Liability for His or Her Own Acts

Finally, regardless of the type of sale contemplated by the parties (whether a warranty sale, non-warranty sale, or sale at buyer's peril and risk), Article 2503 articulates an important limitation: "In all those cases the seller is liable for an eviction that is occasioned by his own act, and any agreement to the contrary is null." La. Civ. Code art. 2503. In those cases where the eviction was caused by the actions of the seller, any attempt to waive or otherwise modify the warranty against eviction will be without effect—the buyer will always have a remedy.

Notes and Questions

In light of the foregoing discussion, answer the following hypotheticals:

i. Seller conveys Blackacre to Buyer. The Act of Sale expressly designates the transaction as a "non-warranty" sale. Unbeknownst to either party, Neighbor, the owner of a tract of land adjoining Blackacre, acquired a 10-foot by

50-foot strip of land at the boundary of the two tracts by acquisitive prescription three years before the sale. Upon learning of the eviction, Buyer seeks recourse against Seller. To what recovery, if any, is Buyer entitled?

    ii. Seller conveys Blackacre to Buyer 1. The Act of Sale states: "The parties agree that this sale is made without warranty of title and without any recourse of any kind against Seller." Buyer 1 fails to record the Act of Sale. Days after the sale to Buyer 1, Seller again conveys Blackacre, this time to Buyer 2, who records the Act of Sale in the conveyance records of the parish where Blackacre is located. Upon learning of the recordation, Buyer 1 seeks recourse against Seller. To what recovery, if any, is Buyer 1 entitled?

D. The Buyer's Right of Subrogation

Article 2503 provides: "The buyer is subrogated to the rights in warranty of the seller against other persons, even when the warranty is excluded." LA. CIV. CODE art. 2503. Under this Article, the buyer who is evicted may seek recourse against not only his or her own seller, but also against any other seller in the chain of title who sold the thing in breach of the warranty. Recall that subrogation is defined as "the substitution of one person to the rights of another." LA. CIV. CODE art. 1825. Under Article 2503, a buyer who is evicted is automatically substituted to the rights of his or her seller against that seller's seller. The case below explores this concept.

Hoggatt v. Halcomb
250 So. 2d 471 (La. App. 2 Cir. 1971)

PRICE, Judge.

This appeal is taken from a judgment by the district court sustaining a peremptory exception of no cause or right of action. This decision in favor of a third party defendant was based upon the court's opinion that a call in warranty cannot go indiscriminately against any prior vendor in the chain of title, as it is a personal action which will lie only against the vendee's immediate vendor with whom he has privity of contract.

On June 2, 1959, plaintiffs, Wilton E. Hoggatt, et al., filed a petition for a judgment declaring them sole owners of a tract of land in Franklin Parish, entitled to peaceful and undisturbed possession thereof.

The named defendant in the above petition, Roy S. Halcomb, answered the petition, denying plaintiff owned the property in question and asserting that he acquired ownership thereof by purchase from Concordia Bank & Trust Company, or, alternatively, by ten or thirty years acquisitive prescription by his own possession and that of his authors in title.

Halcomb also filed a third party demand against Dr. Russell U. Fairbanks and J. B. Weston, alleging that each has warranted the title to the property and should be called to defend his title or to respond in damages in the event of an eviction. Halcomb's vendor, Concordia Bank & Trust Company, acquired the property by foreclosure from Weston, who had previously purchased it from Dr. Fairbanks. Halcomb did not join the bank as a defendant in this third party action.

In response to the third party demand, Dr. Fairbanks filed an exception of prematurity on May 22, 1970, alleging that he could not be called as a warrantor of title until Halcomb's remedies against Weston, an intervening vendor, have been exhausted.

Subsequently, Dr. Fairbanks filed exceptions of no cause or right of action urging that a vendee must proceed in an orderly manner through his own vendor back through the chain of title, and cannot indiscriminately select any prior vendor for suit. He also plead the prescription of ten years *liberandi causa* under Article 3544 [R.C.C. 3499] of the La. Civil Code on the theory that his vendee, Weston, held the property for more than ten years before its seizure by Concordia Bank & Trust Company.

Judgment was rendered in the district court sustaining the exception of no cause or right of action. The trial judge held that a call in warranty cannot be directed against any prior vendor through which the title of the present holder was derived, but that the vendee must resort to the vendor with which he has privity.

From the above judgment Halcomb has taken this appeal.

The following codal articles are pertinent to our decision of whether prior vendors may be cited in warranty:

"Art. 2475. [R.C.C. 2475] The seller is bound to two principal obligations, that of delivering and that of warranting the thing which he sells."

"Art. 2476. [R.C.C. 2475] The warranty respecting the seller has two objects; the first is the buyer's peaceable possession of the thing sold, and the second is the hidden defects of the thing sold or its redhibitory vices."

"Art. 2501. [R.C.C. 2501] Although at the time of the sale no stipulations have been made respecting the warranty, the seller is obliged, of course, to warrant the buyer against the eviction suffered by him from the totality or part of the thing sold, and against the charges claimed on such thing, which were not declared at the time of the sale."

"Art. 2503. [R.CC 2503] The parties may, by particular agreement, add to the obligation of warranty, which results of right from the sale, or diminish its effect; they may even agree that the seller shall not be subject to any warranty.

But whether warranty be excluded or not the buyer shall become subrogated to the seller's rights and actions in warranty against all others."

"Art. 2517. [R.C.C. 2517] The purchaser threatened with eviction, who wishes to preserve his right of warranty against his vendor, should notify the latter in time of the interference which he has experienced.

This notification is usually given by calling in the vendor to defend the action which has been instituted against the purchaser."

In *Smith v. Wilson*, 11 Rob. 522, 523 (1845), the Court stated:

"The general rule now settled is, that the party evicted can sue only his own immediate warrantor; but there is clearly an exception, when the party so evicted has been subrogated to the action of warranty by his vendor."

In 1924, subsequent to the above decision, Article 2503 (*supra*) of the Louisiana Civil Code [R.CC 2503] was amended to incorporate the exception provided in *Smith v. Wilson* into the purview of this article. The buyer is now subrogated to the seller's rights and actions in warranty against all others even where there has been no express stipulation to that effect, and regardless of whether the immediate seller warrants title.

Several years after this amendment, the Louisiana Supreme Court decided the case of *Carpenter v. Herndon*, 173 La. 239, 136 So. 577 (1931), in which it noted by way of dictum that Act No. 116 of 1924 (amending article 2503 [R.CC 2503]) was an enactment of the view of French authorities that a buyer can proceed against any preceding seller in the chain of title by an action in warranty.

Two earlier cases have recognized the right of a vendee to proceed against a remote vendor, *Johnston v. Bell*, 6 Mart. (N.S.) 384 (1828), and *Town of Vinton v. Lyons*, 131 La. 673, 60 So. 54 (1912). The later case of *McEachern v. Plauche Lumber & Construction Co.*, 220 La. 696, 57 So.2d 405 (1952), cited by appellee as reaching a contrary result to the cases just cited is not inconsistent in our understanding. In the *McEachern* case the court merely held the obligation of warranty of vendor in a chain of title is not an obligation in solido. In this action Halcomb has not prayed for an in solido judgment against Weston and Fairbanks but has alleged he should have a monetary judgment in the event of an eviction against Weston *and/ or* Fairbanks.

In the event defendants are unable to successfully defend the title and an eviction is ordered, we recognize the obligation to respond in damages varies among the vendors in the chain of title in accordance with the consideration for various sales in the chain. However, as no judgment can be rendered against any vendor for more than the purchase price and other incidentals allowed under La.C.C. article 2506 [R.C.C. 2506], we do not see any prejudice to anyone by allowing more than one vendor to be joined in the same call in warranty. To do so would prevent a multiplicity of actions.

In filing the exception of prescription Fairbanks relies on the provisions of La.C.C. article 3544 [R.C.C. 3499] with the assumption the period begins to run at the time of his sale to Weston. He further assumes that as Weston retained the property for over ten years that any action in warranty against him prescribes at the end of this period, and as Halcomb merely is subrogated to whatever rights are possessed by Weston, then the right of warranty has prescribed to him also.

Under the prevailing jurisprudence the prescriptive period does not begin to run until knowledge of a contrary claim is possessed by the vendee. *Whitten v. Monkhouse*, 29 So. 800 (La.App.2d Cir. 1947); *Gage v. Heins*, 197 So.2d 699 (La. App.4th Cir., 1967).

As the date on which Halcomb first became aware of the contrary claim to his title to the property in dispute is not reflected by the record, and as the trial court did not pass on the exception of prescription, we do not find it proper for us to pass on this issue at this time.

For the foregoing reasons the judgment appealed from is hereby reversed, and the exceptions of no cause or right of action are hereby overruled. It is further ordered that this case be remanded to the Fifth Judicial District Court for the Parish of Franklin for further proceedings in accordance with the law and not inconsistent with the views expressed herein.

Costs of this appeal are to be paid by appellee.

Notes and Questions

1. As the foregoing case makes clear, the right of subrogation permits the buyer a cause of action not only against his or her own seller, but against more remote sellers in the chain of title with whom the buyer lacks contractual privity. The buyer may proceed against any seller in the chain of title who owned the property during a time when a third person held a superior right.

2. The Civil Code does not provide a special period of liberative prescription for the buyer's action against the seller for breach of the warranty against eviction. Thus, the general rule for personal actions applies, and the buyer's action is subject to a liberative prescription of 10 years. *See* LA. CIV. CODE art. 3499. When does this prescription begin to run?

3. While it is clear under Article 2503 that a buyer who has suffered an eviction may step into the shoes of his or her seller and proceed against more remote sellers in the chain of title, the extent of the liability of those remote sellers is less clear. Two factors may impact the liability of a remote seller in the chain of title: (1) differences between the price paid by the buyer to the seller and that paid by the seller to the remote seller; and (2) modifications of the warranty against eviction agreed upon by the buyer and the seller or by the seller and the remote seller.

Consider first the complexities introduced by differences between the price paid by the buyer to the seller and that paid by the seller to the remote seller. Assume that Seller 1 is not the true owner of Blackacre, but nonetheless sells Blackacre to Seller 2 in a full warranty sale for $100,000. Seller 2 then sells Blackacre to Buyer in a full warranty sale for $150,000. After the sale, Buyer learns that Third Person is the true owner of Blackacre. It is clear that Buyer may proceed against Seller 2 for the return of the price paid by Buyer ($150,000) and other remedies allowed by law as discussed above. It is also clear that Buyer may proceed against the more remote seller, Seller 1. Less clear is the remedy to which Buyer is entitled from Seller 1 with regard to the purchase price: will Buyer recover the price paid by Buyer to Seller 2 ($150,000) or the price paid by Seller 2 to Seller 1 ($100,000)? While no case has yet directly addressed this issue, some scholars have argued that the Buyer is restricted in his or her recovery against Seller 1 to the price paid by Seller 2, as subrogation involves the "substitution" of Buyer to Seller 2's rights against Seller 1. Moreover, those same scholars have argued that the difference between the price paid by Buyer and that paid by Seller 2 cannot be recovered from Seller 1 as "damages" because no seller is liable for an increase in the value of the thing sold. *See* 24 Dian Tooley-Knoblett & David Gruning, Louisiana Civil Law Treatise, Sales § 10:40 (2017).

What would be the result if the value of Blackacre had decreased, rather than increased, over time? Assume that Seller 1 sold Blackacre to Seller 2 in a full warranty sale for $150,000, and Seller 2 later sold to Buyer for $100,000. It is clear that Buyer could recover $100,000 from Seller 2, but what amount can Buyer recover from Seller 1? If Buyer is fully substituted to the rights of Seller 2 against Seller 1, will Buyer receive a windfall? Again, while no case has yet addressed this issue, scholars who have considered this problem have concluded that a buyer is limited in his or her recovery against a remote seller to the *lesser* of what his or her seller could have recovered from the remote seller and what the buyer could have recovered from his or her own seller. *See* 24 Dian Tooley-Knoblett & David Gruning, Louisiana Civil Law Treatise, Sales § 10:40 (2017).

Consider now the complexity introduced by modifications of the warranty against eviction. Two hypotheticals illustrate the difficulties here. First, assume that Seller 1 sells Blackacre to Seller 2 in a non-warranty sale. Seller 2 then sells Blackacre to Buyer in a full warranty sale. After the sale, Buyer learns that Third Person is the true owner of Blackacre. It is clear that Buyer may proceed against Seller 1 for a return of the price, because Seller 1 would have been liable to Seller 2 for the return of the price. Is Seller 1 also liable to Buyer for damages? The answer should be "no" given that Seller 1 sold to Seller 2 by non-warranty sale, and Buyer, through subrogation, is substituted to (and limited by) the rights of Seller 2.

Now assume that whereas Seller 1 sold Blackacre to Seller 2 in a full warranty sale, Seller 2 sold to Buyer in a non-warranty sale. It is clear that Buyer may proceed against Seller 2 for breach of the warranty against eviction and, by virtue of the non-warranty sale, may recover only the price paid. With respect to Seller 1, Article 2503 expressly provides that the buyer's right to subrogation exists "even when the warranty is excluded." La. Civ. Code art. 2503. Thus, it is clear that Buyer may also proceed against Seller 1 for the return of the price. May Buyer also proceed against Seller 1 for damages? Why or why not? How would Buyer's recovery against Seller 1 be affected if the sale from Seller 2 to Buyer had been made "at Buyer's peril and risk"?

422   9 · THE WARRANTY AGAINST EVICTION

E. Quitclaim Deeds

La. Civ. Code art. 2502

The "quitclaim deed" is a form of conveyance at common law according to which the seller conveys to the buyer only whatever interest in the estate the seller may have at the time of the conveyance, without any guarantee that the seller has any interest at all. The quitclaim deed is a convenient tool for conveying one's rights in a thing to another when one is uncertain about what rights, if any, one might have.

The quitclaim deed has long been utilized in Louisiana and, in 1995, was recognized in the revision of the Title on Sales with the adoption of Article 2502, which provides in part: "A person may transfer to another whatever rights to a thing he may then have, without warranting the existence of any such rights. In such a case the transferor does not owe restitution of the price to the transferee in case of eviction . . . ." LA. CIV. CODE art. 2502. The Civil Code does not use the common law terminology of "quitclaim" but instead properly characterizes the quitclaim deed as an assignment of rights. A transferor who quitclaims to another does not sell the thing itself, but instead sells whatever rights to thing the transferor may have at the time of the transaction. Given this explanation, do you see why the quitclaim is exempt from the warranty against eviction?

One can tell the difference between a sale and a mere quitclaim by looking to the language used in the parties' agreement. Does the transferor intend to sell the property to the transferee or is the former merely transferring the chance of rights in the property, without attesting to their existence or extent? It does not take much imagination to understand how vague and ambiguous language can lead to a lack of clarity as to the parties' true intentions.

Significantly, the public records doctrine interacts differently with quitclaim deeds than with other types of transfers (like sales and donations). The case below considers this interaction.

Simmesport State Bank v. Roy

614 So. 2d 265 (La. App. 3 Cir. 1993)

DOMENGEAUX, Chief Judge

Simmesport State Bank filed this action to annul a quitclaim deed which was granted by Leonard R. Tanner and Lucy Tanner to Jack R. Roy and Jean Roy, all of whom were named as defendants. The quitclaim deed purportedly conveyed to the Roys an interest in a piece of land located in Avoyelles Parish. All parties filed motions for summary judgment. The trial judge granted summary judgment in favor of the Bank, declaring the quitclaim deed at issue to be null, void, and of no effect. The trial judge also granted summary judgment in favor of the Tanners, dismissing them from the litigation.

The Roys have appealed the judgment in favor of the Bank, and we affirm the trial court's decision; the judgment in favor of the Tanners has not been appealed.

The record reveals the following undisputed facts. In 1988, the Tanners went into bankruptcy. Simmesport State Bank was one of their creditors. Pursuant to a bankruptcy court order authorizing a trustee's consensual sale, the property at issue was sold to the Bank on September 14, 1988. Officials at the Bank, however, did not record the deed until August 8, 1991, probably through inadvertence.

In May of 1991, the Roys purchased the property at a tax sale. Jack Roy then checked the mortgage and conveyance records and discovered that the Tanners were the record owners of the property. While the tax assessment was still listed under the Tanners' names, the tax records did contain a reference to Simmesport State Bank. (Apparently, the tax notices for 1988, 1989, and 1990 were sent to the Tanners who forwarded them to the Bank. The Bank paid the 1988 and 1989 taxes but neglected to pay the 1990 taxes.) Jack Roy also learned from his research that a mortgage executed by the Tanners in favor of the Bank had been cancelled. When Roy talked to the Tanners, he was told they no longer owned the property because they had lost it to the Bank as a result of their bankruptcy. The Tanners showed Roy the pertinent papers evidencing the trustee's consensual sale.

Roy explained to the Tanners that he was in the process of buying the property for delinquent taxes, and he requested that they execute a quitclaim deed in his favor in exchange for $500.00. The Tanners were reluctant to execute the quitclaim deed, but after making sure they were not doing anything wrong, and were not guaranteeing title to property which they did not own, they decided to execute the deed and accept the $500.00 payment. Roy immediately filed the deed in the Avoyelles Parish conveyance records on August 5, 1991.

On August 7, 1991, Roy informed the Bank that he had purchased the property at a tax sale. Upon reviewing their records for this property, officials at the Bank discovered that the deed from the trustee's consensual sale had never been recorded. The Bank then recorded the deed on August 8, whereupon the quitclaim deed in favor of the Roys was discovered. The Bank successfully redeemed the tax sale and instituted this suit on August 20, 1991, to annul the quitclaim deed.

The Bank asserts ownership of the subject property based upon the well established principle that a quitclaim deed is one which purports to convey, and is understood to convey, nothing more than the interest in the property described of which the grantor is possessed, if any, at the time, rather than the property itself. *Waterman v. Tidewater Associated Oil Co.*, 213 La. 588, 35 So. 2d 225 (1947). The Bank contends that because the Tanners owned no interest in the property at the time they executed the quitclaim deed, the deed transferred nothing and is essentially null and void.

The Roys assert ownership based on the public records doctrine, codified at La. R.S. 9:2721 and 9:2756 [R.C.C. 3338–3353], which requires that all contracts affecting immovable property must be recorded in order to affect third parties. The Roys cite *Dallas v. Farrington*, 490 So. 2d 265 (La. 1986) for the long established rule that because recordation is essential for effectiveness against third parties, actual knowledge by third parties of unrecorded interests is immaterial. 490 So.2d at 269, citing *McDuffie v. Walker*, 125 La. 152, 51 So. 100 (La. 1909).

The issue before us, as the trial judge pointed out in his well reasoned oral opinion, which was transcribed, is how the law applicable to quitclaim deeds is affected by the public records doctrine. In other words, in applying the law that a vendor in a quitclaim deed sells only that interest which the vendor owns at the time of the sale, a determination must be made as to what the vendor owned, but is that determination restricted to what is contained in the public records? Or can the determination be based on facts outside of the public records?

There is no question in the present case that the trustee's sale was a valid transfer of property between the Tanners and the Bank. There is also no question that the sale could have no effect on third parties until it was recorded three years after the fact in 1991. But what effect does an unrecorded sale have on a quitclaim deed which, by its very nature, transfers only an interest in property, not the property itself? The trial judge held that what is contained in the public records is not determinative of the interest held by a vendor to a quitclaim deed. He found that an unrecorded sale has the same effect as a recorded sale on the validity of a quitclaim deed. The Tanners, therefore, had no interest in the property at the time they executed the deed.

We find the trial judge's analysis to be correct. There is nothing in the jurisprudence which requires that a determination of the interest held by a vendor to a quitclaim deed must depend on what is contained in the public records. The Tanners lost their interest in the subject property when it was sold to the Bank. Therefore, they had no interest to convey when they executed the quitclaim deed. We agree with the century old case of *Benton v. Sentell*, 50 La.Ann. 869, 24 So. 297 (1898), which stated:

> "We think that a quitclaim deed reaches only to interests actually owned at that time by the party executing it; that it is of no effect whatever as to interests already gone. In the very nature of things, there is a great difference between an act of sale or donation and a quitclaim deed. It is true that through the latter interests in property may be acquired, for the party quitclaiming is ordinarily estopped from subsequently asserting rights which had been by him relinquished. A person undertaking to sell warrants the existence of and his ownership of the thing sold, and is bound to make the warranty good, but a party quitclaiming, carries out precisely what he undertook to do in simply abstaining from disturbing or questioning the rights of those in whose favor he has renounced."

24 So. at 301.

In this appeal, the Roys argue that a decision affirming the trial court's judgment would serve only to imperil or erode the public records doctrine. This argument is without merit. Our decision is based on the unique characteristics of a quitclaim deed and its inherent independence from what is contained in the public records. Indeed, more often than not, a quitclaim deed is obtained from persons who are *not* record owners, but who may have an ownership interest nonetheless. In order to protect himself from the uncertainty of the situation, such a vendor will transfer whatever interest he has, but only without any warranty of title. Hence, the quitclaim deed is utilized.

The Roys' reliance on the rule that unrecorded transfers of immovable property cannot affect third parties is misplaced. The focus, instead, must be on the deed which the Roys hold; it is a deed that contains no warranty of title and transfers nothing but an interest in property, the ownership of which had previously been lost. The purported interest, therefore, is nonexistent, and the deed itself is null and void and of no effect. There are many instances where a quitclaim deed does constitute a valid transfer of property because the vendor does, in fact, own an interest which can be transferred. See, *Osborn v. Johnston*, 322 So.2d 112 (La. 1975); *Clifton v. Liner*, 552 So.2d 407 (La. App. 1st Cir. 1989); *Sabourin v. Jilek*, 128 So.2d 698 (La. App. 4th Cir. 1961); *Armstrong v. Bates*, 61 So.2d 466 (La. App. 1st Cir. 1952). This, however, is not such a case, and we therefore affirm the trial court's ruling.

Finally, we note that in the instant case, both the vendor and the vendee to the quitclaim deed knew of the trustee's consensual sale to the Bank. Further, the vendee knew that sale had not been recorded. The vendee attempted to take advantage of the situation by obtaining a quitclaim deed. The questions of fraud and bad faith are relevant generally to a determination of whether a third party purchaser is entitled to the protection afforded by the public records doctrine. *American Legion v. Morel*, 577 So.2d 346 (La. App. 1st Cir. 1991), writ denied, 580 So.2d 924 (La. 1991). However, in the instant case, the question of fraud is not before us as the Bank did not allege fraud and the trial court pointed out that he was not making a finding of fraud. Our decision likewise is not based on any finding of fraud or bad faith, but rather, on the conclusion that the law governing quitclaim deeds does not support the position advocated by the Roys.

For the foregoing reasons, the judgment of the trial court is affirmed at appellants' costs.

AFFIRMED.

Notes and Questions

1. Transfers via quitclaim may not be rescinded for lesion, even if the price paid by the buyer is less than one half the fair market value of the rights that are ultimately conveyed. *See* LA. CIV. CODE art. 2502. Given the nature of a quitclaim, this is a logical rule. After all, the transferor is not selling a corporeal immovable. Instead, the seller is assigning whatever rights he or she may (or may not) have in a corporeal immovable. Thus, what the seller has transferred—the right to the property—is properly classified as an incorporeal immovable to which lesion is clearly inapplicable under Article 2589. *See* LA. CIV. CODE art. 470 ("Rights and actions that apply to immovable things are incorporeal immovables.").

2. Quitclaim deeds do not give rise to a presumption of bad faith on the part of the transferee, and they qualify as a just title for purposes of acquisitive prescription.

La. Civ. Code art. 2502. As explained in comment (d), the fact that a sale occurs by quitclaim does not necessarily indicate that the buyer lacked faith in the seller's title. La. Civ. Code art. 2502 cmt. d.

3. The exemption of quitclaim deeds from the warranty against eviction comes along with an exemption from the so-called "after-acquired title doctrine." As Article 2502 states, "If the transferor [by quitclaim deed] acquires ownership of the thing after having transferred his rights to it, the after-acquired title of the transferor does not inure to the benefit of the transferee." La. Civ. Code art. 2502. The after-acquired title doctrine is the subject of the following Part.

F. Doctrine of After-Acquired Title

The doctrine of after-acquired title is a jurisprudentially-recognized doctrine that, while uncodified, rests on the central principles that underlie the warranty against eviction. This doctrine provides that when a seller who has conveyed something that he or she does not own later acquires ownership of that thing, the seller's rights vest automatically in the buyer, thereby curing the eviction.

St. Landry Oil & Gas Co. v. Neal
118 So. 24 (La. 1928)

Overton, J.

In January, 1919, Emma Garrett and others executed a mineral lease on 5 acres of land in the parish of Claiborne to J. M. Eastham, who, on October 6, 1919, assigned the lease to T. S. Neal, one of the defendants in this case. In December of the same year, Neal assigned the lease to the St. Landry Oil & Gas Company, Inc., the plaintiff herein. The consideration for this assignment was $10,000 cash and $15,000, to be paid out of a certain part of the oil produced from the land. In November, 1920, Neal assigned to W. F. Reynolds a one-third interest in the credit portion of the consideration, stipulated in the assignment to plaintiff, and Reynolds transferred this one-third interest to the Commercial National Bank of Shreveport. In May, 1920, plaintiff assigned a one-half interest in the lease acquired by it to the Tulsa Oil & Gas Company, under a contract by which plaintiff was to pay a certain part of the cost of production. Two wells were drilled on the property under this contract, one of which produced nothing and the other $39,563.99 of oil, which was sold to the Standard Oil Company of Louisiana.

In August, 1920, Emma Garrett, the widow of William Garrett, and various others, including plaintiff, instituted a suit against the heirs of Thornton Bridgeman and his widow to have recognized as valid a correction made in a deed from the Bridgemans to Garrett, and, in the alternative, to reform two deeds to Garrett by correcting the description of the property therein conveyed. In that case judgment was rendered recognizing the Bridgemans as the owners of the land upon which Emma Garrett and others had granted the lease that was acquired by plaintiff.

Within two months after the foregoing judgment became final, the defendant Neal, who had transferred the lease to plaintiff, obtained from the Bridgemans, who had been decreed the owners of the land, a ratification and confirmation of the lease, executed by Emma Garrett and others to his assignor. Neal had the act of confirmation recorded, and notified plaintiff of its execution and recordation, but plaintiff refused to accepted [sic] the confirmation.

Some months after the foregoing act of confirmation was executed, plaintiff, urging that it had been evicted by the judgment declaring that the Bridgemans, and not Emma Garrett and others, were the owners of the land upon which the lease was granted, instituted the present suit to recover from Neal the $10,000 paid by it to Neal as the cash portion of the consideration for the assignment of the lease; to recover from him $7,500, one-half of the cost paid by it for drilling a well; also to recover from him $3,353.39, the cost of operations and production incurred by it, and also to annul and rescind the obligation, contracted by it, to pay the credit portion of the consideration for the assignment of the lease made to it by Neal. As Neal had assigned a one-third interest in that part of the consideration to Reynolds, who had assigned that third to the Commercial National Bank, that bank was made a party to the suit.

The defense is that, when Neal obtained the ratification from the Bridgemans, the ratification immediately accrued to plaintiff, and gave him a perfect title to the lease, thereby destroying any right plaintiff might have had to rescind the sale of the lease to it, and recover the purchase price with damages.

Ordinarily, where one sells the property of another-and the rule is equally applicable to the granting or sale of mineral leases-and later acquires title to the property sold by him, the title vests immediately in his vendee. *Bonin v. Eyssaline*, 12 Mart. (O. S.) 185, 227; *McGuire v. Amelung*, 12 Mart. (O. S.) 649; *Woods v. Kimbal*, 5 Mart. (N. S.) 246; *Fenn v. Rils*, 9 La. 95, 100; *Stokes v. Shakleford*, 12 La. 170; *Lee v. Ferguson*, 5 La. Ann. 532; *New Orleans v. Riddell*, 113 La. 1051, 37 So. 966; *Wolff v. Carter*, 131 La. 667, 60 So. 52; *Brewer v. New Orleans Land Co.*, 154 La. 446, 97 So. 605.

The foregoing rule admits of exceptions. The first case, in this jurisdiction, in which it was considered when, and under what circumstances, the after-acquired title of the vendor vests in his vendee and when it does not, is the case of *Bonin v. Eyssaline*, supra, 12 Mart. (O. S.) 185, 227. In that case, the plaintiff, who was still in possession of the property sold him, discovered the nullity of his title, and gave public notice that he would sue his vendor for the rescission of the sale. His vendor took steps to acquire title to the property, and acquired it. Thereafter the plaintiff brought his suit to rescind the sale. The question was raised as to whether, and when, an after-acquired title vests in the vendee of the one acquiring it. The court, in passing upon the question, which was raised by defendant in order to defeat the suit for rescission, expressed the view that, while it was inclined to think that an after-acquired title vested in the vendee of the one acquiring it, if it was acquired at any time prior to final judgment rescinding the sale, yet held that it clearly did so, where the title was acquired prior to the institution of the suit to rescind, and, as the title in that case was so acquired, rejected the demand for rescission.

The same question arose in the case of *Hale v. City of New Orleans*, supra, 18 La. Ann. 321. In that case it appeared that the city of New Orleans sold to Thomas Hale certain real estate. In a suit instituted by A. and F. Remy, the Remys were adjudged the owners of the property. Hale then sued to rescind the sale made to him by the city of New Orleans, and to recover the purchase price. The city then acquired the title of the Remys, and urged that the new title acquired accrued to Hale, and hence that his title was perfect. But Hale resisted this contention, and it was held that, having instituted his suit to rescind before the acquisition by his vendor of the newly acquired title, and having thereby evinced his intention not to accept any such title, it could not be held in the face of these facts that the title vested in him.

A similar question arose in the case of *Brewer v. New Orleans Land Co.*, supra, 154 La. 446, 97 So. 605, in which the facts are similar, in essential respects to those in the *Hale* Case. In that case, as in the *Hale* Case, the suit to rescind was instituted prior to the acquisition of the newly acquired title, and the same ruling was made, as was made in the *Hale* Case, or, in other words, it was there ruled that the new title did not accrue to the plaintiffs therein, and defeat their suit to rescind.

While there are expressions in the *Hale* Case and in the *Brewer* Case, and especially in the former, that are suggestive that it is wholly optional with one who has purchased from a person without title whether he will accept an after-acquired title, yet these expressions must be considered in connection with the particular facts of those cases. In either instance the plaintiffs therein might have accepted the after-acquired titles, but, due to their suits to rescind, they had the right to refuse those titles and continue with their suits.

In our view, at least in the absence of an actual eviction working substantial injury, where one purchases from another without title before a suit to rescind is commenced, the title thus acquired vests immediately in the vendee of the one acquiring it, and the vendee cannot sue for a rescission of the sale by which he purchased. He should not then be permitted to sue, because his vendor, under these circumstances, would have fulfilled all of his obligations to him. However, after he has instituted suit to rescined [sic], his suit cannot be defeated by a title acquired by his vendor after the institution of the suit. [T]he new title does not vest in him then, unless he accepts it, for he cannot be forced to retract his steps and dismiss his suit by an after occurrence.

* * * * *

For the reasons assigned, the judgment appealed from is annulled and set aside, plaintiff's demands are now rejected, the reconventional demand of the Commercial National Bank is rejected, and that of said Neal for the remaining two-thirds of said $15,000 is dismissed as of nonsuit; plaintiff to pay the costs in both courts.

O'Niell, C. J., takes no part.

Notes and Questions

1. The after-acquired title doctrine sensibly cures an eviction before it can be asserted, thereby avoiding the unnecessary expense and delay of litigation. Note that the after-acquired title doctrine operates in transactions other than sales. Indeed, *St. Landry Oil & Gas Co. v. Neal* involved the application of the doctrine in the context of the granting of a mineral lease. As this case illustrates, the doctrine does not apply without limitation. While the after-acquired title doctrine typically operates to automatically vest title in the buyer once it is acquired by the seller, if the buyer has already instituted a lawsuit against the seller on account of the eviction, then the buyer will not be forced to accept perfect title. Instead, the buyer may either accept the after-acquired title (and thereby extinguish the lawsuit) or continue the litigation and seek whatever remedy is available under the warranty against eviction.

2. Does the after-acquired title doctrine apply to a non-warranty sale? A sale at the buyer's peril and risk? Quitclaim deeds? In *Waterman v. Tidewater Associated Oil Co.*, 35 So. 2d 225 (La. 1947), the Louisiana Supreme Court observed that the after-acquired title doctrine has typically only been recognized as applying in cases where the vendor has warranted title to the conveyed property—i.e., full warranty sales. *See also Wells v. Blackman*, 46 So. 437, 444 (La. 1908) (holding the same). The issue before the court in *Waterman* was whether the doctrine of after-acquired title applies to quitclaim deeds. According to the Court,

> [I]t is quite manifest that the doctrine of after-acquired title should not be expanded to include a quit-claim deed, primarily for the reason that a conveyance of that character transfers only the present interest of the vendor in the land and does not convey the property. . . . This being so, there is no reason why the vendor should not thereafter acquire title even though it be adverse to the vendee holding under the deed.

Waterman, 35 So. 2d at 233–34. With respect to the non-warranty sale, the Court stated in dicta:

> To hold that the title [the seller] acquires inures to his grantee is really nothing more than an enforcement of the grantor's obligation to deliver good title. And it may even be proper to extend application of the doctrine to a sale without warranty where the land conveyed is adequately described. In such a case, it might be argued that the vendor would be precluded from subsequently acquiring an adverse title to the prejudice of the vendee under Article [2503] of the Civil Code . . . .

Id. at 233. The Court did not consider whether the after-acquired title doctrine could apply to a sale at the buyer's peril and risk. Does the rationale offered by the

Court for extending the after-acquired title doctrine to non-warranty sales apply also to sales at the buyer's peril and risk? Why or why not? Note that while the application of the doctrine of after-acquired title to non-warranty sales and sales at the buyer's peril and risk remains unsettled in the jurisprudence, leading commentators express the view that the doctrine should apply "to any sale in which the seller is bound to return the price in the event of an eviction." 24 DIAN TOOLEY-KNOBLETT & DAVID GRUNING, LOUISIANA CIVIL LAW TREATISE, SALES § 10:39 (2017).

Chapter 10

The Warranty Against Redhibitory Defects

In addition to delivering the thing sold and warranting ownership and peaceful possession of the thing (discussed in Chapters 8: Delivery and 9: The Warranty Against Eviction, respectively), the seller also warrants the absence of hidden defects in the thing and that the thing is fit for its intended use. LA. CIV. CODE art. 2475. This Chapter focuses on the final obligations of the seller: the warranty against hidden defects and the warranty of fitness.

A. In General

La. Civ. Code arts. 2520–2521, 2530, 2541

For a buyer to make a claim for breach of the warranty against redhibition, several things must be shown. First, the defect in question must be redhibitory. A defect is redhibitory when (1) it renders the thing useless or its use so inconvenient that it must be presumed that a buyer would not have bought the thing had the buyer known of the defect; or (2) without rendering the thing totally useless, it diminishes its usefulness or value so that it must presumed that a buyer would still have bought it but for a lesser price. LA. CIV. CODE art. 2520. The defectiveness of the thing sold is a factual determination for the trier of fact. *Guillot v. Doughty*, 142 So. 3d 1034 (La. App. 1 Cir. 2014). The type of redhibitory defect will dictate whether the buyer is entitled to rescission of the sale or a reduction in price, *id.*, and that determination is also factual in nature. *Hernandez v. Chisesi Investments, L.L.C.*, 164 So. 3d 912 (La. App. 5 Cir. 2014). Note, however, that a buyer may choose to seek only reduction of the price even when the redhibitory defect is such as to give the buyer the right to obtain rescission of the sale. LA. CIV. CODE art. 2541. Likewise, in an action for rescission because of a redhibitory defect, the court may limit the buyer's remedy to a reduction of the price. *Id.*

Second, the warranty applies only to defects that are hidden — there is no warranty for defects that were known to the buyer or should have been discovered by a reasonably prudent buyer of such things. LA. CIV. CODE art. 2521. Finally, the defect must exist at the time of delivery, which is presumed if the defect appears within three days of delivery. LA. CIV. CODE art. 2530. The cases below address these elements of a redhibition claim.

Dage v. Obed

917 So. 2d 713 (La. App. 2 Cir. 2005)

Before BROWN, WILLIAMS, and PEATROSS, JJ.

BROWN, C.J.

Larry Eldon Dage, Jr. and his wife, Kathy Edward Dage, filed suit against John and Janiece Obed, Frank Ricks d/b/a All Phase Service Company, Inc., and American Exterminating Company on May 30, 2001. The Dages alleged that they purchased a commercial property located at 215 Trenton Street, West Monroe, Louisiana, for $147,500 from the Obeds on May 30, 2000. Plaintiffs sought a diminution in the purchase price of the building because of redhibitory defects. The suit against American Exterminating Company was dismissed before trial, and the suit against Frank Ricks and All Phase Service Company, Inc. was dismissed the morning of trial, leaving only the claim against the Obeds. The trial court rendered judgment ordering a $35,000 quanti minoris price reduction. Defendants have appealed.

Facts

In the months of April and May of 2000, plaintiffs considered purchasing the building at 215 Trenton Street owned by defendants and used as an antique mall. Plaintiffs' intent was to operate a beauty parlor in part of the building. They inspected the property three times. Plaintiffs noticed signs of an old leak in the rear men's bathroom, but were assured each time by John Obed that a new roof had been recently installed.

Plaintiffs reviewed a number of reports. Prince and Company issued an inspection report that stated that there were no signs of active leaks, there was water damage to ceiling tiles from previous leaks, and the roof had been replaced ten years earlier. Prince and Company were hired to make this inspection by the Kellys, a couple previously interested in buying the property. The Kellys did not purchase the property because Obed refused to make any repairs, wanting to sell the building "as is."

Obed's disclosure form stated that the building "has had a leak" and that the roof was one year old. Prior to purchase, plaintiffs hired Frank Ricks to inspect the building, which he did on May 5, 2000. Ricks' initial report indicated structural damage to the rafters under the flat roof area, and opined that some of the damage was severe. Ricks strongly recommended that a structural engineer make an inspection. Ricks mentioned that John Obed had not allowed him on the roof. After plaintiffs called Obed and repeated what Ricks had said, Obed arranged for Ricks to inspect the roof. Ricks made a second inspection, and, in a supplemental report on May 21, 2000, observed that the roof was sound but that the sheeting wasn't installed properly so that water would run off at a slower rate than it would if the sheeting were correctly installed.

As noted above, Obed had used the building as an antique mall, wherein certain vendors would rent space to sell their wares. Larry Dage testified that Obed requested that the Dages not communicate with the vendors or employees at the site, as they might become nervous that the building was changing ownership. Prior to purchase, plaintiffs were never in the building during or soon after it rained. Cathy Dage testified that she looked at the building with her husband and that Obed told her that the building had a "perfectly good new roof." Although she saw stains, she did not observe wetness.

Obed's asking price for the building was $150,000. Plaintiffs countered with $140,000 and two conditions. The first was a non-compete agreement for antique stores, as Obed owned several other buildings in the area, and the second was a one-year warranty on the roof, which had been a condition of the previous buyers interested in purchasing the building. Eventually plaintiffs and defendants settled on a price of $147,500, including the non-compete clause but not the warranty on the roof. Plaintiffs testified that they felt comfortable dropping the one-year roof warranty after Obed explained to them that a new roof was warrantied for 30 to 50 years by the roof installers.

Plaintiffs hired Randy Stephenson to remodel in the rear of the building for the beauty salon in September and October of 2000. After tearing out the rear men's bathroom, the Dages and Stephenson discovered a fiberglass bathtub with a PVC drain pipe in the original ceiling above the bathroom.

Obed contends that plaintiffs' carpenter, Randy Stephenson, tore out a supporting wall resulting in the roof dropping four inches. Stephenson testified that the roof had leaked before he began remodeling the men's bathroom and that he did not remove any load bearing walls. Further, Stephenson testified that there are no load bearing walls to remove in the building, as the structure is covered by a truss roof which is carried by both walls on the exterior of the building. The walls in the rear men's bathroom did not go all the way to the roof, but only high enough to support the storage loft directly above. Stephenson commented that buildings like the one at issue are essentially only roofs with the parapet walls being of secondary value.

Plaintiffs testified that it only rained once during the summer of 2000 and that there may have been a small leak in the rear men's bathroom during that rain. It rained more in September and October 2000, when the Dages observed an increase in the leakage, as well as additional leakage along the right side of the building. The leaks worsened in December and in early January 2001, prompting plaintiffs to ask John Obed for the name of the company that had installed the roof.

Charlie Hood was admitted as an expert witness in roofing. He first inspected the building in question at plaintiffs' request in early 2001 and at that time took many photographs. Hood believed the material used to cover the roof to be "regular roll roofing," which is very cheap and generally lasts only two years before cracking and leaking. If the material were indeed "modified roll roofing," it would still crack soon after installation from bending to the wind, as "modified roll roofing" is supposed to be "laid flat and sealed." Here it was simply laid flat.

Hood tore out the layers of roll roofing above the rear men's bathroom and discovered rotten decking underneath, which he replaced with new wood. Additionally, Hood noted a serious problem with the roof in that the rain caught in a 3,000 square foot area would be forced through a drainage hole the size of a baseball. The drainage hole was reduced in size due to the roll roofing.

Hood also pointed out that one serious cause of leakage was due to a spot where two sheets, presumably roofing sheets, overlapped. Tar was used as a flashing for the overlap, and when the tar cracked, water poured into the building, rotting several of the joists. Tar is a poor material for flashing, and Hood opined that when tar is used for flashing, leakage is inevitable. This area is at the base of an unused water tower, which Hood stated should have been removed, as any projection on a roof is a potential source of leakage. Hood also discovered that the electrical pipes were coated with spray foam, which is bad protection, and Hood testified that he would have used a boot made up to go around the pipes and then filled with tar.

Charlie Hood noted the generally poor state of the roof, believing it to be amateur work. Hood also observed that there were numerous leaks, due to the use of tar, and opined that the longest the tar could hope to last would be two years, if applied properly. Hood stated that it would be difficult to just patch the roof up without removing most of it and starting over. Hood estimated the cost to replace the roof would be in the range of $35,000, assuming no other damage existed under the roof. Hood testified that he gives a 12-year warranty on material and a 2-year warranty on labor.

Evelyn Lolley testified that she began working for defendant as a cashier in October of 1998, two years before plaintiffs purchased the building. From the beginning Lolley knew of a leak at the bar, leaks in the electrical cabinet, coat closet, and the back window, as well as heavy leaks in the restroom area where they kept tubs to catch the water. She testified that she also used buckets to catch the water that were as tall as Lolley's waist, and she was five feet tall. The buckets and tubs had to be brought out whenever it rained, almost filling all the way and becoming far too heavy for her to lift. Lolley also noticed a PVC pipe in the men's bathroom when she cleaned at the end of the day. Lolley was told by Obed not to discuss anything with prospective buyers.

Evelyn Lolley testified that the roof leaks as much after plaintiffs purchased the building as it did before, but noted that because of a dry spell the leakage wasn't noticeable until September. According to Lolley, the remodeling in the rear of the building had no impact on the amount of leakage. Lolley stated that the Dages were surprised and angry when the roof leaked in their salon. On cross exam, Lolley testified that she did not recall a hail storm in 1998 or 1999 that, according to John Obed, damaged many roofs on Trenton Street.

John Obed testified that after the hail storm in 1998 or 1999, he hired Bob Chandler to repair the roof damage. Chandler employed both of defendants' sons and people from City of Faith, a halfway house, to rebuild the roof. The job cost the

$23,000 the Obeds received from the insurance company for a new roof and took two to three months to complete. There were leaks immediately, but either Chandler or one of defendant's sons tarred the spots, and the leakage stopped. Obed did not know if Chandler, an insurance adjuster, had any training or experience in roof repair or installation.

Obed testified that he told plaintiffs that he had put a 26-gauge metal roof on a year before, and that it should last from 30 to 40 years. Obed verified the sales agreement document, his signature on the document, and the passage, "sold as is for a total consideration."

Obed testified that he visited the building frequently after the sale, and that he and Chandler observed that the ceiling had dropped four inches, likely due to the remodeling work. Obed believed that the wall removed by Stephenson caused the leaks. The Dages and their carpenter deny the existence of any load bearing walls in the building, and they likewise dispute that the ceiling dropped any distance.

Ann McClendon worked as the broker for the sale of the building. McClendon testified that she explained to the plaintiffs what it means to buy a property "as is."

The trial court found that the building possessed a redhibitory defect that diminished the usefulness and/or the value of the building to such a degree that plaintiffs would have bought the building but for a lesser price. The court used Hood's estimate of $35,000 for repairs as the source for its damage award. The Obeds have timely appealed from the trial court's judgment, arguing that plaintiffs knew or should have known of, or should have further investigated the roof's defect.

Discussion

Louisiana Civil Code art. 2520 provides:

> The seller warrants the buyer against redhibitory defects, or vices, in the thing sold.
>
> A defect is redhibitory when it renders the thing useless, or its use so inconvenient that it must be presumed that a buyer would not have bought the thing had he known of the defect. The existence of such a defect gives a buyer the right to obtain rescission of the sale.
>
> A defect is redhibitory also when, without rendering the thing totally useless, it diminishes its usefulness or its value so that it must be presumed that a buyer would still have bought it but for a lesser price. The existence of such a defect limits the right of a buyer to a reduction of the price.

La. C.C. art. 2521 provides:

> The seller owes no warranty for defects in the thing that were known to the buyer at the time of the sale, or for defects that should have been discovered by a reasonably prudent buyer of such things.

* * * * *

"[T]he 'as is' stipulation, especially in the sale of a used thing, means that the thing is not warranted to be in perfect condition and free of all defects which prior usage and age may cause." *Bond v. Broadway,* 607 So.2d 865, 867 (La.App. 2d Cir.1992). The trial court found that the roof was defective. With this ruling, we agree; however, the outcome of this case depends on the buyers' knowledge or what a prudent buyer should have discovered.

In *Lemaire v. Breaux,* 00-1826 (La.App. 5th Cir.04/11/01), 788 So.2d 498, 501-503, the court held that when a purchaser observes stained ceiling tiles and receives a strong recommendation for a roof inspection from her own real estate agent, but said purchaser ignored the strong recommendation for a roof inspection and proceeds with the purchase, a redhibitory claim based upon a leaking roof must fail. If the defect is apparent and could have been discovered by simple inspection, plaintiff has a duty to make a further investigation. A failure to do so waives the right to sue in quanti minoris. *Pursell v. Kelly,* 244 La. 323, 152 So.2d 36 (1963); and *Caple v. Green,* 545 So.2d 1222, (La.App. 2d Cir.1989)

As noted above, Frank Ricks performed the inspection of the building for plaintiffs before they purchased the building. Ricks did not go on the roof during the initial inspection. Ricks observed that the rafters on the underside of the roof were rotten, and that they needed to be repaired. Ricks prepared a report that *"strongly recommended"* plaintiffs hire a structural engineer to inspect the building and that the deteriorated wood be repaired.

Ricks testified that when Obed allowed him onto the roof, he did not actually walk over the roof, as Obed was afraid it would could [sic] cause leaks, but that he was allowed to view the roof from a small flat area. Ricks could tell that there had been serious leaking in the past due to fallen ceiling tiles, rusted ceiling tiles, rotten woodwork in the bathroom, and fallen stucco, all of which Ricks told to the plaintiffs.

Plaintiffs were advised to make sure that the roof was good. Thereafter, defendants dropped the price by $2,500, and plaintiffs dropped the one-year warranty for the roof. A reasonably prudent buyer would have been on notice that the roof was a problem and insured its soundness under the circumstances of this case. A reasonably prudent buyer would have asked for the warranty documents. The trial court based its opinion on the fact that the roof presented a redhibitory defect; however, such a defect was apparent by any reasonable inspection and in this case, made known to the buyer. The trial court's opinion was clearly in error and manifestly erroneous.

Conclusion

For the reasons set forth above, the judgment of the trial court is reversed and judgment ordered in favor of defendants, dismissing plaintiffs' action. Costs are assessed against plaintiffs.

REVERSED AND RENDERED.

Notes and Questions

1. Note that in the foregoing case the parties had included a provision that the Dages were buying the property "as is." However, such a provision does not constitute a waiver of the warranty against redhibitory defects and as such, did not foreclose the plaintiffs' claim. Waivers are discussed in detail in Part D below.

2. Article 2521 negates the warranty for defects which were "known to the buyer at the time of the sale," or for defects that "should have been discovered by a reasonably prudent buyer of such things." LA. CIV. CODE art. 2521. Was the defect in *Dage* known to the buyer at the time of the sale? Should it have been discovered by a reasonably prudent buyer? What obligation does a buyer have to conduct an inspection of the thing prior to the sale? *See also* LA. CIV. CODE art. 2521 cmt. d.

3. As discussed above, to assert a claim for redhibition, the buyer must not have known of the defect in the thing sold. Thus, the buyer who successfully asserts a claim in redhibition may also assert claims for error and fraud. While these claims can be asserted in conjunction with one another, remember that they are distinct theories with their own rules, remedies, and prescriptive periods. For example, while a buyer claiming redhibition must satisfy the requirements discussed above, one asserting unilateral error must show that the error "concerns a cause without which the obligation would not have been incurred and that cause was known or should have been known to the other party." LA. CIV. CODE art. 1949. One asserting fraud must show "a misrepresentation or a suppression of the truth made with the intention either to gain an unjust advantage for one party or to cause a loss or inconvenience to the other." LA. CIV. CODE art. 1953. Also, success on certain claims of redhibition and all claims of fraud allows the aggrieved party to recover attorney fees, whereas success on claims of error does not. Furthermore, claims for error and fraud are subject to a five-year prescriptive period, commencing from the discovery of the error or fraud. LA. CIV. CODE art. 2032. The prescriptive periods for redhibition claims are different and are discussed in Subpart B.2.c below.

4. In cases of multiple sellers, the warranty against redhibitory defects is owed by each seller in proportion to his or her interest. LA. CIV. CODE art. 2538. In cases of multiple buyers, all must concur in an action for rescission because of a redhibitory defect; for an action for a reduction of price, however, one of multiple buyers may bring it in proportion to his or her interest. *Id.* These rules also apply if the thing with a redhibitory defect is transferred, inter vivos or mortis causa, to multiple successors. *Id.*

5. Judicial sales resulting from a seizure are not subject to the rules on redhibition. LA. CIV. CODE art. 2537. In other words, there is no warranty against redhibitory defects on property that is foreclosed upon and sold at an auction. Note, though, that the rule applies only to judicial sales resulting from seizure; it does not apply to other sales held under the supervision of the court (i.e., partition and successions proceedings). Also note that the warranty against eviction is implied in all judicial sales resulting from seizure.

Royal v. Cook

984 So. 2d 156 (La. App. 4 Cir. 2008)

(Court composed of Judge Max N. Tobias, Jr., Judge Edwin A. Lombard, Judge Leon A. Cannizzaro, Jr.).

Max N. Tobias, Jr., Judge.

The defendant, Patsy Cook ("Cook"), appeals the trial court's judgment in favor of Debra and Joel Royal ("the Royals") on their claim for redhibition and breach of contract. After reviewing the record, we affirm the trial court's judgment.

BACKGROUND

On 21 July 2003, Cook sold to the Royals a home located at 121 Rho Street in Belle Chasse, Louisiana, (the "property"). The Royals, having moved from Puerto Rico, were relocating to Belle Chasse for work-related reasons. After Joel Royal made an initial walk-through of the home, the parties entered into an Agreement to Purchase/Sell the property (the "Agreement") on 9 May 2003. The Agreement, which did not contain an "as is" clause, granted the Royals the right to have the property inspected prior to purchase; if the inspection revealed deficiencies, the Royals were given the right to advise Cook of the deficiencies and request that they be remedied. After notification, Cook had the option to either remedy or refuse to remedy the deficiencies. If Cook refused to remedy the deficiencies, the Royals could accept the property in its then present (deficient) condition or void the Agreement.

* * * * *

[Following the purchase of the property,] [o]n 19 July 2004, the Royals filed the instant suit against Cook and GNOHS alleging redhibition, breach of contract, fraud, and damages arising out of the sale of the property. Following a two-day bench trial, the trial court rendered judgment in favor of the Royals and against Cook as follows: $20,244.00, with legal interest from date of judicial demand until paid, for rodent infestation and remediation; $7,545.00 for attorney's fees and court costs; and $8,432.00 for breach of contract. This appeal followed.

DISCUSSION

* * * * *

Redhibition Claim

* * * * *

In Louisiana, "[t]he seller warrants the buyer against redhibitory defects or vices in the thing sold." La. C.C. art. 2520. A defect is redhibitory when it "renders the thing useless, or its use so inconvenient that it must be presumed that the buyer would not have bought the thing had he known of the defect." *Id.* The existence of this type of redhibitory defect provides the buyer with the right to obtain rescission of the sale. *Id.* A thing can also contain a redhibitory defect when the defect "diminishes its usefulness or its value so that it must be presumed the buyer would still have bought it, but for a lesser price." *Id.* This type of redhibitory defect limits the right of a buyer to seek a reduction of the price. *Id.* Pursuant to La. C.C. art. 2530, the warranty extends only to defects that exist at the time of delivery, and there is a presumption that the defect existed at delivery if the defect appears within three days of delivery. Proof that a redhibitory defect existed at the time of sale [sic][±] can be made by direct or circumstantial evidence giving rise to a reasonable inference that the defect existed at the time of sale. *Boos v. Benson Jeep-Eagle Co., Inc.*, 98-1424, p. 3 (La.App. 4 Cir. 6/24/98), 717 So.2d 661, 663. Further, under La. C.C. art. 2521, the seller owes no warranty for defects that were known to the buyer at the time of the sale or for defects that should have been discovered by a reasonably prudent buyer. La. C.C. art. 2522 requires that the buyer must give the seller notice of a redhibitory defect and allow time for the seller to repair the defect; however, if the seller has actual knowledge of the defect, then no notice is required.

While the Royals' petition asserts a claim for a rescission of the sale, and in the alternative, a reduction in the purchase price, our review of the record indicates that the Royals' claim in redhibition is actually limited to a claim for a reduction in the purchase price. The Royals alleged redhibitory defects in the water heater, air conditioner, dishwasher, carpet (stains), kitchen plumbing, backyard swing, and living room wall (resulting from a hole). The trial court concluded that these problems did not constitute redhibitory defects in the home as the Royals or GNOHS either had, or should have had, notice of these issues from the pre-sale inspection of the home. These rulings by the trial court are not at issue on appeal; the only redhibition claim at issue herein involves rat infestation.

1. The Rodent Problem

Cook avers the trial court erred in determining that rodent infestation constitutes a defect entitling the Royals to recover under a theory of redhibition because there was no evidence that the house was "structurally unsound," that repairs were needed, or that repairs were made, which Cook contends must be established in redhibitory actions involving the sale of real estate. Additionally, Cook contends that, to the extent a rodent problem did exist,[5] the trial court erred in finding that the problem was not apparent on ordinary inspection prior to purchase, precluding recovery in redhibition.

While we recognize that prior decisions from this court have looked at "structural soundness" in determining the measure of an award in an action for reduction in purchase price due to a redhibitory defect, no requirement exists that the buyer prove the defect renders the property structurally unsound in order to recover in a redhibitory action against the seller as contained in Book III, Title VII, Chapter 9 of the Louisiana Civil Code entitled, "Redhibition." Further, while section (d) of the

---

± [Note the court's misstatement of the law on this point — a redhibitory defect need not exist at the time of the sale but must exist at the time of delivery. *See* La. Civ. Code art. 2530. *Eds.*]

5. Cook contends that, while she previously experienced a problem with rats in the attic in or about 1987–1988, the problem was completely eradicated long before the sale of the property in July 2003.

Revision Comments following La. C.C. art. 2541 states that "[i]n sales of immovable property the amount to be awarded is the amount necessary to convert an unsound structure into a sound one," this comment neither defines what constitutes a redhibitory defect, nor has the effect of law as to calculating the reduction in price of an immovable resulting from a redhibitory defect. As noted *above,* La. C.C. art. 2520 specifically defines a redhibitory defect as follows: "[a] defect is redhibitory . . . when . . . it diminishes [the thing's] value so that it must be presumed that a buyer would still have bought it but for a lesser price." Thus, the issue before us is whether the rodent problem diminished the value of the home such that the Royals would have purchased the property, but for a lesser price.

The evidence established an abundance of rat feces was discovered in and beneath the attic insulation and in the walls of the property within days of the act of sale, and that the Royals personally witnessed several rats hop onto the roof of the property, enter the attic through the eves, and heard the rats scurrying about in the attic. Thereafter, the Royals placed rat traps in the attic. They testified that they caught at least 10 rats, and removed approximately 20 dead rats and carcasses in various stages of decomposition from underneath the insulation and attic floor decking. Further, the record contains evidence that repairs were made and that steps were taken by the Royals to clean and disinfect the affected areas, and remediating any bio-hazard caused by the decaying rats and rat feces. They also obtained an estimate to disinfect the walls and other affected areas. Moreover, Joel and Debra Royal each testified that, had they known that a rat problem existed in the attic and walls prior to their purchase of the property, they would not have gone through with the act of sale. The record also contains testimony that in attempting to sell the property, upon disclosing to prospective buyers of the previous rodent infestation, the Royals had received no viable offers to purchase as of the time of trial.

The trial court, citing La. C.C. art. 2520, determined that "rodent infestation, in any form, could diminish the value of a home such that the buyer might have still bought it, but for a lower price." We agree with this conclusion. This court takes judicial notice that rodents can gnaw through wood, electrical wiring, sheetrock, et cetera, causing an imperfection or redhibitory defect in real property within the meaning of La. C.C. art. 2520. Based on our review of the evidence, we cannot say that the decision of the trial court finding that the rat infestation at issue constituted a vice or defect in the property was manifestly erroneous or clearly wrong.

However, not all redhibitory vices or defects justify rescission or reduction of the price. Apparent defects, which the buyer can discover through a simple inspection, are excluded from the seller's legal warranty. La. C.C. art. 2521. A defect is apparent if a reasonably prudent buyer, acting under similar circumstances, would discover it through a simple inspection of the property. *David v. Thibodeaux,* 04-0976, p. 3 (La.App. 1 Cir. 5/11/05), 916 So.2d 214, 217. Factors to be considered in determining whether an inspection is reasonable include knowledge and expertise of the buyer, the opportunity for inspection, and assurances made by the seller. *Crowe v. Laurie,* 98-0648, p. 6 (La.App. 1 Cir. 2/19/99), 729 So.2d 703, 707-708. Whether a defect is apparent to the buyer of a home by reasonable inspection is a question of fact. *See David*, 04-0976, p. 3, 916 So.2d at 217.

In the instant case, Cook avers that the Royals, seasoned home buyers, failed to conduct a reasonable inspection of the property prior to sale, which would have revealed a rodent problem in the attic necessitating further inspection. The record reveals that, at the time of the execution of the Agreement, the Royals were stationed and residing in Puerto Rico. Joel Royal had come to Belle Chasse in May 2003 on military orders, and while there, looked to purchase a house for his family due to his impending reassignment to the area. He testified that he first viewed Cook's house with an agent and that Cook was not present. Candles were burning in the home. During this initial visit, Mr. Royal testified that his main objective was to ascertain whether the floor plan and square footage of the home would accommodate his family's needs. He briefly viewed the house a second time prior to his return to Puerto Rico. Despite his request that no artificial fragrances be used, again candles were burning. On one of the two visits, Mr. Royal briefly looked at the attic, but he did so to determine if it had storage space. He did not notice any fecal matter or smell a foul odor. Mr. Royal's testimony was that Cook was not present on this second occasion. According to Mr. Royal, he briefly met Cook for the first time at the agent's office for purposes of signing the Agreement.

The Royals retained GNOHS to perform the professional inspection of the property prior to sale. Under the circumstances, we find it was not unreasonable for the Royals to rely on the professional services of an inspection company (rather than their own) to inspect the property for possible defects or deficiencies. This professional inspection included an inspection of the attic, which noted that the insulation was thinning and needed to be replaced. The GNOHS report, however, was devoid of any mention of observable rodent feces or the presence of rat poison bags in the attic suggestive of rodent infestation. Further, the record establishes that the rat carcasses, which were found in various stages of decomposition by the Royals after the act of sale when they were removing the attic insulation, as well as different bags of rat poison, were nestled and/or covered up by insulation alone, or by plywood decking (forming the attic floor) covering the insulation. Testimony and photographs further show that extensive amounts of rodent feces were in the walls and behind baseboards in several areas; this was discovered by the Royals within days of moving in after they commenced renovations.

The trial court concluded that the Royals "did not know of the rodent infestation and that a reasonably prudent buyer would not have known of the infestation," because "the extent of the infestation was clearly hidden to a reasonably prudent buyer." The trial court further determined that "most reasonably prudent buyers would not remove baseboards or open walls to see if rodents and/or rodent feces are located in those places." The record supports the trial court's finding. We are also of the opinion that the rodent infestation could not have been discovered by simple inspection. It was necessary to remove the attic insulation, baseboards, and drywall to see the damage. Accordingly, we do not find that the trial court was manifestly erroneous or clearly wrong in its finding that the rodent infestation constituted a redhibitory defect that was not apparent to the Royals prior to the act of sale.[12]

* * * * *

Notes and Questions

1. The court in *Royal* articulates a set of factors to be considered in determining whether an inspection is reasonable. What are those factors? According to those factors, did the buyer in this case conduct a reasonable inspection of the property? Why or why not?

2. Both *Dage* and *Royal* explored the buyers' actual or constructive knowledge of the defects at issue. The issue of the buyer's knowledge is frequently litigated. Another case that addressed the buyer's knowledge of a redhibitory defect was *Hancock v. Lauzon*, 161 So. 3d 957 (La. App. 2 Cir. 2015). In that case, after allegedly one instance of flooding, the sellers installed a sump pump on the property. When listing the property for sale, the sellers noted this fact. However, on the property disclosure statement, they checked "no" in response to the question whether the property had ever experienced flooding, water intrusion, accumulation, or drainage problems. After the sale, the property flooded eight times and upon the installation of a second sump pump, the buyers discovered an eight-inch french drain and a concrete drainage ditch that had been covered by rocks and debris in the back of the property. The drainpipe was not visible or noticeable until they began digging out the area to install the second sump pump. The buyers sued in redhibition, and the sellers filed motions for summary judgment, alleging that the defect was apparent given the slope of the land and the MLS listing. The appellate court reversed the trial court's grant of summary judgment, noting that the sellers' disclosure statement was inconsistent with their actions in installing a sump pump. The court noted the existence of material issues of fact as to whether the sellers were truthful in their disclosure and also whether the buyers, without inspecting the property immediately after a rainstorm, could reasonably have discovered the drainage defect.

3. The Louisiana Residential Property Disclosure Act (RPDA) requires sellers of residential immovable property to furnish purchasers with a Property Disclosure Document. *See* La. Rev. Stat. §§ 9:3195–3200. This disclosure is generally required for any transfer of an interest in immovable property (including sales, exchanges, bond for deed contracts, leases with option to purchase, or any other options to purchase), although numerous transactions are exempted from its reach (including court-ordered transfers, transfers made by a succession representative, and transfers between co-owners, blood relatives, and spouses, among others). La. Rev. Stat. § 9:3197. The Louisiana Real Estate Commission is charged with the responsibility

---

12. We reject Cook's argument that the stench from the attic (which, because of the burning candles at the time of the inspections, was not detected by Mrs. Royal until after moving into the home) or the thinning attic insulation required the Royals to investigate further by actually lifting the insulation in order to discover the rodent problem. * * *

of promulgating a form Property Disclosure Document. LA. REV. STAT. §9:3198. While sellers are not required to use this form, the disclosure statement prepared by the seller must meet the minimum requirements of the form prepared by the Real Estate Commission. *Id.* The Property Disclosure Document requires sellers to disclose the existence of numerous defects and conditions in the property including (but not limited to) the existence of servitudes burdening the property, the occurrence of flooding, past or current infestations of termites or other wood-destroying insects, structural defects and defects in the plumbing, water, gas, sewerage, electrical, or heating and cooling systems and appliances. *Id.* Disclosure of a defect in the Property Disclosure Document may place the buyer on notice of the existence of the defect, thereby defeating the buyer's redhibition claim. *See, e.g., Newton v. Dongieux,* 145 So. 3d 478, 484 (La. App. 5 Cir. 2014).

Additionally, a seller's misrepresentation in the Property Disclosure Document may expose the seller to liability in redhibition as a bad faith seller, as well as to liability for fraud. *Stutts v. Melton,* 130 So. 3d 808, 814 (La. 2013). However, even if the seller affirmatively misrepresents the existence of defects in the Property Disclosure Document, a buyer who either knew or should have known of the defects will be foreclosed from recovering under either theory. *See, e.g., Louapre v. Booher,* 216 So. 3d 1044, 1053 (La. App. 4 Cir. 2016); *Vanek v. Seeber,* 29 So. 3d 582, 587–88 (La. App. 1 Cir. 2009).

4. It is typical in real estate sales that the buyer will obtain a professional inspection of the property to be purchased. In the event that the home inspector fails to give correct information to the buyer, the buyer may sue the inspector. Note, however, that no such action "whether based in tort, breach of contract, or otherwise . . . shall be brought unless filed in a court of competent jurisdiction and proper venue within one year from the date the act, omission, or neglect is alleged to have occurred." LA. REV. STAT. §9:5608.

Rey v. Cuccia

298 So. 2d 840 (La. 1974)

TATE, Justice.

The buyer ("Rey") sues to recover the purchase price paid for a camper trailer, alleging that, because of redhibitory defect, it had come apart after a short period of use. Made defendant are the seller ("Cuccia") and manufacturer ("Yellowstone") of the trailer. The court of appeal affirmed the trial court's dismissal of the action, 284 So.2d 66 (La.App.4th Cir. 1973), certiorari granted, 288 So.2d 352 (La.1974).

1.

The plaintiff Rey purchased the trailer from Cuccia on May 27, 1971, and drove it to his home, a distance of less than ten miles. It was not used again until June 4, eight days later, when Rey and his family drove to Dauphin Island, Alabama, a distance of 125 miles. On the return trip to New Orleans two days later, the trailer commenced swerving back and forth on the highway. After stopping, Rey found that the trailer body had come loose from its frame, the frame was buckled, and the right rear of the trailer body was down toward the ground.

At the time of this serious breakage, the trailer had been used in total for just slightly over 200 miles, all on major paved highways.

The previous courts held that the buyer had failed to prove that any redhibitory defect had caused the break-up of the trailer so soon after its purchase. They felt that, since the collapse occurred just four miles after the buyer's wife commenced driving the vehicle, it is likely that her inexperience may have been the cause of the mishap.

In our opinion, the previous courts held the buyer to too strict a burden in rejecting his proof of a redhibitory defect as the cause of the break-up during normal use of the recently purchased trailer. Further, as we shall note, there is absolutely no evidence that the driving of the buyer's wife contributed to the collapse.

2.

In Louisiana sales, the seller is bound by an implied warranty that the thing sold is free of hidden defects and is reasonably fit for the product's intended use. Civil Code Articles 2475 [R.C.C. 2475], 2476 [R.C.C. 2475], 2520 [R.C.C. 2520]; *Media Production Consultants, Inc. v. Mercedes-Benz of North America, Inc.,* 262 La. 80, 262 So.2d 377 (1972). The seller, of course, can limit this warranty by declaring to the buyer the hidden defects at the time of the sale, Article 2522 [R.C.C. 2521], or can otherwise limit his obligations as seller, providing he do so clearly and unambiguously, Article 2474 [R.C.C. 2474 & 2548].

A redhibitory defect entitling the buyer to annul the sale is some defect in the manufacture or design of a thing sold "'which renders it either absolutely useless, or its use so inconvenient and imperfect, that it must be supposed that the buyer would not have purchased it, had he known of the vice.'" Article 2520 [R.C.C. 2520]. Upon proof of such a defect, the buyer is entitled to annul the sale and recover the purchase price, rather than being limited to recovering the cost of curing any such substantial defects. *Prince v. Paretti Pontiac Company, Inc.,* 281 So.2d 112 (La.1973).

The buyer must prove that the defect existed before the sale was made to him. Article 2530 [R.C.C. 2530]. However, if he proves that the product purchased is not reasonably fit for its intended use, it is sufficient that he prove that the object is thus defective, without his being required to prove the exact or underlying cause for its malfunction. *J.B. Beaird Co. v. Burris Bros.,* 216 La. 655, 44 So.2d 693 (1949); *Crawford v. Abbott Automobile Co., Ltd.,* 157 La. 59, 101 So. 871 (1924); *Stumpf v. Metairie Motor Sales, Inc.,* 212 So.2d 705 (La.App.4th Cir. 1968); *Fisher v. City Sales and Service,* 128 So.2d 790 (La.App.3d Cir. 1961).

The buyer may prove the existence of redhibitory defects at the time of the sale not only by direct evidence of eyewitnesses, but also by circumstantial evidence giving rise to the reasonable inference that the defect existed at the time of the sale. *Fisher v. City Sales and Service,* 128 So.2d 790 (La.App.3d Cir. 1961); *Mattes v. Heintz,*

69 So.2d 924 (La.App.Orl.1954); *Standard Motor Car Co. v. St. Amant*, 134 So. 279) La.App.1st Cir. 1931). As stated in *Jordan v. Travelers Insurance Co.*, 257 La. 995, 245 So.2d 151, 155: "* * * proof by direct or circumstantial evidence is sufficient to constitute a preponderance when, taking the evidence as a whole, such proof shows the fact or causation sought to be proved is more probable than not."

If the defect appears within three days following the sale, it is presumed to have existed before the sale. Article 2537 [R.C.C. 2530]. However, even where the defect appears more than three days after the sale (as here, when it appeared on the second day of use, buy ten days after the sale), if it appears soon after the thing is put into use, a reasonable inference may arise, in the absence of other explanation or intervening cause shown, that she [sic] defect existed at the time of the sale.[±] *Andries v. Nelson*, 46 So.2d 333 (La.App.1st Cir. 1950); *Standard Motor Car Co. v. St. Amant*, 134 So. 279 (La.App.1st Cir. 1931). See, for similar principle, when a constructed thing fails shortly after being put into use. *Joyner v. Aetna Casualty & Surety Co.*, 259 La. 660, 251 So.2d 166 (1971).

3.

Tested by these standards, the buyer Rey met his burden of proving that a redhibitory defect existed at the time of the sale. We find no difficulty in holding the seller Cuccia liable for such redhibitory defect. (The liability of the manufacturer Yellowstone presents a more difficult issue. See part 5 below of this opinion.)

Rey purchased the 18-foot 2700-pound camper trailer from Cuccia on May 27, 1961. The price of $2510.15 included the installation, at Cuccia's direction and order, of a trailer hitch on the Rey automobile which would be used to haul the trailer. Improper installation of this hitch, as will be noted, is one of the factors assigned as causing the break-up of the trailer.

As earlier stated, the trailer breakage occurred when the vehicle had been used slightly more than 200 miles, all on good paved roads. The buyer Rey had driven the vehicle to an Alabama park, a distance of some 125 miles, and for about 80 miles of the return trip, all without incident. Three-to-four miles before the accident, he and his wife changed as drivers of the automobile hauling the trailer, in order to give her some experience preparatory to a vacation trip planned for later that summer.

Mrs. Rey drove slowly, at a speed of 30-35 mph, in the right-hand lane of the Interstate highway. When another vehicle passed on her left, the trailer behind her immediately began to swing, pulling the car first to the left, then right, and then left again. The wife held the wheel straight, controlling the tandem of car and trailer, and brought it to a slow stop in the right emergency lane off the travel-lanes. At no time did the vehicles leave the highway surface. Other testimony established that neither the husband nor wife hit anything in the road while driving, nor was the trailer ever involved in any other untoward incident.

± [Note that the defect must exist at delivery under current law. *Eds.*]

When the vehicle stopped, it was discovered that the trailer-body had pulled loose from the frame, that the frame was buckled, and that the right rear of the body dragged toward the ground. Other damage had occurred due to buckling and wrenching of the exterior and interior of the trailer. A repair estimate totaled $1,338.18, without including all the damages involved.

By a mechanic witness, the buyer Rey made some effort to prove, as cause of the incident, that the process of spot-welding the trailer body to the frame was inadequate; that the spot-welds, even if correctly done, were too far apart (18 inches) to hold the body on the frame under stress. Three to five spot-welds had, in fact, broken. The mechanic's opinion was that the frame had collapsed over the wheel, and the body had come loose from the frame, because of some structural deficiency in the rear of the trailer.

As the previous courts held, the preponderance of the evidence does not prove a structural deficiency or inadequate number of spot-welds to be the cause of the trailer break-up. (On the other hand, it does not negative the possibility that the particular three-to-five spot-welds which came loose had individually been defectively done.)

The failure to prove inadequate welding to be the cause of the trailer break-up does not defeat the buyer's cause of action. If the purchased vehicle breaks up soon after it is put into use, then this in itself (in the absence of other cause shown) may be evidence of a redhibitory defect, without the buyer being held to prove the specific cause of the vehicle's break-up.

The chief thrust of the defense against this redhibitory action is the suggestion that the vehicle-collapse occurred because Mrs. Rey, an inexperienced trailer-hauler, may have swung too sharply in an overcompensation of the sway caused when a vehicle passed her.[1] However, the uncontradicted evidence established that no such overcompensation took place. The opinion that the incident and break-up [m]ight have been caused by such driver reaction is negated by the clear testimony that the wife did not so react and that there was no misuse of the trailer during its short period of use by either of the drivers.[2]

---

1. The defendants' witnesses testify that this might cause too sharp a shift of stress and weight, causing the vehicle body to 'bottom' on the wheel-axis as the spring flexed, resulting in a severe impact which caused the body to come loose from the frame as well as the other damage.

2. If indeed the trailer was so sensitive to sway when used by an inexperienced driver, this itself might be a redhibitory defect. As the dissenting judge in the court of appeal stated, 284 So.2d 72: "Even if driver reaction to unexpected sway contributed to the trailer collapse in the present case, the manufacturer who knew of this possible hazard was obliged to warn its prospective users (who were not aware of the hazard). Absent this warning, a normal driver reaction should be considered normal use. The manufacturer did not offer the trailer for sale only to persons experienced in driving trailers. If the normal reaction of an inexperienced driver resulted in a collapsed trailer, then the manufacturer should not be allowed to defend on the basis that the trailer collapsed in abnormal use."

Since no abnormal and unforeseeable use or other intervening cause is proved, the collapse of the trailer during normal and foreseeable use, after only 200 miles or so after the dale, raises the strong inference that the trailer would not have collapsed in the absence of a latent defect.

Additionally, the evidence of the manufacturer's expert indicates, as a possible cause of the break-up, an improper installation of the trailer hitch on the automobile by Cuccia part of the sales transaction. Installed at 24 inches above the ground, rather than at 18 inches as specified by the manufacturer's manual, such improperly installed trailer-hitch could have caused or contributed to sway and to abnormal stresses and strains during use of the trailer.

We therefore hold that the circumstantial evidence clearly proves, at least against the seller Cuccia, that a redhibitory defect existed at the time of the sale of the trailer, which included Cuccia's installation of the trailer hitch.

4.

The buyer's case against the manufacturer Yellowstone is not as clear. In the first place, the improper hitch-installation by the seller Cuccia may cast into doubt whether any other underlying redhibitory defect existed at the time the manufacturer delivered the trailer to Cuccia. In the second place, Yellowstone had sold the trailer to Cuccia more than a year before Cuccia sold it to Rey—although the evidence shows that, during Cuccia's possession, the trailer was not used except occasionally to move it from one part of Cuccia's lot to another, the inference is not as strong that the defect existed at the time the manufacturer Yellowstone transferred the vehicle to the seller Cuccia, as it is that the defect existed at the time of the sale, just ten days before the defect appeared after slightly over 200 miles of use.

Preliminarily, we should observe that we find no merit to the manufacturer's contention that it could not be held liable directly to the buyer for a redhibitory defect existing at the time is sold that vehicle to Cuccia. In so contending, the manufacturer relies upon the lack of privity between it and the ultimate buyer, Rey, and on the circumstance that its own sale had occurred more than a year before the resale by Cuccia to Rey and before the breakage.

When the sale is annulled for a redhibitory defect resulting from the original manufacture, the purchaser can recover the pecuniary loss resulting from the unusable thing sold from the manufacturer as well as the seller. *Media Productions Consultant v. Mercedes-Benz of N.A., Inc.*, cited above. As there stated, 262 La. 80, 262 So.2d 377: "Louisiana has aligned itself with the consumer-protection rule, by allowing a consumer without privity to recover, whether the suit be strictly in tort or upon implied warranty." In effect, the consumer's cause of action, which is based upon the breach of the sale's implied warranty, is enforceable directly against the manufacturer, who himself is by law bound to the same implied warranty.

The consumer's action is enforceable against the manufacturer at the same time and at least within the same year following the sale to the consumer, Article 2534 [R.C.C. 2534], as it is enforceable against the seller. The manufacturer is presumed to know of the defect in the thing made by him. *Radalec, Incorporated v. Automatic Firing Corp.*, 228 La. 116, 81 So.2d 830 (1955); *Tuminello v. Mawby*, 220 La. 733, 57 So.2d 666 (1952); *George v. Shreveport Cotton Oil Co.*, 114 La. 498, 38 So. 432 (1905). The one-year limitation on redhibitory actions does not apply where the seller (manufacturer) had knowledge of the defect buy [sic] failed to declare it at the time of the sale. Article 2534 [R.C.C. 2534]. In such instance, the consumer may institute the action to recover for the redhibitory defect within the year following his discovery of it. Article 2546 [R.C.C. 2534].

5.

The chief witness relied upon by Yellowstone was Lawrence Drudge, Yellowstone's production manager. He was qualified as an expert in the repair and supervision of repairs for such trailers.

He testified that he found no fault in the construction or design of the camper trailer. He did testify that the trailer hitch was improperly installed on the Rey automobile at 24 inches from the ground.

The Yellowstone manual specified that it should be installed 18 inches from the ground, and Drudge testified that in no case should it be more than 19 or 19½ inches from the ground. The reason is that a higher installation would cause a difference in the weight distribution between the two vehicles, tending to exaggerate any sway. This, of course, would cause more than normal stresses and strains and would tend, on the sway, to cause the body to compress the spring on one side or the other more deeply than if the hitch were installed at the proper height.

The witness opined that the damages to the Rey trailer were similar to those which resulted from severe swaying. The witness listed as principal causes of undue sway of a trailer which result in the need for repairs: (1) an improper hitch from towing vehicle to trailer (as here); (2) high winds; (3) the suction effect caused by high speed vehicles passing, which tends to result in overcompensation by the driver; and (4) "the biggest one we have found" is inexperience of the driver of the towing vehicle.

By the last, he explained, he meant that an inexperienced driver tended to steer the opposite way the trailer was swaying, causing it to sway back. This then may result in the driver's steering the opposite way, causing an accentuated sway back again, eventually causing the trailer body to rock over hard and sometimes to "bottom out" (the impact of the body drives the wheel through the wheel well) and, perhaps, wrench loose, similar to the damage which resulted in the present case.

The substance of Drudge's testimony is that the damage resulted when the trailer bottomed out due to severe swaying.

We may note at this point that the Yellowstone owner's guide furnished with the vehicle does not warn against such hazards, nor does the manual's suggestion as to installation of the trailer hitch ("'The top of the hitch should be 18 from the ground on most models.'") warn about the dire consequences resulting, according to Drudge, if the trailer is installed at higher than 18 inches. No other witness than Drudge testified as to this danger, and there is no evidence that the seller Cuccia had any reason to appreciate any undue hazard to result from installing the trailer-hitch six inches higher than recommended "'for most models'".

Under cross-examination, Drudge also admitted that the damage found could have resulted if, as the vehicle was swaying, the frame came loose and the trailer body fell on the wheel well.

Considering the evidence as a whole, we conclude that the preponderance of the evidence proves that the trailer break-up resulted from a defect in construction or design which existed at the time the manufacturer Yellowstone sold the trailer to the seller Cuccia.

The evidence indicates that, until it collapsed after 200 miles of use, it had been kept on Cuccia's lot without any use, except a move 50 or 75 feet or so to make room for another trailer. As previously noted, driver mal-use is not proven to be a cause of the collapse of the trailer.[3]

Cuccia's improper installation of the trailer hitch may have contributed to the severe swaying and to unusual stresses and strains during the 200 miles of customer use. Nevertheless, Yellowstone should not be exonerated from liability for defective functioning of the camper-trailer because a trailer-hitch, necessarily contemplated by a sale of the camper-trailer, was installed six inches higher than weakly recommended by the manual. There is no warning that there might be such damage occasioned as was here by the failure to so install the hitch. If the trailer were so constructed that such a slight deviation from a recommended procedure of installation of the hitch would cause this type of damage, then this constitutes a defect for which the manufacturer would be responsible, absent at least some warning of the danger involved.

The evidence, in effect, negatives any other than a redhibitory defect in the manufacture or design of the trailer as the cause of the break-up of the trailer, even though Cuccia's improper installation of the trailer-hitch may have contributed to the vehicle's malfunctioning.

6.

Under the 1968 amendment to Article 2545 [R.C.C. 2545]: "The seller, who knows the vice of the thing he sells and omits to declare it, besides the restitution of price and repayment of the expenses, *including reasonable attorneys' fees*, is answerable to the buyer in damages." (Italics ours.) A manufacturer is presumed to know of the defects of the products he sells. In this instance, the retailer Cuccia, who ordered

---

3. Indeed, if such should happen within four miles, because another vehicle passed an inexperienced driver, such condition should be a redhibitory defect in itself, in the absence of strong warning by the manufacturer that the vehicle was sold only for use to experienced drivers, not to the general public, or of strong caution of the dangers involved in driving on the highways when passed by other vehicles.

the installation of the trailer hitch as part of his sale of the product, is presumed to know of the defect in this installation. Therefore, both Cuccia and Yellowstone are liable for such attorneys' fees.

The evidence in the record justifies an award of attorneys['] [sic] fees in the amount of one thousand dollars.

Conclusion

The buyer is therefore entitled to recover the sum of $2510.15, the purchase price of the vehicle, plus $1,000 attorneys' fees. The buyer is entitled to recover this amount from the seller and the manufacturer as solidarily liable.

Accordingly, there will be judgment in favor of the plaintiff, Armand J. Rey, and against the defendants, Robert E. Cuccia and Yellowstone, Inc., holding them liable in the amount of three thousand five hundred and ten and 15/100 ($3,510.15) dollars, together with all costs and legal interest thereon from date of judicial demand, conditioned upon the return of the camper-trailer to Cuccia.

Reversed and rendered.

SUMMERS, J., dissents for the reasons assigned.

MARCUS, J., recused.

SUMMERS, Justice (dissenting).

Both lower courts found, and I agree, that there is no evidence to establish any inherent defect or vice in the trailer. Each of the courts below attributed the accident to the suction effect caused by a high speed vehicle passing, which tends to result in over compensation by the driver. They found that Mrs. Rey was inexperienced and over-reacted to the swaying caused by the passing vehicle. This conclusion is corroborated by the absence of incident during the first 125 miles of the trip during which Mr. Rey, an experienced driver, was at the wheel. The laborious effort of the Court's opinion to de-emphasize these facts is unconvincing to say the least. The case presents nothing buy a factual question. This Court is not warranted in overruling both courts on this record. I agree with the opinion of the Court of Appeal. See 284 So.2d 71. I would uphold that adjudication.

Notes and Questions

1. Note that the buyer in *Rey* brought suit against both his immediate vendor and the manufacturer of the trailer. Louisiana's law of redhibition provides that the buyer is subrogated to the seller's claims against other persons (including the seller's own seller). *See* LA. CIV. CODE art. 2548. The topic of subrogation is discussed in Part E. of this Chapter.

2. Note that current law clearly requires that the defect exist at the time of *delivery* and also clearly provides for a presumption in the event that the defect appears within three days of delivery. LA. CIV. CODE art. 2530. Prior law required that the defect exist at the time of the *sale*, so of course, older jurisprudence will recite that rule. Unfortunately, some recent cases erroneously do so, as well. For additional

cases addressing the timing of the existence of the defect, see *Cadiere v. Wholesale Autoplex, L.L.C.*, 2015 WL 3613154 (La. App. 1 Cir. 2015), and *Arant v. Wal-Mart Stores, Inc.*, 2015 WL 1419335 (W.D. La. 2015).

The court in *Rey* expounded upon the three-day rule in Article 2530 to hold that even where the defect appears more than three days after the sale, if it appears soon after the thing is put into use, a reasonable inference may arise, in the absence of other explanation or intervening cause shown, that the defect existed at the requisite time. The Louisiana First Circuit Court of Appeal went even further in *Griffin v. Coleman Oldsmobile, Inc.*, 424 So. 2d 1116 (La. App. 1 Cir. 1982), holding that defects appearing more than three days after the sale may be inferred to have pre-existed the sale when such defects usually do not result from ordinary use. 424 So. 2d at 1118. It appears that the redactors of the 1995 Sales revision intended to preserve the courts' expansive approach. *See* La. Civ. Code art. 2530 cmt. c.

3. What, according to the court in *Rey*, is the plaintiff's burden of proof with respect to the defect? Must the buyer prove the cause of the underlying defect? Is it sufficient to show merely that a defect exists?

4. Note also that the Court in *Rey* referred to the warranty against redhibition and the warranty of fitness for use interchangeably. However, under current law, the warranty against redhibitory defects is not synonymous with the warranty of fitness. The latter is discussed in Subpart F.5 below.

B. Seller's Good or Bad Faith

In the event that a buyer has a valid claim for breach of the warranty against redhibitory defects, it must be determined whether the seller is in good or bad faith. This determination affects the seller's right to notice and opportunity for repair, the buyer's remedies, and the prescriptive period applicable to the redhibition claim. The buyer bears the burden of proving the seller's bad faith. *Guillot v. Doughty*, 142 So. 3d 1034 (La. App. 1 Cir. 2014). Subpart 1 below provides insight as to how to determine whether a seller is in good or bad faith. Subpart 2 discusses why that determination is significant.

1. Determining the Good or Bad Faith of the Seller
La. Civ. Code arts. 2531, 2545

Louisiana Civil Code Article 2531 addresses the liability of a seller "who did not know that the thing he sold had a defect." La. Civ. Code art. 2531. Although the Civil Code does not expressly identify such a seller as one in "good faith," doctrine and commentary refer to a seller who is ignorant of the defect in this manner. *See* 24 Dian Tooley-Knoblett & David Gruning, Louisiana Civil Law Treatise, Sales § 11:11, n.1 (2017). Louisiana Civil Code Article 2545 addresses the liability of a seller "who knows that the thing he sells has a defect but omits to declare it" or one "who declares that the thing has a quality that he knows it does not have." La. Civ.

CODE art. 2545. Again, while the term is not used in the Civil Code, doctrine and commentary refer to sellers such as these as "bad faith" sellers. 24 DIAN TOOLEY-KNOBLETT & DAVID GRUNING, LOUISIANA CIVIL LAW TREATISE, SALES § 11:11, n.1 (2017). Article 2545 also provides that a seller is "deemed to know that the thing he sells has a redhibitory defect when he is a manufacturer of that thing." LA. CIV. CODE art. 2545. Note that the word "deemed" is not synonymous with a presumption. Presumptions are rebuttable; a "deeming" is not. Thus, the manufacturer can never be in good faith if a defect in fact exists. LA. CIV. CODE art. 2545 cmt b. The case below provides an illustration of a bad faith seller deemed to know of the defect.

Bearly v. Brunswick Mercury Marine Div.

888 So. 2d 309 (La. App. 2 Cir. 2004)

CARAWAY, J.

Plaintiff seeks return of the purchase price of a boat and motor from the wholesaler of the boat and motor. Plaintiff alleged that the defendant manufacturer outfitted its product with another manufacturer's motor which was incompatible for use with the boat. Plaintiff alleged that the defendant knew of the motor's incompatibility at the time of its assembly with the boat, but that it marketed the boat wholesale to plaintiff's marine dealer despite the defective condition. Defendant challenged plaintiff's ability to prove its advance knowledge of the defect with a motion for summary judgment which was granted by the trial court. Finding that defendant's knowledge of the defect is immaterial to plaintiff's claim under either our products liability law or in redhibition, we reverse.

Facts

Plaintiff, Floyd Bearly, purchased a Ranger boat and Mercury motor from Reeves Marine ("Reeves"), a boat retailer. Bearly alleged that he immediately began experiencing problems with the motor which necessitated returning to Reeves for repair work on several occasions. He filed suit against Brunswick, Mercury Marine Division ("Brunswick"), the manufacturer of the motor, and Wood Manufacturing Company, d/b/a Ranger Boats ("Ranger"), the manufacturer of the boat. Bearly sought return of the purchase price, unspecified damages, and attorney fees.

The pertinent allegations of Bearly's petition are as follows:

9.

In the time spent trying to continually repair the broken and cracked reeds in the Mercury Boat, Petitioner has discovered that whenever the Mercury Motor is idling around, the reeds in the Motor get blown out or cracked. Petitioner has even spoken with representatives of Brunswick and members of its racing team, and they have indicated to him that this type of Mercury Motor on this type of Ranger Boat will not work properly.

* * *

20.

Petitioner was informed by representatives of Brunswick Corporation that the representatives of Wood were well aware of the fact that this particular Mercury motor was not a suitable design for this type of Ranger Boat, but that Wood decided to go ahead and market this Mercury Motor and Ranger Boat together anyway.

21.

Petitioner alleges that Wood knew of the design problem with the Mercury Motor for this particular Ranger Boat prior to the sale of the Mercury Motor and Ranger Boat to Petitioner, but Wood failed to take any actions to solve it.

Ranger filed an answer and incidental demand, generally denying the allegations made by Bearly and countering that Brunswick indemnify Ranger for any damages arising from Bearly's suit.

After discovery, Ranger filed a motion for summary judgment based on a lack of evidence supporting the allegation that Ranger knew the Mercury motor and the Ranger boat were incompatible but marketed them together anyway. Ranger offered the supporting affidavit of Bill Beatty, a technical account manager for Brunswick when Bearly's problems arose. Beatty averred that he never told Bearly the Mercury motor was not suitable for the Ranger boat.

Ranger also attached Brunswick's answers to interrogatories denying that its representatives or employees ever told Bearly the Mercury motor would not work properly in tandem with the Ranger boat, or that Ranger was aware of any such incompatibility. Brunswick also denied the existence of any internal documents so indicating.

Bearly's opposition included his own affidavit and answers to interrogatories describing conversations with three different Brunswick representatives who allegedly informed him of such incompatibility. The affidavit also stated that Beatty told Bearly he had informed Ranger of the problem. The affidavit of Kevin Parker, a mechanic at Reeves, describing several telephone conversations with Brunswick's employee Randy Hankwitz was also submitted. Hankwitz informed Parker that the motor was a performance engine, not suitable for extended idling, and thus unsuitable for the bass boat.

After the hearing, the trial court granted Ranger's motion for summary judgment and dismissed Bearly's claims against it. The trial court determined that since the affidavits of Bearly and Parker were based upon the hearsay statements of others regarding Ranger's knowledge of the alleged defect, Bearly had not shown that he could meet his burden of proof at trial. Bearly appeals the judgment on the grounds that his opposition affidavits established genuine issues of material fact based upon the personal knowledge of the affiants.

Discussion

Our review of the parties' briefs to this court and the trial court reveals the glaring omission of any discussion of the cause of action existing between Bearly and Ranger. Instead, the parties debated in a vacuum whether there was undisputed evidence that Brunswick had notified Ranger that the Mercury motor was incompatible for installation on the boat Ranger marketed wholesale to Reeves. Since we find that Ranger, as the alleged assembler of the two products, may be responsible under the Louisiana Products Liability Act (La. R.S. 9:2800.51, *et seq.*) (the "LPLA") or in redhibition (La. C.C. arts. 2520, *et seq.*) *without actual knowledge* of its defectively assembled product, the issue of its knowledge contested in this summary judgment proceeding is not dispositive of the case.

* * * * *

The two redhibition articles of the Civil Code which directly address manufacturers are Articles 2531 and 2545. Regarding the seller without knowledge of the defect, Article 2531 provides:

> A seller who is held liable for a redhibitory defect has an action against the manufacturer of the defective thing, if the defect existed at the time the thing was delivered by the manufacturer to the seller, for any loss the seller sustained because of the redhibition. Any contractual provision that attempts to limit, diminish or prevent such recovery by a seller against the manufacturer shall have no effect.

Article 2545 further provides that a seller, who is also the manufacturer of the product, is deemed to know that the thing he sells has a redhibitory defect and he is liable in redhibition.

Regardless of these limited articles, our highest court, in dealing with a clear redhibitory claim, pronounced the following in the landmark decision in *Media Production Consultants, Inc. v. Mercedes-Benz of North America, Inc.*, 262 La. 80, 262 So.2d 377, 381 (La.1972):

> Louisiana has aligned itself with the consumer-protection rule, by allowing a consumer without privity to recover, whether the suit be strictly in tort or upon implied warranty. We see no reason why the rule should not apply to the pecuniary loss resulting from the purchase of a new automobile that proves unfit for use because of latent defects.

[Citations omitted.] In *Rey v. Cuccia, supra,* the court confirmed that the *Media* conclusion was indeed a ruling regarding the scope of redhibition and that "the purchaser can recover the pecuniary loss resulting from the unusable thing sold from the manufacturer as well as the seller." *Id.* at 845.

The 1993 Revision Comments to Article 2545, again, written after the enactment of the LPLA, reflect that *Media*'s and *Rey*'s broad interpretation of the Code's redhibition principles still apply to a manufacturer who is not the immediate vendor of the plaintiff/vendee. Comment (i) states that "the assembler of things manufactured by another is a seller in bad faith." Comment (d) states that "the buyer may bring action against all sellers in the chain of sales back to the primary manufacturer to rescind a sale for breach of implied warranty." *See also*, La. C.C. art. 2548. The jurisprudence cited in support of the Revision Comments reflects that Ranger, as an alleged assembler/manufacturer without direct privity with Bearly, is nevertheless subject to claims in redhibition. *Spillers v. Montgomery Ward & Co., Inc.,* 294 So.2d 803 (La.1974); *Womack and Adcock v. 3M Business Products Sales, Inc.,* 316 So.2d 795 (La.App. 1st Cir.1975); see also, *LeGros v. ARC Services, Inc.,* 03-918 (La.App. 3d Cir.2/25/04), 867 So.2d 63 and *De Atley v. Victoria's Secret Catalogue, LLC,* 04-0661 (La.App. 4th Cir.5/14/04), 876 So.2d 112.

From this authority, Bearly's petition reflects the allegation of a cause of action in redhibition. Accordingly, because of the manufacturer's presumed knowledge of the defect under the jurisprudential interpretation of Article 2545, Ranger's actual knowledge of the alleged defect is immaterial to Bearly's claim.

* * * * *

Notes and Questions

1. As discussed in *Bearly*, the definition of "manufacturer" is broadly understood for purposes of redhibition. Although the term is not defined in the Civil Code articles on redhibition, it is defined in the Louisiana Products Liability Act (LPLA) and includes those who produce, construct, and design products as well as persons who hold themselves out as manufacturers of a product, those who exercise control or influence over the design or construction of a product, those who incorporate parts into a final product, and even domestic sellers of foreign-produced goods. *See* La. Rev. Stat. § 9:2800.53(1). The interaction between the LPLA and the law of redhibition is complex and is further discussed in Subpart G.1 of this Chapter.

2. The LPLA (and its definitions of "manufacturer") are not applicable to immovable property. For purposes of sales involving immovables, the term "manufacturer" has been given context by the jurisprudence. Comment (e) to Louisiana Civil Code Article 2545 indicates that a vendor-builder of a residence is a manufacturer, citing to *Cox v. Moore,* 367 So. 2d 424 (La. App. 2 Cir. 1979). La. Civ. Code art. 2545 cmt. e. However, recent jurisprudence clarifies that "[t]he mere label of 'general contractor' is not equivalent to 'manufacturer' under Article 2545." *Newton v. Dongieux,* 145 So. 3d 478, 483 (La. App. 5 Cir. 2014). The court in *Newton* noted that "if a vendor-builder has any type of engineering or construction knowledge or is in the business of building or developing homes for sale, it is more likely that he will be considered a manufacturer." *Id.* at 483. Absent that knowledge, the vendor-builder will not. While comment (h) to Article 2545 indicates that the developer of a subdivision is a "manufacturer" of the lots thereon, this statement must be understood in light of the effects of the New Home Warranty Act, which significantly limits the application of redhibition in sales of new homes. See Subpart G.3 below for further discussion of the New Home Warranty Act and its relationship with redhibition.

3. The classification of a seller who does not know and is not deemed to know of the defect but who *should have known* of the defect is not clear under the Louisiana Civil Code. Certainly, neither Louisiana Civil Code Article 2534 nor Louisiana Civil Code Article 2545 mentions that type of seller, a fact that some commentators suggest should bar extending the label of "bad faith seller" to such a seller. *See, e.g.,* 24 DIAN TOOLEY-KNOBLETT & DAVID GRUNING, LOUISIANA CIVIL LAW TREATISE, SALES § 11:11 (2017). That said, some courts have labeled a seller who should have known of the defect as a bad faith seller. In an unpublished opinion, Judge Fallon of the Louisiana Eastern District, exercising his *Erie* duty to apply Louisiana law, noted that while the Louisiana Supreme Court has not yet definitively answered the question, "neither has it left the question entirely open." *In re Chinese Manufactured Drywall Products Liability Litigation*, 2012 WL 5878730 (E.D. La. 2012) at *7. As he explained, "The Court has not yet used the phrase 'knew or should have known' in an opinion that also applied that standard but it has used the phrase" (citing *Spillers v. Montgomery Ward & Co.*, 294 So. 2d 803, 807 (La. 1974)). Judge Fallon also pointed out that the Louisiana Supreme Court has "denied writs or affirmed appellate courts that have both articulated and applied a 'knew or should have known' standard." (citing and quoting *Picolo v. Flex-A-Bed, Inc.*, 466 So. 2d 652, 654 (La. App. 5 Cir. 1985), *writ denied*, 467 So. 2d 1134 (1985); *Coleman Oldsmobile, Inc. v. Newman & Associates, Inc.*, 477 So. 2d 1155, 1158 (La. 1985), *writ denied*, 481 So. 2d 1334 (1986); *Harris v. Atlanta Stove Works, Inc.*, 428 So. 2d 1040, 1043 (La. App. 1 Cir.1983), *writ denied*, 434 So. 2d 1106 (1983); *Lacey v. Baywood Truck & Machinery*, 381 So. 2d 863, 866 (La. App. 1 Cir.1980), *aff'd sub nom. Capital Bank and Trust Co. v. Lacey*, 393 So. 2d 668 (1981)).

4. In many real estate transactions, the seller and/or the buyer employ real estate agents to guide them through the purchase process. The seller's real estate agent is a mandatary for the seller, *Louisiana Hand & Upper Extremity Institute, Inc. v. City of Shreveport*, 781 So. 2d 685 (La. App. 2 Cir. 2001), and as such, representations made by the agent may be imputed to the seller. *See, e.g.,* LA. CIV. CODE art. 3010; *Morehead Mfg. Co. v. Howard's D.G.S., Inc., Odorless Cleaners*, 172 So. 549, 552 (La. App. 2 Cir. 1937). Thus, if the seller's agent misrepresents the condition of the property to the buyer, the misrepresentation may result in a designation of the seller as one in bad faith. *See* LA. CIV. CODE art. 2545; 24 DIAN TOOLEY-KNOBLETT & DAVID GRUNING, LOUISIANA CIVIL LAW TREATISE, SALES § 11:14 (2017). Furthermore, real estate agents owe a duty to relay accurate information about the property they are selling, and the buyer may independently sue the seller's agent for breach of this duty under theories like fraud or negligent misrepresentation. *See, e.g., Bailey v. Delacruz*, 143 So. 3d 1220 (La. App. 2 Cir. 2014). For example, in *Waddles v. Lacour*, 950 So. 2d 937 (La. App. 3 Cir. 2007), the real estate agent failed to inform the buyer that the home he was buying had once been a mobile home. The agent had no actual knowledge of this fact, but she had received three calls from neighbors inquiring whether the home used to be a mobile home. The seller, when confronted by the agent, said that there had been a mobile home on the property but that it was gone. The agent

admitted that she was suspicious but that she believed the seller. The court held that she violated her duty to the buyer because she did not tell him about the three calls.

5. Note also that some jurisprudence suggests that a seller who has a reasonable basis to believe that a defect has been remedied is not in bad faith by virtue of failing to inform a buyer of the remedied defect. *See, e.g., Landry v. Williamson*, 2014 WL 3555934 (La. App. 1 Cir. 2014) (unpublished).

2. Significance of Good or Bad Faith of the Seller
La. Civ. Code arts. 2522, 2531, 2545, 2534

Whether a seller who has breached the warranty against redhibitory defects is in good or bad faith is significant for several reasons. Those reasons are discussed below.

a. Buyer's Remedies

One reason that determining the good or bad faith of a seller is significant is that this determination has a profound effect on the buyer's remedies. A seller in good faith is bound only to repair, remedy, or correct the defect. La. Civ. Code art. 2531. However, if the seller cannot or does not do this, he or she must return to the buyer the price with interest from the time it was paid, along with reimbursement for the reasonable expenses incurred in the sale and those incurred for the preservation of the thing. *Id.* A good faith seller is also entitled to a credit for the buyer's use of the thing or the fruits it has yielded if they were of some value to the buyer. *Id.*

The remedies for a buyer who purchased from a bad faith seller differ significantly. Like the good faith seller, a seller in bad faith must return to the buyer the price with interest from the time it was paid, along with reimbursement for the reasonable expenses incurred in the sale and those incurred for the preservation of the thing. La. Civ. Code art. 2545. However, unlike the good faith seller, a seller in bad faith is also liable for damages and reasonable attorney fees. *Id.* Note that these damages may include those of a nonpecuniary nature if the criteria for such damages set forth in Louisiana Civil Code Article 1998 are established. La. Civ. Code art. 2545 cmt. j. Also, unlike the good faith seller, a seller in bad faith is not necessarily entitled to a credit for the buyer's use of the thing and the fruits the thing might have yielded; instead, the bad faith seller *may* be entitled to the credit. *Id.* That decision lies within the discretion of the court. La. Civ. Code art. 2545 cmt. g.

b. Seller's Right to Notice and Opportunity to Repair

Another reason that classification of a seller as one in good or bad faith is significant is because this classification determines the seller's right to notice and an opportunity to repair. As noted in Louisiana Civil Code Article 2522, a good faith seller is entitled to notice and an opportunity to repair. La. Civ. Code art. 2522. Article 2522 also provides that a buyer who fails to give that notice suffers diminution of the warranty to the extent the seller can show that the defect could have been repaired or that the repairs would have been less burdensome, had he or she received timely notice. *Id.* In contrast, a bad faith seller with actual knowledge is entitled to neither notice nor the opportunity to repair. LA. CIV. CODE art. 2522. However, a manufacturer who does not have knowledge of the defect, as one who is only deemed to know of the defects in its product, is entitled to notice. *See* LA. CIV. CODE arts. 2522 cmt. b, 2531 cmt. c, 2545 cmt. f. Admittedly, allowing the manufacturer who does not have knowledge of the defect the right to notice seems incongruous with the general rule that a seller in bad faith has no right to make repairs. While the manufacturer who is entitled to notice may not have a *right* to repair, such notice at least provides the manufacturer with an opportunity to offer to make repairs (if economically and practically feasible) and helps to ensure that other items produced by the same manufacturer do not contain the same or similar defects.

Note also that providing notice to the seller of the defect's existence serves to shift the risk of loss for destruction of the thing by a fortuitous event. More specifically, if the thing is destroyed by a fortuitous event before the buyer gives the seller notice of the existence of a redhibitory defect that would have given rise to rescission of the sale, the loss is borne by the buyer. LA. CIV. CODE art. 2532. Thus, although not all sellers are entitled to notice under Article 2522, the buyer would be wise to provide notice to any seller, regardless of the seller's actual knowledge of the defect.

The case below discusses the consequences of the failure of the buyer to give timely notice to a seller in good faith.

David v. Thibodeaux

916 So. 2d 214 (La. App. 1 Cir. 2005)

Before: GUIDRY, GAIDRY, and McCLENDON, JJ.

GUIDRY, J.

In this redhibition action, defendant, Concepcion St. Romain Thibodeaux, appeals the trial court's judgment, ordering rescission of the April 26, 2000 Act of Sale of certain immovable property to plaintiffs, Joseph and Pamela David. For the following reasons, we reverse.

FACTS AND PROCEDURAL HISTORY

On April 26, 2000, Joseph and Pamela David purchased immovable property, including a single-family residence, in Lakeland, Louisiana from Mrs. Thibodeaux for the purchase price of $175,000.00. According to the Act of Sale, Joseph David paid $125,000.00 in cash, and executed a promissory note in favor of Mrs. Thibodeaux for the remaining $50,000.00. Prior to the sale, the Davids conducted several visual inspections of the premises. Additionally, a wood destroying insect report (WDIR) and a property condition disclosure statement were obtained. The property condition disclosure statement indicated that termite damage was discovered and repaired in 1990. Further, according to the WDIR, old termite damage and/or scars were discovered in three locations of the home. However, Mrs. Thibodeaux showed the Davids the three locations and explained that the termite problem had been taken care of and the damages had been repaired.

After moving into the home, the Davids discovered extensive active termite infestation and damage. Thereafter, the Davids filed a petition to rescind the sale and for damages, and in the alternative, for a reduction in the purchase price. Following a trial held on February 4, 5, 7, and 28, 2003, the trial court rendered judgment on May 13, 2003, ordering rescission of the Act of Sale. Mrs. Thibodeaux appeals from this judgment.

DISCUSSION

Generally, the seller of a home impliedly warrants to the buyer that it is free from redhibitory vices or defects. La. C.C. art. 2520. A defect is redhibitory, entitling the buyer to rescind the sale, when it renders the home useless, or makes its use so inconvenient that it must be presumed that the buyer would not have bought the home had he known of the defect. La. C.C. arts. 2520. A defect is also redhibitory, entitling the buyer to reduction of the price, when, without rendering the home totally useless, it diminishes its usefulness or its value so that it must be presumed that a buyer would still have bought it but for a lesser price. La. C.C. art. 2520.

However, not all redhibitory vices or defects justify rescission or reduction of the price. Apparent defects, which the buyer can discover through a simple inspection, are excluded from the seller's legal warranty. La. C.C. art. 2521. A defect is apparent if a reasonably prudent buyer, acting under similar circumstances, would discover it through a simple inspection of the property. A simple inspection is more than a casual observation; it is an examination of the article by the buyer with a view of ascertaining its soundness. *Amend v. McCabe,* 95-0316, p. 9 (La.12/1/95), 664 So.2d 1183, 1188. Factors considered in determining whether an inspection is reasonable include the knowledge and expertise of the buyer, the opportunity for inspection, and assurances made by the seller. *Crow v. Laurie,* 98-0648, p. 6 (La. App. 1st Cir.2/19/99), 729 So.2d 703, 707-708.

Whether termite damage is apparent to the buyer of a home by reasonable inspection is a question of fact. *See McMorris v. Marcotte Builders, L.L.C.,* 98-2302, p. 6 (La. App. 1st Cir.12/28/99), 756 So.2d 424, 428, *writ denied,* 00-0664 (La.4/20/00), 760 So.2d 1158. Typically, when *all* of the termite damage is concealed within the home's structure (e.g., walls and floors) it is considered unapparent because it is not discoverable by a simple inspection. *Amend,* 95-0316 at p. 10, 664 So.2d at 1188. In such situations, there is no obligation on the part of the buyer to inspect further. On the other hand, when *some* of the termite damage is detectable by a simple inspection, the buyer has a duty to investigate further. If he chooses to purchase the home without further investigation, he waives the right to sue for rescission or reduction based upon the termite damage. *Amend,* 95-0316 at p. 10, 664 So.2d at 1188. However, if the seller represents that suspected defects have been corrected, and simple inspection establishes these representations to be accurate, the buyer need not investigate further. *Estopinal v. Bourshie*, 420 So.2d 749, 751-752 (La.App. 4th Cir.1982); *see also Caple v. Green*, 545 So.2d 1222, 1227 (La.App. 2nd Cir.1989) and *Perrin v. Kuehne*, 97-196, p. 10 (La.App. 5th Cir.12/10/97), 704 So.2d 839, 844, *writ denied*, 98-0022 (La.2/20/98), 709 So.2d 786.

In the instant case, the Davids made at least four visual inspections of the home. According to the Davids, Mrs. Thibodeaux was present during each inspection, and controlled their access/view of the home. Additionally, Morris Bergeron performed a professional inspection on April 14, 2000. According to the Davids, nothing from their inspection or from Mr. Bergeron's report caused any alarm, and all the notations made by Mr. Bergeron appeared to be "cosmetic."

Additionally, on April 14, 2000, Joseph David reviewed a copy of the WDIR, which noted three locations where old termite damage and/or scars were discovered. Mr. David testified that he asked Mrs. Thibodeaux for further explanation of the notations on the WDIR. Mrs. Thibodeaux brought him to all three areas listed on the WDIR and told him that the termites and damage had been taken care of and that it was not a problem anymore, the spots being just old scars.[2] Further, the property condition disclosure statement received by the Davids indicated that termite damage was discovered and repaired in 1990. Mr. David testified that based on his visual inspection, the WDIR prepared by Terminix, Mr. Bergeron's report, and the assurances made by Mrs. Thibodeaux, he felt satisfied that there was old damage that had been repaired, and that he did not see anything to suggest that there was still a problem.

According to the Davids' testimony, it was not until the outside, wooden deck collapsed in July 2000 and Mrs. David's hand went through the basement wall while moving boxes in August 2000 that they suspected something was wrong. In September 2000, the Davids hired Gary Morris to perform a structural inspection of the home, at which time some of the walls and flooring were removed, revealing hidden, active termite infestation and damage. Additionally, the Davids hired Louis Faxon, an architect, who inspected the home twice. According to Mr. Faxon, evidence of termite damage had been covered up. Both experts testified that some damage was initially observable, but that did not mean a layperson buying a home would recognize it as a problem like a home inspector or architect would. From our review of the entire record, we cannot find that the trial court manifestly erred or was clearly wrong in determining that the active termites and termite damage were a latent defect.

Mrs. Thibodeaux, however, also asserts that according to La. C.C. art. 2531, she is only bound to repair, remedy, or correct the defect; therefore, the trial court erred

---

2. These representations were apparently not considered material misrepresentations, as the trial court specifically found that Mrs. Thibodeaux did not have actual knowledge of active terminate infestation and was not in bad faith. Rather, the trial court indicated that Mrs. Thibodeaux operated under the assumption and/or hoped that the termites and damage had in fact been taken care of in pursuit of her contract with Terminix.

in ordering rescission of the sale. Louisiana Civil Code article 2522 provides that a buyer must give the seller notice of the existence of a redhibitory defect within sufficient time to allow the seller the opportunity to make the required repairs. "A buyer who fails to give that notice suffers diminution of the warranty to the extent the seller can show that the defect could have been repaired." However, this notice is not required when the seller has actual knowledge of the existence of a redhibitory defect. La. C.C. art. 2522. Additionally, La. C.C. art. 2531 provides, in part, that "[a] seller who did not know that the thing he sold had a defect is only bound to repair, remedy, or correct the defect. If he is unable or fails so to do, he is then bound to return the price to the buyer." Together, these codal provisions state that the right to an opportunity to repair is a condition precedent to rescission if the seller is in good faith. *See Jordan v. LeBlanc and Broussard Ford. Inc.*, 332 So.2d 534, 538 (La.App. 3rd Cir.1976). The buyer has the burden of establishing that the seller was given the opportunity to repair the defect. *Pratt v. Himel Marine, Inc.*, 01-1832 (La.App. 1st Cir.6/21/02), 823 So.2d 394, *writ denied*, 02-2128 (La.11/1/02), 828 So.2d 571. If the buyer fails to establish that he gave notice of the defect to the seller, he is not entitled to rescission of the sale. However, such failure to give notice does not preclude the buyer from obtaining reduction of the price. *See Coleman Oldsmobile, Inc. v. Newman and Associates, Inc.*, 477 So.2d 1155, 1160 (La.App. 1st Cir.1985), *writ denied*, 481 So.2d 1334 (La.1986); *see also Dunn v. Pauratore*, 387 So.2d 1227 (La.App. 1st Cir.1980) and *Coffin v. Laborde*, 393 So.2d 915 (La.App. 4th Cir.), *writ denied*, 396 So.2d 915 (La.1981) (finding that notice and an opportunity to repair are not prerequisites to maintain a suit in quanti minoris).

In the instant case, the trial court specifically found that Mrs. Thibodeaux did not have actual knowledge and was not in bad faith. Therefore, in order to obtain rescission of the sale, the Davids had to show that they notified Mrs. Thibodeaux of the redhibitory defect, thereby affording her an opportunity to repair it. From our review of the record, we do not find any evidence that the Davids gave Mrs. Thibodeaux notice of the existence of the redhibitory defect. Rather, the Davids elected to file suit, seeking rescission, or alternatively, reduction of the purchase price on the basis that Mrs. Thibodeaux had actual knowledge. Therefore, because the Davids did not establish that they notified Mrs. Thibodeaux of the redhibitory defect, the trial court erred in awarding rescission of the sale.

However, as stated above, failure to give notice does not preclude the buyer from obtaining reduction of the purchase price. In an action for reduction of the purchase price, the amount to be awarded is the difference between the sale price and the price that a reasonable buyer would have paid if he had known of the defect. In the case of immovable property, the amount to be awarded is the amount necessary to convert the unsound structure into a sound one. A principle element in formulating a reduction of the purchase price is the cost of repairs. *Lemonier v. Coco*, 237 La. 760, 765-66, 112 So.2d 436, 438-39 (La.1959); *Sanders v. Earnest*, 34,656, p. 29 (La.App. 2nd Cir.7/24/01), 793 So.2 393, 409; *see also Lemoine v. Hebert*, 395 So.2d 353 (La.App. 1st Cir.1980).

At trial of this matter, the testimony of three experts was introduced. The Davids introduced the testimony of Garry Morris, who performed a structural inspection of the home, and Louis Faxon. The trial court specifically found Mr. Morris's testimony not to be credible and also found that his estimated repair costs were extraordinarily high. Additionally, the trial court specifically found that the standards set by Mr. Faxon were very high, in that he thought the only way to remedy the defects was to tear the house down and start over, and that his estimate for repair costs was also high. Mrs. Thibodeaux introduced the testimony of Kenneth Jones. Mr. Jones inspected the home and testified that he prepared an estimate of repairs in the amount of $25,622.00. Mr. Jones stated that this amount estimated the cost to repair the existing damage, and included mark ups to take into account contingencies, such as undiscovered damage. The trial court considered Mr. Jones's repair estimate to be realistic and we agree. As such, we grant the Davids a reduction in the purchase price, in the amount of $25,622.00, subject to a credit of $24,000.00 in favor of Mrs. Thibodeaux for the award arising from the arbitration with Terminix.

CONCLUSION

For the foregoing reasons, the judgment of the trial court, ordering rescission of the sale, return of the purchase price, and cancellation of the promissory note is reversed. We grant the Davids a reduction in the purchase price, in the amount of $25,622.00, subject to a credit of $24,000.00 in favor of Mrs. Thibodeaux for the award arising from the arbitration with Terminix, for a net judgment of $1,622.00, together with legal interest. All costs of this appeal are to be borne equally, one-half assessed to Concepcion St. Romain Thibodeaux, and one-half assessed to Joseph and Pamela David.

REVERSED AND RENDERED.

McCLENDON, J., concurs and assigns reasons.

McCLENDON, J., concurs.

The majority's analysis is premised on the seller's lack of knowledge of active termite infestations. I respectfully disagree with that interpretation of the trial court's finding, and concur in the result.

In oral reasons, the trial court specifically found, as follows: "she did fail to disclose some things that had the Davids known, they would not have made the purchase of this home." The trial court further stated: "[i]t may have slipped her mind, whatever . . . she didn't strike me as being the type of person that would be evil or dishonest." Thus, the trial court did not find that she did not know, but rather that she "may" have forgotten, or that she did not have evil intentions in not revealing the infestations. In a footnote, the majority also seems to admit that Mrs. Thibodeaux had some knowledge, but she either assumed that the active termite problem was eliminated, or she "hoped" it was. Although she may have thought Terminix remedied the post 1990 problems, a seller with knowledge is not relieved of the duty to disclose active termite infestations based on hopes that the problem may have been eliminated. In addition, as documentary proof of knowledge, the record contains post 1990 reports of active infestations signed for by the seller, Mrs. Thibodeaux. While rescission is the usual remedy under such circumstances, facts peculiar to this case require a reduction in price.

If a buyer would have been willing to buy at a lesser price, the remedy is a reduction in price under Louisiana Civil Code article 2520. In the purchase agreement, both Mrs. Thibodeaux and the Davids agreed that if active termite infestation was found, the seller would provide treatment at her expense. Although the purchase agreement does not control the issue before this court, and the seller failed to advise the buyers of the active infestations, the agreement provides insight into what the buyers were willing to accept if the active termite problems had been revealed. More importantly, Louisiana Civil Code article 2532 charged the buyers seeking return with being prudent administrators, and thus, subject to a return of the thing, the house and property, in the same or like condition. However, in this case, the buyers made significant changes to the property, including removal of a pool, pool house, deck, and fence, and breached their fiduciary duty by allowing the house to deteriorate while in their care. For these reasons, the Davids must bear responsibility for their acts that damaged the property, and the just remedy is a reduction in price. *See delaVergne v. delaVergne*, 514 So.2d 186, 192 (La.App. 4 Cir.1987), *writ denied*, 519 So.2d 118 (La.1988).

Notes and Questions

Per the *David* court above, the buyer must give notice to a good faith seller if the buyer is asserting a claim for rescission. However, such notice is not required as a prerequisite for a claim for a reduction of the price. Although this distinction is not evidenced in the Civil Code, as *David* illustrates, it is firmly rooted in the jurisprudence. Note also that the majority in *David* found the seller to have been in good faith. Do you agree with this assessment? Why or why not?

c. Applicable Prescriptive Period

A final reason that the distinction between a good faith and a bad faith seller is important is prescription. A good faith seller, as a general rule, is subject to a prescriptive period of four years from delivery of the thing or one year from the buyer's discovery of the defect, whichever occurs first. LA. CIV. CODE art. 2534(A)(1). That said, if the thing in question is a residential or commercial immovable, a claim for redhibition against a good faith seller prescribes one year from delivery. LA. CIV. CODE art. 2534(A)(2). In contrast, a seller in bad faith is subject to a prescriptive period of one year from the buyer's discovery of the defect. LA. CIV. CODE art. 2534(B). Under any scenario, "prescription is interrupted when the seller accepts the thing for repairs and commences anew from the day he tenders it back to the buyer or notifies the buyer of his refusal or inability to make the required repairs." LA. CIV. CODE art. 2534(C). According to the jurisprudence, this rule regarding interruption of prescription "applies not only to physical repairs but to verbal or written statements that lead a buyer to believe that the defects will be remedied."

Robertson v. Jimmy Walker Chrysler-Plymouth, Inc., 368 So. 2d 747, 750-751 (La. App. 3 Cir. 1979); *Weaver v. Fleetwood Homes of Mississippi, Inc.*, 327 So. 2d 172, 177 (La. App. 3 Cir. 1976); *Seeman v. Clearview Dodge Sales, Inc.*, 467 So. 2d 1332, 1333 (La. App. 5 Cir. 1985); *Blue v. Schoen*, 556 So. 2d 1364 1368 (La. App. 4 Cir. 1990). The rationale behind this extension of the rule is that the seller's statements lull the buyer "into a false sense of security[,]" such that interruption of prescription is appropriate. *Id.* at 751. Note that some cases mandate that the verbal or written communication must "reasonably lead" the buyer to believe that defects would be remedied. *Southwest Louisiana Hosp. Ass'n v. BASF Const. Chemicals, LLC*, 947 F. Supp. 2d 661, 688–89 (W.D. La. 2013).

Note that comment b to Article 2534 states that "an action in redhibition prescribes ten years from the time of perfection of the sale, regardless of whether the seller was in good or bad faith." LA. CIV. CODE art. 2534 cmt. b. Given the rules provided in the text of Article 2534, this statement is clearly incorrect.

C. Obligations of the Buyer

La. Civ. Code art. 2532

A buyer of a thing containing a redhibitory defect has certain obligations to fulfill. If the buyer obtains rescission because of the defect, he or she must return the thing to the seller once any claims or judgments arising from the defect are satisfied. LA. CIV. CODE art. 2532. Furthermore, the buyer must take care of the thing as a prudent administrator. *Id.* For example, in *David v. Thibodeaux*, 916 So. 2d 214 (La. App. 1 Cir. 2005), the concurring judge noted that the duty to act as a prudent administrator under Article 2532 required that the buyers who bought the property subject to a redhibitory defect return the thing "in the same or like condition." *Id.* at 221. In that case, the buyers violated Article 2532 because they "made significant changes to the property, including removal of a pool, pool house, deck, and fence, and breached their fiduciary duty by allowing the house to deteriorate while in their care." *Id.*

In the event that the thing in question is destroyed because of the redhibitory defect, the loss is borne by the seller, and the buyer may bring the action for breach even after the destruction has occurred. LA. CIV. CODE art. 2532. However, if the thing is destroyed by a fortuitous event, who bears the loss depends upon whether it occurred before or after the buyer gave notice of the defect. If the fortuitous event destroys the thing "before the buyer gives the seller notice of the existence of a redhibitory defect that would have given rise to a rescission of the sale, the loss is borne by the buyer." *Id.* However, if the fortuitous event destroys the thing after such notice is given, "the loss is borne by the seller, except to the extent the buyer has insured that loss." *Id.* The seller who returns the price or a part thereof "is subrogated to the buyer's right against third persons who may be liable for the destruction of the thing." *Id.*

D. Waiver of Warranty Against Redhibitory Defects

La. Civ. Code art. 2548

The rules governing the warranty against redhibitory defects are suppletive and as a result, as a general rule, may be altered by the parties' agreement. In fact, the parties may agree to an exclusion or limitation of the warranty against redhibitory defects, but according to Article 2548 the terms of any such exclusion or limitation must be clear and unambiguous and must be brought to the attention of the buyer. La. Civ. Code art. 2548. Additionally, the jurisprudence requires that if the Act of Sale is in writing, the waiver must also be in writing. *Creger v. Robertson*, 542 So. 2d 1090, 1095 (La. App. 2 Cir. 1989); *Williston v. Nolan*, 888 So. 2d 950, 952 (La. App. 1 Cir. 2010). Furthermore, even if the waiver satisfies these requirements, it is unenforceable nonetheless if the seller has declared that the thing has a quality that he knew it did not have. La. Civ. Code art. 2548. The cases below address the rules regarding waivers of the warranty against redhibitory defects.

Shelton v. Standard/700 Associates

798 So. 2d 60 (La. 2001)

Knoll, Judge

This writ concerns whether the sellers of a condominium were properly granted summary judgment against the buyer, where the buyer alleged fraud in the inducement of a contract of sale waiving all warranties and rights to sue in redhibition. Finding that there is an absence of factual support to show fraud, which is essential to the buyer's claim, we affirm.

FACTS AND PROCEDURAL HISTORY

On September 4, 1996, the plaintiff, J. Elise Shelton, purchased a condominium from defendant Standard/700 Associates. The condominium, designated as Unit 617, is located on the top floor of a building at 700 South Peters Street in the City of New Orleans. The condominium was sold "as is where is," without any warranties or right to sue in redhibition.

Two months after the sale, on or about November 13 or 14 of 1996, water began to leak through the ceiling of the condominium, causing damage to the interior of the condominium and plaintiff's personal property. After several failed attempts by defendant Standard/700 Associates to repair the roof of the building, on April 17, 1997, plaintiff filed suit. In her petition for damages, plaintiff alleged the leaks were caused by a swimming pool, a hot tub, and planters located on the roof of the building. Seeking rescission of the sale, plaintiff further alleged the condominium contained a redhibitory defect insofar as the leaks rendered the condominium useless or, alternatively, its use so inconvenient that plaintiff would not have bought the condominium had she known of the defect.

In a supplemental and amending petition, plaintiff pled fraud and inducement, alleging that defendants had knowledge of the condition of the roof, but intentionally concealed this information from plaintiff prior to purchase. Plaintiff specifically alleged that, prior to the act of sale, defendant Ms. Margaret Aldon Lovelace Guichard, the sales agent for defendant Standard/700 Associates, "unequivocally vouched for the soundness of the roof of the subject condominium complex" and stated there had been no previous leaks.

After answering plaintiff's original petition and amended petition, defendants moved for summary judgment, contending that plaintiff effectively waived the warranty against redhibitory defects when plaintiff entered the contract of sale containing the "as is where is" clause. Defendants relied on the following language contained in the act of sale:

> NOTWITHSTANDING ANYTHING HEREIN TO THE CONTRARY, THE UNIT DESCRIBED HEREIN IS SOLD AND PURCHASED "AS IS WHERE IS", WITHOUT ANY WARRANTY OR REPRESENTATION WHATSOEVER WITH RESPECT TO THE CONDITION OR REMAINING USEFUL LIFE OF SUCH CONDOMINIUM UNIT OR WITH RESPECT TO ANY OF THE COMMON ELEMENTS OF THE CONDOMINIUM, OR ANY OF THEIR COMPONENTS OR PARTS OR CONTENTS, AND WITHOUT WARRANTY WHATSOEVER WITH RESPECT TO THE FITNESS OF ANY CONDOMINIUM UNIT OF THE COMMON ELEMENTS FOR ANY PARTICULAR OR GENERAL USE OR PURPOSE AND NO REPRESENTATION OR WARRANTIES WITH RESPECT TO ANY OF THE FOREGOING ARE MADE, ALL OF THEM BEING EXPRESSLY DISCLAIMED.

> PURCHASER HEREBY WAIVES ANY RIGHT TO SUE IN REDHIBITION OR FOR RETURN OR REDUCTION OF THE PURCHASE PRICE OR ANY PART THEREOF AS A RESULT OF THE CONDITION OF THE UNIT OR UNITS DESCRIBED HEREIN OR THE CONDOMINIUM.

After a hearing, the trial court granted defendants' motion. On appeal, the Fourth Circuit affirmed. *Shelton v. Standard/700 Associates,* 2000-0227 (La.App. 4th Cir.1/31/01), 778 So.2d 1265. In reaching its holding, the court of appeal relied on two findings. First, the court of appeal found no defect existed in the condominium at the time of delivery. Consequently, the court of appeal determined there was no redhibitory defect in the condominium. LSA-C.C. art. 2530. Second, the court of appeal found that plaintiff waived her right to sue for redhibitory defects.

DISCUSSION

The issue before us does not concern the "as is where is" waiver of warranties plaintiff signed. It is the allegation of fraud that prompted this court to grant this writ, as fraud in the inducement of a contract cannot be waived.

Plaintiff can only obtain relief from the harsh consequences of the waiver she signed if she can show fraud in the inducement of the contract. As such, our discussion will address the body of law pertaining to fraud in the inducement of a contract of sale.

It is clear that a seller warrants his buyer against redhibitory defects, or vices, in the thing sold. LSA-C.C. art. 2520. It is equally clear, however, that this warranty may be excluded or limited per LSA-C.C. art. 2548, which provides, in pertinent part:

The parties may agree to an exclusion or limitation of the warranty against redhibitory defects. The terms of the exclusion or limitation must be clear and unambiguous and must be brought to the attention of the buyer.

While an exclusion or limitation of the warranty against redhibitory defects is usually effective, LSA-C.C. art. 2548 further provides that "[a] buyer is not bound by an otherwise effective exclusion or limitation of the warranty when the seller has declared that the thing has a quality that he knew it did not have." Under this article, an otherwise effective exclusion or limitation of the warranty against redhibitory defects is not effective if the seller commits fraud, as defined in the civil code, upon the buyer. Thus, although the warranty against redhibitory defects may be excluded or limited, a seller cannot contract against his own fraud and relieve himself of liability to fraudulently induced buyers. *See Roby Motors Co. v. Price,* 173 So. 793, 796 (La.App. 2nd Cir.1937). Indeed, such a contract would be contra bonos mores and unenforceable.

A contract is formed by the consent of the parties. LSA-C.C. art. 1927. However, consent may be vitiated by error, fraud, or duress. LSA-C.C. art. 1948. "Fraud is a misrepresentation or a suppression of the truth made with the intention either to obtain an unjust advantage for one party or to cause a loss or inconvenience to the other. Fraud may also result from silence or inaction." LSA-C.C. art. 1953. "Error induced by fraud need not concern the cause of the obligation to vitiate consent, but it must concern a circumstance that has substantially influenced that consent." LSA-C.C. art. 1955.

Nevertheless, fraud does not vitiate consent when the party against whom the fraud was directed could have ascertained the truth without difficulty, inconvenience, or special skill. However, this exception does not apply when a relation of confidence has reasonably induced a party to rely on the other's assertions or representations. LSA-C.C. art. 1954.

In pleading fraud, the circumstances constituting fraud must be alleged with particularity. LSA-C.C.P. art. 856. However, fraud need only be proven by a preponderance of the evidence and may be established by circumstantial evidence. LSA-C.C. art. 1957.

In sum, there are three basic elements to an action for fraud against a party to a contract: (1) a misrepresentation, suppression, or omission of true information; (2) the intent to obtain an unjust advantage or to cause damage or inconvenience to another; and (3) the error induced by a fraudulent act must relate to a circumstance substantially influencing the victim's consent to (a cause of) the contract.

* * * * *

After carefully studying the documents plaintiff filed in opposition to summary judgment, we find that plaintiff failed to produce factual support sufficient to establish that she would be able to prove her allegation of fraud at trial. Notably, plaintiff herself conceded in deposition that defendant Ms. Guichard, the sales agent for defendant Standard/700 Associates, who represented defendants throughout the sales negotiations, and who in fact managed the condominium building, may never have known about any prior problems involving leaks in the roof of the condominium building. This admission certainly belies plaintiff's allegation of fraud because it underscores defendants' lack of intent to obtain an unjust advantage or to cause damage or inconvenience to plaintiff. In her deposition, plaintiff further stated that if Ms. Guichard was unaware of the prior leak problems, surely "somebody there knew about it." This statement is pure speculation which falls far short of plaintiff's burden on summary judgment to produce factual support sufficient to establish that she would be able to satisfy her evidentiary burden of proof at trial. Moreover, the repair and maintenance records which plaintiff relies on fail to raise a genuine issue of material fact regarding fraud. Indeed, the records evidencing the extent and amount of repairs made on the roof *after the date of sale* are irrelevant to plaintiff's fraud allegation. The records evidencing the extent and amount of repairs made on the roof *before the date of sale* are relevant, but such repairs were so infrequent and inconsequential that these records also fail to raise a genuine issue of material fact regarding plaintiff's fraud allegation.

Furthermore, the three affidavits submitted by plaintiff in opposition to summary judgment fail to raise a genuine issue of material fact regarding fraud. The first affidavit executed by plaintiff merely recounts and expounds on allegations made in plaintiff's original petition and amended petition. The second affidavit executed by plaintiff, referred to as a supplemental affidavit, contains irrelevant information regarding plaintiff's continuing problems with the leaky roof. The affidavit of Ms. Carita Boutte merely corroborates an alleged conversation between plaintiff and Ms. Guichard, wherein Ms. Guichard allegedly told plaintiff that "there had never been any reported leak in the roof of 700 S. Peters."

Finally, Ms. Guichard's deposition fails to support plaintiff's allegation of fraud. Indeed, Ms. Guichard denies having any knowledge of any roof leaks prior to September 4, 1996, the date of the act of sale.

In conclusion, we find plaintiff's conjectural allegations of fraud are too speculative. Plaintiff has failed to produce factual support sufficient to establish that she would be able to satisfy her evidentiary burden of proof at trial. Summary judgment was properly granted in defendants' favor. Accordingly, the judgment of the court of appeal is affirmed.

AFFIRMED.

JOHNSON, J., dissents and assigns reasons.

JOHNSON, J., dissenting.

Summary judgment is inappropriate in this case because material issues of fact exist as to plaintiff's allegations of fraud. Summary judgment is not intended to be used as a vehicle to circumvent a trial on the merits, and it may not be used to dispense with a case that is difficult to prove. *Serigne v. Ivker*, 95-1538 (La.App. 4 Cir. 2/15/96), 669 So.2d 1335.

In this case, defendants vouched for the soundness of the roof and denied that there had been any previous leaks prior to the Act of Sale. Yet, it is apparent from the record that defendants had experienced problems with the roof. In fact, in the three years prior to plaintiff's purchase, defendant spent in excess of $5,000.00 on roof repairs, the last of which occurred eight months before plaintiff's purchase. Further, despite the "as is where is" warranty, defendants spent several months (January of 1997 through March of 1997) attempting to repair the roof after plaintiff moved into the condominium.

Because I believe that plaintiff should have been given the opportunity to prove to a trier of fact that defendants misrepresented or suppressed the truth about the problems with the roof, I respectfully dissent.

Notes and Questions

1. What language could be employed in a waiver to ensure that its terms are "clear and unambiguous"? Case law is clear that a simple "as is" clause is insufficient to satisfy the standard for wavier. *Wilks v. Ramsey Auto Brokers, Inc.*, 132 So. 3d 1009, 1014–15 (La. App. 2 Cir. 2014). Courts explain that the reason behind this is that such a clause "only notifies the buyer that the thing being sold is not in perfect condition or that it is not free of all defects which prior usage and age may cause." *Larimer v. Harper*, 773 So. 2d 218, 221 (La. App. 4 Cir. 2000). Furthermore, courts are seemingly reluctant to enforce waivers and have suggested that in order to waive the warranty against redhibitory defects, the contract must use the word "redhibition." *Wilks*, 132 So. 3d at 1014–15.

2. How might a sales contract clearly show that the waiver was brought to the buyer's attention? In *Linch Intern. Trucks, Inc. v. Pierre*, 434 So. 2d 1225, 1227 (La. App. 1 Cir. 1983), the buyer signed the waiver without reading it, and no evidence was offered that the importance of the document was called to the buyer's attention or that its contents were explained to the buyer; the court held the waiver to be ineffective. By contrast, in *Boos v. Benson Jeep-Eagle Co., Inc.*, 717 So. 2d 661, 663–65 (La. App. 4 Cir. 1998), the buyers signed two waivers, one in the purchase order and one in the finance contract. The one in the purchase order was denominated with the caption "disclaimer of warranty" in all capital letters in bold print and was printed at the bottom of the purchase order and set apart from the rest of the page. The buyers signed the line directly below the waiver. The court held that this waiver called sufficient attention to the waiver to satisfy the requirements of Article 2548. The waiver in the finance agreement contained another waiver of rights at the bottom of the page, set apart from the other provisions and signed by the buyers, but it did not denominate it as such. The court suggested that it, too, was valid, but

stated: "Should either form of the waiver be deemed insufficient standing alone to attract the attention of the buyers, the cumulative impact of both together would be sufficient." *Id.* at 655.

3. Note that it is not sufficient that a waiver of redhibition be included in a purchase agreement; it must be included in the Act of Sale. *See, e.g., Moore v. Dupart,* 785 So. 2d 207, 211 (La. App. 4 Cir. 2001). What if the waiver is not included in the purchase agreement? Can a vendor demand that such a waiver then be included in the Act of Sale? *See, e.g., Mitchell v. Popiwchak,* 677 So. 2d 1050 (La. App. 4 Cir. 1996).

4. Article 2548 provides that an otherwise valid waiver will not be enforceable if the seller has declared that the thing has a quality that he knew it did not have. LA. CIV. CODE art. 2548. Does this mean that the seller must affirmatively make such a declaration in order to lose the benefit of an otherwise valid waiver? In *Royal v. Cook,* 984 So. 2d 156 (La. App. 4 Cir. 2008) (excerpted above), the court answered that question with a resounding "no." Per Article 1953, fraud is defined as "a misrepresentation or a *suppression* of the truth with the intention to either obtain an unjust advantage to one party or to cause loss or inconvenience to the other." LA. CIV. CODE art. 1953 (emphasis added). Additionally, the article provides that inaction or silence may also constitute fraud. *Id.* Thus, because the seller knew of the rodent problem and failed to disclose it, she concealed the redhibitory defect from the buyer. Such concealment, the court decided, was fraudulent, and therefore negated the buyer's (otherwise valid) waiver of the warranty against redhibitory defects. Additionally, the court found the seller to be a bad faith seller and thus, not entitled to notice or an opportunity to repair. Ultimately, fraud negates an otherwise valid waiver of redhibition, and fraud includes both lies of commission and lies of omission. Thus, not only is a seller who declares the thing to have a quality it does not have fraudulent, so is a seller who fails to disclose a known defect.

5. The Louisiana Supreme Court's recent opinion in *Valobra v. Nelson,* 136 So. 3d 793 (La. 2014) (per curium), illustrates the importance of the seller accurately and honestly completing the Residential Property Disclosure Document. In that case, the sellers completed a property disclosure document that required them to check one of three boxes when answering questions regarding defects in the property: "yes," "no," or "no knowledge." The sellers checked the "no" box for numerous defects which the buyers later alleged existed at the time of delivery. Once the buyers filed suit, the sellers asserted the buyers' waiver of the warranty against redhibitory defects, which was included in the Act of Sale. In response, the buyer alleged that the sellers fraudulently induced the waiver through misrepresentation, and thus, the waiver was negated. The sellers filed an exception of no cause of action, claiming that they were never in a position to know of any defects as a result of the fact that, as co-trustees of trusts that came to co-own the property following the death of one of the former residents, they never resided there. The court denied the sellers' exception, ruling that the buyers had a cause of action to challenge the validity

of the waiter, presumably by proving that the sellers had committed fraud — not in the misrepresentation of the existence of defects, but in the misrepresentation of their level of knowledge about potential defects. According to the Court,

> We do not believe that a seller can represent a thing to have no defects in order to procure a waiver of redhibition and then claim that they were not in a position to know whether there were defects or not, as alleged by the plaintiffs, while using the waiver of redhibition to require the buyer to prove actual knowledge of the defect by the seller rather than merely the thing sold contained a defect which rendered it useless (regardless of the seller's knowledge of same). Sellers cannot avoid their representation of no defects by claiming "we really didn't know."

Id. at 795. This case stands for the proposition that fraud in the inducement of the waiver can arise from a seller's misrepresentations regarding the *extent* of his or her knowledge of a redhibitory defect, and not merely misrepresentations regarding the existence of defects. Note that at the time of the sale at issue in *Valobra*, the Property Disclosure Document required the seller to disclose any defects and conditions by checking boxes marked "yes," "no," or "no knowledge." It has recently been revised, effective as of January 1, 2018, to require the seller to disclose any defects and conditions by checking boxes marked either "yes" or "no knowledge." *See Property Disclosure Document for Residential Real Estate*, available at https://www.lrec.state.la.us /files/01-01-2018%20Property%20Disclosure%20Letter.pdf. Do you see why? What are the effects of this revision?

6. Note that "any contractual provision that attempts to limit, diminish or prevent" redhibition claims against a manufacturer "shall have no effect." LA. CIV. CODE art. 2531.

7. In light of the foregoing case and notes, can a bad faith seller ever secure a waiver of the warranty against redhibitory defects?

E. The Buyer's Right to Subrogation

1. In General

La. Civ. Code arts. 2548, 2531

Article 2548 provides that "[t]he buyer is subrogated to the rights in warranty of the seller against other persons, even when the warranty is excluded." LA. CIV. CODE art. 2548. This language reproduces verbatim Article 2503, which, as is discussed in Chapter 9: The Warranty Against Eviction, provides that the buyer is subrogated to the seller's rights with respect to the warranty against eviction. Whereas the buyer's right of subrogation was introduced to the law of eviction in 1924, the subrogation rule of redhibition was not enacted until 1993. Prior to that time, it was left to the courts to determine whether a buyer was subrogated to the seller's rights in redhibition.

The Louisiana Supreme Court addressed the issue of subrogation in the following seminal case. Consider carefully the rationales for the buyer's right of subrogation provided by the majority and concurring opinions.

Media Production Consultants, Inc. v. Mercedes-Benz of North America, Inc.
262 So. 2d 377 (La. 1972)

SANDERS, Justice.

We granted certiorari to review a decision of the Fourth Circuit Court of Appeal denying the purchaser of an imported Mercedes-Benz automobile warranty rights against Mercedes-Benz of North America, Inc., the American distributor that supplied the automobile to the dealer. We reverse.

On April 30, 1968, Media Production Consultants, Inc., a public relations firm, purchased a new 1968 Mercedes-Benz automobile from Cookie's Auto Sales, Inc., in Baton Rouge. The automobile had been manufactured in Germany by Daimler-Benz Aktiengesellschaft, a German corporation. The manufacturer transferred the automobile at the factory to Daimler-Benz of North America, the American importer, with warranty covering defects in materials and workmanship. At the American port of entry, the importer transferred the automobile to Mercedes-Benz of North America, Inc. (MBNA), the distributor. MBNA inspected the automobile and, at its vehicle distribution center, prepared it for sale to a dealer. It was later sold to Cookie's Auto Sales, Inc., a dealer holding a franchise from MBNA. The Claims Policies and Procedures Manual, which MBNA furnished to Cookie's, contains the following warranty:

> "'Seller [MBNA] warrants (except as hereinafter provided) each part of each new Mercedes-Benz motor vehicle sold by dealer and operated in North America; i.e., the U.S.A. and Canada (including each part of any accessory or equipment thereon manufactured by Daimler-Benz A.G. or supplied by Mercedes-Benz of North America, Inc.) to be free from defects in material and workmanship under normal use and service until such motor vehicle has been operated for a distance of 24,000 miles or for a period of 24 months from the date of delivery to the original purchaser or from the date of initial operation, whichever event shall first occur.

> "'Seller's obligation under this warranty is limited to the replacement or repair at Seller's option, without charge for installation at Seller's place of business, of such parts as shall be returned to and acknowledged by Seller to be defective.'"

> . . . (Specific exclusions omitted.)

> "'This warranty is expressly in lieu of all other warranties and representations, expressed or implied, and of all other obligations or liabilities on the part of the Seller, Mercedes-Benz of North America, Inc. and Daimler-Benz

of North America, Inc. and Daimler-Benz A.G. Seller neither assumes nor authorizes any other person to assume for it any other liability in connection with such motor vehicle.'"[2]

Cookie's sold the automobile to Media. The Mercedes-Benz Owner's Service Policy delivered with automobile contained a warranty that the vehicle was "'free from defects in material and workmanship.'" In it the dealer agreed to replace or repair defective parts. The Service Policy also contains the following provision:

> "'This warranty is expressly in lieu of all other warranties and representations, expressed or implied, and of all other obligations or liabilities on the part of Dealer, Mercedes-Benz of North America, Inc., and Daimler-Benz A. G. Dealer neither assumes nor authorizes any other person to assume for it any other liability in connection with such motor vehicle.'"

The cover of the Mercedes-Benz Service policy bore the inscription: Mercedes-Banz [sic] of North America, Inc, Service Department, 158 Linwood Plaza, Fort Lee, New Jersey. To validate the warranty, the customer was requested to fill in and mail a card captioned "'Important—Warranty'" to MBNA.

The purchaser also received a manual describing the automobile and giving its specifications, bearing the inscription, Mercedes-Benz of North America, Inc.

Immediately after the purchase, Media found the automobile unsuitable for use. Among the defects were a peeling off of the interior trim, interior lights that did not burn, transmission problems, stalling in traffic, a defective air conditioner, excessive brake squeal, deterioration of rear window channels, uncorrectable vibration, and paint deficiencies.

After futile efforts to obtain correction of the deficiencies, Media surrendered the car to an authorized dealer and filed this suit.

Both lower courts found the vehicle so defective as to require an avoidance of the sale. Accordingly, the sale was set aside with judgment against Cookie's, the dealer, for the purchase price. The judgment is now final but unexecuted. It is conceded that the dealer is no longer in business.

The question before us is whether or not the automobile buyer can recover from the distributor.

---

2. The four-page dealership contract executed by MBNA and Cookie's Auto Sales, Inc. contains the following italicized paragraph: "*Twelfth: EXCEPT AS EXPRESSLY STATED IN SUBPARAGRAPH (N) OF PARAGRAPH 10 AND SUBPARAGRAPH (H) OF PARAGRAPH 11 of the STANDARD PROVISIONS OF THE DEALER AGREEMENT, MBNA MAKES NO WARRANTIES WHATSOEVER, EXPRESS OR IMPLIED, AS TO PERFORMANCE, CHARACTERISTICS, SPECIFICATIONS, OR CONDITION OF MERCEDES-BENZ PASSENGER CARS OR MERCEDES-BENZ PARTS TO BE SUPPLIED BY IT TO THE DEALER, INCLUDING BUT NOT LIMITED TO THE MERCHANTABILITY OR FITNESS FOR ANY PARTICULAR PURPOSE AND ASSUMES NO LIABILITY WHATSOEVER, WHETHER FOR DIRECT, INDIRECT, OR CONSEQUENTIAL DAMAGES, OR IN ANY OTHER WAY IN CONNECTION WITH SUCH PERFORMANCE, CHARACTERISTICS, SPECIFICATIONS, OR CONDITION.*"

The Court of Appeal held that no express or implied warranty ran from MBNA to Media, the purchaser, and denied recourse against the distributor. In our opinion, this disposition is unsound.

Two warranty obligations are inherent in every sale, the warranty of merchantable title and the warranty of reasonable fitness for the product's intended use. LSA-C.C. Arts. 2475, 2476 [R.C.C. 2475].±

The jurisprudence is well settled that warranty limitation provisions in automobile manuals and similar documents delivered with the vehicle have no effect upon the statutory warranty of fitness. [Citations omitted.] Hence, despite the warranty limitation in the Owner's Service Policy, Media has not renounced the warranty of fitness.

More difficult is the question of whether Mercedes-Benz of North America can be held liable for a breach of the implied warranty.

MBNA asserts that it has no liability in warranty to Media, because it is neither the seller nor manufacturer of the automobile and has no contract with the purchaser.

Media asserts that MBNA occupies the position of manufacturer and, under sound legal theory, no privity of contract is required for a consumer to bring an action in warranty against a manufacturer of a defective product, relying upon *Penn v. Inferno Mfg. Corp.*, La.App., 199 So.2d 210, *cert. denied* 251 La 27, 202 So.2d 649 (1967); *Marine Ins. Co. v. Strecker*, 234 La. 522, 100 So.2d 493 (1958); *MacPherson v. Buick Motor Co.*, 217 N.Y. 382, 111 N.E. 1050, L.R.A.1916F, 696.

The maker of Media's vehicle is a foreign corporation, not qualified to do business in the United States. In its distribution agreement, MBNA assumes the total responsibility for marketing the cars in the United States and for selling, servicing, and establishing franchise dealerships. Its name appears upon the Dealers Claims Policies and Procedures Manual, the owner's service policy, and the owner's automobile manual.

It operates a vehicle distribution center and inspects, adjusts, and prepares the automobiles for placement in the hands of a dealer for retail sale.

Insofar as the American consumer is concerned, MBNA occupies the position of manufacturer. We hold, therefore, that the liability of MBNA to the American consumer is that of the manufacturer of a defective vehicle. *See Penn v. Inferno Mfg. Corp.*, supra; *Carney v. Sears, Roebuck & Co.*, 309 F.2d 300 (1962); Restatement (Second) of Torts § 400, Comment (C); 65 C.J.S. Negligence § 100(3), p. 1114.

± [Note that although the Court speaks of the "warranty of merchantable title" and the warranty of "reasonable fitness for the product's specific use," the Civil Code articles to which the Court cites reference the warranties of "peaceful possession" (i.e., eviction) and "hidden defects of the thing sold or . . . redhibitory vices." *Eds.*]

MBNA strongly relies upon the absence of privity between it and the purchaser. The question of no privity, no liability is the traditional rule that held sway for many years. Beginning with the landmark decision of *MacPherson v. Buick Motor Co.*, *supra*, in 1916, however, the privity requirement has been eliminated in product liability cases. *See, e.g., Henningsen v. Bloomfield Motors, Inc.*, 327 N.J. 358, 161 A.2d 69 (1960); *Jacob E. Decker & Sons, Inc. v. Capps*, 139 Tex. 609, 164 S.W.2d 828 (1942).

Louisiana has aligned itself with the consumer-protection rule, by allowing a consumer without privity to recover, whether the suit be strictly in tort or upon implied warranty. *Marine Ins. Co. v. Strecker, supra*; *LeBlanc v. Louisiana Coca Cola Bottling Co.*, 221 La. 919, 60 So.2d 873 (1952).[3]

We see no reason why the rule should not apply to the pecuniary loss resulting from the purchase of a new automobile that proves unfit for use because of latent defects.

The Legislature has declared that the distribution and sale of motor vehicles in Louisiana vitally affect the public interest. *See* LSA-R.S. 32:1251. By placing automobiles on the market, the supplier represents to the public that the vehicles are suitable for use. The intervention of a franchised dealer should not mitigate that responsibility. The dealer serves only as a conduit for marketing the automobiles.

The pecuniary loss resulting from an unusable vehicle is recoverable when there is an *express* warranty without privity. [Citations omitted.] Although there is a split of authority on the question, we find no adequate reason for not applying the same rule and allowing recovery when there is an Implied warranty without privity. [Citations omitted.]

We hold, therefore, that Mercedes-Benz of North America, Inc. is solidarily liable with Cookie's Auto Sales, Inc. [sic] for the price of the automobile and other allowable expenses.

The Court of Appeal has never reviewed the amount of recovery, since it affirmed the trial court's dismissal of the suit. Hence, the case should be remanded to that court for fixing of the amount of the award. *See Felt v. Price*, 240 La. 966, 126 So.2d 330 (1961).

For the reasons assigned, the judgment of the Court of Appeal is reversed and judgment is rendered in favor of plaintiff, Media Production Consultants, Inc., and against the defendant, Mercedes-Benz of North America, Inc., in such amount as may hereafter be fixed, said judgment to be in solido with that rendered against Cookie's Auto Sales, Inc. The case is remanded to the Court of Appeal, Fourth Circuit, for the fixing of the award. All costs are taxed against the defendant.

DIXON, Justice (concurring).

---

3. Under French law, the right to sue the original vendor for breach of warranty of quality is transmitted with the object of the sale. Hec, Commentaire the orique et pratique du Code civil X (1897) No. 154, p. 209; Baudry-Lacantinerie et Saignat, Traite the orique et pratique de droit civil XVII, De la vente et de l'e change (2E e d. 1900) No. 432, pp. 368-369; 14 Tul.L.Rev. 471.

I fully concur in the opinion of the majority.

An additional reason available to the plaintiff is that it was subrogated to the rights of warranty of Cookie's Auto Sales, Inc. Cookie could have waived all its rights against MBNA; the warranty of quality could have been waived but was not. The waiver must be specific. C.C. 1764 [R.C.C. 2474, 2548]; Note, 4 Tul.L.Rev. 285; *see also* C.C. 2503 [R.C.C. 2503].

The limitations that MBNA attempted to place on its warranty as quoted in footnote 2 of the majority opinion did not serve as a waiver of all rights of warranty by Cookie. MBNA did not say that it sold cars to Cookie without Any warranty whatsoever, express or implied. MBNA modified the "'no warranty'" clause to limit it to performance, characteristics, specifications and conditions, including merchantability and fitness for a particular purpose. The warranty of quality of C.C. 2520 [R.C.C. 2520] (against redhibitory vices which might render a car absolutely useless or its use so imperfect and inconvenient that it would not have been knowingly purchased) was not mentioned.

This dealership contract was obviously prepared by MBNA. If any ambiguity exists as to the interpretation of limitations placed on the no warranty clause, it must be construed against MBNA. As this court said in *Radalec, Incorporated v. Automatic Firing Corporation*, 228 La. 116, 123, 81 So.2d 830, 833:

> "Under Article 2476 [R.C.C. 2474, 2458] of the Civil Code, the warranty against hidden defects and redhibitory vices is implied in every contract of sale unless expressly excluded, see *Nelson v. M.C.M. Truck Lines*, 209 La. 582, 25 So.2d 236, and Article 2474 [R.C.C. 2474] declares that 'The seller is bound to explain himself clearly respecting the extent of his obligation: any obscure or ambiguous clause is construed against him'. Accordingly, even if it be liberally conceded that the defendant actually intended to restrict its entire liability to a replacement of parts, it would still be responsible, as the alleged limitation in the contract does not plainly signify such an aim."

Under C.C. 2503 [R.C.C. 2503], the buyer is subrogated to the seller's rights and actions in warranty. If C.C. 2503 [R.C.C. 2503] is applicable, plaintiff Media is subrogated to Cookie's rights against MBNA. C.C. 2503 [R.C.C. 2503] should be applicable, even though found in the section of the code dealing with warranty against eviction. This court recognized its applicability in dicta in *McEachern v. Plauche Lumber & Construction Co., Inc.*, 220 La. 696, 57 So.2d 405, 408. *See also* 14 Tul.L.Rev. 470; 23 Tul.L.Rev. 119, 140.

This principle of subrogation, long recognized as applicable to the warranty of quality, should be available to plaintiff.

Notes and Questions

1. Recall that subrogation is "the substitution of one person for the rights of another." LA. CIV. CODE art. 1825. As in the case of eviction, in the context of

redhibition subrogation permits the buyer to exercise the rights of his or her seller against more remote sellers in the chain of title. Without the operation of this rule, of course, the principle of privity of contract would prevent the buyer from asserting a breach of contract claim against anyone but his or her own seller. The right of subrogation is of critical importance when a judgment against the buyer's immediate seller would be insufficient to make the buyer whole, as when the seller is insolvent or cannot be located. Rather than restricting the buyer's recovery to suit against his or her seller alone, the buyer is entitled to bring a claim against remote sellers in the chain of title in addition to, or in lieu of, the immediate seller.

2. While the buyer's right of subrogation has been codified by Article 2548, some questions remain regarding the extent of the buyer's recovery against remote sellers in the chain of title. Specifically, the buyer's recovery against an individual seller in the chain of title is likely dependent upon (1) the good or bad faith of that seller and (2) the price paid to that seller by his buyer.

The difficulties surrounding the extent of the buyer's recovery are best illustrated through a hypothetical. Consider the following example:

> Manufacturer, the manufacturer of an automobile, sells to Dealer, the retailer, for $30,000. Dealer then sells to Consumer, the end-buyer, for $35,000. Consumer later discovers a number of significant defects that were both hidden and present at the time of delivery from Manufacturer to Dealer. Dealer does not hold itself out as the manufacturer of the automobile and has no knowledge of the existence of any defects.

First, consider how the good or bad faith of the seller impacts that seller's liability. Dealer is a good faith seller—one who did know that the thing sold had a defect. On the other hand, Manufacturer, who is "deemed" to have knowledge of the defect, is a seller in bad faith. Dealer, as a good faith seller, is liable for the return of the price, plus interest and expenses, but not damages or attorney fees. In contrast, Manufacturer, as a bad faith seller, is liable not only for the return of the price, plus interest and expenses, but also damages and attorney fees.

While it is clear that Dealer could seek the return of the price, damages, and attorney fees from Manufacturer, it is less clear whether Consumer is entitled to recover damages and attorney fees from Manufacturer when Consumer could not have recovered those damages from Dealer—Consumer's own vendor. Presumably, when Consumer is subrogated to Dealer's rights against Manufacturer, Consumer acquires the same rights that Dealer would have against Manufacturer, which of course includes the right to damages and attorney fees owing to Manufacturer's bad faith. Moreover, given that Manufacturer is a bad faith seller, allowing Consumer to recover damages and attorney fees is consistent with the "consumer protection" approach of the Louisiana jurisprudence. On the other hand, given that Consumer could not recover damages and attorney fees from Dealer—Consumer's own seller—to allow Consumer that recovery against Manufacturer provides Consumer with a windfall of sorts. Is this result desirable?

Second, consider how the price paid to the seller impacts that seller's liability. In the hypothetical above, Manufacturer sold to Dealer for $30,000, and Dealer subsequently sold to Consumer for $35,000. In a suit against Dealer, Consumer could recover the full price that he paid to Dealer—$35,000. Whether Consumer can recover that sum from Manufacturer is less clear. Arguably, by occupying Dealer's position, Consumer is limited to the sum that Dealer could recover from Manufacturer. Since Dealer paid only $30,000, the "price" Manufacturer owes to Dealer is that sum and no more. Nevertheless, Consumer has a strong argument supporting a claim for the full $35,000. Recall that Manufacturer is a seller in "bad faith," liable to Dealer not only for the price but also damages. From Dealer's perspective, the difference between the price paid by Dealer to the Manufacturer and the price paid by Consumer to Dealer is characterized as "lost profits"—a recoverable element of damage resulting from any breach of contract claim. *See* LA. CIV. CODE art. 1995. Note too that the buyer's ability to collect as damages the increase in value of the thing sold differs between redhibition and eviction. Whereas the eviction rule, Article 2506, expressly forecloses the characterization as damages "any increase in value of the thing," no such limitation is stated in the provisions governing the action in redhibition. Thus, since the articles on redhibition do not foreclose recovery for increase in value, this appears to be an allowable element of the buyer's damages against a bad faith seller in the chain of title. However, without clear legislative or jurisprudential rules on the topic of subrogation, it remains unclear whether a remote seller is liable to return a price greater than that received from his or her own buyer.

3. Article 2548 provides for the buyer's right of subrogation "even when the warranty has been excluded." LA. CIV. CODE art. 2548. This language leads inexorably to the conclusion that even if the warranty has been waived by the buyer vis-à-vis the buyer's immediate seller, the buyer may nonetheless step into the seller's shoes to seek recourse against more remote sellers in the chain of title. Presumably, however, the buyer has no claim against any seller in the chain of title who sold the thing subject to a valid and enforceable waiver of the warranty against redhibitory defects. Recall, however, that waivers protect only good faith sellers; an otherwise valid waiver has no effect against a bad faith seller, including a manufacturer. *See* LA. CIV. CODE arts. 2531, 2548.

4. Is the buyer subrogated to the seller's claims against persons other than sellers in the chain of title? For instance, what if the defect in the thing sold is caused by the fault of someone other than a manufacturer or seller, such as contractor whose work resulted in a defect, or a lessee who caused damage to the property prior to the sale? Article 2548 states that the buyer is subrogated to the rights "in warranty" of the seller against other persons, thus signaling that the buyer does not acquire the right to assert actions of the seller that are not premised on breach of warranty. LA. CIV. CODE art. 2548. In addition, the Louisiana Supreme Court has made clear that while a buyer has a claim in redhibition against a former owner for hidden damage to the thing sold, the buyer does not, absent express conventional assignment

or subrogation, acquire the former owner's claims against persons outside of the chain of title for damage caused by their fault. *See Eagle Pipe & Supply, Inc. v. Hess*, 79 So. 3d 246 (La. 2011) (holding that a purchaser of land contaminated with radioactive material, absent express conventional assignment, was not subrogated to the seller's claims against oil and trucking companies allegedly responsible for the contamination).

2. The Nature of the Sellers' Liability: Solidary or Not?

Given that all sellers in the chain of title, including the manufacturer, are potentially liable to the buyer in redhibition, a question arises regarding the nature of sellers' liability. Recall that under the general principles of obligations law, "[w]hen an obligation binds more than one obligor to one obligee . . . the obligation may be several, joint, or solidary." La. Civ. Code art. 1786.

For decades, the conventional wisdom has held that sellers in the chain of title are *solidarily* liable. The first pronouncement of solidarity came in 1972, when the Louisiana Supreme Court announced in *Media Production Consultants, Inc. v. Mercedez-Benz of North American, Inc.* that the dealer-manufacturer was liable *in solido* with the buyer's immediate vendor. 262 So. 2d 377, 381 (1972). And although the Civil Code does not provide explicitly for solidarity, comment (c) to Article 2545 affirmatively states that "the manufacturer and the seller are solidarily liable to the buyer for the return of the price." La. Civ. Code art. 2545 cmt. c. *See also* 24 Dian Tooley-Knoblett & David Gruning, Louisiana Civil Law Treatise, Sales § 11:31 (2017) (discussing historical treatment of sellers as solidarily liable).

When multiple obligors are bound solidarily, each is liable for the whole performance. *See* La. Civ. Code art. 1794. Applied in the context of redhibition, this general principle suggests that each seller in the chain of title is liable for the full extent of the buyer's recovery. However, given that the liability of an individual seller in the chain of title varies depending upon (1) the good or bad faith of that seller and (2) the price paid to that seller by his vendee, it is doubtful that the general principle of solidarity can be applied to *every* redhibition claim. Consider the following example:

> Andrea sells a house to Beau for $200,000, who in turn sells to Constance for $225,000. At the time of delivery from Andrea to Beau, the house was infested with termites. While Andrea did not know of the termite infestation prior to the sale to Beau, Beau had discovered the infestation prior to the sale to Constance and failed to disclose it.

On these facts, Andrea is a seller in good faith; Beau, in contrast, is in bad faith. In a suit against Beau, Constance may recover the full price paid ($225,000), damages, and attorney fees. Against Andrea, however, Constance is likely limited to the price paid by Beau ($200,000). Assuming that Andrea is liable for no more than $200,000, it cannot be the case that Andrea is liable solidarily with Beau for the full extent of Beau's performance. Rather, at best, Andrea and Beau are solidarily bound for the full extent of Andrea's performance ($200,000), while Beau is jointly (or perhaps severally) bound for the remainder ($25,000, damages, and attorney fees).

Recent jurisprudence has recognized another challenge to the conventional wisdom of solidarity among sellers in the chain of title: comparative fault. Comparative fault was introduced into Louisiana's tort law in 1996. According to Article 2323, "In any action for damages where a person suffers injury, death, or loss, the degree or percentage of fault of all persons causing or contributing to the injury, death, or loss shall be determined . . . ." LA. CIV. CODE art. 2323. This language effectively abolishes solidary liability among tortfeasors (although Article 2324 carves out an exception for liability resulting from "intentional" or "willful" acts, which remain solidary in nature).

Following Article 2323's amendment, a question emerged regarding the extent to which the regime of comparative fault may be applicable to actions involving breach of contract, and more specifically, to actions for breach of the warranty against redhibitory vices and defects. While the placement of Article 2323 in Title V of Book III ("Obligations Arising Without Agreement") may seem to foreclose the application of comparative fault to contractual liability, Article 2323 is not so obviously restricted in scope. The article itself provides: "The provisions of [this Article] shall apply to any claim for recovery of damages for injury, death, or loss asserted under *any law or legal doctrine or theory of liability, regardless of the basis of liability.*" LA. CIV. CODE art. 2323 (emphasis added). According to some courts, this language prohibits a finding that sellers in the chain of title are solidarily liable for the damage suffered by the buyer, and instead mandates that fault be apportioned among the manufacturer, intermediate sellers, and ultimate vendor.

As of the publication of this Textbook, Louisiana's appellate courts are split on the issue of whether comparative fault applies to actions in redhibition and thus eradicates solidary liability. The Second Circuit has held that Article 2323 is applicable to actions in redhibition and have thus concluded that solidary liability is inapplicable to sellers in redhibition. *Hampton v. Cappaert Manufactured Housing, Inc.*, 839 So. 2d 363 (La. App. 2 Cir. 2003). In contrast, the Third and Fourth Circuits have held that Article 2323 applies only to actions in tort and does not apply in an action in redhibition because such actions are based on the law of contract; thus, solidary liability is applicable to redhibition claims in those circuits. *See Touro Infirmary v. Sizeler Architects*, 900 So. 2d 200 (La. App. 4 Cir. 2005), *writs denied* 901 So. 2d 1093 (La. 2005), 920 So. 2d 232 (La. 2006); *Justiss Oil Co., Inc. v. Oil Country Tubular Corp.*, 216 So. 3d 346 (La. App. 3 Cir. 2017). Opinions from the First Circuit are conflicting, with some deciding that Article 2323 applies to redhibition claims, foreclosing solidary liability, *see Petroleum Rental Tools v. Hal Oil & Gas Co., Inc.*, 701 So. 2d 213 (La. App. 1 Cir. 1997), *writ dismissed* 706 So. 2d 982 (La. 1998), and others deciding that Article 2323 does not apply in redhibition, allowing for solidary liability. *See, e.g., Hoffman v. B & G, Inc.*, 215 So. 3d 273, 282 (La. App. 1 Cir. 2017).

In 2008, the Louisiana Supreme Court granted writs in a case that provided an opportunity for the Court to resolve the circuit split definitively. As you read the following opinion, consider whether the Louisiana Supreme Court has, in fact, clarified the nature of the liability of sellers in the chain of title.

Aucoin v. Southern Quality Homes, LLC

984 So. 2d 685 (La. 2008)

VICTORY, J.

* * * * *

FACTS AND PROCEDURAL HISTORY

Kelly G. Aucoin ("plaintiff") purchased a mobile home and land from Southern Quality Homes, LLC (the "seller") on July 6, 2001 for $93,980.00. The mobile home had been delivered to Southern Quality Homes' lot by Dynasty Homes (the "manufacturer") in January, 2000. A pre-occupancy inspection report listed numerous defects in regard to the mobile home; however, Southern Quality Homes assured plaintiff they were minor and would be repaired. Plaintiff alleged that after the delivery and set-up of the mobile home, he and his wife, Cindy, began to experience problems with the home. The Aucoins contacted Southern Quality Homes and Dynasty Homes numerous times regarding these defects, and several attempts at repair were made by the manufacturer.

Plaintiff ultimately filed suit against Southern Quality Homes and Dynasty Homes, alleging redhibitory defects and seeking to hold the two defendants solidarily liable for rescission of the sale, including the price of the land, damages and expenses. At trial, the plaintiff presented expert witness testimony that the principal defect in the home was a moisture problem that caused a proliferation of mold, and that the manufacturer was responsible for several defects that related to the infiltration of moisture, including improper installation of the vinyl vapor barrier, improper sealing of the marriage line, improper fastening and installation of the roof and roof shingles, improper installation of vinyl siding, and improper installation of drywall on the ceiling. The plaintiff also produced a document dated October 17, 2000, wherein Southern Quality Homes requested service from Dynasty Homes because the ceiling in the master bedroom had a leak and needed repair, indicating that defects relating to the moisture problem were present in the home when the home was delivered by the manufacturer to the seller.

The trial court found in favor of the plaintiff, relying heavily on the above mentioned testimony of the plaintiff's expert witnesses.

* * * * *

[T]he trial court inspected the home and noted the following:

> "[t]he Court visually walked through the home at the request of all counsel and was especially troubled by the obvious condition of the siding having deflections or bowing, and the fact that the underside of the home had not

been sealed properly. The Court was not able to get on the roof and look at the roof problems described by Mr. Mallet nor was the Court able to get in the attic and notice the improper sealing problems mentioned by Mr. Mallet. However, the Court finds his testimony to be credible and accepts his testimony on these issues. The 'gap' between the wall and the ceiling was obvious. You could actually see light from outside through the crack."

The trial court concluded that:

[t]he main and principle [sic] defect in this mobile home is the moisture problem causing the mold and eventual deterioration of the home. The main cause of the moisture problem, the Court finds, is the improper sealing of the marriage lines in the roof and underside of the home and top plate. The construction defects in the home show poor quality workmanship throughout, and though some problems are minor and are easily repaired, taken as a whole, the plaintiffs have satisfied their burden under the redhibition articles.

Recognizing that the seller had filed for bankruptcy, the trial court held the manufacturer and the seller solidarily liable for these redhibitory defects. Finally, the trial court held the manufacturer liable for nonpecuniary damages under La. C.C. art. 1998, finding a "significant nonpecuniary interest in the fact that the Aucoins decided to upgrade and buy this new mobile home to satisfy their desire to achieve the American dream and to have a new, much finer home so that they could live more comfortably, worry free, and entertain family and friends." The total damages awarded were the $93,980.00 purchase price for the home and land, $4,190.33 for closing costs, $1,000 for dirt work, $25,000 for mental pain and suffering, $25,000 in attorney fees, $25,000 in expert fees, $288.18 for medical bills, $285.00 for prescription bills, and $6,446.13 for insurance and taxes.

The court of appeal affirmed the trial court's judgment. *Aucoin v. Southern Quality Homes, LLC*, 06-979 (La.App. 3 Cir. 2/28/07), 953 So.2d 856. The court of appeal rejected the manufacturer's argument that the 1996 amendments to La. C.C. arts. 2323 and 2324 applied to redhibition and instead chose to rely on "the clear legislative intent expressed in La. Civ.Code art. 2545 to hold manufacturers and sellers generally solidarily bound to help protect consumers." 953 So.2d at 861. The court of appeal further found that "[i]n order for Dynasty not to be held solidarily bound with Southern Quality, it must show that the redhibitory defects present in the home sold to Aucoin were solely caused by Southern Quality." *Id.* The court of appeal found no manifest error in the trial court's factual finding that both the seller and manufacturer were at fault in causing the redhibitory defect. *Id.* at 862. The court of appeal likewise rejected the manufacturer's other arguments, finding that the manufacturer was liable for improper setup and sealing of the home; that damages, including the cost of the land, closing costs, and mental pain and suffering were appropriate; and that the expert fees awarded were not excessive. *Id.* at 863. We granted Dynasty Homes' writ application to determine whether it is liable for the redhibitory defects in this mobile home, and, if so, the appropriate damages thereunder. *Aucoin v. Southern Quality Homes, LLC*, 07-1014 (La.6/29/07), 959 So.2d 516.

DISCUSSION

The statutory law relative to redhibition is contained in Title VII of the Louisiana Civil Code governing "Sale." La. C.C. art. 2520 states the warranty against redhibitory defects as follows:

> The seller warrants the buyer against redhibitory defects, or vices, in the thing sold.
>
> A defect is redhibitory when it renders the thing useless, or its use so inconvenient that it must be presumed that a buyer would not have bought the thing had he known of the defect. The existence of such a defect gives a buyer the right to obtain rescission of the sale.
>
> A defect is redhibitory also when, without rendering the thing totally useless, it diminishes its usefulness or its value so that it must be presumed that a buyer would still have bought it but for a lesser price. The existence of such a defect limits the right of a buyer to a reduction of the price.[8]

La. C.C. art. 2530 provides in pertinent part that "[t]he warranty against redhibitory defects covers only defects that exist at the time of delivery."

The extent of a seller's liability to a buyer for breaching this warranty depends on whether the seller knew, or did not know, of the defect. La. C.C. art. 2531 provides:

> A seller who did not know that the thing he sold had a defect is only bound to repair, remedy, or correct the defect. If he is unable or fails so to do, he is then bound to return the price to the buyer with interest from the time it was paid, and to reimburse him for the reasonable expenses occasioned by the sale, as well as those incurred for the preservation of the thing, less the credit to which the seller is entitled if the use made of the thing, or the fruits it has yielded, were of some value to the buyer.
>
> A seller who is held liable for a redhibitory defect has an action against the manufacturer of the defective thing, if the defect existed at the time the thing was delivered by the manufacturer to the seller, for any loss the seller sustained because of the redhibition. Any contractual provision that attempts to limit, diminish or prevent such recovery by a seller against the manufacturer shall have no effect.

---

8. The Louisiana Products Liability Act, enacted in 1988, provides that it "establishes the exclusive theories of liability for manufacturers for damages caused by their products." La. R.S. 9:2800.52. However, the LPLA defines "damage" by explicitly excluding amounts recoverable under redhibition for damage to the product and economic loss arising from a deficiency in or loss of use of the product. La. R.S. 9:2800.53(5). Thus, while the LPLA is the exclusive remedy against manufacturers for damages resulting from a defective product, a manufacturer can still be liable for damages in redhibition.

On the other hand, the liability of a seller who knows of the defect is greater:

> A seller who knows that the thing he sells has a defect but omits to declare it, or a seller who declares that the thing has a quality that he knows it does not have, is liable to the buyer for the return of the price with interest from the time it was paid, for the reimbursement of the reasonable expenses occasioned by the sale and those incurred for the preservation of the thing, and also for damages and reasonable attorney fees. If the use made of the thing, or the fruits it might have yielded, were of some value to the buyer, such a seller may be allowed credit for such use or fruits.
>
> A seller is deemed to know that the thing he sells has a redhibitory defect when he is a manufacturer of that thing.

La. C.C. art. 2545.

In *Young v. Ford Motor Co., Inc.*, 595 So.2d 1123 (La.1992), we explained the Roman origins of the redhibitory action and that its purpose was to protect buyers from latent defects undisclosed by corrupt dealers. "This important aspect of our current law on sales (i.e., this system of implied warranty against latent defects and vices) was fully incorporated into Louisiana law." *Id. (See e.g.,* Louisiana Civil Code of 1808, Art. 66 and Art. 71) "The purpose of the redhibition action in Louisiana, as was the case in Roman law, has been to restore the *status quo.*" *Id.* (Citing Floyd W. Lewis, Comment, *Warranty of Quality in Louisiana: Extent of Recovery under the Implied-In-Law Warranty*, 23 Tul. L.Rev. 130, 131 (1948); *Savoie v. Snell*, 213 La. 823, 35 So.2d 745, 746 (1948). "The seller in good faith had only to restore the purchase price paid and any expenses incurred (Article 2509, La. Civil Code of 1825), while the seller in bad faith was also liable in damages. Article 2523, La. Civil Code of 1825)." *Id.* Thus, an action in redhibition entitles the buyer to annul the sale and recover the purchase price, rather than being limited to recovering the cost of curing any such substantial defects. *Rey v. Cuccia*, 298 So.2d 840 (La.1974); *Prince v. Paretti Pontiac Co., Inc.*, 281 So.2d 112 (La.1973).

Although the code articles on redhibition appear to only allow a suit by a buyer against a "seller" for redhibitory defects, this Court held in *Media Production Consultants, Inc. v. Mercedes-Benz of North America, Inc.*, 262 La. 80, 262 So.2d 377 (1972), that the buyer could recover directly from the manufacturer for breach of warranty, despite the fact that there was no privity of contract between them. In *Media Production*, the Court stated:

> Louisiana has aligned itself with the consumer-protection rule, by allowing a consumer without privity to recover, whether the suit be strictly in tort or upon implied warranty. *Marine Ins. Co. v. Strecker*, 234 La. 522, 100 So.2d 493 (1958); *LeBlanc v. Louisiana Coco Cola Bottling Co.*, 221 La. 919, 60 So.2d 873 (1952).
>
> We see no reason why the rule should not apply to the pecuniary loss resulting from the purchase of a new automobile that proves unfit for use because of latent defects. The pecuniary loss resulting from an unusable

vehicle is recoverable when there is an Express warranty without privity. [Cites omitted.] Although there is a split of authority on the question, we find no adequate reason for not applying the same rule and allowing recovery when there is an Implied [sic] warranty without privity. [Cites omitted.]

262 So.2d at 380-81. After this analysis, the Court held "that Mercedes-Benz of North America, Inc. [the manufacturer], is solidarily liable with [the seller] for the price of the automobile and other allowable expenses." *Id.*

Two years later, in *Rey v. Cuccia*, supra, this Court relied on *Media Productions* to hold the manufacturer of a trailer solidarily liable with the seller for a redhibitory defect which existed at the time the manufacturer sold the trailer to the seller. *See also Womack and Adcock v. 3M Business Products Sales, Inc.*, 316 So.2d 795 (La. App. 1 Cir.1975) (holding that "since the now famous case of *Media Pro. . . .* , the buyer's action for breach of implied warranty has been extended to all sellers in the chain of sales back to the primary manufacturer"). The Court in *Rey* held that "[t]he consumer's action is enforceable against the manufacturer at the same time and at least within the same year following the sale to the consumer, Article 2534, as it is enforceable against the seller." 298 So.2d at 845. The Court further held that because the manufacturer is presumed to know of defects, the one-year limitation of Article 2534 does not apply and the consumer may institute the action to recover for the redhibitory defect within the year following his discovery of it. *Id.* (Citing La. C.C. art. 2546).

Although *Media Production* and *Rey* held the manufacturer and seller were solidarily liable for the defects at issue, we need not reach the correctness of that issue, as we find that the manufacturer is independently liable under those cases for redhibitory defects that existed at the time of delivery to the seller.[12]

Under La. C.C. art. 2520, the seller warrants the product he sells to be free of redhibitory defects, and under La. C.C. art. 2531, the seller is liable to the buyer even for redhibitory defects he was not aware of, including those that were the fault of the manufacturer. In such a case, the seller is responsible for correcting the defect, or, if he is unable to do so, he must return the purchase price with interest, plus reimburse the buyer for his reasonable expenses; however, he has an action against the manufacturer for any defects which "existed at the time the thing was delivered by the manufacturer to the seller." La. C.C. art. 2531. On the other hand, while a buyer

---

12. Since the 1996 amendments to La. C.C. arts. 2323 and 2324, courts of appeal have split on the issue of whether La. C.C. arts. 2323 and 2324 apply to abolish solidary liability in redhibition cases. The First and Second Circuits have held that these articles apply to a redhibition suit. *Petroleum Rental Tools, Inc. v. Hal Oil & Gas, Co., Inc.*, 95, 1820 (La.App. 1 Cir. 8/22/97), 701 So.2d 213, *writ dismissed*, 97-3088 (La.2/10/98), 706 So.2d 982; *Hampton v. Cappaert Manufactured Housing, Inc.*, 36,773 (La.App. 2 Cir. 1/29/03), 839 So.2d 363. On the other hand, the Fourth Circuit has held that La. C.C. art. 2323 applies only to "actions based in tort" and that a redhibition suit is a contractual action, not a tort action. *Touro Infirmary v. Sizeler Architects*, 04-0634 (La.App. 4 Cir. 3/23/05), 900 So.2d 200, 205, *writs denied*, 04-2114 (La.5/6/05), 901 So.2d 1093 and 05-1315 (La.1/13/06), 920 So.2d 232.

may sue a manufacturer directly for redhibitory defects, the manufacturer is liable but only for defects "resulting from the original manufacture" of the product. *Rey v. Cuccia, supra* at 845.[13]

Thus, whether the manufacturer is solidarily liable with the seller for redhibitory defects is immaterial in this case, as the manufacturer is directly liable for redhibitory defects resulting from the original manufacture of the product. In this case, although the lower courts held that the manufacturer and seller were solidarily liable for the redhibitory defects, the trial court found, and the court of appeal affirmed, that the redhibitory defects were manufacturing defects, for which the manufacturer would be independently liable.

* * * * *

The manufacturer next argues that the trial court erred in holding it liable for the cost of the land and closing costs. It is undisputed that the manufacturer sold only the home to the seller, while the seller sold the home and land to the buyer for $93,980.00. The Third Circuit affirmed the trial court's holding by applying La. C.C. art. 2540, which provides that "[w]hen more than one thing are sold together as a whole so that the buyer would not have bought one thing without the other or others, a redhibitory defect in one of such things gives rise to redhibition for the whole." The court of appeal's holding was in error.

As early as 1894, this Court held that the principles contained in La. C.C. art. 2540 (1870) apply "only when the things sold are dependent upon each other, so that the defect of one renders the other useless and without value." *C.S. Burt Co. v. Laplace*, 46 La. Ann. 722, 15 So. 293 (La.1894). In this case, there was no evidence presented that defects in plaintiff's home rendered the land useless and without value such that plaintiff will be prevented from using the land in the future. Further, the manufacturer had nothing to do with the development and sale of the land to plaintiff. There is simply no legal basis under Louisiana law for holding the manufacturer of a mobile home liable for the rescission of the sale of the land simply because it was sold jointly with the home by the seller. Further, such a holding could lead to absurd results. For example, if plaintiff had purchased 100 acres of valuable land for $1,000,000 as part of a package deal with a defective $50,000 mobile home from a seller, it would be absurd to hold the manufacturer of the mobile home liable to the plaintiff for the value of the land. Thus, we find that the lower courts erred in holding the manufacturer liable for the purchase price of the land and closing costs associated with the land.

---

13. While *Media Productions, supra*, did state that the manufacturer was solidarily liable with the seller, neither *Media Productions, supra*, nor *Rey* held a manufacturer liable for defects caused by the seller. Further, *Media Productions* was not technically a redhibition case, but was a product liability case involving a breach of the warranty of reasonable fitness for the product's intended use under La. C.C. art. 2475.

Next, the manufacturer argues that the lower courts erred in awarding mental pain and suffering damages in this redhibition suit. First, the manufacturer argues that mental pain and suffering damages in this case are not allowed under the standards enunciated in *Young* for the award of nonpecuniary damages in a redhibition case. In addition, the manufacturer argues that the Louisiana Product Liability Act (the "LPA") provides the exclusive means of recovery for such damages, and plaintiff dismissed his LPA claim at the beginning of trial.

La. C.C. art. 1998 provides:

> Damages for nonpecuniary loss may be recovered when the contract, because of its nature, is intended to gratify a nonpecuniary interest and, because of the circumstances surrounding the formation or the nonperformance of the contract, the obligor knew, or should have known, that his failure to perform would cause that kind of loss.

> Regardless of the nature of the contract, these damages may be recovered also when the obligor intended, through his failure, to aggrieve the feelings of the obligee.

In *Young, supra*, where this Court was faced with the issue of whether nonpecuniary damages were awardable in a redhibitory action, we held:

> ... under Article 1998, which is the controlling article for the type of damages referred to by the redhibition articles (specifically Article 2545), if it can be established that the obligee intended-and if the nature of the contract supports this contention-to gratify a significant nonpecuniary interest by way of the contract, and that the obligor either knew or should have known that failure to perform would cause nonpecuniary loss to the obligee, then the requirements for recovery of nonpecuniary damages are satisfied.

595 So.2d at 1133.

The court of appeal found that the plaintiff proved a nonpecuniary interest by his testimony that he formerly lived in a small, 30-year-old mobile home and that he was purchasing this home to entertain family and friends and to live "the American Dream." However, as we stated in *Young*, the obligee must intend "to gratify a significant nonpecuniary interest by way of the contract," and the obligor must or should know that failure to perform would cause nonpecuniary loss. Regardless of whether plaintiff has or has not proven that he intended to gratify a significant nonpecuniary interest, he presented no evidence that the manufacturer knew or should have known that his failure to perform would cause nonpecuniary loss.[14] Further, there

---

14. Based on this ruling, we do not reach the issue of whether nonpecuniary damages are precluded in redhibition by the LPA.

was no evidence presented that the manufacturer "intended, though his failure, to aggrieve the feelings of the obligee" as required by La. C.C. art. 1998. Thus, we find that the lower courts erred in awarding damages for mental pain and suffering and the associated costs of medical bills and prescriptions.

⋆ ⋆ ⋆ ⋆ ⋆

CONCLUSION

The manufacturer is directly liable to the buyer for redhibitory defects which exist at the time the manufacturer sold and delivered the product to the seller. In this case, the lower courts did not err in finding redhibitory defects existed for which the manufacturer was responsible and in holding the manufacturer liable for damages pursuant to La. C.C. art. 2545. However, in its assessment of these damages, the lower courts erred in several respects. First, the manufacturer is only liable for the return of the purchase price of the mobile home with interest from the time it was paid and for reimbursement of the reasonable expenses occasioned by the sale and those incurred for the preservation of the mobile home, plus reasonable attorney fees as were properly awarded by the lower courts. The price of the land should not be included in this amount because the evidence did not show that the requirements of La. C.C. art. 2540 were met. Accordingly, on remand, the trial court must determine what amount of the $93,980.00 was for the mobile home and what was for the land, and what amount of the closing costs and dirt work were associated with the mobile home itself. The $25,000 attorney fee award was appropriate and should not be disturbed. In addition, the lower courts erred in awarding $25,000.00 in mental pain and suffering damages because the plaintiff failed to show that the manufacturer knew or should have known that its failure to perform his obligations would result in nonpecuniary losses. Finally, the trial court did not abuse its discretion in awarding $25,000.00 in expert witness fees, but did err in awarding $20,000.00 of that amount as damages bearing interest from the date of judicial demand. On remand, the trial court must tax the entire $25,000.00 as costs bearing interest from the date of judgment.

DECREE

For the reasons expressed herein, the judgment of the court of appeal is affirmed in part and reversed in part and the case is remanded to the trial court for further proceedings.

AFFIRMED IN PART; REVERSED IN PART; REMANDED TO TRIAL COURT.

KNOLL, Justice, dissents in part and assigns reasons.

KNOLL, Justice, dissenting in part.

I agree with the majority that the manufacturer is directly liable for redhibitory defects resulting from the manufacture of the mobile home under La. Civ.Code art. 2545, and under the facts of this case, the manufacturer is so liable. However, I find the majority errs in reversing the trial court's award of $25,000 for mental pain and suffering in nonpecuniary damages.

The majority is correct that this court held:

> [U]nder Article 1998, which is the controlling article for the type of damages referred to by the redhibition articles (specifically Article 2545), if it can be established that the obligee intended—and if the nature of the contract supports this contention—to gratify a significant nonpecuniary interest by way of the contract, and that the obligor either knew or should have known that failure to perform would cause nonpecuniary loss to the obligee, then the requirements for recovery of nonpecuniary damages are satisfied.

Young v. Ford Motor Co., Inc., 595 So.2d 1123, 1133 (La.1992).

The majority finds the lower courts erred in awarding nonpecuniary damages because the plaintiff presented no evidence that the manufacturer knew or should have known that his failure to perform would cause nonpecuniary loss. Although the majority is correct that there was no evidence presented concerning whether the manufacturer, Dynasty Homes, knew or should have known that its failure to perform would cause nonpecuniary loss to the plaintiff, that should not end our inquiry.

Louisiana Civil Code article 1998 provides:

> Damages for nonpecuniary loss may be recovered when the contract, because of its nature, is intended to gratify a nonpecuniary interest and, because of the circumstances surrounding the formation or the nonperformance of the contract, the obligor knew, or should have known, that his failure to perform would cause that kind of loss.

> Regardless of the nature of the contract, these damages may be recovered also when the obligor intended, through his failure, to aggrieve the feelings of the obligee.

In written reasons awarding nonpecuniary damages, the trial court stated:

> In holding the manufacturer *in solido* for redhibition under Article 2520, the Court finds the decision of the Third Circuit in *Beasley v. Ed's Mobile Home[s], Inc.*, 824 So.2d 383 (La.App. 3rd Cir.2002) instructive. The Court further finds that, as in the *Ed's Mobile Home* case, *the buyer is entitled to non-pecuniary damages based on the manufacturer's bad faith. That bad faith was due in part to the home being sold as a new home when the manufacturer knew that the home had previous damage and "moisture problems" in the ceiling. It likewise was in bad faith because it knew or should have known when the complaints were made by the plaintiff that the home had not been sealed properly and yet took no steps whatsoever to make the house secure and sealed. The manufacturer continues to downplay the problems with the mobile home as cosmetic only, and continues to attempt to argue that since the home was supposedly built in accordance with the National Manufactured Housing and Construction and Safety Standards, that it has no defects.* (emphasis added)

Although the trial court stated elsewhere in its written reasons that nonpecuniary damages were owed as the plaintiff sufficiently proved his significant nonpecuniary interest in purchasing the home, the court further made a specific finding that the manufacturer was in bad faith because it knew of and concealed from the plaintiff the facts that the mobile home had leaked and had water and ceiling damage before the sale. The second paragraph of La. Civ.Code art. 1998 provides an express exception to the requirement of a nonpecuniary purpose of the contract. That paragraph states:

> Regardless of the nature of the contract, these damages may be recovered *also* when the obligor intended, *through his failure*, to aggrieve the feelings of the obligee. (emphasis added).

In my view, finding a manufacturer in *intentional* bad faith is sufficient to prove the manufacturer "intended, through his failure, to aggrieve the feelings of the" purchaser. In this case, it is clear the plaintiff's repeated demands to the manufacturer to repair the defective mobile home fell upon deaf ears and aggrieved the plaintiff. Thus, I find the trial court was correct in awarding nonpecuniary damages.

The trial court, relying upon *Ducote v. Perry's Auto World, Inc.*, 98-1972 (La. Ct. App. 1 Cir. 11/5/99), 745 So.2d 229, held where there is intentional bad faith, nonpecuniary damages are also allowed. Relying upon *Beasley v. Ed's Mobile Homes, Inc.*, 01-1549 (La. Ct. App. 3 Cir. 4/17/02), 824 So.2d 383, *writ denied*, 02-1408 (La.9/20/02), 825 So.2d 1170 and *Ducote, supra*, the trial court found Dynasty Homes, because of its intentional bad faith, owed nonpecuniary damages to the plaintiff.

In *Beasley*, the plaintiff purchased a double-wide mobile home. The mobile home contained defects on the date of sale and still had the defects at the time of delivery. The manufacturer authorized a repairperson to submit an estimate of the cost to repair the mobile home; the estimated cost was $5,140. The manufacturer would not approve the repairs because the cost was over $5,000, even though the plaintiff offered to pay the difference of $140 if it would mean the home would be repaired. The trial court awarded judgment in favor of the plaintiff, including $30,000 in general damages.

Affirming the award of general damages in that case, the appellate court observed the evidence did not satisfy the *Young* requirement that the contract was entered into to satisfy a significant nonpecuniary interest. *Beasley*, 01-1549 at p. 9, 824 So.2d at 388. The court further observed that La. Civ.Code art. 1998 provides an express exception to the requirement of a nonpecuniary purpose, and that the record showed the manufacturer engaged in intentional bad faith in failing to make the proper repairs and in failing to approve repair of the home in the amount of $5,140 when plaintiff offered to pay $140. *Beasley*, 01-1549 at p. 10, 824 So.2d at 389. The manufacturer's failure to repair, knowing that the home was uninhabitable in its defective condition, constituted intentional bad faith on the manufacturer's part. *Id.* Relying upon *Ducote*, wherein the First Circuit found that although the purchase of a used automobile was primarily pecuniary in nature, due to the seller's intentional bad faith in failing to inform the buyer of a known defect in addition to failing to repair the vehicle the exception of article 1998 was applicable, the *Beasley* court upheld the award of general damages. *Id.* Although the manufacturer is imputed with bad faith, the record showed the manufacturer engaged in intentional bad faith and thus its bad faith was not merely imputed due to its position as manufacturer of a mobile home. *Beasley*, 01-1549 at p. 10, 824 So.2d at 388-89. Where intentional bad faith on the part of the manufacturer is proven, plaintiff should be awarded nonpecuniary damages.

In this case, the trial court found the cost to repair this mobile home would greatly exceed the value of the home. The record is replete with evidence of the failure of the manufacturer to repair the home, which it knew was damaged even before the sale. Regardless of whether plaintiff proved he intended to gratify a significant nonpecuniary interest and that the obligor knew or should have known his failure to perform would cause nonpecuniary loss to the plaintiff, Dynasty Homes's *intentional* bad faith in selling a damaged mobile home as new and then failing to take any steps to secure and seal the home renders it liable for nonpecuniary damages pursuant to the exception of La. Civ.Code art. 1998. For these reasons, I respectfully dissent from that part of the opinion which reverses the award for mental pain and suffering damages.

Notes and Questions

1. Rather than addressing directly the circuit split over the application of comparative fault principles to redhibition claims, the *Aucoin* Court sidestepped the issue entirely and ruled instead that the manufacturer was "independently liable" to the buyer. Is this language consistent with a finding of solidary liability, joint liability, or both? What do you think is the correct resolution of the question? Which arguments in favor of solidarity do you find more compelling: those rooted in principles of statutory interpretation, or those rooted in the policy of buyer protection? For additional discussion and analysis, see Elizabeth A. Spurgeon, Comment, *All for One or Every Man for Himself? What Is Left of Solidarity in Redhibition*, 70 La. L. Rev. 1227 (2010).

2. Assuming that sellers in the chain of title are solidarily liable for the buyer's losses, a question remains regarding the rights of the sellers against one another as co-solidary obligors. The general rule among co-solidary obligors is that each is liable for his share or "virile portion" of the debt owed to the obligee. La. Civ. Code art. 1804. And, absent special circumstances, a solidary obligor who renders the whole performance to the obligee may claim the virile portion of each of the other obligors in contribution. *Id.* Applied in the context of redhibition, these rules suggest that if one seller in the chain of title satisfies the buyer's claim, that seller may proceed against other sellers in the chain of title (including the manufacturer) for contribution. However, as leading scholars have pointed out, the traditional contribution rules fit poorly with the overall scheme of redhibition, under which each

seller in the chain of title has a claim against his or her own vendor for the return of the price, and potentially damages and attorney fees. 24 DIAN TOOLEY-KNOBLETT & DAVID GRUNING, LOUISIANA CIVIL LAW TREATISE, SALES § 11:31, n.5 (2017). Indeed, the legal relationship of sellers in the chain of title suggests that indemnification, not contribution, is the appropriate means of dividing the liability of the sellers between themselves. After all, Article 2531 *explicitly* recognizes the right of a seller held liable in redhibition to be indemnified by the manufacturer of the defective thing if the defect existed at the time the thing was delivered by the manufacturer to the seller. *See* LA. CIV. CODE art. 2531; *id.* cmt. (b).

At least one Louisiana court has held that a seller is not entitled to indemnification from the manufacturer where the loss is attributable to the seller's own fault. *Wheeler v. Clearview Dodge Sales,* 462 So. 2d 1298 (La. App. 5 Cir. 1985) involved the sale of a customized van. The van was manufactured by Chrysler Corporation (Chrysler) and bought and customized by Gladiator, Inc., who sold the vehicle to the dealer, Clearview Dodge Sales (Clearview), who in turn sold the van to the Wheelers. When the van exhibited multiple defects, including a transmission problem, the Wheelers returned the van to the dealership for repairs and, after attempts at repairs were unsuccessful, filed suit against Chrysler and Clearview. Clearview filed a third-party action against Chrysler, and both Clearview and Chrysler filed third-party demands against Gladiator. A jury trial resulted in the dismissal of Chrysler and Gladiator; Clearview was cast in judgment for the return of the Wheeler's price plus damages. On appeal, Clearview argued *inter alia* that if the judgment against Clearview were upheld, Clearview's third-party judgments against Chrysler and/or Gladiator must be maintained. Although the Louisiana Fifth Circuit Court of Appeal reduced the award of damages after finding that Clearview was a good faith seller, the court refused to award any indemnification from other sellers in the chain of title. According to the court:

> Indemnification has been denied the seller where the loss is caused by his own fault. [Internal citation omitted.] Failure to remedy easily repairable defects, the seller's dilatory actions or tardiness in repairing the vices, or where the seller's negligence is a substantial factor in aggravating or maintaining the defaults have been held to constitute fault such as to bar the seller's recovery from the manufacturer. [Internal citations omitted.]

> In this case, the evidence shows that the seller was dilatory and tardy in repairing the various defects they argue were easily repairable. Some of the problems were in fact corrected; however whether the van's transmission problem was corrected as alleged by the appellant's witness is suspect as the van was neither returned nor was an offer made to return the supposedly repaired van to the appellees.

> Consequently, we find that the jury did not err in failing to grant indemnity to appellant, as the losses sustained herein by appellant were caused by its own fault in failing to repair the vehicle in a reasonable time and manner.

Id. at 1303–1304.

3. The dispute in *Aucoin* raised several important aspects of the law of redhibition other than the nature of the sellers' liability, and with respect to those issues, the Court provides helpful guidance for future courts. Review the opinion carefully and answer the following questions:

    i. The Aucoins purchased not only a mobile home, but also the tract of land on which the home was situated, from Southern Quality Homes, LLC (Southern). The manufacturer, Dynasty Homes (Dynasty), sold the mobile home, but not the land, to Southern. Are the Aucoins entitled to rescission of the sale *of the land*? If so, is Dynasty responsible for the return of the price *of the land*? Why or why not? *See* La. Civ. Code art. 2540.

    ii. The Aucoins claimed that they suffered nonpecuniary damages as a result of the defects in their mobile home. Are nonpecuniary losses ever compensable in an action for redhibition? Are the Aucoins in particular entitled to recover nonpecuniary damages, and if so, from whom? *See* La. Civ. Code art. 1998.

F. Distinction from Breach of Contract

The seller's obligation to warrant against redhibitory defects must be contrasted with other obligations regarding the quality of the thing sold. Two such obligations are recognized by the Louisiana Civil Code and jurisprudence: the warranty of fitness and the obligation to deliver a thing of the kind or quality specified in the contract. These warranties were inserted in the redhibition articles as part of the 1995 revision. Although the comments to the relevant Code articles claim that they do not change the law, some question the accuracy of that statement. *See* George L. Bilbe, *Redhibition and Implied Warranties Under the 1993 Revision of the Louisiana Law of Sales*, 54 La. L. Rev. 125 (1993). The warranties are addressed in the materials that follow.

1. Warranty of Fitness

La. Civ. Code art. 2524

In addition to the warranty against redhibitory defects, the Civil Code recognizes a second implied warranty of quality: the implied warranty of fitness. The warranty of fitness is actually twofold. First, in every sale, "[t]he thing sold must be reasonably fit for its ordinary use." La. Civ. Code art. 2524. Second, in some cases only, the thing must also be fit for the particular use the buyer intends for the thing. Under Article 2524, the seller warrants the thing is fit for the buyer's intended use only when two criteria are satisfied: (1) the seller has reason to know the particular use the buyer intends for the thing, or the buyer's particular purpose for buying the thing, and (2) the seller has reason to know that the buyer is relying on the seller's skill or judgment in selecting it. La. Civ. Code art. 2524.

While the buyer's claim for breach of the warranty against redhibitory vices and defects is governed by its own legal regime including specialized rules governing available remedies, notice requirements, and applicable prescriptive periods, the Civil Code provides that the buyer's claim for breach of the warranty of fitness is "governed by the general rules of conventional obligations." *Id.* In some ways, the remedies afforded to the buyer for breach of the warranty of fitness are more generous than those afforded for breach of the warranty against vices and defects. For example, while a seller in good faith is limited in liability to return of the price plus interest from the time it was paid and reimbursement of expenses occasioned by the sale and for the preservation of the thing, a seller found liable or breach of the warranty of fitness will be liable for dissolution and damages, even if he or she did not know at the time of the sale that the thing was unfit. *Cf.* La. Civ. Code art. 2532 *with* La. Civ. Code arts. 1994–1996.

The following case addresses the distinction between the warranty of fitness for ordinary use and the warranty against redhibitory defects and also underscores the importance of properly classifying the buyer's claim in warranty.

Cunard Line Ltd. v. Datrix, Inc.

926 So. 2d 109 (La. App. 3 Cir. 2006)

Peters, J.

Cunard Line Limited Co. (Cunard) purchased lighting systems from Datrex, Inc. (Datrex) for installation on its cruise ships. Subsequently, Cunard filed the instant suit against Datrex for damages and attorney fees in connection with alleged problems with the lighting systems. Datrex filed an exception of prescription, which the trial court granted. Cunard has appealed. At issue in this appeal is whether the one-year prescriptive period for redhibitory defects applies or the ten-year prescriptive period for conventional obligations applies. For the following reasons, we affirm the trial court's grant of the exception of prescription.

DISCUSSION OF THE RECORD

Cunard owns a fleet of cruise ships. In order to comply with International Maritime Organization (IMO) regulations requiring the installation of lighting devices to mark passenger escape routes and exits, Cunard sought to equip its cruise ships with low-location lighting (LLL) systems. Datrex was in the business of selling LLL systems, and it advertised, marketed, and promoted its lighting systems to the cruise ship industry.

Datrex submitted proposals to Cunard for several of its cruise ships, which proposals included information about Datrex's system, recommendations, materials estimates, and the cost of the system. Beginning in 1996 through early 1997, Cunard sent purchase orders to Datrex for the LLL systems for four of its ships, and Datrex supplied the systems to Cunard.

However, according to Cunard, there were "numerous delays" by Datrex in delivering the system components, but the systems were delivered sometime before late

1997. Regarding installation of the LLL systems, Cunard and Datrex had agreed that Cunard would pay additional compensation to Datrex for any installation services provided by Datrex, including the training of Cunard's employees to install the LLL systems. However, Cunard chose to install the LLL systems on the four ships at issue without any assistance from Datrex.

On March 14, 2002, Cunard filed the instant petition for damages and attorney fees against Datrex, alleging that, following delivery and installation of the LLL systems, "numerous problems immediately developed, including, but not limited to, shorting out." In fact, according to its petition, Cunard was aware of these problems by late 1997. Cunard also alleged that the Coast Guard found the LLL systems to be "non-compliant with safety standards."

Prior to the filing of Cunard's suit, Datrex attempted to address Cunard's problems with the systems. According to David Mills, Datrex's executive vice president, his inspection of the systems revealed "some very serious issues with installation" which could have been avoided had Cunard accepted the installation training offered by Datrex. Mr. Mills indicated that proper installation was crucial in order for the LLL systems to work properly. In fact, Mr. Mills testified that Datrex sold the LLL system to Cunard for installation on a fifth ship owned by Cunard and that Cunard paid for installation training for that system; Datrex has not been sued over the system installed on that ship, nor has it been sued on LLL systems sold to other customers.

Datrex ceased its repair efforts in May of 1999. Cunard alleged in its petition that it was compelled to contract with another company to have the Datrex LLL system removed and another LLL system installed on its ships.

Datrex responded to Cunard's petition by filing various pleadings, including an exception of prescription. In its exception, Datrex asserted that Cunard's claims were barred by the one-year prescriptive period applicable to redhibition and tort claims. Cunard opposed the exception on the basis that the ten-year prescriptive period for contract claims was applicable.

A hearing was held on the exception, and Datrex submitted testimonial and documentary evidence, including Cunard's opposition to the exception and attached exhibits; Cunard presented no evidence. The trial court found that the contract between Cunard and Datrex constituted primarily a contract of sale such that the claim was subject to the one-year prescriptive period for redhibition actions. Thus, the trial court granted Datrex's exception of prescription and dismissed Cunard's claims. Cunard then filed a motion for new trial, which the trial court denied. Cunard has appealed.

OPINION

Louisiana Civil Code Article 2520 provides:

> The seller warrants the buyer against redhibitory defects, or vices, in the thing sold.

A defect is redhibitory when it renders the thing useless, or its use so inconvenient that it must be presumed that a buyer would not have bought the thing had he known of the defect. The existence of such a defect gives a buyer the right to obtain rescission of the sale.

A defect is redhibitory also when, without rendering the thing totally useless, it diminishes its usefulness or its value so that it must be presumed that a buyer would still have bought it but for a lesser price. The existence of such a defect limits the right of a buyer to a reduction of the price.

Importantly, an action for redhibition against a seller prescribes in one year from the day the defect was discovered by the buyer, unless the seller did not know of the existence of a defect in the thing sold, in which case the action prescribes in four years from the day delivery of the thing was made to the buyer or one year from the day the defect was discovered by the buyer, whichever occurs first. La.Civ.Code art. 2534. Thus, under La.Civ.Code art. 2534, Cunard's claims have prescribed, and Cunard does not argue otherwise.

Rather, on appeal, Cunard argues that La.Civ.Code art. 2524 provides an alternative cause of action for defective products along with an additional prescriptive period of ten years. Louisiana Civil Code Article 2524 provides:

The thing sold must be reasonably fit for its ordinary use.

When the seller has reason to know the particular use the buyer intends for the thing, or the buyer's particular purpose for buying the thing, and that the buyer is relying on the seller's skill or judgment in selecting it, the thing sold must be fit for the buyer's intended use or for his particular purpose.

If the thing is not so fit, the buyer's rights are governed by the general rules of conventional obligations.

(Emphasis added.)

Under the rules of conventional obligations, La.Civ.Code art. 3499 provides that "a personal action is subject to a liberative prescription of ten years."

Specifically, Cunard contends on appeal that it alleged in its petition that the Datrex LLL system was unsuitable for ordinary use in a cruise ship. Further, Cunard contends that it alleged that it relied on Datrex's skill in selecting the LLL system and that Datrex was aware of Cunard's particular purpose for the LLL system, i.e., compliance with IMO regulations. Thus, Cunard argues that these allegations bring its claim within the ambit of La.Civ.Code art. 2524.

Cunard did assert in its petition that the LLL systems were "unsuitable for ordinary use in a cruise ship," but it based this assertion on the "defective design and/ or installation" of the systems. Additionally, Cunard alleged in its petition that it "did in fact rely upon DATREX'S skill, judgment and representations regarding the" LLL systems, but again it asserted that the systems were "defective." Regardless of the language in which Cunard couched its cause of action, it is evident that Cunard's cause of action arose out of the allegedly defective condition of the LLL systems. Importantly, Cunard did not contend that a properly functioning Datrex LLL system would fail to meet either IMO requirements or Cunard's needs or purposes. Rather, essentially, Cunard alleged that the Datrex LLL systems at issue were not suitable for ordinary use or for Cunard's intended use or particular purpose because they were defective.

Thus, the issue before us is whether La.Civ.Code art. 2524 is intended to encompass the warranty against redhibitory defects so as to provide an additional cause of action for defective products. This issue is res nova for us.

A law shall be applied as written and no further interpretation made in search of the legislature's intent, when the law is clear and unambiguous and its application does not lead to absurd consequences. La.Civ.Code art. 9; *Mallard Bay Drilling, Inc. v. Kennedy*, 04-1089 (La.6/29/05), 914 So.2d 533. It is presumed that no words or provisions in a statute were used unnecessarily and that every word and provision in a statute was intended to serve some useful purpose. *Id.* Conversely, it is not presumed that the legislature intended any part of a statute to be meaningless, redundant, or useless or that it inserted idle, meaningless, or superfluous language in a statute. *Id.* Additionally, courts have a duty, if possible, to adopt a statutory construction that harmonizes and reconciles the statute with other statutory provisions. *Id.* Finally, courts should avoid a statutory construction that creates an inconsistency, when a reasonable interpretation can be adopted that will carry out the legislature's intention and that does not do violence to the plain words of the statute. *Id.*

Louisiana Civil Code Article 2524, regarding fitness for ordinary use and/or for a particular use or purpose, was added by 1993 La. Acts No. 841, § 1, effective January 1, 1995. Revision Comment (a) to the Article states: "The Louisiana jurisprudence has recognized the existence of [the seller's obligation of delivering to the buyer a thing that is reasonably fit for its ordinary use] although, in most instances, *it has been confused with the warranty against redhibitory vices.*" (Emphasis added.) Further, Revision Comment (b) to La.Civ.Code art. 2524 provides: "Under this Article when the thing sold is not fit for its ordinary use, *even though it is free from redhibitory defects,* the buyer may seek dissolution of the sale and damages, or just damages, under the general rules of conventional obligations. The buyer's action in such a case is one for breach of contract and not the action arising from the warranty against redhibitory defects." (Emphasis added.)

It is apparent that the legislature intended by Act 841 to address and clarify any confusion between the warranty against redhibitory defects and the warranty of fitness for ordinary use and/or for a particular use or purpose by enacting La.Civ. Code art. 2524 as a separate and distinct Article from La.Civ.Code art. 2520. It would appear superfluous or redundant for the legislature to have enacted two warranty statutes addressing the same subject matter, with no mention or indication of its reasoning for the overlap, such as to provide for an election of remedies and prescriptive periods. In fact, Act 841 additionally enacted La.Civ.Code art. 2529, which provides: "When the thing the seller has delivered, though in itself free from redhibitory defects, is not of the kind or quality specified in the contract or represented by the seller, the rights of the buyer are governed by other rules of sale and conventional obligations." Thus, it appears that the legislature intended to separate and categorize three different types of warranties applicable to sales rather than to have all such warranties defaulted into the category of the warranty against redhibitory defects. Accordingly, we conclude that La.Civ.Code art. 2524 applies to a situation in which the cause of action is based, not on the defective nature of the thing at issue, but on its fitness for ordinary use and/or for a particular use or purpose.

Because Cunard's cause of action is based on the allegedly defective nature of the LLL systems, it is limited to the prescriptive period for redhibitory defects and may not avail itself of the ten-year prescriptive period for conventional obligations. Thus, the trial court did not err in granting Datrex's exception of prescription.

DISPOSITION

For the foregoing reasons, we affirm the judgment of the trial court granting Datrex, Inc.'s exception of prescription. We assess costs of this appeal to Cunard Line Limited Co.

AFFIRMED.

Notes and Questions

1. Not every court faced with the issue has held that the warranty against redhibitory defects and the warranty of fitness for ordinary use are mutually exclusive. For example, the United States District Court for the Western District of Louisiana has refused to find the two warranties mutually exclusive, instead holding that as long as the prescriptive period for the redhibition claim has not expired, nothing precludes a plaintiff from bringing an additional claim under Article 2524. *See, e.g., Justiss Oil Co., Inc. v. T3 Energy Services, Inc.*, 2011 WL 539135 (W.D. La. 2011); *Southwest La. Hosp. Ass'n v. BASF Const. Chemicals, LLC*, 947 F. Supp. 2d 661 (W.D. La. 2013). The Eastern District recently concurred in this approach, though in an unreported opinion. *Cassidy v. Ford Motor Co.*, 2016 WL 687621 *3 (E.D. La. 2/19/2016). The Louisiana Supreme Court has yet to take up the matter.

2. The Civil Code's distinction between the warranty against redhibitory defects and the warranty of fitness for ordinary use suggests that there must exist cases in which a thing sold is unfit for its *ordinary* use, yet is not defective. However, it is difficult to imagine such a case. While it is easy to see how a non-defective lighting system may be unfit for the *particular* purpose of installation on cruise ships, it is nearly impossible to conceive of a lighting system that does not produce light, and yet suffers from neither defect nor vice. Can you think of an example of a thing that, though not defective, is not fit for its *ordinary* use?

3. The *Datrix* court stated that the prescriptive period applicable to the buyer's claim for breach of the warranty of fitness is the ten-year period applicable to personal actions. *See* LA. CIV. CODE art. 3499. However, this premise is not universally accepted. One leading authority, characterizing a failure of fitness as a failure of cause, suggests that the appropriate period is the five-year period for annulment of

a relatively null contract, as stated in Article 2032. *See* Alain Levassuer & David Gruning, Louisiana Law of Sale & Lease: A Précis, § 4.1.4(A)(1) (LexisNexis 3d. ed. 2015).

4. Unlike the warranty of fitness for ordinary use, the warranty of fitness for particular use is not implied in every sale. Rather, it applies only when the seller either knows or has reason to know both (1) the buyer's particular use for the thing and (2) that the buyer is relying on the seller's skill or judgment in selecting it. La. Civ. Code art. 2524. As the following case makes clear, these prerequisites are difficult to satisfy.

Downs v. Hammett Properties, Inc.

899 So. 2d 792 (La. App. 2 Cir. 2005)

Stewart, J.

Shirley Downs ("Downs") appeals from a judgment dismissing her redhibition action against Hammett Properties, Inc. and Timothy W. Hammett. We affirm.

FACTS

According to her September 18, 2002, petition, Ms. Downs sought to buy a piece of property in Ouachita Parish suitable for subdivision into four tracts to be used for homes for herself and each of her three children in 2001. She alleged that she informed Timothy Hammett, president of Hammett Properties, Inc., of her intention to subdivide the property in this manner. On November 21, 2001, Ms. Downs executed an act of exchange with Hammett Properties, Inc., wherein she exchanged her existing house in West Monroe and a note for $13,000.00 for a 3.947-acre tract in Calhoun, Louisiana.

Subsequent to the exchange, Ms. Downs learned of a Ouachita Parish ordinance that restricted the subdivision of her land to tracts with a minimum size of 1.25 acres each. This restriction made it impossible to subdivide the four-acre tract into four lots. In her petition, she alleged that Timothy Hammett and Hammett Properties, Inc., knew of this ordinance and did not disclose it to her. She sued Timothy Hammett individually as well as Hammett Properties, Inc., and sought damages, attorney fees, and legal interest.

* * * * *

DISCUSSION

* * * * *

Ms. Downs' petition alleged that Hammett and Hammett Properties knew of the alleged Ouachita Parish ordinance and knew that the ordinance made the property not suitable for her intended use, but sold her the property anyway. No party has produced a copy of or identified the ordinance in question. Defendants asserted in their answer that "upon information and belief, the subject immovable property is fit for its ordinary use and is legally susceptible to being sub-divided into four or more residential lots." In brief, they acknowledge that a Parish ordinance requires a lot of at least 1.25 acres for a residence that relies on a mechanical sewage disposal system. Presumably this is Ouachita Parish Ordinance Sec. 21.5-127(4), which provides:

> (4) Where the use of individual disposal systems is approved by the Ouachita Parish Police Jury and the Ouachita Parish Health Unit each lot so served shall be of a size and shape to accommodate the necessary length of filter field at a safe distance from and at a lower elevation than the proposed building. Such lot shape and size shall conform to the standards set forth in Article VI.

> In the absence of an acceptable effluent drainage course and/or easements from adjacent property owners, a minimum of 1.25 acres shall be required for all new developments utilizing individual sewage technology that generates an effluent.

Redhibitory defects are defined in La. C.C. art. 2520 which provides:

> The seller warrants the buyer against redhibitory defects, or vices, in the thing sold.

> A defect is redhibitory when it renders the thing useless, or its use so inconvenient that it must be presumed that a buyer would not have bought the thing had he known of the defect. The existence of such a defect gives a buyer the right to obtain rescission of the sale.

> A defect is redhibitory also when, without rendering the thing totally useless, it diminishes its usefulness or its value so that it must be presumed that a buyer would still have bought it but for a lesser price. The existence of such a defect limits the right of a buyer to a reduction of the price.

An ordinance that restricts the subdivision of property is not a "defect" or "vice" in the "thing sold" within the meaning of this article; it is merely a restriction on the use of the property. Consequently, it is unnecessary to apply La. C.C. art. 2521, which states that a seller owes no warranty for defects that a reasonably prudent buyer of such things should have discovered. A "defect" or "vice" has been described as a "physical imperfection or deformity, a lacking of a necessary component or level of quality." *Williams v. Louisiana Machinery Company, Inc.*, 387 So.2d 8, 11 (La. App. 3d Cir.1980). Further, the property may be suitable for many uses upon which such an ordinance has no impact.

However, La. C.C. art. 2524 provides:

> The thing sold must be reasonably fit for its ordinary use.

> When the seller has reason to know the particular use the buyer intends for the thing, or the buyer's particular purpose for buying the thing, and that the buyer is relying on the seller's skill or judgment in selecting it, the thing sold must be fit for the buyer's intended use or for his particular purpose. If the thing is not so fit, the buyer's rights are governed by the general rules of conventional obligations.

Ms. Downs did not allege in her petition that she relied on the skill or judgment of the seller or its agent in selecting the tract that she bought (although the defendants' answer asserted that she did not so rely). However, the law recognizes a cause of action against the seller when such reliance exists. Although the public is presumed to know the law, see *Miles v. Kilgore*, 191 So. 556 (La.App. 2d Cir.1939), in some circumstances a person may rely on the advice or assertions of others. *See, e.g.,* La. C.C. art.1954, which provides:

> Fraud does not vitiate consent when the party against whom the fraud was directed could have ascertained the truth without difficulty, inconvenience, or special skill.

> This exception does not apply when a relation of confidence has reasonably induced a party to rely on the other's assertions or representations.

Nonetheless, whatever subdivision regulations or ordinances existed concerning the subject property were matters of public record and easily and equally attainable by the plaintiff prior to the execution of the act of exchange. Whether or not the defendants may have been aware of the existence of these ordinances is immaterial as this is not the type of information relative to the essential quality of the land so as to require an affirmative declaration on the part of the defendant. In other words, this alleged failure to apprise Ms. Downs of the existing ordinance and regulation is not a redhibitory vice.

* * * * *

CONCLUSION

The judgment of the district court is affirmed at appellant's cost.

AFFIRMED.

Notes and Questions

1. The court in *Downs* suggests that Article 1954 should be read *in pari materia* with Article 2524 to preclude an action for breach of the warranty of fitness for particular use when the buyer could have easily discovered that the thing sold was not fit for the buyer's particular purpose. Thus, even if the seller has reason to know of the buyer's particular use for the thing *and* that the buyer is relying on the seller to select a thing for that use, the seller is not responsible when the buyer should have known that the thing would not be so fit.

2. The *Downs* court cites prior jurisprudence defining a "vice" or "defect" as "a 'physical imperfection or deformity, a lacking of a necessary component or level of quality.'" *Downs*, 899 So. 2d 792, 796 (citing *Williams v. Louisiana Machinery Company, Inc.,* 387 So. 2d 8, 11 (La. App. 3d Cir. 1980)). These cases suggest that absent a physical defect, the warranty against redhibition does not apply to a buyer's claim that the thing sold was not as it should be. Consider the cases in the foregoing Parts of this Chapter in which the plaintiffs prevailed in their redhibition claims. Did the alleged vices or defects in those cases meet this definition?

3. The Civil Code is silent regarding waiver of the warranty of fitness. Can the warranty of fitness, whether for ordinary use or particular use, be waived? If so, how? Prior to the 1995 Sales revision, Louisiana courts held that, like the warranty against redhibitory defects, the warranty of fitness could not be waived in the absence of a clear, unambiguous and express agreement. *See e.g., Bo-Pic Foods, Inc. v. Polyflex Film & Converting, Inc.*, 665 So. 2d 787 (La. App. 1 Cir. 1995).

Authority for this approach remains after the revision. Article 2474 places an affirmative obligation on the seller to "clearly express the extent of his obligations arising from the contract," and provides that "any obscurity or ambiguity in that expression must be interpreted against the seller." La. Civ. Code art. 2474. By the express terms of this article, a waiver of any implied warranty must be strictly construed. In addition, given that the warranty of fitness and the warranty against redhibitory defects are so closely related, argument may be made that the special rules governing waiver of redhibition should apply by analogy to the warranty of fitness. On the other hand, given that the buyer's rights resulting from breach of the warranty of fitness are governed by the general rules of conventional obligations rather than the rules on redhibition, argument may also be made that the special rules governing waiver of redhibition are *not* applicable to fitness claims. The Louisiana Supreme Court has yet to address the matter.

If you were representing a seller in a sales transaction, how would you advise your client to minimize his or her liability to the greatest extent possible? Consider the suggestions of the leading Louisiana practice manual on real estate transactions:

Practice Tip: If representing the seller, it is advisable to obtain not only a waiver of the warranty against redhibitory defects, but also against any other implied warranties, such as the warranty of fitness for ordinary use or for the buyer's intended use. Furthermore, it is advisable to expand the scope of the waiver to include other matters that may not technically constitute redhibitory defects, such as zoning or other regulatory matters that may impact upon the buyer's intended use of the property.

Practice Tip: In order for the waiver of implied warranties against redhibitory defects and the warranty of fitness for ordinary use to be effective, the waiver should be included in both the purchase agreement and the act of sale. If the waiver is not part of the purchase agreement, it cannot thereafter be included in the act of sale without the purchaser's consent. *See Mitchell v. Popiwchak*, 677 So. 2d 1050 (La. Ct. App. 4th Cir. 1996). Furthermore, it is common practice to have the waiver placed in bold print or on a separate addendum in the purchase agreement initialed or signed by the purchaser. It is also advisable to include in the purchase agreement the language that will be used in the act of sale to waive the implied warranties. The seller has the burden of proving that the waiver was brought to the attention of the purchaser. The closing attorney should discuss the waiver with the purchaser at the closing and ascertain that the purchaser is aware of the contents of the waiver and explain that the purchaser is waiving any right to rescind the sale or reduce the purchase price because of redhibitory defects. Otherwise, the purchaser, particularly in a residential consumer transaction, may argue that he or she was not aware of the waiver and the waiver may be disregarded. *Mitchell v. Popiwchak*, 677 So. 2d 1050, 1053 (La. Ct. App. 4th Cir. 1996).

1 Peter S. Title, Louisiana Practice Series, Louisiana Real Estate Transactions § 10:104 (2017–18 ed.).±

2. Difference in Kind or Quality

La. Civ. Code art. 2529

The foregoing materials should make clear that the introduction of the warranty of fitness into the Civil Code brought a "classification problem" into the law of sales that did not previously exist. That is, since the 1995 revision of the Sales Title, courts are faced with the task of deciding whether a buyer's complaint about the thing sold stems from a "defect" or the fact that the thing is "unfit" for use. Complicating the matter still further, the Civil Code insists on distinguishing problems of redhibition and fitness from a *third* category of deficiency: failure of the thing sold to conform to the specifications of the contract. According to Article 2529: "When the thing the seller has delivered, though in itself free from redhibitory defects, is not of the kind or quality specified in the contract or represented by the seller, the rights of the buyer are governed by other rules of sale and conventional obligations." La. Civ. Code art. 2529.

The following case addresses the question of whether a buyer's claim is properly classified as a redhibition claim or a breach of the obligation to deliver a thing in conformity with an express warranty as to quality.

PPG Industries, Inc. v. Industrial Laminates Corp.

664 F.2d 1332 (5th Cir. 1982)

Clark, Chief Judge:

The sole issue in this diversity case involving defective construction materials is which prescriptive period is applicable to plaintiff's cause of action under Louisiana law. We agree that the action was properly treated as one in redhibition calling for a one-year period.

Plaintiff PPG Industries, Inc. was a subcontractor for the construction of a building in Baton Rouge, Louisiana. As part of its contract with the general contractor, PPG agreed to install spandrel panels on the curtain wall of the building. PPG contracted in turn with the defendant, Industrial Laminates Corporation, for a supply of spandrel panels meeting certain specifications. Industrial Laminates

---

± Reproduced with permission of Thomson Reuters.

manufactured and delivered the panels to the job-site where they were installed by PPG. After installing the panels and paying the contract price for them, PPG discovered that the panels were delaminating. Industrial Laminates acknowledged this failure and sent replacement panels, the last of which was received in March 1976. PPG removed the defective panels and installed the replacement panels. Upon completion of the contract in March 1977 the owner of the building, pursuant to a release and agreement with PPG, withheld $51,487.29 from PPG because of construction losses associated with the defective panels. One year later, on March 8, 1978, PPG filed suit against Industrial Laminates seeking $51,487.29 for the sum withheld by the owner, $23,000.00 for the extra labor cost incurred in replacing the defective panels, and $25,512.31 for interest lost on all the funds withheld by the owner over the duration of these events.

The district court granted summary judgment for defendant, holding that the cause of action under Louisiana law was one in redhibition, and therefore barred by a one-year period of prescription. La.Civ.Code Ann. art. 2534 [R.C.C. 2534] provides that a redhibitory action must be instituted within a year, at the farthest, commencing from the date of the sale. This limitation does not apply where the seller had knowledge of the vice and neglected to declare it to the purchaser, *ibid*. Louisiana law imputes such knowledge to the manufacturer. *E.g. Phillipe v. Browning Arms Co.*, 395 So.2d 310, 318 n.15 (La.1981) (on rehearing). The one year period does not begin to run in such cases until the discovery of the vice. La.Civ.Code Ann. art. 2546 [R.C.C. 2534]. *Cotton States Chemical Co. v. Larrison Enterprises, Inc.*, 342 So.2d 1212, 1214-15 (La.App.1977). In any case, the one year period does not begin to run until the seller abandons his attempts to repair. *E.g. Weaver v. Fleetwood Homes of Mississippi*, 327 So.2d 172, 176-77 (La.App.1976). Here, the defect was discovered in 1973. However, Industrial Laminates continued efforts to repair until March, 1976. Thus, if this is an action in redhibition, the action would have prescribed March 1977, a year before suit was filed.

On appeal the plaintiff urges two main points: (1) that the suit is founded on an express warranty contained in the purchase order so that the ten-year prescriptive period to an action for breach of contract applies; and (2) that PPG's action is one for indemnity from Industrial Laminates, and as such is governed by the ten-year prescription for actions in quasi-contract.

PPG relied heavily on *Delta Refrigeration Co. v. Upjohn Co.*, 432 F.Supp. 124 (W.D.La.1977), *aff'd* 575 F.2d 879 (5th Cir. 1977), *cert. denied*, 439 U.S. 984, 99 S. Ct. 574, 58 L.Ed.2d 655 (1978), for its argument that a suit founded on an express warranty is one for breach of contract and not redhibition. In *Delta Refrigeration* the plaintiff sued the manufacturer of a polyurethane spray foam used for building insulation upon discovering that the foam's flame and heat resistance was not as great as that represented by the manufacturer's advertisements. The complaint in that action was held not time barred as a redhibitory action:

> Here, Upjohn represented that its CPA 425 was flame-retardant and self-extinguishing, claims which the facts of this case show are not so, and

were held to be misleading and unfair . . . The thrust of plaintiff's claim is to recover, not for a hidden defect, a redhibitory vice; instead, it is to be awarded damages for breach of the express warranties Upjohn made when it sold the chemicals. Therefore, the proper prescriptive period is founded in La. R.C.C. art. 3544-ten years-not the one-year period provided by Art. 2534.

432 F.Supp. at 127. The district court in the present case declined to follow *Delta Refrigeration*. It reasoned that under a correct interpretation of Louisiana law there is no difference to prescription of an action in redhibition whether it is predicated upon an express warranty or on the warranty implied by law in all sales. The district court misapprehended the holding in *Delta Refrigeration* to be broader than it is. However, the legal reasoning expressed in *Delta Refrigeration* and that used by the district court in this case can be harmonized.

The district court correctly stated that the presence of an express warranty does not convert an action for redhibition into an action for breach of contract, nor does it alter the one-year prescription for redhibitory suits. Indeed, the Louisiana statutes explicitly recognize that breach of an express warranty gives rise to an action in redhibition where the declaration by the seller as to the product's qualities forms the principal motive for the purchase. La.Civ.Code Ann. art. 2529 [No Corresponding Article]. So too, the courts in Louisiana have held unequivocally that actions based on a breach of warranty against defects are to be brought in redhibition instead of as a breach of contract. *See Molbert Bros. Poultry & Egg Co. v. Montgomery*, 261 So.2d 311, 314 (La.App.1972) and cases cited therein. *See also Austin v. North American Forest*, 656 F.2d 1076, 1083 (5th Cir. 1981). *Delta Refrigeration* does not challenge this fundamental Louisiana law nor does it hold that where an action in redhibition involves an express warranty the prescription period for breach of contract applies. Rather the district court there held and we affirmed that the action simply wasn't one in redhibition since it did not seek to recover for a hidden, or redhibitory defect. 432 F.Supp. at 127. There was no allegation that the foam was defectively manufactured. Rather the facts showed that even "state of the art" foam did not possess the requisite flame-retardant qualities. On this basis the court apparently reasoned that the foam contained no defect and hence redhibition would not lie.

* * * * *

That this action is one in redhibition under Louisiana law is easily discerned. Redhibition is the remedy when the defect in the thing sold renders it absolutely useless or its use so inconvenient and imperfect that it must be supposed that the buyer would not have purchased the thing had he known of the vice. La.Civ.Code Ann. art. 2520 [R.C.C. 2520]. *See Ark.-La.-Tex. Builders & Realty, Inc. v. Hoge*, 344 So.2d 90 (La.App.1977); *Riche v. Krestview Mobile Homes, Inc.*, 375 So.2d 133 (La. App.1979); *Womack and Adcock v. 3M Business Products Sales, Inc.*, 316 So.2d 795 (La.App.1975). The following are examples of redhibitory vices: a cracked engine block, *Leson Chevrolet Co. v. Barbier*, 173 So.2d 50 (La.App.1962) (1967); termite damage, *Pursell v. Kelly*, 139 So.2d 12 (La.App.1962), *aff'd* 244 La. 323, 152 So.2d 36

(1963); an inadequate building foundation, *Sterbcow v. Peres*, 222 La. 850, 64 So.2d 195 (1953); a contaminated popsicle, *Roniger v. Borden, Inc.*, 309 So.2d 756 (La. App.1975). Without question the district court correctly concluded that the delamination of the spandrel wall panels, which were only valuable if they stayed intact, fits squarely into the definition of redhibition under Louisiana law.

PPG cites, besides *Delta Refrigeration*, several Louisiana cases where express contractual obligations supposedly mandated application of the prescriptive period for breach of contract. These cases are likewise easily distinguishable.

* * * * *

S.H. Hanville Lumber and Export Co. v. C-B Lumber Co., 52 So.2d 61 (La. App.1951) cited by PPG is inapplicable because there the plaintiff's complaint was not that the defendant's lumber contained a hidden defect, but that the defendant sent grade "D" lumber instead of grade "C". Where the plaintiff's claim is based on the defendant's failure to supply the correct type of material, rather than a defect in the material itself, an action for breach of contract will lie, *Victory Oil Co. v. Perret*, 183 So.2d 360, 363 (La.App.1966). Here PPG received the correct type of material.

PPG argues that since the panels were not readily separable and could not be returned to the seller in avoidance of the sale, redhibition will not lie because the statute envisions the return by the buyer of movable or separable objects. This argument is without merit. Redhibition encompasses those situations where the product cannot be returned. *Molbert Bros. Poultry & Egg Co. v. Montgomery*, 261 So.2d 311, 314 (La.App.1972); *Frank Brigsten, Inc. v. Swegel*, 258 So.2d 579 (La.App.1972). For example, in *Frank Brigsten* the buyer was not required to return defective bricks which had already been installed.

* * * * *

The judgment of the district court is AFFIRMED.

Notes and Questions

1. Article 2529 makes clear that the seller's failure to deliver a thing of the kind or quality specified in the contract is governed by "other rules of sale and conventional obligations" rather than the rules of redhibition. LA. CIV. CODE art. 2529. Recall that the buyer's failure to deliver a thing of the kind or quality specified in the contract is governed by various provisions of the sales title, including Article 2585 (setting forth general remedies for seller's failure to deliver the thing sold), Article 2489 (requiring seller to deliver the thing sold in the condition expected by the parties), and Articles 2603–2612 (requiring seller to deliver things of the same kind, quality, or quantity agreed by the parties and setting forth the rights of the parties upon the seller's failure to perform).

2. Recall that Article 2545 includes among bad faith sellers in redhibition "a seller who declares that the thing has a quality that he knows it does not have." LA. CIV. CODE art. 2545. This language suggests that a seller who intentionally breaches an express warranty of quality is liable to the buyer in redhibition—not breach of

contract—even if the thing sold is not defective. It is unclear why the Civil Code would mandate entirely distinct causes of action against sellers who misrepresent the qualities of things sold intentionally rather than negligently or innocently. The legislative history of the sales revision does not reveal any particular motive behind this approach. *See* 24 DIAN TOOLEY-KNOBLETT & DAVID GRUNING, LOUISIANA CIVIL LAW TREATISE, SALES § 11:14 (2017). Article 2545 may be more sensibly reconciled with Articles 2524 and 2529 if the language regarding a seller's knowing declaration of the thing's quality is read narrowly to apply only when the seller knowingly makes an affirmative misrepresentation designed to conceal a *defect* in the thing sold.

3. Some recent cases have raised questions about the relationship between the seller's obligation to deliver a thing conforming to the contract and other obligations of the seller. See, for example, *Thibodeaux v. Kaufman Trailers, Inc.*, 108 So. 3d 1283, 1287 (La. App. 3 Cir. 2013), a case involving the sale of a trailer in which the buyer ordered a trailer with a deck width of 102 inches and received a trailer with a deck width of 99 inches. Although the facts of the case seem to raise an issue of conformity—not a redhibitory defect—the court affirmed the trial court's judgment granting rescission of the sale under the law of redhibition.

Consider also *Swoboda v. SMT Properties, L.L.C.*, 975 So. 2d 691 (La. App. 2 Cir. 2008), a case that involved the claims of homebuyers Thomas and Karen Swoboda against their seller, who was also the contractor responsible for placement and construction of the house. The subdivision was subject to a declaration of covenants and building restrictions requiring a setback of at least ten feet from the interior, or side, property lines of each lot. During construction of the home eventually purchased by the Swobodas, the contractor allowed forty percent of the foundation to be improperly placed across the property line onto the adjacent lot. Instead of demolishing the foundation upon learning of the mistake, the contractor purchased the adjacent lot, which the developer of the subdivision agreed to "resubdivide." After the resubdivision plat was filed in the public records, the developer of the subdivision agreed to grant verbal variances reducing the side setback from ten feet, as required by the declaration of covenants, to five feet for both resubdivided lots. The variances were never reduced to writing, were not reflected on the re-subdivision plat, and were not a matter of public record. After the house was completed, the contractor allowed a portion of the bricked flower bed, two sprinkler heads and some sod to be improperly placed across the revised property line onto the neighboring property.

While the Swobodas were informed of the resubdivision of the lot prior to the purchase, they were not informed of the setback variances or encroachments onto the neighboring property. They learned of the problems close to a year after the sale, when a prospective purchaser of the neighboring lot ordered a survey of the property. The Swobodas attempted to buy a strip of land from the adjacent landowner in order to remedy the noncompliance with the declaration of covenants, but the adjacent landowner was unwilling to sell. As a result, the Swobodas bought the entire adjacent lot for $49,950. The Swobodas then brought suit against the contractor for damages, including the purchase price of the adjacent lot, interest, and attorney fees.

Affirming the trial court's award of damages to the Swobodas, the court reasoned as follows:

> The declaration of covenants expressly stated that any waiver, or variance, of the setback requirement must be "in writing." Thus, the verbal variance granted to defendant allowing the house on Lot 122 to be built five feet from the property line was not a valid waiver of the requirement for a setback of ten feet. In addition, the defendant never disclosed to plaintiffs the existence of any such variance. Consequently, at the time of sale the defendant represented that the house complied with the setback of ten feet required in the declaration of covenants. Based upon this record, we cannot say the trial court erred in concluding that pursuant to Article 2529, the defendant breached its duty to plaintiffs by delivering a house that was actually only five feet from the property line. The court found that such a deviation was material to plaintiff's decision to buy their home and this finding was not clearly wrong.

Id. at 694.

Do you agree with the court's assessment that the seller's conduct amounted to breach of the obligation to deliver a thing conforming in "kind and quality" to the contract? How, if at all, is this case similar to *Guthrie v. Rudy Brown Builders, Inc.*, 416 So. 2d 590 (La. App. 5 Cir. 1982), reproduced in Chapter 9: The Warranty Against Eviction?

4. A final thought on the distinction between redhibition and breach of contract: does any meaningful distinction really exist between nonconforming things, things unfit for the buyer's particular use, and defective things? The current framework of Louisiana's law of sales requires not only that distinctions be made among these types of problems, but also imposes significant consequences on the proper classification of a particular buyer's grievance. Modern civil law authorities tend to downplay the distinctions between defective things, unfit things, and non-conforming things. For more discussion of the modern civil law trend, see 24 DIAN TOOLEY-KNOBLETT & DAVID GRUNING, LOUISIANA CIVIL LAW TREATISE, SALES § 11:46 (2017). Should Louisiana law move toward a more unified approach to these problems?

G. Other Remedies

Beyond the Civil Code Title on Sale, Louisiana law is replete with potential remedies for buyers who discover that the things they have purchased are lacking in quality or safety. While some of these remedies may be cumulated with those provided by the law of sales, others are either exclusive or semi-exclusive theories of recovery and thus displace the law of sales either entirely or in part. Some of these remedies, and their relationship to the law of sales, are examined briefly below.

1. Louisiana Products Liability Act

The Louisiana Products Liability Act (LPLA) governs manufacturers' liability for defective products. The LPLA is situated outside of the Civil Code, within Title 9 of the Louisiana Revised Statutes. *See* La. Rev. Stat. §§ 9:2800.51–9:2800.58. When the LPLA was enacted in 1998, one of its primary goals was to clarify the extent to which a manufacturer's liability for defective products was governed by the law of sale rather than the law of delict. Two provisions of the LPLA in particular address this issue:

§ 2800.52. Scope of this Chapter

This Chapter establishes the exclusive theories of liability for manufacturers for damage caused by their products. A claimant may not recover from a manufacturer for damage caused by a product on the basis of any theory of liability that is not set forth in this Chapter.

* * * * *

§ 2800.53. Definitions

The following terms have the following meanings for the purpose of this Chapter:

* * * * *

(5) "Damage" means all damage caused by a product, including survival and wrongful death damages, for which Civil Code Articles 2315, 2315.1 and 2315.2 allow recovery. "Damage" includes damage to the product itself and economic loss arising from a deficiency in or loss of use of the product only to the extent that Chapter 9 of Title VII of Book III of the Civil Code, entitled "Redhibition," does not allow recovery for such damage or economic loss. Attorneys' fees are not recoverable under this Chapter.

The meaning and significance of these provisions is addressed by the case that follows.

De Atley v. Victoria's Secret Catalogue, LLC

876 So. 2d 112 (La. App. 4 Cir. 2004)

Max N. Tobias, Jr., Judge.

Relators, Cheri Pink, Inc. ("Cheri Pink") and Victoria's Secret Catalogue, L.L.C. n/k/a Victoria's Secret Direct, LLC ("Victoria's Secret"), have filed substantially similar writ applications objecting to the denial of their peremptory exceptions of no cause of action and prescription by the trial court. For the reasons below, we grant the writ, but deny relief, and remand the matter for further proceedings.

This matter involves a suit for bodily injury arising out of a fire that occurred on 8 January 2001 at the home of the respondents Carol Chilton De Atley and Ronald R. De Atley. The fire started when Ms. De Atley's cotton flannel dress caught on fire from the nearby gas fireplace, causing severe bodily injury.

On 21 September 2001, the respondents filed suit seeking damages under the Louisiana Products Liability Act ("LPLA"), La. R.S. 9:2800.51 *et seq.* The respondents allege that the dress worn by Ms. De Atley, which had been purchased from a Victoria's Secret catalog in December 1999, was unreasonably dangerous in various respects pursuant to the LPLA. Cheri Pink is alleged to have sold the dress to Victoria's Secret for retail sale.

On 11 December 2003, the respondents filed a third amended and supplemental petition which added for the first time a claim in redhibition. In response to this amended and supplemental petition, the relators filed the exceptions at issue. Both were denied by the trial court.

The relators contend that the exception of no cause of action should be granted and the claim for redhibition dismissed on the basis that the LPLA provides the exclusive theories of liability against manufacturers for their allegedly defective products. Alternatively, the relators contend that the exception of prescription should be granted because the redhibition claim constitutes a completely distinct and separate cause of action from the products liability claim and, therefore, does not relate back to the filing of the original petition so as to interrupt prescription.

* * * * *

On the merits of the applications, we first address the issue of whether the exclusivity provision of the LPLA prohibits the respondents' claim of redhibition. The LPLA, enacted in 1988 "establishes the exclusive theories of liability for manufacturers for damages caused by their products." La. R.S. 9:2800.52. The statute defines "damage" as follows:

> "Damage" means all damage caused by a product, including survival and wrongful death damages, for which Civil Code Articles 2315, 2315.1 and 2315.2 allow recovery. "Damage" includes damage to the product itself and economic loss arising from a deficiency in or loss of use of the product only to the extent that Chapter 9 of Title VII of Book III of the Civil Code, entitled "Redhibition [La. C.C. art. 2520 et seq.]," does not allow recovery for such damage or economic loss. Attorneys' fees are not recoverable under this Chapter.

La. R.S. 9:2800.53(5).

Thus, the statute defines "damage" by explicitly excluding amounts recoverable under redhibition for damage to the product and other economic loss. Courts have interpreted the LPLA as preserving redhibition as a cause of action only to the extent the claimant seeks to recover the value of the product or other economic loss. *See Pipitone v. Biomatrix, Inc.,* 288 F.3d 239, 251 (5th Cir.2002); Thomas C. Galligan, Jr., *Contortions Along the Boundary Between Contracts and Torts,* 69 Tulane L.Rev. 457, 489–91 (1994). Thus, we conclude that the respondents have a cause of action for redhibition for economic loss only and not for personal injury claims.

The remedies for a claim under the LPLA and one in redhibition are different in a number of ways. The LPLA is the exclusive remedy against a manufacturer and does not allow for the recovery of attorney's fees, while attorney's fees are recoverable from the manufacturer in a redhibition claim pursuant to La. C.C. art. 2545. However, attorney's fees may be awarded only:

> [I]nsofar as those fees relate to the recovery of purely economic loss. This is because much of the proof of a "vice" for redhibition recovery overlaps with proof of a defective product for tort purposes. However, courts in such suits should be careful to realistically allocate recovery costs between the personal injury and economic loss portions of the claim.

Frank L. Maraist & Thomas C. Galligan, Jr., *Louisiana Tort Law* § 15–6 (1996) (citations omitted).

Thus, it will be for the trial court to determine what of the respondents' claims constitute pure economic loss and what damages for which La. C.C. arts. 2315, 2315.1, and 2315.2 allow recovery. Attorney's fees would only be recoverable for the pure economic loss and not for the damages recovered pursuant to the LPLA.[2]

* * * * *

Notes and Questions

1. Besides the possibility for recovering attorney fees, additional strategic reasons may motivate an aggrieved buyer to assert a claim in redhibition alongside a claim under the LPLA. For example, assume the buyer of a defective product, who is a Louisiana citizen, wishes to maintain a lawsuit against the manufacturer in state court rather than federal court. Assume further that whereas the "manufacturer" of a product subject to suit under the LPLA is not a citizen of the state of Louisiana, the distributor of the product is a Louisiana citizen. In a case like this one, joinder of the distributor is necessary to defeat federal diversity jurisdiction and maintain suit in Louisiana state court. *See* 42 U.S.C. § 1332 (setting forth requirements for federal diversity jurisdiction). Under the LPLA, while a distributor *may* qualify as a "manufacturer," not every distributor is properly so classified. *See* LA. REV. STAT. § 9:5800.53(1). Thus, the redhibition claim against the distributor provides a mechanism by which the plaintiff-buyer ensures state court jurisdiction over the lawsuit. Since the introduction of the warranty of fitness, litigants have utilized both warranties as a mechanism for defeating the removal of a products liability suit to federal court. *See, e.g., Badon v. RJR Nabisco,*

---

2. It would be inappropriate for the respondents to argue for an overly broad definition of economic loss under the redhibition claim for the sole purpose to recover attorney's fees for damages that clearly fall under the LPLA. Damages recoverable under the LPLA include pain and suffering, medical expenses, damage to property, other than to the product itself, and loss of consortium, to name a few. *See* John Kennedy, *A Primer on the Louisiana Products Liability Act*, 49 La. L.Rev. 565, 579-80 (1989). On the other hand, economic loss would include the cost of the product, and the loss of income or profits resulting from the loss of or inability to use the product as intended. Respondents' reliance on *Andry v. Murphy Oil USA, Inc.*, 97-0793, 97-0800 (La.App. 4 Cir. 4/1/98), 710 So.2d 1126, for the proposition that medical expenses are economic losses, is misplaced. That statement by the court was pure dicta. In addition, the LPLA specifically references La. C.C. art. 2315, under which medical expenses for personal injuries are typically recovered.

Inc., 236 F.3d 282, 287 (5th Cir. 2000) (granting plaintiffs' motion to remand where plaintiffs, who were cigarette smokers, brought breach of warranty and LPLA claims against cigarette manufacturers, wholesalers, and distributers).

2. The term "manufacturer" is broadly defined by the LPLA. In addition to "a person or entity who is in the business of manufacturing a product for placement into trade or commerce," the term includes:

> (a) A person or entity who labels a product as his own or who otherwise holds himself out to be the manufacturer of the product.

> (b) A seller of a product who exercises control over or influences a characteristic of the design, construction or quality of the product that causes damage.

> (c) A manufacturer of a product who incorporates into the product a component or part manufactured by another manufacturer.

> (d) A seller of a product of an alien manufacturer if the seller is in the business of importing or distributing the product for resale and the seller is the alter ego of the alien manufacturer.

LA. REV. STAT. § 9:2800.53(1) Recall that the term "manufacturer" is not defined in the Civil Code for purposes of redhibition. However, Louisiana courts have broadly construed the term. *See, e.g., Bearly v. Brunswick Mercury Marine Div.*, 888 So. 2d 309 (La. App. 2 Cir. 2004) (finding the assembler of a boat and motor whose combination caused damage to both the boat and the motor a "manufacturer" under both the LPLA and the law of redhibition); *Media Prod. Consultants, Inc. v. Mercedes-Benz of North America, Inc.*, 262 So. 2d 377 (La. 1972) (holding that domestic dealer of automobile manufactured outside of United States was a "manufacturer" for purposes of redhibition).

2. Lemon Law

Like many states, Louisiana has enacted a "Lemon Law"—a consumer protection statute providing for the rights of a buyer of a motor vehicle that suffers from defects that cannot be repaired. Specifically, Louisiana's Lemon Law places a duty on the manufacturer to repair any "nonconformity" with an express warranty, provided that the consumer "reports the nonconformity to the manufacturer or any of its authorized motor vehicle dealers and makes the motor vehicle available for repair before the expiration of the warranty period or during a period of one year following the date of the original delivery of the motor vehicle to a consumer, whichever is the earlier date." LA. REV. STAT. § 51:1941. If the motor vehicle is not repaired after four or more attempts within the earlier of the express warranty period or one year from the date of original delivery to a consumer, or is out of service due to repairs for a cumulative total of ninety or more calendar days during the warranty period, the manufacturer must either replace the motor vehicle or refund the purchase price plus costs associated with the sale, minus a credit for the consumer's use of the vehicle. LA. REV. STAT. § 51:1944.

Significantly, the Lemon Law's enforcement mechanism is limited to *express* warranties regarding the condition or fitness for use of the vehicle. La. Rev. Stat. § 51:1941(5). The enactment's primary intention, then, is to ensure that express warranties are not dishonored by manufacturers. Given the Lemon Law was designed to *supplement* existing legal remedies available to buyers, a buyer with rights under the Lemon Law is not foreclosed from bringing any other action against the manufacturer that may otherwise be available, including an action in redhibition. La. Rev. Stat. § 51:1946; *Young v. Ford Motor Co., Inc.*, 595 So. 2d 1123, 1125 (La. 1992). The conclusion that the buyer's right to enforce implied warranties is not impacted by the Lemon Law is particularly significant given that the latter regime provides that if the manufacturer has established an informal settlement dispute procedure, the consumer is required to utilize the procedure prior to receiving a replacement vehicle or refund. La. Rev. Stat. § 1944(D). These informal dispute resolution procedures in no way impact the buyers' right to assert any claim arising from other law.

A few final notes on the scope of the Lemon Law are as follows. First, the Lemon Law is applicable not only to "motor vehicles" (defined to include cars, vans, and trucks) but also motor homes. La. Rev. Stat. § 51:1941(6). Second, while the protections of the Lemon Law are restricted to "consumers," the term "consumer" is broadly defined to include (1) "[t]he purchaser . . . of a new motor vehicle normally used for personal, family, or household purposes . . . ," (2) any subsequent purchaser to whom the vehicle is transferred during the express warranty period, (3) a person to whom the motor vehicle is leased, and (4) "any other person entitled to enforce the warranty." La. Rev. Stat. § 51:1941(2). Third, the Lemon Law covers any "nonconformity" of the vehicle to an express warranty, including "any specific or generic defect or malfunction, or any defect or condition which substantially impairs the use, market value or both of a motor vehicle." La. Rev. Stat. § 51:1941(7). Thus, the protections of the Lemon Law are fairly far-reaching.

3. New Home Warranty Act

In 1986, the Louisiana legislature enacted a special statutory regime governing the warranty obligations of builders of new residential structures. This statutory regime is known as the "New Home Warranty Act" (NHWA) and is situated within Title 9 of the Louisiana Revised Statutes. *See* La. Rev. Stat. §§ 9:3141–9:3150.

The NHWA sets forth a series of warranties owed by the builder of a home to the buyer and subsequent purchasers (collectively referred to in the NHWA as the "owner"). The warranties are organized according to the time periods for which they are applicable and are grouped into three categories: one-year warranties, two-year warranties, and five-year warranties. For one year, the builder warrants that the home will be "free from any defect due to noncompliance with the building standards or due to other defects in materials or workmanship not regulated by building standards." La. Rev. Stat. § 9:3144(A)(1). For two years, the builder warrants that "the plumbing, electrical, heating, cooling, and ventilating systems exclusive of any appliance, fixture, and equipment will be free from any defect due to noncompliance with the building standards or other defects in material or workmanship not regulated by building standards." La. Rev. Stat. § 9:3144(A)(2). And, for five years, the builder warrants that "the home will be free from major structural defects due to noncompliance with the building standards or due to other defects in materials or workmanship not regulated by building standards." La. Rev. Stat. § 9:3144(A)(3). The warranty periods begin to run on the date of the sale to the initial purchaser or the date of first occupancy. La. Rev. Stat. § 9:3142(7). The right of a buyer or subsequent purchaser to proceed against the builder is governed by a peremptive period of thirty days after the expiration of the relevant warranty period. La. Rev. Stat. § 9:3146. Because the periods are peremptive, they may not be renounced, interrupted, or suspended, La. Civ. Code art. 3461, nor may they be extended by an agreement between the builder and the owner. See La Civ. Code art. 3505.

The NHWA also includes numerous exclusions, listing nearly twenty categories of defects and items of damage not covered by any warranty unless the parties expressly agree otherwise in writing. La. Rev. Stat. §§ 9:3144(B)(1)–(19). The exclusions are substantial and include discrete types of damage such as mold damage and insect damage as well as broad categories of damage including bodily injury, damage to personal property, and consequential damages. Id. Although these exclusions are extensive, the warranties that are provided may not be waived by the owner or limited by the builder if the home is a single or multiple family dwelling to be occupied by the owner as his or her home. La. Rev. Stat. § 9:3144(C).

Perhaps most significantly, the NHWA includes an exclusiveness provision which states as follows:

> This Chapter provides the exclusive remedies, warranties, and peremptive periods as between builder and owner relative to home construction and no other provisions of law relative to warranties and redhibitory vices and defects shall apply. Nothing herein shall be construed as affecting or limiting any warranty of title to land or improvements.

La. Rev. Stat. § 9:3150. The exclusiveness provision has been the subject of much litigation. The following case illustrates some of the difficulties with its application.

Stutts v. Melton
130 So. 3d 808 (La. 2013)

Victory, J.

We granted this writ application to determine whether the New Home Warranty Act ("NHWA"), La. R.S. 9:3141 et seq., provides the exclusive remedy between a home builder and a purchaser of residential property, where the builder failed to disclose known defects in the home in a Residential Property Disclosure Statement. After reviewing the record and the applicable law, we reverse the judgment of the court of appeal and hold that the purchasers are not limited to the provisions of the NHWA under the facts of this case.

FACTS AND PROCEDURAL HISTORY

Chad Melton was the builder of a residential home in Walker, Louisiana. Construction was completed in December of 2004. Chad and his wife, Lauren, (the "Meltons") were the first occupants of the home and lived there for approximately nine months before selling the home to James and Lisa Stutts (the "Stutts") on September 30, 2005. On September 26, 2005, in conjunction with the sale of the property, the Meltons gave the Stutts a Residential Property Disclosure Form in conformity with the Residential Property Disclosure Act, La. R.S. 9:3196 *et seq.* (the "RPDA"), which stated that there were no known defects in the roof. However, the Meltons had previously discovered color bleeding on the walls due to a defect in the roof and entered into a settlement agreement with the roofing manufacturer, Atlas Roofing Corporation, sixty days prior to selling the house to the Stutts for replacement of the roof. Pursuant to the settlement agreement, Atlas paid the Meltons $13,600.00 for a replacement roof. Rather than replace the roof, the Meltons kept the money, cleaned the color bleeding on the walls and driveway, and installed gutters to prevent further color bleeding.

In the summer of 2006, the Stutts noticed color bleeding on the walls, which was determined to be the result of defective roofing materials. The Stutts contacted Atlas, who told them that the Meltons had previously discovered the defect and entered into a settlement agreement with them to pay for a replacement roof, which exhausted all rights under warranty against Atlas. The Stutts filed suit against the Meltons, claiming that the roof's defective condition was not apparent at the time of the sale, and that the Meltons committed fraud by not disclosing the defective condition of the roof in the Residential Property Disclosure Statement and by covering up the defective condition of the roof rather than replacing the roof. The Stutts' suit against the Meltons prayed for the cost of replacing the roof, or the amount which the Meltons received in the settlement with Atlas, plus costs for additional repairs related to the defective roof, legal interest, and attorney fees.

The Stutts filed a motion for summary judgment on their fraud claim, presenting undisputed material facts which they claimed proved the Meltons committed fraud under La. C.C. art. 1953. The Meltons opposed the motion, arguing that the NHWA provides the exclusive remedy for the Stutts. The trial court granted the Stutts' motion for summary judgment, finding the Meltons liable to the Stutts under the RPDA. After a bench trial, the trial judge found the Meltons guilty of civil fraud and awarded damages of $15,503.55, plus $12,000 in attorney fees. The Meltons appealed and the court of appeal reversed both the summary judgment and the money judgment, finding that the Stutts' sole remedy was provided by the NHWA and that any claims under the NHWA were untimely. *Stutts v. Melton,* 12–0438 (La.App. 1 Cir. 12/21/12), 2012 WL 6677905 [unpublished opinion]. Two judges dissented. We granted the Stutts' writ application. *Stutts v. Melton,* 13–0557 (La.5/17/13), 118 So.3d 373.

DISCUSSION

The NHWA provides mandatory warranties for the purchasers of new homes in Louisiana. La. R.S. 9:3141. The specific mandatory warranties provided by the builder to the purchaser are:

A. Subject to the exclusions provided in Subsection B of this Section, every builder warrants the following to the owner:

(1) One year following the warranty commencement date, the home will be free from any defect due to noncompliance with the building standards or due to other defects in materials or workmanship not regulated by building standards.

(2) Two years following the warranty commencement date, the plumbing, electrical, heating, cooling, and ventilating systems exclusive of any appliance, fixture, and equipment will be free from any defect due to noncompliance with the building standards or due to other defects in materials or workmanship not regulated by building standards.

(3) Five years following the warranty commencement date, the home will be free from major structural defects[3] due to noncompliance with the building standards or due to other defects in materials or workmanship not regulated by building standards.

La. R.S. 9:3144(A). La. R.S. 9:3146 provides a peremptive period of thirty days after the expiration of the appropriate time period provided in La. R.S. 9:3144 to enforce any warranty. An owner has a cause of action against the builder who fails to perform as required by the warranties for actual damages, including attorney fees and court costs arising out of the violation. La. R.S. 9:3149. However, the NHWA "provides the exclusive remedies, warranties, and peremptive periods as between builder and owner relative to home construction and no other provisions of law relative to warranties and redhibitory vices and defects shall apply." La. R.S. 9:3150. Based on this exclusivity provision, the Meltons argue, and the court of appeal agreed, that the Stutts can have no other cause of action against them arising from the defective roof other than under the NHWA. Under the NHWA, the defective roof would amount to "noncompliance with the building standards or due to other defects in materials or workmanship not regulated by building standards," which is subject to a one-year warranty, and which must be brought thirty days from the expiration of the one-year period. La. R.S. 9:3144(A)(1) and 9:3146. Thus, the court of appeal found that the Stutts' claim was perempted as it was brought outside of that peremptive period.

The Stutts' petition did not allege any claims under the NHWA, but instead claimed the Meltons were liable under the RPDA and for fraud. The RPDA applies to

---

3. Foot Note Text Missing

"the transfer of any interest in residential property, whether by sale, exchange, bond for deed, lease with option to purchase, or any other option to purchase, including transactions in which the assistance of a real estate licensee is utilized and those in which such assistance is not utilized." La. R.S. 9:3197(A). The RPDA does not apply to "transfers of newly constructed residential real property, which has never been occupied." La. R.S. 9:3197(B)(5). This was a sale of residential property, and while the property was newly constructed, it had been occupied by the builder, making the provisions of the RPDA applicable to the sale. If the Meltons had sold the property to the Stutts upon completion of the home and had never lived in it, they would not have had to comply with the RPDA.

Pursuant to the RPDA, "the seller of a residential real property shall complete a property disclosure document in a form prescribed by the Louisiana Real Estate Commission . . . which discloses, at a minimum, known defects in the residential real property." La. R.S. 9:3198(A)(1). This form is known as the Residential Property Disclosure Statement. In completing the form, "[t]he seller shall complete the property disclosure document in good faith to the best of the seller's belief and knowledge as of the date the disclosure is completed and signed by the seller . . . ." La. R.S. 9:3198(B)(1). The form contains a section entitled "Structure" and the seller must answer affirmatively if there are any defects in various parts of the house, including the roof. In the case of a newly constructed home that had been occupied, the purpose of requiring a Residential Property Disclosure Statement is so that the seller/builder can disclose any defects that he becomes aware of since occupying the house.

In this Residential Property Disclosure Statement, the Meltons stated that the roof was free of any defects. A "known defect" is defined as a "condition found within the property that was actually known by the seller and that results in any of the following: (a) has a substantial adverse effect on the value of the property; (b) significantly impairs the health or safety of future occupants of the property; or (c) if not repaired, removed, or replaced, significantly shortens the expected normal life of the premises." La. R.S. 9:3196(1). After a trial on the merits, the trial court found that the Stutts proved that the misrepresentation on the Residential Property Disclosure Statement regarding the condition of the roof had a "significant adverse effect on the value of the property."

The liability of the seller for lying on the Residential Property Disclosure Statement is expressed in the negative, as follows:

> A seller shall not be liable for any error, inaccuracy, or omission of any information required to be delivered to the purchaser in a property disclosure document if either of the following conditions exists:
>
> (1) The error, inaccuracy, or omission was not a willful misrepresentation according to the best of the seller's information, knowledge, and belief.
>
> (2) The error, inaccuracy, or omission was based on information provided by a public body or by another person with a professional license or special knowledge who provided a written or oral report or opinion that the

seller reasonably believed to be correct and which was transmitted by the seller to the purchaser.

La. R.S. 9:3198(E). Though the RPDA provides that the seller is not liable for errors, inaccuracies, or misrepresentations that were not willful misrepresentations, it does not state the extent to which a seller is liable for willful misrepresentations. Thus, the Meltons argue that the RPDA does not provide a private cause of action under La. R.S. 9:3198(E) or by virtue of La. R.S. 9:3198(D), which provides:

> A property disclosure document shall not be considered as a warranty by the seller. The information contained within the property disclosure document is for disclosure purposes only and is not intended to be a part of any contract between the purchaser and seller.

We disagree with the Melton's argument. By specifically excepting from liability a seller who makes an error or omission that is not a willful misrepresentation, the only reasonable interpretation of that statute is that a seller who makes a willful misrepresentation is liable. Liability can be found in the fraud articles as the RPDA also provides that "[t]his chapter shall not limit or modify any obligation between buyers and sellers created by any other statute or that may exist in law." La. R.S. 9:3200. As a sale of real estate is a contract, the law of contracts, including fraud, applies to this case by virtue of La. R.S. 9:3200.

Thus, while the NHWA "provides the exclusive remedies, warranties, and peremptive periods as between builder and owner relative to home construction and no other provisions of law relative to warranties and redhibitory vices and defects shall apply," the NHWA does not immunize a seller from other contract law provisions the seller is to follow in connection with the sale of the home. Further, as noted earlier, a Residential Property Disclosure Statement is not required with most newly constructed homes. La. R.S. 9:3197(B)(5) (the RPDA does not apply to "transfers of newly constructed residential real property, which has never been occupied"). However, where the builder has lived in the home and later sells it, the RPDA applies and the seller is required to fill out the Residential Property Disclosure Statement, disclosing any known defects that has arisen during the time period that the seller occupied the home. Any action claiming the seller made a fraudulent misrepresentation on the statement is not a claim "relative to home construction" under La. R.S. 9:3150; it is a claim that the seller has knowingly misrepresented that the home has a quality which he knows it not to have. In this case, a roof free from defects.

"Fraud is a misrepresentation or a suppression of the truth made with the intention either to obtain an unjust advantage for one party or to cause a loss or inconvenience to the other." La. C.C. art. 1953. "Fraud may also result from silence or inaction." *Id.* The trial court found that by misrepresenting the condition of the roof on the Residential Property Disclosure Statement, "the Stutts have satisfied by a preponderance of the evidence the existence of fraud under Civil Code Article 1953." Here, the Meltons knew about the condition of the roof, as they had made a previous claim that the roof was defective and needed to be totally replaced. After they were paid to have the roof replaced on the condition that they actually replace the roof, they did not. Instead, they made a knowing misrepresentation that the existing roof was free from any defects, and then covered up the evidence of the defect, i.e., the color bleeding on the walls. Thus, we find that there is a reasonable factual basis for the trial court's finding that the Meltons committed fraud as defined by La. C.C. art. 1953.

The next issue concerns damages, specifically, whether the seller can be held liable for attorney fees in this case. Louisiana courts have long held that attorney fees are not allowed except where authorized by statute or contract. *Sher v. Lafayette Ins. Co.*, 07–2441 (La.4/8/08), 988 So.2d 186, 201; *Rivet v. State, Dept. of Transp. and Development*, 96–0145 (La.9/5/96), 680 So.2d 1154; *State, Dept. of Transp. and Development v. Williamson*, 597 So.2d 439, 441 (La.1992).

Fraud vitiates consent, La. C.C.P. art. 1948, and thus is grounds for rescission. *See* La. C.C. art. 2031 ("A contract is relatively null when it violates a rule intended for the protection of private parties, as when a party lacked capacity or did not give free consent at the time the contract was made.") As vitiation of consent is grounds for rescission, La. C.C. art. 1958 provides that "[t]he party against whom rescission is granted because of fraud is liable for damages and attorney fees." Here, the Stutts are not seeking rescission of the sale of their home, although, under the facts of this case and the findings of the trial court, they would have been entitled to it. They are only seeking the replacement value of the roof; in effect, they are seeking rescission of the sale of the roof. Thus, the issue is, when fraud has been proven but the defendant chooses not to seek rescission of the entire sales contract, is he nonetheless entitled to attorney fees?

While La. C.C. art. 1958 allows attorney fees against a party "whom rescission is granted because of fraud," it is the only code article that allows "damages" of any kind for fraud. There is no provision in the Civil Code for an award of damages where fraud is committed in the formation of a contract, but the plaintiff does not seek rescission of the contract. Although we have long held that attorney fees are not authorized unless provided by statute, this case is different in that no statute specifically provides damages for fraud in this case. Surely, the legislature did not intend the victim of fraud to go uncompensated for attorney fees, or for that matter, any damages at all, unless he seeks rescission of the entire contract. And, if La. C.C. art. 1958 is interpreted to mean that the plaintiff is only entitled to damages and not attorney fees, then the fraudulent defendant is essentially being treated as a good faith obligor, who is only liable for damages that were foreseeable at the time the contract was made. La. C.C. art. 1996. This is contrary to law as "[i]t should be clear that in Louisiana the liability of an obligor who committed fraud in failing to perform his obligation, rather than just acting in bad faith, would, for greater reasons, be at least as extensive as the liability of an obligor in bad faith." Saul Litvinoff, *6 Louisiana Civil Law Treatise: The Law of Obligations, Part II, Putting in Default and Damages*, § 5.20, p. 133 (1999). Further, in our view, the intent of the legislation providing attorney fees when the obligor has committed fraud is to punish the fraudulent conduct, regardless of whether the obligee seeks rescission of the contract. As Professor Litvinoff has pointed out, "the Louisiana Civil Code provides that when rescission of a contract is granted against a party because of his fraud, that party is liable for damages *and* attorney fees, which seems to intimate that such fees are not damages but something else, and in the context of such a serious wrong as fraud that something else sounds with penalty overtones." Litvinoff, *supra*, § 12.30, p. 371.

Pursuant to La. C.C. art. 4, "[w]hen no rule for a particular situation can be derived from legislation or custom, the court is bound to proceed according to equity." "To decide equitably, resort is made to justice, reason, and prevailing usages." La. C.C. art. 4. Comparable articles are found in the sales articles of the Civil Code. Particularly, the sales articles on redhibition provide that a seller who knows of a defect but fails to declare it is liable for return of the price paid plus interest, reimbursement of reasonable expenses occasioned by the sale and those incurred for the preservation of the thing, damages and reasonable attorney fees. La. C.C. art. 2545. We note that the Revision Comments to La. C.C. art. 2520 provide "[t]he Articles on redhibition do not apply to hidden defects discovered in a new home governed by the New Home Warranty Act, R.S. 9:3141–3150." La. C.C. art. 2520 (Official Revision Comment (e) (1993)). However, as we have held, the NHWA does not provide the exclusive remedy to the Stutts because the Meltons also committed fraud in violating the RPDA, which does not fall within the NHWA. Another important provision of these sales articles is that they specify that "a buyer may choose to seek only reduction of the price even when the redhibitory defect is such as to give him the right to obtain rescission of the sale." La. C.C. art. 2541. We also note that the comments to La. C.C. art. 2545 explain that "this provision [Article 2545] does not preclude an action for fraud against such a seller whenever the requirements of Art.1953 are met." La. C.C. art. 2545 (Official Revision Comment (a) (1993)). Thus, while this is not technically a claim for damages under La. C.C. art. 2545, the elements of the Stutts' fraud claim are essentially the same, if not more egregious. Therefore, in order to provide an equitable remedy, it is reasonable and just to assume the legislature intended at least the same type of damages for fraud where rescission of the entire sale is not sought. Accordingly, we find that the Stutts are entitled to attorney fees in this case.

CONCLUSION

The NHWA provides the "exclusive remedies, warranties, and peremptive periods as between builder and owner relative to home construction," but, when the new home is occupied by the builder for some time period before being sold, the builder/seller must also comply with the provisions of the RPDA. This requires the builder/seller to disclose of any known defects in the home, including those which he becomes aware of during his occupancy. Under the RPDA, the seller is liable for any willful misrepresentations on the Residential Property Disclosure Statement. A claim that the seller violated the provisions of the RPDA is not a claim "relative to home construction," but is a fraud claim. This liability is separate and apart from any liability that may arise under the NHWA. As the RPDA does not "limit or modify any obligation between buyers and sellers created by any other statute or that may exist in law," a seller can be liable for fraud for violating the RPDA. In this case, the trial court found the Meltons committed fraud by making a willful misrepresentation of a known defect and this was not manifest error.

Regarding damages, La. C.C. art. 1958 provides that "[t]he party against whom rescission is granted because of fraud is liable for damages and attorney fees." Pursuant to the findings of the trial court, the Meltons could have sought rescission of the sales contract, but they did not. They seek the cost of a new roof plus attorney fees. Although we have long held that attorney fees are not awarded unless authorized by statute or contract, this case is distinguishable in that the fraud articles do not address an award of damages for fraud at all where rescission of the contract is not sought. Thus, we resort to equity in determining what sort of damages are awardable in this case. We find that in mandating that a fraudulent party be liable for attorney fees in Article 1958, the legislature was attempting to punish the fraud, regardless of whether rescission is sought. Further, when the Stutts purchased this home, they were misled to believe that they were purchasing a new roof with a lengthy warranty and no known defects. In seeking the costs of a new roof, they are essentially asking for rescission of the contract as to the roof. In addition, the comparable articles on redhibition also award attorney fees where the seller "declares the thing has a quality that he knows it does not have . . . ." Accordingly, the Meltons are liable for damages for their fraud even though the Stutts are only seeking a new roof, and these damages include attorney fees.

DECREE

For the reasons stated herein, the judgment of the court of appeal is reversed and the trial court judgment is reinstated. The case is remanded to the trial court for further proceedings regarding any additional attorney fees incurred since the time of that judgment.

REVERSED; TRIAL COURT JUDGMENT REINSTATED; REMANDED.

WEIMER, Justice, concurs and assigns reasons.

WEIMER, J., concurring.

I agree with the majority's conclusion that the Residential Property Disclosure Act ("RPDA") provides a private cause of action against a seller who makes a willful misrepresentation in a Residential Property Disclosure Statement. I also agree that the plaintiffs/purchasers are entitled to an award of damages and attorney fees for the defendants' breach of their obligations under the RPDA. However, I do not believe it is necessary to resort to equity to reach this conclusion. Because the cause of action is one arising out of a sale and because, as the majority recognizes, the New Home Warranty Act does not provide the exclusive remedy available to the plaintiffs since the defendants also violated the RPDA, I believe the articles on redhibition, and particularly La. C.C. arts. 2541 and 2545, apply to allow the plaintiffs to recover the damages, including attorney fees, they seek.

Notes and Questions

1. The NHWA includes a statement of purpose, which provides as follows:

> The legislature finds a need to promote commerce in Louisiana by providing clear, concise, and mandatory warranties for the purchasers and occupants of new homes in Louisiana and by providing for the use of homeowners' insurance as additional protection for the public against defects in the construction of new homes. This need can be met by providing a warranty for a new home purchaser defining the responsibility of the builder to that purchaser and subsequent purchasers during the warranty periods provided herein. The warranty, which is mandatory in most cases, shall apply whether or not building code regulations are in effect in the location of the structure, thereby promoting uniformity of defined building standards. Additionally, all provisions of this Chapter shall apply to any defect although there is no building standard directly regulating the defective workmanship or materials.

La. Rev. Stat. § 9:3141. Based on the foregoing, why do you think the NHWA was enacted? Who benefits more by its enactment: builders or buyers of new homes?

2. The NHWA applies only to claims of owners against "builders" of new homes. The term "builder" is defined by the statutory regime as "any person, corporation, partnership, limited liability company, joint venture, or other entity which constructs a home, or addition thereto, including a home occupied initially by its builder as his residence." La. Rev. Stat. § 9:3134(1). One court has suggested that the traditional distinction between the contract of sale and the contract to build, which was addressed in detail in Chapter 1: The Nature of the Contract of Sale, should govern whether the NHWA is applicable to a given transaction. *See Garner v. Louisiana Housing, Inc.*, 798 So. 2d 295 (La. App. 4 Cir. 2001).

3. The NHWA's exclusiveness provision unquestionably displaces *implied* warranties of quality. Does it also prevent the parties from agreeing to *express* warranties of quality that derogate from the NHWA?

4. The NHWA does not apply to the sale of manufactured homes. *See Dalme v. Blockers Manufactured Homes, Inc.*, 779 So. 2d 1014 (La. App. 3 Cir. 2001). However, sales of manufactured homes are subject to the Uniform Standards Code for Manufactured Housing (USCMH), set forth in La. Rev. Stat. §§ 51:911.21–51:911.46. The standards contained within the USCMH are not exclusive; therefore, they do not foreclose a claim in redhibition. *Dalme*, 779 So. 2d at 1024. Instead, the standards set forth by the USCMH are to be considered in establishing whether or not a defect exists in the manufactured home. *See* La. Rev. Stat. § 51:911.23 (providing that the standards "shall be considered in establishing and determining whether or not a defect exists" in "any redhibitory action brought against the seller of a manufactured home or mobile home").

Chapter 11

Obligations of the Buyer

Like every bilateral contract, a contract of sale entails correlative obligations for the buyer and seller. Chapters 8 through 10 discussed the seller's obligations of delivery and warranties, respectively; this Chapter covers the buyer's obligations.

A. The Buyer's Two Obligations

La. Civ. Code arts. 2549, 2553–2555, 2561–2564

The buyer has two obligations: to pay the price and to take delivery of the thing. LA. CIV. CODE art. 2549.

As a matter of suppletive law, the buyer must pay the price at the time and place of delivery. LA. CIV. CODE art. 2550. Of course, the parties may contract for the payment at any time and place. *Id.* If the buyer fails to pay the price in a timely fashion, the buyer owes interest on the price from the time it was due. LA. CIV. CODE art. 2553. That said, the buyer's obligation to pay the price is correlative to the seller's obligations. Recall, for instance, that a buyer who is evicted may withhold the price that has not yet been paid. LA. CIV. CODE arts. 2557–60.

The buyer must also take delivery of the thing sold after it is tendered. LA. CIV. CODE arts. 2549, 2555. This obligation is correlative to the seller's obligation to deliver the thing. *Id.* Therefore, if the seller, without justification, refuses to deliver the thing, the buyer is relieved of the obligation to take delivery.

B. The Seller's Remedies for the Buyer's Failure to Perform

A buyer who fails to pay the price or take delivery has failed to perform. *See* LA. CIV. CODE art. 1994 (providing that a failure to perform includes nonperformance). Upon such a breach, the seller is entitled to the remedies of specific performance or dissolution and if applicable, damages. *See generally* LA. CIV. CODE arts. 1986, 1994, 2013.

1. Specific Performance and the Vendor's Privilege

La. Civ. Code arts. 1986, 3217, 3249, 3271

A seller's demand for specific performance is an attempt to obtain the performance for which the buyer is obligated, i.e., the payment of the price or the taking of delivery. The availability of specific performance for failure to perform an obligation is detailed in Article 1986.

When the breach of contract is a result of the buyer's failure to pay the price of the thing sold, the seller, in some cases, has a mechanism that provides a greater chance of actually recovering the price: a security device. Ultimately, a security device provides the seller with an interest in the secured property, such that upon the buyer's default of the obligation to pay the price, the seller may have the property seized and sold to recoup the price. A security device elevates the seller into the position of a secured creditor.

Security devices may be obtained via contract between the buyer and seller or by operation of law. Louisiana law grants a security device to sellers—the vendor's privilege. A privilege is defined as a right, which the nature of debt gives to a creditor, and which entitles him to be preferred before other creditors, even those who have mortgages. La. Civ. Code art. 3186. The law grants the vendor's privilege over the thing sold to an unpaid seller in every credit sale. La Civ. Code arts. 3217(7), 3249(1). This privilege is an accessory because it secures the buyer's obligation to perform and assists the seller in collecting the price. Such a privilege exists regardless of the nature of the property sold—movable or immovable.

In the event that the property on which the vendor's privilege exists is immovable, in order to affect third persons, the sale must be filed in the *mortgage* records of the parish in which the immovable is located and must note that the price has not been fully paid or that the buyer has not yet fully performed. La. Civ. Code arts. 3271, 3346. A vendor's privilege on movable property is only effective as long as the property remains in the possession of the purchaser, La. Civ. Code art. 3227, and thus, the unpaid seller may not assert the vendor's privilege over movable property against a third person.

Notes and Questions

1. The discussion above centers on the buyer's failure to pay the price of the thing sold. Of course, the buyer's failure to take delivery is also a breach of contract. When the thing sold is immovable, failure to take delivery is not really an issue. This is because delivery of an immovable is deemed to take place upon execution of the writing that transfers its ownership. La. Civ. Code art. 2447.

2. When the buyer fails to take delivery of movable property, the seller may request court authority to put the things out of the seller's possession and at the buyer's risk. La. Civ. Code art. 2612. In such a case, the seller must give the buyer notice of the time at which the things will leave the seller's possession. *Id.*

2. Dissolution

La. Civ. Code arts. 2561–2564

Dissolution is a separate and alternative remedy available to a seller whose buyer has failed to perform. La. Civ. Code art. 2561. According to the law of conventional obligations, it is within the court's discretion either to grant dissolution or to grant the buyer additional time within which to perform. *See* LA. CIV. CODE art. 2013. The law of sales deviates slightly from this approach, in that judicial discretion is granted only when the sale is of immovable property. LA. CIV. CODE arts. 2562, 2564. Furthermore, in exercising its discretion, the court may only allow the buyer an additional 60 days within which to pay. LA. CIV. CODE art. 2562. In the event that this happens and the buyer does not perform within the extended time, the court must dissolve the sale.

A court's discretion to award additional time for performance is subject to additional legislative and jurisprudential limitations. First, according to Article 2562, judicial discretion is not permitted if the seller is in danger of losing both the price and the thing. *Id.* The "danger" referenced in Article 2562 is more than a mere possibility of losing the thing and the price, and the court should consider the ability of the buyer to make payment. LA. CIV. CODE art. 2562 cmts. b and c. In addition, eminent scholar Professor Saúl Litvinoff warned against the casual dissolution of contracts and suggested that courts consider the following in deciding whether to grant this remedy: (1) the extent and gravity of the failure to perform; (2) the nature of the obligor's fault; (3) the good or bad faith of the parties involved; and (4) the surrounding economic circumstances that may make the dissolution opportune or not. 6 SAÚL LITVINOFF, LOUISIANA CIVIL LAW TREATISE, OBLIGATIONS § 2:14 (1975). Louisiana courts have adopted Professor Litvinoff's suggested analysis as a jurisprudential test for determining whether dissolution is, according to the circumstances, appropriate. *See Waseco Chemical & Supply Co. v. Bayou State Corp.*, 371 So. 2d 305 (La. App. 2 Cir. 1979).

For example, in *Robertson v. Buoni*, 504 So. 2d 860 (La. 1987) the plaintiff sold a piece of immovable property to the defendants. The buyers agreed to pay an $8,000 deposit, assume the balance of an existing mortgage held by Jefferson Savings & Loan, and execute a $40,000 promissory note in the seller's favor for the balance of the purchase price. The buyers paid the deposit but nothing else. When the seller tried to collect, she could not locate the buyers. To avoid foreclosure (because she did not have sufficient funds with which to bid on the property), the seller continued to pay the mortgage payments and taxes, despite the fact that the property was now in the buyers' names. Eventually, the seller sued for dissolution. Applying the *Waseco* factors, the Court proclaimed that dissolution was both warranted and just. As to the first factor, the Court found the extent and gravity of the failure to perform to be "quite extreme." *Robertson*, 504 So. 2d at 863. It noted that the buyers' failure to pay caused the seller to lose her property and her equity in it and to suffer substantial financial losses in paying the mortgage and taxes and legal fees. As to the second factor, the Court ruled that the nature of the buyer's fault "goes to the very heart of the purpose of the contract." *Id.* As to the third factor, the Court decided that the seller was in good faith, and it further highlighted the fact that the buyers defaulted on their obligation and left the area without notice. Finally, the Court found no economic circumstances that would make dissolution inopportune and in fact, found dissolution "quite opportune" given that the seller had been paying the mortgage and taxes on the property for three and a half years. *Id.*

Dissolution may also occur extrajudicially in the event that the parties include an express dissolution clause in their contract. A dissolution clause provides for a contract to be deemed dissolved upon a party's failure to perform certain obligations. LA. CIV. CODE art. 2017. Thus, its purpose is to avoid the need for judicial intervention. However, even when the contract of sale contains an express dissolution clause, the right to extrajudicial dissolution is not absolute. Article 2563 dictates that even if the contract of sale of an immovable contains an express dissolution clause for failure to pay the price, the buyer is still allowed to pay (despite the clause) for as long as the seller has not given the buyer notice that he or she is availing himself of the clause or has not filed a suit to dissolve the contract. LA. CIV. CODE art. 2563. In other words, the buyer may avoid dissolution by paying the price before being put into default. LA. CIV. CODE art. 2563 cmt. a.

The right to sue for dissolution may be lost if the seller expressly waives it or if it has prescribed. A claim for dissolution prescribes, as a general rule, after ten years. LA. CIV. CODE art. 3499. However, if a promissory note or other instrument has been given for the price, the right to dissolution prescribes at the same time and in the same period as the note or other instrument. LA. CIV. CODE art. 2561.

Dissolution of a contract of sale carries many effects. Recall Article 2018: "Upon dissolution of a contract, the parties shall be restored to the situation that existed before the contract was made." LA. CIV. CODE art. 2018. As a general rule, then, ownership of the property is restored to the seller, and the buyer is excused from paying the price. If the buyer has paid any part of the price, that part is returned to him with interest. LA. CIV. CODE art. 2561 cmt. e. The buyer is accountable to the seller for the fair rental value of the property during the buyer's possession. *Groner Apts. v. Controlled Bldg. Sys.*, 432 So. 2d 1142 (La. App. 3 Cir. 1983). Courts have held that the term "fair rental value" is synonymous with the "fruits" and "revenues" derived from the property. *Id.*

The seller may or may not have the ability to assert the right of dissolution against third persons. According to Article 2021:

> Dissolution of a contract does not impair the rights acquired through an onerous contract by a third party in good faith. If the contract involves immovable property, the principles of recordation apply to a third person acquiring an interest in the property whether by onerous or gratuitous title.

LA. CIV. CODE art. 2021. Thus, the seller's right to dissolution vis-à-vis third persons hinges on whether the thing in question is movable or immovable. If the thing in question is movable, the seller has no right of dissolution as to third persons who have acquired rights in the thing both in good faith and by onerous title; instead, the seller will be allowed damages only. If the thing in question is immovable, the public records doctrine prevails regardless of whether the third person acquired rights in the thing by onerous or gratuitous title and regardless of whether the third person is in good faith. *See* LA. CIV. CODE arts. 2021, 2561 cmt. g. Thus, a third person who purchases or acquires other real rights in the property from the buyer is entitled to rely on the absence of any indication in the public records that the seller has the right to dissolve. For example, if a recorded Act of Sale indicates that the price has been paid, a third person who acquires the property from the buyer is protected against an action for dissolution by the seller who, contrary to the recitals of the act, was in fact not paid. *See* LA. CIV. CODE art. 2561 cmt. g. In contrast, if the recorded Act of Sale indicates that the sale was a credit sale or otherwise notifies third persons that the buyer has not fully performed his or her obligations, then the seller's action to dissolve is preserved against third persons.

Notes and Questions

1. If the right to dissolve a sale for nonpayment of the purchase price or for other nonperformance under Article 2013 exists by virtue of law in every sale, how is this right different from a "sale with the right of redemption" covered in Chapter 7: Effects of the Contract of Sale? How is it different from a "conditional sale" covered in the same Chapter?

2. *See* Article 2591 for the rules regarding dissolution in the event that the seller has assigned the right to the price.

3. Damages

A buyer who fails to perform the contract of sale is liable for the expenses incurred by the seller for the preservation of the thing and for other damages of the seller. LA. CIV. CODE art. 2555. These damages could include compensatory, moratory, and/or nonpecuniary damages. *See generally* LA. CIV. CODE arts. 1989, 1994–04. Of course, the seller is bound to mitigate damages. LA. CIV. CODE art. 2002.

The cases below illustrate the proper method of calculation of damages upon the buyer's breach of contract.

Friedman Iron & Supply Co. v. J.B. Beaird Co.

63 So. 2d 144 (La. 1952)

On Rehearing

PONDER, Justice.

The plaintiff contends that we erred in using the market value of scrap steel at the date of the trial as a criterion in determining whether it had suffered a loss or been deprived of a profit as a result of the defendant's breach of contract. The plaintiff takes the position that the true measure of damages is the difference between the contract price and the market price of the scrap steel on the date the contract was breached.

The defendant purchased 500 tons of scrap steel from the plaintiff at a price of $41 per gross ton, to be delivered in carload lots on specified dates between April 4 and June 6, 1949. On March 8, 1949, prior to the delivery of the scrap steel, the defendant notified the plaintiff, by letter, that it was cancelling the order in its entirety.

On March 12th, the plaintiff requested the defendant to accept the scrap steel and the defendant thereafter refused to accept it or pay the purchase price. In this suit the plaintiff is seeking to recover damages for the breach of the contract.

Under the provisions of Article 1934, LSA-Civil Code, [R.C.C. 1995–1997] the damages due the plaintiff for the defendant's breach of the contract is the amount of the loss the plaintiff has sustained and the profit of which it has been deprived, except, in the absence of fraud or bad faith, the defendant is liable only for such damages as were contemplated or may have reasonably been supposed to have entered into the contemplation of the parties at the time the contract was entered into. It is presumed, in the sale of personal property, that the parties contemplated the difference between the contract price of the thing sold and the market value at the time and place at which it was to be delivered when they entered into the contract. *Robinson Lumber Company v. W.O. & C.G. Burton*, 128 La. 120, 54 So. 582 and the authorities cited therein. This court has on numerous occasions pointed out that the measure of damages for the breach of a contract of sale, where no fraud is shown, is the difference between the contract price and the market price of the goods on the *date of the breach*. See *Interstate Electric Company v. Frank Adam Electric Company*, 173 La. 103, 136 So. 283 and the authorities cited therein to that effect. This rule of law is based on solid grounds because neither a plaintiff nor a defendant should be permitted to select the market value of a date different from that on which the contract was breached for the purpose of determining whether any loss was suffered or profit deprived to the detriment of either party.

The facts in this case amply demonstrate the reasonableness of and the necessity for this rule. The defendant breached its contract when it saw the market for scrap steel was rapidly declining. At the time the suit was tried, more than a year after the contract had been breached, the price for scrap steel had advanced in excess of the price called for in the contract. The record shows that scrap steel had continued to decline for more than two months after the contract was breached but it does not show when the prices took an upward trend. If the suit had been tried at an earlier date when the market price of steel might have been on the further decline, the defendant's liability would have been greater if the value of the steel at the date of the trial was to be used as a criterion in determining whether the plaintiff had suffered a loss or been deprived of a profit. If such were to be used as a criterion, the rights of the parties would depend on conditions arising at an uncertain future date. In fact, it would leave the rights of the parties uncertain and encourage litigants to jockey for a trial on a date when the market was favorable. The rule, that the measure of damages for the breach of the sale of personal property is the difference between the contract price and the market price at the date of the breach of the contract, is a salutary one and does not depend on uncertain events that may occur sometime in the future.

There is dispute in the evidence as to the date the contract was breached but we have arrived at the conclusion that the plaintiff received notice of the cancellation of the contract on March 9, 1949. This is borne out by the fact that the plaintiff consulted attorneys as to its rights under the contract within three or four days after that date. While there is dispute as to the market value of the scrap steel on March 9th, we have reached the conclusion that the testimony produced by the plaintiff, based on the trade journal "The Iron Age", which is the accepted trade journal of the iron and steel industry, that the price quotations for scrap steel listed from date to date therein are accepted in the trade as being reliable and authentic and that they serve as a basis for the buying and selling of scrap steel. This publication bases its prices on the Pittsburgh market, which is the center of the buying and consuming of scrap steel, and, of course, if these prices are to be the guide it is necessary to deduct the freight charges from Shreveport to Pittsburgh in order to determine the value of this scrap steel now located in Shreveport. On March 9, 1949, No. 1 scrap steel was listed at $36.50 to $37 per ton and phosphate steel was listed at $42 to $43 per ton. The scrap steel specified in the contract involved herein is a type of scrap especially selected and prepared for small electric furnaces similar to that of defendant's which has no premium value to large mills and according to the testimony of the expert witness, who testified in behalf of the plaintiff, it is bought and sold in the market as No. 1 steel except when there exists a scarcity of scrap steel which compels the Pittsburgh buyer to pay the premium low phosphate price in order to obtain the scrap steel. At the time the contract was breached, the market was declining rapidly and a seller could only expect to receive the prevailing price of No. 1 steel. The highest price for No. 1 steel at Pittsburgh on the date of the breach was $37 per ton and the cost of freight to ship it to the Pittsburgh market on that date was $13.3248 per ton. Under the contract the defendant was to pay $41 per ton for the scrap steel. At the date of the breach of the contract, the steel was worth $37 per ton at Pittsburgh. Deducting the freight charges from Shreveport to Pittsburgh of $13.3248, the steel would have had a market value at Shreveport of $23.6752 per ton. The contract price called for $41 per ton. After deducting the present market value at Shreveport, the plaintiff suffered a loss of $17.3248 per ton on the steel. The contract calling for 500 tons, the loss suffered by the defendant would be $8,662.40. The plaintiff is entitled to recover this amount as it is the difference between the contract price and the market value of the steel at the date the contract was breached.

Under the provisions of Articles 1932 [No Corresponding Article] and 1933 [R.C.C. 1989], LSA-Civil Code, damages are due from the moment that there is an active violation of the contract and the creditor is not under obligation to place the debtor in default, but when the breach is passive only it is necessary to place the debtor in default.[±] Irrespective of whether the cancellation of the contract is considered as an active violation or a passive violation of the contract, there would be

---

± [The distinction between active and passive breach was eliminated as part of the 1984 revision to the law of obligations in general. Only in the event that one claims moratory damages is a putting in default required. LA. CIV. CODE art. 1989. Eds.]

no necessity to place the defendant in default because it would have been a vain and useless thing after the defendant had notified the plaintiff that it did not intend to comply with the contract by ordering its cancellation.

For the reasons assigned, the decree heretofore handed down is reversed and set aside. The judgment of the district court is reversed and set aside. It is ordered, adjudged and decreed that there be judgment in favor of the plaintiff and against the defendant in the sum of $8,662.40 with legal interest from judicial demand. All costs to be paid by the defendant. The right to apply for a rehearing is reserved to defendant.

HAMITER and HAWTHORNE, JJ., dissent.

* * * * *

Notes and Questions

In the case above, the court held that the proper measure of damages in the event of the buyer's breach is the difference between the contract price and the market price on the date of breach. Observe the method by which the court calculated the market price. First, the court referred to an industry journal indicating the market price of scrap steel on the date of the breach in Pittsburgh, Pennsylvania. Second, the court deducted the costs of shipping the steel from Shreveport (the location where the steel was located and where the contract with the defendant was to take place) to Pittsburgh. Do you see why the court deducted freight costs? To resell the scrap steel on the Pittsburgh market at a price of $41 per ton would require the seller to first ship the steel to Pittsburgh at a price of approximately $13 per ton. Ultimately, as a result of the additional costs associated with shipping, the steel was worth less in Shreveport than in Pittsburgh.

Elazab v. Bryant

203 So. 2d 834 (La. App. 4 Cir. 1967)

McBRIDE, Judge.

Originally this suit involved a claim by plaintiffs against their vendors for the rescission of the sale of 2209 Roosevelt Boulevard, Parish of Jefferson, on the ground of redhibition. During the trial the suit was terminated by compromise, the nature of which was somewhat unusual. On September 24, 1965, defendant William Bryant, in open court, made a verbal offer to compromise the suit by personally agreeing to purchase 2209 Roosevelt Boulevard from plaintiffs on the following terms and conditions: The sale for the price of $20,214.83 to be without warranty by the sellers as to the soundness of the buidings [sic], the act of sale to be passed before purchaser's notary within 60 days. Plaintiffs verbally accepted the "compromise" offer to Bryant and agreed to sell to him on such terms. It was further mutually agreed that whereas the property was then in a damaged condition as a result of hurricane Betsy, the pending claim which plaintiffs had against their windstorm insurer for the amount of the loss would be assigned to Bryant.

As reflected by the stenographic notes of evidence, all parties and the trial judge considered the litigation fully compromised by virtue of the offer to buy and agreement to sell.

On October 16, 1965, before the termination of the 60-day period in which Bryant was to take title, plaintiffs entered into a written agreement of sale with J.O. Kuebel whereunder they would purchase from him Lot 50 with improvements of Macque Subdivision for $37,000 and Kuebel was to purchase from them 2209 Roosevelt Boulevard "Subject to the conditions listed on the reverse side hereof", the pertinent portions of such conditions reading thusly:

> "1. After 45 days J. O. Kuebel agrees to purchase from Mr. and Mrs. Maneer E. Elazab their residence located at #2209 Roosevelt Blvd., Kenner, Louisiana, for the sum of Eighteen Thousand Seven Hundred Twenty Dollars ($18,720.00). This purchase agreement will be null and void should Mr. and Mrs. Elazab, the owner, decide to pay in cash $18,720 towards the purchase of 193 Macque St. to cancel this paragraph of the agreement. It is further agreed and understood that the agreement to purchase 193 Macque Street is final and definite and that the owners, Mr. and Mrs. Elazab, at their option can either sell 2209 Roosevelt Blvd. for his own account or sell to J. O. Kuebel for the price and sum as agreed $18,720.00 when passing the act of sale of 193 Macque Street, Harahan, Louisiana.

> "3. The Dixie Homestead has an appraisal on 2209 Roosevelt Blvd. of $20,800 less $1,800.00 for storm damage or an appraisal of $19,000.00 as is. Since the amount of $1,800 is covered by insurance they will require the Storm Damages repaired. It is understood Mr. Elazab will complete these repairs as listed on the appraised report, before title is exchanged, and likewise all work at 193 Macque St. shall be completed by J.O. Kuebel."

On November 24, 1965 (one day subsequent to the termination of the 60-day period within which Bryant was to take title) plaintiffs filed a rule against Bryant reciting that he did not take title to 2209 Roosevelt Boulevard as per his agreement and seeking "* * * a judgment * * * against William Bryant, in their favor in a sum that is just, fair and equitable by virtue of the pleadings and most especially the stipulations hereinabove referred to."

There was no objection whatever made on behalf of Bryant as to the form of procedure invoked by plaintiffs or as to time at which the rule was filed, and the matter was contradictorily tried on December 3, 1965, evidence being adduced on behalf of all parties. Upon termination of the trial, the judge below made the rule absolute and rendered judgment in favor of plaintiffs (movers) and against Bryant for the sum of $1498.83, which is the exact difference between the amount for which Bryant had offered to buy 2209 Roosevelt Boulevard and the amount for which plaintiffs sold said property to Kuebel under their agreement with him. As part of the evidence appears a certified copy of a notarial act of sale wherein plaintiffs sold 2209 Roosevelt Boulevard to Joseph Kuebel for $18,720, said act being dated *December 1, 1965*, which was a time subsequent to the filing of the rule for judgment against Bryant.

Bryant has perfected this appeal from said judgment rendered against him on the rule.

Pretermitting all contentions of appellant Bryant, our opinion is that the judgment appealed from is clearly erroneous and must be reversed for the simple reason movers in rule were not damaged to any extent by the failure of Bryant to purchase 2209 Roosevelt Boulevard.

As pointed out, the trial judge measured the "damages" by computing the difference between the price Bryant had offered to pay and the amount for which movers sold to Kuebel. This formula is not the proper method for measuring any damages movers sustained, but even if that formula is utilized movers have proved no loss. It was error to accept the figure of $20,214.83 as the amount for which Bryant was obligated to buy the property. It is not to be overlooked that movers at the time of their agreement with Bryant then had a pending claim against their windstorm insurer for the amount of damages inflicted upon the property by the hurricane. Under the agreement not only was Bryant to receive title to the property for the $20,214.83, but he was also to become the assignee of movers' claim against the insurer. The amount of such claim can be gleaned from the record as there appears in the condition on the reverse side of the subsequent agreement of sale between movers and Kuebel a stipulation that the storm loss was $1800. To ascertain what price Bryant was to pay for the property 'as is' we should deduct the $1800 from the gross purchase price of $20,214.83 (which Bryant was to pay in consideration of both the transfer of title and the assignment of the insurance claim) which would leave a net purchase price for the property of $18,414.83 which is several hundred dollars less than the $18,720 for which Kuebel bought. Clearly, movers were not damaged by Bryant's failure to take title because the purchase price paid by Kuebel exceeded that net amount they would have received from Bryant had he taken title.

The proper measure of damages for a buyer's breach of an executory contract of sale is the difference between the contract and the market price. R.C.C. art. 2555 [R.C.C. 2555]; *Mutual Rice Co. v. Star Bottling Works*, 163 La. 159, 111 So. 661; *Washburn Crosby Co. v. Riccobono*, 162 La. 698, 111 So. 65; *Wertham Bag Co. v. Roanoke Mercantile Co.*, 157 La. 312, 102 So. 412; *Shushan Bros. v. Vilensky*, 12 La.App. 183, 124 So. 562; *Cyrus W. Scott Mfg. Co. v. Stoma*, 10 La.App. 469, 121 So. 335 and *Belle Alliance Co. v. International Molasses Co.*, 8 Orleans App. 176.

In *Friedman Iron & Supply Co. v. J.B. Beaird Co.*, 222 La. 627, 63 So.2d 144, the Supreme Court said on rehearing:

> "Under the provisions of Article 1934, LSA-Civil Code [R.C.C. 1995], the damages due the plaintiff for the defendant's breach of the contract is the amount of the loss the plaintiff has sustained and the profit of which it has been deprived * * *. This court has on numerous occasions pointed out that the measure of damages for the breach of a contract of sale, where no fraud

is shown, is the difference between the contract price and the market price of the goods on the *date of the breach*. See *Interstate Electric Company v. Frank Adam Electric Company*, 173 La. 103, 136 So. 283 and the authorities cited therein to that effect." (Italics theirs).

In the above cited cases the subject of the sale was movable property; however, the measure of damages for a vendee's neglect to obtain delivery of the thing sold is identical whether the object of the sale be movable property or an immovable. This clearly appears from footnote 3 in *Womack v. Sternberg*, 247 La. 566, 172 So.2d 682, in which case the Supreme Court was concerned with measuring the damages due for the failure of a party to exchange real estate in accordance with his contract. The Court held that the rules governing a contract of sale apply as well to the contract of exchange and pointed out in the footnote:

> "The Civil Code does not make any distinction between movables and immovables with respect to the damages due for breach of contract of sale and there appears to be no good reason why the jurisprudence respecting movables should not apply to all kinds of property. See *Du Bell v. Union Central Life Ins. Co.*, 211 La. 167, 29 So.2d 709."

As to the measure of damages for a breach of a contract of exchange, the Court said:

> "* * * it is readily seen that the damages due to the creditor for the profit of which he has been deprived by reason of the breach is and can only be one item of damage—viz., the difference between the market value of the thing he was to give and the thing or things he was to receive in exchange."

The jurisprudence of this state defines "market value" and sets forth how it should be determined. The market value of the property is the price which would be agreed upon at a voluntary sale between an owner willing to sell and a purchaser willing to buy. The preferred yardstick in the determination of the value of property is evidence of sales of similar or comparable properties in the vicinity. Where, however, the record contains no satisfactory evidence of sales of property comparable to that involved, the ascertainment of the true value must be sought from a consideration of other factors and circumstances. The opinion of expert witnesses qualified and accepted is ofttimes given effect on the question of value of property if and when such opinion appears to be well grounded. *Housing Authority of New Orleans v. Waters*, 233 La. 259, 96 So.2d 560; *Mississippi River Bridge Authority v. Curry*, 232 La. 140, 94 So.2d 9; *State Through Dept. of Highways v. Madden*, La.App., 139 So.2d 21; *State Through Dept. of Highways v. Ebrecht*, La.App., 135 So.2d 624; *State Through Dept. of Highways v. Boyer*, La.App., 130 So.2d 738, and many other cases.

In this case we have no evidence of sales of similar or comparable property in the vicinity nor do we have any expert testimony as to the value of 2209 Roosevelt Boulevard. However, there is in the record a certain bit of evidence which we believe should be accepted as determinative of the market value. We refer to the recital contained in condition (3) appearing on the reverse side of the October 15, 1965 agreement of sale between movers and Kuebel which sets forth the appraisal of the property as being $20,800 "* * * less $1,800.00 for storm damage or an appraisal of $19,000 as is." This appraisal was made by the Dixie Homestead Association and was concurred in and approved by movers and inserted in their contract with Kuebel.

Nothing appears in the record to show, at the time Kuebel accepted title, whether the storm damage had been repaired, but that is of no moment. The two appraisals, $20,800 after repairs and the figure of $19,000 'as is' must be accepted as the market values. This being so, the net amount Bryant was to pay is less than either market value and Bryant's purchase price and any difference between the two is in favor of Bryant and not in favor of movers.

It is apparent that movers sold their property to Kuebel for less than the market price.

For the above and foregoing reasons, the judgment appealed from is reversed; it is now ordered, adjudged and decreed that the rule filed by appellees on November 26, 1965, be dismissed; appellees are condemened [sic] to pay the costs in both courts.

Reversed.

4. Other Remedies

La. Civ. Code arts. 2022, 2487, 2611–2612, 2614

In certain situations, the law allows additional remedies to the seller beyond the ones detailed above. For example, the seller may withhold delivery of the thing until the buyer has paid the price. La. Civ. Code arts. 2487, 2022.

Furthermore, if the thing sold is movable, "[t]he seller may stop delivery of the things in the possession of a carrier or other depositary when he learns that the buyer will not perform the obligations arising from the contract or is insolvent." La. Civ. Code art. 2614. Thus, in the event that the buyer indicates an unwillingness to pay the price or take delivery, the seller may stop delivery of the things while they are in transit. Note, however, that this rule admits of some exceptions depending on the form of the bill of lading. See, e.g., La. Civ. Code art. 2614 cmts. c & d.

Additionally, for sales of movables, Article 2612 provides that if the buyer neglects to take delivery, the seller may request court authority to put the things out of the seller's possession and at the buyer's risk. La. Civ. Code art. 2612. In such a situation, the seller must give the buyer notice of the time at which the things will leave the possession of the seller. Id. This article protects the seller in that it allows the seller to shift the risk of loss to the buyer upon the buyer's failure to take delivery. Once the seller gives the requisite notice to the buyer, the buyer is put into default, and the risk of loss shifts. Id.

The seller also has the right to resell the movable thing still in his or her possession upon the buyer's failure to perform. La. Civ. Code art. 2611. This right is subject to certain limitations. For example, the seller who chooses to resell must do so within a reasonable time and in good faith. Id. Unless the things are perishable or subject to rapid decline in value, the seller must also give the buyer reasonable notice of any public sale at which the things will be resold or of the intention to resell the things at a private sale. *Id.* In the event that the seller utilizes the right to resell, the seller is entitled to recover the difference between the contract price and the resale price. *Id.* This presupposes that the resale price is lower than the contract price. If the converse is true, the seller recovers nothing from the buyer (as there is no loss to be recouped), but the seller does not owe the buyer the profit made on the resale. LA. CIV. CODE art. 2611 cmt. d. The seller is allowed to enjoy the windfall. The seller may also recover other damages, less the expenses saved as a result of the buyer's failure to perform. LA. CIV. CODE art. 2611. As a general rule, the seller is not obligated to resell, but if the things are perishable or subject to a rapid decline in value, the seller does have a duty to resell in order to comply with his or her obligations of good faith and mitigation of damages. LA. CIV. CODE art. 2611 cmt. e.

Read the case below for an illustration of the seller's rights upon the buyer's failure to perform.

Leon Godchaux Clothing Co. v. De Buys

120 So. 539 (App. Orleans 1929)

JONES, J.

This is an attachment suit brought on January 5, 1928, against defendant, alleged to be a resident of the city of Los Angeles, for the sum of $169.68, the unpaid purchase price of two dresses sold and delivered by plaintiff to defendant. The itemized account attached to plaintiff's petition and made a part thereof reads as follows:

May 2/27	1 Dress.	$99.50
	1 Dress.	69.50
	Postage & Ins....................	.68
		$169.68

A curator ad hoc was appointed to represent the absent defendant and a writ of attachment issued and interrogatories were duly served on Stafford, Derbes & Roy, Inc., a local real estate firm. It answered that it did not know the defendant, but that it had sold on the 15th day of January, 1926, to defendant, 104 lots of ground in the parish of Jefferson, for the sum of $8,112, and had received a cash payment of $1,100, with mortgage notes for the balance. Defendant had, since that time, made an additional payment of $1,500, leaving a balance due of $5,181, with interest.

The curator ad hoc filed an answer on January 14, denying the allegations on information and belief.

On March 1, 1928, the defendant filed exceptions to the citation and to the attachment, which exceptions were overruled, and later, on April 4, 1928, defendant answered denying the allegations of plaintiff's petition specifically.

There was judgment for plaintiff as prayed, recognizing plaintiff's lien, and ordering that the property held by the garnishee be sold and petitioner's claim be paid by preference out of the proceeds.

Defendant has appealed to this court.

The evidence shows that on May 2, 1927, defendant, after trying on several dresses at plaintiff's store without satisfaction, ordered the two dresses, the price of which is herein claimed, to be sent down from New York City. Though defendant was told at the time that it would take two or three weeks to make delivery of the dresses, she insisted on ordering them. Accordingly the order was at once telegraphed by plaintiff to the manufacturing firm with which it did business in New York, and shortly thereafter the order was confirmed by letter. In about three weeks the dresses were received by plaintiff in this city, and an unsuccessful attempt was made to deliver them at the residence which defendant had given in this city. On the next day the woman who had sold the dresses telephoned defendant's alleged residence and was told that defendant had left for Los Angeles. Thereupon plaintiff secured defendant's address in Los Angeles and sent the dresses to her in that city by parcel post C.O.D. They were refused, and were returned to New Orleans. After an exchange of letters between plaintiff and defendant, plaintiff sent the dresses parcel post C.O.D. again to defendant in Los Angeles, but they were again refused. After another unsuccessful attempt had been made to deliver them in this city, this suit was filed.

Plaintiff's manager testifies that the dresses conformed in all respects to the order.

In this court defendant argues vehemently that plaintiff has not followed the right procedure. The dresses, she contends, should have been sold, and defendant should then have been sued for the loss occasioned by her breach of the contract. In support of this contention, she cites articles 1934 [R.C.C. 1995] and 2555 [R.C.C. 2555], *H.T. Cottam & Co. v. Moises*, 149 La. 305, 88 So. 916, and many other decisions of the appellate courts of this state.

It is thus seen that defendant contends that the sole remedy of a seller, where the buyer refuses to take delivery of movable goods, is a suit for damages after selling the goods. Such a contention is not sustained by the authorities. The case most relied on by defendant is that of *H.T. Cottam & Co. v. Moises, supra*, where merchandise had been sold by the grocery firm of Cottam Company to purchasers in South America, in which the Supreme Court held that the seller may sell the goods at auction or at private sale, and then sue for the balance. All the other decisions are in cases where sales had been made and damages sued for, but not one of them sustains his contention that the *sole* remedy is a suit for damages after sale of the article. Such is not the law of Louisiana.

If the vendee refuses to accept delivery, the vendor becomes the "negotiorum gestor" of the vendee, and must administer the thing sold like a good administrator. If the thing sold is of a perishable nature, he must sell it within a reasonable time and credit the vendee with the proceeds of sale and sue for the balance of the price; but, if the thing sold is not perishable, he may pursue one of two courses in order to minimize the loss on both sides–either sell it, or hold it and take reasonable care of it. *Gilly et al. v. Henry*, 8 Mart. (O.S.) 416, 13 Am. Dec. 291; *White v. Kearney*, 9 Rob. 495; Id., 2 La. Ann. 639; *Benton v. Bidault*, 6 La. Ann. 30; *Judd Oil Co. v. Kearney*, 14 La. Ann. 352; Pothier's Contract of Sale, § 280. But the course above indicated fixes the amount of the vendor's claim only when he chooses to sue for damages. He may elect between one of these actions. When the vendee fails to accept delivery of the thing sold, the vendor, according to Louisiana law, may sue him for the price (R.C.C. 2549 [R.C.C. 2549]), or for the rescission of the sale (R.C.C. 2561 [R.C.C. 2561]), or for damages (R.C.C. 2555 [R.C.C. 2555]).

R.C.C. 1799 [No Corresponding Article]: "It is a presumption of law that in every contract each party has agreed to confer on the other the right of judicially enforcing the performance of the agreement, unless the contrary be expressed, or may be implied."

R.C.C. 1926 [R.C.C. 1986]: "On the breach of any obligation to do or not to do, the obligee is entitled either to damages, or, in cases which permit it, to a specific performance of the contract, at his option, or he may require the dissolution of the contract, and in all these cases damages may be given where they have accrued according to the rules established in the following section."

R.C.C. 1927 [R.C.C. 1986]: "In ordinary cases, the breach of such a contract entitles the party aggrieved only to damages, but where this would be an inadequate compensation, and the party has the power of performing the contract, he may be constrained to a specific performance by means prescribed in the laws which regulate the practice of the courts."

R.C.C. 2046 [R.C.C. 2013]: "A resolutory condition is implied in all commutative contracts, to take effect, in case either of the parties do not comply with his engagements; in this case the contract is not dissolved of right; the party complaining of a breach of the contract may either sue for its dissolution, with damages, or, if the circumstances of the case permit, demand a specific performance."

R.C.C. 2549 [R.C.C. 2549]: "The obligations of the buyer are: 1. To pay the price of sale. 2. To receive delivery of the thing and to remove it, if it be an object which requires removal, and to indemnify the seller for what he has expended in preserving it for him."

R.C.C. 2551 [No Corresponding Article]: "On failure of the buyer to pay the price, the seller may compel him to do it, by offering to deliver the thing to him, if that has not been already done."

It is only where the thing sold is perishable that the law makes it the duty of the vendor to sell the thing, on the principle that the creditor must use every means to minimize his own loss and that of the debtor. In every other case, where the thing is not perishable, the right is optional with the creditor. In the present case the burden was on the defendant to prove that a sale for a reasonable price could have been effected by the plaintiff at private or at public sale, and within a reasonable time. The defense has offered no evidence on that point, and the presumption is it could not be done, since defendant's dresses had to be sent from New York.

The articles of our Code are taken almost literally from the Code Napoleon. The authors say that the duty of the vendor to sell or sue for specific performance is optional with vendor.

See volume XVII, G. Baudry-Lacantinerie et L. Saignat, pp. 525 and 526:

> "Then if the buyer neglects to take delivery of the thing within the delay fixed, the sale is dissolved of right and without demand for the benefit of the vendor. The latter may, therefore, without recourse to the courts, and without putting the buyer in default, consider the sale as not having taken place, and dispose of the thing while preserving the right to demand damages according to Article 1184 (R.C.C. 2046 [R.C.C. 2013], 2047 [R.C.C. 2013]). But this is for him simply an option (a faculty), the sale is dissolved of right and to the advantage of the vendor, says Article 1657 [No corresponding article]; the latter may, therefore, if he prefers it, require, by the rules of law, the execution of the contract which is perhaps advantageous to him."

Such was the interpretation given to R.C.C. art. 2551 [No Corresponding Article], by this court on rehearing in the case of *L'Hote Lumber Mfg. Co. v. Dugue*, 2 Orl. App. 308, where the plaintiff obtained judgment against the defendant for the price of lumber, delivery of which the defendant refused to accept or to pay for.

The last expression of the Supreme Court on this point is found in the very recent case of *Mutual Rice Co. of La. v. Star Bottling Works*, 163 La. 159, 111 So. 661. In the last paragraph of its decision, the court uses the following words:

> "It is argued on behalf of appellant that, according to articles 2551 [R.C.C. No corresponding article], 2556 [R.C.C. 2612], and 2462 [R.C.C. 2620, 2623] of the Civil Code, when a buyer breaches the contract of sale, the seller has the option either to resell the property and bring an action in damages for the difference between the contract price and the price actually received, or to demand specific performance by tendering the property at the stipulated time and place of delivery and suing for the contract price. The right to demand specific performance in such cases is not appropriate to a sale of merchantable goods, like sugar, which is quoted every day on the commercial exchanges throughout the world, because in such case it is the duty of the seller to lighten his loss—or avoid it altogether if possible—by selling the goods on the open market as soon as practicable after the contract has been breached."

The court here distinctly recognizes that the seller has the option either to resell the property and bring an action in damages for loss, or to demand specific performance. In this case the plaintiff has exercised the option of suing for specific performance after it had taken every possible step to comply with its contract, and defendant had prevented it from doing so.

For above reasons, the judgment appealed from is affirmed.

Chapter 12

Contracts Preparatory to Sale

Parties frequently engage in pre-sale transactions that contemplate that a sale may take place in the future but that do not immediately bind the parties to the obligations of a contract of sale. These pre-sale contracts serve a number of functions. Some of these agreements serve to lock in a certain price or certain terms for a potential sale in the future. Some of these agreements give the potential buyer the ability to inspect the property before ultimately taking the final step of becoming owner. And some of these agreements give the potential buyer the peace of mind of knowing that if a neighbor ever decides to sell his or her property that it will be offered for purchase to the potential buyer first.

Louisiana law recognizes three pre-sale agreements: the option contract, the contract to sell, and the right of first refusal. These agreements are referred to collectively in the Civil Code as "agreements preparatory to the sale." The following Parts describe and explore these different contracts and explain how they are used in everyday transactions.

A. Option To Buy or Sell

La. Civ. Code arts. 2620–2622, 2590

The Civil Code defines an "option" as "a contract whereby a party gives to another the right to accept an offer to sell, or to buy, a thing within a stipulated time." La. Civ. Code art. 2620. Like all agreements preparatory to the sale, this contract does not involve an immediate sale, but instead it allows the holder of the option the right to purchase specified property from the seller at a later time. Importantly, the choice is entirely that of the holder of the right—he or she may decide to exercise the right and acquire the property or not. In this way, the option contract is unilateral in nature. *See* La. Civ Code. art. 1907.

The option contract has a number of uses, particularly in the context of real estate development. Consider the following scenario in which an option contract is commonly used. Charlotte, a residential real estate developer, wants to purchase a 100-acre tract of land in Bossier Parish. At this point in time, Charlotte only wants to develop the front 30 acres of the tract (and, indeed, can only afford to purchase about 30 acres), but she is worried that if she does not purchase the entire 100 acres now that the property owner may later sell the remaining 70 acres to someone else before she is ready to purchase it herself. To remedy this problem, Charlotte purchases 30 acres and also secures an option whereby she can elect to purchase some or all of the remaining 70 acres at a later time. In doing so, Charlotte obtains the property she needs to begin her development (30 acres), and she also gains the security of knowing that she can purchase the remaining 70 acres when she has the funds necessary to do so. Importantly, although Charlotte has the *right* to purchase the remaining 70 acres, she is not *bound* to do so unless she exercises her option. The property owner, on the other hand, is unconditionally bound to sell the 70 acres if Charlotte chooses to exercise her right. This process of purchasing different pieces of real estate through the use of option contracts is known as "phasing." Phasing is commonly used in real estate development because it allows the developer to control costs and act conservatively in implementing the development plan. Phasing also prevents a property owner from selling the property to a third person who might, through his or own use of the property, affect the value of the developer's project.

The following excerpt of the *Exposé des Motifs* accompanying the 1995 revision of the Title of Sales explains both the history of the option contract in Louisiana law and the current provisions of the Civil Code that govern this preparatory agreement. Before reading this excerpt, carefully read Articles 2620 through 2622 and the comments thereto.

Louisiana State Law Institute, Proposed Louisiana Civil Code Revision of Sales 64–67 (1992) (Exposé des Motifs)

THE OPTION: GENERAL PRINCIPLES

Louisiana courts have not been consistent in providing a definition of option under Louisiana law. A line of decisions defines the option as: "an offer, which upon acceptance, ripens into a binding contract to buy and sell, and such contract must be specific as to the thing, price and terms." *McGill v. Gem Builders, Inc.*, 393 So. 2d 409, 411 (La. App. 1st Cir. 1980); *Herring v. Pollock*, 339 So. 2d 510 (La. App. 2d Cir. 1976); *McMikle v. O'Neal*, 207 So. 2d 922 (La. App. 2d Cir. 1968). Other decisions have, on the other hand, labeled the option as a contract. *Deville v. Opelousas General Hospital*, 432 So. 2d 1131 (La. App. 3d Cir. 1983); *Rogers v. Metrailer*, 432 So. 2d 390 (La. App. 1st Cir. 1983); *Moresi v. Burleigh et al.*, 170 La. 270, 127 So. 624 (La. 1930). In *Rogers v. Metrailer*, the court defined the option as: "an agreement by which one binds himself to perform a certain act, usually to transfer property, for a stipulated price within a designated time, leaving it to the discretion of the person to whom the option is given to accept upon the terms specified." 432 So. 2d 391.

While former Civil Code Article 2462 (1870) (as amended by Act 249 of 1910) introduced the notion of the option to buy into the Louisiana Civil Code, that code did not contain a definition of option in general until the revision of the law of obligations in 1984. Current Article 1933 of the Louisiana Civil Code provides: "An option is a contract whereby the parties agree that the offeror is bound by his offer for a specified period of time and that the offeree may accept within that time."

Thus, Article 1933 has adopted the contract notion of the option. The characterization of the option as a contract rather than as a mere offer is very significant. While a contract may be assigned and gives rise to rights and obligations to the heirs and legatees of the parties to it, an offer expires at the death of the offeror, does not pass to the heirs or legatees of the offeree, and cannot be assigned. It should also be noted that the nontransferability rule applies even with respect to irrevocable offers. See official comment "b" to Article 1933 of the Louisiana Civil Code.

Revised Article 2620 preserves the definition of the option as a contract. It also adopts the rule developed by the Louisiana jurisprudence that prohibits perpetual options. Thus, under the revised Article, the option must specify "a stipulated time" as its term.

Revised Article 2620 also recognizes the fact that the option must be sufficiently specific with respect to the thing offered for sale and the price that must be paid therefor to allow for a contract to sell—and, eventually a perfect sale—to be completed upon the optionee's election to exercise the option.

Revised Article 2620 also makes it quite clear that its provisions are applicable to options to buy and sell. The source article—Article 2462 of the Louisiana Civil Code of 1870—was incomplete and confusing on this score.

TIME WHEN OPTION BECOMES EFFECTIVE

Revised Article 2621 provides, first of all, that the acceptance of an option is effective when received by the optionor. That result parallels the one reached under Article 1934 of the Louisiana Civil Code for irrevocable offers. *Bankston v. Estate of Bankston*, 401 So. 2d 436 (La. App. 1st Cir. 1981), and other cases holding that an acceptance of an option is effective when notification thereof is sent to the offeror are overruled. The same approach is taken by the Restatement of Contracts, Second Section 63(b) (1981).

Like the source article—Article 2462 of the Louisiana Civil Code of 1870—revised Article 2621 provides that, upon acceptance, the option turns into a contract to sell. Thus, an act of sale would still be needed in order to perfect the sale. While the requirement of a further act following acceptance of the option seems indispensable for immovables, it would also appear to make perfect sense for the transfer of certain movables, such as a drilling rig or shares of stock. At any rate, this is not a mandatory rule, and the parties are always at liberty to provide otherwise in their agreement. See La.C.C. Arts. 7 (rev. 1987), 1983 (rev. 1984).

The second paragraph of revised Article 2621 provides that a rejection of an option terminates the option. Thus, under that Article, upon the optionee's rejection the option terminates, regardless of whether the time stipulated for exercise of the option has expired. The weight of authority at common law is to the effect that an option, supported by consideration, does not expire upon the optionee's rejection. See *J.R. Stone Co. v. Keate*, 576 P.2d 1285 (Utah, 1978); *Ryder v. Wescoat*, 535 S.W.2d 269 (Mo. Ct. of App. 1976); *Humble Oil & Refining Co. v. Westside Inv. Corp.*, 428 S.W.2d 92 (Texas, 1968). The Restatement of Contracts has codified that rule thusly: ". . . the power of acceptance under the option contract is not terminated by rejection or counter-offer . . . unless the requirements are met for the discharge of a contractual duty." Restatement of Contracts, Second, Section 37 (1981). However, at least one commentator believes that it is quite doubtful whether the same result would obtain under the U.C.C., particularly where the optionor has relied on the rejection. See Farnsworth, Contracts 175 (1982). At civil law, the solution given by the revised Article may be justified through application of general principles. Thus, upon rejection of the option the optionee has taken a juridical position that he cannot change without violating the overriding principle of good faith. See C.C. Arts. 1759, 1983 (rev. 1984). The optionee is precluded from attempting to exercise the option thereafter by the principle of *venire contra factum proprium*. [Emphasis added].

WARRANTY OF THE ASSIGNOR OF AN OPTION

Under revised Article 2622, the assignor of an option warrants the existence of the option but does not warrant that the person who granted it can be required to make a final sale. The revised Article changes the interpretation and application of the law made by the jurisprudence in *Ratcliff v. McIlhenny*, 102 So. 878 (1925) and its progeny, since the Article provides that, if the grantor of the option proves unable to make a final sale when the option is exercised by its assignee, the assignee has against the assignor the same rights as a buyer without warranty has against his seller; that is, the assignee of the option may recover whatever he gave for the assignment, but he may not recover other damages from the assignor.

In *Lemoine v. City of Shreveport*, 184 La. 221, 165 So. 873 (1936), the defendant had assigned to the plaintiff without recourse a promissory note secured by a mortgage on immovable property. Upon the plaintiff's inability to execute a judgment on the note, he demanded from the defendant a return of the purchase price of the note plus attorney's fees as stipulated in the note. The court held that although the plaintiff was entitled to a return of the purchase price for breach of warranty, he had no right to recover attorney's fees as stipulated in the note, since the note was issued without recourse.

* * * * *

In addition to the real estate development context, option contracts are often utilized in the context of commercial leases. In such a situation, the lease agreement includes an option granted by the lessor to the lessee that allows the lessee to choose to purchase the leased property at a later time. Of course, the lessee may also choose not to purchase the property by not exercising the option. The case below presents an option in the context of a commercial lease.

Federal Work Ready, Inc. v. Wright
193 So. 3d 1217 (La. App. 4 Cir. 2016)

ROLAND L. BELSOME, Judge.

This appeal is taken from the trial court's partial grant of summary judgment in favor of Federal Work Ready, Inc. (FWC).

FWC as lessee of a commercial property maintained that it had a valid Purchase Option provision within the lease that it properly executed and the lessors, Barry Wright and Millicent Wright (collectively the Wrights) refused to sell the property. In response, FWC filed a Petition for Specific Performance, Damages, Declaratory Judgment, and Injunctive Relief. Once the Wrights filed an answer to the petition, FWC moved for a summary judgment. After a hearing on the matter, the trial court partially granted the motion for summary judgment. This appeal followed.

* * * * *

Discussion

The Wrights contend that the trial court erred in granting summary judgment in favor of FWR because there are contested issues of material fact. We disagree. This is a matter of contract interpretation and therefore a question of law subject to *de novo* review.

Beginning on November 14, 2011, pursuant to a lease agreement, FWR leased commercial property located at 3620 Chestnut Street, New Orleans from the Wrights. On December 5, 2012, FWR and the Wrights executed a First Amendment to Lease Agreement (Amendment). Section IV of the Amendment provided FWR with an option to purchase. The Amendment, which contained other non-pertinent sections, was signed by Barry R. Wright and Millie Wright as lessors and Jeff Rose as director and authorized agent for FWR the lessee. Section IV of the Amendment, titled "Option To Purchase", read:

> The Parties hereby expressly acknowledge and agree that Lessee or Additional Lessee shall have a two-year option to purchase the Leased Premises (the "Purchase Option") for a purchase price of Three Hundred and Twenty Thousand Dollars and NO/100 Cents ($320,000.00 U.S.) (the "Purchase Price"), which Purchase Option exercise period shall commence on January 1, 2013, and terminate on December 31[,] 2014 (the "Option Period"). In consideration for the Purchase Option, Lessee or Additional Lessee or their designee shall pay to Lessor or Lessor's designee(s) upon execution of this Amendment a sum of One Hundred Thousand Dollars and NO/1OO Cents ($100,000.00 U.S.) in certified United States funds (the "Option Price"), which Option Price shall also count as pre-paid rent under the Lease for the next 24 months through to December 31[,] 2014, the end of the Option Period. Should Lessee or Additional Lessee fail to exercise the Purchase Option timely during the Option Period, then the obligation to resume payment of the monthly rental amount pursuant to the terms of the Lease shall arise effective as of the first month after the Option Period has ended.

> Lessee or Additional Lessee may exercise the Purchase Option at any time during the Option Period by written notice to Lessor in accordance with the process outlined under the heading "NOTICES" in the Lease. Lessee or Additional Lessee shall be obligated to consummate the purchase

of the Leased Premises within sixty (60) days after delivery of its written notice to Lessor to exercise the Purchase Option or else Lessor's obligation to honor such Purchase Option shall thereafter be null and void.

According to Civil Code art. 2620, an option to buy or to sell "is a contract whereby a party gives to another the right to accept an offer to sell, or to buy, a thing within a stipulated time." Additionally, the "option must set forth the thing and the price, and meet the formal requirements of the sale it contemplates." [*Id.*] In this case, the Amendment clearly provides a valid option to purchase which met all formal requirements.

In opposition to FWR's motion for summary judgment, Barry Wright filed an affidavit declaring that the intention of the parties was for the option to purchase to be contingent on him securing a release of the property from the bank and that the $100,000.00 was just pre-paid rent. However, there is nothing in the contract noting any such contingency and the option to purchase expressly states that the $100,000.00 pre-payment of rent was in consideration for the purchase option. Further, the Civil Code dictates that "[c]ontracts have the effect of law for the parties." [La. Civ. Code art. 1983]. If the words of the contract are clear, unambiguous, and lead to no absurd consequences, the court need not look beyond the contract language to determine the true intent of the parties. [La. Civ. Code art. 2046].

Therefore, we find no error in the trial court's ruling as to the existence of a valid option to purchase.

Furthermore, on November 14, 2014, pursuant to the provisions of the purchase option, FWR, through counsel, provided the Wrights with written notification of its intent to exercise the purchase option. FWR requested a closing date of December 22, 2014. That letter was sent via certified mail but was not claimed by the Wrights and ultimately returned to sender. Thereafter, FWR had a private process server hand deliver the November 14, 2014 letter to Barry Wright.

The Wrights did not respond to the letter and another letter was sent on December 18, 2014 via certified mail and the same letter was sent out via United States Postal Service on December 19, 2014. The letters read the same as the November letter notifying the Wrights of FWR's desire to exercise the purchase option provided in the amended lease. Like the first, the second certified mail letter was also returned as unclaimed.

"The acceptance or rejection of an offer contained in an option is effective when received by the grantor." [La. Civ. Code art. 2621]. Based on the record, FWR timely notified the Wrights of its intent to exercise the purchase option in accordance with the lease requirements. Therefore, we find no error with the trial court's finding that Federal Work Ready, Inc. properly exercised the purchase option.

For these reasons, the writ is denied.

APPEAL CONVERTED TO WRIT; WRIT DENIED

Notes and Questions

1. Based on your reading of Louisiana Civil Code Article 2620 and the *FWI v. Wright* case above, what are the prerequisites that must be satisfied in order to validly form an option contract? Note that Article 2620 states that an option must "meet the formal requirements of the sale it contemplates." LA. CIV. CODE art. 2620. What are those requirements? *See* LA. CIV. CODE arts. 1839, 2440.

2. Does an option contract require the giving of "consideration"? The precursor to Article 2620 provided that "[o]ne may purchase the right, or option to accept or reject, within a stipulated time, an offer or promise to sell, after the purchase of such option, for *any consideration* therein stipulated . . . ." LA. CIV. CODE art. 2462 (1870) (emphasis added). Some Louisiana courts interpreted this article to mean that an option contact required that consideration (as that term is understood at common law) be given. This interpretation flies in the face of Louisiana contract law, which allows one to bind himself to a gratuitous contract for the benefit of the other party without obtaining a return advantage. LA. CIV. CODE art. 1910. Comments (a) and (h) to Article 2620 make clear that, under the revision, the requirement of consideration is not required, if it ever was. LA. CIV. CODE art. 2620 cmts. a, h.

3. How does the grantee exercise the option? In other words, how may the grantee accept the offer contained in the option contract? Read Louisiana Civil Code Article 2521. Note that acceptance of the offer contained in the option contract transforms the option into a contract to sell. LA. CIV. CODE art. 2621 cmt. b. By contrast, if the grantee rejects the offer, the option is terminated. The same is not true if the grantee provides a counteroffer. LA. CIV. CODE art. 2621.

4. Finally, note that an option contract is heritable and may be assigned provided that the parties do not intend otherwise. LA. CIV. CODE art. 2620 cmt. i. In the event of an assignment, the assignor warrants only the existence of the option; the assignor does not warrant that the grantor of the option can be required to make a final sale. LA. CIV. CODE art. 2622. If the grantor fails to make a final sale, the assignee has against the assignor the same rights as a buyer without warranty has against the seller. *Id.* In other words, the assignee occupies the same position as would a buyer in a non-warranty sale who succeeds on a claim for breach of the warranty of eviction. (To review the rights of a buyer in a non-warranty sale, see Chapter 9: The Warranty Against Eviction, Subpart C: Modification of the Warranty.) This means that the assignee may recover whatever was given for the assignment. *See* LA. CIV. CODE art. 2622 cmts. a, b.

Delcambre v. Dubois

263 So. 2d 96 (La. App. 3 Cir. 1972)

CULPEPPER, Judge.

This is a suit for specific performance of an alleged "counter letter", whereby plaintiff contends defendants granted him the right to repurchase certain real property. When this case was previously before us, 236 So.2d 249, we found the agreement in question ambiguous and remanded the matter for parol evidence to show the intent of the parties. Pursuant to this remand, the testimony of the attorney who drew the instrument and of some of the parties was taken. The district judge has now granted specific performance ordering defendants to convey the property to plaintiff upon payment of the specified price. Defendants appealed.

The substantial issue is whether the alleged "counter letter" is an option to repurchase, which is unenforceable since it does not stipulate a time within which to accept or reject the promise to sell.

The general facts are that plaintiff and defendants inherited approximately 4300 acres of land and owned it in indivision. In 1963, when there was no oil production from the property, plaintiff had mortgaged his interest, was being sued by his creditors and was heavily in debt. The other heirs were afraid plaintiff's creditors would seize his interest and force a partition. So they agreed that plaintiff would sell to the other heirs his interest in the 4300 acres, as well as certain other smaller tracts which he owned, in consideration of their assuming the mortgages and judgments which totaled over $60,000. To accomplish this purpose, their attorney drew a cash sale by which plaintiff conveyed to defendants the property in question for a stated cash consideration, represented by their assumption of these indebtednesses.

Contemporaneous with the sale, the parties signed a separate instrument, the one in dispute here, in which defendants granted to plaintiff "the right and option to repurchase from the said appearers, all of that certain property sold and conveyed unto them by act" (then follows the description of the cash sale). This secret agreement provides further that should plaintiff "exercise said option to repurchase the said property sold by him to the said appearers, that he will pay to them as the repurchase price thereof, all sums of money expended by appearers and paid to him as the purchase price of said property (then follows a description of certain mortgages and judgments) . . . which have been made necessary in order for appearers to protect a good and merchantable title in and to said properties."

In 1968, oil had been discovered on the property owned in indivision. Plaintiff sought to repurchase his interest. When defendants refused to sell, the present suit followed.

* * * * *

Plaintiff argues first that the counter letter in this case provides for a reciprocal agreement to buy and sell, under LSA-C.C. Article 2462, paragraph 1 [R.C.C. 2623], which reads as follows:

> "A promise to sell, when there exists a reciprocal consent of both parties
> as to the thing, the price and terms, and which, if it relates to immovables,
> is in writing, so far amounts to a sale, as to give either party the right to
> enforce specific performance of same."

This argument has no merit. The language of the agreement shows, clearly there was no agreement by plaintiff to repurchase the property. He was not obligated to accept defendants' promise to sell. Since there was no reciprocal consent to sell and to buy, there is no right to specific performance.

Plaintiff next contends that the counter letter provided an option, under LSA-C.C. Article 2462, second paragraph [R.C.C. 2620], which reads as follows:

"One may purchase the right, or option to accept or reject, within a stipulated time, an offer or promise to sell, after the purchase of such option, for any consideration therein stipulated, such offer, or promise cannot be withdrawn before the time agreed upon; and should it be accepted within the time stipulated, the contract or agreement to sell, evidenced by such promise and acceptance, may be specifically enforced by either party. (As amended by Acts 1910, No. 249; Acts 1910, 2nd Ex.Sess., No. 3; Acts 1920, No. 27)."

It is the position of defendants that there is no option, since the agreement does not stipulate a time for plaintiff to accept or reject defendants' offer to sell. Our jurisprudence establishes a public policy in this state against holding property out of commerce, *Gueno v. Medlenka*, 238 La. 1081, 117 So.2d 817; *Freed Realty Co. v. Singer*, 12 La.App. 369, 126 So. 74; *Bristo v. Christine Oil & Gas Co.*, 139 La. 312, 71 So. 521; *Chicago Mill & Lumber Co. v. Ayer Timber Co.*, La.App., 131 So.2d 635; and *Wright v. DeFatta*, La.App., 142 So.2d 489. The statutory basis of this jurisprudence is found in LSA-C.C. Articles 488 [R.C.C. 477] and 491 [R.C.C. 477], which define ownership as the right to use, enjoy and dispose of one[']s property in the most unlimited manner. Obligations which cause property to be perpetually inalienable are contrary to our notion of ownership and therefore against public policy. See also Planiol, Vol. 1, Part 2, No. 2344 for a discussion of the prohibition against clauses of perpetual inalienability.

* * * * *

For the reasons assigned, the judgment appealed is reversed and set aside. It is now ordered adjudged and decreed that there be judgment herein in favor of defendants and against the plaintiff, rejecting his demands. All costs in the district court, as well as the costs of this appeal, are assessed against the plaintiff.

[Dissenting opinions omitted, Eds.]

ON REHEARING

MILLER, Judge.

On application for rehearing, the court found applicable certain civil code articles not presented by counsel or the trial court. Additional briefs were requested and filed. We now conclude that the act of sale and the counter letter (both described in our original opinion) constitute a sale of real estate with the right of redemption. LSA-C.C. Articles 2567 [R.C.C. 2567], 2568 [R.C.C. 2568] and Planiol vol. 2, no. 1574 are applicable and require that we reverse our decision and affirm the trial court.

"Art. 2567 [R.C.C. 2567]. The right of redemption is an agreement or paction, by which the vendor reserves to himself the power of taking back the thing sold by returning the price paid for it."

"Art. 2568 [R.C.C. 2568]. The right of redemption cannot be reserved for a time exceeding ten years.

If a term, exceeding that, has been stipulated in the agreement, it shall be reduced to the term of ten years."

Planiol, vol. 2, no. 1574, in pertinent part states: '* * * This delay also applies when the parties have not fixed any.'

A real and reasonably adequate consideration must be paid by the vendee (*Marbury v. Colbert*, 105 La. 467, 29 So. 871 (1901)) and the vendee must have actual possession of the land in order for these articles to apply. *Woods v. Stoma*, 242 So.2d 320 (La.App. 2 Cir. 1970). In such cases, ownership passes to the vendee subject to a condition of redemption or *vente à réméré*. *Jackson v. Golson*, 91 So.2d 394, 399 (La. App. 2 Cir. 1956).

The right of redemption may be set forth in a written counter letter. *Baker v. Patton*, 191 La. 784, 186 So. 336 (1939). The price of redemption must be determinate (*Hutchings v. Field*, 10 La. 237 (1836)) but may include costs and still be acceptable. Planiol, vol. 2, no. 1579. As to the delay for redemption, LSA-C.C. Art. 2568 [R.C.C. 2568] states that the delay may not be stipulated to exceed 10 years and will be reduced to 10 years if it does. However, if no delay has been stipulated, the 10 year limitation automatically applies. Planiol, vol. 2, no. 1574. This is only logical in that if vendor is accorded, by law, a 10 year period for redemption in a situation where there is contractual intent to Limit his right to a term in excess of 10 years, he should be accorded at least this much time, by law, where no intent has been manifested to limit the term of his right of redemption.

Vendor must reserve the right to redeem. If vendee grants an option to repurchase, this will not be a sale with the right of redemption. *Glover v. Abney*, 160 La. 175, 106 So. 735 (1935). In *Glover*, one of two vendors was granted the right not only to reacquire his own part of the property transferred to vendee, but also the right to acquire the part transferred by his co-vendor. Therefore this vendor assumed the role of a non-vendor (third person) in relation to his co-vendor's property and the court found the whole counter letter to be an option.

However, the characterization of the counter letter as an option or a *vente à réméré* is not meant to depend upon whether the vendee, in the counter letter, says "I grant" or whether the vendor says "I reserve." See *Baker v. Patton*, 191 La. 784, 186 So. 336 (1939) where both vendors participated in the counter letter to the extent of their respective original conveyances-each assuming the role of a prior vendor in respect thereto. The counter letter read in pertinent part:

"H.E. Patton (vendee) agrees and hereby binds and obligates himself, his heirs and assigns, to retransfer the above described property to the said J.H. Baker and J.P. Baker (vendees) . . . ." (Inserts added.) 186 So. 336, 337.

The court found this to be a sale with a right of redemption.

Planiol, vol. 2, no. 1573 offers insight, pertinent to the case at hand, regarding the nature of a sale a *à rémére*:

> "This kind of sale is especially useful to persons who have need of money and who wish to procure it by selling their property, without however, losing the hope of getting it back someday . . . he who sells *à rémére* first sells his property and does not recover it unless he is in a position to reimburse the funds which he received at the time."

The apparent purpose of the sale by plaintiff to his co-owners was to prevent plaintiff's creditors from acquiring plaintiff's interest in their land and thereby prevent a possible partition by licitation. The land was effectively transferred to defendants to place it out of the creditors reach and in return, defendants paid off these creditors. Plaintiff was granted the right to redeem the land when he could reimburse his brothers and sisters for these expenditures.

The intent of the parties to the contract falls within the classic confines of a sale with a right of redemption as set forth in Planiol, vol. 2, no. 1573.

* * * * *

The counter letter, which sets forth plaintiff's right of reacquisition, seems to be written in terms of a right granted by vendees and not retained by vendor, but as pointed out in *Baker v. Patton*, 191 La. 784, 186 So. 336 (1939), when the obvious intention of the parties is to create a sale with the right of redemption, the form of the counter letter will not prevent the judicial implementation of that purpose. See also *Harper v. Citizens' Bank*, 51 La.Ann. 511, 25 So. 466 (1899), and *Keough v. Meyers*, 43 La.Ann. 952, 9 So. 913 (1891).

* * * * *

The trial court's judgment is now affirmed. Costs of this appeal are assessed to defendants. All parties are granted the right to apply for a rehearing.

Affirmed.

DOMENGEAUX, Judge (concurs).

I adhere to the expressions contained in my dissenting opinion on the argued hearing, and for the reasons contained therein concur in the result reached on rehearing.

CULPEPPER, Judge (dissenting).

I cannot agree there was a sale with a right of redemption. An essential element of such a contract is that the vendor must [r]eserve the right to repurchase. If, on the contrary, the right to repurchase is granted by the vendee, the contract is an option and not a sale with a right of redemption. This fundamental distinction between an option and a sale with a right of redemption was recognized in *Pitts v. Lewis*, 7 La.Ann. 552 as follows:

> "It is elementary that there is no *vente à rémére* unless the right to take back the property, on refunding the price, be stipulated in the act of sale, so as to

form one of the reservations of it, and that if it is appended by a subsequent act to a sale originally pure and simple, it is either a resale or a promise to sell."

* * * * *

The counter-letter at issue here provides in pertinent part that the defendants "do by these presents agree, grant, and deliver unto Howard Delcambre, the right and option to repurchase from the said appearers . . . ." Furthermore, the counter-letter states "and the said Howard Delcambre declared and agreed that should he exercise said option to repurchase the said property sold by him to the said appearers . . . ." From this we see that the language used in the instrument clearly states that it is an option granted to the plaintiff to purchase the property, and not a right reserved by him to redeem the property.

In addition to the clear language of the contract, the parole testimony of the parties and of the attorney who drew the instrument shows they intended the counter-letter to be an option. The attorney says it was his purpose to draw an option. He does not mention a sale with a right of redemption. It is apparent that the parties and their attorney understood it was a contract of option.

I agree the court should consider the entire factual situation, rather than the mere words "grant" or "reserve", in determining whether there is a sale with a right of redemption. However, the facts in this case show clearly that the parties intended an option and that neither they nor their attorney even thought of a sale with a right of redemption.

The majority opinion states "The intent of the parties to the contract falls within the classic confines of a sale with a right of redemption" as set forth in Planiol, Vol. 2, No. 1573. The citation from Planiol reads as follows:

> "This kind of sale is especially useful to persons who have need of money, and who wish to procure it by selling their property, without however, losing the hope of getting it back some day. It is a transaction analogous to the loan on the mortgage, with this difference that its elements are present in an inverse chronological order: the person who borrows by mortgaging his immovable provisionally retains the ownership, and does not lose it unless he is unable to reimburse the loan when it becomes due; he who sells *à rémére* first sells his property and does not recover it unless he is in a position to reimburse the funds which he received at the time.
>
> "The sale with the right of redemption is a bad system of credit: it was useful for centuries before the establishment of the modern mortgage system. In our day, there is hardly any reason for its retention, and it often conceals usurious contracts of land, but the dangers which it presents because of the employment made of them can only be studied in connection with the loan of money and pledge (*infra*, Nos. 2071 and 2460)."

Of course, in the present case the basic situation was that the plaintiff was badly in need of money and he wished to procure it without losing his property, or at least the hope of getting it back some day. The parties had a choice of at least three security devices: (1) A mortgage, (2) sale with an option to repurchase and (3) sale with a right of redemption. Counsel for defendant argues it was an attempted option and counsel for plaintiff argues it was either a sale with a right of redemption or a pignorative (mortgage) contract.

The choice of security device was very important, because each is subject to different rules which produce substantially different legal effects. For instance, in the present case, although there was no oil production from the large tract of marsh land at the time of the agreement, oil was discovered soon thereafter and large sums of royalty have been paid to the defendants. If the agreement were a mortgage, then of course the plaintiff would retain these royalties. Also, if the agreement were a sale with a right of redemption, the plaintiff would be entitled to the restoration of the royalty under LSA-C.C. Article 2578 [R.C.C. 2578]. See *Harang v. Bowie Lumber Company*, 145 La. 96, 81 So. 769 (1919) and *Elder v. Ellerbe*, 135 La. 990, 66 So. 337 (1914) which hold that mineral royalties, like timber, are not classified as fruits which defendants could retain under LSA-C.C. Article 2575 [R.C.C. 2575].

However, if the security device chosen were a valid option, then of course the defendants would have enjoyed the full rights of ownership of the property until the option was exercised, and defendants would retain these mineral royalties.

Another substantial difference in these security devices which may be material in the present case, is that under LSA-C.C. Article 2587 [R.C.C. 2587], "The vendor who exercises the right of redemption, is bound to reimburse to the purchaser, not only the purchase money, but also the expenses resulting from necessary repairs, those which have attended the sale, and the price of the improvements which have increased the value of the estate, up to that increased value." Of course, the plaintiff in the present case did not plead that this was a sale with a right of redemption, and hence legal issues pertinent to this type of transaction were not at issue and no evidence was introduced in that regard. This in itself is sufficient reason that we should not decide the case on that basis. It may be that the defendants made necessary repairs or that they made improvements to the property which have increased its value, in which event, they are entitled to allege and prove reimbursement for these amounts.

Finally, the holding that this is a sale with a right of redemption is in direct conflict with the established jurisprudence that delivery of corporeal possession is an absolute requirement of a sale with a right of redemption, *Woods v. Stoma*, 242 So.2d 320 (La.App.2d Cir. 1970) and the cases cited therein. In the present case, the property consists of three principal tracts: (1) the 4300 acres of marshland; (2) plaintiff's home, and (3) the property on which plaintiff operates his fuel dock business. Although the evidence may be sufficient to show that defendants took actual possession of the 4300 acres of marshland, it is conceded by all parties that plaintiff has never parted with corporeal possession of the other two tracts, i.e., his home place and his business place. The retention by plaintiff of possession of these two tracts is not only another factor indicating the parties did not intend a sale with a right of redemption, but absolutely negates such a transaction as to them.

In an effort to overcome the effect of the rule regarding the transfer of actual possession, the majority cites *Brooks v. Broussard*, 136 La. 380, 67 So. 65 (1915), for the proposition that retention by the vendor of a small portion of land relative to the whole, does not negate the validity of a sale with a right of redemption. I have carefully read the *Brooks* case and do not find it contains such a holding. The facts were that Broussard owned a 233 acre tract of land which was heavily encumbered. He sold the property to Brooks in consideration of the purchaser assuming the encumbrances. In a subsequent counter-letter, it was agreed that Broussard had the "option" to repurchase the land within a year, and that Broussard could continue to live on the place and raise a crop. When Broussard failed to make the required payments on time, Brooks sued for recognition of his title. The issue was whether the transaction was a sale or a mortgage. The court held it was a sale, and that Brooks was the owner. The court did not hold that it was a sale with a right of redemption. It could not, since Broussard remained in possession. The court merely mentioned in passing that even if the transaction had been a sale with a right of redemption, Broussard did not exercise his redemption by paying on time.

In conclusion, it is simply not fair to these defendants to say that since the plaintiff needed money and wanted to [use] his property as security to obtain a loan, the transaction must be construed as a sale with a right of redemption. There are at least two other security devices, mortgage and sale with an option to repurchase, which could have been used. I think it is obvious that the parties intended to use an option, which would have been much more advantageous to defendants. The court should not in effect say that since a sale with a right of redemption would be legal, that is what the parties should have used. Who knows what the parties would have done, if they had known about a sale with a right of redemption and its legal effects.

For the reasons assigned, I respectfully dissent.

Notes and Questions

1. In what ways does a sale with the right of redemption vary from a sale in which the buyer grants the seller the option to repurchase the property? How did the court determine the nature of the contract at issue in the foregoing case? Note that this case predates the 1995 revision of the law of sales. Would the result be the same under current law?

2. As the foregoing case makes clear, the proper classification of an agreement to reconvey the property as a sale with a right of redemption or an option to repurchase the property has important consequences. For one thing, Louisiana courts historically have interpreted the Civil Code articles on options to require that, as opposed to a right of redemption, an option must contain a stipulated term. *See* La. Civ. Code arts. 1933 & 2623. Thus, while an option with no stipulated term is absolutely null, when the parties fail to state a term for the right of redemption, the

law supplies maximum terms depending on whether the thing sold is movable or immovable. In addition, the maximum terms allowed by law for rights of redemption affecting movables differ from the maximum terms allowed for options affecting movables. While an option contract involving a movable thing is subject to no maximum term, a right of redemption involving a movable thing may not exceed five years. *See* La. Civ. Code art. 2568.

3. You may recall from Chapter 5: Price that the sale of a corporeal immovable may be rescinded on grounds of lesion beyond moiety when the price paid is less than one-half of the fair market value of the corporeal immovable sold, La. Civ. Code art. 2589, and that typically, the immovable is evaluated according to the state in which it was at the time of the sale. La. Civ. Code art. 2590. How does the concept of lesion apply — if at all — when the contract of sale is preceded by an option contract? First, if the option is exercised and a claim for lesion asserted, the property must be evaluated in the state in which it was at the time of the option contract. La. Civ. Code art. 2590. Furthermore, an option to purchase an immovable cannot be attacked on the ground of lesion before there is an attempt to exercise the option. *Farris v. Interstate Enterprises, Inc.*, 270 So. 2d 230 (La. App. 1 Cir. 1972).

B. Contract to Sell

La. Civ. Code arts. 2623–2624

Of the three contracts preparatory to sale, none enjoys such widespread and frequent use as the contract to sell. This contract, according to Louisiana Civil Code Article 2623, is "[a]n agreement whereby one party promises to sell and the other party promises to buy a thing at a later time, or upon the happening of a condition, or upon the performance of some obligation by either party." La. Civ. Code art. 2623. Thus, the contract to sell does not involve an immediate sale, but instead it contemplates a future sale following the completion of a waiting period, the occurrence of contingencies, or both. The contract to sell, also referred to in the Civil Code as the bilateral promise of sale, is known by practitioners as the "purchase agreement" or the "buy/sell" agreement.

By entering into a contract to sell, the buyer shows the seller a degree of seriousness about a potential contract of sale, all the while reserving the right to back out of the deal if the property proves to be unsuitable for the buyer's needs or if other contingencies are not met. An example illustrates why these contracts are useful. Consider a scenario in which Betty desires to purchase a new home and begins looking in various neighborhoods across the city. She finally settles on a single-story brick house that is owned by Susie and listed for sale at a price of $230,000. It would certainly be possible for Betty and Susie to enter a contract of sale that would thereby immediately transfer ownership of the house to Betty and entitle Susie to payment of the purchase price. However, as you might imagine, there are likely some additional things Betty might want to know about the house other than what a simple tour from the realtor and perusal of the realtor's website might provide. For one, she will want to make sure the roof and foundation are in good condition. Additionally, if Betty is like most residential homebuyers, she does not have $230,000 in cash. Rather, she will need to arrange to borrow that amount of money from a bank before proceeding with the final sale. Moreover, if Betty already has an existing home loan, she may wish to sell her current residence and relieve herself of any loan associated with that house prior to incurring a new one.

It is certainly true that Susie could simply allow Betty access to the home for purposes of making these inspections and could also give her some time to sell her home and arrange for new financing, but what would happen if, during this period, Susie sold the house to someone else? Under that scenario, Betty would have expended a great deal of time and money only to then end up with no recourse against Susie. The contract to sell solves this problem. By virtue of the contract to sell, Susie must sell the property to Betty and cannot sell the property to anyone other than Betty, and Betty is bound to purchase the property. However, the obligations to buy and sell may be made conditional on inspections, financing, and other events that allow both parties to walk away from the deal if the conditions are not met. Because both parties to the contract to sell incur obligations, the agreement is bilateral in nature. *See* LA. CIV. CODE art. 1908.

The following excerpts provide an overview of how Louisiana law contemplates the contract to sell. Before reading these materials, carefully read Articles 2623 and 2624 and the comments thereto.

Louisiana State Law Institute, Proposed Louisiana Civil Code Revision of Sales 67–69 (1992) (Exposé des Motifs)

CONTRACT TO SELL: GENERAL PRINCIPLES

The expression "contract to sell" has been adopted by Louisiana courts. A contract to sell is an agreement to buy and sell where the parties are looking forward to a sale to take place in the future, but which is not yet a sale and does not transfer ownership. See Litvinoff, *"Of the Promise of Sale and Contract to Sell,"* 34 LA. L. REV. 1017, 1068 (1974); *Bornemann v. Richards*, 245 La. 851, 151 So. 2d 741 (1964); *Scott v. Apgar*, 238 La. 29, 113 So. 2d 457 (1959); *Davis v. McCain*, 171 La. 1011, 132 So. 758 (1931); *Buckman v. Stafford, Derbes & Roy, Inc.*, 167 La. 540, 119 So. 701 (1929).

The notion of the contract to sell in Louisiana law arose from Article 2462 of the Civil Code of 1870, and is the same as a bilateral promise of sale. See Smith, *"An Analytical Discussion of the Promise of Sale and Related Subjects, Including Earnest Money,"* 20 LA. L. REV. 522, 529 (1960). Revised Article 2623 codifies the expression "contract to sell", but also preserves the notion of a bilateral promise of sale.

DEPOSIT AND EARNEST MONEY

One of the strongest presumptions in Louisiana law is that any sum paid by the buyer in connection with a contract to sell is earnest money,—that is, a sum of money given by the buyer to the seller with the understanding that the buyer may validly recede from the contract by forfeiting that sum. That presumption has traditionally applied unless the parties specifically stipulated to the contrary. See Litvinoff, *"Of the Promise of Sale and the Contract to Sell,"* 34 LA. L. REV. 1017, 1073-1074 (1974). The presumption obtains even when the sum paid is referred to by the parties as money given to bind the contract or as payment on account of the purchase price. See *Maloney v. Aschaffenburg*, 143 La. 509, 78 So. 761 (1917); *Haeuser v. Schiro*, 235 La. 909, 106 So. 2d 306 (1958); *Ducuy v. Falgoust*, 228 La. 533, 83 So. 2d 118 (1955); *McCain v. Hicks*, 150 La. 43, 90 So. 506 (1922). That jurisprudentially-created presumption had no basis in the legislation and, in many cases, was in fact contrary to the intention of the parties. Moreover, it frequently led to unconscionable and impractical results.

Revised Article 2624 abandons the presumption favoring earnest adopted by Louisiana courts for one more in tune with the presumptive intention of the parties. Thus, under the draft article a sum of money paid in connection with a contract to sell is presumed to be a deposit towards the purchase of the thing involved. However, where the evidence indicates that the parties intended the sum paid to be earnest money the presumption of deposit does not apply.

One of the most significant prior decisions on earnest money was that in the case of *Ducuy v. Falgoust*, 228 La. 533, 83 So. 2d 118 (1955), where a seller sued for specific performance of a contract to sell immovable property. On original hearing, the Louisiana Supreme Court held that the seller had to return to the buyer "the deposit," since the seller's title was unmerchantable. Upon the buyer's application, the court granted a rehearing limited to the issue of whether the buyer was entitled to double the "deposit" as liquidated damages.

After a detailed examination of "earnest money" under Roman and French law, the court proceeded to determine whether the deposit involved in *Ducuy* was earnest money under Article 2463 of the Louisiana Civil Code of 1870. The language used in the contract to sell provided that: "In the event . . . the vendor does not comply with this agreement to sell within the time specified, purchaser shall have the right either to demand the return of double the deposit, or specific performance." In the court's view, such a clause negatived any presumption that the deposit was intended by the parties as earnest money. According to the court: "Thus, it may be seen that the parties did not intend the deposit as earnest. It was not given for the purpose of securing to the parties the privilege of withdrawing from the contract, for neither was free to withdraw. Both specifically reserved to themselves the right to demand specific performance, at their option." 83 So. 2d at 122-123. []

Although the above-quoted language suggests that the court would have ordered specific performance of the contract to sell therein involved, it did not do so, since it found that a cloud on the seller's title furnished grounds for dissolving the contract to sell. With respect to the remedy to which the buyer became entitled as a result of the seller's failure to deliver merchantable title, the court stated: "Consequently, inasmuch as the plaintiffs cannot specifically comply with the agreement they entered into, being without a valid and merchantable title to convey, the defendant is entitled to the return of the $780 deposited by him, plus an equal amount as stipulated damages." 83 So. 2d at 124.

The *Ducuy* court's assumption that a reservation of specific performance is necessary in order to make that remedy available in cases where a deposit is given in connection with a contract of sale is totally unwarranted. Nowhere in the law is there a basis for establishing the presumption in favor of earnest money which underlies that conclusion. The obligation to perform the contract to sell arises by virtue of the contract itself, there being no need for a specific reservation to that effect. See C.C. Art. 1986, 2046 (rev. 1984).

In addition, the court's characterization of the deposit in *Ducuy* as a "stipulated damages" sum was totally unwarranted. That is so because, first of all, the court made a specific factual finding that the buyer had given the sum involved as a deposit on the purchase price and not as earnest money. Thus, Article 2463 of the Louisiana Civil Code of 1870 was inapplicable to that situation, either directly or by analogy. Secondly, there was no basis in that case for presuming that it was the intention of the parties for the sum deposited to constitute a stipulated damages figure.

Accordingly, in instances where the sum given by the buyer in connection with an agreement to purchase is indeed a deposit on the purchase price, the buyer, in instances where the seller is unable or unwilling to transfer good title to the property, should be allowed to recover whatever damages he has actually sustained as a result of the seller's breach. On the other hand, in instances where the sum given in connection with an agreement to purchase is, in fact, earnest money, it makes perfect sense to regard this sum as liquidated damages when one of the parties is unable to perform for reasons other than a fortuitous event. Revised Article 2624 follows that approach.

1 Peter S. Title, *Louisiana Practice Series, Louisiana Real Estate Transactions* §§ 9:47–9:59 (2017–18 ed.)[±]

CHAPTER 9. PURCHASE AGREEMENTS

II. PURCHASE AGREEMENT PROVISIONS

§ 9:47. Deposits and earnest money — Form of deposit

A seller should insist that at least part of the deposit be in cash, since a cash deposit demonstrates seriousness on the part of the purchaser and motivates the purchaser to take title. If the purchaser gives a note for all or part of the purchase price, the note should be non-negotiable so that the seller cannot negotiate it to a holder in due course. The note should also provide that it is payable only in accordance with the terms of the contract to sell.

± Reproduced with permission of Thomson Reuters.

§ 9:48. Deposits and earnest money—Effect of failure to make deposit

Purchase agreements often provide that if the purchaser fails to make the required deposit, his failure to do so will not void the agreement but will be considered a breach. If the purchase agreement contains such a provision and the purchaser appears at the act of sale ready to buy the property and tender the purchase price, the seller cannot refuse to deliver title on the ground that the purchaser failed to make the required deposit. *Membreno v. Ponder*, 417 So. 2d 1257 (La. Ct. App. 1st Cir. 1982), *writ denied*, 423 So. 2d 1146 (La. 1982). If the purchase agreement does not contain a provision that the failure to made the deposit does not void the agreement, the seller might have a remedy of dissolution of the contract to sell for failure to make the required deposit but the seller would first have to serve on the purchaser a notice to perform within a certain time with a warning that, unless the deposit was furnished within that time, the contract shall be deemed dissolved. The time allowed for that purpose must be reasonable according to the circumstances. La. Civ. Code Ann. Art[.] 2015. In *Membreno*, the court noted that the seller had never made demand on the purchaser for the deposit.

§ 9:49. Deposits and earnest money—Deposit and specific performance

The effect of a deposit on the right of specific performance was changed by Article 2624 of the Civil Code, effective January 1, 1995. To understand that article, a discussion of the prior jurisprudence is necessary.

§ 9:50. Deposits and earnest money—Deposit and specific performance—Right to specific performance where deposit was given under prior jurisprudence

Under the Civil Code of 1870, if a deposit was required at the time the contract was executed, in the absence of a contrary stipulation the deposit was considered "earnest money," and neither the seller nor the purchaser could demand specific performance of the contract if either, without cause, receded from the agreement. Article 2463 of the Civil Code of 1870 provided that:

> If the promise to sell has been made with the giving of earnest, each of the contracting parties is at liberty to recede from the promise; to wit: he who has given the earnest, by forfeiting it; and he who has received it, by returning the double.

While Article 2462 of the Civil Code of 1870 provided that either party could demand specific performance of a contract to sell, Article 2463 of the Civil Code of 1870 negated this remedy where earnest money was given and thus allowed the contracting parties to retain the liberty to withdraw from the contract by forfeiting a set sum, without liability for specific performance. *Lulich v. Robin*, 466 So. 2d 780 (La. Ct. App. 4th Cir. 1985). It was not necessary that the deposit or payment given by the purchaser be specifically designated as earnest money in order for that deposit or payment to preclude the remedy of specific performance. A deposit given in accordance with a contract to sell was presumed to be earnest money unless it was clearly specified to the contrary. *Mexic Bros., Inc. v. Sauviac*, 191 So. 2d 873 (La.

Ct. App. 4th Cir. 1966). The deposit was considered earnest money even if it was agreed that it would be applied to the purchase price. *Southern Pac. Transp. Co. v. Port-O-Call, Inc.*, 314 So. 2d 755 (La. Ct. App. 4th Cir. 1975), writ denied, 318 So. 2d 45 (La. 1975). Thus, the giving of a deposit had the effect of precluding either party from obtaining specific performance in the absence of contrary agreement. *Trestman v. L. & B. Inv. Corp.*, 499 So. 2d 735 (La. Ct. App. 4th Cir. 1986). Parties could negate the presumption that a deposit was earnest money by specifically providing in the contract that the deposit was not to be considered earnest money (*Southern Pac. Transp. Co. v. Port-O-Call, Inc.*, 314 So. 2d 755 (La. Ct. App. 4th Cir. 1975), writ denied, 318 So. 2d 45 (La. 1975), at 759) or by providing that either the vendor or purchaser had the remedy of specific performance in event of breach of the contract. *Ducuy v. Falgoust*, 228 La. 533, 83 So. 2d 118 (1955); *see also Mason v. Coen*, 449 So. 2d 1195 (La. Ct. App. 2d Cir. 1984). Standard-form contracts usually negated the presumption of earnest money, and the presumption of earnest money did not apply if the deposit was not required by the contract to sell. If a deposit was not required by the contract to sell and was made after the execution of the contract, it was not considered earnest money but rather simply a partial payment of the purchase price and did not prevent either party from seeking specific performance. *Stipelcovich v. Mike Persia Chevrolet Co., Inc.*, 391 So. 2d 582 (La. Ct. App. 4th Cir. 1980

* * * * *

§ 9:51. Deposits and earnest money — Deposit and specific performance — Right to specific performance when deposit is given under present Article 2624

Article 2624 of the Civil Code, effective January 1, 1995, made an important change in the rule stated in the preceding section. Under Article 2624, a sum given by the buyer to the seller in connection with a contract to sell is regarded as a deposit on account of the price, unless the parties expressly provide otherwise. If the parties stipulate that a sum given by the buyer to the seller is earnest money, either party may recede from the contract; the buyer who chooses to recede must forfeit the earnest money, and the seller who so chooses must return the earnest money plus an equal amount. When earnest money has been given and a party fails to perform for reasons other than a fortuitous event, that party will be regarded as receding from the contract. Under the new rule of Article 2624, therefore, when the parties' intention is that a sum of money be given as earnest, they must clearly express that intention. Under prior jurisprudence (which was no longer controlling when Article 2624 became effective), the presumption was exactly the opposite; a deposit given in accordance with a contract to sell was presumed to be earnest money unless it was clearly specified to the contrary, and therefore if such a deposit was given neither party could obtain specific performance. Article 2624 also legislatively overrules *Haeuser v. Schiro*, 235 La. 909, 106 So. 2d 306 (1958) (*see* 9:53); under the article, a deposit made at the time of exercising an option is not to be regarded as earnest money. La Civ Code Ann art 2624 Cmt (a).

§ 9:52. Suspensive conditions in the purchase agreement

Contracts to sell often contain suspensive conditions on the obligations of either the seller or purchaser, i.e., the seller or purchaser, as applicable, is not obligated unless a certain event occurs. *See* La Civ Code Ann art 1767 for a definition of a suspensive condition. In real estate contracts, such conditions are often referred to as "contingencies." A common suspensive condition on the seller's obligation to sell is the requirement for court approval when the real estate is owned by a succession. More often, suspensive conditions qualify the purchaser's obligation to purchase the property. The obligation of the purchaser may be conditioned on his ability to secure, within a certain period of time, approvals from governmental authorities for the construction of certain improvements, for zoning variances, or for other waivers. *See Alliance Financial Services, Inc. v. Cummings*, 526 So. 2d 324 (La. Ct. App. 4th Cir. 1988), writ not considered, 531 So. 2d 465 (La. 1988). A "predication" clause, which conditions the purchaser's obligation to buy on the sale of other property that he owns, is another suspensive condition that is particularly common in residential transactions. Another common suspensive condition found in purchase agreements are inspections clauses and "contingency periods" and "due diligence" periods, which give the purchaser a period of time to inspect the property and examine records pertaining to the property, such as leases, and allow the purchaser to cancel the contract within that period by notice to the seller. Another contingency often found in purchase agreements is that the purchaser's obligation to purchase the property is subject to receipt of an appraisal of the property indicating that the market value of the property is no less than the sales price or other agreed upon amount.

§ 9:53. Suspensive conditions in the purchase agreement — Sale subject to financing

The most common suspensive condition found in contracts to sell is that which makes the sale subject to the ability of the purchaser to obtain financing for all or part of the sales price. If a sale is made subject to the purchaser's ability to obtain mortgage financing, a purchase agreement should specify the amount of the mortgage loan, the interest rate, terms of repayment, discount points if any, and any other particular requirements of the loan. The purchaser may even stipulate that a loan will be made only from a particular type of financial institution as the only acceptable financing. *See Katz v. Chatelain*, 321 So. 2d 802 (La. Ct. App. 4th Cir. 1975). Any seller financing for all or part of the purchase price, and the terms of the financing, should also be set forth clearly. Purchase agreements typically provide that the failure of the purchaser to obtain financing under the terms specified in the contract will render the agreement null and entitle the purchaser to return of the deposit.

§ 9:54. Suspensive conditions in the purchase agreement — Sale subject to financing — Effect of purchaser's inability to secure loan

When a purchaser, through no fault of his own, is unable to obtain the loan upon which the loan agreement is conditioned, the obligations imposed by the agreement are not binding upon the parties; the agreement is null and the parties are released from their obligations to perform. *Bacon v. Ford*, 522 So. 2d 1232 (La. Ct. App. 4th Cir. 1988), *writ denied*, 523 So. 2d 1340 (La. 1988).

§ 9:55. Suspensive conditions in the purchase agreement — Sale subject to financing — Requirements of good faith effort by purchaser to secure loan or fulfill other suspensive condition

A party has an implied obligation to put forth a good faith effort to fulfill a suspensive condition. *Alliance Financial Services, Inc. v. Cummings*, 526 So. 2d 324, 327 (La. Ct. App. 4th Cir. 1988), writ not considered, 531 So. 2d 465 (La. 1988). Thus, a purchaser has the implied obligation to make a good faith effort to obtain financing and thereby fulfill the condition. The penalty imposed on a purchaser who does not make a good faith effort to obtain a mortgage loan necessary to fulfill a condition in the contract to sell is that the condition which was not fulfilled because of the purchaser's fault is deemed waived by the purchaser and the condition is considered as fulfilled. *Dapremont v. Crossley*, 367 So. 2d 127 (La. Ct. App. 4th Cir. 1979), writ denied, 369 So. 2d 710 (La. 1979); La Civ Code Ann art 1772. The condition is considered as fulfilled, and the purchase agreement is not null and void, if the purchaser's inability to obtain a mortgage loan is due to his inability to furnish the cash down payment, i.e., the amount that is not subject to mortgage financing. *Farnsworth/Samuel Ltd. v. Cervini*, 492 So. 2d 1245 (La. Ct. App. 4th Cir. 1986), *writ denied*, 497 So. 2d 316 (La. 1986).

§ 9:56. Suspensive conditions in the purchase agreement — Sale subject to financing — Requirements of good faith effort by purchaser to secure loan or fulfill other suspensive Condition — Evidence of good faith effort

Whether or not a party has made a good faith effort to obtain financing or fulfill a different suspensive condition depends on the facts and circumstances peculiar to each case. In *Liuzza v. Panzer*, 333 So. 2d 689 (La. Ct. App. 4th Cir. 1976), the prospective purchaser's application to one homestead did not constitute a good faith effort to obtain financing when it appeared that financing was available from other lending agencies. On the other hand, in *Katz v. Chatelain*, 321 So. 2d 802 (La. Ct. App. 4th Cir. 1975), it was held that the purchaser's single application to a loan association constituted a good faith effort since the appraisal was made by the Central Appraisal Bureau used by all of the homesteads in the New Orleans area where the real estate was located. Under the circumstances that existed in *Katz v. Chatelain*, since all homesteads used the same appraisal, a denial of a loan by one homestead based on that appraisal necessarily would result in a denial of the loan by other homesteads. A purchaser is not required to obtain financing on terms that are different from those stated in the purchase agreement.

§ 9:57. Suspensive conditions in the purchase agreement — Sale subject to financing — Requirements of good faith effort by purchaser to secure loan or fulfill other suspensive condition — Effect of showing that condition could probably not be fulfilled

If the purchaser alleges that the condition would not have been fulfilled even if he had made a good faith effort to fulfill it, can the purchaser be exempted from liability if he made no effort to fulfill the condition? The purchaser made such an allegation in *Riverfront Investors Group v. Chavez*, 644 So. 2d 247 (La. Ct. App. 4th Cir. 1994), reh'g denied, (Nov. 15, 1994) and writ not considered, 649 So. 2d 416 (La. 1995). In that case, the purchase agreement provided that the purchaser's obligation to purchase the property was subject to obtaining all appropriate permits and licenses for its intended use and the purchaser agreed to apply for them. The purchaser contended that it was excused from making a good faith effort to obtain the permits and licenses because the chance of obtaining them was remote in light of political opposition to a zoning concession that would have been necessary for them to be issued. The court rejected the purchaser's defense; the purchaser was required to make a good faith effort to obtain the permits and licenses. While the law does not require the purchaser to do a vain thing, an unlikely thing is not synonymous with a vain thing, the court held.

§ 9:58. Suspensive conditions in the purchase agreement — Sale subject to financing — Requirements of good faith effort by purchaser to secure loan or fulfill other suspensive condition — Loan by seller if purchaser cannot secure loan

Many purchase agreements provide that the seller can obtain financing for the purchaser or can even finance the sale himself if the purchaser is unable to obtain a loan. A purchaser is not, however, obligated to accept a loan offered by the seller that is inconsistent with that contemplated in the agreement to purchase. *Thaly v. Namer,* 496 So. 2d 1211 (La. Ct. App. 5th Cir. 1986); *Katz v. Chatelain*, 321 So. 2d 802 (La. Ct. App. 4th Cir. 1975). If a "homestead" or Federal Housing Authority loan is contemplated, alternative financing must be repayable on a long-term basis similar to that offered by long-term lending institutions. *Antonini v. Thrifty-Nifty Homes*, 76 So. 2d 564 (La. Ct. App., Orleans 1955).

§ 9:59. Suspensive conditions in the purchase agreement — Sale subject to financing — Waiver of financing condition

A provision in a purchase agreement conditioning the sale on the purchaser's ability to make a mortgage loan is a suspensive condition for the sole benefit of the purchaser, who may waive the condition. *Felder v. Terry*, 351 So. 2d 244 (La. Ct. App. 4th Cir. 1977), writ denied, 353 So. 2d 1046 (La. 1978). The seller is presumed to be interested only in getting the purchase price regardless of the source. Even if the purchase agreement provides that the agreement is null and void should the purchaser not obtain financing, the purchaser is entitled to decline financing and decide to pay all cash for the property without attempting to make a loan. In that event, the seller cannot rely on the nullity of the agreement because of the purchaser's failure to obtain financing, and must comply with his obligation to deliver title.

Notes and Questions

1. What are the prerequisites for a valid contract to sell? Must a contract to sell be made in any particular form? *See* LA. CIV CODE arts. 1839, 2440.

2. Based on the foregoing reading, what conditions are commonly contemplated by the parties in a contract to sell? Which conditions favor the buyer? The seller? Both parties? What are the parties' obligations with respect to ensuring that conditions are fulfilled?

Consider the following hypothetical. Annie is in the market for her first home and finds one that she would like to buy. The house is owned by Bob, and the price is $250,000. Annie and Bob enter into a purchase agreement in which they agree that Annie will buy the house if she qualifies for a loan for the entire purchase price at an interest rate no higher than 4%. After entering the agreement, Annie's grandmother dies, leaving her home to Annie, and as a result, Annie decides that she does not want to buy Bob's house after all and never applies for the home loan. When Annie informs Bob of this, he avers that Annie has breached their purchase agreement. Annie responds that the condition in the contract—that she obtain a loan for $250,000 at an interest rate no higher than 4%—was not fulfilled. Thus, she argues, she does not have to go through with the sale and has not breached the purchase agreement. Who is correct? Read Civil Code Article 1772.

3. Article 2623 provides that the contract to sell "gives either party the right to demand specific performance." LA. CIV. CODE art. 2623. Note that the payment of "earnest money" in connection with a contract to sell negates the right to specific performance. What is "earnest money" and how does it differ from a "deposit?" What are the rights of the parties when "earnest money" is paid?

4. Recall that, under the law of Obligations in General, when performance of an obligation becomes impossible due to the occurrence of a fortuitous event, the obligation is extinguished and nonperformance is excused. Impossibility of performance likewise extinguishes the obligations of the parties to a contract to sell. Before reading the following case, which illustrates the application of the law governing impossibility of performance in this context, carefully read Articles 1873 through 1878 and the comments thereto.

Payne v. Hurwitz
978 So. 2d 1000 (La. App. 1 Cir. 2008)

GAIDRY, J.

The prospective purchasers of a home under a purchase agreement sued the prospective seller, alleging the seller's noncompliance with the agreement and refusal to consummate the sale. The trial court rendered judgment in favor of the prospective purchasers for the return of their deposit, a contractual penalty, and attorney fees, expenses, and costs. The seller appeals and the prospective purchasers have answered his appeal, asserting error by the trial in failing to grant them specific performance. For the following reasons, we amend the judgment to grant the prospective purchasers specific performance, vacate the awards for the deposit return and contractual penalty, affirm the judgment in all other respects, and remand the case for further proceedings.

FACTS AND PROCEDURAL BACKGROUND

The plaintiffs, Wesley Payne and Gwendolyn Payne (the Paynes), decided to purchase a smaller home, and in July 2005 began searching for one. Using the Internet, they eventually located a home for sale at 4018 Willow Lane in Madisonville, Louisiana. The owner was Keefe Hurwitz. After viewing the home, the Paynes made an offer that was acceptable to Mr. Hurwitz, and a purchase agreement for the price of $241,500.00 was signed on August 22, 2005. On the same date, the Paynes wrote a check in the amount of $1,000.00, representing the required deposit, made payable to Houlemarde Realty, the real estate agency representing Mr. Hurwitz. The purchase agreement provided for a closing date for execution of the act of sale of September 26, 2005, or sooner if mutually agreed. However, it also provided for an automatic extension of the closing date for up to sixty days in the event repairs were necessary.

On August 29, 2005, Hurricane Katrina made landfall, causing extensive damage to property in southeast Louisiana, including Madisonville. Mr. Hurwitz's home sustained substantial roof damage from the hurricane winds and a fallen tree, as well as water damage to the sheetrock, windows, and other interior fixtures of the left side of the home. The costs of repair were estimated by Mr. Hurwitz, a self-employed contractor with experience as an insurance adjuster, at approximately $60,000.00.

Due to disruption of electronic communications systems and mail service following the hurricane, the Paynes, who had evacuated to Kansas City, Missouri, experienced considerable difficulty in contacting Mr. Hurwitz regarding the status of the sale of the home. On September 9, 2005, they hand-delivered a letter containing their contact information to Michelle Poliski, Mr. Hurwitz's wife, and attempted to contact Mr. Hurwitz by e-mail directed to Angela Houlemarde, Mr. Hurwitz's agent. The Paynes also contacted their loan officer, who suggested that they ask the lender's title attorney to attempt to contact Mr. Hurwitz regarding the status of the closing date and a proposed extension of that date, as authorized by the agreement.

On September 20, 2005, Mr. Hurwitz e-mailed the lender's title attorney, acknowledging a conversation of that date and stating:

> Per our conversation today I was blunt that the house was in need of major repair due to storm damage. It will take months to get this work completed. I will not be interested in selling for the same amount when and if I decide to sell my house. Naturally the house goes up in value each day. Your client states on the contract a sale for cash. That means no bank loan or approval is needed. I understand that Katrina was an inconvenance [sic] to every one[.] I'm sorry at this time I cannot afford to sell my house under the previous terms and conditions or the present status of my house and my life at this time. I thank you for your understanding. KH

On October 3, 2005, the Paynes filed a petition seeking specific performance and damages, alleging that Mr. Hurwitz breached the terms of the purchase agreement.

On October 28, 2005, Mr. Hurwitz answered the petition, alleging that the agreement was unenforceable due to Hurricane Katrina and that his performance was impossible due *to force majeure*. He also alleged that the property could not be repaired within the automatic sixty-day extension for closing, or by November 24, 2005.

The matter was tried on May 8, 2006. At the conclusion of the trial, the trial court took the matter under advisement after ordering the submission of posttrial memoranda. On September 11, 2006, the trial court issued its judgment, incorporating its written reasons. The court ruled in favor of the Paynes, awarding them the return of their $1,000.00 deposit and an equal amount representing a contractual penalty, as well as costs, fees, expenses and reasonable attorney fees, as provided in the agreement.

The Paynes answered the appeal, seeking amendment of the trial court's judgment to grant them the alternative remedy of specific performance in lieu of the return of their deposit and the contractual penalty.

ASSIGNMENTS OF ERROR

Mr. Hurwitz designates four assignments of error on the part of the trial court:

(1) The trial court erred in determining that he breached the terms and conditions of the purchase agreement;

(2) The trial court erred in determining that the home could have been repaired in time to accomplish the closing;

(3) The trial court erred in determining that the obligation was not rendered null and void due to *force majeure* or an "Act of God"; and

(4) The trial court erred in determining that he was in bad faith under the terms and conditions of the purchase agreement.

In their answer to the appeal, the Paynes assign the following error on the part of the trial court:

(5) The trial court erred in holding that the Paynes were required to set a closing or to "put the seller in default," in order to be entitled to the remedy of specific performance authorized by the terms of the purchase agreement.

DISCUSSION

The purchase agreement at issue was signed by the Paynes on August 19, 2005 and presented in the form of an offer, and was accepted and signed by Mr. Hurwitz on August 22, 2005. It consisted of a two-page form agreement entitled "Agreement to Purchase or Sell," and bore language stating that it was produced through the use of a computer software program. The first page, bearing the parties' signatures, confirmed that the Paynes' offer was submitted to Angela Houlemarde, Mr. Hurwitz's designated real estate agent. The purchase agreement contained the following provision relating to the effect of necessary title work or repairs upon the date of the act of sale:

CURATIVE WORK/REPAIRS In the event curative work in connection with the title is required, and/or if repairs are a requirement for obtaining the loan(s) upon which this agreement is conditioned, the parties agree to and do extend the date for passing the Act of Sale to a date not more than fifteen (15) days following completion of curative work/repairs; but in no event shall extension exceed sixty (60) days without the written consent of all parties.[3]

The purchase agreement also included the following pertinent provisions:

BREACH OF AGREEMENT BY SELLER In the event SELLER fails to comply with this agreement, for any reason other than inability to deliver a merchantable title, within the time specified, PURCHASER shall have the right to demand specific performance; or, at PURCHASER's option, PURCHASER shall have the right to demand the return of his deposit in full, plus an equal amount to be paid as penalty by SELLER. In either event, PURCHASER shall have the right to recover any costs and/or fees, including expenses and reasonable attorney's fees, incurred as a result of this agreement or breach thereof.

. . .

DEADLINES Time is of the essence and all deadlines are final except where modifications, changes, or extensions are made in writing and signed by all parties.

Mr. Hurwitz testified at trial that no repairs had been made by the original scheduled closing date of September 26, 2005. According to Mr. Hurwitz, the roof repair began on October 21, 2005, and was completed on October 28, 2005. He received the final supplemental check from his insurer for the estimated cost of repairs on November 15, 2005. He also testified that additional needed repairs were still incomplete at the time of trial.

Louisiana Civil Code article 2623 sets forth the requisite elements of a contract to sell, or purchase agreement:

An agreement whereby one party promises to sell and the other promises to buy a thing at a later time, or upon the happening of a condition, or upon performance of some obligation by either party, is a bilateral promise of sale or contract to sell. Such an agreement gives either party the right to demand specific performance.

A contract to sell must set forth the thing and the price, and meet the formal requirements of the sale it contemplates.

---

3. The record confirms that the Paynes obtained financing for the purchase from a lender, but there is no evidence that the loan was conditioned upon any repairs. Regardless of whether or not the Paynes' loan was conditioned upon repairs being made, the parties have conceded the applicability of the extension provision.

Delivery of an immovable is deemed to take place upon execution of the writing that transfers its ownership. La. C.C. art. 2477. Louisiana Civil Code article 2489 expresses the obligation of the seller as to the condition of the thing sold at time of delivery:

> The seller must deliver the thing sold in the condition that, at the time of the sale, the parties expected, or should have expected, the thing to be in at the time of delivery, according to its nature.

Under article 2489, the seller must care for and preserve the thing sold as a reasonably prudent administrator, in accordance with the overriding obligation of good faith. La. C.C. art. 2489. Revision Comments-1993, (b). Thus, Mr. Hurwitz as seller bore the risk of any damage to the home pending the sale, and had the legal duty to restore it to its expected condition prior to delivery to the buyers. As the obligor in that respect, the extensions provided for in the "Curative Work/Repairs" provision of the purchase agreement were primarily for his benefit as seller, to assist him in fulfilling that obligation.

Our Civil Code provides that "[a]n obligor is not liable for his failure to perform when it is caused by a fortuitous event that makes performance impossible." La. C.C. art. 1873. A fortuitous event is one that, at the time the contract was made, could not have been reasonably foreseen. La. C.C. art. 1875. Our jurisprudence uses the terms "fortuitous event" and *force majeure* (irresistible force) interchangeably. La. C.C. art. 1873, Revisions Comments-1984, (c). *Force majeure* is defined as "an event or effect that can be neither anticipated nor controlled." Black's Law Dictionary 673-74 8th ed.2004). It includes such acts of nature as floods and hurricanes. *Id.* It is essentially synonymous with the common law concept of "act of God," and the latter term has also found its way into our jurisprudence. *See Saden v. Kirby*, 94-0854, p. (La.9/5/95), 660 So.2d 423, 428; *Bass v. Aetna Ins. Co.*, 370 So.2d 511, 513 n. 1 (La.1979); and *A. Brousseau & Co. v. Ship Hudson*, 11 La.Ann. 427 (La.1856). The parties concede, as we do, that Hurricane Katrina undoubtedly was a *force majeure*. But this is only part of the contractual defense of impossibility of performance.

To relieve an obligor of liability, a fortuitous event must make the performance truly impossible. La. C.C. art. 1873, Revision Comments-1984, (d). The nonperformance of a contract is not excused by a fortuitous event where it may be carried into effect, although not in the manner contemplated by the obligor at the time the contract was entered into. *Dallas Cooperage & Woodenware Co. v. Creston Hoop Co.*, 161 La. 1077, 1078-79, 109 So. 844 (La.1926). In other words, if the fortuitous event prevents the obligor from performing his obligation in the manner contemplated at the time of contracting, he must pursue reasonable alternatives to render performance in a different manner before he can take advantage of the defense of impossibility. *West v. Cent La. Limousine Serv., Inc.*, 03-373, p. 2 (La.App. 3rd Cir.10/1/03), 856 So.2d 203, 205. An obligor is not released from his duty to perform under a contract by the mere fact that such performance has been made more difficult or more burdensome by a fortuitous event. *Schenck v. Capri Constr. Co.*, 194 So.2d 378, 380

(La.App. 4th Cir.1967). The fortuitous event must pose an insurmountable obstacle in order to excuse the obligor's nonperformance. Saúl Litvinoff, *Louisiana Civil Law Treatise: The Law of Obligations,* § 16.17, at 476 (2nd ed.2001).

The leading commentator cited above has also made the following observations relevant to the situation of this case:

> A question arises when a fortuitous event prevents the timely performance of an obligation without making that performance impossible in an absolute sense. That is the case of a fortuitous event of limited duration that temporarily prevents the use of but does not destroy the means on which the obligor was counting in order to perform the obligation . . . .
>
> If the obligation is [such] that a delayed performance is still useful to the obligee, then the obligor remains bound to perform once the impediment ceases and owes no damages for the delay caused by the fortuitous event.

Id., § 16.62.

Louisiana Civil Code article 1759 provides that good faith governs the conduct of both the obligor and the obligee in whatever pertains to the obligation. Similarly, La. C.C. art. 1983 provides that contracts, or conventional obligations, must be performed in good faith. Thus, a party to a contract has an implied obligation to put forth a good faith effort to fulfill the conditions of the contract. *Bond v. Allemand,* 632 So.2d 326, 328 (La.App. 1st Cir.1993), *writ denied,* 94-0718 (La.4/29/04), 637 So.2d 468.

The recent case of *Associated Acquisitions, L.L.C. v. CarboneProperties of Audubon, L.L.C.,* 07-0120 (La.App. 4th Cir.7/11/07), 962 So.2d 1102, also arose in the aftermath of Hurricane Katrina. The defendant in that case also urged the defense of *force majeure* in an effort to excuse its nonperformance. The court there rejected the defense, observing that under settled Louisiana jurisprudence, "a party is obliged to perform a contract entered into by him if performance be possible at all, and regardless of any difficulty he might experience in performing it." *Id.,* 07-0120 at p. 9, 962 So.2d at 1107, citing *Picard Const. Co. v. Bd. of Comm'rs of Caddo Levee Dist.,* 161 La. 1002, 1007, 109 So. 816, 818 (La.1926). The court concluded: "the unexpected and unforeseen damage of Hurricane Katrina does not change the agreement between these parties; therefore, this is an agreement which can still be performed." *Id.* 07-0120 at p. 9, 962 So.2d at 1107-08.

Here, the only possible obstacle to Mr. Hurwitz's performance under the purchase agreement was a temporal one: the completion of the necessary repairs and the closing within the automatic sixty-day deadline or any additional extension agreeable to the parties. The Paynes, as obligees, unequivocally expressed their willingness to agree to the latter extension, but Mr. Hurwitz did not, and preemptively rejected the consummation of the agreement as impossible of performance even before the expiration of the automatic sixty-day extension. Mr. Hurwitz could certainly have rendered performance in a different manner, that is, at a later time based upon a mutual written extension of the closing deadline. We agree with the trial court's conclusion that the real basis of Mr. Hurwitz's failure to perform was volitional in nature, rather than the type of insurmountable obstacle necessary to invoke the defense of *force majeure*. The determination of whether performance was truly impossible was a factual one, and the trial court expressly concluded in its reasons that Mr. Hurwitz was disingenuous in his explanation regarding the availability of materials and delay in repairs.[5] Being based upon a reasonable credibility assessment, the trial court's conclusion cannot be manifestly erroneous.

In summary, we conclude that none of Mr. Hurwitz's assignments of error have merit. As to the Paynes' assignment of error, however, we conclude that there is merit. Louisiana Civil Code article 1986 provides:

> **Upon an obligor's failure to perform an obligation to deliver a thing,** or not to do an act, *or to execute an instrument, the court shall grant specific performance* plus damages for delay if the obligee so demands. If specific performance is impracticable, the court may allow damages to the obligee.
>
> Upon a failure to perform an obligation that has another object, such as an obligation to do, the granting of specific performance is at the discretion of the court.

The factual situation before us clearly falls within the mandatory relief provided in the first paragraph of the article, rather than the discretionary relief authorized by the second paragraph. Additionally, both La. C.C. art. 2623 (relating to purchase agreements) and the express terms of the purchase agreement at issue grant the Paynes the right to seek specific performance. The record does not support a finding that specific performance is impracticable as a remedy under the circumstances of this case.

The trial court based its finding that the Paynes were not entitled to specific performance because they "failed to demand specific performance as provided for in the [c]ontract by setting a closing date or otherwise . . . putting [Mr. Hurwitz] in default." We agree with the Paynes that the trial court erred in that regard as a matter of law. Putting the obligor in default is not a prerequisite to filing suit for specific performance because in such a case the judicial demand itself amounts to a putting in default. La. C.C. art.1989, Revision Comments-1984, (d). And even if a putting in default might somehow be considered a prerequisite to obtaining specific performance, our jurisprudence holds that "there is no need for a putting in default

---

5. The trial court also observed that although Mr. Hurwitz testified that he had "fired" his real estate agent, Ms. Houlemarde, before Hurricane Katrina, and never listed the home for sale after the hurricane, testimony from another real estate agent at trial confirmed that the home was listed for sale as of September 29, 2005, on the MLS (Multi-Listing Service) accessible to realtors, with a new price of $287,000.00. That agent also testified that as of April 28, 2006, Ms. Houlemarde was still shown as the listing agent, with the home's price at $287,000.00. The trial court also pointedly expressed its belief that Mr. Hurwitz did not feel obligated to fulfill his contractual obligations after the hurricane, and "thereby could profit from Katrina's destruction by insisting on a higher sales price."

of a seller who has advised the buyer that he, the seller, will not appear to execute the final act of sale at the time fixed for that purpose." Saúl Litvinoff, *Louisiana Civil Law Treatise: The Law of Obligations, Part II: Putting in Default and Damages,* § 1.18 (1999). Similarly, if the seller simply refuses to agree to the fixing of a mutually acceptable date for the closing, and affirmatively repudiates his obligation to sell under a purchase agreement, it is quite clear that there is no requirement for a putting in default as a prerequisite to seeking specific performance. *See id.,* § 1.19 at 23. Such is the situation here. We conclude that the Paynes are entitled to specific performance under the facts before us, and will amend the judgment in their favor to grant them that relief.

DECREE

The judgment of the trial court is amended to vacate the award of $2,000.00, representing the return of the deposit of $1,000.00 and the penalty of $1,000.00, and in lieu thereof to grant the plaintiffs-appellees, Wesley Payne and Gwendolyn Payne, specific performance of the Agreement to Purchase and Sell, and to order the defendant, Keefe Hurwitz, to sell the immovable property to the plaintiffs-appellees for the sum of TWO HUNDRED FORTY-ONE THOUSAND FIVE HUNDRED AND NO/100 DOLLARS ($241,500), in default of which the trial court shall render a judgment that shall stand for the act, pursuant to Louisiana Civil Code article 1988. In all other respects, the judgment is affirmed. This matter is further remanded to the trial court for the entry of an order setting a convenient date and time for the execution of the act of sale, or the entry of a judgment that shall stand for the act. All costs of this appeal are assessed to the defendant-appellant, Keefe Hurwitz.

ANSWER TO APPEAL MAINTAINED; JUDGMENT AMENDED AND, AS AMENDED, AFFIRMED; CASE REMANDED.

McDonald, J., concurs and assigns reasons.

McClendon, J., concurs with the result and assigns reasons.

McDonald, J., concurring:

Under the facts of this case, Mr. Hurwitz was obligated to make a good faith effort to repair the property. He breached the contract when he unilaterally and erroneously concluded that Hurricane Katrina relieved him of his obligation, as evidenced by his e-mail of September 20, 2005 stating that he was no longer willing to sell the house. Mr. Hurwitz did not offer any evidence regarding the extent of the damage to the house or the time required to repair it. Although he testified that some of the repairs still had not been made at the time of the trial, the trial court found his testimony "disingenuous," and I agree with this opinion's conclusion that the failure to repair was volitional. The purchase agreement allowed the buyer to demand specific performance if the seller was in default. The buyer has made such a demand and there is no reason not to grant it. Therefore, I agree with the result reached, and respectfully concur in the opinion.

McClendon, J., concurs and assigns reasons.

After reviewing the particular facts of this case, I believe that the seller by virtue of his e-mail dated September 20, 2005 to the closing attorney, defaulted on the purchase agreement. Based on that finding, the application and ramifications of the 60 day provision need not be addressed. Although specific performance may not be the correct or appropriate remedy in all default cases following a devastating hurricane, such as Hurricane Katrina, the buyer herein was entitled to pray for specific performance pursuant to the clear language of the purchase agreement, and answered the appeal seeking an order of specific performance. For these reasons, I respectfully concur.

Notes and Questions

Consider the following provision, enacted in 2006. What purpose does it serve? When does the prescriptive period announced by this provision begin to run?

La. Rev. Stat. § 9:5645. Prescription of actions involving contract to sell or transfer immovable property

An action for the breach or other failure to perform a contract for the sale, exchange, or other transfer of an immovable is prescribed in five years.

Note that this provision, by its own terms, applies to a failure to perform "a contract *for the sale, exchange, or other transfer*" of an immovable. Is its application limited to contracts to sell? Might it also apply to options? To rights of first refusal?

C. Right of First Refusal

La. Civ. Code arts. 2625–2627

The final contract preparatory to sale is the right of first refusal. This contract is described in the Civil Code as one in which a party agrees "that he will not sell a certain thing without first offering it to a certain person." La. Civ. Code art. 2625. The right of first refusal, like the other preparatory contracts described above, does not involve an immediate sale. Rather, it is an agreement by which the grantor promises to make an offer to sell a thing to a potential buyer, if (and only if) the grantor decides to sell.

As the excerpt below explains, the holder of a right of first refusal plays a rather passive role. Unlike the holder of an option contract, who enjoys the power to elect to purchase the property subject to the right, the holder of a right of first refusal has no power to compel a sale. Rather, the holder of the right of first refusal must wait until the owner desires to divest himself or herself of the property. It is then and only then that the holder of the right may acquire the property due to the fact that (as the name suggests) the owner must first offer the property for sale to the holder of the right before the owner can convey the property to anyone else. However, if the owner does not wish to part with the property during the term of the right of first refusal, then the holder of the right of first refusal has no right to act unilaterally with regard to the property. For instance, if Adam holds a right of first refusal on Blackacre, which is owned by Ben, Adam must wait until Ben wishes to sell the property before Adam can acquire it. While it is true that Ben cannot sell Blackacre to anyone else without first offering the property for sale to Adam, if Ben never wishes to sell Blackacre, then Adam will never come to own the property.

The following excerpt expounds further upon this particular type of pre-sale contract.

Louisiana State Law Institute, Proposed Louisiana Civil Code Revision of Sales 69–70 (1992) (Exposé des Motifs)

RIGHT OF FIRST REFUSAL: GENERAL PRINCIPLES

A right of first refusal, or *pacte de préférence*, may be defined as "a promise whereby the promisor obligates himself to give the promisee a first choice to make a certain transaction should the promisor ever decide to make that transaction." See Litvinoff, *"Consent Revisited: Offer Acceptance Option Right of First Refusal and Contracts of Adhesion in the Revision of the Louisiana Law of Obligations,"* 47 LA. L. REV. 753 (1987). See also 2 LITVINOFF, OBLIGATIONS 187–188 (1975). Thus, in the law of sales, a right of first refusal is a promise to offer a first chance to buy a thing to another when and if the seller desires to sell that thing.

Promises involving rights of first refusal, or preemption, were once fairly common in situations where the vendor of a thing wished to preserve the opportunity of repurchasing it in the future if the vendee ever wanted to put it up for sale. Thus, Article 1072 of the Civil Code of Austria provides: "A person who sells property upon the condition that the buyer must offer it for sale to him in the event that the buyer wishes to sell it again has a right of preemption."

While there exist certain similarities between the option and the right of first refusal, upon closer scrutiny it seems quite clear that there are marked differences between the two types of agreement. Thus, while the grantor of an option to buy is unconditionally bound to sell the thing to the optionee from the time the optionee elects to accept the offer contained in the option, the grantor of a right of first refusal is only conditionally bound: all that the promisor of a right of first refusal promises is to offer the property to the promisee if the promisor ever wishes to sell it. See Litvinoff, *"Consent Revisited: Offer Acceptance Option Right of First Refusal and Contracts of Adhesion in the Revision of the Louisiana Law of Obligations,"* 47 LA. L. REV. 753-754 (1987).

Revised Article 2625 defines the right of first refusal as an agreement whereby a party commits himself not to "sell a certain thing without first offering it to a certain person." That Article makes it crystal clear that the right of first refusal may be enforced by specific performance.

* * * * *

Notes and Questions

The case that follows addresses the distinction between a right of first refusal and an option. Differentiating between the two contracts is often challenging for students new to the law of sales. Before reading this case, carefully read Articles 2625 and 2526 and the comments thereto.

Robichaux v. Boutte

492 So. 2d 521 (La. App. 3 Cir. 1986)

STOKER, Judge.

The essential question in this case is whether a vendor of immovable property granted the vendees a right of refusal or an option to purchase certain other property as a part of the conveyance.

The defendants, Lance F. Gauthier and Madeline Champagne Gauthier, appeal a judgment of this court overruling their peremptory exceptions of liberative prescription and nonjoinder of indispensable parties and the granting of the plaintiff's motion for partial summary judgment. We affirm the judgment of the trial court.

FACTS

By credit deed dated May 19, 1966, the defendant, Verla Lavergne Boutte (now deceased), conveyed to the plaintiffs a 50.83-acre tract of land on Louisiana Highway 347 in St. Martin Parish. In addition to that conveyance of property, the deed provided as follows, that:

> "It is understood and agreed that should Vendors and their heirs, at any time in the future, desire to sell and convey the property on which is presently situated their residence and shown on Plat annexed to this sale as "Mrs. George Boutte", that Vendee and his heirs are to be given the first preference in the purchase thereof, that is, upon determination of said sale, the same shall be offered to Vendee and/or his heirs for an amount equal to the highest bonafide [sic] offer received by Vendor and Vendee and his heirs, to be given a period of ten (10) days in which to notify Vendor that they desire to purchase said property at the offered price and upon a rejection of said offer to sell Vendors are not to convey the same at a lesser price without again offering the same to Vendee or his heirs."

Mrs. Boutte also conveyed to plaintiffs any right of repurchase which she may have had with regard to certain property conveyed earlier to Junius Willis. Both the vendor's residence property and the Junius Willis' property consist of tracts located partially in front of the property sold to plaintiffs. Acquisition of either or both of these tracts would increase plaintiff's frontage.

The consideration recited in the sale was the sum of $30,000, of which $7,000 was paid in cash with the remainder to be paid in 12 consecutive annual installments.

On March 15, 1979 the plaintiffs received a letter from Mrs. Boutte by certified mail which read in pertinent part as follows:

"I have this day received an offer from Mr. Lance Gauthier to purchase my present residence on the terms and conditions as are contained in his letter offer, a duplicate original of which I enclose herewith. As you recall, and in my sale to you of other property owned by me dated June 19, 1966, recorded same date, in Book 546, Folio 363, under No. 135672 of the Conveyance Records of St. Martin Parish, Louisiana, I had agreed that I would not convey my residence to anyone before offering the same to you under the terms and conditions of the highest bonafide [sic] offer which I may receive. I have made no determination to dispose of this property, however, in view of the offer received, you are requested to advise in writing and within ten (10) days as provided for in the above mentioned sale, whether you would be interested in purchasing my property described in said offer for the price and under the terms and conditions set forth in Mr. Gauthier's offer."

The letter was signed by Mrs. Boutte and a copy of the signed offer from Mr. Gauthier was attached.

The plaintiffs did not respond in writing to this letter. On March 28, 1979 Mrs. Boutte sold the property to her nephew, Lance Gauthier, for the stated sum of $20,000, of which $14,000 was paid in cash with the remaining sum due to be paid in 12 semi-annual installments of $500. This balance due was evidenced by a promissory note in the amount of $6,000. In the contract of sale Mrs. Boutte reserved in her favor a usufruct over the property; and the defendants agreed to maintain and repair the property while she and her husband lived there.

PLEADINGS AND PROCEDURAL HISTORY

Thereafter, on March 13, 1980 the plaintiffs filed a petition seeking to have the sale to the Gauthiers rescinded and demanding specific performance of their right of first refusal. * * * Ultimately, the plaintiffs filed a motion for partial summary judgment limited to the issues of rescission and specific performance. The trial court's granting of the partial summary judgment is the subject of this appeal. After the trial court rendered judgment in favor of the plaintiffs and dismissing the defendant's motion, the defendants filed a motion for rehearing. Defendants also filed peremptory exceptions of prescription and nonjoinder of indispensable parties. The motion for rehearing was granted, but the trial court maintained its judgment in favor of plaintiffs. The exceptions filed by defendants were dismissed by the trial court.

ISSUES ON APPEAL

The issues presented in this appeal are substantially as follows:

1. Was the trial court correct in granting plaintiff's motion for partial summary judgment;

2. Was the right of first refusal subject to a plea of 10 years liberative prescription; and,

3. Were the heirs of Verla Boutte indispensable parties to this litigation.

Defendants-appellants discuss numerous other issues, which are factual in nature. In light of our affirmance of the trial court's granting of the partial summary judgment, only brief reference will be made to those issues.

THE RIGHT OF FIRST REFUSAL

The trial court's ruling on the validity of the right of first refusal was correct. Defendants maintain that the right granted to the plaintiffs was an option unsupported by consideration, having no specified term, and was therefore invalid as not in accord with LSA-C.C. art. 2462 [R.C.C. 2620, 2623]. We disagree with that contention. In dealing with the very same argument in *Crawford v. Deshotels,* 359 So.2d 118, 121-22 (La.1978), the Supreme Court said:

> "Relator's second contention is that, even if the agreement between McDaniel and Crawford is founded upon a valid consideration, the portion of that agreement here at issue, an option, is invalid on other grounds.
>
> The clause of the contract or quitclaim is fully related hereinabove. Pertinently it provides:
>
> "if ever a bona fide offer is made and should [McDaniel] desiring to sell . . . [she] is herein obligated to offer to [Crawford] the first chance to buy same at the bona fide offer."
>
> Relator contends that the agreement cannot be enforced because it is an option in perpetuity and contrary to the public policy of Louisiana as expressed in Article 2462 of the Civil Code [R.C.C. 2620, 2623]. That article provides:
>
> > A promise to sell, when there exists a reciprocal consent of both parties as to the thing, the price and terms, and which, if it relates to immovables, is in writing, so far amounts to a sale, as to give either party the right to enforce specific performance of same.
> >
> > One may purchase the right, or option to accept or reject, *within a stipulated time,* an offer or promise to sell, after the purchase of such option, for any consideration therein stipulated, such offer, or promise can not [sic] be withdrawn before the time agreed upon; and should it be accepted within the time stipulated, the contract or agreement to sell, evidenced by such promise and acceptance, may be specifically enforced by either party. [emphasis provided]

This Court has applied Civil Code Article 2462 [R.C.C. 2620, 2623], when pertinent, and held void an option for an indefinite time. *Becker and Assoc., Inc. v. Lou-Ark Equipment Rental Co., Inc.,* 331 So.2d 474 (La.1976); *Bristo v. Christine Oil & Gas Co.,* 139 La. 312, 71 So. 521 (1916); *Clark v. Dixon,* 254 So.2d 482 (La.App.3d Cir.1971).

The article and the jurisprudence on which relator relies, however, are not applicable here, for there is not here following "the purchase of such option"—or in this case entry of the contract-a continuing right or option to accept (or reject) an extant offer or promise to sell—as contemplated by Article 2462 [R.C.C. 2620, 2623]. Rather there is here what is more commonly described as a right of first refusal, or as the contract says, a right to be afforded a "first chance to buy" at a price equal to any bona fide offer which McDaniel should receive and be interested in accepting. Thus, the stipulated time requirement of Article 2462 [R.C.C. 2620, 2624] is not applicable.

The only case in the jurisprudence directly on point is *Price v. Town of Ruston*, 171 La. 985, 132 So. 653 (La.1931) wherein this Court rejected a contention similar to relators with the following language:

> "There is no merit in the appellant's argument that the option was null for want of a stipulation limiting the time within which it might be exercised. The stipulation limiting the time was that the option would be available whenever the Elks Lodge might desire to sell the property, meaning whenever it might become necessary for Mrs. Price or her heirs or assigns to prevent the title to the third story of the Price building from passing to someone else." 171 La. at 993, 132 So. at 656.

For the foregoing reasons there is no merit to relator's contention that the pertinent clause of the contract is null and void in violation of Civil Code Article 2462."

See also *Keene v. Williams,* 423 So.2d 1065 (La.1983) and *Terrell v. Messenger,* 428 So.2d 1241 (La.App.3d Cir.1983), *writ denied,* 433 So.2d 709 (La.1983).

As the trial court correctly noted, the right granted to plaintiffs did not involve a "continuing offer to sell." It was rather a unilateral promise by the grantor not to accept any offer made to her for purchase of the property without first offering it to plaintiffs. Therefore, Mrs. Boutte could decide at any time to sell and was obligated only to offer the property to the plaintiffs first at the same price which a third person was willing to pay by way of a bona fide offer.

The trial court in its reasons for granting a partial summary judgment said:

> "Defendants argue that Mrs. Boutte of legal necessity used the language in her letter of March 14, 1979 that "I have made no determination to dispose of this property", because she was legally precluded from making such determination until she determined whether Mr. Robichaux would accept her offer. That is simply not so. She certainly could have determined to sell the property; it is only that she could not determine to sell it to defendants until she learned whether or not Mr. Robichaux would exercise his right. All Mrs. Boutte would have had to do was substitute the letter "a" for the word "no" in the above-quoted language to insure a document which unquestionably would have passed legal muster. . . . had Mr. Robichaux

responded affirmatively, the matter might still have ended up in court because, had Mrs. Boutte then refused to sell to him, he might have sued to enforce his right. In such event, the undersigned would have held for Mrs. Boutte, concluding that the language of her letter did not obligate her to sell to anyone, so that she was not bound by Mr. Robichaux's affirmative response."

Professor Saul Litvinoff in his article *Offer and Acceptance in Louisiana: A comparative Analysis: Part I-Offer*, 28 La. L. Rev. 1, 3 (1967), discussed the elements of an offer. He said:

"An offer is a proposal to do something or to refrain from doing something in return for a counter-promise, an act, or forebearance. To be considered properly as such, the offer must fulfill the following three requirements clearly established in the Louisiana Civil Code:

"(a) The design to give the other party the right of concluding the contract by his assent.

"(b) The offeror's intention to obligate himself.

"(c) A serious intent.

"When requirement (a) is absent, the proposition cannot be considered an offer, but an invitation to negotiate, or an expression of willingness to receive an offer from the other party. The intention required under (b) must be that of creating a legal obligation-and not one in the moral sense or a duty in conscience. Requirement (c) will exclude, as a real offer, a proposition made in jest, as a part of a game, or at the peak of an argument. It is, however, necessary that the joke or game be in accord with the circumstances or usages; otherwise, if the addressee of such a proposition could have reason to assume it to be a real offer, his acceptance would create a contract." (Citations omitted.)

Analyzing Mrs. Boutte's letter in light of these requirements, we agree that the letter contained no offer to the plaintiffs. Because she stated that she had made no determination to sell, the plaintiffs could not have bound Mrs. Boutte to sell by treating the letter as an offer and responding to it with a written acceptance. It was clear from her statement that she did not intend to obligate herself to sell her property at any amount. The letter did not contain a serious intention to be bound or to contract with the plaintiffs. The proposal sent by Mrs. Boutte to plaintiffs did not firmly reflect the intent of the author to enter into a contract. See *Eames v. James*, 452 So.2d 384 (La.App.3d Cir.1984), *writ denied* 458 So.2d 123 (La.1984) and *Terrebonne v. Louisiana Ass'n of Educators*, 444 So.2d 206 (La.App. 1st Cir.1983), *writ denied*, 445 So.2d 1232 (La.1984).

The trial court went on to say in its reasons for judgment that:

"Agreements legally entered into have the effect of laws on those who have formed them. They cannot be revoked, unless by mutual consent of the parties, or for causes acknowledged by law. They must be performed in good faith." LSA-C.C. art. 1901 [R.C.C. 1983].

"The right of first refusal is referred to in the civil law as a "*pacte de préférence*" (right of pre-emption). Language used by authorities indicates clearly that a firm offer to sell by the obligor must be made before any obligation attaches. See *Litvinoff, Louisiana Civil Law Treatise, Obligations,* Book 2, Secs. 104 and 108. Note especially the following language at p. 188:

"A '*pacte de préférence*' is certainly not a sale since the prospective vendee's consent cannot exist until the vendor *offers to sell* him the thing." (emphasis added)

and

"'In regard to contractual requirements . . . a *pacte de préférence* is governed by the same rules as *unilateral promises of sale*," (emphasis added)

"Acceptance of the offer creates a binding obligation. LSA-C.C. art. 1803 [No Corresponding Article]. While there was no acceptance in the instant matter, there can be no acceptance until there is an offer, and no offer was made by Mrs. Boutte herein."

The defendants sought to show by affidavits what Mrs. Boutte's intentions were with reference to any contemplated sale of the property. The affidavits were given by third parties and the trial court rejected them as hearsay. Mrs. Boutte had died in the meanwhile. However, even if she had not been deceased, and even though the matter came up on motion for summary judgment, Mrs. Boutte's alleged intentions are not material. Her letter was so explicitly worded that, assuming parol evidence would have been admissible to contradict it, her supposed intent could not have altered the plain import of her letter declarations.

The cases of *Price v. Town of Ruston,* 171 La. 985, 132 So. 653 (1931); *Crawford v. Deshotels,* 359 So.2d 118 (La.1978); and *Terrell v. Messenger,* 428 So.2d 1241 (La. App.3d Cir.1983), *writ denied* 433 So.2d 709 (La.1983), all dealing with breaches of contracts granting a right of first refusal, indicate that specific performance is the appropriate remedy in such cases. The trial court was correct in ordering specific performance.

We discern from the record that the trial court determined that a partial summary judgment would be advantageous to all parties, because it would settle the issues of rescission of sale and specific performance before the court proceeded to consider other issues. As we have noted, Mrs. Boutte is deceased and her heirs have transferred their rights to the defendants. No provision has been made to condition any transfer to plaintiffs upon tender of payment by plaintiffs to defendants. All that the trial court's judgment provides for is rescission of the sale from Mrs. Boutte to defendants. Tr. 359-360. Defendants are the only parties who may now transfer the property to plaintiffs unless the trial court makes provision for transfer in a judgment. As this case will go back to the trial court for completion of this litigation, we will not attempt to deal with them or make the appropriate provision. We direct that the trial court give consideration to these matters upon remand.

PRESCRIPTION

Alternatively, appellants argue that the right of first refusal is subject to a plea of 10 years liberative prescription as defined in LSA-C.C. art. 3447. The Civil Code defines three types of prescription in Article 3445: acquisitive, liberative, and prescription of nonuse. Liberative prescription operates to bar certain actions as a result of the inaction of those persons possessing a right of action for a period of time. For liberative prescription to be operative, a right or cause of action must exist in order for prescription to run.

Appellants contend that the plaintiffs had 10 years within which to exercise their right of first refusal. The only opportunity in favor of the plaintiffs to exercise the right would arise upon Mrs. Boutte's determination to sell. Accordingly, there was no action for them to enforce until such time as Mrs. Boutte made a determination to sell, and they were not accorded the right of first refusal.

The trial court was correct in relying on *Orleans Parish School Board v. Pittman Construction Company*, 261 La. 665, 260 So.2d 661 (1972) and *Wilkinson v. Wilkinson*, 323 So.2d 120 (La.1975) as authority for the overruling of the defendants' exception of prescription. The trial court stated in its reasons for judgment:

"[T]hat until a right of action accrues, the prescription period doesn't start running. This right of first refusal was granted in 1966. Obviously, the Plaintiffs in this case didn't have a right to bring an action based on it in 1967 or in 1969. So, for that reason, the prescriptive period could not have begun at those times. The cause of action accrued on March 14, 1979 [sic] when Mrs. Boutte sold the property involved. The instant litigation was filed March 13, 1980, less than a year after that. That was within the prescriptive period."

We find defendants' prescription argument to be without merit.

INDISPENSABLE PARTY ISSUE

The trial court found that the heirs of Verla Boutte were not indispensable parties and overruled the defendants' exception directed to that issue. We agree with the trial court.

The alleged indispensable parties had conveyed their rights in this litigation to the remaining defendants, the Gauthiers. A certain document styled Sale and Agreement With Power of Attorney was entered into between Mrs. Boutte's heirs and the defendant, Lance Gauthier, on January 12, 1981. This instrument was recorded in the Conveyance Records of the Clerk of Court for St. Martin Parish. By that act the heirs did:

"Grant, Bargain, Sell, Convey, Transfer, Assign, Set-over and Deliver to and unto LANCE F. GAUTHIER, the husband of Madeline Champagne, with whom he lives and abides, of lawful age, whose mailing address is Rt. 3, Box

842, St. Martinville, Louisiana 70582, domiciled in and a resident of the Parish of St. Martin, Louisiana, who is the nephew of Decedent, Mrs. Verla Lavergne Boutte, (hereinafter referred to as Purchaser, Obligor or Agent), who is here present [sic] accepting [sic] purchasing and acquiring for himself, his heirs, successors and assigns and acknowledging delivery hereby of all of the assets, rights, rights of action, defenses to pending suits and claims, which belonged to the Decedent, Mrs. Verla Lavergne Boutte [sic] and which she died possessed of and now belonging to her estate . . . ."

The act goes on to list the assets of Mrs. Boutte's estate with particularity.

It is apparent from a reading of the instrument that Mrs. Boutte's heirs relinquished all claims and interests in and to her estate. They can therefore have no possible interest in the estate which would require that they be joined in the instant suit for an equitable and proper adjudication of this matter.

This argument is without merit.

OTHER ISSUES

As to the other issues concerning the use of parol evidence briefed by the defendants, we find that the trial court's rulings as to these issues were correct, but the facts sought to be established were irrelevant to a determination of the issues of law involved in this case and presented no genuine issue of material fact warranting discussion herein.

Additionally, defendants have appealed the trial court's denial of their own motion for summary judgment. LSA-C.C.P. art. 968 provides in pertinent part that:

"An appeal does not lie from the court's refusal to render any judgment on the pleadings or summary judgment."

CONCLUSION

Accordingly, the judgment of the trial court in favor of the plaintiffs, Roland Robichaux and Ida Judice Robichaux, and against defendants, Lance F. Gauthier and Madeline Champagne Gauthier, overruling the exceptions of liberative prescription and nonjoinder of indispensable parties and denying the motion for rehearing on the judgment granting plaintiff's motion for partial summary judgment and denying defendants' motion for summary judgment is hereby affirmed. This case is remanded to the trial court for further proceedings.

The costs of this appeal are assessed against the appellants.

AFFIRMED AND REMANDED.

Notes and Questions

1. What are the prerequisites for a right of first refusal? Must a right of first refusal be made in any particular form? *See* La. Civ. Code arts. 1839, 2440.

2. The foregoing case involves the difficulty of distinguishing between a right of first refusal and an option. It can also be difficult to distinguish between a right of

first refusal and sale with the right of redemption. The First Circuit grappled with this in the case of *Travis v. Heirs of Felker*, 482 So. 2d 5 (La. App. 1 Cir. 1985). In that case, Travis sold some property to her sister in 1959, and the Act of Sale contained the following provision: "It is understood and agreed that the Vendor (Mrs. Bernice Martin Travis) has the right to buy her interest back if ever sold . . . ." *Id.* at 5. After her sister died, one of her heirs sold part of the property, and the succession administrator made application to sell another part of it. Travis sued to enforce the provision in 1979. The trial court classified the contract as a sale with the right of redemption. The appellate court disagreed. It explained that in a sale with the right of redemption, the vendor holds the choice to take the thing back, while the vendee has no choice. Such was not the situation in the case at bar. Here, the Act of Sale did not give Travis the unqualified right to demand the return of the property; instead, it gave her the right to buy it back "if ever sold." This, the court held, made the agreement a right of first refusal. This case was decided prior to the 1995 revision. Read carefully Article 2628, which in 1995 introduced a time limitation for options and rights of first refusal concerning immovables. Under that article, would Travis' right of first refusal be enforceable? Why or why not?

2. Consider Article 2627, which sets forth the manner in which a right of first refusal is exercised by the holder of the right. Once the grantor of the right makes an offer to the grantee, the latter may accept the offer (thereby converting the contract into a contract to sell) or may either reject the offer or simply allow the offer to expire. The time for expiration varies depending upon whether the thing subject to the right is movable or immovable. If the thing is movable, the holder must accept the offer within ten days. If the thing is immovable, the holder has thirty days within which to accept the offer. La. Civ. Code art. 2627. Note that these terms are suppletive in nature and may be altered by the agreement of the parties.

If the grantee does not accept the offer to sell, the grantor is free to sell to a third person. However, Article 2627 makes clear that "[u]nless the grantor concludes a final sale, or a contract to sell, with a third person within six months, the right of first refusal subsists in the grantee who failed to exercise it when the offer was made to him." La. Civ. Code art. 2627. What is the purpose of this rule?

3. Note that unlike Article 2620, which defines an option as a contract involving a "stipulated time," Article 2625 does not require that a right of first refusal contain a term for performance. Nor has Louisiana jurisprudence required a right of first refusal to contain a term. This is so despite the admonition in Article 2628 comment (b) that "[a] right of first refusal or an option to buy for a perpetual or indefinite term is null." La. Civ. Code art. 2628. Do the distinctions between rights of first refusal and options justify a different rule with respect to the requirement of a term? Why or why not?

4. While a right of first refusal need not contain a term as a prerequisite for validity, as indicated above in Note 2, Article 2628 does set forth a maximum term for a right of first refusal affecting immovable property. The time limitations set forth in Article 2628 are addressed more fully in the following Part.

D. Effects of Contracts Preparatory to the Sale

La. Civ. Code arts. 2628–2630

1. Time Limitations

As discussed above, option contracts require a term for performance. This is so because of public policy concerns about holding property out of commerce. When property is subject to an option, the grantor may not sell the property to anyone other than the grantee. Moreover, while the grantee has the right to purchase the property, he or she is not bound to do so. If the grantee never exercises the right, the property is never sold. Indefinite or perpetual options could, thus, take property out of commerce altogether. Moreover, the owner of property burdened by an option is unlikely to make any improvements to it during the term of the option. Option contracts require a stipulated price, which often reflects the current or projected market value of the property. Any improvements not contemplated in the agreed-upon price would reduce the owner's profit. As a result, property subject to an indefinite or perpetual option may eventually fall into complete disrepair.

In recognition of these public policy concerns, the Civil Code not only requires a specified term for all option contracts, it provides a maximum term for any option or right of first refusal affecting immovable property. Article 2628 provides:

> An option or a right of first refusal that concerns an immovable thing may not be granted for a term longer than ten years. If a longer time for an option or a right of first refusal has been stipulated in a contract, that time shall be reduced to ten years. Nevertheless, if the option or right of first refusal is granted in connection with a contract that gives rise to obligations of continuous or periodic performance, an option or a right of first refusal may be granted for as long a period as required for the performance of those obligations.

La. Civ. Code art. 2628. This article contains several discrete rules. First, it provides a general rule that the duration of a right of first refusal or an option contract affecting immovable property may not exceed ten years. Second, it provides that if the parties agree to a term longer than ten years, a court may reduce the term to achieve compliance with the law. Lastly, it provides an important exception for rights of first refusal or options which are granted in connection with so-called "obligations of continuous or periodic performance." *Id.* For these agreements, the 10-year rule is negated, and the duration of the right of first refusal or option may be for as long as required for the performance of those obligations.

The most common example of a contract involving "obligations of continuous or periodic performance" with which an option or right of first refusal may be granted is a lease. For instance, Owner may lease Blackacre to Lessee for 30 years and also provide that at any time during the lease or at the end of the lease Lessee may elect to purchase the property from Owner by paying a specified amount. The parties have essentially entered into two contracts—a lease of the property and an option to purchase the property. Under the general rule articulated in the first sentence of Article 2628, the option, because it affects immovable property, could normally exist for no longer than 10 years; however, because the option is connected to a contract of continuous and periodic performance (i.e., the lease) then the option's term may extend for as long as the performance under the lease requires (which would be a full 30 years).

Civil Code article 2628 was enacted as part of the sales law revision in 1995. Consider the following case that was decided *before* the enactment of article 2628.

Becker and Associates, Inc. v. Lou-Ark Equipment Rentals Co.
331 So. 2d 474 (La. 1976)

DENNIS, Justice.

These consolidated cases present a suit by a lessee of heavy equipment against its lessor for the specific performance of an option to purchase the equipment and a suit by the lessor to recover the movable property and accrued rental from the lessee.

Lou-Ark Equipment Rentals Co., Inc., applicant herein, by a written agreement dated July 13, 1971, leased to respondent, Becker and Associates, Inc., a 45 ton crawler crane at a rental of $2,000.00 per 30 calendar days plus sales tax, for a minimum lease period of 30 days. On the same date the parties executed and made part of the lease a written agreement granting Becker the option to purchase the equipment, which provided that 99% [o]f the rental paid for the crane would apply toward the purchase price and that the value of the equipment would be determined "by an independent appraiser or by mutual agreement."

Becker paid Lou-Ark rental in accordance with the terms of the lease from July, 1971 through February, 1973, totaling $41,200.00 including taxes. In January and February, 1973, Becker informed Lou-Ark of its desire to exercise the option. At the request of Becker the value of the crane was estimated by two different appraisers, both of whom determined it was worth $40,000.00. It is disputed whether Lou-Ark agreed to the designation of either appraiser as an "independent appraiser" for purposes of determining the value of the property under the option. When Becker called upon Lou-Ark to sell the crane for the price of $40,000.00, Lou-Ark refused.

Becker filed suit against Lou-Ark for a declaratory judgment of ownership and alternatively for specific performance. It deposited $412 including taxes into the registry of the court as the balance between the appraisal value of the equipment and 99% [o]f the amount it had paid Lou-Ark as rent. Lou-Ark brought suit against Becker seeking to be declared owner of the crane, for its return and for $12,000.00 accrued rent, as well as future rent, interest and attorney's fees.

The two suits were consolidated for trial; the district court rendered judgment for Lou-Ark, and Becker appealed. The court of appeal reversed, set aside the lower court decrees and rendered judgment for Becker ordering specific performance of the option to purchase. 314 So.2d 553 (La.App.4th Cir. 1975). Upon application of Lou-Ark, we granted writs. 318 So.2d 55 (La.1975).

Lou-Ark contends that the option agreement was null and void because it was without a fixed or definite term as required by Article 2462 of the La. Civil Code [R.C.C. 2620, 2623], which, in pertinent part, provides:

> "One may·purchase the right, or option to accept or reject, within a stipulated time, an offer or promise to sell, after the purchase of such option, for any consideration therein stipulated, such offer, or promise cannot be withdrawn before the time agreed upon; and should it be accepted within the time stipulated, the contract or agreement to sell, evidenced by such promise and acceptance, may be specifically enforced by either party."

In enforcing this provision we have held that perpetual options which would take property out of commerce are prohibited because they violate the doctrine of ownership established by the La. Civil Code.

The option agreement itself sets forth no time limit within which the offer to sell the property must be accepted. Nevertheless, the court of appeal held that the option stated a time within which it was to be exercised, because, being part of the same agreement as the lease, Becker could elect to exercise its right of option to purchase the leased property at any time during a thirty-day rental period for which the rent had been paid.

Had the lease contract provided a definite term we would agree with the decision below, because the failure to expressly state a termination date in an option agreement made part of a lease having a definite term does not render the option invalid if the time for its acceptance is necessarily limited by the term of the lease. However, upon careful inspection, we find that the lease between Becker and Lou-Ark was not for a definite term but was dependent upon the will of the parties for its duration.

The lease instrument provided for a "rental rate" of $2,000.00 plus tax "per 30 calendar days." The "rental period" was described as beginning on July 13, 1971, and ending when the equipment is received by the Owner at their warehouse or on the date Bill of Lading is issued covering the return of the Equipment to the Owner. Additionally, a "termination of agreement" clause provided that the lessor shall have the right to take possession of the equipment five days after the lessee's default on any payment. Therefore, the parties agreed to methods by which the lease could be terminated, but they did not agree upon a definite term for the lease.

Because no time for the duration of the lease was agreed on by the parties, it was subject to termination in accordance with La.C.C. art. 2686 [R.C.C.2727, 2728], which provides:

> "The parties must abide by the agreement as fixed at the time of the lease. If no time for its duration has been agreed on, the party desiring to put an end to it must give notice in writing to the other, at least ten days before the expiration of the month, which has begun to run."

Thus, in addition to the methods provided by the lease contract, the lease could be terminated by either party by the giving of notice in writing to the other, at least ten days before the expiration of the month.

The court of appeal apparently concluded that by operation of law a new 30-day lease was confected each month. Thus, the court reasoned that the option to purchase terminated upon the expiration of each 30-day rental period and was effectively limited thereby. We find, however, that the premise of the court of appeal decision was erroneous and at variance with the jurisprudence concerning month to month leases.

Under La.C.C. art. 2686 [R.C.C. 2727, 2728], the presumed continuance of a lease by operation of law from month to month, resulting from holding over without notice, is called a "tacit reconduction." The effect of such a continuance is not to constitute a new lease each month or even to renew the old one, but rather to continue the original lease. Accordingly, the month to month lease in the instant case did not terminate each month but endured continuously until put to an end in the manner provided by La.C.C. art. 2686 [R.C.C. 2727, 2728] or by the lease contract.

Since there were no provisions in either the lease or the option itself limiting its duration, the option was null and void for failure to stipulate a time period for the acceptance of the promise to sell. La.C.C. art. 2462 [R.C.C. 2620, 2623].

Accordingly, the judgment of the court of appeal must be set aside. However, we cannot fully reinstate the trial court's judgment because its conclusion that Lou-Ark is entitled to enforcement of the lease contract, including award of attorney's fees, was also erroneous. It is well settled under our Civil Code and the jurisprudence interpreting it that when one of the parties errs in perceiving the very nature of the contract into which he enters, the contract cannot be enforced against him. La.C.C. art. 1841 [No Corresponding Article] states:

> "Error as to the nature of the contract will render it void.
>
> "The nature of the contract is that which characterizes the obligation which it creates. Thus, if the party receives property, and from error or ambiguity in the words accompanying the delivery, believes that he has purchased, while he who delivers intends."

See also Baker v. Baker, 209 La. 1041, 26 So.2d 132 (1946); *Green v. McDade*, 17 So.2d 637 (La.App.2nd Cir. 1944). In both cases, the courts refused to enforce a purported contract of sale against an owner of property who intended only to offer it as security.

As stated at Pothier, 1 Obligations, Part 1, Art. III, s 1, n. 17, the source of our present Civil Code art. 1841 [No Corresponding Article]:

> "Error is the greatest defect that can occur in a contract, for agreements can only be formed by the consent of the parties, and there can be no consent when the parties are in an error respecting the object of their agreement. * * *

"There if a person intends to sell me anything, and I intend to receive it by way of loan or gift, there is neither sale, no loan, nor gift. If a person intends to sell me a thing, and I intend to buy or receive a donation of another, there is neither sale nor donation."

In the instant case, Becker's officers mistakenly believed that it was entering into a rental agreement with an option to purchase. In fact, the option was null for lack of a specified time within which to accept the offer of sale. We are convinced from the evidence that Becker would not have entered the transaction if its officers had been aware that the contract consisted of a mere lease of the equipment. Thus, Becker erred as to the nature of the contract, and the lease agreement should not be enforced against it.

However, the principle of unjust enrichment, embodied in our Civil Code art. 1965 [R.C.C. 2298] requires that Lou-Ark be compensated in the amount of the fair rental value of the equipment for the period it was in Becker's possession. Accordingly, it is necessary that we remand the case to the trial court to determine precisely this value. The court of appeal judgment is set aside and the case is remanded to the trial court for further proceedings consistent with the views expressed herein.

Reversed and remanded.

Notes and Questions

1. The Court in *Becker* indicated that an option granted in connection with a lease, though lacking a specified term, may still be enforceable for the duration of the lease. But note that the court said it would *only* apply this rule if the lease was subject to a "definite" term. As you will see in the Chapters on the contract of lease that follow, lease terms may be fixed or indeterminate. A lease term is fixed when the parties agree that the lease will terminate at a designated date or upon the occurrence of a designated event. LA. CIV. CODE art. 2678. In all other cases, a lease term is indeterminate. *Id.* The month-to-month lease in *Becker* was an indeterminate lease, as the parties contemplated that the lease would continue indefinitely, in month-long intervals, until one of the parties provided notice of an intent to terminate the agreement. Because the lease in *Becker* did not have a definite end-point, the option was absolutely null.

After having read *Becker*, carefully re-read Article 2628. Is the new Article consistent with the pre-revision jurisprudence, or does it change the law? As you consider the answer to this question, carefully read the comments to Article 2628. Also consider whether permitting an option to exist for an indefinite period furthers or frustrates the public policy upon which Article 2628 is founded.

2. In *Buller v. Clark*, 7 So. 3d 167 (La. App. 3d Cir. 2009), the Louisiana Third Circuit Court of Appeal had the opportunity to address the issue of what qualifies as an obligation for continuous and periodic performance. In that case, the parties to the litigation jointly purchased a piece of property that included a commercial building. As part of their agreement, each gave the other a right of first refusal in

the event that either decided to sell her interest in the property. Also, as part of their agreement, they stipulated that together they would share equally in the expenses of maintaining the property and in covering the cost of insurance and property taxes. Just over ten years after the purchase, Clark sold her interest to someone other than Buller, and Buller immediately brought suit to enforce the right of first refusal. Clark argued that the right of first refusal was no longer in effect when she sold her share (i.e., it was beyond the maximum 10-year period provided by law). Buller, on the other hand, argued that the right should last longer because, under article 2628, it was connected to an obligation of continuous and periodic performance — the co-ownership agreement specifying the periodic payment of taxes and insurance.

The court ultimately rejected Buller's argument on two grounds. First, it held, without explanation, that "an agreement to share expenses is not the kind of obligation contemplated in the language of the exception [found in Article 2628]." 7 So. 3d at 169. Second, the court stated that "[i]n any event, it is very clear that the right of first refusal cannot be indefinite and any continuing obligation that would extend the right would itself have to have a *definite term or ending date*." *Id*. Under this latter holding, an obligation for continuous and periodic performance must have "an ending date." *Id*.

3. Does Article 2628 mandate a change for the historical treatment of options lacking stipulated terms? Recall that historically, courts have held that an option with a perpetual or indefinite term is absolutely null. The article clearly contemplates that a court can reduce a term exceeding ten years to the statutory maximum; can a court *supply* the maximum term as the term for an option that lacks a term altogether? Consider the following case.

Youngblood v. Rosedale Dev. Co.

911 So. 2d 418 (La. App. 2 Cir. 2005)

BROWN, C.J.

Plaintiffs, Ray Oden Youngblood, James Dee Youngblood, III, and Mary Anne Youngblood Shemwell, filed this lawsuit for a declaratory judgment. Rosedale Development Company, LLC ("Rosedale"), was named as defendant. Defendant's predecessors purchased 15 acres out of an undeveloped 363-acre tract from plaintiffs. An option to purchase the remaining acreage provided a three-year term and that "a partial exercise (of at least 12 acres) or any subsequent partial exercise shall have the effect of extending this option for an additional (3) year period." Plaintiffs claimed that this provision created an endless stream of three-year extensions that is prohibited by law. A stipulation of facts was agreed to by both sides. The trial court ruled in favor of defendant and plaintiffs have appealed. We reverse and render judgment reducing the term of the option to ten years.

Facts and Procedural History

Plaintiffs owned 363 undeveloped acres north of Bossier City off Airline Drive. On June 26, 1996, a group of developers purchased 15 acres for $12,000 per acre with the intent to build a residential subdivision. If successful, they contemplated buying more land from plaintiffs and eventually hoped to develop all of plaintiffs' land in stages. In furtherance of this plan, the developers obtained from plaintiffs an option to purchase the remaining 348 acres at the same price per acre adjusted by a change in the Consumer Price Index. The term of the option was three years; however, it provided for a partial exercise of the option as follows:

> It is understood and agreed that Purchaser may exercise its option on a portion of the Optioned Property, provided however that no such partial exercise shall be for less than twelve (12) acres. Such a partial exercise or any subsequent partial exercise shall have the effect of extending this option for an additional three (3) year period from the closing date of the property upon which the option has last been exercised.

In December 1996, the developers assigned and transferred all their rights under the agreement to defendant, Rosedale. Over the next six years and within each three-year period provided for, defendant partially exercised the option four times, purchasing approximately 56 acres. The last purchase was on March 8, 2002. On April 21, 2004, defendant gave plaintiffs notice of its intent to again exercise the option and purchase an additional 16.23 acres of land. Plaintiffs refused to sell the land. On June 24, 2004, plaintiffs filed this petition to declare the option null. Defendant filed an answer and the parties submitted the case on a joint stipulation of facts.

In a written opinion, the trial court held that the right to extend the stipulated time period three years from each purchase of twelve acres or more was not in violation of Louisiana Civil Code article 2628, which limits any option contract for immovable property to a maximum term of ten years. The court noted that this article allows an exception for a contract that gives rise to obligations of continuous or periodic performance. Plaintiffs have appealed from this judgment.

Discussion

Because options to buy immovable property restrict the free flow of commerce, the legislature imposed as a contractual limitation a maximum term of ten years. Therefore, Louisiana Civil Code article 2628 provides:

> An option . . . that concerns an immovable thing may not be granted for a term longer than ten years. If a longer time for an option . . . has been stipulated in a contract, that time shall be reduced to ten years. Nevertheless, if the option . . . is granted in connection with a contract that gives rise to obligations of continuous or periodic performance, an option . . . may be granted for as long a period as required for the performance of those obligations.

In this case, the exception is inapplicable. Never did the original purchasers of the first 15 acres of land, nor the defendant when it purchased land by means of the option to buy, obligate themselves to the development of the whole or any part of the 363 acres of land. There is no agreement or contract to the ultimate development by increments, nor any requirement of the defendant to purchase any additional acreage. Since the contract to buy was not granted "in connection with a contract that gives rise to obligations of continuous or periodic performance," then it cannot fall into the exception stipulated in Louisiana Civil Code article 2628.

According to the clear language of the option at issue, unhampered by the ten year limitation mandated by Louisiana Civil Code article 2628, defendant could purchase 12 acres every three years until achieving complete ownership of the estate, thus leaving the last 12-acre plot out of the stream of commerce for approximately 73 years. Plaintiffs argue that this is beyond their life span, and it was not their intention when they made the contract to tie up the property beyond their natural lives. Plaintiffs cite the 1993 Revision Comments to Article 2620, which provides:

> Under this Article, an option for a perpetual or indefinite term is null. *See Crawford v. Deshotels et al.*, 359 So.2d 118 (La.1978); *Becker and Assoc., Inc. v. Lou-Ark Equipment Rentals, Inc.*, 331 So.2d 474 (La.1976); *Bristo v. Christine Oil & Gas Co.*, 139 La. 312, 71 So. 521 (1916).

The language and intention of the Louisiana Civil Code is clear and unambiguous on the issue of term limits for options to buy immovable property. In this case, the term provided in the contract was for three years, which could be extended every three years, well beyond the ten-year limitation. Louisiana Civil Code article 2628 states that if the term for an option to buy exceeds ten years, it shall be reduced to ten years. Plaintiffs, however, ask that the option be declared null and void. This would be a drastic measure that would not give any effect to the intent of the parties. We find that the trial court was in error when it failed to reduce the term of the option to buy to ten years, or June 26, 2006.

Conclusion

For reasons set forth above, the judgment of the trial court is reversed.

IT IS HEREBY ORDERED, ADJUDGED and DECREED that judgment be rendered declaring the option to purchase in favor of defendant, Rosedale Development Company, L.L.C., is valid for a term of ten years to expire on June 26, 2006. Costs are assessed one-half to plaintiffs and one-half to defendant.

REVERSED and RENDERED

Notes and Questions

As the cases above illustrate, the issue of time limitations for contracts preparatory to the sale is a complex one, and the governing rules are not uniform across all such contracts. Remember that an option contract must have a term or else it is null, whereas neither a contract to sell nor a right of first refusal needs a term. That said, when a term is included in an option or a right of first refusal, in the event that the object of the contract is immovable property, the maximum term length is ten years, absent the situation in which the right is granted in connection with a contract for continuous or periodic performance.

2. Effects as to Third Persons

It is often essential to determine whether a party may enforce a contract preparatory to a sale against a third person who has acquired rights in the property that is the object of that contract. For example, what would happen if Beau secured an option to purchase from Sal, but Sal sells the thing in question to someone else, Terry? Does Beau have the right to reclaim the property from Terry? If not, does Beau have any rights against Sal? To answer these inquiries, the Civil Code provides clear rules governing the effects of preparatory contracts vis-à-vis third persons, and they hinge, first and foremost, on whether the property in question is movable or immovable.

If the property subject to the preparatory agreement is movable, the contract is effective against third persons who, "at the time of acquisition of a conflicting right, had actual knowledge of that transaction." LA. CIV. CODE art. 2629. A simple example illustrates the application of this rule. Beau secures an option to purchase a drilling rig from Sal. Prior to the expiration of the option, Sal sells the drilling rig to Terry, who was completely unaware of Beau's option. Upon learning of the sale to Terry, Beau seeks specific performance of his option. Because Terry lacked "actual knowledge" of Beau's right to the rig, Terry will remain secure in his ownership, with the result that Sal will be required to pay damages to Beau due to his failure to perform the option.

If the property subject to the preparatory agreement is immovable then, naturally, the public records doctrine dictates the rights of the parties. According to Article 2629: "a preparatory contract 'is effective against third persons only from the time the instrument that contains it is filed for registry in the parish where the immovable is located.'" LA. CIV. CODE art. 2629. Again, a simple example illustrates the rule. Beau enters into a contract to buy a residential home located in St. Tammany Parish from Sal. Beau files the agreement in the conveyance records of St. Tammany Parish. Prior to the expiration of the agreement, Sal sells the home to Terry, who was unaware of Beau's option. Upon learning of the sale to Terry, Beau seeks specific performance of his option. Even though Terry did not know of Beau's right to the home, Beau will prevail in his action because his right in the home was evidenced in the public records. Note that Terry is not entirely without recourse. The warranty against eviction, covered in detail in Chapter 9: The Warranty Against Eviction, will govern his rights against Sal.

In 2007, special legislation was enacted requiring contracts to buy or sell immovable property to be reinscribed in the conveyance records on an annual basis. As you read the following provision, consider whether this provision may also be applicable to options or rights of first refusal.

La. Rev. Stat. § 5609. Contracts to buy or sell; peremption of the effect of recordation; prescription for actions

A. The effect of recording in the conveyance records of a contract to buy or sell an immovable shall cease one year from the date of its recordation, unless prior thereto one of the parties to the contract causes it to be reinscribed in the same manner as the reinscription of a mortgage as provided by Article 3362 of the Civil Code. Such a reinscription shall continue the effect of recordation for one year and its effect may be renewed from time to time thereafter in the same manner. Except as provided in Paragraph B, the effect of recordation shall thereafter cease upon the lapse of any continuous twelve-month period during which the contract is not reinscribed.

B. The filing of a notice of lis pendens of a suit to enforce a recorded contract to buy or sell the immovable that is then effective as provided in Paragraph A shall continue the effect of recordation in the manner and to the extent prescribed by Articles 3751 through 3753 of the Code of Civil Procedure, and reinscription of the contract shall thereafter not be required or have effect.

C. A contract recorded pursuant to Paragraph A shall be canceled from the records by the recorder upon the written request of any person after the effect of its inscription has ceased as herein provided or as provided by Article 3753 of the Code of Civil Procedure.

3. Indivisibility of the Right

An additional note on contracts preparatory to sale concerns the indivisibility of the rights of the holders when the rights belong to more than one person. According to Article 2630, "The right to exercise an option and the right of first refusal are indivisible." LA. CIV. CODE art. 2630. As a result, "[w]hen either of such rights belongs to more than one person all of them must exercise the right." *Id.* According to comment (b), "[T]he indivisibility of the right protects the grantor of the option, as it prevents one grantee from attempting to exercise the option for the part of the thing that may correspond to his share. Among grantees, if one of them refuses to exercise the option, the others may exercise the right to buy the whole thing provided that the refusal is final and clearly evinced." *Id.* at cmt. b.

E. Duty to Deliver Merchantable Title

A final topic that must be discussed in the context of contracts preparatory to the sale is that of warranty. As you may remember from earlier Chapters, the contract of sale carries with it certain warranties. One of them is the warranty against eviction which, as discussed in Chapter 9: The Warranty Against Eviction, protects the buyer from loss of, or danger of losing the whole or part of the thing sold because of a third person's right that existed at the time of the sale. A similar warranty is implied in connection with a contract to sell: the warranty of merchantable title. That warranty and its parameters are discussed in the case below.

Young v. Stevens

209 So. 2d 25 (La. 1967)

SUMMERS, Justice.

Presented for determination as the principal question in this suit is whether the title to certain real estate is merchantable. On March 9, 1965, by written agreement designated 'Agreement to Purchase or Sell', Mrs. Helen W. Stevens offered and agreed to sell for $24,750 the premises referred to as: '1228 Arabella Street, Single, Two Story On grounds measuring about 40' × 120' or as per title.' The sale was to be on terms of credit and was conditioned on the ability of the purchaser to obtain a satisfactory loan, as detailed in the agreement. Latter & Blum, Inc., was designated in the agreement as the real estate agent for the transaction.

Norman L. Young agreed to purchase the property and signed the acceptance on March 10, 1965. As required by the agreement, he deposited $2,475 with the seller's agent, which was 10 percent of the purchase price.

The agreement further provided that:

'The seller shall deliver to purchaser a merchantable title, and his inability to deliver such title within the time stipulated herein shall render this contract null and void, reserving unto purchaser the right to demand the return of the deposit from the holder thereof, and reserving unto agent the right to recover commission.

'Either party hereto who fails, for any reason whatsoever, to comply with the terms of this offer, if accepted, is obligated and agrees to pay the agent's commission and all reasonable attorney's fees and costs incurred by the other party, and/or agent in enforcing their respective rights.'

The prospective lending agency in this transaction, The Carruth Mortgage Corporation, caused a survey of the premises to be made for the account of the purchaser Young on May 4, 1965. The lot was surveyed as Lot "X" fronting on Arabella Street in Square 44, Hurstville, Sixth District of the city of New Orleans, said square being bounded by Nashville Ave., Prytania St., Arabella St. and Perrier St. The survey revealed the following encroachments:

1. A concrete drive strip belonging to Mrs. James Van Buren Gresham, the adjoining property owner, encroaching onto the lot in question from the property on the Prytania Street side to the extent of one foot at the intersection of the Prytania Street side property line at Arabella Street and tapering back in diminishing width to a point on the Prytania Street side property line about 25 feet distant from the front of the lot on Arabella Street.

2. A fence belonging to the adjoining property owner, Mrs. James Van Buren Gresham, encroaching onto the property on the Prytania Street side commencing about half way back from the front of the lot, to the extent of

1 foot 3 inches, and tapering down to the property line about two thirds of the distance from Arabella Street to the rear of the lot.

3. A fence encroachment at the rear of the lot onto the adjoining lot in the rear to the extent of 10 inches 6 lines near the Prytania Street side of the lot and tapering down to 3 inches to 5 lines towards the Perrier Street side.

4. A fence encroachment onto the adjoining property on part of the Perrier Street side to the extent of 6 inches 0 lines.

Being of the opinion that the driveway and other encroachments made title to the property unmerchantable, the purchaser Young notified the seller Mrs. Stevens that he considered the contract void. But Mrs. Stevens was unwilling to declare the purchase agreement null and void or to return his deposit; nor was she able to clear the encroachments revealed by the survey. Young then instituted suit against Mrs. Stevens and the agent Latter & Blum for the return of his deposit with interest, attorneys fees and costs. Mrs. Stevens answered admitting the encroachments, but she denied that they rendered her title unmerchantable. She asked for the forfeiture of Young's deposit of $2,475, for attorneys fees and for costs of the proceedings.

Mrs. James Van Buren Gresham, the adjoining property owner, steadfastly refused to remove the encroaching driveway or fence on the Prytania Street side of the lot in question. Mrs. Stevens therefore asserted a third-party demand against her for indemnification in the event it should be held that the encroachments rendered the property unmerchantable.

Latter & Blum answered and set forth its position as a stakeholder of the deposit. It also prayed for judgment against Young for its commission of $1,485, together with attorneys fees in the amount of $500 with interest and costs.

A motion for summary judgment was tried upon a joint stipulation of facts. Whereupon the trial court dismissed plaintiff's suit and declared Mrs. Stevens to be entitled to the deposit, less the amount due the real estate agent. This result made an adjudication of the third party demand unnecessary.

The Court of Appeal reversed the judgment and declared that plaintiff was entitled to the refund of his deposit and to attorneys fees and costs; it held that Latter & Blum would have to proceed against the seller and defendant Mrs. Stevens for its commission; and it remanded the cause for further proceedings to permit the prosecution of defendant's third party demand against Mrs. Gresham. (190 So.2d 264.)

Certiorari was granted on the application of Mrs. Stevens.

Property has a merchantable title when it can be readily sold or mortgaged in the ordinary course of business by reasonable persons familiar with the facts and questions involved. *Roberts v. Medlock*, 148 So. 474 (La.App.1933). "(O)ne should not be made to accept a title tendered as good, valid and binding unless it is entirely legal from every point of view." *Bodcaw Lumber v. White,* 121 La. 715, 721, 46 So. 782, 784 (1908). The promisee in a contract to sell is not called upon to accept a title which may reasonably suggest litigation. *Marsh v. Lorimer,* 164 La. 175, 113 So. 808 (1927).

And while the amount involved may be small, "it cannot be said that because of this fact the danger of litigation is not serious. No one can be forced to buy a lawsuit * * *" *Rodriguez v. Shroder,* 77 So.2d 216, 224 (La.App.1955). *See* Patton on Titles § 46 et seq. (2d ed. 1957); 92 C.J.S. Vendor and Purchaser §§ 209, 211 (1955); 55 Am.Jur. Vendor and Purchaser §§ 252, 253, 254 (1946).

The encroachments upon the property in this case undoubtedly suggest litigation; for the purchaser could not take peaceful possession of the entire property if part of it is occupied by Mrs. Gresham, who, the record shows, refuses to surrender the controverted strips. No circumstance more clearly suggests litigation than this fact. Truly, Young would be buying a lawsuit, or he would have to take less footage than the agreement calls for, either condition being a violation of the requirement that he be furnished a merchantable title. In like manner, a person buying property whose improvements encroach upon his neighbor is likely to sustain a law suit to defend his right to possession of the property sold to him beyond his title. *Kay v. Carter,* 243 La. 1095, 150 So.2d 27 (1963); *DeSalvo v. Doll,* 209 La. 1063, 26 So.2d 140 (1946); *Jacobs v. Freyhan,* 156 La. 585, 100 So. 726 (1924); *Schroeder v. Krushevski,* 186 So.2d 640 (La.App.1966); *Clesi, Inc. v. Quaglino,* 137 So.2d 500 (La.App.1962); *Papalia v. Hartson,* 52 So.2d 775 (La.App.1951).

The same result obtains, therefore, whether the adjoining property owner's improvements encroach upon the property to be sold or whether the property to be sold encroaches onto the adjoining property. What makes the title unmerchantable in either instance (and both occur here) is not necessarily the extent of the encroachment, but the fact that it suggests litigation. The law will not require Young to assume Mrs. Stevens' controversy with her neighbor.

Indeed, the prospect of litigation is the very circumstance which would destroy the principal cause of a contract to purchase a home. A person buying a home wants, above all, peaceful occupancy among peaceful neighbors. Selling him property which will probably bring on a lawsuit is contrary to that motive and furnishes a basis for nullifying the contract. La. Civil Code art. 1823 (1870) [R.C.C. 1949, 2032].

It will not do in such a case to contend, as Mrs. Stevens does here, that the encroachments are de minimis. To begin with the encroachments consume about 1/40th of the lot area. This is significant. But what is more noteworthy is the fact that, until this time, no one has been able to remove the objectionable encroachments without a lawsuit, not even the vendor Mrs. Stevens who advances the contention that they are insignificant.

We are able to distinguish the authorities relied upon by Mrs. Stevens. Insofar as we deem it appropriate to discuss those distinctions, we make these observations: *Hunley v. Ascani,* 174 La. 712, 141 So. 385 (1932) deals with discrepancies in the quantity of ground between the dimensions given in a contract to purchase and sell and in the dimensions in the title sought to be conveyed pursuant thereto. The case does not involve an encroachment which suggests litigation. *Scurria v. Russo,* 134 So.2d 679 (La.App.1961) likewise has to do with a shortage in the area of the property contracted to be sold, not with an encroachment suggesting litigation. *O'Reilly v. Poche,* 162 So.2d 787 (La.App.1964), and *Werk v. Leland University,* 155 La. 971, 99 So. 716 (1924) simply recognize the established proposition that where there is a conflict between the calls in a deed and a survey referred to in the deed the survey governs. We conclude that the title in question is not merchantable.

The pertinent part of the 'Agreement to Purchase or Sell', quoted in the beginning of this opinion, entitles the purchaser to a return of his deposit when the seller is unable to convey a merchantable title.

The allowance of $500 attorneys fees to Mr. Young is amply supported by the record before us and the work performed under the eye of the Court.

For the reasons assigned the judgment of the Court of Appeal is affirmed and is recast as follows:

It is hereby ordered that Latter & Blum, Inc., return to Norman Lind Young the sum of $2,475 deposited in connection with the contract in question.

It is further ordered, adjudged and decreed that there be judgment herein in favor of plaintiff Norman Lind Young and against Mrs. Helen W. Stevens in the sum of $500 as attorneys fees, with legal interest from date of judicial demand until paid, together with legal interest on the deposit of $2,475 from date of judicial demand until paid, and for all costs of these proceedings.

It is further ordered, adjudged and decreed that this case be remanded to the trial court for further proceedings in connection with Mrs. Stevens' third party petition against Mrs. Gresham, and for a determination of such additional issues as the nature of the case may require.

* * * * *

Notes and Questions

1. The warranty of merchantable title is not mentioned in the Louisiana Civil Code, but the jurisprudence has long recognized it. 24 DIAN TOOLEY-KNOBLETT & DAVID GRUNING, LOUISIANA CIVIL LAW TREATISE, SALES § 5:41 (2017). This warranty may be express or implied. For example, in *Young*, the parties' agreement specifically provided that the seller was required to deliver merchantable title. That said, under Louisiana law, even in the absence of such an express provision, the duty of the seller to deliver merchantable title exists.

2. Who carries the burden of establishing the merchantability (or lack thereof) of the property to be sold and what exactly must this person show? Does the extent of the encroachment affect the buyer's claim?

3. What are the consequences of a seller's breach of the warranty of merchantable title? The court in *Young* cites a jurisprudential rule that when the seller fails to deliver merchantable title, the buyer can refuse to execute the Act of Sale. In other words, the seller's failure to deliver merchantable title amounts to a breach of contract, and the buyer may regard the contract as extrajudicially dissolved.

Presumably, the buyer may also recover any damages incurred as a result of the seller's failure to perform. *See* La. Civ. Code art. 1994. These default remedies may be altered by the parties' agreement. For example, in *Young*, the parties' agreement stated that in case of the seller's failure to deliver merchantable title, the agreement would be "null and void," the buyer would be entitled to the return of the deposit, and the seller required to pay the buyer's legal fees.

4. As mentioned above, the warranty of merchantable title is similar to the warranty against eviction. While both protect against competing claims to the property, they are distinguishable. The most important difference is that the warranty of merchantable title attaches to a contract *to sell*, whereas the warranty against eviction attaches to a contract *of sale*. Knowing that, should a buyer be allowed to invoke the warranty of merchantability after the sale is concluded? Why or why not? It is worth noting that leading commentators have opined that Louisiana courts have eroded the distinction between these two warranties, a development that they characterize as "disturbing," "inappropriate," and "clearly wrong." *See* 24 Dian Tooley-Knoblett & David Gruning, Louisiana Civil Law Treatise, Sales §§ 5:44, 10:15 (2017).

Part II

Lease

Chapter 13

The Nature and Essential Elements of the Contract of Lease

La. Civ. Code arts. 2668–2672
A. Introduction

Revision of the Lease Title was recently undertaken by the Louisiana Law Institute as part of its ongoing revision of the Louisiana Civil Code. This project began in 1992 and was completed in 2004. Act Number 821 of 2004 became effective January 1, 2005. Title IX of Book III of the Louisiana Civil Code, "Of Lease," previously defined the contract of lease broadly to include both the lease of things and the lease of industry. The revision affects only the lease of things. Provisions governing the lease of industry are found in Chapter 5 of Title IX, Louisiana Civil Code Articles 2745 through 2777 and are not covered in this Textbook.

Louisiana Civil Code Article 2668 defines lease as "a synallagmatic [or bilateral] contract by which one party, the lessor, binds himself to give to the other party, the lessee, the use and enjoyment of a thing for a term in exchange for a rent that the lessee binds himself to pay." La. Civ. Code art. 2668. This article makes clear that, like a sale, a lease is a bilateral, commutative contract in which the obligations of the parties are correlative. *See* La. Civ. Code arts. 1908, 1911. The lessor is bound to give to the lessee the use and enjoyment of a thing, and in exchange, the lessee is bound to pay rent. Note that the lease obligates the lessor to give "the use and enjoyment of a thing"—there is no transfer of ownership or other real right. La. Civ. Code art. 2668. A contract of lease gives the lessee personal rights over the leased thing; it does not create real rights in the thing. In addition, because each of the parties in a lease obtains an advantage in exchange for his or her obligation, the lease is onerous in nature. *See* La. Civ. Code art. 1909. If the parties enter into a *gratuitous* contract whereby one of them gives the other the use of a thing without receiving rent in return, the contract is properly classified as a "loan for use" and is governed by the Title on Loan rather than the rules continued in the Title on Lease. *See* La. Civ. Code arts. 2891–2913.

Depending on the agreed use of the leased thing, a lease is characterized by the Civil Code as residential, agricultural, mineral, commercial, or consumer. La. Civ. Code art. 2671. A lease is residential when the thing is to be occupied as a dwelling, agricultural when the thing is a predial estate to be used for agricultural purposes, mineral when the thing is to be used for the production of minerals, commercial when the thing is to be used for business or commercial purposes, and consumer when the thing is a movable intended for the lessee's personal or familial use outside his trade or profession. *Id.* These classifications are important because they are used occasionally to determine the rules applicable to the term of the lease and the parties' obligations. Note that Louisiana Civil Code Article 2672 provides that mineral leases are governed by the Mineral Code, La. Civ. Code art. 2672, and, under that body of law, are defined as real rights. *See* La. Rev. Stat. § 31:2. Because of the specialized treatment of mineral leases under Louisiana law, the rules specific to mineral leases are not covered in this Textbook.

B. Essential Elements of the Contract of Lease

A lease is, first and foremost, a contract. Thus, like any contract, a lease requires capacity, consent, object, and cause for its formation. *See generally* La. Civ. Code arts. 1918–82. Furthermore, a lease requires certain elements set forth in the Title on Lease. The essential elements of the contract of lease are addressed in detail in the Subparts that follow.

1. Consent to Lease

La. Civ. Code art. 2668

According to Louisiana Civil Code Article 2668, "The consent of the parties *as to* the thing and the rent is essential but not necessarily sufficient for a contract of lease." La. Civ. Code art. 2668 (emphasis added). In other words, consent as to these things is required, but this, alone, will not necessarily mean that a contract of lease has been formed. If, for example, the parties do not intend to be bound until they agree on the other terms to the contract, then there will be no lease unless and until they agree on those terms. Likewise, if the parties intend to be bound upon their agreement as to a "thing" and a "rent," the contract may not actually be one of lease if the right the parties intend to convey is a real right, like, for example, a usufruct. This is true even if the parties label their agreement a "lease."

Faroldi v. Nungesser

144 So. 2d 568 (La. App. 4 Cir. 1962)

Ayres, Judge.

By this action, plaintiffs seek to recover of the defendant the sum of $276 allegedly due as rent on certain of plaintiffs' property occupied by the defendant. The defense is there was no contract of lease upon which a claim for rent may be predicated. From a judgment in favor of plaintiffs, as prayed for, defendant appealed.

The factual situation upon which plaintiffs' claim for rent is predicated may be briefly stated. Plaintiffs, as the owners of Lots 48 and 49, Square 428, 2d District, of the City of New Orleans, on August 18, 1959, sold a portion thereof to the State of Louisiana for right-of-way purposes in connection with the construction of an interstate highway. Plaintiffs retained that portion of the lots fronting 50.04 feet on Catina Street, 62.95 feet in width in the rear, by a depth of 58.04 feet on Homedale Avenue, and 20.20 feet on Florida Avenue. The State, however, acquired, by the sale, the improvements located partially on the property acquired by it and partially on the portion retained by plaintiffs.

The improvements as purchased by the State were sold by it to the defendant in December, 1959, without a specified time for removal. Defendant, at the time of his purchase, was unaware that plaintiffs had retained a portion of the realty and, consequently, was unaware of the fact that the improvements were located partially on plaintiffs' property. Through subsequent correspondence, defendant's counsel advised plaintiffs' counsel the improvements would be removed by April 30, 1960. Notwithstanding the fact that the defendant had promptly, on making his purchase of the improvements, instructed a house-moving concern to move them, delays were encountered due to the number of houses to be moved and, in this particular case, to the presence of trees for which permission to cut had to be obtained. The removal, however, was carried out on June 9, 1960.

In the meantime, plaintiffs had requested of defendant, by letter, that the improvements be removed from their property on or prior to April 1, 1960, or, in the event said improvements had not been removed by that date, that the defendant pay rental at the rate of $120 per month. The record does not establish that defendant in any wise or manner assented to plaintiffs' proposition or agreed to pay rent in any amount. For the period from April 1 to June 9, 1960, plaintiffs charged defendant rent in the sum of $276.

No claim, alternately or otherwise, predicated on a basis of a quantum meruit is made.

The legal proposition advanced in brief by plaintiffs, in justification of their claim, is that the use of their land by the defendant permits the recovery of rent under the relationship of lessor and lessee (or in quasi contract). This proposition, for the reasons hereinafter assigned, is, in our opinion, untenable.

A lease in a contract imposing reciprocal obligations on the parties by which one party gives to the other the enjoyment of a thing at a fixed price. LSA-C.C. Art. 2669 [R.C.C. 2668]. To a contract of lease, there are three absolute essentials; namely, the thing forming the subject matter of the contract, the price for its enjoyment, and the consent or agreement of the parties. LSA-C.C. Art. 2670 [R.C.C. 2668]; *Caldwell v. Turner*, 129 La. 19, 55 So. 695; *Myers v. Burke*, La.App.1st Cir., 1939, 189 So. 482. Thus, there can be no contract of lease in the absence of a stipulation or agreement between the parties as to the amount of rent to be paid. LSA-C.C. Art. 2671 [R.C.C. 2675–2676]; *McCain v. McCain Bros.*, 165 La. 884, 116 So. 221; *Weaks Supply Co. v. Werdin*, La.App.2d Cir., 1933, 147 So. 838. Two parties are necessary in order to form a contract, one proposing something and the other accepting and agreement to it;

and the will of both parties must unite on the same. LSA-C.C. Art. 1798 [R.C.C. 1927]; *Succession of Aurianne*, 219 La. 701, 53 So.2d 901; *Superior Merchandise Corporation v. Oser*, La.App.Orleans, 1942, 8 So.2d 770.

The terms of plaintiffs' letter to the defendant, upon which they rely as fixing the amount of rent allegedly due them, were, as heretofore pointed out, neither accepted nor agreed to by the defendant. Consequently, there clearly was no meeting of the minds of the parties, and, hence, no contract. LSA-C.C. Art. 1798 [R.C.C. 1927]; *Collins v. Louisiana State Lottery Co.*, 43 La.Ann. 9, 9 So. 27. Plaintiffs' letter to defendant, without an acceptance of the proposal made, is insufficient to constitute a contract between the parties. *Hearne v. De Generes*, La.App.2d Cir., 1932, 144 So. 194.

Thus, the unity of will necessary for the formation of a contract is not present here.

Nor will occupancy alone imply a relationship of lessor and lessee. *Terzia v. The Grand Leader*, 176 La. 151,145 So. 363; *Weaks Supply Co. v. Werdin, supra; Jordan v. Mead*, 19 La.Ann. 101; *Blanchard v. Davidson*, 7 La.Ann. 654.

At most, all that can be inferred from the record is that defendant was the mere occupant of plaintiffs' property, and, as we have pointed out, it has been repeatedly held that the proof of mere occupancy alone is insufficient to establish the relationship of lessor and lessee.

As heretofore observed, no basis of recovery under a quasi contract or on a quantum meruit has been alleged or established. Particularly noted is the fact that plaintiffs' petition fails to allege and the record is devoid of any proof as to the rental value of plaintiffs' property which was occupied by the defendant. One cannot, under such circumstances, where there is no lease, sue for an arbitrary amount. The value of the use or occupancy of the property must be established by the evidence.

The conclusion is therefore inescapable that plaintiffs have failed to establish their claim to that degree of legal certainty and by a preponderance of the evidence which would entitle them to judgment.

Therefore, the judgment appealed is annulled, avoided, reversed and set aside; and

It is now Ordered, Adjudged and Decreed that plaintiffs-appellees' demands be, and they are hereby, rejected and their suit dismissed at their cost.

Reversed.

Notes and Questions

1. Did the parties in *Faroldi* enter into a contract of lease? Why or why not? The court observed that "no basis of recovery under a quasi contract or on a quantum meruit has been alleged or established." 144 So. 2d at 570. Recall that quantum meruit is "simply a measure of compensation or price unstated in a contract," i.e., a

method of calculating the compensation that should be paid to a party to a contract when the parties did not agree to a precise price or method of payment. *See Morphy, Makofsky & Masson, Inc. v. Canal Place 2000*, 538 So. 2d 569, 574 (La. 1989). In such a case, the amount owed to the party is a "reasonable sum" in return for what is given. *Id.* Read carefully Article 2676 (discussed further below in Subpart B.3). Can the rent in a lease ever be fixed through quantum meruit? Why or why not? Recall also that quasi-contractual obligations arise in the absence of a contract. For example, under Article 2298, even in the absence of an agreement, "[a] person who has been enriched without cause at the expense of another person is bound to compensate that person." La. Civ. Code art. 2298. Was the plaintiff in *Faroldi* entitled to compensation for enrichment without cause? Why or why not?

2. The Civil Code contemplates that the parties may enter into a "contract *to* lease," whereby the parties agree to enter into a lease at a future time. According to Article 2670, "A contract to enter into a lease at a future time is enforceable by either party if there was agreement as to the thing to be leased and the rent, unless the parties understood that the contract would not be binding until reduced to writing or until its other terms were agreed upon." La. Civ. Code art. 2670.

2. The Thing
La. Civ. Code arts. 2673–2674; *cf.* 2904–2905

As a general rule, all things susceptible of ownership may be the object of a contract of lease. La. Civ. Code art. 2673. This includes both corporeals and incorporeals, as well as movables and immovables. *Id.* Recall that common things like the air and the high seas are not susceptible of ownership. *See* La. Civ. Code art. 449. Things that cannot be used without being destroyed by that very use (i.e., consumable things) and things prohibited by law cannot be the object of a lease. La. Civ. Code art. 2673. A purported "lease" of consumable things is properly characterized as a loan for consumption, defined as "a contract by which a person, the lender, delivers consumable things to another, the borrower, who binds himself to return to the lender an equal amount of things of the same kind and quality." La. Civ. Code art. 2904. In such a contract, unlike a lease, the borrower becomes the owner of the thing lent and bears the risk of loss of that thing. La. Civ. Code art. 2905.

Significantly, a lease may be binding on the parties even if the lessor does not own the leased thing. La. Civ. Code art. 2674. In other words, the lessor's ownership of the thing is not an essential element of the contract of lease. This seemingly simple rule must not be overlooked, as it has significant consequences for the parties that will be addressed in the Chapters that follow. Note that while the lessor's ownership of the leased thing is not a prerequisite to a valid contract under suppletive law, the parties may agree that the lease is binding only for so long as the lessor is owner. *See* La. Civ. Code art. 2674 cmt. c.

3. The Rent

La. Civ. Code arts. 2675–2677; *cf.* 2891

Rent is an essential element of a contract of lease. *See* La. Civ. Code art. 2668. However, unlike the price in a contract of sale, which must be in money, La. Civ. Code art. 2439, in a contract of lease "[t]he rent may consist of money, commodities, fruits, services, or other performances sufficient to support an onerous contract." La. Civ. Code art. 2675. Because of the onerous nature of the contract of lease, the amount of rent must be serious and not out of proportion to the thing's value. *See* La. Civ. Code art. 2675 cmt. b.

Similar to the contract of sale, the rent may be fixed by the parties in a sum either certain or determinable through a method agreed by them; likewise, it may be fixed by a third person designated by them. La. Civ. Code art. 2676. However, if the agreed method proves unworkable or the designated person is unwilling or unable to fix the rent, then there is no lease. *Id.* Note that this is a departure from the rules for the contract of sale, under which the court may determine the price in the event that the parties fail to agree on or appoint a third person or if the one appointed is unable or unwilling to make a determination. *See* La. Civ. Code art. 2465. By contrast, if the rent has been established initially and is subject to *redetermination* by a third person or through a method agreed to by the parties but the third person is unwilling or unable to fix the rent or the agreed method proves unworkable, the court may either fix the rent or provide a similar method in accordance with the intent of the parties. La. Civ. Code art. 2676.

4. The Term

La. Civ. Code arts. 2678–2680

The definition of lease provides that the lease shall be "for a term," and Article 2678 echoes this requirement. *See* La. Civ. Code arts. 2668, 2678. It is fundamental to the nature of a lease that the contract cannot be perpetual. *See* La. Civ. Code art. 2678. This is a rule of public policy designed in part to prevent parties from taking property out of commerce indefinitely. In addition, the rule is designed to prevent parties from binding themselves (or their successors) permanently. Thus, a lease for a perpetual term is absolutely null. *See* La. Civ. Code art. 2678 cmt. a.

The term of a lease may be classified under two different schemes: (1) conventional or legal; and (2) fixed or indeterminate. *See id.* These schemes are discussed in the Subparts that follow.

a. Conventional vs. Legal Terms

Article 2678 recognizes that the duration of a lease "may be agreed to by the parties or supplied by law." La. Civ. Code art. 2678. A term that is supplied by the parties' agreement is known as a "conventional" term. Parties are generally free to designate the duration of their lease in any manner they wish; however, the parties' contractual freedom is limited in that the term of the lease may not exceed 99 years. LA. CIV. CODE art. 2679. This rule of public policy is designed not only to prevent parties from taking property out of commerce for too long but also to prevent parties from binding themselves for a period that exceeds their ability to anticipate the risk of changing circumstances. *See* LA. CIV. CODE art. 2679 cmt. a. Said another way, a lease with a term in excess of 99 years differs very little from a perpetual lease. If the parties provide for a term longer than 99 years or include an option to extend the term to more than 99 years, the lease is not invalid; instead, the term shall be reduced to the maximum term provided by law. LA. CIV. CODE art. 2679 and cmt. b.

The parties to the lease may choose not to supply a term, and their failure to do so will not necessarily invalidate the lease. As long as the parties do not intend to create a perpetual lease, the term of the lease will be supplied by law. Such a term is known as a "legal" term. The duration of a legal term is supplied by Article 2680. Because all legal terms are also "indeterminate" terms, the terms supplied by Article 2680 are discussed further below.

b. Fixed vs. Indeterminate Terms

A term may be either "fixed" or "indeterminate." A term is "fixed" when the parties agree that the lease will terminate at a designated date or upon the occurrence of a designated event. LA. CIV. CODE art. 2678. The lease of an apartment for one year is a fixed term lease, as is the lease of a piece of industrial equipment for 30 days. Importantly, while a fixed term lease must have a designated end-point that is certain to occur, the precise timing of that end-point need not be known by the parties at the time of their agreement. *See* LA. CIV. CODE art. 2678 cmt. d. For example, the lease of an apartment until the death of the lessee has a fixed term because the duration of the lease is tied to a designated event (i.e., the death of the lessee).

Article 2678 provides that in all cases in which the term of the lease is not fixed, the term is "indeterminate." LA. CIV. CODE art. 2678. When the term of the lease is indeterminate, the termination date is not fixed in advance but depends on the will of the parties subsequently expressed. *See* LA. CIV. CODE art. 2678 cmt. e. Said another way, an indeterminate term lease continues indefinitely until one of the parties expresses a desire that the lease terminate. As will be discussed further in Chapter 15: Termination and Dissolution of the Lease, notice to terminate an indeterminate term lease must be given in proper time and form in order to be effective. *See* LA. CIV. CODE arts. 2678 cmt. c; 2727–2729.

Indeterminate term leases are referred to in the common law as "periodic" leases. Although the term "periodic" is not used in the Civil Code, the designation is helpful because it makes clear that indeterminate term leases continue indefinitely for successive periods of time. An indeterminate lease may be year-to-year, month-to-month, week-to-week, day-to-day, or even hour-by-hour. If the indeterminate term is agreed to by the parties (i.e., conventional), the parties may choose *any* incremental period for their lease, provided that the first period does not exceed 99 years. (A lease for 100-year-to-100-year intervals would be reduced to 99-year-to-99-year intervals for public policy reasons.) Note that a lease for a shorter indeterminate term, such as a year-to-year lease, that is allowed by the parties through their acquiescence to last longer than 99 years does not violate the law. *See* La. Civ. Code art. 2679 cmt. c.

If the indeterminate term is supplied by law (i.e., legal), then the duration of the lease will be determined by its object pursuant to Article 2680. That article sets forth the rules for establishing the duration of legal indeterminate terms:

(1) An agricultural lease shall be from year to year.

(2) Any other lease of an immovable, or a lease of a movable to be used as a residence, shall be from month to month.

(3) A lease of other movables shall be from day to day, unless the rent was fixed by longer or shorter periods, in which case the term shall be one such period, not to exceed one month.

La. Civ. Code art. 2680. Note also that that the parties to the lease may agree that the duration of the lease will depend solely on the will of the lessor or the lessee, without specifying a maximum fixed term for their lease. When this occurs, the lease is regarded as indeterminate, and the legal terms supplied by Article 2680 apply. *See* La. Civ. Code art. 2679.

5. Form

La. Civ. Code art. 2681

There is no particular form requirement for a contract of lease. In fact, the Code specifically provides that "[a] lease may be made orally or in writing." La. Civ. Code art. 2681. Particularly noteworthy is the fact that this rule applies even to immovable property—an oral lease of an immovable is a perfectly valid lease (at least as between the parties). This is because the rights conveyed by a contract of lease are of a personal nature; a lease does not convey ownership or any other real right. Thus, a lease is not a "transfer of an immovable" which under the Louisiana Civil Code nearly always requires a writing. La. Civ. Code arts. 1839, 2440.

As discussed below, there are additional requirements to make a lease valid against third persons. *Id.*

C. Effects Against Third Persons

While a lease is enforceable between the parties upon their consent, additional requirements must be satisfied in order for leases to have effects against third persons. As is the case with sales, the rules governing the effects of a lease against third persons differ depending upon whether the leased thing is movable or immovable.

1. Immovables

La. Civ. Code arts. 2681, 3338, 3343

While the lease of an immovable is binding on the parties to the lease irrespective of whether it is oral or written, to be effective against third persons, the contract of lease must be properly recorded. *See* LA. CIV. CODE arts. 3338(2), 2681. Recordation must be made in the parish where the immovable is located. LA. CIV. CODE art. 3346. In addition, although a lease of an immovable is not a conveyance, recordation must be made in the conveyance records. *Id.* (providing that instruments creating or relating to mortgages or privileges over immovables or to the pledge of the lessor's rights in the lease of an immovable and its rents are recorded in the mortgage records; *all other* instruments are recorded in the conveyance records). Consistent with the general principles of the law of registry, an unrecorded lease of an immovable has no effect on third persons, even if the third person has actual knowledge of the lease. *See, e.g., Murray v. Le Blanc*, 6 Orl. App. 387, 387 (La. App. 1909).

Of course, in order to be recorded, the lease must be in writing. Furthermore, like in a contract of sale, the contract of lease must contain an adequate property description in order to have effects against third persons. *Allen v. George*, 110 So. 2d 587, 594 (La. App. 1 Cir. 1959). Thus, while the lease of an immovable need not be in writing to be enforceable between the parties, a writing is a practical necessity for recordation. Note, however, that the parties may choose to record a notice of lease instead of their entire contract of lease. *See* LA. REV. STAT. § 9:2742. A notice of lease must contain: (i) the names, addresses, and signatures of the parties; (ii) the date of execution; (iii) a brief description of the leased property; (iv) the term; (v) any renewal or purchase options; and (vi) a reference to the existence of an option, right of first refusal, or other agreement of the lessor to transfer the leased premises. *Id.*

Many leases contain an option by which the parties may extend the term of the lease beyond the original term agreed upon by the parties. Indeed, Article 2725 acknowledges the enforceability of such agreements, providing: "If the lease contract contains an option to extend the term and the option is exercised, the lease continues for the term and under the other provisions stipulated in the option." LA. CIV. CODE art. 2725. Consider whether the exercise of an option to extend must be recorded in the public records in order to have effects against third persons. Article 3339 provides that "the exercise of an option ... evidenced by a recorded instrument [is] effective as to a third person although not evidenced of record." LA. CIV. CODE art. 3339. Thus, if a lease containing an option to renew is properly recorded, the exercise of the option to renew need not be recorded to be effective against third persons. Take, for example, a lease of a commercial building for a term of five years which contains a clause permitting the lessee to renew the lease for an additional five-year term, provided the lessee notifies the lessor of his or her intention to renew in writing within thirty days of the expiration of the first term. As long as this lease is properly recorded in the conveyance records of the parish where the commercial building is located, the lease is effective against third persons not only for the initial five-year term, but (if the option is properly exercised) for the additional five-year term as well.

While an unrecorded lease has no effect against a "third person," recall that a "third person" is one who is not a party to the lease or one who is not personally bound by an instrument. La. Civ. Code art. 3343. In contrast, "[a] person who by contract assumes an obligation . . . is not a third person with the respect to the obligation or right or to the instrument creating or establishing it." *Id.* Thus, one who purchases immovable property and agrees to assume the lessor's obligations under the lease is not a third person to the lease; rather, the unrecorded lease is binding on this purchaser. Additionally, "[a] person who . . . is bound by contract to recognize a right is not a third person with respect to the . . . right or to the instrument creating or establishing it." *Id.* Thus, one who purchases an immovable under a contract providing that the sale is "subject to" the lease is not a third person to the lease, either. Instead, this purchaser is bound by his agreement to recognize the lessee's rights under the unrecorded lease.

The following case addresses the rights of a purchaser of immovable property that was burdened by an unrecorded lease at the time of the sale.

Motwani v. Fun Centers, Inc.

388 So. 2d 1173 (La. App. 4 Cir. 1980)

Samuel, Judge.

Plaintiffs, Kishore V. Motwani, Giani V. Gethwani, wife of/and Verhomal J. Motwani, owners of certain immovable property located at 227–233 Bourbon Street in New Orleans, filed suit to evict defendants, Fun Centers, Inc. and its sublessee, Playgirl Shops of America, Inc. The basis of plaintiffs' suit is that the written lease to Fun Centers, Inc. was not registered in the public records of Orleans Parish.

Following trial in the district court, there was judgment denying plaintiffs' eviction attempt apparently on the basis that plaintiffs knew about the lease and subjected themselves to it upon purchase of the property in suit. Plaintiffs have appealed from that judgment.

The record shows that on May 6, 1976, the then owners of the property in question leased a portion of it to Fun Centers, Inc. This lease was not registered in the conveyance records of Orleans Parish. On January 21, 1977 Fun Centers, Inc. in turn subleased the premises to Playgirl Shops of America, Inc. with the permission of the owners. This sublease was registered in the conveyance records.

On December 12, 1977, the property was sold to Mr. and Mrs. Nick Karno and Mr. and Mrs. Frank Caracci. On the same date the purchasers executed a document titled "Assignment of Lease, Rents and Profits" in favor of the National American Bank in New Orleans as additional security for the bank in the event of a default on purchasers' mortgage. The assignment of the lease specifically referred to the original lease to Fun Centers, Inc. and the sublease to Playgirl Shops of America, Inc., and the assignment was registered in the conveyance records of Orleans Parish.

Playgirl Shops of America, Inc., the sublessee, used the trade name "Disco Stop". On December 14, 1977 Verhomal J. Motwani, plaintiff herein, executed an agreement to purchase from Karno and Caracci the property subject to the lease, and in the agreement to purchase plaintiffs acknowledged the existence of a lease in favor of Disco Stop and two other lessees. The testimony indicates copies of the leases were furnished to Motwani before he purchased the property.

On February 24, 1978, plaintiffs took title to the property from the Karnos and the Caraccis, and in the act of sale the vendors warranted they had not alienated the property except for the assignment of lease, rents, and profits which they had previously made in favor of the National American Bank. On the same date and before the same notary public, plaintiffs executed their own assignment of lease, rents, and profits to the National American Bank, which assignment specifically acknowledged and assigned the lease of Playgirl Shops of America, Inc. and referred to it as follows:

> "That certain lease and sublease by Charles J. Napoli and John J. Elms, Jr., Joyce Elms Roche and Regina Elms Mauberret to Playgirl Shops of America, Inc. covering that part of the first floor of 227-233 Bourbon as shown in lease approximately 1033 square feet."

In their original brief, plaintiffs based their position almost entirely on the public records doctrine which states that the public records are dispositive of the rights of purchasers of immovable property regardless of their actual knowledge of adverse rights of third persons in or to the property. This doctrine was intended to protect innocent third parties who have no knowledge of the existence of any rights and/or claims against property, and allows them to take free and clear of any such unrecorded claims. The doctrine has been enforced even where the purchaser had actual knowledge of the outstanding unrecorded claims. However, the public records doctrine is not pertinent to the present case under its facts.

Defendants rely on *Brown v. Johnson*, in which the court stated that all persons have constructive notice of the existence and contents of recorded instruments affecting immovable property, and when such an instrument contains language which fairly places a purchaser on inquiry as to the title and he does not avail himself of the means and facilities at hand to obtain knowledge of the true facts, he is to be considered as having purchased the property at his own risk and peril. However, we likewise need not consider this exception to the public records doctrine because of facts found by us.

The record is clear that in the act of sale by which plaintiffs acquired title to the property the assignment of the lease by their vendors to the National American Bank of New Orleans was made the subject of an exception to unincumbered [sic] title. More important, however, is the fact that plaintiffs on the same day of their acquisition themselves executed an assignment of the same lease in favor of the same bank in order to furnish the lending bank additional security for its loan. Hence, the plaintiffs, with full knowledge, expressly assumed the lease obligations of their vendors and simultaneously acknowledged this assumption by means of an assignment of the lease to the bank. Because plaintiffs contractually assumed the obligation of the lease, the lease became their obligation and the Public Records Doctrine was rendered inapplicable.

A similar case, *Stanley v. Orkin Exterminating Co., Inc.*, was decided by the First Circuit. In that case, Orkin entered into a written lease with the owner of the property but failed to record it. The owner subsequently sold the property to a Mr. and Mrs. Owens, who orally acknowledged the lease in favor of Orkin and accepted monthly rental payments from it. Eventually Stanley, the plaintiff, entered into a written agreement to purchase the property from Mr. and Mrs. Owens, and the agreement to purchase provided the sale of the property was subject to the Orkin lease. The sale to Stanley did not mention the lease, and he brought eviction proceedings against Orkin claiming the sale was free from the lease because he only intended to honor a recorded lease. Plaintiff testified he knew Owens intended to sell subject to the Orkin lease, and he acknowledged he was given a copy of the lease at the signing of the purchase agreement. The First Circuit held for Orkin, stating the public records doctrine was not applicable to the facts before it. The court found that the intent of the parties throughout the entire transaction was that the property was sold subject to the Orkin lease and this intention was expressly stated in the purchase agreement and impliedly agreed to by Stanley's accepting monthly rental payments from Orkin.

In a supplemental brief, plaintiffs contend that defendants could avail themselves of plaintiffs' actions only upon a showing that these actions constituted a stipulation pour autrui. The argument is without merit. Plaintiffs cannot use a known lease for their benefit by assigning it to a bank in order to obtain financing and later claim they did not have knowledge of the tenant or of the lease from which the assignment was derived. Having made the lease their own, they are obliged to maintain defendants in peaceable possession of the premises.

For the reasons assigned, the judgment appealed from is affirmed.

AFFIRMED.

Notes and Questions

1. The court in the foregoing case held that the plaintiffs "assumed" the unrecorded lease between the sellers and their lessee. After reading about the distinction between a purchaser's "assumption" of an unrecorded lease and a purchaser's agreement to buy "subject to" an unrecorded lease, do you agree with the court's analysis? What consequences, if any, does the distinction have for the lessee? For the sublessee?

2. The court in *Motwani* cites to a previous decision in *Stanley v. Orkin Exterminating Co., Inc.*, 360 So. 2d 225 (La. App. 1 Cir. 1978). In that case, the court held that a buyer of an immovable was bound by an assumption agreement in the contract to sell even though the Act of Sale did not contain any language regarding the buyer's assumption of unrecorded leases. The accuracy of this statement is questionable; rather, it is well-accepted that "the act of sale represents 'the conclusion of the negotiation process and embodies the final expression of the parties' intent.'" *Long-Fork, L.L.C. v. Petite Riviere, L.L.C.*, 987 So. 2d 831, 837 (La. App. 3 Cir. 2008) (quoting *Esplanade Management, Ltd. v. Sajare Interests*, 498 So. 2d 289, 292 (La. App. 4 Cir. 1986)). An in-depth discussion of the requirements of a valid and enforceable assumption agreement appears in the following Part. After reading that material, consider whether the *Stanley* court was nevertheless correct in concluding, based upon the parties' negotiations, that the buyer "impliedly" assumed the seller's obligations under the lease. At the very least, did the buyer purchase the property "subject to" the lessee's rights?

3. Louisiana courts have long held that a buyer of an immovable burdened with an unrecorded lease who accepts rent from the lessee "ratifies" the unrecorded lease and becomes bound thereby, even without expressly assuming the obligations of the lessor or agreeing to recognize the lease. *See Pirkle & Williams v. Shreveport Jitney Jungle*, 140 So. 837 (La. App. 2 Cir. 1932).

2. Movables

The Civil Code does not specify the circumstances under which a lease of movables becomes effective against third persons. To determine when a lease of movables has effects against persons other than the parties to the lease, it is essential to recall that a lease is a contract by which the lessor gives to the lessee the use and enjoyment of a thing, but by which no real rights are transferred. Like any other contract that does not involve the transfer of a real right, the lease of a movable has no effects against third persons other than those who agree by contract with the lessor or lessee to assume the lessor's obligations under the lease or to acquire rights in the object of the lease "subject to" the lessee's rights.

D. Transfer of Interest by Lessor or Lessee
La. Civ. Code arts. 2711–2713

Oftentimes, the factual circumstances of one or both of the parties change after they have confected the contract of lease. Some changes of circumstance potentially affect the relationship between the parties and their relationship with third persons. On the lessor's side of the equation, the change in circumstance may be that the lessor transfers his or her interest in the leased thing; in other words, the lessor may alienate the property that is being leased. Or the change of circumstance may be that the lessor transfers his or her interest in the contract of lease itself. On the lessee's side of the equation, the change of circumstance may be that the lessee transfers his or her interest in the lease via an assignment, subleases the leased thing, or encumbers the lease. These topics are discussed in the Subparts below.

1. By Lessor

As noted above, two potential situations exist regarding a lessor's transfer of interest: transfer of interest in the leased thing and transfer of interest in the contract of lease.

a. Transfer of the Interest in the Leased Thing

If the lessor transfers the leased thing, the lease does not terminate unless the lessor and lessee agreed to the contrary. LA. CIV. CODE art. 2711. Assuming no contrary agreement, the lease is still fully enforceable between the lessor and the lessee, and both are bound by the obligations and entitled to the rights under the lease, despite the lessor's transfer of the thing to a third person. If the lease is on an immovable and is recorded, the third person is bound by the lease and may not evict the lessee. LA. CIV. CODE art. 2711 cmt. c.

If the lease is not recorded, the transferee of immovable property is not bound by the lease unless (as described above) the lessee assumed the lessor's obligations under the lease, purchased the property "subject to" unrecorded leases, or accepted rent from the lessee. LA. CIV. CODE art. 2712. A transferee who is not bound by the lease may evict the lessee at any time. Should the transferee do so, Louisiana Civil Code Article 2712 provides: "In the absence of a contrary provision in the lease contract, the lessee has an action against the lessor for any loss the lessee sustained as a result of the transfer." LA. CIV. CODE art. 2712. This article recognizes that the lessor whose transfer of the leased thing caused the lessee to lose peaceful possession has breached the lessor's warranty obligation to the lessee under Louisiana Civil Code Article 2700 (discussed in more detail in Chapter 14: The Obligations of the Lessor and the Lessee).

b. Transfer of Interest in the Lease

As delineated above, when a lessor transfers the leased thing to another, the lease remains enforceable between the lessor and the lessee. However, because the lease entails personal rather than real obligations, the lessor's rights and obligations in the lease do not pass with the thing to the transferee absent a contrary agreement between the transferee and the lessor. A transfer of the leased property that is not accompanied by a transfer of the lessor's interest in the lease may result in a difficult situation for the lessor, lessee, and third person. For one thing, the third person — now owner of the property — is not entitled to collect the rent under the contract of lease because the third person is not a party to that contract. Nonetheless, property law provides that the owner of a thing is entitled to natural and civil fruits of the thing — like, for example, rent. *See* La. Civ. Code art. 483. This means that contractually, the lessee must pay rent to the lessor, but the lessor, per property law, must turn over the rent to the transferee. Further, although the lessor is now obligated to pay rent to the transferee, the lessor — not the transferee — remains bound to perform the obligations of the lessor (which, as is discussed in Chapter 14: The Obligations of the Lessor and the Lessee, may be extensive). Thus, oftentimes, the lessor who transfers the leased thing will also transfer his or her interest in the contract of lease — both his or her *rights* and *duties* under the lease — to the transferee.

Transfer of the lessor's *rights* under the lease requires a conventional subrogation. Recall that conventional subrogation may be accomplished either through an agreement between the obligor and the third person or between the obligee and the third person. *See* La. Civ. Code arts. 1827–28. In this context, conventional subrogation is accomplished through an agreement between the lessor (the obligee) and the third person who is acquiring ownership of the property subject to the lease. This conventional subrogation is governed by the rules on assignment of rights. *See* La. Civ. Code arts. 1827, 2642. The lessee is not required to consent to this agreement, *see* La. Civ. Code art. 1827, but it is not enforceable against the lessee until the lessee is given notice of it. *See* La. Civ. Code art. 2643. Thus, if the lessor's rights under the lease have been transferred to a third person without the lessee's knowledge, the lessee may continue to render performance to the original lessor (through the payment of rent or otherwise) until such time as the lessee is notified of the assignment of rights.

Transfer of the lessor's *duties* under the lease requires an assumption. Recall that assumption may occur in one of two ways: through an agreement between the obligor and the third person, or through an agreement between the obligee and a third person. *See* La. Civ. Code arts. 1821, 1823. The most common method by which the lessor's obligations are transferred to another is through an agreement between the lessor and a third person who is purchasing the leased thing. To be enforceable by the *lessee* against the third person, the assumption must be made in writing. La. Civ. Code art. 1821. However, the assumption need not be written to be enforceable between the *lessor* and the third person. Moreover, the lessee need not consent to the assumption for it to be enforceable between the lessor and the third person, and the lessee's consent does not release the lessor, unless the lessee agrees to a novation. *Id.* Significantly, the unreleased lessor remains solidarily bound with the new lessor. *Id.* Thus, unless the lessee consents to a substitution of the transferee for the original lessor, *both* the original lessor and the transferee are bound to perform the lessor's obligations.

Recall that an assumption differs from a "subject to" clause (discussed above) in that a third person who assumes the contract of lease becomes a lessor under the lease, while a third person who merely purchases a leased thing "subject to" a lease, though precluded from evicting the lessee, is not otherwise bound by the contract of lease.

A final note on transfer of the lease relates to terminology. In practice, the transfer of a lease is commonly referred to as an "assignment" of the lease. While legally speaking an "assignment" would transfer only the lessor's rights in the lease, assignment agreements nearly always include not only a conventional assignment of rights, but also language by which the third person assumes the lessor's obligations under the lease. Typically, the parties specify that while the third person is bound to the lessor's obligations from the time of the agreement, the third person is not responsible for any default of the original lessor that occurred prior to the assignment of rights. *See, e.g.,* 2 Peter S. Title, Louisiana Practice Series, Louisiana Real Estate Transactions § 18:111 (2017–18 ed.).

2. By Lessee

Because the lessee has no ownership right in the leased thing, the only transfer that may be made by the lessee is the transfer of his or her interest in the contract of lease. Unless the parties to the lease agree otherwise, the lessee may sublease the leased thing or assign or encumber his or her rights in the lease. La. Civ. Code art. 2713. The article contemplates three different transfers of the lessee's interest: a sublease, an assignment, and an encumbrance.

A sublease envisions a situation whereby the lessor leases the thing to the lessee, and then the lessee leases the same thing to another person. Once the lessee subleases the interest in the lease to another, two different contracts of lease exist: one between the lessor and lessee (the original lease) and one between the lessee and the third person (the sublease under which the lessee of the original lease is the sublessor and the third person is the sublessee). Under the original lease, the lessor and the lessee are entitled to rights and obligations; the same is true of the sublessor and sublessee under the sublease. However, the lessor and the sublessee are not in privity of contract with one another; thus, neither is entitled to any contractual rights or owes any contractual obligations vis-à-vis the other.

An assignment of the lessee's interest in the lease, in contrast, envisions a situation whereby the lessee transfers both rights and obligations in the original lease to a third person. Although Article 2713 refers to this arrangement as an "assignment," legally speaking, both an assignment of the lessee's rights in the lease (i.e., conventional subrogation), and an assumption of the lessee's duties takes place. Under this arrangement, the assignee steps into the shoes of the lessee, such that the lessor and the assignee are in privity of contract. The assignee's assumption of the obligations of the lease is enforceable by the original lessor as long as the agreement is in writing. *See* La. Civ. Code art. 1821. And, the assignment of the original lessee's rights to the assignee is effective against the original lessor upon notice. Importantly, when an assignment occurs, both the original lessee and the assignee are solidarily bound as obligors under the lease. *See* La. Civ. Code art. 1823.

An encumbrance is typically a situation where the lessee mortgages his or her interest in the lease to a creditor as security for a debt. In the event the lessee defaults on that debt, the creditor may seize and sell the lessee's interest in the lease.

These three rights are allowed as a matter of suppletive law, but the parties may expressly prohibit them. LA. CIV. CODE art. 2713. In the event that the parties prohibit one of these rights, the provision doing so will be deemed to prohibit the others as well. *Id.* In all other respects, any provision prohibiting one of these rights will be strictly construed against the lessor. *Id.*

Note, also, that the doctrine of abuse of rights has been raised in connection with the parties' ability, per Article 2713, to prohibit the lessee from subleasing, assigning, or encumbering the lease interest. The abuse of rights doctrine provides that the holder of a right "may not exercise that right to the detriment of another simply for the sake of exercising it." *Lilawanti Enterprises, Inc. v. Walden Book Co., Inc.*, 670 So. 2d 558, 561 (La. App. 4 Cir. 1996). The doctrine is "applied only in limited circumstances because its application renders unenforceable one's otherwise judicially protected rights." *Truschinger v. Pak*, 513 So. 2d 1151, 1154 (La. 1987). The genesis of this civil law doctrine is French jurisprudence and doctrine, and it has been recognized in numerous civil law jurisdictions. The Louisiana Supreme Court recognized it expressly for the first time in the 1977 case of *Morse v. J. Ray McDermott & Co., Inc.*, 344 So. 2d 1353 (La. 1977), and the following case illustrates its application in the context of Article 2713.

Illinois Central Gulf Railroad Co. v. International Harvester Co.

368 So. 2d 1009 (La. 1979)

DENNIS, Justice.

In this case we are called upon to decide two principal issues: Did the lessor by its silence and acceptance of rentals under the circumstances of this case impliedly consent to a sublease and a modification of the lease clause restricting the tenant's use and occupation of the premises? Should the court, by applying the doctrine of abuse of rights to the facts of this case, refuse to enforce the lessor's right under the lease contract to withhold permission from the lessee to enter a sublease with a third party?

Illinois Central Gulf Railroad Company (Illinois Central) leased two contiguous parcels of land on Poydras Street in New Orleans to International Harvester Company (Harvester) in 1960 and 1961 for the continued operation of a truck sales and service business which it had established on the same site in 1936. The lease contracts provided that the leases would terminate in 1986. Between 1971 and 1975 the Louisiana Superdome was constructed directly across the street from the leased premises. Consequently, the market value of the property subject to the leases increased in value significantly. Harvester constructed a new building on the leased premises in 1972 but moved its sales and service business from the property in 1974.

On January 17, 1975 Harvester requested Illinois Central's permission to sublease the premises 1601 Poydras Corporation for use as a parking garage. Illinois Central refused and counter-proposed that the leases be cancelled. Harvester once again requested permission to sublease but ultimately offered to cancel the leases for a cash payment. Several months later, on August 27, 1975, Harvester subleased the premises to 1601 Poydras Corporation without notice to Illinois Central. The sublease contract was not recorded until almost nine months after its confection. In September, 1975 Illinois Central's real estate manager learned that a public parking business was being operated on the premises. In October of 1975 the Illinois Central real estate manager wrote Harvester and, without referring to the parking operation, requested a conference for the purpose of reaching an amicable solution without litigation. Harvester replied by letter within a few days tacitly refusing to confer and stating its intention to continue with the leases. Following this exchange of letters there was no communication between the parties for approximately sixteen months during which Illinois Central continued to accept monthly rent payments from Harvester. In March of 1977 one of Illinois Central's officers complained by telephone to Harvester about a problem existing on the leased premises. Harvester responded by letter on April 21, 1977 that because it had been denied consent to sublease it was continuing to operate under the terms and conditions of the lease.

After further discussions and unsuccessful settlement negotiations Illinois Central filed this eviction suit in December, 1977, and deposited in court all rents received after November 23, 1977. Illinois Central alleged that Harvester had violated the lease contracts by subletting the premises without the lessor's written consent and by using the premises for purposes not authorized by the leases. After trial of the summary proceeding, the district court rendered judgment ordering Harvester to vacate the premises, remove all improvements and deliver possession to Illinois Central. The court of appeal reversed the judgment holding that Illinois Central's silence for sixteen months and acceptance of rental payments for twenty-six months after gaining knowledge of the operation of a parking business on the premises constituted a waiver of its rights under the leases to reject the sublease and to restrict the use of the property. *Illinois Central Gulf Railroad Company v. International Harvester Company,* 360 So.2d 628 (La.App. 4th Cir. 1978). We granted a writ of certiorari to consider the issues of law raised by the court of appeal opinion.

The leases between Illinois Central and Harvester, in pertinent part, provide:

> "It is further agreed by the Lessee, that said premises shall be used and occupied exclusively as a site for (a motor truck sales and service station and warehouse) (a storage space).
>
> "* * *
>
> "It is further agreed by the Lessee, not to underlet said premises, or any part thereof, or assign this Lease, without the written consent of the Lessor, first had and obtained."

The contract further provided that, upon the lessee's default in keeping any agreement, the lessor would have the right to terminate the lease.

Implied Consent to Modify Leases

It is uncontroverted that Harvester did not obtain written or express consent before subletting the premises and converting it to a parking garage. The court of appeal, however, found that Illinois Central, by its silence and inaction, had impliedly assented to the sublease and altered use of the premises. The intermediate court's treatment of the issue raises the question of whether a lessor's mere silence in the face of proposals and actions contrary to the lease contract by his lessee constitutes assent to the modification of the contract.

Every contract or modification of a previously concluded agreement requires the concurrence of the consent of the parties. La.C.C. arts. 1766 [No Corresponding Article], 1779(2) [No Corresponding Article], 1798 [R.C.C. 1927]. Consent results from a free and deliberate exercise of the will of each party where the intent has been mutually communicated or implied, La.C.C. art. 1819 [R.C.C. 1934, 1948], and accepted by the party to whom a proposal is made. La.C.C. arts. 1798 [R.C.C. 1927], 1800 [No Corresponding Article].

Consent may be given either expressly or by implication, La.C.C. arts. 1780 [No Corresponding Article], 1811 [No Corresponding Article], but the cases in which consent is implied are particularly determined by law. La.C.C. art. 1781 [No Corresponding Article]. According to the civil code, consent may be implied in the following instances:

> "... when it is manifested by actions, even by silence or by inaction, in cases in which they can from the circumstances be supposed to mean, or by legal presumption are directed to be considered as evidence of an assent." La.C.C. art. 1811 [No Corresponding Article].

> "* * *

> "(W)hen (actions without words) are done under circumstances that naturally imply a consent to such contract ...." La.C.C. art. 1816 [R.C.C. 1927]. See also, La.C.C. art. 1817 [R.C.C. 1927, 1942].

Thus, except in those instances in which the statutory law creates a legal presumption, the mere silence of an offeree should not, in principle, be considered as involving acceptance on his part. His consent can result from silence, however, when combined with other facts or acts so as to imply or indicate his consent unequivocally. 1 Civil Law Translations Aubry & Rau, Obligations, s 343, p. 307 (1965). See, *Governor Claiborne Apartments, Inc. v. Attaldo,* 256 La. 218, 235 So.2d 574 (1970). In cases where the law does not expressly create a legal presumption of consent from certain facts, it is left to the discretion of the judge to determine if consent is to be implied from the particular circumstances of the case. La.C.C. art. 1818 [No Corresponding Article]; *Pooler Bldg. Mats. Inc. v. Hogan,* 244 So.2d 62 (La.App. 1st Cir. 1971).

The civil code and statutes do not provide that any legal presumption of consent shall arise from a lessor's silence and acceptance of rent. Compare, e.g., La.C.C. arts.

2295 [R.C.C. 2292-2293], 2688-89 [R.C.C. 2721-2723], 2933 [R.C.C. 2927], 3145-46 [R.C.C. 3136, 3157]. Accordingly, the question to be resolved in this part of the case is essentially factual, i.e., whether the judge exercised sound discretion in determining that Illinois Central's consent to a modification of the lease contract was not unequivocally implied from its silence and inaction under the particular circumstances of the instant case. In his brief dictated reasons for judgment the trial judge found that there had been no showing of consent to the sublease and that Illinois Central's objections and attempts at amicable settlement negated its consent to allow the premises to be used as a parking garage.

We agree with the trial judge's conclusions. There is no showing that Illinois Central unequivocally consented to modify the leases so as to permit a sublease to 1601 Poydras Corporation or to allow the operation of a parking garage on the premises. On the contrary, Illinois Central declined Harvester's proposal for such an amendment of the leases and offered instead to cancel the leases. Harvester's requests for Illinois Central's permission, followed by Harvester's alternative offer to cancel the leases for a cash payment, show that the will of the parties had not united on a modification of the leases. The acceptance of rentals and delay in filing eviction proceedings by the railroad company were not necessarily inconsistent with an intent to enforce the leases as written. Although disputed, there is evidence of record that Illinois Central had no definite knowledge until shortly before filing suit that Harvester had entered a sublease. The fact that Illinois Central, like Harvester, was a large corporation headquartered in Chicago, with extensive national real estate holdings tends to indicate that its delay was due to lack of information and inattention rather than its assent to a modification of the leases. Illinois Central presented testimony from its officers that there was never an intention to accept any modification of the contracts permitting a sublease to 1601 Poydras Corporation or the operation of a parking business on the premises. They attributed the railroad company's lengthy delay and silence to a combination of factors including changes in corporate management, the large number of leases under management, and the desire to avoid litigation. The trial judge apparently found these witnesses to be credible. Considering that he heard and saw the witnesses and that the other circumstances of the case do not unequivocally indicate that the railroad consented to a modification of the leases, we conclude that the trial judge exercised sound discretion in finding that Illinois Central's consent was not to be implied from the evidence of the case.

Harvester has cited a number of decisions in support of its argument that Illinois Central condoned its violations of the lease contracts by accepting rent for many months after learning of the parking garage operation on the premises. *Arms v. Rodriguez*, 232 La. 951, 95 So.2d 616 (1957); *Canal Realty & Improvement Co. v. Pailet*, 217 La. 376, 46 So.2d 303 (1950); *Trichel v. Donovan*, 138 La. 985, 71 So. 130 (1916); *Blanchard v. Shrimp Boats of Louisiana, Inc.*, 305 So.2d 748 (La.App. 4th Cir. 1974); *Moore v. Bannister*, 269 So.2d 291 (La.App. 4th Cir. 1972); *Major v. Hall*, 251 So.2d 444 (La.App. 1st Cir. 1971); *Jourdan v. Randall*, 190 So.2d 469 (La.App. 1st Cir.

13 · THE NATURE AND ESSENTIAL ELEMENTS OF THE CONTRACT OF LEASE 621

1966). In these cases the appellate courts made factual determinations that the lessor either impliedly consented to a modification of the lease or forgave a breach of the lease. However, a factual determination relating to a party's intention or consent in a particular case, even by an appellate court, does not establish a rule of law for other cases. We interpret the authorities relied upon by Harvester as holdings based on the same legal principles as the instant opinion but reaching different results founded upon different evidentiary records. The appellate opinions in those cases, and the opinion in the instant case, should not be construed as creating legal presumptions of consent beyond those set forth in the civil code or other statutes. It is the function of the legislature to formulate new legal presumptions. The proper role of the court, in cases where statutory legal presumptions are not applicable, is to determine if consent is to be implied from the particular circumstances of the case. La.C.C. arts. 1811 [No Corresponding Article], 1818 [No Corresponding Article].

Accordingly, we conclude that the court of appeal erred in reversing the trial court's finding of fact with respect to whether the lessor impliedly consented to the sublease or the change in use of the premises.

Abuse of Lessor's Right to Withhold Permission to Sublease

Harvester contends alternatively that, if Illinois Central did not consent to its sublease to 1601 Poydras Corporation, the lessor's exercise of its right to withhold its consent was abusive under the facts of the instant case and therefore should not be enforced judicially.

Article 2725 [R..C.C. 2713] of the Louisiana Civil Code provides that the lessor may by contract prohibit the lessee from entering a sublease:

"The lessee has the right to underlease, or even to cede his lease to another person, unless this power has been expressly interdicted.

"The interdiction may be for the whole, or for a part; and this clause is always construed strictly."

The article is not clear as to whether a clause expressly interdicting the lessee's right to sublease is to be construed strictly for or against the lessee. However, this Court has said that "(t)he language is taken literally from the Napoleon Code; and the interpretation which it appears to have uniformly received in France . . . is that the prohibition must be construed strictly against the lessee." *Cordeviolle v. Redon*, 4 La.Ann. 40 (1849).

Harvester points out, however, that the leases in the instant case do not absolutely prohibit subleasing but merely require the prior written consent of the lessor. Consequently, Harvester contends, Illinois Central's refusal of consent should not be judicially enforced if in light of all the circumstances it was an abusive exercise of the lessor's contractual right. See, 2 Colin et Capitant, Droit civil Francais, No. 1041 at 690 (10th ed. 1948); Josserand D.P. 1923.2.172.

This Court expressly recognized the doctrine of abuse of rights in *Morse v. J. Ray McDermott & Co., Inc.*, 344 So.2d 1353 (La.1977), and has employed a similar analysis in earlier decisions. *Higgins Oil & Fuel Co. v. Guaranty Oil Co.*, 145 La. 233, 82 So. 206 (1919); *Onorato v. Maestri*, 173 La. 375, 137 So. 67 (1931).

Nevertheless, the doctrine of abuse of rights has been invoked sparingly in Louisiana and we must look to other civilian jurisdictions for its full articulation. The doctrine is the product of a French jurisprudential and doctrinal movement which has expanded into most of the civil law jurisdictions "to the point of becoming a widely accepted principle of the Civil Law." Cueto-Rua, *Abuse of Rights*, 35 La.L.Rev. 965, 967 (1975). See, generally, Catala and Weir, *Delict and Torts: A Study in Parallel (Part II)*, 38 Tul.L.Rev. 221 (1964); Herman, *Classical Social Theories and the Doctrine of Abuse of Right*, 37 La.L.Rev. 747 (1977); Maynard, *Abuse of Rights in France and Quebec*, 34 La.L.Rev. 993 (1974); Comment, 7 Tul.L.Rev. 426 (1933). The main body of French case law on abuse of rights is based on article 1382 of the French Civil Code, which is very similar in wording to article 2315 of the Louisiana Civil Code. In its origin, the abuse of rights doctrine was applied to prevent the holder of rights or powers from exercising those rights exclusively for the purpose of harming another, but today most courts in civil law jurisdictions will find an act abusive if the predominant motive for it was to cause harm. See, Cueto-Rua, *supra*, at 990-91; Catala and Weir, *supra*, at 222-26. The doctrine has been applied where an intent to harm was not proven, if it was shown that there was no serious and legitimate interest in the exercise of the right worthy of judicial protection. See, Cueto-Rua, *supra*, at 992-96; Catala and Weir, *supra*, at 230-34. Protection or enforcement of a right has been denied when the exercise of the right is against moral rules, good faith or elementary fairness. See, Cueto-Rua, *supra*, at 996-99. Another criteria, espoused originally by the French scholar Louis Josserand, would require an examination of the purpose for which the right was granted. If the holder of the right exercised the right for a purpose other than that for which the right was granted, then he may have abused the right. See, Cueto-Rua, *supra*, at 1000-1003; Catala and Weir, *supra*, at 227-29; Herman, *supra*, at 754-55.

The foregoing principles seem to be the main criteria which have been formulated for applying the abuse of rights doctrine. These tests have met with varying degrees of acceptance in the civil law jurisdictions, and it should be kept in mind that the entire doctrine is in a state of flux. As Professor Cueto-Rua observes:

> " * * * The doctrine of abuse of rights is in the making, it is 'in fieri.' It is an important juridical-political element of modern civil law doctrine. Although there are still pending important questions concerning its scope as well as criteria for the definition of abusive use of rights, this we may safely say now: it will be difficult for a holder of an individual right, in most of the civil law jurisdictions today, to exercise such right to the detriment of other parties, just for the sheer sake of exercising it. At least a 'serious and legitimate interest' will have to be shown in order to justify the exercise of its right."

After evaluating the conduct of the parties in the present case under the jurisprudential and doctrinal tests, we conclude that judicial enforcement of Illinois

Central's right to withhold permission for the sublease and change of use proposed by Harvester would not sanction an abuse of right. Illinois Central did not withhold its consent with a predominant intent to harm Harvester. Instead, the record reflects that it refused to grant permission for the purpose of attempting to negotiate a cancellation of the leases with Harvester. The railroad company's motive and intent were openly and honestly stated in its reply to Harvester's sublease proposal:

> "Land values have risen so dramatically since the renewal of these leases that we are now receiving an inequitable rental compared to the present day market.
>
> "In view of the existing conditions, rather than approve a sublease, we suggest as an alternative cancellation of both agreements subject to the terms contained in each."

Since the property involved has greatly appreciated in value, reducing rental revenues to an inadequate level, Illinois Central's withholding of its immediate consent to a sublease for purposes of negotiating a cancellation was certainly based on a serious and legitimate motive.

Moreover, it cannot be said that Illinois Central's refusal to consent to the sublease was adamant or irrevocable; and it does not appear that Harvester was insistent upon its request for permission. Harvester wrote two letters seeking its lessor's consent to the parking lot sublease, but in a third letter it offered to cancel the leases for a cash settlement of $69,886. From these letters it appears that Illinois Central could not have withheld its consent for more than ninety-eight days, and the record reflects that the parties' oral negotiations had shifted from sublease to cancellation much earlier. After this, Harvester never again requested permission to sublease; nor did it seek judicial relief from Illinois Central's alleged abusive conduct. Instead, during the time that its offer to cancel the leases apparently was still open, Harvester entered a sublease with 1601 Poydras Corporation without further notice to its lessor.

We cannot say that Illinois Central exercised its right to withhold consent to a sublease for a purpose other than that for which it was granted. The record is devoid of evidence of the parties' intention in placing the clause in the leases. It cannot be assumed that the lessor merely sought by the clause to protect itself against an objectionable subtenant. The parties likely would have limited the interdiction to subleases with objectionable sublessees if this had been the lessor's only concern. Moreover, in the instant case, the lessee sought to do more than merely substitute an acceptable subtenant for itself; it sought as well to change the use of the premises from a truck retail outlet to a parking garage. Furthermore, Josserand's purpose-of-the-right test has not been generally accepted in the civil law jurisdictions. Cueto-Rua, *supra*, at 1002-1005; Catala and Weir, *supra*, at 228.

The exercise of the right to withhold consent was plainly not against moral rules, good faith or elementary fairness. Nor did Illinois Central act without any regard for the interest of Harvester. The railroad company candidly disclosed its motives and intent, bargained in good faith, and offered significant concessions in an attempt to reach a settlement with Harvester.

In summary, we do not find that Illinois Central's conduct falls within any of the definitions of abusive use of rights. The withholding of consent to a sublease was for a relatively brief period of time, not done for the sheer sake of exercising the right, but done for the purpose of attempting to carry on actual good faith negotiations for cancellation of the lease, in which the lessor had a serious and legitimate interest under the circumstances, and the lessee did not pursue its rights vigorously by insisting on a sublease or by proceeding against the lessor judicially before violating the agreements of the lease.

Dissolution of the Leases

Finally, Harvester argues that the trial court abused its discretion by evicting the lessee under the circumstances of the instant case. It relies on Louisiana Civil Code article 2711 [R.C.C. 2686], which, in pertinent part, provides:

> "If the lessee makes another use of the thing than that for which it was intended, and if any loss is thereby sustained by the lessor, the latter may obtain the dissolution of the lease."

Under this article the dissolution of a lease because a tenant has put the premises to a use for which it was not intended requires a showing of loss by the lessor and rests within the discretion of the court. *New Orleans and Carrollton R. Co. v. Darms*, 39 La.Ann. 766, 2 So. 230 (1887); *Stoltz v. McConnell*, 202 So.2d 451 (La.App. 4th Cir.), Cert. denied, 251 La. 231, 203 So.2d 559 (1967); *Arbo v. Jankowski*, 39 So.2d 458 (La. App. Orl.Cir.1949). If unauthorized use of the premises were the only basis for dissolution proven in the instant case we might agree that a less drastic remedy would be more appropriate.

However, the sublease from Harvester to 1601 Poydras Corporation was in violation of clauses contained in the leases expressly prohibiting underletting without the lessor's prior consent. The right to demand a dissolution of the lease is given reciprocally to landlord and tenant if either violates the contract. La.C.C. art. 2729 [R.C.C. 2719]. Unlike the right to dissolve a lease under La.C.C. art. 2711 [R.C.C. 2686] for use of the premises for an unintended purpose, Article 2729 [R.C.C. 2719] does not require a showing of actual damage, and our courts have fully enforced the lessor's right to dissolve the lease for subletting the premises in contravention of the contract of lease. *Bryan v. French*, 20 La.Ann. 366 (1868); *Cordeviolle v. Redon*, 4 La.Ann. 40 (1849); *Reed v. Ross*, 12 La.App. 619, 126 So. 923 (2d Cir. 1930). Accordingly, we conclude that the trial judge did not abuse his discretion but reached the correct result in dissolving the leases.

For the reasons assigned, the judgment of the court of appeal is reversed and the judgment of the trial court is reinstated at the cost of the defendant.

REVERSED: JUDGMENT OF TRIAL COURT REINSTATED.

MARCUS, J., dissents and assigns reasons.

MARCUS, Justice (dissenting).

Under the facts of this case, I consider that Illinois Central impliedly consented to the sublease and change in the use of the premises. Accordingly, I respectfully dissent.

Notes and Questions

1. According to the Louisiana Supreme Court in the *Illinois Central Railroad* case, what are the "main criteria" for applying the abuse of rights doctrine?

2. Why did the Court hold that Illinois Central Railroad had not abused its contractual right to withhold consent to the sublease? What did the Court find to be Illinois Central Railroad's motives in withholding consent to the sublease?

3. A number of abuse of rights claims asserted by lessees in connection with Article 2713 have failed because the lessor has succeeded in showing economic reasons for the withholding of consent to a sublease. *See, e.g.*, *Lilawanti Enterprises, Inc. v. Walden Book Co.*, 670 So. 2d 558 (La. App. 4 Cir. 1996); *Truschinger v. Pak*, 513 So. 2d 1151 (La. 1987).

4. Note that some leases provide that the while the lessee may not sublease without consent of the lessor, the lessor may not "unreasonably" withhold consent. This was the situation presented in *Caplan v. Latter & Blum, Inc.*, 468 So. 2d 1188 (La. 1985). In this case, Dr. Caplan withheld consent to a sublease in order to negotiate a new lease with Latter & Blum on more favorable terms. Although this is precisely the factual scenario in *Illinois Central* (in which the Louisiana Supreme Court held that the lessor did not abuse its rights), the Court ruled to the contrary in *Caplan* (finding the lessor did abuse its rights) because the withholding was "unreasonable." The Court explained that while the facts were the same, it reached a different conclusion in *Caplan* because the lessee "had guarded against that contingency [that the lessor would withhold consent to the sublease] by the insert in the printed lease form which prohibited Dr. Caplan from unreasonably withholding his consent to an underlease." *Id.* at 1191.

Chapter 14

Obligations of the Lessor and the Lessee

A. Introduction

La. Civ. Code arts. 2682–2683

The Civil Code sets forth a number of "principal obligations" owed by the lessor and the lessee. According to Article 2682, the lessor owes three principal obligations: "(1) [t]o deliver the thing to the lessee; (2) [t]o maintain the thing in a condition suitable for the purpose for which it was leased; and (3) [t]o protect the lessee's peaceful possession for the duration of the lease." LA. CIV. CODE art. 2682. Under Article 2683, the lessee, in turn, is bound: "(1) [t]o pay the rent in accordance with the agreed terms; (2) [t]o use the thing as a prudent administrator and in accordance with the purpose for which it was leased; and (3) [t]o return the thing at the end of the lease in a condition that is the same as when it was delivered to him, except for normal wear or as otherwise provided [by law]." LA. CIV. CODE art. 2683. This Chapter will explore each of these obligations in detail.

The obligations above are implied by suppletive law, meaning they arise in every lease by default. Some, but not all, of the obligations of the parties may be modified by contract. The extent to which the obligations of the parties may be altered by the parties' agreement is a matter of fundamental importance. As will be shown in the materials that follow, the parties' contractual freedom is not governed by a single set of rules; rather, the matter of contractual modification of the default regime must be studied on an obligation-by-obligation basis.

The consequences of the parties' failure to perform their obligations are governed by the law of conventional obligations. As you will recall, when a party to a contract fails to perform any obligation—whether arising from suppletive law or the parties' contract—this may lead to dissolution, either judicial or extrajudicial. See LA. CIV. CODE arts. 2719, 2013–2024. Depending upon the circumstances, specific performance may be appropriate in lieu of dissolution. See LA. CIV. CODE arts. 1986–1988. In either case, the party who fails to perform may be liable for damages. See LA. CIV. CODE arts. 1994–2003. The consequences of the parties' failure to perform their obligations are explored both in this Chapter and in Chapter 15: Termination and Dissolution of the Lease.

B. The Lessor's Obligations

1. To Deliver

La. Civ. Code arts. 2684–2685

The first principal obligation of the lessor is to "deliver the thing to the lessee." LA. CIV. CODE art. 2682(1). As provided by Article 2684: "The lessor is bound to deliver the thing at the agreed time and in good condition suitable for the purpose for which it was leased." LA. CIV. CODE art. 2684. Under this article, delivery consists of three distinct obligations: (1) delivering the agreed thing; (2) at the agreed time; and (3) in good condition. *See* LA. CIV. CODE art. 2684 cmt. b. Of these three obligations, the most frequently litigated is the lessor's obligation to deliver the thing "in good condition." The following case presents an example of a dispute involving this issue.

Hinds v. Poo-Yies Inc.

520 So. 2d 1016 (La. App. 3 Cir. 1987)

DOMENGEAUX, Judge.

Cyril Hinds and Helen L. Hinds, as lessors of the property located at 4300 Johnston Street in Lafayette, Louisiana, instituted these proceedings against Poo-Yie's, Inc. to recover rent, interest and taxes allegedly due under a written lease agreement. The Hinds named as additional defendants: (1) Herbert Hebert; and (2) Louis Bordelon. Hebert and Bordelon were stockholders in Poo-Yie's and had executed personal guarantees in favor of the lessors guaranteeing the obligations of the corporation.

At trial, the parties orally stipulated to the amount of rent, interest, taxes and attorney's fees due. The parties agreed that the rent, $2,350.00 per month, had not been paid for the period July 1, 1984 to November 10, 1984 and that the total amount unpaid was $12,533.00. The parties stipulated that $1,467.00 in interest was unpaid as of November 10, 1984 and that according to the lease, interest was to accrue subsequent to November 10, 1984, at the rate of twelve percent per annum. The parties concluded their stipulations by stating that the lessees had not paid taxes due under the lease in the amount of $2,715.42 and that the lease provided for attorney's fees of twenty-five percent should the services of an attorney become necessary to enforce performance.

Subsequent to entering the stipulations into the record, Cyril Hinds took the witness stand. Hinds' testimony authenticated the lease exhibited to the court by his attorney. The plaintiffs, thereafter, moved for the introduction of the lease into evidence and then rested their case relying solely on the stipulations and the lease agreement.

The defendants rebutted the plaintiff's case-in-chief by presenting evidence that the leased premises were in need of repair at the commencement of the lease and that according to La.Civ.Code art. 2694 (1870) [R.C.C. 2694] they were entitled to a credit up to the cost of the repairs. The defendants called to testify in support of their case: (1) Hebert, one of the owners of Poo-Yie's; (2) Chester Alleman, an electrician who had performed electrical repair work; (3) Kenneth Bernard, a plumber who had undertaken plumbing repairs; and (4) Robert Mashburn, the tenant who had immediately preceded Poo-Yie's in the premises. Testimony by the witnesses established that at the commencement of the lease, the premises were in need of considerable electrical, plumbing, flooring and roofing repairs.

The trial court rendered judgment in favor of the plaintiff-lessors and against the defendants, Poo-Yie's, Hebert and Bordelon, in solido, in the amount of $15,248.42, with interest accruing at the rate of twelve percent per annum from November 10, 1984 until paid and attorney's fees of twenty-five percent. The court then rendered judgment in favor of the defendant Poo-Yie's and against the lessors in the amount of $8,778.00. The trial judge in his reasons for judgment concluded that the repairs made by the defendant corporation were indispensable, that it had paid a reasonable price for the repairs and that the lessee was entitled to deduct the cost of the repairs from the rent.

The lessors have appealed and assign four errors. The lessors contend: (1) the trial court incorrectly interpreted the lease when it concluded that the lessors had not waived the obligation of delivering the premises in good condition and free from repairs; (2) the trial court erred in permitting the defendants to violate the parol evidence rule by allowing the introduction of testimony which varied the terms of the lease; (3) the trial court erred in permitting the defendants to expand the pleadings at trial, over objection, to include testimony addressing the condition of the leased premises at the commencement of the lease; and (4) the trial court erred when it determined that the lessee had given proper notice of the need for the repairs to the lessors prior to undertaking the repair work and deducting the cost of the repairs from the rent.

The lessors' initial issue on appeal calls into question the trial court's interpretation of the lease agreement. The lessors submit that they expressly waived the implied obligation of La.Civ.Code art. 2693 (1870) [R.C.C. 2684] to "deliver the thing in good condition and free from any repair." They cite the following lease provisions in support of their position:

VII.

(a) It is the intention of the lessor and the lessee that the rent herein specified during both terms of this lease shall be net to the landlord in each year during the term of this lease, that all costs, expenses, obligations of every kind relating to the leased property except as otherwise specifically provided in this lease which may arise or become due during the term of this lease shall be paid by the lessee and that the lessor shall be indemnified by the lessee against such costs, expenses and obligations.

(b) The lessee shall at his own expense make all necessary repairs, and replacements to the leased property and to the pipes, heating and cooling systems, plumbing system, window glass, fixtures and all other appliances and appurtenances belonging to or used in connection with the leased premises. The lessor shall be responsible for repairs to the roof and foundation caused by normal deterioration. Lessor shall not be responsible for repairs to the roof or foundation caused by fire, wind, storm or other casualty. Should lessee desire to insure against such causes, at its sole cost and expense Lessor agrees to participate in obtaining but not in paying for such insurance.

and

X.

(a) Lessor will not be responsible for damage caused by leaks in the roof, by bursting of pipes, by freezing or otherwise, or by any vice or defects of the leased property or the consequences thereof except in the case of positive neglect or failure to take action toward the remedying of such defects within reasonable time after having written notice from lessee of such defects and the damage caused thereby. Should lessee fail to promptly so notify lessor in writing of any such defect, lessee will become responsible for any damage resulting to lessor or other parties.

We have read the lease in its entirety and applying the Civil Code articles governing the interpretation of contracts, La.Civ.Code arts. 2045 et seq., we do not believe that the trial court erred.

The cardinal rule of contractual interpretation is to endeavor to ascertain the intentions of the parties at the moment the agreement was executed. La.Civ.Code art. 2045 (1984). We are unable to conclude from our review of the agreement that the lessors were relieved of their obligation to deliver the premises in good condition and free from repairs. We believe that a more correct interpretation of the lease is that the lessee only assumed the obligation of making specific repairs which might become necessary during the term of the lease.

Analogous to the instant case is the First Circuit decision in *Moity v. Guillory*, 430 So.2d 1243 (La.App. 1st Cir.1983), *writ denied*, 437 So.2d 1148 (La.1983). The court in *Moity* held, inter alia, that "[a]lthough the lessee assumed the obligation to maintain the leased premises after the lease commenced, such contractual provisions did not relieve the lessor of his responsibility for defects in the premises which existed prior to the commencement of the lease." *Id.* at 1246.

* * * * *

In the final issue raised on appeal, the lessors contend that the lessee failed to provide them with notice of the needed repairs as required by article 2694 [R.C.C. 2694]. La.Civ.Code art. 2694 [R.C.C. 2694], *supra*, provides in its entirety:

> *If the lessor do not make the necessary repairs* in the manner required in the preceding article, *the lessee may call on him to make them.* If he refuse or neglect to make them, the lessee may himself cause them to be made, and

deduct the price from the rent due, on proving that the repairs were indispensable, and that the price which he has paid was just and reasonable. (Emphasis added).

The trial judge, in awarding the lessee a credit on the rent due for the repairs made, concluded that the lessees had given the lessors notice of the needed repairs. Subsequent to our review of the record, we are unable to entirely agree.

Our review indicates that the lessors were only apprised of the need to repair the roof and the floor. The record does not reveal that they were ever informed of the need to repair the electrical wiring or the plumbing.

Hebert repeatedly stated that the lessors were informed of all the necessary repairs prior to the work being undertaken. He stated, however, that he only spoke with Cyril Hinds about the roof and the floor. Hebert continuously attempted, over the lessors' hearsay objections, to state that Bordelon informed the lessors of the need to repair the plumbing and electrical wiring. The trial judge correctly sustained the lessors' objections.

Despite Hebert's allegations that Bordelon notified the lessors of the needed repairs, Bordelon did not take the witness stand. It can only be presumed from Bordelon's unexplained absence from trial that his testimony would have been unfavorable. *Clifton Upholstery Company v. Kayjun Industries, Inc.,* 254 So.2d 514 (La.App. 3rd Cir.1971), and *Gulf States Utilities Company v. Guidry,* 183 So.2d 122 (La.App. 4th Cir.1986).

We must, therefore, amend the lower court judgment. Poo-Yie's is only entitled to a credit of $729.00 on the rent due, $514.00 for roofing repairs and $215.00 for flooring repairs.

Accordingly, the judgment of the district court is amended so as to reduce the award in favor of the lessee, Poo-Yie's to the sum of $729.00. In all other respects the judgment of the district court is affirmed.

Costs on appeal are assessed 80% to defendants-lessee and 20% to plaintiffs-lessors.

AFFIRMED AS AMENDED.

Notes and Questions

1. The Civil Code does not define the precise contours of whether a thing delivered is in "good condition suitable for the purpose for which it was leased." Whether the lessor has complied with the obligation to deliver is a question of fact that must be determined by reference to the purpose for which the thing was leased, whether as expressly set forth in the lease or as implied by the nature or destination of the thing itself. *See* LA. CIV. CODE art. 2684 cmt. b.

2. The lessor's obligation to deliver the thing in "good condition" is a matter of suppletive law that may be altered by the parties' agreement. For example, where the need for repairs is apparent and the lessee takes the thing "as is," a court will

find that the lessor owes no obligation with respect to those items of repair. George M. Armstrong, Jr., Louisiana Landlord and Tenant Law § 7.21 (1992). (Note, however, that if the leased property is not merely in need of repair but suffers from "vices or defects" then the lessor's obligations are much harder to modify or exclude. *See infra* Subpart B.2.) The lease in *Hinds* contained language indicating that the lessee assumed responsibility for making repairs to the leased premises. Why did the court find that the parties had *not* modified the lessor's obligation to deliver the thing?

3. In addition, the parties can modify the lessor's obligation to deliver the thing "at the agreed time," for example by providing that a delay in delivery of possession will entitle the lessee to a remission of the rent. *See Weil v. Segura*, 151 So. 639 (1933).

4. It seems axiomatic that while the parties may agree to modifications of the lessor's obligation to deliver the thing "in good condition" and "at the agreed time," the obligation of the lessor to deliver possession of the leased thing to the lessee is nonwaivable — the use and possession of the thing is the lessee's principal cause for contracting. *See* La. Civ. Code art. 2668.

5. When the leased thing is an immovable, one aspect of the obligation to deliver the agreed thing is a requirement that the lessor deliver the full extent of the immovable promised. According to Article 2685, "If the leased thing is an immovable and its extent differs from that which was agreed upon, the rights of the parties with regard to such discrepancy are governed by the provisions of the Title 'Sale.'" La. Civ. Code art. 2685. Recall that the seller's obligation to deliver the full extent of an immovable sold is governed by Articles 2491 through 2498. This obligation of the seller is addressed in detail in Chapter 8: Delivery.

2. To Maintain and Warrant Against Vices and Defects

The second principal obligation of the lessor is to "maintain the thing in a condition suitable for the purpose for which it was leased." La. Civ. Code art. 2682(2). This obligation of the lessor involves two closely related but distinct duties: (1) the obligation to make repairs that become necessary during the lease, and (2) the obligation to warrant that the thing is suitable for the purpose for which it was leased and that it is free of vices or defects that prevent its use for that purpose. Each of these duties will be explored in the subparts that follow.

a. Lessor's Responsibility for Repairs
La. Civ. Code arts. 2690–2694

The lessor's duty to maintain the leased thing principally involves the responsibility to make needed repairs to the leased thing for the duration of the lease. According to Article 2691, "During the lease, the lessor is bound to make all repairs that become necessary to maintain the thing in a condition suitable for the purpose for which it was leased, except those for which the lessee is responsible." La. Civ.

CODE art. 2691. The lessee, in turn, is obliged "to repair damage to the thing caused by his fault or that of persons who, with his consent, are on the premises or use the thing, and to repair any deterioration resulting from his or their use to the extent it exceeds the normal or agreed use of the thing." LA. CIV. CODE art. 2692. Thus, the lessee bears responsibility only for damage attributable to his or her own fault or that of persons accountable to him or her. All other repairs are, by default, the responsibility of the lessor.

If the lessor fails to make repairs that become necessary, the rights of the lessee are governed in part by the general law of conventional obligations, meaning that the lessee may seek dissolution of the lease or specific performance and damages. *See generally* LA. CIV. CODE arts. 1986–2024. In addition, the lessee enjoys a remedy made available by the Title on Lease which is known informally as "repair-and-deduct." Article 2694 provides:

> If the lessor fails to perform his obligation to make necessary repairs within a reasonable time after demand by the lessee, the lessee may cause them to be made. The lessee may demand immediate reimbursement of the amount expended for the repair or apply that amount to the payment of rent, but only to the extent that the repair was necessary and the expended amount reasonable.

LA. CIV. CODE art. 2694. Under this article, the lessee may have necessary repairs made and deduct from the rent the cost of making those repairs if three prerequisites are satisfied: (1) the lessor fails to make the repair within a reasonable time after demand by the lessee; (2) the repair was necessary; and (3) the amount spent by the lessee in making the repair was reasonable.

The following case addresses another important limitation on the lessee's right to repair-and-deduct.

Davilla v. Jones

436 So. 2d 507 (La. 1983)

DIXON, Chief Justice

Plaintiff lessor, Antoinette Davilla, filed a rule to evict defendant lessee, Lowell F. Jones, on September 23, 1981, alleging nonpayment of rent due. Defendant answered, asserting a right to withhold the rent in order to make necessary repairs to the property. The trial judge granted the rule to evict and the defendant took a suspensive appeal. The court of appeal reversed, 418 So.2d 724, finding that the dealings between this lessee and lessor relative to withholding the rent to make necessary wall repairs prevented the lessor from evicting the lessee. We granted lessor's application for writs. 422 So.2d 151 (La.1982).

Davilla and Jones signed a five year lease for part of a building at 333–335 Bourbon Street beginning in 1974, with an option to renew for five additional years. The monthly rent for the primary term was $500; the rent for the renewal period was

$720. The lease provided that the lessee was responsible for all maintenance and repairs, excluding the roof and exterior walls, which were the responsibility of the lessor.

On February 4, 1981 Jones wrote to Davilla complaining of continuing problems with water leakage through the roof and the exterior walls. The letter noted that lessee's previous requests to the lessor to repair the property remained unanswered and formally demanded that the repairs be made. The letter advised that if repairs were not commenced within two weeks, "we will have no choice but to move on our own to secure the proper repair of these premises, which are absolutely necessary, and to secure such repair at a reasonable cost. We will, in turn, deduct the cost of these expenses from such future rental as is necessary to reimburse our expenses herein."

Jones testified that in response to the letter, a roofing contractor, Mr. Shaw, was sent to the property at the lessor's request. He examined the building with the lessee and stated he could not give a firm price, but would quote to the lessor on a materials and labor basis only. Repairs were subsequently undertaken by Mr. Shaw with the roofing work completed in mid-April at a cost of $2500. Jones had not paid the rent due for March or for April. He testified:

> "When he got near the end of completion of the roofing work I said to the man, 'Now, let's get on the rest of the job.' And he said, 'I can't do the rest of the job. That's not my type of work.' And I said, 'Well, have you advised the lessor that you're not doing all of the work that needs to be done?', he said, 'Advise the lessor that I won't be able to do everything.'"

On April 22, 1981 Jones wrote Davilla saying that Mr. Shaw would not be completing the job and advising the lessor that he would continue to withhold the rent until enough was accumulated to employ his own contractor.

Discussions continued between Davilla and Jones concerning repairs to the exterior walls. At the same time, the tenant next door at 333 Bourbon (Ellwest Theatre) was also negotiating with Davilla. As part of those negotiations Ellwest agreed to pay the maintenance and repair costs for the entire 333–335 Bourbon Street building. On April 27, 1981 Jones wrote to Davilla acknowledging their telephone conversation:

> "As you requested, I will get in touch with one or more contractors for prices on the north wall maintenance work . . . I understand that you do not wish to get involved in this project beyond the work that you already have employed Mr. Shaw to do, and that you will convey to Ellwest for payment any invoice from any contractor."

The rent due for May was not paid. On May 21 Jones forwarded to Davilla an estimate of $30,850 he had obtained from a contractor to repair the leaking walls. The letter stated: "This letter confirms our understanding that the necessary exterior wall maintenance is to be done, that we will deduct the cost from our rent payments, and that you will collect in full from Ellwest under your current rental agreement with them."

On June 1, 1981 letters were exchanged between Davilla and Jones. Jones forwarded another estimate in the amount of $36,736 and recognized Davilla's prompt need for bids for the repairs as part of lessor's negotiations with Ellwest. The letter continued:

> "The heavy rains at 4 a.m. today once again brought in so much water through the exterior walls that we had to sweep it off the floor before starting today's business. Hence, you can see there is some urgency about doing this work and unless we hear otherwise from you within a week we shall assume that you want us to have the job done and deduct from rent payments."

Davilla's June 1 letter read:

> "This letter is to confirm our conversation on Monday June 1, 1981. I Elizabeth A. Davilla do request that you do not give a work crew permission to start work at 333–35 Bourbon Street. I would like to get at least one more reasonable estimate, after which time I will take necessary action in getting the work completed. But you must allow me a reasonable amount of time. SO I DO NOT AUTHORIZE THE WORK BE STARTED AT THIS TIME."

The record indicates that the lessor contacted two additional contractors for prices, and that at least one of them visited the property, though no further bids were received, and no further repair work has been done by either lessor or lessee.

On July 10, 1981 a notice to vacate for nonpayment of rent totaling $3600 was personally served on Jones. The Rule to Evict Tenant was not filed in court until September 23, 1981 and was not heard until October 9.

The essence of the contract of lease is the enjoyment of a thing in exchange for a price. C.C. 2669 [R.C.C. 2668]. The lessee is bound to use the thing as a good administrator, for the intended use, and to pay the rent on the agreed terms. C.C. 2710 [R.C.C. 2683]. The lessee may be expelled from the property if he fails to pay the rent when due. C.C. 2712 [R.C.C. 2704].

The lessor is bound by the very nature of the contract to deliver the thing to the lessee and maintain it in sufficiently good condition. C.C. 2692 [R.C.C. 2682]. The Civil Code makes provision for the division of the responsibility to repair between the lessor and lessee (C.C. 2693) [R.C.C. 2691] but the parties by agreement may reallocate the responsibility among themselves. C.C. 11 [R.C.C. 7]. Under the contract of lease between Davilla and Jones, the lessor was responsible for repairs to the roof and exterior walls.

The lessee asserted as a defense to the Rule to Evict Tenant that he was entitled to withhold the rent from the lessor because the lessor failed to make necessary repairs to the premises. C.C. 2694 [R.C.C. 2694] provides:

> "If the lessor do not make the necessary repairs in the manner required . . . the lessee may call on him to make them. If he refuse or neglect to make

them, the lessee may himself cause them to be made, and deduct the price from the rent due, on proving that the repairs were indispensable, and that the price which he has paid was just and reasonable."

The lessee argues that demand was properly made on the lessor to make the repairs, yet all of the repairs were not made. Lessee further argues that he did not make the wall repairs himself because he was prevented from doing so by the lessor. He therefore contends that his withholding of the rent was proper under C.C. 2694 [R.C.C. 2694] and, consequently, eviction in this case would deprive him of the right to repair and deduct provided by the Civil Code.

The right of the lessee to apply the rent due to repairs arises only after the lessor has refused or neglected to make the repairs upon demand by the lessee. *Brignac v. Boisdore,* 288 So.2d 31 (La.1973). In *Mullen v. Kerlec,* 115 La. 783, 785, 40 So. 46 (1905), this court stated:

> "The Civil Code seems plain enough that the right of the lessee to make indispensable repairs at the expense of the lessor arises only after calling on the lessor to make such repairs and after his refusal or neglect to make them. We do not think that the lessee can be permitted to anticipate the refusal of the lessor to repair and on that ground refuse to pay the rent when due."

Jones' February 4 demand letter gave the lessor two weeks within which to commence repairs. Jones' testimony indicates the demand was complied with:

> "On the 14th day of the month, the 14th day after mailing of the letter I was called upon by a man who presented himself as the roofer who had been sent to me by the lessor."

The roofer indicated that he would quote a price. He thereafter began the work. It was not until mid-April, after two months rent had already been withheld, that Jones learned that this contractor would not complete the entire job, and he notified the lessor. Jones forwarded the first bid he obtained for the wall work to the lessor with the understanding that the contractor would be paid by Ellwest Theatre. It was not until the letter of May 21 that there is any indication in the record that Jones would have to pay for the work himself, after another month's rent had been withheld.

There is no evidence in the record that Davilla refused to make the repairs. The June 1 letter relied on by defendant was not a refusal to make the repairs. Davilla's statement, "So I do not authorize the work to be started at this time" is not a refusal to complete the work where in the previous sentences Davilla had stated that one more estimate was desired and then work would be completed within a reasonable time. Neither do the actions of the lessor show neglect of the obligation to make the repairs. The lessor responded to each of the lessee's letters and was taking steps toward the completion of the repairs by negotiating with Ellwest and by arranging with the lessee to secure bids. The lessor's cautious approach to the repairs was justified by their high cost.

In any event, the June 1 letter relied on by Jones comes too late to support his withholding the rent previously due. Jones argues to this court that the eviction is inequitable since Davilla led Jones to believe that the repairs would be made, and, after asking for a reasonable amount of time in which to complete the repairs, moved to have Jones evicted. However, Jones offers no justification for his withholding the rent prior to the June 1 letter. His demand for the repairs was being met. C.C. 2694 [R.C.C. 2694] gives the lessee the right to withhold rent only to apply it to the cost of the repairs. A lessee may not anticipate refusal or neglect to make the repairs or withhold rent to apply economic pressure on a lessor.

The judgment of the court of appeal is reversed, and the judgment of the district court is reinstated, all at the cost of the respondent.

LEMMON, J., dissents for the reasons assigned by the court of appeal.

Notes and Questions

1. Some early decisions held that because the lessee has this "repair-and-deduct" right, the lessee is not entitled to dissolution of the lease when the lessor fails to make repairs if the rent is sufficient for the lessee to have them made. *See, e.g., Scudder v. Paulding*, 4 Rob. 428, 1843 WL 1438 (La. 1843). This approach has not been followed in modern cases, though it has not been expressly repudiated. Is this approach consistent with the overall approach of the Civil Code to the obligations of the parties to the lease? As a matter of policy, should the lessee be required to make repairs if the cost of doing so does not exceed the rent?

2. In addition to the obligation to repair, the lessor has a *right* to make certain repairs. Article 2693 provides that "[i]f during the lease the thing requires a repair that cannot be postponed until the end of the lease, the lessor has the right to make that repair even if this causes the lessee to suffer inconvenience or loss of use of the thing." LA. CIV. CODE art. 2693. This article provides an exception to the general rule that during the lease, the lessor can take no action that disturbs the lessee's peaceful possession of the thing. *See* LA. CIV. CODE art. 2700; Subpart B.3, *infra*. If the lessor avails himself of the right to make such repairs, the lessee may obtain a reduction or abatement of the rent or dissolution of the lease. LA. CIV. CODE art. 2693. The extent of the lessee's remedy depends upon "all of the circumstances" surrounding the needed repair, including "each party's fault or responsibility for the repair, the length of the repair period, and the extent of the loss of use." *Id.*

3. Like the lessor's obligation to deliver the thing in good condition, the lessor's obligation to make repairs that become necessary during the lease may be altered by the agreement of the parties. Contractual provisions shifting the responsibility for some or all repairs are quite common, particularly in commercial leases of immovable property. In practice, commercial leases are of two types—the "gross" lease and the "net" lease. A gross lease is one in which the lessor pays for property taxes, insurance on the land and building, and maintenance. A net lease, on the other hand, is one in which some or all of these responsibilities are shifted to

the lessee. Consider the following description of "net" leases provided by a leading practice guide:

> Net leases themselves are of various kinds, depending on the amount of responsibility assumed by the lessee. A "net lease, excepting for taxes, insurance and outside repairs," as its name indicates, means that the lessee maintains and operates the leased premises but does not have responsibility for property taxes, insurance on the building, and any structural repairs. A "net-net" lease provides that the lessee pays for operating expenses, maintenance costs, insurance, real estate taxes, and so on. Finally, the so-called "triple net" lease, which is typically a long-term lease, requires that the lessee pay for all expenses during the term of the lease as if the lessee were owner of the property, such as property taxes, insurance, and all maintenance and repairs, including structural repairs.

2 Peter S. Title, Louisiana Real Estate Transactions § 18:32 (2017-18 ed.).[±] "Structural" repairs of the sort referenced in the last sentence tend to fall under the ambit of the lessor's warranty against vices and defects, which is addressed in the materials that follow.

b. Lessor's Warranty Against Vices and Defects
La. Civ. Code arts. 2696–2699, 2004

Related to the lessor's obligation to make repairs is the lessor's warranty against vices and defects in the leased thing. As provided by Article 2696, "The lessor warrants the lessee that the thing is suitable for the purpose for which it was leased and that it is free of vices or defects that prevent its use for that purpose." La. Civ. Code art. 2696. This warranty is a close cousin of the warranty against redhibitory defects in the law of sales; however, it is considerably broader than the seller's warranty in several important respects. First, the warranty applies to defects present in the property at the inception of the lease *and* those that arise after delivery of the thing to the lessee, provided they are not attributable to the fault of the lessee. La. Civ. Code art. 2696. Second, there is no requirement that a defect be "hidden" as is the case under the law of redhibition—the warranty applies regardless of whether the defect was known to the parties. However, if the lessee knows of a vice or defect and fails to notify the lessor, the lessee's recovery for breach of the warranty "may be reduced accordingly." La. Civ. Code art. 2697. Third, in residential leases, the protections of the warranty extend to "all persons who reside in the premises in accordance with the lease." La. Civ. Code art. 2698. This exception to the general rule of contractual privity provides the spouse, children, and roommates of a residential lessee with a direct right of action against a lessor who breaches the warranty.

When the lessor breaches the warranty against vices or defects, the lessee is afforded the same rights as when the lessor fails to make necessary repairs to the

---

± Reproduced with permission of Thomson Reuters.

thing. That is, the lessee may seek specific performance or dissolution of the lease and damages or may avail himself of the right to repair-and-deduct. While the lessee's remedies for breach of warranty may be the same as for the lessor's failure to repair, the two obligations are not identical. The following case distinguishes the warranty from the obligation to repair.

Reed v. Classified Parking System
232 So. 2d 103 (La. App. 2 Cir. 1970)

Bolin, Judge.

Plaintiffs, Robert B. Reed, Rutledge H. Deas, Jr., and Shreve-Park, Inc., bring this action to cancel their sublease with defendant, Classified Parking System, affecting The Auto Hotel, a multistoried parking garage at 520 Edwards Street in Shreveport, Louisiana. Defendant answered in the nature of a general denial and filed a third-party demand against Mr. and Mrs. John B. Hutchinson, original lessors and owners of the premises, asking for cancellation in the event plaintiffs are entitled to such relief in the main demand. The Hutchinsons answered with a general denial and by way of a reconventional demand against Classified and a third-party demand against plaintiffs, demand reimbursement for the cost of repairing the roof and replacing the main electrical panel of the premises and judgment directing Classified and plaintiffs to place the man-lift system in an operable condition and to so maintain it during the term of the lease. Numerous exceptions were filed by all the parties and referred to the merits. The trial court rendered judgment overruling all the exceptions of no cause and right of action filed by plaintiffs and Classified; rejected the principal demand and third-party demand for cancellation; rejected demands of the Hutchinsons for reimbursement for the roofing and electrical work; granted the Hutchinsons' demands against Classified and plaintiffs, in solido, ordering them to install an operable man-lift system in the premises within ninety days and, in the alternative, a money judgment in the amount of $5,373, the cost of a new man-lift installed; and granted a like award to Classified and against plaintiffs as to the man-lift. From that judgment plaintiffs and defendant Classified have appealed, and the Hutchinsons have answered the appeal seeking a reversal insofar as their demands as to the roofing and electrical work were rejected. The exceptions have been abandoned and are not before this court on appeal.

The stipulation of facts in the record show that the Hutchinsons operated The Auto Hotel from the date of its construction in 1930 until 1956. By instrument dated May 15, 1956, the Hutchinsons leased the premises to Classified Parking System, a Texas corporation, for the purpose of operating an automobile parking and storage garage. By instrument dated December 1, 1958, Classified subleased the premises to the plaintiffs for the same purpose.

The man-lift, presently located in the leased premises, was installed when the building was constructed in 1930, although parts have been replaced from time to time. The man-lift was in use from that time until December of 1964, when it became inoperable. The man-lift has become completely inoperative and cannot be used. A workable man-lift is required for the operation of a first-class automobile parking and storage garage as contemplated by the lease and sublease. Almost all of the component parts of the man-lift, except the electric motor, would have to be replaced to put the man-lift in working condition, including some of the lead shields which are sunk into the various concrete floors and which are designed to hold the iron bolts fastening the frame support braces.

The roof of the leased premises leaked prior to the date of the lease to Classified in 1956. The roof continued to leak and was leaking at the time of the sublease in 1958. However, plaintiffs had no notice of the leaking condition at the time the sublease was executed. While the roof presented no particular problem at first, the situation became progressively worse and finally became acute shortly before January of 1963. In September of 1963, the Hutchinsons had a hot-mix asphalt topping placed on the roof parking area which improved the situation temporarily. The asphalt began cracking within two weeks from the completion of the job, and the leakage of water has grown progressively worse. About a month after completion, water was still dripping down to the seventh floor, and is now leaking down to the fifth floor. At the same time the Hutchinsons had a new electrical panel installed in the premises. The panel then in use was installed when the building was erected, and had become damaged as a result of the water leaking into the electrical system. The installation of the new electrical panel restored some of the electric lights on the various floors; however, at the present time there are no lights at all on the seventh floor. In addition, shorts occur in the various electrical circuits from time to time causing the circuit breakers to cut off the electricity on the circuits affected. In many instances the electric light fixtures have rusted and corroded as a result of the leaking water and cannot be used.

Because of the leakage, many parked automobiles have been damaged which plaintiffs were obligated to repair. The details surrounding the damage to these automobiles will be noted later in this opinion.

As we view the record there are three issues on appeal:

1. Is the man-lift worn out or only in need of extensive repairs, and, if the former, on whom does the obligation of replacement fall?

2. Does the work which is necessary to maintain an adequate roof on the building constitute ordinary repairs, structural repairs or reconstruction, and, if the second, on whom does the obligation fall?

3. If either or both of the above obligations fall to the Hutchinsons, is the building so untenantable that it cannot be used for that which it was intended, thereby entitling the lessee and sub-lessees to cancellation of the lease and sublease, respectively?

Responsibility for the man-lift rests on the interpretation of Articles 12 and 14 of the lease (sublease). Article 12 of the lease (sublease) provides

"This lease covers not only the real property described herein but also all equipment and fixtures (but specifically excluded are the inventories) now in the premises and used by the sub-lessors in connection with the operation of the parking business. Sub-lessee agrees that all similar equipment and any other equipment in use in the business at the time of the termination of this lease, as well as all fixtures and improvements added to or made by the sub-lessee during the term, shall become the property of the sub-lessors without further compensation."

Article 14 of the lease (sublease) provides:

"Sub-lessee shall operate and maintain, during the entire term of this lease, a first-class parking and storage garage on the demised premises and it shall maintain on said leased premises adequate equipment and personnel to render first-class service at all times. It shall conduct its automobile storage business on such premises in a manner designated to produce the maximum gross storage revenue therefrom. Sub-lessee agrees, as part of the consideration of this lease, that it obligates itself not to divert any storage business from the leased premises so long as there is available in the leased premises a vacant car stall or space."

Under the above lease provisions it is the duty of the sub-lessee (lessee) to make the necessary repairs to all equipment used in the leased premises, including the man-lift. However, for this court to hold that the word maintain includes the obligation to replace worn out equipment would be to give the lease clauses a broader interpretation than was intended by the parties. The lease states that the sub-lessor (lessor) shall own all fixtures and improvements without compensation upon termination of the lease, but we are unable to find any language to the effect the sub-lessee (lessee) must replace worn out equipment as a result of reasonable wear and tear during the term of the lease.

Upon careful study of the record we find the preponderance of both expert and lay testimony establishes the man-lift was worn out in 1964, when it was retired from operation. The apparatus had been in operation since 1930, almost fifteen years beyond its expected life span.

Therefore, plaintiffs' liability only arises if they were negligent in their care and maintenance of the man-lift during the term of the lease. The trial judge in his reasons for judgment held the plaintiffs were negligent in caring for the man-lift from 1961 to 1964 due to the inexperience of Mr. Humphries, an employee of the plaintiff. We cannot agree with these conclusions. Plaintiff attempted to contract three companies for performance of routine maintenance. It is obvious by their refusal they felt the man-lift was beyond any condition to be repaired, needed to be replaced, and they could not stand behind any work on the apparatus. Such a conclusion is substantiated by the cancellation of insurance coverage in 1963. Only when these attempts failed did plaintiffs allow Mr. Humphries to perform the necessary maintenance and repairs as they were needed. On these facts, we conclude the plaintiffs were not negligent in the manner in which they cared for the man-lift. The obligation was on the Hutchinsons and not on the sub-lessees to furnish new equipment to the premises. Indeed, the parties stipulated a workable man-lift was essential to the operation of a first-class parking garage.

The resolution of the issue concerning the condition of the roof of the building hinges upon the proper interpretation and application of Article 5 of the sublease (and lease) which provides:

> "* * * The sub-lessee (lessee) accepts the demised premises in the condition in which they now are, and agrees to keep them at a good state of repair during the term of this lease, a reasonable wear and tear excepted. It is specifically agreed that the sub-lessors (lessors) shall not be liable or responsible for any repairs whatsoever."

Whether clauses of this nature obligate the sub-lessees to make ordinary repairs, extraordinary repairs, or structural repairs is immaterial to the facts of this case as such clauses are not so broad as to encompass structural defects. *Fazzio v. Riverside Realty Company*, 232 La. 794, 95 So.2d 315 (1957). Although the sub-lessee accepts the demised premises in the condition in which they now are, he is still entitled to the warranty protection afforded him by Articles 2692 [R.C.C. 2582] and 2695 [R.C.C. 2696] of the Louisiana Civil Code. *Brunies v. Police Jury of Parish of Jefferson*, 237 La. 227, 110 So.2d 732 (1959); *Knapp v. Guerin*, 144 La. 754, 81 So. 302 (1919); *Bennett v. Southern Scrap Material Co.*, 121 La. 204, 46 So. 211 (1908); *Pierce v. Hedden*, 105 La. 294, 29 So. 734 (1901).

The roof of the parking garage, as it was originally constructed in 1930, is known technically as a rib-slab type of roof. The roof consists of a series of concrete joists and an inner deck of homogenous concrete cast monolithically with the joists. The concrete inner deck is overlaid with a waterproof tar composition membrane, several inches thick. Over this membrane is the outer wearing surface consisting of a two and one-half inch layer of concrete poured in sections which are separated by expansion joints filled with tar to allow for expansion and contraction of the concrete. This outer wearing layer is the exposed parking surface.

Since the waterproofing membrane cannot be seen or inspected without removing the concrete outer wearing surface, its condition at a given time can only be inferred from the surrounding circumstances. At the trial, witnesses who testified as experts on the roof were of the opinion even with the best of care and maintenance, in time it would be necessary to replace the waterproofing membrane. The membrane could not be expected to last more than thirty years, and difficulties could be expected after fifteen years.

Therefore, it was incumbent upon the Hutchinsons under their implied warranty to replace the waterproofing membrane in the roof and thereby correct the structural defect. Notwithstanding the temporary repairs in 1963, which were unsuccessful in that they provided relief for only a short time, the Hutchinsons have done nothing to correct the situation resulting in great damage to the premises.

In light of the above facts, plaintiffs, sub-lessees, have two courses of action available to them. Article 2694 [R.C.C. 2694] of the Louisiana Civil Code provides:

> "If the lessor do not make the necessary repairs in the manner required in the preceding article, the lessee may call on him to make them. If he refuse or neglect to make them, the lessee may himself cause them to be made, and deduct the price from the rent due, on proving that the repairs were indispensable, and that the price which he has paid was just and reasonable."

However, while they have the privilege or option under Article 2694 to perform repairs which are the responsibility of the lessors, that is not the exclusive remedy available. *Boutte v. New Orleans Terminal Co.*, 139 La. 945, 72 So. 513 (1916); *Landry v. Monteleone*, 150 La. 546, 90 So. 919 (1922). The lessee, sub-lessees in this case, may sue for cancellation of the lease. Article 2729 [R.C.C. 2719] of the Louisiana Civil Code provides:

> "The neglect of the lessor or lessee to fulfill his engagements, may also give cause for a dissolution of the lease, in the manner expressed concerning contracts in general, except that the judge cannot order any delay of the dissolution."

In order to justify a cancellation of the lease, the lessee must show the lessor has failed or refused to comply with his obligations for which he contracted in the lease. The plaintiffs have affirmatively proved. In addition, the lessee must prove that he has been seriously disturbed in his possession or that the premises no longer serve for the use for which they were leased. See LSA-C.C. Art. 2692: *Young v. Eddy*, 86 So.2d 243 (La.App. 1 Cir.1956); *Lacour v. Myer*, 98 So.2d 308 (La.App. 1 Cir.1957); *LaNasa v. Winkler*, 144 So.2d 489 (La.App. 4 Cir.1962).

The record in this case shows by 1962 the defect in the roof began to manifest itself. Chunks of concrete began to spall and fall from the ceilings of the premises in the area around the steel reinforcing bars embedded in the concrete joists. Following a rain, water began to drip down from the ceilings inside the premises onto cars parked in the garage, carrying along an alkaline substance which could not be washed off. The cars had to be cleaned with a compound, washed and polished. Drippage onto a windshield had to be removed before it dried or permanent damage resulted. Failures in the electrical system occurred, leaving the building without lighting in certain areas. The falling chunks of concrete create hazards to life and property.

On the basis of the above facts, proved by a preponderance of the evidence, we conclude the sublessees were subjected to much more than mere inconvenience and are entitled to a dissolution of the sublease. In a like manner, Classified Parking System, sub-lessor, is entitled to a cancellation of its original lease with the Hutchinsons, original lessors.

For the reasons assigned the judgment is annulled and set aside and it is now ordered, adjudged and decreed that the judgment read as follows:

It is hereby ordered, adjudged and decreed that all exceptions filed on behalf of plaintiffs, Robert B. Reed, Rutledge H. Deas, Jr., and Shreve-Park, Inc., and on behalf of defendant, Classified Parking System, be and they are hereby overruled.

It is further ordered, adjudged and decreed that there be judgment in favor of petitioners, Robert B. Reed, Rutledge H. Deas, Jr., and Shreve-Park, Inc., and against defendant, Classified Parking System, cancelling the aforesaid sublease from defendant to Robert B. Reed and Rutledge H. Deas, Jr., dated December 1, 1958, pertaining to the following described premises, to-wit:

> 520 Edwards Street-North 78 feet of Lots 6, 7 and 8, Block 32, of the City of Shreveport, Caddo Parish, Louisiana, together with buildings and improvements thereon,

and decreeing the same to be of no further force and effect.

It is further ordered, adjudged and decreed that there be judgment in favor of defendant, Classified Parking System, and against John B. Hutchinson and Bessie Lee Hutchinson cancelling the lease dated May 15, 1956, pertaining to the following described premises, to-wit:

> 520 Edwards Street-North 78 Feet of Lots 6, 7 and 8, Block 32, of the City of Shreveport, Caddo Parish, Louisiana, together with buildings and improvements thereon,

and decreeing the same to be of no further force and effect.

It is further ordered, adjudged and decreed that the reconventional demand against Classified Parking System by John B. Hutchinson and Bessie Lee Hutchinson for reimbursement of the Lachle Electric Company bill of $198.93 in connection with installing a new electrical panel in the premises, and for reimbursement of the Industrial Roofing and Sheet Metal Works bill of $3,734.00 in connection with roofing work, be and they are hereby rejected; and likewise the third-party demands of John B. Hutchinson and Bessie Lee Hutchinson against plaintiffs, Robert B. Reed, Rutledge H. Deas, Jr., and Shreve-Park, Inc., for reimbursement of the said Lachle Electric Company and Industrial Roofing and Sheet Metal Works bills be and they are hereby rejected.

It is further ordered, adjudged and decreed that the reconventional demand of John B. Hutchinson and Bessie Lee Hutchinson against Classified Parking System, and their third-party demand against Robert B. Reed, Rutledge H. Deas, Jr., and Shreve-Park, Inc., ordering defendant and plaintiffs to have a man-lift in operation in the premises, be and they are hereby rejected.

It is further ordered, adjudged and decreed that the third-party demand of Classified Parking System against Robert B. Reed, Rutledge H. Deas, Jr., and Shreve-Park, Inc., ordering plaintiffs to have a man-lift in operation in the premises, be and it is hereby rejected.

It is further ordered, adjudged and decreed that all costs of these proceedings be taxed to and paid by John B. Hutchinson and Bessie Lee Hutchinson.

Reversed and rendered.

Notes and Questions

1. The foregoing case makes clear that a provision in the lease that shifts the responsibility to make repairs from the lessor to the lessee does not necessarily effect a waiver of the lessor's obligation to warrant against vices or defects in the leased thing. If the parties shift the lessor's obligation to repair to the lessee, but do not modify the lessor's warranty obligations, the lessor is still responsible for vices and defects in the thing. After reading *Reed*, can you articulate the distinction between a "mere repair" and a "vice or defect"? Consider the following hypotheticals:

    i. In a lease of a warehouse, Lessor and Lessee agree that Lessee shall make "all necessary repairs required at present, and which may be required during the term of the lease, at Lessee's own cost." Shortly after taking possession of the premises, Lessee discovers that the beams holding up the structure are rotten from age and dry rot. Who is responsible for repairing or replacing the beams — Lessor or Lessee? *See Bennett v. Southern Scrap Material Co.,* 46 So. 211 (La. 1908).

    ii. Lessor and Lessee agree in the lease of a store building that Lessee will be responsible for all repairs. Following a severe rainstorm, a large canopy overhanging the front of the building collapsed. The principal cause of the canopy's collapse was that an iron supporting rod holding up the store canopy was pulled loose from the rotted piece of lumber to which it was attached by the additional weight of approximately five tons of water collected on top of the canopy after two days of downpour. Who is responsible for repairing or replacing the canopy and the damage caused by the canopy's collapse — Lessor or Lessee? *See Green v. Southern Furniture Co.,* 94 So. 2d 508 (La. App. 1 Cir. 1957).

2. Although the warranty against vices and defects may be modified or excluded by the parties to the lease, the parties' contractual freedom is subject to several important limitations, set forth in Article 2699:

The warranty provided in the preceding articles [Articles 2696–2698] may be waived, but only by clear and unambiguous language that is brought to the attention of the lessee.

Nevertheless, a waiver of warranty is ineffective:

    (1) To the extent it pertains to vices or defects of which the lessee did not know and the lessor knew or should have known;

    (2) To the extent it is contrary to the provisions of Article 2004.

    (3) In a residential or consumer lease, to the extent it purports to waive the warranty for vices or defects that seriously affect health or safety.

LA. CIV. CODE art. 2699. Similar to waivers of the seller's warranty against redhibitory defects, a waiver of the lessor's warranty against vices and defects must be clear and unambiguous and pointed out to the lessee at the time of the formation of the lease. Also similar to the law governing redhibition waivers, under Article 2699(1), an otherwise valid waiver is invalid if procured through fraud on the part of the lessor. *Cf.* LA. CIV. CODE art. 2548. The requirements for a valid waiver of the warranty against redhibitory defects are covered in detail in Chapter 10: The Warranty Against Redhibitory Defects.

Article 2699(2)'s prohibition on waivers "contrary to the provisions of Article 2004" requires some exploration. Recall that Article 2004 provides the general rules governing limitations or exclusions of contractual liability, announcing the nullity of two types of exculpatory provisions. First, "[a]ny clause is null that, in advance, excludes or limits the liability of one party for intentional or gross fault that causes damage to the other party." LA. CIV. CODE art. 2004 para. 1. When this limitation is read *in pari materia* with Article 2699, it is clear that an otherwise valid waiver of the warranty against vices and defects shall have no effect if the lessor's failure to remedy the defect amounts to intentional or gross fault. Second, "[a]ny clause is null that, in advance, excludes or limits the liability of one party for causing physical injury to the other party." LA. CIV. CODE art. 2004 para. 2. Read together with Article 2699, this provision makes clear that an otherwise valid warranty waiver will not shield the lessor from liability for physical injury caused to a person protected by the warranty (i.e., the lessee or a person residing in the premises in accordance with the lease).±

Finally, Article 2699(3) articulates a limitation on warranty waivers which, "in residential or consumer" leases, would shield the lessor from liability for defects that "seriously affect health or safety." LA. CIV. CODE art. 2699(3). As indicated by comment (g) to Article 2699, this limitation is premised on an acknowledgment that residential and consumer lessees suffer from a lack of bargaining power vis-à-vis their lessors. LA. CIV. CODE art. 2699 cmt. g. The warranty against vices and defects provides residential and consumer lessees with basic safety and habitability, and for that reason, the lessor's liability for defects that might injure those interests may not be excluded.

Also potentially applicable to a waiver of the lessor's warranty against vices and defects is Louisiana Revised Statutes section 9:3221 ("R.S. 9:3221"). The significance of this provision cannot be fully understood without an appreciation of the lessor's delictual liability for vices and defects in the thing leased, and the relationship of that liability to the lessor's contractual obligations. These topics are addressed in the materials that follow.

± It should be noted that although Article 2548 does not explicitly reference Article 2004 and its applicability to waivers of the warranty against redhibitory defects, the limitations of Article 2004 are also applicable to redhibition waivers by virtue of general principals of statutory interpretation.

c. Lessor's Delictual Liability for Vices and Defects
La. Civ. Code arts. 660, 2317.1, 2322; La. Rev. Stat. § 9:3221

Louisiana Revised Statutes § 9:3221. Assumption of responsibility by lessee; liability of owner.

Notwithstanding the provisions of Louisiana Civil Code Article 2699, the owner of premises leased under a contract whereby the lessee assumes responsibility for their condition is not liable for injury caused by any defect therein to the lessee or anyone on the premises who derives his right to be thereon from the lessee, unless the owner knew or should have known of the defect or had received notice thereof and failed to remedy it within a reasonable time.

* * * * *

Melissa T. Lonegrass, *The Anomalous Interaction Between Code and Statute: Lessor's Warranty and Statutory Waiver*
88 TUL. L. REV. 423, 442–447 (2015)
(Internal Citations Omitted)

[A] lessor is answerable in delict (tort) for the condition of the leased premises in his capacity as owner or custodian of the thing leased. Under article 2317.1, which deals with liability for "custody" or "garde" of a thing, the lessor of a building is "answerable for damage occasioned by its ruin, vice, or defect." Article 2322, addressing the responsibility of an owner of a building, imposes liability for "damage occasioned by its ruin, when this is caused by neglect to repair it, or when it is the result of a vice or defect in its original construction." Also applicable is article 660 (formerly 670), which appears in the title of the Civil Code dealing with legal servitudes, and which provides that an "owner is bound to keep his buildings in repair so that neither their fall nor that of any part of their materials may cause damage to a neighbor or to a passerby." Together, these provisions make the lessor who is also the owner or custodian of the property responsible not only to his tenant, but to anyone who is injured by a defect in the premises.

Article 2697 makes clear that the lessor's contractual warranty imposes a strict liability standard — the lessor is liable for damage caused by a vice or defect in the leased thing regardless of whether the lessor knew of those defects. Thus, in order to recover damages for breach of this warranty, the lessee must prove only that a defect existed and that the defect caused damages. Historically, the lessor's delictual liability as owner or custodian was also assessed according to a strict liability standard. However, in 1996, the Louisiana legislature introduced landmark legislation eliminating the strict liability formerly imposed on property owners and replacing it with liability for negligence only. The new provisions contain parallel language making clear that an owner or custodian is liable "only upon a showing that he knew or, in the exercise of reasonable care, should have known of the ruin, vice, or defect which caused the damage, that the damage could have been prevented by the exercise of reasonable care, and that he failed to exercise such reasonable care." In contrast to this change, the articles providing for the lessor's contractual liability were left untouched. Thus, while the lessor's delictual responsibilities as owner or custodian of a building are now assessed according to a negligence standard, a lessor's liability in contract remains strict.

The contractual and delictual obligations are imposed upon the lessor concurrently, so that an injured lessee may recover under either theory, or both. However, an injured lessee is most likely to allege a violation of the lessor's contractual responsibilities. This has been the case historically and remains true under current law, likely because the contractual action is generally far more advantageous to the lessee. As noted above, the lessor is strictly liable for a breach of the warranty against vices and defects, while liability in tort lies in negligence alone. Additionally, the lessee's breach of warranty claim is subject to a generous ten-year period of prescription, as opposed to the one-year period applicable to delictual claims. Moreover, Louisiana courts have traditionally awarded damages for all types of harm resulting from breach of the lessor's contractual warranty, including damages for economic loss, loss of property, personal injury, and nonpecuniary damages for mental anguish, anxiety, and worry.

While an injured lessee is entitled to recover under either contract or tort principles, when third parties to the lease claim damage resulting from defects in the premises, tort is generally the only theory of recovery available. The warranty, being contractual in nature, traditionally extended only to the lessee. Thus, under prior law, a nonsignatory to the lease who was injured on the premises was restricted to a tort claim against the lessor. The distinction between the contract and tort claims, particularly the disparity in the standard of liability, was a source of serious potential unfairness, especially for the lessee's spouse and children who resided in the house but who did not sign the lease contract. To remedy this unfairness, article 2698 was revised in 2005 to extend the lessor's contractual obligations to "all persons who reside in the premises in accordance with the lease." However, other invitees and passersby remain outside of the protective scope of the contractual warranty and are limited to claims in tort only.

A paradigmatic example best illustrates the operation of the foregoing principles. Assume that a residential lessee executes a lease for a house. The lessee moves into the premises with his wife and minor child, neither of whom are signatories to the lease. Shortly after the family moves in, the house catches fire. The lessee, his wife, and his child suffer serious injuries. All of their possessions are destroyed. A friend who was visiting their home is injured. An investigation reveals that faulty wiring located inside of the walls of the house caused the fire. Under these facts, the lessor is potentially liable both in contract and in tort. First, the faulty wiring constitutes a defect for which the lessor is answerable in contract. The strict nature of the warranty against vices and defects imposes responsibility on the lessor even if he was unaware of the danger. The lessee is entitled to damages for his injuries and other losses, as are his family members. They have ten years in which to sue. The lessor's liability is not the same with respect to the family friend, however. Her rights arise from the law of delict rather than the contract that exists between the lessor and the lessee. Thus, her claim lies in negligence and requires that she show the lessor's lack of reasonable care. Additionally, the family friend must sue within one year or risk forfeiting her claim.

* * * * *

Notes and Questions

As discussed in the foregoing excerpt, prior to 1996, the lessor's delictual liability for vices and defects in the leased thing was strict liability. In 1926, the Louisiana Supreme Court held that although the lessee could assume the risk of harm resulting from a vice or defect in the lease agreement, a contractual provision allocating responsibility for the condition of the thing to the lessee did not alleviate the lessor's responsibility to third persons who were not parties to the lease. *Klein v. Young*, 111 So. 495, 496–97 (1926). This decision produced a harsh result for landlords. While a lessor's liability to his or her *lessee* could be avoided by the lessee's assumption of responsibility for the condition of the premises, the owner's liability to *third persons* was unaffected by such a stipulation, even though the lessor had no obligation vis-à-vis the lessee to maintain the premises in a safe condition. The result was even more unfair when the complaining party was the child or spouse of the lessee, entitled to sue the lessor in tort despite a clause in the lease absolving the lessor of the obligation to maintain the premises.

In 1932, the Louisiana legislature enacted a statute designed to overrule *Klein* and lessen the potential liability of a lessor-owner to third persons to the lease. In effect, the statute served to shield lessors who shifted responsibility for the premises to their lessees from the unforgiving standards of strict liability. R.S. 9:3221 remains substantially unchanged today, and provides as follows:

> [T]he owner of premises leased under a contract whereby the lessee assumes responsibility for their condition is not liable for injury caused by any defect therein to the lessee or anyone else on the premises who derives his right to be thereon from the lessee, unless the owner knew or should have known of the defect or had received notice thereof and failed to remedy it within a reasonable time.

La. Rev. Stat. §9:3221. Although R.S. 9:3221 was designed to overrule *Klein* and increase protections for *lessors*, Louisiana courts eventually applied the statute to protect *lessees* by using it to hold warranty waivers invalid when the lessor knew or should have known of a defect in the leased premises. As you read the case that follows, recall that Article 2699, which currently articulates substantial limitations for waivers of the warranty against vices and defects, was not enacted until 2005.

Tassin v. Slidell Mini-Storage, Inc.

396 So. 2d 1261 (La. 1981)

Marcus, Justice.

Mr. and Mrs. Byron Tassin and Jacqueline Carr instituted this action for damages sustained to furniture and related items stored in units leased by them in a storage facility known as Slidell Mini-Storage, Inc. Made defendants were Slidell Mini-Storage, Inc., Sidney Tiblier III and Rodney Zeringue, owners of the storage facility, and their insurer, Aetna Insurance Company. Also named defendants were Stovall Construction Company, contractor of the storage facility, and Overhead Door Company, installer of the doors of the facility.

Defendants (owners/lessors) and their insurer answered generally denying the allegations of the petition and further answered by affirmatively asserting no liability on their part on the ground that the contracts entered into between plaintiffs and Slidell Mini-Storage explicitly provided that Slidell Mini- Storage would not be responsible for any loss caused by water.

The trial judge found that the damage to the goods was caused by water that found its way into the leased units. He further held that despite the clause in each agreement exculpating the lessor for the loss of property stored on the premises caused by "water," the owners of the storage facility were nevertheless liable to plaintiffs under La. R.S. 9:3221 since they knew or should have known that the doors on the units were defective inasmuch as they would not withstand the heavy rains and thunderstorms that are common, natural phenomena in southeast Louisiana. Further finding that plaintiffs clearly proved the amount of damages to their property, he rendered judgment in favor of Mr. and Mrs. Tassin for $4,802 and in favor of Jacqueline Carr for $3,140 and against Slidell Mini-Storage. He further dismissed all third party demands. Slidell Mini-Storage and Aetna were the only parties to appeal. Plaintiffs did not answer the appeal. The court of appeal reversed, finding that the clause in each lease exculpating the lessor for loss of property by water controlled and precluded the imposition of liability on Slidell Mini-Storage. The court further held that, even assuming that La. R.S. 9:3221 was applicable, there was no evidence in the record supportive of a finding that Slidell Mini-Storage knew or should have known of the alleged defect. Upon plaintiffs' application, we granted certiorari to review the correctness of this decision.

The record reflects that plaintiffs entered into identical warehouse lease agreements with Slidell Mini-Storage. The Tassin lease, executed by Byron Tassin, was for unit 16 and was dated April 29, 1976. The Carr lease, executed by Alfred E. Carr, Jr. as agent for his daughter, Jacqueline Carr, was for unit 15 and was dated February 16, 1977. Each agreement contained the following provision under "2. Insurance":

> Insurance on property stored on said premises for loss caused by fire, water, theft, Acts of God, or otherwise, shall be obtained at Depositor's option and

> expense and Warehouseman shall not be responsible for any such losses, whatsoever.

Both Mr. Tassin and Mr. Carr testified that they read the contracts in their entirety including the clause regarding insurance; however, no insurance was obtained on the goods stored in the warehouse.

Subsequent to the execution of the agreements, plaintiffs moved furniture and related items into the units for storage. Upon opening their respective units on or about March 11, 1977, plaintiffs found them to be very damp and most of the items were mildewed and discolored. Ms. Carr and her father testified that items in the back of the unit were sitting in approximately two to three inches of water. Mr. Carr noted that there was no water in the front by the door.

Mr. Carr, qualified as an expert in the building industry, testified that the over-head doors on storage units 15 and 16 did not close flush with the concrete slab flooring despite the rubber stripping on the bottom of the doors, thereby leaving a gap between the door and concrete of about one-fourth inch when the doors were fully closed and locked. Photographs received in evidence revealed that a person could reach a hand and part of an arm under the door and into the unit even when the door was fully closed and locked. Further testimony by Mr. Carr and other wit-nesses as well as photographs taken of the area showed the concrete slabs of these particular units sloped toward the back of the units. Mr. Carr opined that the cause of the water getting into the unit was the fact that the "door did not seal properly" and that water that entered by rain or otherwise would remain on the floor because the "slab was not level, or sloping toward the front." Testimony by several witnesses as well as certified National Weather Service records indicated that while there was considerable rainfall and thunderstorms during the three weeks prior to March 11, 1977, the weather conditions were not unusual for that time of the year in southeast Louisiana. Defendants offered testimony to the effect that the concrete flooring and overhead doors of the mini-storage units including 15 and 16 were not defectively constructed. Mr. Tiblier, one of the owners of the facility, testified that he had never received any complaints of water damage from any of the tenants either prior or subsequent to the commencement of this suit.

It is clear that the relationship existing between plaintiffs and Slidell Mini-Storage pursuant to the warehouse agreements was one of lease and is therefore governed by the rights and obligations under Louisiana law pertaining to lease agreements. La.Civ.Code art. 2695 [R.C.C. 2696] provides:

> The lessor guarantees the lessee against all the vices and defects of the thing, which may prevent its being used even in case it should appear he knew nothing of the existence of such vices and defects, at the time the lease was made, and even if they have arisen since, provided they do not arise from the fault of the lessee; and if any loss should result to the lessee from the vices and defects the lessor shall be bound to indemnify him for the same.

Nevertheless, the owner can shift responsibility for [the] condition of the premises including liability for injury caused by any defect therein to the lessee pursuant to La. R.S. 9:3221.

However, the codal articles and statutes defining the rights and obligations of lessors and lessees are not prohibitory laws which are unalterable by contractual agreement, but are simply intended to regulate the relationship between lessor and lessee when there is no contractual stipulation imposed in the lease. *General Leasing Co. v. Leda Towing Co., Inc.*, 286 So.2d 802 (La.App. 4th Cir. 1973), *cert. denied*, 290 So.2d 334 (La.1974). All things that are not forbidden by law may become the subject of or the motive for contracts and, when legally entered into, the contracts have the effect of law between the parties who have made them. La.Civ.Code arts. 1764 [No Corresponding Article], 1901 [R.C.C. 1983]. Our jurisprudence is that the usual warranties and obligations imposed under the codal articles and statutes dealing with lease may be waived or otherwise provided for by contractual agreement of the parties as long as such waiver or renunciation does not affect the rights of others and is not contrary to the public good. *Louisiana National Leasing Corp. v. A.D.F. Services, Inc.*, 377 So.2d 92 (La.1979); *Klein v. Young*, 163 La. 59, 111 So. 495 (1926); *General Leasing Co. v. Leda Towing Co., Inc., supra*. We must therefore determine if the warehouse agreements in the instant case containing the exculpating clauses effectively relieved owners/lessors of liability to plaintiffs imposed under Louisiana lease law for damages to plaintiffs, goods stored on the leased premises.

First, we are convinced that the damage to plaintiffs' property was caused by water that entered and remained in the storage units due to defects in the structure. Plaintiffs proved by a preponderance of the evidence that the doors and concrete flooring of storage units 15 and 16 were such as to allow water to blow or seep into the units. The doors did not close properly and the concrete sloped to the rear rather than to the front. Moreover, we consider that the clause in each lease agreement clearly and unambiguously transferred liability of the owners/lessors for loss caused by water to property stored on the premises to the lessees including water loss caused by a vice or defect in the premises. The lessees assumed this responsibility by freely entering into the warehouse agreements, thereby dispensing with the implied warranty in their favor established by La.Civ.Code art. 2695 [R.C.C. 2696].

Although plaintiffs assumed responsibility for water damage caused by a vice or defect in the premises, we are convinced that the owners/lessors knew or should have known that the storage units were defective in that they did not secure against the entering of water into the units resulting from rain normally occurring in southeast Louisiana. It should have been obvious to them that, since the doors did not close flush with the concrete flooring which sloped to the rear, water would enter the units and cause damage to property located therein. Moreover, since the units did not contain shelving, they should have been aware that property would be placed on the flooring and would be affected by any water that might enter and accumulate in the units.

Under the circumstances, even though the lessees assumed responsibility for water damage caused by a vice or defect in the premises, La.R.S. 9:3221 did not relieve the owners/lessors of the responsibility imposed on them by La.Civ.Code art. 2695 [R.C.C. 2696] because they should have known of the defects in the premises. This is the conclusion reached by the trial judge. We are unable to say that it is clearly wrong. *Arceneaux v. Domingue,* 365 So.2d 1330 (La.1980). To the contrary, we consider that the record fully supports this conclusion. Accordingly, we must reverse the judgment of the court of appeal and reinstate that of the trial judge.

DECREE

For the reasons assigned, the judgment of the court of appeal is reversed and the judgment of the district court is reinstated and made the judgment of this court. All costs of this appeal are assessed against Slidell Mini-Storage, Inc.

Notes and Questions

Following *Tassin* and continuing through the enactment of Article 2699 in 2005, Louisiana courts consistently applied R.S. 9:3221 to regulate not only the lessor's delictual liability, but also the lessor's warranty against vices and defects. The introduction of Article 2699, with its many limitations on waivers of the lessor's warranty, raises an obvious question regarding the continued applicability of R.S. 9:3221 to a lessee's breach of warranty claims. The redactors of the 2005 revision of the Title on Lease attempted to address the relationship between the two provisions in comment (h) to Article 2699:

> Civil Code Article 2699 (Rev. 2004) deals with the contractual obligations between the parties rather than with the delictual or quasi-delictual obligations that one party may incur vis a vis the other party, or vis a vis third parties. Consequently, Civil Code Article 2699 (Rev. 2004) does not supersede the provisions of R.S. 9:3221 which provides for delictual or quasi-delictual obligations incurred as a result of injury occurring in the leased premises. Section 3 of this Act amends and reenacts R.S. 9:3221 to provide that the amendment and reenactment of Civil Code Article 2699 does not change the law of R.S. 9:3221.

LA. CIV. CODE art. 2699 cmt. h. As indicated in comment (h), the same legislation that introduced Article 2699 also amended R.S. 9:3221, so that it now reads as follows:

> *Notwithstanding the provisions of Civil Code Article 2699,* the owner of premises leased under a contract whereby the lessee assumes responsibility for their condition is not liable for injury caused by any defect therein to the lessee or anyone else on the premises who derives his right to be thereon from the lessee, unless the owner knew or should have known of the defect or had received notice thereof and failed to remedy it within a reasonable time.

LA. REV. STAT. § 9:3221. Having read *Tassin v. Slidell Mini-Storage,* do you agree with the assertion in comment (h) that R.S. 9:3221 is applicable to the lessor's delictual and quasi-delictual obligations only? Assuming that the assertion is correct, what effect does R.S. 9:3221 have now that the lessor's delictual obligations are governed by a negligence standard rather than strict liability? Is a lessor's delictual liability in any way impacted by the existence (or not) of a provision in the lease shifting responsibility for the condition of the premises to the lessee? The following case is representative of the attempts of courts to rationalize the law following the 2005 revision of Article 2699 and R.S. 9:3221.

Stuckey v. Riverstone Residential SC, LP

21 So. 3d 970 (La. App. 1 Cir. 2009)

GAIDRY, J.

The tenants of an apartment appeal the trial court's summary judgment dismissing their claims for damages against the apartment complex owner. For the following reasons, we affirm the trial court's judgment.

FACTUAL AND PROCEDURAL BACKGROUND

On February 11, 2005, the plaintiff, Ashley Stuckey, executed an apartment lease for Apartment No. 2907 of the Jefferson Lakes Apartments, an apartment complex owned by the defendant, The Lakes Limited Partnership (The Lakes), and managed by the defendant, Riverstone Residential SC, LP (Riverstone). The term of the lease was from the date of signing to August 30, 2005, and on a month-to-month basis thereafter. Apartment No. 2907 was a two-floor or townhouse apartment, with two bedrooms and two bathrooms on the second floor. In addition to Ashley Stuckey, her minor son, Austin Stuckey, and her mother Crystal Stuckey, resided in the apartment.

Maintenance records showed that prior tenants of the apartment had reported a number of intermittent water leaks, in various locations of the apartment, from February 1998 through December 2004. In April 2005, Ashley Stuckey complained to the apartments' property manager on two occasions of a leak in one of the upstairs bathrooms. After repairs were attempted, Ms. Stuckey delivered a handwritten letter to the property manager, in which she complained about the continuing leak and the accumulation of a "black substance" on the air conditioning vents. She expressed her concern that there might be "a possible mold problem," and claimed that "we have all been sick with symptoms that are associated with mold exposure." The property manager promptly contacted Ashley Stuckey upon receiving the letter to discuss the situation.

* * * * *

On February 13, 2006, the plaintiffs filed a petition for damages, naming The Lakes and Riverstone as defendants. They alleged that while residing in the apartment from February 12 through June 24, 2005, they and Austin were exposed to toxigenic molds due to the defendants' negligence and fault. They also alleged that on April 6, 2005, Crystal Stuckey reported a hole in a bathroom wall that was leaking water into the living room downstairs, that fungus was growing in that hole, and that another hole was present in the ceiling of Austin's bedroom. It was alleged that water damage and visible mold on the ceiling were also reported to the property manager. Because the reported problems were allegedly not remedied, the plaintiffs again notified the property manager by telephone on April 20, 2005 of the hole in the bathroom wall, after which some repairs to the living room ceiling were made. However, according to the petition, the bathroom leak was not addressed. The plaintiffs claimed that the water leaks resulted in the growth of the toxigenic molds, which caused them and Austin to suffer various health problems due to that exposure, including bronchial infections, persistent nose bleeds, headaches, nausea, and other conditions.

The defendants answered the petition, denying their liability, but admitting that a leak in an upstairs bathroom was reported around April 15, 2005. The defendants also raised various affirmative defenses, including the plaintiffs' contributory negligence and fault, the provisions of the lease agreement, and the plaintiffs' failure to mitigate their damages. They further asserted a reconventional demand against Ashley Stuckey for unpaid rent, attorney fees and costs, and any property damage attributable to her failure to promptly notify the defendants of any water damage or mold contamination.

In her answer to the reconventional demand, Ashley Stuckey generally denied its allegations, except to admit the allegation that she vacated the apartment around June 27, 2005. She further alleged that the "mold problems" were reported to Riverstone within a month of her moving into the apartment, and that she made oral and written requests to have those problems addressed.

On October 8, 2007, the defendants filed a motion for summary judgment on the grounds that the terms of the lease served to absolve them of any liability for damages related to mold or mildew.

* * * * *

The defendants' motion for summary judgment was eventually heard on March 17, 2008. Following the formal introduction of evidence and oral argument, the trial court ruled in favor of the defendants, finding that the defendants were not liable by virtue of La. R.S. 9:3221. On April 10, 2008, the trial court signed the summary judgment, dismissing the plaintiffs' claims with prejudice. The plaintiffs now appeal that judgment.

ASSIGNMENTS OF ERROR

We summarize the plaintiffs' assignments of error as follows:

1. The trial court erred in granting the defendants' motion for summary judgment, as there are genuine issues of material fact as to the defendants' actual or constructive knowledge of the defects.

2. The trial court committed legal error in granting the defendants' motion, as the defendants did not prove entitlement to judgment as a matter of law, based upon the following:

(a) The purported waiver of warranty in the lease agreement is invalid and unenforceable under La. C.C. arts.2004 and 2699, as it was not clear and unambiguous, not clearly brought to Ashley Stuckey's attention, and purports to immunize the defendants from delictual liability in advance of the occurrence of the tort;

(b) The plaintiffs proved a *prima facie* case of liability; and

(c) The defendants failed to remedy the defect, the toxigenic mold, after acquiring actual knowledge of its presence.

* * * * *

DISCUSSION

Legal Principles

Louisiana Civil Code article 2696 establishes the lessor's warranty against vices or defects in the leased thing:

> The lessor warrants the lessee that the thing is suitable for the purpose for which it was leased and that it is free from vices or defects that prevent its use for that purpose. This warranty also extends to vices or defects that arise after the delivery of the thing and are not attributable to the fault of the lessee.

Louisiana Civil Code article 2697 further provides that:

> The warranty provided in the preceding Article also encompasses vices or defects that are not known to the lessor. However, if the lessee knows of such vices or defects and fails to notify the lessor, the lessee's recovery for breach of warranty may be reduced accordingly.

Louisiana Civil Code article 2699 provides for the lessee's waiver of the warranty against vices or defects in certain circumstances:

> The warranty provided in the preceding Articles may be waived, but only by clear and unambiguous language that is brought to the attention of the lessee.

> Nevertheless, a waiver of warranty is ineffective:

> (1) To the extent it pertains to vices or defects of which the lessee did not know and the lessor knew or should have known;

> (2) To the extent it is contrary to the provisions of Article 2004;

> (3) In a residential or consumer lease, to the extent it purports to waive the warranty for vices or defects that seriously affect health or safety.

Louisiana Revised Statutes 9:3221 provides:

> *Notwithstanding the provisions of Louisiana Civil Code Article 2699,* the owner of premises leased under a contract whereby the lessee assumes responsibility for their condition is not liable for injury caused by any defect therein to the lessee or anyone on the premises who derives his right to be thereon from the lessee, *unless the owner knew or should have known of the*

defect or had received notice thereof and failed to *remedy it within a reasonable time.* (Emphasis added.)

The emphasized introductory phrase of the last-cited statute was added effective January 1, 2005, as part of the same act that amended and reenacted La. C.C. art. 2699. Although La. C.C. art. 2699 and La. R.S. 9:3221 are *in pari materia,* article 2699 deals with the contractual obligations between the parties to the lease, rather than with delictual obligations that may arise related to the leased property. *See* La. C.C. art. 2699, Revision Comments—2004, (h). Thus, La. C.C. art. 2699 does not supersede the provisions of La. R.S. 9:3221 that govern and allocate such delictual obligations between the parties. *Id.* Louisiana Revised Statutes 9:3221 is a statutory exception to the strict liability of La. C.C. art. 2696, and is expressly recognized as not subject to the provisions of La. C.C. art. 2699.

Louisiana Civil Code article 2004 provides that "[a]ny clause [in a contract] is null that, in advance, excludes or limits the liability of one party for causing physical injury to the other party." However, its provisions do not supersede La. R.S. 9:3221. La. C.C. art.2004, Revision Comments—1984, (f).

We therefore conclude that the trial court did not commit legal error in finding La. R.S. 9:3221 legally applicable to the facts of this case.

The Terms of the Lease Agreement

The initial term of the lease agreement was for a period of slightly over six months, ending August 30, 2005, with monthly rent of $685.00. Paragraph 11, although primarily directed to the subject of insurance, also contains language relevant to the issues presented:

> 11. ___Insurance.___ Owner recommends that Resident secure Renter's insurance to help protect Resident and Resident's property. Owner is not responsible for, and will not provide fire or casualty insurance for, the personal property of Resident or occupants of the Unit . . . . *Neither Owner nor Owner's managing agent shall be liable to Resident, other occupants of the Unit or their respective guests for any damage, injury or loss to person or property (furniture, jewelry, clothing, etc.) from . . . flood, water leaks, rain, . . . or other occurrences unless such damage, injury, or loss is caused exclusively by the negligence of Owner* . . . . (Emphasis added.)

Paragraph 17 of the lease agreement is captioned "Delivery of Unit," and concludes with the following provision:

> TO THE FULLEST EXTENT ALLOWED BY APPLICABLE LAW, OWNER EXPRESSLY DISCLAIMS ANY AND ALL WARRANTIES, WHETHER EXPRESS OR IMPLIED RELATING TO THE UNIT OR ANY FURNITURE, FURNISHINGS, EQUIPMENT OR APPLIANCES, IF ANY, IN THE UNIT INCLUDING, BUT NOT LIMITED TO, WARRANTIES OF FITNESS FOR A PARTICULAR PURPOSE, MERCHANTABILITY, HABITABILITY OR SUITABILITY.

Finally, and most importantly for our purposes, Paragraph 26(a) specifically provides the following:

> ***Mold & Mildew*** *Resident(s) acknowledges that the apartment is located in a State which has a climate conducive to the growth of mold and mildew.* It is, therefore, necessary to provide proper ventilation and *dehumidification* to the apartment to minimize the growth of mold and mildew. The only effective method to properly condition the air is to operate the heating and/or air conditioning ventilation system at all times throughout the year, even during those times when outside temperatures are moderate. *Please understand that Management is not responsible for any injury, illness, harm or damage to the apartment or any person or property caused by or arising from, in* <u>whole</u> *or in part, mold or mildew.* (Emphasis added.)

It is certainly open to question whether the first and second paragraphs quoted above sufficiently express the intent that Ashley Stuckey assumed general responsibility for the condition of the apartment for purposes of La. R.S. 9:3221. We note that the first paragraph's stated title, "Insurance," and its context might suggest that it relates only to responsibility for securing insurance. At any rate, we conclude that Paragraph 26(a) clearly and adequately expresses the parties' intent that, as between them, the responsibility for any condition or defect involving mold or mildew in the apartment would rest upon Ashley Stuckey, for purposes of application of La. R.S. 9:3221. The paragraph describes necessary preventative measures, the operation of the apartment's individual heating and air conditioning system, obviously within the primary control and responsibility of the resident tenant, and specifically and unambiguously provides that the lessor will have no responsibility for mold or mildew in the apartment.

As previously noted, La. R.S. 9:3221 operates as an express statutory exception to La. C.C. art. 2699 where the lessee assumes responsibility for the condition of leased premises. Where the language of a provision transferring delictual liability under La. R.S. 9:3221 is clear and unambiguous, the law does not require that the provision be brought to the lessee's attention or explained to him. *Greely v. OAG Properties, LLC*, 44,240, p. 4 (La.App. 2nd Cir.5/13/09), 12 So.3d 490, 494. *See also Ford v. Bienvenu*, 00–2376, pp. 6–9 (La.App. 4th Cir.8/29/01), 804 So.2d 64, 68–70, *writ denied*, 01–2688 (La.12/14/01), 804 So.2d 639. Thus, La. C.C. art. 2699's requirement that a waiver of the lessor's warranty against vices or defects be brought to the attention of the lessee does not apply to a provision transferring responsibility for purposes of La. R.S. 9:3221.

The deposition testimony of Ashley Stuckey and Connie Stuckey was generally corroborative of the allegations of their petition regarding the reporting of the water leak in the bathroom. In her affidavit and deposition, Ashley Stuckey denied that anyone on behalf of the defendants fixed the leak after it was initially reported, a disputed point between the parties. In her deposition, Ashley Stuckey confirmed that she did not observe any black substance on any air conditioning vent upon moving in, and described herself as "excited" to be moving into the "very white apartment."

The deposition of Connie Campbell, Riverstone's property manager for the apartment complex, was filed in the record. She testified that she had been employed in that capacity since March 2000, and that during that time there had been no complaints of mold in Apartment No. 2907, other than that of Ashley Stuckey on May 6, 2005. When she and Riverstone's maintenance supervisor inspected the apartment on May 6, 2005, she observed a circular water stain, about two feet in diameter, on the living room ceiling. A representative of Guaranty Systems, a specialty cleaning contractor, also inspected the air conditioning vents on May 9, 2005, and verbally reported to Ms. Campbell that no evidence of mold was found. A technician of Air Environmental Services, an environmental testing service, reported that his inspection of May 10, 2005 found no toxic mold, and that mold levels with the apartment were no higher than those outside the apartment. Ms. Campbell did acknowledge in her deposition that no professional remediation for mold was performed at the apartment between April 6, 2005, and June 27, 2005, when the plaintiffs vacated it.

The deposition of Ralph Oby, Riverstone's maintenance supervisor, was also filed in the record. Although he acknowledged that he inspected Apartment No. 2907 following the May 2005 complaint of suspected mold, he testified that he observed only what appeared to be water stains, and that he never suspected mold in the apartment. Because he never suspected the actual presence of mold, he did not institute any remediation steps. He further confirmed that the Guaranty Systems representative who inspected the apartment verbally reported that no mold was present in the apartment, and agreed that there were only water stains. However, the representative recommended that an environmental testing company be consulted. Mr. Oby conceded that generally, if a water problem in an apartment is not corrected within 48 hours, there is a "significant potential" for the growth of mold. Another maintenance worker, Mr. Aubin, was deposed. He described repair work to fix the leaks, but denied ever observing any condition suggestive of the presence of mold in the apartment. He also acknowledged various discussions with Mr. Oby at different times concerning conditions that might lead to development of mold, but he denied knowing of any actual mold problems or issues in the apartment complex.

The plaintiffs filed the affidavit of Brandon Phillips, the employee of Envirotest, Inc., in charge of testing performed at the request of the plaintiffs' attorney. Mr. Phillips's affidavit was dated March 6, 2008 and filed with the trial court on March 10, 2008. According to Mr. Phillips's affidavit, the on-site testing was performed on June 14, 2005. The report referenced in his affidavit shows that the third-party testing laboratory received the samples on June 15, 2005, and issued its certificate of analysis and analysis summary on June 23, 2005. In his affidavit, Mr. Phillips attested to the following:

> 8. I am of the opinion that a responsible landlord, who is responsible for the maintenance of the Jefferson Place Apartments, should have known of the existence of this mold in sufficient time to properly remediate this mold . . . .

9. . . . Ordinarily, a lay person is incapable of determining the difference between mold and dust, as microscopic analysis may be necessary to determine the contents of the dust.

10. I am of the opinion that a responsible, prudent landlord . . . should have known what the preconditions for mold were and should have been aware of the significant risk of the development of mold in this apartment unit, due to the fact that there had been multiple complaints of water leaks . . . between 1998 and 2005.

Significantly, although he made reference to the reported prior water leaks in his affidavit, Mr. Phillips did not attribute the presence of mold to those leaks; instead, he described "the underlying problem in this apartment which caused the growth of the mold" as "humidity." Even more significantly, neither the affidavit nor the analysis report show that any of the direct transfer samples (taken from surfaces) were obtained from the actual locations of reported water leaks. Mr. Phillips expressed the opinion that "[a]lthough mold may develop in a 48 hour period, based upon [his] experience, the extent of the mold growth found *inside of the heating and air conditioning vents* . . . would not have developed to the extent [he] observed . . . on 6/14/05." (Emphasis added.) He also stated: "[I]t is my opinion evidence [sic] that there has been a *humidity problem* within the apartment which has been in existence since 1998." (Emphasis added.) He did not describe the factual bases of that opinion, such as the basis for 1998 being the year the "humidity problem" began. There is nothing in the affidavit evidencing or suggesting that the results of the testing or any of Mr. Phillips's described conclusions were communicated to the defendants prior to June 23, 2005 at the earliest.

Finally, as pointed out by the defendants, there was no factual foundation set forth in the affidavit that Mr. Phillips was competent to express conclusory opinions relating to the standard of care of a "responsible landlord," responsible for apartment maintenance. Whether the defendants had the obligation to maintain the apartment and to repair reported problems is not determinative of their duties for purposes of tort liability under the standards imposed by La. R.S. 9:3221. There is a distinction between liability for damages occasioned by defects in leased premises and who has the obligation to repair such defects. *Hebert v. Neyrey*, 445 So.2d 1165, 1168 n. 3 (La.1984).

The plaintiffs contend on appeal that Ms. Campbell, as property manager of the complex, should have performed a "reasonable inspection" of Apartment No. 2907 prior to leasing it to Ashley Stuckey. In the first place, the record does not affirmatively show that the defendants failed to inspect the apartment prior to the plaintiffs' occupancy. As the parties alleging that circumstance as a basis for the defendants' negligence, the plaintiffs would bear that burden at trial. Secondly, the record confirms that Ashley Stuckey herself inspected the apartment, signed the required apartment move-in inspection form acknowledging that all items were in good condition, and reported no problems with it prior to occupancy. Most importantly, however, the jurisprudence interpreting La. R.S. 9:3221 does not support the imposition of a duty on the part of a lessor to inspect conditions over which a lessee has assumed responsibility.

* * * * *

The plaintiffs' opposition affidavits do not show that the defendants knew or should have known of any unusual "humidity problem" with Apartment No. 2907, nor any unusual potential for mold or mildew beyond that typical to Louisiana's climate. At best, the plaintiffs put forth evidence suggestive of the possibility that the defendants should have known of the *potential* for the development of mold or mildew. But such evidence simply does not rise to evidence creating a genuine issue of material fact on the issue of whether the defendants should have known or received adequate notice of the *presence* or even probability of development of mold or mildew, the defect of which the plaintiffs complain.

We agree with the trial court's conclusions that the defendants did not know and did not have reason to know of the alleged mold until their receipt of Ashley Stuckey's letter of May 6, 2005, and that upon receiving such notice, the defendants sought to investigate and remedy the claimed condition within a reasonable time. *See, e.g., Meyers v. Drewes,* 196 So.2d 607, 611 (La.App. 4th Cir.1967). The plaintiffs do not dispute that the defendants even offered them the use of another apartment while the report of suspected mold was being investigated. The failure of the plaintiffs to meet their burden of proof on this element is fatal to their opposition to summary judgment.

The judgment of the trial court is affirmed. All costs of this appeal are assessed to the plaintiffs-appellants, Ashley Stuckey and Crystal Stuckey.

AFFIRMED.

GUIDRY, J., dissents.

Melissa T. Lonegrass, *The Anomalous Interaction Between Code and Statute: Lessor's Warranty and Statutory Waiver*

88 Tul. L. Rev..423, 477–481 (2015)

(Internal Citations Omitted)

Numerous conclusions can be drawn from the foregoing discussion of R.S. 9:3221 and its relationship with the Civil Code. First, it is apparent that the current state of the law governing contractual waivers of the lessor's responsibility for defective premises is untenable. Although clauses purporting to shift responsibility from the lessor to the lessee are included in both residential and commercial leases as a matter of course, their enforceability is highly questionable. It is unknown whether these clauses, as a prerequisite to their enforceability, must be specifically brought to the attention of the lessee at the time of the formation of the lease or whether their mere inclusion in a signed standard form contract is sufficient. It is uncertain whether the parties to a lease may agree that the lessor will bear no responsibility for defects in the premises as long as he remains in good faith, or whether a lessor retains the responsibility to timely repair defects that become known even after the lessee has agreed to accept responsibility for maintenance. It is unclear whether a waiver, if otherwise enforceable, will shield a lessor from liability for his tenant's personal injuries or from other damage caused by a defect that poses a serious risk to the tenant's health and safety. One cannot predict with confidence whether a waiver's enforceability will vary if the lessee seeks damages versus other forms of relief, or if the action is based in tort or contract. In fact, there is little about the legal regime governing waivers of the lessor's warranty that is clear other than the fact that this narrow area of the law is highly unsettled.

The predictability and certainty of lessor liability are essential to ensure a functioning rental market in this state. Louisiana property owners are potentially exposed to tremendous liability for latent defects, and fear of high damage awards may drive up the price of space and liability insurance, or dissuade the risk averse from entering the market at all. At the same time, important public policy concerns militate against the absolute enforceability of exculpatory clauses, particularly in residential leases, even if the end result is a marginal inflation of the cost of leased property. Moreover, litigation involving the lessor's obligation to maintain property free of vices and defects is plentiful. Because of the clear need to balance the concerns of lessors and lessees, one would expect the rules governing lessor liability to be clearly and thoughtfully articulated, leaving little to no question regarding whether and to what extent that liability can be contractually altered by the parties to a lease. Why, then, is this not the case?

The answer to this question is not a simple one. The problem is not necessarily one of legislative inaction. The Civil Code has long contained provisions that delineate the standards by which parties can contractually alter obligations implied by law. But those articles and the principles contained within them have been forced to compete with legislation existing outside of the framework of the Code—a special interest statute enacted over eighty years ago to solve a problem that today no longer exists. For decades, R.S. 9:3221 has been interpreted broadly and dynamically, contrary to established principles of interpretation applicable to statutory law, and as a result has been allowed to directly contradict Civil Code directives governing the power of lessor and lessee to allocate between themselves responsibility for leased premises. Even worse, the full reach of the statute has been misunderstood repeatedly by the redactors of the rolling revision, resulting in a jumbled body of law that is today nearly impossible to apply sensibly.

The best course of action to rectify the confusion wrought by the interaction between R.S. 9:3221 and the Civil Code is the complete repeal of the statutory provision. In its absence, Louisiana Civil Code article 2699 would properly govern the enforceability and effects of warranty waivers executed between lessors and lessees. Thus, the Code would require that waivers be drawn in clear and unambiguous language and brought to the attention of the lessee. The Code would preclude waivers of defects of which the lessor knew or should have known, and of which the lessee was unaware, at the time of the lease, but would not prevent the parties from waiving liability for defects of which the parties later became aware. Finally, the Code would prevent the enforceability of a waiver to insulate lessors from liability for personal injuries or, in the case of residential or consumer leases, defects posing a threat to health or safety. Significantly, although repeal of the statute would work to significantly improve the law governing a lessor's contractual responsibility to his tenant, it would present little substantive change in the law of torts, where a lessor's responsibility is today predicated solely on his negligence, even in cases involving attempted waivers. And yet, repeal of the statute would bring clarity to this area of the law as well, by removing the source of courts' confusion regarding the effect of waivers on tort claims.

Without the statute's repeal, courts are hindered in their power to bring sense to law governing warranty waivers. Courts could theoretically rectify the conflict between Code and statute by applying R.S. 9:3221 only to a lessor's tort responsibilities according to its original purpose and the direction of comment (h) to article 2699. This approach admits a number of weaknesses, however. *Tassin* and its progeny—a line of cases that now amounts to jurisprudence constante—must be abruptly renounced. Furthermore, although courts are free to find that laws have been impliedly repealed in appropriate cases, courts may be reluctant to find the statute repealed by implication, particularly in light of the fact that it was reenacted in 2005. To restrict R.S. 9:3221 to tort claims between lessors and third parties would be to read the statute into obsolescence; as discussed above, the statute no longer has any practical effect when applied to tort claims of that type. The enactment, interpretation, application, and revision of R.S. 9:3221 reveal just one example of the methodological difficulties posed by statutory law in Louisiana. As the Civil Code Ancillaries continue to be used as a "dumping place" for special interest legislation, and as the rolling revision continues to undertake repeated and piecemeal reform of isolated areas of private law, conflict between Code and statute is bound to occur, likely with increasing frequency. The interaction between R.S. 9:3221 and the Civil Code may be anomalous, but it should not be mistaken for an isolated occurrence. Rather, there are a great many lessons to be learned from this cautionary tale about the drafting and interpretation of statutory law, its placement within the hierarchy of the sources of law in this state, the proper placement within code and statute of legislative rules and standards, and the attention that must be given to statutory law throughout the revision process.

3. Lessor's Warranty of Peaceful Possession
La. Civ. Code arts. 2700–2702

The third principal obligation of the lessor is "[t]o protect the lessee's peaceful possession for the duration of the lease." LA. CIV. CODE art. 2682(3). The scope of the warranty of peaceful possession is set forth in Article 2700. First, in every lease, the lessor warrants the lessee's "peaceful possession of the leased thing against any disturbance caused by a person who asserts ownership, or right to possession of, or any other right in the thing." LA. CIV. CODE art. 2700. During the lease, the lessor must not interfere with the lessee's use and possession of the thing leased and must also defend and protect the lessee's possession against disturbances caused by third persons who claim a right in the leased thing.

In the event of a disturbance, the lessee is bound to call the lessor in warranty so that the lessor may take any steps necessary to protect the lessee's possession. LA. CIV. CODE art. 2701. Breach of the warranty of peaceful possession is governed by the general law of Conventional Obligations, meaning that the lessee is entitled to dissolution of the lease and damages resulting from interruption of the lease. Louisiana courts have held that if the disturbance is not severe, the lessee may be entitled to a reduction in the rent in lieu of dissolution. *Weil v. Segura*, 151 So. 639 (1933). In addition, if the lessor fails to take necessary steps to protect the lessee's possession, the lessee may file any appropriate action against the person who caused the disturbance, including, if appropriate, a possessory action. *See* LA. CIV. CODE art. 2701; *id.* at cmt. b.

Similar to the warranty against eviction, the warranty of peaceful possession generally does not extend to disturbances caused by third persons who have no right of possession or ownership of the leased property, including trespassers. LA. CIV. CODE art. 2702. If a disturbance by such a person occurs, the lessee may file any appropriate action against that person, but the lessor is not bound to take any action on the lessee's behalf. *Id.* An exception to this limitation exists in residential leases: there, the warranty encompasses a disturbance caused by "a person who, with the lessor's consent, has access to the thing or occupies adjacent property belonging to the lessor." LA. CIV. CODE art. 2700; *see also Kennan v. Flannigan*, 103 So. 30 (La. 1925) (landlord's failure to suppress noisy tenant resulted in breach of warranty of peaceful possession to adjacent tenants — noisy tenants played a Victrola from 8 p.m. until 2 or 3 a.m. and held parties at which "drunken merrymakers indulged in loud and obscene language").

The following case explores the meaning of the term "disturbance" as it is used in the Civil Code articles governing the warranty of peaceful possession.

Union Bank v. Cottonport Ins. Exchange

630 So. 2d 975 (La. App. 3 Cir. 1994)

WOODARD, Judge.

This appeal arises out of a suit by the assignee of a lease interest to recover rent payments allegedly due under the lease agreement.

FACTS

Plaintiff, The Union Bank, held a promissory note executed by Avoyelles Insurance Agency. The note was secured by a mortgage on an office building in Hessmer, Louisiana. Avoyelles leased the office building to defendant, Cottonport Insurance Exchange, for a three year term beginning May 1, 1988. The lease agreement also contained an option to purchase, which was never exercised. Both the lease agreement and the mortgage were properly recorded, however the mortgage was superior to the lease.

Avoyelles defaulted on the note with the Bank, and on September 28, 1989, the Bank filed a petition for executory process to enforce the mortgage. An order permitting the seizure and sale of the office building was signed October 21, 1989.

Three days later, a representative from the Bank went to the office building. He was accompanied by a sheriff's deputy. When they arrived at the office building they met Cottonport's representative, Mr. Jerry Guillory. Mr. Guillory testified that he was told the men had come to seize the building. The Bank, however, was apparently unaware of Avoyelles' lease agreement with Cottonport. Upon learning of the lease agreement, the Bank representative made a phone call and then left, telling Mr. Guillory they would come back later.

Believing that the property could be seized at any time, Mr. Guillory vacated the building and moved his offices to another location. Cottonport discontinued paying the monthly rent at this time.

On October 27, 1989, two representatives from the Bank made an inventory and took measurements of the office building. For several months after this, the Bank did nothing with the property. On April 3, 1990, the Bank entered into a *dation en paiement* with Avoyelles where Avoyelles transferred the building, along with its interest in the lease, to the Bank. [Emphasis added]

On October 5, 1990, the Bank filed this lawsuit against Cottonport to enforce the lease. The Bank sued to collect past due rent and all other rent due under the lease acceleration clause. Cottonport claimed it owed nothing because the lease was terminated when Cottonport's peaceful possession was disturbed by the threat of seizure of the property.

The trial court found that the petition for executory process and the signed order for seizure of the property were a disturbance of Cottonport's peaceful possession of the leased premises. The trial court found the lease was terminated and rendered judgment in favor of Cottonport. It is from this judgment that the Bank appeals, assigning as error the trial court's finding that Cottonport's peaceful possession was disturbed. We reverse.

DISTURBANCE OF PEACEABLE POSSESSION

A lessor is obligated to maintain the lessee in peaceable possession of the premises during the continuance of the lease. La.C.C. art. 2692 [R.C.C. 2682]; *T.D. Bickham Corp. v. Hebert,* 432 So.2d 228 (La.1983). In *Henry Rose Mercantile & Mfg. Co. v. Stearns,* 154 La. 946, 98 So. 429 (La.1923), the Supreme Court found that a lessor suing for rent due under a lease must exercise care in executing a writ of seizure so that the lessee's possession is not unnecessarily disturbed. A lessor has breached its obligation to maintain the lessee in peaceable possession if a disturbance is such that the lessee can no longer use the premises for the purposes intended. *Shreveport*

Plaza Assoc. v. L.R. Resources, 557 So.2d 1067 (La.App. 2 Cir.1990); see also *Bowers v. Greene*, 386 So.2d 920 (La.App. 3 Cir.), writ denied, 390 So.2d 202 (La.1980); *Salim v. Louisiana State Board of Education*, 289 So.2d 554 (La.App. 3 Cir.), writ denied, 293 So.2d 177 (La.1974).

In the case *sub judice*, an order was signed for the seizure and sale of the property, however no actual seizure ever took place. Cottonport was never denied access to the building and was never told to vacate the premises. A sheriff's deputy visited the leased premises for approximately fifteen minutes on October 24, 1989, and bank representatives took an inventory of the building for approximately thirty minutes on October 27, 1989. A necessary temporary or insignificant disturbance is not grounds for the abrogation of a lease. *Friendly Finance, Inc. v. Cefalu Realty Investment, Inc.*, 278 So.2d 584 (La.App. 1 Cir.), writ denied, 281 So.2d 747 (La.1973).

Cottonport was never prevented from using the premises for its intended purposes. Although Cottonport vacated the building, it did so by its own choice. We therefore find that the trial court erred in concluding that Cottonport's peaceable possession was disturbed. The Petition for Executory Process and order for the seizure and sale of the property did not disturb Cottonport's peaceable possession, thus, Cottonport breached the lease agreement when it ceased paying rent. We, therefore, reverse the judgment of the trial court dismissing the demands of The Union Bank.

Notes and Questions

1. Can the warranty of peaceful possession be limited or excluded by the parties? Although the Civil Code is silent on this point, it is widely accepted that the warranty cannot be waived in its entirety given that the undisturbed use and possession of the thing is the lessee's principal cause in the lease. *See* LA. CIV. CODE art. 2699 cmt. a; *Entergy Louisiana, Inc. v. Kennedy*, 859 So. 2d 74, 80–81 (La. App. 1 Cir. 2003); 2 PETER S. TITLE, LOUISIANA REAL ESTATE TRANSACTIONS § 18:21 (2017-8 ed.). The parties may, however, modify the lessor's obligations under this warranty, for example by providing that the lessor may enter the premises in order to make inspections or repairs after prior notice to the lessee, place "for rent" or "for sale" signs on the property, and show the property to prospective lessees or buyers. *See, e.g., Succession of Marx v. Schornstein*, 169 So. 93 (La. Ct. App., Orleans 1936); *Hartz v. Stauffer*, 111 So. 794 (La. 1927). The lessor and lessee may also agree that contractors employed by the lessor may enter the premises. *See Cross v. Breland*, 185 So. 542 (La. App. Orleans 1941). Presumably the parties may also agree that the lessee will tolerate noise and other disturbances caused by occupants of adjacent property belonging to the lessor.

2. Recall that if the owner-lessor of an immovable transfers the leased property to a third person and the lease is not recorded, the transferee is not bound by the lease. LA. CIV. CODE art. 2712. However, as long as the parties do not agree otherwise, the lessee may have an action against the lessor for any loss sustained as a result of the transfer. *Id; see also Black Water Marsh, LLC v. Roger C. Ferriss Properties, Inc.*, 2017

WL 5900748 (La. App. 3 Cir. 2017). Of course, the parties may agree that the lease will terminate if the lessor transfers the leased thing to a third person. In such a case, the lessor is not liable for any damage suffered by the lessee as long as the lessor gives sufficient notice of the termination of the lease. *See* LA. CIV. CODE arts. 2712 cmt. (d), 2718.

3. In the following case, the Louisiana Supreme Court considered whether a lessor should bear any liability for damage to the lessee's person or property caused by the criminal activity of third persons.

Potter v. First Federal Savings & Loan Ass'n of Scotlandville
615 So. 2d 318 (La. 1993)

ORTIQUE, Justice

A month after plaintiff allegedly complained to the assistant manager of her apartment complex about the inadequacy of the lighting in the complex's parking lot and was assured that the burned out floodlights would be replaced and the lighting system upgraded, plaintiff was raped and robbed in the poorly lit parking lot by an unknown assailant. The Trial Court granted summary judgment dismissing her suit for damages with prejudice in favor of defendants, the owner/lessor of the apartment complex and its managerial company. The Appellate Court affirmed, primarily based upon its determination that a lessor is not liable to its lessees for the intentional torts of third persons based upon LSA-C.C. art. 2703 [R.C.C. 2702]. We granted writ of certiorari to consider whether article 2703 [R.C.C. 2702] immunizes the lessor from liability precluding the lessee from pursuing tort and/or breach of contract claims against the lessor, despite allegations of the lessor's fault, when the intervening cause of the harm is the conduct of a third person who is not claiming a possessory right to the leased property.

We find that the lessee's right to seek redress from the lessor on claims that the lessor breached obligations *ex contractu* and *ex delicto* are unaffected by article 2703 [R.C.C. 2702]. Article 2703 [R.C.C. 2702] applies only to the premises leased to the lessee and does not grant the lessor absolute immunity. When the lessor is otherwise free from fault, it merely limits the lessor's warranty of peaceful possession, excusing him from guaranteeing the lessee against disturbances caused by third persons not claiming any right to the leased premises. Applying these precepts to the pleadings, affidavits and exhibits of record, we find that all genuine issues of material fact relating to the lessor and manager's duties owed to lessee have not been resolved. We, therefore, vacate the summary judgment and remand for further proceedings.

FACTUAL AND PROCEDURAL HISTORY

On February 8, 1989, Adiana Kathleen Potter ("Potter") was raped and robbed in the poorly lit parking area of Turtle Creek Apartment complex ("Turtle Creek") where she resided. She filed this breach of contract and tort action against the owner/lessor of the apartment complex, First Federal Savings & Loan Association of Scotlandville ("First Federal"); the apartment complex's managerial company,

Kim Knighten and Associates ("Knighten"); and State Farm General Insurance Company ("State Farm"). Potter's petition alleges the exterior of the apartment complex was poorly lit and the complex lacked adequate security. It claims that prior to the occurrence of her rape, the Turtle Creek complex and other apartment complexes in the immediate area had been the subject of repeated burglaries and vandalism, and tenants had complained about the need for additional lighting because the poor lighting conditions invited crime. It alleges Knighten was under contract with First Federal for the management of Turtle Creek, and Knighten obligated itself to take all reasonable measures to ensure the safety of the complex's tenants. It further alleges that First Federal is vicariously liable for the negligent acts of its agent, Knighten; is contractually liable as lessor; and is strictly liable due to its legal garde of the complex as it was in ruin as a result of the burned out exterior lights.

First Federal, Knighten and State Farm moved for summary judgment claiming Potter was not owed any legal duty of protection from unforeseen and unforeseeable intentional criminal acts of a third parties and legal causation was lacking between Potter's damages and the allegedly inadequate lighting. Kim Knighten's deposition and affidavit and Potter's deposition accompanied the motion. The memorandum in support concluded Potter's petition must be dismissed due to the lessor's immunity from liability pursuant to article 2703 [R.C.C. 2702], the absence of a duty owed to Potter to provide security or lighting and the lack of causation.

Defendants' uncontested material facts acknowledged the absence of a written lease between Potter and First Federal, Knighten and/or Turtle Creek. It declared no warranties or guarantees concerning safety were made by Kim Knighten to Potter. However, it did not state Knighten's other employees had not made warranties to Potter. Defendants' statement of uncontested material facts also asserted Kim Knighten was unaware of any crimes against persons occurring at the Turtle Creek complex and of any information which would have led her to believe that Potter's rape was foreseeable. It stated Kim Knighten was not aware of any specific complaints by Potter with regard to the lighting in the parking areas, but it did not indicate that Knighten had not received complaints from other tenants or that Potter had not raised such complaints to other Knighten employees. In her deposition, Kim Knighten testified that complaints about burned out exterior lights were responded to within one and a one-half days of the complaint. Yet, she admitted that, subsequent to the rape of Potter, the electrician replaced at least a dozen (12) flood-light bulbs out of a total of twenty-six (26) and the complex's exterior lighting was upgraded.

The deposition of Potter indicated she mainly dealt with James Coussins ("Coussins"), Knighten's assistant manager. She arranged with Coussins to obtain and sign a copy of the lease; however, he failed to produce it. She testified she complained to Coussins once or twice about the complex's exterior lighting being so inadequate that at night she could not differentiate between her automobile and someone else's vehicle. Speaking about a conversation she had with Coussins three or four weeks prior to the attack, Potter testified:

> When I had complained about the lights, I knew that several complaints were before mine; and he assured me that it was being taken care of. And he said that Kim [Knighten] had arranged to have more powerful lights and more number of lights put out, and that to me was satisfactory.

Potter's opposition to the motion insisted article 2703 [R.C.C. 2702] is irrelevant to her causes of action against defendants for breach of contract, negligence and strict liability. Potter urged that causation from the lack of security or foreseeability of the criminal act was a question of fact, inappropriate for summary judgment. Her opposition was supported by the affidavits of Erin Spaht, Karen Seibert and Frank J. Panepinto, CPP.

The affidavits of both Spaht and Seibert averred they had complained to Coussins about the poor lighting. They both described the lighting as "dark as an unilluminated room with a single window at night" and it was "impossible to distinguish colors in the parking lot." Spaht averred she left notes for Knighten and talked to her in person concerning the poor lighting problem. Seibert's affidavit also recounted that she had informed Coussins about her dog causing an unknown male to jump up from behind a car in the parking lot. He told her he was just smoking a cigarette. Panepinto, a Certified Protection Professional, averred that sufficient lighting is a deterrent to crime and the lighting at the time of the rape was insufficient. He considered Turtle Creek a high crime area as in 1988, its surrounding 11 block area had 80 burglaries, 21 simple batteries, 4 aggravated batteries, 4 aggravated assaults, 43 suspicious persons, 5 prowlers, 1 robbery, 1 crime against nature, 1 peeping tom and 60 thefts from automobiles.

Following a hearing, the Trial Court declared First Federal and Knighten did not have legal duty to protect Potter from the harm she sustained. It, therefore, granted defendants' motion for summary judgment and dismissed Potter's petition with prejudice. The Appellate Court affirmed. *Potter v. First Fed. Sav. & Loan Ass'n of Scotlandville*, 602 So.2d 1070 (La.App. 1st Cir.1992). It determined that a lessor is not liable to its lessees for the intentional torts of third persons because article 2703 [R.C.C. 2702] applies to torts committed by third persons on premises leased to the lessee and on premises to which the lessee has access. It also determined Potter could not prevail under the theory of strict liability and footnoted that she could not prevail under LSA-C.C. art. 2315 negligence. The dissenting judge found article 2703 [R.C.C. 2702] inapplicable because the attack occurred in the complex's common area and found summary judgment improper as genuine issues of material fact remained.

From this adverse judgment, Potter sought writ from this court. We granted certiorari, 607 So.2d 547 (La.1992), to examine whether article 2703 [R.C.C. 2702] immunizes the lessor from liability precluding the lessee from pursuing tort and/or breach of contract claims against the lessor, despite allegations of the lessor's fault, when the intervening cause of the harm is the conduct of a third person who is not claiming a possessory right to the leased property.

THE LIMITED PROTECTION AFFORDED A LESSOR UNDER ARTICLE 2703 [R.C.C. 2702]

To prevent their misapplication, the articles of the Civil Code must not be read in isolation. See LSA-C.C. art. 13. Codal articles must be read together, as an integrated whole. *See Reynolds v. Egan*, 123 La. 294, 48 So. 940, 946 (1908).

The lessor's duties *ex contractu* are set forth in the parties' contract of lease; in Title IX of the Civil Code, *Of Lease*, art. 2669 *et seq.* [R.C.C. 2668–2729]; and in Title III of the Civil Code, *Obligations in General*, art. 1756 *et seq.* The lessor's duties *ex delicto* are also provided by the Civil Code. For example, LSA-C.C. arts. 670, 2315, 2316, 2317, 2332. As a result, the duties of a lessor may have more than one source, as in the case of a negligent breach of a contractual obligation, in which case causes of action lie for both the breach and the negligence. *Gray & Co., Inc. v. Ranger Ins. Co.*, 292 So.2d 829, 830 (La.App. 1st Cir.1974). The existence of the lessor/lessee relationship and contractual remedies, therefore, does not preclude lessor liability for breach of duties *ex delicto. Bunge Corp. v. GATX Corp.*, 557 So.2d 1376 (La.1990), *reh'g den.; Federal Ins. Co. v. Insurance Co. of N. America*, 262 La. 509, 263 So.2d 871 (1972); *Thompson v. Cane Gardens Apts.*, 442 So.2d 1296 (La.App. 3d Cir.1983).

Under the rules *Of Lease*, a lease is a bilateral contract by which one party binds himself to grant to the other the enjoyment of a thing during a certain time, for a certain stipulated price which the other party binds himself to pay. LSA-C.C. arts. 2669 [R.C.C. 2668], 2674 [R.C.C. 2668]. From the nature of the contract of lease, the lessor is bound, without any clause to that effect, to maintain the thing in a condition such as to serve the use for which it was hired and to cause the lessee to be in peaceable possession of the thing during the continuation of the lease. LSA-C.C. art. 2692 [R.C.C. 2682]. These are warranties implied in every contract of lease. Failure of the lessor to fulfill either of these obligations is a breach of contract and may cause a finding of constructive eviction of the lessee. Comment, *The Louisiana Law of Lease*, 39 Tul.L.Rev. 798, 821 (1965); *Cf. Keenan v. Flanigan*, 157 La. 749, 103 So. 30 (1925); *Gayle v. Auto-Lec Stores*, 174 La. 1044, 142 So. 258 (1932); *Credithrift of America, Inc. v. Sinclair*, 430 So.2d 822 (La.App. 5th Cir.1983).

Even though the nature of the lease contract binds the lessor to maintain the lessee in peaceable possession of the thing during the continuation of the lease via article 2692 [R.C.C. 2682], there:

> might well be that *in some given case the lessor would be unable to comply with his obligations and yet be free from fault.* The law, therefore, deals equitably with both parties under special circumstances. Under some circumstances it limits the relief of the lessee to a reduction of rent; . . . under others, *absolving the lessor of all blame, it requires the lessee to bring his action against third parties troubling or disturbing his rights.*

Where the rights of the lessee are disturbed by third parties not claiming any right to the premises, *and* under circumstances which bring the case under the provisions of article 2703 [R.C.C. 2702], the lessor is protected from attack by the lessee under its express terms. *Reynolds v. Egan*, 48 So. at 946-947. (emphasis added)

Thus, to protect the lessor when he is free from fault, article 2703 provides that the *lessor is not bound to guarantee* the lessee against disturbances caused by persons not claiming any right to the premises;[6] but in that case the lessee has a right of action for damages sustained against the person occasioning the disturbance. *Dixie Homestead Ass'n v. Intravia*, 145 So. 561 (La.App.Orl.1933); *Robicheaux v. Roy*, 352 So.2d 766, 767 (La.App. 3d Cir.1977), *writ den.*, 354 So.2d 207 (La.1978). Simply stated, the lessor's implied warranty of peaceful possession does not extend to disturbances by third persons not claiming any right to the leasehold. *Dixie Homestead Ass'n v. Intravia, supra; Keenan v. Flanigan*, 157 La. 749, 103 So. 30, 37 (1925) ["a lessor is not bound to warrant his lessee against a disturbance caused by a person who does not claim under covenant with lessor, a right to be in a position to carry on the disturbance; e.g., a lessor is not responsible for a disturbance inflicted upon his lessee by a trespasser"]; *see also Credithrift of America, Inc. v. Sinclair, supra.*

This principle is clarified by article 2704 [R.C.C. 2701] which sets forth that, if the persons by whom those acts of disturbance have been committed, pretend to have a right to the thing leased, the lessee shall call his lessor in warranty. LSA-C.C. art. 2704 [R.C.C. 2701]; *Bright v. Bell*, 113 La. 1078, 37 So. 976, 980 (1905) ["It is true that the lessor is not bound to guaranty the lessee against disturbances caused by persons not claiming any right to the premises, but he is bound to protect the lessee in quiet enjoyment of the property leased as against persons who set up such claims; and in either case the possession of the lessee being possession of the lessor, the disturbance of one is necessarily the disturbance of the other."]; *see* 1 Aubry & Rau, Civil Law Translations § 310, Obligations (6th ed. 1965). *Disturbances* as used in articles 2703 and 2704 [R.C.C. 2701], then, refers to disturbances of the lessee's possession by third persons in the context of the lessor's implied contractual warranties of article 2692. [R.C.C. 2682].[8] *See Cornelius v. Housing Authority of New Orleans*, 539 So.2d 1250, 1251 (La.App. 4th Cir.1989), *writ den.*, 544 So.2d 404 (La.1989).

---

6. "According to the French, the lessee alone must defend against such disturbances because they result from his negligence in not taking better care of the thing leased, or from activity directed against him personally, as distinguished from claims of right to the thing leased which ultimately concern the lessor. The disturbances for which the lessee has his own action include not only intentional acts, but also negligent acts which result in injury to the premises." Comments, *Disturbance of the Lessee's Possession in Louisiana*, 29 La.L.Rev. 101, 112 (1968) (citations omitted).

8. Relative to the warranty to maintain the condition of the thing leased, a lessor may be held liable where he assumes an implied or express obligation to provide security maintenance to the lessee and a breach of that obligation is the proximate cause of a tort committed by a third person. *U.S. Fidelity & Guar. Ins. Co. v. Burns Itern. Sec. Serv., Inc.*, 468 So.2d 662 (La.App. 4th Cir.1985), *writ den.*, 470 So.2d 882 (La.1985); *See also* 59 Tul.L.Rev. at 729-731; *Gant v. Flint-Goodridge Hospital of Dillard University*, 359 So.2d 279 (La.App. 4th Cir.1978), dissent 356 So.2d at 281, *writ not*

The lessee's right to seek redress from his lessor on claims that the lessor breached obligations *ex contractu* and *ex delicto*, therefore, are unaffected by the provisions of article 2703. *Cf. Day v. Castilow*, 407 So.2d 510 (La.App. 4th Cir.1981). Article 2703 [R.C.C. 2702] does not impede the lessee's action for breach of contract against his lessor when the lessor is charged with fault. *Reynolds v. Egan*, 123 La. 294, 48 So. 940, 948 (1908); Comments, *Landlord Liability—Obligation to Maintain Adequate Security—A Comparative Study*, 59 Tul.L.Rev. 701, 729-731 (1985). Nor does article 2703 [R.C.C. 2702] preclude the lessee's tort action against the lessor for injuries he sustained from intervening acts of a third person when the lessor's negligence or breach of other tort duties was a cause in fact and a legal cause of the lessee's injuries. Case law to the contrary maintaining article 2703 [R.C.C. 2702] absolves the lessor from liability for the lessee's damages when a third person not claiming any right to the premises commits an intentional tort against the lessee, notwithstanding a breach of contract or tort fault by the lessor, inaccurately overstates the legal consequences of article 2703 [R.C.C. 2702]. For example, *Gant v. Flint-Goodridge Hospital of Dillard University*, 359 So.2d 279 (La.App. 4th Cir.1978), *writ not consid.*, 362 So.2d 581 (La.1978); *Reilly v. Fairway View II Assoc. Ltd. Partnership*, 544 So.2d 73 (La.App. 1st Cir.1989). As a matter of law, article 2703 [R.C.C. 2702] merely limits the lessor's warranty of peaceful possession, when the lessor is free from fault, excusing him from guaranteeing the lessee against disturbances caused by third persons not claiming any right to the premises. Parenthetically, by implication it applies only to the property leased to lessee and not to common areas or areas to which the lessee has only access, but not a possessory right.

In the instant case, plaintiff's right to proceed is not based upon the efficacy or ineffectiveness of article 2703 [R.C.C. 2702]. Jurisprudence which gives to article 2703 [R.C.C. 2702] a meaning of absolute immunity is overreaching and overbroad. If plaintiff is able to establish facts sufficient to evoke the principles enumerated heretofore, she has a remedy at law.

PROPRIETY OF SUMMARY JUDGMENT

* * * * *

Applying the foregoing criteria, as a matter of law, First Federal, Knighten and State Farm are not entitled to summary judgment. The lower courts erred in concluding that article 2703 [R.C.C. 2702] absolved First Federal and Knighten from liability. As a consequence, their review of the issues presented and of the merits of the motion was impeded. Reviewing the summary judgment evidence in light of the lessor's lack of immunity, we find the evidence on record reveals genuine issues exist regarding whether First Federal and Knighten owed Potter contractual and/or tort

---

consid., 362 So.2d 581 (La.1978). In *Thompson v. Cane Garden Apts.*, 442 So.2d 1296 (La.App. 3d Cir.1983), the allegations that, lessor expressly warranted a security guard was on duty and the lease contract provided lessor would maintain the premises in a decent and safe condition, yet as a result of the breach of the obligation an intruder gained access to plaintiff lessees' apartment, assaulting them, stated causes of action in contract and tort.

duties to maintain adequate exterior lighting, to keep the complex in a reasonably safe condition and/or to provide her a reasonably safe place. *See generally Roberts v. Benoit*, 605 So.2d 1032, 1050 (La.1992) (on reh'g); *Harris v. Pizza Hut, Inc.*, 455 So.2d 1364 (La.1984).

Potter's deposition indicates she spoke to Coussins once or twice about the lighting being so inadequate that at night she could not differentiate between her automobile and someone else's vehicle. Weeks prior to the attack, Coussins assured her the exterior lights were, "being taken care of. And . . . Kim had arranged to have more powerful lights and more number of lights put out." Since Potter's alleged lease is an oral one, Coussins' assurances could have modified the terms of the contract of lease, creating an express or implied contractual duty to maintain adequate lighting in the parking area. *See* note 8, *supra*.

Relative to this contractual duty to maintain adequate lighting, the implied warranty of habitability and the tort duty to maintain the property in a reasonably safe condition, the evidence conflicted on the speed at which Knighten replaced burned out flood lights. Defendants' statement of uncontested facts maintained that the bulbs were replaced within one and one-half days of Knighten's receipt of tenant complaints. Potter's deposition and Seibert and Spaht's affidavits, however, evince that inadequate lighting from burned out floodlights was a continuous problem and tenant complaints on the issue were not attended to promptly. Potter's position is supported by Knighten's admission that after the rape, it was necessary to replace 12 of the 26 floodlight bulbs.

Germane to the foreseeability of a criminal attack on Potter, Seibert's affidavit recounted that she had informed Coussins about her dog finding an unknown male behind a car in the parking lot, causing him to jump up from where he was seemingly lurking. Genuine issues, therefore, exist as to whether a dangerous condition was created from inadequate lighting, whether the inadequate lighting encouraged criminal attacks and/or enhanced their foreseeability, and/or, if there was a breach of a duty owed to Potter, whether that breach was causally connected to her damages.

Based upon these illustrative issues, defendants did not meet their burden of establishing an absence of genuine issues of material fact. Their affidavits, depositions and exhibits defendants introduced in support of their motion failed to meet the exacting burden required for summary judgment, thus, they are not entitled to judgment as a matter of law.

DECREE

For the reasons assigned, the summary judgment rendered in favor of First Federal, Knighten and State Farm is vacated and the case is remanded for further proceedings. Costs are assessed against defendant/respondents.

VACATED AND REMANDED.

CALOGERO, C.J., concurs and assigns reasons.

WATSON, J., joins in the opinion and adds brief concurring reasons.

WATSON, Justice, concurring.

The court of appeal erred in considering only Civil Code art. 2703 [R.C.C. 2702]. This is an art. 2315 (negligence) and art. 2317 (strict liability) case. I respectfully concur.

CALOGERO, Chief Justice, concurring.

There are genuine issues of material fact concerning defendant's alleged negligence. The majority is correct concerning the court of appeal's misapplication of Civil Code Article 2703 [R.C.C. 2702].

Notes and Questions

The lessor's warranty of peaceful possession governs the extent to which a lessor is liable to the lessee for disturbances of the lessee's use and possession caused by the lessor or third persons. What rules govern the lessor's liability *to third persons* for disturbances caused *by the lessee*? According to the Louisiana Supreme Court, the lessor's responsibility for disturbances to third persons caused by the lessee's use and possession of the premises falls under Article 667 of the Civil Code. *Yokum v. 615 Bourbon Street, L.L.C.*, 977 So. 2d 859 (La. 2008). That article provides: "Although a proprietor may do with his estate whatever he pleases, still he cannot make any work on it, which may deprive his neighbor of the liberty of enjoying his own, or which may be the cause of any damage to him." LA. CIV. CODE art. 667. A "proprietor" whose "works" cause damage to his neighbor is answerable "only upon a showing that he knew, or in the exercise of reasonable care, should have known that his works would cause damage, that the damage could have been prevented by the exercise of reasonable care, and that he failed to exercise such reasonable care." *Id.* In *Yokum*, residents of the French Quarter in New Orleans brought suit against the owner-lessor of a building located on Bourbon Street, complaining that the bar operated by the lessee interfered with their enjoyment of their home. Without deciding that the owner-lessor in question was responsible for the plaintiffs' damages, the court held that an owner-lessor with full knowledge of the potentially harmful effects of the lessee's activities may be answerable for any damage the lessee causes. 977 So. 2d 859, 875–76 (La. 2008).

C. The Lessee's Obligations

The lessee's obligations under Article 2683 are: "(1) [t]o pay the rent in accordance with the agreed terms; (2) [t]o use the thing as a prudent administrator and in accordance with the purpose for which it was leased; and (3) [t]o return the thing at the end of the lease in a condition that is the same as when it was delivered to him, except for normal wear or as otherwise provided [by law]." LA. CIV. CODE art. 2683. Each of these obligations is addressed in detail below.

1. To Pay Rent
La. Civ. Code arts. 2703–2710

The lessee is obligated to pay the rent when and where it is due. La. Civ. Code arts. 2683(1), 2703. In the absence of a contrary agreement of the parties, usage, or custom, the rent is due at the beginning of the term. La. Civ. Code art. 2703(1). In residential and commercial leases, rent is frequently payable at shorter intervals, usually on a monthly basis. When rent is payable by intervals shorter than the term, the rent is due at the beginning of each interval unless the parties agree otherwise. *Id.* In a common example, Lessor leases an apartment to Lessee for one year (January 1 to December 31, 2019) with total rent set at $12,000, and Lessor and Lessee agree that rent will be paid in $1000 increments on the first day of each month.

With respect to where the rent must be paid, the Civil Code provides that the rent is payable at the address provided by the lessor and, in the absence thereof, at the address of the lessee. *Id.*

If the lessee fails to pay the rent when due, the lessor's rights are governed by the Title on Conventional Obligations or Contracts, under which the lessor may seek dissolution of the lease and damages. La. Civ. Code art. 2704. Dissolution of leases is addressed further in Chapter 15: Termination and Dissolution of the Lease.

2. To Use the Thing as a Prudent Administrator and in Accordance with the Lease
La. Civ. Code arts. 2686–2689

The lessee is required to use the thing "as a prudent administrator" and "in accordance with the purpose for which it was leased." La. Civ. Code art. 2683(2). If the lessee uses the thing for an improper purpose or in a manner that may cause damage to the thing, the lessor may seek dissolution of the lease or injunctive relief and, in either case, damages. La. Civ. Code art. 2686. The lessee is answerable also for any damage to the thing caused by his or her fault or that of a person who is on the premises or uses the thing with the lessee's consent. La. Civ. Code art. 2687. The following seminal Louisiana Supreme Court case addresses the determination of whether the lessee's use of the thing is proper.

New Orleans & C.R. Co. v. Darms
2 So. 230 (La. 1887)

Fenner, J.

This action invokes the remedy of injunction to prevent the improper use of property leased by plaintiff to defendant, and seeks to annul the lease on the ground of such improper use. The use complained of is the establishment of a bar-room or coffee-house and a gaming-house. The evidence clearly establishes that, some months after taking possession of the leased premises, the defendant did fit up and open a public bar-room for the sale of spirituous drinks, with a room attached, provided with card-tables, where visitors played cards for drinks.

Article 2710 Civil Code [R.C.C. 2683] provides: "the lessee is bound—*First*, to enjoy the thing leased, as a good administrator, *according to the use for which it was intended by the lease; second*, to pay the rents at the terms agreed on." It is not necessary that the use according to which the thing is to be enjoyed should be expressed in the lease; nor does it follow, if the lease is silent as to the use, that the lessee may make of the thing leased any use which he pleases. On the contrary, this court used the following language in a case of this sort: "the lease is silent as to the destination or object to which the building was to be affected. The inference is that the parties intended that it should be used for one of the purposes to which it had previously been put, etc.; the question of determination to be determined according to surrounding circumstances." *Murrell v. Jackson*, 33 La. Ann. 1342. In an earlier case the court said: "the evidence establishes that the plaintiff's right of action was well founded; that the store rented to defendant was never intended by plaintiff to be used as a kitchen; that no such use was in contemplation at the time the lease was contracted," etc. *Caffin v. Scott*, 7 Rob. (La.) 205.

We quote these decisions to show that, notwithstanding some difference between the language of our article and that of the corresponding article of the French Code, 1729, they have been construed as substantially identical in meaning, and hence that the French authorities are fully applicable. Those authorities are quite unanimous in support of the doctrine announced by Marcade in the following language: "the destination of the thing will be sometimes fixed by the agreement; but often the contract will be silent in this respect; and it is then by the situation of the place, by the use to which the thing had been previously put, and by the character under which the lessee presents himself, that the destination shall be gathered. That destination, in whatever manner it shall appear, the lessee is bound to respect. Thus, not only shall the lessee, in default of an express stipulation, not be permitted to establish in a private dwelling a house of prostitution or gambling house, but he cannot transform a private apartment into a restaurant or coffee-house, a club, nor a private house into an inn or hotel." 6 Marcade, 459; 3 Delvincourt, 192; 17 Duranton, No. 98; Duvergier Louage, No. 308; 25 Laurent, No. 257.

It is held that the establishment of a house of prostitution or of a gaming house would in no case be sustained, unless the lessor has positive knowledge that such was the use for which the lessee rented the premises. Duvergier, No. 402; Troplong, No. 302.

In a lease which authorized the lessee to sublease, "*a qui bon lui sembler a ou lui plaira*," it was still held that he could not sublease to one who would use the thing in a manner contrary to its destination. Poth. Louage, No. 281; Troplong, Louage, No. 1276; Duvergier, Louage, No. 391.

Now, in the instant case, the evidence shows that the building leased was contiguous to the depot and stables of plaintiff, at the corner of Napoleon and St. Charles avenues, and was built to serve as a boarding-house and lodging house for drivers and other employees; that it had been used to some extent for that purpose, and had never been otherwise used, except, partially, as business offices; that plaintiff had received numerous offers to rent it as a bar-room and coffee-house, at much higher rent than was paid by defendant, but had always refused; that no bar-room or other place for sale of spirituous liquors had ever been permitted; that defendant, prior to the lease, had kept a private market not far from this place, in which business he had been engaged for many years, and that he had never kept a bar-room or coffee-house; that, when he applied to rent the place, he asked permission to open a private market there, which was at first refused, and only granted after discussion and intervention of friends; that for the first three months of the lease he used the house simply for the purpose of a private market, and for offices and lodgings, and that it was only after that time that he indicated his purpose of opening the bar-room; and finally that, as soon as plaintiff heard of such purpose, it promptly protested against and prohibited it.

The foregoing surrounding circumstances would be amply sufficient to establish that the opening of a bar-room in the house was contrary to "the use for which it was intended by the lease." But, in addition thereto, the plaintiff offers evidence to prove that, during the negotiations for the lease, defendant was expressly notified that under no circumstances would the selling of spirituous liquors be permitted on the premises. This evidence was rejected on the ground that parol evidence was inadmissible to contradict or vary a written contract.

We think the ruling was error, and that the evidence fell within the familiar exception to the general rule which admits parol, in order to ascertain the nature and qualities of the subject-matter of the contract, *e.g.*, to identify or define the extent of the premises leased or sold, when not sufficiently described in the written contract, and the like. 1 Greenl. Ev. §§ 286, 298a; *Sargent v. Adams*, 3 Gray, 72; *Falcon v. Boucherville*, 1 Rob. (La.) 337; *Moore v. Hampton*, 3 La. Ann. 193; *D'Aquin v. Barbour*, 4 La. Ann. 411; *Corbett v. Costello*, 8 La. Ann. 427; *McLeroy v. Duckworth*, 13 La. Ann. 410.

In this case the use of the premises is the cause or consideration of the conduct; and we have shown that, in the silence of the contract as to the nature and kind of use contemplated between the parties, resort must be had to parol evidence of the surrounding circumstances to ascertain the intentions and define the rights of the parties. No circumstance could be of so much significance as the express notice given to the lessee that a certain use, foreign to the destination of the premises, would not be allowed. The evidence is found in the record, and although, perhaps, unnecessary to our decision, we may give it effect, and it confirms the conclusions arrived at.

Plaintiff claims a dissolution of the lease under article 2711 of the Code [R.C.C. 2686], which provides: "If the lessee makes another use of the thing than that for which it was intended, and if any loss is thereby sustained by the lessor, the latter may obtain the dissolution of the lease." In this case, the improper use was stopped by the injunction almost as soon as it had begun, and the lessor has suffered no loss. Under the similar article 1729 of the French Code it is held that the right to dissolution for this cause is not absolute, but is left to the discretion of the court according to the circumstances. Troplong, Louage, No. 316; Duvergier, Louage, No. 107.

We think in this case the right of plaintiff will be sufficiently vindicated by perpetuating the injunction, without dissolving the lease, which runs for five years. It is therefore ordered, adjudged, and decreed that the verdict and judgment appealed from be annulled and set aside; and that there be judgment in favor of plaintiff, and against defendant, perpetuating the injunction granted therein, and rejecting the reconventional demand of defendant; defendant to pay all costs in the lower court and of this appeal.

Rehearing refused May 28, 1887.

Notes and Questions

1. According to Article 2688, "The lessee is bound to notify the lessor without delay when the thing has been damaged or requires repair, or when his possession has been disturbed by a third person." La. Civ. Code art. 2688. If the lessee fails to give the lessee notice of disturbances or needed repairs, the lessor is entitled to recover any damages sustained as a result of the lessee's failure to perform. *Id.*

2. "The lessor is bound to pay all taxes, assessments, and other charges that burden the thing, except those that arise from the use of the thing by the lessee." La. Civ. Code art. 2689. Thus, while the lessor generally owes the property taxes assessed to leased premises, the lessee is responsible for utilities.

3. Return of the Thing in the Same Condition
La. Civ. Code arts. 2686, 2691–2692

According to Article 2683, the lessee is required "[t]o return the thing at the end of the lease in a condition that is the same as when the thing was delivered to him, except for normal wear and tear or as otherwise provided [by law]." La. Civ. Code art. 2683. This provision requires the lessee to relinquish possession of the thing upon the termination of the lease. Although generally the lessee must deliver the thing in the same condition as he or she received it, this obligation is tempered by the rules governing the parties' respective obligations to make repairs to the thing that become necessary during the lease. As discussed in Subpart B.2.a, above, the lessor is generally bound to make all repairs, except those for which the lessee is responsible. La. Civ. Code art. 2691. The lessee, in turn, is responsible for damage to the thing caused by his fault or by the fault of persons who are on the premises or use the thing with the lessee's consent. La. Civ. Code art. 2692. The lessee is also responsible for any deterioration resulting from the lessee's use of the thing that exceeds "the normal or agreed use," or "normal wear and tear." *Id.*

D. Attachments, Additions & Improvements

La. Civ. Code arts. 2690, 2695

During the lease, the lessor may not make any alternations or improvements to the leased thing unless the parties agree otherwise. *See* LA. CIV. CODE art. 2690. Any attempt of the lessor to make unauthorized alterations or improvements to the thing could amount to a breach of the implied warranty of peaceful possession. *See* LA. CIV. CODE art. 2700.

The lessee, however, is generally free to make improvements to the leased property absent an agreement of the parties to the contrary, provided that the lessee restores the property to the condition in which it was received at the termination of the lease. LA. CIV. CODE art. 2695. If the lessee does not remove the improvements, the lessor may either (a) appropriate ownership of the improvements by reimbursing the lessee for their cost or for the enhanced value of the leased thing, whichever is less; or (b) demand that the lessee remove the improvements within a reasonable time and restore the leased thing to its former condition. *Id.* If the lessor opts to demand that the lessee remove the improvements, and the lessee fails to do so, the lessor may then either (a) remove the improvements and restore the leased thing to its former condition at the expense of the lessee or (b) appropriate ownership of the improvements without any obligation of reimbursement to the lessee. *Id.* Appropriation of the improvement by the lessor may only be accomplished by providing additional notice by certified mail to the lessee after expiration of the time given the lessee to remove the improvements. *Id.* Unless and until the lessor appropriates ownership of them, the improvements remain the property of the lessee. *Id.* As owner, the lessee is solely responsible for any harm caused by the improvements. *Id.*

E. Security Devices

The law recognizes two security devices that protect the lessor against the eventuality that the lessee may fail to perform his or her obligations: the lessor's privilege and the security deposit.

1. Lessor's Privilege

La. Civ. Code arts. 2707–2710, 3219; La. Code Civ. Proc. arts. 3571–3576

In leases of immovables, the lessor enjoys a privilege over the lessee's movables that are found in or upon the leased property. LA. CIV. CODE arts. 2707, 3219. This privilege secures the lessee's implied obligations and any obligations that are specifically provided by the parties' agreement. The lessor's privilege arises automatically by virtue of the parties' agreement, and the contract of lease need not be written for the privilege to be enforceable between the parties. Rather, even when the lease is unwritten and unrecorded, the lessor's privilege remains in effect for the duration of the lease.

All movable property belonging to the lessee that is located in or on the leased property is subject to the privilege. LA. CIV. CODE art. 2707. In addition, the movable property of a sublessee is also subject to the lessor's privilege, but "only to the extent that the sublessee is indebted to his sublessor at the time the lessor exercises his right." LA. CIV. CODE art. 2708. Even the movable property belonging to third parties is subject to the lessor's privilege, but only if the lessor does not know that those movable items did not belong to the lessee. LA. CIV. CODE art. 2709. If the property of a third person is seized under the lessor's privilege, the third person may recover the movable by establishing his ownership prior to the judicial sale in the manner provided by Article 1092 of the Code of Civil Procedure. *Id.* If the third person fails to do so, the movable may be sold as though it belonged to the lessee. *Id.*

To enforce the lessor's privilege, the lessor may seize the movables on which he or she has a privilege while they are in or upon the leased property, and for fifteen days after they have been removed if they remain the property of the lessee and can be identified. LA. CIV. CODE art. 2710. The lessor may enforce this privilege against movables that have been seized by the sheriff or other officer of the court, without the necessity of a further seizure thereof, as long as the movables or the proceeds therefrom remain in the custody of the officer. *Id.*

The lessor may not utilize self-help to enforce the privilege; rather, seizure is accomplished using the writ of sequestration. LA. CODE CIV. PROC. arts. 3571–3576. When used to enforce a lessor's privilege, the writ of sequestration issues without the furnishing of security. LA. CODE CIV. PROC. art. 3575. Significantly, the lessor may seize property of the lessee *before* the rent is due "if the lessor has good reason to believe that the lessee will remove the property subject to the lessee's privilege." LA. CODE CIV. PROC. art. 3572.

2. Security Deposit

La. Rev. Stat. §§ 9:3251–3254

The lessor may require that the lessee furnish a security deposit to secure the performance of the lessee's obligations. In residential leases, security deposits are governed by the Security Deposits Law, which is found in Title 9 of the Revised Statutes and reproduced below. According to these provisions, the lessor must return the deposit within one month of the date the lease terminates. LA. REV. STAT. § 9:3251. However, the lessor may retain the entire deposit or a portion of it to remedy a lessee's failure to perform, such as nonpayment of rent or damage to the premises. *Id.* If the lessee retains all or a portion of the deposit, the lessor must furnish to the lessee an itemized statement accounting for the retention. *Id.* If the lessor fails to return the deposit within thirty days of written demand for a refund, the lessee may claim, in addition to the return of the amount of the deposit wrongfully retained, damages in the amount of three hundred dollars or twice the amount of the portion of the security deposit wrongfully retained, whichever is greater. La. Rev. Stat. § 9:3252. In addition, the court may award attorney fees and costs to the prevailing party. La. Rev. Stat. § 9:3253. The rights of a residential lessee under the Security Deposits Law are nonwaivable. La. Rev. Stat. § 9:3254. The statutes cited are reproduced below.

Louisiana Revised Statutes § 9:3251. Lessee's deposit to secure lease; retention by lessor; conveyance of leased premises; itemized statement by lessor

A. Any advance or deposit of money furnished by a tenant or lessee to a landlord or lessor to secure the performance of any part of a written or oral lease or rental agreement shall be returned to the tenant or lessee of residential or dwelling premises within one month after the lease shall terminate, except that the landlord or lessor may retain all or any portion of the advance or deposit which is reasonably necessary to remedy a default of the tenant or to remedy unreasonable wear to the premises. If any portion of an advance or deposit is retained by a landlord or lessor, he shall forward to the tenant or lessee, within one month after the date the tenancy terminates, an itemized statement accounting for the proceeds which are retained and giving the reasons therefor. The tenant shall furnish the lessor a forwarding address at the termination of the lease, to which such statements may be sent.

B. In the event of a transfer of the lessor's interest in the leased premises during the term of a lease, the transferor shall also transfer to his successor in interest the sum deposited as security for performance of the lease and the transferor shall then be relieved of further liability with respect to the security deposit. The transferee shall be responsible for the return of the lessee's deposit at the termination of the lease, as set forth in Subsection A of this Section.

C. Paragraph A of this Section shall not apply when the tenant abandons the premises, either without giving notice as required or prior to the termination of the lease.

Louisiana Revised Statutes § 9:3252. Damages; venue

A. The willful failure to comply with R.S. 9:3251 shall give the tenant or lessee the right to recover any portion of the security deposit wrongfully retained and three hundred dollars or twice the amount of the portion of the security deposit wrongfully retained, whichever is greater, from the landlord or lessor, or from the lessor's successor in interest. Failure to remit within thirty days after written demand for a refund shall constitute willful failure.

B. An action for the recovery of such damages may be brought in the parish of the lessor's domicile or in the parish where the property is situated.

Louisiana Revised Statutes § 9:3253. Costs and attorney's fees

In an action brought under R.S. 9:3252, the court may in its discretion award costs and attorney's fees to the prevailing party.

Louisiana Revised Statutes § 9:3254. Waiver of tenant's rights prohibited

Any waiver of the right of a tenant under this part shall be null and void.

Chapter 15

Termination and Dissolution of the Lease

Leases do not go on forever—at some point all leases come to an end. A lease may terminate for any number of reasons: by the arrival of a fixed term, by notice of one of the parties to a lease with an indeterminate term, by expropriation or destruction of the leased thing, or through dissolution upon one party's failure to perform. The rules governing the duration of leases and the methods by which they are terminated are the subject of this Chapter.

A. The Arrival of the Term

Given that the term of a lease sets forth the period of its duration, one might think that upon the arrival of the term, the lease simply terminates. However, as the following Subparts demonstrate, the precise duration of a term and the method by which a lease terminates depend upon whether the term is fixed or indeterminate and, in addition, often depends upon the conduct of the parties to the lease.

1. Indeterminate Term Leases
La. Civ. Code arts. 2727–2729

Recall that when the term of the lease is indeterminate, the termination date is not fixed in advance but depends on the will of the parties subsequently expressed. *See* La. Civ. Code art. 2678 cmt. e. An indeterminate term lease, therefore, continues indefinitely until one of the parties expresses a desire to terminate the lease. Importantly, once a party gives proper notice of termination, the lease does not necessarily end immediately; instead, termination of an indeterminate term lease usually occurs at the close of a particular period. Thus, a month-to-month lease that begins on January 1 can terminate at the *end* of any month (e.g., February 28, March 31, or April 30), provided that proper notice is given. Absent special circumstances, such a lease will not terminate on a date that falls within the middle of any month.

The precise timing of the termination of an indeterminate term lease depends upon the application of Articles 2727 through 2729, which set forth the time and form requirements for notice of termination. Read those articles carefully; then read the following case which illustrates the application of these rules.

683

Herring v. Breedlove

64 So. 2d 441 (La. 1953)

HAWTHORNE, Justice.

Plaintiff Jolly F. Herring instituted this suit seeking to recover damages in the sum of $10,576.07 from Edward C. Breedlove. The lower court dismissed his suit on an exception of no cause or right of action, and he appealed to the Court of Appeal, Second Circuit, which transferred the case to this court because it lacked appellate jurisdiction.

In considering the exception which was sustained by the lower court, all well pleaded allegations of plaintiff's petition must be accepted as true. The material allegations are as follows:

In December of 1945 plaintiff discussed with defendant the possibility of obtaining a lease on a filling station owned by the defendant in Natchitoches, Louisiana. In January of 1946 Breedlove, the defendant, advised plaintiff that, if he wanted to take over the filling station, he could do so as of February 1, 1946. Plaintiff requested a written lease, but was informed by the defendant that one was not necessary, and that he, plaintiff, could have a lease on the filling station as long as he wanted it provided he "ran it right". Thereafter, relying on the representations of Breedlove, the plaintiff and his wife gave up their employment in Houston, Texas, where he was earning approximately $4,000 per annum and his wife $1,000, and moved to Natchitoches in order to run the filling station. He operated the filling station during the months of February and March, 1946, and during March made a net profit of $489.13. On April 5 he received a written notice from the defendant to vacate the premises and deliver possession at the end of the month. On the same day defendant executed a written contract of lease of the filling station to the Billups Petroleum Company, effective May 1, 1946. In view of the fact that plaintiff had no written contract from Breedlove but only a verbal lease, he was forced to vacate the premises and on April 30, 1946, turned them over to Billups Petroleum Company.

Plaintiff itemized his damages as follows: For loss of his job in Texas and loss of his wife's employment in Texas and loss of anticipated profit of this filling station during the next two years had he been permitted to operate it for this period of time, $10,000; for expenses in moving to Louisiana, $125; for loss in the value of the filling station equipment purchased by him which he would be forced to sell at 50 per cent of its cost, $451.07—or a total of $10,576.07.

Under the allegations of plaintiff's petition he had a verbal lease of the filling station, but he does not allege that the lease had a fixed duration. On the contrary, his allegations show that its duration was not fixed, for he alleged that defendant had told him he "could have a lease on the filling station as long as he wanted, provided that he "ran it right". Since the verbal contract between the plaintiff and the defendant for the renting of the filling station did not fix the duration of the lease, the law provides that it shall be considered as having been made by the month, under

Article 2685 of the LSA-Civil Code [R.C.C. 2680]: "If the renting of a house or other edifice, or of an apartment, has been made without fixing its duration, the lease shall be considered to have been made by the month."

According to plaintiff's allegations he was damaged because, after occupying the leased premises for only two months under the verbal lease, defendant gave him notice to vacate and deliver possession, but defendant had a right to do this under Article 2686 of the Code [R.C.C. 2727–2728], which provides: "* * * If no time for its [the lease's] duration has been agreed on, the party desiring to put an end to it must give notice in writing to the other, at least ten days before the expiration of the month, which has begun to run." Since no time for the lease's duration had been agreed upon by these parties, either had the legal right to terminate the lease at the expiration of any month by complying with the provisions of the above quoted article.

Plaintiff in brief states that the whole theory of his case is that the defendant made representations to him upon which he relied, and caused him to suffer the damages claimed, citing in support thereof Article 2315 of the LSA-Civil Code. The damages to plaintiff were caused by termination of the lease contract by the defendant, but the defendant under the allegations of the petition has a legal right to end the lease, and consequently is not responsible in damages.

For the reasons assigned, the judgment appealed from is affirmed at appellant's costs.

* * * * *

Notes and Questions

1. Since *Herring v. Breedlove* was decided, Article 1967 has been amended to codify the doctrine of detrimental reliance. As the article provides, "A party may be obligated by a promise when he knew or should have known that the promise would induce the other party to rely on it to his detriment and the other party was reasonable in so relying." La. Civ. Code art. 1967. Would the outcome of *Herring* be any different today? Why or why not?

2. As the foregoing case makes clear, notice of termination of a month-to-month lease must be given ten calendar days before the end of the month. *See* La. Civ. Code art. 2728. If notice is given but is not timely, then the notice will be effective for the following month. Consider, for example, a month-to-month lease made on January 1. If the lessee gives notice to terminate the lease on March 25, the lease will terminate on April 30 (the last day of April).

3. Proper application of Article 2728 requires that the article be read *in pari materia* with Article 1784: "When the term for performance of an obligation is not marked by a specific date but is rather a period of time, the term begins to run on the day . . . after the occurrence of the event that marks the beginning of the term, and it includes the last day of the period." La. Civ. Code art. 1784. In light of this rule, what is the *last day* on which notice may be given to ensure that a month-to-month lease that began on January 1 terminates on the last day of April (April 30)?

4. The 10-day notice period for terminating a month-to-month lease is not applicable to all leases. In a lease whose term is measured by a period longer than a month, the notice period is 30 calendar days. LA. CIV. CODE art. 2728(1). To terminate a year-to-year lease that began on January 1, notice must be given no later than December 1 of any given year. In a lease with a term that is measured by a period equal to or longer than a week but shorter than a month, the notice period is 5 calendar days. LA. CIV. CODE art. 2728(3). To ensure that a week-to-week lease that began on Monday, January 1 terminates on Sunday, January 28, notice must be given no later than Tuesday, January 23. In a lease with a term that is measured by a period shorter than a week, the notice period is "any time prior to the expiration of that period." LA. CIV. CODE art. 2728(4). Thus, to ensure that a day-to-day lease of a backhoe that began on Monday, January 1 terminates on Friday, January 5, notice must be given no later than the end of the day on Friday, January 5. Query: when is the "end of the day" in this context? *See* LA. CIV. CODE art. 1794 cmt. b.

5. Consider the purpose of the notice requirements described above. The periods are designed to provide the parties with adequate time to take care of their affairs before the lease comes to an end. The residential lessee who receives a notice of termination from the lessor will need time to move his or her belongings and find another place to live. The residential lessor who receives the notice from the lessee will need time to find another lessee, particularly if the lessor relies upon rental payments as income or to make mortgage loan payments on the property. Consider whether the 10-day notice period is sufficient to settle such matters. Should the period be lengthened, at least in residential leases? What period of time do you think would be sufficient for the parties to put their affairs in order?

6. In addition to being timely, notice of termination must also be made in proper form. Article 2729 provides that "[i]f the leased thing is an immovable or a movable used as a residence, the notice of termination shall be in writing. It may be oral in all other cases." LA. CIV. CODE art. 2729. In addition, the lessee's timely "surrender of possession" of the leased thing to the lessor shall also constitute notice. *Id.* Thus, if the lessee of an apartment in a month-to-month lease surrenders possession of the premises and returns the keys to the lessor at least ten days prior to the end of the month, the lease terminates at the end of the month even if the lessee has not notified the lessor of termination in writing. Note that "surrender of possession" is not the same as "abandonment," which, as discussed in Part E of this Chapter, may amount to breach of the lease.

2. Fixed Term Leases

La. Civ. Code arts. 2720–2726, 2728

a. General Rule

Recall that when the term of a lease is fixed, its end point is either a designated date or the occurrence of a designated event. LA. CIV. CODE art. 2678. In general, "[a] lease with a fixed term terminates upon the expiration of that term, without need of notice . . . ." LA. CIV. CODE art. 2720. Thus, a one-year lease of an apartment executed on January 1 comes to an end on December 31 of the same year. Neither party to the lease is required to give notice of termination to avoid continuing obligations under the contract.

b. Exceptions

There exist several exceptions to the general rule that a fixed term lease terminates at the expiration of its term. Article 2720 recognizes two of these: reconduction and extension. In both of these cases, the lease continues beyond the designated end point. Another exception is that the parties may amend the term of the lease, an eventuality recognized in Article 2726. A final exception is a special rule, announced in Article 2718, that applies to a fixed term lease in which the parties have agreed that either party may terminate the lease "at will" prior to the designated end point. Each of these four exceptions to the general rule is discussed in the materials that follow.

i. Reconduction

La. Civ. Code arts. 2720–2724

The term "reconduction" is not defined in the Civil Code, and it is best understood through the facts that give rise to it and its effects. Reconduction of a fixed term lease takes place when the lessee remains in possession for a period of time following the expiration of the term, without notice to vacate or terminate or other opposition from the lessor. When a fixed term lease is reconducted, it continues beyond the designated end point as an indeterminate term lease. *See* LA. CIV. CODE art. 2724. The concept of reconduction is known as "holdover" in the common law, a term that perhaps more accurately describes the situation at hand: the parties allow the lessee to "hold over" beyond the term of the lease, and through their inaction, the lease is extended. Because reconduction involves the inaction of the parties rather than their express consent, reconduction is frequently referred to as "tacit" reconduction.

The rules for reconduction can seem confusing and difficult due to the fact that they are very specific and somewhat complex. These rules can be understood more easily if one keeps in mind that a reconduction analysis always involves a two-step process. First, one must determine whether reconduction has occurred at all—that is, whether the lessee remained in unopposed possession of the leased thing for the requisite time. The time periods for reconduction differ depending upon whether the lease is agricultural and, if not agricultural, upon the length of the original fixed term of the lease. *See* LA. CIV. CODE art. 2721. Second, if reconduction has occurred, one must then determine what the new, reconducted term of the lease will be. While the new term is always indeterminate, the period will vary, again depending upon whether the lease is agricultural or, if not agricultural, upon the length of the original fixed term in the lease. *See* LA. CIV. CODE arts. 2722–23.

Consider the first inquiry: how long must the lessee remain in unopposed possession for reconduction to occur? The answer is governed by Civil Code article 2721. In the case of an agricultural lease, the lessee must remain in possession for thirty days beyond the expiration of the fixed term. La. Civ. Code art. 2721(1). In the case of a non-agricultural lease with a fixed term longer than a week, the lessee must remain in possession for at least one week beyond the expiration of the fixed term. La. Civ. Code art. 2721(2). And, in the case of a non-agricultural lease with a fixed term equal to or shorter than a week, the lessee must remain in possession for at least one day beyond the expiration of the fixed term. La. Civ. Code art. 2721(3).

Consider the following common hypothetical: Lessor and Lessee agree to a one-year lease of an apartment on January 1. On December 31 of the same year, Lessee does not vacate the premises, and Lessor does not communicate to Lessee that Lessee's right to possession has ended. On January 10, Lessor calls Lessee on the telephone and demands that Lessee vacate the premises immediately. Has the lease come to an end or has it been reconducted through Lessee's unopposed possession? Because this lease is residential (non-agricultural) with a one-year fixed term (a fixed term longer than a week), Lessee must remain in possession for at least one week beyond the expiration of the fixed term for the lease to be reconducted. As a result of Lessee remaining in possession until January 10 (more than one week after the fixed term expired), the lease is reconducted as an indeterminate term lease.

Consider now the second inquiry: once a lease has been reconducted, what is the new indeterminate term? Articles 2722 and 2723 provide the answer. As stated above, while the new term is always indeterminate, the period will vary, again depending upon whether the lease is agricultural or, if not agricultural, the length of the original fixed term in the lease. Under Article 2722, the new term of a reconducted agricultural lease is year-to-year, unless the parties intended a different term which, according to local custom or usage, is observed in leases of the same type. La. Civ. Code art. 2722. Article 2723 provides three different terms for reconducted non-agricultural leases. In the case of a lease with a fixed term of a month or longer, the term of the reconducted lease is month-to-month. La. Civ. Code art. 2723(1). In the case of a lease with a fixed term of at least a day but shorter than a month, the term of the reconducted lease is day-to-day. La. Civ. Code art. 2723(2). And, in the case of a lease with a fixed term that shorter than a day, the term of the reconducted lease is equal to the expired term. La. Civ. Code art. 2723(3).

Returning to the hypothetical above regarding the reconducted residential lease: what is its new indeterminate term? Because the lease was residential (non-agricultural), Article 2723 applies. And, because the fixed term of the lease was one year (one month or longer), the new term of the lease is month-to-month.

Once a lease has been reconducted, how is the reconducted lease properly terminated? Because all reconducted leases are indeterminate term leases, the rules governing termination of indeterminate term leases, described above in Subpart A.1, apply. As provided by Article 2727, the party seeking to terminate the lease must provide notice to that effect to the other party. The timeliness of that notice is governed by Article 2728, which sets forth different time periods depending upon the length of the indeterminate term. Finally, recall that under Article 2729 if the leased thing is an immovable or a movable used as a residence, the notice generally must be made in writing.

Again, returning to the hypothetical above, Lessor contacted Lessee on January 10 and demanded that Lessee vacate the premises. Was this notice sufficient to terminate the lease? Because the term of the reconducted lease is a month-to-month lease, the earliest date upon which the lease can be terminated is January 31. In addition, to terminate the lease, Lessor must provide timely notice to Lessee. And, because the reconducted lease is a month-to-month lease, notice must be given at least ten calendar days before the end of the month. Finally, because this is a lease of an immovable, that notice must be given in writing. Here, although Lessor gave Lessee notice of Lessor's desire to terminate the lease on January 10 (more than ten days before the end of the month), which was timely, the fact that the notice was verbal rather than written precludes its effectiveness.

A final consideration is this: what are the terms of a reconducted lease? Article 2724 provides: "When reconduction occurs, all provisions of the lease continue . . . ." La. Civ. Code art. 2724. Considering again the hypothetical above, assume that the parties' lease shifted all responsibility for repairs to the Lessee. If in January the pipes burst as a result of a freeze, Lessee bears the duty of repair, not Lessor, per the parties' agreement.

ii. Extension/Renewal

La. Civ. Code arts. 2720, 2725

Article 2720 recognizes "extension" of the lease as an exception to the general rule that a fixed term lease terminates upon the expiration of its term. "Extension" is a term of art that refers to the lengthening of the term of the lease through the operation of an option to extend the term that is contained in the parties' agreement. As Article 2725 provides, "If the lease contract contains an option to extend the term and the option is exercised, the lease continues for the term and under the other provisions stipulated in the option." La. Civ. Code art. 2725.

Under prior law, the concept of extension was referred to as "renewal" of the lease. See id. cmt. a. Many attorneys and courts still refer to options to extend the term of a lease as "options to renew." The term "renew" is misleading because it suggests that the lease, following exercise of the option, is a "new" lease. This is not the case, however. Article 2725 makes clear that the original lease "continues" (much in the same manner as a reconducted lease). Thus, the terms of the original lease apply to the extent they are not modified by the option to extend.

A frequently litigated issue involving leases that contain options to extend is whether the lessee properly exercised the option. Consider the following hypothetical: Lessor and Lessee agree to the lease of a commercial building for a fixed term of one year commencing on January 1. The lease contains an option to extend the lease for an additional one-year term, provided the Lessee gives written notice to the Lessor of his intent to exercise the option at least 30 days prior to the expiration of the original term. On December 15, Lessee sends written notice to the Lessor of his intent to exercise the option. On December 31 of the same year, Lessee does not vacate the premises, and Lessor does not communicate to Lessee that Lessee's right to possession has ended. Instead, the parties do nothing. On January 10, Lessor contacts Lessee and demands that he vacate the premises immediately. Has the lease come to an end? Has it been extended through the Lessee's exercise of the option to extend? Has it been reconducted through Lessee's unopposed possession? As the following cases demonstrate, the rights of the parties in circumstances such as these depend entirely upon the details of the parties' conduct.

Le Blanc v. Barielle

25 So. 2d 638 (La. App. Orl. Cir. 1946)

JANVIER, Judge.

Plaintiff is the owner of a certain piece of property in the Parish of Jefferson which, with the buildings on it, constitutes an automobile tourist court. The property is known as "The Wigwam Village No. 3" and is located at No. 4800 Airline Highway. On December 14, 1943, LeBlanc and defendant, Alphonse N. Barielle, entered into a written agreement of lease by which the property was to be taken over by Barielle as tenant for a period commencing on January 1, 1944, and terminating on December 31, 1944. The monthly rental was fixed at $125 and the lease contained a paragraph reading as follows:

> "The Lessee, Alphonse N. Barielle, has signified an intention to construct and erect additional facilities on the property described above, at his own expense, for a trailer court on the rear of said portion of ground, to cost a minimum of Fifteen hundred and no/100 ($1500.00) Dollars. In consideration of his erecting said improvements, and in the event they are made before January 1, 1945, the said Lessor does hereby grant unto the said Lessee the right of renewing the said lease presently in existence between them for a three year period beginning January 1, 1945, and running through December 31, 1947 on the same terms and conditions as the present lease. It is specifically understood between the Lessor and the Lessee that in the event that the additions and improvements are not constructed by the Lessee before January 1, 1945, that this option shall be of no force and effect, and shall be absolutely null and void. If the Lessee does construct the facilities as contemplated, it is hereby agreed that they shall belong to the Lessor in their entirety at the termination of this lease or any renewal thereof."

The lessee took over the property and operated it during the year 1944 and prior to December 31, 1944, he expended considerably more than the $1,500 stipulated for in the above quoted paragraph. It is not denied that the money was properly expended in accordance with the provisions of that paragraph.

During the year 1944 he at no time gave notice, either orally or in writing, that he intended to exercise the right given to him to renew the lease for the additional years to December 31, 1947. However, after the expiration of the original term of the lease he continued to occupy the property and to pay the stipulated monthly rental.

On October 18, 1945, LeBlanc, through his attorney, gave written notice to Barielle to vacate the leased property on November 1, 1945, and, when Barielle failed to comply, LeBlanc, on November 16, 1945, brought this suit praying that Barielle be ordered to vacate the property and to deliver it to LeBlanc. Barielle answered admitting the execution of the lease and that he had occupied the property from the commencement of the lease, and averring that he had spent more than $2,000 in erecting the additional facilities called for in that paragraph of the lease which we have already quoted, and averring also that at no time had LeBlanc informed him that he, LeBlanc, considered that the lease had terminated in spite of the fact that he, Barielle, continued to occupy the property for ten months after the expiration of the original term of the lease and to pay the stipulated monthly rental therefor.

Barielle averred that the acceptance by LeBlanc of the monthly rental for ten months after the expiration of the original term of the lease had constituted "an express and implied renewal and extension of said lease for the full period as set forth in the provision thereof hereinabove recited * * *."

In the court below there was judgment dismissing LeBlanc's suit and he has appealed.

It is the contention of Barielle that it was not necessary that he expressly give notice to LeBlanc of his desire to renew the lease for the additional three years, he maintaining that by the expenditure of the $1,500 required by the quoted paragraph of the lease, the extension was automatically effected.

The lease does not so stipulate. It is not provided that the expenditure of the $1,500 should, in itself, being about an extension of the lease. All that the said expenditure would accomplish according to the language employed would be to obtain for Barielle the right or option to extend the said lease if he so desired. We see no other possible interpretation. It is not stated that the expenditure of the money would affect the renewal but merely that by making the said expenditure Barielle would have "the right of renewing the said lease." In the last sentence of the paragraph, the said "right of renewing" is referred to as an "option."

We think it almost unnecessary to state that if an option is to be exercised action by the one to whom it is granted is necessary.

For several reasons it will not do to say that by remaining in the property Barielle tacitly gave notice of his intention to exercise the option. The notice of intention to exercise an option to renew a lease must be given before the expiration of the original term. That is exactly what was held in *Cappiello v. Hingle, et al*, 170 La. 295, 127 So. 729. There, the lease contained the following stipulation:

> "* * * 'this lease is made for a period of one year for and in consideration of $100, to be paid by December 20th, 1928; subject to renewal under the same terms and conditions,'* * *."

The lessee took no steps to renew the lease and gave no notice to the lessor until two months after the original term had expired. He then notified the lessor of his intention to renew and tendered the rent for the ensuing year. The lessor objected and the matter found its way into court. The Supreme Court said:

> "* * * 'this tender of the price of a renewal, did not itself operate a renewal, because it came too late for that purpose. For the option to renew a lease must be exercised before the expiration of the lease, otherwise it lapses.' * * *"

Counsel for Barielle argues that in permitting him to remain in the premises, LeBlanc, by his silence and inaction, created the obligation to let him remain for the extended term. He cites Civil Code, Article 1817 [R.C.C. 1927, 1942], which reads as follows:

> "Silence and inaction evidencing assent. — Silence and inaction are also, under some circumstances, the means of showing an assent that creates an obligation; if, after the termination of a lease, the lessee continue in possession, and the lessor be inactive and silent, a complete mutual obligation for continuing the lease, is created by the act of occupancy of the tenant on the one side, and the inaction and silence of the lessor on the other."

But the fact that LeBlanc permitted Barielle to remain in the property cannot be construed as an assent to the extended term provided for in the option, for it seems to be well settled that where a lease which contains an option for a term renewal is allowed to expire, the fact that the lessor does not at once require the lessee to vacate does not constitute acquiescence in the extended term but merely brings about a reconduction under the appropriate articles of our Civil Code — 2689 [R.C.C. 2721, 2723], where a house or a room is involved or 2688 [R.C.C. 2721–2722], in the case of a predial estate. That exact question was considered in *Mossey v. Mead*, 4 La.195. There, the lessee leased his house to a tenant for one year with the agreement that if the tenant required it "he should have the privilege of remaining seven years longer at the same rent." During the original term no notice of intention to take advantage of the option for an extended term was given but after the expiration of the original year, the tenant or his successor was allowed to remain in the property for three years and the lessor accepted the monthly rent each month during those years. It was contended that by accepting the rent money each month for those years after the expiration of the original term, the lessor should be considered as having acquiesced in the extension of the lease for the seven year period. The court held that the acceptance of the rent merely constituted a reconduction in accordance with the articles of the Code and did not bring about the extension for seven years, which could only have been accomplished by actual notice given by the lessee of his intention to renew. In *Dolese v. Barberot*, 9 La.Ann. 352, the Supreme Court reached the same conclusion and there tersely said:

"* * * There having been no agreement between the parties to renew the lease, and the privilege of renewing it either for three or six years accorded to the defendant by an express stipulation not having been exercised by him; the effect of his holding over after the expiration of the term of the original lease was to constitute a tacit re-conduction from month to month."

* * * * *

The proper notice required by C.C. article 2686 [R.C.C. 2727] was given here and therefore the defendant must be required to vacate the property. It is strenuously argued that to require the defendant to vacate brings about a most unfair result because it gives to the plaintiff the right to take over the improvements and additions for which the defendant has paid, and to use them for his benefit without making any payment therefor. This is unfortunate. But it comes from defendant's own failure to take the necessary steps to protect himself against such a result. Suppose the operation of the tourist court had proven unsuccessful and the defendant had found that even after expending the money which he did expend, it was to his advantage to abandon it, since he had not bound himself for the renewal term he could have taken the position that a mere reconduction had been effected and could, himself, have terminated his occupancy and, with it, his obligation to pay rent.

For these reasons it is ordered, adjudged and decreed that the judgment appealed from be and it is annulled, avoided and reversed and that there now be judgment in favor of plaintiff, Pierre Hoa LeBlanc, Jr., and against defendant, Alphonse N. Barielle, ordering and condemning the said Barielle, immediately upon the finality of this decree, to vacate the property and premises known as Wigwam Village No. 3, No. 4800 Airline Highway, Jefferson Parish. Defendant-appellee to pay all costs.

Reversed.

Notes and Questions

1. The court's analysis of the exercise of the option in *LeBlanc* highlighted the importance of following, to the letter, the contract of lease. Although the lessee argued that his conduct (erecting the improvements) constituted an exercise of the option, the court disagreed, drawing a distinction between fulfillment of a condition to create the *right* to extend, on the one hand, and the *exercise of the right* to extend once that condition had occurred, on the other. In the case, the lessee's erection of a minimum of $1,500 in improvements was the condition that, once fulfilled, gave the lessee the right to extend the lease, but because the lessee failed to exercise the option in the precise manner provided in the contract of lease, the court held that the option to extend had not been exercised.

2. In *LeBlanc*, the lessee remained on the property for ten months after the expiration of the original one-year term without complaint from the lessor. Does this conduct serve as a tacit exercise of the option to extend? Why or why not? Does it

serve to reconduct the lease? Why or why not? If yes, was the lessor's notice to the lessee directing him to vacate the premises both timely and proper in form?

3. The lessor in *LeBlanc* accepted rent for the ten months the lessee occupied the premises beyond the expiration of the lease's original term. Does such conduct indicate his consent to the exercise of the option to extend?

Huval v. 4S Const. & Maintenance, Inc.

442 So. 2d 1353 (La. App. 3 Cir. 1983)

FORET, Judge.

4S Construction & Maintenance, Inc. (defendant) appeals from a judgment of the trial court, making Patrick Huval's (plaintiff) rule to evict it from a certain tract of land absolute, and ordering it to vacate the same and deliver possession thereto to plaintiff. We affirm.

Defendant raises the following issues:

(1) Whether the trial court erred in finding that it failed to give sufficient notice to plaintiff of its intention to exercise its option to renew a lease plaintiff had given it on the tract of land.

(2) Whether the trial court erred in finding that plaintiff had not acquiesced in defendant's attempt to exercise its option by cashing a check given him by it.

FACTS

On January 1, 1976, plaintiff and defendant entered into a contract of lease whereby defendant agreed to lease from plaintiff a tract of land described as follows:

That certain lot of land, situated in St. Martin Parish, Louisiana, on the East Side of Bayou Teche, containing one (1) arpent, more or less, and bounded Northerly by the property of Elise Latiolais, Easterly by property of Paul Melancon; Southerly by a public road; and Westerly by property of Lionel Latiolais; see Book 560, folio 412, Entry No. 137424, Conveyance Records of St. Martin Parish, Louisiana.

The primary term of the lease was for a period of five years with the rent set at $300 per year. In addition, defendant was given "the right and option to renew this lease for three additional periods of five years each by giving Lessor written notice of intent to renew sixty days before the expiration of the original five-year term or of any additional five-year terms that the lease is extended". The lease provided that the rent would increase at the rate of $300 per year for each five-year period that it was extended.

NOTICE OF INTENTION TO EXERCISE OPTION

Steve Schexnayder, defendant's President, admitted that defendant failed to give plaintiff written notice of its intent to exercise its option to renew the lease within sixty days of the expiration date of the primary term of the lease. Instead, defendant sent plaintiff a check dated January 26, 1982, made out to him in the amount of $600.[1]

The check was received and negotiated by plaintiff's wife, who endorsed his name thereon. Defendant argues that, by negotiating this check, plaintiff waived his right to written notice of defendant's intention to exercise its option to renew the lease. We disagree.

We adopt the following reasoning of the trial court as our own and find it to be dispositive of this issue:

> "BY THE COURT: I'm going to submit to you that I think that the matter is decided by the case of *Southern Ventures Corporation versus Texaco, Inc.*, which is a Supreme Court case at 372 So.2nd, 1228 [(La.1979)], which involved a lease with an option to renew where a written notice was required not later than sixty (60) days before the expiration of the primary term; exactly the same situation that we have here. Written notice was in fact given but it was given nine (9) days before the expiration of the primary term rather than sixty (60) days before. The lessor did nothing. The lessee remained on the property, continued to make rental payments. The lessor accepted the rental payments. But, the Supreme Court held that the late notice was not sufficient under the terms of the lease, and therefore, the lease expired at the end of its primary term and what they had thereafter was a tenancy by consent, if you will, rather than an extension of the original lease."

Governor Claiborne Apartments, Inc. v. Attaldo, 235 So. 2d 574 (La. 1970), expressed the law relative to occupancy of leased premises after the lease expires, referring to the appropriate code articles:

> "Under our Civil Code provisions based on these articles of the Code Napoleon, legal reconduction takes place when a fixed-term lease expires and the lessee without opposition continues to occupy the premises for more than a week. The reconducted lease is actually a continuation of the lease under the same terms and conditions except that the fixed term or period of duration in the old lease is voided and the reconducted lease is considered to be

---

1. Defendant notes that the lease contains the following provision and argues that since plaintiff failed to send it notice by certified or registered mail of its failure to provide written notice to him of its intention to renew the lease, its sending of the $600 check to plaintiff and the subsequent negotiation of that check constitutes sufficient notice of its intent to re-new:

> "LESSEE shall not be deemed to have defaulted in the payment of any rental during the five year term of the lease or any renewal of the lease until fifteen days after LESSEE shall have received from LESSOR notice by registered or certified mail of LESSEE'S failure to make such payment. The lease or renewal of the lease shall continue in full effect if LESSEE shall tender the payment within fifteen days after the receipt of such notice; however, it will owe to LESSOR a penalty of ten (10) per cent of the rental due for that year."

We agree with the trial court's conclusion that this provision has nothing to do with the method whereby defendant was to exercise its option to renew the lease.

by the month. La.Civ.Code Arts. 2689 [R.C.C. 2721, 2723], 2685 [R.C.C. 2680], 2686 [R.C.C. 2627, 2628]." (Footnote omitted.)

In further support of its position that plaintiff waived his right to written notice of its intention to renew the lease, defendant cites the case of *Lingle v. Wainwright*, 39 So.2d 843 (La.1949). We find *Lingle* to be distinguishable on its facts.

In *Lingle,* plaintiff's predecessor had leased the premises to defendant by written contract for a primary term of one year at a monthly rental of $250. Under the terms of the lease, defendant had the privilege of renewing the lease for four additional years under the same conditions (except that the monthly rent was increased) provided he notified the plaintiff of his intention to renew on or before March 1, 1946. Defendant failed to timely notify plaintiff of his intention to renew. However, on April 22, 1946, defendant wrote a letter to plaintiff expressing his desire to renew the lease under all the terms and conditions as stated therein. Plaintiff conceded that this notice was duly received. Plaintiff did not protest or inform defendant that the renewal would not be granted because the notice had not been given on or before March 1, 1946. Instead, he remained silent and accepted from defendant the increased rental of $650 per month provided for in the renewal clause of the lease from May 15, 1946, through March, 1947. It wasn't until March 28, 1947, that plaintiff made his initial complaint in the form of a ten-day notice for defendant to vacate the premises.

Noting these facts, *Lingle* held, on page 844, that:

"We think it clear that the actions of plaintiff constitute a waiver of his right to insist that notice of renewal be given on or before March 1, 1946. While it is generally held that an option to renew a lease, provided notice is given at or before a specified time of the intention to exercise the privilege, is a condition precedent which must be complied with within the stipulated time (see Annotation, 27 A.L.R. 981 and cases there cited), it is equally well settled that such a provision is for the benefit of the lessor and therefore the notice itself, or any other matter going to the sufficiency thereof, may be waived." 51 C.J.S., Landlord & Tenant, §62, page 611, citing *Polizzotto v. D'Agostino,* 170 La. 932, 129 So. 534, 536 [(1930)], where the court said:

"And, further, that, having accepted and acted on said notice as being sufficient, the defendant thereafter cannot be heard to raise the question of the technical informality of the notice, or complete want of notice."

In the action *sub judice,* defendant never sent plaintiff written notice of its intention to renew the lease until after February 16, 1982. On that date, plaintiff had his attorney write a letter to defendant in which he stated that it would be allowed to occupy the leased premises for an additional year because plaintiff's wife had erroneously negotiated the check sent him by it. However, defendant would not be allowed to occupy the leased premises for any greater length of time because it had failed to provide plaintiff with timely written notice of its intention to renew the lease. Thus, in the case before us, plaintiff informed defendant that it would not be allowed to renew the lease before he received written notice of its intention to renew.

It is our opinion that plaintiff did not waive his right to timely written notice of defendant's intent to renew the lease.

ALLEGED VERBAL AGREEMENT TO RENEW

Defendant contends that it and plaintiff entered into a verbal agreement to renew the above mentioned lease. Defendant relies on *Wahlder v. Tiger Stop, Inc.,* 391 So.2d 535 (La.App. 3 Cir.1980), writ denied, 396 So.2d 1351 (La.1981), as authority for the proposition that parol evidence is admissible to prove that a written lease may be modified by a subsequent oral agreement between the parties. Indeed, *Wahlder* stands as authority for this proposition even though the written lease provides that modifications must be agreed to in writing to be valid.

Defendant argues that the evidence shows that the parties did enter into a verbal agreement for renewal of the lease. Steve Schexnayder testified that he had a conversation with plaintiff some time in the latter part of 1981, in which he told plaintiff that defendant was going to exercise its option to renew the lease. He stated that plaintiff agreed to the renewal. He further stated that plaintiff sent someone to pick up the $600 check dated January 26, 1982, although he could not remember who this person was.

Plaintiff testified that he could remember no such conversation having taken place. He further denied telling Schexnayder that he would send someone to pick up the above mentioned check. He did remember talking to Schexnayder about entering into a *new* lease that would provide for higher rental payments, but stated that both were drinking in a bar at the time and that it was hard for each of them to understand what the other was saying because loud music was being played. Plaintiff insisted that no agreement was entered into by the parties at this time.

While assent to a contract may be implied, that implication must be established and cannot be presumed. Defendant's burden was to establish a lease for a fixed term. It had to prove a meeting of the minds of the contracting parties that their relationship as lessor and lessee was for the alleged fixed term, by either express language or by circumstances (action or inaction) that necessarily implied the proposition.

The trial court found that defendant had failed to prove that any verbal agreement was entered into by the parties for renewal of the lease, and we agree with this finding.

DECREE

For the above and foregoing reasons, the judgment of the trial court is affirmed.

All costs of this appeal are assessed against defendant-appellant.

AFFIRMED.

Notes and Questions

1. In light of the foregoing cases, is there a universal method by which to exercise an option to extend a lease?

2. The *Huval* court discussed the case of *Lingle v. Wainwright*, 39 So. 2d 843 (La. 1949). How is that case distinguishable from *Huval*? How is it distinguishable from *LeBlanc*? In answering these questions, pay careful attention to what amount of rent the lessor accepted. Also, pay careful attention to the timing of the lessee's notice of an intention to renew as compared to the timing of the lessor's notice of an intention to evict the lessee.

3. The *Huval* court also discussed the case of *Wahlder v. Tiger Stop, Inc.,* 391 So. 2d 535 (La. App. 3 Cir. 1980). In that case, Wahlder leased to Wansley a lot and building known locally as the Tiger Stop, a convenience store. The primary term of the lease began November 1, 1978, and it expired one year later on November 1, 1979. The lease provided that Wansley had the right to extend the lease one year at a time for up to seven years, or through November 1, 1986, provided he notify Wahlder in writing of his desire to exercise an option at least two months prior to the end of each term. On October 22, 1979, ten days before the primary term expired, Wansley suddenly remembered that he had to actively extend the lease to remain in the leased premises. He telephoned Wahlder, explained to him that he had forgotten about the written notice requirement, and informed Wahlder that he desired to extend the lease for one year. Wahlder verbally agreed to an extension of the lease, but the following day, he telephoned Wansley, attempted to rescind his earlier verbal agreement to extend the lease period, and instructed Wansley to vacate the premises upon the expiration of the primary term of the lease. When Wahlder refused, Wansley instituted eviction proceedings. The district court refused to evict Wahlder, finding that the parties' oral agreement constituted an effective exercise of the extension option. The appellate court agreed. According to the court:

> It is a well-settled principle of our law that a written contract may be modified, abrogated or revoked by a subsequent oral agreement if the original contract is not one required by law to be in writing. A contract of lease is not required by law to be in writing. Therefore, parol evidence is admissible to prove the written lease was modified by a subsequent oral agreement between the parties. This is true even though the written contract provides that modifications must be agreed to in writing to have validity. In the instant case, the written lease provided that lessor (plaintiff) be given written notice at least sixty days prior to the expiration of the primary term if lessee wished to extend the lease for an extra year. However, defendant (lessee) called plaintiff ten days before the primary term and expressed a desire to renew the lease . . . . Once the lease was modified or altered by subsequent parol agreement, renewing the lease through November 1, 1979, that part of the written lease requiring sixty day written notice was effectively waived or abrogated with respect to the first option period. Thus, the parties remain bound under all the terms of the original lease, with the exception that the first option was renewed orally. Unless the parties express a different intent, all future options (second through seventh) must be exercised in the manner prescribed by the original lease.

Id. at 537–38 (internal citations omitted). How is *Wahlder* distinguishable from *Huval*? Note the impact of the parol evidence rule on the question of whether a lessee has validly exercised an option to renew. *See* LA. CIV. CODE art. 1848.

4. Consider a contract of lease that provides that the lessee has the "option to renew this lease on the then agreed upon terms for three (3) years." Is this an option to extend the lease? If not, how would you characterize it? The Second Circuit addressed this question in *Walters v. Greer*, 726 So. 2d 1094 (La. App. 2 Cir. 1999) and held that the provision was not an option to extend; instead, it was an option to negotiate an extension.

5. Remember, as mentioned in the introduction to this Subpart, that an extended lease is a continuation of the existing lease. However, this does not mean that every provision of the existing lease continues. As Article 2725 provides, the exercise of an option to extend leads to a continuation of the lease "for the term and under the other provisions stipulated *in the option*." LA. CIV. CODE art. 2725 (emphasis added).

6. Recall that while an option to extend a lease must be properly recorded in order to have effects against third persons, the *exercise* of an option that is evidenced by a recorded instrument is effective against third persons although not evidenced of record. *See* LA. CIV. CODE art. 3339. Consider the following hypothetical. Lessor and Lessee execute and properly record a written lease of a shopping center for a term of five years beginning on January 1, 2014. The parties' agreement contains a clause permitting the lessee to renew the lease for an additional five-year term provided the lessee notifies the lessor of the intention to renew in writing within thirty days of the expiration of the first term. Assume that Lessee exercises the option as required by the recorded lease agreement by sending a letter on November 15, 2018, notifying Lessor of Lessee's intent to exercise the option to renew. The letter is never recorded in the public records. In January of 2019, Lessor sells the leased property to Third Person, who neither assumes nor purchases subject to the lease. Is Third Person bound to honor the lease? Why or why not?

iii. Amendment

La. Civ. Code arts. 1879–1881, 2726

Parties to a lease frequently amend the contract after its original execution. This is particularly common in the context of commercial leases. Consider, for example, a situation in which a Lessor and Lessee have agreed to the lease of a commercial building at a rent of $10,000/year and for a term of 5 years, ending on December 31, 2023. Assume that during the fourth year of the lease, the parties agree that the lease will not terminate until 2030. Have the parties, through their agreement, entered into a new lease? Or have they simply modified the terms of their original contract? As Article 2726 makes clear, the answer to this question depends upon whether the parties intended a "novation" of their original lease. LA. CIV. CODE art. 2726.

Novation, you will recall, is the extinguishment of an original obligation accomplished by the substitution of a new one. LA. CIV. CODE art. 1879. Novation takes place when the parties' substitute a "new performance" or a "new cause" for that of their original obligation. LA. CIV. CODE art. 1881. However, if any substantial part of the original performance is still owed, there is no novation. *Id.* Moreover, mere modification of an obligation, made without the intention to extinguish it, does not effect a novation. *Id.* Most importantly, the intention to extinguish the original obligation must be clear and unequivocal; it is never presumed. LA. CIV. CODE art. 1880.

Article 2726 was enacted in response to the fact that prior to the 2005 revision of the law of lease, courts did not always properly apply the law of novation in the context of leases. *See* LA. CIV. CODE art. 2726 cmt. The following case, which predates the lease revision, considers the effect of the parties' agreement to modify the term of the lease. How, if at all, would Article 2726 have impacted the court's decision?

Waller Oil Co. v. Brown

528 So. 2d 584 (La. App. 2 Cir. 1988)

NORRIS, Judge.

This is a suit for breach of a lease contract that was allegedly reconducted. The lessor, Waller Oil Co. Inc., sued the lessee, Loyd T. Brown, d/b/a The Sound Company, for damages due to a fire on the leased premises. Waller alleged that Brown failed to carry fire insurance, in violation of the lease. The case went to jury trial and yielded a verdict that Brown had breached a contractual duty and Waller had sustained damage as a result. Judgment was entered accordingly and Brown appeals, raising three issues:

(1) Whether the doctrine of reconduction applied to the case.

(2) Whether the lessor's failure to notify the lessee promptly of default in the latter's obligation to maintain fire insurance estopped the lessor from claiming damages.

(3) Assuming the lease was in effect and the insurance clause had not been waived, was the penalty for lessee's breach the cost of the insurance or the amount of the fire loss.

Finding merit in the first argument, we reverse.

FACTS

In April 1978, Waller Oil Company executed a contract of lease with Brown, covering a portion of a commercial building in Minden. The lease had a term of seven years, from July 1, 1978 to June 30, 1985, at a monthly rental of $500. The lease also contained an option to renew for an additional seven years under the same terms and conditions. The lease further imposed on Brown the duty of procuring and maintaining fire and extended coverage insurance on the premises for its full insurable value during the time of the lease. Waller was obligated to notify Brown promptly and in writing of any default except payment of rent; upon notification, Brown would have 20 days to cure the default, after which Waller was authorized to effect the cure and charge the cost to Brown as part of the rent.

Sometime in June 1985, shortly before the contract was to expire, Brown telephoned Mr. Waller, president of Waller Oil, to inform him specifically that he would
not exercise the option to renew. Waller admitted this and testified that it was not in
the parties' best interests for Brown to vacate immediately, as Waller planned to be
out of state on business until September. After discussion, both parties agreed that
Brown would continue to rent the premises for a term not exceeding three months.[1]
Brown asked if he would have to pay a higher rent; Waller said no. They therefore reached a verbal agreement whereby Brown would stay in the store at the same
monthly rent he had been paying. No other provisions of the lease were discussed
or settled. Three months later, in September, Brown again telephoned Waller to say
he had still not found a new location. Waller had not yet found a new lessee, so
they verbally agreed that Brown would stay another month, through October. Once
again, nothing was discussed except the term and the rent. On October 28, a fire
engulfed the building, causing substantial damage. Brown was not at fault in causing the damage.

Waller learned that Brown was not carrying fire insurance the day after the fire.
An insurance agent testified he could have sold Brown fire insurance on the leased
premises for the term of the lease. Waller also presented evidence concerning the
cost of repairing the building and his legal expenses. At the time of trial, he had not
repaired the building.

Brown testified he was not aware of the fire insurance clause in the original lease
contract and that he never maintained the coverage. He also testified about his conversations with Waller in June and September 1985; his testimony was substantially
the same as Waller's. Other witnesses also testified about Brown's intention not to
renew the lease.

As noted, the jury found in response to special interrogatories that Brown had
a duty under the lease to provide fire insurance and that Brown's failure to do so
made him liable for the property damage. The court entered judgment in favor of
Waller for $16,500 for the cost of repairs, $500 for lost rent and $4,000 for attorney
fees. Brown has appealed.

DISCUSSION

Brown's first argument is that his lease was not reconducted at the end of
June 1985. Tacit reconduction is the continuation of a lease after the expiration of
its term by operation of law. LSA-C.C. arts. 2688 [R.C.C. 2721, 2722], 2689 [R.C.C.
2721, 2723]. In *Ashton Realty Co. v. Prowell*, 165 La. 328, 115 So. 579 (1928), the
supreme court interpreted the principle of reconduction as follows:

> [I]f both parties to the lease remain silent and inactive for the space of one
> month [one week, under art. 2689 [R.C.C. 2721, 2723] after the expira-
> tion of the lease, they shall be presumed to have acquiesced in, and tacitly

---

1. Brown testified he wanted to take the premises only until he could find a new location, but
ultimately their understanding was for three months.

consented to, a renewal of the lease for another year [another month, under article 2689 [R.C.C. 2721, 2723]. It has no application whatever when either party has clearly announced his intention *not to renew* the lease on the same terms or for a full year, for the purpose of the law is not to *force* a contract upon parties unwilling to contract, but merely to establish a rule of evidence, or presumption, as to their intention in the premises. 115 So. at 581.

We have closely examined the evidence in this case. It is abundantly clear that the parties were not "silent and inactive," such as would activate the presumption of reconduction. Rather, toward the end of the term Brown communicated to his lessor that he would not renew the existing lease. Waller never denied he understood Brown's intention to terminate the lease. This testimony from the parties themselves shows that both agreed that the old lease would expire. Aware that the written lease would have no effect, they reached an oral agreement as to the basic elements of a new lease: the thing leased and the price. LSA-C.C. arts. 2670 [R.C.C. 2668], 2683 [R.C.C. 2681]. Later, they reached yet another new agreement. There would be little point in striking these new agreements unless the old one was considered abandoned. Furthermore, the term of the first new agreement was different from that of the typical reconducted lease. The parties' stated intent not to be bound by the expired lease, together with their consent to the new leases, undermines the jury's implicit finding that the old lease was reconducted and that Brown was bound by it. This finding is manifestly erroneous. *Arceneaux v. Domingue*, 365 So.2d 1330 (La.1978).

Since *Ashton Realty, supra*, the courts have repeatedly held that evidence of intent not to renew the old lease circumvents the presumption of art. 2689 and renders it inapplicable. *Prisock v. Boyd*, 199 So.2d 373 (La.App. 2d Cir.1967); *Misse v. Dronet*, 493 So.2d 271 (La.App. 3d Cir.1986); *Metzler v. Rising T Racing Stables*, 461 So.2d 1219 (La.App. 1st Cir.1984); *Rosedale Rental Inc. v. Fransen*, 427 So.2d 620 (La.App. 5th Cir.1983); *Eames v. Goodwin*, 337 So.2d 909 (La.App. 3d Cir.1976). These cases reiterate that when one party expresses an intent not to renew, tacit reconduction does not apply.

We are aware of the facts in other cases cited in brief that might arguably distinguish them from the instant case. For instance, in *Rosedale Rental Inc. v. Fransen, supra*, the lessors showed their intent not to reconduct by seeking judicial termination of the lease and eviction of the lessee. Such an expression of intent is strong and persuasive. In *Kogos v. Lemann*, 285 So.2d 548 (La.App. 4th Cir.1973), writ denied 288 So.2d 648 (La.1974), and *Jacobi v. Toomer*, 164 So.2d 610 (La.App. 3d Cir.1964), the original lease agreements contained clauses stating that if the lessee retained possession of the leased premises after expiration of the term, then reconduction would not occur. The parties' stated intent was bound to be upheld. LSA-C.C. art. 1971 [R.C.C. 2037]. In the instant case, the parties' intent was also clearly stated and admitted at trial. They agreed that the written lease would end on its termination date and not be renewed. LSA-C.C. art. 1906 [No Corresponding Article]. Their will was expressed just as well by oral agreement as by the instigation of legal process or by written contract. The parties' subsequent dealings were wholly independent of the lease agreement. The evidence in the instant case will not support the presumption of reconduction.

Because there was no reconduction, the parties are bound by the terms of their new agreement. As already noted, they had agreed on a thing and a price. LSA-C.C. art. 2670 [R.C.C. 2668]. Nothing more is necessary to the confection of a valid lease. There was no agreement as to fire insurance coverage. In the absence of such an agreement, the lessee is not liable for the loss. LSA-C.C. art. 2723 [R.C.C. 2687]; *Gen'l Acc., Fire & Life Assur. v. Glenn*, 261 So.2d 78 (La.App. 3d Cir.1972); Litvinoff, Smith's Materials on the Louisiana Law of Sales and Leases (1st ed., 1978), 468. Furthermore, silence as to a particular issue in the agreement must be construed against the lessor. *Exxon Corp. of Robichaux*, 393 So.2d 224 (La.App. 1st Cir.1980), writ denied 397 So.2d 1358 (La.1981). This rule of interpretation would require imposing on the lessor, not the lessee, the burden of carrying fire insurance. *Metzler v. Rising T Racing Stables, supra*. Brown was not obligated under the new agreement to carry it.

In sum, Brown was not bound by the terms of the written contract, which would have obligated him to carry fire insurance but had admittedly expired. The original contract was not reconducted and the new contract did not impose the obligation on him. For these reasons, the jury's verdict and the trial court's judgment are reversed. The plaintiff's claims are dismissed. Costs of appeal are assessed to appellee, Waller Oil Co. Inc.

REVERSED

FRED W. JONES, JR., J., dissents and assigns written reasons.

FRED W. JONES, JR., Judge, dissenting:

Under the reasoning of the majority, the lessor released the lessee from all obligations under the lease (except for payment of rent) simply because the lessee did not choose to remain on the lease premises another seven years. The essence of tacit reconduction is legally presumed continuation of the old agreement under all the same conditions except for duration. The "express intent to the contrary," which is jurisprudentially required to defeat reconduction, contemplates more than mere repudiating the original term of duration, as occurred here. Thus, in the absence of any evidence in the record tending to show either party's desire to be free of any obligations under this lease except for the seven year term, the lessee's continued occupancy tacitly reconducted the original agreement on a monthly basis.

According to Waller, prior to expiration of the written lease the lessee telephoned the witness and stated that he did not wish to exercise his option to renew the lease because he expected to sell his business in three or four months. Lessor voiced no objection to lessee remaining on the lease premises for that period of time. It was agreed that the lessee would continue occupying the building for three months, through September 1985, at the same rental. No other changes in the lease were discussed. The lessee contacted the lessor again in late September, requesting that he be allowed to remain for an additional month. The lessor agreed.

Defendant Brown testified concerning his lack of knowledge about the insurance clause in the lease and his consequent failure to procure that insurance. His testimony concerning his expressed intent not to renew the lease and remaining on the premises on a monthly basis after the expiration was substantially the same as Waller's.

After considering the evidence, the jury answered affirmatively to the following interrogatories:

> 1) Did defendant Loyd T. Brown have a duty under a lease agreement to provide fire insurance on the building owned by plaintiff, Waller Oil Co., Inc.?
>
> 2) If so, did the failure of the defendant to provide fire insurance cause defendant to be liable to plaintiff for the damage resulting from the fire?

Tacit reconduction of a lease is a continuation of the lease after the expiration of its term by operation of law. In Louisiana, tacit reconduction requires that the lease has expired, that the lessee remain in possession for more than one week, and that the lessor consent to the lessee remaining in possession or not have given notice to vacate. La.C.C. Art. 2689 [R.C.C. 2721, 2723]; 39 Tulane Law Review 798, 813–814; *Governor Claiborne Apartments, Inc. v. Attaldo*, 256 La. 218, 235 So.2d 574 (1970); *Misse v. Dronet*, 493 So.2d 271 (La.App. 3d Cir.1986).

The reconducted lease is a continuation of the original lease under the same terms and conditions except that the fixed term or period of duration of the old lease is voided and the reconducted lease is considered to be by the month. *Comegys v. Shreveport Kandy Kitchens*, 162 La. 103, 110 So. 104 (1926); *Weaks Supply v. Werdin*, 147 So. 838 (La.App. 2d Cir.1933).

A lease is presumed to be reconducted on a monthly basis if the lessee continues in possession for more than one week beyond the term of the lease. The purpose of this presumption is not to force a contract upon unwilling parties, but merely to establish a rule of evidence, or presumption, as to their intention when a contrary intent has not been expressed. The presumption is inapplicable, however, in the face of a clear intention of the parties to the contrary. [Citations omitted.]

In *Kogos v. Lemann, supra*, and *Jacobi v. Toomer, supra*, the leases contained clauses providing that retention of possession of the leased premises by lessee with lessor's permission beyond the expiration of the term would not reconduct the lease. The courts therefore found that the presumption of reconduction was rendered inoperable by this clearly expressed intention to the contrary.

In several of the cited cases, one of the parties to the lease was seeking to end the contractual relationship altogether after the expiration of the lease. In *Prisock v. Boyd, supra*, evidence that the landlord did not intend to renew the original lease or create a new lease with the tenant, and that the tenant had notice of this within 30 days of the expiration of the lease, supported a finding that tacit reconduction had not occurred.

Similarly, in *Ashton Realty Co. v. Prowell, supra*, our Supreme Court found the lessee's remaining on the premises beyond the expiration of the lease had not reconducted the lease where the lessor sued the lessee to obtain possession of the premises after giving him notice to vacate.

Eames v. Goodwin, supra, upon which defendant relies, was an eviction action in which the court held that the predial lease, which had been reconducted twice previously, was not subject to reconduction a third time when the landowner terminated the lease by verbally notifying defendants in advance of expiration that he intended to farm his tract the following year.

In *Rosedale Rental, Inc. v. Fransen*, 427 So.2d 620 (La.App. 5th Cir.1983), another eviction suit, the continued occupancy of the premises by the lessee was held not to constitute reconduction since the lessor had obtained a judgment terminating the lease and ordering the lessee evicted. He failed to enforce the judgment, however, and a new monthly lease was created when he allowed the lessee to remain for two and one half years.

Divincenti v. Redondo, 486 So.2d 959 (La.App. 1st Cir.1986) is another case in which the court concluded the lease was not continued through reconduction when the lessee remained in possession after expiration. There, the parties had unsuccessfully attempted to negotiate a new lease during the final month of the primary term. The negotiations involved terms, which were substantially different from those in the original lease. This was also an eviction action, and although there was no formal demand to vacate, the court found the negotiations to be clear evidence of an intent not to continue the lease under the same terms.

Furthermore, in *Misse v. Dronet, supra*, the third circuit affirmed the trial court's determination that a month-to-month continuation of the prior agreement constituted reconduction. Significantly, special note was taken of the fact that the same rent was paid during the "hold-over" period as had been paid under the original agreement. In contrast, see *Maxwell, Inc. v. Mack Trucks, Inc.*, 172 So.2d 297 (La. App. 4th Cir.1965), writ refused, 247 La. 717, 174 So.2d 131 (1974), where, after the expiration of a written lease, the owner and lessee of the premises agreed orally to a short extension on different terms (different rental and portion of premises subject to lease was changed) and acted under such agreement. The court there found that the lessee had not remained in possession after the expiration of the term within the meaning of the lease, and thus reconduction had not occurred.

The lessee in *Talambas v. Louisiana State Board of Education, supra*, was not in actual possession of the leased premises beyond the expiration date of the lease. In that case, the Louisiana State Board of Education entered into a series of agreements with plaintiff to lease a meat processing facility in which to conduct vocational training for meat cutting. The meatcutting course lasted six months, and at the end of each term, the school closed. As each new class was organized, a new lease was signed.

On the final day of the last lease contracted by the parties, the instructor told the lessor that he would not return as an instructor, but that he thought a new instructor would arrive for the next class. This instructor locked the doors of the building before leaving and kept the keys. Furniture and equipment belonging to the school were left in the building. When a new instructor did not arrive after some time, the lessor began trying to find out if the lessee planned to sign a new lease, so that if not, he could rent to another. The lessor allowed the building to remain unused for some 36 months, after which he filed an action for damages for loss of use and deterioration of the building.

The third circuit reversed the lower court's finding that the lease had been tacitly reconducted by defendant's continued possession of the premises after the lease expired. Agreeing with the lower court's determination that the lessee had remained in possession after the lease expired, the court held that the evidence did not support the presumption that the parties had intended the lease to continue month to month for 36 months, in view of the fact that the longest period of time previously elapsing between leases was 20 days, and defendant had not paid any rent after the expiration of the last six month lease.

In contrast to these cases, a finding of reconduction in the present cause does not operate to force a contract on anyone, as both parties obviously desired that the contractual relationship continue on a monthly basis after the expiration of the term. The record is devoid of any evidence supporting an intention on the part of either party to change any terms of the written lease except for the 7 year term.

Moreover, in *Garner v. Perrin*, 403 So.2d 814 (La.App. 2d Cir.1981), this court held that a written lease continued (was reconducted) on a month-to-month basis where the record did not support a conclusion that the lessor opposed possession of the leased premises by the tenant during the week after the lease expired.

In light of this jurisprudence, it appears that where a fixed-term lease expires and the lessee without opposition continues to occupy the premises for more than a week, and there is no evidence of an intent by either party to change any provision of the lease other than its duration, the lease is reconducted. Consequently, I would hold that the lease in this case was reconducted or continued with its same conditions, except for the term.

For these reasons, I respectfully dissent.

Notes and Questions

1. Do you agree with the majority's position that the parties entered into a new lease through their renegotiation of the term or with the dissent's position that the lease was reconducted? Consider the possibility that neither position is correct. Was the lease instead amended? How would a finding that the lease was "amended" have affected the outcome in this case?

2. Does a change in rent result in a new lease? One court considered this issue, holding in *Weaks Supply Co. v. Werdin*, 147 So. 838 (La. App. 2 Cir. 1933), that a

change in rent automatically results in a new lease. Is this finding correct under the law of novation? *See* La. Civ. Code arts. 1881, 2726 cmt.

iv. Termination at Will

La. Civ. Code art. 2718

The parties to a fixed term lease may agree that one or both of them will have the ability to unilaterally terminate the lease at some point prior to the expiration of the fixed term. While this right is referred to in practice as the right of "termination at will," the parties usually agree that termination will take place following notice given by one of the parties. For example, Lessor and Lessee may agree, in a ten-year lease of a shopping center, that either party may terminate the lease at any time prior to the expiration of the term by giving sixty days' notice to the other party.

Termination-at-will clauses are generally enforceable. However, the parties are not entirely free to contract for any notice period that they desire. Instead, Article 2718 provides that "[a] lease in which one or both parties have reserved the right to terminate the lease before the end of the term may be so terminated by giving the notice specified in the lease contract *or* the notice provided in Articles 2727 through 2729, *whichever period is longer.*" La. Civ. Code art. 2718 (emphasis added). The application of this rule requires the understanding that the parties to a fixed term lease that contains a termination-at-will clause have agreed to two *alternative* terms: one that is fixed and conventional and one that is legal and indeterminate. If a party with the right to terminate at will does so, termination is governed by the rules on indeterminate term leases. Thus, one must determine the length of the indeterminate term supplied by law per Article 2680 and then determine how notice is properly given for a lease with a term of that length per Articles 2727 through 2729. If the parties' agreement provides for a longer notice period than that proscribed by law, the parties' agreement controls. If the parties' agreement provides for a shorter period than the legal period, then the legal period controls. Presumably also the form requirements specified by Article 2729 may not be altered by the parties' agreement.

Returning to the example of the shopping center lease described above, consider the application of the rule announced in Article 2718. To determine the enforceability of the parties' agreement that the lease may be terminated by sixty days' written notice, one must first determine the duration of the indeterminate term supplied by law. Under Article 2680, because the lease is a non-agricultural lease of an immovable, the term of the lease is month-to-month. Next, one must determine the proper method of termination for such a lease. Under Articles 2727 through 2729, written notice must be provided by the party seeking to terminate the lease at least ten calendar days before the end of the month. Because the parties' agreement provides for a longer notice period than that proscribed by law, the parties' agreement controls, and notice must be given by sixty days' written notice.

Note that the parties may not altogether exclude notice of termination. Article 2718 makes clear that "[t]he right to receive this notice may not be renounced in advance." La. Civ. Code art. 2718.

B. Expropriation, Loss, and Destruction

La. Civ. Code arts. 2693, 2714–2715

As discussed in Part A above, termination of a lease may be tied to the term of the lease. However, not every termination of a lease results from the arrival of its term. This Part discusses the circumstances under which the expropriation, loss, or destruction (total and partial) of the leased thing may bring an end to the lease and how those events affect the parties.

Louisiana Civil Code Articles 2714 and 2715 provide the rules for expropriation, loss, and destruction of the leased thing. Note that the rules for total destruction, loss, and expropriation are not the same as those addressing partial destruction, loss, and expropriation; the two sets of rules have different effects on the lease and the parties to it (as discussed below).

Article 2714 states that "[i]f the leased thing is lost or totally destroyed, without the fault of either party, or if it is expropriated, the lease terminates and neither party owes damages to the other." La. Civ. Code art. 2714. This article contemplates two effects of total loss, destruction, or expropriation: termination of the lease and the possibility that one of the parties may owe damages to the other for his or her fault.

First, with respect to termination, note that in any of the scenarios mentioned in Article 2714, performance is impossible, leading to a failure of cause. La. Civ. Code art. 2714 cmt. b. This means in any case of total loss, destruction, or expropriation, the lease terminates, and this is true regardless of the parties' fault (or lack thereof). *Id.* Hence, termination under this article is referred to as one "of right" or one "by operation of law." La. Civ. Code art. 2714 cmt. d.

Second, with respect to damages, Article 2714 provides that if the loss or destruction occurs "without the fault of either party," although the lease terminates of right, "neither party owes damages to the other." La. Civ. Code art. 2714. If, on the other hand, the loss or destruction is attributable to the fault of a party, then that party owes damages to the other. La. Civ. Code art. 2714 cmt. b. In such a case, the lease still terminates due to impossibility of performance. *Id.* (referencing La. Civ. Code art. 1876). Note also that Louisiana jurisprudence provides that in the event of a total expropriation, a lessee is allowed to demand compensation from the expropriating authority if such compensation is otherwise due. La. Civ. Code art. 2714 cmt. c.

In the event of a partial destruction, loss, or expropriation, or other substantial impairment of use of the leased thing, as long as the lessee was not at fault, he or she may, according to the circumstances of both parties, obtain a diminution of the rent or a dissolution of the lease, whichever is more appropriate under the circumstances. La. Civ. Code art. 2715. If the lessor was at fault, the lessee may also demand damages. *Id.* Note, though, that if the substantial impairment of the use of the thing was caused by circumstances external to the thing, the lessee is entitled to dissolution of the lease but not diminution of the rent. *Id.* Such external circumstances are those out of the lessor's control and include, for example, a neighbor who raised his or her walls, intercepting the light of the house leased and zoning or other governmental restrictions that substantially limit the use of the leased thing. LA. CIV. CODE art. 2715 cmt. c.

In the event of a partial destruction, the parties' rights are governed also by Articles 2693 and 2694—the provisions addressing the parties' rights and obligations concerning repairs. Article 2693, you will recall, provides that if the thing requires a repair that cannot be postponed until the end of the lease, the lessor has the right to repair even if it causes inconvenience or loss of use to the lessee. LA. CIV. CODE art. 2693. The article also provides that the lessee may obtain a reduction or abatement of rent or dissolution of the lease, depending on the circumstances, including the fault of each party or responsibility for the repair, the length of the repair period, and the extent of the loss of use. *Id.* If the lessor does not make repairs within a reasonable time after demand by the lessee, the lessee may cause them to be made and seek reimbursement of the amount for the repair or deduct the amount from the rent. LA. CIV. CODE art. 2694.

Whether a lessee is entitled to dissolution of the lease or mere diminution of the rent is a question that is frequently litigated following partial destruction of leased premises. The following case explores this question in detail.

Bossier Center, Inc. v. Palais Royal, Inc.

385 So. 2d 886 (La. App. 2 Cir. 1980)

JASPER E. JONES, Judge.

A violent tornado which struck Bossier City on December 3, 1978, is the underlying cause of these consolidated cases. The Bossier Center, Inc. (Center) leased premises in its shopping center to Palais Royal (Palais) whose clothing store was heavily damaged by the tornadic forces. Shortly after the tornado, Jay Kline, President of Palais Royal, informed the Center that Palais Royal would be vacating the premises because it elected to declare the lease to be null due to the extensive damage sustained by the leased premises in the tornado. Palais filed a declaratory judgment action seeking a determination that the lease was ended because of the damages done to the leased premises by the tornado. The Center filed a separate suit against Palais to accelerate the rental payments for the remaining years of the lease and for loss of revenue, future loss of revenue, merchants' dues, and damages to the leased premises caused by Palais while moving from the building. The cases were consolidated for trial.

The trial court held Palais did not have the right to cancel the lease because although the premises were seriously damaged, they were not partially destroyed. The trial court found Center was not entitled to accelerate the rent installments because of its failure to repair the leased premises. It also held Center did not prove it was entitled to damages, either in the form of lost income or reimbursement for any alleged damage done to the premises. Both parties appeal.

On December 19, 1974 the Center leased 20,500 sq. ft. to Palais within its shopping center to be used as a men's, ladies', and children's ready-to-wear clothing store. The lease period was ten years. The Palais area was remodeled by the Center in preparation for occupancy by Palais at a cost of approximately $275,000. Palais then spent about $150,000 on decorative and merchandising fixtures.

Palais was severely damaged by the tornado. Part of the roof was blown off and other portions were so severely damaged that over ⅓ of the roof had to be replaced at a cost of almost $50,000. The wind and rain destroyed substantially all Palais' merchandise and stock. The floor was inundated and there was substantial evidence that all parquet wood flooring and carpeting would have to be replaced. The electrical system was heavily damaged and one electrical contractor would not guarantee the system unless he replaced all wiring and fixtures. The air conditioning units located on top of the building were heavily damaged. The ceiling tile and insulation were blown out or exposed to rain, humidity, and moisture. One witness testified that much of the interior sheet rock walls would have to be totally replaced because of water damage. The large sign in front of the store was razed by the tornadic gusts.

The issues on appeal are (1) did Palais establish the leased premises were partially destroyed and for that reason it was entitled to cancel the lease? (2) if the lease is not subject to cancellation is the Center required to repair the premises as a condition precedent to accelerating all unpaid rent? and (3) did Center prove it was entitled to recover damages from Palais?

LSA-C.C. art. 2697 [R.C.C. 2714, 2715] provides:

"If, during the lease, the thing be totally destroyed by an unforeseen (unforeseen) event, or it be taken for a purpose of public utility, the lease is at an end. If it be only destroyed in part, the lessee may either demand a diminution of the price, or a revocation of the lease. In neither case has he any claim of damages."

LSA-C.C. art. 2700 [R.C.C. 2693] states:

"If, during the continuance of the lease, the thing leased should be in want of repairs, and if those repairs cannot be postponed until the expiration of the lease, the tenant must suffer such repairs to be made, whatever be the inconvenience he undergoes thereby, and though he be deprived either totally or in part of the use of the thing leased to him during the making of the repairs. But in case such repairs should continue for a longer time than one month, the price of the rent shall be lessened in proportion to the time during which the repairs have continued, and to the parts of the tenement for the use of which the lessee has thereby been deprived.

And the whole of the rent shall be remitted, if the repairs have been of such nature as to oblige the tenant to leave the house or the room and to take another house, while that which he had leased was repairing."

A review of these two Articles establish that where partial reconstruction is required to the leased premises, the lease may be cancelled but if only repairs are necessary the lease may not be subject to cancellation. The lessee is given the exclusive right to cancel the lease if the premises are partially destroyed. See *Chivleatto v. Family Furniture & Appliance Center*, 196 So. 2d 298 (La.App. 4th Cir. 1967).

The distinction to be drawn between a partial destruction requiring reconstruction and a mere damage requiring only repair has been considered many times in our jurisprudence in cases involving deterioration, fire, floods, and other *cas fortuit*. The jurisprudence allows expert testimony as to the extent of restoration (whether repairs or reconstruction is required) to help distinguish between injury and partial destruction. See XXX Tulane Law Review 474. The case law sets out other criteria to be used to determine whether a partial destruction or a mere injury has occurred, such as (1) length of time the repairs would take, (2) the partial or absolute deprivation of lessee's use of the premises, (3) the length of time lessee would be displaced, (4) damage done to the lessee's stock, goods and merchandise, (5) the amount paid by the insurer of the building to the insured (as compared with the value of the building prior to damage), (6) the cost of repairs to the premises (as compared with the total value of the pre-damaged premises), and (7) to what degree and which parts of the building are damaged. [Citations omitted.]

All the cases cited turn on the individual facts and circumstances. They variously found partial destruction and terminated the lease or concluded only damage not amounting to a destruction had occurred and refused to end the lease, but all used one or more of the above criteria in making this determination.

In *Meyer v. Henderson, supra*, damage that was construed as partial destruction entitling a lessee to demand cancellation was described as follows:

> "But when the partial destruction has been of such a nature as to menace discomfort to the tenant during the entire term; to cause the tenant to abandon the premises, in order that repairs may be made; when the premises are no longer suitable for the purposes for which they were leased, in such cases it is clear that the lease should be annulled. The partial destruction of the building leased by plaintiffs from defendants made it entirely unfit for the purposes for which it was leased. It was a wreck. It was not habitable. It was unfit for the storage of goods and merchandise. The necessary repairs to it required some months for their completion." *Meyer*, supra, 16 So. at 729-730.

The court here annulled the lease which had two years remaining of its term.

The Center offered testimony of numerous witnesses who qualified as experts in construction, all of whom minimized the effect of the tornado upon the leased premises. The purpose of this testimony was to establish there had been no partial destruction of the leased premises. This evidence was offered to establish only repairs were necessary for the restoration of the premises which Palais was required to endure under the provisions of LSA-C.C. art. 2700 [R.C.C. 2693].

The testimony of the two architects offered by Palais and Center was inconclusive on the issue of repair versus reconstruction.

Pictures in evidence revealed a large hole in the roof (testified by one of Center's experts to be 750 sq. ft.) where the entire roof structure was blown away. Other pictures show large holes in the roof and extensive areas where only a few pieces of sheet iron across steel beams remain, the wind having removed the zonite and other material used in the construction of the roof. Pictures also establish extensive electrical conduit and light fixture damage. These photographs also reveal extensive air condition conduit damage and substantial destruction to interior ceilings. The testimony of Palais' witnesses, who included electrical, air conditioning, and acoustical tile contractors, further established the scope and extent of the damage. The preponderance of the evidence established almost total destruction to ⅓ of the roof, substantial damage to the floor, interior ceiling, walls, electrical and air conditioning system.

The totality of the damage ($200,000 plus) in relation to the value of the building ($1,000,000 plus) shows 20% or more of this modern retail store was destroyed, exclusive of $150,000 interior decorating costs incorporated into the leased premises by Palais, all of which were destroyed. The leased structure and component parts of it essential to the operation of a modern clothing store were so extensively damaged that Palais would have been totally evicted from the premises for four to seven months while the necessary rebuilding of its store was being accomplished.

We conclude that because of the severity and nature of the damages, with the resulting total eviction of the premises for some months (because of the time required for restoration), a partial destruction of the leased premises has occurred. Partial reconstruction will be necessary within the contemplation of LSA-C.C. art. 2697 [R.C.C. 2714, 2715] rather than only repairs which are referred to in LSA-C.C. art. 2700 [R.C.C. 2693]. This conclusion is not incompatible with the factual findings of the trial judge as reflected by the following quote from his reasons for judgment:

> "There is no question but that the leased premise were severely damaged. Part of the roof was blown off and the wind and rain substantially ruined all the merchandise belonging to Palais Royal. Much of the floor was completely under water. Much of the ceiling tile was either blown out, displaced, or exposed to moisture. There was damage to the electrical system and the air conditioning units which were located on top of the building, a large display sign in front of the building was blown away. Substantial damage was done to the interior and cost of repair 'approximately $150,000 to $250,000' and that the total value of the leased premises is approximately $ 1,125,000 . . . .
>
> The evidence also shows that it will take approximately two to four months for the necessary repairs to be made to the lease premises and that another two to three months would be required by Palais Royal for repairs

by its design specialist. Thus the premises would not be ready to use for several months."

The only error made by the trial judge was he concluded the building was structurally sound and he characterized the havoc wrought by the tornado as severe damage when he should have found it was partial destruction.

In the case of *Caffin v. Redon* and *Brunies v. Police Jury of Parish of Jefferson, supra,* substantial replacement of weight-bearing walls was construed to be reconstruction of "partially destroyed" leased premises within the contemplation of LSA-C.C. art. 2697 [R.C.C. 2714, 2715]. We find the roof of Palais analogous to the walls in those cases. It is the top of the four sides of a building and its function is no less important than is the purpose served by the walls. The roof is essential to the protection of all the interior of the building and no doubt the partial destruction of the roof of Palais subjected the interior of the building to the winds and rain of the tornado resulting in a substantial portion of the other damage described.

Palais is entitled to have the lease cancelled under the provisions of LSA-C.C. art. 2697 [R.C.C. 2714, 2715] and therefore we find no need to decide its contention that it is entitled to have the lease cancelled under the provisions of LSA-C.C. art. 2699 [R.C.C. 2715].

Because the lease is a nullity due to Palais' election to terminate, the Center is not entitled to the acceleration of the unpaid rent installments.

The trial judge found that the Center failed to establish any of the damages sought by it and the evidence fully supports this factual determination.

The judgment appealed in *Palais Royal, Inc. v. Bossier Center, Inc.*, No. 14,167, is REVERSED and we render judgment therein cancelling the lease.

The judgment appealed in *Bossier Center, Inc. v. Palais Royal, Inc.*, No. 14,166, rejecting plaintiff's demands for rent and damages is AFFIRMED.

All costs in these consolidated cases in the trial court and on appeal are assessed against Bossier Center, Inc.

Notes and Questions

1. Did the court in the case above allow for dissolution of the lease or did it grant some other remedy? Why did the court reach the conclusion that it did?

2. Given the changes to the law of lease, are the cases decided under prior law still instructive? Why or why not? How, if at all, would the court's analysis differ if the facts of the *Palais* case arose under current law?

3. In *Chivleatto v. Family Furniture & Appliance Center,* 196 So. 2d 298 (La. App. 4 Cir. 1967), Hurricane Betsy caused extensive damage to the leased premises. Although the lessor began repairs, seven weeks after the hurricane, he notified the lessee that the lease was terminated. The lessee argued that the lessor had no right to cancel the lease. The lessor, in turn, pointed to the following provision in the

contract of lease: "Should the property be destroyed or materially damaged so as to render it wholly unfit for occupancy by fire or other unforeseen [sic] event not due to any fault or neglect of lessee, then lessee shall be entitled to a credit for the unexpired term of the lease and any unmatured rent notes shall be cancelled." *Id.* at 299. The Fourth Circuit agreed with the trial court that the quoted provision gives the lessee only, and not the lessor, the right to cancel the lease. The court also analyzed whether the same result would occur under the default rules of the Civil Code and stated that it did; in other words, only the lessee has the right to dissolution in the case of partial eviction unless the parties provide otherwise. Read Article 2715 carefully; do you see why? Of course, in a total destruction, the lease terminates as a matter of law, meaning neither party is required to request that the court grant dissolution of the lease. *See* La. Civ. Code art. 2714.

C. Termination of Lease Granted by Usufructuary

La. Civ. Code arts. 568.2, 2716

As discussed in Chapter 13: The Nature and Essential Elements of the Contract of Lease, one need not own the thing in order to lease it. La. Civ. Code art. 2674. Thus, a usufructuary may grant a lease over the thing on which he or she enjoys a usufruct. How, if at all, does the termination of the usufruct affect the lease? The answer to that question depends upon what sort of rights the naked owner granted to the usufructuary.

Recall, first, that because a lease always involves a nonconsumable thing (*see* La. Civ. Code art. 2673), the rights of a usufructuary are subject to the rules governing usufructs of nonconsumables. According to that regime, a usufructuary does not have the right to dispose of the thing subject to the usufruct unless that right has been specifically granted to him or her. La. Civ. Code art. 568. Recall also that the right to dispose of a nonconsumable thing includes the right to lease it. *Id.*

If the usufructuary has not been granted the right to dispose of the thing subject to the usufruct, then rights of the parties are governed by Article 2716. That article provides that "[a] lease granted by a usufructuary terminates upon the termination of the usufruct." La. Civ. Code art. 2716. In such a case, if the usufructuary-lessor failed to disclose that he or she was a usufructuary, the usufructuary-lessor is liable to the lessee for any loss caused by the termination of the lease. If, on the other hand, the usufructuary-lessor did disclose that status, then the lessee has no remedy. Of course, the rule of Article 2716 does not apply in the event that the naked owner confirms or ratifies the lease, in which case, the lease continues beyond the termination of the usufruct. La. Civ. Code art. 568.2 cmt. a.

If, in contrast, the usufructuary has been granted the right to dispose of the thing subject to the usufruct, then Article 568.2 (added in 2010) applies. That article provides: "The right to dispose of a nonconsumable thing includes the right to lease the thing for a term that extends beyond the termination of the usufruct." La. Civ. Code art. 568.2. Thus, a usufructuary who has been granted the right to dispose of the nonconsumable may lease the thing for a term beyond the life of the usufruct that burdens it. Stated another way, the lease does not terminate upon the termination of the usufruct. Note, though, that in such a case, "[i]f, at the termination of the usufruct, the thing remains subject to the lease, the usufructuary is accountable to the naked owner for any diminution in the value of the thing at that time attributable to the lease." *Id.*

Ultimately, then, unless the naked owner has granted to the usufructuary the right to dispose of a nonconsumable thing, the lease will terminate contemporaneously with the termination of the usufruct. If such a right was granted by the naked owner to the usufructuary, the lease will not terminate contemporaneously with the termination of the usufruct unless the parties to the lease so agreed.

D. Death of Lessor or Lessee

La. Civ. Code art. 2717

Article 2717 provides that the lease does not terminate upon the death of either party, even a juridical person that ceases to exist. La. Civ. Code art. 2717. This is true because the obligations created by a contract of lease are heritable, not strictly personal, and therefore, they may be enforced against the successors of the lessor or the lessee. La. Civ. Code art. 2717 cmt. a; *see also* La. Civ. Code arts. 1765–66.

E. Dissolution for Party's Failure to Perform

La. Civ. Code art. 2719

When a party to the lease fails to perform his or her obligations under the lease or under the provisions of the Louisiana Civil Code, the other party may obtain dissolution of the lease pursuant to the provisions found in the Title on Conventional Obligations or Contracts. La. Civ. Code art. 2719. This includes the provisions on both judicial and extrajudicial dissolution. La. Civ. Code art. 2719 cmt. b. Following a general discussion of the right to dissolution in the event of a party's nonperformance, this Part will explore the *alternative* to dissolution: specific performance. As will be shown by the materials that follow, an obligee may seek either dissolution or enforcement of the lease, but not both.

1. The Right to Dissolution

Failure to perform is defined by the Civil Code as nonperformance, defective performance, or delay in performance. La. Civ. Code art. 1994. However, even under those circumstances, dissolution is not allowed when the obligor has substantially performed, and the part not performed does not substantially impair the interest of the obligee. La, Civ. Code art. 2014. Thus, a lease may not be dissolved for minor violations. La. Civ. Code art. 2719 cmt. c.

Furthermore, in an action involving judicial dissolution, the obligor may be granted, according to the circumstances, additional time to perform. La. Civ. Code art. 2013. In the jurisprudence involving leases, courts have referred to the judicial discretion permitted by this article as the "judicial control" of leases and have further defined that phrase as "an equitable doctrine by which the courts will deny cancellation of the lease when the lessee's breach is of minor importance, is caused by no fault of his own, or is based on a good faith mistake of fact." *KM, Inc. v. Weil Cleaners, Inc.*, 185 So. 3d 112, 118 (La. App. 2 Cir. 2016). In other words, even if a lessee breaches the lease, which would seemingly give the lessor the right to dissolve the lease, courts may decline to grant the remedy of dissolution. *Id.* (quoting *Ergon, Inc. v. Allen*, 593 So. 2d 438 (La. App. 2 Cir. 1992)). In making the decision whether to grant a request for judicial dissolution of a contract, courts often consider the guidance of Professor Saúl Litvinoff on the matter:

> For this purpose the court takes into consideration the extent and gravity of the failure to perform alleged by the complaining party, the nature of the obligor's fault, the good or bad faith of the parties involved, and also the surrounding economic circumstances that may make the dissolution opportune or not.

See Waseco Chemical & Supply Co. v. Bayou State Oil Corp., 371 So. 2d 305, 308–09 (La. App. 2 Cir. 1979) (quoting 7 Saúl Litvinoff, Louisiana Civil Law Treatise, Obligations § 270, at 509 (1975)). While courts have not always relied explicitly on these factors in the context of leases, the jurisprudence has firmly established that dissolution of leases is not favored and should be ordered only when the lessor is clearly entitled to it. *See, e.g., Tolar v. Spillers*, 2 So. 3d 560, 563–64 (La. App. 2 Cir. 2009) (issuing injunction rather than granting dissolution); *KM, Inc. v. Weil Cleaners, Inc.*, 185 So. 3d 112 (La. App. 2 Cir. 2016) (refusing to dissolve the lease despite lessee's failure to timely pay rent, given that the lessor never demanded the past due rent and never gave the lessee the opportunity to pay before taking action to terminate the lease and evict him, and also given that by the time of trial, the lessee had performed its obligation of paying the past-due rent and associated late fees, as well as the following month's rent); *cf. Western Sizzlin Corp. v. Greenway*, 821 So. 2d 594, 601 (La. App. 2 Cir. 2002) (finding lessee's failure to maintain the premises as required by lease agreement sufficiently egregious to justify dissolution and eviction of lessee); *Select Properties, Ltd. v. Rando*, 453 So. 2d 980 (La. App. 4 Cir. 1984) (granting dissolution for the lessee's failure to obtain the insurance required by the contract of lease).

Read the case below to see an example of a situation in which a court may exercise its judicial control over the dissolution of a lease.

Edwards v. Standard Oil Co. of Louisiana

144 So. 430 (La. 1932)

St. Paul, Justice.

Plaintiff alleges that on August 1, 1930, he leased to defendant, for a filling station, certain premises in Ponchatoula, La., for a period of two years, with privilege of renewal for two years more; the monthly rental being one cent per gallon of gasoline or oil sold from said premises, and being payable on the 15th day of the month following that in which the oil was sold; that the rent due July 15, 1931, was not paid when it became due; that plaintiff was "tendered a check for $35.19 [amount of said rent] on the 21st of the month"; that on the same day plaintiff returned said check; and that, "by reason of the non-payment of the rent when due," he is entitled (due notice having been given defendant) to have said defendant vacate the premises and deliver possession thereof to him.

I.

The lease does not set forth where the rent is to be paid; and the petition does not allege, but on the contrary inferentially negatives that any demand for payment was ever made on defendant. And the fact is that a check for the amount of the rent was mailed by defendant to its agent at Ponchatoula on July 10th; but, owing to some oversight, or perhaps some fault in mail deliveries, it did not reach plaintiff until July 21st, as aforesaid.

The district court gave judgment for plaintiff as prayed for; and the Court of Appeal affirmed the judgment. 141 So. 513.

II.

Article 2712, Rev. Civ. Code [R.C.C. 2704], declares that "The lessee may be expelled from the property if he fails to pay the rent when it becomes due."

But "Incivile est, nisi tota lege prospecta, una aliqua particula ejus proposita, judicare vel respondere," a laconic as old as the seven hills of Rome, which Corpus Juris correctly translates as meaning, "It is improper, unless the whole law has been examined, to give judgment or advice upon a view of a single clause of it."

And article 2157, Rev. Civ. Code [R.C.C. 1862], provides, that "The payment must be made in the place specified in the agreement. If the place be not thus specified, the payment, in case of a certain and determinate substance, must be made in the place where was, at the time of the agreement, the thing which is the object of it. These two cases excepted, the payment must be made at the dwelling of the debtor."

Hence, it is a rule that, "where the lease is silent as to where the rent shall be paid, the payment is to be made either at the leased premises or at the domicile of the debtor, and this presupposes, of course, that the lessor is to call for his rent." *Saxton v. Para Rubber Co.*, 166 La. 308, 117 So. 235, 237. So that, "where * * * there is no specification in the lease as to the place where the rent should be paid, the law prescribes that 'payment must be made at the dwelling of the debtor.' * * * R.C.C.,

2157 [R.C.C. 1862] [hence]. By formally tendering the rent after maturity, but prior to default and to the filing of this action, the defendant effectively stripped the landlord of his right to cancel the lease on the ground alleged." *Lafayette Realty Co. v. Joseph Puglia*, 10 Orleans App. 105.

Moreover, where "defendant was offered its money, and could have had it before it even brought suit to annul the contract [lease]," he cannot annul the lease for alleged nonpayment of the rent. "Our law does not contemplate that contracts shall be annulled by one party, where the other is able and willing to perform his own part of it as soon as demanded of him." *Hemsing v. Wiener-Loeb Grocery Co.*, 157 La. 189, 102 So. 303, 304.

Hence, although "it is true that ordinarily a lessor may dissolve a lease for failure on the part of the lessee to pay the rent promptly when due, [nevertheless] the right to dissolve a lease is subject to judicial control according to circumstances." [Citations omitted.]

DECREE

For the reasons assigned, the judgment of the district court, and that of the Court of Appeal affirming the same, are reversed and set aside, and it is now ordered that the demand of the plaintiff be rejected at his cost in all courts.

Notes and Questions

1. Courts frequently exercise judicial control to refuse dissolution when the lessee, though acting in good faith, fails to pay rent on time. As noted by the court in *Plunkett v. D & L Family Pharmacy, Inc.*, 562 So. 2d 1048 (La. App. 3 Cir. 1990): "Louisiana has never followed a dogmatic rule requiring the mechanical application of a general rule that a lessor may dissolve a lease for failure on the part of lessee to pay rent promptly when due." *Id.* at 1053 (quoting *Touchet v. Humble Oil and Refining Co.*, 191 F.Supp. 291 (W.D. La. 1960). In *Belvin v. Sikes*, 2 So. 2d 65 (La. App. 2 Cir. 1941), the lessee failed to pay the full amount of rent due to a misunderstanding about the amount owed, and that misunderstanding was caused by an error in a receipt provided by the lessor. In *Baham v. Faust*, 333 So. 2d 261 (La. App. 1 Cir. 1976), dissolution was refused when rent was eight days late and the lease provided no place for payment. In *Housing Authority of the City of Lake Charles v. Minor*, 355 So. 2d 271 (La. App. 3 Cir. 1977), the rent was paid timely with a third-party check from the lessee's employer, but the check was returned for insufficient funds. In *Tullier v. Tanson Enterprises, Inc.*, 359 So. 2d 654 (La. App. 1 Cir. 1978), *overruled on other grounds*, 367 So. 2d 773 (La. 1979), the rent was late due to a malfunction in the bank's transmittal device. In *Atkinson v. Richeson*, 393 So. 2d 801 (La. App. 2 Cir. 1981), the rent was 15 days late because the lessee believed his wife had paid the rent. In each of these cases, the court refused to grant dissolution of the lease. The doctrine of judicial control does not, however, prevent dissolution in all cases of late payment of rent. In fact, the general rule employed by courts is that, absent special circumstances, late payment of rent justifies immediate dissolution of the lease. *Ergon, Inc. v. Allen*, 593 So. 2d 438, 440 (La. App. 2 Cir. 1992).

2. If the lessor has frequently accepted late rent from the lessee without complaint, the lessor will not be permitted to dissolve the lease because of a late payment. *Himbola Manor Apts. v. Allen*, 315 So. 2d 790, 792–93 (La. App. 3 Cir. 1975). According to the court in *Himbola*, the acceptance of late rent is a "custom" which, "by acquiescence of the parties, has the effect of altering the original contract in respect to punctuality of rent payments." *Id.* In order to hold the lessee to the explicit terms of the lease, the lessor must notify the lessee that the lessor intends to strictly enforce the lease and collect the rent when it is due. *Id.* at 793.

3. Although many of the cases addressing the doctrine of judicial control involve the lessee's failure to timely pay rent, the doctrine applies to other failures to perform, as well. For example, in *Rogers v. Restructure Petroleum Marketing Svces.*, 811 So. 2d 1154 (La. App. 3 Cir. 2002), the court addressed the doctrine in the context of the lessee's failure to perform the contractual obligation of making repairs. The court decided to grant the lessor's request for dissolution, noting that the contractual provision dictating the repairs was "not of minor importance, but was a major factor in maintaining the lease." *Id.* at 1159. By contrast, in *Karno v. Bourbon Burlesque Club, Inc.*, 931 So. 2d 1111 (La. App. 4 Cir. 2006), the lessee failed to comply with all laws and ordinances as required by a provision in the lease contract. The court, exercising its power of judicial control, refused the lessor's request for dissolution of the lease, finding that the lessee's violations were merely "technical." *Id.* at 1117.

4. A lessor who wishes to regain possession as a result of a lessee's failure to pay rent or perform some other obligation under the lease may institute an action for summary eviction, which is governed by Articles 4701 through 4735 of the Code of Civil Procedure. As Code of Civil Procedure Article 4701 makes clear, a lessor may institute eviction proceedings not only for nonpayment of rent, but whenever the lessee's right of occupancy has ceased, whether "because of the termination of the lease by expiration of its term, action by the lessor [e.g., notice to terminate], nonpayment of rent, or *for any other reason*." LA. CODE CIV. PROC. art. 4701 (emphasis added). Eviction proceedings are generally initiated by delivering to the lessee a "notice to vacate," which informs the lessee that the lessor considers the lessee's right of occupancy to have ceased and which gives the lessee at least five days to vacate the premises. *Id.* However, the lessee's right to the notice to vacate may be (and often is) waived in the lease. *Id.* Moreover, in an indeterminate lease, a notice to terminate satisfies the requirement of a notice to vacate. *Id.* If the lessee fails to comply with the notice to vacate or if the right to such notice has been waived, the lessor may file a rule to show cause why the lessee should not be ordered to deliver possession of the premises to the lessor. LA. CODE CIV. PROC. art. 4731. The hearing on the rule may be set as soon as three days after service on the lessee, and at the hearing, the lessee may present any defense the lessee may have to dissolution of the lease. LA. CODE CIV. PROC. art. 4732. If the court determines that the lessor is entitled to the relief sought, or if the lessee fails to answer or to appear, the court is required to render "immediately" a judgment ordering the

lessee to deliver possession of the premises. *Id.* If the lessee fails to comply with the judgment within twenty-four hours, the court is required to issue a warrant directing the sheriff to deliver possession of the premises to the lessor or owner, often through the removal of the lessee's property from the premises. La. Code Civ. Proc. arts. 4733–34. The lessee may appeal an order of eviction, but appeal does not suspend the execution of the judgment unless the defendant "answered the rule under oath, pleading an affirmative defense entitling him to retain possession of the premises, and the appeal has been applied for and the appeal bond filed within twenty-four hours after the rendition of the judgment of eviction." La. Code Civ. Proc. art. 4735.

5. The lessor generally may not engage in self-help to obtain possession, even when the lease has been extrajudicially dissolved or judicial dissolution of the lease is appropriate. La. Code Civ. Proc. art. 4731. Instead, the lessor must resort to judicial process to retake possession of the leased property. *See Richard v. Broussard*, 495 So. 2d 1291 (La. 1986). However, if the lessor has a "reasonable belief that the lessee . . . has abandoned the premises," the lessor may retake possession without judicial process. La. Code Civ. Proc. art. 4731. Indicia of abandonment include "a cessation of business activity or residential occupancy, returning keys to the premises, and removal of equipment, furnishings, or other movables from the premises." *Id.*

6. Recall that a contract of lease is commutative, meaning that the performance of the obligation of each party is correlative to the performance of the other. La. Civ. Code art. 1911. As a result, either party may refuse to perform his or her obligation if the other has failed to perform or does not offer to perform at the same time, if the performances are due simultaneously. La. Civ. Code art. 2022.

7. Although *Edwards* and the foregoing notes focus predominantly on the *lessor's* right to dissolve, Article 2719 makes clear that either party to the lease has the right to dissolution in the event of the other party's failure to perform. If, for example, the leased thing contains vices and defects that prevent it from being used for the purpose for which it was leased or if the lessee's peaceful possession is disturbed, the lessee may, according to the circumstances, demand dissolution of the lease. The following case addresses the right of the lessee to dissolve the lease in the event of a breach of the warranty against vices and defects.

Purnell v. Dugue
129 So. 178 (Orl. Cir. 1930)

Janvier, Judge.

Plaintiff, owner of an apartment which was rented to and occupied by defendant, seeks to recover on twelve rent notes, each for the sum of $70.

Defendant had occupied the apartment for two years, under a written lease for the term of three years, when, during the early days of October, shortly after the commencement of the third year, he abandoned the premises.

He admits that he signed the notes and executed the lease, but refuses to pay them, and bases his refusal on the assertion that the heating system with which the apartment was provided was inadequate and that it was impossible, during the winter months, to raise the temperature sufficiently high to make the premises habitable.

Plaintiff denies that the heating system was inadequate and also denies that she, as the owner of the apartment, was under any obligation to provide a heating apparatus of any particular size or type and contends that, as the heating system, such as it was, was in proper working order, her duty as landlord was fully complied with, and that she did not guarantee, and that, as a matter of law, an owner is not called upon to guarantee, that an apartment can be heated to any particular temperature.

It thus appears that two questions are presented:

One of fact, viz., was the heating apparatus adequate and capable of heating the apartment to a reasonable temperature? And the other of law, viz., is it the duty of a landlord who rents an apartment containing a heating system to see to it that the system will maintain a reasonable temperature?

The question of fact is the more easily disposed of, so we will consider that first.

The testimony of Mrs. Dugue, defendant's wife, and of defendant himself, of their servant and of a gentleman who was a frequent visitor in the apartment and who later married defendant's niece, is to the effect that, during the two winters the apartment was occupied, they were never able to maintain on cold days a reasonable temperature. A physician who treated Mrs. Dugue states that he, on one occasion when he called upon her professionally, found the rooms very cold and that he kept his overcoat on.

Various heating experts who examined the heaters testified that they were entirely inadequate and could not furnish sufficient heat for rooms so large as those composing the apartment and the figures given by one of these experts with reference to the cubic capacity of the rooms and the heating capacity of the heaters show that in order to heat the place in accordance with what is recognized in this climate as proper practice there would have been required heaters either almost double in size, or practically double in number.

Against this evidence, we find but little testimony and that of a rather negative character.

Mrs. Poitevent, who occupied the premises after Mr. and Mrs. Dugue left, states that the heaters were sufficient for her needs, except that sometimes she had to employ oil heaters to supplement the regularly installed heating system. Mrs. Dugue, defendant's wife, stated that she on several occasions had tried the use of oil heaters, but that she was subject to headaches and that the effect of the oil heater increased her headaches to such an extent that she had to discontinue their use.

Other persons occupying various other apartments in the same building state that their respective heating systems are and were adequate, but the fact is that only one of the other apartments was at all similar in size and arrangement to that involved here, and the tenant of that one demanded and received at least one additional heater.

We are thoroughly convinced from the evidence that the apartment could not be even reasonably comfortably heated because of the inadequate heating system, and that the defendant and his wife were most uncomfortable during the winters they occupied the place.

We now approach the question of law to which we have referred. Plaintiff maintains that a tenant who has the opportunity of seeing and examining the type of heaters or radiators contained in an apartment cannot complain if those heaters or radiators, when working properly and to their full capacity, are not able to heat the leased premises to a comfortable temperature; in other words that a landlord does not warrant that his premises can be heated to any particular temperature, even to a reasonable temperature, but merely that such heaters as he furnished have no mechanical defects and will operate. We are told of the far-reaching effects which will attend a holding that a landlord warrants the efficiency of his heating system and that, if we so hold, all leases of houses containing only old-fashioned open grates may be immediately broken. We do not believe that any such dire result will follow a decision that a landlord, who furnishes a modern apartment without open fires, but containing what seems to be a modern heating system, warrants to his tenant that that system is of sufficient size and efficiency to maintain a reasonably comfortable temperature.

In *Scudder v. Marsh*, 224 Ill. App. 355 we find a case involving facts strikingly similar to those presented here. The property leased was a two- story dwelling.

A heating system was contained in the dwelling but as the court found:

"In November, when the weather became cold, the furnace failed to heat the dwelling although it was run properly with a good fire; the average temperature in the rooms was from 48 to 56 degrees. Defendant's children became ill and a physician found the room so cold that his breath congealed in every room. He examined the furnace and describes it as in full blast; an experienced man in heating plants examined the furnace at this time and testified that it was only 60 per cent. adequate to furnish sufficient heat for the building."

The court said:

"The insufficiency of the furnace cannot be determined by merely looking at it, especially by one not expert in the matter of furnaces, and its inadequacy in heating capacity can only be determined by an investigation by an expert and by an actual experience with it in cold weather. Do such circumstances amount to a constructive eviction by the landlord justifying the removal from the premises of the tenant and his discharge from any obligation to pay rent thereafter?

"Plaintiff invokes the general rule of caveat emptor which throws upon the lessee the responsibility of examining as to the existence of defects and providing against their consequences. Experience, however, has shown that under circumstances like these under consideration, the strict application of this rule tends to work an injustice upon the tenant. From the very nature of the case, it would be almost impossible for a tenant by merely looking at a furnace in the summer time to have any informed judgment or opinion as to its heating sufficiency."

We have quoted somewhat at length from the opinion in the above case because of its remarkable similarity both of fact and in legal principle.

In the case of the building containing only open grates, the tenant sees and knows just what he is leasing and it cannot be said that he is given any warranty as to the efficiency of open grates. But such is not the case where the lease covers a modern apartment containing a heating system, the efficiency of which the ordinary layman can tell nothing about except after actual use. In such case it is only reasonable in the tenant to suppose that that system will not only operate, but will operate efficiently.

The various cases in which we and other courts have held that the abrogation of written leases is not favored meet with our entire approval, but in all such cases it was held that, where an abrogation is justified by the facts and the law, it should not be denied.

Here we think both the law and the facts warrant us in holding that defendant was within his rights in abandoning the premises.

Plaintiff complains that, as the written lease makes no mention of a heating system, to allow evidence to be introduced showing that the system was insufficient, is to permit the varying of a written contract by parol. We do not think so. All modern apartments contain heating systems and it is contemplated in any such lease, whether actually written into it or not, that, where an apartment contains a heating system, as a matter of fact that system is included in the lease and the reasonable adequacy of that system is warranted. That even plaintiff interpreted her lease as including a heating system is evidenced by her many promises that she would remedy the defect by the installation of additional heaters.

It was held in *Bliss v. Clark*, 104 Misc. Rep. 543, 172 N.Y.S. 112, that even in the absence of a covenant to furnish heat if "the means of furnishing the heat are in the control of the landlord, the lessee of a living apartment may, for failure of landlord to furnish proper heat, abandon the premises. * * *"

The court in discussing such covenants as are impliedly contained in certain leases, even though not expressly set forth therein, said:

"An entirely different situation, however, arises where, as in the case at bar, there is a lease of the premises with no covenant on the part of the landlord to furnish heat, although the means of furnishing heat are within the control of the landlord. In such a case there is an implication created by the court that a failure to supply heat furnished sufficient reason for an abandonment of the premises by the tenant and a refusal to pay rent. *Berlinger v. MacDonald*, 149 App. Div. 6, 133 N.Y.S. 522; *Tallman v. Murphy*, 120 N.Y. 345, 24 N.E. 716. Originally, the courts created an implication that in a lease there is implied a covenant for quiet enjoyment. *Noke's Case*, 4 Coke R. 80b; *Andrews' Case of Gray's Inn, Croke, Eliz.* 214, 674. Whatever may have given rise originally to the implication of this covenant by the court, the doctrine is now too well established to be doubted, either in this country or in England. *Brady v. Cartwright*, 22 L.J. Ex. 285; *Budd-Scott v. Daniel*, 2 K.B. 351; *Mack v. Patchin*, 42 N.Y. 171, 1 Am. Rep. 506. The implied covenant to supply heat is a part of the covenant of quiet enjoyment, and thus an implied covenant for quiet enjoyment has given rise to this implied covenant to furnish heat."

We think that the reasoning above set forth is sound and is applicable here and that, as we have stated, where a leased dwelling contains a supposedly modern heating system, there is implied a warranty, even if it be not expressed, that that system is reasonably adequate.

Plaintiff also contends that the installation of additional heaters would have cost only about $35 or $40 and that therefore defendant should have installed them himself and would have been entitled to deduct the cost thereof from the rent due or to become due. Civ. Code, article 2694 [R.C.C. 2694]. We do not think that either the right or the duty of a tenant requires that he go so far as to tamper with the piping and fundamental structure of his landlord's building; his right is limited to the making of repairs and, in our judgment, does not include the right to remedy defects which were in the building when he first went into possession of it.

If the repairs became necessary without fault on the part of the landlord and did not result from an original defect, possibly the tenant should make them under the article of the Code referred to, but here the defect is an original one and is due to the owner's neglect. In *Denman v. Lopez*, 12 La. Ann. 824, the Supreme Court said: "In the case at bar there was no original or latent defect in the building."

In *Caffin v. Redon*, 6 La. Ann. 487, the controversy was decided in favor of the lessee because of an original defect in the construction of the building, and it was held that the lessee had the right to demand the dissolution of the lease.

The fact that the installation of additional heaters was not so simple a matter as is now suggested is evidenced by the fact that, though plaintiff undoubtedly promised on many occasions to add the additional heaters necessary, she failed to do so, apparently considering it a matter more costly than she cared to undertake.

It is therefore ordered, adjudged, and decreed that the judgment appealed from be, and it is, annulled, avoided, and reversed, and that there now be judgment in favor of defendant and against plaintiff, dismissing this suit at her cost.

Reversed.

Notes and Questions

In the foregoing case, the lessor argued that the lessee improperly abandoned the premises. When doing so is not justified as a result of the lessor's failure to perform, the lessee's relinquishment of possession of the premises, when coupled with the failure to pay rent and perform other obligations under the lease, amounts to a breach of the lease which entitles the lessor to dissolution. La. Civ. Code art. 2719. In addition, if the lessee of an immovable abandons the premises, the lessor may retake possession without first engaging in a judicial proceeding. La. Code Civ. Proc. art. 4731.

Not every relinquishment of possession results in a breach of the lease, however. First, recall that when the lease is indeterminate, the lessee may give proper notice to terminate the lease through "surrender of possession to the lessor" at the appropriate time. La. Civ. Code art. 2729. If the lessee's surrender of possession is not accompanied by an element of nonperformance—e.g., failing to pay rent or causing damage to the premises, then the relinquishment of possession alone does not amount to nonperformance. Even in a fixed term lease, a lessee's failure to occupy leased premises is not in and of itself a failure to perform, provided the lessee continues to pay rent and perform its other obligations under the lease. Nevertheless, if the parties' agreement requires the lessee to remain in possession of the premises, termination of occupancy will result in a breach of the lease. For example, the lessor of space in a shopping center may require lessees to remain in continuous operation of the leased premises.

2. Specific Performance and Related Remedies

As discussed in the Subpart above, dissolution is, in certain cases, an available remedy for a party's failure to perform its obligations under the contract of lease, and dissolution will terminate the contract. An alternative remedy that a party may seek in response to a failure of the other party to perform is specific performance. This Subpart discusses the basics of specific performance, as well as other concepts that are associated with specific performance in the context of lease.

a. Specific Performance

Specific performance requires that the obligor perform in kind; in other words, it allows the obligee to obtain "that which by virtue of the obligation he was entitled to expect." 5 Saúl Litvinoff, Louisiana Civil Law Treatise, Obligations § 1.7 (1975). Thus, specific performance is an *alternative* remedy to dissolution. The rules on specific performance are found in the Title on Conventional Obligations. Specifically, Article 1986 provides when the failure to perform involves an obligation *to do*, the granting of specific performance lies within the discretion of the court. La. Civ. Code art. 1986. However, by contrast, if the failure to perform involves an obligation *to deliver a thing*, or *not to do an act*, or *to execute an instrument*, the court shall award specific performance unless specific performance is impracticable, in which case the court may allow damages to the obligee instead. *Id.*

Ultimately, outside of the context of an obligation to do, specific performance is the preferred remedy unless it is "impracticable." Determining the parameters of impracticability has been the focus of many Louisiana judicial opinions. In *J. Weingarten, Inc. v. Northgate Mall, Inc.*, 404 So. 2d 896 (La. 1981), the Louisiana Supreme Court provided needed guidance on that issue. Northgate had subleased space in a shopping center to Weingarten, and after some time, Northgate undertook a $4 million renovation of the shopping center in an area that was reserved to Weingarten under the lease for customer parking. Weingarten sought to specifically enforce the lease, asking the court to order Northgate to tear down the building that it had constructed in breach of its obligation "not to do" something, i.e., "not to infringe on plaintiff's contractual rights over areas reserved for parking by the lease." *Id.* at 899. The Court refused to do so and set forth four instances in which specific performance would be "impracticable": (1) where it is impossible; (2) where it would be greatly disproportionate in cost to the actual damage caused; (3) where it is no longer in the obligee's interest; or (4) where it would render a substantial negative effect upon the interests of third parties. *Id.* at 901. Employing the aforementioned analysis, the Court noted:

> In view of the great disparity between the cost of specific relief and the damages caused by the contractual breach, the magnitude of the economic and energy waste that would result from the building's destruction, the substantial hardship which would be imposed on individuals who are not parties to the contract or to this litigation, and the potential negative effect upon the community, the circumstances and nature of this case do not permit specific performance.

Id. at 897.

Comment (b) to Article 1986 also notes that specific performance is impracticable "when it requires the continuous supervision of the court." La. Civ. Code art. 1986 cmt. b. *Sizeler Property Investors, Inc. v. Gordon Jewelry Corp.*, 544 So. 2d 53 (La. App. 4 Cir. 1989), provides an example of such a situation. In that case, the lessor sought specific performance against the lessee who had closed its store that had been located on the leased premises; the lessor wanted the court to order the lessee to reopen the store per the continuing operations provisions in the contract of lease. The court refused to do so, relying on the comment and deciding that such a remedy would be "virtually impossible" under the circumstances because it "clearly requires not only the reorganization of a no longer existing business, but supervision by the court of the reopening and running of the business as well." *Id.* at 55.

b. Accelerated Rental

A common issue that arises when a lease is breached by the lessee is the extent of the lessor's right to collect rent. If a lessor seeks dissolution of the lease, the lessor is entitled to collect any *past* rent that the lessee has failed to pay; however, the lessor is not entitled to collect any *future* rent — i.e., rent corresponding to the remainder of the term following dissolution. If the lessor wishes to collect future rent, then enforcement, rather than dissolution, of the lease is required.

Recall that although rent is, by default, due at the beginning of the lease, parties usually provide suspensive terms for individual rent payments, allowing rent to be payable in shorter intervals (in which case the rent is due at the beginning of each interval). LA. CIV. CODE art. 2703. In a common example, Lessor leases an apartment to Lessee for one year (January 1 to December 31, 2019) with total rent set at $12,000. However, Lessor and Lessee agree that rent will be paid in $1000 increments on the first day of each month.

In the hypothetical above, because Lessee is bound to pay rent in monthly intervals, each payment is due on the first day of each month. In general, Lessor cannot require Lessee to pay rent earlier than the time it is due, even if Lessee has in some way failed to perform his or her obligations under the lease. However, in many instances, the contract of lease will contain an acceleration clause, which allows the lessor to accelerate future rent payments upon the lessee's failure to perform his or her obligations under the lease. Acceleration clauses are allowed under Article 1807, which provides that "[t]he parties may provide that the failure of the obligor to perform one or more items shall allow the obligee to demand the immediate performance of all the remaining items." LA. CIV. CODE art. 1807. Returning again to the hypothetical above, assume that the lease in question contained an acceleration clause. Assume also that Lessee paid the rent payments that were due January 1, 2019, and February 1, 2019. However, Lessee failed to pay the rent that was due on March 1, 2019. The Lessor may invoke the acceleration clause and require that Lessee pay both the March 1, 2019, rent in the amount of $1000 and the entire balance of the rent due for the remaining nine months of the lease (April through December of 2019) in the amount of $9000.

Acceleration clauses have another important effect: they alter the time at which prescription begins to run on the lessee's obligation to pay rent. When rent is due at monthly intervals, the obligation to pay rent is a conjunctive obligation. Article 1807 defines a conjunctive obligation as one that "binds the obligor to multiple items of performance that may be separately rendered or enforced." LA. CIV. CODE art. 1807. In the hypothetical above, the multiple items of performance are the monthly rent payments. Article 1807 goes on to provide that in such a case, "each item is regarded as the object of a separate obligation." *Id.* Because each rent payment is the object of a separate obligation per Article 1807, each payment is subject to its own prescriptive period (three years from the date it was due, per LA. CIV. CODE art. 3493). If Lessee pays the first two months of rent when each is due (January 1, 2019, and February 1, 2019) but does not pay the next two months of rent (March 1, 2019, and April 1, 2019), then, under the general rule, Lessor's right to sue for the March rent prescribes on March 1, 2022, whereas Lessor's right to sue for the April rent prescribes on

April 1, 2022. However, if Lessor accelerates future rent in accordance with an acceleration clause on March 1, then all rent payments for the remainder of the term becomes due immediately, and prescription runs on all payments from that time.

c. Reletting the Premises

Another question that arises when the lessee fails to perform his or her obligations under the lease is whether the lessor may retake possession of the leased premises while simultaneously enforcing the lease against the lessee through the collection of future rent. The Louisiana Supreme Court has stated, as a general rule, that "if the lessor elects to *enforce* the lease, he may obtain a money judgment against the lessee based on the terms of the lease agreement, but the lease remains in effect and the lessee retains the right of occupancy for the remainder of the term of the lease." *Richard v. Broussard*, 495 So. 2d 1291, 1293 (La. 1986). Under the general rule, then, the lessor cannot both enforce the lease (and collect future rent for the remainder of the lease) and also retake possession; instead, these remedies are mutually exclusive. Indeed, as a general rule, retaking possession of the premises while the lease is ongoing would amount to breach of the warranty against peaceful possession. However, Louisiana courts recognize a significant exception to this general rule: if the lessee has unjustifiably abandoned the premises, then the lessor may, under certain circumstances, both retake possession of the premises and collect future rent from the lessee.

The following case addresses the rights of the lessor in the case of the lessee's abandonment.

Sunbelt Security Services, Inc. v. Delahoussaye

572 So. 2d 598 (La. App. 4 Cir. 1990)

Williams, Judge.

This is an appeal from a judgment on a lease in favor of defendants/lessors, Gerard J. and Gary J. Delahoussaye d/b/a Twin Investments (hereinafter "lessors"), and against plaintiffs/lessees, Sunbelt Security Services, Inc., and third party defendant, Anthony J. Montelaro, in solido. The judgment was in the amount of $43,800.00, representing accelerated rentals due under the lease, plus 15% attorney fees, with costs and interest from the date of judicial demand.

Lessees appeal, contending that the trial court erred 1) in failing to rescind the contract of lease based on error in the cause of the original contract; 2) in failing to declare the lease an absolute nullity because the contract had as its object an illegal object; 3) in failing to hold that the lessors violated warranties of peaceable possession and fitness for intended use, which would have entitled lessees to terminate the lease and vacate the premises; 4) in not holding that the lessors are barred from recovery even if lessees did unjustifiably default on the lease, since the premises became unfit for its intended use by the fault of the lessors; 5) in failing to find that the lease was terminated upon reletting the premises or renovating the property after Sunbelt's abandonment and, alternatively, in failing to credit lessees with the full amounts received by lessors in reletting the premises subsequent to lessees' vacating the premises; and 6) in failing to award lessees damages sustained when they were forced to vacate the premises as well as attorney fees due to lessors' bad faith failure to perform.

* * * * *

We hold that, under the facts of this case, the lack of a permit to convert the leased premises into an office pursuant to the City Code of New Orleans and the New Orleans Building Code did not vitiate the consent of the lessees. We also hold that the contract of lease did not have an illegal object which would nullify the contract under LSA-C.C. article 2030. Further, we hold that the lessors' failure to secure a permit to convert the leased premises into an office immediately upon disapproval of lessees' application for an occupational license did not constitute cause sufficient to justify lessees' abandonment of the premises in this case. Next, we hold that the lease was not terminated by the reletting or renovation of the premises upon Sunbelt's abandonment so long as Sunbelt's right of occupancy remained under the lease, although Sunbelt is entitled to a credit for rentals received by lessors in reletting the premises. We remand for a determination of whether Sunbelt's right of occupancy was usurped by post-abandonment renovations to the property and for a determination of the total amount of rentals received from reletting the premises.

As to Montelaro's appeal, we hold that the trial court erred in holding Montelaro solidarily liable as surety on the lease, where Montelaro expressly signed the lease in the capacity of President of Sunbelt and not in his individual capacity.

Accordingly, we affirm in part [. . .] and remand for further proceedings consistent with this opinion.

FACTS

On April 23, 1985, the parties to this litigation entered into a written lease of commercial property located at 4631 S. Carrollton Avenue in New Orleans for a five year term commencing May 1, 1985 and ending April 30, 1990. The lease, which contained an escalating rent schedule, twice designated that the leased premises were for "Office space only."

Lessees occupied the premises at the start of the lease and began operation of their business. On January 27, 1987, lessees filed with the City a renewal application for their occupational license authorized by LSA-R.S. 47:341 et seq. and required under Chapter 70 of the New Orleans City Code. The record shows that the City issued a 1987 occupational license on February 11, 1987 entitling lessees to operate a business at the address shown, but that the address shown was 4006 Canal Street. The City subsequently disapproved lessees' application for an occupational license at the Carrollton Avenue address.

On February 19, 1987, the City sent to lessees and to the Delahoussayes a letter confirming the disapproval and informing them of the reason, i.e., converting a residence into an office without first securing a permit, which constitutes a violation of the New Orleans Building Code. Before a permit could issue, it was required that three sets of plans and specifications be submitted. The lessees were given until March 2, 1987 to comply with the Code requirements, under penalty of fine and/or imprisonment, and were given the recommendation to "(c)ease operation of unauthorized business." Douglas Emmer, Vice President of Sunbelt, testified that he immediately contacted the lessors to notify them of the problem and also requested of the City an extension for compliance. On March 4, 1987 the City granted lessees' request for an extension until March 31, 1987.

On March 11, 1987, before the expiration of the extension granted by the City, lessees sent written notice to lessors that they were terminating the lease effective April 11, 1987. Lessees vacated the premises at the end of March and returned the keys to lessors on May 2, 1987.

Gerard Delahoussaye of Twin Investments testified that he began attempts to rectify the problem immediately upon receipt of the City's February 19 letters. Specifically, Delahoussaye met with Charles Cochran, Chief Building Inspector, in an effort to obtain an extension of time. On March 18, 1987, he met with Paul May, the Zoning Administrator for the Department of Safety & Permits, and Michael Centineo, Chief Building Inspector for the same department, in an attempt to cure the problem. Delahoussaye testified that he obtained an additional extension until June 2, 1987 to comply with the regulations. It is not clear when or if the required permit was obtained.

After Sunbelt returned the keys, lessors leased the property to various third persons. However, Delahoussaye testified that lessees were at no time prohibited from re-entering the premises. The premises were leased to the campaign of Judge Steven R. Plotkin from August to October 1987 and to the campaign of Judge Patrick M. Schott from August to September 1988. Further, Sunbelt asserts that two additional leases entered into were discovered after the trial, particularly a third lease to Success Seminars, Inc. from February through May 1989 and a fourth lease to a beauty parlor beginning in 1989 and apparently continuing to date.

Sunbelt filed suit on April 2, 1987, alleging fraud and error and praying for rescission of the lease and damages in the amount of $11,280.00. Defendants reconvened, alleging that the lessees were in default and praying for acceleration of rentals due or, alternatively, for specific performance [. . .] The case was tried before a Commissioner, who ruled in favor of defendants in the amount of $2,900.00 [. . .] Although the trial court initially signed a judgment affirming the Commissioner's recommendation, the court later set aside that judgment as premature, granted a new trial, and ultimately held in favor of defendants in the full amount of $43,800.00 plus attorney fees, costs and interest.

* * * * *

ASSIGNMENT OF ERROR NO. 1

First, Sunbelt contends that because the lessors did not have the required permit there was error as to the principal cause of the contract, specifically, use of the building as an office, which vitiates Sunbelt's consent and entitles them to rescind the contract. This assignment is without merit.

The Louisiana Civil Code articles on vices of consent to a contract provide that consent may be vitiated by error, fraud or duress, LSA-C.C. article 1948, and that error vitiates consent only when it concerns a cause without which the obligation would not have been incurred and that cause was known or should have been known to the other party, LSA-C.C. article 1949. *See also Don Smart & Associates—Century 21 v. Lanier Business Products*, 551 So.2d 665, 670 (La.App. 1st Cir.1989). LSA-C.C. article 1947 [sic, Article 1967] defines cause as ". . . the reason why a party obligates himself."

Louisiana jurisprudence has held that a lease should be rescinded based on error in the principal cause of the contract where a license to operate a particular business could not be obtained, *Marcello v. Bussiere*, 284 So.2d 892 (La.1973); *Guaranty Savings Assurance Co. v. Uddo*, 386 So.2d 670 (La.App. 1st Cir.1980), writ den. 389 So.2d 1126 (La.1980), or where property which was the subject of an option agreement contained a zoning classification inconsistent with the use intended by the prospective purchasers, *C.H. Boehmer Sales Agency v. Russo*, 99 So.2d 475 (La.App. Orl.1958).

In *Marcello v. Bussiere, supra*, defendants agreed to sub-lease a bar-lounge which they believed to be an on-going enterprise when, in fact, it had been closed for six months due to revocation of its alcoholic beverage license. After the defendants began renovation of the premises, they were informed that they could not obtain an alcoholic beverage license ". . . in view of the attitude of the Gretna officials toward (the business's) reputation." *Id*. at 895. The court concluded that there was an error in the principal cause of the contract since the defendants received no on-going business and could not secure a license to operate.

Similarly, in *Guaranty Savings Assurance Co. v. Uddo, supra*, the lessee contracted to lease certain property for the establishment of a restaurant and adjoining lounge, a motive clearly communicated to the lessor. Despite this, the lessor failed to inform the lessee that the property was not zoned for a lounge and that it had a prior history of neighborhood opposition to any use which would permit the serving of alcohol from the premises. When the lessee applied for the liquor permit, he was met with "solid opposition from city and civic officials," obstacles which he concluded were "insurmountable." *Id*. at 672. He also learned that under no circumstances would he likely obtain a rezoning of the property. The court granted rescission of the contract.

In the instant case, the reason lessees obligated themselves under the lease was to obtain use of the premises for office space, a cause clearly indicated in the lease itself. Further, this cause was known by the lessors, who not only advertised the premises as office space but also drafted the lease. Nonetheless, under the particular facts of this case, we conclude that there was not an error in cause which would vitiate consent.

Unlike *Marcello v. Bussiere, supra*, and *Guaranty Savings Assurance Co. v. Uddo, supra*, the lessees in this case did not show that there was an incurable defect which would unreasonably delay or prevent the issuance of the use and occupancy license. The record shows that the required permit could easily issue upon submission of three sets of plans and specifications for conversion of the premises. Further, the testimony of Michael Centineo, Chief Building Inspector for the Department of Safety and Permits, indicated that the City would not pursue legal action against a tenant notified of a violation unless that tenant continued to occupy the premises without contacting the City. That was clearly not the case here.

The lessors began efforts to cure the problem immediately upon receipt of the City's February 19, 1987 notice and of the lessees' complaint shortly thereafter. Upon the lessees' request, the City granted an extension of time until March 31, 1987 to comply with the regulations. The lessors then requested an additional extension until June 2, 1987, which the testimony of Gerard Delahoussaye shows was granted. Throughout this period, the lessors met with various City officials concerning the problem.

The fact that the lessors were first apprised of a problem in August 1986 when their own application for an occupational license was disapproved pending submission of plans and specifications does not establish unreasonable delay or inability to secure a license. Delahoussaye testified that, upon disapproval of the 1986 license, he contacted the Department of Safety and Permits by phone and believed the problem was cured, as he did not receive another notice until February, 1987.

After considering all of the facts of this case, we conclude that there was no error in the principal cause of the contract which would vitiate lessees' consent. Moreover, even if there were error, Sunbelt is not entitled to rescission since the record shows that the lessors were willing to perform the contract as intended by Sunbelt, specifically, to comply with the regulations which would enable Sunbelt to obtain their use and occupancy license. LSA-C.C. article 1951. *See also* Litvinoff, *Vices of Consent, Error, Fraud, Duress and an Epilogue on Lesion*, 50 La.L.Rev. 1, 39 (1989). Accordingly, lessees' first assignment of error is without merit.

ASSIGNMENT OF ERROR NO. 2

Next, Sunbelt argues that the contract of lease is an absolute nullity under LSA-C.C. article 2030 because its object, use as an office, was illegal under local law. This argument is without merit.

LSA-C.C. article 2030 provides:

> A contract is absolutely null when it violates a rule of public order, as when the object of a contract is illicit or immoral. A contract that is absolutely null may not be confirmed.

Absolute nullity may be invoked by any person or may be declared by the court on its own initiative.

The official revision comment to this article states that it codifies the jurisprudential rule that a contract which contravenes the public order is absolutely null.

Lessees' reliance on this article is strained, at best. Operation of the leased premises as an office is not in derogation of municipal law, but merely requires that a permit to convert that particular premises from residential to commercial use be secured first. That lessees did not have the required permit and were disallowed their 1987 occupational license pending acquisition of that permit does not render the contract violative of public order and absolutely null. This assignment is without merit.

ASSIGNMENT OF ERROR NO. 3

Next, Sunbelt argues that the lessors violated their implied warranties of peaceable possession and fitness for intended use, which entitled lessees to unilaterally terminate the lease. We disagree.

LSA-C.C. article 2692 [R.C.C. 2682] enumerates the obligations arising from the nature of the contract of lease:

> The lessor is bound from the very nature of the contract, and without any clause to that effect:
>
> 1. To deliver the thing leased to the lessee.
>
> 2. To maintain the thing in a condition such as to serve for the use for which it is hired.
>
> 3. To cause the lessee to be in a peaceable possession of the thing during the continuance of the lease.

In support of their argument that they were entitled to terminate the lease as a result of deprivation of peaceable possession and unfitness of the thing for its intended use, lessees cite *Mecca Realty, Inc. v. New Orleans Health Corp.*, 389 So.2d 403 (La.App. 4th Cir.1980). In that case, the leased premises contained electrical wiring deficiencies which failed to meet City Code requirements. When electrical service was discontinued due to the defect, lessee abandoned the premises. Lessor filed suit, alleging damages resulting from the abandonment. In ruling for the lessee, this Court reasoned that the electrical problem was a pre-existing condition for which the lessor was responsible under LSA-C.C. article 2695 [R.C.C. 2692, 2697]. The lessor's failure to remedy the defect resulted in the loss of electrical service and therefore constituted a violation of LSA-C.C. article 2692(2) [R.C.C. 2682], entitling lessees to vacate. Sunbelt argues that, under *Mecca Realty*, lessors' noncompliance with the building code constituted a violation of the warranty of peaceable possession and rendered the premises unfit for their intended use.

Unlike *Mecca Realty*, the landlords in the instant case commenced curative action immediately upon receipt of the February 19 notice. Extensions for compliance were granted by the City beyond the date Sunbelt abandoned the premises, and the testimony of Michael Centineo indicated that the City would take no legal action during this period as long as curative efforts were being made. Sunbelt had no problems with the building as did the lessee in *Mecca Realty* when the electrical deficiencies persisted and electrical service was discontinued. Sunbelt was never locked out, evicted or ordered to abandon the premises. Under these facts, we cannot say that Sunbelt's peaceable possession was disturbed or that the premises were unfit for their intended use so as to warrant lessees' abandonment of the premises.

We note that Louisiana jurisprudence has long recognized an implied warranty of compliance with building code requirements. But while nonconformity entitles the lessee to obviation of that nonconformity, the jurisprudence indicates that the lessee is not entitled to vacate the premises unless the noncompliance with building code requirements threatens the tenant's safety or welfare. *See Chagnard v. Schiro*, 166 So. 496 (La.App.Orl.1936); Armstrong, *The Implied Warranty of Habitability: Louisiana Institution, Common Law Innovation*, 46 La.L.Rev. 195, 211-212 (1985); Hersbergen, *Consumer Protection*, 49 La.L.Rev. 315, 322 n. 43 (1988).

In the instant case, Sunbelt introduced into evidence an April 20, 1987 "letter of requirement" by Bhola Dhume, Chief Plan Examiner for the City, to architect Mark Ripple regarding the Carrollton Avenue property. The letter lists the requirements for the plans and specifications to be submitted for the permit and references some fire-restrictive standards. However, the record does not establish that Sunbelt's safety was threatened by the noncompliance with the code requirement that a permit be obtained prior to conversion of the premises from residential to commercial use. Thus, we conclude that Sunbelt failed to show that it was entitled to vacate the premises because of noncompliance with building code requirements.

Accordingly, for the reasons cited, Sunbelt's third assignment of error is without merit.

ASSIGNMENTS OF ERROR NO. 4 AND 6

Next, Sunbelt contends that even if the abandonment was not justified under the law, defendants should not recover because it was by their own fault that lessees defaulted on the lease. According to Sunbelt, lessors' failure to secure the permit constitutes fault which not only bars their recovery but also renders them liable for damages and attorney fees. These assignments of error are without merit.

As detailed above, the nonconformity with the building code requirement entitled lessees to correction of the nonconformity. However, in view of the lessors' immediate attempts to cure the problem, the extensions for compliance which were granted by the City, and our holding that the premises were not unfit for their intended use, we conclude that the lessees were not entitled to rescission of the lease, damages or attorney fees, and that the lessors are not barred from recovery.

ASSIGNMENT OF ERROR NO. 5

Next, Sunbelt argues that the lessors improperly engaged in self-help and thereby terminated the lease when they relet the premises following Sunbelt's abandonment.

(There is no dispute that the lessors entered into four separate leases after Sunbelt vacated the premises. The third and fourth leases, not part of the record, were for terms extending beyond and commencing after the trial of this matter.) In the alternative, Sunbelt asserts that the lessors terminated the lease by remodeling the premises as a beauty salon under the fourth post-abandonment lease. Alternatively, Sunbelt contends that any judgment against them for future rentals must be credited with amounts received from reletting the premises.

In *Richard v. Broussard*, 495 So.2d 1291 (La.1986), the Louisiana Supreme Court set forth the remedies available to a lessor when a lessee defaults on a lease. That Court stated:

> Generally, when a lessee defaults on a lease agreement, the lessor has two options available: he may sue to *cancel* the lease and to recover accrued rentals due, or he may sue to *enforce* the lease and to recover both accrued rentals and future accelerated rentals (if the lease contains an acceleration clause). These remedies are mutually exclusive. . . . If the lessor elects to *cancel* the lease, the lease is terminated and the lessor is entitled to return into possession, but he forfeits the right to all future rentals. On the other hand, if the lessor elects to *enforce* the lease, he may obtain a money judgment against the lessee based on the terms of the lease agreement, but the lease remains in effect and the lessee retains the right of occupancy for the remainder of the term of the lease. . . . However, when the lessee breaches the lease by abandoning the premises, the lessor has the right to take possession of the premises as agent for the lessee and to relet the premises to a third party without canceling the lease or relieving the lessee of his obligations under the lease contract.

Id. at 1293.

The Court noted that, although a lessor generally must resort to the judicial process to take possession of the premises, there is an established jurisprudential exception which allows a lessor to engage in self-help when the lessee has unjustifiably abandoned the premises. *Id.* at 1293 n. 1, citing *Bunel of New Orleans, Inc. v. Cigali*, 348 So.2d 993 (La.App. 4th Cir.1977). In such a case, the lessor may rent the property to other tenants without thereby canceling the lease or impairing his recourse against the lessee and is bound to credit the lessee for any amounts received from reletting the premises. *Sliman v. Fish*, 177 La. 38, 147 So. 493, 495 (1933). *See also Shank-Jewella v. Diamond Gallery*, 535 So.2d 1207, 1212 (La.App. 2d Cir.1988); *Preen v. LeRuth*, 430 So.2d 825, 827 (La.App. 5th Cir.1983).

The contract of lease in the instant case incorporated these remedies:

> Should the premises be vacated or abandoned by Lessee because of ejectment for breach hereof, or otherwise, or should the Lessee begin to remove personal property or goods to the prejudice of the Lessor's lien, then the rent for the unexpired term, with Attorney's fees, shall at once become due and exigible, and Lessor, at his option, has the right to cancel the lease, or

re-enter and let said premises for such price and on such terms as may be immediately obtainable and apply the net amount realized to the payment of the rent.

Under the principles enunciated above and the terms of the contract, the lessors in the instant case had the right to re-enter the premises and relet the property "for such price and on such terms as may be immediately obtainable" upon abandonment by the lessees, with the lessees remaining liable for unpaid rentals less the amount received from reletting the premises.

However, while a lessor may take reasonable steps necessary to relet the property, including refurbishing the premises to attract new tenants, the lessor may not alter the premises to the extent that they cannot be used for the purpose for which they were originally leased. In such a case, the lessor's act ceases to be for the account of the lessee, as it effectively terminates the lessee's ability to re-occupy the premises under the lease. Compare *Richard v. Broussard*, *supra* [occupation of the premises by lessors themselves effectively usurped the lessees right to occupy the premises]; *Weil v. Segura*, 178 La. 421, 151 So. 639 (1933) [sale of abandoned premises terminated the lessees right to occupancy].

The record in the instant case contains no evidence of the work, if any, done to the premises after the abandonment by the lessees or of the full amounts received from the third and fourth leases. Therefore, we remand this case to the trial court for taking of evidence of these leases and the amounts received therefrom, and also for a determination of whether the lessees' right to occupy the premises was effectively usurped by renovation of the premises under the third or fourth lease.

* * * * *

For the foregoing reasons, we affirm in part and reverse in part the judgment of the trial court. Further, we remand for the taking of evidence on the third and fourth post-abandonment leases and a determination of 1) the amounts received there under and 2) whether Sunbelt's right of occupancy was usurped by renovations to the premises.

AFFIRMED IN PART; REVERSED IN PART AND REMANDED

Notes and Questions

1. As discussed in *Sunbelt*, the lessor may *both* sue to enforce a lease and collect future rent *and* retake possession of the premises for purposes of re-letting it to another lessee. Why is this permitted? What limitations are placed on the lessor's right to re-let? Why are these limitations in place? Notice that if this right is exercised, the lessor re-lets the premises as an "agent" of the lessee.

2. Consider the following hypothetical. Lessor leased a convenience store and parking lot to Lessee for a term of ten years beginning on January 1, 2018, at a rent of $1,000 per month, due on the first day of each month. The contract of lease contains an acceleration clause. In December of 2018, Lessee failed to pay rent and

unjustifiably abandoned the leased premises; Lessor sent notice of the acceleration of rent to the Lessee on January 15, 2019. In May of 2019, Lessor rented the premises to someone else for a five-year term at a rent of $750 per month. If Lessor sues Lessee to collect both past and future rent, to how much rent will Lessor be entitled? Consider specifically the questions that follow. To how much rent is Lessor entitled from the time of Lessee's breach on December 1, 2018, until the start of the new lease in May of 2019? To how much rent is Lessor entitled during the term of the new lease? To how much rent is Lessor entitled after the new lease expires?

3. In the event of the lessee's abandonment of the leased premises, the lessor *may*, in most instances, obtain possession of the leased thing and re-let it to a third person. But *must* he or she do so? In other words, does the obligation of a lessor to mitigate his damages, *see* LA. CIV. CODE art. 2002, extend to a duty to re-let? The following case considers this issue.

Dixie Services, LLC v. R&B Falcon Drilling USA, Inc.

955 So. 2d 214 (La. App. 4 Cir.)

DENNIS R. BAGNERIS, SR., Judge.

The issue in this case is whether the Lessees of commercial property located in Plaquemines Parish are liable to Lessor for unpaid rent and damages. In the consolidation of this case, the issue is whether the district court erred considering a Motion to Assess Costs and Fix Attorney Fees. We affirm in part and reverse in part.

FACTS AND PROCEDURAL HISTORY

In November 1997, Dixie Services, LLC (hereinafter "Dixie"), as Lessor, and R&B Falcon Drilling USA, Inc. (formerly Falcon Workover Company, Inc. and hereinafter referred to as "Falcon") as Lessee, entered into a lease ("Lease") of real property located at 230 Gunther Lane, Belle Chasse, Louisiana. The Lease had an initial term of five (5) years, commencing on November 15, 1997 and continuing through November 14, 2002. A monthly rental of $6,500.00 was due during the primary term of five years.

The primary term of the Lease automatically renewed for a single, additional five (5) year period, unless Falcon timely elected to *not* renew the Lease. The terms of any renewal term were to be identical to those contained in the Lease and in place during the initial term, except for an increase in the rents, commensurate with an index for inflation. In order to limit the Lease to its primary term and avoid the single renewal term, Falcon was required to provide written notice of cancellation to Dixie at least one hundred and twenty (120) days prior to the end of the primary term. Specifically, the Lease granted to Lessee, the ". . . right and privilege of canceling this Lease at the end of the primary term or any renewal period (if applicable) by notifying Lessor in writing by certified mail at least one hundred and twenty (120) days prior to the expiration of the primary term or any renewal period (if applicable)."

Falcon vacated the leased premises in February 1999. Thereafter, on March 29, 1999, Falcon entered into a sublease with Marine Specialties, Inc. ("Marine Specialties") ("Sublease") for the building and parking lot of the leased premises. The Sublease was for a one year term commencing April 1, 1999 and terminating on March 31, 2000 with a rental of $3,740 per month. Dixie acknowledged and accepted the terms of the Sublease including those pertaining to reduced rent and its limited term. Marine Specialties and Falcon executed one renewal to extend the Sublease through November 14, 2002 at an increased rent of $4,000.00 per month. Following expiration of the Sublease, Marine Specialties has continued to occupy the Leased premises on a month-to-month basis. Falcon continued to accept the monthly rental payments from Marine Specialties until Marine Specialties vacated the premises in August 2003. None of the payments were forwarded to Dixie.

Falcon, via certified mail dated July 30, 2002, advised Dixie of its election to cancel the lease. Because this notice was sent less than 120 days prior to the lease's expiration date of November 14, 2002, Dixie informed Falcon that the notice was deficient and that the monthly rental payments should continue for an additional five years or until November 14, 2007. However, Falcon stopped making rental payments at the expiration of the initial term and Dixie notified Falcon that they were in default of the lease on November 15, 2002. The building has remained vacant since Marine Specialties moved out in August 2003.

On January 3, 2003, Dixie filed suit against Falcon to accelerate all of the rent due under the terms of the lease. On November 19, 2003, Dixie filed its First Supplemental and Amending Petition alleging that Falcon and Marine Specialties had caused damage to the leased premises by failing to maintain the property, and sought damages against both defendants for the damage thus caused. On March 23, 2004, Dixie filed its Second Supplemental and Amending Petition seeking payment of the real estate taxes due and owing under the lease from the defendants.

After a two-day bench trial, the trial court rendered a judgment in favor of Dixie and against Falcon in the amount of $164,893.02 for 21.5 months of rent at the rate of $7,294.65 per month, and 21.5 months of unpaid property taxes. The trial court also rendered judgment in favor of Dixie and against Marine Specialties in the sum of $15,154.00 for damages sustained by the leased premises during the term of the lease in question. Thereafter, Dixie filed a Motion to Assess Costs and Fix Attorney's Fees. Although the Motion to Assess Costs was heard on June 16, 2005, no judgment has yet been rendered.

Dixie now appeals this final judgment. On appeal, Dixie alleges the following assignments of error: (1) the trial court erred in finding that it had a duty to mitigate its damages; (2) the trial court erred in failing to award it rent and taxes for the property at issue for the entire five year term of the renewal of the lease; and (3) the trial court erred in failing to award it attorneys fees against Falcon and Marine Specialties as provided for under the terms of the lease.

Falcon filed an answer to the appeal alleging the following assignments of error: (1) the trial court erred in ruling that it did not timely and/or properly cancel/terminate the Lease at issue; (2) the trial court erred in applying the Louisiana law of mitigation, in quantifying Dixie's failure to mitigate and in its award of past due rents to Dixie; and (3) the trial court erred in failing to hold Marine Specialties liable to Falcon and/or jointly and severally liable with Falcon to Dixie.

Marine Specialties filed a brief alleging the following four assignments of error: (1) the trial court erred in awarding damages against it based upon its obligations under the Sublease in the amount of $1,928.00 dollars to replace curbing in the parking lot; (2) the trial court erred in awarding damages against it based upon its obligations under the Sublease in the amount of $1,221.00 to replace damaged grating; (3) the trial court erred in awarding damages against it based upon its obligations under the Sublease in the amount of $4,300.00 to repair two of the metal doors and replace one metal door; and (4) the trial court erred in awarding damages against it based upon its obligations under the Sublease in the amount of $7,705.00 to restore the premises to its original condition by removal of the office.

* * * * *

DIXIE'S ISSUE # 1: WHETHER THE TRIAL COURT ERRED IN FINDING THAT DIXIE HAD A DUTY TO MITIGATE ITS DAMAGES

Dixie argues that the trial court committed legal error when it found that Dixie had a duty to mitigate its damages when Falcon abandoned the leased premises without lawful cause. Dixie maintains that since Falcon abandoned the premises without cause and failed to pay rent, it violated the terms of the lease and accelerated all rents due.

Falcon argues that Dixie was expressly informed that it had every intention to cancel the lease and not return to the leased premises.

> "An obligee must make reasonable efforts to mitigate the damage caused by the obligor's failure to perform. When an obligee fails to make these efforts, the obligor may demand that the damages be accordingly reduced." LSA-C.C. art. 2002.

An injured party has a duty to mitigate his damages. *Rogers v. Nelson Dodge Inc.*, 407 So.2d 443, 447 (La.App. 3d Cir.1981). However, that duty only requires that the injured party take *reasonable* steps to minimize the consequences of the injury. The standard by which these steps are judged is that of a reasonable man under like circumstances. *See Philippe v. Browning Arms Co.*, 395 So.2d 310, 318 (La.1980) and *Lawyers Title Ins. Co. v. Carey Hodges & Associates Inc.* 358 So.2d 964, 968 (La.App. 1 Cir.1978); *Easterling v. Halter Marine, Inc.*, 470 So.2d 221, 223 (La.App. 4 Cir.1985).

In the instant matter the district court granted Dixie unpaid rent "up to the time of trial". On April 22, 2004, the parties stipulated that Dixie could attempt to re-lease the property without waiving its claim to accelerated rental payments, yet as of the trial date of September 1, 2004, the property had not been leased. The record reflects that Dixie knew that Marine Specialists were only going to remain on the property until it purchased its own facility. Both Dixie and Falcon offered evidence that Dixie attempted to re-lease the property. The district court, in its Reasons for Judgment, concluded, "The placing of a sign in front of a property on a dead-end street and relying on "word of mouth" notice to potential lessees is not reasonable so as to obligate Falcon for rent until 2007."

We cannot conclude that the district court erred in determining that Dixie's efforts to mitigate were somewhat unreasonable when Dixie knew that Falcon had no intention of remaining on the property although its actual written notice was untimely. We find that the district court recognized in all fairness the duty of Dixie to mitigate and relied on Dixie's efforts (or lack thereof) in calculating damages. There is no error in this regard.

DIXIE'S ISSUE # 2: WHETHER THE TRIAL COURT ERRED IN FAILING TO AWARD DIXIE RENT AND TAXES FOR THE PROPERTY AT ISSUE FOR THE ENTIRE FIVE-YEAR TERM OF THE RENEWAL OF THE LEASE

Dixie argues that it is entitled to a judgment for the accelerated rent for the entire term of the lease form November 14, 2002 through November 14, 2007, at a rate of $7,294.65 per month, for a total of $437,679. The district court awarded Dixie the "sum of ONE HUNDRED SIXTY-FOUR THOUSAND EIGHT HUNDRED NINETY-THREE AND 00/100 ($164,893.02) DOLLARS, representing 21.5 months of rental at the rate of $7,294.65 per month, with interest at the rate of 12% on the unpaid rent, plus unpaid taxes at the rate of $255.81 per month for 21.5 months and $2,558.11 for 2002, together with legal interest from the date of judicial demand until paid, plus 92% of the costs incurred in this matter."

The district court determined that even though Falcon's intention not to renew the lease resulted in another five-year term by law, the acceleration of payment would be an unfair and a huge financial gain for Dixie, or a "windfall."

The facts and the law presented by the parties in the instant matter reflect that the district court took a fair approach. This Court has a long stated history as to the appellate review in determining whether the trier of fact is in error.

> When there is evidence before the trier of fact which, upon its reasonable evaluation of credibility, furnishes a reasonable factual basis for the trial court's finding, on review the appellate court should not disturb this factual finding in the absence of manifest error. Stated another way, the reviewing court must give great weight to factual conclusion of the trier of fact; there is conflict in the testimony, reasonable evaluations of credibility and reasonable inferences of fact should not be disturbed upon review, even though the appellate court may feel that its own evaluations and inferences are as reasonable. The reason for this well-settled principle of review is based not only upon the trial court's better capacity to evaluate live witnesses (as compared with the appellate court's access only to cold record),

but also upon the proper allocation of trial and appellate functions between the respective courts.

Martin v. Graves, 343 So.2d 1212, 1213 (La.App. 4 Cir.1977) quoting *Canter v. Koehring Co.,* 283 So.2d 716, 724 (La.1993).

This Court finds no error by the district court in calculating damages in an amount feasible to the parties in the interest of fairness especially considering that Dixie had a duty to mitigate and Falcon had a duty to provide substantial notice of termination of the lease.

There was no error by the district court.

* * * * *

Notes and Questions

According to the Louisiana Fourth Circuit in *Dixie Services,* the lessor's obligation to mitigate damages includes the duty to re-let. Some other circuits agree. *See, e.g., Shank-Jewella v. Diamond Gallery,* 535 So. 2d 1207 (La. App. 2 Cir. 1988). However, cases from the Louisiana Fifth Circuit have yielded a different conclusion. *See, e.g., Meadowcrest Professional Bldg. Partnership v. Toursarkissian,* 1 So. 3d 555 (La. App. 5 Cir. 2008) (citing *BP Venture v. Stucki,* 562 So. 2d 461 (La. App. 5 Cir. 1990)).

Index